D0380881

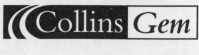

English
Thesaurus

Collins Gem

English Thesaurus

Collins Gem

An Imprint of HarperCollinsPublishers

First Edition 1987

Second Edition 1994

Third Edition 1999
Reprinted 1999 (twice), 2000
Latest reprint 2001

10 9 8 7 6 5

© HarperCollins Publishers 1987, 1994, 1999

The HarperCollins Gem website address is
www.collins-gem.com

ISBN 0-00-710917-2

A catalogue record for this book
is available from the British Library.

Typeset by Stewart C. Russell

Printed and bound in Great Britain by
Omnia Books Ltd, Glasgow, G64

EDITORIAL STAFF

FOREWORD

Collins Gem Thesaurus, which was first published in 1987, has proved itself to be an immensely popular language resource. It allows you to look up a word and find a wide selection of alternatives that can replace it. It is, therefore, tremendously helpful when you are trying to find different ways of expressing yourself, as well as being an invaluable aid for crosswords and puzzles.

Collins thesauruses have always been designed to give the user as much help as possible in finding the right word for any occasion. Collins pioneered the A-Z arrangement of main entry words. This lets you go straight to any word without having to resort to an index, just as if you were looking up a word in a dictionary. This arrangement is continued in this new edition, but the number of main entry words has been increased, thus giving you an even greater chance of finding the word you want. At the same time, the list of alternative words (synonyms) for each main entry word has been reviewed so that the most helpful alternatives are included in each case. The new edition also takes account of recent changes in the language, with new terms like *gridlock*, *nerd*, and *Internet* included as main entry words for the first time, and words like *wannabe*, *stakeholder*, and *luvvie* being found among the synonyms.

This new edition further demonstrates Collins' commitment to helping the user. As part of an innovative design, key synonyms have been underlined and placed first in each list. This layout enables you to see immediately which sense of the word is referred to. This is particularly helpful when a main entry word has a number of different senses. It also gives you an idea of which synonym is the closest alternative to the word you have looked up.

These innovations mean that **Collins Gem Thesaurus** continues to provide the user with a treasury of useful words arranged in the most helpful format possible.

HOW TO USE THIS BOOK

Main Entry Words

Main entry words are printed in large bold type. They are arranged in alphabetical order, so you can go straight to the word for which you want to find an alternative.

> **absolute**
>
> **absolutely**
>
> **absolution**

When the main entry word has been borrowed from a foreign language, it is given in italics.

> *femme fatale*

Parts of Speech

The part of speech of each main entry word is indicated in italic letters.

> **famine** *noun*

The symbol ♦ is used to indicate that the following sense or senses of the main entry word refer to a different part of speech.

> **farm** *noun* **1** <u>smallholding</u> ... ♦ *verb*
> **2** <u>cultivate</u>

Sometimes the synonyms that are given can refer to more than one part of speech.

> **tweak** *verb, noun* <u>twist</u>, jerk, pinch,
> pull, squeeze

Synonyms

The alternative words for the headword are listed in alphabetical order, except for the most useful synonym, which is placed first and underlined to give it special prominence.

> **fertilizer** *noun* <u>compost</u>, dressing,
> dung, manure

When a word has more than one sense, separate numbered lists of synonyms are given for each sense.

HOW TO USE THIS BOOK

> **field** *noun* **1** <u>meadow</u>, grassland,
> green, lea (*poetic*), pasture
> **2** <u>competitors</u>, applicants,
> candidates, competition, contestants,
> entrants, possibilities, runners
> **3** <u>speciality</u>, area, department, discipline,
> domain, line, province, territory

When a synonym has been borrowed from a foreign language, it is given in italics.

> **flower** *noun* ... **2** <u>elite</u>, best, cream,
> *crème de la crème*, pick

Phrases and Idioms

Short idiomatic phrases are given in small bold type and included under the most appropriate main entry word from the phrase. Such phrases appear after other senses of the main entry word which refer to the same part of speech.

> **fort** *noun* **1** <u>fortress</u>, blockhouse,
> camp, castle, citadel, fortification,
> garrison, stronghold **2 hold the
> fort** <u>stand in</u>, carry on, keep things
> on an even keel, take over the reins

When a particular sense of a word is usually found only in a certain phrase, that phrase is shown.

> **mince** *verb* **1** <u>cut</u>, chop, crumble,
> grind, hash **2** *As in* **mince one's
> words** <u>tone down</u>, moderate,
> soften, spare, weaken

Cross-references

Cross-references to other main entry words are shown in small capital letters.

> **enquire** *see* INQUIRE

HOW TO USE THIS BOOK

Labels

Many words and senses are labelled to indicate that their use is restricted to a certain subject, a certain geographical area, or a certain style of language.

> **overture** noun **1** Music ...
>
> **scupper** verb Brit. slang ...
>
> **wimp** noun Informal ...

An italic label in brackets refers only to the synonym preceding it, and gives you guidance about the appropriate context for using that particular alternative to the main entry word.

> **faint** ... ♦ verb **4** <u>pass out</u>, black out,
> collapse, flake out (*informal*), keel
> over (*informal*), lose consciousness,
> swoon (*literary*)

A a

abandon *verb* **1** <u>leave</u>, desert, forsake, strand **2** <u>give up</u>, relinquish, surrender, yield ♦ *noun* **3** <u>wildness</u>, recklessness

abandonment *noun* <u>leaving</u>, dereliction, desertion, forsaking

abashed *adjective* <u>embarrassed</u>, ashamed, chagrined, disconcerted, dismayed, humiliated, mortified, shamefaced, taken aback

abate *verb* <u>decrease</u>, decline, diminish, dwindle, fade, lessen, let up, moderate, relax, slacken, subside, weaken

abbey *noun* <u>monastery</u>, convent, friary, nunnery, priory

abbreviate *verb* <u>shorten</u>, abridge, compress, condense, contract, cut, reduce, summarize

abbreviation *noun* <u>shortening</u>, abridgment, contraction, reduction, summary, synopsis

abdicate *verb* <u>give up</u>, abandon, quit, relinquish, renounce, resign, step down (*informal*)

abdication *noun* <u>giving up</u>, abandonment, quitting, renunciation, resignation, retirement, surrender

abduct *verb* <u>kidnap</u>, carry off, seize, snatch (*slang*)

abduction *noun* <u>kidnapping</u>, carrying off, seizure

aberration *noun* <u>oddity</u>, abnormality, anomaly, defect, irregularity, lapse, peculiarity, quirk

abet *verb* <u>help</u>, aid, assist, connive at, support

abeyance *noun* **in abeyance** <u>shelved</u>, hanging fire, on ice (*informal*), pending, suspended

abhor *verb* <u>hate</u>, abominate, detest, loathe, shrink from, shudder at

abhorrent *adjective* <u>hateful</u>, abominable, disgusting, distasteful, hated, horrid, loathsome, offensive, repulsive

abide *verb* <u>tolerate</u>, accept, bear, endure, put up with, stand, suffer

abide by *verb* <u>obey</u>, agree to, comply with, conform to, follow, observe, submit to

abiding *adjective* <u>everlasting</u>, continuing, enduring, lasting, permanent, persistent, unchanging

ability *noun* <u>skill</u>, aptitude, capability, competence, expertise, proficiency, talent

abject *adjective* **1** <u>miserable</u>, deplorable, forlorn, hopeless, pitiable, wretched **2** <u>servile</u>, cringing, degraded, fawning, grovelling, submissive

ablaze *adjective* <u>on fire</u>, aflame, alight, blazing, burning, fiery, flaming, ignited, lighted

able *adjective* <u>capable</u>, accomplished, competent, efficient, proficient, qualified, skilful

able-bodied *adjective* <u>strong</u>, fit, healthy, robust, sound, sturdy

abnormal *adjective* <u>unusual</u>, atypical, exceptional, extraordinary, irregular, odd, peculiar, strange, uncommon

abnormality noun oddity, deformity, exception, irregularity, peculiarity, singularity, strangeness

abode noun home, domicile, dwelling, habitat, habitation, house, lodging, pad (slang), quarters, residence

abolish verb do away with, annul, cancel, destroy, eliminate, end, eradicate, put an end to, quash, rescind, revoke, stamp out

abolition noun ending, cancellation, destruction, elimination, end, extermination, termination, wiping out

abominable adjective terrible, despicable, detestable, disgusting, hateful, horrible, horrid, repulsive, revolting, vile

abort verb 1 terminate (a pregnancy), miscarry 2 stop, arrest, axe (informal), call off, check, end, fail, halt, terminate

abortion noun termination, deliberate miscarriage, miscarriage

abortive adjective failed, fruitless, futile, ineffectual, miscarried, unsuccessful, useless, vain

abound verb be plentiful, flourish, proliferate, swarm, swell, teem, thrive

abounding adjective plentiful, abundant, bountiful, copious, full, profuse, prolific, rich

about preposition 1 regarding, as regards, concerning, dealing with, on, referring to, relating to 2 near, adjacent to, beside, circa (used with dates), close to, nearby

♦ adverb 3 nearly, almost, approaching, approximately, around, close to, more or less, roughly

above preposition over, beyond, exceeding, higher than, on top of, upon

abrasion noun Medical graze, chafe, scrape, scratch, scuff, surface injury

abrasive adjective 1 unpleasant, caustic, cutting, galling, grating, irritating, rough, sharp 2 rough, chafing, grating, scraping, scratchy

abreast adjective 1 alongside, beside, side by side 2 abreast of informed about, acquainted with, au courant with, au fait with, conversant with, familiar with, in the picture about, in touch with, keeping one's finger on the pulse of, knowledgeable about, up to date with, up to speed with

abridge verb shorten, abbreviate, condense, cut, decrease, reduce, summarize

abroad adverb overseas, in foreign lands, out of the country

abrupt adjective 1 sudden, precipitate, quick, surprising, unexpected 2 curt, brusque, gruff, impatient, rude, short, terse

abscond verb flee, clear out, disappear, escape, make off, run off, steal away

absence noun 1 nonattendance, absenteeism, truancy 2 lack, deficiency, need, omission, unavailability, want

absent adjective 1 missing, away, elsewhere, gone, nonexistent,

out, unavailable
2 absent-minded, blank, distracted, inattentive, oblivious, preoccupied, vacant, vague
♦ *verb* **3 absent oneself** stay away, keep away, play truant, withdraw

absent-minded *adjective* vague, distracted, dreaming, forgetful, inattentive, preoccupied, unaware

absolute *adjective* **1** total, complete, outright, perfect, pure, sheer, thorough, utter **2** supreme, full, sovereign, unbounded, unconditional, unlimited, unrestricted

absolutely *adverb* totally, completely, entirely, fully, one hundred per cent, perfectly, utterly, wholly

absolution *noun* forgiveness, deliverance, exculpation, exoneration, mercy, pardon, release

absolve *verb* forgive, deliver, exculpate, excuse, let off, pardon, release, set free

absorb *verb* **1** soak up, consume, digest, imbibe, incorporate, receive, suck up, take in **2** preoccupy, captivate, engage, engross, fascinate, rivet

absorbed *adjective* **1** preoccupied, captivated, engrossed, fascinated, immersed, involved, lost, rapt, riveted, wrapped up **2** digested, assimilated, incorporated, received, soaked up

absorbent *adjective* permeable, porous, receptive, spongy

absorbing *adjective* fascinating, captivating, engrossing, gripping, interesting, intriguing, riveting, spellbinding

absorption *noun* **1** soaking up, assimilation, consumption, digestion, incorporation, sucking up **2** concentration, fascination, immersion, intentness, involvement, preoccupation

abstain *verb* refrain, avoid, decline, deny (oneself), desist, fast, forbear, forgo, give up, keep from

abstemious *adjective* self-denying, ascetic, austere, frugal, moderate, sober, temperate

abstention *noun* refusal, abstaining, abstinence, avoidance, forbearance, refraining, self-control, self-denial, self-restraint

abstinence *noun* self-denial, abstemiousness, avoidance, forbearance, moderation, self-restraint, soberness, teetotalism, temperance

abstinent *adjective* self-denying, abstaining, abstemious, forbearing, moderate, self-controlled, sober, temperate

abstract *adjective* **1** theoretical, abstruse, general, hypothetical, indefinite, notional, recondite ♦ *noun* **2** summary, abridgment, digest, epitome, outline, précis, résumé, synopsis ♦ *verb* **3** summarize, abbreviate, abridge, condense, digest, epitomize, outline, précis, shorten **4** remove, detach, extract, isolate, separate, take away, take out, withdraw

abstraction *noun* **1** idea, concept, formula, generalization, hypothesis, notion, theorem,

theory, thought
2 absent-mindedness, absence,
dreaminess, inattention,
pensiveness, preoccupation,
remoteness, woolgathering

abstruse *adjective* obscure,
arcane, complex, deep,
enigmatic, esoteric, recondite,
unfathomable, vague

absurd *adjective* ridiculous, crazy
(*informal*), farcical, foolish,
idiotic, illogical, inane,
incongruous, irrational,
ludicrous, nonsensical,
preposterous, senseless, silly,
stupid, unreasonable

absurdity *noun* ridiculousness,
farce, folly, foolishness,
incongruity, joke, nonsense,
silliness, stupidity

abundance *noun* plenty,
affluence, bounty, copiousness,
exuberance, fullness, profusion

abundant *adjective* plentiful,
ample, bountiful, copious,
exuberant, filled, full, luxuriant,
profuse, rich, teeming

abuse *noun* **1** ill-treatment,
damage, exploitation, harm,
hurt, injury, maltreatment,
manhandling **2** insults, blame,
castigation, censure, defamation,
derision, disparagement,
invective, reproach, scolding,
vilification **3** misuse,
misapplication ♦ *verb* **4** ill-treat,
damage, exploit, harm, hurt,
injure, maltreat, misuse, take
advantage of **5** insult, castigate,
curse, defame, disparage,
malign, scold, vilify

abusive *adjective* **1** insulting,
censorious, defamatory,
disparaging, libellous, offensive,

reproachful, rude, scathing
2 harmful, brutal, cruel,
destructive, hurtful, injurious,
rough

abysmal *adjective* terrible,
appalling, awful, bad, dire,
dreadful

abyss *noun* pit, chasm, crevasse,
fissure, gorge, gulf, void

academic *adjective* **1** scholarly,
bookish, erudite, highbrow,
learned, literary, studious
2 hypothetical, abstract,
conjectural, impractical, notional,
speculative, theoretical ♦ *noun*
3 scholar, academician, don,
fellow, lecturer, master,
professor, tutor

accede *verb* **1** agree, accept,
acquiesce, admit, assent,
comply, concede, concur,
consent, endorse, grant
2 inherit, assume, attain, come
to, enter upon, succeed, succeed
to (*as heir*)

accelerate *verb* speed up,
advance, expedite, further,
hasten, hurry, quicken

acceleration *noun* speeding up,
hastening, hurrying, quickening,
stepping up (*informal*)

accent *noun* **1** pronunciation,
articulation, brogue, enunciation,
inflection, intonation,
modulation, tone **2** emphasis,
beat, cadence, force, pitch,
rhythm, stress, timbre ♦ *verb*
3 emphasize, accentuate, stress,
underline, underscore

accentuate *verb* emphasize,
accent, draw attention to,
foreground, highlight, stress,
underline, underscore

accept *verb* **1** receive, acquire,

gain, get, obtain, secure, take
2 <u>agree to</u>, admit, approve,
believe, concur with, consent to,
cooperate with, recognize

acceptable *adjective* <u>satisfactory</u>,
adequate, admissible, all right,
fair, moderate, passable, tolerable

acceptance *noun* 1 <u>accepting</u>,
acquiring, gaining, getting,
obtaining, receipt, securing,
taking 2 <u>agreement</u>,
acknowledgement, acquiescence,
admission, adoption, approval,
assent, concurrence, consent,
cooperation, recognition

accepted *adjective* <u>agreed</u>,
acknowledged, approved,
common, conventional,
customary, established, normal,
recognized, traditional

access *noun* <u>entrance</u>, admission,
admittance, approach, entry,
passage, path, road

accessibility *noun* 1 <u>handiness</u>,
availability, nearness, possibility,
readiness 2 <u>approachability</u>,
affability, cordiality, friendliness,
informality 3 <u>openness</u>,
susceptibility

accessible *adjective* 1 <u>handy</u>,
achievable, at hand, attainable,
available, near, nearby,
obtainable, reachable
2 <u>approachable</u>, affable,
available, cordial, friendly,
informal 3 <u>open</u>, exposed, liable,
susceptible, vulnerable,
wide-open

accessory *noun* 1 <u>addition</u>,
accompaniment, adjunct,
adornment, appendage,
attachment, decoration, extra,
supplement, trimming
2 <u>accomplice</u>, abettor, assistant,

associate (*in crime*), colleague,
confederate, helper, partner

accident *noun* 1 <u>misfortune</u>,
calamity, collision, crash,
disaster, misadventure, mishap
2 <u>chance</u>, fate, fluke, fortuity,
fortune, hazard, luck

accidental *adjective*
<u>unintentional</u>, casual, chance,
fortuitous, haphazard,
inadvertent, incidental, random,
unexpected, unforeseen,
unlooked-for, unplanned

accidentally *adverb*
<u>unintentionally</u>, by accident, by
chance, fortuitously,
haphazardly, inadvertently,
incidentally, randomly,
unwittingly

acclaim *verb* 1 <u>praise</u>, applaud,
approve, celebrate, cheer, clap,
commend, exalt, hail, honour,
salute ♦ *noun* 2 <u>praise</u>,
acclamation, applause, approval,
celebration, commendation,
honour, kudos

acclamation *noun* <u>praise</u>,
acclaim, adulation, approval,
ovation, plaudit, tribute

acclimatization *noun*
<u>adaptation</u>, adjustment,
habituation, inurement,
naturalization

acclimatize *verb* <u>adapt</u>,
accommodate, accustom, adjust,
get used to, habituate, inure,
naturalize

accolade *noun* <u>praise</u>, acclaim,
applause, approval,
commendation, compliment,
ovation, recognition, tribute

accommodate *verb* 1 <u>house</u>,
cater for, entertain, lodge, put
up, shelter 2 <u>help</u>, aid, assist,

oblige, serve **3** <u>adapt</u>, adjust, comply, conform, fit, harmonize, modify, reconcile, settle

accommodating *adjective* <u>helpful</u>, considerate, cooperative, friendly, hospitable, kind, obliging, polite, unselfish, willing

accommodation *noun* <u>housing</u>, board, digs (*Brit. informal*), house, lodging(s), quarters, shelter

accompaniment *noun* **1** <u>supplement</u>, accessory, companion, complement **2** <u>backing music</u>, backing

accompany *verb* **1** <u>go with</u>, attend, chaperon, conduct, convoy, escort, hold (someone's) hand **2** <u>occur with</u>, belong to, come with, follow, go together with, supplement

accompanying *adjective* <u>additional</u>, associated, attached, attendant, complementary, related, supplementary

accomplice *noun* <u>helper</u>, abettor, accessory, ally, assistant, associate, collaborator, colleague, henchman, partner

accomplish *verb* <u>do</u>, achieve, attain, bring about, carry out, complete, effect, execute, finish, fulfil, manage, perform, produce

accomplished *adjective* <u>skilled</u>, expert, gifted, masterly, polished, practised, proficient, talented

accomplishment *noun* **1** <u>completion</u>, bringing about, carrying out, conclusion, execution, finishing, fulfilment, performance **2** <u>achievement</u>, act, coup, deed, exploit, feat, stroke, triumph

accord *noun* **1** <u>agreement</u>, conformity, correspondence, harmony, rapport, sympathy, unison ♦ *verb* **2** <u>fit</u>, agree, conform, correspond, harmonize, match, suit, tally

accordingly *adverb* **1** <u>appropriately</u>, correspondingly, fitly, properly, suitably **2** <u>consequently</u>, as a result, ergo, hence, in consequence, so, therefore, thus

according to *adverb* **1** <u>as stated by</u>, as believed by, as maintained by, in the light of, on the authority of, on the report of **2** <u>in keeping with</u>, after, after the manner of, consistent with, in accordance with, in compliance with, in line with, in the manner of

accost *verb* <u>approach</u>, buttonhole, confront, greet, hail

account *noun* **1** <u>description</u>, explanation, narrative, report, statement, story, tale, version **2** *Commerce* <u>statement</u>, balance, bill, books, charge, invoice, reckoning, register, score, tally **3** <u>importance</u>, consequence, honour, note, significance, standing, value, worth ♦ *verb* **4** <u>consider</u>, count, estimate, judge, rate, reckon, regard, think, value

accountability *noun* <u>responsibility</u>, answerability, chargeability, culpability, liability

accountable *adjective* <u>responsible</u>, amenable, answerable, charged with, liable, obligated, obliged

accountant *noun* <u>auditor</u>, bean counter (*informal*), book-keeper

account for verb explain, answer for, clarify, clear up, elucidate, illuminate, justify, rationalize

accredited adjective authorized, appointed, certified, empowered, endorsed, guaranteed, licensed, official, recognized

accrue verb increase, accumulate, amass, arise, be added, build up, collect, enlarge, flow, follow, grow

accumulate verb collect, accrue, amass, build up, gather, hoard, increase, pile up, store

accumulation noun collection, build-up, gathering, heap, hoard, increase, mass, pile, stack, stock, stockpile, store

accuracy noun exactness, accurateness, authenticity, carefulness, closeness, correctness, fidelity, precision, strictness, truthfulness, veracity

accurate adjective exact, authentic, close, correct, faithful, precise, scrupulous, spot-on (Brit. informal), strict, true, unerring

accurately adverb exactly, authentically, closely, correctly, faithfully, precisely, scrupulously, strictly, to the letter, truly, unerringly

accursed adjective 1 cursed, bewitched, condemned, damned, doomed, hopeless, ill-fated, ill-omened, jinxed, unfortunate, unlucky, wretched 2 hateful, abominable, despicable, detestable, execrable, hellish, horrible

accusation noun charge, allegation, complaint, denunciation, incrimination, indictment, recrimination

accuse verb charge, blame, censure, denounce, impeach, impute, incriminate, indict

accustom verb adapt, acclimatize, acquaint, discipline, exercise, familiarize, train

accustomed adjective 1 usual, common, conventional, customary, established, everyday, expected, habitual, normal, ordinary, regular, traditional 2 used, acclimatized, acquainted, adapted, familiar, familiarized, given to, in the habit of, trained

ace noun 1 Cards, dice, etc. one, single point 2 Informal expert, champion, dab hand (Brit. informal), master, star, virtuoso, wizard (informal) ♦ adjective 3 Informal excellent, awesome (slang), brilliant, fine, great, outstanding, superb

ache verb 1 hurt, pain, pound, smart, suffer, throb, twinge ♦ noun 2 pain, hurt, pang, pounding, soreness, suffering, throbbing

achieve verb attain, accomplish, acquire, bring about, carry out, complete, do, execute, fulfil, gain, get, obtain, perform

achievement noun accomplishment, act, deed, effort, exploit, feat, feather in one's cap, stroke

acid adjective 1 sour, acerbic, acrid, pungent, tart, vinegary 2 sharp, biting, bitter, caustic, cutting, harsh, trenchant, vitriolic

acidity noun 1 sourness, acerbity, pungency, tartness 2 sharpness, bitterness, harshness

acknowledge verb 1 <u>accept</u>, admit, allow, concede, confess, declare, grant, own, profess, recognize, yield 2 <u>greet</u>, address, hail, notice, recognize, salute 3 <u>reply to</u>, answer, notice, react to, recognize, respond to, return

acknowledged adjective <u>accepted</u>, accredited, approved, confessed, declared, professed, recognized, returned

acknowledgment noun 1 <u>acceptance</u>, admission, allowing, confession, declaration, profession, realization, yielding 2 <u>greeting</u>, addressing, hail, hailing, notice, recognition, salutation, salute 3 <u>appreciation</u>, answer, credit, gratitude, reaction, recognition, reply, response, return, thanks

acquaint verb <u>tell</u>, disclose, divulge, enlighten, familiarize, inform, let (someone) know, notify, reveal

acquaintance noun 1 <u>associate</u>, colleague, contact 2 <u>knowledge</u>, awareness, experience, familiarity, fellowship, relationship, understanding

acquainted with adjective <u>familiar with</u>, alive to, apprised of, au fait with, aware of, conscious of, experienced in, informed of, knowledgeable about, versed in

acquiesce verb <u>agree</u>, accede, accept, allow, approve, assent, comply, concur, conform, consent, give in, go along with, submit, yield

acquiescence noun <u>agreement</u>, acceptance, approval, assent, compliance, conformity,

consent, giving in, obedience, submission, yielding

acquire verb <u>get</u>, amass, attain, buy, collect, earn, gain, gather, obtain, receive, secure, win

acquisition noun 1 <u>possession</u>, buy, gain, prize, property, purchase 2 <u>acquiring</u>, attainment, gaining, procurement

acquisitive adjective <u>greedy</u>, avaricious, avid, covetous, grabbing, grasping, predatory, rapacious

acquit verb 1 <u>clear</u>, discharge, free, liberate, release, vindicate 2 <u>behave</u>, bear, comport, conduct, perform

acquittal noun <u>clearance</u>, absolution, deliverance, discharge, exoneration, liberation, release, relief, vindication

acrid adjective <u>pungent</u>, bitter, caustic, harsh, sharp, vitriolic

acrimonious adjective <u>bitter</u>, caustic, irascible, petulant, rancorous, spiteful, splenetic, testy

acrimony noun <u>bitterness</u>, harshness, ill will, irascibility, rancour, virulence

act noun 1 <u>deed</u>, accomplishment, achievement, action, exploit, feat, performance, undertaking 2 <u>law</u>, bill, decree, edict, enactment, measure, ordinance, resolution, statute 3 <u>performance</u>, routine, show, sketch, turn 4 <u>pretence</u>, affectation, attitude, front, performance, pose, posture, show ♦ verb 5 <u>do</u>, carry out, enact, execute, function, operate, perform, take effect,

work **6** <u>perform</u>, act out,
impersonate, mimic, play, play
or take the part of, portray,
represent

act for verb <u>stand in for</u>, cover
for, deputize for, fill in for,
replace, represent, substitute for,
take the place of

acting noun **1** <u>performance</u>,
characterization, impersonation,
performing, playing, portrayal,
stagecraft, theatre ♦ adjective
2 <u>temporary</u>, interim, pro tem,
provisional, substitute, surrogate

action noun **1** <u>deed</u>,
accomplishment, achievement,
act, exploit, feat, performance
2 <u>lawsuit</u>, case, litigation,
proceeding, prosecution, suit
3 <u>energy</u>, activity, force,
liveliness, spirit, vigour, vim,
vitality **4** <u>movement</u>, activity,
functioning, motion, operation,
process, working **5** <u>battle</u>, clash,
combat, conflict, contest,
encounter, engagement, fight,
skirmish, sortie

activate verb <u>start</u>, arouse,
energize, galvanize, initiate,
mobilize, move, rouse, set in
motion, stir

active adjective **1** <u>busy</u>, bustling,
hard-working, involved,
occupied, on the go (informal),
on the move, strenuous
2 <u>energetic</u>, alert, animated,
industrious, lively, quick,
sprightly, spry, vigorous **3** <u>in
operation</u>, acting, at work,
effectual, in action, in force,
operative, working

activist noun <u>militant</u>, organizer,
partisan

activity noun **1** <u>action</u>,

animation, bustle, exercise,
exertion, hustle, labour, motion,
movement **2** <u>pursuit</u>, hobby,
interest, pastime, project, scheme

actor noun <u>performer</u>, actress,
luvvie (informal), player, Thespian

actress noun <u>performer</u>, actor,
leading lady, player, starlet,
Thespian

actual adjective <u>definite</u>, concrete,
factual, physical, positive, real,
substantial, tangible

actually adverb <u>really</u>, as a
matter of fact, indeed, in fact, in
point of fact, in reality, in truth,
literally, truly

acumen noun <u>judgment</u>,
astuteness, cleverness, ingenuity,
insight, intelligence, perspicacity,
shrewdness

acute adjective **1** <u>serious</u>, critical,
crucial, dangerous, grave,
important, severe, urgent
2 <u>sharp</u>, excruciating, fierce,
intense, piercing, powerful,
severe, shooting, violent
3 <u>perceptive</u>, astute, clever,
insightful, keen, observant,
sensitive, sharp, smart

acuteness noun **1** <u>seriousness</u>,
gravity, importance, severity,
urgency **2** <u>perceptiveness</u>,
astuteness, cleverness,
discrimination, insight,
perspicacity, sharpness

adamant adjective <u>determined</u>,
firm, fixed, obdurate, resolute,
stubborn, unbending,
uncompromising

adapt verb <u>adjust</u>, acclimatize,
accommodate, alter, change,
conform, convert, modify,
remodel, tailor

adaptability noun flexibility, changeability, resilience, versatility

adaptable adjective flexible, adjustable, changeable, compliant, easy-going, plastic, pliant, resilient, versatile

adaptation noun
1 acclimatization, familiarization, naturalization 2 conversion, adjustment, alteration, change, modification, transformation, variation, version

add verb 1 count up, add up, compute, reckon, total, tot up 2 include, adjoin, affix, append, attach, augment, supplement

addendum noun addition, appendage, appendix, attachment, extension, extra, postscript, supplement

addict noun 1 junkie (informal), fiend (informal), freak (informal) 2 fan, adherent, buff (informal), devotee, enthusiast, follower, nut (slang)

addicted adjective hooked (slang), absorbed, accustomed, dedicated, dependent, devoted, habituated

addiction noun dependence, craving, enslavement, habit, obsession

addition noun 1 inclusion, adding, amplification, attachment, augmentation, enlargement, extension, increasing 2 extra, addendum, additive, appendage, appendix, extension, gain, increase, increment, supplement 3 counting up, adding up, computation, totalling, totting up 4 in addition (to) as well (as),

additionally, also, besides, into the bargain, moreover, over and above, to boot, too

additional adjective extra, added, fresh, further, new, other, spare, supplementary

address noun 1 location, abode, dwelling, home, house, residence, situation, whereabouts 2 speech, discourse, dissertation, lecture, oration, sermon, talk ♦ verb 3 speak to, approach, greet, hail, talk to 4 address (oneself) to concentrate on, apply (oneself) to, attend to, devote (oneself) to, engage in, focus on, take care of

add up verb count up, add, compute, count, reckon, total, tot up

adept adjective 1 skilful, able, accomplished, adroit, expert, practised, proficient, skilled, versed ♦ noun 2 expert, dab hand (Brit. informal), genius, hotshot (informal), master

adequacy noun sufficiency, capability, competence, fairness, suitability, tolerability

adequate adjective enough, competent, fair, satisfactory, sufficient, tolerable, up to scratch (informal)

adhere verb stick, attach, cleave, cling, fasten, fix, glue, hold fast, paste

adherent noun supporter, admirer, devotee, disciple, fan, follower, upholder

adhesive adjective 1 sticky, clinging, cohesive, gluey, glutinous, tenacious ♦ noun 2 glue, cement, gum, paste

adieu noun goodbye, farewell, leave-taking, parting, valediction

adjacent adjective next, adjoining, beside, bordering, cheek by jowl, close, near, neighbouring, next door, touching

adjoin verb connect, border, join, link, touch

adjoining adjective connecting, abutting, adjacent, bordering, neighbouring, next door, touching

adjourn verb postpone, defer, delay, discontinue, interrupt, put off, suspend

adjournment noun postponement, delay, discontinuation, interruption, putting off, recess, suspension

adjudicate verb judge, adjudge, arbitrate, decide, determine, mediate, referee, settle, umpire

adjudication noun judgment, arbitration, conclusion, decision, finding, pronouncement, ruling, settlement, verdict

adjust verb alter, accustom, adapt, make conform, modify

adjustable adjective alterable, adaptable, flexible, malleable, modifiable, movable

adjustment noun 1 alteration, adaptation, modification, redress, regulation, tuning 2 acclimatization, orientation, settling in

ad-lib verb improvise, busk, extemporize, make up, speak off the cuff, wing it (informal)

administer verb 1 manage, conduct, control, direct, govern, handle, oversee, run, supervise

2 give, apply, dispense, impose, mete out, perform, provide

administration noun management, application, conduct, control, direction, government, running, supervision

administrative adjective managerial, directorial, executive, governmental, organizational, regulatory, supervisory

administrator noun manager, bureaucrat, executive, official, organizer, supervisor

admirable adjective excellent, commendable, exquisite, fine, laudable, praiseworthy, wonderful, worthy

admiration noun regard, amazement, appreciation, approval, esteem, praise, respect, wonder

admire verb 1 respect, appreciate, approve, esteem, look up to, praise, prize, think highly of, value 2 marvel at, appreciate, delight in, take pleasure in, wonder at

admirer noun 1 suitor, beau, boyfriend, lover, sweetheart, wooer 2 fan, devotee, disciple, enthusiast, follower, partisan, supporter

admissible adjective permissible, acceptable, allowable, passable, tolerable

admission noun 1 entrance, acceptance, access, admittance, entrée, entry, initiation, introduction 2 confession, acknowledgment, allowance, declaration, disclosure, divulgence, revelation

admit verb 1 <u>confess</u>, acknowledge, declare, disclose, divulge, own, reveal 2 <u>allow</u>, agree, grant, let, permit, recognize 3 <u>let in</u>, accept, allow, give access, initiate, introduce, receive, take in

admonish verb <u>reprimand</u>, berate, chide, rebuke, scold, slap on the wrist, tell off (*informal*)

adolescence noun 1 <u>youth</u>, boyhood, girlhood, minority, teens 2 <u>youthfulness</u>, childishness, immaturity

adolescent adjective 1 <u>young</u>, boyish, girlish, immature, juvenile, puerile, teenage, youthful ♦ noun 2 <u>youth</u>, juvenile, minor, teenager, youngster

adopt verb 1 <u>foster</u>, take in 2 <u>choose</u>, assume, espouse, follow, maintain, take up

adoption noun 1 <u>fostering</u>, adopting, taking in 2 <u>choice</u>, appropriation, assumption, embracing, endorsement, espousal, selection, taking up

adorable adjective <u>lovable</u>, appealing, attractive, charming, cute, dear, delightful, fetching, pleasing

adore verb <u>love</u>, admire, cherish, dote on, esteem, exalt, glorify, honour, idolize, revere, worship

adoring adjective <u>loving</u>, admiring, affectionate, devoted, doting, fond

adorn verb <u>decorate</u>, array, embellish, festoon

adornment noun <u>decoration</u>, accessory, embellishment, festoon, frill, frippery, ornament, supplement, trimming

adrift adjective 1 <u>drifting</u>, afloat, unanchored, unmoored 2 <u>aimless</u>, directionless, goalless, purposeless ♦ adverb 3 <u>wrong</u>, amiss, astray, off course

adroit adjective <u>skilful</u>, adept, clever, deft, dexterous, expert, masterful, neat, proficient, skilled

adulation noun <u>worship</u>, fawning, fulsome praise, servile flattery, sycophancy

adult noun 1 <u>grown-up</u>, grown or grown-up person (man or woman), person of mature age ♦ adjective 2 <u>fully grown</u>, full grown, fully developed, grown-up, mature, of age, ripe

advance verb 1 <u>progress</u>, come forward, go on, hasten, make inroads, proceed, speed 2 <u>benefit</u>, further, improve, prosper 3 <u>suggest</u>, offer, present, proffer, put forward, submit 4 <u>lend</u>, pay beforehand, supply on credit ♦ noun 5 <u>progress</u>, advancement, development, forward movement, headway, inroads, onward movement 6 <u>improvement</u>, breakthrough, gain, growth, progress, promotion, step 7 <u>loan</u>, credit, deposit, down payment, prepayment, retainer 8 <u>advances</u> overtures, approach, approaches, moves, proposals, proposition ♦ adjective 9 <u>prior</u>, beforehand, early, forward, in front 10 <u>in advance</u> beforehand, ahead, earlier, previously

advanced adjective <u>foremost</u>, ahead, avant-garde, forward, higher, leading, precocious, progressive

advancement noun promotion, betterment, gain, improvement, preferment, progress, rise

advantage noun benefit, ascendancy, dominance, good, help, lead, precedence, profit, superiority, sway

advantageous adjective
1 beneficial, convenient, expedient, helpful, of service, profitable, useful, valuable, worthwhile 2 superior, dominant, dominating, favourable

adventure noun escapade, enterprise, experience, exploit, incident, occurrence, undertaking, venture

adventurer noun 1 mercenary, charlatan, fortune-hunter, gambler, opportunist, rogue, speculator 2 hero, daredevil, heroine, knight-errant, traveller, voyager

adventurous adjective daring, bold, daredevil, enterprising, intrepid, reckless

adversary noun opponent, antagonist, competitor, contestant, enemy, foe, rival

adverse adjective unfavourable, contrary, detrimental, hostile, inopportune, negative, opposing

adversity noun hardship, affliction, bad luck, disaster, distress, hard times, misfortune, reverse, trouble

advert noun Brit. informal advertisement, ad (informal), announcement, blurb, commercial, notice, plug (informal), poster

advertise verb publicize, announce, inform, make known, notify, plug (informal), promote, tout

advertisement noun advert (Brit. informal), ad (informal), announcement, blurb, commercial, notice, plug (informal), poster

advice noun guidance, counsel, help, opinion, recommendation, suggestion

advisability noun wisdom, appropriateness, aptness, desirability, expediency, fitness, propriety, prudence, suitability

advisable adjective wise, appropriate, desirable, expedient, fitting, politic, prudent, recommended, seemly, sensible

advise verb 1 recommend, admonish, caution, commend, counsel, prescribe, suggest, urge 2 notify, acquaint, apprise, inform, make known, report, tell, warn

adviser noun guide, aide, confidant, consultant, counsellor, helper, mentor, right-hand man

advisory adjective advising, consultative, counselling, helping, recommending

advocate verb 1 recommend, advise, argue for, campaign for, champion, commend, encourage, promote, propose, support, uphold ♦noun 2 supporter, campaigner, champion, counsellor, defender, promoter, proponent, spokesman, upholder 3 Law lawyer, attorney, barrister, counsel, solicitor

affable adjective friendly, amiable,

amicable, approachable,
congenial, cordial, courteous,
genial, pleasant, sociable, urbane

affair noun 1 <u>event</u>, activity,
business, episode, happening,
incident, matter, occurrence
2 <u>relationship</u>, amour, intrigue,
liaison, romance

affect[1] verb 1 <u>influence</u>, act on,
alter, bear upon, change,
concern, impinge upon, relate to
2 <u>move</u>, disturb, overcome,
perturb, stir, touch, upset

affect[2] verb <u>put on</u>, adopt, aspire
to, assume, contrive, feign,
imitate, pretend, simulate

affectation noun <u>pretence</u>, act,
artificiality, assumed manners,
façade, insincerity, pose,
pretentiousness, show

affected adjective <u>pretended</u>,
artificial, contrived, feigned,
insincere, mannered, phoney or
phony (informal), put-on,
unnatural

affecting adjective <u>moving</u>,
pathetic, pitiful, poignant, sad,
touching

affection noun <u>fondness</u>,
attachment, care, feeling,
goodwill, kindness, liking, love,
tenderness, warmth

affectionate adjective <u>fond</u>,
attached, caring, devoted,
doting, friendly, kind, loving,
tender, warm-hearted

affiliate verb <u>join</u>, ally,
amalgamate, associate, band
together, combine, incorporate,
link, unite

affinity noun 1 <u>attraction</u>,
fondness, inclination, leaning,
liking, partiality, rapport,

sympathy 2 <u>similarity</u>, analogy,
closeness, connection,
correspondence, kinship,
likeness, relationship,
resemblance

affirm verb <u>declare</u>, assert, certify,
confirm, maintain, pronounce,
state, swear, testify

affirmation noun <u>declaration</u>,
assertion, certification,
confirmation, oath,
pronouncement, statement,
testimony

affirmative adjective <u>agreeing</u>,
approving, assenting,
concurring, confirming,
consenting, corroborative,
favourable, positive

afflict verb <u>torment</u>, distress,
grieve, harass, hurt, oppress,
pain, plague, trouble

affliction noun <u>suffering</u>,
adversity, curse, disease,
hardship, misfortune, ordeal,
plague, scourge, torment, trial,
trouble, woe

affluence noun <u>wealth</u>,
abundance, fortune, opulence,
plenty, prosperity, riches

affluent adjective <u>wealthy</u>, loaded
(slang), moneyed, opulent,
prosperous, rich, well-heeled
(informal), well-off, well-to-do

afford verb 1 As in **can afford**
spare, bear, manage, stand,
sustain 2 <u>give</u>, offer, produce,
provide, render, supply, yield

affordable adjective <u>inexpensive</u>,
cheap, economical, low-cost,
moderate, modest, reasonable

affront noun 1 <u>insult</u>, offence,
outrage, provocation, slap in the
face (informal), slight, slur ♦ verb

2 offend, anger, annoy, displease, insult, outrage, provoke, slight

aflame adjective burning, ablaze, alight, blazing, fiery, flaming, lit, on fire

afoot adverb going on, abroad, brewing, current, happening, in preparation, in progress, on the go (informal), up (informal)

afraid adjective **1** scared, apprehensive, cowardly, faint-hearted, fearful, frightened, nervous **2** sorry, regretful, unhappy

afresh adverb again, anew, newly, once again, once more, over again

after adverb following, afterwards, behind, below, later, subsequently, succeeding, thereafter

aftermath noun effects, aftereffects, consequences, end result, outcome, results, sequel, upshot, wake

again adverb **1** once more, afresh, anew, another time **2** also, besides, furthermore, in addition, moreover

against preposition **1** beside, abutting, facing, in contact with, on, opposite to, touching, upon **2** opposed to, anti (informal), averse to, hostile to, in defiance of, in opposition to, resisting, versus **3** in preparation for, in anticipation of, in expectation of, in provision for

age noun **1** time, date, day(s), duration, epoch, era, generation, lifetime, period, span **2** old age, advancing years, decline (of life), majority, maturity, senescence,

senility, seniority ♦ verb **3** grow old, decline, deteriorate, mature, mellow, ripen

aged adjective old, ancient, antiquated, antique, elderly, getting on, grey

agency noun **1** business, bureau, department, office, organization **2** Old-fashioned medium, activity, means, mechanism

agenda noun list, calendar, diary, plan, programme, schedule, timetable

agent noun **1** representative, envoy, go-between, negotiator, rep (informal), surrogate **2** worker, author, doer, mover, operator, performer **3** force, agency, cause, instrument, means, power, vehicle

aggravate verb **1** make worse, exacerbate, exaggerate, increase, inflame, intensify, magnify, worsen **2** Informal annoy, bother, get on one's nerves (informal), irritate, nettle, provoke

aggravation noun **1** worsening, exacerbation, exaggeration, heightening, increase, inflaming, intensification, magnification **2** Informal annoyance, exasperation, gall, grief (informal), hassle (informal), irritation, provocation

aggregate noun **1** total, accumulation, amount, body, bulk, collection, combination, mass, pile, sum, whole ♦ adjective **2** total, accumulated, collected, combined, composite, cumulative, mixed ♦ verb **3** combine, accumulate, amass, assemble, collect, heap, mix, pile

aggression noun **1** hostility,

antagonism, belligerence, destructiveness, pugnacity
2 attack, assault, injury, invasion, offensive, onslaught, raid

aggressive *adjective* **1** hostile, belligerent, destructive, offensive, pugnacious, quarrelsome **2** forceful, assertive, bold, dynamic, energetic, enterprising, militant, pushy (*informal*), vigorous

aggressor *noun* attacker, assailant, assaulter, invader

aggrieved *adjective* hurt, afflicted, distressed, disturbed, harmed, injured, unhappy, wronged

aghast *adjective* horrified, amazed, appalled, astonished, astounded, awestruck, confounded, shocked, startled, stunned

agile *adjective* **1** nimble, active, brisk, lithe, quick, sprightly, spry, supple, swift **2** acute, alert, bright (*informal*), clever, lively, quick-witted, sharp

agility *noun* nimbleness, litheness, liveliness, quickness, suppleness, swiftness

agitate *verb* **1** upset, disconcert, distract, excite, fluster, perturb, trouble, unnerve, worry **2** stir, beat, convulse, disturb, rouse, shake, toss

agitation *noun* **1** turmoil, clamour, commotion, confusion, disturbance, excitement, ferment, trouble, upheaval **2** turbulence, convulsion, disturbance, shaking, stirring, tossing

agitator *noun* troublemaker, agent provocateur, firebrand,

instigator, rabble-rouser, revolutionary, stirrer (*informal*)

agog *adjective* eager, avid, curious, enthralled, enthusiastic, excited, expectant, impatient, in suspense

agonize *verb* suffer, be distressed, be in agony, be in anguish, go through the mill, labour, strain, struggle, worry

agony *noun* suffering, anguish, distress, misery, pain, throes, torment, torture

agree *verb* **1** consent, assent, be of the same opinion, comply, concur, see eye to eye **2** get on (together), coincide, conform, correspond, match, tally

agreeable *adjective* **1** pleasant, delightful, enjoyable, gratifying, likable *or* likeable, pleasing, satisfying, to one's taste **2** consenting, amenable, approving, complying, concurring, in accord, onside (*informal*), sympathetic, well-disposed, willing

agreement *noun* **1** assent, agreeing, compliance, concord, concurrence, consent, harmony, union, unison **2** correspondence, compatibility, conformity, congruity, consistency, similarity **3** contract, arrangement, bargain, covenant, deal (*informal*), pact, settlement, treaty, understanding

agricultural *adjective* farming, agrarian, country, rural, rustic

agriculture *noun* farming, cultivation, culture, husbandry, tillage

aground *adverb* beached, ashore, foundered, grounded, high and dry, on the rocks, stranded, stuck

ahead *adverb* **1** <u>in front</u>, at an advantage, at the head, before, in advance, in the lead, leading, to the fore, winning

aid *noun* **1** <u>help</u>, assistance, benefit, encouragement, favour, promotion, relief, service, support ◆ *verb* **2** <u>help</u>, assist, encourage, favour, promote, serve, subsidize, support, sustain

aide *noun* <u>assistant</u>, attendant, helper, right-hand man, second, supporter

ailing *adjective* <u>ill</u>, indisposed, infirm, poorly, sick, under the weather (*informal*), unwell, weak

ailment *noun* <u>illness</u>, affliction, complaint, disease, disorder, infirmity, malady, sickness

aim *verb* **1** <u>intend</u>, attempt, endeavour, mean, plan, point, propose, seek, set one's sights on, strive, try ◆ *noun* **2** <u>intention</u>, ambition, aspiration, desire, goal, objective, plan, purpose, target

aimless *adjective* <u>purposeless</u>, directionless, pointless, random, stray

air *noun* **1** <u>atmosphere</u>, heavens, sky **2** <u>wind</u>, breeze, draught, zephyr **3** <u>manner</u>, appearance, atmosphere, aura, demeanour, impression, look, mood **4** <u>tune</u>, aria, lay, melody, song ◆ *verb* **5** <u>publicize</u>, circulate, display, exhibit, express, give vent to, make known, make public, reveal, voice **6** <u>ventilate</u>, aerate, expose, freshen

airborne *adjective* <u>flying</u>, floating, gliding, hovering, in flight, in the air, on the wing

airing *noun* **1** <u>ventilation</u>, aeration, drying, freshening **2** <u>exposure</u>, circulation, display, dissemination, expression, publicity, utterance, vent

airless *adjective* <u>stuffy</u>, close, heavy, muggy, oppressive, stifling, suffocating, sultry

airs *plural noun* <u>affectation</u>, arrogance, haughtiness, hauteur, pomposity, pretensions, superciliousness, swank (*informal*)

airy *adjective* **1** <u>well-ventilated</u>, fresh, light, open, spacious, uncluttered **2** <u>light-hearted</u>, blithe, cheerful, high-spirited, jaunty, lively, sprightly

aisle *noun* <u>passageway</u>, alley, corridor, gangway, lane, passage, path

alacrity *noun* <u>eagerness</u>, alertness, enthusiasm, promptness, quickness, readiness, speed, willingness, zeal

alarm *noun* **1** <u>fear</u>, anxiety, apprehension, consternation, fright, nervousness, panic, scare, trepidation **2** <u>danger signal</u>, alarm bell, alert, bell, distress signal, hooter, siren, warning ◆ *verb* **3** <u>frighten</u>, daunt, dismay, distress, give (someone) a turn (*informal*), panic, scare, startle, unnerve

alarming *adjective* <u>frightening</u>, daunting, distressing, disturbing, scaring, shocking, startling, unnerving

alcoholic *noun* **1** <u>drunkard</u>, dipsomaniac, drinker, drunk, inebriate, tippler, toper, wino (*informal*) ◆ *adjective* **2** <u>intoxicating</u>, brewed, distilled, fermented, hard, strong

alcove noun <u>recess</u>, bay, compartment, corner, cubbyhole, cubicle, niche, nook

alert adjective 1 <u>watchful</u>, attentive, awake, circumspect, heedful, observant, on guard, on one's toes, on the lookout, vigilant, wide-awake ♦ noun 2 <u>warning</u>, alarm, signal, siren ♦ verb 3 <u>warn</u>, alarm, forewarn, inform, notify, signal

alertness noun <u>watchfulness</u>, attentiveness, heedfulness, liveliness, vigilance

alias adverb 1 <u>also known as</u>, also called, otherwise, otherwise known as ♦ noun 2 <u>pseudonym</u>, assumed name, nom de guerre, nom de plume, pen name, stage name

alibi noun <u>excuse</u>, defence, explanation, justification, plea, pretext, reason

alien adjective 1 <u>foreign</u>, exotic, incongruous, strange, unfamiliar ♦ noun 2 <u>foreigner</u>, newcomer, outsider, stranger

alienate verb <u>set against</u>, disaffect, estrange, make unfriendly, turn away

alienation noun <u>setting against</u>, disaffection, estrangement, remoteness, separation, turning away

alight[1] verb 1 <u>get off</u>, descend, disembark, dismount, get down 2 <u>land</u>, come down, come to rest, descend, light, perch, settle, touch down

alight[2] adjective 1 <u>on fire</u>, ablaze, aflame, blazing, burning, fiery, flaming, lighted, lit 2 <u>lit up</u>, bright, brilliant, illuminated, shining

align verb 1 <u>ally</u>, affiliate, agree, associate, cooperate, join, side, sympathize 2 <u>line up</u>, even up, order, range, regulate, straighten

alignment noun 1 <u>alliance</u>, affiliation, agreement, association, cooperation, sympathy, union 2 <u>lining up</u>, adjustment, arrangement, evening up, order, straightening up

alike adjective 1 <u>similar</u>, akin, analogous, corresponding, identical, of a piece, parallel, resembling, the same ♦ adverb 2 <u>similarly</u>, analogously, correspondingly, equally, evenly, identically, uniformly

alive adjective 1 <u>living</u>, animate, breathing, in the land of the living (*informal*), subsisting 2 <u>in existence</u>, active, existing, extant, functioning, in force, operative 3 <u>lively</u>, active, alert, animated, energetic, full of life, vital, vivacious

all adjective 1 <u>the whole of</u>, every bit of, the complete, the entire, the sum of, the totality of, the total of 2 <u>every</u>, each, each and every, every one of, every single 3 <u>complete</u>, entire, full, greatest, perfect, total, utter ♦ adverb 4 <u>completely</u>, altogether, entirely, fully, totally, utterly, wholly ♦ noun 5 <u>whole amount</u>, aggregate, entirety, everything, sum total, total, totality, utmost

allegation noun <u>claim</u>, accusation, affirmation, assertion, charge, declaration, statement

allege verb <u>claim</u>, affirm, assert, charge, declare, maintain, state

alleged adjective 1 <u>stated</u>,

affirmed, asserted, declared, described, designated **2** <u>supposed</u>, doubtful, dubious, ostensible, professed, purported, so-called, unproved

allegiance noun <u>loyalty</u>, constancy, devotion, faithfulness, fidelity, obedience

allegorical adjective <u>symbolic</u>, emblematic, figurative, symbolizing

allegory noun <u>symbol</u>, fable, myth, parable, story, symbolism, tale

allergic adjective <u>sensitive</u>, affected by, hypersensitive, susceptible

allergy noun <u>sensitivity</u>, antipathy, hypersensitivity, susceptibility

alleviate verb <u>ease</u>, allay, lessen, lighten, moderate, reduce, relieve, soothe

alley noun <u>passage</u>, alleyway, backstreet, lane, passageway, pathway, walk

alliance noun <u>union</u>, affiliation, agreement, association, coalition, combination, confederation, connection, federation, league, marriage, pact, partnership, treaty

allied adjective <u>united</u>, affiliated, associated, combined, connected, in league, linked, related

allocate verb <u>assign</u>, allot, allow, apportion, budget, designate, earmark, mete, set aside, share out

allocation noun <u>assignment</u>, allotment, allowance, lot, portion, quota, ration, share

allot verb <u>assign</u>, allocate, apportion, budget, designate, earmark, mete, set aside, share out

allotment noun **1** <u>plot</u>, kitchen garden, patch, tract **2** <u>assignment</u>, allocation, allowance, grant, portion, quota, ration, share, stint

all-out adjective <u>total</u>, complete, exhaustive, full, full-scale, maximum, thoroughgoing, undivided, unremitting, unrestrained

allow verb **1** <u>permit</u>, approve, authorize, enable, endure, let, sanction, stand, suffer, tolerate **2** <u>give</u>, allocate, allot, assign, grant, provide, set aside, spare **3** <u>acknowledge</u>, admit, concede, confess, grant, own

allowable adjective <u>permissible</u>, acceptable, admissible, all right, appropriate, suitable, tolerable

allowance noun **1** <u>portion</u>, allocation, amount, grant, lot, quota, ration, share, stint **2** <u>concession</u>, deduction, discount, rebate, reduction

allow for verb <u>take into account</u>, consider, make allowances for, make concessions for, make provision for, plan for, provide for, take into consideration

alloy noun **1** <u>mixture</u>, admixture, amalgam, blend, combination, composite, compound, hybrid ♦ verb **2** <u>mix</u>, amalgamate, blend, combine, compound, fuse

all right adjective **1** <u>satisfactory</u>, acceptable, adequate, average, fair, O.K. or okay (informal), standard, up to scratch (informal) **2** <u>O.K. or okay</u> (informal), healthy, safe, sound, unharmed, uninjured, well, whole

allude verb refer, hint, imply, intimate, mention, suggest, touch upon

allure noun 1 attractiveness, appeal, attraction, charm, enchantment, enticement, glamour, lure, persuasion, seductiveness, temptation ♦ verb 2 attract, captivate, charm, enchant, entice, lure, persuade, seduce, tempt, win over

alluring adjective attractive, beguiling, captivating, come-hither, fetching, glamorous, seductive, tempting

allusion noun reference, casual remark, hint, implication, innuendo, insinuation, intimation, mention, suggestion

ally noun 1 partner, accomplice, associate, collaborator, colleague, friend, helper ♦ verb 2 unite, associate, collaborate, combine, join, join forces, unify

almighty adjective 1 all-powerful, absolute, invincible, omnipotent, supreme, unlimited 2 Informal great, enormous, excessive, intense, loud, severe, terrible

almost adverb nearly, about, approximately, close to, just about, not quite, on the brink of, practically, virtually

alone adjective by oneself, apart, detached, isolated, lonely, only, on one's tod (slang), separate, single, solitary, unaccompanied

aloof adjective distant, detached, haughty, remote, standoffish, supercilious, unapproachable, unfriendly

aloud adverb out loud, audibly, clearly, distinctly, intelligibly, plainly

already adverb before now, at present, before, by now, by then, even now, heretofore, just now, previously

also adverb too, additionally, and, as well, besides, further, furthermore, in addition, into the bargain, moreover, to boot

alter verb change, adapt, adjust, amend, convert, modify, reform, revise, transform, turn, vary

alteration noun change, adaptation, adjustment, amendment, conversion, difference, modification, reformation, revision, transformation, variation

alternate verb 1 change, act reciprocally, fluctuate, interchange, oscillate, rotate, substitute, take turns ♦ adjective 2 every other, alternating, every second, interchanging, rotating

alternative noun 1 choice, option, other (of two), preference, recourse, selection, substitute ♦ adjective 2 different, alternate, another, other, second, substitute

alternatively adverb or, as an alternative, if not, instead, on the other hand, otherwise

although conjunction though, albeit, despite the fact that, even if, even though, notwithstanding, while

altogether adverb 1 completely, absolutely, fully, perfectly, quite, thoroughly, totally, utterly, wholly 2 on the whole, all in all, all things considered, as a whole,

collectively, generally, in general
3 in total, all told, everything
included, in all, in sum, taken
together

altruistic *adjective* selfless,
benevolent, charitable, generous,
humanitarian, philanthropic,
public-spirited, self-sacrificing,
unselfish

always *adverb* continually,
consistently, constantly,
eternally, evermore, every time,
forever, invariably, perpetually,
repeatedly, without exception

amalgamate *verb* combine, ally,
blend, fuse, incorporate,
integrate, merge, mingle, unite

amalgamation *noun*
combination, blend, coalition,
compound, fusion, joining,
merger, mixture, union

amass *verb* collect, accumulate,
assemble, compile, gather,
hoard, pile up

amateur *noun* nonprofessional,
dabbler, dilettante, layman

amateurish *adjective*
unprofessional, amateur,
bungling, clumsy, crude,
inexpert, unaccomplished

amaze *verb* astonish, alarm,
astound, bewilder, dumbfound,
shock, stagger, startle, stun,
surprise

amazement *noun* astonishment,
admiration, bewilderment,
confusion, perplexity, shock,
surprise, wonder

amazing *adjective* astonishing,
astounding, breathtaking,
eye-opening, overwhelming,
staggering, startling, stunning,
surprising

ambassador *noun*
representative, agent, consul,
deputy, diplomat, envoy, legate,
minister

ambiguity *noun* vagueness,
doubt, dubiousness,
equivocation, obscurity,
uncertainty

ambiguous *adjective* unclear,
dubious, enigmatic, equivocal,
inconclusive, indefinite,
indeterminate, obscure, vague

ambition *noun* **1** enterprise,
aspiration, desire, drive,
eagerness, longing, striving,
yearning, zeal **2** goal, aim,
aspiration, desire, dream, hope,
intent, objective, purpose, wish

ambitious *adjective* enterprising,
aspiring, avid, eager, hopeful,
intent, purposeful, striving,
zealous

ambivalent *adjective* undecided,
contradictory, doubtful,
equivocal, in two minds,
uncertain, wavering

amble *verb* stroll, dawdle,
meander, mosey (*informal*),
ramble, saunter, walk, wander

ambush *noun* **1** trap, lying in
wait, waylaying ◆ *verb* **2** trap,
attack, bushwhack (*U.S.*),
ensnare, surprise, waylay

amenable *adjective* receptive,
able to be influenced,
acquiescent, agreeable, open,
persuadable, responsive,
susceptible

amend *verb* change, alter,
correct, fix, improve, mend,
modify, reform, remedy, repair,
revise

amendment *noun* **1** change,

alteration, correction,
emendation, improvement,
modification, reform, remedy,
repair, revision **2** alteration,
addendum, addition,
attachment, clarification

amends plural noun As in **make
amends for** compensation,
atonement, recompense, redress,
reparation, restitution, satisfaction

amenity noun facility, advantage,
comfort, convenience, service

amiable adjective pleasant,
affable, agreeable, charming,
congenial, engaging, friendly,
genial, likable or likeable, lovable

amicable adjective friendly,
amiable, civil, cordial, courteous,
harmonious, neighbourly,
peaceful, sociable

amid, amidst preposition in the
middle of, among, amongst, in
the midst of, in the thick of,
surrounded by

amiss adverb **1** wrongly,
erroneously, improperly,
inappropriately, incorrectly,
mistakenly, unsuitably **2** As in
take (something) amiss as an
insult, as offensive, out of turn,
wrongly ♦ adjective **3** wrong,
awry, faulty, incorrect, mistaken,
untoward

ammunition noun munitions,
armaments, explosives, powder,
rounds, shells, shot

amnesty noun general pardon,
absolution, dispensation,
forgiveness, immunity, remission
(of penalty), reprieve

amok, amuck adverb As in **run
amok** madly, berserk,
destructively, ferociously, in a
frenzy, murderously, savagely,

uncontrollably, violently, wildly

among, amongst preposition
1 in the midst of, amid, amidst,
in the middle of, in the thick of,
surrounded by, together with,
with **2** in the group of, in the
class of, in the company of, in
the number of, out of **3** to each
of, between

amorous adjective loving, erotic,
impassioned, in love, lustful,
passionate, tender

amount noun quantity, expanse,
extent, magnitude, mass,
measure, number, supply,
volume

amount to verb add up to,
become, come to, develop into,
equal, mean, total

ample adjective plenty, abundant,
bountiful, copious, expansive,
extensive, full, generous, lavish,
plentiful, profuse

amplify verb **1** explain, develop,
elaborate, enlarge, expand, flesh
out, go into detail **2** increase,
enlarge, expand, extend,
heighten, intensify, magnify,
strengthen, widen

amply adverb fully, abundantly,
completely, copiously,
generously, profusely, richly

amputate verb cut off, curtail,
lop, remove, separate, sever,
truncate

amuck see AMOK

amuse verb entertain, charm,
cheer, delight, interest, please,
tickle

amusement noun
1 entertainment, cheer,
enjoyment, fun, merriment,
mirth, pleasure **2** entertainment,

diversion, game, hobby, joke, pastime, recreation, sport

amusing adjective funny, comical, droll, enjoyable, entertaining, humorous, interesting, witty

anaemic adjective pale, ashen, colourless, feeble, pallid, sickly, wan, weak

anaesthetic noun 1 painkiller, analgesic, anodyne, narcotic, opiate, sedative, soporific ♦ adjective 2 pain-killing, analgesic, anodyne, deadening, dulling, numbing, sedative, soporific

analogy noun similarity, comparison, correlation, correspondence, likeness, parallel, relation, resemblance

analyse verb 1 examine, evaluate, investigate, research, test, work over 2 break down, dissect, divide, resolve, separate, think through

analysis noun examination, breakdown, dissection, inquiry, investigation, scrutiny, sifting, test

analytic, analytical adjective rational, inquiring, inquisitive, investigative, logical, organized, problem-solving, systematic

anarchic adjective lawless, chaotic, disorganized, rebellious, riotous, ungoverned

anarchist noun revolutionary, insurgent, nihilist, rebel, terrorist

anarchy noun lawlessness, chaos, confusion, disorder, disorganization, revolution, riot

anatomy noun 1 examination, analysis, dissection, division, inquiry, investigation, study

2 structure, build, composition, frame, framework, make-up

ancestor noun forefather, forebear, forerunner, precursor, predecessor

ancient adjective old, aged, antique, archaic, old-fashioned, primeval, primordial, timeworn

ancillary adjective supplementary, additional, auxiliary, extra, secondary, subordinate, subsidiary, supporting

and conjunction also, along with, as well as, furthermore, in addition to, including, moreover, plus, together with

anecdote noun story, reminiscence, short story, sketch, tale, urban legend, yarn

angel noun 1 divine messenger, archangel, cherub, seraph 2 Informal dear, beauty, darling, gem, jewel, paragon, saint, treasure

angelic adjective 1 pure, adorable, beautiful, entrancing, lovely, saintly, virtuous 2 heavenly, celestial, cherubic, ethereal, seraphic

anger noun 1 rage, annoyance, displeasure, exasperation, fury, ire, outrage, resentment, temper, wrath ♦ verb 2 madden, annoy, displease, enrage, exasperate, gall, incense, infuriate, outrage, rile, vex

angle¹ noun 1 intersection, bend, corner, crook, edge, elbow, nook, point 2 point of view, approach, aspect, outlook, perspective, position, side, slant, standpoint, viewpoint

angle² verb fish, cast

angry adjective <u>furious</u>, annoyed, cross, displeased, enraged, exasperated, incensed, infuriated, irate, mad (*informal*), outraged, resentful

angst noun <u>anxiety</u>, apprehension, unease, worry

anguish noun <u>suffering</u>, agony, distress, grief, heartache, misery, pain, sorrow, torment, woe

animal noun 1 <u>creature</u>, beast, brute 2 *Applied to a person* brute, barbarian, beast, monster, savage, wild man ♦ adjective 3 <u>physical</u>, bestial, bodily, brutish, carnal, gross, sensual

animate verb 1 <u>enliven</u>, energize, excite, fire, inspire, invigorate, kindle, move, stimulate ♦ adjective 2 <u>living</u>, alive, alive and kicking, breathing, live, moving

animated adjective <u>lively</u>, ebullient, energetic, enthusiastic, excited, passionate, spirited, vivacious

animation noun <u>liveliness</u>, ebullience, energy, enthusiasm, excitement, fervour, passion, spirit, verve, vivacity, zest

animosity noun <u>hostility</u>, acrimony, antipathy, bitterness, enmity, hatred, ill will, malevolence, malice, rancour, resentment

annals plural noun <u>records</u>, accounts, archives, chronicles, history

annex verb 1 <u>seize</u>, acquire, appropriate, conquer, occupy, take over 2 <u>join</u>, add, adjoin, attach, connect, fasten

annihilate verb <u>destroy</u>, abolish, eradicate, exterminate, extinguish, obliterate, wipe out

announce verb <u>make known</u>, advertise, broadcast, declare, disclose, proclaim, report, reveal, tell

announcement noun <u>statement</u>, advertisement, broadcast, bulletin, communiqué, declaration, proclamation, report, revelation

announcer noun <u>presenter</u>, broadcaster, commentator, master of ceremonies, newscaster, newsreader, reporter

annoy verb <u>irritate</u>, anger, bother, displease, disturb, exasperate, get on one's nerves (*informal*), hassle (*informal*), madden, molest, pester, plague, trouble, vex

annoyance noun 1 <u>irritation</u>, anger, bother, hassle (*informal*), nuisance, trouble 2 <u>nuisance</u>, bore, bother, drag (*informal*), pain (*informal*)

annoying adjective <u>irritating</u>, disturbing, exasperating, maddening, troublesome

annual adjective <u>yearly</u>, once a year, yearlong

annually adverb <u>yearly</u>, by the year, once a year, per annum, per year

annul verb <u>invalidate</u>, abolish, cancel, declare or render null and void, negate, nullify, repeal, retract

anoint verb <u>consecrate</u>, bless, hallow, sanctify

anomalous adjective <u>unusual</u>, abnormal, eccentric, exceptional, incongruous, inconsistent, irregular, odd, peculiar

anomaly noun <u>irregularity</u>, abnormality, eccentricity, exception, incongruity, inconsistency, oddity, peculiarity

anonymous adjective <u>unnamed</u>, incognito, nameless, unacknowledged, uncredited, unidentified, unknown, unsigned

answer verb 1 <u>reply</u>, explain, react, resolve, respond, retort, return, solve ♦ noun 2 <u>reply</u>, comeback, defence, explanation, reaction, rejoinder, response, retort, return, riposte, solution

answerable adjective, usually with **for** or **to** <u>responsible</u>, accountable, amenable, chargeable, liable, subject, to blame

answer for verb <u>be responsible for</u>, be accountable for, be answerable for, be chargeable for, be liable for, be to blame for

antagonism noun <u>hostility</u>, antipathy, conflict, discord, dissension, friction, opposition, rivalry

antagonist noun <u>opponent</u>, adversary, competitor, contender, enemy, foe, rival

antagonistic adjective <u>hostile</u>, at odds, at variance, conflicting, incompatible, in dispute, opposed, unfriendly

antagonize verb <u>annoy</u>, anger, get on one's nerves (informal), hassle (informal), irritate, offend

anthem noun 1 <u>hymn</u>, canticle, carol, chant, chorale, psalm 2 <u>song of praise</u>, paean

anthology noun <u>collection</u>, compendium, compilation,

miscellany, selection, treasury

anticipate verb <u>expect</u>, await, foresee, foretell, hope for, look forward to, predict, prepare for

anticipation noun <u>expectation</u>, expectancy, foresight, forethought, premonition, prescience

anticlimax noun <u>disappointment</u>, bathos, comedown (informal), letdown

antics plural noun <u>clowning</u>, escapades, horseplay, mischief, playfulness, pranks, tomfoolery, tricks

antidote noun <u>cure</u>, countermeasure, remedy

antipathy noun <u>hostility</u>, aversion, bad blood, dislike, enmity, hatred, ill will

antiquated adjective <u>obsolete</u>, antique, archaic, dated, old-fashioned, out-of-date, passé

antique noun 1 <u>period piece</u>, bygone, heirloom, relic ♦ adjective 2 <u>vintage</u>, antiquarian, classic, olden 3 <u>old-fashioned</u>, archaic, obsolete, outdated

antiquity noun 1 <u>old age</u>, age, ancientness, elderliness, oldness 2 <u>distant past</u>, ancient times, olden days, time immemorial

antiseptic adjective 1 <u>hygienic</u>, clean, germ-free, pure, sanitary, sterile, uncontaminated ♦ noun 2 <u>disinfectant</u>, germicide, purifier

antisocial adjective 1 <u>unsociable</u>, alienated, misanthropic, reserved, retiring, uncommunicative, unfriendly, withdrawn 2 <u>disruptive</u>, antagonistic, belligerent, disorderly, hostile, menacing, rebellious, uncooperative

antithesis noun <u>opposite</u>, contrary, contrast, converse, inverse, reverse

anxiety noun <u>uneasiness</u>, angst, apprehension, concern, foreboding, misgiving, nervousness, tension, trepidation, worry

anxious adjective **1** <u>uneasy</u>, apprehensive, concerned, fearful, in suspense, nervous, on tenterhooks, tense, troubled, worried **2** <u>eager</u>, desirous, impatient, intent, itching, keen, yearning

apart adverb **1** <u>to pieces</u>, asunder, in bits, in pieces, to bits **2** <u>separate</u>, alone, aside, away, by oneself, isolated, to one side **3** **apart from** <u>except for</u>, aside from, besides, but, excluding, not counting, other than, save

apartment noun <u>room</u>, accommodation, flat, living quarters, penthouse, quarters, rooms, suite

apathetic adjective <u>uninterested</u>, cool, indifferent, passive, phlegmatic, unconcerned

apathy noun <u>lack of interest</u>, coolness, indifference, inertia, nonchalance, passivity, torpor, unconcern

apex noun <u>highest point</u>, crest, crown, culmination, peak, pinnacle, point, summit, top

apiece adverb <u>each</u>, for each, from each, individually, respectively, to each

aplomb noun <u>self-possession</u>, calmness, composure, confidence, level-headedness,

poise, sang-froid, self-assurance, self-confidence

apocryphal adjective <u>dubious</u>, doubtful, legendary, mythical, questionable, unauthenticated, unsubstantiated

apologetic adjective <u>regretful</u>, contrite, penitent, remorseful, rueful, sorry

apologize verb <u>say sorry</u>, ask forgiveness, beg pardon, express regret

apology noun **1** <u>defence</u>, acknowledgment, confession, excuse, explanation, justification, plea **2** As in **an apology for mockery**, caricature, excuse, imitation, travesty

apostle noun **1** <u>evangelist</u>, herald, messenger, missionary, preacher **2** <u>supporter</u>, advocate, champion, pioneer, propagandist, proponent

apotheosis noun <u>deification</u>, elevation, exaltation, glorification, idealization, idolization

appal verb <u>horrify</u>, alarm, daunt, dishearten, dismay, frighten, outrage, shock, unnerve

appalling adjective <u>horrifying</u>, alarming, awful, daunting, dreadful, fearful, frightful, horrible, shocking, terrifying

apparatus noun **1** <u>equipment</u>, appliance, contraption (informal), device, gear, machinery, mechanism, tackle, tools **2** <u>organization</u>, bureaucracy, chain of command, hierarchy, network, setup (informal), structure, system

apparent adjective **1** <u>obvious</u>,

discernible, distinct, evident, manifest, marked, unmistakable, visible 2 <u>seeming</u>, ostensible, outward, superficial

apparently *adverb* <u>it appears that</u>, it seems that, on the face of it, ostensibly, outwardly, seemingly, superficially

apparition *noun* <u>ghost</u>, chimera, phantom, spectre, spirit, wraith

appeal *verb* 1 <u>plead</u>, ask, beg, call upon, entreat, pray, request 2 <u>attract</u>, allure, charm, entice, fascinate, interest, please, tempt ♦ *noun* 3 <u>plea</u>, application, entreaty, petition, prayer, request, supplication 4 <u>attraction</u>, allure, beauty, charm, fascination

appealing *adjective* <u>attractive</u>, alluring, charming, desirable, engaging, winsome

appear *verb* 1 <u>come into view</u>, be present, come out, come to light, crop up (*informal*), emerge, occur, show up (*informal*), surface, turn up 2 <u>look (like or as if)</u>, occur, seem, strike one as

appearance *noun* 1 <u>arrival</u>, coming, emergence, introduction, presence 2 <u>look</u>, demeanour, expression, figure, form, looks, manner, mien (*literary*) <u>impression</u>, front, guise, illusion, image, outward show, pretence, semblance

appease *verb* 1 <u>pacify</u>, calm, conciliate, mollify, placate, quiet, satisfy, soothe 2 <u>ease</u>, allay, alleviate, calm, relieve, soothe

appeasement *noun* 1 <u>pacification</u>, accommodation, compromise, concession, conciliation, mollification,

placation 2 <u>easing</u>, alleviation, lessening, relieving, soothing

appendage *noun* <u>attachment</u>, accessory, addition, supplement

appendix *noun* <u>supplement</u>, addendum, addition, adjunct, appendage, postscript

appetite *noun* <u>desire</u>, craving, demand, hunger, liking, longing, passion, relish, stomach, taste, yearning

appetizing *adjective* <u>delicious</u>, appealing, inviting, mouthwatering, palatable, succulent, tasty, tempting

applaud *verb* <u>clap</u>, acclaim, approve, cheer, commend, compliment, encourage, extol, praise

applause *noun* <u>ovation</u>, accolade, approval, big hand, cheers, clapping, hand, praise

appliance *noun* <u>device</u>, apparatus, gadget, implement, instrument, machine, mechanism, tool

applicable *adjective* <u>appropriate</u>, apt, fitting, pertinent, relevant, suitable, useful

applicant *noun* <u>candidate</u>, claimant, inquirer

application *noun* 1 <u>request</u>, appeal, claim, inquiry, petition, requisition 2 <u>effort</u>, commitment, dedication, diligence, hard work, industry, perseverance

apply *verb* 1 <u>request</u>, appeal, claim, inquire, petition, put in, requisition 2 <u>use</u>, bring to bear, carry out, employ, exercise, exert, implement, practise, utilize 3 <u>put on</u>, cover with, lay on, paint, place, smear, spread on **4** be relevant, be applicable, be appropriate, bear upon, be fitting, fit, pertain, refer, relate **5 apply oneself** try, be diligent, buckle down (*informal*), commit oneself, concentrate, dedicate oneself, devote oneself, persevere, work hard

appoint *verb* **1** assign, choose, commission, delegate, elect, name, nominate, select **2** decide, allot, arrange, assign, choose, designate, establish, fix, set **3** equip, fit out, furnish, provide, supply

appointed *adjective* **1** assigned, chosen, delegated, elected, named, nominated, selected **2** decided, allotted, arranged, assigned, chosen, designated, established, fixed, set **3** equipped, fitted out, furnished, provided, supplied

appointment *noun* **1** meeting, arrangement, assignation, date, engagement, interview, rendezvous **2** selection, assignment, choice, election, naming, nomination **3** job, assignment, office, place, position, post, situation **4 appointments** fittings, fixtures, furnishings, gear, outfit, paraphernalia, trappings

apportion *verb* divide, allocate, allot, assign, dispense, distribute, dole out, ration out, share

apportionment *noun* division, allocation, allotment, assignment, dispensing, distribution, doling out, rationing out, sharing

apposite *adjective* appropriate,

applicable, apt, fitting, pertinent, relevant, suitable, to the point

appraisal *noun* assessment, estimate, estimation, evaluation, judgment, opinion

appraise *verb* assess, estimate, evaluate, gauge, judge, rate, review, value

appreciable *adjective* significant, considerable, definite, discernible, evident, marked, noticeable, obvious, pronounced, substantial

appreciate *verb* **1** value, admire, enjoy, like, prize, rate highly, respect, treasure **2** be aware of, perceive, realize, recognize, sympathize with, take account of, understand **3** be grateful for, be appreciative, be indebted, be obliged, be thankful for, give thanks for **4** increase, enhance, gain, grow, improve, rise

appreciation *noun* **1** gratitude, acknowledgment, gratefulness, indebtedness, obligation, thankfulness, thanks **2** awareness, admiration, comprehension, enjoyment, perception, realization, recognition, sensitivity, sympathy, understanding **3** increase, enhancement, gain, growth, improvement, rise

appreciative *adjective* **1** grateful, beholden, indebted, obliged, thankful **2** aware, admiring, enthusiastic, respectful, responsive, sensitive, sympathetic, understanding

apprehend *verb* **1** arrest, capture, catch, nick (*slang, chiefly Brit.*), seize, take prisoner **2** understand, comprehend, conceive, get the picture, grasp, perceive, realize, recognize

apprehension noun **1** anxiety, alarm, concern, dread, fear, foreboding, suspicion, trepidation, worry **2** arrest, capture, catching, seizure, taking **3** awareness, comprehension, grasp, perception, understanding

apprehensive adjective anxious, concerned, foreboding, nervous, uneasy, worried

apprentice noun trainee, beginner, learner, novice, probationer, pupil, student

approach verb **1** move towards, come close, come near, draw near, near, reach **2** make a proposal to, appeal to, apply to, make overtures to, sound out **3** set about, begin work on, commence, embark on, enter upon, make a start, undertake ◆ noun **4** coming, advance, arrival, drawing near, nearing **5** often plural proposal, advance, appeal, application, invitation, offer, overture, proposition **6** access, avenue, entrance, passage, road, way **7** way, manner, means, method, style, technique **8** likeness, approximation, semblance

approachable adjective **1** friendly, affable, congenial, cordial, open, sociable **2** accessible, attainable, reachable

appropriate adjective **1** suitable, apt, befitting, fitting, pertinent, relevant, to the point, well-suited ◆ verb **2** seize, commandeer, confiscate, impound, take possession of, usurp **3** steal, embezzle, filch, misappropriate,

pilfer, pocket **4** set aside, allocate, allot, apportion, assign, devote, earmark

approval noun **1** consent, agreement, assent, authorization, blessing, endorsement, permission, recommendation, sanction **2** favour, acclaim, admiration, applause, appreciation, esteem, good opinion, praise, respect

approve verb **1** favour, admire, commend, have a good opinion of, like, praise, regard highly, respect **2** agree to, allow, assent to, authorize, consent to, endorse, pass, permit, recommend, sanction

approximate adjective **1** close, near **2** rough, estimated, inexact, loose ◆ verb **3** come close, approach, border on, come near, reach, resemble, touch, verge on

approximately adverb almost, about, around, circa (used with dates), close to, in the region of, just about, more or less, nearly, roughly

approximation noun guess, conjecture, estimate, estimation, guesswork, rough calculation, rough idea

apron noun pinny (informal), pinafore

apt adjective **1** inclined, disposed, given, liable, likely, of a mind, prone, ready **2** appropriate, fitting, pertinent, relevant, suitable, to the point **3** gifted, clever, quick, sharp, smart, talented

aptitude noun **1** tendency, inclination, leaning, predilection, proclivity, propensity **2** gift, ability, capability, faculty, intelligence, proficiency, talent

arable *adjective* productive, farmable, fertile, fruitful

arbiter *noun* **1** judge, adjudicator, arbitrator, referee, umpire **2** authority, controller, dictator, expert, governor, lord, master, pundit, ruler

arbitrary *adjective* random, capricious, chance, erratic, inconsistent, personal, subjective, whimsical

arbitrate *verb* settle, adjudicate, decide, determine, judge, mediate, pass judgment, referee, umpire

arbitration *noun* settlement, adjudication, decision, determination, judgment

arbitrator *noun* judge, adjudicator, arbiter, referee, umpire

arc *noun* curve, arch, bend, bow, crescent, half-moon

arcade *noun* gallery, cloister, colonnade, portico

arcane *adjective* mysterious, esoteric, hidden, occult, recondite, secret

arch[1] *noun* **1** curve, archway, dome, span, vault **2** curve, arc, bend, bow, hump, semicircle ◆ *verb* **3** curve, arc, bend, bow, bridge, span

arch[2] *adjective* playful, frolicsome, mischievous, pert, roguish, saucy, sly, waggish

archaic *adjective* **1** old, ancient, antique, bygone, olden (*archaic*), primitive **2** old-fashioned, antiquated, behind the times,

obsolete, outmoded, out of date, passé

archetypal *adjective* **1** typical, classic, ideal, model, standard **2** original, prototypic or prototypical

archetype *noun* **1** standard, model, paradigm, pattern, prime example **2** original, prototype

architect *noun* designer, master builder, planner

architecture *noun* **1** design, building, construction, planning **2** structure, construction, design, framework, make-up, style

archive *noun* **1** record office, museum, registry, repository **2** archives records, annals, chronicles, documents, papers, rolls

arctic *adjective Informal* freezing, chilly, cold, frigid, frozen, glacial, icy

Arctic *adjective* polar, far-northern, hyperborean

ardent *adjective* **1** passionate, amorous, hot-blooded, impassioned, intense, lusty **2** enthusiastic, avid, eager, keen, zealous

ardour *noun* **1** passion, fervour, intensity, spirit, vehemence, warmth **2** enthusiasm, avidity, eagerness, keenness, zeal

arduous *adjective* difficult, exhausting, fatiguing, gruelling, laborious, onerous, punishing, rigorous, strenuous, taxing, tiring

area *noun* **1** region, district, locality, neighbourhood, zone **2** part, portion, section, sector **3** field, department, domain, province, realm, sphere, territory

arena noun **1** ring, amphitheatre, bowl, enclosure, field, ground, stadium **2** sphere, area, domain, field, province, realm, sector, territory

argue verb **1** discuss, assert, claim, debate, dispute, maintain, reason, remonstrate **2** quarrel, bicker, disagree, dispute, fall out (informal), fight, squabble

argument noun **1** quarrel, clash, controversy, disagreement, dispute, feud, fight, row, squabble **2** discussion, assertion, claim, debate, dispute, plea, questioning, remonstration **3** reason, argumentation, case, defence, dialectic, ground(s), line of reasoning, logic, polemic, reasoning

argumentative adjective quarrelsome, belligerent, combative, contentious, contrary, disputatious, litigious, opinionated

arid adjective **1** dry, barren, desert, parched, sterile, torrid, waterless **2** boring, dreary, dry, dull, tedious, tiresome, uninspired, uninteresting

arise verb **1** happen, begin, emerge, ensue, follow, occur, result, start, stem **2** Old-fashioned get up, get to one's feet, go up, rise, stand up, wake up

aristocracy noun upper class, elite, gentry, nobility, patricians, peerage, ruling class

aristocrat noun noble, aristo (informal), grandee, lady, lord, patrician, peer, peeress

aristocratic noun upper-class, blue-blooded, elite, gentlemanly, lordly, noble, patrician, titled

arm¹ noun upper limb, appendage, limb

arm² verb Especially with weapons equip, accoutre, array, deck out, furnish, issue with, provide, supply

armada noun fleet, flotilla, navy, squadron

armaments plural noun weapons, ammunition, arms, guns, materiel, munitions, ordnance, weaponry

armed adjective carrying weapons, equipped, fitted out, primed, protected

armistice noun truce, ceasefire, peace, suspension of hostilities

armour noun protection, armour plate, covering, sheathing, shield

armoured adjective protected, armour-plated, bombproof, bulletproof, ironclad, mailed, steel-plated

arms plural noun **1** weapons, armaments, firearms, guns, instruments of war, ordnance, weaponry **2** heraldry, blazonry, crest, escutcheon, insignia

army noun **1** soldiers, armed force, legions, military, military force, soldiery, troops **2** vast number, array, horde, host, multitude, pack, swarm, throng

aroma noun scent, bouquet, fragrance, odour, perfume, redolence, savour, smell

aromatic adjective fragrant, balmy, perfumed, pungent, redolent, savoury, spicy, sweet-scented, sweet-smelling

around preposition **1** surrounding, about, encircling, enclosing, encompassing, on all sides of,

on every side of
2 approximately, about, circa
(*used with dates*), roughly
♦ *adverb* **3** everywhere, about, all
over, here and there, in all
directions, on all sides,
throughout, to and fro **4** near,
at hand, close, close at hand,
nearby, nigh (*archaic or dialect*)

arouse *verb* **1** stimulate, excite,
incite, instigate, provoke, spur,
stir up, summon up, whip up
2 awaken, rouse, waken, wake up

arrange *verb* **1** plan, construct,
contrive, devise, fix up, organize,
prepare **2** agree, adjust, come to
terms, compromise, determine,
settle **3** put in order, classify,
group, line up, order, organize,
position, sort **4** adapt,
instrument, orchestrate, score

arrangement *noun* **1** *often plural*
plan, organization, planning,
preparation, provision, schedule
2 agreement, adjustment,
compact, compromise, deal,
settlement, terms **3** order,
alignment, classification, form,
organization, structure, system
4 adaptation, instrumentation,
interpretation, orchestration,
score, version

array *noun* **1** arrangement,
collection, display, exhibition,
formation, line-up, parade,
show, supply **2** *Poetic* clothing,
apparel, attire, clothes, dress,
finery, garments, regalia ♦ *verb*
3 arrange, display, exhibit,
group, parade, range, show
4 dress, adorn, attire, clothe,
deck, decorate, festoon

arrest *verb* **1** capture,
apprehend, catch, detain, nick

(*slang, chiefly Brit.*), seize, take
prisoner **2** stop, block, delay,
end, inhibit, interrupt, obstruct,
slow, suppress **3** grip, absorb,
engage, engross, fascinate, hold,
intrigue, occupy ♦ *noun*
4 capture, bust (*informal*), cop
(*slang*), detention, seizure
5 stopping, blockage, delay,
end, hindrance, interruption,
obstruction, suppression

arresting *adjective* striking,
engaging, impressive, noticeable,
outstanding, remarkable,
stunning, surprising

arrival *noun* **1** coming, advent,
appearance, arriving, entrance,
happening, occurrence, taking
place **2** newcomer, caller,
entrant, incomer, visitor

arrive *verb* **1** come, appear,
enter, get to, reach, show up
(*informal*), turn up **2** *Informal*
succeed, become famous, make
good, make it (*informal*), make
the grade (*informal*)

arrogance *noun* conceit,
disdainfulness, haughtiness,
high-handedness, insolence,
pride, superciliousness, swagger

arrogant *adjective* conceited,
disdainful, haughty,
high-handed, overbearing,
proud, scornful, supercilious

arrow *noun* **1** dart, bolt, flight,
quarrel, shaft (*archaic*) **2** pointer,
indicator

arsenal *noun* armoury,
ammunition dump, arms depot,
ordnance depot, stockpile, store,
storehouse, supply

art *noun* skill, craft, expertise,
ingenuity, mastery, virtuosity

artful *adjective* cunning, clever,

crafty, shrewd, sly, smart, wily

article noun **1** piece, composition, discourse, essay, feature, item, paper, story, treatise **2** thing, commodity, item, object, piece, substance, unit **3** clause, item, paragraph, part, passage, point, portion, section

articulate adjective **1** expressive, clear, coherent, eloquent, fluent, lucid, well-spoken ♦ verb **2** express, enunciate, pronounce, say, speak, state, talk, utter, voice

artifice noun **1** trick, contrivance, device, machination, manoeuvre, stratagem, subterfuge, tactic **2** cleverness, ingenuity, inventiveness, skill

artificial adjective **1** synthetic, man-made, manufactured, non-natural, plastic **2** fake, bogus, counterfeit, imitation, mock, sham, simulated **3** insincere, affected, contrived, false, feigned, forced, phoney or phony (informal), unnatural

artillery noun big guns, battery, cannon, cannonry, gunnery, ordnance

artisan noun craftsman, journeyman, mechanic, skilled workman, technician

artistic adjective creative, aesthetic, beautiful, cultured, elegant, refined, sophisticated, stylish, tasteful

artistry noun skill, brilliance, craftsmanship, creativity, finesse, mastery, proficiency, virtuosity

artless adjective
1 straightforward, frank, guileless, open, plain **2** natural, plain, pure, simple, unadorned,

unaffected, unpretentious

as conjunction **1** when, at the time that, during the time that, just as, while **2** in the way that, in the manner that, like **3** what, that which **4** since, because, considering that, seeing that **5** for instance, like, such as ♦ preposition **6** being, in the character of, in the role of, under the name of

ascend verb move up, climb, go up, mount, scale

ascent noun **1** rise, ascending, ascension, climb, mounting, rising, scaling, upward movement **2** upward slope, gradient, incline, ramp, rise, rising ground

ascertain verb find out, confirm, determine, discover, establish, learn

ascetic noun **1** monk, abstainer, hermit, nun, recluse ♦ adjective **2** self-denying, abstinent, austere, celibate, frugal, puritanical, self-disciplined

ascribe verb attribute, assign, charge, credit, impute, put down, refer, set down

ashamed adjective embarrassed, distressed, guilty, humiliated, mortified, remorseful, shamefaced, sheepish, sorry

ashen adjective pale, colourless, grey, leaden, like death warmed up (informal), pallid, wan, white

ashore adverb on land, aground, landwards, on dry land, on the beach, on the shore, shorewards, to the shore

aside adverb **1** to one side, apart, beside, on one side, out of the way, privately, separately, to the side ♦ *noun* **2** interpolation, parenthesis

asinine *adjective* stupid, fatuous, foolish, idiotic, imbecilic, moronic, senseless

ask *verb* **1** inquire, interrogate, query, question, quiz **2** request, appeal, beg, demand, plead, seek **3** invite, bid, summon

askew *adverb* **1** crookedly, aslant, awry, obliquely, off-centre, to one side ♦ *adjective* **2** crooked, awry, cockeyed (*informal*), lopsided, oblique, off-centre, skewwhiff (*Brit. informal*)

asleep *adjective* sleeping, dormant, dozing, fast asleep, napping, slumbering, snoozing (*informal*), sound asleep

aspect *noun* **1** feature, angle, facet, side **2** position, outlook, point of view, prospect, scene, situation, view **3** appearance, air, attitude, bearing, condition, demeanour, expression, look, manner

asphyxiate *verb* suffocate, choke, smother, stifle, strangle, strangulate, throttle

aspiration *noun* aim, ambition, desire, dream, goal, hope, objective, wish

aspire *verb* aim, desire, dream, hope, long, seek, set one's heart on, wish

aspiring *adjective* hopeful, ambitious, eager, longing, wannabe (*informal*), would-be

ass *noun* **1** donkey, moke (*slang*) **2** fool, blockhead, halfwit, idiot, jackass, numbskull *or* numskull,

oaf, twit (*informal, chiefly Brit.*)

assail *verb* attack, assault, fall upon, lay into (*informal*), set upon

assailant *noun* attacker, aggressor, assailer, assaulter, invader

assassin *noun* murderer, executioner, hatchet man (*slang*), hit man (*slang*), killer, liquidator, slayer

assassinate *verb* murder, eliminate (*slang*), hit (*slang*), kill, liquidate, slay, take out (*slang*)

assault *noun* **1** attack, charge, invasion, offensive, onslaught ♦ *verb* **2** attack, beset, fall upon, lay into (*informal*), set about, set upon, strike at

assemble *verb* **1** gather, amass, bring together, call together, collect, come together, congregate, meet, muster, rally **2** put together, build up, connect, construct, fabricate, fit together, join, piece together, set up

assembly *noun* **1** gathering, collection, company, conference, congress, council, crowd, group, mass, meeting **2** putting together, building up, connecting, construction, piecing together, setting up

assent *noun* **1** agreement, acceptance, approval, compliance, concurrence, consent, permission, sanction ♦ *verb* **2** agree, allow, approve, consent, grant, permit

assert *verb* **1** state, affirm, declare, maintain, profess, pronounce, swear **2** insist upon, claim, defend, press, put forward, stand up for, stress, uphold **3 assert oneself** be **forceful**, exert one's influence, make one's presence felt, put oneself forward, put one's foot down (*informal*)

assertion noun **1** statement, claim, declaration, pronouncement **2** insistence, maintenance, stressing

assertive adjective confident, aggressive, domineering, emphatic, feisty (*informal, chiefly U.S. & Canad.*), forceful, positive, insistent, pushy (*informal*), strong-willed

assess verb **1** judge, appraise, estimate, evaluate, rate, size up (*informal*), value, **2** evaluate, fix, impose, levy, rate, tax, value

assessment noun **1** judgment, appraisal, estimate, evaluation, rating, valuation **2** evaluation, charge, fee, levy, rating, toll, valuation

asset noun **1** benefit, advantage, aid, blessing, boon, feather in one's cap, help, resource, service **2 assets** property, capital, estate, funds, goods, money, possessions, resources, wealth

assiduous adjective diligent, hard-working, indefatigable, industrious, persevering, persistent, unflagging

assign verb **1** select, appoint, choose, delegate, designate, name, nominate **2** give, allocate, allot, apportion, consign, distribute, give out, grant **3** attribute, accredit, ascribe, put down

assignation noun **1** secret

meeting, clandestine meeting, illicit meeting, rendezvous, tryst (*archaic*) **2** selection, appointment, assignment, choice, delegation, designation, nomination

assignment noun **1** task, appointment, commission, duty, job, mission, position, post, responsibility

assimilate verb **1** learn, absorb, digest, incorporate, take in **2** adjust, adapt, blend in, mingle

assist verb help, abet, aid, cooperate, lend a helping hand, serve, support

assistance noun help, aid, backing, cooperation, helping hand, support

assistant noun helper, accomplice, aide, ally, colleague, right-hand man, second, supporter

associate verb **1** connect, ally, combine, identify, join, link, lump together **2** mix, accompany, consort, hobnob, mingle, socialize ♦ noun **3** partner, collaborator, colleague, confederate, co-worker **4** friend, ally, companion, comrade, mate (*informal*)

association noun **1** group, alliance, band, club, coalition, federation, league, organization, society **2** connection, blend, combination, joining, juxtaposition, mixture, pairing, union

assorted adjective various, different, diverse, miscellaneous, mixed, motley, sundry, varied

assortment noun variety, array,

choice, collection, jumble, medley, mixture, selection

assume verb **1** take for granted, believe, expect, fancy, imagine, infer, presume, suppose, surmise, think **2** take on, accept, enter upon, put on, shoulder, take over **3** put on, adopt, affect, feign, imitate, impersonate, mimic, pretend to, simulate

assumed adjective **1** false, bogus, counterfeit, fake, fictitious, made-up, make-believe **2** taken for granted, accepted, expected, hypothetical, presumed, presupposed, supposed, surmised

assumption noun **1** presumption, belief, conjecture, guess, hypothesis, inference, supposition, surmise **2** taking on, acceptance, acquisition, adoption, entering upon, putting on, shouldering, takeover, taking up **3** taking, acquisition, appropriation, seizure, takeover

assurance noun **1** assertion, declaration, guarantee, oath, pledge, promise, statement, vow, word **2** confidence, boldness, certainty, conviction, faith, nerve, poise, self-confidence

assure verb **1** promise, certify, confirm, declare confidently, give one's word to, guarantee, pledge, swear, vow **2** convince, comfort, embolden, encourage, hearten, persuade, reassure **3** make certain, clinch, complete, confirm, ensure, guarantee, make sure, seal, secure

assured adjective **1** confident,

certain, poised, positive, self-assured, self-confident, sure of oneself **2** certain, beyond doubt, confirmed, ensured, fixed, guaranteed, in the bag (slang), secure, settled, sure

astonish verb amaze, astound, bewilder, confound, daze, dumbfound, stagger, stun, surprise

astonishing adjective amazing, astounding, bewildering, breathtaking, brilliant, sensational (informal), staggering, stunning, surprising

astonishment noun amazement, awe, bewilderment, confusion, consternation, surprise, wonder, wonderment

astounding adjective amazing, astonishing, bewildering, breathtaking, brilliant, impressive, sensational (informal), staggering, stunning, surprising

astray adjective, adverb off the right track, adrift, amiss, lost, off, off course, off the mark, off the subject

astute adjective intelligent, canny, clever, crafty, cunning, perceptive, sagacious, sharp, shrewd, subtle

asylum noun **1** refuge, harbour, haven, preserve, retreat, safety, sanctuary, shelter **2** Old-fashioned mental hospital, hospital, institution, madhouse (informal), psychiatric hospital

atheism noun nonbelief, disbelief, godlessness, heathenism, infidelity, irreligion, paganism, scepticism, unbelief

atheist noun nonbeliever, disbeliever, heathen, infidel, pagan, sceptic, unbeliever

athlete noun sportsperson, competitor, contestant, gymnast, player, runner, sportsman, sportswoman

athletic adjective fit, active, energetic, muscular, powerful, strapping, strong, sturdy

athletics plural noun sports, contests, exercises, gymnastics, races, track and field events

atmosphere noun 1 air, aerosphere, heavens, sky 2 feeling, ambience, character, climate, environment, mood, spirit, surroundings, tone

atom noun particle, bit, dot, molecule, speck, spot, trace

atone verb, usually with for make amends, compensate, do penance, make redress, make reparation, make up for, pay for, recompense, redress

atonement noun amends, compensation, penance, recompense, redress, reparation, restitution

atrocious adjective 1 cruel, barbaric, brutal, fiendish, infernal, monstrous, savage, vicious, wicked 2 Informal shocking, appalling, detestable, grievous, horrible, horrifying, terrible

atrocity noun 1 cruelty, barbarity, brutality, fiendishness, horror, savagery, viciousness, wickedness 2 act of cruelty, abomination, crime, evil, horror, outrage

attach verb 1 connect, add, couple, fasten, fix, join, link, secure, stick, tie 2 put, ascribe,

assign, associate, attribute, connect

attached adjective 1 spoken for, accompanied, engaged, married, partnered 2 **attached to** fond of, affectionate towards, devoted to, full of regard for

attachment noun 1 fondness, affection, affinity, attraction, liking, regard 2 accessory, accoutrement, extension, extra, fitting, fixture, supplement

attack verb 1 assault, invade, lay into (informal), raid, set upon, storm, strike (at) 2 criticize, abuse, blame, censure, have a go (at) (informal), put down, vilify ♦ noun 3 assault, campaign, charge, foray, incursion, invasion, offensive, onslaught, raid, strike 4 criticism, abuse, blame, censure, denigration, stick (slang), vilification 5 bout, convulsion, fit, paroxysm, seizure, spasm, stroke

attacker noun assailant, aggressor, assaulter, intruder, invader, raider

attain verb achieve, accomplish, acquire, complete, fulfil, gain, get, obtain, reach

attainment noun achievement, accomplishment, completion, feat

attempt verb 1 try, endeavour, seek, strive, undertake, venture ♦ noun 2 try, bid, crack (informal), effort, go (informal), shot (informal), stab (informal), trial

attend verb 1 be present, appear, frequent, go to, haunt, put in an appearance, show oneself, turn up, visit 2 look after, care for, mind, minister to, nurse, take care of, tend **3** pay attention, hear, heed, listen, mark, note, observe, pay heed **4 attend to** apply oneself to, concentrate on, devote oneself to, get to work on, look after, occupy oneself with, see to, take care of

attendance noun **1** presence, appearance, attending, being there **2** turnout, audience, crowd, gate, house, number present

attendant noun **1** assistant, aide, companion, escort, follower, guard, helper, servant ♦ adjective **2** accompanying, accessory, associated, concomitant, consequent, related

attention noun **1** concentration, deliberation, heed, intentness, mind, scrutiny, thinking, thought **2** notice, awareness, consciousness, consideration, observation, recognition, regard **3** care, concern, looking after, ministration, treatment

attentive adjective **1** intent, alert, awake, careful, concentrating, heedful, mindful, observant, studious, watchful **2** considerate, courteous, helpful, kind, obliging, polite, respectful, thoughtful

attic noun loft, garret

attire noun clothes, apparel, costume, dress, garb, garments, outfit, robes, wear

attitude noun **1** disposition, approach, frame of mind, mood, opinion, outlook, perspective, point of view, position, stance **2** position, pose, posture, stance

attract verb appeal to, allure, charm, draw, enchant, entice,

lure, pull (informal), tempt

attraction noun appeal, allure, charm, enticement, fascination, lure, magnetism, pull (informal), temptation

attractive adjective appealing, alluring, charming, fair, fetching, good-looking, handsome, inviting, lovely, pleasant, pretty, tempting

attribute verb **1** ascribe, assign, charge, credit, put down to, refer, set down to, trace to ♦ noun **2** quality, aspect, character, characteristic, facet, feature, peculiarity, property, trait

attune verb accustom, adapt, adjust, familiarize, harmonize, regulate

audacious adjective **1** daring, bold, brave, courageous, fearless, intrepid, rash, reckless **2** cheeky, brazen, defiant, impertinent, impudent, insolent, presumptuous, shameless

audacity noun **1** daring, boldness, bravery, courage, fearlessness, nerve, rashness, recklessness **2** cheek, chutzpah (U.S. & Canad. informal), effrontery, impertinence, impudence, insolence, nerve

audible adjective clear, detectable, discernible, distinct, hearable, perceptible

audience noun **1** spectators, assembly, crowd, gallery, gathering, listeners, onlookers, turnout, viewers **2** interview, consultation, hearing, meeting, reception

aura noun air, ambience, atmosphere, feeling, mood, quality, tone

auspicious adjective favourable, bright, encouraging, felicitous, hopeful, promising

austere adjective **1** stern, forbidding, formal, serious, severe, solemn, strict **2** ascetic, abstemious, puritanical, self-disciplined, sober, solemn, strait-laced, strict **3** plain, bleak, harsh, simple, spare, Spartan, stark

austerity noun **1** sternness, formality, inflexibility, rigour, seriousness, severity, solemnity, stiffness, strictness **2** asceticism, puritanism, self-denial, self-discipline, sobriety **3** plainness, simplicity, starkness

authentic adjective genuine, actual, authoritative, bona fide, legitimate, pure, real, true-to-life, valid

authenticity noun genuineness, accuracy, certainty, faithfulness, legitimacy, purity, truthfulness, validity

author noun **1** writer, composer, creator **2** creator, architect, designer, father, founder, inventor, originator, producer

authoritarian adjective **1** strict, autocratic, dictatorial, doctrinaire, dogmatic, severe, tyrannical ♦ noun **2** disciplinarian, absolutist, autocrat, despot, dictator, tyrant

authoritative adjective **1** reliable, accurate, authentic, definitive, dependable, trustworthy, valid **2** commanding, assertive, imperious, imposing, masterly, self-assured

authority noun **1** power, command, control, direction, influence, supremacy, sway, weight **2** usually plural powers that be, administration, government, management, officialdom, police, the Establishment **3** expert, connoisseur, judge, master, professional, specialist

authorization noun permission, a blank cheque, approval, leave, licence, permit, warrant

authorize verb **1** empower, accredit, commission, enable, entitle, give authority **2** permit, allow, approve, give authority for, license, sanction, warrant

autocracy noun dictatorship, absolutism, despotism, tyranny

autocrat noun dictator, absolutist, despot, tyrant

autocratic adjective dictatorial, absolute, all-powerful, despotic, domineering, imperious, tyrannical

automatic adjective **1** mechanical, automated, mechanized, push-button, self-propelling **2** involuntary, instinctive, mechanical, natural, reflex, spontaneous, unconscious, unwilled

autonomous adjective self-ruling, free, independent, self-determining, self-governing, sovereign

autonomy noun independence, freedom, home rule, self-determination, self-government, self-rule, sovereignty

auxiliary adjective **1** supplementary, back-up, emergency, fall-back, reserve, secondary, subsidiary, substitute

2 supporting, accessory, aiding, ancillary, assisting, helping ♦ noun **3** backup, reserve **4** helper, assistant, associate, companion, subordinate, supporter

avail verb **1** benefit, aid, assist, be of advantage, be useful, help, profit ♦ noun **2** benefit, advantage, aid, good, help, profit, use

availability noun accessibility, attainability, handiness, readiness

available adjective accessible, at hand, at one's disposal, free, handy, on tap, ready, to hand

avalanche noun **1** snow-slide, landslide, landslip **2** flood, barrage, deluge, inundation, torrent

avant-garde adjective progressive, experimental, ground-breaking, innovative, pioneering, unconventional

avarice noun greed, covetousness, meanness, miserliness, niggardliness, parsimony, stinginess

avaricious adjective grasping, covetous, greedy, mean, miserly, niggardly, parsimonious, stingy

avenge verb get revenge for, get even for (informal), get one's own back, hit back, punish, repay, retaliate

avenue noun street, approach, boulevard, course, drive, passage, path, road, route, way

average noun **1** usual, mean, medium, midpoint, norm, normal, par, standard **2 on average** usually, as a rule, for the most part, generally,

normally, typically ♦ adjective **3** usual, commonplace, fair, general, normal, ordinary, regular, standard, typical **4** mean, intermediate, median, medium, middle ♦ verb **5** make on average, balance out to, be on average, do on average, even out to

averse adjective opposed, disinclined, hostile, ill-disposed, loath, reluctant, unwilling

aversion noun hatred, animosity, antipathy, disinclination, dislike, hostility, revulsion, unwillingness

avert verb **1** turn away, turn aside **2** ward off, avoid, fend off, forestall, frustrate, preclude, prevent, stave off

aviator noun pilot, aeronaut, airman, flyer

avid adjective **1** enthusiastic, ardent, devoted, eager, fanatical, intense, keen, passionate, zealous **2** insatiable, grasping, greedy, hungry, rapacious, ravenous, thirsty, voracious

avoid verb **1** refrain from, dodge, duck (out of) (informal), eschew, fight shy of, shirk **2** prevent, avert **3** keep away from, bypass, dodge, elude, escape, evade, shun, steer clear of

avoidance noun evasion, dodging, eluding, escape, keeping away, shunning, steering clear

avowed adjective **1** declared, open, professed, self-proclaimed, sworn **2** confessed, acknowledged, admitted

await verb **1** wait for, abide, anticipate, expect, look for, look forward to, stay for **2** be in store

for, attend, be in readiness for,
be prepared for, be ready for,
wait for

awake *adjective* **1** not sleeping,
aroused, awakened, aware,
conscious, wakeful, wide-awake
2 alert, alive, attentive, aware,
heedful, observant, on the
lookout, vigilant, watchful ♦ *verb*
3 wake up, awaken, rouse, wake
4 alert, arouse, kindle, provoke,
revive, stimulate, stir up

awaken *verb* **1** awake, arouse,
revive, rouse, wake **2** alert,
kindle, provoke, stimulate, stir up

awakening *noun* waking up,
arousal, revival, rousing,
stimulation, stirring up

award *verb* **1** give, bestow,
confer, endow, grant, hand out,
present ♦ *noun* **2** prize,
decoration, gift, grant, trophy

aware *adjective* **1** aware of,
knowing about, acquainted with,
conscious of, conversant with,
familiar with, mindful of
2 informed, enlightened, in the
picture, knowledgeable

awareness *noun* knowledge,
consciousness, familiarity,
perception, realization,
recognition, understanding

away *adverb* **1** off, abroad,
elsewhere, from here, from
home, hence **2** at a distance,
apart, far, remote **3** aside, out of
the way, to one side
4 continuously, incessantly,
interminably, relentlessly,
repeatedly, uninterruptedly,
unremittingly ♦ *adjective* **5** not
present, abroad, absent,
elsewhere, gone, not at home,
not here, out

awe *noun* **1** wonder, admiration,
amazement, astonishment,
dread, fear, horror, respect,
reverence, terror ♦ *verb*
2 impress, amaze, astonish,
frighten, horrify, intimidate,
stun, terrify

awesome *adjective* awe-inspiring,
amazing, astonishing,
breathtaking, formidable,
impressive, intimidating, stunning

awful *adjective* **1** terrible,
abysmal, appalling, deplorable,
dreadful, frightful, ghastly,
horrendous **2** *Obsolete*
awe-inspiring, awesome,
fearsome, majestic, solemn

awfully *adverb* **1** badly,
disgracefully, dreadfully,
reprehensibly, unforgivably,
unpleasantly, woefully,
wretchedly **2** *Informal* very,
dreadfully, exceedingly,
exceptionally, extremely, greatly,
immensely, terribly

awkward *adjective* **1** clumsy,
gauche, gawky, inelegant,
lumbering, uncoordinated,
ungainly **2** unmanageable,
clunky (*informal*), cumbersome,
difficult, inconvenient,
troublesome, unwieldy
3 embarrassing, delicate,
difficult, ill at ease, inconvenient,
uncomfortable

awkwardness *noun*
1 clumsiness, gawkiness,
inelegance, ungainliness
2 unwieldiness, difficulty,
inconvenience **3** embarrassment,
delicacy, difficulty, inconvenience

axe *noun* **1** hatchet, adze,
chopper **2** the axe *Informal* the
sack (*informal*), dismissal,

termination, the boot (*slang*), the chop (*slang*) ♦ *verb* **3** *Informal* cut back, cancel, dismiss, dispense with, eliminate, fire (*informal*), get rid of, remove, sack (*informal*)

axiom *noun* principle, adage, aphorism, dictum, maxim, precept, truism

axiomatic *adjective* self-evident, accepted, assumed, certain, given, granted, manifest, understood

axis *noun* pivot, axle, centre line, shaft, spindle

axle *noun* shaft, axis, pin, pivot, rod, spindle

B b

babble *verb* **1** gabble, burble, chatter, jabber, prattle, waffle (*informal, chiefly Brit.*) **2** gibber, gurgle ♦ *noun* **3** gabble, burble, drivel, gibberish, waffle (*informal, chiefly Brit.*)

baby *noun* **1** infant, babe, babe in arms (*Scot.*), child, newborn child ♦ *adjective* **2** small, little, mini, miniature, minute, teeny-weeny, tiny, wee

babyish *adjective* childish, foolish, immature, infantile, juvenile, puerile, sissy, spoiled

back *noun* **1** rear, end, far end, hind part, hindquarters, reverse, stern, tail end **2** behind one's back secretly, covertly, deceitfully, sneakily, surreptitiously ♦ *verb* **3** move back, back off, backtrack, go back, retire, retreat, reverse, turn tail, withdraw **4** support,

advocate, assist, champion, endorse, promote, sponsor ♦ *adjective* **5** rear, end, hind, hindmost, posterior, tail **6** previous, delayed, earlier, elapsed, former, overdue, past

backbiting *noun* slander, bitchiness (*slang*), cattiness (*informal*), defamation, disparagement, gossip, malice, scandalmongering, spitefulness

backbone *noun* **1** *Medical* spinal column, spine, vertebrae, vertebral column **2** strength of character, character, courage, determination, fortitude, grit, nerve, pluck, resolution

backbreaking *adjective* exhausting, arduous, crushing, gruelling, hard, laborious, punishing, strenuous

back down *verb* give in, accede, admit defeat, back-pedal, concede, surrender, withdraw, yield

backer *noun* supporter, advocate, angel (*informal*), benefactor, patron, promoter, second, sponsor, subscriber

backfire *verb* fail, boomerang, disappoint, flop (*informal*), miscarry, rebound, recoil

background *noun* history, circumstances, culture, education, environment, grounding, tradition, upbringing

backing *noun* support, aid, assistance, encouragement, endorsement, moral support, patronage, sponsorship

backlash *noun* reaction, counteraction, recoil, repercussion, resistance, response, retaliation

backlog noun <u>build-up</u>, accumulation, excess, hoard, reserve, stock, supply

back out verb, often with **of** <u>withdraw</u>, abandon, cancel, give up, go back on, resign, retreat

backslide verb <u>relapse</u>, go astray, go wrong, lapse, revert, slip, stray, weaken

backslider noun <u>relapser</u>, apostate, deserter, recidivist, recreant, renegade, turncoat

back up verb <u>support</u>, aid, assist, bolster, confirm, corroborate, reinforce, second, stand by, substantiate

backward adjective <u>slow</u>, behind, dull, retarded, subnormal, underdeveloped, undeveloped

backwards, backward adverb <u>towards the rear</u>, behind, in reverse, rearward

bacteria plural noun <u>microorganisms</u>, bacilli, bugs (slang), germs, microbes, pathogens, viruses

bad adjective 1 <u>inferior</u>, defective, faulty, imperfect, inadequate, poor, substandard, unsatisfactory 2 <u>harmful</u>, damaging, dangerous, deleterious, detrimental, hurtful, ruinous, unhealthy 3 <u>evil</u>, corrupt, criminal, immoral, mean, sinful, wicked, wrong 4 <u>naughty</u>, disobedient, mischievous, unruly 5 <u>rotten</u>, decayed, mouldy, off, putrid, rancid, sour, spoiled 6 <u>unfavourable</u>, adverse, distressing, gloomy, grim, troubled, unfortunate, unpleasant

badge noun <u>mark</u>, brand, device, emblem, identification, insignia, sign, stamp, token

badger verb <u>pester</u>, bully, goad, harass, hound, importune, nag, plague, torment

badinage noun <u>wordplay</u>, banter, mockery, pleasantry, repartee, teasing

badly adverb 1 <u>poorly</u>, carelessly, imperfectly, inadequately, incorrectly, ineptly, wrongly 2 <u>unfavourably</u>, unfortunately, unsuccessfully 3 <u>severely</u>, deeply, desperately, exceedingly, extremely, greatly, intensely, seriously

baffle verb <u>puzzle</u>, bewilder, confound, confuse, flummox, mystify, nonplus, perplex, stump

bag noun 1 <u>container</u>, receptacle, sac, sack ♦ verb 2 <u>catch</u>, acquire, capture, kill, land, shoot, trap

baggage noun <u>luggage</u>, accoutrements, bags, belongings, equipment, gear, paraphernalia, suitcases, things

baggy adjective <u>loose</u>, bulging, droopy, floppy, ill-fitting, oversize, roomy, sagging, slack

bail noun Law <u>security</u>, bond, guarantee, pledge, surety, warranty

bail out see BALE OUT

bait noun 1 <u>lure</u>, allurement, attraction, decoy, enticement, incentive, inducement, snare, temptation ♦ verb 2 <u>tease</u>, annoy, bother, harass, hassle (informal), hound, irritate, persecute, torment, wind up (Brit. slang)

baked adjective <u>dry</u>, arid, desiccated, parched, scorched, seared, sun-baked, torrid

balance noun 1 <u>stability</u>,

composure, equanimity, poise, self-control, self-possession, steadiness **2** equilibrium, correspondence, equity, equivalence, evenness, parity, symmetry **3** remainder, difference, residue, rest, surplus ♦ *verb* **4** stabilize, level, match, parallel, steady **5** compare, assess, consider, deliberate, estimate, evaluate, weigh **6** *Accounting* calculate, compute, settle, square, tally, total

balcony *noun* **1** terrace, veranda **2** upper circle, gallery, gods

bald *adjective* **1** hairless, baldheaded, depilated **2** plain, blunt, direct, forthright, straightforward, unadorned, unvarnished

balderdash *noun* nonsense, claptrap (*informal*), drivel, garbage (*informal*), gibberish, hogwash, hot air (*informal*), rubbish

baldness *noun* **1** hairlessness, alopecia (*Pathology*), baldheadedness **2** plainness, austerity, bluntness, severity, simplicity

bale out, bail out *verb* **1** *Informal* help, aid, relieve, rescue, save (someone's) bacon (*informal, chiefly Brit.*) **2** escape, quit, retreat, withdraw

balk, baulk *verb* **1** recoil, evade, flinch, hesitate, jib, refuse, resist, shirk, shrink from **2** foil, check, counteract, defeat, frustrate, hinder, obstruct, prevent, thwart

ball *noun* sphere, drop, globe, globule, orb, pellet, spheroid

ballast *noun* counterbalance, balance, counterweight,

equilibrium, sandbag, stability, stabilizer, weight

balloon *verb* swell, billow, blow up, dilate, distend, expand, grow rapidly, inflate, puff out

ballot *noun* vote, election, poll, polling, voting

ballyhoo *noun* *Informal* fuss, babble, commotion, hubbub, hue and cry, hullabaloo, noise, racket, to-do

balm *noun* **1** ointment, balsam, cream, embrocation, emollient, lotion, salve, unguent **2** comfort, anodyne, consolation, curative, palliative, restorative, solace

balmy *adjective* mild, clement, pleasant, summery, temperate

bamboozle *verb* *Informal* **1** cheat, con (*informal*), deceive, dupe, fool, hoodwink, swindle, trick **2** puzzle, baffle, befuddle, confound, confuse, mystify, perplex, stump

ban *verb* **1** prohibit, banish, bar, block, boycott, disallow, disqualify, exclude, forbid, outlaw ♦ *noun* **2** prohibition, boycott, disqualification, embargo, restriction, taboo

banal *adjective* unoriginal, hackneyed, humdrum, mundane, pedestrian, stale, stereotyped, trite, unimaginative

band¹ *noun* **1** ensemble, combo, group, orchestra **2** gang, body, company, group, party, posse (*informal*)

band² *noun* strip, belt, bond, chain, cord, ribbon, strap

bandage *noun* **1** dressing, compress, gauze, plaster ♦ *verb* **2** dress, bind, cover, swathe

bandit noun robber, brigand, desperado, highwayman, marauder, outlaw, thief

bane noun plague, bête noire, curse, nuisance, pest, ruin, scourge, torment

bang noun 1 explosion, clang, clap, clash, pop, slam, thud, thump 2 blow, bump, cuff, knock, punch, smack, stroke, whack ♦ verb 3 hit, belt (informal), clatter, knock, slam, strike, thump 4 explode, boom, clang, resound, thump, thunder ♦ adverb 5 hard, abruptly, headlong, noisily, suddenly 6 straight, precisely, slap, smack

banish verb 1 expel, deport, eject, evict, exile, outlaw 2 get rid of, ban, cast out, discard, dismiss, oust, remove

banishment noun expulsion, deportation, exile, expatriation, transportation

banisters plural noun railing, balusters, balustrade, handrail, rail

bank[1] noun 1 storehouse, depository, repository 2 store, accumulation, fund, hoard, reserve, reservoir, savings, stock, stockpile ♦ verb 3 save, deposit, keep

bank[2] noun 1 mound, banking, embankment, heap, mass, pile, ridge 2 side, brink, edge, margin, shore ♦ verb 3 pile, amass, heap, mass, mound, stack 4 tilt, camber, cant, heel, incline, pitch, slant, slope, tip

bank[3] noun row, array, file, group, line, rank, sequence, series, succession

bankrupt adjective insolvent,

broke (informal), destitute, impoverished, in queer street, in the red, ruined, wiped out (informal)

bankruptcy noun insolvency, disaster, failure, liquidation, ruin

banner noun flag, colours, ensign, pennant, placard, standard, streamer

banquet noun feast, dinner, meal, repast, revel, treat

banter verb 1 joke, jest, kid (informal), rib (informal), taunt, tease ♦ noun 2 joking, badinage, jesting, kidding (informal), repartee, teasing, wordplay

baptism noun Christianity christening, immersion, purification, sprinkling

baptize verb Christianity purify, cleanse, immerse

bar noun 1 rod, paling, palisade, pole, rail, shaft, stake, stick 2 obstacle, barricade, barrier, block, deterrent, hindrance, impediment, obstruction, stop 3 public house, boozer (Brit., Austral. & N.Z. informal), canteen, counter, inn, pub (informal, chiefly Brit.), saloon, tavern, watering hole (facetious slang) ♦ verb 4 fasten, barricade, bolt, latch, lock, secure 5 obstruct, hinder, prevent, restrain 6 exclude, ban, black, blackball, forbid, keep out, prohibit

Bar noun the Bar Law barristers, body of lawyers, counsel, court, judgment, tribunal

barb noun 1 dig, affront, cut, gibe, insult, sarcasm, scoff, sneer 2 point, bristle, prickle, prong, quill, spike, spur, thorn

barbarian noun 1 <u>savage</u>, brute, yahoo 2 <u>lout</u>, bigot, boor, philistine

barbaric adjective 1 <u>uncivilized</u>, primitive, rude, wild 2 <u>brutal</u>, barbarous, coarse, crude, cruel, fierce, inhuman, savage

barbarism noun <u>savagery</u>, coarseness, crudity

barbarous adjective 1 <u>uncivilized</u>, barbarian, brutish, primitive, rough, rude, savage, uncouth, wild 2 <u>brutal</u>, barbaric, cruel, ferocious, heartless, inhuman, monstrous, ruthless, vicious

barbed adjective 1 <u>cutting</u>, critical, hostile, hurtful, nasty, pointed, scathing, unkind 2 <u>spiked</u>, hooked, jagged, prickly, spiny, thorny

bare adjective 1 <u>naked</u>, nude, stripped, unclad, unclothed, uncovered, undressed, without a stitch on (informal) 2 <u>plain</u>, bald, basic, sheer, simple, stark, unembellished 3 <u>simple</u>, austere, spare, spartan, unadorned, unembellished

barefaced adjective 1 <u>obvious</u>, blatant, flagrant, open, transparent, unconcealed 2 <u>shameless</u>, audacious, bold, brash, brazen, impudent, insolent

barely adverb <u>only just</u>, almost, at a push, by the skin of one's teeth, hardly, just, scarcely

bargain noun 1 <u>agreement</u>, arrangement, contract, pact, pledge, promise 2 <u>good buy</u>, (cheap) purchase, discount, giveaway, good deal, reduction, snip (informal), steal (informal)
♦ verb 3 <u>negotiate</u>, agree, contract, covenant, promise, stipulate, transact

barge noun <u>canal boat</u>, flatboat, lighter, narrow boat

bark[1] noun, verb <u>yap</u>, bay, growl, howl, snarl, woof, yelp

bark[2] noun <u>covering</u>, casing, cortex (Anatomy, botany), crust, husk, rind, skin

barmy adjective Slang <u>insane</u>, crazy, daft (informal), foolish, idiotic, nuts (slang), out of one's mind, stupid

barracks plural noun <u>camp</u>, billet, encampment, garrison, quarters

barrage noun 1 <u>torrent</u>, burst, deluge, hail, mass, onslaught, plethora, stream 2 Military <u>bombardment</u>, battery, cannonade, fusillade, gunfire, salvo, shelling, volley

barren adjective 1 <u>infertile</u>, childless, sterile 2 <u>unproductive</u>, arid, desert, desolate, dry, empty, unfruitful, waste

barricade noun 1 <u>barrier</u>, blockade, bulwark, fence, obstruction, palisade, rampart, stockade ♦ verb 2 <u>bar</u>, block, blockade, defend, fortify, obstruct, protect, shut in

barrier noun 1 <u>barricade</u>, bar, blockade, boundary, fence, obstacle, obstruction, wall 2 <u>hindrance</u>, difficulty, drawback, handicap, hurdle, obstacle, restriction, stumbling block

barter verb <u>trade</u>, bargain, drive a hard bargain, exchange, haggle, swap, swop, traffic

base[1] noun 1 <u>bottom</u>, bed, foot, foundation, pedestal, rest, stand, support 2 <u>basis</u>, core, essence,

heart, key, origin, root, source
3 centre, camp, headquarters,
home, post, settlement, starting
point, station ♦ *verb* **4** found,
build, construct, depend, derive,
establish, ground, hinge **5** place,
locate, post, station

base² *adjective* **1** dishonourable,
contemptible, despicable,
disreputable, evil, immoral,
shameful, sordid, wicked
2 counterfeit, alloyed, debased,
fake, forged, fraudulent, impure

baseless *adjective* unfounded,
groundless, unconfirmed,
uncorroborated, ungrounded,
unjustified, unsubstantiated,
unsupported

bash *verb* **1** *Informal* hit, belt
(*informal*), smash, sock (*slang*),
strike, wallop (*informal*) ♦ *noun*
2 *Informal* attempt, crack
(*informal*), go (*informal*), shot
(*informal*), stab (*informal*), try

bashful *adjective* shy, blushing,
coy, diffident, reserved, reticent,
retiring, timid

basic *adjective* essential,
elementary, fundamental, key,
necessary, primary, vital

basically *adverb* essentially, at
heart, fundamentally, inherently,
in substance, intrinsically,
mostly, primarily

basics *plural noun* essentials,
brass tacks (*informal*),
fundamentals, nitty-gritty
(*informal*), nuts and bolts
(*informal*), principles, rudiments

basis *noun* foundation, base,
bottom, footing, ground,
groundwork, support

bask *verb* lie in, laze, loll, lounge,
relax, sunbathe, swim in

bass *adjective* deep, deep-toned,
low, low-pitched, resonant,
sonorous

bastard *noun* **1** *Informal, offensive*
rogue, blackguard, miscreant,
reprobate, scoundrel, villain,
wretch **2** illegitimate child, love
child, natural child

bastion *noun* stronghold,
bulwark, citadel, defence,
fortress, mainstay, prop, rock,
support, tower of strength

bat *noun, verb* hit, bang, smack,
strike, swat, thump, wallop
(*informal*), whack

batch *noun* group, amount,
assemblage, bunch, collection,
crowd, lot, pack, quantity, set

bath *noun* **1** wash, cleansing,
douche, scrubbing, shower,
soak, tub ♦ *verb* **2** wash, bathe,
clean, douse, scrub down,
shower, soak

bathe *verb* **1** swim **2** wash,
cleanse, rinse **3** cover, flood,
immerse, steep, suffuse

baton *noun* stick, club, crook,
mace, rod, sceptre, staff,
truncheon, wand

batten *verb, usually with* **down**
fasten, board up, clamp down,
cover up, fix, nail down, secure,
tighten

batter *verb* beat, buffet, clobber
(*slang*), pelt, pound, pummel,
thrash, wallop (*informal*)

battery *noun* artillery, cannon,
cannonry, gun emplacements,
guns

battle *noun* **1** fight, action,
attack, combat, encounter,
engagement, hostilities, skirmish
2 conflict, campaign, contest,

crusade, dispute, struggle ♦ *verb*
3 struggle, argue, clamour,
dispute, fight, lock horns, strive,
war

battlefield *noun* battleground,
combat zone, field, field of
battle, front

battleship *noun* warship,
gunboat, man-of-war

batty *adjective* crazy, daft
(*informal*), dotty (*slang, chiefly
Brit.*), eccentric, mad, odd,
peculiar, potty (*Brit. informal*),
touched

bauble *noun* trinket, bagatelle,
gewgaw, gimcrack, knick-knack,
plaything, toy, trifle

baulk *see* BALK

bawdy *adjective* rude, coarse,
dirty, indecent, lascivious,
lecherous, lewd, ribald, salacious,
smutty

bawl *verb* **1** cry, blubber, sob,
wail, weep **2** shout, bellow, call,
clamour, howl, roar, yell

bay[1] *noun* inlet, bight, cove, gulf,
natural harbour, sound

bay[2] *noun* recess, alcove,
compartment, niche, nook,
opening

bay[3] *verb* howl, bark, clamour,
cry, growl, yelp

bazaar *noun* **1** fair,
bring-and-buy, fête, sale of work
2 market, exchange, marketplace

be *verb* exist, be alive, breathe,
inhabit, live

beach *noun* shore, coast, sands,
seashore, seaside, water's edge

beached *adjective* stranded,
abandoned, aground, ashore,
deserted, grounded, high and
dry, marooned, wrecked

beacon *noun* signal, beam,
bonfire, flare, lighthouse, sign,
watchtower

bead *noun* drop, blob, bubble,
dot, droplet, globule, pellet, pill

beady *adjective* bright, gleaming,
glinting, glittering, sharp, shining

beak *noun* **1** bill, mandible, neb
(*archaic or dialect*), nib **2** *Slang*
nose, proboscis, snout

beam *noun* **1** smile, grin **2** ray,
gleam, glimmer, glint, glow,
shaft, streak, stream **3** rafter,
girder, joist, plank, spar, support,
timber ♦ *verb* **4** smile, grin
5 radiate, glare, gleam, glitter,
glow, shine **6** send out,
broadcast, emit, transmit

bear *verb* **1** support, have, hold,
maintain, possess, shoulder,
sustain, uphold **2** carry, bring,
convey, hump (*Brit. slang*),
move, take, transport **3** produce,
beget, breed, bring forth,
engender, generate, give birth
to, yield **4** tolerate, abide, allow,
brook, endure, permit, put up
with (*informal*), stomach, suffer

bearable *adjective* tolerable,
admissible, endurable,
manageable, passable,
sufferable, supportable,
sustainable

bearer *noun* carrier, agent,
conveyor, messenger, porter,
runner, servant

bearing *noun* **1** *usually with* on *or*
upon relevance, application,
connection, import, pertinence,
reference, relation, significance
2 manner, air, aspect, attitude,
behaviour, demeanour,
deportment, posture

bearings *plural noun* position,

aim, course, direction, location, orientation, situation, track, way, whereabouts

bear out verb <u>support</u>, confirm, corroborate, endorse, justify, prove, substantiate, uphold, vindicate

beast noun 1 <u>animal</u>, brute, creature 2 <u>brute</u>, barbarian, fiend, monster, ogre, sadist, savage, swine

beastly adjective <u>unpleasant</u>, awful, disagreeable, horrid, mean, nasty, rotten

beat verb 1 <u>hit</u>, bang, batter, buffet, knock, pound, strike, thrash 2 <u>flap</u>, flutter 3 <u>throb</u>, palpitate, pound, pulsate, quake, thump, vibrate 4 <u>defeat</u>, conquer, outdo, overcome, overwhelm, surpass, vanquish ◆noun 5 <u>throb</u>, palpitation, pulsation, pulse 6 <u>route</u>, circuit, course, path, rounds, way 7 <u>rhythm</u>, accent, cadence, metre, stress, time

beaten adjective 1 <u>stirred</u>, blended, foamy, frothy, mixed, whipped, whisked 2 <u>defeated</u>, cowed, overcome, overwhelmed, thwarted, vanquished

beat up verb Informal <u>assault</u>, attack, batter, beat the living daylights out of (informal), knock about or around, thrash

beau noun 1 Chiefly U.S. <u>boyfriend</u>, admirer, fiancé, lover, suitor, sweetheart 2 <u>dandy</u>, coxcomb, fop, gallant, ladies' man

beautiful adjective <u>attractive</u>, charming, delightful, exquisite, fair, fine, gorgeous, handsome, lovely, pleasing

beautify verb <u>make beautiful</u>, adorn, decorate, embellish, festoon, garnish, glamorize, ornament

beauty noun 1 <u>attractiveness</u>, charm, comeliness, elegance, exquisiteness, glamour, grace, handsomeness, loveliness 2 <u>belle</u>, good-looker, lovely (slang), stunner (informal)

becalmed adjective <u>still</u>, motionless, settled, stranded, stuck

because conjunction <u>since</u>, as, by reason of, in that, on account of, owing to, thanks to

beckon verb <u>gesture</u>, bid, gesticulate, motion, nod, signal, summon, wave at

become verb 1 <u>come to be</u>, alter to, be transformed into, change into, develop into, grow into, mature into, ripen into 2 <u>suit</u>, embellish, enhance, fit, flatter, set off

becoming adjective 1 <u>appropriate</u>, compatible, fitting, in keeping, proper, seemly, suitable, worthy 2 <u>flattering</u>, attractive, comely, enhancing, graceful, neat, pretty, tasteful

bed noun 1 <u>bedstead</u>, berth, bunk, cot, couch, divan 2 <u>plot</u>, area, border, garden, patch, row, strip 3 <u>bottom</u>, base, foundation, groundwork

bedevil verb 1 <u>torment</u>, afflict, distress, harass, plague, trouble, vex, worry 2 <u>confuse</u>, confound

bedlam noun <u>pandemonium</u>, chaos, commotion, confusion, furore, tumult, turmoil, uproar

bedraggled *adjective* messy, dirty, dishevelled, disordered, muddied, unkempt, untidy

bedridden *adjective* confined to bed, confined, flat on one's back, incapacitated, laid up (*informal*)

bedrock *noun* **1** bottom, bed, foundation, rock bottom, substratum, substructure **2** basics, basis, core, essentials, fundamentals, nuts and bolts (*informal*), roots

beefy *adjective Informal* brawny, bulky, hulking, muscular, stocky, strapping, sturdy, thickset

befall *verb Archaic or literary* happen, chance, come to pass, fall, occur, take place, transpire (*informal*)

befitting *adjective* appropriate, apposite, becoming, fit, fitting, proper, right, seemly, suitable

before *preposition* **1** ahead of, in advance of, in front of **2** earlier than, in advance of, prior to **3** in the presence of, in front of ◆ *adverb* **4** previously, ahead, earlier, formerly, in advance, sooner **5** in front, ahead

beforehand *adverb* in advance, ahead of time, already, before, earlier, in anticipation, previously, sooner

befriend *verb* help, aid, assist, back, encourage, side with, stand by, support, welcome

beg *verb* **1** scrounge, cadge, seek charity, solicit charity, sponge on, touch (someone) for (*slang*) **2** implore, beseech, entreat, petition, plead, request, solicit

beggar *noun* tramp, bag lady

(*chiefly U.S.*), bum (*informal*), down-and-out, pauper, vagrant

beggarly *adjective* poor, destitute, impoverished, indigent, needy, poverty-stricken

begin *verb* **1** start, commence, embark on, initiate, instigate, institute, prepare, set about **2** happen, appear, arise, come into being, emerge, originate, start

beginner *noun* novice, amateur, apprentice, learner, neophyte, starter, trainee, tyro

beginning *noun* **1** start, birth, commencement, inauguration, inception, initiation, onset, opening, origin, outset **2** seed, fount, germ, root

begrudge *verb* resent, be jealous, be reluctant, be stingy, envy, grudge

beguile *verb* **1** fool, cheat, deceive, delude, dupe, hoodwink, mislead, take for a ride (*informal*), trick **2** charm, amuse, distract, divert, engross, entertain, occupy

beguiling *adjective* charming, alluring, attractive, bewitching, captivating, enchanting, enthralling, intriguing

behave *verb* **1** act, function, operate, perform, run, work **2** conduct oneself properly, act correctly, keep one's nose clean, mind one's manners

behaviour *noun* **1** conduct, actions, bearing, demeanour, deportment, manner, manners, ways **2** action, functioning, operation, performance

behind *preposition* **1** after, at the

back of, at the heels of, at the rear of, following, later than **2** causing, at the bottom of, initiating, instigating, responsible for **3** supporting, backing, for, in agreement, on the side of
♦ *adverb* **4** after, afterwards, following, in the wake (of), next, subsequently **5** overdue, behindhand, in arrears, in debt
♦ *noun* **6** *Informal* bottom, butt (*U.S. & Canad. informal*), buttocks, posterior

behold *verb Archaic or literary* look at, observe, perceive, regard, survey, view, watch, witness

beholden *adjective* indebted, bound, grateful, obliged, owing, under obligation

being *noun* **1** existence, life, reality **2** nature, entity, essence, soul, spirit, substance **3** creature, human being, individual, living thing

belated *adjective* late, behindhand, behind time, delayed, late in the day, overdue, tardy

belch *verb* **1** burp (*informal*), hiccup **2** emit, discharge, disgorge, erupt, give off, spew forth, vent

beleaguered *adjective* **1** harassed, badgered, hassled (*informal*), persecuted, pestered, plagued, put upon, vexed **2** besieged, assailed, beset, blockaded, hemmed in, surrounded

belief *noun* **1** trust, assurance, confidence, conviction, feeling, impression, judgment, notion, opinion **2** faith, credo, creed, doctrine, dogma, ideology,

principles, tenet

believable *adjective* credible, authentic, imaginable, likely, plausible, possible, probable, trustworthy

believe *verb* **1** accept, be certain of, be convinced of, credit, depend on, have faith in, rely on, swear by, trust **2** think, assume, gather, imagine, judge, presume, reckon, speculate, suppose

believer *noun* follower, adherent, convert, devotee, disciple, supporter, upholder, zealot

belittle *verb* disparage, decry, denigrate, deprecate, deride, scoff at, scorn, sneer at

belligerent *adjective*
1 aggressive, bellicose, combative, hostile, pugnacious, unfriendly, warlike, warring
♦ *noun* **2** fighter, combatant, warring nation

bellow *noun, verb* shout, bawl, cry, howl, roar, scream, shriek, yell

belly *noun* **1** stomach, abdomen, corporation (*informal*), gut, insides (*informal*), paunch, potbelly, tummy ♦ *verb* **2** swell out, billow, bulge, fill, spread, swell

bellyful *noun* surfeit, enough, excess, glut, plateful, plenty, satiety, too much

belonging *noun* relationship, acceptance, affinity, association, attachment, fellowship, inclusion, loyalty, rapport

belongings *plural noun* possessions, accoutrements, chattels, effects, gear, goods, paraphernalia, personal property, stuff, things

belong to verb 1 be the property of, be at the disposal of, be held by, be owned by 2 be a member of, be affiliated to, be allied to, be associated with, be included in

beloved adjective dear, admired, adored, darling, loved, pet, precious, prized, treasured, worshipped

below preposition 1 lesser, inferior, subject, subordinate 2 less than, lower than ♦ adverb 3 lower, beneath, down, under, underneath

belt noun 1 waistband, band, cummerbund, girdle, girth, sash 2 Geography zone, area, district, layer, region, stretch, strip, tract

bemoan verb lament, bewail, deplore, grieve for, mourn, regret, rue, weep for

bemused adjective puzzled, at sea, bewildered, confused, flummoxed, muddled, nonplussed, perplexed

bench noun 1 seat, form, pew, settle, stall 2 worktable, board, counter, table, trestle table, workbench 3 the bench court, courtroom, judges, judiciary, magistrates, tribunal

benchmark noun reference point, criterion, gauge, level, measure, model, norm, par, standard, yardstick

bend verb 1 curve, arc, arch, bow, lean, turn, twist, veer ♦ noun 2 curve, angle, arc, arch, bow, corner, loop, turn, twist

beneath preposition 1 under,

below, lower than, underneath 2 inferior to, below, less than 3 unworthy of, unbefitting ♦ adverb 4 underneath, below, in a lower place

benefactor noun supporter, backer, donor, helper, philanthropist, sponsor, well-wisher

beneficial adjective helpful, advantageous, benign, favourable, profitable, useful, valuable, wholesome

beneficiary noun recipient, heir, inheritor, payee, receiver

benefit noun 1 help, advantage, aid, asset, assistance, favour, good, profit ♦ verb 2 help, aid, assist, avail, enhance, further, improve, profit

benevolent adjective kind, altruistic, benign, caring, charitable, generous, philanthropic

benign adjective 1 kindly, amiable, friendly, genial, kind, obliging, sympathetic 2 Medical harmless, curable, remediable

bent adjective 1 curved, angled, arched, bowed, crooked, hunched, stooped, twisted 2 bent on determined to, disposed to, fixed on, inclined to, insistent on, predisposed to, resolved on, set on ♦ noun 3 inclination, ability, aptitude, leaning, penchant, preference, propensity, tendency

bequeath verb leave, bestow, endow, entrust, give, grant, hand down, impart, pass on, will

bequest noun legacy, bestowal, endowment, estate, gift, inheritance, settlement

berate verb scold, castigate, censure, chide, criticize, harangue, rebuke, reprimand, reprove, tell off (informal), upbraid

bereavement noun loss, affliction, death, deprivation, misfortune, tribulation

bereft adjective deprived, devoid, lacking, parted from, robbed of, wanting

berserk adverb crazy, amok, enraged, frantic, frenzied, mad, raging, wild

berth noun 1 bunk, bed, billet, hammock 2 Nautical anchorage, dock, harbour, haven, pier, port, quay, wharf ♦ verb 3 Nautical anchor, dock, drop anchor, land, moor, tie up

beseech verb beg, ask, call upon, entreat, Implore, plead, pray, solicit

beset verb plague, bedevil, harass, pester, trouble

beside preposition 1 next to, abreast of, adjacent to, alongside, at the side of, close to, near, nearby, neighbouring 2 beside oneself distraught, apoplectic, at the end of one's tether, demented, desperate, frantic, frenzied, out of one's mind, unhinged

besides adverb 1 too, also, as well, further, furthermore, in addition, into the bargain, moreover, otherwise, what's more ♦ preposition 2 apart from, barring, excepting, excluding, in addition to, other than, over and above, without

besiege verb 1 surround, blockade, encircle, hem in, lay

siege to, shut in 2 harass, badger, harry, hassle (informal), hound, nag, pester, plague

besotted adjective infatuated, doting, hypnotized, smitten, spellbound

best adjective 1 finest, foremost, leading, most excellent, outstanding, pre-eminent, principal, supreme, unsurpassed ♦ adverb 2 most highly, extremely, greatly, most deeply, most fully ♦ noun 3 finest, cream, crème de la crème, elite, flower, pick, prime, top

bestial adjective brutal, barbaric, beastly, brutish, inhuman, savage, sordid

bestow verb present, award, commit, give, grant, hand out, impart, lavish

bet noun 1 gamble, long shot, risk, speculation, stake, venture, wager ♦ verb 2 gamble, chance, hazard, risk, speculate, stake, venture, wager

betoken verb indicate, bode, denote, promise, represent, signify, suggest

betray verb 1 be disloyal, be treacherous, be unfaithful, break one's promise, double-cross (informal), inform on or against, sell out (informal), stab in the back 2 give away, disclose, divulge, expose, let slip, reveal, uncover, unmask

betrayal noun 1 disloyalty, deception, double-cross (informal), sell-out (informal), treachery, treason, trickery 2 giving away, disclosure, divulgence, revelation

better adjective 1 superior,

excelling, finer, greater, higher-quality, more desirable, preferable, surpassing **2** well, cured, fully recovered, on the mend (*informal*), recovering, stronger ♦ *adverb* **3** in a more excellent manner, in a superior way, more advantageously, more attractively, more competently, more effectively **4** to a greater degree, more completely, more thoroughly ♦ *verb* **5** improve, enhance, further, raise

between *preposition* amidst, among, betwixt, in the middle of, mid

beverage *noun* drink, liquid, liquor, refreshment

bevy *noun* group, band, bunch (*informal*), collection, company, crowd, gathering, pack, troupe

bewail *verb* lament, bemoan, cry over, deplore, grieve for, moan, mourn, regret

beware *verb* be careful, be cautious, be wary, guard against, heed, look out, mind, take heed, watch out

bewilder *verb* confound, baffle, bemuse, confuse, flummox, mystify, nonplus, perplex, puzzle

bewildered *adjective* confused, at a loss, at sea, baffled, flummoxed, mystified, nonplussed, perplexed, puzzled

bewitch *verb* enchant, beguile, captivate, charm, enrapture, entrance, fascinate, hypnotize

bewitched *adjective* enchanted, charmed, entranced, fascinated, mesmerized, spellbound, under a spell

beyond *preposition* **1** past, above,

apart from, at a distance, away from, over **2** exceeding, out of reach of, superior to, surpassing

bias *noun* **1** prejudice, favouritism, inclination, leaning, partiality, tendency ♦ *verb* **2** prejudice, distort, influence, predispose, slant, sway, twist, warp, weight

biased *adjective* prejudiced, distorted, one-sided, partial, slanted, weighted

bicker *verb* quarrel, argue, disagree, dispute, fight, row (*informal*), squabble, wrangle

bid *verb* **1** offer, proffer, propose, submit, tender **2** say, call, greet, tell, wish **3** tell, ask, command, direct, instruct, order, require ♦ *noun* **4** offer, advance, amount, price, proposal, sum, tender **5** attempt, crack (*informal*), effort, go (*informal*), stab (*informal*), try

bidding *noun* order, beck and call, command, direction, instruction, request, summons

big *adjective* **1** large, enormous, extensive, great, huge, immense, massive, substantial, vast **2** important, eminent, influential, leading, main, powerful, prominent, significant **3** grown-up, adult, elder, grown, mature **4** generous, altruistic, benevolent, gracious, magnanimous, noble, unselfish

bighead *noun* Informal boaster, braggart, know-all (*informal*)

bigheaded *adjective* boastful, arrogant, cocky, conceited, egotistic, immodest, overconfident, swollen-headed

bigot *noun* fanatic, racist,

sectarian, zealot

bigoted adjective <u>intolerant</u>, biased, dogmatic, narrow-minded, opinionated, prejudiced, sectarian

bigotry noun <u>intolerance</u>, bias, discrimination, dogmatism, fanaticism, narrow-mindedness, prejudice, sectarianism

bigwig noun Informal <u>important person</u>, big shot (informal), celebrity, dignitary, mogul, personage, somebody, V.I.P.

bill[1] noun 1 <u>charges</u>, account, invoice, reckoning, score, statement, tally 2 <u>proposal</u>, measure, piece of legislation, projected law 3 <u>advertisement</u>, bulletin, circular, handbill, handout, leaflet, notice, placard, poster 4 <u>list</u>, agenda, card, catalogue, inventory, listing, programme, roster, schedule ◆ verb 5 <u>charge</u>, debit, invoice 6 <u>advertise</u>, announce, give advance notice of, post

bill[2] noun <u>beak</u>, mandible, neb (archaic or dialect), nib

billet verb 1 <u>quarter</u>, accommodate, berth, station ◆ noun 2 <u>quarters</u>, accommodation, barracks, lodging

billow noun 1 <u>wave</u>, breaker, crest, roller, surge, swell, tide ◆ verb 2 <u>surge</u>, balloon, belly, puff up, rise up, roll, swell

bind verb 1 <u>secure</u>, fasten, hitch, lash, stick, strap, tie, wrap 2 <u>oblige</u>, compel, constrain, engage, force, necessitate, require ◆ noun 3 Informal <u>nuisance</u>, bore, difficulty, dilemma, drag (informal), pain in

the neck (informal), quandary, spot (informal)

binding adjective <u>compulsory</u>, indissoluble, irrevocable, mandatory, necessary, obligatory, unalterable

binge noun Informal <u>bout</u>, bender (informal), feast, fling, orgy, spree

biography noun <u>life story</u>, account, curriculum vitae, CV, life, memoir, profile, record

birth noun 1 <u>childbirth</u>, delivery, nativity, parturition 2 <u>ancestry</u>, background, blood, breeding, lineage, parentage, pedigree, stock

bisect verb <u>cut in two</u>, cross, cut across, divide in two, halve, intersect, separate, split

bit[1] noun <u>piece</u>, crumb, fragment, grain, morsel, part, scrap, speck

bit[2] noun <u>curb</u>, brake, check, restraint, snaffle

bitchy adjective Informal <u>spiteful</u>, backbiting, catty (informal), mean, nasty, snide, vindictive

bite verb 1 <u>cut</u>, chew, gnaw, nip, pierce, pinch, snap, tear, wound ◆ noun 2 <u>wound</u>, nip, pinch, prick, smarting, sting, tooth marks 3 <u>snack</u>, food, light meal, morsel, mouthful, piece, refreshment, taste

biting adjective 1 <u>piercing</u>, bitter, cutting, harsh, penetrating, sharp 2 <u>sarcastic</u>, caustic, cutting, incisive, mordant, scathing, stinging, trenchant, vitriolic

bitter adjective 1 <u>sour</u>, acid, acrid, astringent, harsh, sharp, tart, unsweetened, vinegary 2 <u>resentful</u>, acrimonious, begrudging, hostile, sore, sour, sullen **3** freezing, biting, fierce, intense, severe, stinging

bitterness noun **1** sourness, acerbity, acidity, sharpness, tartness **2** resentment, acrimony, animosity, asperity, grudge, hostility, rancour, sarcasm

bizarre adjective strange, eccentric, extraordinary, fantastic, freakish, ludicrous, outlandish, peculiar, unusual, weird, zany

blab verb tell, blurt out, disclose, divulge, give away, let slip, let the cat out of the bag, reveal, spill the beans (informal)

black adjective **1** dark, dusky, ebony, jet, raven, sable, swarthy **2** hopeless, depressing, dismal, foreboding, gloomy, ominous, sad, sombre **3** angry, furious, hostile, menacing, resentful, sullen, threatening **4** wicked, bad, evil, iniquitous, nefarious, villainous ♦verb **5** boycott, ban, bar, blacklist

blacken verb **1** darken, befoul, begrime, cloud, dirty, make black, smudge, soil **2** discredit, defame, denigrate, malign, slander, smear, smirch, vilify

blackguard noun scoundrel, bastard (offensive), bounder (old-fashioned Brit. slang), rascal, rogue, swine, villain

blacklist verb exclude, ban, bar, boycott, debar, expel, reject, snub

black magic noun witchcraft, black art, diabolism, necromancy, sorcery, voodoo, wizardry

blackmail noun **1** threat,

extortion, hush money (slang), intimidation, ransom ♦verb **2** threaten, coerce, compel, demand, extort, hold to ransom, intimidate, squeeze

blackness noun darkness, duskiness, gloom, murkiness, swarthiness

blackout noun
1 unconsciousness, coma, faint, loss of consciousness, oblivion, swoon **2** noncommunication, censorship, radio silence, secrecy, suppression, withholding news

black sheep noun disgrace, bad egg (old-fashioned informal), dropout, ne'er-do-well, outcast, prodigal, renegade, reprobate, wastrel

blame verb **1** hold responsible, accuse, censure, chide, condemn, criticize, find fault with, reproach ♦noun
2 responsibility, accountability, culpability, fault, guilt, liability, onus

blameless adjective innocent, above suspicion, clean, faultless, guiltless, immaculate, impeccable, irreproachable, perfect, unblemished, virtuous

blameworthy adjective reprehensible, discreditable, disreputable, indefensible, inexcusable, iniquitous, reproachable, shameful

bland adjective dull, boring, flat, humdrum, insipid, tasteless, unexciting, uninspiring, vapid

blank adjective **1** unmarked, bare, clean, clear, empty, plain, void, white **2** expressionless, deadpan, empty, impassive, poker-faced

(*informal*), vacant, vague ♦ *noun*
3 empty space, emptiness, gap,
nothingness, space, vacancy,
vacuum, void

blanket *noun* **1** cover, coverlet,
rug **2** covering, carpet, cloak,
coat, layer, mantle, sheet ♦ *verb*
3 cover, cloak, coat, conceal,
hide, mask, obscure, suppress

blare *verb* sound out, blast,
clamour, clang, resound, roar,
scream, trumpet

blarney *noun* flattery,
blandishment, cajolery, coaxing,
soft soap (*informal*), spiel, sweet
talk (*informal*), wheedling

blasé *adjective* indifferent,
apathetic, lukewarm,
nonchalant, offhand,
unconcerned

blaspheme *verb* curse, abuse,
damn, desecrate, execrate,
profane, revile, swear

blasphemous *adjective*
irreverent, godless, impious,
irreligious, profane, sacrilegious,
ungodly

blasphemy *noun* irreverence,
cursing, desecration, execration,
impiety, profanity, sacrilege,
swearing

blast *noun* **1** explosion, bang,
burst, crash, detonation,
discharge, eruption, outburst,
salvo, volley **2** gust, gale, squall,
storm, strong breeze, tempest
3 blare, blow, clang, honk, peal,
scream, toot, wail ♦ *verb* **4** blow
up, break up, burst, demolish,
destroy, explode, put paid to,
ruin, shatter

blastoff *noun* launch, discharge,
expulsion, firing, launching,
liftoff, projection, shot

blatant *adjective* obvious, brazen,
conspicuous, flagrant, glaring,
obtrusive, ostentatious, overt

blaze *noun* **1** fire, bonfire,
conflagration, flames **2** glare,
beam, brilliance, flare, flash,
gleam, glitter, glow, light,
radiance ♦ *verb* **3** burn, fire,
flame **4** shine, beam, flare, flash,
glare, gleam, glow

bleach *verb* whiten, blanch, fade,
grow pale, lighten, wash out

bleak *adjective* **1** exposed, bare,
barren, desolate, unsheltered,
weather-beaten, windswept
2 dismal, cheerless, depressing,
discouraging, dreary, gloomy,
grim, hopeless, joyless, sombre

bleary *adjective* dim, blurred,
blurry, foggy, fuzzy, hazy,
indistinct, misty, murky

bleed *verb* **1** lose blood, flow,
gush, ooze, run, shed blood,
spurt **2** draw or take blood,
extract, leech **3** *Informal* extort,
drain, exhaust, fleece, milk,
squeeze

blemish *noun* **1** mark, blot,
defect, disfigurement, fault, flaw,
imperfection, smudge, stain,
taint ♦ *verb* **2** stain, damage,
disfigure, impair, injure, mar,
mark, spoil, sully, taint, tarnish

blend *verb* **1** mix, amalgamate,
combine, compound, merge,
mingle, unite **2** go well,
complement, fit, go with,
harmonize, suit ♦ *noun*
3 mixture, alloy, amalgamation,
combination, compound,
concoction, mix, synthesis, union

bless *verb* **1** sanctify, anoint,
consecrate, dedicate, exalt,
hallow, ordain **2** grant, bestow,

favour, give, grace, provide

blessed adjective holy, adored, beatified, divine, hallowed, revered, sacred, sanctified

blessing noun **1** benediction, benison, commendation, consecration, dedication, grace, invocation, thanksgiving **2** approval, backing, consent, favour, good wishes, leave, permission, sanction, support **3** benefit, favour, gift, godsend, good fortune, help, kindness, service, windfall

blight noun **1** curse, affliction, bane, contamination, corruption, evil, plague, pollution, scourge, woe **2** disease, canker, decay, fungus, infestation, mildew, pest, pestilence, rot ♦ verb **3** frustrate, crush, dash, disappoint, mar, ruin, spoil, undo, wreck

blind adjective **1** sightless, eyeless, unseeing, unsighted, visionless **2** unaware of, careless, heedless, ignorant, inattentive, inconsiderate, indifferent, insensitive, oblivious, unconscious of **3** unreasoning, indiscriminate, prejudiced ♦ noun **4** cover, camouflage, cloak, façade, feint, front, mask, masquerade, screen, smoke screen

blindly adverb **1** thoughtlessly, carelessly, heedlessly, inconsiderately, recklessly, senselessly **2** aimlessly, at random, indiscriminately, instinctively

blink verb **1** wink, bat, flutter **2** flicker, flash, gleam, glimmer, shine, twinkle, wink ♦ noun **3 on the blink** Slang not working

(properly), faulty, malfunctioning, out of action, out of order, playing up

bliss noun joy, beatitude, blessedness, blissfulness, ecstasy, euphoria, felicity, gladness, happiness, heaven, nirvana, paradise, rapture

blissful adjective joyful, ecstatic, elated, enraptured, euphoric, happy, heavenly (informal), rapturous

blister noun sore, abscess, boil, carbuncle, cyst, pimple, pustule, swelling

blithe adjective heedless, careless, casual, indifferent, nonchalant, thoughtless, unconcerned, untroubled

blitz noun attack, assault, blitzkrieg, bombardment, campaign, offensive, onslaught, raid, strike

blizzard noun snowstorm, blast, gale, squall, storm, tempest

bloat verb puff up, balloon, blow up, dilate, distend, enlarge, expand, inflate, swell

blob noun drop, ball, bead, bubble, dab, droplet, globule, lump, mass

bloc noun group, alliance, axis, coalition, faction, league, union

block noun **1** piece, bar, brick, chunk, hunk, ingot, lump, mass **2** obstruction, bar, barrier, blockage, hindrance, impediment, jam, obstacle ♦ verb **3** obstruct, bung up (informal), choke, clog, close, plug, stem the flow, stop up **4** stop, bar, check, halt, hinder, impede, obstruct, thwart

blockade noun <u>stoppage</u>, barricade, barrier, block, hindrance, impediment, obstacle, obstruction, restriction, siege

blockage noun <u>obstruction</u>, block, impediment, occlusion, stoppage

blockhead noun <u>idiot</u>, chump (informal), dunce, fool, nitwit, numbskull or numskull, thickhead, twit (informal, chiefly Brit.)

bloke noun Informal <u>man</u>, chap, character (informal), fellow, guy (informal), individual, person

blond, blonde adjective <u>fair</u>, fair-haired, fair-skinned, flaxen, golden-haired, light, tow-headed

blood noun 1 <u>lifeblood</u>, gore, vital fluid 2 <u>family</u>, ancestry, birth, descent, extraction, kinship, lineage, relations

bloodcurdling adjective <u>terrifying</u>, appalling, chilling, dreadful, fearful, frightening, hair-raising, horrendous, horrifying, scaring, spine-chilling

bloodshed noun <u>killing</u>, blood bath, blood-letting, butchery, carnage, gore, massacre, murder, slaughter, slaying

bloodthirsty adjective <u>cruel</u>, barbarous, brutal, cut-throat, ferocious, gory, murderous, savage, vicious, warlike

bloody adjective 1 <u>bloodstained</u>, bleeding, blood-soaked, blood-spattered, gaping, raw 2 <u>cruel</u>, ferocious, fierce, sanguinary, savage

bloom noun 1 <u>flower</u>, blossom, blossoming, bud, efflorescence, opening (of flowers) 2 <u>prime</u>, beauty, flourishing, freshness, glow, health, heyday, lustre, radiance, vigour ♦ verb 3 <u>blossom</u>, blow, bud, burgeon, open, sprout 4 <u>flourish</u>, develop, fare well, grow, prosper, succeed, thrive, wax

blossom noun 1 <u>flower</u>, bloom, bud, floret, flowers ♦ verb 2 <u>flower</u>, bloom, burgeon 3 <u>grow</u>, bloom, develop, flourish, mature, progress, prosper, thrive

blot noun 1 <u>spot</u>, blotch, mark, patch, smear, smudge, speck, splodge 2 <u>stain</u>, blemish, defect, fault, flaw, scar, spot, taint ♦ verb 3 <u>stain</u>, disgrace, mark, smirch, smudge, spoil, spot, sully, tarnish 4 <u>soak up</u>, absorb, dry, take up 5 <u>blot out</u> a <u>obliterate</u>, darken, destroy, eclipse, efface, obscure, shadow b <u>erase</u>, cancel, expunge

blow[1] verb 1 <u>carry</u>, buffet, drive, fling, flutter, move, sweep, waft 2 <u>exhale</u>, breathe, pant, puff 3 <u>play</u>, blare, mouth, pipe, sound, toot, trumpet, vibrate

blow[2] noun 1 <u>knock</u>, bang, clout (informal), punch, smack, sock (slang), stroke, thump, wallop (informal), whack 2 <u>setback</u>, bombshell, calamity, catastrophe, disappointment, disaster, misfortune, reverse, shock

blow out verb 1 <u>put out</u>, extinguish, snuff 2 <u>burst</u>, erupt, explode, rupture, shatter

blow up verb 1 <u>explode</u>, blast, blow sky-high, bomb, burst, detonate, rupture, shatter

2 <u>inflate</u>, bloat, distend, enlarge, expand, fill, puff up, pump up, swell 3 *Informal* <u>lose one's temper</u>, become angry, erupt, fly off the handle (*informal*), hit the roof (*informal*), rage, see red (*informal*)

bludgeon noun 1 <u>club</u>, cosh (*Brit.*), cudgel, truncheon ♦ verb 2 <u>club</u>, beat up, cosh (*Brit.*), cudgel, knock down, strike 3 <u>bully</u>, bulldoze (*informal*), coerce, force, railroad (*informal*), steamroller

blue adjective 1 <u>azure</u>, cerulean, cobalt, cyan, navy, sapphire, sky-coloured, ultramarine 2 <u>depressed</u>, dejected, despondent, downcast, low, melancholy, sad, unhappy 3 <u>smutty</u>, indecent, lewd, obscene, risqué, X-rated (*informal*)

blueprint noun 1 <u>plan</u>, design, draft, outline, pattern, pilot scheme, prototype, sketch

blues plural noun 1 <u>depression</u>, doldrums, dumps (*informal*), gloom, low spirits, melancholy, unhappiness

bluff[1] verb 1 <u>deceive</u>, con, delude, fake, feign, mislead, pretend, pull the wool over someone's eyes ♦ noun 2 <u>deception</u>, bluster, bravado, deceit, fraud, humbug, pretence, sham, subterfuge

bluff[2] noun 1 <u>precipice</u>, bank, cliff, crag, escarpment, headland, peak, promontory, ridge ♦ adjective 2 <u>hearty</u>, blunt, blustering, genial, good-natured, open, outspoken, plain-spoken

blunder noun 1 <u>mistake</u>, bloomer

(*Brit. informal*), clanger (*informal*), faux pas, gaffe, howler (*informal*), indiscretion 2 <u>error</u>, fault, inaccuracy, mistake, oversight, slip, slip-up (*informal*) ♦ verb 3 <u>make a mistake</u>, botch, bungle, err, put one's foot in it (*informal*), slip up (*informal*) 4 <u>stumble</u>, bumble, flounder

blunt adjective 1 <u>dull</u>, dulled, edgeless, pointless, rounded, unsharpened 2 <u>forthright</u>, bluff, brusque, frank, outspoken, plain-spoken, rude, straightforward, tactless ♦ verb 3 <u>dull</u>, dampen, deaden, numb, soften, take the edge off, water down, weaken

blur verb 1 <u>make indistinct</u>, cloud, darken, make hazy, make vague, mask, obscure ♦ noun 2 <u>indistinctness</u>, confusion, fog, haze, obscurity

blurt out verb <u>exclaim</u>, disclose, let the cat out of the bag, reveal, spill the beans (*informal*), tell all, utter suddenly

blush verb 1 <u>turn red</u>, colour, flush, go red (as a beetroot), redden, turn scarlet ♦ noun 2 <u>reddening</u>, colour, flush, glow, pink tinge, rosiness, rosy tint, ruddiness

bluster verb 1 <u>roar</u>, bully, domineer, hector, rant, storm ♦ noun 2 <u>hot air</u> (*informal*), bluff, bombast, bravado

blustery adjective <u>gusty</u>, boisterous, inclement, squally, stormy, tempestuous, violent, wild, windy

board noun 1 <u>plank</u>, panel, piece of timber, slat, timber 2 <u>directors</u>, advisers, committee,

conclave, council, panel, trustees
3 meals, daily meals, provisions,
victuals ♦ *verb* **4** get on, embark,
enter, mount **5** lodge, put up,
quarter, room

boast *verb* **1** brag, blow one's
own trumpet, crow, strut,
swagger, talk big (*slang*), vaunt
2 possess, be proud of,
congratulate oneself on, exhibit,
flatter oneself, pride oneself on,
show off ♦ *noun* **3** brag, avowal

boastful *adjective* bragging,
cocky, conceited, crowing,
egotistical, full of oneself,
swaggering, swollen-headed,
vaunting

bob *verb* duck, bounce, hop,
nod, oscillate, waggle, wobble

bode *verb* portend, augur, be an
omen of, forebode, foretell,
predict, signify, threaten

bodily *adjective* physical, actual,
carnal, corporal, corporeal,
material, substantial, tangible

body *noun* **1** physique, build,
figure, form, frame, shape
2 torso, trunk **3** corpse, cadaver,
carcass, dead body, remains, stiff
(*slang*) **4** organization,
association, band, bloc,
collection, company,
confederation, congress,
corporation, society **5** main part,
bulk, essence, mass, material,
matter, substance

boffin *noun Brit. informal* expert,
brainbox, egghead, genius,
intellectual, inventor, mastermind

bog *noun* marsh, fen, mire,
morass, quagmire, slough,
swamp, wetlands

bogey *noun* bugbear, bête noire,
bugaboo, nightmare

bogus *adjective* fake, artificial,
counterfeit, false, forged,
fraudulent, imitation, phoney *or*
phony (*informal*), sham

bohemian *adjective*
1 unconventional, alternative,
artistic, arty (*informal*), left bank,
nonconformist, offbeat,
unorthodox ♦ *noun*
2 nonconformist, beatnik,
dropout, hippy, iconoclast

boil[1] *verb* bubble, effervesce, fizz,
foam, froth, seethe

boil[2] *noun* pustule, blister,
carbuncle, gathering, swelling,
tumour, ulcer

boisterous *adjective* unruly,
disorderly, loud, noisy, riotous,
rollicking, rowdy, unrestrained,
vociferous, wild

bold *adjective* **1** fearless,
adventurous, audacious, brave,
courageous, daring, enterprising,
heroic, intrepid, valiant
2 impudent, barefaced, brazen,
cheeky, confident, forward,
insolent, rude, shameless

bolster *verb* support, augment,
boost, help, reinforce, shore up,
strengthen

bolt *noun* **1** bar, catch, fastener,
latch, lock, sliding bar **2** pin,
peg, rivet, rod ♦ *verb* **3** run
away, abscond, dash, escape,
flee, fly, make a break (for it),
run for it **4** lock, bar, fasten,
latch, secure **5** gobble, cram,
devour, gorge, gulp, guzzle,
stuff, swallow whole, wolf

bomb *noun* **1** explosive, device,
grenade, mine, missile,
projectile, rocket, shell, torpedo
♦ *verb* **2** blow up, attack, blow
sky-high, bombard, destroy,

shell, strafe, torpedo

bombard verb 1 *bomb*, assault, blitz, fire upon, open fire, pound, shell, strafe 2 *attack*, assail, beset, besiege, harass, hound, pester

bombardment noun *bombing*, assault, attack, barrage, blitz, fusillade, shelling

bombastic adjective *grandiloquent*, grandiose, high-flown, inflated, pompous, verbose, wordy

bona fide adjective *genuine*, actual, authentic, honest, kosher (*informal*), legitimate, real, true

bond noun 1 *fastening*, chain, cord, fetter, ligature, manacle, shackle, tie 2 *tie*, affiliation, affinity, attachment, connection, link, relation, union 3 *agreement*, contract, covenant, guarantee, obligation, pledge, promise, word ♦ verb 4 *hold together*, bind, connect, fasten, fix together, glue, paste

bondage noun *slavery*, captivity, confinement, enslavement, imprisonment, subjugation

bonus noun *extra*, dividend, gift, icing on the cake, plus, premium, prize, reward

bony adjective *thin*, emaciated, gaunt, lean, scrawny, skin and bone, skinny

book noun 1 *work*, publication, title, tome, tract, volume 2 *notebook*, album, diary, exercise book, jotter, pad ♦ verb 3 *reserve*, arrange for, charter, engage, make reservations, organize, programme, schedule 4 *note*, enter, list, log, mark down, put down, record,

register, write down

booklet noun *brochure*, leaflet, pamphlet

boom verb 1 *bang*, blast, crash, explode, resound, reverberate, roar, roll, rumble, thunder 2 *flourish*, develop, expand, grow, increase, intensify, prosper, strengthen, swell, thrive ♦ noun 3 *bang*, blast, burst, clap, crash, explosion, roar, rumble, thunder 4 *expansion*, boost, development, growth, improvement, increase, jump, upsurge, upswing, upturn

boon noun *benefit*, advantage, blessing, favour, gift, godsend, manna from heaven, windfall

boorish adjective *loutish*, churlish, coarse, crude, oafish, uncivilized, uncouth, vulgar

boost noun 1 *help*, encouragement, praise, promotion 2 *rise*, addition, expansion, improvement, increase, increment, jump ♦ verb 3 *increase*, add to, amplify, develop, enlarge, expand, heighten, raise 4 *advertise*, encourage, foster, further, hype, plug (*informal*), praise, promote

boot verb *kick*, drive, drop-kick, knock, punt, put the boot in(to) (*slang*), shove

booty noun *plunder*, gains, haul, loot, prey, spoils, swag (*slang*), takings, winnings

border noun 1 *frontier*, borderline, boundary, line, march 2 *edge*, bounds, brink, limits, margin, rim, verge ♦ verb 3 *edge*, bind, decorate, fringe, hem, rim, trim

bore¹ verb *drill*, burrow, gouge

out, mine, penetrate, perforate, pierce, sink, tunnel

bore² verb **1** tire, be tedious, fatigue, jade, pall on, send to sleep, wear out, weary ♦ noun **2** nuisance, anorak (informal), pain (informal), yawn (informal)

bored adjective fed up, listless, tired, uninterested, wearied

boredom noun tedium, apathy, ennui, flatness, monotony, sameness, tediousness, weariness, world-weariness

boring adjective uninteresting, dull, flat, humdrum, mind-numbing, monotonous, tedious, tiresome

borrow verb **1** take on loan, cadge, scrounge (informal), touch (someone) for (slang), use temporarily **2** steal, adopt, copy, obtain, plagiarize, take, usurp

bosom noun **1** breast, bust, chest ♦ adjective **2** intimate, boon, cherished, close, confidential, dear, very dear

boss¹ noun head, chief, director, employer, gaffer (informal, chiefly Brit.), leader, manager, master, supervisor

boss² noun stud, knob, point, protuberance, tip

boss around verb Informal domineer, bully, dominate, oppress, order, push around (slang)

bossy adjective domineering, arrogant, authoritarian, autocratic, dictatorial, hectoring, high-handed, imperious, overbearing, tyrannical

botch verb **1** spoil, blunder, bungle, cock up (Brit. slang),

make a pig's ear of (informal), mar, mess up, screw up (informal) ♦ noun **2** mess, blunder, bungle, cock-up (Brit. slang), failure, hash, pig's ear (informal)

bother verb **1** trouble, alarm, concern, disturb, harass, hassle (informal), inconvenience, pester, plague, worry ♦ noun **2** trouble, difficulty, fuss, hassle (informal), inconvenience, irritation, nuisance, problem, worry

bottleneck noun hold-up, block, blockage, congestion, impediment, jam, obstacle, obstruction, snarl-up (informal, chiefly Brit.)

bottle up verb suppress, check, contain, curb, keep back, restrict, shut in, trap

bottom noun **1** lowest part, base, bed, depths, floor, foot, foundation **2** underside, lower side, sole, underneath **3** buttocks, backside, behind (informal), posterior, rear, rump, seat ♦ adjective **4** lowest, last

bottomless adjective unlimited, boundless, deep, fathomless, immeasurable, inexhaustible, infinite, unfathomable

bounce verb **1** rebound, bob, bound, jump, leap, recoil, ricochet, spring ♦ noun **2** Informal life, dynamism, energy, go (informal), liveliness, vigour, vivacity, zip (informal) **3** springiness, elasticity, give, recoil, resilience, spring

bound¹ adjective **1** tied, cased, fastened, fixed, pinioned, secured, tied up **2** certain, destined, doomed, fated, sure

3 <u>obliged</u>, beholden, committed, compelled, constrained, duty-bound, forced, pledged, required

bound[2] *verb* <u>limit</u>, confine, demarcate, encircle, enclose, hem in, restrain, restrict, surround

bound[3] *verb, noun* <u>leap</u>, bob, bounce, gambol, hurdle, jump, skip, spring, vault

boundary *noun* <u>limits</u>, barrier, border, borderline, brink, edge, extremity, fringe, frontier, margin

boundless *adjective* <u>unlimited</u>, endless, immense, incalculable, inexhaustible, infinite, unconfined, untold, vast

bounds *plural noun* <u>boundary</u>, border, confine, edge, extremity, limit, rim, verge

bountiful *adjective Literary*
1 <u>plentiful</u>, abundant, ample, bounteous, copious, exuberant, lavish, luxuriant, prolific
2 <u>generous</u>, liberal, magnanimous, open-handed, prodigal, unstinting

bounty *noun Literary*
1 <u>generosity</u>, benevolence, charity, kindness, largesse *or* largess, liberality, philanthropy
2 <u>reward</u>, bonus, gift, present

bouquet *noun* **1** <u>bunch of flowers</u>, buttonhole, corsage, garland, nosegay, posy, spray, wreath **2** <u>aroma</u>, fragrance, perfume, redolence, savour, scent

bourgeois *adjective* <u>middle-class</u>, conventional, hidebound, materialistic, traditional

bout *noun* **1** <u>period</u>, fit, spell, stint, term, turn **2** <u>fight</u>, boxing

match, competition, contest, encounter, engagement, match, set-to, struggle

bow[1] *verb* **1** <u>bend</u>, bob, droop, genuflect, nod, stoop **2** <u>give in</u>, acquiesce, comply, concede, defer, kowtow, relent, submit, succumb, surrender, yield ♦ *noun* **3** <u>bending</u>, bob, genuflexion, kowtow, nod, obeisance

bow[2] *noun Nautical* <u>prow</u>, beak, fore, head, stem

bowels *plural noun* **1** <u>guts</u>, entrails, innards (*informal*), insides (*informal*), intestines, viscera, vitals **2** <u>depths</u>, belly, core, deep, hold, inside, interior

bowl[1] *noun* <u>basin</u>, dish, vessel

bowl[2] *verb* <u>throw</u>, fling, hurl, pitch

box[1] *noun* **1** <u>container</u>, carton, case, casket, chest, pack, package, receptacle, trunk ♦ *verb* **2** <u>pack</u>, package, wrap

box[2] *verb* <u>fight</u>, exchange blows, spar

boxer *noun* <u>fighter</u>, prizefighter, pugilist, sparring partner

boy *noun* <u>lad</u>, fellow, junior, schoolboy, stripling, youngster, youth

boycott *verb* <u>embargo</u>, ban, bar, black, exclude, outlaw, prohibit, refuse, reject

boyfriend *noun* <u>sweetheart</u>, admirer, beau, date, lover, man, suitor

boyish *adjective* <u>youthful</u>, adolescent, childish, immature, juvenile, puerile, young

brace *noun* **1** <u>support</u>, bolster, bracket, buttress, prop, reinforcement, stay, strut, truss ♦ *verb* **2** <u>support</u>, bolster, buttress, fortify, reinforce, steady, strengthen

bracing adjective <u>refreshing</u>, brisk, crisp, exhilarating, fresh, invigorating, stimulating

brag verb <u>boast</u>, blow one's own trumpet, bluster, crow, swagger, talk big (slang), vaunt

braggart noun <u>boaster</u>, bigmouth (slang), bragger, show-off (informal)

braid verb <u>interweave</u>, entwine, interlace, intertwine, lace, plait, twine, weave

brainless adjective <u>stupid</u>, foolish, idiotic, inane, mindless, senseless, thoughtless, witless

brains plural noun <u>intelligence</u>, intellect, sense, understanding

brainwave noun <u>idea</u>, bright idea, stroke of genius, thought

brainy adjective Informal <u>intelligent</u>, bright, brilliant, clever, smart

brake noun 1 <u>control</u>, check, constraint, curb, rein, restraint ♦ verb 2 <u>slow</u>, check, decelerate, halt, moderate, reduce speed, slacken, stop

branch noun 1 <u>bough</u>, arm, limb, offshoot, shoot, spray, sprig 2 <u>division</u>, chapter, department, office, part, section, subdivision, subsection, wing

brand noun 1 <u>label</u>, emblem, hallmark, logo, marker, mark, sign, stamp, symbol, trademark 2 <u>kind</u>, cast, class, grade, make, quality, sort, species, type, variety ♦ verb 3 <u>mark</u>, burn, burn in, label, scar, stamp 4 <u>stigmatize</u>, censure, denounce, discredit, disgrace, expose, mark

brandish verb <u>wave</u>, display, exhibit, flaunt, flourish, parade, raise, shake, swing, wield

brash adjective <u>bold</u>, brazen, cocky, impertinent, impudent, insolent, pushy (informal), rude

bravado noun <u>swagger</u>, bluster, boastfulness, boasting, bombast, swashbuckling, vaunting

brave adjective 1 <u>courageous</u>, bold, daring, fearless, heroic, intrepid, plucky, resolute, valiant ♦ verb 2 <u>confront</u>, defy, endure, face, stand up to, suffer, tackle, withstand

bravery noun <u>courage</u>, boldness, daring, fearlessness, fortitude, heroism, intrepidity, mettle, pluck, spirit, valour

brawl noun 1 <u>fight</u>, affray (Law), altercation, clash, dispute, fracas, fray, melee or mêlée, punch-up (Brit. informal), rumpus, scuffle, skirmish ♦ verb 2 <u>fight</u>, scrap (informal), scuffle, tussle, wrestle

brawn noun <u>muscle</u>, beef (informal), might, muscles, power, strength, vigour

brawny adjective <u>muscular</u>, beefy (informal), hefty (informal), lusty, powerful, strapping, strong, sturdy, well-built

brazen adjective <u>bold</u>, audacious, barefaced, brash, defiant, impudent, insolent, shameless, unabashed, unashamed

breach noun 1 <u>nonobservance</u>, contravention, infraction, infringement, noncompliance, transgression, trespass, violation 2 <u>crack</u>, cleft, fissure, gap, opening, rift, rupture, split

bread noun 1 <u>food</u>, fare,

nourishment, sustenance **2** *Slang* money, cash, dough (*slang*)

breadth noun **1** width, broadness, latitude, span, spread, wideness **2** extent, compass, expanse, range, scale, scope

break verb **1** separate, burst, crack, destroy, disintegrate, fracture, fragment, shatter, smash, snap, split, tear **2** disobey, breach, contravene, disregard, infringe, renege on, transgress, violate **3** reveal, announce, disclose, divulge, impart, inform, let out, make public, proclaim, tell **4** stop, abandon, cut, discontinue, give up, interrupt, pause, rest, suspend **5** weaken, demoralize, dispirit, subdue, tame, undermine **6** *Of a record, etc.* beat, better, exceed, excel, go beyond, outdo, outstrip, surpass, top ♦ noun **7** division, crack, fissure, fracture, gap, hole, opening, split, tear **8** rest, breather (*informal*), hiatus, interlude, intermission, interruption, interval, let-up (*informal*), lull, pause, respite **9** *Informal* stroke of luck, advantage, chance, fortune, opening, opportunity

breakable adjective fragile, brittle, crumbly, delicate, flimsy, frail, frangible, friable

breakdown noun collapse, disintegration, disruption, failure, mishap, stoppage

break down verb **1** collapse, come unstuck, fail, seize up, stop, stop working **2** be overcome, crack up (*informal*),

go to pieces

break-in noun burglary, breaking and entering, robbery

break off verb **1** detach, divide, part, pull off, separate, sever, snap off, splinter **2** stop, cease, desist, discontinue, end, finish, halt, pull the plug on, suspend, terminate

break out verb begin, appear, arise, commence, emerge, happen, occur, set in, spring up, start

breakthrough noun development, advance, discovery, find, invention, leap, progress, quantum leap, step forward

break up verb **1** separate, dissolve, divide, divorce, part, scatter, sever, split **2** stop, adjourn, disband, dismantle, end, suspend, terminate

breast noun bosom, bust, chest, front, teat, udder

breath noun respiration, breathing, exhalation, gasp, gulp, inhalation, pant, wheeze

breathe verb **1** inhale and exhale, draw in, gasp, gulp, pant, puff, respire, wheeze **2** whisper, murmur, sigh

breather noun *Informal* rest, break, breathing space, halt, pause, recess, respite

breathless adjective **1** out of breath, gasping, gulping, panting, short-winded, spent, wheezing **2** excited, eager, on tenterhooks, open-mouthed, with bated breath

breathtaking adjective amazing, astonishing, awe-inspiring, exciting, impressive, magnificent, sensational, stunning (*informal*), thrilling

breed *verb* **1** reproduce, bear, bring forth, hatch, multiply, procreate, produce, propagate **2** bring up, cultivate, develop, nourish, nurture, raise, rear **3** produce, arouse, bring about, cause, create, generate, give rise to, stir up ◆ *noun* **4** variety, pedigree, race, species, stock, strain, type **5** kind, brand, sort, stamp, type, variety

breeding *noun* **1** upbringing, ancestry, cultivation, development, lineage, nurture, raising, rearing, reproduction, training **2** refinement, conduct, courtesy, cultivation, culture, polish, sophistication, urbanity

breeze *noun* **1** light wind, air, breath of wind, current of air, draught, gust, waft, zephyr ◆ *verb* **2** move briskly, flit, glide, hurry, pass, sail, sweep

breezy *adjective* **1** windy, airy, blowy, blustery, fresh, gusty, squally **2** carefree, blithe, casual, easy-going, free and easy, jaunty, light-hearted, lively, sprightly

brevity *noun* **1** shortness, briefness, impermanence, transience, transitoriness **2** conciseness, crispness, curtness, economy, pithiness, succinctness, terseness

brew *verb* **1** make (*beer*), boil, ferment, infuse (*tea*), soak, steep, stew **2** develop, foment, form, gather, start, stir up ◆ *noun* **3** drink, beverage, blend, concoction, infusion, liquor,

mixture, preparation

bribe *verb* **1** buy off, corrupt, grease the palm or hand of (*slang*), pay off (*informal*), reward, suborn ◆ *noun* **2** inducement, allurement, backhander (*slang*), enticement, kickback (*U.S.*), pay-off (*informal*), sweetener (*slang*)

bribery *noun* buying off, corruption, inducement, palm-greasing (*slang*), payola (*informal*)

bric-a-brac *noun* knick-knacks, baubles, curios, ornaments, trinkets

bridal *adjective* matrimonial, conjugal, connubial, marital, marriage, nuptial, wedding

bridge *noun* **1** arch, flyover, overpass, span, viaduct ◆ *verb* **2** connect, join, link, span

bridle *noun* **1** curb, check, control, rein, restraint ◆ *verb* **2** get angry, be indignant, bristle, draw (oneself) up, get one's back up, raise one's hackles, rear up

brief *adjective* **1** short, ephemeral, fleeting, momentary, quick, short-lived, swift, transitory ◆ *noun* **2** summary, abridgment, abstract, digest, epitome, outline, précis, sketch, synopsis ◆ *verb* **3** inform, advise, explain, fill in (*informal*), instruct, keep posted, prepare, prime, put (someone) in the picture (*informal*)

briefing *noun* instructions, conference, directions, guidance, information, preparation, priming, rundown

briefly *adverb* shortly, concisely,

hastily, hurriedly, in a nutshell, in brief, momentarily, quickly

brigade noun group, band, company, corps, force, organization, outfit, squad, team, troop, unit

brigand noun bandit, desperado, freebooter, gangster, highwayman, marauder, outlaw, plunderer, robber

bright adjective 1 shining, brilliant, dazzling, gleaming, glowing, luminous, lustrous, radiant, shimmering, vivid 2 intelligent, astute, aware, clever, inventive, quick-witted, sharp, smart, wide-awake 3 sunny, clear, cloudless, fair, limpid, lucid, pleasant, translucent, transparent, unclouded

brighten verb make brighter, gleam, glow, illuminate, lighten, light up, shine

brightness noun 1 shine, brilliance, glare, incandescence, intensity, light, luminosity, radiance, vividness 2 intelligence, acuity, cleverness, quickness, sharpness, smartness

brilliance, brilliancy noun 1 brightness, dazzle, intensity, luminosity, lustre, radiance, sparkle, vividness 2 talent, cleverness, distinction, excellence, genius, greatness, inventiveness, wisdom 3 splendour, éclat, glamour, grandeur, illustriousness, magnificence

brilliant adjective 1 shining, bright, dazzling, glittering, intense, luminous, radiant, sparkling, vivid 2 splendid,

celebrated, famous, glorious, illustrious, magnificent, notable, outstanding, superb 3 intelligent, clever, expert, gifted, intellectual, inventive, masterly, penetrating, profound, talented

brim noun 1 rim, border, brink, edge, lip, margin, skirt, verge ◆ verb 2 be full, fill, fill up, hold no more, overflow, run over, spill, well over

bring verb 1 take, bear, carry, conduct, convey, deliver, escort, fetch, guide, lead, transfer, transport 2 cause, contribute to, create, effect, inflict, occasion, produce, result in, wreak

bring about verb cause, accomplish, achieve, create, effect, generate, give rise to, make happen, produce

bring off verb accomplish, achieve, carry off, execute, perform, pull off, succeed

bring up verb 1 rear, breed, develop, educate, form, nurture, raise, support, teach, train 2 mention, allude to, broach, introduce, move, propose, put forward, raise

brink noun edge, border, boundary, brim, fringe, frontier, limit, lip, margin, rim, skirt, threshold, verge

brisk adjective lively, active, bustling, busy, energetic, quick, sprightly, spry, vigorous

briskly adverb quickly, actively, apace, efficiently, energetically, promptly, rapidly, readily, smartly

bristle noun 1 hair, barb, prickle, spine, stubble, thorn, whisker ◆ verb 2 stand up, rise, stand on

bristly adjective hairy, prickly, rough, stubbly

brittle adjective fragile, breakable, crisp, crumbling, crumbly, delicate, frail, frangible, friable

broach verb 1 bring up, introduce, mention, open up, propose, raise the subject, speak of, suggest, talk of, touch on 2 open, crack, draw off, pierce, puncture, start, tap, uncork

broad adjective 1 wide, ample, expansive, extensive, generous, large, roomy, spacious, vast, voluminous, widespread 2 general, all-embracing, comprehensive, encyclopedic, inclusive, sweeping, wide, wide-ranging

broadcast noun 1 transmission, programme, show, telecast ◆ verb 2 transmit, air, beam, cable, put on the air, radio, relay, show, televise 3 make public, advertise, announce, circulate, proclaim, publish, report, spread

broaden verb expand, develop, enlarge, extend, increase, spread, stretch, supplement, swell, widen

broad-minded adjective tolerant, free-thinking, indulgent, liberal, open-minded, permissive, unbiased, unbigoted, unprejudiced

broadside noun attack, assault, battering, bombardment, censure, criticism, denunciation, diatribe

brochure noun booklet, advertisement, circular, folder,

handbill, hand-out, leaflet, mailshot, pamphlet

broke adjective Informal penniless, bankrupt, bust (informal), down and out, impoverished, insolvent, in the red, ruined, short, skint (Brit. slang)

broken adjective 1 smashed, burst, fractured, fragmented, ruptured, separated, severed, shattered 2 interrupted, discontinuous, erratic, fragmentary, incomplete, intermittent, spasmodic 3 not working, defective, imperfect, kaput (informal), on the blink (slang), out of order 4 imperfect, disjointed, halting, hesitating, stammering

brokenhearted adjective heartbroken, desolate, devastated, disconsolate, grief-stricken, inconsolable, miserable, sorrowful, wretched

broker noun dealer, agent, factor, go-between, intermediary, middleman, negotiator

bronze adjective reddish-brown, brownish, chestnut, copper, rust, tan

brood noun 1 offspring, clutch, family, issue, litter, progeny ◆ verb 2 think upon, agonize, dwell upon, mope, mull over, muse, ponder, ruminate

brook noun stream, beck, burn, rill, rivulet, watercourse

brother noun 1 sibling, blood brother, kin, kinsman, relation, relative 2 monk, cleric, friar

brotherhood noun 1 fellowship, brotherliness, camaraderie, companionship, comradeship, friendliness, kinship **2** <u>association</u>, alliance, community, fraternity, guild, league, order, society, union

brotherly adjective <u>kind</u>, affectionate, altruistic, amicable, benevolent, cordial, fraternal, friendly, neighbourly, philanthropic, sympathetic

browbeat verb <u>bully</u>, badger, coerce, dragoon, hector, intimidate, ride roughshod over, threaten, tyrannize

brown adjective **1** <u>brunette</u>, auburn, bay, bronze, chestnut, chocolate, coffee, dun, hazel, sunburnt, tan, tanned, tawny, umber ♦ verb **2** <u>fry</u>, cook, grill, sauté, seal, sear

browse verb **1** <u>skim</u>, dip into, examine cursorily, flip through, glance at, leaf through, look round, look through, peruse, scan, survey **2** <u>graze</u>, eat, feed, nibble

bruise verb **1** <u>discolour</u>, damage, injure, mar, mark, pound ♦ noun **2** <u>discoloration</u>, black mark, blemish, contusion, injury, mark, swelling

brunt noun <u>full force</u>, burden, force, impact, pressure, shock, strain, stress, thrust, violence

brush¹ noun **1** <u>broom</u>, besom, sweeper **2** <u>encounter</u>, clash, conflict, confrontation, skirmish, tussle ♦ verb **3** <u>clean</u>, buff, paint, polish, sweep, wash **4** <u>touch</u>, flick, glance, graze, kiss, scrape, stroke, sweep

brush² noun <u>shrubs</u>, brushwood, bushes, copse, scrub, thicket, undergrowth

brush off verb Slang <u>ignore</u>, disdain, dismiss, disregard, reject, repudiate, scorn, snub, spurn

brush up verb <u>revise</u>, bone up (informal), cram, go over, polish up, read up, refresh one's memory, relearn, study

brusque adjective <u>curt</u>, abrupt, discourteous, gruff, impolite, sharp, short, surly, terse

brutal adjective **1** <u>cruel</u>, bloodthirsty, heartless, inhuman, ruthless, savage, uncivilized, vicious **2** <u>harsh</u>, callous, gruff, impolite, insensitive, rough, rude, severe

brutality noun <u>cruelty</u>, atrocity, barbarism, bloodthirstiness, ferocity, inhumanity, ruthlessness, savagery, viciousness

brute noun **1** <u>savage</u>, barbarian, beast, devil, fiend, monster, sadist, swine **2** <u>animal</u>, beast, creature, wild animal ♦ adjective **3** <u>mindless</u>, bodily, carnal, fleshly, instinctive, physical, senseless, unthinking

bubble noun **1** <u>air ball</u>, bead, blister, blob, drop, droplet, globule ♦ verb **2** <u>foam</u>, boil, effervesce, fizz, froth, percolate, seethe, sparkle **3** <u>gurgle</u>, babble, burble, murmur, ripple, trickle

bubbly adjective **1** <u>lively</u>, animated, bouncy, elated, excited, happy, merry, sparky **2** <u>frothy</u>, carbonated, effervescent, fizzy, foamy, sparkling

buccaneer noun <u>pirate</u>, corsair, freebooter, privateer, sea-rover

buckle noun **1** <u>fastener</u>, catch, clasp, clip, hasp ♦ verb **2** <u>fasten</u>, clasp, close, hook, secure

3 distort, bend, bulge, cave in, collapse, contort, crumple, fold, twist, warp

bud noun 1 shoot, embryo, germ, sprout ♦verb 2 develop, burgeon, burst forth, grow, shoot, sprout

budding adjective developing, beginning, burgeoning, embryonic, fledgling, growing, incipient, nascent, potential, promising

budge verb move, dislodge, push, shift, stir

budget noun 1 allowance, allocation, cost, finances, funds, means, resources ♦verb 2 plan, allocate, apportion, cost, estimate, ration

buff[1] adjective 1 yellowish-brown, sandy, straw, tan, yellowish ♦verb 2 polish, brush, burnish, rub, shine, smooth

buff[2] noun Informal expert, addict, admirer, aficionado, connoisseur, devotee, enthusiast, fan

buffer noun safeguard, bulwark, bumper, cushion, fender, intermediary, screen, shield, shock absorber

buffet[1] noun snack bar, brasserie, café, cafeteria, refreshment counter, sideboard

buffet[2] verb batter, beat, bump, knock, pound, pummel, strike, thump, wallop (informal)

buffoon noun clown, comedian, comic, fool, harlequin, jester, joker, wag

bug noun 1 Informal illness, disease, infection, lurgy (informal), virus 2 fault, defect, error, flaw, glitch, gremlin ♦verb

3 Informal annoy, bother, disturb, get on one's nerves (informal), hassle (informal), irritate, pester, vex 4 tap, eavesdrop, listen in, spy

bugbear noun pet hate, bane, bête noire, bogey, dread, horror, nightmare

build verb 1 construct, assemble, erect, fabricate, form, make, put up, raise ♦noun 2 physique, body, figure, form, frame, shape, structure

building noun structure, domicile, dwelling, edifice, house

build-up noun increase, accumulation, development, enlargement, escalation, expansion, gain, growth

bulbous adjective bulging, bloated, convex, rounded, swelling, swollen

bulge noun 1 swelling, bump, hump, lump, projection, protrusion, protuberance 2 increase, boost, intensification, rise, surge ♦verb 3 swell out, dilate, distend, expand, project, protrude, puff out, stick out

bulk noun 1 size, dimensions, immensity, largeness, magnitude, substance, volume, weight 2 main part, better part, body, lion's share, majority, mass, most, nearly all, preponderance

bulky adjective large, big, cumbersome, heavy, hulking, massive, substantial, unwieldy, voluminous, weighty

bulldoze verb demolish, flatten, level, raze

bullet noun projectile, ball,

missile, pellet, shot, slug

bulletin *noun* <u>announcement</u>, account, communication, communiqué, dispatch, message, news flash, notification, report, statement

bully *noun* 1 <u>persecutor</u>, browbeater, bully boy, coercer, intimidator, oppressor, ruffian, tormentor, tough ◆ *verb* 2 <u>persecute</u>, browbeat, coerce, domineer, hector, intimidate, oppress, push around (*slang*), terrorize, tyrannize

bulwark *noun* 1 <u>fortification</u>, bastion, buttress, defence, embankment, partition, rampart 2 <u>defence</u>, buffer, guard, mainstay, safeguard, security, support

bumbling *adjective* <u>clumsy</u>, awkward, blundering, bungling, incompetent, inefficient, inept, maladroit, muddled

bump *verb* 1 <u>knock</u>, bang, collide (with), crash, hit, slam, smash into, strike 2 <u>jerk</u>, bounce, jolt, rattle, shake ◆ *noun* 3 <u>knock</u>, bang, blow, collision, crash, impact, jolt, thud, thump 4 <u>lump</u>, bulge, contusion, hump, nodule, protuberance, swelling

bumper *adjective* <u>exceptional</u>, abundant, bountiful, excellent, jumbo (*informal*), massive, whopping (*informal*)

bumpkin *noun* <u>yokel</u>, country bumpkin, hick (*informal, chiefly U.S. & Canad.*), hillbilly, peasant, rustic

bumptious *adjective* <u>cocky</u>, arrogant, brash, conceited, forward, full of oneself,

overconfident, pushy (*informal*), self-assertive

bumpy *adjective* <u>rough</u>, bouncy, choppy, jarring, jerky, jolting, rutted, uneven

bunch *noun* 1 <u>number</u>, assortment, batch, bundle, clump, cluster, collection, heap, lot, mass, pile 2 <u>group</u>, band, crowd, flock, gang, gathering, party, team ◆ *verb* 3 <u>group</u>, assemble, bundle, cluster, collect, huddle, mass, pack

bundle *noun* 1 <u>bunch</u>, assortment, batch, collection, group, heap, mass, pile, stack ◆ *verb* 2 <u>with out, off, into, etc.</u> push, hurry, hustle, rush, shove, throw, thrust

bundle up *verb* <u>wrap up</u>, swathe

bungle *verb* <u>mess up</u>, blow (*slang*), blunder, botch, foul up, make a mess of, muff, ruin, spoil

bungling *adjective* <u>incompetent</u>, blundering, cack-handed (*informal*), clumsy, ham-fisted (*informal*), inept, maladroit

bunk, bunkum *noun* <u>nonsense</u>, balderdash, baloney (*informal*), garbage (*informal*), hogwash, hot air (*informal*), moonshine, poppycock (*informal*), rubbish, stuff and nonsense, twaddle

buoy *noun* 1 <u>marker</u>, beacon, float, guide, signal ◆ *verb* 2 <u>buoy up</u> <u>encourage</u>, boost, cheer, cheer up, hearten, keep afloat, lift, raise, support, sustain

buoyancy *noun* 1 <u>lightness</u>, weightlessness 2 <u>cheerfulness</u>, animation, bounce (*informal*), good humour, high spirits, liveliness

buoyant *adjective* **1** floating, afloat, light, weightless **2** cheerful, carefree, chirpy (*informal*), happy, jaunty, light-hearted, upbeat (*informal*)

burden *noun* **1** load, encumbrance, weight **2** trouble, affliction, millstone, onus, responsibility, strain, weight, worry ♦ *verb* **3** weigh down, bother, handicap, load, oppress, saddle with, tax, worry

bureau *noun* **1** office, agency, branch, department, division, service **2** desk, writing desk

bureaucracy *noun*
1 government, administration, authorities, civil service, corridors of power, officials, the system **2** red tape, officialdom, regulations

bureaucrat *noun* official, administrator, civil servant, functionary, mandarin, officer, public servant

burglar *noun* housebreaker, cat burglar, filcher, pilferer, robber, sneak thief, thief

burglary *noun* breaking and entering, break-in, housebreaking, larceny, robbery, stealing, theft, thieving

burial *noun* interment, entombment, exequies, funeral, obsequies

buried *adjective* **1** interred, entombed, laid to rest **2** hidden, concealed, private, sequestered, tucked away

burlesque *noun* **1** parody, caricature, mockery, satire, send-up (*Brit. informal*), spoof (*informal*), takeoff (*informal*), travesty ♦ *verb* **2** satirize, ape,

caricature, exaggerate, imitate, lampoon, make a monkey out of, make fun of, mock, parody, ridicule, send up (*Brit. informal*), spoof (*informal*), take off (*informal*), take the piss out of (*taboo slang*), travesty

burly *adjective* brawny, beefy (*informal*), big, bulky, hefty, hulking, stocky, stout, sturdy, thickset, well-built

burn *verb* **1** be on fire, be ablaze, blaze, flame, flare, glow, go up in flames, smoke **2** set on fire, char, ignite, incinerate, kindle, light, parch, scorch, sear, singe, toast **3** be passionate, be angry, be aroused, be inflamed, fume, seethe, simmer, smoulder

burning *adjective* **1** intense, ardent, eager, fervent, impassioned, passionate, vehement **2** crucial, acute, compelling, critical, essential, important, pressing, significant, urgent, vital **3** blazing, fiery, flaming, flashing, gleaming, glowing, illuminated, scorching, smouldering

burnish *verb* polish, brighten, buff, furbish, glaze, rub up, shine, smooth

burrow *noun* **1** hole, den, lair, retreat, shelter, tunnel ♦ *verb* **2** dig, delve, excavate, hollow out, scoop out, tunnel

burst *verb* **1** explode, blow up, break, crack, puncture, rupture, shatter, split, tear apart **2** rush, barge, break, break out, erupt, gush forth, run, spout ♦ *noun* **3** explosion, bang, blast, blowout, break, crack, discharge, rupture, split **4** rush, gush, gust,

outbreak, outburst, outpouring,
spate, spurt, surge, torrent
♦ *adjective* 5 <u>ruptured</u>, flat,
punctured, rent, split

bury *verb* 1 <u>inter</u>, consign to the
grave, entomb, inhume, lay to
rest 2 <u>embed</u>, engulf, submerge
3 <u>hide</u>, conceal, cover,
enshroud, secrete, stow away

bush *noun* 1 <u>shrub</u>, hedge, plant,
shrubbery, thicket 2 **the bush**
<u>the wild</u>, backwoods, brush,
scrub, scrubland, woodland

bushy *adjective* <u>thick</u>, bristling,
fluffy, fuzzy, luxuriant, rough,
shaggy, unruly

busily *adverb* <u>actively</u>,
assiduously, briskly, diligently,
energetically, industriously,
purposefully, speedily, strenuously

business *noun* 1 <u>trade</u>,
bargaining, commerce, dealings,
industry, manufacturing, selling,
transaction 2 <u>establishment</u>,
company, concern, corporation,
enterprise, firm, organization,
venture 3 <u>profession</u>, career,
employment, function, job, line,
occupation, trade, vocation,
work 4 <u>concern</u>, affair,
assignment, duty, pigeon
(*informal*), problem,
responsibility, task

businesslike *adjective* <u>efficient</u>,
methodical, orderly, organized,
practical, professional,
systematic, thorough,
well-ordered

businessman *noun* <u>executive</u>,
capitalist, employer,
entrepreneur, financier,
industrialist, merchant,
tradesman, tycoon

bust[1] *noun* <u>bosom</u>, breast, chest,
front, torso

bust[2] *Informal* ♦ *verb* 1 <u>break</u>,
burst, fracture, rupture 2 <u>arrest</u>,
catch, raid, search ♦ *adjective*
3 **go bust** <u>go bankrupt</u>, become
insolvent, be ruined, fail

bustle *verb* 1 <u>hurry</u>, fuss, hasten,
rush, scamper, scurry, scuttle
♦ *noun* 2 <u>activity</u>, ado,
commotion, excitement, flurry,
fuss, hurly-burly, stir, to-do

bustling *adjective* <u>busy</u>, active,
buzzing, crowded, full,
humming, lively, swarming,
teeming

busy *adjective* 1 <u>occupied</u>, active,
employed, engaged, hard at
work, industrious, on duty,
rushed off one's feet, working
2 <u>lively</u>, energetic, exacting, full,
hectic, hustling ♦ *verb* 3 <u>occupy</u>,
absorb, employ, engage,
engross, immerse, interest

busybody *noun* <u>nosy parker</u>
(*informal*), gossip, meddler,
snooper, stirrer (*informal*),
troublemaker

but *conjunction* 1 <u>however</u>,
further, moreover, nevertheless,
on the contrary, on the other
hand, still, yet ♦ *preposition*
2 <u>except</u>, bar, barring,
excepting, excluding,
notwithstanding, save, with the
exception of ♦ *adverb* 3 <u>only</u>,
just, merely, simply, singly, solely

butcher *noun* 1 <u>murderer</u>,
destroyer, killer, slaughterer,
slayer ♦ *verb* 2 <u>slaughter</u>, carve,
clean, cut, cut up, dress, joint,
prepare 3 <u>kill</u>, assassinate, cut
down, destroy, exterminate,
liquidate, massacre, put to the
sword, slaughter, slay

butt[1] noun 1 <u>end</u>, haft, handle, hilt, shaft, shank, stock 2 <u>stub</u>, fag end (*informal*), leftover, tip

butt[2] noun <u>target</u>, Aunt Sally, dupe, laughing stock, victim

butt[3] verb, noun 1 With or of the head or horns <u>knock</u>, bump, poke, prod, push, ram, shove, thrust ♦ verb 2 **butt in** <u>interfere</u>, chip in (*informal*), cut in, interrupt, intrude, meddle, put one's oar in, stick one's nose in

butt[4] noun <u>cask</u>, barrel

buttonhole verb <u>detain</u>, accost, bore, catch, grab, importune, take aside, waylay

buttress noun 1 <u>support</u>, brace, mainstay, prop, reinforcement, stanchion, strut ♦ verb 2 <u>support</u>, back up, bolster, prop up, reinforce, shore up, strengthen, sustain, uphold

buxom adjective <u>plump</u>, ample, bosomy, busty, curvaceous, healthy, voluptuous, well-rounded

buy verb 1 <u>purchase</u>, acquire, get, invest in, obtain, pay for, procure, shop for ♦ noun 2 <u>purchase</u>, acquisition, bargain, deal

by preposition 1 <u>via</u>, by way of, over 2 <u>through</u>, through the agency of 3 <u>near</u>, along, beside, close to, next to, past ♦ adverb 4 <u>near</u>, at hand, close, handy, in reach 5 <u>past</u>, aside, away, to one side

bygone adjective <u>past</u>, antiquated, extinct, forgotten, former, lost, of old, olden

bypass verb <u>go round</u>, avoid, circumvent, depart from, detour round, deviate from, get round, give a wide berth to, pass round

bystander noun <u>onlooker</u>, eyewitness, looker-on, observer, passer-by, spectator, watcher, witness

byword noun <u>saying</u>, adage, maxim, motto, precept, proverb, slogan

C c

cab noun <u>taxi</u>, hackney carriage, minicab, taxicab

cabal noun 1 <u>clique</u>, caucus, conclave, faction, league, party, set 2 <u>plot</u>, conspiracy, intrigue, machination, scheme

cabin noun 1 <u>room</u>, berth, compartment, quarters 2 <u>hut</u>, chalet, cottage, lodge, shack, shanty, shed

cabinet noun <u>cupboard</u>, case, chiffonier, closet, commode, dresser, escritoire, locker

Cabinet noun <u>council</u>, administration, assembly, counsellors, ministry

cad noun Old-fashioned, informal <u>scoundrel</u>, bounder (*old-fashioned Brit. slang*), heel (*slang*), rat (*informal*), rotter (*slang, chiefly Brit.*)

caddish adjective <u>ungentlemanly</u>, despicable, ill-bred, low, unmannerly

café noun <u>snack bar</u>, brasserie, cafeteria, coffee bar, coffee shop, lunchroom, restaurant, tearoom

cage noun <u>enclosure</u>, pen, pound

cagey, cagy adjective Informal

wary, careful, cautious, chary, discreet, guarded, noncommittal, shrewd, wily

cajole *verb* persuade, coax, flatter, seduce, sweet-talk (*informal*), wheedle

cake *noun* 1 block, bar, cube, loaf, lump, mass, slab ♦ *verb* 2 encrust, bake, coagulate, congeal, solidify

calamitous *adjective* disastrous, cataclysmic, catastrophic, deadly, devastating, dire, fatal, ruinous, tragic

calamity *noun* disaster, cataclysm, catastrophe, misadventure, misfortune, mishap, ruin, tragedy, tribulation

calculate *verb* 1 work out, compute, count, determine, enumerate, estimate, figure, reckon 2 plan, aim, design, intend

calculated *adjective* deliberate, considered, intended, intentional, planned, premeditated, purposeful

calculating *adjective* scheming, crafty, cunning, devious, Machiavellian, manipulative, sharp, shrewd, sly

calculation *noun* 1 working out, answer, computation, estimate, forecast, judgment, reckoning, result 2 planning, contrivance, deliberation, discretion, foresight, forethought, precaution

calibre *noun* 1 worth, ability, capacity, distinction, merit, quality, stature, talent 2 diameter, bore, gauge, measure

call *verb* 1 name, christen,

describe as, designate, dub, entitle, label, style, term 2 cry, arouse, hail, rouse, shout, yell 3 phone, ring up (*informal, chiefly Brit.*), telephone 4 summon, assemble, convene, gather, muster, rally ♦ *noun* 5 cry, hail, scream, shout, signal, whoop, yell 6 summons, appeal, command, demand, invitation, notice, order, plea, request 7 need, cause, excuse, grounds, justification, occasion, reason

call for *verb* 1 require, demand, entail, involve, necessitate, need, occasion, suggest 2 fetch, collect, pick up

calling *noun* profession, career, life's work, mission, trade, vocation

call on *verb* visit, drop in on, look in on, look up, see

callous *adjective* heartless, cold, hard-bitten, hardened, hardhearted, insensitive, uncaring, unfeeling

callow *adjective* inexperienced, green, guileless, immature, naive, raw, unsophisticated

calm *adjective* 1 cool, collected, composed, dispassionate, relaxed, sedate, self-possessed, unemotional 2 still, balmy, mild, quiet, serene, smooth, tranquil, windless ♦ *noun* 3 peacefulness, hush, peace, quiet, repose, serenity, stillness ♦ *verb* 4 quieten, hush, mollify, placate, relax, soothe

calmness *noun* 1 coolness, composure, cool (*slang*), equanimity, impassivity, poise, sang-froid, self-possession 2 peacefulness, calm, hush,

quiet, repose, restfulness,
serenity, stillness, tranquillity

camouflage noun **1** disguise,
blind, cloak, concealment, cover,
mask, masquerade, screen,
subterfuge ♦ verb **2** disguise,
cloak, conceal, cover, hide,
mask, obfuscate, obscure,
screen, veil

camp¹ noun camp site, bivouac,
camping ground, encampment,
tents

camp² adjective Informal
effeminate, affected, artificial,
mannered, ostentatious,
posturing

campaign noun operation,
attack, crusade, drive,
expedition, movement,
offensive, push

canal noun waterway, channel,
conduit, duct, passage,
watercourse

cancel verb **1** call off, abolish,
abort, annul, delete, do away
with, eliminate, erase, expunge,
obliterate, repeal, revoke
2 cancel out make up for,
balance out, compensate for,
counterbalance, neutralize,
nullify, offset

cancellation noun
abandonment, abolition,
annulment, deletion, elimination,
repeal, revocation

cancer noun growth, corruption,
malignancy, pestilence, sickness,
tumour

candid adjective honest, blunt,
forthright, frank, open,
outspoken, plain,
straightforward, truthful

candidate noun contender,

applicant, claimant, competitor,
contestant, entrant, nominee,
runner

candour noun honesty,
directness, forthrightness,
frankness, openness,
outspokenness,
straightforwardness, truthfulness

canker noun disease, bane,
blight, cancer, corruption,
infection, rot, scourge, sore, ulcer

cannon noun gun, big gun, field
gun, mortar

canny adjective shrewd, astute,
careful, cautious, clever,
judicious, prudent, wise

canon noun **1** rule, criterion,
dictate, formula, precept,
principle, regulation, standard,
statute, yardstick **2** list,
catalogue, roll

canopy noun awning, covering,
shade, sunshade

cant¹ noun **1** hypocrisy, humbug,
insincerity, lip service, pretence,
pretentiousness,
sanctimoniousness **2** jargon,
argot, lingo, patter, slang,
vernacular

cant² verb tilt, angle, bevel,
incline, rise, slant, slope

cantankerous adjective
bad-tempered, choleric,
contrary, disagreeable, grumpy,
irascible, irritable, testy, waspish

canter noun **1** jog, amble,
dogtrot, lope ♦ verb **2** jog,
amble, lope

canvass verb **1** campaign,
electioneer, solicit, solicit votes
2 poll, examine, inspect,
investigate, scrutinize, study
♦ noun **3** poll, examination,

investigation, scrutiny, survey, tally

cap verb Informal beat, better, crown, eclipse, exceed, outdo, outstrip, surpass, top, transcend

capability noun ability, capacity, competence, means, potential, power, proficiency, qualification(s), wherewithal

capable adjective able, accomplished, competent, efficient, gifted, proficient, qualified, talented

capacious adjective spacious, broad, commodious, expansive, extensive, roomy, sizable or sizeable, substantial, vast, voluminous, wide

capacity noun 1 size, amplitude, compass, dimensions, extent, magnitude, range, room, scope, space, volume 2 ability, aptitude, aptness, capability, competence, facility, genius, gift 3 function, office, position, post, province, role, sphere

cape noun headland, head, peninsula, point, promontory

caper noun 1 escapade, antic, high jinks, jape, lark (informal), mischief, practical joke, prank, stunt ◆ verb 2 dance, bound, cavort, frolic, gambol, jump, skip, spring, trip

capital noun 1 money, assets, cash, finances, funds, investment(s), means, principal, resources, wealth, wherewithal ◆ adjective 2 principal, cardinal, major, prime, vital 3 Old-fashioned first-rate, excellent, fine, splendid, sterling, superb

capitalism noun private

enterprise, free enterprise, laissez faire or laisser faire, private ownership

capitalize on verb take advantage of, benefit from, cash in on (informal), exploit, gain from, make the most of, profit from

capitulate verb give in, come to terms, give up, relent, submit, succumb, surrender, yield

caprice noun whim, fad, fancy, fickleness, impulse, inconstancy, notion, whimsy

capricious adjective unpredictable, changeful, erratic, fickle, fitful, impulsive, inconsistent, inconstant, mercurial, variable, wayward, whimsical

capsize verb overturn, invert, keel over, tip over, turn over, turn turtle, upset

capsule noun 1 pill, lozenge, tablet 2 Botany pod, case, receptacle, seed case, sheath, shell, vessel

captain noun leader, boss, chief, commander, head, master, skipper

captivate verb charm, allure, attract, beguile, bewitch, enchant, enrapture, enthral, entrance, fascinate, infatuate, mesmerize

captive noun 1 prisoner, convict, detainee, hostage, internee, prisoner of war, slave ◆ adjective 2 confined, caged, enslaved, ensnared, imprisoned, incarcerated, locked up, penned, restricted, subjugated

captivity noun confinement,

bondage, custody, detention, imprisonment, incarceration, internment, slavery

capture verb 1 <u>catch</u>, apprehend, arrest, bag, collar (informal), secure, seize, take, take prisoner ♦ noun 2 <u>catching</u>, apprehension, arrest, imprisonment, seizure, taking, taking captive, trapping

car noun 1 <u>vehicle</u>, auto (U.S.), automobile, jalopy (informal), machine, motor, motorcar, wheels (informal) 2 U.S. & Canad. (railway) carriage, buffet car, cable car, coach, dining car, sleeping car, van

carcass noun <u>body</u>, cadaver (Medical), corpse, dead body, framework, hulk, remains, shell, skeleton

cardinal adjective <u>principal</u>, capital, central, chief, essential, first, fundamental, key, leading, main, paramount, primary

care verb 1 <u>be concerned</u>, be bothered, be interested, mind ♦ noun 2 <u>caution</u>, attention, carefulness, consideration, forethought, heed, management, pains, prudence, vigilance, watchfulness 3 <u>protection</u>, charge, control, custody, guardianship, keeping, management, supervision 4 <u>worry</u>, anxiety, concern, disquiet, perplexity, pressure, responsibility, stress, trouble

career noun 1 <u>occupation</u>, calling, employment, life's work, livelihood, pursuit, vocation ♦ verb 2 <u>rush</u>, barrel (along) (informal, chiefly U.S. & Canad.), bolt, dash, hurtle, race, speed, tear

care for verb 1 <u>look after</u>, attend, foster, mind, minister to, nurse, protect, provide for, tend, watch over 2 <u>like</u>, be fond of, desire, enjoy, love, prize, take to, want

carefree adjective <u>untroubled</u>, blithe, breezy, cheerful, easy-going, halcyon, happy-go-lucky, light-hearted

careful adjective 1 <u>cautious</u>, chary, circumspect, discreet, prudent, scrupulous, thoughtful, thrifty 2 <u>thorough</u>, conscientious, meticulous, painstaking, particular, precise

careless adjective 1 <u>slapdash</u>, cavalier, inaccurate, irresponsible, lackadaisical, neglectful, offhand, slipshod, sloppy (informal) 2 <u>negligent</u>, absent-minded, forgetful, hasty, remiss, thoughtless, unthinking 3 <u>nonchalant</u>, artless, casual, unstudied

carelessness noun <u>negligence</u>, indiscretion, irresponsibility, laxity, neglect, omission, slackness, sloppiness (informal), thoughtlessness

caress verb 1 <u>stroke</u>, cuddle, embrace, fondle, hug, kiss, neck (informal), nuzzle, pet ♦ noun 2 <u>stroke</u>, cuddle, embrace, fondling, hug, kiss, pat

caretaker noun <u>warden</u>, concierge, curator, custodian, janitor, keeper, porter, superintendent, watchman

cargo noun <u>load</u>, baggage, consignment, contents, freight, goods, merchandise, shipment

caricature noun 1 <u>parody</u>, burlesque, cartoon, distortion, farce, lampoon, satire, send-up

(*Brit. informal*), takeoff (*informal*), travesty ♦ *verb* 2 **parody**, burlesque, distort, lampoon, mimic, mock, ridicule, satirize, send up (*Brit. informal*), take off (*informal*)

carnage *noun* **slaughter**, blood bath, bloodshed, butchery, havoc, holocaust, massacre, mass murder, murder, shambles

carnal *adjective* **sexual**, erotic, fleshly, lascivious, lewd, libidinous, lustful, sensual

carnival *noun* **festival**, celebration, fair, fête, fiesta, gala, holiday, jamboree, jubilee, merrymaking, revelry

carol *noun* **song**, chorus, ditty, hymn, lay

carp *verb* **find fault**, cavil, complain, criticize, pick holes, quibble, reproach

carpenter *noun* **joiner**, cabinet-maker, woodworker

carriage *noun* 1 **vehicle**, cab, coach, conveyance 2 **bearing**, air, behaviour, comportment, conduct, demeanour, deportment, gait, manner, posture

carry *verb* 1 **transport**, bear, bring, conduct, convey, fetch, haul, lug, move, relay, take, transfer 2 **win**, accomplish, capture, effect, gain, secure

carry on *verb* 1 **continue**, endure, keep going, last, maintain, perpetuate, persevere, persist 2 *Informal* **make a fuss**, create (*slang*), misbehave, raise Cain

carry out *verb* **perform**, accomplish, achieve, carry

through, effect, execute, fulfil, implement, realize

carton *noun* **box**, case, container, pack, package, packet

cartoon *noun* 1 **drawing**, caricature, comic strip, lampoon, parody, satire, sketch, takeoff (*informal*) 2 **animation**, animated cartoon, animated film

cartridge *noun* 1 **shell**, charge, round 2 **container**, capsule, case, cassette, cylinder, magazine

carve *verb* **cut**, chip, chisel, engrave, etch, hew, mould, sculpt, slice, whittle

cascade *noun* 1 **waterfall**, avalanche, cataract, deluge, downpour, falls, flood, fountain, outpouring, shower, torrent ♦ *verb* **flow**, descend, fall, flood, gush, overflow, pitch, plunge, pour, spill, surge, teem, tumble

case[1] *noun* 1 **instance**, example, illustration, occasion, occurrence, specimen 2 **situation**, circumstance(s), condition, context, contingency, event, position, state 3 *Law* **lawsuit**, action, dispute, proceedings, suit, trial

case[2] *noun* 1 **container**, box, canister, carton, casket, chest, crate, holder, receptacle, suitcase, tray 2 **covering**, capsule, casing, envelope, jacket, sheath, shell, wrapper

cash *noun* **money**, brass (*Northern English dialect*), coinage, currency, dough (*slang*), funds, notes, ready money, silver

cashier[1] *noun* **teller**, bank clerk, banker, bursar, clerk, purser, treasurer

cashier² verb dismiss, discard, discharge, drum out, expel, give the boot to (slang)

casket noun box, case, chest, coffer, jewel box

cast noun 1 actors, characters, company, dramatis personae, players, troupe 2 type, complexion, manner, stamp, style ♦ verb 3 choose, allot, appoint, assign, name, pick, select 4 give out, bestow, deposit, diffuse, distribute, emit, radiate, scatter, shed, spread 5 form, found, model, mould, set, shape 6 throw, fling, hurl, launch, pitch, sling, thrust, toss

caste noun class, estate, grade, order, rank, social order, status, stratum

castigate verb reprimand, berate, censure, chastise, criticize, lambast(e), rebuke, scold

cast-iron adjective certain, copper-bottomed, definite, established, fixed, guaranteed, settled

castle noun fortress, chateau, citadel, keep, palace, stronghold, tower

cast-off adjective 1 unwanted, discarded, rejected, scrapped, surplus to requirements, unneeded, useless ♦ noun 2 reject, discard, failure, outcast, second

castrate verb neuter, emasculate, geld

casual adjective 1 careless, blasé, cursory, lackadaisical, nonchalant, offhand, relaxed, unconcerned 2 occasional, accidental, chance, incidental, irregular, random, unexpected 3 informal, non-dressy, sporty

casualty noun victim, death, fatality, loss, sufferer, wounded

cat noun feline, kitty (informal), moggy (slang), puss (informal), pussy (informal), tabby

catacombs plural noun vault, crypt, tomb

catalogue noun 1 list, directory, gazetteer, index, inventory, record, register, roll, roster, schedule ♦ verb 2 list, accession, alphabetize, classify, file, index, inventory, register, tabulate

catapult noun 1 sling, slingshot (U.S.) ♦ verb 2 shoot, heave, hurl, pitch, plunge, propel

catastrophe noun disaster, adversity, calamity, cataclysm, fiasco, misfortune, tragedy, trouble

catcall noun jeer, boo, gibe, hiss, raspberry, whistle

catch verb 1 seize, clutch, get, grab, grasp, grip, lay hold of, snatch, take 2 capture, apprehend, arrest, ensnare, entrap, snare 3 discover, catch in the act, detect, expose, find out, surprise, take unawares, unmask 4 contract, develop, get, go down with, incur, succumb to, suffer from 5 make out, comprehend, discern, get, grasp, hear, perceive, recognize, sense, take in ♦ noun 6 fastener, bolt, clasp, clip, latch 7 Informal drawback, disadvantage, fly in the ointment, hitch, snag, stumbling block, trap, trick

catching adjective infectious, communicable, contagious, transferable, transmittable

catch on verb Informal underline, comprehend, find out, get the picture, grasp, see, see through, twig (Brit. informal)

catchword noun slogan, byword, motto, password, watchword

catchy adjective memorable, captivating, haunting, popular

categorical adjective absolute, downright, emphatic, explicit, express, positive, unambiguous, unconditional, unequivocal, unqualified, unreserved

category noun class, classification, department, division, grade, grouping, heading, section, sort, type

cater verb provide, furnish, outfit, purvey, supply

cattle plural noun cows, beasts, bovines, livestock, stock

catty adjective spiteful, backbiting, bitchy (informal), malevolent, malicious, rancorous, shrewish, snide, venomous

cause noun 1 origin, agent, beginning, creator, genesis, mainspring, maker, producer, root, source, spring 2 reason, basis, grounds, incentive, inducement, justification, motivation, motive, purpose 3 aim, belief, conviction, enterprise, ideal, movement, principle ◆ verb 4 produce, bring about, create, generate, give rise to, incite, induce, lead to, result in

caustic adjective 1 burning, acrid, astringent, biting, corroding, corrosive, mordant, vitriolic 2 sarcastic, acrimonious, cutting, pungent, scathing, stinging, trenchant, virulent, vitriolic

caution noun 1 care, alertness, carefulness, circumspection, deliberation, discretion, forethought, heed, prudence, vigilance, watchfulness 2 warning, admonition, advice, counsel, injunction ◆ verb 3 warn, admonish, advise, tip off, urge

cautious adjective careful, cagey (informal), chary, circumspect, guarded, judicious, prudent, tentative, wary

cavalcade noun parade, array, march-past, procession, spectacle, train

cavalier adjective haughty, arrogant, disdainful, lofty, lordly, offhand, scornful, supercilious

cavalry noun horsemen, horse, mounted troops

cave noun hollow, cavern, cavity, den, grotto

cavern noun cave, hollow, pothole

cavernous adjective deep, hollow, sunken, yawning

cavity noun hollow, crater, dent, gap, hole, pit

cease verb stop, break off, conclude, discontinue, end, finish, halt, leave off, refrain, terminate

ceaseless adjective continual, constant, endless, eternal, everlasting, incessant, interminable, never-ending, nonstop, perpetual, unremitting

cede verb surrender, concede, hand over, make over, relinquish, renounce, resign, transfer, yield

celebrate verb 1 rejoice,

celebrated commemorate, drink to, keep, kill the fatted calf, observe, put the flags out, toast **2** _perform_, bless, honour, solemnize

celebrated _adjective_ _well-known_, acclaimed, distinguished, eminent, famous, illustrious, notable, popular, prominent, renowned

celebration _noun_ **1** _party_, festival, festivity, gala, jubilee, merrymaking, red-letter day, revelry **2** _performance_, anniversary, commemoration, honouring, observance, remembrance, solemnization

celebrity _noun_ **1** _personality_, big name, big shot (_informal_), dignitary, luminary, star, superstar, V.I.P. **2** _fame_, distinction, notability, prestige, prominence, renown, reputation, repute, stardom

celestial _adjective_ _heavenly_, angelic, astral, divine, ethereal, spiritual, sublime, supernatural

celibacy _noun_ _chastity_, continence, purity, virginity

cell _noun_ **1** _room_, cavity, chamber, compartment, cubicle, dungeon, stall **2** _unit_, caucus, core, coterie, group, nucleus

cement _noun_ **1** _mortar_, adhesive, glue, gum, paste, plaster, sealant ♦ _verb_ **2** _stick together_, attach, bind, bond, combine, glue, join, plaster, seal, unite, weld

cemetery _noun_ _graveyard_, burial ground, churchyard, God's acre, necropolis

censor _verb_ _cut_, blue-pencil, bowdlerize, expurgate

censorious _adjective_ _critical_, captious, carping, cavilling, condemnatory, disapproving, disparaging, fault-finding, hypercritical, scathing, severe

censure _noun_ **1** _disapproval_, blame, condemnation, criticism, obloquy, rebuke, reprimand, reproach, reproof, stick (_slang_) ♦ _verb_ **2** _criticize_, blame, castigate, condemn, denounce, rap over the knuckles, rebuke, reprimand, reproach, scold, slap on the wrist

central _adjective_ **1** _middle_, inner, interior, mean, median, mid **2** _main_, chief, essential, focal, fundamental, key, primary, principal

centralize _verb_ _unify_, concentrate, condense, incorporate, rationalize, streamline

centre _noun_ **1** _middle_, core, focus, heart, hub, kernel, midpoint, nucleus, pivot ♦ _verb_ **2** _focus_, cluster, concentrate, converge, revolve

ceremonial _adjective_ **1** _ritual_, formal, liturgical, ritualistic, solemn, stately ♦ _noun_ **2** _ritual_, ceremony, formality, rite, solemnity

ceremonious _adjective_ _formal_, civil, courteous, deferential, dignified, punctilious, solemn, stately, stiff

ceremony _noun_ **1** _ritual_, commemoration, function, observance, parade, rite, service, show, solemnities **2** _formality_, ceremonial, decorum, etiquette, niceties, pomp, propriety, protocol

certain _adjective_ **1** _sure_, assured,

confident, convinced, positive, satisfied **2** <u>known</u>, conclusive, incontrovertible, irrefutable, true, undeniable, unequivocal **3** <u>inevitable</u>, bound, definite, destined, fated, inescapable, sure **4** <u>fixed</u>, decided, definite, established, settled

certainly adverb <u>definitely</u>, assuredly, indisputably, indubitably, surely, truly, undeniably, undoubtedly, without doubt

certainty noun **1** <u>sureness</u>, assurance, confidence, conviction, faith, positiveness, trust, validity **2** <u>fact</u>, reality, sure thing (informal), truth

certificate noun <u>document</u>, authorization, credential(s), diploma, licence, testimonial, voucher, warrant

certify verb <u>confirm</u>, assure, attest, authenticate, declare, guarantee, testify, validate, verify

chafe verb **1** <u>rub</u>, abrade, rasp, scrape, scratch **2** <u>be annoyed</u>, be impatient, fret, fume, rage, worry

chaff[1] noun <u>waste</u>, dregs, husks, refuse, remains, rubbish, trash

chaff[2] verb <u>tease</u>, mock, rib (informal), ridicule, scoff, taunt

chain noun **1** <u>link</u>, bond, coupling, fetter, manacle, shackle **2** <u>series</u>, progression, sequence, set, string, succession, train ♦ verb **3** <u>bind</u>, confine, enslave, fetter, handcuff, manacle, restrain, shackle, tether

chairman noun <u>director</u>, chairperson, chairwoman, master of ceremonies, president, speaker, spokesman

challenge noun **1** <u>test</u>, confrontation, provocation, question, trial, ultimatum ♦ verb **2** <u>test</u>, confront, defy, dispute, object to, question, tackle, throw down the gauntlet

chamber noun **1** <u>room</u>, apartment, bedroom, compartment, cubicle, enclosure, hall **2** <u>council</u>, assembly, legislative body, legislature

champion noun **1** <u>winner</u>, conqueror, hero, title holder, victor **2** <u>defender</u>, backer, guardian, patron, protector, upholder ♦ verb **3** <u>support</u>, advocate, back, commend, defend, encourage, espouse, fight for, promote, uphold

chance noun **1** <u>probability</u>, likelihood, odds, possibility, prospect **2** <u>opportunity</u>, occasion, opening, time **3** <u>luck</u>, accident, coincidence, destiny, fate, fortune, providence **4** <u>risk</u>, gamble, hazard, jeopardy, speculation, uncertainty ♦ verb **5** <u>risk</u>, endanger, gamble, hazard, jeopardize, stake, try, venture, wager

change noun **1** <u>alteration</u>, difference, innovation, metamorphosis, modification, mutation, revolution, transformation, transition **2** <u>variety</u>, break (informal), departure, diversion, novelty, variation **3** <u>exchange</u>, conversion, interchange, substitution, swap, trade ♦ verb **4** <u>alter</u>, convert, modify, mutate, reform, reorganize, restyle, shift, transform, vary **5** <u>exchange</u>, barter, convert, interchange, replace, substitute, swap, trade

changeable adjective variable, erratic, fickle, inconstant, irregular, mobile, mutable, protean, shifting, unsettled, unstable, volatile, wavering

channel noun 1 route, approach, artery, avenue, course, means, medium, path, way 2 passage, canal, conduit, duct, furrow, groove, gutter, route, strait ♦ verb 3 direct, conduct, convey, guide, transmit

chant verb 1 sing, carol, chorus, descant, intone, recite, warble ♦ noun 2 song, carol, chorus, melody, psalm

chaos noun disorder, anarchy, bedlam, confusion, disorganization, lawlessness, mayhem, pandemonium, tumult

chaotic adjective disordered, anarchic, confused, deranged, disorganized, lawless, riotous, topsy-turvy, tumultuous, uncontrolled

chap noun Informal fellow, bloke (Brit. informal), character, guy (informal), individual, man, person

chaperone noun 1 escort, companion ♦ verb 2 escort, accompany, attend, protect, safeguard, shepherd, watch over

chapter noun 1 section, clause, division, episode, part, period, phase, stage, topic

character noun 1 nature, attributes, calibre, complexion, disposition, personality, quality, temperament, type 2 reputation, honour, integrity, rectitude, strength, uprightness 3 role, part, persona, portrayal

4 eccentric, card (informal), oddball (informal), original 5 symbol, device, figure, hieroglyph, letter, mark, rune, sign

characteristic noun 1 feature, attribute, faculty, idiosyncrasy, mark, peculiarity, property, quality, quirk, trait ♦ adjective 2 typical, distinctive, distinguishing, idiosyncratic, individual, peculiar, representative, singular, special, symbolic, symptomatic

characterize verb identify, brand, distinguish, indicate, mark, represent, stamp, typify

charade noun pretence, fake, farce, pantomime, parody, travesty

charge verb 1 accuse, arraign, blame, impeach, incriminate, indict 2 rush, assail, assault, attack, stampede, storm 3 fill, load 4 Formal command, bid, commit, demand, entrust, instruct, order, require ♦ noun 5 price, amount, cost, expenditure, expense, outlay, payment, rate, toll 6 accusation, allegation, imputation, indictment 7 rush, assault, attack, onset, onslaught, sortie, stampede 8 care, custody, duty, office, responsibility, safekeeping, trust 9 ward 10 instruction, command, demand, direction, injunction, mandate, order, precept

charisma noun charm, allure, attraction, lure, magnetism, personality

charismatic adjective charming, alluring, attractive, enticing, influential, magnetic

charitable adjective 1 tolerant, considerate, favourable, forgiving, humane, indulgent, kindly, lenient, magnanimous, sympathetic, understanding 2 generous, beneficent, benevolent, bountiful, kind, lavish, liberal, philanthropic

charity noun 1 donations, assistance, benefaction, contributions, endowment, fund, gift, hand-out, help, largesse or largess, philanthropy, relief 2 kindness, altruism, benevolence, compassion, fellow feeling, generosity, goodwill, humanity, indulgence

charlatan noun fraud, cheat, con man (informal), fake, impostor, phoney or phony (informal), pretender, quack, sham, swindler

charm noun 1 attraction, allure, appeal, fascination, magnetism 2 spell, enchantment, magic, sorcery 3 talisman, amulet, fetish, trinket ◆ verb 4 attract, allure, beguile, bewitch, captivate, delight, enchant, enrapture, entrance, fascinate, mesmerize, win over

charming adjective attractive, appealing, captivating, cute, delightful, fetching, likable or likeable, pleasing, seductive, winsome

chart noun 1 table, blueprint, diagram, graph, map, plan ◆ verb 2 plot, delineate, draft, map out, outline, shape, sketch

charter noun 1 document, contract, deed, licence, permit, prerogative ◆ verb 2 hire, commission, employ, lease, rent

3 authorize, sanction

chase verb 1 pursue, course, follow, hunt, run after, track 2 drive away, drive, expel, hound, put to flight ◆ noun 3 pursuit, hunt, hunting, race

chasm noun gulf, abyss, crater, crevasse, fissure, gap, gorge, ravine

chaste adjective pure, immaculate, innocent, modest, simple, unaffected, undefiled, virtuous

chasten verb subdue, chastise, correct, discipline, humble, humiliate, put in one's place, tame

chastise verb 1 scold, berate, castigate, censure, correct, discipline, upbraid 2 Old-fashioned beat, flog, lash, lick (informal), punish, scourge, whip

chastity noun purity, celibacy, continence, innocence, maidenhood, modesty, virginity, virtue

chat noun 1 talk, chatter, chinwag (Brit. informal), conversation, gossip, heart-to-heart, natter, tête-à-tête ◆ verb 2 talk, chatter, gossip, jaw (slang), natter

chatter noun 1 prattle, babble, blather, chat, gab (informal), gossip, natter ◆ verb 2 prattle, babble, blather, chat, gab (informal), gossip, natter, rabbit (on) (Brit. informal), schmooze (slang)

cheap adjective 1 inexpensive, bargain, cut-price, economical, keen, low-cost, low-priced, reasonable, reduced 2 inferior, common, poor, second-rate, shoddy, tatty, tawdry, two a penny, worthless **3** *Informal* despicable, contemptible, mean

cheapen *verb* **1** degrade, belittle, debase, demean, denigrate, depreciate, devalue, discredit, disparage, lower

cheat *verb* **1** deceive, beguile, con (*informal*), defraud, double-cross (*informal*), dupe, fleece, fool, mislead, rip off (*slang*), swindle, trick ◆ *noun* **2** deceiver, charlatan, con man (*informal*), double-crosser (*informal*), shark, sharper, swindler, trickster **3** deception, deceit, fraud, rip-off (*slang*), scam (*slang*), swindle, trickery

check *verb* **1** examine, inquire into, inspect, investigate, look at, make sure, monitor, research, scrutinize, study, test, vet **2** stop, delay, halt, hinder, impede, inhibit, limit, obstruct, restrain, retard ◆ *noun* **3** examination, inspection, investigation, once-over (*informal*), research, scrutiny, test **4** stoppage, constraint, control, curb, damper, hindrance, impediment, limitation, obstacle, obstruction, restraint

cheek *noun Informal* impudence, audacity, chutzpah (*U.S. & Canad. informal*), disrespect, effrontery, impertinence, insolence, lip (*slang*), nerve, temerity

cheeky *adjective* impudent, audacious, disrespectful, forward, impertinent, insolent, insulting, pert, saucy

cheer *verb* **1** applaud, acclaim,

clap, hail **2** cheer up, brighten, buoy up, comfort, encourage, gladden, hearten, uplift ◆ *noun* **3** applause, acclamation, ovation, plaudits

cheerful *adjective* happy, buoyant, cheery, chirpy (*informal*), enthusiastic, jaunty, jolly, light-hearted, merry, optimistic, upbeat (*informal*)

cheerfulness *noun* happiness, buoyancy, exuberance, gaiety, geniality, good cheer, good humour, high spirits, jauntiness, light-heartedness

cheerless *adjective* gloomy, bleak, desolate, dismal, drab, dreary, forlorn, miserable, sombre, woeful

cheer up *verb* **1** comfort, encourage, enliven, gladden, hearten, jolly along (*informal*) **2** take heart, buck up (*informal*), perk up, rally

cheery *adjective* cheerful, breezy, carefree, chirpy (*informal*), genial, good-humoured, happy, jovial, upbeat (*informal*)

chemist *noun* pharmacist, apothecary (*obsolete*), dispenser

cherish *verb* **1** cling to, cleave to, encourage, entertain, foster, harbour, hold dear, nurture, prize, sustain, treasure **2** care for, comfort, hold dear, love, nurse, shelter, support

chest *noun* box, case, casket, coffer, crate, strongbox, trunk

chew *verb* bite, champ, chomp, crunch, gnaw, grind, masticate, munch

chewy *adjective* tough, as tough as old boots, leathery

chic adjective stylish, elegant, fashionable, smart, trendy (*Brit. informal*)

chide verb Old-fashioned scold, admonish, berate, censure, criticize, lecture, rebuke, reprimand, reproach, reprove, tell off (*informal*)

chief noun 1 head, boss (*informal*), captain, commander, director, governor, leader, manager, master, principal, ruler ♦ adjective 2 primary, foremost, highest, key, leading, main, predominant, pre-eminent, premier, prime, principal, supreme, uppermost

chiefly adverb 1 especially, above all, essentially, primarily, principally 2 mainly, in general, in the main, largely, mostly, on the whole, predominantly, usually

child noun youngster, babe, baby, bairn (*Scot.*), infant, juvenile, kid (*informal*), offspring, toddler, tot

childbirth noun child-bearing, confinement, delivery, labour, lying-in, parturition, travail

childhood noun youth, boyhood or girlhood, immaturity, infancy, minority, schooldays

childish adjective immature, boyish or girlish, foolish, infantile, juvenile, puerile, young

childlike adjective innocent, artless, guileless, ingenuous, naive, simple, trusting

chill noun 1 cold, bite, coldness, coolness, crispness, frigidity, nip, rawness, sharpness ♦ verb 2 cool, freeze, refrigerate 3 dishearten, dampen, deject, depress, discourage, dismay ♦ adjective

4 cold, biting, bleak, chilly, freezing, frigid, raw, sharp, wintry

chilly adjective 1 cool, brisk, crisp, draughty, fresh, nippy, penetrating, sharp 2 unfriendly, frigid, hostile, unresponsive, unsympathetic, unwelcoming

chime verb, noun ring, clang, jingle, peal, sound, tinkle, toll

china noun pottery, ceramics, crockery, porcelain, service, tableware, ware

chink noun opening, aperture, cleft, crack, cranny, crevice, fissure, gap

chip noun 1 scratch, fragment, nick, notch, shard, shaving, sliver, wafer ♦ verb 2 nick, chisel, damage, gash, whittle

chirp verb chirrup, cheep, peep, pipe, tweet, twitter, warble

chivalrous adjective courteous, bold, brave, courageous, gallant, gentlemanly, honourable, valiant

chivalry noun courtesy, courage, gallantry, gentlemanliness, knight-errantry, knighthood, politeness

choice noun 1 option, alternative, range, pick, preference, say 2 selection, range, variety ♦ adjective 3 best, elite, excellent, exclusive, prime, rare, select

choke verb 1 strangle, asphyxiate, gag, overpower, smother, stifle, suffocate, suppress, throttle 2 block, bar, bung, clog, congest, constrict, obstruct, stop

choose verb pick, adopt, designate, elect, opt for, prefer, select, settle upon

choosy adjective Informal fussy,

discriminating, faddy, fastidious, finicky, particular, picky (*informal*), selective

chop *verb* cut, cleave, fell, hack, hew, lop, sever

chore *noun* task, burden, duty, errand, job

chortle *verb, noun* chuckle, cackle, crow, guffaw

chorus *noun* 1 choir, choristers, ensemble, singers, vocalists 2 refrain, burden, response, strain 3 unison, accord, concert, harmony

christen *verb* 1 baptize 2 name, call, designate, dub, style, term, title

Christmas *noun* festive season, Noel, Xmas (*informal*), Yule (*archaic*), Yuletide (*archaic*)

chronicle *noun* 1 record, account, annals, diary, history, journal, narrative, register, story ♦ *verb* 2 record, enter, narrate, put on record, recount, register, relate, report, set down, tell

chubby *adjective* plump, buxom, flabby, podgy, portly, rotund, round, stout, tubby

chuck *verb* Informal throw, cast, fling, heave, hurl, pitch, sling, toss

chuckle *verb* laugh, chortle, crow, exult, giggle, snigger, titter

chum *noun* Informal friend, companion, comrade, crony, mate (*informal*), pal (*informal*)

chunk *noun* piece, block, dollop (*informal*), hunk, lump, mass, nugget, portion, slab

churlish *adjective* rude, brusque, harsh, ill-tempered, impolite, sullen, surly, uncivil

churn *verb* stir up, agitate, beat, convulse, swirl, toss

cinema *noun* films, big screen (*informal*), flicks (*slang*), motion pictures, movies, pictures

cipher *noun* 1 code, cryptograph 2 nobody, nonentity

circle *noun* 1 ring, disc, globe, orb, sphere 2 group, clique, club, company, coterie, set, society ♦ *verb* 3 go round, circumnavigate, circumscribe, encircle, enclose, envelop, ring, surround

circuit *noun* course, journey, lap, orbit, revolution, route, tour, track

circuitous *adjective* indirect, labyrinthine, meandering, oblique, rambling, roundabout, tortuous, winding

circular *adjective* 1 round, ring-shaped, rotund, spherical 2 orbital, circuitous, cyclical ♦ *noun* 3 advertisement, notice

circulate *verb* 1 spread, broadcast, disseminate, distribute, issue, make known, promulgate, publicize, publish 2 flow, gyrate, radiate, revolve, rotate

circulation *noun* 1 bloodstream 2 flow, circling, motion, rotation 3 distribution, currency, dissemination, spread, transmission

circumference *noun* boundary, border, edge, extremity, limits, outline, perimeter, periphery, rim

circumstance *noun* event, accident, condition, contingency, happening, incident, occurrence, particular, respect, situation

circumstances *plural noun* situation, means, position, state, state of affairs, station, status

cistern *noun* tank, basin, reservoir, sink, vat

citadel *noun* fortress, bastion, fortification, keep, stronghold, tower

cite *verb* quote, adduce, advance, allude to, enumerate, extract, mention, name, specify

citizen *noun* inhabitant, denizen, dweller, resident, subject, townsman

city *noun* town, conurbation, metropolis, municipality

civic *adjective* public, communal, local, municipal

civil *adjective* 1 civic, domestic, municipal, political 2 polite, affable, courteous, obliging, refined, urbane, well-mannered

civilization *noun* 1 culture, advancement, cultivation, development, education, enlightenment, progress, refinement, sophistication 2 society, community, nation, people, polity

civilize *verb* cultivate, educate, enlighten, refine, sophisticate, tame

civilized *adjective* cultured, educated, enlightened, humane, polite, sophisticated, tolerant, urbane

claim *verb* 1 assert, allege, challenge, insist, maintain, profess, uphold 2 demand, ask, call for, insist, need, require
♦ *noun* 3 assertion, affirmation, allegation, pretension, privilege,

protestation 4 demand, application, call, petition, request, requirement 5 right, title

clairvoyant *noun* 1 psychic, diviner, fortune-teller, visionary
♦ *adjective* 2 psychic, extrasensory, second-sighted, telepathic, visionary

clamber *verb* climb, claw, scale, scramble, scramble, shin

clammy *adjective* moist, close, damp, dank, sticky, sweaty

clamour *noun* noise, commotion, din, hubbub, outcry, racket, shouting, uproar

clamp *noun* 1 vice, bracket, fastener, grip, press ♦ *verb* 2 fasten, brace, fix, make fast, secure

clan *noun* family, brotherhood, faction, fraternity, group, society, tribe

clandestine *adjective* secret, cloak-and-dagger, concealed, covert, furtive, private, stealthy, surreptitious, underground

clap *verb* applaud, acclaim, cheer

clarification *noun* explanation, elucidation, exposition, illumination, interpretation, simplification

clarify *verb* explain, clear up, elucidate, illuminate, interpret, make plain, simplify, throw or shed light on

clarity *noun* clearness, definition, limpidity, lucidity, precision, simplicity, transparency

clash *verb* 1 conflict, cross swords, feud, grapple, lock horns, quarrel, war, wrangle 2 crash, bang, clang, clank, clatter, jangle, jar, rattle ♦ *noun*

3 conflict, brush, collision, confrontation, difference of opinion, disagreement, fight, showdown (*informal*)

clasp *noun* 1 fastening, brooch, buckle, catch, clip, fastener, grip, hook, pin 2 grasp, embrace, grip, hold, hug ♦ *verb* 3 grasp, clutch, embrace, grip, hold, hug, press, seize, squeeze 4 fasten, connect

class *noun* 1 group, category, division, genre, kind, set, sort, type ♦ *verb* 2 classify, brand, categorize, designate, grade, group, label, rank, rate

classic *adjective* 1 definitive, archetypal, exemplary, ideal, model, quintessential, standard 2 typical, characteristic, regular, standard, time-honoured, usual 3 best, consummate, finest, first-rate, masterly, world-class 4 lasting, abiding, ageless, deathless, enduring, immortal, undying ♦ *noun* 5 standard, exemplar, masterpiece, model, paradigm, prototype

classical *adjective* fine, elegant, harmonious, refined, restrained, symmetrical, understated, well-proportioned

classification *noun* categorization, analysis, arrangement, grading, sorting, taxonomy

classify *verb* categorize, arrange, catalogue, grade, pigeonhole, rank, sort, systematize, tabulate

classy *adjective Informal* high-class, elegant, exclusive, posh (*informal, chiefly Brit.*), stylish, superior, top-drawer, up-market

clause *noun* section, article, chapter, condition, paragraph, part, passage

claw *noun* 1 nail, pincer, talon, tentacle ♦ *verb* 2 scratch, dig, lacerate, maul, rip, scrape, tear

clean *adjective* 1 pure, flawless, fresh, immaculate, impeccable, spotless, unblemished, unsullied 2 hygienic, antiseptic, decontaminated, purified, sterile, sterilized, uncontaminated, unpolluted 3 moral, chaste, decent, good, honourable, innocent, pure, respectable, upright, virtuous 4 complete, conclusive, decisive, entire, final, perfect, thorough, total, unimpaired, whole ♦ *verb* 5 cleanse, disinfect, launder, purge, purify, rinse, sanitize, scour, scrub, wash

cleanse *verb* clean, absolve, clear, purge, purify, rinse, scour, scrub, wash

cleanser *noun* detergent, disinfectant, purifier, scourer, soap, solvent

clear *adjective* 1 certain, convinced, decided, definite, positive, resolved, satisfied, sure 2 obvious, apparent, blatant, comprehensible, conspicuous, distinct, evident, manifest, palpable, plain, pronounced, recognizable, unmistakable 3 transparent, crystalline, glassy, limpid, pellucid, see-through, translucent 4 bright, cloudless, fair, fine, light, luminous, shining, sunny, unclouded 5 unobstructed, empty, free, open, smooth, unhindered, unimpeded 6 unblemished, clean, immaculate, innocent, pure, untarnished ♦ verb **7** unblock, disentangle, extricate, free, loosen, open, rid, unload **8** pass over, jump, leap, miss, vault **9** brighten, break up, lighten **10** clean, cleanse, erase, purify, refine, sweep away, tidy (up), wipe **11** absolve, acquit, excuse, exonerate, justify, vindicate **12** gain, acquire, earn, make, reap, secure

clear-cut *adjective* straightforward, black-and-white, cut-and-dried (*informal*), definite, explicit, plain, precise, specific, unambiguous, unequivocal

clearly *adverb* obviously, beyond doubt, distinctly, evidently, markedly, openly, overtly, undeniably, undoubtedly

clergy *noun* priesthood, churchmen, clergymen, clerics, holy orders, ministry, the cloth

clergyman *noun* minister, chaplain, cleric, man of God, man of the cloth, padre, parson, pastor, priest, vicar

clever *adjective* intelligent, bright, gifted, ingenious, knowledgeable, quick-witted, resourceful, shrewd, smart, talented

cleverness *noun* intelligence, ability, brains, ingenuity, quick wits, resourcefulness, shrewdness, smartness

cliché *noun* platitude, banality, commonplace, hackneyed phrase, stereotype, truism

client *noun* customer, applicant, buyer, consumer, patient, patron, shopper

clientele *noun* customers, business, clients, following, market, patronage, regulars, trade

cliff *noun* rock face, bluff, crag, escarpment, overhang, precipice, scar, scarp

climactic *adjective* crucial, critical, decisive, paramount, peak

climate *noun* weather, temperature

climax *noun* culmination, height, highlight, high point, peak, summit, top, zenith

climb *verb* ascend, clamber, mount, rise, scale, shin up, soar, top

climb down *verb* **1** descend, dismount **2** back down, eat one's words, retract, retreat

clinch *verb* settle, conclude, confirm, decide, determine, seal, secure, set the seal on, sew up (*informal*)

cling *verb* stick, adhere, clasp, clutch, embrace, grasp, grip, hug

clinical *adjective* unemotional, analytic, cold, detached, dispassionate, impersonal, objective, scientific

clip[1] *verb* **1** trim, crop, curtail, cut, pare, prune, shear, shorten, snip ♦ *noun, verb* **2** *Informal* smack, clout (*informal*), cuff, knock, punch, strike, thump, wallop (*informal*), whack

clip[2] *verb* attach, fasten, fix, hold, pin, staple

clique *noun* group, cabal, circle, coterie, faction, gang, set

cloak *noun* **1** cape, coat, mantle, wrap ♦ *verb* **2** cover, camouflage, conceal, disguise, hide, mask, obscure, screen, veil

clog verb obstruct, block, congest, hinder, impede, jam

close[1] verb 1 shut, bar, block, lock, plug, seal, secure, stop up 2 end, cease, complete, conclude, finish, shut down, terminate, wind up 3 connect, come together, couple, fuse, join, unite ♦ noun 4 end, completion, conclusion, culmination, denouement, ending, finale, finish

close[2] adjective 1 near, adjacent, adjoining, at hand, cheek by jowl, handy, impending, nearby, neighbouring, nigh 2 intimate, attached, confidential, dear, devoted, familiar, inseparable, loving 3 careful, detailed, intense, minute, painstaking, rigorous, thorough 4 compact, congested, crowded, dense, impenetrable, jam-packed, packed, tight 5 stifling, airless, heavy, humid, muggy, oppressive, stuffy, suffocating, sweltering 6 secretive, private, reticent, secret, taciturn, uncommunicative 7 mean, miserly, stingy

closed adjective 1 shut, fastened, locked, out of service, sealed 2 exclusive, restricted 3 finished, concluded, decided, ended, over, resolved, settled, terminated

cloth noun fabric, material, textiles

clothe verb dress, array, attire, cover, drape, equip, fit out, garb, robe, swathe

clothes plural noun clothing, apparel, attire, costume, dress, garb, garments, gear (informal), outfit, wardrobe, wear

clothing noun clothes, apparel, attire, costume, dress, garb, garments, gear (informal), outfit, wardrobe, wear

cloud noun 1 mist, gloom, haze, murk, vapour 2 obscure, becloud, darken, dim, eclipse, obfuscate, overshadow, shade, shadow, veil 3 confuse, disorient, distort, impair, muddle, muddy the waters

cloudy adjective 1 dull, dim, gloomy, leaden, louring or lowering, overcast, sombre, sunless 2 opaque, muddy, murky

clout Informal ♦ noun 1 influence, authority, power, prestige, pull, weight ♦ verb 2 hit, clobber (slang), punch, sock (slang), strike, thump, wallop (informal)

clown noun 1 comedian, buffoon, comic, fool, harlequin, jester, joker, prankster ♦ verb 2 play the fool, act the fool, jest, mess about

club noun 1 association, company, fraternity, group, guild, lodge, set, society, union 2 stick, bat, bludgeon, cosh (Brit.), cudgel, truncheon 3 verb 3 beat, bash, batter, bludgeon, cosh (Brit.), hammer, pummel, strike

clue noun indication, evidence, hint, lead, pointer, sign, suggestion, suspicion, trace

clueless adjective stupid, dim, dozy (Brit. informal), dull, half-witted, simple, slow, thick, unintelligent, witless

clump noun 1 cluster, bunch, bundle, group, mass ♦ verb 2 stomp, lumber, plod, thud, thump, tramp

clumsy adjective awkward,

bumbling, gauche, gawky, ham-fisted (*informal*), lumbering, maladroit, ponderous, uncoordinated, ungainly, unwieldy

cluster noun 1 <u>gathering</u>, assemblage, batch, bunch, clump, collection, group, knot ♦ verb 2 <u>gather</u>, assemble, bunch, collect, flock, group

clutch verb <u>seize</u>, catch, clasp, cling to, embrace, grab, grasp, grip, snatch

clutches plural noun <u>power</u>, claws, control, custody, grip, hands, keeping, possession, sway

clutter verb 1 <u>litter</u>, scatter, strew ♦ noun 2 <u>untidiness</u>, confusion, disarray, disorder, hotchpotch, jumble, litter, mess, muddle

coach noun 1 <u>bus</u>, car, carriage, charabanc, vehicle 2 <u>instructor</u>, handler, teacher, trainer, tutor ♦ verb 3 <u>instruct</u>, drill, exercise, prepare, train, tutor

coalesce verb <u>blend</u>, amalgamate, combine, fuse, incorporate, integrate, merge, mix, unite

coalition noun <u>alliance</u>, amalgamation, association, bloc, combination, confederation, conjunction, fusion, merger, union

coarse adjective 1 <u>rough</u>, crude, homespun, impure, unfinished, unpolished, unprocessed, unpurified, unrefined 2 <u>vulgar</u>, earthy, improper, indecent, indelicate, ribald, rude, smutty

coarseness noun 1 <u>roughness</u>, crudity, unevenness 2 <u>vulgarity</u>, bawdiness, crudity, earthiness,

indelicacy, ribaldry, smut, uncouthness

coast noun 1 <u>shore</u>, beach, border, coastline, seaboard, seaside ♦ verb 2 <u>cruise</u>, drift, freewheel, glide, sail, taxi

coat noun 1 <u>fur</u>, fleece, hair, hide, pelt, skin, wool 2 <u>layer</u>, coating, covering, overlay ♦ verb 3 <u>cover</u>, apply, plaster, smear, spread

coax verb <u>persuade</u>, allure, cajole, entice, prevail upon, sweet-talk (*informal*), talk into, wheedle

cocktail noun <u>mixture</u>, blend, combination, mix

cocky adjective <u>overconfident</u>, arrogant, brash, cocksure, conceited, egotistical, full of oneself, swaggering, vain

code noun 1 <u>cipher</u>, cryptograph 2 <u>principles</u>, canon, convention, custom, ethics, etiquette, manners, maxim, regulations, rules, system

cogent adjective <u>convincing</u>, compelling, effective, forceful, influential, potent, powerful, strong, weighty

cogitate verb <u>think</u>, consider, contemplate, deliberate, meditate, mull over, muse, ponder, reflect, ruminate

coherent adjective 1 <u>consistent</u>, logical, lucid, meaningful, orderly, organized, rational, reasoned, systematic 2 <u>intelligible</u>, articulate, comprehensible

coil verb <u>wind</u>, curl, loop, snake, spiral, twine, twist, wreathe, writhe

coin noun 1 <u>money</u>, cash,

change, copper, silver, specie ♦ *verb* **2** <u>invent</u>, create, fabricate, forge, make up, mint, mould, originate

coincide *verb* **1** <u>occur simultaneously</u>, be concurrent, coexist, synchronize **2** <u>agree</u>, accord, concur, correspond, harmonize, match, square, tally

coincidence *noun* **1** <u>chance</u>, accident, fluke, happy accident, luck, stroke of luck **2** <u>coinciding</u>, concurrence, conjunction, correlation, correspondence

coincidental *adjective* <u>chance</u>, accidental, casual, fluky (*informal*), fortuitous, unintentional, unplanned

cold *adjective* **1** <u>chilly</u>, arctic, bleak, cool, freezing, frigid, frosty, frozen, icy, wintry **2** <u>unfriendly</u>, aloof, distant, frigid, indifferent, reserved, standoffish ♦ *noun* **3** <u>coldness</u>, chill, frigidity, frostiness, iciness

cold-blooded *adjective* <u>callous</u>, dispassionate, heartless, ruthless, steely, stony-hearted, unemotional, unfeeling

collaborate *verb* **1** <u>work together</u>, cooperate, join forces, participate, play ball (*informal*), team up **2** <u>conspire</u>, collude, cooperate, fraternize

collaboration *noun* <u>teamwork</u>, alliance, association, cooperation, partnership

collaborator *noun* **1** <u>co-worker</u>, associate, colleague, confederate, partner, team-mate **2** <u>traitor</u>, fraternizer, quisling, turncoat

collapse *verb* **1** <u>fall down</u>, cave in, crumple, fall, fall apart at the seams, give way, subside **2** <u>fail</u>, come to nothing, fold, founder, go belly-up (*informal*) ♦ *noun* **3** <u>falling down</u>, cave-in, disintegration, falling apart, ruin, subsidence **4** <u>failure</u>, downfall, flop, slump **5** <u>faint</u>, breakdown, exhaustion, prostration

collar *verb* Informal <u>seize</u>, apprehend, arrest, capture, catch, grab, nab (*informal*), nail (*informal*)

colleague *noun* <u>fellow worker</u>, ally, assistant, associate, collaborator, comrade, helper, partner, team-mate, workmate

collect *verb* **1** <u>assemble</u>, cluster, congregate, convene, converge, flock together, rally **2** <u>gather</u>, accumulate, amass, assemble, heap, hoard, save, stockpile

collected *adjective* <u>calm</u>, composed, cool, poised, self-possessed, serene, unperturbed, unruffled

collection *noun* **1** <u>accumulation</u>, anthology, compilation, heap, hoard, mass, pile, set, stockpile, store **2** <u>group</u>, assembly, assortment, cluster, company, crowd **3** <u>contribution</u>, alms, offering, offertory

collective *adjective* <u>combined</u>, aggregate, composite, corporate, cumulative, joint, shared, unified, united

collide *verb* **1** <u>crash</u>, clash, come into collision, meet head-on **2** <u>conflict</u>, clash

collision *noun* **1** <u>crash</u>, accident, bump, impact, pile-up (*informal*), prang (*informal*), smash **2** <u>conflict</u>, clash, confrontation, encounter, opposition, skirmish

colloquial adjective informal, conversational, demotic, everyday, familiar, idiomatic, vernacular

colony noun settlement, community, dependency, dominion, outpost, possession, province, satellite state, territory

colossal adjective huge, enormous, gigantic, immense, mammoth, massive, monumental, prodigious, vast

colour noun 1 hue, colorant, dye, paint, pigment, shade, tint ♦ verb 2 paint, dye, stain, tinge, tint 3 blush, flush, redden

colourful adjective 1 bright, brilliant, multicoloured, psychedelic, variegated 2 interesting, distinctive, graphic, lively, picturesque, rich, vivid

colourless adjective 1 drab, achromatic, anaemic, ashen, bleached, faded, wan, washed out 2 uninteresting, characterless, dreary, dull, insipid, lacklustre, vapid

column noun 1 pillar, obelisk, post, shaft, support, upright 2 line, cavalcade, file, procession, rank, row

coma noun unconsciousness, oblivion, stupor, trance

comb verb 1 untangle, arrange, dress, groom 2 search, forage, hunt, rake, ransack, rummage, scour, sift

combat noun 1 fight, action, battle, conflict, contest, encounter, engagement, skirmish, struggle, war, warfare ♦ verb 2 fight, defy, do battle with, oppose, resist, withstand

combatant noun fighter, adversary, antagonist, enemy, opponent, soldier, warrior

combination noun 1 mixture, amalgamation, blend, coalescence, composite, connection, mix 2 association, alliance, coalition, confederation, consortium, federation, syndicate, union

combine verb join together, amalgamate, blend, connect, integrate, link, merge, mix, pool, unite

come verb 1 move towards, advance, approach, draw near, near 2 arrive, appear, enter, materialize, reach, show up (informal), turn up (informal) 3 happen, fall, occur, take place 4 result, arise, emanate, emerge, flow, issue, originate 5 reach, extend 6 be available, be made, be offered, be on offer, be produced

come about verb happen, arise, befall, come to pass, occur, result, take place, transpire (informal)

come across verb find, bump into (informal), chance upon, discover, encounter, meet, notice, stumble upon, unearth

comeback noun 1 Informal return, rally, rebound, recovery, resurgence, revival, triumph 2 response, rejoinder, reply, retaliation, retort, riposte

come back verb return, reappear, recur, re-enter

comedian noun comic, card (informal), clown, funny man, humorist, jester, joker, wag, wit

comedown noun 1 decline,

deflation, demotion, reverse
2 *Informal* disappointment,
anticlimax, blow, humiliation,
letdown

comedy noun humour, farce,
fun, hilarity, jesting, joking, light
entertainment

comeuppance noun *Informal*
punishment, chastening, deserts,
due reward, recompense,
retribution

comfort noun **1** luxury, cosiness,
ease, opulence, snugness,
wellbeing **2** relief, compensation,
consolation, help, succour,
support ♦ verb **3** console,
commiserate with, hearten,
reassure, soothe

comfortable adjective **1** relaxing,
agreeable, convenient, cosy,
homely, pleasant, restful, snug
2 happy, at ease, at home,
contented, gratified, relaxed,
serene **3** *Informal* well-off,
affluent, in clover (*informal*),
prosperous, well-to-do

comforting adjective consoling,
cheering, consolatory,
encouraging, heart-warming,
reassuring, soothing

comic adjective **1** funny, amusing,
comical, droll, farcical,
humorous, jocular, witty ♦ noun
2 comedian, buffoon, clown,
funny man, humorist, jester,
wag, wit

comical adjective funny, amusing,
comic, droll, farcical, hilarious,
humorous, priceless, side-splitting

coming adjective **1** approaching,
at hand, forthcoming, imminent,
impending, in store, near, nigh
♦ noun **2** arrival, advent, approach

command verb **1** order, bid,

charge, compel, demand, direct,
require **2** have authority over,
control, dominate, govern,
handle, head, lead, manage,
rule, supervise ♦ noun **3** order,
commandment, decree,
demand, directive, instruction,
requirement, ultimatum
4 authority, charge, control,
government, management,
mastery, power, rule, supervision

commandeer verb seize,
appropriate, confiscate,
requisition, sequester, sequestrate

commander noun officer, boss,
captain, chief, commanding
officer, head, leader, ruler

commanding adjective
controlling, advantageous,
decisive, dominant, dominating,
superior

commemorate verb remember,
celebrate, honour, immortalize,
pay tribute to, salute

commemoration noun
remembrance, ceremony,
honouring, memorial service,
tribute

commence verb begin, embark
on, enter upon, initiate, open,
originate, start

commend verb praise, acclaim,
applaud, approve, compliment,
extol, recommend, speak highly
of

commendable adjective
praiseworthy, admirable,
creditable, deserving, estimable,
exemplary, laudable,
meritorious, worthy

commendation noun praise,
acclaim, acclamation,
approbation, approval, credit,
encouragement, good opinion,

panegyric, recommendation

comment noun 1 remark, observation, statement 2 note, annotation, commentary, explanation, exposition, illustration ♦ verb 3 remark, mention, note, observe, point out, say, utter 4 annotate, elucidate, explain, interpret

commentary noun 1 narration, description, voice-over 2 notes, analysis, critique, explanation, review, treatise

commentator noun 1 reporter, special correspondent, sportscaster 2 critic, annotator, interpreter

commerce noun trade, business, dealing, exchange, traffic

commercial adjective 1 mercantile, trading 2 materialistic, mercenary, profit-making

commiserate verb sympathize, console, feel for, pity

commission noun 1 duty, errand, mandate, mission, task 2 fee, cut, percentage, rake-off (slang), royalties 3 committee, board, commissioners, delegation, deputation, representatives ♦ verb 4 appoint, authorize, contract, delegate, depute, empower, engage, nominate, order, select

commit verb 1 do, carry out, enact, execute, perform, perpetrate 2 put in custody, confine, imprison

commitment noun 1 dedication, devotion, involvement, loyalty 2 responsibility, duty, engagement, liability, obligation, tie

common adjective 1 average, commonplace, conventional, customary, everyday, familiar, frequent, habitual, ordinary, regular, routine, standard, stock, usual 2 popular, accepted, general, prevailing, prevalent, universal, widespread 3 collective, communal, popular, public, social 4 vulgar, coarse, inferior, plebeian

commonplace adjective 1 everyday, banal, common, humdrum, mundane, obvious, ordinary, run-of-the-mill, widespread ♦ noun 2 cliché, banality, platitude, truism

common sense noun good sense, gumption (Brit. informal), horse sense, level-headedness, native intelligence, prudence, sound judgment, wit

commotion noun disturbance, disorder, excitement, furore, fuss, hue and cry, rumpus, tumult, turmoil, upheaval, uproar

communal adjective public, collective, general, joint, shared

commune noun community, collective, cooperative, kibbutz

commune with verb contemplate, meditate on, muse on, ponder, reflect on

communicate verb make known, convey, declare, disclose, impart, inform, pass on, proclaim, transmit

communication noun 1 passing on, contact, conversation, correspondence, dissemination, link, transmission 2 message, announcement, disclosure, dispatch, information, news, report, statement, word

communicative *adjective* talkative, chatty, expansive, forthcoming, frank, informative, loquacious, open, outgoing, voluble

Communism *noun* socialism, Bolshevism, collectivism, Marxism, state socialism

Communist *noun* socialist, Bolshevik, collectivist, Marxist, Red (*informal*)

community *noun* society, brotherhood, commonwealth, company, general public, people, populace, public, residents, state

commuter *noun* daily traveller, straphanger (*informal*), suburbanite

compact[1] *adjective* 1 closely packed, compressed, condensed, dense, pressed together, solid, thick 2 brief, compendious, concise, succinct, terse, to the point ♦ *verb* 3 pack closely, compress, condense, cram, stuff, tamp

compact[2] *noun* agreement, arrangement, bargain, bond, contract, covenant, deal, pact, treaty, understanding

companion *noun* 1 friend, accomplice, ally, associate, colleague, comrade, consort, mate (*informal*), partner 2 escort, aide, assistant, attendant, chaperon, squire

companionship *noun* fellowship, camaraderie, company, comradeship, conviviality, esprit de corps, friendship, rapport, togetherness

company *noun* 1 business, association, concern,

corporation, establishment, firm, house, partnership, syndicate 2 group, assembly, band, collection, community, crowd, gathering, party, set 3 guests, callers, party, visitors

comparable *adjective* 1 on a par, a match for, as good as, commensurate, equal, equivalent, in a class with, proportionate, tantamount 2 similar, akin, alike, analogous, cognate, corresponding, cut from the same cloth, of a piece, related

comparative *adjective* relative, by comparison, qualified

compare *verb* 1 weigh, balance, contrast, juxtapose, set against 2 *usually with* with be on a par with, approach, bear comparison, be in the same class as, be the equal of, compete with, equal, hold a candle to, match 3 **compare to** liken to, correlate to, equate to, identify with, mention in the same breath as, parallel, resemble

comparison *noun* 1 contrast, distinction, juxtaposition 2 similarity, analogy, comparability, correlation, likeness, resemblance

compartment *noun* section, alcove, bay, berth, booth, carriage, cubbyhole, cubicle, locker, niche, pigeonhole

compass *noun* range, area, boundary, circumference, extent, field, limit, reach, realm, scope

compassion *noun* sympathy, condolence, fellow feeling, humanity, kindness, mercy, pity, sorrow, tender-heartedness, tenderness, understanding

compassionate adjective
sympathetic, benevolent,
charitable, humane,
humanitarian, kind-hearted,
merciful, pitying, tender-hearted,
understanding

compatibility noun harmony,
affinity, agreement, concord,
empathy, like-mindedness,
rapport, sympathy

compatible adjective
harmonious, adaptable,
congruous, consistent, in
harmony, in keeping, suitable

compel verb force, coerce,
constrain, dragoon, impel, make,
oblige, railroad (informal)

compelling adjective
1 fascinating, enchanting,
enthralling, gripping, hypnotic,
irresistible, mesmeric,
spellbinding 2 pressing, binding,
coercive, imperative, overriding,
peremptory, unavoidable, urgent
3 convincing, cogent,
conclusive, forceful, irrefutable,
powerful, telling, weighty

compensate verb 1 recompense,
atone, make amends, make
good, refund, reimburse,
remunerate, repay 2 cancel
(out), balance, counteract,
counterbalance, make up for,
offset, redress

compensation noun
recompense, amends,
atonement, damages,
reimbursement, remuneration,
reparation, restitution, satisfaction

compete verb contend, be in the
running, challenge, contest,
fight, strive, struggle, vie

competence noun ability,

capability, capacity, expertise,
fitness, proficiency, skill, suitability

competent adjective able,
adequate, capable, fit, proficient,
qualified, suitable

competition noun 1 rivalry,
opposition, strife, struggle
2 contest, championship, event,
head-to-head, puzzle, quiz,
tournament 3 opposition,
challengers, field, rivals

competitive adjective
1 cut-throat, aggressive,
antagonistic, at odds,
dog-eat-dog, opposing, rival
2 ambitious, combative

competitor noun contestant,
adversary, antagonist,
challenger, opponent, rival

compilation noun collection,
accumulation, anthology,
assemblage, assortment, treasury

compile verb put together,
accumulate, amass, collect, cull,
garner, gather, marshal, organize

complacency noun
self-satisfaction, contentment,
satisfaction, smugness

complacent adjective
self-satisfied, contented, pleased
with oneself, resting on one's
laurels, satisfied, serene, smug,
unconcerned

complain verb find fault,
bemoan, bewail, carp, deplore,
groan, grouse, grumble, lament,
moan, whine, whinge (informal)

complaint noun 1 criticism,
charge, grievance, gripe
(informal), grouse, grumble,
lament, moan, protest 2 illness,
affliction, ailment, disease,
disorder, malady, sickness, upset

complement noun
1 completion, companion,
consummation, counterpart,
finishing touch, rounding-off,
supplement 2 total, aggregate,
capacity, entirety, quota, totality,
wholeness ♦ verb 3 complete,
cap (informal), crown, round off,
set off

complementary adjective
completing, companion,
corresponding, interdependent,
interrelating, matched, reciprocal

complete adjective 1 total,
absolute, consummate, outright,
perfect, thorough,
thoroughgoing, utter 2 finished,
accomplished, achieved,
concluded, ended 3 entire, all,
faultless, full, intact, plenary,
unbroken, whole ♦ verb 4 finish,
close, conclude, crown, end,
finalize, round off, settle, wrap
up (informal)

completely adverb totally,
absolutely, altogether, entirely,
every inch, fully, hook, line and
sinker, in full, lock, stock and
barrel, one hundred per cent,
perfectly, thoroughly, utterly,
wholly

completion noun finishing, bitter
end, close, conclusion,
culmination, end, fruition,
fulfilment

complex adjective 1 compound,
composite, heterogeneous,
manifold, multifarious, multiple
2 complicated, convoluted,
elaborate, intricate, involved,
labyrinthine, tangled, tortuous
♦ noun 3 structure, aggregate,
composite, network,
organization, scheme, system

4 Informal obsession, fixation,
fixed idea, idée fixe, phobia,
preoccupation

complexion noun 1 skin, colour,
colouring, hue, pigmentation,
skin tone 2 nature, appearance,
aspect, character, guise, light,
look, make-up

complexity noun complication,
elaboration, entanglement,
intricacy, involvement,
ramification

complicate verb make difficult,
confuse, entangle, involve,
muddle, ravel

complicated adjective 1 difficult,
involved, perplexing,
problematic, puzzling,
troublesome 2 involved,
complex, convoluted, elaborate,
intricate, labyrinthine

complication noun
1 complexity, confusion,
entanglement, intricacy, web
2 problem, difficulty, drawback,
embarrassment, obstacle, snag

compliment noun 1 praise,
bouquet, commendation,
congratulations, eulogy, flattery,
honour, tribute ♦ verb 2 praise,
commend, congratulate, extol,
flatter, pay tribute to, salute,
speak highly of

complimentary adjective
1 flattering, appreciative,
approving, commendatory,
congratulatory, laudatory 2 free,
courtesy, donated, gratis,
gratuitous, honorary, on the
house

compliments plural noun
greetings, good wishes, regards,
remembrances, respects,
salutation

comply verb <u>obey</u>, abide by, acquiesce, adhere to, conform to, follow, observe, submit, toe the line

component noun **1** <u>part</u>, constituent, element, ingredient, item, piece, unit ♦ *adjective* **2** <u>constituent</u>, inherent, intrinsic

compose verb **1** <u>put together</u>, build, comprise, constitute, construct, fashion, form, make, make up **2** <u>create</u>, contrive, devise, invent, produce, write **3** <u>calm</u>, collect, control, pacify, placate, quiet, soothe **4** <u>arrange</u>, adjust

composed adjective <u>calm</u>, at ease, collected, cool, level-headed, poised, relaxed, sedate, self-possessed, serene, unflappable

composition noun **1** <u>creation</u>, compilation, fashioning, formation, formulation, making, production, putting together **2** <u>design</u>, arrangement, configuration, formation, layout, make-up, organization, structure **3** <u>essay</u>, exercise, literary work, opus, piece, treatise, work

composure noun <u>calmness</u>, aplomb, equanimity, poise, sang-froid, self-assurance, self-possession, serenity

compound noun **1** <u>combination</u>, alloy, amalgam, blend, composite, fusion, medley, mixture, synthesis ♦ *verb* **2** <u>combine</u>, amalgamate, blend, intermingle, mix, synthesize, unite **3** <u>intensify</u>, add to, aggravate, augment, complicate, exacerbate, heighten, magnify, worsen ♦ *adjective* **4** <u>complex</u>,

composite, intricate, multiple

comprehend verb <u>understand</u>, apprehend, conceive, fathom, grasp, know, make out, perceive, see, take in

comprehensible adjective <u>understandable</u>, clear, coherent, conceivable, explicit, intelligible, plain

comprehension noun <u>understanding</u>, conception, discernment, grasp, intelligence, perception, realization

comprehensive adjective <u>broad</u>, all-embracing, all-inclusive, blanket, complete, encyclopedic, exhaustive, full, inclusive, thorough

compress verb <u>squeeze</u>, abbreviate, concentrate, condense, contract, crush, press, shorten, squash

comprise verb **1** <u>be composed of</u>, consist of, contain, embrace, encompass, include, take in **2** <u>make up</u>, compose, constitute, form

compromise noun **1** <u>give-and-take</u>, accommodation, adjustment, agreement, concession, settlement, trade-off ♦ *verb* **2** <u>meet halfway</u>, adjust, agree, concede, give and take, go fifty-fifty (*informal*), settle, strike a balance **3** <u>dishonour</u>, discredit, embarrass, expose, jeopardize, prejudice, weaken

compulsion noun **1** <u>urge</u>, drive, necessity, need, obsession, preoccupation **2** <u>force</u>, coercion, constraint, demand, duress, obligation, pressure, urgency

compulsive adjective <u>irresistible</u>,

compelling, driving, neurotic, obsessive, overwhelming, uncontrollable, urgent

compulsory adjective obligatory, binding, de rigueur, forced, imperative, mandatory, required, requisite

compute verb calculate, add up, count, enumerate, figure out, reckon, tally, total

comrade noun companion, ally, associate, colleague, co-worker, fellow, friend, partner

con Informal ♦ noun 1 swindle, deception, fraud, scam (slang), sting (informal), trick ♦ verb 2 swindle, cheat, deceive, defraud, double-cross (informal), dupe, hoodwink, rip off (slang), trick

concave adjective hollow, indented

conceal verb hide, bury, camouflage, cover, disguise, mask, obscure, screen

concede verb 1 admit, accept, acknowledge, allow, confess, grant, own 2 give up, cede, hand over, relinquish, surrender, yield

conceit noun 1 self-importance, arrogance, egotism, narcissism, pride, swagger, vanity 2 Archaic fancy, fantasy, image, whim, whimsy

conceited adjective self-important, arrogant, bigheaded (informal), cocky, egotistical, full of oneself, immodest, narcissistic, too big for one's boots or breeches, vain

conceivable adjective imaginable, believable, credible, possible, thinkable

conceive verb 1 imagine, believe, comprehend, envisage, fancy, suppose, think, understand 2 think up, contrive, create, design, devise, formulate 3 become pregnant, become impregnated

concentrate verb 1 focus one's attention on, be engrossed in, put one's mind to, rack one's brains 2 focus, bring to bear, centre, cluster, converge 3 gather, accumulate, cluster, collect, congregate, huddle

concentrated adjective 1 intense, all-out (informal), deep, hard, intensive 2 condensed, boiled down, evaporated, reduced, rich, thickened, undiluted

concentration noun 1 single-mindedness, absorption, application, heed 2 focusing, bringing to bear, centralization, centring, consolidation, convergence, intensification 3 convergence, accumulation, aggregation, cluster, collection, horde, mass

concept noun idea, abstraction, conception, conceptualization, hypothesis, image, notion, theory, view

conception noun 1 idea, concept, design, image, notion, plan 2 impregnation, fertilization, germination, insemination

concern noun 1 worry, anxiety, apprehension, burden, care, disquiet, distress 2 importance, bearing, interest, relevance 3 business, affair, interest, job, responsibility, task 4 business, company, corporation, enterprise, establishment, firm, organization ♦ *verb* **5** <u>worry</u>, bother, disquiet, distress, disturb, make anxious, perturb, trouble **6** <u>be relevant to</u>, affect, apply to, bear on, interest, involve, pertain to, regard, touch

concerned *adjective* **1** <u>involved</u>, active, implicated, interested, mixed up, privy to **2** <u>worried</u>, anxious, bothered, distressed, disturbed, troubled, uneasy, upset

concerning *preposition* <u>regarding</u>, about, apropos of, as regards, on the subject of, re, relating to, respecting, touching, with reference to

concession *noun* **1** <u>grant</u>, adjustment, allowance, boon, compromise, indulgence, permit, privilege, sop **2** <u>conceding</u>, acknowledgment, admission, assent, confession, surrender, yielding

conciliate *verb* <u>pacify</u>, appease, clear the air, mediate, mollify, placate, reconcile, soothe, win over

conciliation *noun* <u>pacification</u>, appeasement, mollification, placation, reconciliation, soothing

conciliatory *adjective* <u>pacifying</u>, appeasing, mollifying, pacific, peaceable, placatory

concise *adjective* <u>brief</u>, compendious, condensed, laconic, pithy, short, succinct, terse

conclude *verb* **1** <u>decide</u>, assume, deduce, gather, infer, judge, surmise, work out **2** <u>end</u>, cease, close, complete, finish, round

off, terminate, wind up **3** <u>accomplish</u>, bring about, carry out, effect, pull off

conclusion *noun* **1** <u>decision</u>, conviction, deduction, inference, judgment, opinion, verdict **2** <u>end</u>, bitter end, close, completion, ending, finale, finish, result, termination **3** <u>outcome</u>, consequence, culmination, end result, result, upshot

conclusive *adjective* <u>decisive</u>, clinching, convincing, definite, final, irrefutable, ultimate, unanswerable

concoct *verb* <u>make up</u>, brew, contrive, devise, formulate, hatch, invent, prepare, think up

concoction *noun* <u>mixture</u>, blend, brew, combination, compound, creation, preparation

concrete *adjective* **1** <u>specific</u>, definite, explicit **2** <u>real</u>, actual, factual, material, sensible, substantial, tangible

concur *verb* <u>agree</u>, acquiesce, assent, consent

condemn *verb* **1** <u>disapprove</u>, blame, censure, damn, denounce, reproach, reprove, upbraid **2** <u>sentence</u>, convict, damn, doom, pass sentence on

condemnation *noun* **1** <u>disapproval</u>, blame, censure, denunciation, reproach, reproof, stricture **2** <u>sentence</u>, conviction, damnation, doom, judgment

condensation *noun* **1** <u>distillation</u>, liquefaction, precipitate, precipitation **2** <u>abridgment</u>, contraction, digest, précis, synopsis **3** <u>concentration</u>, compression, consolidation, crystallization, curtailment, reduction

condense verb 1 <u>abridge</u>, abbreviate, compress, concentrate, epitomize, shorten, summarize 2 <u>concentrate</u>, boil down, reduce, thicken

condensed adjective 1 <u>abridged</u>, compressed, concentrated, shortened, shrunken, slimmed-down, summarized 2 <u>concentrated</u>, boiled down, reduced, thickened

condescend verb 1 <u>patronize</u>, talk down to 2 <u>lower oneself</u>, bend, deign, humble or demean oneself, see fit, stoop

condescending adjective <u>patronizing</u>, disdainful, lofty, lordly, snobbish, snooty (informal), supercilious, superior, toffee-nosed (slang, chiefly Brit.)

condition noun 1 <u>state</u>, circumstances, lie of the land, position, shape, situation, state of affairs 2 <u>requirement</u>, limitation, prerequisite, proviso, qualification, restriction, rider, stipulation, terms 3 <u>health</u>, fettle, fitness, kilter, order, shape, state of health, trim 4 <u>ailment</u>, complaint, infirmity, malady, problem, weakness ♦ verb 5 <u>accustom</u>, adapt, equip, prepare, ready, tone up, train, work out

conditional adjective <u>dependent</u>, contingent, limited, provisional, qualified, subject to, with reservations

conditions plural noun <u>circumstances</u>, environment, milieu, situation, surroundings, way of life

condone verb <u>overlook</u>, excuse, forgive, let pass, look the other way, make allowance for, pardon, turn a blind eye to

conduct noun 1 <u>behaviour</u>, attitude, bearing, demeanour, deportment, manners, ways 2 <u>management</u>, administration, control, direction, guidance, handling, organization, running, supervision ♦ verb 3 <u>carry out</u>, administer, control, direct, handle, manage, organize, preside over, run, supervise 4 <u>behave</u>, acquit, act, carry, comport, deport 5 <u>accompany</u>, convey, escort, guide, lead, steer, usher

confederacy noun <u>union</u>, alliance, coalition, confederation, federation, league

confer verb 1 <u>discuss</u>, consult, converse, deliberate, discourse, talk 2 <u>grant</u>, accord, award, bestow, give, hand out, present

conference noun <u>meeting</u>, colloquium, congress, consultation, convention, discussion, forum, seminar, symposium

confess verb 1 <u>admit</u>, acknowledge, come clean (informal), concede, confide, disclose, divulge, own up 2 <u>declare</u>, affirm, assert, confirm, profess, reveal

confession noun <u>admission</u>, acknowledgment, disclosure, exposure, revelation, unbosoming

confidant, confidante noun <u>close friend</u>, alter ego, bosom friend, crony, familiar, intimate

confide verb 1 <u>tell</u>, admit, confess, disclose, divulge, impart, reveal, whisper **2** *Formal* entrust, commend, commit, consign

confidence noun **1** trust, belief, credence, dependence, faith, reliance **2** self-assurance, aplomb, assurance, boldness, courage, firmness, nerve, self-possession **3 in confidence** in secrecy, between you and me (and the gatepost), confidentially, privately

confident adjective **1** certain, convinced, counting on, positive, satisfied, secure, sure **2** self-assured, assured, bold, dauntless, fearless, self-reliant

confidential adjective secret, classified, hush-hush (*informal*), intimate, off the record, private, privy

confidentially adverb in secret, behind closed doors, between ourselves, in camera, in confidence, personally, privately, sub rosa

confine verb restrict, cage, enclose, hem in, hold back, imprison, incarcerate, intern, keep, limit, shut up

confinement noun **1** imprisonment, custody, detention, incarceration, internment, porridge (*slang*) **2** childbirth, childbed, labour, lying-in, parturition

confines plural noun limits, boundaries, bounds, circumference, edge, precincts

confirm verb **1** prove, authenticate, bear out, corroborate, endorse, ratify, substantiate, validate, verify **2** strengthen, buttress, establish,

fix, fortify, reinforce

confirmation noun **1** proof, authentication, corroboration, evidence, substantiation, testimony, validation, verification **2** sanction, acceptance, agreement, approval, assent, endorsement, ratification

confirmed adjective long-established, chronic, dyed-in-the-wool, habitual, hardened, ingrained, inveterate, seasoned

confiscate verb seize, appropriate, commandeer, impound, sequester, sequestrate

confiscation noun seizure, appropriation, forfeiture, impounding, sequestration, takeover

conflict noun **1** opposition, antagonism, difference, disagreement, discord, dissension, friction, hostility, strife **2** battle, clash, combat, contest, encounter, fight, strife, war ♦ verb **3** be incompatible, be at variance, clash, collide, differ, disagree, interfere

conflicting adjective incompatible, antagonistic, clashing, contradictory, contrary, discordant, inconsistent, opposing, paradoxical

conform verb **1** comply, adapt, adjust, fall in with, follow, obey, toe the line **2** agree, accord, correspond, harmonize, match, suit, tally

conformist noun traditionalist, stick-in-the-mud (*informal*), yes man

conformity noun compliance, conventionality, observance, orthodoxy, traditionalism

confound verb bewilder, astound, baffle, confuse, dumbfound, flummox, mystify, nonplus, perplex

confront verb face, accost, challenge, defy, encounter, oppose, stand up to, tackle

confrontation noun conflict, contest, encounter, fight, head-to-head, set-to (informal), showdown (informal)

confuse verb 1 mix up, disarrange, disorder, jumble, mingle, muddle, ravel 2 bewilder, baffle, bemuse, faze, flummox, mystify, nonplus, perplex, puzzle 3 disconcert, discompose, disorient, fluster, rattle (informal), throw off balance, unnerve, upset

confused adjective 1 bewildered, at sea, baffled, disorientated, flummoxed, muddled, nonplussed, perplexed, puzzled, taken aback 2 disordered, chaotic, disorganized, higgledy piggledy (informal), in disarray, jumbled, mixed up, topsy-turvy, untidy

confusing adjective bewildering, baffling, contradictory, disconcerting, misleading, perplexing, puzzling, unclear

confusion noun 1 bewilderment, disorientation, mystification, perplexity, puzzlement 2 disorder, chaos, commotion, jumble, mess, muddle, shambles, turmoil, untidiness, upheaval

congenial adjective 1 pleasant, affable, agreeable, companionable, favourable, friendly, genial, kindly 2 compatible, kindred, like-minded, sympathetic, well-suited

congenital adjective inborn, immanent, inbred, inherent, innate, natural

congested adjective 1 overcrowded, crowded, teeming 2 clogged, blocked-up, crammed, jammed, overfilled, overflowing, packed, stuffed

congestion noun 1 overcrowding, crowding 2 clogging, bottleneck, jam, surfeit

congratulate verb compliment, pat on the back, wish joy to

congratulations plural noun, interjection good wishes, best wishes, compliments, felicitations, greetings

congregate verb come together, assemble, collect, convene, converge, flock, gather, mass, meet

congregation noun assembly, brethren, crowd, fellowship, flock, multitude, throng

congress noun meeting, assembly, conclave, conference, convention, council, legislature, parliament

conjecture noun 1 guess, hypothesis, shot in the dark, speculation, supposition, surmise, theory ♦ verb 2 guess, hypothesize, imagine, speculate, suppose, surmise, theorize

conjugal adjective marital, bridal, connubial, married, matrimonial, nuptial, wedded

conjure verb perform tricks, juggle

conjure up verb bring to mind, contrive, create, evoke, produce as if by magic, recall, recollect

conjuror, conjurer noun magician, illusionist, sorcerer, wizard

connect verb link, affix, attach, couple, fasten, join, unite

connected adjective linked, affiliated, akin, allied, associated, combined, coupled, joined, related, united

connection noun 1 association, affinity, bond, liaison, link, relationship, relevance, tie-in 2 link, alliance, association, attachment, coupling, fastening, junction, tie, union 3 contact, acquaintance, ally, associate, friend, sponsor

connivance noun collusion, abetting, complicity, conspiring, tacit consent

connive verb 1 conspire, collude, cook up (informal), intrigue, plot, scheme 2 connive at turn a blind eye to, abet, disregard, let pass, look the other way, overlook, wink at

connoisseur noun expert, aficionado, appreciator, authority, buff (informal), devotee, judge

conquer verb 1 defeat, beat, crush, get the better of, master, overcome, overpower, overthrow, quell, subjugate, vanquish 2 seize, acquire, annex, obtain, occupy, overrun, win

conqueror noun winner, conquistador, defeater, master, subjugator, vanquisher, victor

conquest noun 1 defeat, mastery, overthrow, rout, triumph, victory 2 takeover, annexation, coup, invasion, occupation, subjugation

conscience noun principles, moral sense, scruples, sense of right and wrong, still small voice

conscientious adjective thorough, careful, diligent, exact, faithful, meticulous, painstaking, particular, punctilious

conscious adjective 1 aware, alert, alive to, awake, responsive, sensible, sentient 2 deliberate, calculated, intentional, knowing, premeditated, self-conscious, studied, wilful

consciousness noun awareness, apprehension, knowledge, realization, recognition, sensibility

consecrate verb sanctify, dedicate, devote, hallow, ordain, set apart, venerate

consecutive adjective successive, in sequence, in turn, running, sequential, succeeding, uninterrupted

consensus noun agreement, assent, common consent, concord, general agreement, harmony, unanimity, unity

consent noun 1 agreement, acquiescence, approval, assent, compliance, go-ahead (informal), O.K. or okay (informal), permission, sanction ◆ verb 2 agree, acquiesce, allow, approve, assent, concur, permit

consequence noun 1 result, effect, end result, issue, outcome, repercussion, sequel, upshot 2 importance, account, concern, import, moment, significance, value, weight

consequent adjective following, ensuing, resultant, resulting, subsequent, successive

consequently adverb as a result, accordingly, ergo, hence, subsequently, therefore, thus

conservation noun protection, guardianship, husbandry, maintenance, preservation, safeguarding, safekeeping, saving, upkeep

conservative adjective 1 traditional, cautious, conventional, die-hard, hidebound, reactionary, sober ♦ noun 2 traditionalist, reactionary, stick-in-the-mud (informal)

Conservative adjective 1 Tory, right-wing ♦ noun 2 Tory, right-winger

conserve verb protect, hoard, husband, keep, nurse, preserve, save, store up, take care of, use sparingly

consider verb 1 think, believe, deem, hold to be, judge, rate, regard as 2 think about, cogitate, contemplate, deliberate, meditate, ponder, reflect, ruminate, turn over in one's mind, weigh 3 bear in mind, keep in view, make allowance for, reckon with, remember, respect, take into account

considerable adjective large, appreciable, goodly, great, marked, noticeable, plentiful, sizable or sizeable, substantial

considerably adverb greatly, appreciably, markedly, noticeably, remarkably,

significantly, substantially, very much

considerate adjective thoughtful, attentive, concerned, kindly, mindful, obliging, patient, tactful, unselfish

consideration noun 1 thought, analysis, deliberation, discussion, examination, reflection, review, scrutiny 2 factor, concern, issue, point 3 thoughtfulness, concern, considerateness, kindness, respect, tact 4 payment, fee, recompense, remuneration, reward, tip

considering preposition taking into account, in the light of, in view of

consignment noun shipment, batch, delivery, goods

consist verb 1 consist of be made up of, amount to, be composed of, comprise, contain, embody, include, incorporate, involve 2 consist in lie in, be expressed by, be found or contained in, inhere in, reside in

consistency noun 1 texture, compactness, density, firmness, thickness, viscosity 2 constancy, evenness, regularity, steadfastness, steadiness, uniformity

consistent adjective 1 unchanging, constant, dependable, persistent, regular, steady, true to type, undeviating 2 agreeing, coherent, compatible, congruous, consonant, harmonious, logical

consolation noun comfort, cheer, encouragement, help, relief, solace, succour, support

console verb comfort, calm,

cheer, encourage, express
sympathy for, soothe

consolidate verb 1 strengthen,
fortify, reinforce, secure, stabilize
2 combine, amalgamate,
federate, fuse, join, unite

consort verb 1 associate,
fraternize, go around with, hang
about, around or out with, keep
company, mix ♦ noun 2 spouse,
companion, husband, partner,
wife

conspicuous adjective 1 obvious,
blatant, clear, evident,
noticeable, patent, salient
2 noteworthy, illustrious,
notable, outstanding, prominent,
remarkable, salient, signal,
striking

conspiracy noun plot, collusion,
intrigue, machination, scheme,
treason

conspirator noun plotter,
conspirer, intriguer, schemer,
traitor

conspire verb 1 plot, contrive,
intrigue, machinate, manoeuvre,
plan, scheme 2 work together,
combine, concur, contribute,
cooperate, tend

constant adjective 1 continuous,
ceaseless, incessant,
interminable, nonstop,
perpetual, sustained, unrelenting
2 unchanging, even, fixed,
invariable, permanent, stable,
steady, uniform, unvarying
3 faithful, devoted, loyal,
stalwart, staunch, true,
trustworthy, trusty

constantly adverb continuously,
all the time, always, continually,
endlessly, incessantly,
interminably, invariably,

nonstop, perpetually

consternation noun dismay,
alarm, anxiety, distress, dread,
fear, trepidation

constituent noun 1 voter,
elector 2 component, element,
factor, ingredient, part, unit
♦ adjective 3 component, basic,
elemental, essential, integral

constitute verb make up,
compose, comprise, establish,
form, found, set up

constitution noun 1 health,
build, character, disposition,
physique 2 structure,
composition, form, make-up,
nature

constitutional adjective
1 statutory, chartered, vested
♦ noun 2 walk, airing, stroll, turn

constrain verb 1 force, bind,
coerce, compel, impel,
necessitate, oblige, pressurize
2 restrict, check, confine,
constrict, curb, restrain, straiten

constraint noun 1 restriction,
check, curb, deterrent,
hindrance, limitation, rein
2 force, coercion, compulsion,
necessity, pressure, restraint

construct verb build, assemble,
compose, create, fashion, form,
make, manufacture, put
together, shape

construction noun 1 building,
composition, creation, edifice
2 Formal interpretation,
explanation, inference, reading,
rendering

constructive adjective helpful,
positive, practical, productive,
useful, valuable

consult verb ask, compare notes,

confer, pick (someone's) brains, question, refer to, take counsel, turn to

consultant noun specialist, adviser, authority

consultation noun seminar, appointment, conference, council, deliberation, dialogue, discussion, examination, hearing, interview, meeting, session

consume verb 1 eat, devour, eat up, gobble (up), put away, swallow 2 use up, absorb, dissipate, exhaust, expend, spend, squander, waste 3 destroy, annihilate, demolish, devastate, lay waste, ravage 4 often passive obsess, absorb, dominate, eat up, engross, monopolize, preoccupy

consumer noun buyer, customer, purchaser, shopper, user

consummate verb 1 complete, accomplish, conclude, crown, end, finish, fulfil ♦ adjective 2 skilled, accomplished, matchless, perfect, polished, practised, superb, supreme 3 complete, absolute, conspicuous, extreme, supreme, total, utter

consumption noun 1 using up, depletion, diminution, dissipation, exhaustion, expenditure, loss, waste 2 Old-fashioned tuberculosis, T.B.

contact noun 1 communication, association, connection 2 touch, contiguity 3 acquaintance, connection ♦ verb 4 get or be in touch with, approach, call, communicate with, reach, speak to, write to

contagious adjective infectious,

catching, communicable, spreading, transmissible

contain verb 1 hold, accommodate, enclose, have capacity for, incorporate, seat 2 include, comprehend, comprise, consist of, embody, embrace, involve 3 restrain, control, curb, hold back, hold in, keep a tight rein on, repress, stifle

container noun holder, receptacle, repository, vessel

contaminate verb pollute, adulterate, befoul, corrupt, defile, infect, stain, taint, tarnish

contamination noun pollution, contagion, corruption, defilement, impurity, infection, poisoning, taint

contemplate verb 1 think about, consider, deliberate, meditate, muse over, ponder, reflect upon, ruminate (upon) 2 consider, envisage, expect, foresee, intend, plan, think of 3 look at, examine, eye up, gaze at, inspect, regard, stare at, study, survey, view

contemporary adjective 1 coexisting, concurrent, contemporaneous 2 modern, à la mode, current, newfangled, present, present-day, recent, up-to-date ♦ noun 3 peer, fellow

contempt noun scorn, derision, disdain, disregard, disrespect, mockery, neglect, slight

contemptible adjective despicable, detestable, ignominious, measly, paltry, pitiful, shameful, worthless

contemptuous adjective scornful, arrogant,

condescending, derisive, disdainful, haughty, sneering, supercilious, withering

contend verb **1** compete, clash, contest, fight, jostle, strive, struggle, vie **2** argue, affirm, allege, assert, dispute, hold, maintain

content[1] noun **1** meaning, essence, gist, significance, substance **2** amount, capacity, load, measure, size, volume

content[2] adjective **1** satisfied, agreeable, at ease, comfortable, contented, fulfilled, willing to accept ♦ verb **2** satisfy, appease, humour, indulge, mollify, placate, please ♦ noun **3** satisfaction, comfort, contentment, ease, gratification, peace of mind, pleasure

contented adjective satisfied, comfortable, content, glad, gratified, happy, pleased, serene, thankful

contentious adjective argumentative, bickering, captious, cavilling, disputatious, quarrelsome, querulous, wrangling

contentment noun satisfaction, comfort, content, ease, equanimity, fulfilment, happiness, peace, pleasure, serenity

contents plural noun constituents, elements, ingredients, load

contest noun **1** competition, game, match, tournament, trial **2** struggle, battle, combat, conflict, controversy, dispute, fight ♦ verb **3** dispute, argue, call in or into question, challenge,

debate, doubt, object to, oppose, question **4** compete, contend, fight, strive, vie

contestant noun competitor, candidate, contender, entrant, participant, player

context noun **1** circumstances, ambience, conditions, situation **2** frame of reference, background, connection, framework, relation

contingency noun possibility, accident, chance, emergency, event, eventuality, happening, incident

continual adjective constant, frequent, incessant, interminable, recurrent, regular, repeated, unremitting

continually adverb constantly, all the time, always, forever, incessantly, interminably, nonstop, persistently, repeatedly

continuation noun **1** continuing, perpetuation, prolongation, resumption **2** addition, extension, furtherance, postscript, sequel, supplement

continue verb **1** remain, abide, carry on, endure, last, live on, persist, stay, survive **2** keep on, carry on, go on, maintain, persevere, persist in, stick at, sustain **3** resume, carry on, pick up where one left off, proceed, recommence, return to, take up

continuing adjective lasting, enduring, in progress, ongoing, sustained

continuity noun sequence, cohesion, connection, flow, progression, succession

continuous adjective constant,

extended, prolonged, unbroken, unceasing, undivided, uninterrupted

contraband noun 1 <u>smuggling</u>, black-marketing, bootlegging, trafficking ♦ adjective 2 <u>smuggled</u>, banned, bootleg, forbidden, hot (informal), illegal, illicit, prohibited, unlawful

contract noun 1 <u>agreement</u>, arrangement, bargain, commitment, covenant, pact, settlement ♦ verb 2 <u>agree</u>, bargain, come to terms, commit oneself, covenant, negotiate, pledge 3 <u>shorten</u>, abbreviate, curtail, diminish, dwindle, lessen, narrow, reduce, shrink, shrivel 4 <u>catch</u>, acquire, be afflicted with, develop, get, go down with, incur

contraction noun <u>shortening</u>, abbreviation, compression, narrowing, reduction, shrinkage, shrivelling, tightening

contradict verb <u>deny</u>, be at variance with, belie, challenge, controvert, fly in the face of, negate, rebut

contradiction noun <u>denial</u>, conflict, contravention, incongruity, inconsistency, negation, opposite

contradictory adjective <u>inconsistent</u>, conflicting, contrary, incompatible, opposed, opposite, paradoxical

contraption noun Informal <u>device</u>, apparatus, contrivance, gadget, instrument, mechanism

contrary noun 1 <u>opposite</u>, antithesis, converse, reverse ♦ adjective 2 <u>opposed</u>, adverse, clashing, contradictory, counter,

discordant, hostile, inconsistent, opposite, paradoxical 3 <u>perverse</u>, awkward, cantankerous, difficult, disobliging, intractable, obstinate, stroppy (Brit. slang), unaccommodating

contrast noun 1 <u>difference</u>, comparison, disparity, dissimilarity, distinction, divergence, foil, opposition ♦ verb 2 <u>differentiate</u>, compare, differ, distinguish, oppose, set in opposition, set off

contribute verb 1 <u>give</u>, add, bestow, chip in (informal), donate, provide, subscribe, supply 2 **contribute to** be partly responsible for, be conducive to, be instrumental in, help, lead to, tend to

contribution noun <u>gift</u>, addition, donation, grant, input, offering, subscription

contributor noun <u>giver</u>, donor, patron, subscriber, supporter

contrite adjective <u>sorry</u>, chastened, conscience-stricken, humble, penitent, regretful, remorseful, repentant, sorrowful

contrivance noun 1 <u>device</u>, apparatus, appliance, contraption, gadget, implement, instrument, invention, machine, mechanism 2 <u>plan</u>, intrigue, machination, plot, ruse, scheme, stratagem, trick

contrive verb 1 <u>bring about</u>, arrange, effect, manage, manoeuvre, plan, plot, scheme, succeed 2 <u>devise</u>, concoct, construct, create, design, fabricate, improvise, invent, manufacture

contrived adjective <u>forced</u>,

artificial, elaborate, laboured, overdone, planned, strained, unnatural

control noun **1** power, authority, charge, command, guidance, management, oversight, supervision, supremacy **2** restraint, brake, check, curb, limitation, regulation ♦ verb **3** have power over, administer, command, direct, govern, handle, have charge of, manage, manipulate, supervise **4** restrain, check, constrain, contain, curb, hold back, limit, repress, subdue

controls plural noun instruments, console, control panel, dash, dashboard, dials

controversial adjective disputed, at issue, contentious, debatable, disputable, open to question, under discussion

controversy noun argument, altercation, debate, dispute, quarrel, row, squabble, wrangling

convalescence noun recovery, improvement, recuperation, rehabilitation, return to health

convalescent adjective recovering, getting better, improving, mending, on the mend, recuperating

convene verb gather, assemble, bring together, call, come together, congregate, convoke, meet, summon

convenience noun **1** availability, accessibility, advantage, appropriateness, benefit, fitness, suitability, usefulness, utility **2** appliance, amenity, comfort, facility, help, labour-saving device

convenient adjective **1** useful, appropriate, fit, handy, helpful,

labour-saving, serviceable, suitable, timely **2** nearby, accessible, at hand, available, close at hand, handy, just round the corner, within reach

convention noun **1** custom, code, etiquette, practice, propriety, protocol, tradition, usage **2** agreement, bargain, contract, pact, protocol, treaty **3** assembly, conference, congress, convocation, council, meeting

conventional adjective **1** ordinary, accepted, customary, normal, orthodox, regular, standard, traditional, usual **2** unoriginal, banal, hackneyed, prosaic, routine, run-of-the-mill, stereotyped

converge verb come together, coincide, combine, gather, join, meet, merge

conversation noun talk, chat, conference, dialogue, discourse, discussion, gossip, tête-à-tête

converse[1] verb talk, chat, commune, confer, discourse, exchange views

converse[2] noun **1** opposite, antithesis, contrary, obverse, other side of the coin, reverse ♦ adjective **2** opposite, contrary, counter, reverse, reversed, transposed

conversion noun **1** change, metamorphosis, transformation **2** adaptation, alteration, modification, reconstruction, remodelling, reorganization

convert verb **1** change, alter, transform, transpose, turn **2** adapt, apply, customize, modify, remodel, reorganize,

restyle, revise **3** reform, convince, proselytize ♦ *noun*
4 neophyte, disciple, proselyte

convex *adjective* rounded, bulging, gibbous, protuberant

convey *verb* **1** communicate, disclose, impart, make known, relate, reveal, tell **2** carry, bear, bring, conduct, fetch, guide, move, send, transport

convict *verb* **1** find guilty, condemn, imprison, pronounce guilty, sentence ♦ *noun*
2 prisoner, criminal, culprit, felon, jailbird, lag (*slang*)

conviction *noun* **1** belief, creed, faith, opinion, persuasion, principle, tenet, view
2 confidence, assurance, certainty, certitude, firmness, reliance

convince *verb* persuade, assure, bring round, prevail upon, satisfy, sway, win over

convincing *adjective* persuasive, cogent, conclusive, credible, impressive, plausible, powerful, telling

convulse *verb* shake, agitate, churn up, derange, disorder, disturb, twist, work

convulsion *noun* spasm, contraction, cramp, fit, paroxysm, seizure

cool *adjective* **1** cold, chilled, chilly, nippy, refreshing **2** calm, collected, composed, relaxed, sedate, self-controlled, self-possessed, unemotional, unruffled **3** unfriendly, aloof, distant, indifferent, lukewarm, offhand, standoffish, unenthusiastic, unwelcoming
♦ *verb* **4** chill, cool off, freeze,

lose heat, refrigerate ♦ *noun*
5 *Slang* calmness, composure, control, poise, self-control, self-discipline, self-possession, temper

cooperate *verb* work together, collaborate, combine, conspire, coordinate, join forces, pool resources, pull together

cooperation *noun* teamwork, collaboration, combined effort, esprit de corps, give-and-take, unity

cooperative *adjective* **1** helpful, accommodating, obliging, onside (*informal*), responsive, supportive **2** shared, collective, combined, joint

coordinate *verb* bring together, harmonize, integrate, match, organize, synchronize, systematize

cope *verb* **1** manage, carry on, get by (*informal*), hold one's own, make the grade, struggle through, survive **2** cope with deal with, contend with, grapple with, handle, struggle with, weather, wrestle with

copious *adjective* abundant, ample, bountiful, extensive, full, lavish, plentiful, profuse

copy *noun* **1** reproduction, counterfeit, duplicate, facsimile, forgery, imitation, likeness, model, replica ♦ *verb*
2 reproduce, counterfeit, duplicate, replicate, transcribe
3 imitate, ape, emulate, follow, mimic, mirror, repeat

cord *noun* rope, line, string, twine

cordial *adjective* warm, affable, agreeable, cheerful, congenial, friendly, genial, hearty, sociable

cordon noun 1 <u>chain</u>, barrier, line, ring ♦ verb 2 **cordon off** <u>surround</u>, close off, encircle, enclose, fence off, isolate, picket, separate

core noun <u>centre</u>, crux, essence, gist, heart, kernel, nub, nucleus, pith

corner noun 1 <u>angle</u>, bend, crook, joint 2 <u>space</u>, hideaway, hide-out, nook, retreat ♦ verb 3 <u>trap</u>, run to earth 4 As in **corner the market** <u>monopolize</u>, dominate, engross, hog (slang)

corny adjective Slang <u>unoriginal</u>, hackneyed, old-fashioned, old hat, stale, stereotyped, trite

corporation noun 1 <u>business</u>, association, corporate body, society 2 <u>town council</u>, civic authorities, council, municipal authorities 3 Informal <u>paunch</u>, beer belly (informal), middle-age spread (informal), potbelly, spare tyre (Brit. slang), spread (informal)

corps noun <u>team</u>, band, company, detachment, division, regiment, squadron, troop, unit

corpse noun <u>body</u>, cadaver, carcass, remains, stiff (slang)

correct adjective 1 <u>true</u>, accurate, exact, faultless, flawless, O.K. or okay (informal), precise, right 2 <u>proper</u>, acceptable, appropriate, fitting, kosher (informal), O.K. or okay (informal), seemly, standard ♦ verb 3 <u>rectify</u>, adjust, amend, cure, emend, redress, reform, remedy, right 4 <u>punish</u>, admonish, chasten, chastise, chide, discipline, rebuke, reprimand, reprove

correction noun 1 <u>rectification</u>, adjustment, alteration, amendment, emendation, improvement, modification 2 <u>punishment</u>, admonition, castigation, chastisement, discipline, reformation, reproof

correctly adverb <u>rightly</u>, accurately, perfectly, precisely, properly, right

correctness noun 1 <u>truth</u>, accuracy, exactitude, exactness, faultlessness, fidelity, preciseness, precision, regularity 2 <u>decorum</u>, civility, good breeding, propriety, seemliness

correspond verb 1 <u>be consistent</u>, accord, agree, conform, fit, harmonize, match, square, tally 2 <u>communicate</u>, exchange letters, keep in touch, write

correspondence noun 1 <u>letters</u>, communication, mail, post, writing 2 <u>relation</u>, agreement, coincidence, comparison, conformity, correlation, harmony, match, similarity

correspondent noun 1 <u>letter writer</u>, pen friend or pal 2 <u>reporter</u>, contributor, journalist

corresponding adjective <u>related</u>, analogous, answering, complementary, equivalent, matching, reciprocal, similar

corridor noun <u>passage</u>, aisle, alley, hallway, passageway

corroborate verb <u>support</u>, authenticate, back up, bear out, confirm, endorse, ratify, substantiate, validate

corrode verb <u>eat away</u>, consume, corrupt, erode, gnaw, oxidize, rust, wear away

corrosive adjective <u>corroding</u>,

caustic, consuming, erosive, virulent, vitriolic, wasting, wearing

corrupt adjective 1 <u>dishonest</u>, bent (slang), bribable, crooked (informal), fraudulent, unprincipled, unscrupulous, venal 2 <u>depraved</u>, debased, degenerate, dissolute, profligate, vicious 3 <u>distorted</u>, altered, doctored, falsified ◆ verb 4 <u>bribe</u>, buy off, entice, fix (informal), grease (someone's) palm (slang), lure, suborn 5 <u>deprave</u>, debauch, pervert, subvert 6 <u>distort</u>, doctor, tamper with

corruption noun 1 <u>dishonesty</u>, bribery, extortion, fraud, shady dealings (informal), unscrupulousness, venality 2 <u>depravity</u>, decadence, evil, immorality, perversion, vice, wickedness 3 <u>distortion</u>, doctoring, falsification

corset noun <u>girdle</u>, belt, bodice

cosmetic adjective <u>beautifying</u>, nonessential, superficial, surface

cosmic adjective <u>universal</u>, stellar

cosmopolitan adjective 1 <u>sophisticated</u>, broad-minded, catholic, open-minded, universal, urbane, well-travelled, worldly-wise ◆ noun 2 <u>man or woman of the world</u>, jet-setter, sophisticate

cost noun 1 <u>price</u>, amount, charge, damage (informal), expense, outlay, payment, worth 2 <u>loss</u>, damage, detriment, expense, harm, hurt, injury, penalty, sacrifice, suffering ◆ verb 3 <u>sell at</u>, come to, command a price of, set (someone) back (informal) 4 <u>lose</u>, do disservice

to, harm, hurt, injure

costly adjective 1 <u>expensive</u>, dear, exorbitant, extortionate, highly-priced, steep (informal), stiff 2 <u>damaging</u>, catastrophic, deleterious, disastrous, harmful, loss-making, ruinous

costs plural noun <u>expenses</u>, budget, outgoings, overheads

costume noun <u>outfit</u>, apparel, attire, clothing, dress, ensemble, garb, livery, uniform

cosy adjective <u>snug</u>, comfortable, comfy (informal), homely, intimate, sheltered, tucked up, warm

cottage noun <u>cabin</u>, chalet, hut, lodge, shack

cough noun 1 <u>frog or tickle in one's throat</u>, bark, hack ◆ verb 2 <u>clear one's throat</u>, bark, hack

council noun <u>governing body</u>, assembly, board, cabinet, committee, conference, congress, convention, panel, parliament

counsel noun 1 <u>advice</u>, direction, guidance, information, recommendation, suggestion, warning 2 <u>legal adviser</u>, advocate, attorney, barrister, lawyer, solicitor ◆ verb 3 <u>advise</u>, advocate, exhort, instruct, recommend, urge, warn

count verb 1 <u>add (up)</u>, calculate, compute, enumerate, number, reckon, tally, tot up 2 <u>matter</u>, be important, carry weight, rate, signify, tell, weigh 3 <u>consider</u>, deem, judge, look upon, rate, regard, think 4 <u>take into account or consideration</u>, include, number among ◆ noun 5 <u>calculation</u>, computation, enumeration, numbering, poll, reckoning, sum, tally

counter verb **1** retaliate, answer, hit back, meet, oppose, parry, resist, respond, ward off ♦ adverb **2** opposite to, against, at variance with, contrariwise, conversely, in defiance of, versus

counteract verb act against, foil, frustrate, negate, neutralize, offset, resist, thwart

counterbalance verb offset, balance, compensate, make up for, set off

counterfeit adjective **1** fake, bogus, false, forged, imitation, phoney or phony (informal), sham, simulated ♦ noun **2** fake, copy, forgery, fraud, imitation, phoney or phony (informal), reproduction, sham ♦ verb **3** fake, copy, fabricate, feign, forge, imitate, impersonate, pretend, sham, simulate

countermand verb cancel, annul, override, repeal, rescind, retract, reverse, revoke

counterpart noun opposite number, complement, equal, fellow, match, mate, supplement, tally, twin

countless adjective innumerable, endless, immeasurable, incalculable, infinite, legion, limitless, myriad, numberless, untold

count on or **upon** verb depend on, bank on, believe (in), lean on, pin one's faith on, reckon on, rely on, take for granted, take on trust, trust

country noun **1** nation, commonwealth, kingdom, people, realm, state **2** territory,

land, region, terrain **3** people, citizens, community, inhabitants, nation, populace, public, society **4** countryside, backwoods, farmland, green belt, outback (Austral. & N.Z.), provinces, sticks (informal)

countryside noun country, farmland, green belt, outback (Austral. & N.Z.), outdoors, sticks (informal)

count up verb add, reckon up, sum, tally, total

county noun province, shire

coup noun masterstroke, accomplishment, action, deed, exploit, feat, manoeuvre, stunt

couple noun **1** pair, brace, duo, two, twosome ♦ verb **2** link, connect, hitch, join, marry, pair, unite, wed, yoke

coupon noun slip, card, certificate, ticket, token, voucher

courage noun bravery, daring, fearlessness, gallantry, heroism, mettle, nerve, pluck, resolution, valour

courageous adjective brave, bold, daring, fearless, gallant, gritty, intrepid, lion-hearted, stouthearted, valiant

courier noun **1** guide, representative **2** messenger, bearer, carrier, envoy, runner

course noun **1** classes, curriculum, lectures, programme, schedule **2** progression, development, flow, movement, order, progress, sequence, unfolding **3** route, direction, line, passage, path, road, track, trajectory, way **4** racecourse, cinder track, circuit

5 underline, behaviour, conduct, manner, method, mode, plan, policy, programme **6** period, duration, lapse, passage, passing, sweep, term, time **7 of course** naturally, certainly, definitely, indubitably, needless to say, obviously, undoubtedly, without a doubt ♦ verb **8** run, flow, gush, race, speed, stream, surge **9** hunt, chase, follow, pursue

court noun **1** law court, bar, bench, tribunal **2** courtyard, cloister, piazza, plaza, quad (informal), quadrangle, square, yard **3** palace, hall, manor **4** royal household, attendants, cortege, entourage, retinue, suite, train ♦ verb **5** woo, date, go (out) with, run after, serenade, set one's cap at, take out, walk out with **6** cultivate, curry favour with, fawn upon, flatter, pander to, seek, solicit **7** invite, attract, bring about, incite, prompt, provoke, seek

courteous adjective polite, affable, attentive, civil, gallant, gracious, refined, respectful, urbane, well-mannered

courtesy noun **1** politeness, affability, civility, courteousness, gallantry, good manners, graciousness, urbanity **2** favour, indulgence, kindness

courtier noun attendant, follower, squire

courtly adjective ceremonious, chivalrous, dignified, elegant, formal, gallant, polished, refined, stately, urbane

courtyard noun yard, enclosure, quad, quadrangle

cove noun bay, anchorage, inlet, sound

covenant noun **1** promise, agreement, arrangement, commitment, contract, pact, pledge ♦ verb **2** promise, agree, contract, pledge, stipulate, undertake

cover verb **1** clothe, dress, envelop, put on, wrap **2** overlay, coat, daub, encase, envelop **3** submerge, engulf, flood, overrun, wash over **4** conceal, cloak, disguise, enshroud, hide, mask, obscure, shroud, veil **5** travel over, cross, pass through or over, traverse **6** protect, defend, guard, shield **7** report, describe, investigate, narrate, relate, tell of, write up ♦ noun **8** covering, canopy, case, coating, envelope, jacket, lid, top, wrapper **9** disguise, façade, front, mask, pretext, screen, smoke screen, veil **10** protection, camouflage, concealment, defence, guard, shelter, shield **11** insurance, compensation, indemnity, protection, reimbursement

covering adjective **1** explanatory, accompanying, descriptive, introductory ♦ noun **2** cover, blanket, casing, coating, layer, wrapping

cover-up noun concealment, complicity, conspiracy, front, smoke screen, whitewash (informal)

cover up verb conceal, draw a veil over, hide, hush up, suppress, sweep under the carpet, whitewash (informal)

covet verb long for, aspire to,

crave, desire, envy, lust after, set one's heart on, yearn for

covetous adjective <u>envious</u>, acquisitive, avaricious, close-fisted, grasping, greedy, jealous, rapacious, yearning

coward noun <u>wimp</u> (informal), chicken (slang), scaredy-cat (informal), yellow-belly (slang)

cowardice noun <u>faint-heartedness</u>, fearfulness, spinelessness, weakness

cowardly adjective <u>faint-hearted</u>, chicken (slang), craven, fearful, scared, soft, spineless, timorous, weak, yellow (informal)

cowboy noun <u>cowhand</u>, cattleman, drover, gaucho (S. American), herdsman, rancher, stockman

cower verb <u>cringe</u>, draw back, flinch, grovel, quail, shrink, tremble

coy adjective <u>shy</u>, bashful, demure, modest, reserved, retiring, shrinking, timid

crack verb 1 <u>break</u>, burst, cleave, fracture, snap, splinter, split 2 <u>snap</u>, burst, crash, detonate, explode, pop, ring 3 <u>give in</u>, break down, collapse, give way, go to pieces, lose control, succumb, yield 4 Informal <u>hit</u>, clip (informal), clout (informal), cuff, slap, smack, whack 5 <u>solve</u>, decipher, fathom, get the answer to, work out ◆ noun 6 <u>snap</u>, burst, clap, crash, explosion, pop, report 7 <u>break</u>, chink, cleft, cranny, crevice, fissure, fracture, gap, rift 8 Informal <u>blow</u>, clip (informal), clout (informal), cuff, slap, smack, whack 9 Informal <u>joke</u>,

dig, funny remark, gag (informal), quip, wisecrack, witticism ◆ adjective 10 Slang <u>first-class</u>, ace, choice, elite, excellent, first-rate, hand-picked, superior, world-class

crackdown noun <u>suppression</u>, clampdown, crushing, repression

cracked adjective <u>broken</u>, chipped, damaged, defective, faulty, flawed, imperfect, split

cradle noun 1 <u>crib</u>, bassinet, cot, Moses basket 2 <u>birthplace</u>, beginning, fount, fountainhead, origin, source, spring, wellspring ◆ verb 3 <u>hold</u>, lull, nestle, nurse, rock, support

craft noun 1 <u>occupation</u>, business, employment, handicraft, pursuit, trade, vocation, work 2 <u>skill</u>, ability, aptitude, art, artistry, expertise, ingenuity, know-how (informal), technique, workmanship 3 <u>vessel</u>, aircraft, boat, plane, ship, spacecraft

craftsman noun <u>skilled worker</u>, artisan, maker, master, smith, technician, wright

craftsmanship noun <u>workmanship</u>, artistry, expertise, mastery, technique

crafty adjective <u>cunning</u>, artful, calculating, devious, sharp, shrewd, sly, subtle, wily

crag noun <u>rock</u>, bluff, peak, pinnacle, tor

cram verb 1 <u>stuff</u>, compress, force, jam, pack in, press, shove, squeeze 2 <u>overeat</u>, glut, gorge, satiate, stuff 3 <u>study</u>, bone up (informal), mug up (slang), revise, swot

cramp[1] noun spasm, ache, contraction, convulsion, pain, pang, stitch, twinge

cramp[2] verb restrict, constrain, hamper, handicap, hinder, impede, inhibit, obstruct

cramped adjective closed in, confined, congested, crowded, hemmed in, overcrowded, packed, uncomfortable

cranny noun crevice, chink, cleft, crack, fissure, gap, hole, opening

crash noun 1 collision, accident, bump, pile-up (informal), prang (informal), smash, wreck 2 smash, bang, boom, clang, clash, clatter, din, racket, thunder 3 collapse, debacle, depression, downfall, failure, ruin ♦ verb 4 collide, bump (into), crash-land (an aircraft), drive into, have an accident, hit, plough into, wreck 5 collapse, be ruined, fail, fold, fold up, go belly up (informal), go bust (informal), go to the wall, go under 6 hurtle, fall headlong, give way, lurch, overbalance, plunge, topple

crass adjective insensitive, boorish, gross, indelicate, oafish, stupid, unrefined, witless

crate noun container, box, case, packing case, tea chest

crater noun hollow, depression, dip

crave verb 1 long for, desire, hanker after, hope for, lust after, want, yearn for 2 Informal beg, ask, beseech, entreat, implore, petition, plead for, pray for, seek, solicit, supplicate

craving noun longing, appetite, desire, hankering, hope, hunger, thirst, yearning, yen (informal)

crawl verb 1 creep, advance slowly, inch, slither, worm one's way, wriggle, writhe 2 grovel, creep, fawn, humble oneself, toady 3 be full of, be alive, be overrun (slang), swarm, teem

craze noun fad, enthusiasm, fashion, infatuation, mania, rage, trend, vogue

crazy adjective 1 Informal ridiculous, absurd, foolish, idiotic, ill-conceived, ludicrous, nonsensical, preposterous, senseless 2 fanatical, devoted, enthusiastic, infatuated, mad, passionate, wild (informal) 3 insane, crazed, demented, deranged, mad, nuts (slang), out of one's mind, unbalanced

creak verb squeak, grate, grind, groan, scrape, scratch, screech

cream noun 1 lotion, cosmetic, emulsion, essence, liniment, oil, ointment, paste, salve, unguent 2 best, crème de la crème, elite, flower, pick, prime ♦ adjective 3 off-white, yellowish-white

creamy adjective smooth, buttery, milky, rich, soft, velvety

crease noun 1 line, corrugation, fold, groove, ridge, wrinkle ♦ verb 2 wrinkle, corrugate, crumple, double up, fold, rumple, screw up

create verb 1 make, compose, devise, formulate, invent, originate, produce, spawn 2 cause, bring about, lead to, occasion 3 appoint, constitute, establish, install, invest, make, set up

creation noun 1 making, conception, formation,

generation, genesis, procreation
2 setting up, development,
establishment, formation,
foundation, inception,
institution, production
3 invention, achievement,
brainchild (*informal*), concoction,
handiwork, magnum opus, *pièce
de résistance*, production
4 universe, cosmos, nature, world

creative *adjective* imaginative,
artistic, clever, gifted, ingenious,
inspired, inventive, original,
visionary

creativity *noun* imagination,
cleverness, ingenuity, inspiration,
inventiveness, originality

creator *noun* maker, architect,
author, designer, father,
inventor, originator, prime mover

creature *noun* **1** living thing,
animal, beast, being, brute
2 person, human being,
individual, man, mortal, soul,
woman

credentials *plural noun*
certification, authorization,
document, licence, papers,
passport, reference(s), testimonial

credibility *noun* believability,
integrity, plausibility, reliability,
trustworthiness

credible *adjective* **1** believable,
conceivable, imaginable, likely,
plausible, possible, probable,
reasonable, thinkable **2** reliable,
dependable, honest, sincere,
trustworthy, trusty

credit *noun* **1** praise, acclaim,
acknowledgment, approval,
commendation, honour, kudos,
recognition, tribute **2** As in **be a
credit to** source of satisfaction or
pride, feather in one's cap,

honour **3** prestige, esteem, good
name, influence, position,
regard, reputation, repute,
standing, status **4** belief,
confidence, credence, faith,
reliance, trust **5 on credit** on
account, by deferred payment,
by instalments, on hire-purchase,
on (the) H.P., on the slate
(*informal*), on tick (*informal*)
♦ *verb* **6** believe, accept, have
faith in, rely on, trust **7** credit
with attribute to, ascribe to,
assign to, impute to

creditable *adjective* praiseworthy,
admirable, commendable,
honourable, laudable, reputable,
respectable, worthy

credulity *noun* gullibility, blind
faith, credulousness, naïveté

creed *noun* belief, articles of
faith, catechism, credo, doctrine,
dogma, principles

creek *noun* **1** inlet, bay, bight,
cove, firth *or* frith (*Scot.*) **2** *U.S.,
Canad., Austral., & N.Z.* stream,
bayou, brook, rivulet, runnel,
tributary, watercourse

creep *verb* **1** sneak, approach
unnoticed, skulk, slink, steal,
tiptoe **2** crawl, glide, slither,
squirm, wriggle, writhe ♦ *noun*
3 *Slang* bootlicker (*informal*),
crawler (*slang*), sneak,
sycophant, toady

creeper *noun* climbing plant,
rambler, runner, trailing plant,
vine (*chiefly U.S.*)

creeps *plural noun* **give one the
creeps** *Informal* disgust, frighten,
make one's hair stand on end,
make one squirm, repel, repulse,
scare

creepy *adjective Informal*

disturbing, eerie, frightening, hair-raising, macabre, menacing, scary (*informal*), sinister

crescent *noun* meniscus, new moon, sickle

crest *noun* 1 top, apex, crown, highest point, peak, pinnacle, ridge, summit 2 tuft, comb, crown, mane, plume 3 emblem, badge, bearings, device, insignia, symbol

crestfallen *adjective* disappointed, dejected, depressed, despondent, discouraged, disheartened, downcast, downhearted

crevice *noun* gap, chink, cleft, crack, cranny, fissure, hole, opening, slit

crew *noun* 1 (ship's) company, hands, (ship's) complement 2 team, corps, gang, posse, squad 3 *Informal* crowd, band, bunch (*informal*), gang, horde, mob, pack, set

crib *noun* 1 *Informal* translation, key 2 cradle, bassinet, bed, cot 3 manger, rack, stall ◆ *verb* 4 *Informal* copy, cheat, pirate, plagiarize, purloin, steal

crime *noun* 1 offence, felony, misdeed, misdemeanour, transgression, trespass, unlawful act, violation 2 lawbreaking, corruption, illegality, misconduct, vice, wrongdoing

criminal *noun* 1 lawbreaker, convict, crook (*informal*), culprit, felon, offender, sinner, villain ◆ *adjective* 2 unlawful, corrupt, crooked (*informal*), illegal, illicit, immoral, lawless, wicked, wrong 3 *Informal* disgraceful, deplorable, foolish, preposterous,

ridiculous, scandalous, senseless

cringe *verb* 1 shrink, cower, draw back, flinch, recoil, shy, wince 2 grovel, bootlick (*informal*), crawl, creep, fawn, kowtow, pander to, toady

cripple *verb* 1 disable, hamstring, incapacitate, lame, maim, paralyse, weaken 2 damage, destroy, impair, put out of action, put paid to, ruin, spoil

crippled *adjective* disabled, handicapped, incapacitated, laid up (*informal*), lame, paralysed

crisis *noun* 1 critical point, climax, crunch (*informal*), crux, culmination, height, moment of truth, turning point 2 emergency, deep water, dire straits, meltdown (*informal*), panic stations (*informal*), plight, predicament, trouble

crisp *adjective* 1 crunchy, brittle, crispy, crumbly, firm, fresh 2 clean, neat, smart, spruce, tidy, trim, well-groomed, well-pressed 3 bracing, brisk, fresh, invigorating, refreshing

criterion *noun* standard, bench mark, gauge, measure, principle, rule, test, touchstone, yardstick

critic *noun* 1 judge, analyst, authority, commentator, connoisseur, expert, pundit, reviewer 2 fault-finder, attacker, detractor, knocker (*informal*)

critical *adjective* 1 crucial, all-important, decisive, pivotal, precarious, pressing, serious, urgent, vital 2 disparaging, captious, censorious, derogatory, disapproving, fault-finding, nagging, nit-picking (*informal*), scathing 3 analytical, discerning, discriminating, fastidious, judicious, penetrating, perceptive

criticism noun **1** fault-finding, bad press, censure, character assassination, disapproval, disparagement, flak (informal), stick (slang) **2** analysis, appraisal, appreciation, assessment, comment, commentary, critique, evaluation, judgment

criticize verb find fault with, carp, censure, condemn, disapprove of, disparage, knock (informal), put down, slate (informal)

croak verb squawk, caw, grunt, utter or speak huskily, wheeze

crook noun Informal criminal, cheat, racketeer, robber, rogue, shark, swindler, thief, villain

crooked adjective **1** bent, curved, deformed, distorted, hooked, irregular, misshapen, out of shape, twisted, warped, zigzag **2** at an angle, askew, awry, lopsided, off-centre, skewwhiff (Brit. informal), slanting, squint, uneven **3** Informal dishonest, bent (slang), corrupt, criminal, fraudulent, illegal, shady (informal), underhand, unlawful

croon verb sing, hum, purr, warble

crop noun **1** produce, fruits, gathering, harvest, reaping, vintage, yield ♦ verb **2** cut, clip, lop, pare, prune, shear, snip, trim **3** graze, browse, nibble

crop up verb Informal happen, appear, arise, emerge, occur, spring up, turn up

cross verb **1** go across, bridge, cut across, extend over, move across, pass over, span, traverse **2** intersect, crisscross, intertwine **3** oppose, block, impede, interfere, obstruct, resist **4** interbreed, blend, crossbreed, cross-fertilize, cross-pollinate, hybridize, intercross, mix, mongrelize ♦ noun **5** crucifix, rood **6** crossroads, crossing, intersection, junction **7** mixture, amalgam, blend, combination **8** trouble, affliction, burden, grief, load, misfortune, trial, tribulation, woe, worry ♦ adjective **9** angry, annoyed, grumpy, ill-tempered, in a bad mood, irascible, put out, short **10** transverse, crosswise, diagonal, intersecting, oblique

cross-examine verb question, grill (informal), interrogate, pump, quiz

cross out or **off** verb strike off or out, blue-pencil, cancel, delete, eliminate, score off or out

crouch verb bend down, bow, duck, hunch, kneel, squat, stoop

crow verb gloat, blow one's own trumpet, boast, brag, exult, strut, swagger, triumph

crowd noun **1** multitude, army, horde, host, mass, mob, pack, swarm, throng **2** group, bunch (informal), circle, clique, lot, set **3** audience, attendance, gate, house, spectators ♦ verb **4** flock, congregate, gather, mass, stream, surge, swarm, throng **5** squeeze, bundle, congest, cram, pack, pile

crowded adjective packed, busy, congested, cramped, full, jam-packed, swarming, teeming

crown noun **1** coronet, circlet, diadem, tiara **3** laurel wreath, garland, honour, laurels, prize, trophy, wreath **3** high point, apex, crest, pinnacle, summit, tip, top ◆ verb **4** honour, adorn, dignify, festoon **5** cap, be the climax or culmination of, complete, finish, perfect, put the finishing touch to, round off, top **6** Slang strike, belt (informal), biff (slang), box, cuff, hit over the head, punch

Crown noun **1** monarchy, royalty, sovereignty **2** monarch, emperor or empress, king or queen, ruler, sovereign

crucial adjective **1** Informal vital, essential, high-priority, important, momentous, pressing, urgent **2** critical, central, decisive, pivotal

crucify verb execute, persecute, torment, torture

crude adjective **1** primitive, clumsy, makeshift, rough, rough-and-ready, rudimentary, unpolished **2** vulgar, coarse, dirty, gross, indecent, obscene, smutty, tasteless, uncouth **3** unrefined, natural, raw, unprocessed

crudely adverb vulgarly, bluntly, coarsely, impolitely, roughly, rudely, tastelessly

crudity noun **1** roughness, clumsiness, crudeness **2** vulgarity, coarseness, impropriety, indecency, indelicacy, obscenity, smuttiness

cruel adjective **1** brutal, barbarous, callous, hard-hearted, heartless, inhumane, malevolent, sadistic, spiteful, unkind, vicious **2** merciless, pitiless, ruthless, unrelenting

cruelly adverb **1** brutally, barbarously, callously, heartlessly, in cold blood, mercilessly, pitilessly, sadistically, spitefully **2** bitterly, deeply, fearfully, grievously, monstrously, severely

cruelty noun brutality, barbarity, callousness, depravity, fiendishness, inhumanity, mercilessness, ruthlessness, spitefulness

cruise noun **1** sail, boat trip, sea trip, voyage ◆ verb **2** sail, coast, voyage **3** travel along, coast, drift, keep a steady pace

crumb noun bit, fragment, grain, morsel, scrap, shred, soupçon

crumble verb **1** disintegrate, collapse, decay, degenerate, deteriorate, fall apart, go to pieces, go to wrack and ruin, tumble down **2** crush, fragment, granulate, grind, pound, powder, pulverize

crumple verb **1** crush, crease, rumple, screw up, scrumple, wrinkle **2** collapse, break down, cave in, fall, give way, go to pieces

crunch verb **1** chomp, champ, chew noisily, grind, munch ◆ noun **2** Informal critical point, crisis, crux, emergency, moment of truth, test

crusade noun campaign, cause, drive, movement, push

crush verb **1** squash, break, compress, press, pulverize, squeeze **2** overcome, conquer, overpower, overwhelm, put down, quell, stamp out, subdue **3** humiliate, abash, mortify, put down (slang), quash, shame

♦ *noun* 4 <u>crowd</u>, huddle, jam

crust *noun* <u>layer</u>, coating, covering, shell, skin, surface

crusty *adjective* 1 <u>crispy</u>, hard 2 <u>irritable</u>, cantankerous, cross, gruff, prickly, short-tempered, testy

cry *verb* 1 <u>weep</u>, blubber, shed tears, snivel, sob 2 <u>shout</u>, bawl, bellow, call out, exclaim, howl, roar, scream, shriek, yell ♦ *noun* 3 <u>weeping</u>, blubbering, snivelling, sob, sobbing, weep 4 <u>shout</u>, bellow, call, exclamation, howl, roar, scream, screech, shriek, yell 5 <u>appeal</u>, plea

cry off *verb Informal* <u>back out</u>, excuse oneself, quit, withdraw

cub *noun* <u>young</u>, offspring, whelp

cuddle *verb* <u>hug</u>, bill and coo, cosset, embrace, fondle, pet, snuggle

cudgel *noun* <u>club</u>, baton, bludgeon, cosh (*Brit.*), stick, truncheon

cue *noun* <u>signal</u>, catchword, hint, key, prompting, reminder, sign, suggestion

cul-de-sac *noun* <u>dead end</u>, blind alley

culminate *verb* <u>end up</u>, climax, close, come to a climax, come to a head, conclude, finish, wind up

culmination *noun* <u>climax</u>, acme, conclusion, consummation, finale, peak, pinnacle, zenith

culpable *adjective* <u>blameworthy</u>, at fault, found wanting, guilty, in the wrong, to blame, wrong

culprit *noun* <u>offender</u>, criminal, evildoer, felon, guilty party,

miscreant, transgressor, wrongdoer

cult *noun* 1 <u>sect</u>, clique, faction, religion, school 2 <u>devotion</u>, idolization, worship

cultivate *verb* 1 <u>farm</u>, plant, plough, tend, till, work 2 <u>develop</u>, foster, improve, promote, refine 3 <u>court</u>, dance attendance upon, run after, seek out

cultivation *noun* 1 <u>farming</u>, gardening, husbandry, planting, ploughing, tillage 2 <u>development</u>, encouragement, fostering, furtherance, nurture, patronage, promotion, support

cultural *adjective* <u>artistic</u>, civilizing, edifying, educational, enlightening, enriching, humane, liberal

culture *noun* 1 <u>civilization</u>, customs, lifestyle, mores, society, way of life 2 <u>refinement</u>, education, enlightenment, good taste, sophistication, urbanity 3 <u>farming</u>, cultivation, husbandry

cultured *adjective* <u>refined</u>, educated, enlightened, highbrow, sophisticated, urbane, well-informed, well-read

culvert *noun* <u>drain</u>, channel, conduit, gutter, watercourse

cumbersome *adjective* <u>awkward</u>, bulky, burdensome, heavy, unmanageable, unwieldy, weighty

cunning *adjective* 1 <u>crafty</u>, artful, devious, Machiavellian, sharp, shifty, sly, wily 2 <u>skilful</u>, imaginative, ingenious ♦ *noun* 3 <u>craftiness</u>, artfulness, deviousness, guile, slyness, trickery 4 <u>skill</u>, artifice, cleverness, ingenuity, subtlety

cup noun **1** <u>mug</u>, beaker, bowl, chalice, goblet, teacup **2** <u>trophy</u>

cupboard noun <u>cabinet</u>, press

curb noun **1** <u>restraint</u>, brake, bridle, check, control, deterrent, limitation, rein ♦ verb **2** <u>restrain</u>, check, control, hinder, impede, inhibit, restrict, retard, suppress

cure verb **1** <u>make better</u>, correct, ease, heal, mend, relieve, remedy, restore **2** <u>preserve</u>, dry, pickle, salt, smoke ♦ noun **3** <u>remedy</u>, antidote, medicine, nostrum, panacea, treatment

curiosity noun **1** <u>inquisitiveness</u>, interest, nosiness (informal), prying, snooping (informal) **2** <u>oddity</u>, freak, novelty, phenomenon, rarity, sight, spectacle, wonder

curious adjective **1** <u>inquiring</u>, inquisitive, interested, questioning, searching **2** <u>inquisitive</u>, meddling, nosy (informal), prying **3** <u>unusual</u>, bizarre, extraordinary, mysterious, novel, odd, peculiar, rare, strange, unexpected

curl verb **1** <u>twirl</u>, bend, coil, curve, loop, spiral, turn, twist, wind ♦ noun **2** <u>twist</u>, coil, kink, ringlet, spiral, whorl

curly adjective <u>curling</u>, crinkly, curled, frizzy, fuzzy, wavy, winding

currency noun **1** <u>money</u>, coinage, coins, notes **2** <u>acceptance</u>, circulation, exposure, popularity, prevalence, vogue

current adjective **1** <u>present</u>, contemporary, fashionable, in

fashion, in vogue, present-day, trendy (Brit. informal), up-to-date **2** <u>prevalent</u>, accepted, common, customary, in circulation, popular, topical, widespread ♦ noun **3** <u>flow</u>, course, draught, jet, progression, river, stream, tide, undertow **4** <u>mood</u>, atmosphere, feeling, tendency, trend, undercurrent

curse verb **1** <u>swear</u>, blaspheme, cuss (informal), take the Lord's name in vain **2** <u>damn</u>, anathematize, excommunicate ♦ noun **3** <u>oath</u>, blasphemy, expletive, obscenity, swearing, swearword **4** <u>denunciation</u>, anathema, ban, excommunication, hoodoo (informal), jinx **5** <u>affliction</u>, bane, hardship, plague, scourge, torment, trouble

cursed adjective <u>damned</u>, accursed, bedevilled, doomed, ill-fated

curt adjective <u>short</u>, abrupt, blunt, brief, brusque, gruff, monosyllabic, succinct, terse

curtail verb <u>cut short</u>, cut back, decrease, diminish, dock, lessen, reduce, shorten, truncate

curtain noun <u>hanging</u>, drape (chiefly U.S.)

curve noun **1** <u>bend</u>, arc, curvature, loop, trajectory, turn ♦ verb **2** <u>bend</u>, arc, arch, coil, hook, spiral, swerve, turn, twist, wind

curved adjective <u>bent</u>, arched, bowed, rounded, serpentine, sinuous, twisted

cushion noun **1** <u>pillow</u>, beanbag, bolster, hassock, headrest, pad ♦ verb **2** <u>soften</u>, dampen,

cushy *adjective Informal* easy,
comfortable, soft, undemanding

custody *noun* 1 safekeeping,
care, charge, keeping,
protection, supervision
2 imprisonment, confinement,
detention, incarceration

custom *noun* 1 tradition,
convention, policy, practice,
ritual, rule, usage 2 habit,
practice, procedure, routine,
way, wont 3 customers,
patronage, trade

customary *adjective* usual,
accepted, accustomed, common,
conventional, established,
normal, ordinary, routine,
traditional

customer *noun* client, buyer,
consumer, patron, purchaser,
regular (*informal*), shopper

customs *plural noun* duty, import
charges, tariff, tax, toll

cut *verb* 1 penetrate, chop,
pierce, score, sever, slash, slice,
slit, wound 2 divide, bisect,
dissect, slice, split 3 trim, clip,
hew, lop, mow, pare, prune,
shave, snip 4 abridge,
abbreviate, condense, curtail,
delete, shorten 5 reduce,
contract, cut back, decrease,
diminish, lower, slash, slim
(down) 6 shape, carve, chisel,
engrave, fashion, form, sculpt,
whittle 7 hurt, insult, put down,
snub, sting, wound 8 *Informal*
ignore, avoid, cold-shoulder,
slight, spurn, turn one's back on
♦ *noun* 9 incision, gash,
laceration, nick, slash, slit, stroke,
wound 10 reduction, cutback,
decrease, fall, lowering, saving

11 *Informal* share, percentage,
piece, portion, section, slice
12 style, fashion, look, shape

cutback *noun* reduction, cut,
decrease, economy, lessening,
retrenchment

cut down *verb* 1 fell, hew, level,
lop 2 reduce, decrease, lessen,
lower

cute *adjective* appealing,
attractive, charming, delightful,
engaging, lovable, sweet,
winning, winsome

cut in *verb* interrupt, break in,
butt in, intervene, intrude

cut off *verb* 1 separate, isolate,
sever 2 interrupt, disconnect,
intercept

cut out *verb* stop, cease, give up,
refrain from

cutthroat *adjective*
1 competitive, dog-eat-dog,
fierce, relentless, ruthless,
unprincipled ♦ *noun* 2 murderer,
assassin, butcher, executioner,
hit man (*slang*), killer

cutting *adjective* hurtful,
acrimonious, barbed, bitter,
caustic, malicious, sarcastic,
scathing, vitriolic, wounding

cycle *noun* era, circle, period,
phase, revolution, rotation

cynic *noun* sceptic, doubter,
misanthrope, misanthropist,
pessimist, scoffer

cynical *adjective* sceptical,
contemptuous, derisive,
distrustful, misanthropic,
mocking, pessimistic, scoffing,
scornful, unbelieving

cynicism *noun* scepticism,
disbelief, doubt, misanthropy,
pessimism

D d

dab verb 1 pat, daub, stipple, tap, touch ♦ noun 2 spot, bit, drop, pat, smudge, speck 3 pat, flick, stroke, tap, touch

dabble verb 1 play at, dip into, potter, tinker, trifle (with) 2 splash, dip

daft adjective Informal, chiefly Brit. 1 foolish, absurd, asinine, crackpot (informal), crazy, idiotic, silly, stupid, witless 2 crazy, crackers (Brit. slang), demented, deranged, insane, nuts (slang), touched, unhinged

dagger noun knife, bayonet, dirk, stiletto

daily adjective 1 everyday, diurnal, quotidian ♦ adverb 2 every day, day by day, once a day

dainty adjective delicate, charming, elegant, exquisite, fine, graceful, neat, petite, pretty

dam noun 1 barrier, barrage, embankment, obstruction, wall ♦ verb 2 block up, barricade, hold back, obstruct, restrict

damage verb 1 harm, hurt, impair, injure, ruin, spoil, weaken, wreck ♦ noun 2 harm, destruction, detriment, devastation, hurt, injury, loss, suffering 3 Informal cost, bill, charge, expense

damages plural noun Law compensation, fine, reimbursement, reparation, satisfaction

damaging adjective harmful,

deleterious, detrimental, disadvantageous, hurtful, injurious, ruinous

dame noun noblewoman, baroness, dowager, grande dame, lady, peeress

damn verb 1 condemn, blast, censure, criticize, denounce, put down 2 sentence, condemn, doom

damnation noun condemnation, anathema, damning, denunciation, doom

damned adjective 1 doomed, accursed, condemned, lost 2 Slang detestable, confounded, hateful, infernal, loathsome

damp adjective 1 moist, clammy, dank, dewy, drizzly, humid, soggy, sopping, wet ♦ noun 2 moisture, dampness, dankness, drizzle ♦ verb 3 moisten, dampen, wet 4 damp down reduce, allay, check, curb, diminish, inhibit, pour cold water on, stifle

dampen verb 1 reduce, check, dull, lessen, moderate, restrain, stifle 2 moisten, make damp, spray, wet

damper noun As in put a damper on discouragement, cold water (informal), hindrance, restraint, wet blanket (informal)

dance verb 1 prance, hop, jig, skip, sway, trip, whirl ♦ noun 2 ball, disco, discotheque, hop (informal), knees-up (Brit. informal), social

dancer noun ballerina, Terpsichorean

danger noun peril, hazard, jeopardy, menace, pitfall, risk, threat, vulnerability

dangerous adjective **1** hang, flap, hang
breakneck, chancy (informal),
hazardous, insecure, precarious,
risky, unsafe, vulnerable

dangerously adverb perilously,
alarmingly, hazardously,
precariously, recklessly, riskily,
unsafely

dangle verb **1** hang, flap, hang
down, sway, swing, trail **2** wave,
brandish, flaunt, flourish

dapper adjective neat, natty
(informal), smart, soigné or
soignée, spruce, spry, trim,
well-groomed, well turned out

dare verb **1** risk, hazard, make
bold, presume, venture
2 challenge, defy, goad,
provoke, taunt, throw down the
gauntlet ♦ noun **3** challenge,
provocation, taunt

daredevil noun **1** adventurer,
desperado, exhibitionist,
madcap, show-off (informal),
stunt man ♦ adjective **2** daring,
adventurous, audacious, bold,
death-defying, madcap, reckless

daring adjective **1** brave,
adventurous, audacious, bold,
daredevil, fearless, intrepid,
reckless, venturesome ♦ noun
2 bravery, audacity, boldness,
bottle (Brit. slang), courage,
fearlessness, nerve (informal),
pluck, temerity

dark adjective **1** dim, dingy,
murky, shadowy, shady, sunless,
unlit **2** black, dark-skinned,
dusky, ebony, sable, swarthy
3 gloomy, bleak, dismal, grim,
morose, mournful, sad, sombre
4 evil, foul, infernal, sinister, vile,
wicked **5** secret, concealed,

hidden, mysterious ♦ noun
6 darkness, dimness, dusk,
gloom, murk, obscurity,
semi-darkness **7** night, evening,
nightfall, night-time, twilight

darken verb make dark, blacken,
dim, obscure, overshadow

darkness noun dark, blackness,
duskiness, gloom, murk,
nightfall, shade, shadows

darling noun **1** beloved, dear,
dearest, love, sweetheart,
truelove ♦ adjective **2** beloved,
adored, cherished, dear,
precious, treasured

darn verb **1** mend, cobble up,
patch, repair, sew up, stitch
♦ noun **2** mend, invisible repair,
patch, reinforcement

dart verb dash, fly, race, run,
rush, shoot, spring, sprint, tear

dash verb **1** rush, bolt, fly, hurry,
race, run, speed, sprint, tear
2 throw, cast, fling, hurl, slam,
sling **3** crash, break, destroy,
shatter, smash, splinter
4 frustrate, blight, foil, ruin,
spoil, thwart, undo ♦ noun
5 rush, dart, race, run, sortie,
sprint, spurt **6** little, bit, drop,
hint, pinch, soupçon, sprinkling,
tinge, touch **7** style, brio, élan,
flair, flourish, panache, spirit,
verve

dashing adjective **1** bold,
debonair, gallant, lively, spirited,
swashbuckling **2** stylish, elegant,
flamboyant, jaunty, showy,
smart, sporty

data noun information, details,
facts, figures, statistics

date noun **1** time, age, epoch,
era, period, stage
2 appointment, assignation,

engagement, meeting, rendezvous, tryst **3** partner, escort, friend ♦ **verb 4** put a date on, assign a date to, fix the period of **5** become old-fashioned, be dated, show one's age **6 date from** *or* **date back to** come from, bear a date of, belong to, exist from, originate in

dated *adjective* old-fashioned, obsolete, old hat, outdated, outmoded, out of date, passé, unfashionable

daub *verb* smear, coat, cover, paint, plaster, slap on (*informal*)

daunting *adjective* intimidating, alarming, demoralizing, disconcerting, discouraging, disheartening, frightening, off-putting (*Brit. informal*), unnerving

dauntless *adjective* fearless, bold, doughty, gallant, indomitable, intrepid, resolute, stouthearted, undaunted, unflinching

dawdle *verb* waste time, dally, delay, drag one's feet *or* heels, hang about, idle, loaf, loiter, trail

dawn *noun* **1** daybreak, aurora (*poetic*), cockcrow, crack of dawn, daylight, morning, sunrise, sunup **2** beginning, advent, birth, emergence, genesis, origin, rise, start ♦ *verb* **3** grow light, break, brighten, lighten **4** begin, appear, develop, emerge, originate, rise, unfold **5 dawn on** *or* **upon** hit, become apparent, come into one's head, come to mind, occur, register (*informal*), strike

day *noun* **1** twenty-four hours, daylight, daytime **2** point in

time, date, time **3** time, age, epoch, era, heyday, period, zenith

daybreak *noun* dawn, break of day, cockcrow, crack of dawn, first light, morning, sunrise, sunup

daydream *noun* **1** fantasy, dream, fancy, imagining, pipe dream, reverie, wish ♦ *verb* **2** fantasize, dream, envision, fancy, imagine, muse

daylight *noun* sunlight, light of day, sunshine

daze *verb* **1** stun, benumb, numb, paralyse, shock, stupefy ♦ *noun* **2** shock, bewilderment, confusion, distraction, stupor, trance, trancelike state

dazed *adjective* shocked, bewildered, confused, disorientated, dizzy, muddled, punch-drunk, staggered, stunned

dazzle *verb* **1** impress, amaze, astonish, bowl over (*informal*), overpower, overwhelm, take one's breath away **2** blind, bedazzle, blur, confuse, daze ♦ *noun* **3** splendour, brilliance, glitter, magnificence, razzmatazz (*slang*), sparkle

dazzling *adjective* splendid, brilliant, glittering, glorious, scintillating, sensational (*informal*), sparkling, stunning, virtuoso

dead *adjective* **1** deceased, defunct, departed, extinct, late, passed away, perished **2** not working, inactive, inoperative, stagnant, unemployed, useless **3** numb, inert, paralysed **4** total, absolute, complete, outright, thorough, unqualified, utter

5 *Informal* exhausted, dead beat (*informal*), spent, tired, worn out **6** boring, dull, flat, uninteresting ♦ *noun* **7** middle, depth, midst ♦ *adverb* **8** *Informal* exactly, absolutely, completely, directly, entirely, totally

deaden *verb* reduce, alleviate, blunt, cushion, diminish, dull, lessen, muffle, smother, stifle, suppress, weaken

deadline *noun* time limit, cutoff point, limit, target date

deadlock *noun* impasse, dead heat, draw, gridlock, stalemate, standoff, standstill, tie

deadlocked *adjective* even, equal, level, neck and neck

deadly *adjective* **1** lethal, dangerous, death-dealing, deathly, fatal, malignant, mortal **2** *Informal* boring, dull, mind-numbing, monotonous, tedious, tiresome, uninteresting, wearisome

deadpan *adjective* expressionless, blank, impassive, inexpressive, inscrutable, poker-faced, straight-faced

deaf *adjective* **1** hard of hearing, stone deaf, without hearing **2** oblivious, indifferent, unconcerned, unhearing, unmoved

deafen *verb* make deaf, din, drown out, split *or* burst the eardrums

deafening *adjective* ear-piercing, booming, ear-splitting, overpowering, piercing, resounding, ringing, thunderous

deal *noun* **1** *Informal* agreement, arrangement, bargain, contract, pact, transaction, understanding **2** amount, degree, extent, portion, quantity, share ♦ *verb* **3** sell, bargain, buy and sell, do business, negotiate, stock, trade, traffic

dealer *noun* trader, merchant, purveyor, supplier, tradesman, wholesaler

deal out *verb* distribute, allot, apportion, assign, dispense, dole out, give, mete out, share

deal with *verb* **1** handle, attend to, cope with, get to grips with, manage, see to, take care of, treat **2** be concerned with, consider

dear *noun* **1** beloved, angel, darling, loved one, precious, treasure ♦ *adjective* **2** beloved, cherished, close, favourite, intimate, precious, prized, treasured **3** expensive, at a premium, costly, high-priced, overpriced, pricey (*informal*)

dearly *adverb* **1** very much, extremely, greatly, profoundly **2** at great cost, at a high price

dearth *noun* scarcity, deficiency, inadequacy, insufficiency, lack, paucity, poverty, shortage, want

death *noun* **1** dying, demise, departure, end, exit, passing **2** destruction, downfall, extinction, finish, ruin, undoing

deathly *adjective* deathlike, ghastly, grim, pale, pallid, wan

debacle *noun* disaster, catastrophe, collapse, defeat, fiasco, reversal, rout

debase *verb* degrade, cheapen, devalue, lower, reduce

debatable *adjective* doubtful,

arguable, controversial, dubious, moot, problematical, questionable, uncertain

debate noun 1 <u>discussion</u>, argument, contention, controversy, dispute ♦ verb 2 <u>discuss</u>, argue, dispute, question 3 <u>consider</u>, deliberate, ponder, reflect, ruminate, weigh

debauchery noun <u>depravity</u>, dissipation, dissoluteness, excess, indulgence, intemperance, lewdness, overindulgence

debonair adjective <u>elegant</u>, charming, courteous, dashing, refined, smooth, suave, urbane, well-bred

debrief verb <u>interrogate</u>, cross-examine, examine, probe, question, quiz

debris noun <u>remains</u>, bits, detritus, fragments, rubble, ruins, waste, wreckage

debt noun 1 <u>debit</u>, commitment, liability, obligation 2 **in debt** <u>owing</u>, in arrears, in the red (informal), liable

debtor noun <u>borrower</u>, mortgagor

debunk verb Informal <u>expose</u>, cut down to size, deflate, disparage, mock, ridicule, show up

debut noun <u>introduction</u>, beginning, bow, coming out, entrance, first appearance, initiation, presentation

decadence noun <u>degeneration</u>, corruption, decay, decline, deterioration, dissipation, dissolution

decadent adjective <u>degenerate</u>, corrupt, decaying, declining, dissolute, immoral, self-indulgent

decapitate verb <u>behead</u>, execute, guillotine

decay verb 1 <u>decline</u>, crumble, deteriorate, disintegrate, dwindle, shrivel, wane, waste away, wither 2 <u>rot</u>, corrode, decompose, perish, putrefy ♦ noun 3 <u>decline</u>, collapse, degeneration, deterioration, fading, failing, wasting, withering 4 <u>rot</u>, caries, decomposition, gangrene, putrefaction

decease noun Formal <u>death</u>, demise, departure, dying, release

deceased adjective <u>dead</u>, defunct, departed, expired, former, late, lifeless

deceit noun <u>dishonesty</u>, cheating, chicanery, deception, fraud, lying, pretence, treachery, trickery

deceitful adjective <u>dishonest</u>, deceptive, false, fraudulent, sneaky, treacherous, two-faced, untrustworthy

deceive verb <u>take in</u> (informal), cheat, con (informal), dupe, fool, hoodwink, mislead, swindle, trick

deceiver noun <u>liar</u>, cheat, con man (informal), double-dealer, fraud, impostor, swindler, trickster

decency noun <u>respectability</u>, civility, correctness, courtesy, decorum, etiquette, modesty, propriety

decent adjective 1 <u>reasonable</u>, adequate, ample, fair, passable, satisfactory, sufficient, tolerable 2 <u>respectable</u>, chaste, decorous, modest, proper, pure 3 <u>proper</u>, appropriate, becoming, befitting, fitting, seemly, suitable 4 Informal <u>kind</u>, accommodating, courteous, friendly, generous, gracious, helpful, obliging, thoughtful

deception noun 1 trickery, cunning, deceit, fraud, guile, legerdemain, treachery 2 trick, bluff, decoy, hoax, illusion, lie, ruse, subterfuge

deceptive adjective misleading, ambiguous, deceitful, dishonest, false, fraudulent, illusory, unreliable

decide verb reach or come to a decision, adjudge, adjudicate, choose, conclude, determine, make up one's mind, resolve

decidedly adverb definitely, clearly, distinctly, downright, positively, unequivocally, unmistakably

decimate verb devastate, ravage, wreak havoc on

decipher verb figure out (informal), crack, decode, deduce, interpret, make out, read, solve

decision noun 1 judgment, arbitration, conclusion, finding, resolution, ruling, sentence, verdict 2 decisiveness, determination, firmness, purpose, resolution, resolve, strength of mind or will

decisive adjective 1 influential, conclusive, critical, crucial, fateful, momentous, significant 2 resolute, decided, determined, firm, forceful, incisive, strong-minded, trenchant

deck verb decorate, adorn, array, beautify, clothe, dress, embellish, festoon

declaim verb 1 orate, harangue,

hold forth, lecture, proclaim, rant, recite, speak 2 **declaim against** protest against, attack, decry, denounce, inveigh, rail

declaration noun 1 statement, acknowledgment, affirmation, assertion, avowal, disclosure, protestation, revelation, testimony 2 announcement, edict, notification, proclamation, profession, pronouncement

declare verb 1 state, affirm, announce, assert, claim, maintain, proclaim, profess, pronounce, swear, utter 2 make known, confess, disclose, reveal, show

decline verb 1 lessen, decrease, diminish, dwindle, ebb, fade, fall off, shrink, sink, wane 2 deteriorate, decay, degenerate, droop, languish, pine, weaken, worsen 3 refuse, abstain, avoid, reject, say 'no', turn down ♦ noun 4 lessening, downturn, drop, dwindling, falling off, recession, slump 5 deterioration, decay, degeneration, failing, weakening, worsening

decode verb decipher, crack, decrypt, interpret, solve, unscramble, work out

decompose verb rot, break up, crumble, decay, fall apart, fester, putrefy

decor noun decoration, colour scheme, furnishing style, ornamentation

decorate verb 1 adorn, beautify, embellish, festoon, grace, ornament, trim 2 do up (informal), colour, furbish, paint, paper, renovate, wallpaper 3 pin a medal on, cite, confer an honour on *or* upon

decoration *noun* **1** adornment, beautification, elaboration, embellishment, enrichment, ornamentation, trimming **2** ornament, bauble, frill, garnish, trimmings **3** medal, award, badge, ribbon, star

decorative *adjective* ornamental, beautifying, fancy, nonfunctional, pretty

decorous *adjective* proper, becoming, correct, decent, dignified, fitting, polite, seemly, well-behaved

decorum *noun* propriety, decency, dignity, etiquette, good manners, politeness, protocol, respectability

decoy *noun* **1** lure, bait, enticement, inducement, pretence, trap ◆ *verb* **2** lure, deceive, ensnare, entice, entrap, seduce, tempt

decrease *verb* **1** lessen, cut down, decline, diminish, drop, dwindle, lower, reduce, shrink, subside ◆ *noun* **2** lessening, contraction, cutback, decline, dwindling, falling off, loss, reduction, subsidence

decree *noun* **1** law, act, command, edict, order, proclamation, ruling, statute ◆ *verb* **2** order, command, demand, ordain, prescribe, proclaim, pronounce, rule

decrepit *adjective* **1** weak, aged, doddering, feeble, frail, infirm **2** worn-out, battered, beat-up (*informal*), broken-down, dilapidated, ramshackle, rickety, run-down, tumbledown, weather-beaten

decry *verb* condemn, belittle, criticize, denigrate, denounce, discredit, disparage, put down, run down

dedicate *verb* **1** devote, commit, give over to, pledge, surrender **2** inscribe, address

dedicated *adjective* devoted, committed, enthusiastic, purposeful, single-minded, wholehearted, zealous

dedication *noun* **1** devotion, adherence, allegiance, commitment, faithfulness, loyalty, single-mindedness, wholeheartedness **2** inscription, address, message

deduce *verb* conclude, draw, gather, glean, infer, reason, take to mean, understand

deduct *verb* subtract, decrease by, knock off (*informal*), reduce by, remove, take away, take off

deduction *noun* **1** subtraction, decrease, diminution, discount, reduction, withdrawal **2** conclusion, assumption, finding, inference, reasoning, result

deed *noun* **1** action, achievement, act, exploit, fact, feat, performance **2** *Law* document, contract, title

deep *adjective* **1** wide, bottomless, broad, far, profound, unfathomable, yawning **2** mysterious, abstract, abstruse, arcane, esoteric, hidden, obscure, recondite, secret **3** intense, extreme, grave, great, profound, serious (*informal*), unqualified **4** absorbed, engrossed, immersed, lost, preoccupied, rapt **5** dark, intense, rich, strong, vivid **6** low, bass, booming, low-pitched, resonant, sonorous ♦ *noun* **7 the deep** *Poetic* ocean, briny (*informal*), high seas, main, sea

deepen *verb* intensify, grow, increase, magnify, reinforce, strengthen

deeply *adverb* **1** thoroughly, completely, gravely, profoundly, seriously, severely, to the core, to the heart, to the quick **2** intensely, acutely, affectingly, distressingly, feelingly, mournfully, movingly, passionately, sadly

deface *verb* vandalize, damage, deform, disfigure, mar, mutilate, spoil, tarnish

de facto *adverb* **1** in fact, actually, in effect, in reality, really ♦ *adjective* **2** actual, existing, real

defame *verb* slander, bad-mouth (*slang, chiefly U.S. & Canad.*), cast aspersions on, denigrate, discredit, disparage, knock (*informal*), libel, malign, smear

default *noun* **1** failure, deficiency, dereliction, evasion, lapse, neglect, nonpayment, omission ♦ *verb* **1** fail, dodge, evade, neglect

defeat *verb* **1** beat, conquer, crush, master, overwhelm, rout, trounce, vanquish, wipe the floor with (*informal*) **2** frustrate, baffle, balk, confound, foil, get the better of, ruin, thwart ♦ *noun* **3** conquest, beating, overthrow, pasting (*slang*) **4** frustration, failure, rebuff, reverse, setback, thwarting

defeatist *noun* **1** pessimist, prophet of doom, quitter ♦ *adjective* **2** pessimistic

defect *noun* **1** imperfection, blemish, blotch, error, failing, fault, flaw, spot, taint ♦ *verb* **2** desert, abandon, change sides, go over, rebel, revolt, walk out on (*informal*)

defection *noun* desertion, apostasy, rebellion

defective *adjective* faulty, broken, deficient, flawed, imperfect, not working, on the blink (*slang*), out of order

defector *noun* deserter, apostate, renegade, turncoat

defence *noun* **1** protection, cover, guard, immunity, resistance, safeguard, security, shelter **2** shield, barricade, bulwark, buttress, fortification, rampart **3** argument, excuse, explanation, justification, plea, vindication **4** *Law* plea, alibi, denial, rebuttal, testimony

defenceless *adjective* helpless, exposed, naked, powerless, unarmed, unguarded, unprotected, vulnerable, wide open

defend *verb* **1** protect, cover, guard, keep safe, preserve, safeguard, screen, shelter, shield **2** support, champion, endorse, justify, speak up for, stand up for, stick up for (*informal*), uphold, vindicate

defendant *noun* the accused, defence, offender, prisoner at the bar, respondent

defender *noun* **1** protector, bodyguard, escort, guard **2** supporter, advocate, champion, sponsor

defensive adjective <u>on guard</u>, on the defensive, protective, uptight (informal), watchful

defer[1] verb <u>postpone</u>, delay, hold over, procrastinate, put off, put on ice, shelve, suspend

defer[2] verb <u>comply</u>, accede, bow, capitulate, give in, give way to, submit, yield

deference noun <u>respect</u>, attention, civility, consideration, courtesy, honour, politeness, regard, reverence

deferential adjective <u>respectful</u>, ingratiating, obedient, obeisant, obsequious, polite, reverential, submissive

defiance noun <u>resistance</u>, confrontation, contempt, disobedience, disregard, insolence, insubordination, opposition, rebelliousness

defiant adjective <u>resisting</u>, audacious, bold, daring, disobedient, insolent, insubordinate, mutinous, provocative, rebellious

deficiency noun 1 <u>lack</u>, absence, dearth, deficit, scarcity, shortage 2 <u>failing</u>, defect, demerit, fault, flaw, frailty, imperfection, shortcoming, weakness

deficient adjective 1 <u>lacking</u>, inadequate, insufficient, meagre, scant, scarce, short, skimpy, wanting 2 <u>unsatisfactory</u>, defective, faulty, flawed, impaired, imperfect, incomplete, inferior, weak

deficit noun <u>shortfall</u>, arrears, deficiency, loss, shortage

define verb 1 <u>describe</u>,

characterize, designate, explain, expound, interpret, specify, spell out 2 <u>mark out</u>, bound, circumscribe, delineate, demarcate, limit, outline

definite adjective 1 <u>clear</u>, black-and-white, cut-and-dried (informal), exact, fixed, marked, particular, precise, specific 2 <u>certain</u>, assured, decided, guaranteed, positive, settled, sure

definitely adverb <u>certainly</u>, absolutely, categorically, clearly, positively, surely, undeniably, unmistakably, unquestionably, without doubt

definition noun 1 <u>explanation</u>, clarification, elucidation, exposition, statement of meaning 2 <u>sharpness</u>, clarity, contrast, distinctness, focus, precision

definitive adjective 1 <u>final</u>, absolute, complete, conclusive, decisive 2 <u>authoritative</u>, exhaustive, perfect, reliable, ultimate

deflate verb 1 <u>collapse</u>, empty, exhaust, flatten, puncture, shrink 2 <u>humiliate</u>, chasten, disconcert, dispirit, humble, mortify, put down (slang), squash 3 Economics <u>reduce</u>, depress, devalue, diminish

deflect verb <u>turn aside</u>, bend, deviate, diverge, glance off, ricochet, swerve, veer

deflection noun <u>deviation</u>, bend, divergence, swerve

deform verb 1 <u>distort</u>, buckle, contort, gnarl, mangle, misshape, twist, warp 2 <u>disfigure</u>, deface, maim, mar, mutilate, ruin, spoil

deformity noun abnormality, defect, disfigurement, malformation

defraud verb cheat, con (informal), diddle (informal), embezzle, fleece, pilfer, rip off (slang), swindle, trick

deft adjective skilful, adept, adroit, agile, dexterous, expert, neat, nimble, proficient

defunct adjective 1 dead, deceased, departed, extinct, gone 2 obsolete, bygone, expired, inoperative, invalid, nonexistent, out of commission

defy verb 1 resist, brave, confront, disregard, flout, scorn, slight, spurn

degenerate adjective 1 depraved, corrupt, debauched, decadent, dissolute, immoral, low, perverted ♦ verb 2 worsen, decay, decline, decrease, deteriorate, fall off, lapse, sink, slip

degradation noun 1 disgrace, discredit, dishonour, humiliation, ignominy, mortification, shame 2 deterioration, decline, degeneration, demotion, downgrading

degrade verb 1 disgrace, debase, demean, discredit, dishonour, humble, humiliate, shame 2 demote, downgrade, lower

degrading adjective demeaning, dishonourable, humiliating, infra dig (informal), shameful, undignified, unworthy

degree noun stage, grade, notch, point, rung, step, unit

deity noun god, divinity, goddess, godhead, idol, immortal, supreme being

dejected adjective downhearted, crestfallen, depressed, despondent, disconsolate, disheartened, downcast, glum, miserable, sad

dejection noun low spirits, depression, despair, despondency, doldrums, downheartedness, gloom, melancholy, sadness, sorrow, unhappiness

de jure adverb legally, by right, rightfully

delay verb 1 put off, defer, hold over, postpone, procrastinate, shelve, suspend 2 hold up, bog down, detain, hinder, hold back, impede, obstruct, set back, slow up 3 putting off, deferment, postponement, procrastination, suspension 4 hold-up, hindrance, impediment, interruption, interval, setback, stoppage, wait

delegate noun 1 representative, agent, ambassador, commissioner, deputy, envoy, legate ♦ verb 2 entrust, assign, consign, devolve, give, hand over, pass on, transfer 3 appoint, accredit, authorize, commission, depute, designate, empower, mandate

delegation noun 1 deputation, commission, contingent, embassy, envoys, legation, mission 2 devolution, assignment, commissioning, committal

delete verb remove, cancel, cross out, efface, erase, expunge, obliterate, rub out, strike out

deliberate adjective 1 intentional,

calculated, conscious, planned, prearranged, premeditated, purposeful, wilful 2 <u>unhurried</u>, careful, cautious, circumspect, measured, methodical, ponderous, slow, thoughtful ◆verb 3 <u>consider</u>, cogitate, consult, debate, discuss, meditate, ponder, reflect, think, weigh

deliberately adverb <u>intentionally</u>, by design, calculatingly, consciously, in cold blood, knowingly, on purpose, wilfully, wittingly

deliberation noun 1 <u>consideration</u>, calculation, circumspection, forethought, meditation, reflection, thought 2 <u>discussion</u>, conference, consultation, debate

delicacy noun 1 <u>fineness</u>, accuracy, daintiness, elegance, exquisiteness, lightness, precision, subtlety 2 <u>fragility</u>, flimsiness, frailty, slenderness, tenderness, weakness 3 <u>treat</u>, dainty, luxury, savoury, titbit 4 <u>fastidiousness</u>, discrimination, finesse, purity, refinement, sensibility, taste 5 <u>sensitivity</u>, sensitiveness, tact

delicate adjective 1 <u>fine</u>, deft, elegant, exquisite, graceful, precise, skilled, subtle 2 <u>subtle</u>, choice, dainty, delicious, fine, savoury, tender 3 <u>fragile</u>, flimsy, frail, slender, slight, tender, weak 4 <u>considerate</u>, diplomatic, discreet, sensitive, tactful

delicately adverb 1 <u>finely</u>, daintily, deftly, elegantly, exquisitely, gracefully, precisely, skilfully, subtly 2 <u>tactfully</u>,

diplomatically, sensitively

delicious adjective <u>delectable</u>, appetizing, choice, dainty, mouthwatering, savoury, scrumptious (informal), tasty, toothsome

delight noun 1 <u>pleasure</u>, ecstasy, enjoyment, gladness, glee, happiness, joy, rapture ◆verb 2 <u>please</u>, amuse, charm, cheer, enchant, gratify, thrill 3 **delight in** <u>take pleasure in</u>, appreciate, enjoy, feast on, like, love, relish, revel in, savour

delighted adjective <u>pleased</u>, ecstatic, elated, enchanted, happy, joyous, jubilant, overjoyed, thrilled

delightful adjective <u>pleasant</u>, agreeable, charming, delectable, enchanting, enjoyable, pleasurable, rapturous, thrilling

delinquent noun <u>criminal</u>, culprit, lawbreaker, miscreant, offender, villain, wrongdoer

delirious adjective 1 <u>mad</u>, crazy, demented, deranged, incoherent, insane, raving, unhinged 2 <u>ecstatic</u>, beside oneself, carried away, excited, frantic, frenzied, hysterical, wild

delirium noun 1 <u>madness</u>, derangement, hallucination, insanity, raving 2 <u>frenzy</u>, ecstasy, fever, hysteria, passion

deliver verb 1 <u>carry</u>, bear, bring, cart, convey, distribute, transport 2 <u>hand over</u>, commit, give up, grant, make over, relinquish, surrender, transfer, turn over, yield 3 <u>give</u>, announce, declare, present, read, utter 4 <u>release</u>, emancipate, free, liberate, loose, ransom, rescue, save 5 <u>strike</u>,

administer, aim, deal, direct, give, inflict, launch

deliverance noun release, emancipation, escape, liberation, ransom, redemption, rescue, salvation

delivery noun 1 handing over, consignment, conveyance, dispatch, distribution, surrender, transfer, transmission 2 speech, articulation, elocution, enunciation, intonation, utterance 3 childbirth, confinement, labour, parturition

delude verb deceive, beguile, dupe, fool, hoodwink, kid (informal), mislead, take in (informal), trick

deluge noun 1 flood, cataclysm, downpour, inundation, overflowing, spate, torrent 2 rush, avalanche, barrage, flood, spate, torrent ♦ verb 3 flood, douse, drench, drown, inundate, soak, submerge, swamp 4 overwhelm, engulf, inundate, overload, overrun, swamp

delusion noun misconception, error, fallacy, false impression, fancy, hallucination, illusion, misapprehension, mistake

de luxe adjective luxurious, costly, exclusive, expensive, grand, opulent, select, special, splendid, superior

delve verb research, burrow, explore, ferret out, forage, investigate, look into, probe, rummage, search

demagogue noun agitator, firebrand, rabble-rouser

demand verb 1 request, ask, challenge, inquire, interrogate,

question 2 require, call for, cry out for, entail, involve, necessitate, need, want 3 claim, exact, expect, insist on, order ♦ noun 4 request, inquiry, order, question, requisition 5 need, call, claim, market, requirement, want

demanding adjective difficult, challenging, exacting, hard, taxing, tough, trying, wearing

demarcation noun delimitation, differentiation, distinction, division, separation

demean verb lower, abase, debase, degrade, descend, humble, stoop

demeanour noun behaviour, air, bearing, carriage, comportment, conduct, deportment, manner

demented adjective mad, crazed, crazy, deranged, frenzied, insane, maniacal, unbalanced, unhinged

demise noun 1 failure, collapse, downfall, end, fall, ruin 2 Euphemistic death, decease, departure

democracy noun self-government, commonwealth, republic

democratic adjective self-governing, autonomous, egalitarian, popular, populist, representative

demolish verb 1 knock down, bulldoze, destroy, dismantle, flatten, level, raze, tear down 2 defeat, annihilate, destroy, overthrow, overturn, undo, wreck

demolition noun knocking down, bulldozing, destruction, explosion, levelling, razing, tearing down, wrecking

demon noun **1** evil spirit, devil, fiend, ghoul, goblin, malignant spirit **2** wizard, ace (informal), fiend, master

demonic, demoniac, demoniacal adjective **1** devilish, diabolic, diabolical, fiendish, hellish, infernal, satanic **2** frenzied, crazed, frantic, frenetic, furious, hectic, maniacal, manic

demonstrable adjective provable, evident, irrefutable, obvious, palpable, self-evident, unmistakable, verifiable

demonstrate verb **1** prove, display, exhibit, indicate, manifest, show, testify to **2** show how, describe, explain, illustrate, make clear, teach **3** march, parade, picket, protest, rally

demonstration noun **1** march, mass lobby, parade, picket, protest, rally, sit-in **2** explanation, description, exposition, presentation, test, trial **3** proof, confirmation, display, evidence, exhibition, expression, illustration, testimony

demoralize verb dishearten, deject, depress, discourage, dispirit, undermine, unnerve, weaken

demote verb downgrade, degrade, kick downstairs (slang), lower in rank, relegate

demur verb **1** object, balk, dispute, hesitate, protest, refuse, take exception, waver ♦ noun **2** As in without demur objection, compunction, dissent, hesitation, misgiving, protest, qualm

demure adjective shy, diffident, modest, reserved, reticent, retiring, sedate, unassuming

den noun **1** lair, cave, cavern, haunt, hide-out, hole, shelter **2** Chiefly U.S. study, cubbyhole, hideaway, retreat, sanctuary, sanctum

denial noun **1** negation, contradiction, dissent, renunciation, repudiation, retraction **2** refusal, prohibition, rebuff, rejection, repulse, veto

denigrate verb disparage, bad-mouth (slang, chiefly U.S. & Canad.), belittle, knock (informal), malign, rubbish (informal), run down, slander, vilify

denomination noun **1** religious group, belief, creed, persuasion, school, sect **2** unit, grade, size, value

denote verb indicate, betoken, designate, express, imply, mark, mean, show, signify

denounce verb condemn, accuse, attack, censure, denunciate, revile, stigmatize, vilify

dense adjective **1** thick, close-knit, compact, condensed, heavy, impenetrable, opaque, solid **2** Informal stupid, dozy (Brit. informal), dull, obtuse, slow-witted, stolid, thick

density noun tightness, bulk, compactness, consistency, denseness, impenetrability, mass, solidity, thickness

dent noun **1** hollow, chip, crater, depression, dimple, dip, impression, indentation, pit ♦ verb **2** make a dent in, gouge, hollow, press in, push in

deny verb 1 contradict, disagree with, disprove, rebuff, rebut, refute 2 refuse, begrudge, disallow, forbid, reject, turn down, withhold 3 renounce, disclaim, disown, recant, repudiate, retract

depart verb 1 leave, absent (oneself), disappear, exit, go, go away, quit, retire, retreat, withdraw 2 deviate, differ, digress, diverge, stray, swerve, turn aside, vary, veer

department noun section, branch, bureau, division, office, station, subdivision, unit

departure noun 1 leaving, exit, exodus, going, going away, leave-taking, removal, retirement, withdrawal 2 divergence, deviation, digression, variation 3 shift, change, difference, innovation, novelty, whole new ball game (informal)

depend verb 1 trust in, bank on, count on, lean on, reckon on, rely upon, turn to 2 be determined by, be based on, be contingent on, be subject to, be subordinate to, hang on, hinge on, rest on, revolve around

dependable adjective reliable, faithful, reputable, responsible, staunch, steady, sure, trustworthy, trusty, unfailing

dependant noun relative, child, minor, protégé, subordinate

dependent adjective 1 relying on, defenceless, helpless, reliant, vulnerable, weak 2 dependent on or upon determined by, conditional on, contingent on, depending on, influenced by,

subject to

depict verb 1 draw, delineate, illustrate, outline, paint, picture, portray, sketch 2 describe, characterize, narrate, outline, represent

depiction noun representation, delineation, description, picture, portrayal, sketch

deplete verb use up, consume, drain, empty, exhaust, expend, impoverish, lessen, reduce

deplorable adjective 1 regrettable, grievous, lamentable, pitiable, sad, unfortunate, wretched 2 disgraceful, dishonourable, reprehensible, scandalous, shameful

deplore verb disapprove of, abhor, censure, condemn, denounce, object to, take a dim view of

deploy verb position, arrange, set out, station, use, utilize

deployment noun position, arrangement, organization, spread, stationing, use, utilization

deport verb 1 expel, banish, exile, expatriate, extradite, oust 2 deport yourself behave, acquit oneself, act, bear oneself, carry oneself, comport oneself, conduct oneself, hold oneself

depose verb 1 remove from office, demote, dethrone, dismiss, displace, oust 2 Law testify, avouch, declare, make a deposition

deposit verb 1 put, drop, lay, locate, place 2 store, bank, consign, entrust, lodge ♦ noun 3 down payment, instalment, part payment, pledge, retainer, security, stake **4** sediment, accumulation, dregs, lees, precipitate, silt

depot noun **1** storehouse, depository, repository, warehouse **2** Chiefly U.S. & Canad. bus station, garage, terminus

depraved adjective corrupt, degenerate, dissolute, evil, immoral, sinful, vicious, vile, wicked

depravity noun corruption, debauchery, evil, immorality, sinfulness, vice, wickedness

depreciate verb **1** devalue, decrease, deflate, lessen, lose value, lower, reduce **2** disparage, belittle, denigrate, deride, detract, run down, scorn, sneer at

depreciation noun **1** devaluation, deflation, depression, drop, fall, slump **2** disparagement, belittlement, denigration, deprecation, detraction

depress verb **1** sadden, deject, discourage, dishearten, dispirit, make despondent, oppress, weigh down **2** lower, cheapen, depreciate, devalue, diminish, downgrade, lessen, reduce **3** press down, flatten, level, lower, push down

depressed adjective **1** low-spirited, blue, dejected, despondent, discouraged, dispirited, downcast, downhearted, fed up, sad, unhappy **2** poverty-stricken, deprived, disadvantaged, needy, poor, run-down **3** lowered,

cheapened, depreciated, devalued, weakened **4** sunken, concave, hollow, indented, recessed

depressing adjective bleak, discouraging, disheartening, dismal, dispiriting, gloomy, harrowing, sad, saddening

depression noun **1** low spirits, dejection, despair, despondency, downheartedness, dumps (informal), gloominess, melancholy, sadness, the blues **2** recession, economic decline, hard or bad times, inactivity, slump, stagnation **3** hollow, bowl, cavity, dent, dimple, dip, indentation, pit, valley

deprivation noun **1** withholding, denial, dispossession, expropriation, removal, withdrawal **2** want, destitution, distress, hardship, need, privation

deprive verb withhold, bereave, despoil, dispossess, rob, strip

deprived adjective poor, bereft, destitute, disadvantaged, down at heel, in need, lacking, needy

depth noun **1** deepness, drop, extent, measure **2** insight, astuteness, discernment, penetration, profoundness, profundity, sagacity, wisdom

deputation noun delegation, commission, embassy, envoys, legation

deputize verb stand in for, act for, take the place of, understudy

deputy noun substitute, delegate, legate, lieutenant, number two, proxy, representative, second-in-command, surrogate

deranged adjective mad, crazed,

crazy, demented, distracted, insane, irrational, unbalanced, unhinged

derelict adjective 1 abandoned, deserted, dilapidated, discarded, forsaken, neglected, ruined ♦ noun 2 tramp, bag lady, down-and-out, outcast, vagrant

deride verb mock, disdain, disparage, insult, jeer, ridicule, scoff, scorn, sneer, taunt

derisory adjective ridiculous, contemptible, insulting, laughable, ludicrous, outrageous, preposterous

derivation noun origin, beginning, foundation, root, source

derive from verb come from, arise from, emanate from, flow from, issue from, originate from, proceed from, spring from, stem from

derogatory adjective disparaging, belittling, defamatory, offensive, slighting, uncomplimentary, unfavourable, unflattering

descend verb 1 move down, drop, fall, go down, plummet, plunge, sink, subside, tumble 2 slope, dip, incline, slant 3 lower oneself, degenerate, deteriorate, stoop 4 **be descended** originate, be handed down, be passed down, derive, issue, proceed, spring 5 **descend on** attack, arrive, invade, raid, swoop

descent noun 1 coming down, drop, fall, plunge, swoop 2 slope, declivity, dip, drop, incline, slant 3 ancestry, extraction, family tree, genealogy, lineage, origin,

parentage 4 decline, degeneration, deterioration

describe verb 1 relate, depict, explain, express, narrate, portray, recount, report, tell 2 trace, delineate, draw, mark out, outline

description noun 1 account, depiction, explanation, narrative, portrayal, report, representation, sketch 2 kind, brand, category, class, order, sort, type, variety

descriptive adjective graphic, detailed, explanatory, expressive, illustrative, pictorial, picturesque, vivid

desert[1] noun wilderness, solitude, waste, wasteland, wilds

desert[2] verb abandon, abscond, forsake, jilt, leave, leave stranded, maroon, quit, strand, walk out on (informal)

deserted adjective abandoned, derelict, desolate, empty, forsaken, neglected, unoccupied, vacant

deserter noun defector, absconder, escapee, fugitive, renegade, runaway, traitor, truant

desertion noun abandonment, absconding, apostasy, betrayal, defection, dereliction, escape, evasion, flight, relinquishment

deserve verb merit, be entitled to, be worthy of, earn, justify, rate, warrant

deserved adjective well-earned, due, earned, fitting, justified, merited, proper, rightful, warranted

deserving adjective worthy, commendable, estimable, laudable, meritorious, praiseworthy, righteous

design verb **1** plan, draft, draw, outline, sketch, trace **2** create, conceive, fabricate, fashion, invent, originate, think up **3** intend, aim, mean, plan, propose, purpose ♦ noun **4** plan, blueprint, draft, drawing, model, outline, scheme, sketch **5** arrangement, construction, form, organization, pattern, shape, style **6** intention, aim, end, goal, object, objective, purpose, target

designate verb **1** name, call, dub, entitle, label, style, term **2** appoint, assign, choose, delegate, depute, nominate, select

designation noun name, description, label, mark, title

designer noun creator, architect, deviser, inventor, originator, planner

desirable adjective **1** worthwhile, advantageous, advisable, beneficial, good, preferable, profitable **2** attractive, adorable, alluring, fetching, glamorous, seductive, sexy (informal)

desire verb **1** want, crave, hanker after, hope for, long for, set one's heart on, thirst for, wish for, yearn for ♦ noun **2** wish, aspiration, craving, hankering, hope, longing, thirst, want **3** lust, appetite, libido, passion

desist verb stop, break off, cease, discontinue, end, forbear, leave off, pause, refrain from

desolate adjective **1** uninhabited, bare, barren, bleak, dreary, godforsaken, solitary, wild **2** miserable, dejected,

despondent, disconsolate, downcast, forlorn, gloomy, wretched ♦ verb **3** lay waste, depopulate, despoil, destroy, devastate, lay low, pillage, plunder, ravage, ruin **4** deject, depress, discourage, dishearten, dismay, distress, grieve

desolation noun **1** ruin, destruction, devastation, havoc **2** bleakness, barrenness, isolation, solitude **3** misery, anguish, dejection, despair, distress, gloom, sadness, woe, wretchedness

despair noun **1** despondency, anguish, dejection, depression, desperation, gloom, hopelessness, misery, wretchedness ♦ verb **2** lose hope, give up, lose heart

despairing adjective hopeless, dejected, desperate, despondent, disconsolate, frantic, grief-stricken, inconsolable, miserable, wretched

despatch see DISPATCH

desperado noun criminal, bandit, lawbreaker, outlaw, villain

desperate adjective **1** reckless, audacious, daring, frantic, furious, risky **2** grave, drastic, extreme, urgent

desperately adverb **1** gravely, badly, dangerously, perilously, seriously, severely **2** hopelessly, appallingly, fearfully, frightfully, shockingly

desperation noun **1** recklessness, foolhardiness, frenzy, impetuosity, madness, rashness **2** misery, agony, anguish, despair, hopelessness, trouble, unhappiness, worry

despicable adjective
contemptible, detestable,
disgraceful, hateful, mean,
shameful, sordid, vile, worthless,
wretched

despise verb look down on,
abhor, detest, loathe, revile,
scorn

despite preposition in spite of,
against, even with, in the face
of, in the teeth of,
notwithstanding, regardless of,
undeterred by

despondency noun dejection,
depression, despair, desperation,
gloom, low spirits, melancholy,
misery, sadness

despondent adjective dejected,
depressed, disconsolate,
disheartened, dispirited,
downhearted, glum, in despair,
sad, sorrowful

despot noun tyrant, autocrat,
dictator, oppressor

despotic adjective tyrannical,
authoritarian, autocratic,
dictatorial, domineering,
imperious, oppressive

despotism noun tyranny,
autocracy, dictatorship,
oppression, totalitarianism

destination noun journey's end,
haven, resting-place, station,
stop, terminus

destined adjective fated, bound,
certain, doomed, intended,
meant, predestined

destiny noun fate, doom,
fortune, karma, kismet, lot,
portion

destitute adjective penniless,
down and out, impoverished,
indigent, insolvent, moneyless,

penurious, poor, poverty-stricken

destroy verb ruin, annihilate,
crush, demolish, devastate,
eradicate, shatter, wipe out,
wreck

destruction noun ruin,
annihilation, demolition,
devastation, eradication,
extermination, havoc, slaughter,
wreckage

destructive adjective damaging,
calamitous, catastrophic, deadly,
devastating, fatal, harmful,
lethal, ruinous

detach verb separate, cut off,
disconnect, disengage, divide,
remove, sever, tear off, unfasten

detached adjective 1 separate,
disconnected, discrete,
unconnected 2 uninvolved,
disinterested, dispassionate,
impartial, impersonal, neutral,
objective, reserved, unbiased

detachment noun 1 indifference,
aloofness, coolness,
nonchalance, remoteness,
unconcern 2 impartiality,
fairness, neutrality, objectivity
3 Military unit, body, force,
party, patrol, squad, task force

detail noun 1 point, aspect,
component, element, fact,
factor, feature, particular, respect
2 fine point, nicety, particular,
triviality 3 Military party,
assignment, body, detachment,
duty, fatigue, force, squad ♦ verb
4 list, catalogue, enumerate,
itemize, recite, recount, rehearse,
relate, tabulate 5 appoint,
allocate, assign, charge,
commission, delegate, send

detailed adjective comprehensive,
blow-by-blow, exhaustive, full,

intricate, minute, particular, thorough

detain verb 1 delay, check, hinder, hold up, impede, keep back, retard, slow up (or down) 2 hold, arrest, confine, intern, restrain

detect verb 1 notice, ascertain, identify, note, observe, perceive, recognize, spot 2 discover, find, track down, uncover, unmask

detective noun investigator, cop (slang), gumshoe (U.S. slang), private eye, private investigator, sleuth (informal)

detention noun imprisonment, confinement, custody, incarceration, quarantine

deter verb discourage, dissuade, frighten, inhibit from, intimidate, prevent, put off, stop, talk out of

detergent noun cleaner, cleanser

deteriorate verb decline, degenerate, go downhill (informal), lower, slump, worsen

determination noun tenacity, dedication, doggedness, fortitude, perseverance, persistence, resolve, single-mindedness, steadfastness, willpower

determine verb 1 settle, conclude, decide, end, finish, ordain, regulate 2 find out, ascertain, detect, discover, learn, verify, work out 3 decide, choose, elect, make up one's mind, resolve

determined adjective resolute, dogged, firm, intent, persevering, persistent, single-minded, steadfast, tenacious, unwavering

deterrent noun discouragement, check, curb, disincentive, hindrance, impediment, obstacle, restraint

detest verb hate, abhor, abominate, despise, dislike intensely, loathe, recoil from

detonate verb explode, blast, blow up, discharge, set off, trigger

detour noun diversion, bypass, indirect course, roundabout way

detract verb lessen, devaluate, diminish, lower, reduce, take away from

detriment noun damage, disadvantage, disservice, harm, hurt, impairment, injury, loss

detrimental adjective damaging, adverse, deleterious, destructive, disadvantageous, harmful, prejudicial, unfavourable

devastate verb destroy, demolish, lay waste, level, ravage, raze, ruin, sack, wreck

devastating adjective overwhelming, cutting, overpowering, savage, trenchant, vitriolic, withering

devastation noun destruction, demolition, desolation, havoc, ruin

develop verb 1 advance, evolve, flourish, grow, mature, progress, prosper, ripen 2 form, breed, establish, generate, invent, originate 3 expand, amplify, augment, broaden, elaborate, enlarge, unfold, work out

development noun 1 growth, advance, evolution, expansion, improvement, increase, progress, spread 2 event, happening, incident, occurrence, result, turn of events, upshot

deviant adjective 1 perverted, kinky (slang), sick (informal), twisted, warped ♦ noun 2 pervert, freak, misfit

deviate verb differ, depart, diverge, stray, swerve, veer, wander

deviation noun departure, digression, discrepancy, disparity, divergence, inconsistency, irregularity, shift, variation

device noun 1 gadget, apparatus, appliance, contraption, implement, instrument, machine, tool 2 ploy, gambit, manoeuvre, plan, scheme, stratagem, trick, wile

devil noun 1 the Devil Satan, Beelzebub, Evil One, Lucifer, Mephistopheles, Old Nick (informal), Prince of Darkness 2 brute, beast, demon, fiend, monster, ogre, terror 3 scamp, rascal, rogue, scoundrel 4 person, beggar, creature, thing, wretch

devilish adjective fiendish, atrocious, damnable, detestable, diabolical, hellish, infernal, satanic, wicked

devious adjective 1 sly, calculating, deceitful, dishonest, double-dealing, insincere, scheming, surreptitious, underhand, wily 2 indirect, circuitous, rambling, roundabout

devise verb work out, conceive, construct, contrive, design, dream up, formulate, invent, think up

devoid adjective lacking, bereft,

deficient, destitute, empty, free from, wanting, without

devote verb dedicate, allot, apply, assign, commit, give, pledge, reserve, set apart

devoted adjective dedicated, ardent, committed, constant, devout, faithful, loyal, staunch, steadfast, true

devotee noun enthusiast, adherent, admirer, aficionado, buff (informal), disciple, fan, fanatic, follower, supporter

devotion noun 1 dedication, adherence, allegiance, commitment, constancy, faithfulness, fidelity, loyalty 2 love, affection, attachment, fondness, passion 3 devoutness, godliness, holiness, piety, reverence, spirituality 4 devotions prayers, church service, divine office, religious observance

devour verb 1 eat, consume, gobble, gulp, guzzle, polish off (informal), swallow, wolf 2 destroy, annihilate, consume, ravage, waste, wipe out 3 enjoy, read compulsively or voraciously, take in

devout adjective religious, godly, holy, orthodox, pious, prayerful, pure, reverent, saintly

dexterity noun 1 skill, adroitness, deftness, expertise, finesse, nimbleness, proficiency, touch 2 cleverness, ability, aptitude, ingenuity

diabolical adjective Informal dreadful, abysmal, appalling, atrocious, hellish, outrageous, shocking, terrible

diagnose verb identify, analyse,

determine, distinguish, interpret, pinpoint, pronounce, recognize

diagnosis noun **1** examination, analysis, investigation, scrutiny **2** opinion, conclusion, interpretation, pronouncement

diagonal adjective slanting, angled, cross, crossways, crosswise, oblique

diagonally adverb aslant, at an angle, cornerwise, crosswise, obliquely

diagram noun plan, chart, drawing, figure, graph, representation, sketch

dialect noun language, brogue, idiom, jargon, patois, provincialism, speech, vernacular

dialogue noun conversation, communication, conference, discourse, discussion

diary noun journal, appointment book, chronicle, daily record, engagement book, Filofax (Trademark)

dicky adjective Brit. informal weak, fluttery, shaky, unreliable, unsound, unsteady

dictate verb **1** speak, read out, say, utter **2** order, command, decree, demand, direct, impose, lay down the law, pronounce ♦noun **3** command, decree, demand, direction, edict, fiat, injunction, order **4** principle, code, law, rule

dictator noun absolute ruler, autocrat, despot, oppressor, tyrant

dictatorial adjective **1** absolute, arbitrary, autocratic, despotic, totalitarian, tyrannical, unlimited, unrestricted **2** domineering,

authoritarian, bossy (informal), imperious, oppressive, overbearing

dictatorship noun absolute rule, absolutism, authoritarianism, autocracy, despotism, totalitarianism, tyranny

diction noun pronunciation, articulation, delivery, elocution, enunciation, fluency, inflection, intonation, speech

dictionary noun wordbook, glossary, lexicon, vocabulary

die verb **1** pass away, breathe one's last, croak (slang), expire, give up the ghost, kick the bucket (slang), peg out (informal), perish, snuff it (slang) **2** dwindle, decay, decline, fade, sink, subside, wane, wilt, wither **3** stop, break down, fade out or away, fail, fizzle out, halt, lose power, peter out, run down **4** be dying long, ache, be eager, desire, hunger, pine for, yearn

die-hard noun reactionary, fanatic, old fogey, stick-in-the-mud (informal)

diet¹ noun **1** food, fare, nourishment, nutriment, provisions, rations, sustenance, victuals **2** regime, abstinence, fast, regimen ♦verb **3** slim, abstain, eat sparingly, fast, lose weight

diet² noun council, chamber, congress, convention, legislature, meeting, parliament

differ verb **1** be dissimilar, contradict, contrast, depart from, diverge, run counter to, stand apart, vary **2** disagree, clash, contend, debate, demur, dispute, dissent, oppose, take exception, take issue

difference noun 1 <u>dissimilarity</u>, alteration, change, contrast, discrepancy, disparity, diversity, variation, variety 2 <u>disagreement</u>, argument, clash, conflict, contretemps, debate, dispute, quarrel 3 <u>remainder</u>, balance, rest, result

different adjective 1 <u>unlike</u>, altered, changed, contrasting, disparate, dissimilar, divergent, inconsistent, opposed 2 <u>various</u>, assorted, diverse, miscellaneous, sundry, varied 3 <u>unusual</u>, atypical, distinctive, extraordinary, peculiar, singular, special, strange, uncommon

differentiate verb 1 <u>distinguish</u>, contrast, discriminate, make a distinction, mark off, separate, set off or apart, tell apart 2 <u>make different</u>, adapt, alter, change, convert, modify, transform

difficult adjective 1 <u>hard</u>, arduous, demanding, formidable, laborious, onerous, strenuous, uphill 2 <u>problematical</u>, abstruse, baffling, complex, complicated, intricate, involved, knotty, obscure 3 <u>hard to please</u>, demanding, fastidious, fussy, perverse, refractory, unaccommodating

difficulty noun 1 <u>laboriousness</u>, arduousness, awkwardness, hardship, strain, strenuousness, tribulation 2 <u>predicament</u>, dilemma, embarrassment, hot water (informal), jam (informal), mess, plight, quandary, trouble 3 <u>problem</u>, complication, hindrance, hurdle, impediment,

obstacle, pitfall, snag, stumbling block

diffidence noun <u>shyness</u>, bashfulness, hesitancy, insecurity, modesty, reserve, self-consciousness, timidity

diffident adjective <u>shy</u>, bashful, doubtful, hesitant, insecure, modest, reserved, self-conscious, timid, unassertive, unassuming

dig verb 1 <u>excavate</u>, burrow, delve, hollow out, mine, quarry, scoop, tunnel 2 <u>investigate</u>, delve, dig down, go into, probe, research, search with out or up <u>find</u>, discover, expose, uncover, unearth, uproot 4 <u>poke</u>, drive, jab, prod, punch, thrust ♦ noun 5 <u>poke</u>, jab, prod, punch, thrust 6 <u>cutting remark</u>, barb, crack (slang), gibe, insult, jeer, sneer, taunt, wisecrack (informal)

digest verb 1 <u>ingest</u>, absorb, assimilate, dissolve, incorporate 2 <u>take in</u>, absorb, consider, contemplate, grasp, study, understand ♦ noun 3 <u>summary</u>, abridgment, abstract, epitome, précis, résumé, synopsis

digestion noun <u>ingestion</u>, absorption, assimilation, conversion, incorporation, transformation

dignified adjective <u>distinguished</u>, formal, grave, imposing, noble, reserved, solemn, stately

dignitary noun <u>public figure</u>, bigwig (informal), high-up (informal), notable, personage, pillar of society, V.I.P., worthy

dignity noun 1 <u>decorum</u>, courtliness, grandeur, gravity, loftiness, majesty, nobility, solemnity, stateliness 2 <u>honour</u>, eminence, importance, rank, respectability, standing, status **3** <u>self-importance</u>, pride, self-esteem, self-respect

digress verb <u>wander</u>, depart, deviate, diverge, drift, get off the point or subject, go off at a tangent, ramble, stray

digression noun <u>departure</u>, aside, detour, deviation, divergence, diversion, straying, wandering

dilapidated adjective <u>ruined</u>, broken-down, crumbling, decrepit, in ruins, ramshackle, rickety, run-down, tumbledown

dilate verb <u>enlarge</u>, broaden, expand, puff out, stretch, swell, widen

dilatory adjective <u>time-wasting</u>, delaying, lingering, procrastinating, slow, sluggish, tardy, tarrying

dilemma noun <u>predicament</u>, difficulty, mess, plight, problem, puzzle, quandary, spot (informal)

dilettante noun <u>amateur</u>, aesthete, dabbler, trifler

diligence noun <u>application</u>, attention, care, industry, laboriousness, perseverance

diligent adjective <u>hard-working</u>, assiduous, attentive, careful, conscientious, industrious, painstaking, persistent, studious, tireless

dilute verb **1** <u>water down</u>, adulterate, cut, make thinner, thin (out), weaken **2** <u>reduce</u>, attenuate, decrease, diffuse, diminish, lessen, mitigate, temper, weaken

dim adjective **1** <u>poorly lit</u>, cloudy,

dark, grey, overcast, shadowy, tenebrous **2** <u>unclear</u>, bleary, blurred, faint, fuzzy, ill-defined, indistinct, obscured, shadowy **3** Informal <u>stupid</u>, dense, dozy (Brit. informal), dull, dumb (informal), obtuse, slow on the uptake (informal), thick **4** <u>take a dim view</u> disapprove, be displeased, be sceptical, look askance, reject, suspect, take exception, view with disfavour ♦ verb **5** <u>dull</u>, blur, cloud, darken, fade, obscure

dimension noun, often plural <u>measurement</u>, amplitude, bulk, capacity, extent, proportions, size, volume

diminish verb **1** <u>decrease</u>, curtail, cut, lessen, lower, reduce, shrink **2** <u>dwindle</u>, decline, die out, recede, subside, wane

diminutive adjective <u>small</u>, little, mini, miniature, minute, petite, tiny, undersized

din noun **1** <u>noise</u>, clamour, clatter, commotion, crash, pandemonium, racket, row, uproar ♦ verb **2** <u>din (something) into (someone)</u> instil, drum into, go on at, hammer into, inculcate, instruct, teach

dine verb <u>eat</u>, banquet, feast, lunch, sup

dingy adjective <u>dull</u>, dark, dim, drab, dreary, gloomy, murky, obscure, sombre

dinner noun <u>meal</u>, banquet, feast, main meal, repast, spread (informal)

dip verb **1** <u>plunge</u>, bathe, douse, duck, dunk, immerse **2** <u>slope</u>, decline, descend, drop (down), fall, lower, sink, subside ♦ noun

3 plunge, douche, drenching, ducking, immersion, soaking **4 bathe**, dive, plunge, swim **5 hollow**, basin, concavity, depression, hole, incline, slope **6 drop**, decline, fall, lowering, sag, slip, slump

dip into *verb* sample, browse, glance at, peruse, skim

diplomacy *noun*
1 statesmanship, international negotiation, statecraft **2 tact**, artfulness, craft, delicacy, discretion, finesse, savoir-faire, skill, subtlety

diplomat *noun* negotiator, conciliator, go-between, mediator, moderator, politician, tactician

diplomatic *adjective* tactful, adept, discreet, polite, politic, prudent, sensitive, subtle

dire *adjective* **1** disastrous, awful, calamitous, catastrophic, horrible, ruinous, terrible, woeful **2 desperate**, critical, crucial, drastic, extreme, now or never, pressing, urgent **3 grim**, dismal, dreadful, fearful, gloomy, ominous, portentous

direct *adjective* **1 straight**, nonstop, not crooked, shortest, through, unbroken, uninterrupted **2 immediate**, face-to-face, first-hand, head-on, personal **3 honest**, candid, frank, open, plain-spoken, straight, straightforward, upfront (*informal*) **4 explicit**, absolute, blunt, categorical, downright, express, plain, point-blank, unambiguous, unequivocal ♦ *verb* **5 control**, conduct, guide, handle, lead, manage, oversee,

run, supervise **6 order**, bid, charge, command, demand, dictate, instruct **7 guide**, indicate, lead, point in the direction of, point the way, show **8 address**, label, mail, route, send **9 aim**, focus, level, point, train

direction *noun* **1 way**, aim, bearing, course, line, path, road, route, track **2 management**, administration, charge, command, control, guidance, leadership, order, supervision

directions *plural noun* instructions, briefing, guidance, guidelines, plan, recommendation, regulations

directive *noun* order, command, decree, edict, injunction, instruction, mandate, regulation, ruling

directly *adverb* **1 straight**, by the shortest route, exactly, in a beeline, precisely, unswervingly, without deviation **2 honestly**, openly, plainly, point-blank, straightforwardly, truthfully, unequivocally **3 at once**, as soon as possible, forthwith, immediately, promptly, right away, straightaway

director *noun* controller, administrator, chief, executive, governor, head, leader, manager, supervisor

dirge *noun* lament, dead march, elegy, funeral song, requiem, threnody

dirt *noun* **1 filth**, dust, grime, impurity, muck, mud **2 soil**, clay, earth, loam **3 obscenity**, indecency, pornography, sleaze, smut

dirty adjective **1** filthy, foul, grimy, grubby, messy, mucky, muddy, polluted, soiled, unclean **2** dishonest, crooked, fraudulent, illegal, treacherous, unfair, unscrupulous, unsporting **3** obscene, blue, indecent, pornographic, salacious, sleazy, smutty **4** As in **a dirty look** angry, annoyed, bitter, choked, indignant, offended, resentful, scorching ♦ verb **5** soil, blacken, defile, foul, muddy, pollute, smirch, spoil, stain

disability noun **1** handicap, affliction, ailment, complaint, defect, disorder, impairment, infirmity, malady **2** incapacity, inability, unfitness

disable verb **1** handicap, cripple, damage, enfeeble, immobilize, impair, incapacitate, paralyse **2** disqualify, invalidate, render or declare incapable

disabled adjective handicapped, crippled, incapacitated, infirm, lame, paralysed, weakened

disadvantage noun **1** harm, damage, detriment, disservice, hurt, injury, loss, prejudice **2** drawback, downside, handicap, inconvenience, nuisance, snag, trouble

disagree verb **1** differ (in opinion), argue, clash, cross swords, dispute, dissent, object, quarrel, take issue with **2** conflict, be dissimilar, contradict, counter, differ, diverge, run counter to, vary **3** make ill, bother, discomfort, distress, hurt, nauseate, sicken, trouble, upset

disagreeable adjective **1** nasty,

disgusting, displeasing, distasteful, objectionable, obnoxious, offensive, repugnant, repulsive, unpleasant **2** rude, bad-tempered, churlish, difficult, disobliging, irritable, surly, unpleasant

disagreement noun **1** incompatibility, difference, discrepancy, disparity, dissimilarity, divergence, incongruity, variance **2** argument, altercation, clash, conflict, dispute, dissent, quarrel, row, squabble

disallow verb reject, disavow, dismiss, disown, rebuff, refuse, repudiate

disappear verb **1** vanish, evanesce, fade away, pass, recede **2** cease, die out, dissolve, evaporate, leave no trace, melt away, pass away, perish

disappearance noun vanishing, departure, eclipse, evanescence, evaporation, going, melting, passing

disappoint verb let down, disenchant, disgruntle, dishearten, disillusion, dismay, dissatisfy, fail

disappointed adjective let down, cast down, despondent, discouraged, disenchanted, disgruntled, dissatisfied, downhearted, frustrated

disappointing adjective unsatisfactory, depressing, disconcerting, discouraging, inadequate, insufficient, sad, sorry

disappointment noun **1** frustration, chagrin, discontent, discouragement, disenchantment, disillusionment, dissatisfaction, regret **2** letdown, blow, calamity, choker (*informal*), misfortune, setback

disapproval *noun* displeasure, censure, condemnation, criticism, denunciation, dissatisfaction, objection, reproach

disapprove *verb* condemn, deplore, dislike, find unacceptable, frown on, look down one's nose at (*informal*), object to, reject, take a dim view of, take exception to

disarm *verb* **1** render defenceless, disable **2** win over, persuade, set at ease **3** demilitarize, deactivate, demobilize, disband

disarmament *noun* arms reduction, arms limitation, de-escalation, demilitarization, demobilization

disarming *adjective* charming, irresistible, likable *or* likeable, persuasive, winning

disarrange *verb* disorder, confuse, disorganize, disturb, jumble (up), mess (up), scatter, shake (up), shuffle

disarray *noun* **1** confusion, disorder, disorganization, disunity, indiscipline, unruliness **2** untidiness, chaos, clutter, hotchpotch, jumble, mess, muddle, shambles

disaster *noun* catastrophe, adversity, calamity, cataclysm, misfortune, ruin, tragedy, trouble

disastrous *adjective* terrible, calamitous, cataclysmic, catastrophic, devastating, fatal, ruinous, tragic

disbelief *noun* scepticism,

distrust, doubt, dubiety, incredulity, mistrust, unbelief

discard *verb* get rid of, abandon, cast aside, dispense with, dispose of, drop, dump (*informal*), jettison, reject, throw away or out

discharge *verb* **1** release, allow to go, clear, free, liberate, pardon, set free **2** dismiss, cashier, discard, expel, fire (*informal*), oust, remove, sack (*informal*) **3** fire, detonate, explode, let loose (*informal*), let off, set off, shoot **4** pour forth, dispense, emit, exude, give off, leak, ooze, release **5** carry out, accomplish, do, execute, fulfil, observe, perform **6** pay, clear, honour, meet, relieve, satisfy, settle, square up ♦ *noun* **7** release, acquittal, clearance, liberation, pardon **8** dismissal, demobilization, ejection **9** firing, blast, burst, detonation, explosion, report, salvo, shot, volley **10** emission, excretion, ooze, pus, secretion, seepage, suppuration

disciple *noun* follower, adherent, apostle, devotee, pupil, student, supporter

disciplinarian *noun* authoritarian, despot, martinet, stickler, taskmaster, tyrant

discipline *noun* **1** training, drill, exercise, method, practice, regimen, regulation **2** punishment, castigation, chastisement, correction **3** self-control, conduct, control, orderliness, regulation, restraint, strictness **4** field of study, area, branch of knowledge, course,

curriculum, speciality, subject
♦ verb 5 <u>train</u>, bring up, drill,
educate, exercise, prepare
6 <u>punish</u>, bring to book,
castigate, chasten, chastise,
correct, penalize, reprimand,
reprove

disclose verb **1** <u>make known</u>,
broadcast, communicate,
confess, divulge, let slip, publish,
relate, reveal **2** <u>show</u>, bring to
light, expose, lay bare, reveal,
uncover, unveil

disclosure noun <u>revelation</u>,
acknowledgment, admission,
announcement, confession,
declaration, divulgence, leak,
publication

discolour verb <u>stain</u>, fade, mark,
soil, streak, tarnish, tinge

discomfort noun **1** <u>pain</u>, ache,
hurt, irritation, malaise, soreness
2 <u>uneasiness</u>, annoyance,
distress, hardship, irritation,
nuisance, trouble

disconcert verb <u>disturb</u>, faze,
fluster, perturb, rattle (informal),
take aback, unsettle, upset, worry

disconcerting adjective
<u>disturbing</u>, alarming, awkward,
bewildering, confusing,
distracting, embarrassing,
off-putting (Brit. informal),
perplexing, upsetting

disconnect verb <u>cut off</u>, detach,
disengage, divide, part, separate,
sever, take apart, uncouple

disconnected adjective <u>illogical</u>,
confused, disjointed, incoherent,
jumbled, mixed-up, rambling,
unintelligible

disconsolate adjective
<u>inconsolable</u>, crushed, dejected,
desolate, forlorn, grief-stricken,

heartbroken, miserable, wretched

discontent noun <u>dissatisfaction</u>,
displeasure, envy, regret,
restlessness, uneasiness,
unhappiness

discontented adjective
<u>dissatisfied</u>, disaffected,
disgruntled, displeased,
exasperated, fed up, unhappy,
vexed

discontinue verb <u>stop</u>, abandon,
break off, cease, drop, end, give
up, quit, suspend, terminate

discord noun **1** <u>disagreement</u>,
conflict, dissension, disunity,
division, friction, incompatibility,
strife **2** <u>disharmony</u>, cacophony,
din, dissonance, harshness,
jarring, racket, tumult

discordant adjective
1 <u>disagreeing</u>, at odds, clashing,
conflicting, contradictory,
contrary, different, incompatible
2 <u>inharmonious</u>, cacophonous,
dissonant, grating, harsh, jarring,
shrill, strident

discount verb **1** <u>leave out</u>, brush
off (slang), disbelieve, disregard,
ignore, overlook, pass over
2 <u>deduct</u>, lower, mark down,
reduce, take off ♦ noun
3 <u>deduction</u>, concession, cut,
rebate, reduction

discourage verb **1** <u>dishearten</u>,
dampen, deject, demoralize,
depress, dispirit, intimidate,
overawe, put a damper on **2** <u>put
off</u>, deter, dissuade, inhibit,
prevent, talk out of

discouraged adjective <u>put off</u>,
crestfallen, deterred,
disheartened, dismayed,
dispirited, downcast, down in
the mouth, glum

discouragement noun 1 loss of confidence, dejection, depression, despair, despondency, disappointment, dismay, downheartedness 2 deterrent, damper, disincentive, hindrance, impediment, obstacle, opposition, setback

discouraging adjective disheartening, dampening, daunting, depressing, disappointing, dispiriting, off-putting (Brit. informal), unfavourable

discourse noun 1 conversation, chat, communication, dialogue, discussion, seminar, speech, talk 2 speech, dissertation, essay, homily, lecture, oration, sermon, treatise ♦ verb 3 hold forth, expatiate, speak, talk

discourteous adjective rude, bad-mannered, boorish, disrespectful, ill-mannered, impolite, insolent, offhand, ungentlemanly, ungracious

discourtesy noun 1 rudeness, bad manners, disrespectfulness, impertinence, impoliteness, incivility, insolence 2 insult, affront, cold shoulder, kick in the teeth (slang), rebuff, slight, snub

discover verb 1 find, come across, come upon, dig up, locate, turn up, uncover, unearth 2 find out, ascertain, detect, learn, notice, perceive, realize, recognize, uncover

discovery noun 1 finding, detection, disclosure, exploration, location, revelation, uncovering 2 breakthrough, find, innovation, invention, secret

discredit verb 1 disgrace, bring into disrepute, defame, dishonour, disparage, slander, smear, vilify 2 doubt, challenge, deny, disbelieve, discount, dispute, distrust, mistrust, question ♦ noun 3 disgrace, dishonour, disrepute, ignominy, ill-repute, scandal, shame, stigma

discreditable adjective disgraceful, dishonourable, ignominious, reprehensible, scandalous, shameful, unworthy

discreet adjective tactful, careful, cautious, circumspect, considerate, diplomatic, guarded, judicious, prudent, wary

discrepancy noun disagreement, conflict, contradiction, difference, disparity, divergence, incongruity, inconsistency, variation

discretion noun 1 tact, carefulness, caution, consideration, diplomacy, judiciousness, prudence, wariness 2 choice, inclination, pleasure, preference, volition, will

discriminate verb 1 show prejudice, favour, show bias, single out, treat as inferior, treat differently, victimize 2 differentiate, distinguish, draw a distinction, segregate, separate, tell the difference

discriminating adjective discerning, cultivated, fastidious, particular, refined, selective, tasteful

discrimination noun 1 prejudice, bias, bigotry, favouritism, intolerance, unfairness 2 discernment, judgment, perception, refinement, subtlety, taste

discuss verb <u>talk about</u>, argue, confer, consider, converse, debate, deliberate, examine

discussion noun <u>talk</u>, analysis, argument, conference, consultation, conversation, debate, deliberation, dialogue, discourse

disdain noun 1 <u>contempt</u>, arrogance, derision, haughtiness, scorn, superciliousness ♦ verb 2 <u>scorn</u>, deride, disregard, look down on, reject, slight, sneer at, spurn

disdainful adjective <u>contemptuous</u>, aloof, arrogant, derisive, haughty, proud, scornful, sneering, supercilious, superior

disease noun <u>illness</u>, affliction, ailment, complaint, condition, disorder, infection, infirmity, malady, sickness

diseased adjective <u>sick</u>, ailing, infected, rotten, sickly, unhealthy, unsound, unwell, unwholesome

disembark verb <u>land</u>, alight, arrive, get off, go ashore, step out of

disenchanted adjective <u>disillusioned</u>, cynical, disappointed, indifferent, jaundiced, let down, sick of, soured

disenchantment noun <u>disillusionment</u>, disappointment, disillusion, rude awakening

disengage verb <u>release</u>, disentangle, extricate, free, loosen, set free, unloose, untie

disentangle verb <u>untangle</u>, disconnect, disengage, extricate, free, loose, unravel

disfavour noun <u>disapproval</u>, disapprobation, dislike, displeasure

disfigure verb <u>damage</u>, blemish, deface, deform, distort, mar, mutilate, scar

disgorge verb <u>vomit</u>, discharge, eject, empty, expel

disgrace noun 1 <u>shame</u>, degradation, dishonour, disrepute, ignominy, infamy, odium, opprobrium 2 <u>stain</u>, blemish, blot, reproach, scandal, slur, stigma ♦ verb 3 <u>bring shame upon</u>, degrade, discredit, dishonour, humiliate, shame, sully, taint

disgraceful adjective <u>shameful</u>, contemptible, detestable, dishonourable, disreputable, ignominious, scandalous, shocking, unworthy

disgruntled adjective <u>discontented</u>, annoyed, displeased, dissatisfied, grumpy, irritated, peeved, put out, vexed

disguise verb 1 <u>hide</u>, camouflage, cloak, conceal, cover, mask, screen, shroud, veil 2 <u>misrepresent</u>, fake, falsify ♦ noun 3 <u>costume</u>, camouflage, cover, mask, screen, veil 4 <u>façade</u>, deception, dissimulation, front, pretence, semblance, trickery, veneer

disguised adjective <u>in disguise</u>, camouflaged, covert, fake, false, feigned, incognito, masked, undercover

disgust noun 1 <u>loathing</u>, abhorrence, aversion, dislike, distaste, hatred, nausea,

repugnance, repulsion, revulsion
♦ *verb* 2 <u>sicken</u>, displease, nauseate, offend, put off, repel, revolt

disgusted *adjective* <u>sickened</u>, appalled, nauseated, offended, repulsed, scandalized

disgusting *adjective* <u>sickening</u>, foul, gross, loathsome, nauseating, offensive, repellent, repugnant, revolting

dish *noun* 1 <u>bowl</u>, plate, platter, salver 2 <u>food</u>, fare, recipe

dishearten *verb* <u>discourage</u>, cast down, deject, depress, deter, dismay, dispirit, put a damper on

dishevelled *adjective* <u>untidy</u>, bedraggled, disordered, messy, ruffled, rumpled, tousled, uncombed, unkempt

dishonest *adjective* <u>deceitful</u>, bent (*slang*), cheating, corrupt, crooked (*informal*), disreputable, double-dealing, false, lying, treacherous

dishonesty *noun* <u>deceit</u>, cheating, chicanery, corruption, fraud, treachery, trickery, unscrupulousness

dishonour *verb* 1 <u>shame</u>, debase, debauch, defame, degrade, discredit, disgrace, sully ♦ *noun* 2 <u>shame</u>, discredit, disgrace, disrepute, ignominy, infamy, obloquy, reproach, scandal 3 <u>insult</u>, abuse, affront, discourtesy, indignity, offence, outrage, sacrilege, slight

dishonourable *adjective* 1 <u>shameful</u>, contemptible, despicable, discreditable, disgraceful, ignominious, infamous, scandalous 2 <u>untrustworthy</u>, blackguardly,

corrupt, disreputable, shameless, treacherous, unprincipled, unscrupulous

disillusioned *adjective* <u>disenchanted</u>, disabused, disappointed, enlightened, undeceived

disinclination *noun* <u>reluctance</u>, aversion, dislike, hesitance, objection, opposition, repugnance, resistance, unwillingness

disinclined *adjective* <u>reluctant</u>, averse, hesitating, loath, not in the mood, opposed, resistant, unwilling

disinfect *verb* <u>sterilize</u>, clean, cleanse, decontaminate, deodorize, fumigate, purify, sanitize

disinfectant *noun* <u>antiseptic</u>, germicide, sterilizer

disinherit *verb Law* <u>cut off</u>, disown, dispossess, oust, repudiate

disintegrate *verb* <u>break up</u>, break apart, crumble, fall apart, go to pieces, separate, shatter, splinter

disinterest *noun* <u>impartiality</u>, detachment, fairness, neutrality

disinterested *adjective* <u>impartial</u>, detached, dispassionate, even-handed, impersonal, neutral, objective, unbiased, unprejudiced

disjointed *adjective* <u>incoherent</u>, confused, disconnected, disordered, rambling

dislike *verb* 1 <u>be averse to</u>, despise, detest, disapprove, hate, loathe, not be able to bear *or* abide *or* stand, object to, take a dim view of ♦ *noun* **2** aversion, animosity, antipathy, disapproval, disinclination, displeasure, distaste, enmity, hostility, repugnance

dislodge *verb* displace, disturb, extricate, force out, knock loose, oust, remove, uproot

disloyal *adjective* treacherous, faithless, false, subversive, traitorous, two-faced, unfaithful, untrustworthy

disloyalty *noun* treachery, breach of trust, deceitfulness, double-dealing, falseness, inconstancy, infidelity, treason, unfaithfulness

dismal *adjective* gloomy, bleak, cheerless, dark, depressing, discouraging, dreary, forlorn, sombre, wretched

dismantle *verb* take apart, demolish, disassemble, strip, take to pieces

dismay *verb* **1** alarm, appal, distress, frighten, horrify, paralyse, scare, terrify, unnerve **2** disappoint, daunt, discourage, dishearten, disillusion, dispirit, put off ♦ *noun* **3** alarm, anxiety, apprehension, consternation, dread, fear, horror, trepidation **4** disappointment, chagrin, discouragement, disillusionment

dismember *verb* cut into pieces, amputate, dissect, mutilate, sever

dismiss *verb* **1** sack (*informal*), axe (*informal*), cashier, discharge, fire (*informal*), give notice to, give (someone) their marching orders, lay off, remove **2** let go, disperse, dissolve, free, release, send away **3** put out of one's mind, banish, discard, dispel,

disregard, lay aside, reject, set aside

dismissal *noun* the sack (*informal*), expulsion, marching orders (*informal*), notice, removal, the boot (*slang*), the push (*slang*)

disobedience *noun* defiance, indiscipline, insubordination, mutiny, noncompliance, nonobservance, recalcitrance, revolt, unruliness, waywardness

disobedient *adjective* defiant, contrary, disorderly, insubordinate, intractable, naughty, refractory, undisciplined, unruly, wayward

disobey *verb* refuse to obey, contravene, defy, disregard, flout, ignore, infringe, rebel, violate

disorder *noun* **1** untidiness, chaos, clutter, confusion, disarray, jumble, mess, muddle, shambles **2** disturbance, commotion, riot, turmoil, unrest, unruliness, uproar **3** illness, affliction, ailment, complaint, disease, malady, sickness

disorderly *adjective* **1** untidy, chaotic, confused, disorganized, higgledy-piggledy (*informal*), jumbled, messy, shambolic (*informal*) **2** unruly, disruptive, indiscipline, lawless, riotous, rowdy, tumultuous, turbulent, ungovernable

disorganized *adjective* muddled, chaotic, confused, disordered, haphazard, jumbled, unsystematic

disown *verb* deny, cast off, disavow, disclaim, reject, renounce, repudiate

disparage verb run down, belittle, denigrate, deprecate, deride, malign, put down, ridicule, slander, vilify

dispassionate adjective
1 unemotional, calm, collected, composed, cool, imperturbable, serene, unruffled **2** objective, detached, disinterested, fair, impartial, impersonal, neutral, unbiased, unprejudiced

dispatch, despatch verb
1 send, consign, dismiss, hasten **2** carry out, discharge, dispose of, finish, perform, settle **3** murder, assassinate, execute, kill, slaughter, slay ♦ noun **4** message, account, bulletin, communication, communiqué, news, report, story

dispel verb drive away, banish, chase away, dismiss, disperse, eliminate, expel

dispense verb **1** distribute, allocate, allot, apportion, assign, deal out, dole out, share **2** prepare, measure, mix, supply **3** administer, apply, carry out, discharge, enforce, execute, implement, operate **4** dispense with a do away with, abolish, brush aside, cancel, dispose of, get rid of **b** do without, abstain from, forgo, give up, relinquish

disperse verb **1** scatter, broadcast, diffuse, disseminate, distribute, spread, strew **2** break up, disband, dissolve, scatter, separate

dispirited adjective disheartened, crestfallen, dejected, depressed, despondent, discouraged, downcast, gloomy, glum, sad

displace verb **1** move, disturb,

misplace, shift, transpose **2** replace, oust, succeed, supersede, supplant, take the place of

display verb **1** show, demonstrate, disclose, exhibit, expose, manifest, present, reveal **2** show off, flash (informal), flaunt, flourish, parade, vaunt ♦ noun **3** exhibition, array, demonstration, presentation, revelation, show **4** show, flourish, ostentation, pageant, parade, pomp, spectacle

displease verb annoy, anger, irk, irritate, offend, pique, put out, upset, vex

displeasure noun annoyance, anger, disapproval, dissatisfaction, distaste, indignation, irritation, resentment

disposable adjective
1 throwaway, biodegradable, nonreturnable **2** available, consumable, expendable

disposal noun **1** throwing away, discarding, dumping (informal), ejection, jettisoning, removal, riddance, scrapping **2 at one's disposal** available, at one's service, consumable, expendable, free for use

dispose verb arrange, array, distribute, group, marshal, order, place, put

dispose of verb **1** get rid of, destroy, discard, dump (informal), jettison, scrap, throw out or away, unload **2** deal with, decide, determine, end, finish with, settle

disposition noun **1** character, constitution, make-up, nature, spirit, temper, temperament

2 tendency, bent, bias, habit, inclination, leaning, proclivity, propensity **3** arrangement, classification, distribution, grouping, ordering, organization, placement

disproportion noun inequality, asymmetry, discrepancy, disparity, imbalance, lopsidedness, unevenness

disproportionate adjective unequal, excessive, inordinate, out of proportion, unbalanced, uneven, unreasonable

disprove verb prove false, contradict, discredit, expose, give the lie to, invalidate, negate, rebut, refute

dispute noun **1** disagreement, altercation, argument, conflict, feud, quarrel **2** argument, contention, controversy, debate, discussion, dissension ♦ verb **3** doubt, challenge, contest, contradict, deny, impugn, question, rebut **4** argue, clash, cross swords, debate, quarrel, squabble

disqualification noun ban, elimination, exclusion, ineligibility, rejection

disqualified adjective ineligible, debarred, eliminated, knocked out, out of the running

disqualify verb ban, debar, declare ineligible, preclude, prohibit, rule out

disquiet noun **1** uneasiness, alarm, anxiety, concern, disturbance, foreboding, nervousness, trepidation, worry ♦ verb **2** make uneasy, bother, concern, disturb, perturb, trouble, unsettle, upset, worry

disregard verb **1** ignore, brush aside or away, discount, make light of, neglect, overlook, pass over, pay no heed to, turn a blind eye to ♦ noun **2** inattention, contempt, disdain, disrespect, indifference, neglect, negligence, oversight

disrepair noun dilapidation, collapse, decay, deterioration, ruination

disreputable adjective discreditable, dishonourable, ignominious, infamous, louche, notorious, scandalous, shady (informal), shameful

disrepute noun discredit, disgrace, dishonour, ignominy, ill repute, infamy, obloquy, shame, unpopularity

disrespect noun contempt, cheek, impertinence, impoliteness, impudence, insolence, irreverence, lack of respect, rudeness, sauce

disrespectful adjective contemptuous, cheeky, discourteous, impertinent, impolite, impudent, insolent, insulting, irreverent, rude

disrupt verb **1** disturb, confuse, disorder, disorganize, spoil, upset **2** interrupt, break up or into, interfere with, intrude, obstruct, unsettle, upset

disruption noun disturbance, interference, interruption, stoppage

disruptive adjective disturbing, disorderly, distracting, troublesome, unruly, unsettling, upsetting

dissatisfaction noun discontent, annoyance, chagrin,

disappointment, displeasure, frustration, irritation, resentment, unhappiness

dissatisfied adjective discontented, disappointed, disgruntled, displeased, fed up, frustrated, unhappy, unsatisfied

dissect verb 1 cut up or apart, anatomize, dismember, lay open 2 analyse, break down, explore, inspect, investigate, research, scrutinize, study

disseminate verb spread, broadcast, circulate, disperse, distribute, publicize, scatter

dissension noun disagreement, conflict, discord, dispute, dissent, friction, quarrel, row, strife

dissent verb 1 disagree, differ, object, protest, refuse, withhold assent or approval ◆ noun 2 disagreement, discord, dissension, objection, opposition, refusal, resistance

dissenter noun objector, dissident, nonconformist

dissertation noun thesis, critique, discourse, disquisition, essay, exposition, treatise

disservice noun bad turn, harm, injury, injustice, unkindness, wrong

dissident adjective 1 dissenting, disagreeing, discordant, heterodox, nonconformist ◆ noun 2 protester, agitator, dissenter, rebel

dissimilar adjective different, disparate, divergent, diverse, heterogeneous, unlike, unrelated, various

dissipate verb 1 squander,

consume, deplete, expend, fritter away, run through, spend, waste 2 disperse, disappear, dispel, dissolve, drive away, evaporate, scatter, vanish

dissipation noun 1 dispersal, disappearance, disintegration, dissolution, scattering, vanishing 2 debauchery, dissoluteness, excess, extravagance, indulgence, intemperance, prodigality, profligacy, wantonness, waste

dissociate verb 1 break away, break off, part company, quit 2 separate, detach, disconnect, distance, divorce, isolate, segregate, set apart

dissolute adjective immoral, debauched, degenerate, depraved, dissipated, profligate, rakish, wanton, wild

dissolution noun 1 breaking up, disintegration, division, parting, separation 2 adjournment, discontinuation, end, finish, suspension, termination

dissolve verb 1 melt, deliquesce, fuse, liquefy, soften, thaw 2 end, break up, discontinue, suspend, terminate, wind up

dissuade verb deter, advise against, discourage, put off, remonstrate, talk out of, warn

distance noun 1 space, extent, gap, interval, length, range, span, stretch 2 reserve, aloofness, coldness, coolness, remoteness, restraint, stiffness 3 in the distance far off, afar, far away, on the horizon, yonder ◆ verb 4 distance oneself separate oneself, be distanced from, dissociate oneself

distant adjective 1 far-off, abroad, far, faraway, far-flung, outlying, out-of-the-way, remote 2 apart, dispersed, distinct, scattered, separate 3 reserved, aloof, cool, reticent, standoffish, unapproachable, unfriendly, withdrawn

distaste noun dislike, aversion, disgust, horror, loathing, odium, repugnance, revulsion

distasteful adjective unpleasant, disagreeable, objectionable, offensive, repugnant, repulsive, uninviting, unpalatable, unsavoury

distil verb extract, condense, purify, refine

distinct adjective 1 different, detached, discrete, individual, separate, unconnected, 2 definite, clear, decided, evident, marked, noticeable, obvious, palpable, unmistakable, well-defined

distinction noun
1 differentiation, discernment, discrimination, perception, separation 2 feature, characteristic, distinctiveness, individuality, mark, particularity, peculiarity, quality 3 difference, contrast, differential, division, separation 4 excellence, eminence, fame, greatness, honour, importance, merit, prominence, repute

distinctive adjective characteristic, idiosyncratic, individual, original, peculiar, singular, special, typical, unique

distinctly adverb definitely, clearly, decidedly, markedly, noticeably, obviously, patently, plainly, unmistakably

distinguish verb 1 differentiate, ascertain, decide, determine, discriminate, judge, tell apart, tell the difference 2 characterize, categorize, classify, mark, separate, set apart, single out 3 make out, discern, know, perceive, pick out, recognize, see, tell

distinguished adjective eminent, acclaimed, celebrated, famed, famous, illustrious, noted, renowned, well-known

distort verb 1 misrepresent, bias, colour, falsify, pervert, slant, twist 2 deform, bend, buckle, contort, disfigure, misshape, twist, warp

distortion noun
1 misrepresentation, bias, falsification, perversion, slant 2 deformity, bend, buckle, contortion, crookedness, malformation, twist, warp

distract verb 1 divert, draw away, sidetrack, turn aside 2 amuse, beguile, engross, entertain, occupy

distracted adjective agitated, at sea, flustered, harassed, in a flap (informal), perplexed, puzzled, troubled

distraction noun 1 diversion, disturbance, interference, interruption 2 entertainment, amusement, diversion, pastime, recreation 3 agitation, bewilderment, commotion, confusion, discord, disorder, disturbance

distraught adjective frantic, agitated, beside oneself, desperate, distracted, distressed, out of one's mind, overwrought, worked-up

distress noun 1 worry, grief, heartache, misery, pain, sorrow, suffering, torment, wretchedness 2 need, adversity, difficulties, hardship, misfortune, poverty, privation, trouble ♦ verb 3 upset, disturb, grieve, harass, sadden, torment, trouble, worry

distressed adjective 1 upset, agitated, distracted, distraught, tormented, troubled, worried, wretched 2 poverty-stricken, destitute, down at heel, indigent, needy, poor, straitened

distressing adjective upsetting, disturbing, harrowing, heart-breaking, painful, sad, worrying

distribute verb 1 hand out, circulate, convey, deliver, pass round 2 share, allocate, allot, apportion, deal, dispense, dole out

distribution noun 1 delivery, dealing, handling, mailing, transportation 2 sharing, allocation, allotment, apportionment, division 3 classification, arrangement, grouping, organization, placement

district noun area, locale, locality, neighbourhood, parish, quarter, region, sector, vicinity

distrust verb 1 suspect, be suspicious of, be wary of, disbelieve, doubt, mistrust, question, smell a rat (informal) ♦ noun 2 suspicion, disbelief, doubt, misgiving, mistrust, question, scepticism, wariness

disturb verb 1 interrupt, bother,

butt in on, disrupt, interfere with, intrude on, pester 2 upset, alarm, distress, fluster, harass, perturb, trouble, unnerve, unsettle, worry 3 muddle, disarrange, disorder

disturbance noun 1 interruption, annoyance, bother, distraction, intrusion 2 disorder, brawl, commotion, fracas, fray, rumpus

disturbed adjective 1 Psychiatry unbalanced, disordered, maladjusted, neurotic, troubled, upset 2 worried, anxious, apprehensive, bothered, concerned, nervous, troubled, uneasy, upset

disturbing adjective worrying, alarming, disconcerting, distressing, frightening, harrowing, startling, unsettling, upsetting

disuse noun neglect, abandonment, decay, idleness

ditch noun 1 channel, drain, dyke, furrow, gully, moat, trench, watercourse ♦ verb 2 Slang get rid of, abandon, discard, dispose of, drop, dump (informal), jettison, scrap, throw out or overboard

dither verb 1 Chiefly Brit. vacillate, faff about (Brit. informal), hesitate, hum and haw, shillyshally (informal), teeter, waver ♦ noun 2 Chiefly Brit. flutter, flap (informal), fluster, tizzy (informal)

dive verb 1 plunge, descend, dip, drop, duck, nose-dive, plummet, swoop ♦ noun 2 plunge, jump, leap, lunge, nose dive, spring

diverge verb 1 separate, branch, divide, fork, part, split, spread

2 <u>deviate</u>, depart, digress, meander, stray, turn aside, wander

diverse adjective 1 <u>various</u>, assorted, manifold, miscellaneous, of every description, several, sundry, varied 2 <u>different</u>, discrete, disparate, dissimilar, distinct, divergent, separate, unlike, varying

diversify verb <u>vary</u>, branch out, change, expand, have a finger in every pie, spread out

diversion noun 1 Chiefly Brit. <u>detour</u>, departure, deviation, digression 2 <u>pastime</u>, amusement, distraction, entertainment, game, recreation, relaxation, sport

diversity noun <u>difference</u>, distinctiveness, diverseness, heterogeneity, multiplicity, range, variety

divert verb 1 <u>redirect</u>, avert, deflect, switch, turn aside 2 <u>distract</u>, draw or lead away from, lead astray, sidetrack 3 <u>entertain</u>, amuse, beguile, delight, gratify, regale

diverting adjective <u>entertaining</u>, amusing, beguiling, enjoyable, fun, humorous, pleasant

divide verb 1 <u>separate</u>, bisect, cut (up), part, partition, segregate, split 2 <u>share</u>, allocate, allot, deal out, dispense, distribute 3 <u>cause to disagree</u>, break up, come between, estrange, split

dividend noun <u>bonus</u>, cut (informal), divvy (informal), extra, gain, plus, portion, share, surplus

divine adjective 1 <u>heavenly</u>, angelic, celestial, godlike, holy, spiritual, superhuman, supernatural 2 <u>sacred</u>, consecrated, holy, religious, sanctified, spiritual 3 Informal <u>wonderful</u>, beautiful, excellent, glorious, marvellous, perfect, splendid, superlative ♦ verb 4 <u>infer</u>, apprehend, deduce, discern, guess, perceive, suppose, surmise

divinity noun 1 <u>theology</u>, religion, religious studies 2 <u>god or goddess</u>, deity, guardian spirit, spirit 3 <u>godliness</u>, divine nature, holiness, sanctity

divisible adjective <u>dividable</u>, separable, splittable

division noun 1 <u>separation</u>, cutting up, dividing, partition, splitting up 2 <u>sharing</u>, allotment, apportionment, distribution 3 <u>part</u>, branch, category, class, department, group, section 4 <u>disagreement</u>, difference of opinion, discord, rupture, split, variance

divorce noun 1 <u>separation</u>, annulment, dissolution, split-up ♦ verb 2 <u>separate</u>, disconnect, dissociate, dissolve (marriage), divide, part, sever, split up

divulge verb <u>make known</u>, confess, declare, disclose, let slip, proclaim, reveal, tell

dizzy adjective 1 <u>giddy</u>, faint, light-headed, off balance, reeling, shaky, swimming, wobbly, woozy (informal) 2 <u>confused</u>, at sea, befuddled, bemused, bewildered, dazed, dazzled, muddled

do verb 1 <u>perform</u>, accomplish, achieve, carry out, complete, execute 2 <u>be adequate</u>, be sufficient, cut the mustard, pass muster, satisfy, suffice **3** get ready, arrange, fix, look after, prepare, see to **4** solve, decipher, decode, figure out, puzzle out, resolve, work out **5** cause, bring about, create, effect, produce ♦ noun **6** Informal, chiefly Brit. & N.Z. event, affair, function, gathering, occasion, party

do away with verb **1** kill, exterminate, murder, slay **2** get rid of, abolish, discard, discontinue, eliminate, put an end to, put paid to, remove

docile adjective submissive, amenable, biddable, compliant, manageable, obedient, pliant

docility noun submissiveness, compliance, manageability, meekness, obedience

dock[1] noun **1** wharf, harbour, pier, quay, waterfront ♦ verb **2** moor, anchor, berth, drop anchor, land, put in, tie up **3** Of spacecraft link up, couple, hook up, join, rendezvous, unite

dock[2] verb **1** deduct, decrease, diminish, lessen, reduce, subtract, withhold **2** cut off, clip, crop, curtail, cut short, shorten

doctor noun **1** G.P., general practitioner, medic (informal), medical practitioner, physician ♦ verb **2** change, alter, disguise, falsify, misrepresent, pervert, tamper with **3** add to, adulterate, cut, dilute, mix with, spike, water down

doctrinaire adjective dogmatic, biased, fanatical, inflexible, insistent, opinionated, rigid

doctrine noun teaching, article of

faith, belief, conviction, creed, dogma, opinion, precept, principle, tenet

document noun **1** paper, certificate, record, report ♦ verb **2** support, authenticate, certify, corroborate, detail, substantiate, validate, verify

dodge verb **1** duck, dart, sidestep, swerve, turn aside **2** evade, avoid, elude, get out of, shirk ♦ noun **3** trick, device, ploy, ruse, scheme, stratagem, subterfuge, wheeze (Brit. slang)

dog noun **1** hound, canine, cur, man's best friend, pooch (slang) **2** go to the dogs Informal go to ruin, degenerate, deteriorate, go down the drain, go to pot ♦ verb **3** trouble, follow, haunt, hound, plague, pursue, track, trail

dogged adjective determined, indefatigable, obstinate, persistent, resolute, steadfast, stubborn, tenacious, unflagging, unshakable

dogma noun doctrine, belief, credo, creed, opinion, teachings

dogmatic adjective opinionated, arrogant, assertive, doctrinaire, emphatic, obdurate, overbearing

doldrums noun the doldrums inactivity, depression, dumps (informal), gloom, listlessness, malaise

dole noun **1** Brit. & Austral. informal benefit, allowance, gift, grant, handout ♦ verb **2** dole out give out, allocate, allot, apportion, assign, dispense, distribute, hand out

dollop noun lump, helping, portion, scoop, serving

dolt noun idiot, ass, blockhead, chump (*informal*), clot (*Brit. informal*), dope (*informal*), dunce, fool, oaf

domestic adjective **1** home, family, household, private **2** home-loving, domesticated, homely, housewifely, stay-at-home **3** domesticated, house-trained, pet, tame, trained **4** native, indigenous, internal ♦ noun **5** servant, char (*informal*), charwoman, daily, help, maid

dominant adjective **1** controlling, assertive, authoritative, commanding, governing, ruling, superior, supreme **2** main, chief, predominant, pre-eminent, primary, principal, prominent

dominate verb **1** control, direct, govern, have the whip hand over, monopolize, rule, tyrannize **2** tower above, loom over, overlook, stand head and shoulders above, stand over, survey

domination noun control, ascendancy, authority, command, influence, power, rule, superiority, supremacy

domineering adjective overbearing, arrogant, authoritarian, bossy (*informal*), dictatorial, high-handed, imperious, oppressive, tyrannical

dominion noun **1** control, authority, command, jurisdiction, power, rule, sovereignty, supremacy **2** kingdom, country, domain, empire, realm, territory

don verb put on, clothe oneself in, dress in, get into, pull on, slip on or into

donate verb give, contribute,

make a gift of, present, subscribe

donation noun contribution, gift, grant, hand-out, offering, present, subscription

donor noun giver, benefactor, contributor, donator, philanthropist

doom noun **1** destruction, catastrophe, downfall, fate, fortune, ruin ♦ verb **2** condemn, consign, damn, destine, sentence

doomed adjective condemned, bewitched, cursed, fated, hopeless, ill-fated, ill-omened, luckless, star-crossed

door noun opening, doorway, entrance, entry, exit

dope noun **1** *Slang* drug, narcotic, opiate **2** *Informal* idiot, dimwit (*informal*), dunce, fool, nitwit (*informal*), numbskull or numskull, simpleton, twit (*informal, chiefly Brit.*) ♦ verb **3** drug, anaesthetize, knock out, narcotize, sedate, stupefy

dormant adjective inactive, asleep, hibernating, inert, inoperative, latent, sleeping, slumbering, suspended

dose noun quantity, dosage, draught, measure, portion, potion, prescription

dot noun **1** spot, fleck, jot, mark, point, speck, speckle **2 on the dot** on time, exactly, on the button (*informal*), precisely, promptly, punctually, to the minute ♦ verb **3** spot, dab, dabble, fleck, speckle, sprinkle, stipple, stud

dotage noun senility, decrepitude, feebleness, imbecility, old age, second childhood, weakness

dote on or **upon** verb adore, admire, hold dear, idolize, lavish affection on, prize, treasure

doting adjective adoring, devoted, fond, foolish, indulgent, lovesick

double adjective 1 twice, coupled, dual, duplicate, in pairs, paired, twin, twofold ♦ verb 2 multiply, duplicate, enlarge, grow, increase, magnify ♦ noun 3 twin, clone, dead ringer (slang), Doppelgänger, duplicate, lookalike, replica, spitting image (informal) 4 at or on the double quickly, at full speed, briskly, immediately, posthaste, without delay

double-cross verb betray, cheat, defraud, hoodwink, mislead, swindle, trick, two-time (informal)

doubt noun 1 uncertainty, hesitancy, hesitation, indecision, irresolution, lack of conviction, suspense 2 suspicion, apprehension, distrust, misgiving, mistrust, qualm, scepticism ♦ verb 3 be uncertain, be dubious, demur, fluctuate, hesitate, scruple, vacillate, waver 4 suspect, discredit, distrust, fear, lack confidence in, mistrust, query, question

doubtful adjective 1 unlikely, debatable, dubious, equivocal, improbable, problematic(al), questionable, unclear 2 unsure, distrustful, hesitating, in two minds (informal), sceptical, suspicious, tentative, uncertain, unconvinced, wavering

doubtless adverb 1 certainly, assuredly, indisputably, of

course, surely, undoubtedly, unquestionably, without doubt 2 probably, apparently, most likely, ostensibly, presumably, seemingly, supposedly

dour adjective gloomy, dismal, dreary, forbidding, grim, morose, sour, sullen, unfriendly

dowdy adjective frumpy, dingy, drab, frowzy, old-fashioned, shabby, unfashionable

do without verb manage without, abstain from, dispense with, forgo, get along without, give up, kick (informal)

down adjective 1 depressed, dejected, disheartened, downcast, low, miserable, sad, unhappy ♦ verb 2 Informal swallow, drain, drink (down), gulp, put away, toss off ♦ noun 3 have a down on Informal be antagonistic or hostile to, bear a grudge towards, be prejudiced against, be set against, have it in for (slang)

down-and-out noun 1 tramp, bag lady, beggar, derelict, dosser (Brit. slang), pauper, vagabond, vagrant ♦ adjective 2 destitute, derelict, impoverished, on one's uppers (informal), penniless, short, without two pennies to rub together (informal)

downcast adjective dejected, crestfallen, depressed, despondent, disappointed, disconsolate, discouraged, disheartened, dismayed, dispirited

downfall noun ruin, collapse, comeuppance (slang), destruction, disgrace, fall, overthrow, undoing

downgrade verb demote, degrade, humble, lower or reduce in rank, take down a peg (informal)

downhearted adjective dejected, crestfallen, depressed, despondent, discouraged, disheartened, dispirited, downcast, sad, unhappy

downpour noun rainstorm, cloudburst, deluge, flood, inundation, torrential rain

downright adjective complete, absolute, out-and-out, outright, plain, thoroughgoing, total, undisguised, unqualified, utter

down-to-earth adjective sensible, matter-of-fact, no-nonsense, plain-spoken, practical, realistic, sane, unsentimental

downtrodden adjective oppressed, exploited, helpless, subjugated, subservient, tyrannized

downward adjective descending, declining, earthward, heading down, sliding, slipping

doze verb 1 nap, kip (Brit. slang), nod off (informal), sleep, slumber, snooze (informal) ♦ noun 2 nap, catnap, forty winks (informal), kip (Brit. slang), shuteye (slang), siesta, snooze (informal)

drab adjective dull, dingy, dismal, dreary, flat, gloomy, shabby, sombre

draft noun 1 outline, abstract, plan, rough, sketch, version 2 order, bill (of exchange), cheque, postal order ♦ verb 3 outline, compose, design, draw, draw up, formulate, plan, sketch

drag verb 1 pull, draw, haul, lug, tow, trail, tug 2 drag on or out last, draw out, extend, keep going, lengthen, persist, prolong, protract, spin out, stretch out ♦ noun 3 Slang nuisance, annoyance, bore, bother, pain (informal), pest

dragoon verb force, browbeat, bully, coerce, compel, constrain, drive, impel, intimidate, railroad (informal)

drain noun 1 pipe, channel, conduit, culvert, ditch, duct, sewer, sink, trench 2 reduction, depletion, drag, exhaustion, sap, strain, withdrawal ♦ verb 3 remove, bleed, draw off, dry, empty, pump off or out, tap, withdraw 4 flow out, effuse, exude, leak, ooze, seep, trickle, well out 5 drink up, finish, gulp down, quaff, swallow 6 exhaust, consume, deplete, dissipate, empty, sap, strain, use up

drama noun 1 play, dramatization, show, stage show 2 theatre, acting, dramaturgy, stagecraft 3 excitement, crisis, histrionics, scene, spectacle, turmoil

dramatic adjective 1 theatrical, dramaturgical, Thespian 2 powerful, expressive, impressive, moving, striking, vivid 3 exciting, breathtaking, climactic, electrifying, melodramatic, sensational, suspenseful, tense, thrilling

dramatist noun playwright, dramaturge, screenwriter, scriptwriter

dramatize verb exaggerate, lay it on (thick) (slang), overdo, overstate, play to the gallery

drape verb <u>cover</u>, cloak, fold, swathe, wrap

drastic adjective <u>extreme</u>, desperate, dire, forceful, harsh, radical, severe, strong

draught noun 1 <u>breeze</u>, current, flow, movement, puff 2 <u>drink</u>, cup, dose, potion, quantity

draw verb 1 <u>sketch</u>, depict, design, map out, mark out, outline, paint, portray, trace 2 <u>pull</u>, drag, haul, tow, tug 3 <u>take out</u>, extract, pull out 4 <u>attract</u>, allure, elicit, entice, evoke, induce, influence, invite, persuade 5 <u>deduce</u>, derive, infer, make, take ♦ noun 6 *Informal* <u>attraction</u>, enticement, lure, pull (*informal*) 7 <u>tie</u>, dead heat, deadlock, impasse, stalemate

drawback noun <u>disadvantage</u>, deficiency, difficulty, downside, flaw, handicap, hitch, snag, stumbling block

drawing noun <u>picture</u>, cartoon, depiction, illustration, outline, portrayal, representation, sketch, study

drawn adjective <u>tense</u>, haggard, pinched, stressed, tired, worn

draw on verb <u>make use of</u>, employ, exploit, extract, fall back on, have recourse to, rely on, take from, use

draw out verb <u>extend</u>, drag out, lengthen, make longer, prolong, protract, spin out, stretch, string out

draw up verb 1 <u>draft</u>, compose, formulate, frame, prepare, write out 2 <u>halt</u>, bring to a stop, pull up, stop

dread verb 1 <u>fear</u>, cringe at, have cold feet (*informal*), quail, shrink from, shudder, tremble ♦ noun 2 <u>fear</u>, alarm, apprehension, dismay, fright, horror, terror, trepidation

dreadful adjective <u>terrible</u>, abysmal, appalling, atrocious, awful, fearful, frightful, hideous, horrible, shocking

dream noun 1 <u>vision</u>, delusion, hallucination, illusion, imagination, trance 2 <u>daydream</u>, fantasy, pipe dream 3 <u>ambition</u>, aim, aspiration, desire, goal, hope, wish 4 <u>delight</u>, beauty, gem, joy, marvel, pleasure, treasure ♦ verb 5 <u>have dreams</u>, conjure up, envisage, fancy, hallucinate, imagine, think, visualize 6 <u>daydream</u>, build castles in the air or in Spain, fantasize, stargaze

dreamer noun <u>idealist</u>, daydreamer, escapist, fantasist, utopian, visionary, Walter Mitty

dreamy adjective 1 <u>vague</u>, absent, abstracted, daydreaming, faraway, pensive, preoccupied, with one's head in the clouds 2 <u>impractical</u>, airy-fairy, fanciful, imaginary, quixotic, speculative

dreary adjective <u>dull</u>, boring, drab, humdrum, monotonous, tedious, tiresome, uneventful, wearisome

dregs plural noun 1 <u>sediment</u>, deposit, dross, grounds, lees, residue, residuum, scum, waste 2 <u>scum</u>, good-for-nothings, rabble, ragtag and bobtail, riffraff

drench verb <u>soak</u>, drown, flood, inundate, saturate, souse, steep, swamp, wet

dress noun 1 frock, gown, outfit, robe 2 clothing, apparel, attire, clothes, costume, garb, garments, togs ◆ verb 3 put on, attire, change, clothe, don, garb, robe, slip on or into 4 bandage, bind up, plaster, treat 5 arrange, adjust, align, get ready, prepare, straighten

dressmaker noun seamstress, couturier, tailor

dribble verb 1 run, drip, drop, fall in drops, leak, ooze, seep, trickle 2 drool, drivel, slaver, slobber

drift verb 1 float, be carried along, coast, go (aimlessly), meander, stray, waft, wander 2 pile up, accumulate, amass, bank up, drive, gather ◆ noun 3 pile, accumulation, bank, heap, mass, mound 4 meaning, direction, gist, import, intention, purport, significance, tendency, thrust

drifter noun wanderer, beachcomber, bum (informal), hobo (U.S.), itinerant, rolling stone, vagrant

drill noun 1 boring tool, bit, borer, gimlet 2 training, discipline, exercise, instruction, practice, preparation, repetition ◆ verb 3 bore, penetrate, perforate, pierce, puncture, sink in 4 train, coach, discipline, exercise, instruct, practise, rehearse, teach

drink verb 1 swallow, gulp, guzzle, imbibe, quaff, sip, suck, sup 2 booze (informal), hit the bottle (informal), tipple, tope ◆ noun 3 beverage, liquid,

potion, refreshment 4 alcohol, booze (informal), hooch or hootch (informal, chiefly U.S. & Canad.), liquor, spirits, the bottle (informal) 5 glass, cup, draught

drip verb 1 drop, dribble, exude, plop, splash, sprinkle, trickle ◆ noun 2 drop, dribble, leak, trickle 3 Informal weakling, mummy's boy (informal), namby-pamby, softie (informal), weed (informal), wet (Brit. informal)

drive verb 1 operate, direct, guide, handle, manage, motor, ride, steer, travel 2 goad, coerce, constrain, force, press, prod, prompt, spur 3 push, herd, hurl, impel, propel, send, urge 4 push, hammer, ram, thrust ◆ noun 5 run, excursion, jaunt, journey, outing, ride, spin (informal), trip 6 campaign, action, appeal, crusade, effort, push (informal) 7 initiative, ambition, energy, enterprise, get-up-and-go (informal), motivation, vigour, zip (informal)

drivel noun 1 nonsense, garbage (informal), gibberish, hogwash, hot air (informal), poppycock (informal), rubbish, trash, twaddle, waffle (informal, chiefly Brit.) ◆ verb 2 babble, blether, gab (informal), prate, ramble, waffle (informal, chiefly Brit.)

driving adjective forceful, compelling, dynamic, energetic, sweeping, vigorous, violent

drizzle noun 1 fine rain, Scotch mist ◆ verb 2 rain, shower, spot or spit with rain, spray, sprinkle

droll adjective amusing, comical, entertaining, funny, humorous, jocular, waggish, whimsical

drone verb **1** hum, buzz, purr, thrum, vibrate, whirr **2 drone on** speak monotonously, be boring, chant, intone, spout, talk interminably ♦ noun **3** hum, buzz, murmuring, purr, thrum, vibration, whirring

drool verb **1** dribble, drivel, salivate, slaver, slobber, water at the mouth **2 drool over** gloat over, dote on, gush, make much of, rave about (informal)

droop verb sag, bend, dangle, drop, fall down, hang (down), sink

drop verb **1** fall, decline, descend, diminish, plummet, plunge, sink, tumble **2** drip, dribble, fall in drops, trickle **3** discontinue, axe (informal), give up, kick (informal), quit, relinquish ♦ noun **4** droplet, bead, bubble, drip, globule, pearl, tear **5** dash, mouthful, shot (informal), sip, spot, tot, trace, trickle **6** decrease, cut, decline, deterioration, downturn, fall-off, lowering, reduction, slump **7** fall, descent, plunge

drop off verb **1** set down, deliver, leave, let off **2** Informal fall asleep, doze (off), have forty winks (informal), nod (off), snooze (informal) **3** decrease, decline, diminish, dwindle, fall off, lessen, slacken

drop out verb leave, abandon, fall by the wayside, give up, quit, stop, withdraw

drought noun dry spell, aridity, dehydration, dryness

drove noun herd, collection, company, crowd, flock, horde,

mob, multitude, swarm, throng

drown verb **1** drench, deluge, engulf, flood, go under, immerse, inundate, sink, submerge, swamp **2** overpower, deaden, muffle, obliterate, overcome, overwhelm, stifle, swallow up, wipe out

drowsy adjective **1** sleepy, dopey (slang), dozy, half asleep, heavy, lethargic, somnolent, tired, torpid

drudge noun menial, dogsbody (informal), factotum, servant, skivvy (chiefly Brit.), slave, toiler, worker

drudgery noun menial labour, donkey-work, fag (informal), grind (informal), hard work, labour, skivvying (Brit.), slog, toil

drug noun **1** medication, medicament, medicine, physic, poison, remedy **2** dope (slang), narcotic, opiate, stimulant ♦ verb **3** dose, administer a drug, dope (slang), medicate, treat **4** knock out, anaesthetize, deaden, numb, poison, stupefy

drum verb **1** beat, pulsate, rap, reverberate, tap, tattoo, throb **2 drum into** drive home, din into, hammer away, harp on, instil into, reiterate

drunk adjective **1** intoxicated, drunken, inebriated, legless (informal), merry (Brit. informal), plastered (slang), tipsy, under the influence ♦ noun **2** drunkard, alcoholic, boozer (informal), inebriate, lush (slang), wino (informal)

drunkard noun drinker, alcoholic, dipsomaniac, drunk, lush (slang), tippler, wino (informal)

drunkenness noun intoxication,

alcoholism, bibulousness, dipsomania, inebriation, insobriety, intemperance

dry adjective **1** dehydrated, arid, barren, desiccated, dried up, parched, thirsty **2** dull, boring, dreary, monotonous, plain, tedious, tiresome, uninteresting **3** sarcastic, deadpan, droll, low-key, sly ♦ verb **4** dehydrate, dehumidify, desiccate, drain, make dry, parch, sear

dry out or **up** verb become dry, harden, shrivel up, wilt, wither, wizen

dual adjective twofold, binary, double, duplex, duplicate, matched, paired, twin

dubious adjective **1** suspect, fishy (informal), questionable, suspicious, unreliable, untrustworthy **2** unsure, doubtful, hesitant, sceptical, uncertain, unconvinced, undecided, wavering

duck verb **1** bob, bend, bow, crouch, dodge, drop, lower, stoop **2** plunge, dip, dive, douse, dunk, immerse, souse, submerge, wet **3** Informal dodge, avoid, escape, evade, shirk, shun, sidestep

dud Informal ♦ noun **1** failure, flop (informal), washout (informal) ♦ adjective **2** useless, broken, duff (Brit. informal), failed, inoperative, worthless

dudgeon noun in high dudgeon indignant, angry, choked, fuming, offended, resentful, vexed

due adjective **1** expected, scheduled **2** payable, in arrears, outstanding, owed, owing,

unpaid **3** fitting, appropriate, deserved, justified, merited, proper, rightful, suitable, well-earned ♦ noun **4** right(s), comeuppance (slang), deserts, merits, privilege ♦ adverb **5** directly, dead, exactly, straight, undeviatingly

duel noun **1** single combat, affair of honour **2** contest, clash, competition, encounter, engagement, fight, head-to-head, rivalry ♦ verb **3** fight, clash, compete, contend, contest, lock horns, rival, struggle, vie with

dues plural noun membership fee, charge, charges, contribution, fee, levy

dull adjective **1** boring, dreary, flat, humdrum, monotonous, plain, run-of-the-mill, tedious, uninteresting **2** stupid, dense, dim-witted (informal), dozy (Brit. informal), slow, thick, unintelligent **3** cloudy, dim, dismal, gloomy, leaden, overcast **4** lifeless, apathetic, blank, indifferent, listless, passionless, unresponsive **5** blunt, blunted, unsharpened ♦ verb **6** relieve, allay, alleviate, blunt, lessen, moderate, soften, take the edge off

duly adverb **1** properly, accordingly, appropriately, befittingly, correctly, decorously, deservedly, fittingly, rightfully, suitably **2** on time, at the proper time, punctually

dumb adjective **1** mute, mum, silent, soundless, speechless, tongue-tied, voiceless, wordless **2** Informal stupid, asinine, dense, dim-witted (*informal*), dull, foolish, thick, unintelligent

dumbfounded *adjective* amazed, astonished, astounded, flabbergasted (*informal*), lost for words, nonplussed, overwhelmed, speechless, staggered, stunned

dummy *noun* **1** model, figure, form, manikin, mannequin **2** copy, counterfeit, duplicate, imitation, sham, substitute **3** *Slang* fool, blockhead, dunce, idiot, nitwit (*informal*), numbskull or numskull, oaf, simpleton ♦ *adjective* **4** imitation, artificial, bogus, fake, false, mock, phoney or phony (*informal*), sham, simulated

dump *verb* **1** drop, deposit, fling down, let fall, throw down **2** get rid of, dispose of, ditch (*slang*), empty out, jettison, scrap, throw away or out, tip, unload ♦ *noun* **3** rubbish tip, junkyard, refuse heap, rubbish heap, tip **4** *Informal* pigsty, hole (*informal*), hovel, mess, slum

dunce *noun* simpleton, blockhead, duffer (*informal*), dunderhead, ignoramus, moron, nincompoop, numbskull or numskull, thickhead

dungeon *noun* prison, cage, cell, oubliette, vault

duplicate *adjective* **1** identical, corresponding, matched, matching, twin, twofold ♦ *noun* **2** copy, carbon copy, clone, double, facsimile, photocopy, replica, reproduction ♦ *verb* **3** copy, clone, double, repeat, replicate, reproduce

durability *noun* durableness,

constancy, endurance, imperishability, permanence, persistence

durable *adjective* long-lasting, dependable, enduring, hard-wearing, persistent, reliable, resistant, strong, sturdy, tough

duration *noun* length, extent, period, span, spell, stretch, term, time

duress *noun* pressure, coercion, compulsion, constraint, threat

dusk *noun* twilight, dark, evening, eventide, gloaming (*Scot. or poetic*), nightfall, sundown, sunset

dusky *adjective* **1** dark, dark-complexioned, sable, swarthy **2** dim, cloudy, gloomy, murky, obscure, shadowy, shady, tenebrous, twilit

dust *noun* **1** grime, grit, particles, powder ♦ *verb* **2** sprinkle, cover, dredge, powder, scatter, sift, spray, spread

dusty *adjective* dirty, grubby, sooty, unclean, unswept

dutiful *adjective* conscientious, devoted, obedient, respectful, reverential, submissive

duty *noun* **1** responsibility, assignment, function, job, obligation, role, task, work **2** loyalty, allegiance, deference, obedience, respect, reverence **3** tax, excise, levy, tariff, toll **4 on duty** at work, busy, engaged, on active service

dwarf *verb* **1** tower above or over, diminish, dominate, overshadow ♦ *adjective* **2** miniature, baby, bonsai, diminutive, small, tiny, undersized ♦ *noun* **3** midget, Lilliputian, pygmy *or* pigmy, Tom Thumb

dwell *verb Formal, literary* live, abide, inhabit, lodge, reside

dwelling *noun Formal, literary* home, abode, domicile, habitation, house, lodging, quarters, residence

dwindle *verb* lessen, decline, decrease, die away, diminish, fade, peter out, shrink, subside, taper off, wane

dye *noun* **1** colouring, colorant, colour, pigment, stain, tinge, tint ♦ *verb* **2** colour, pigment, stain, tinge, tint

dying *adjective* expiring, at death's door, failing, *in extremis*, moribund, not long for this world

dynamic *adjective* energetic, forceful, go-ahead, go-getting (*informal*), high-powered, lively, powerful, vital

dynasty *noun* empire, government, house, regime, rule, sovereignty

E e

each *adjective* **1** every ♦ *pronoun* **2** every one, each and every one, each one, one and all ♦ *adverb* **3** apiece, for each, individually, per capita, per head, per person, respectively, to each

eager *adjective* keen, agog, anxious, athirst, avid, enthusiastic, fervent, hungry, impatient, longing

eagerness *noun* keenness,

ardour, enthusiasm, fervour, hunger, impatience, thirst, yearning, zeal

ear *noun* sensitivity, appreciation, discrimination, taste

early *adjective* **1** premature, advanced, forward, untimely **2** primitive, primeval, primordial, undeveloped, young ♦ *adverb* **3** too soon, ahead of time, beforehand, in advance, in good time, prematurely

earmark *verb* set aside, allocate, designate, flag, label, mark out, reserve

earn *verb* **1** make, bring in, collect, gain, get, gross, net, receive **2** deserve, acquire, attain, be entitled to, be worthy of, merit, rate, warrant, win

earnest *adjective* **1** serious, grave, intent, resolute, resolved, sincere, solemn, thoughtful ♦ *noun* **2** As in **in earnest** seriousness, sincerity, truth

earnings *plural noun* income, pay, proceeds, profits, receipts, remuneration, salary, takings, wages

earth *noun* **1** world, globe, orb, planet, sphere **2** soil, clay, dirt, ground, land, turf

earthenware *noun* crockery, ceramics, pots, pottery, terracotta

earthly *adjective* **1** worldly, human, material, mortal, secular, temporal **2** *Informal* possible, conceivable, feasible, imaginable, likely, practical

earthy *adjective* crude, bawdy, coarse, raunchy (*slang*), ribald, robust, uninhibited, unsophisticated

ease noun 1 easiness, effortlessness, facility, readiness, simplicity 2 content, comfort, happiness, peace, peace of mind, quiet, serenity, tranquillity 3 rest, leisure, relaxation, repose, restfulness ♦ verb 4 relieve, alleviate, calm, comfort, lessen, lighten, relax, soothe 5 move carefully, edge, inch, manoeuvre, slide, slip

easily adverb without difficulty, comfortably, effortlessly, readily, smoothly, with ease, with one hand tied behind one's back

easy adjective 1 not difficult, a piece of cake (informal), child's play (informal), effortless, no trouble, painless, plain sailing, simple, straightforward, uncomplicated, undemanding 2 carefree, comfortable, cushy (informal), leisurely, peaceful, quiet, relaxed, serene, tranquil, untroubled 3 tolerant, easy-going, indulgent, lenient, mild, permissive, unoppressive

easy-going adjective relaxed, carefree, casual, easy, even-tempered, happy-go-lucky, laid-back (informal), nonchalant, placid, tolerant, undemanding

eat verb 1 consume, chew, devour, gobble, ingest, munch, scoff (slang), swallow 2 have a meal, dine, feed, take nourishment 3 destroy, corrode, decay, dissolve, erode, rot, waste away, wear away

eavesdrop verb listen in, earwig (informal), monitor, overhear, snoop (informal), spy

ebb verb 1 flow back, go out, recede, retire, retreat, subside,

wane, withdraw 2 decline, decrease, diminish, dwindle, fade away, fall away, flag, lessen, peter out ♦ noun 3 flowing back, going out, low tide, low water, retreat, subsidence, wane, withdrawal

eccentric adjective 1 odd, freakish, idiosyncratic, irregular, outlandish, peculiar, quirky, strange, unconventional ♦ noun 2 crank (informal), character (informal), nonconformist, oddball (informal), weirdo or weirdie (informal)

eccentricity noun oddity, abnormality, caprice, capriciousness, foible, idiosyncrasy, irregularity, peculiarity, quirk

ecclesiastic noun 1 clergyman, churchman, cleric, holy man, man of the cloth, minister, parson, pastor, priest ♦ adjective 2 Also **ecclesiastical** clerical, divine, holy, pastoral, priestly, religious, spiritual

echo noun 1 repetition, answer, reverberation 2 copy, imitation, mirror image, parallel, reflection, reiteration, reproduction ♦ verb 3 repeat, resound, reverberate 4 copy, ape, imitate, mirror, parallel, recall, reflect, resemble

eclipse noun 1 obscuring, darkening, dimming, extinction, shading ♦ verb 2 surpass, exceed, excel, outdo, outshine, put in the shade (informal), transcend

economic adjective 1 financial, commercial, industrial 2 profitable, money-making, productive, profit-making, remunerative, viable 3 Informal

Also **economical** <u>inexpensive</u>,
cheap, low-priced, modest,
reasonable

economical *adjective* **1** <u>thrifty</u>,
careful, frugal, prudent,
scrimping, sparing
2 <u>cost-effective</u>, efficient,
money-saving, sparing,
time-saving

economize *verb* <u>cut back</u>, be
economical, be frugal, draw in
one's horns, retrench, save,
scrimp, tighten one's belt

economy *noun* <u>thrift</u>, frugality,
husbandry, parsimony,
prudence, restraint

ecstasy *noun* <u>rapture</u>, bliss,
delight, elation, euphoria,
fervour, joy, seventh heaven

ecstatic *adjective* <u>rapturous</u>,
blissful, elated, enraptured,
entranced, euphoric, in seventh
heaven, joyous, on cloud nine
(*informal*), overjoyed

eddy *noun* **1** <u>swirl</u>,
counter-current, counterflow,
undertow, vortex, whirlpool
♦ *verb* **2** <u>swirl</u>, whirl

edge *noun* **1** <u>border</u>, boundary,
brink, fringe, limit, outline,
perimeter, rim, side, verge
2 <u>sharpness</u>, bite, effectiveness,
force, incisiveness, keenness,
point **3** *As in* **have the edge on**
<u>advantage</u>, ascendancy,
dominance, lead, superiority,
upper hand **4 on edge** <u>nervous</u>,
apprehensive, edgy, ill at ease,
impatient, irritable, keyed up, on
tenterhooks, tense ♦ *verb*
5 <u>border</u>, fringe, hem **6** <u>inch</u>,
creep, ease, sidle, steal

edgy *adjective* <u>nervous</u>, anxious,
ill at ease, irritable, keyed up, on

edge, on tenterhooks, restive,
tense

edible *adjective* <u>eatable</u>,
digestible, fit to eat, good,
harmless, palatable, wholesome

edict *noun* <u>decree</u>, act,
command, injunction, law,
order, proclamation, ruling

edifice *noun* <u>building</u>,
construction, erection, house,
structure

edify *verb* <u>instruct</u>, educate,
enlighten, guide, improve,
inform, nurture, school, teach

edit *verb* <u>revise</u>, adapt, condense,
correct, emend, polish, rewrite

edition *noun* <u>version</u>, copy,
impression, issue, number,
printing, programme (*TV, Radio*),
volume

educate *verb* <u>teach</u>, civilize,
develop, discipline, enlighten,
improve, inform, instruct, school,
train, tutor

educated *adjective* **1** <u>taught</u>,
coached, informed, instructed,
nurtured, schooled, tutored
2 <u>cultured</u>, civilized, cultivated,
enlightened, knowledgeable,
learned, refined, sophisticated

education *noun* <u>teaching</u>,
development, discipline,
enlightenment, instruction,
nurture, schooling, training,
tuition

educational *adjective* <u>instructive</u>,
cultural, edifying, educative,
enlightening, improving,
informative

eerie *adjective* <u>frightening</u>, creepy
(*informal*), ghostly, mysterious,
scary (*informal*), spooky
(*informal*), strange, uncanny,

unearthly, weird

efface *verb* <u>obliterate</u>, blot out, cancel, delete, destroy, eradicate, erase, rub out, wipe out

effect *noun* **1** <u>result</u>, conclusion, consequence, end result, event, outcome, upshot **2** <u>operation</u>, action, enforcement, execution, force, implementation **3** <u>impression</u>, essence, impact, sense, significance, tenor ♦ *verb* **4** <u>bring about</u>, accomplish, achieve, complete, execute, fulfil, perform, produce

effective *adjective* **1** <u>efficient</u>, active, adequate, capable, competent, productive, serviceable, useful **2** <u>in operation</u>, active, current, in effect, in force, operative **3** <u>powerful</u>, cogent, compelling, convincing, forceful, impressive, persuasive, telling

effects *plural noun* <u>belongings</u>, gear, goods, paraphernalia, possessions, property, things

effeminate *adjective* <u>womanly</u>, camp (*informal*), feminine, sissy, soft, tender, unmanly, weak, womanish

effervescent *adjective* **1** <u>bubbling</u>, carbonated, fizzy, foaming, frothy, sparkling **2** <u>lively</u>, animated, bubbly, ebullient, enthusiastic, exuberant, irrepressible, vivacious

effete *adjective* <u>decadent</u>, dissipated, enfeebled, feeble, ineffectual, spoiled, weak

efficacious *adjective* <u>effective</u>, adequate, efficient, operative, potent, powerful, productive, successful, useful

efficiency *noun* <u>competence</u>, adeptness, capability, economy, effectiveness, power, productivity, proficiency

efficient *adjective* <u>competent</u>, businesslike, capable, economic, effective, organized, productive, proficient, well-organized, workmanlike

effigy *noun* <u>likeness</u>, dummy, figure, guy, icon, idol, image, picture, portrait, representation, statue

effluent *noun* <u>waste</u>, effluvium, pollutant, sewage

effort *noun* **1** <u>exertion</u>, application, elbow grease (*facetious*), endeavour, energy, pains, struggle, toil, trouble, work **2** <u>attempt</u>, endeavour, essay, go (*informal*), shot (*informal*), stab (*informal*), try

effortless *adjective* <u>easy</u>, painless, plain sailing, simple, smooth, uncomplicated, undemanding

effrontery *noun* <u>insolence</u>, arrogance, audacity, brazenness, cheek (*informal*), impertinence, impudence, nerve, presumption, temerity

effusive *adjective* <u>demonstrative</u>, ebullient, expansive, exuberant, gushing, lavish, unreserved, unrestrained

egg on *verb* <u>encourage</u>, exhort, goad, incite, prod, prompt, push, spur, urge

egocentric *adjective* <u>self-centred</u>, egoistic, egoistical, egotistic, egotistical, selfish

egotism, egoism *noun* <u>self-centredness</u>, conceitedness, narcissism, self-absorption,

self-esteem, self-importance, self-interest, selfishness, vanity

egotist, egoist *noun* egomaniac, bighead (*informal*), boaster, braggart, narcissist

egotistic, egotistical, egoistic or **egoistical** *adjective* self-centred, boasting, conceited, egocentric, full of oneself, narcissistic, self-absorbed, self-important, vain

egress *noun Formal* exit, departure, exodus, way out, withdrawal

eject *verb* throw out, banish, drive out, evict, expel, oust, remove, turn out

ejection *noun* expulsion, banishment, deportation, eviction, exile, removal

eke out *verb* be sparing with, economize on, husband, stretch out

elaborate *adjective* 1 detailed, intricate, minute, painstaking, precise, studied, thorough 2 complicated, complex, fancy, fussy, involved, ornamented, ornate ♦ *verb* 3 expand (upon), add detail, amplify, develop, embellish, enlarge, flesh out

elapse *verb* pass, glide by, go by, lapse, roll by, slip away

elastic *adjective* 1 stretchy, plastic, pliable, pliant, resilient, rubbery, springy, supple, tensile 2 adaptable, accommodating, adjustable, compliant, flexible, supple, tolerant, variable, yielding

elated *adjective* joyful, cock-a-hoop, delighted, ecstatic, euphoric, exhilarated, gleeful, jubilant, overjoyed

elation *noun* joy, bliss, delight, ecstasy, euphoria, exhilaration, glee, high spirits, jubilation, rapture

elbow *noun* 1 joint, angle ♦ *verb* 2 push, jostle, knock, nudge, shove

elbow room *noun* scope, freedom, latitude, leeway, play, room, space

elder *adjective* 1 older, first-born, senior ♦ *noun* 2 older person, senior

elect *verb* choose, appoint, determine, opt for, pick, prefer, select, settle on, vote

election *noun* voting, appointment, choice, judgment, preference, selection, vote

elector *noun* voter, constituent, selector

electric *adjective* charged, dynamic, exciting, rousing, stimulating, stirring, tense, thrilling

electrify *verb* startle, astound, excite, galvanize, invigorate, jolt, shock, stir, thrill

elegance *noun* style, dignity, exquisiteness, grace, gracefulness, grandeur, luxury, refinement, taste

elegant *adjective* stylish, chic, delicate, exquisite, fine, graceful, handsome, polished, refined, tasteful

element *noun* 1 component, constituent, factor, ingredient, part, section, subdivision, unit 2 *As in* **in one's element** environment, domain, field, habitat, medium, milieu, sphere

elementary *adjective* simple,

clear, easy, plain, rudimentary, straightforward, uncomplicated

elements *plural noun* **1** basics, essentials, foundations, fundamentals, nuts and bolts (*informal*), principles, rudiments **2** weather conditions, atmospheric conditions, powers of nature

elevate *verb* **1** raise, heighten, hoist, lift, lift up, uplift **2** promote, advance, aggrandize, exalt, prefer, upgrade

elevated *adjective* high-minded, dignified, exalted, grand, high-flown, inflated, lofty, noble, sublime

elevation *noun* **1** promotion, advancement, aggrandizement, exaltation, preferment, upgrading **2** altitude, height

elicit *verb* **1** bring about, bring forth, bring out, bring to light, call forth, cause, derive, evolve, give rise to **2** obtain, draw out, evoke, exact, extort, extract, wrest

eligible *adjective* qualified, acceptable, appropriate, desirable, fit, preferable, proper, suitable, worthy

eliminate *verb* get rid of, cut out, dispose of, do away with, eradicate, exterminate, remove, stamp out, take out

elite *noun* best, aristocracy, cream, crème de la crème, flower, nobility, pick, upper class

elitist *adjective* snobbish, exclusive, selective

elixir *noun* panacea, nostrum

elocution *noun* diction, articulation, declamation, delivery, enunciation, oratory, pronunciation, speech, speechmaking

elongate *verb* make longer, draw out, extend, lengthen, prolong, protract, stretch

elope *verb* run away, abscond, bolt, decamp, disappear, escape, leave, run off, slip away, steal away

eloquence *noun* expressiveness, expression, fluency, forcefulness, oratory, persuasiveness, rhetoric, way with words

eloquent *adjective*
1 silver-tongued, articulate, fluent, forceful, moving, persuasive, stirring, well-expressed **2** expressive, meaningful, suggestive, telling, vivid

elsewhere *adverb* in or to another place, abroad, away, hence (*archaic*), not here, somewhere else

elucidate *verb* clarify, clear up, explain, explicate, expound, illuminate, illustrate, make plain, shed or throw light upon, spell out

elude *verb* **1** escape, avoid, dodge, duck (*informal*), evade, flee, get away from, outrun **2** baffle, be beyond (someone), confound, escape, foil, frustrate, puzzle, stump, thwart

elusive *adjective* **1** difficult to catch, shifty, slippery, tricky **2** indefinable, fleeting, intangible, subtle, transient, transitory

emaciated *adjective* skeletal, cadaverous, gaunt, haggard, lean, pinched, scrawny, thin, undernourished, wasted

emanate verb <u>flow</u>, arise, come forth, derive, emerge, issue, originate, proceed, spring, stem

emancipate verb <u>free</u>, deliver, liberate, release, set free, unchain, unfetter

emancipation noun <u>freedom</u>, deliverance, liberation, liberty, release

embalm verb <u>preserve</u>, mummify

embargo noun 1 <u>ban</u>, bar, boycott, interdiction, prohibition, restraint, restriction, stoppage ♦ verb 2 <u>ban</u>, bar, block, boycott, prohibit, restrict, stop

embark verb 1 <u>go aboard</u>, board ship, take ship 2 **embark on** or **upon** <u>begin</u>, commence, enter, launch, plunge into, set about, set out, start, take up

embarrass verb <u>shame</u>, discomfit, disconcert, distress, fluster, humiliate, mortify, show up (informal)

embarrassed adjective <u>ashamed</u>, awkward, blushing, discomfited, disconcerted, humiliated, mortified, red-faced, self-conscious, sheepish

embarrassing adjective <u>humiliating</u>, awkward, compromising, discomfiting, disconcerting, mortifying, sensitive, shameful, toe-curling (informal), uncomfortable

embarrassment noun 1 <u>shame</u>, awkwardness, bashfulness, distress, humiliation, mortification, self-consciousness, showing up (informal) 2 <u>predicament</u>, bind (informal),

difficulty, mess, pickle (informal), scrape (informal)

embellish verb <u>decorate</u>, adorn, beautify, elaborate, embroider, enhance, enrich, festoon, ornament

embellishment noun <u>decoration</u>, adornment, elaboration, embroidery, enhancement, enrichment, exaggeration, ornament, ornamentation

embezzle verb <u>misappropriate</u>, appropriate, filch, misuse, peculate, pilfer, purloin, rip off (slang), steal

embezzlement noun <u>misappropriation</u>, appropriation, filching, fraud, misuse, peculation, pilfering, stealing, theft

embittered adjective <u>resentful</u>, angry, bitter, disaffected, disillusioned, rancorous, soured, with a chip on one's shoulder (informal)

emblem noun <u>symbol</u>, badge, crest, image, insignia, mark, sign, token

embodiment noun <u>personification</u>, epitome, example, exemplar, expression, incarnation, representation, symbol

embody verb 1 <u>personify</u>, exemplify, manifest, represent, stand for, symbolize, typify 2 <u>incorporate</u>, collect, combine, comprise, contain, include

embolden verb <u>encourage</u>, fire, inflame, invigorate, rouse, stimulate, stir, strengthen

embrace verb 1 <u>hug</u>, clasp,

cuddle, envelop, hold, seize, squeeze, take or hold in one's arms **2** accept, adopt, espouse, seize, take on board, take up, welcome **3** include, comprehend, comprise, contain, cover, encompass, involve, take in ♦ *noun* **4** hug, clasp, clinch (*slang*), cuddle, squeeze

embroil *verb* involve, enmesh, ensnare, entangle, implicate, incriminate, mire, mix up

embryo *noun* germ, beginning, nucleus, root, rudiment

emend *verb* revise, amend, correct, edit, improve, rectify

emendation *noun* revision, amendment, correction, editing, improvement, rectification

emerge *verb* **1** come into view, appear, arise, come forth, emanate, issue, rise, spring up, surface **2** become apparent, become known, come out, come out in the wash, come to light, crop up, transpire

emergence *noun* coming, advent, appearance, arrival, development, materialization, rise

emergency *noun* crisis, danger, difficulty, extremity, necessity, plight, predicament, quandary, scrape (*informal*)

emigrate *verb* move abroad, migrate, move

emigration *noun* departure, exodus, migration

eminence *noun* prominence, distinction, esteem, fame, greatness, importance, note, prestige, renown, repute

eminent *adjective* prominent, celebrated, distinguished, esteemed, famous, high-ranking, illustrious, noted, renowned, well-known

emission *noun* giving off or out, discharge, ejaculation, ejection, exhalation, radiation, shedding, transmission

emit *verb* give off, cast out, discharge, eject, emanate, exude, radiate, send out, transmit

emotion *noun* feeling, ardour, excitement, fervour, passion, sensation, sentiment, vehemence, warmth

emotional *adjective* **1** sensitive, demonstrative, excitable, hot-blooded, passionate, sentimental, temperamental **2** moving, affecting, emotive, heart-warming, poignant, sentimental, stirring, touching

emotive *adjective* sensitive, controversial, delicate, touchy

emphasis *noun* stress, accent, attention, force, importance, priority, prominence, significance, weight

emphasize *verb* stress, accentuate, dwell on, give priority to, highlight, lay stress on, play up, press home, underline

emphatic *adjective* forceful, categorical, definite, insistent, positive, pronounced, resounding, unequivocal, unmistakable, vigorous

empire *noun* kingdom, commonwealth, domain, realm

empirical, empiric *adjective* first-hand, experiential, experimental, observed, practical, pragmatic

employ verb 1 hire, commission, engage, enlist, retain, take on 2 keep busy, engage, fill, make use of, occupy, take up, use up 3 use, apply, bring to bear, exercise, exert, make use of, ply, put to use, utilize ◆ noun 4 As in in the employ of service, employment, engagement, hire

employed adjective working, active, busy, engaged, in a job, in employment, in work, occupied

employee noun worker, hand, job-holder, staff member, wage-earner, workman

employer noun boss (informal), company, firm, gaffer (informal, chiefly Brit.), owner, patron, proprietor

employment noun 1 taking on, engagement, enlistment, hire, retaining 2 use, application, exercise, exertion, utilization 3 job, line, occupation, profession, trade, vocation, work

emporium noun Old-fashioned shop, bazaar, market, mart, store, warehouse

empower verb enable, allow, authorize, commission, delegate, entitle, license, permit, qualify, sanction, warrant

emptiness noun 1 bareness, blankness, desolation, vacancy, vacuum, void, waste 2 purposelessness, banality, futility, hollowness, inanity, meaninglessness, senselessness, vanity, worthlessness 3 insincerity, cheapness, hollowness, idleness

empty adjective 1 bare, blank, clear, deserted, desolate, hollow, unfurnished, uninhabited, unoccupied, vacant, void 2 purposeless, banal, fruitless, futile, hollow, inane, meaningless, senseless, vain, worthless 3 insincere, cheap, hollow, idle ◆ verb 4 evacuate, clear, drain, exhaust, pour out, unload, vacate, void

empty-headed adjective scatterbrained, brainless, dizzy (informal), featherbrained, harebrained, silly, vacuous

emulate verb imitate, compete with, copy, echo, follow, mimic, rival

enable verb allow, authorize, empower, entitle, license, permit, qualify, sanction, warrant

enact verb 1 establish, authorize, command, decree, legislate, ordain, order, proclaim, sanction 2 perform, act out, depict, play, play the part of, portray, represent

enamoured adjective in love, captivated, charmed, enraptured, fond, infatuated, smitten, taken

encampment noun camp, base, bivouac, camping ground, campsite, cantonment, quarters, tents

encapsulate verb sum up, abridge, compress, condense, digest, epitomize, précis, summarize

enchant verb fascinate, beguile, bewitch, captivate, charm, delight, enrapture, enthral, ravish

enchanter noun sorcerer, conjuror, magician, magus, necromancer, warlock, witch, wizard

enchanting adjective fascinating, alluring, attractive, bewitching, captivating, charming, delightful, entrancing, lovely, pleasant

enclose verb 1 surround, bound, encase, encircle, fence, hem in, shut in, wall in 2 send with, include, insert, put in

encompass verb 1 surround, circle, encircle, enclose, envelop, ring 2 include, admit, comprise, contain, cover, embrace, hold, incorporate, take in

encounter verb 1 meet, bump into (informal), chance upon, come upon, confront, experience, face, run across ♦ noun 2 meeting, brush, confrontation, rendezvous 3 battle, clash, conflict, contest, head-to-head, run-in (informal)

encourage verb 1 inspire, buoy up, cheer, comfort, console, embolden, hearten, reassure 2 spur, advocate, egg on, foster, promote, prompt, support, urge

encouragement noun inspiration, cheer, incitement, promotion, reassurance, stimulation, stimulus, support

encouraging adjective promising, bright, cheerful, comforting, good, heartening, hopeful, reassuring, rosy

encroach verb intrude, impinge, infringe, invade, make inroads, overstep, trespass, usurp

encumber verb burden, hamper, handicap, hinder, impede, inconvenience, obstruct, saddle, weigh down

end noun 1 extremity, boundary, edge, extent, extreme, limit, point, terminus, tip 2 finish,

cessation, close, closure, ending, expiration, expiry, stop, termination 3 conclusion, culmination, denouement, ending, finale, resolution 4 remnant, butt, fragment, leftover, oddment, remainder, scrap, stub 5 destruction, death, demise, doom, extermination, extinction, ruin 6 purpose, aim, goal, intention, object, objective, point, reason ♦ verb 7 finish, cease, close, conclude, culminate, stop, terminate, wind up

endanger verb put at risk, compromise, imperil, jeopardize, put in danger, risk, threaten

endearing adjective attractive, captivating, charming, cute, engaging, lovable, sweet, winning

endearment noun loving word, sweet nothing

endeavour Formal ♦ verb 1 try, aim, aspire, attempt, labour, make an effort, strive, struggle, take pains ♦ noun 2 effort, attempt, enterprise, trial, try, undertaking, venture

ending noun finish, cessation, close, completion, conclusion, culmination, denouement, end, finale

endless adjective eternal, boundless, continual, everlasting, incessant, infinite, interminable, unlimited

endorse verb 1 approve, advocate, authorize, back, champion, promote, ratify, recommend, support 2 sign, countersign

endorsement noun 1 approval,

advocacy, approbation, authorization, backing, favour, ratification, recommendation, seal of approval, support **2** <u>signature</u>, countersignature

endow verb <u>provide</u>, award, bequeath, bestow, confer, donate, finance, fund, give

endowment noun <u>provision</u>, award, benefaction, bequest, donation, gift, grant, legacy

endurable adjective <u>bearable</u>, acceptable, sufferable, sustainable, tolerable

endurance noun **1** <u>staying power</u>, fortitude, patience, perseverance, persistence, resolution, stamina, strength, tenacity, toleration **2** <u>permanence</u>, continuity, durability, duration, longevity, stability

endure verb **1** <u>bear</u>, cope with, experience, stand, suffer, sustain, undergo, withstand **2** <u>last</u>, continue, live on, persist, remain, stand, stay, survive

enduring adjective <u>long-lasting</u>, abiding, continuing, lasting, perennial, persistent, steadfast, unfaltering, unwavering

enemy noun <u>foe</u>, adversary, antagonist, competitor, opponent, rival, the opposition, the other side

energetic adjective <u>vigorous</u>, active, animated, dynamic, forceful, indefatigable, lively, strenuous, tireless

energy noun <u>vigour</u>, drive, forcefulness, get-up-and-go (*informal*), liveliness, pep, stamina, verve, vitality

enforce verb <u>impose</u>, administer, apply, carry out, execute, implement, insist on, prosecute, put into effect

engage verb **1** <u>participate</u>, embark on, enter into, join, set about, take part, undertake **2** <u>occupy</u>, absorb, engross, grip, involve, preoccupy **3** <u>captivate</u>, arrest, catch, fix, gain **4** <u>employ</u>, appoint, enlist, enrol, hire, retain, take on **5** *Military* <u>begin battle with</u>, assail, attack, encounter, fall on, join battle with, meet, take on **6** <u>set going</u>, activate, apply, bring into operation, energize, switch on

engaged adjective **1** <u>betrothed</u> (*archaic*), affianced, pledged, promised, spoken for **2** <u>occupied</u>, busy, employed, in use, tied up, unavailable

engagement noun **1** <u>appointment</u>, arrangement, commitment, date, meeting **2** <u>betrothal</u>, troth (*archaic*) **3** <u>battle</u>, action, combat, conflict, encounter, fight

engaging adjective <u>charming</u>, agreeable, attractive, fetching (*informal*), likable *or* likeable, pleasing, winning, winsome

engender verb <u>produce</u>, breed, cause, create, generate, give rise to, induce, instigate, lead to

engine noun <u>machine</u>, mechanism, motor

engineer verb <u>bring about</u>, contrive, create, devise, effect, mastermind, plan, plot, scheme

engrave verb **1** <u>carve</u>, chisel, cut, etch, inscribe **2** <u>fix</u>, embed, impress, imprint, ingrain, lodge

engraving noun <u>carving</u>,

etching, inscription, plate, woodcut

engross verb <u>absorb</u>, engage, immerse, involve, occupy, preoccupy

engrossed adjective <u>absorbed</u>, caught up, enthralled, fascinated, gripped, immersed, lost, preoccupied, rapt, riveted

engulf verb <u>immerse</u>, envelop, inundate, overrun, overwhelm, submerge, swallow up, swamp

enhance verb <u>improve</u>, add to, boost, heighten, increase, lift, reinforce, strengthen, swell

enigma noun <u>mystery</u>, conundrum, problem, puzzle, riddle, teaser

enigmatic adjective <u>mysterious</u>, ambiguous, cryptic, equivocal, inscrutable, obscure, puzzling, unfathomable

enjoy verb **1** <u>take pleasure in or from</u>, appreciate, be entertained by, be pleased with, delight in, like, relish **2** <u>have</u>, be blessed or favoured with, experience, have the benefit of, own, possess, reap the benefits of, use

enjoyable adjective <u>pleasurable</u>, agreeable, delightful, entertaining, gratifying, pleasant, satisfying, to one's liking

enjoyment noun <u>pleasure</u>, amusement, delectation, delight, entertainment, fun, gratification, happiness, joy, relish

enlarge verb **1** <u>increase</u>, add to, amplify, broaden, expand, extend, grow, magnify, swell, widen **2** <u>enlarge on</u> <u>expand on</u>, descant on, develop, elaborate on, expatiate on, give further

details about

enlighten verb <u>inform</u>, advise, cause to understand, counsel, edify, educate, instruct, make aware, teach

enlightened adjective <u>informed</u>, aware, civilized, cultivated, educated, knowledgeable, open-minded, reasonable, sophisticated

enlightenment noun <u>understanding</u>, awareness, comprehension, education, insight, instruction, knowledge, learning, wisdom

enlist verb **1** <u>join up</u>, enrol, enter (into), join, muster, register, sign up, volunteer **2** <u>obtain</u>, engage, procure, recruit

enliven verb <u>cheer up</u>, animate, excite, inspire, invigorate, pep up, rouse, spark, stimulate, vitalize

enmity noun <u>hostility</u>, acrimony, animosity, bad blood, bitterness, hatred, ill will, malice

ennoble verb <u>dignify</u>, aggrandize, elevate, enhance, exalt, glorify, honour, magnify, raise

enormity noun **1** <u>wickedness</u>, atrocity, depravity, monstrousness, outrageousness, vileness, villainy **2** <u>atrocity</u>, abomination, crime, disgrace, evil, horror, monstrosity, outrage **3** Informal <u>hugeness</u>, greatness, immensity, magnitude, vastness

enormous adjective <u>huge</u>, colossal, gigantic, gross, immense, mammoth, massive, mountainous, tremendous, vast

enough adjective **1** <u>sufficient</u>,

abundant, adequate, ample, plenty ♦ *noun* **2** sufficiency, abundance, adequacy, ample supply, plenty, right amount ♦ *adverb* **3** sufficiently, abundantly, adequately, amply, reasonably, satisfactorily, tolerably

enquire SEE INQUIRE

enquiry SEE INQUIRY

enrage *verb* anger, exasperate, incense, inflame, infuriate, madden

enrich *verb* **1** enhance, augment, develop, improve, refine, supplement **2** make rich, make wealthy

enrol *verb* enlist, accept, admit, join up, recruit, register, sign up or on, take on

enrolment *noun* enlistment, acceptance, admission, engagement, matriculation, recruitment, registration

en route *adverb* on or along the way, in transit, on the road

ensemble *noun* **1** whole, aggregate, collection, entirety, set, sum, total, totality **2** outfit, costume, get-up (*informal*), suit **3** group, band, cast, chorus, company, troupe

ensign *noun* flag, banner, colours, jack, pennant, pennon, standard, streamer

ensue *verb* follow, arise, come next, derive, flow, issue, proceed, result, stem

ensure *verb* **1** make certain, certify, confirm, effect, guarantee, make sure, secure, warrant **2** protect, guard, make safe, safeguard, secure

entail *verb* involve, bring about,

call for, demand, give rise to, necessitate, occasion, require

entangle *verb* **1** tangle, catch, embroil, enmesh, ensnare, entrap, implicate, snag, snare, trap **2** mix up, complicate, confuse, jumble, muddle, perplex, puzzle

enter *verb* **1** come or go in or into, arrive, make an entrance, pass into, penetrate, pierce **2** join, commence, embark upon, enlist, enrol, set out on, start, take up **3** record, inscribe, list, log, note, register, set down, take down

enterprise *noun* **1** firm, business, company, concern, establishment, operation **2** undertaking, adventure, effort, endeavour, operation, plan, programme, project, venture **3** initiative, adventurousness, boldness, daring, drive, energy, enthusiasm, resourcefulness

enterprising *adjective* resourceful, adventurous, bold, daring, energetic, enthusiastic, go-ahead, intrepid, spirited

entertain *verb* **1** amuse, charm, cheer, delight, please, regale **2** show hospitality to, accommodate, be host to, harbour, have company, lodge, put up, treat **3** consider, conceive, contemplate, imagine, keep in mind, think about

entertaining *adjective* enjoyable, amusing, cheering, diverting, funny, humorous, interesting, pleasant, pleasurable

entertainment *noun* enjoyment, amusement, fun, leisure activity, pastime, pleasure, recreation, sport, treat

enthral verb fascinate, captivate, charm, enchant, enrapture, entrance, grip, mesmerize

enthusiasm noun keenness, eagerness, fervour, interest, passion, relish, zeal, zest

enthusiast noun lover, aficionado, buff (*informal*), devotee, fan, fanatic, follower, supporter

enthusiastic adjective keen, avid, eager, fervent, passionate, vigorous, wholehearted, zealous

entice verb attract, allure, cajole, coax, lead on, lure, persuade, seduce, tempt

entire adjective whole, complete, full, gross, total

entirely adverb completely, absolutely, altogether, fully, in every respect, thoroughly, totally, utterly, wholly

entitle verb 1 give the right to, allow, authorize, empower, enable, license, permit 2 call, christen, dub, label, name, term, title

entity noun thing, being, creature, individual, object, organism, substance

entourage noun retinue, associates, attendants, company, court, escort, followers, staff, train

entrails plural noun intestines, bowels, guts, innards (*informal*), insides (*informal*), offal, viscera

entrance¹ noun 1 way in, access, door, doorway, entry, gate, opening, passage 2 appearance, arrival, coming in, entry, introduction 3 admission, access,

admittance, entrée, entry, permission to enter

entrance² verb 1 enchant, bewitch, captivate, charm, delight, enrapture, enthral, fascinate 2 mesmerize, hypnotize, put in a trance

entrant noun competitor, candidate, contestant, entry, participant, player

entreaty noun plea, appeal, earnest request, exhortation, petition, prayer, request, supplication

entrenched adjective fixed, deep-rooted, deep-seated, ineradicable, ingrained, rooted, set, unshakable, well-established

entrepreneur noun businessman or businesswoman, impresario, industrialist, magnate, tycoon

entrust verb give custody of, assign, commit, confide, delegate, deliver, hand over, turn over

entry noun 1 way in, access, door, doorway, entrance, gate, opening, passage 2 coming in, appearance, entering, entrance, initiation, introduction 3 admission, access, entrance, entrée, permission to enter 4 record, account, item, listing, note

entwine verb twist, interlace, interweave, knit, plait, twine, weave, wind

enumerate verb list, cite, itemize, mention, name, quote, recite, recount, relate, spell out

enunciate verb 1 pronounce, articulate, enounce, say, sound, speak, utter, vocalize, voice

2 state, declare, proclaim, promulgate, pronounce, propound, publish

envelop verb <u>enclose</u>, cloak, cover, encase, encircle, engulf, shroud, surround, wrap

envelope noun <u>wrapping</u>, case, casing, cover, covering, jacket, wrapper

enviable adjective <u>desirable</u>, advantageous, favoured, fortunate, lucky, privileged, to die for (informal)

envious adjective <u>covetous</u>, green with envy, grudging, jealous, resentful

environment noun <u>surroundings</u>, atmosphere, background, conditions, habitat, medium, setting, situation

environmental adjective <u>ecological</u>, green

environmentalist noun <u>conservationist</u>, ecologist, green

environs plural noun <u>surrounding area</u>, district, locality, neighbourhood, outskirts, precincts, suburbs, vicinity

envisage verb **1** <u>imagine</u>, conceive (of), conceptualize, contemplate, fancy, picture, think up, visualize **2** <u>foresee</u>, anticipate, envision, predict, see

envoy noun <u>messenger</u>, agent, ambassador, courier, delegate, diplomat, emissary, intermediary, representative

envy noun **1** <u>covetousness</u>, enviousness, jealousy, resentfulness, resentment ♦ verb **2** <u>covet</u>, be envious (of), begrudge, be jealous (of), grudge, resent

ephemeral adjective <u>brief</u>, fleeting, momentary, passing, short-lived, temporary, transient, transitory

epidemic noun <u>spread</u>, contagion, growth, outbreak, plague, rash, upsurge, wave

epigram noun <u>witticism</u>, aphorism, bon mot, quip

epilogue noun <u>conclusion</u>, coda, concluding speech, postscript

episode noun **1** <u>event</u>, adventure, affair, escapade, experience, happening, incident, matter, occurrence **2** <u>part</u>, chapter, instalment, passage, scene, section

epistle noun <u>letter</u>, communication, message, missive, note

epitaph noun <u>monument</u>, inscription

epithet noun <u>name</u>, appellation, description, designation, moniker or monicker (slang), nickname, sobriquet, tag, title

epitome noun <u>personification</u>, archetype, embodiment, essence, quintessence, representation, type, typical example

epitomize verb <u>typify</u>, embody, exemplify, illustrate, personify, represent, symbolize

epoch noun <u>era</u>, age, date, period, time

equable adjective <u>even-tempered</u>, calm, composed, easy-going, imperturbable, level-headed, placid, serene, unflappable (informal)

equal adjective **1** <u>identical</u>, alike, corresponding, equivalent, the same, uniform **2** regular, symmetrical, uniform, unvarying **3** even, balanced, evenly matched, fifty-fifty (*informal*), level pegging (*Brit. informal*) **4** fair, egalitarian, even-handed, impartial, just, unbiased **5** **equal to** capable of, competent to, fit for, good enough for, ready for, strong enough, suitable for, up to ♦ *noun* **6** match, counterpart, equivalent, rival, twin ♦ *verb* **7** match, amount to, be tantamount to, correspond to, equate, level, parallel, tie with

equality *noun* **1** sameness, balance, correspondence, equivalence, evenness, identity, likeness, similarity, uniformity **2** fairness, egalitarianism, equal opportunity, parity

equalize *verb* make equal, balance, equal, even up, level, match, regularize, smooth, square, standardize

equate *verb* make or be equal, be commensurate, compare, correspond with or to, liken, mention in the same breath, parallel

equation *noun* equating, comparison, correspondence, parallel

equilibrium *noun* stability, balance, equipoise, evenness, rest, steadiness, symmetry

equip *verb* supply, arm, array, fit out, furnish, kit out, provide, stock

equipment *noun* tools, accoutrements, apparatus, gear, paraphernalia, stuff, supplies, tackle

equitable *adjective* fair, even-handed, honest, impartial, just, proper, reasonable, unbiased

equivalence *noun* equality, correspondence, evenness, likeness, parity, sameness, similarity

equivalent *noun* **1** equal, counterpart, match, opposite number, parallel, twin ♦ *adjective* **2** equal, alike, commensurate, comparable, corresponding, interchangeable, of a piece, same, similar, tantamount

equivocal *adjective* ambiguous, evasive, indefinite, indeterminate, misleading, oblique, obscure, uncertain, vague

era *noun* age, date, day or days, epoch, generation, period, time

eradicate *verb* wipe out, annihilate, destroy, eliminate, erase, exterminate, extinguish, obliterate, remove, root out

erase *verb* wipe out, blot, cancel, delete, expunge, obliterate, remove, rub out

erect *verb* **1** build, construct, put up, raise, set up **2** found, create, establish, form, initiate, institute, organize, set up ♦ *adjective* **3** upright, elevated, perpendicular, pricked-up, stiff, straight, vertical

erode *verb* wear down or away, abrade, consume, corrode, destroy, deteriorate, disintegrate, eat away, grind down

erosion *noun* deterioration, abrasion, attrition, destruction, disintegration, eating away, grinding down, wearing down or away

erotic adjective sexual, amatory, carnal, lustful, seductive, sensual, sexy (informal), voluptuous

err verb make a mistake, blunder, go wrong, miscalculate, misjudge, mistake, slip up (informal)

errand noun job, charge, commission, message, mission, task

erratic adjective unpredictable, changeable, inconsistent, irregular, uneven, unreliable, unstable, variable, wayward

erroneous adjective incorrect, fallacious, false, faulty, flawed, invalid, mistaken, unsound, wrong

error noun mistake, bloomer (Brit. informal), blunder, howler (informal), miscalculation, oversight, slip, solecism

erstwhile adjective former, bygone, late, old, once, one-time, past, previous, sometime

erudite adjective learned, cultivated, cultured, educated, knowledgeable, scholarly, well-educated, well-read

erupt verb 1 explode, belch forth, blow up, burst out, gush, pour forth, spew forth or out, spout, throw off 2 Medical break out, appear

eruption noun 1 explosion, discharge, ejection, flare-up, outbreak, outburst 2 Medical inflammation, outbreak, rash

escalate verb increase, expand, extend, grow, heighten, intensify, mount, rise

escapade noun adventure, antic, caper, prank, scrape (informal), stunt

escape verb 1 get away, abscond, bolt, break free or out, flee, fly, make one's getaway, run away or off, slip away 2 avoid, dodge, duck, elude, evade, pass, shun, slip 3 leak, emanate, exude, flow, gush, issue, pour forth, seep ♦ noun 4 getaway, break, break-out, flight 5 avoidance, circumvention, evasion 6 relaxation, distraction, diversion, pastime, recreation 7 leak, emanation, emission, seepage

escort noun 1 guard, bodyguard, convoy, cortege, entourage, retinue, train 2 companion, attendant, beau, chaperon, guide, partner ♦ verb 3 accompany, chaperon, conduct, guide, lead, partner, shepherd, usher

especial adjective Formal exceptional, noteworthy, outstanding, principal, special, uncommon, unusual

especially adverb exceptionally, conspicuously, markedly, notably, outstandingly, remarkably, specially, strikingly, uncommonly, unusually

espionage noun spying, counter-intelligence, intelligence, surveillance, undercover work

espousal noun support, adoption, advocacy, backing, championing, defence, embracing, promotion, taking up

espouse verb support, adopt, advocate, back, champion, embrace, promote, stand up for, take up, uphold

essay noun **1** composition, article, discourse, dissertation, paper, piece, tract, treatise ◆ verb **2** Formal attempt, aim, endeavour, try, undertake

essence noun **1** fundamental nature, being, core, heart, nature, quintessence, soul, spirit, substance **2** concentrate, distillate, extract, spirits, tincture

essential adjective **1** vital, crucial, important, indispensable, necessary, needed, requisite **2** fundamental, basic, cardinal, elementary, innate, intrinsic, main, principal ◆ noun **3** prerequisite, basic, fundamental, must, necessity, rudiment, sine qua non

establish verb **1** create, constitute, form, found, ground, inaugurate, institute, settle, set up **2** prove, authenticate, certify, confirm, corroborate, demonstrate, substantiate, verify

establishment noun **1** creation, formation, foundation, founding, inauguration, installation, institution, organization, setting up **2** organization, business, company, concern, corporation, enterprise, firm, institution, outfit (informal) **3 the Establishment** the authorities, ruling class, the powers that be, the system

estate noun **1** lands, area, domain, holdings, manor, property **2** Law property, assets, belongings, effects, fortune, goods, possessions, wealth

esteem noun **1** respect, admiration, credit, estimation, good opinion, honour, regard,

reverence, veneration ◆ verb **2** respect, admire, love, prize, regard highly, revere, think highly of, treasure, value **3** Formal consider, believe, deem, estimate, judge, reckon, regard, think, view

estimate verb **1** calculate roughly, assess, evaluate, gauge, guess, judge, number, reckon, value **2** form an opinion, believe, conjecture, consider, judge, rank, rate, reckon, surmise ◆ noun **3** approximate calculation, assessment, ballpark figure (informal), guess, guesstimate (informal), judgment, valuation **4** opinion, appraisal, assessment, belief, estimation, judgment

estimation noun opinion, appraisal, appreciation, assessment, belief, consideration, considered opinion, judgment, view

estuary noun inlet, creek, firth, fjord, mouth

et cetera adverb **1** and so on, and so forth ◆ noun **2** and the rest, and others, and the like, et al.

etch verb cut, carve, eat into, engrave, impress, imprint, inscribe, stamp

etching noun print, carving, engraving, impression, imprint, inscription

eternal adjective **1** everlasting, endless, immortal, infinite, never-ending, perpetual, timeless, unceasing, unending **2** permanent, deathless, enduring, immutable, imperishable, indestructible, lasting, unchanging

eternity noun 1 <u>infinity</u>, ages, endlessness, immortality, perpetuity, timelessness 2 *Theology* <u>the afterlife</u>, heaven, paradise, the hereafter, the next world

ethical adjective <u>moral</u>, conscientious, fair, good, honourable, just, principled, proper, right, upright, virtuous

ethics plural noun <u>moral code</u>, conscience, morality, moral philosophy, moral values, principles, rules of conduct, standards

ethnic, ethnical adjective <u>cultural</u>, folk, indigenous, national, native, racial, traditional

etiquette noun <u>good or proper behaviour</u>, civility, courtesy, decorum, formalities, manners, politeness, propriety, protocol

euphoria noun <u>elation</u>, ecstasy, exaltation, exhilaration, intoxication, joy, jubilation, rapture

evacuate verb <u>clear</u>, abandon, desert, forsake, leave, move out, pull out, quit, vacate, withdraw

evade verb 1 <u>avoid</u>, dodge, duck, elude, escape, get away from, sidestep, steer clear of 2 <u>avoid answering</u>, equivocate, fend off, fudge, hedge, parry

evaluate verb <u>assess</u>, appraise, calculate, estimate, gauge, judge, rate, reckon, size up (*informal*), weigh

evaporate verb 1 <u>dry up</u>, dehydrate, desiccate, dry, vaporize 2 <u>disappear</u>, dematerialize, dissolve, fade

away, melt away, vanish

evasion noun 1 <u>avoidance</u>, dodging, escape 2 <u>deception</u>, equivocation, evasiveness, prevarication

evasive adjective <u>deceptive</u>, cagey (*informal*), equivocating, indirect, oblique, prevaricating, shifty, slippery

eve noun 1 <u>night before</u>, day before, vigil 2 <u>brink</u>, edge, point, threshold, verge

even adjective 1 <u>level</u>, flat, horizontal, parallel, smooth, steady, straight, true, uniform 2 <u>regular</u>, constant, smooth, steady, unbroken, uniform, uninterrupted, unvarying, unwavering 3 <u>equal</u>, comparable, fifty-fifty (*informal*), identical, level, like, matching, neck and neck, on a par, similar, tied 4 <u>calm</u>, composed, cool, even-tempered, imperturbable, placid, unruffled, well-balanced 5 **get even (with)** *Informal* <u>pay back</u>, get one's own back, give tit for tat, reciprocate, repay, requite

evening noun <u>dusk</u>, gloaming (*Scot. or poetic*), twilight

event noun 1 <u>incident</u>, affair, business, circumstance, episode, experience, happening, occasion, occurrence 2 <u>competition</u>, bout, contest, game, tournament

even-tempered adjective <u>calm</u>, composed, cool, imperturbable, level-headed, placid, tranquil, unexcitable, unruffled

eventful adjective <u>exciting</u>, active, busy, dramatic, full, lively, memorable, remarkable

eventual adjective final, concluding, overall, ultimate

eventuality noun possibility, case, chance, contingency, event, likelihood, probability

eventually adverb in the end, after all, at the end of the day, finally, one day, some time, ultimately, when all is said and done

ever adverb 1 at any time, at all, at any period, at any point, by any chance, in any case, on any occasion 2 always, at all times, constantly, continually, evermore, for ever, perpetually

everlasting adjective eternal, endless, immortal, indestructible, never-ending, perpetual, timeless, undying

evermore adverb for ever, always, eternally, ever, to the end of time

every adjective each, all, each one

everybody pronoun everyone, all and sundry, each one, each person, every person, one and all, the whole world

everyday adjective common, customary, mundane, ordinary, routine, run-of-the-mill, stock, usual, workaday

everyone pronoun everybody, all and sundry, each one, each person, every person, one and all, the whole world

everything pronoun all, each thing, the lot, the whole lot

everywhere adverb to or in every place, all around, all over, far and wide or near, high and low, in every nook and cranny, the world over, ubiquitously

evict verb expel, boot out (informal), eject, kick out (informal), oust, remove, throw out, turf out (informal), turn out

evidence noun 1 proof, confirmation, corroboration, demonstration, grounds, indication, sign, substantiation, testimony ♦ verb 2 show, demonstrate, display, exhibit, indicate, prove, reveal, signify, witness

evident adjective obvious, apparent, clear, manifest, noticeable, perceptible, plain, unmistakable, visible

evidently adverb 1 obviously, clearly, manifestly, plainly, undoubtedly, unmistakably, without question 2 apparently, ostensibly, outwardly, seemingly, to all appearances

evil noun 1 wickedness, badness, depravity, malignity, sin, vice, villainy, wrongdoing 2 harm, affliction, disaster, hurt, ill, injury, mischief, misfortune, suffering, woe ♦ adjective 3 wicked, bad, depraved, immoral, malevolent, malicious, sinful, villainous 4 harmful, calamitous, catastrophic, destructive, dire, disastrous, pernicious, ruinous 5 offensive, foul, noxious, pestilential, unpleasant, vile

evoke verb recall, arouse, awaken, call, give rise to, induce, rekindle, stir up, summon up

evolution noun development, expansion, growth, increase, maturation, progress, unfolding, working out

evolve verb develop, expand,

grow, increase, mature, progress, unfold, work out

exact adjective **1** accurate, correct, definite, faultless, precise, right, specific, true, unerring ♦ verb **2** demand, claim, command, compel, extort, extract, force

exacting adjective demanding, difficult, hard, harsh, rigorous, severe, strict, stringent, taxing, tough

exactly adverb **1** precisely, accurately, correctly, explicitly, faithfully, scrupulously, truthfully, unerringly **2** in every respect, absolutely, indeed, precisely, quite, specifically, to the letter

exactness noun precision, accuracy, correctness, exactitude, rigorousness, scrupulousness, strictness, veracity

exaggerate verb overstate, amplify, embellish, embroider, enlarge, overemphasize, overestimate

exaggeration noun overstatement, amplification, embellishment, enlargement, hyperbole, overemphasis, overestimation

exalt verb **1** praise, acclaim, extol, glorify, idolize, set on a pedestal, worship **2** raise, advance, elevate, ennoble, honour, promote, upgrade

exaltation noun **1** praise, acclaim, glorification, idolization, reverence, tribute, worship **2** rise, advancement, elevation, ennoblement, promotion, upgrading

exalted adjective high-ranking, dignified, eminent, grand, honoured, lofty, prestigious

examination noun **1** inspection, analysis, exploration, interrogation, investigation, research, scrutiny, study, test **2** questioning, inquiry, inquisition, probe, quiz, test

examine verb **1** inspect, analyse, explore, investigate, peruse, scrutinize, study, survey **2** question, cross-examine, grill (informal), inquire, interrogate, quiz, test

example noun **1** specimen, case, illustration, instance, sample **2** model, archetype, ideal, paradigm, paragon, prototype, standard **3** warning, caution, lesson

exasperate verb irritate, anger, annoy, enrage, incense, inflame, infuriate, madden, pique

exasperation noun irritation, anger, annoyance, fury, pique, provocation, rage, wrath

excavate verb dig out, burrow, delve, dig up, mine, quarry, tunnel, uncover, unearth

exceed verb **1** surpass, beat, better, cap (informal), eclipse, outdo, outstrip, overtake, pass, top **2** go over the limit of, go over the top, overstep

exceedingly adverb extremely, enormously, exceptionally, extraordinarily, hugely, superlatively, surpassingly, unusually, very

excel verb **1** be superior, beat, eclipse, outdo, outshine, surpass, transcend **2** excel in or at be good at, be proficient in, be skilful at, be talented at, shine at, show talent in

excellence noun high quality, distinction, eminence, goodness, greatness, merit, pre-eminence, superiority, supremacy

excellent adjective outstanding, brilliant, exquisite, fine, first-class, first-rate, good, great, superb, superlative, world-class

except preposition 1 Also **except for** apart from, barring, besides, but, excepting, excluding, omitting, other than, saving, with the exception of ♦ verb 2 exclude, leave out, omit, pass over

exception noun 1 special case, anomaly, deviation, freak, inconsistency, irregularity, oddity, peculiarity 2 exclusion, leaving out, omission, passing over

exceptional adjective 1 special, abnormal, atypical, extraordinary, irregular, odd, peculiar, strange, unusual 2 remarkable, excellent, extraordinary, marvellous, outstanding, phenomenal, prodigious, special, superior

excerpt noun extract, fragment, part, passage, piece, quotation, section, selection

excess noun 1 surfeit, glut, overload, superabundance, superfluity, surplus, too much 2 overindulgence, debauchery, dissipation, dissoluteness, extravagance, intemperance, prodigality

excessive adjective immoderate, disproportionate, exaggerated, extreme, inordinate, overmuch, superfluous, too much, undue,

unfair, unreasonable

exchange verb 1 interchange, barter, change, convert into, swap, switch, trade ♦ noun 2 interchange, barter, quid pro quo, reciprocity, substitution, swap, switch, tit for tat, trade

excitable adjective nervous, emotional, highly strung, hot-headed, mercurial, quick-tempered, temperamental, volatile

excite verb arouse, animate, galvanize, inflame, inspire, provoke, rouse, stir up, thrill

excitement noun agitation, action, activity, animation, commotion, furore, passion, thrill

exciting adjective stimulating, dramatic, electrifying, exhilarating, rousing, sensational, stirring, thrilling

exclaim verb cry out, call out, declare, proclaim, shout, utter, yell

exclamation noun cry, call, interjection, outcry, shout, utterance, yell

exclude verb 1 keep out, ban, bar, boycott, disallow, forbid, prohibit, refuse, shut out 2 leave out, count out, eliminate, ignore, omit, pass over, reject, rule out, set aside

exclusion noun 1 ban, bar, boycott, disqualification, embargo, prohibition, veto 2 elimination, omission, rejection

exclusive adjective 1 sole, absolute, complete, entire, full, total, undivided, whole 2 limited, confined, peculiar, restricted, unique 3 select, chic, cliquish, fashionable, posh (*informal, chiefly Brit.*), restricted, snobbish, up-market

excommunicate *verb* expel, anathematize, ban, banish, cast out, denounce, exclude, repudiate

excruciating *adjective* agonizing, harrowing, insufferable, intense, piercing, severe, unbearable, violent

exculpate *verb* absolve, acquit, clear, discharge, excuse, exonerate, pardon, vindicate

excursion *noun* trip, day trip, expedition, jaunt, journey, outing, pleasure trip, ramble, tour

excusable *adjective* forgivable, allowable, defensible, justifiable, pardonable, permissible, understandable, warrantable

excuse *noun* 1 justification, apology, defence, explanation, grounds, mitigation, plea, reason, vindication ♦ *verb* 2 justify, apologize for, defend, explain, mitigate, vindicate 3 forgive, acquit, exculpate, exonerate, make allowances for, overlook, pardon, tolerate, turn a blind eye to 4 free, absolve, discharge, exempt, let off, release, relieve, spare

execute *verb* 1 put to death, behead, electrocute, guillotine, hang, kill, shoot 2 carry out, accomplish, administer, discharge, effect, enact, implement, perform, prosecute

execution *noun* 1 carrying out, accomplishment, administration, enactment, enforcement, implementation, operation, performance, prosecution

2 killing, capital punishment, hanging

executioner *noun* 1 hangman, headsman 2 killer, assassin, exterminator, hit man (*slang*), liquidator, murderer, slayer

executive *noun* 1 administrator, director, manager, official 2 administration, directorate, directors, government, hierarchy, leadership, management ♦ *adjective* 3 administrative, controlling, decision-making, directing, governing, managerial

exemplary *adjective* 1 ideal, admirable, commendable, excellent, fine, good, model, praiseworthy 2 warning, cautionary

exemplify *verb* show, demonstrate, display, embody, exhibit, illustrate, represent, serve as an example of

exempt *adjective* 1 immune, excepted, excused, free, not liable, released, spared ♦ *verb* 2 grant immunity, absolve, discharge, excuse, free, let off, release, relieve, spare

exemption *noun* immunity, absolution, discharge, dispensation, exception, exoneration, freedom, release

exercise *noun* 1 exertion, activity, effort, labour, toil, training, work, work-out 2 task, drill, lesson, practice, problem 3 use, application, discharge, fulfilment, implementation, practice, utilization ♦ *verb* 4 put to use, apply, bring to bear, employ, exert, use, utilize 5 train, practise, work out

exert *verb* 1 use, apply, bring to

bear, employ, exercise, make use of, utilize, wield **2 exert oneself** <u>make an effort</u>, apply oneself, do one's best, endeavour, labour, strain, strive, struggle, toil, work

exertion noun <u>effort</u>, elbow grease (facetious), endeavour, exercise, industry, strain, struggle, toil

exhaust verb **1** <u>tire out</u>, debilitate, drain, enervate, enfeeble, fatigue, sap, weaken, wear out **2** <u>use up</u>, consume, deplete, dissipate, expend, run through, spend, squander, waste

exhausted adjective **1** <u>worn out</u>, all in (slang), debilitated, done in (informal), drained, fatigued, knackered (slang), spent, tired out **2** <u>used up</u>, consumed, depleted, dissipated, expended, finished, spent, squandered, wasted

exhausting adjective <u>tiring</u>, backbreaking, debilitating, gruelling, laborious, punishing, sapping, strenuous, taxing

exhaustion noun **1** <u>tiredness</u>, debilitation, fatigue, weariness **2** <u>depletion</u>, consumption, emptying, using up

exhaustive adjective <u>thorough</u>, all-embracing, complete, comprehensive, extensive, full-scale, in-depth, intensive

exhibit verb <u>display</u>, demonstrate, express, indicate, manifest, parade, put on view, reveal, show

exhibition noun <u>display</u>, demonstration, exposition, performance, presentation, representation, show, spectacle

exhilarating adjective <u>exciting</u>, breathtaking, enlivening, invigorating, stimulating, thrilling

exhort verb Formal <u>urge</u>, advise, beseech, call upon, entreat, persuade, press, spur

exhume verb Formal <u>dig up</u>, disentomb, disinter, unearth

exigency, exigence noun <u>need</u>, constraint, demand, necessity, requirement

exile noun **1** <u>banishment</u>, deportation, expatriation, expulsion **2** <u>expatriate</u>, deportee, émigré, outcast, refugee ♦ verb **3** <u>banish</u>, deport, drive out, eject, expatriate, expel

exist verb **1** <u>be</u>, be present, endure, live, occur, survive **2** <u>survive</u>, eke out a living, get along or by, keep one's head above water, stay alive, subsist

existence noun <u>being</u>, actuality, life, subsistence

existent adjective <u>in existence</u>, alive, existing, extant, living, present, standing, surviving

exit noun **1** <u>way out</u>, door, gate, outlet **2** <u>departure</u>, exodus, farewell, going, goodbye, leave-taking, retreat, withdrawal ♦ verb **3** <u>depart</u>, go away, go offstage (Theatre), go out, leave, make tracks, retire, retreat, take one's leave, withdraw

exodus noun <u>departure</u>, evacuation, exit, flight, going out, leaving, migration, retreat, withdrawal

exonerate verb <u>clear</u>, absolve, acquit, discharge, exculpate, excuse, justify, pardon, vindicate

exorbitant adjective <u>excessive</u>, extortionate, extravagant, immoderate, inordinate, outrageous, preposterous, unreasonable

exorcise verb drive out, cast out, deliver (from), expel, purify

exotic adjective **1** unusual, colourful, fascinating, glamorous, mysterious, strange, striking, unfamiliar **2** foreign, alien, external, imported, naturalized

expand verb **1** increase, amplify, broaden, develop, enlarge, extend, grow, magnify, swell, widen **2** spread (out), diffuse, stretch (out), unfold, unfurl, unravel, unroll **3** expand on go into detail about, amplify, develop, elaborate on, embellish, enlarge on, expatiate on, expound on, flesh out

expanse noun area, breadth, extent, range, space, stretch, sweep, tract

expansion noun increase, amplification, development, enlargement, growth, magnification, opening out, spread

expansive adjective **1** wide, broad, extensive, far-reaching, voluminous, wide-ranging, widespread **2** talkative, affable, communicative, effusive, friendly, loquacious, open, outgoing, sociable, unreserved

expatriate adjective **1** exiled, banished, emigrant, émigré ♦ noun **2** exile, emigrant, émigré, refugee

expect verb **1** think, assume, believe, imagine, presume, reckon, suppose, surmise, trust **2** look forward to, anticipate, await, contemplate, envisage,

hope for, predict, watch for **3** require, call for, demand, insist on, want

expectant adjective **1** expecting, anticipating, apprehensive, eager, hopeful, in suspense, ready, watchful **2** pregnant, expecting (informal), gravid

expectation noun **1** probability, assumption, belief, conjecture, forecast, likelihood, presumption, supposition **2** anticipation, apprehension, expectancy, hope, promise, suspense

expediency noun suitability, advisability, benefit, convenience, pragmatism, profitability, prudence, usefulness, utility

expedient noun **1** means, contrivance, device, makeshift, measure, method, resort, scheme, stopgap ♦ adjective **2** advantageous, appropriate, beneficial, convenient, effective, helpful, opportune, practical, suitable, useful

expedition noun journey, excursion, mission, quest, safari, tour, trek, voyage

expel verb **1** drive out, belch, cast out, discharge, eject, remove, spew **2** dismiss, ban, banish, drum out, evict, exclude, exile, throw out, turf out (informal)

expend verb Formal spend, consume, dissipate, exhaust, go through, pay out, use (up)

expendable adjective dispensable, inessential, nonessential, replaceable, unimportant, unnecessary

expenditure noun spending,

consumption, cost, expense, outgoings, outlay, output, payment

expense noun <u>cost</u>, charge, expenditure, loss, outlay, payment, spending

expensive adjective <u>dear</u>, costly, exorbitant, extravagant, high-priced, lavish, overpriced, steep (informal), stiff

experience noun 1 <u>knowledge</u>, contact, exposure, familiarity, involvement, participation, practice, training 2 <u>event</u>, adventure, affair, encounter, episode, happening, incident, occurrence ◆ verb 3 <u>undergo</u>, encounter, endure, face, feel, go through, live through, sample, taste

experienced adjective <u>knowledgeable</u>, accomplished, expert, practised, seasoned, tested, tried, veteran, well-versed

experiment noun 1 <u>test</u>, examination, experimentation, investigation, procedure, proof, research, trial, trial run ◆ verb 2 <u>test</u>, examine, investigate, put to the test, research, sample, try, verify

experimental adjective <u>test</u>, exploratory, pilot, preliminary, probationary, provisional, speculative, tentative, trial, trial-and-error

expert noun 1 <u>master</u>, authority, connoisseur, dab hand (Brit. informal), past master, professional, specialist, virtuoso ◆ adjective 2 <u>skilful</u>, adept, adroit, experienced, masterly, practised, professional, proficient, qualified, virtuoso

expertise noun <u>skill</u>, adroitness, command, facility, judgment, know-how (informal), knowledge, mastery, proficiency

expire verb 1 <u>finish</u>, cease, close, come to an end, conclude, end, lapse, run out, stop, terminate 2 <u>breathe out</u>, emit, exhale, expel 3 <u>die</u>, depart, kick the bucket (informal), pass away or on, perish

explain verb 1 <u>make clear or plain</u>, clarify, clear up, define, describe, elucidate, expound, resolve, teach 2 <u>account for</u>, excuse, give a reason for, justify

explanation noun 1 <u>reason</u>, account, answer, excuse, justification, motive, vindication 2 <u>description</u>, clarification, definition, elucidation, illustration, interpretation

explanatory adjective <u>descriptive</u>, illustrative, interpretive

explicit adjective <u>clear</u>, categorical, definite, frank, precise, specific, straightforward, unambiguous

explode verb 1 <u>blow up</u>, burst, detonate, discharge, erupt, go off, set off, shatter 2 <u>disprove</u>, debunk, discredit, give the lie to, invalidate, refute, repudiate

exploit verb 1 <u>take advantage of</u>, abuse, manipulate, milk, misuse, play on or upon 2 <u>make the best use of</u>, capitalize on, cash in on (informal), profit by or from, use, utilize ◆ noun 3 <u>feat</u>, accomplishment, achievement, adventure, attainment, deed, escapade, stunt

exploitation noun <u>misuse</u>, abuse, manipulation

exploration *noun*
1 <u>investigation</u>, analysis, examination, inquiry, inspection, research, scrutiny, search
2 <u>expedition</u>, reconnaissance, survey, tour, travel, trip

exploratory *adjective*
<u>investigative</u>, experimental, fact-finding, probing, searching, trial

explore *verb* 1 <u>investigate</u>, examine, inquire into, inspect, look into, probe, research, search
2 <u>travel</u>, reconnoitre, scout, survey, tour

explosion *noun* 1 <u>bang</u>, blast, burst, clap, crack, detonation, discharge, report 2 <u>outburst</u>, eruption, fit, outbreak

explosive *adjective* 1 <u>unstable</u>, volatile 2 <u>violent</u>, fiery, stormy, touchy, vehement

exponent *noun* 1 <u>advocate</u>, backer, champion, defender, promoter, proponent, supporter, upholder 2 <u>performer</u>, player

expose *verb* 1 <u>uncover</u>, display, exhibit, present, reveal, show, unveil 2 <u>make vulnerable</u>, endanger, imperil, jeopardize, lay open, leave open, subject

exposed *adjective* 1 <u>unconcealed</u>, bare, on display, on show, on view, revealed, uncovered
2 <u>unsheltered</u>, open, unprotected 3 <u>vulnerable</u>, in peril, laid bare, susceptible, wide open

exposure *noun* <u>publicity</u>, display, exhibition, presentation, revelation, showing, uncovering, unveiling

expound *verb* <u>explain</u>, describe, elucidate, interpret, set forth, spell out, unfold

express *verb* 1 <u>state</u>, articulate, communicate, declare, phrase, put into words, say, utter, voice, word 2 <u>show</u>, convey, exhibit, indicate, intimate, make known, represent, reveal, signify, stand for, symbolize ♦ *adjective*
3 <u>explicit</u>, categorical, clear, definite, distinct, plain, unambiguous 4 <u>specific</u>, clear-cut, especial, particular, singular, special 5 <u>fast</u>, direct, high-speed, nonstop, rapid, speedy, swift

expression *noun* 1 <u>statement</u>, announcement, communication, declaration, utterance
2 <u>indication</u>, demonstration, exhibition, manifestation, representation, show, sign, symbol, token 3 <u>look</u>, air, appearance, aspect, countenance, face 4 <u>phrase</u>, idiom, locution, remark, term, turn of phrase, word

expressive *adjective* <u>vivid</u>, eloquent, moving, poignant, striking, telling

expressly *adverb* 1 <u>definitely</u>, categorically, clearly, distinctly, explicitly, in no uncertain terms, plainly, unambiguously
2 <u>specifically</u>, especially, particularly, specially

expulsion *noun* <u>ejection</u>, banishment, dismissal, eviction, exclusion, removal

exquisite *adjective* 1 <u>beautiful</u>, attractive, charming, comely, lovely, pleasing, striking 2 <u>fine</u>, beautiful, dainty, delicate, elegant, lovely, precious
3 <u>intense</u>, acute, keen, sharp

extempore *adverb, adjective* impromptu, ad lib, freely, improvised, offhand, off the cuff (*informal*), spontaneously, unpremeditated, unprepared

extend *verb* 1 make longer, drag out, draw out, lengthen, prolong, spin out, spread out, stretch 2 last, carry on, continue, go on 3 widen, add to, augment, broaden, enhance, enlarge, expand, increase, supplement 4 offer, confer, impart, present, proffer

extension *noun* 1 annexe, addition, appendage, appendix, supplement 2 lengthening, broadening, development, enlargement, expansion, increase, spread, widening

extensive *adjective* wide, broad, far-flung, far-reaching, large-scale, pervasive, spacious, vast, voluminous, widespread

extent *noun* size, amount, area, breadth, expanse, length, stretch, volume, width

extenuating *adjective* mitigating, justifying, moderating, qualifying

exterior *noun* 1 outside, coating, covering, façade, face, shell, skin, surface ♦ *adjective* 2 outside, external, outer, outermost, outward, surface

exterminate *verb* destroy, abolish, annihilate, eliminate, eradicate

external *adjective* 1 outer, exterior, outermost, outside, outward, surface 2 outside, alien, extrinsic, foreign

extinct *adjective* dead, defunct, gone, lost, vanished

extinction *noun* dying out, abolition, annihilation, destruction, eradication, extermination, obliteration, oblivion

extinguish *verb* 1 put out, blow out, douse, quench, smother, snuff out, stifle 2 destroy, annihilate, eliminate, end, eradicate, exterminate, remove, wipe out

extol *verb* praise, acclaim, commend, eulogize, exalt, glorify, sing the praises of

extort *verb* force, blackmail, bully, coerce, extract, squeeze

extortionate *adjective* exorbitant, excessive, extravagant, inflated, outrageous, preposterous, sky-high, unreasonable

extra *adjective* 1 additional, added, ancillary, auxiliary, further, more, supplementary 2 surplus, excess, leftover, redundant, spare, superfluous, unused ♦ *noun* 3 addition, accessory, attachment, bonus, extension, supplement ♦ *adverb* 4 exceptionally, especially, extraordinarily, extremely, particularly, remarkably, uncommonly, unusually

extract *verb* 1 pull out, draw, pluck out, pull, remove, take out, uproot, withdraw 2 derive, draw, elicit, glean, obtain ♦ *noun* 3 passage, citation, clipping, cutting, excerpt, quotation, selection 4 essence, concentrate, distillation, juice

extraneous *adjective* irrelevant, beside the point, immaterial, inappropriate, off the subject, unconnected, unrelated

extraordinary adjective unusual, amazing, exceptional, fantastic, outstanding, phenomenal, remarkable, strange, uncommon

extravagance noun 1 waste, lavishness, overspending, prodigality, profligacy, squandering, wastefulness 2 excess, exaggeration, outrageousness, preposterousness, wildness

extravagant adjective 1 wasteful, lavish, prodigal, profligate, spendthrift 2 excessive, outrageous, over the top (slang), preposterous, reckless, unreasonable

extreme adjective 1 maximum, acute, great, highest, intense, severe, supreme, ultimate, utmost 2 severe, drastic, harsh, radical, rigid, strict, uncompromising 3 excessive, fanatical, immoderate, radical 4 farthest, far-off, most distant, outermost, remotest ♦ noun 5 limit, boundary, edge, end, extremity, pole

extremely adverb very, awfully (informal), exceedingly, exceptionally, extraordinarily, severely, terribly, uncommonly, unusually

extremist noun fanatic, die-hard, radical, zealot

extremity noun 1 limit, border, boundary, edge, extreme, frontier, pinnacle, tip 2 crisis, adversity, dire straits, disaster, emergency, exigency, trouble 3 extremities hands and feet, fingers and toes, limbs

extricate verb free, disengage, disentangle, get out, release, remove, rescue, wriggle out of

extrovert adjective outgoing, exuberant, gregarious, sociable

exuberance noun 1 high spirits, cheerfulness, ebullience, enthusiasm, liveliness, spirit, vitality, vivacity, zest 2 luxuriance, abundance, copiousness, lavishness, profusion

exuberant adjective 1 high-spirited, animated, cheerful, ebullient, energetic, enthusiastic, lively, spirited, vivacious 2 luxuriant, abundant, copious, lavish, plentiful, profuse

exult verb be joyful, be overjoyed, celebrate, jump for joy, rejoice

eye noun 1 eyeball, optic (informal) 2 appreciation, discernment, discrimination, judgment, perception, recognition, taste ♦ verb 3 look at, check out (informal), contemplate, inspect, study, survey, view, watch

eyesight noun vision, perception, sight

eyesore noun mess, blemish, blot, disfigurement, horror, monstrosity, sight (informal)

eyewitness noun observer, bystander, onlooker, passer-by, spectator, viewer, witness

F f

fable noun 1 story, allegory, legend, myth, parable, tale 2 fiction, fabrication, fantasy, invention, tall story (informal), urban legend, yarn (informal)

fabric noun 1 cloth, material, stuff, textile, web 2 framework, constitution, construction, foundations, make-up, organization, structure

fabricate verb 1 make up, concoct, devise, fake, falsify, feign, forge, invent, trump up 2 build, assemble, construct, erect, form, make, manufacture, shape

fabrication noun 1 forgery, concoction, fake, falsehood, fiction, invention, lie, myth 2 construction, assembly, building, erection, manufacture, production

fabulous adjective 1 *Informal* wonderful, brilliant, fantastic (*informal*), marvellous, out-of-this-world (*informal*), sensational (*informal*), spectacular, superb 2 astounding, amazing, breathtaking, inconceivable, incredible, phenomenal, unbelievable 3 legendary, apocryphal, fantastic, fictitious, imaginary, invented, made-up, mythical, unreal

façade noun appearance, exterior, face, front, guise, mask, pretence, semblance, show

face noun 1 countenance, features, mug (*slang*), visage 2 expression, appearance, aspect, look 3 scowl, frown, grimace, pout, smirk 4 façade, appearance, display, exterior, front, mask, show 5 side, exterior, front, outside, surface 6 self-respect, authority, dignity, honour, image, prestige, reputation, standing, status

♦ verb 7 meet, brave, come up against, confront, deal with, encounter, experience, oppose, tackle 8 look onto, be opposite, front onto, overlook 9 coat, clad, cover, dress, finish

faceless adjective impersonal, anonymous, remote

facet noun aspect, angle, face, part, phase, plane, side, slant, surface

facetious adjective funny, amusing, comical, droll, flippant, frivolous, humorous, jocular, playful, tongue in cheek

face up to verb accept, acknowledge, come to terms with, confront, cope with, deal with, meet head-on, tackle

facile adjective superficial, cursory, glib, hasty, shallow, slick

facilitate verb promote, expedite, forward, further, help, make easy, pave the way for, speed up

facility noun 1 skill, ability, adroitness, dexterity, ease, efficiency, effortlessness, fluency, proficiency 2 *often plural* equipment, advantage, aid, amenity, appliance, convenience, means, opportunity, resource

facsimile noun copy, carbon copy, duplicate, fax, photocopy, print, replica, reproduction, transcript

fact noun 1 event, act, deed, *fait accompli*, happening, incident, occurrence, performance 2 truth, certainty, reality

faction noun 1 group, bloc, cabal, clique, contingent, coterie, gang, party, set, splinter group **2** <u>dissension</u>, conflict, disagreement, discord, disunity, division, infighting, rebellion

factor noun <u>element</u>, aspect, cause, component, consideration, influence, item, part

factory noun <u>works</u>, mill, plant

factual adjective <u>true</u>, authentic, correct, exact, genuine, precise, real, true-to-life

faculties plural noun <u>powers</u>, capabilities, intelligence, reason, senses, wits

faculty noun **1** <u>ability</u>, aptitude, capacity, facility, power, propensity, skill **2** <u>department</u>, school

fad noun <u>craze</u>, fashion, mania, rage, trend, vogue, whim

fade verb **1** <u>pale</u>, bleach, discolour, lose colour, wash out **2** <u>dwindle</u>, decline, die away, disappear, dissolve, melt away, vanish, wane

faded adjective <u>discoloured</u>, bleached, dull, indistinct, pale, washed out

fading adjective <u>declining</u>, decreasing, disappearing, dying, on the decline, vanishing

fail verb **1** <u>be unsuccessful</u>, bite the dust, break down, come to grief, come unstuck, fall, fizzle out (informal), flop (informal), founder, miscarry, misfire **2** <u>disappoint</u>, abandon, desert, forget, forsake, let down, neglect, omit **3** <u>give out</u>, conk out (informal), cut out, die, peter out, stop working **4** <u>go bankrupt</u>, become insolvent, close down, fold (informal), go

broke (informal), go bust (informal), go into receivership, go out of business, go to the wall, go under ◆ noun **5** <u>without fail</u> <u>regularly</u>, conscientiously, constantly, dependably, like clockwork, punctually, religiously, without exception

failing noun **1** <u>weakness</u>, blemish, defect, deficiency, drawback, fault, flaw, imperfection, shortcoming ◆ preposition **2** <u>in the absence of</u>, in default of, lacking

failure noun **1** <u>defeat</u>, breakdown, collapse, downfall, fiasco, lack of success, miscarriage, overthrow **2** <u>loser</u>, black sheep, dead duck (slang), disappointment, dud (informal), flop (informal), nonstarter, washout (informal) **3** <u>bankruptcy</u>, crash, downfall, insolvency, liquidation, ruin

faint adjective **1** <u>dim</u>, distant, faded, indistinct, low, muted, soft, subdued, vague **2** <u>slight</u>, feeble, remote, unenthusiastic, weak **3** <u>dizzy</u>, exhausted, giddy, light-headed, muzzy, weak, woozy (informal) ◆ verb **4** <u>pass out</u>, black out, collapse, flake out (informal), keel over (informal), lose consciousness, swoon (literary) ◆ noun **5** <u>blackout</u>, collapse, swoon (literary), unconsciousness

faintly adverb **1** <u>softly</u>, feebly, in a whisper, indistinctly, weakly **2** <u>slightly</u>, a little, dimly, somewhat

fair¹ adjective **1** <u>unbiased</u>, above board, equitable, even-handed, honest, impartial, just, lawful, legitimate, proper, unprejudiced **2** light, blond, blonde, fair-haired, flaxen-haired, towheaded **3** respectable, adequate, average, decent, moderate, O.K. or okay (*informal*), passable, reasonable, satisfactory, tolerable **4** beautiful, bonny, comely, handsome, lovely, pretty **5** fine, bright, clear, cloudless, dry, sunny, unclouded

fair² *noun* carnival, bazaar, festival, fête, gala, show

fairly *adverb* **1** moderately, adequately, pretty well, quite, rather, reasonably, somewhat, tolerably **2** deservedly, equitably, honestly, impartially, justly, objectively, properly, without fear or favour **3** positively, absolutely, really

fairness *noun* impartiality, decency, disinterestedness, equitableness, equity, justice, legitimacy, rightfulness

fairy *noun* sprite, brownie, elf, leprechaun, peri, pixie, Robin Goodfellow

fairy tale *or* **fairy story** *noun* **1** folk tale, romance **2** lie, cock-and-bull story (*informal*), fabrication, fiction, invention, tall story, untruth

faith *noun* **1** confidence, assurance, conviction, credence, credit, dependence, reliance, trust **2** religion, belief, church, communion, creed, denomination, dogma, persuasion **3** allegiance, constancy, faithfulness, fidelity, loyalty

faithful *adjective* **1** loyal,

constant, dependable, devoted, reliable, staunch, steadfast, true, trusty **2** accurate, close, exact, precise, strict, true

faithless *adjective* disloyal, false, fickle, inconstant, traitorous, treacherous, unfaithful, untrue

fake *verb* **1** forge, copy, counterfeit, fabricate, feign, pretend, put on, sham, simulate ♦ *noun* **2** impostor, charlatan, copy, forgery, fraud, hoax, imitation, reproduction, sham ♦ *adjective* **3** artificial, counterfeit, false, forged, imitation, mock, phoney *or* phony (*informal*), sham

fall *verb* **1** descend, cascade, collapse, dive, drop, plummet, plunge, sink, subside, tumble **2** decrease, decline, diminish, drop, dwindle, go down, lessen, slump, subside **3** be overthrown, capitulate, pass into enemy hands, succumb, surrender **4** die, be killed, meet one's end, perish **5** occur, befall, chance, come about, come to pass, happen, take place **6** slope, fall away, incline **7** lapse, err, go astray, offend, sin, transgress, trespass ♦ *noun* **8** descent, dive, drop, nose dive, plummet, plunge, slip, tumble **9** decrease, cut, decline, dip, drop, lessening, lowering, reduction, slump **10** collapse, capitulation, defeat, destruction, downfall, overthrow, ruin **11** lapse, sin, transgression

fallacy *noun* error, delusion, falsehood, flaw, misapprehension, misconception, mistake, untruth

fallible *adjective* imperfect, erring,

frail, ignorant, uncertain, weak

fall out verb argue, clash, come to blows, differ, disagree, fight, quarrel, squabble

fallow adjective uncultivated, dormant, idle, inactive, resting, unplanted, unused

false adjective 1 incorrect, erroneous, faulty, inaccurate, inexact, invalid, mistaken, wrong 2 untrue, lying, unreliable, unsound, untruthful 3 artificial, bogus, counterfeit, fake, forged, imitation, sham, simulated 4 deceptive, deceitful, fallacious, fraudulent, hypocritical, misleading, trumped up

falsehood noun 1 untruthfulness, deceit, deception, dishonesty, dissimulation, mendacity 2 lie, fabrication, fib, fiction, story, untruth

falsify verb forge, alter, counterfeit, distort, doctor, fake, misrepresent, tamper with

falter verb hesitate, stammer, stumble, stutter, totter, vacillate, waver

faltering adjective hesitant, broken, irresolute, stammering, tentative, timid, uncertain, weak

fame noun prominence, celebrity, glory, honour, renown, reputation, repute, stardom

familiar adjective 1 well-known, accustomed, common, customary, frequent, ordinary, recognizable, routine 2 friendly, amicable, close, easy, intimate, relaxed 3 disrespectful, bold, forward, impudent, intrusive, presumptuous

familiarity noun 1 acquaintance,

awareness, experience, grasp, understanding 2 friendliness, ease, informality, intimacy, openness, sociability 3 disrespect, boldness, forwardness, presumption

familiarize verb accustom, habituate, instruct, inure, school, season, train

family noun 1 relations, folk (informal), household, kin, kith and kin, one's nearest and dearest, relatives 2 clan, dynasty, house, race, tribe 3 group, class, genre, network, subdivision, system

famine noun hunger, dearth, scarcity, starvation

famished adjective starving, ravenous, voracious

famous adjective well-known, acclaimed, celebrated, distinguished, eminent, illustrious, legendary, noted, prominent, renowned

fan¹ noun 1 blower, air conditioner, ventilator ♦ verb 2 blow, air-condition, cool, refresh, ventilate

fan² noun supporter, admirer, aficionado, buff (informal), devotee, enthusiast, follower, lover

fanatic noun extremist, activist, bigot, militant, zealot

fanatical adjective passionate, bigoted, extreme, fervent, frenzied, immoderate, obsessive, overenthusiastic, wild, zealous

fanciful adjective unreal, imaginary, mythical, romantic, visionary, whimsical, wild

fancy adjective **1** elaborate, baroque, decorative, embellished, extravagant, intricate, ornamental, ornate ♦ noun **2** whim, caprice, desire, humour, idea, impulse, inclination, notion, thought, urge **3** delusion, chimera, daydream, dream, fantasy, vision ♦ verb **4** suppose, believe, conjecture, imagine, reckon, think, think likely **5** wish for, crave, desire, hanker after, hope for, long for, thirst for, yearn for **6** Informal be attracted to, be captivated by, like, lust after, take a liking to, take to

fantasize verb daydream, dream, envision, imagine

fantastic adjective **1** Informal excellent, awesome (slang), first-rate, marvellous, sensational (informal), superb, wonderful **2** strange, fanciful, grotesque, outlandish **3** unrealistic, extravagant, far-fetched, ludicrous, ridiculous, wild **4** implausible, absurd, cock-and-bull (informal), incredible, preposterous, unlikely

fantasy noun **1** imagination, creativity, fancy, invention, originality **2** daydream, dream, flight of fancy, illusion, mirage, pipe dream, reverie, vision

far adverb **1** a long way, afar, a good way, a great distance, deep, miles **2** much, considerably, decidedly, extremely, greatly, incomparably, very much ♦ adjective **3** remote, distant, faraway, far-flung, far-off, outlying, out-of-the-way

farce noun **1** comedy, buffoonery, burlesque, satire, slapstick **2** mockery, joke, nonsense, parody, sham, travesty

farcical adjective ludicrous, absurd, comic, derisory, laughable, nonsensical, preposterous, ridiculous, risible

fare noun **1** charge, price, ticket money **2** food, provisions, rations, sustenance, victuals ♦ verb **3** get on, do, get along, make out, manage, prosper

farewell noun goodbye, adieu, departure, leave-taking, parting, sendoff (informal), valediction

far-fetched adjective unconvincing, cock-and-bull (informal), fantastic, implausible, incredible, preposterous, unbelievable, unlikely, unrealistic

farm noun **1** smallholding, croft (Scot.), farmstead, grange, homestead, plantation, ranch (chiefly North American) ♦ verb **2** cultivate, plant, work

fascinate verb intrigue, absorb, beguile, captivate, engross, enthral, entrance, hold spellbound, rivet, transfix

fascinating adjective gripping, alluring, captivating, compelling, engaging, engrossing, enticing, intriguing, irresistible, riveting

fascination noun attraction, allure, charm, enchantment, lure, magic, magnetism, pull

fashion noun **1** style, craze, custom, fad, look, mode, rage, trend, vogue **2** method, manner, mode, style, way ♦ verb **3** make, construct, create, forge, form, manufacture, mould, shape

fashionable *adjective* <u>popular</u>, à la mode, chic, in (*informal*), in vogue, modern, stylish, trendy (*Brit. informal*), up-to-date, with it (*informal*)

fast[1] *adjective* **1** <u>quick</u>, brisk, fleet, flying, hasty, nippy (*Brit. informal*), rapid, speedy, swift **2** <u>fixed</u>, close, fastened, firm, immovable, secure, sound, steadfast, tight **3** <u>dissipated</u>, dissolute, extravagant, loose, profligate, reckless, self-indulgent, wanton, wild ♦ *adverb* **4** <u>quickly</u>, hastily, hurriedly, in haste, like lightning, rapidly, speedily, swiftly **5** <u>soundly</u>, deeply, firmly, fixedly, securely, tightly

fast[2] *verb* **1** <u>go hungry</u>, abstain, deny oneself, go without food ♦ *noun* **2** <u>fasting</u>, abstinence

fasten *verb* <u>fix</u>, affix, attach, bind, connect, join, link, secure, tie

fat *adjective* **1** <u>overweight</u>, corpulent, heavy, obese, plump, podgy, portly, rotund, stout, tubby **2** <u>fatty</u>, adipose, greasy, oily, oleaginous ♦ *noun* **3** <u>fatness</u>, blubber, bulk, corpulence, flab, flesh, obesity, paunch

fatal *adjective* **1** <u>lethal</u>, deadly, final, incurable, killing, malignant, mortal, terminal **2** <u>ruinous</u>, baleful, baneful, calamitous, catastrophic, disastrous

fatality *noun* <u>death</u>, casualty, loss, mortality

fate *noun* **1** <u>destiny</u>, chance, divine will, fortune, kismet, nemesis, predestination, providence **2** <u>fortune</u>, cup, horoscope, lot, portion, stars

fated *adjective* <u>destined</u>, doomed, foreordained, inescapable, inevitable, predestined, preordained, sure, written

fateful *adjective* **1** <u>crucial</u>, critical, decisive, important, portentous, significant **2** <u>disastrous</u>, deadly, destructive, fatal, lethal, ominous, ruinous

father *noun* **1** <u>daddy</u> (*informal*), dad (*informal*), old man (*informal*), pa (*informal*), papa (*old-fashioned informal*), pater, pop (*informal*) **2** <u>forefather</u>, ancestor, forebear, predecessor, progenitor **3** <u>founder</u>, architect, author, creator, inventor, maker, originator, prime mover **4** <u>priest</u>, padre (*informal*), pastor ♦ *verb* **5** <u>sire</u>, beget, get, procreate

fatherland *noun* <u>homeland</u>, motherland, native land

fatherly *adjective* <u>paternal</u>, affectionate, benevolent, benign, kindly, patriarchal, protective, supportive

fathom *verb* <u>understand</u>, comprehend, get to the bottom of, grasp, interpret

fatigue *noun* **1** <u>tiredness</u>, heaviness, languor, lethargy, listlessness ♦ *verb* **2** <u>tire</u>, drain, exhaust, knacker (*slang*), take it out of (*informal*), weaken, wear out, weary

fatten *verb* **1** <u>grow fat</u>, expand, gain weight, put on weight, spread, swell, thicken **2** *often with up* <u>feed up</u>, build up, feed, nourish, overfeed, stuff

fatty *adjective* <u>greasy</u>, adipose, fat, oily, oleaginous, rich

fatuous *adjective* <u>foolish</u>, brainless, idiotic, inane, ludicrous, mindless, moronic, silly, stupid, witless

fault *noun* **1** <u>flaw</u>, blemish, defect, deficiency, failing, imperfection, shortcoming, weakness, weak point **2** <u>mistake</u>, blunder, error, indiscretion, lapse, oversight, slip **3** <u>responsibility</u>, accountability, culpability, liability **4 at fault** <u>guilty</u>, answerable, blamable, culpable, in the wrong, responsible, to blame **5 find fault with** <u>criticize</u>, carp at, complain, pick holes in, pull to pieces, quibble, take to task **6 to a fault** <u>excessively</u>, immoderately, in the extreme, overmuch, unduly ♦ *verb* **7** <u>criticize</u>, blame, censure, find fault with, hold (someone) responsible, impugn

faultless *adjective* <u>flawless</u>, correct, exemplary, foolproof, impeccable, model, perfect, unblemished

faulty *adjective* <u>defective</u>, broken, damaged, flawed, impaired, imperfect, incorrect, malfunctioning, out of order, unsound

favour *noun* **1** <u>approval</u>, approbation, backing, good opinion, goodwill, patronage, support **2** <u>good turn</u>, benefit, boon, courtesy, indulgence, kindness, service ♦ *verb* **3** <u>side with</u>, indulge, reward, smile upon **4** <u>advocate</u>, approve, champion, commend, encourage, incline towards, prefer, support

favourable *adjective* **1** <u>advantageous</u>, auspicious, beneficial, encouraging, helpful, opportune, promising, propitious, suitable **2** <u>positive</u>, affirmative, agreeable, approving, encouraging, enthusiastic, reassuring, sympathetic

favourably *adverb* **1** <u>advantageously</u>, auspiciously, conveniently, fortunately, opportunely, profitably, to one's advantage, well **2** <u>positively</u>, approvingly, enthusiastically, helpfully, with approval

favourite *adjective* **1** <u>preferred</u>, best-loved, choice, dearest, esteemed, favoured **2** <u>darling</u>, beloved, blue-eyed boy (*informal*), idol, pet, teacher's pet, the apple of one's eye

fawn[1] *verb*, often with **on** or **upon** <u>curry favour</u>, crawl, creep, cringe, dance attendance, flatter, grovel, ingratiate oneself, kowtow, pander to

fawn[2] *adjective* <u>beige</u>, buff, greyish-brown, neutral

fawning *adjective* <u>obsequious</u>, crawling, cringing, deferential, flattering, grovelling, servile, sycophantic

fear *noun* **1** <u>alarm</u>, apprehensiveness, dread, fright, horror, panic, terror, trepidation **2** <u>bugbear</u>, bête noire, bogey, horror, nightmare, spectre ♦ *verb* **3** <u>be afraid</u>, dread, shake in one's shoes, shudder at, take fright, tremble at **4 fear for** <u>worry about</u>, be anxious about, feel concern for

fearful adjective **1** <u>scared</u>, afraid, alarmed, frightened, jumpy, nervous, timid, timorous, uneasy **2** <u>frightful</u>, awful, dire, dreadful, gruesome, hair-raising, horrendous, horrific, terrible

fearfully adverb **1** <u>nervously</u>, apprehensively, diffidently, timidly, timorously, uneasily **2** <u>very</u>, awfully, exceedingly, excessively, frightfully, terribly, tremendously

fearless adjective <u>brave</u>, bold, courageous, dauntless, indomitable, intrepid, plucky, unafraid, undaunted, valiant

fearsome adjective <u>terrifying</u>, awe-inspiring, daunting, formidable, frightening, horrifying, menacing, unnerving

feasible adjective <u>possible</u>, achievable, attainable, likely, practicable, reasonable, viable, workable

feast noun **1** <u>banquet</u>, dinner, repast, spread (informal), treat **2** <u>festival</u>, celebration, fête, holiday, holy day, red-letter day, saint's day **3** <u>treat</u>, delight, enjoyment, gratification, pleasure ♦ verb **4** <u>eat one's fill</u>, gorge, gormandize, indulge, overindulge, pig out (slang), wine and dine

feat noun <u>accomplishment</u>, achievement, act, attainment, deed, exploit, performance

feathers plural noun <u>plumage</u>, down, plumes

feature noun **1** <u>aspect</u>, characteristic, facet, factor, hallmark, peculiarity, property, quality, trait **2** <u>highlight</u>, attraction, main item, speciality

3 <u>article</u>, column, item, piece, report, story ♦ verb **4** <u>spotlight</u>, emphasize, foreground, give prominence to, play up, present, star

features plural noun <u>face</u>, countenance, lineaments, physiognomy

feckless adjective <u>irresponsible</u>, good-for-nothing, hopeless, incompetent, ineffectual, shiftless, worthless

federation noun <u>union</u>, alliance, amalgamation, association, coalition, combination, league, syndicate

fed up adjective <u>dissatisfied</u>, bored, brassed off (Brit. slang), depressed, discontented, down in the mouth, glum, sick and tired (informal), tired

fee noun <u>charge</u>, bill, payment, remuneration, toll

feeble adjective **1** <u>weak</u>, debilitated, doddering, effete, frail, infirm, puny, sickly, weedy (informal) **2** <u>unconvincing</u>, flimsy, inadequate, insufficient, lame, paltry, pathetic, poor, tame, thin

feebleness noun <u>weakness</u>, effeteness, frailty, infirmity, languor, lassitude, sickliness

feed verb **1** <u>cater for</u>, nourish, provide for, provision, supply, sustain, victual, wine and dine **2** sometimes with **on** <u>eat</u>, devour, exist on, live on, partake of ♦ noun **3** <u>food</u>, fodder, pasturage, provender **4** Informal <u>meal</u>, feast, nosh (slang), repast, spread (informal)

feel verb **1** <u>touch</u>, caress, finger, fondle, handle, manipulate, paw, stroke **2** <u>experience</u>, be aware

of, notice, observe, perceive
3 <u>sense</u>, be convinced, intuit
4 <u>believe</u>, consider, deem, hold,
judge, think ♦ *noun* **5** <u>texture</u>,
finish, surface, touch
6 <u>impression</u>, air, ambience,
atmosphere, feeling, quality,
sense

feeler *noun* **1** <u>antenna</u>, tentacle,
whisker **2** <u>approach</u>, advance,
probe

feeling *noun* **1** <u>emotion</u>, ardour,
fervour, intensity, passion,
sentiment, warmth **2** <u>impression</u>,
hunch, idea, inkling, notion,
presentiment, sense, suspicion
3 <u>opinion</u>, inclination, instinct,
point of view, view **4** <u>sympathy</u>,
compassion, concern, empathy,
pity, sensibility, sensitivity,
understanding **5** <u>sense of touch</u>,
perception, sensation
6 <u>atmosphere</u>, air, ambience,
aura, feel, mood, quality

fell *verb* <u>cut down</u>, cut, demolish,
hew, knock down, level

fellow *noun* **1** <u>man</u>, bloke (*Brit.
informal*), chap (*informal*),
character, guy (*informal*),
individual, person **2** <u>associate</u>,
colleague, companion, comrade,
partner, peer

fellowship *noun* **1** <u>camaraderie</u>,
brotherhood, companionship,
sociability **2** <u>society</u>, association,
brotherhood, club, fraternity,
guild, league, order

feminine *adjective* <u>womanly</u>,
delicate, gentle, ladylike, soft,
tender

femme fatale *noun* <u>seductress</u>,
enchantress, siren, vamp
(*informal*)

fen *noun* <u>marsh</u>, bog, morass,

quagmire, slough, swamp

fence *noun* **1** <u>barrier</u>, barricade,
defence, hedge, palisade,
railings, rampart, wall ♦ *verb*
2 *often with* **in** *or* **off** <u>enclose</u>,
bound, confine, encircle, pen,
protect, surround **3** <u>evade</u>,
dodge, equivocate, flannel (*Brit.
informal*), parry

ferment *noun* <u>commotion</u>,
disruption, excitement, frenzy,
furore, stir, tumult, turmoil,
unrest, uproar

ferocious *adjective* **1** <u>fierce</u>,
predatory, rapacious, ravening,
savage, violent, wild **2** <u>cruel</u>,
bloodthirsty, brutal, ruthless,
vicious

ferocity *noun* <u>savagery</u>,
bloodthirstiness, brutality,
cruelty, fierceness, viciousness,
wildness

ferret out *verb* <u>track down</u>, dig
up, discover, elicit, root out,
search out, trace, unearth

ferry *noun* **1** <u>ferry boat</u>, packet,
packet boat ♦ *verb* **2** <u>carry</u>,
chauffeur, convey, run, ship,
shuttle, transport

fertile *adjective* <u>rich</u>, abundant,
fecund, fruitful, luxuriant,
plentiful, productive, prolific,
teeming

fertility *noun* <u>fruitfulness</u>,
abundance, fecundity,
luxuriance, productiveness,
richness

fertilizer *noun* <u>compost</u>,
dressing, dung, manure

fervent, fervid *adjective* <u>ardent</u>,
devout, earnest, enthusiastic,
heartfelt, impassioned, intense,
vehement

fervour noun intensity, ardour, enthusiasm, excitement, passion, vehemence, warmth, zeal

fester verb 1 decay, putrefy, suppurate, ulcerate 2 intensify, aggravate, smoulder

festival noun 1 celebration, carnival, entertainment, fête, gala, jubilee 2 holy day, anniversary, commemoration, feast, fête, fiesta, holiday, red-letter day, saint's day

festive adjective celebratory, cheery, convivial, happy, jovial, joyful, joyous, jubilant, merry

festivity noun, often plural celebration, entertainment, festival, party

festoon verb decorate, array, deck, drape, garland, hang, swathe, wreathe

fetch verb 1 bring, carry, convey, deliver, get, go for, obtain, retrieve, transport 2 sell for, bring in, earn, go for, make, realize, yield

fetching adjective attractive, alluring, captivating, charming, cute, enticing, winsome

fetish noun 1 fixation, mania, obsession, thing (informal) 2 talisman, amulet

feud noun 1 hostility, argument, conflict, disagreement, enmity, quarrel, rivalry, row, vendetta ♦ verb 2 quarrel, bicker, clash, contend, dispute, fall out, row, squabble, war

fever noun excitement, agitation, delirium, ferment, fervour, frenzy, restlessness

feverish adjective 1 hot, febrile, fevered, flushed, inflamed,
pyretic (Medical) 2 excited, agitated, frantic, frenetic, frenzied, overwrought, restless

few adjective not many, meagre, negligible, rare, scanty, scarcely any, sparse, sporadic

fiasco noun debacle, catastrophe, cock-up (Brit. slang), disaster, failure, mess, washout (informal)

fib noun lie, fiction, story, untruth, white lie

fibre noun 1 thread, filament, pile, strand, texture, wisp 2 essence, nature, quality, spirit, substance 3 As in moral fibre resolution, stamina, strength, toughness

fickle adjective changeable, capricious, faithless, inconstant, irresolute, temperamental, unfaithful, variable, volatile

fiction noun 1 tale, fantasy, legend, myth, novel, romance, story, yarn (informal) 2 lie, cock and bull story (informal), fabrication, falsehood, invention, tall story, untruth, urban legend

fictional adjective imaginary, invented, legendary, made-up, nonexistent, unreal

fictitious adjective false, bogus, fabricated, imaginary, invented, made-up, make-believe, mythical, untrue

fiddle verb 1 fidget, finger, interfere with, mess about or around, play, tamper with, tinker 2 Informal cheat, cook the books (informal), diddle (informal), fix, swindle, wangle (informal) ♦ noun 3 violin 4 Informal fraud, fix, racket, scam (slang), swindle 5 fit as a fiddle healthy, blooming, hale and hearty, in fine fettle, in good form, in good shape, in rude health, in the pink, sound, strong

fiddling *adjective* **1** trivial, futile, insignificant, pettifogging, petty, trifling

fidelity *noun* **1** loyalty, allegiance, constancy, dependability, devotion, faithfulness, staunchness, trustworthiness **2** accuracy, closeness, correspondence, exactness, faithfulness, precision, scrupulousness

fidget *verb* **1** move restlessly, fiddle (*informal*), fret, squirm, twitch ◆ *noun* **2 the fidgets** restlessness, fidgetiness, jitters (*informal*), nervousness, unease, uneasiness

fidgety *adjective* restless, impatient, jittery (*informal*), jumpy, nervous, on edge, restive, twitchy (*informal*), uneasy

field *noun* **1** meadow, grassland, green, lea (*poetic*), pasture **2** competitors, applicants, candidates, competition, contestants, entrants, possibilities, runners **3** speciality, area, department, discipline, domain, line, province, territory ◆ *verb* **4** retrieve, catch, pick up, return, stop **5** deal with, deflect, handle, turn aside

fiend *noun* **1** demon, devil, evil spirit **2** brute, barbarian, beast, ghoul, monster, ogre, savage **3** *Informal* enthusiast, addict, fanatic, freak (*informal*), maniac

fiendish *adjective* wicked, cruel, devilish, diabolical, hellish, infernal, malignant, monstrous, satanic, unspeakable

fierce *adjective* **1** wild, brutal, cruel, dangerous, ferocious, fiery, menacing, savage, vicious **2** strong, furious, howling, inclement, powerful, raging, stormy, tempestuous, violent **3** intense, cut-throat, keen, relentless, strong

fiercely *adverb* ferociously, furiously, passionately, savagely, tempestuously, tigerishly, tooth and nail, viciously, with no holds barred

fiery *adjective* **1** burning, ablaze, afire, aflame, blazing, flaming, on fire **2** excitable, fierce, hot-headed, impetuous, irascible, irritable, passionate

fight *verb* **1** battle, box, clash, combat, do battle, grapple, spar, struggle, tussle, wrestle **2** oppose, contest, defy, dispute, make a stand against, resist, stand up to, withstand **3** engage in, carry on, conduct, prosecute, wage ◆ *noun* **4** conflict, battle, clash, contest, dispute, duel, encounter, struggle, tussle **5** resistance, belligerence, militancy, pluck, spirit

fighter *noun* **1** soldier, fighting man, man-at-arms, warrior **2** boxer, prize fighter, pugilist

fight off *verb* repel, beat off, keep *or* hold at bay, repress, repulse, resist, stave off, ward off

figure *noun* **1** number, character, digit, numeral, symbol **2** amount, cost, price, sum, total, value **3** shape, body, build, frame, physique, proportions **4** diagram, design, drawing, illustration, pattern, representation, sketch

5 character, big name, celebrity, dignitary, personality

6 calculate, compute, count, reckon, tally, tot up, work out

7 *usually with* **in** feature, act, appear, be featured, contribute to, play a part

figurehead *noun* front man, mouthpiece, puppet, titular *or* nominal head

figure out *verb* **1** calculate, compute, reckon, work out **2** understand, comprehend, decipher, fathom, make out, see

filch *verb* steal, embezzle, misappropriate, pilfer, pinch (*informal*), take, thieve, walk off with

file¹ *noun* **1** folder, case, data, documents, dossier, information, portfolio **2** line, column, queue, row ◆*verb* **3** register, document, enter, pigeonhole, put in place, record **4** march, parade, troop

file² *verb* smooth, abrade, polish, rasp, rub, scrape, shape

fill *verb* **1** stuff, cram, crowd, glut, pack, stock, supply, swell **2** saturate, charge, imbue, impregnate, pervade, suffuse **3** plug, block, bung, close, cork, seal, stop **4** perform, carry out, discharge, execute, fulfil, hold, occupy ◆*noun* **5** one's fill sufficient, all one wants, ample, enough, plenty

filler *noun* padding, makeweight, stopgap

fill in *verb* **1** complete, answer, fill out (*U.S.*), fill up **2** *Informal* inform, acquaint, apprise, bring up to date, give the facts *or* background **3** replace, deputize, represent, stand in, sub,

substitute, take the place of

filling *noun* **1** stuffing, contents, filler, inside, insides, padding, wadding ◆*adjective* **2** satisfying, ample, heavy, square, substantial

film *noun* **1** movie, flick (*slang*), motion picture **2** layer, coating, covering, dusting, membrane, skin, tissue ◆*verb* **3** photograph, shoot, take, video, videotape

filter *noun* **1** sieve, gauze, membrane, mesh, riddle, strainer ◆*verb* **2** purify, clarify, filtrate, refine, screen, sieve, sift, strain, winnow **3** trickle, dribble, escape, exude, leak, ooze, penetrate, percolate, seep

filth *noun* **1** dirt, excrement, grime, muck, refuse, sewage, slime, sludge, squalor **2** obscenity, impurity, indecency, pornography, smut, vulgarity

filthy *adjective* **1** dirty, foul, polluted, putrid, slimy, squalid, unclean **2** muddy, begrimed, blackened, grimy, grubby **3** obscene, corrupt, depraved, impure, indecent, lewd, licentious, pornographic, smutty

final *adjective* **1** last, closing, concluding, latest, terminal, ultimate **2** definitive, absolute, conclusive, decided, definite, incontrovertible, irrevocable, settled

finale *noun* ending, climax, close, conclusion, culmination, denouement, epilogue

finalize *verb* complete, clinch, conclude, decide, settle, tie up, work out, wrap up (*informal*)

finally *adverb* **1** eventually, at last, at length, at long last, in the end, lastly, ultimately **2** in

finance noun 1 economics, accounts, banking, business, commerce, investment, money ♦ verb 2 fund, back, bankroll (U.S.), guarantee, pay for, subsidize, support, underwrite

finances plural noun resources, affairs, assets, capital, cash, funds, money, wherewithal

financial adjective economic, fiscal, monetary, pecuniary

find verb 1 discover, come across, encounter, hit upon, locate, meet, recognize, spot, uncover 2 perceive, detect, discover, learn, note, notice, observe, realise ♦ noun 3 discovery, acquisition, asset, bargain, catch, good buy

find out verb 1 learn, detect, discover, note, observe, perceive, realize 2 detect, catch, disclose, expose, reveal, uncover, unmask

fine¹ adjective 1 excellent, accomplished, exceptional, exquisite, first-rate, magnificent, masterly, outstanding, splendid, superior 2 sunny, balmy, bright, clear, clement, cloudless, dry, fair, pleasant 3 satisfactory, acceptable, all right, convenient, good, O.K. or okay (informal), suitable 4 delicate, dainty, elegant, expensive, exquisite, fragile, quality 5 subtle, abstruse, acute, hairsplitting, minute, nice, precise, sharp 6 slender, diaphanous, flimsy, gauzy, gossamer, light, sheer, thin

fine² noun 1 penalty, damages, forfeit, punishment ♦ verb 2 penalize, mulct, punish

finery noun splendour, frippery, gear (informal), glad rags (informal), ornaments, showiness, Sunday best, trappings, trinkets

finesse noun skill, adeptness, adroitness, craft, delicacy, diplomacy, discretion, savoir-faire, sophistication, subtlety, tact

finger verb touch, feel, fiddle with (informal), handle, manipulate, maul, paw (informal), toy with

finish verb 1 stop, cease, close, complete, conclude, end, round off, terminate, wind up, wrap up (informal) 2 consume, devour, dispose of, eat, empty, exhaust, use up 3 destroy, bring down, defeat, dispose of, exterminate, overcome, put an end to, put paid to, rout, ruin 4 perfect, polish, refine 5 coat, gild, lacquer, polish, stain, texture, veneer, wax ♦ noun 6 end, cessation, close, completion, conclusion, culmination, denouement, finale, run-in 7 defeat, annihilation, curtains (informal), death, end, end of the road, ruin 8 surface, lustre, patina, polish, shine, smoothness, texture

finished adjective 1 polished, accomplished, perfected, professional, refined 2 over, closed, complete, done, ended, finalized, through 3 spent, done, drained, empty, exhausted, used up 4 ruined, defeated, done for (informal), doomed, lost, through, undone, wiped out

finite adjective limited, bounded, circumscribed, delimited, demarcated, restricted

fire noun 1 <u>flames</u>, blaze, combustion, conflagration, inferno 2 <u>bombardment</u>, barrage, cannonade, flak, fusillade, hail, salvo, shelling, sniping, volley 3 <u>passion</u>, ardour, eagerness, enthusiasm, excitement, fervour, intensity, sparkle, spirit, verve, vigour ♦verb 4 <u>shoot</u>, detonate, discharge, explode, let off, pull the trigger, set off, shell 5 <u>inspire</u>, animate, enliven, excite, galvanize, impassion, inflame, rouse, stir 6 Informal <u>dismiss</u>, cashier, discharge, make redundant, sack (informal), show the door

firebrand noun <u>rabble-rouser</u>, agitator, demagogue, incendiary, instigator, tub-thumper

fireworks plural noun 1 <u>pyrotechnics</u>, illuminations 2 <u>rage</u>, hysterics, row, storm, trouble, uproar

firm¹ adjective 1 <u>hard</u>, dense, inflexible, rigid, set, solid, solidified, stiff, unyielding 2 <u>secure</u>, embedded, fast, fixed, immovable, rooted, stable, steady, tight, unshakable 3 <u>definite</u>, adamant, inflexible, resolute, resolved, set on, unbending, unshakable, unyielding

firm² noun <u>company</u>, association, business, concern, conglomerate, corporation, enterprise, organization, partnership

firmly adverb 1 <u>securely</u>, immovably, like a rock, steadily, tightly, unflinchingly, unshakably 2 <u>resolutely</u>, staunchly, steadfastly, unchangeably, unwaveringly

firmness noun 1 <u>hardness</u>, inelasticity, inflexibility, resistance, rigidity, solidity, stiffness 2 <u>resolve</u>, constancy, inflexibility, resolution, staunchness, steadfastness

first adjective 1 <u>foremost</u>, chief, head, highest, leading, pre-eminent, prime, principal, ruling 2 <u>earliest</u>, initial, introductory, maiden, opening, original, premier, primordial 3 <u>elementary</u>, basic, cardinal, fundamental, key, primary, rudimentary ♦noun 4 As in **from the first** <u>start</u>, beginning, commencement, inception, introduction, outset, starting point ♦adverb 5 <u>beforehand</u>, at the beginning, at the outset, firstly, initially, in the first place, to begin with, to start with

first-rate adjective <u>excellent</u>, crack (slang), elite, exceptional, first class, outstanding, superb, superlative, top-notch (informal), world-class

fishy adjective 1 Informal <u>suspicious</u>, dodgy (Brit., Austral., & N.Z. informal), dubious, funny (informal), implausible, odd, questionable, suspect, unlikely 2 <u>fishlike</u>, piscatorial, piscatory, piscine

fissure noun <u>crack</u>, breach, cleft, crevice, fault, fracture, opening, rift, rupture, split

fit¹ verb 1 <u>match</u>, accord, belong, conform, correspond, meet, suit, tally 2 <u>prepare</u>, arm, equip, fit out, kit out, provide 3 <u>adapt</u>, adjust, alter, arrange, customize,

modify, shape, tweak (*informal*)
♦ *adjective* **4** appropriate, apt, becoming, correct, fitting, proper, right, seemly, suitable **5** healthy, able-bodied, hale, in good shape, robust, strapping, trim, well

fit² *noun* **1** seizure, attack, bout, convulsion, paroxysm, spasm **2** outbreak, bout, burst, outburst, spell

fitful *adjective* irregular, broken, desultory, disturbed, inconstant, intermittent, spasmodic, sporadic, uneven

fitness *noun* **1** appropriateness, aptness, competence, eligibility, propriety, readiness, suitability **2** health, good condition, good health, robustness, strength, vigour

fitting *adjective* **1** appropriate, apposite, becoming, correct, decent, proper, right, seemly, suitable ♦ *noun* **2** accessory, attachment, component, part, piece, unit

fix *verb* **1** place, embed, establish, implant, install, locate, plant, position, set **2** fasten, attach, bind, connect, link, secure, stick, tie **3** decide, agree on, arrange, arrive at, determine, establish, set, settle, specify **4** repair, correct, mend, patch up, put to rights, see to **5** focus, direct **6** *Informal* manipulate, fiddle (*informal*), influence, rig ♦ *noun* **7** *Informal* predicament, difficulty, dilemma, embarrassment, mess, pickle (*informal*), plight, quandary

fixation *noun* preoccupation, complex, hang-up (*informal*), idée

fixe, infatuation, mania, obsession, thing (*informal*)

fixed *adjective* **1** permanent, established, immovable, rigid, rooted, secure, set **2** intent, resolute, steady, unwavering **3** agreed, arranged, decided, definite, established, planned, resolved, settled

fix up *verb* **1** arrange, agree on, fix, organize, plan, settle, sort out **2** *often with* with provide, arrange for, bring about, lay on

fizz *verb* bubble, effervesce, fizzle, froth, hiss, sparkle, sputter

fizzy *adjective* bubbly, bubbling, carbonated, effervescent, gassy, sparkling

flabbergasted *adjective* astonished, amazed, astounded, dumbfounded, lost for words, overwhelmed, speechless, staggered, stunned

flabby *adjective* limp, baggy, drooping, flaccid, floppy, loose, pendulous, sagging

flag¹ *noun* **1** banner, colours, ensign, pennant, pennon, standard, streamer ♦ *verb* **2** mark, indicate, label, note **3** *sometimes with* down hail, signal, warn, wave

flag² *verb* weaken, abate, droop, fade, languish, peter out, sag, wane, weary, wilt

flagging *adjective* fading, declining, deteriorating, faltering, waning, weakening, wilting

flagrant *adjective* outrageous, barefaced, blatant, brazen, glaring, heinous, scandalous, shameless

flagstone noun <u>paving stone</u>, block, flag, slab

flail verb <u>thrash</u>, beat, thresh, windmill

flair noun 1 <u>ability</u>, aptitude, faculty, feel, genius, gift, knack, mastery, talent 2 <u>style</u>, chic, dash, discernment, elegance, panache, stylishness, taste

flake noun 1 <u>wafer</u>, layer, peeling, scale, shaving, sliver ♦ verb <u>blister</u>, chip, peel (off)

flake out verb <u>collapse</u>, faint, keel over, pass out

flamboyant adjective 1 <u>extravagant</u>, dashing, elaborate, florid, ornate, ostentatious, showy, swashbuckling, theatrical 2 <u>colourful</u>, brilliant, dazzling, glamorous, glitzy (slang)

flame noun 1 <u>fire</u>, blaze, brightness, light 2 Informal <u>sweetheart</u>, beau, boyfriend, girlfriend, heart-throb (Brit.), lover ♦ verb 3 <u>burn</u>, blaze, flare, flash, glare, glow, shine

flaming adjective <u>burning</u>, ablaze, blazing, fiery, glowing, raging, red-hot

flank noun 1 <u>side</u>, hip, loin, thigh 2 <u>wing</u>, side

flap verb 1 <u>flutter</u>, beat, flail, shake, thrash, vibrate, wag, wave ♦ noun 2 <u>flutter</u>, beating, shaking, swinging, swish, waving 3 Informal <u>panic</u>, agitation, commotion, fluster, state (informal), sweat (informal), tizzy (informal)

flare verb 1 <u>blaze</u>, burn up, flicker, glare 2 <u>widen</u>, broaden, spread out ♦ noun 3 <u>flame</u>, blaze,

burst, flash, flicker, glare

flare up verb <u>lose one's temper</u>, blow one's top (informal), boil over, explode, fly off the handle (informal), throw a tantrum

flash noun 1 <u>blaze</u>, burst, dazzle, flare, flicker, gleam, shimmer, spark, streak 2 <u>moment</u>, instant, jiffy (informal), second, split second, trice, twinkling of an eye ♦ adjective 3 Informal <u>ostentatious</u>, tacky (informal), tasteless, vulgar ♦ verb 4 <u>blaze</u>, flare, flicker, glare, gleam, shimmer, sparkle, twinkle 5 <u>speed</u>, dart, dash, fly, race, shoot, streak, whistle, zoom 6 <u>show</u>, display, exhibit, expose, flaunt, flourish

flashy adjective <u>showy</u>, flamboyant, garish, gaudy, glitzy (slang), jazzy (informal), ostentatious, snazzy (informal)

flat¹ adjective 1 <u>even</u>, horizontal, level, levelled, low, smooth 2 <u>dull</u>, boring, dead, lacklustre, lifeless, monotonous, tedious, tiresome, uninteresting 3 <u>absolute</u>, categorical, downright, explicit, out-and-out, positive, unequivocal, unqualified 4 <u>punctured</u>, blown out, burst, collapsed, deflated, empty ♦ adverb 5 <u>completely</u>, absolutely, categorically, exactly, point blank, precisely, utterly 6 <u>flat out</u> at <u>full speed</u>, all out, at full tilt, for all one is worth, hell for leather (informal)

flat² noun <u>apartment</u>, rooms

flatly adverb <u>absolutely</u>, categorically, completely, positively, unhesitatingly

flatness noun 1 <u>evenness</u>, smoothness, uniformity

2 dullness, monotony, tedium

flatten verb level, compress, even out, iron out, raze, smooth off, squash, trample

flatter verb 1 praise, butter up, compliment, pander to, soft-soap (informal), sweet-talk (informal), wheedle 2 suit, become, do something for, enhance, set off, show to advantage

flattering adjective 1 becoming, effective, enhancing, kind, well-chosen 2 ingratiating, adulatory, complimentary, fawning, fulsome, laudatory

flattery noun obsequiousness, adulation, blandishment, fawning, servility, soft-soap (informal), sweet-talk (informal), sycophancy

flaunt verb show off, brandish, display, exhibit, flash about, flourish, parade, sport (informal)

flavour noun 1 taste, aroma, flavouring, piquancy, relish, savour, seasoning, smack, tang, zest 2 quality, character, essence, feel, feeling, style, tinge, tone ♦ verb 3 season, ginger up, imbue, infuse, leaven, spice

flaw noun weakness, blemish, chink in one's armour, defect, failing, fault, imperfection, weak spot

flawed adjective damaged, blemished, defective, erroneous, faulty, imperfect, unsound

flawless adjective perfect, faultless, impeccable, spotless, unblemished, unsullied

flee verb run away, bolt, depart,

escape, fly, make one's getaway, scarper (Brit. slang), take flight, take off (informal), take to one's heels, turn tail

fleet noun navy, armada, flotilla, task force

fleeting adjective momentary, brief, ephemeral, passing, short-lived, temporary, transient, transitory

flesh noun 1 meat, brawn, fat, tissue, weight 2 human nature, carnality, flesh and blood 3 one's own flesh and blood family, blood, kin, kinsfolk, kith and kin, relations, relatives

flexibility noun adaptability, adjustability, elasticity, give (informal), pliability, pliancy, resilience, springiness

flexible adjective 1 pliable, elastic, lithe, plastic, pliant, springy, stretchy, supple 2 adaptable, adjustable, discretionary, open, variable

flick verb 1 strike, dab, flip, hit, tap, touch 2 flick through browse, flip through, glance at, skim, skip, thumb

flicker verb 1 twinkle, flare, flash, glimmer, gutter, shimmer, sparkle 2 flutter, quiver, vibrate, waver ♦ noun 3 glimmer, flare, flash, gleam, spark 4 trace, breath, glimmer, iota, spark

flight¹ noun 1 Of air travel journey, trip, voyage 2 aviation, aeronautics, flying 3 flock, cloud, formation, squadron, swarm, unit

flight² noun escape, departure, exit, exodus, fleeing, getaway, retreat, running away

flimsy adjective 1 fragile, delicate,

frail, insubstantial, makeshift, rickety, shaky 2 <u>thin</u>, gauzy, gossamer, light, sheer, transparent 3 <u>unconvincing</u>, feeble, implausible, inadequate, pathetic, poor, unsatisfactory, weak

flinch verb <u>recoil</u>, cower, cringe, draw back, quail, shirk, shrink, shy away, wince

fling verb 1 <u>throw</u>, cast, catapult, heave, hurl, propel, sling, toss ♦ noun 2 <u>binge</u> (informal), bash, good time, party, rave-up (Brit. slang), spree

flip verb, noun <u>toss</u>, flick, snap, spin, throw

flippancy noun <u>frivolity</u>, impertinence, irreverence, levity, pertness, sauciness

flippant adjective <u>frivolous</u>, cheeky, disrespectful, glib, impertinent, irreverent, offhand, superficial

flirt verb 1 <u>lead on</u>, chat up (informal), make advances, make eyes at, make sheep's eyes at, philander 2 usually with with <u>toy with</u>, consider, dabble in, entertain, expose oneself to, give a thought to, play with, trifle with ♦ noun 3 <u>tease</u>, coquette, heart-breaker, philanderer

flirtatious adjective <u>teasing</u>, amorous, come-hither, coquettish, coy, enticing, flirty, provocative, sportive

float verb 1 <u>be buoyant</u>, hang, hover 2 <u>glide</u>, bob, drift, move gently, sail, slide, slip along 3 <u>launch</u>, get going, promote, set up

floating adjective 1 <u>buoyant</u>, afloat, buoyed up, sailing,

swimming 2 <u>fluctuating</u>, free, movable, unattached, variable, wandering

flock noun 1 <u>herd</u>, colony, drove, flight, gaggle, skein 2 <u>crowd</u>, collection, company, congregation, gathering, group, herd, host, mass ♦ verb 3 <u>gather</u>, collect, congregate, converge, crowd, herd, huddle, mass, throng

flog verb <u>beat</u>, flagellate, flay, lash, scourge, thrash, trounce, whack, whip

flood noun 1 <u>deluge</u>, downpour, inundation, overflow, spate, tide, torrent 2 <u>abundance</u>, flow, glut, profusion, rush, stream, torrent ♦ verb 3 <u>immerse</u>, drown, inundate, overflow, pour over, submerge, swamp 4 <u>engulf</u>, overwhelm, surge, swarm, sweep 5 <u>oversupply</u>, choke, fill, glut, saturate

floor noun 1 <u>tier</u>, level, stage, storey ♦ verb 2 <u>knock down</u>, deck (slang), prostrate 3 Informal <u>bewilder</u>, baffle, confound, defeat, disconcert, dumbfound, perplex, puzzle, stump, throw (informal)

flop verb 1 <u>fall</u>, collapse, dangle, droop, drop, sag, slump 2 Informal <u>fail</u>, come unstuck, fall flat, fold (informal), founder, go belly-up (slang), misfire ♦ noun 3 Informal <u>failure</u>, debacle, disaster, fiasco, nonstarter, washout (informal)

floppy adjective <u>droopy</u>, baggy, flaccid, limp, loose, pendulous, sagging, soft

floral adjective <u>flowery</u>, flower-patterned

florid adjective **1** flushed, blowsy, high-coloured, rubicund, ruddy **2** flowery, baroque, flamboyant, fussy, high-flown, ornate, overelaborate

flotsam noun debris, detritus, jetsam, junk, odds and ends, wreckage

flounder verb fumble, grope, struggle, stumble, thrash, toss

flourish verb **1** prosper, bloom, blossom, boom, flower, grow, increase, succeed, thrive **2** wave, brandish, display, flaunt, shake, wield ♦ noun **3** wave, display, fanfare, parade, show **4** ornamentation, curlicue, decoration, embellishment, plume, sweep

flourishing adjective successful, blooming, going places, in the pink, luxuriant, prospering, rampant, thriving

flout verb defy, laugh in the face of, mock, scoff at, scorn, sneer at, spurn

flow verb **1** run, circulate, course, move, roll **2** pour, cascade, flood, gush, rush, stream, surge, sweep **3** result, arise, emanate, emerge, issue, proceed, spring ♦ noun **4** tide, course, current, drift, flood, flux, outpouring, spate, stream

flower noun **1** bloom, blossom, efflorescence **2** elite, best, cream, crème de la crème, pick ♦ verb **3** blossom, bloom, flourish, mature, open, unfold

flowery adjective ornate, baroque, embellished, fancy, florid, high-flown

flowing adjective **1** streaming, falling, gushing, rolling, rushing, smooth, sweeping **2** fluent, continuous, easy, smooth, unbroken, uninterrupted

fluctuate verb change, alternate, oscillate, seesaw, shift, swing, vary, veer, waver

fluency noun ease, articulateness, assurance, command, control, facility, readiness, slickness, smoothness

fluent adjective smooth, articulate, easy, effortless, flowing, natural, voluble, well-versed

fluff noun **1** fuzz, down, nap, pile ♦ verb **2** Informal spoil, bungle, make a mess off, mess up (informal), muddle

fluffy adjective soft, downy, feathery, fleecy, fuzzy

fluid noun **1** liquid, liquor, solution ♦ adjective **2** liquid, flowing, liquefied, melted, molten, runny, watery

fluke noun lucky break, accident, chance, coincidence, quirk of fate, serendipity, stroke of luck

flurry noun **1** commotion, ado, bustle, disturbance, excitement, flutter, fuss, stir **2** gust, squall

flush[1] verb **1** blush, colour, glow, go red, redden **2** rinse out, cleanse, flood, hose down, wash out ♦ noun **3** blush, colour, glow, redness, rosiness

flush[2] adjective **1** level, even, flat, square, true **2** Informal wealthy, in the money (informal), moneyed, rich, well-heeled (informal), well-off

flushed adjective blushing, crimson, embarrassed, glowing, hot, red, rosy, ruddy

fluster verb 1 upset, agitate, bother, confuse, disturb, perturb, rattle (*informal*), ruffle, unnerve ◆ noun 2 turmoil, disturbance, dither (*chiefly Brit.*), flap (*informal*), flurry, flutter, furore, state (*informal*)

flutter verb 1 beat, flap, palpitate, quiver, ripple, tremble, vibrate, waver ◆ noun 2 vibration, palpitation, quiver, shiver, shudder, tremble, tremor, twitching 3 agitation, commotion, confusion, dither (*chiefly Brit.*), excitement, fluster, state (*informal*)

fly verb 1 take wing, flit, flutter, hover, sail, soar, wing 2 pilot, control, manoeuvre, operate 3 display, flap, float, flutter, show, wave 4 pass, elapse, flit, glide, pass swiftly, roll on, run its course, slip away 5 rush, career, dart, dash, hurry, race, shoot, speed, sprint, tear 6 flee, escape, get away, run for it, skedaddle (*informal*), take to one's heels

flying adjective hurried, brief, fleeting, hasty, rushed, short-lived, transitory

foam noun 1 froth, bubbles, head, lather, spray, spume, suds ◆ verb 2 bubble, boil, effervesce, fizz, froth, lather

focus noun 1 centre, focal point, heart, hub, target ◆ verb 2 concentrate, aim, centre, direct, fix, pinpoint, spotlight, zoom in

foe noun enemy, adversary, antagonist, opponent, rival

fog noun mist, gloom, miasma, murk, peasouper (*informal*), smog

foggy adjective misty, cloudy, dim, hazy, indistinct, murky, smoggy, vaporous

foil[1] verb thwart, balk, counter, defeat, disappoint, frustrate, nullify, stop

foil[2] noun contrast, antithesis, complement

foist verb impose, fob off, palm off, pass off, sneak in, unload

fold verb 1 bend, crease, double over 2 *Informal* go bankrupt, collapse, crash, fail, go bust (*informal*), go to the wall, go under, shut down ◆ noun 3 crease, bend, furrow, overlap, pleat, wrinkle

folder noun file, binder, envelope, portfolio

folk noun people, clan, family, kin, kindred, race, tribe

follow verb 1 come after, come next, succeed, supersede, supplant, take the place of 2 pursue, chase, dog, hound, hunt, shadow, stalk, track, trail 3 accompany, attend, escort, tag along 4 obey, be guided by, conform, heed, observe 5 understand, appreciate, catch on (*informal*), comprehend, fathom, grasp, realize, take in 6 result, arise, develop, ensue, flow, issue, proceed, spring 7 be interested in, cultivate, keep abreast of, support

follower noun supporter, adherent, apostle, devotee, disciple, fan, pupil

following adjective 1 next, consequent, ensuing, later, subsequent, succeeding, successive ◆ noun 2 supporters, clientele, coterie, entourage, fans, retinue, suite, train

folly noun foolishness,
imprudence, indiscretion, lunacy,
madness, nonsense, rashness,
stupidity

fond adjective **1** loving, adoring,
affectionate, amorous, caring,
devoted, doting, indulgent,
tender, warm **2** foolish, deluded,
delusive, empty, naive,
overoptimistic, vain **3** fond of
keen on, addicted to, attached
to, enamoured of, having a soft
spot for, hooked on, into
(informal), partial to

fondle verb caress, cuddle,
dandle, pat, pet, stroke

fondly adverb **1** lovingly,
affectionately, dearly,
indulgently, possessively,
tenderly, with affection
2 foolishly, credulously, naively,
stupidly, vainly

fondness noun **1** liking,
attachment, fancy, love,
partiality, penchant, soft spot,
taste, weakness **2** devotion,
affection, attachment, kindness,
love, tenderness

food noun nourishment, cuisine,
diet, fare, grub (slang), nutrition,
rations, refreshment

fool noun **1** simpleton,
blockhead, dunce, halfwit, idiot,
ignoramus, imbecile (informal),
numbskull or numskull, twit
(informal, chiefly Brit.) **2** dupe, fall
guy (informal), laughing stock,
mug (Brit. slang), stooge (slang),
sucker (slang) **3** clown, buffoon,
harlequin, jester ◆ verb **4** deceive,
beguile, con (informal), delude,
dupe, hoodwink, mislead, take
in, trick

foolhardy adjective rash,

hot-headed, impetuous,
imprudent, irresponsible, reckless

foolish adjective unwise, absurd,
ill-judged, imprudent,
injudicious, senseless, silly

foolishly adverb unwisely,
idiotically, ill-advisedly,
imprudently, injudiciously,
mistakenly, stupidly

foolishness noun stupidity,
absurdity, folly, imprudence,
indiscretion, irresponsibility,
silliness, weakness

foolproof adjective infallible,
certain, guaranteed, safe,
sure-fire (informal), unassailable,
unbreakable

footing noun **1** basis, foundation,
groundwork **2** relationship,
grade, position, rank, standing,
status

footling adjective trivial, fiddling,
hairsplitting, insignificant, minor,
petty, silly, trifling, unimportant

footstep noun step, footfall, tread

forage verb **1** search, cast about,
explore, hunt, rummage, scour,
seek ◆ noun **2** Cattle, etc. fodder,
feed, food, provender

foray noun raid, incursion,
inroad, invasion, sally, sortie,
swoop

forbear verb refrain, abstain,
cease, desist, hold back, keep
from, restrain oneself, stop

forbearance noun patience,
long-suffering, moderation,
resignation, restraint,
self-control, temperance,
tolerance

forbearing adjective patient,
forgiving, indulgent, lenient,
long-suffering, merciful,

moderate, tolerant

forbid verb prohibit, ban, disallow, exclude, outlaw, preclude, rule out, veto

forbidden adjective prohibited, banned, outlawed, out of bounds, proscribed, taboo, vetoed

forbidding adjective threatening, daunting, frightening, hostile, menacing, ominous, sinister, unfriendly

force noun 1 power, energy, impulse, might, momentum, pressure, strength, vigour 2 compulsion, arm-twisting (informal), coercion, constraint, duress, pressure, violence 3 intensity, emphasis, fierceness, vehemence, vigour 4 army, host, legion, patrol, regiment, squad, troop, unit 5 **in force**: a valid, binding, current, effective, in operation, operative, working b in great numbers, all together, in full strength ◆ verb 6 compel, coerce, constrain, dragoon, drive, impel, make, oblige, press, pressurize 7 break open, blast, prise, wrench, wrest 8 push, propel, thrust

forced adjective 1 compulsory, conscripted, enforced, involuntary, mandatory, obligatory 2 false, affected, artificial, contrived, insincere, laboured, stiff, strained, unnatural, wooden

forceful adjective powerful, cogent, compelling, convincing, dynamic, effective, persuasive

forcible adjective 1 violent, aggressive, armed, coercive, compulsory 2 strong,

compelling, energetic, forceful, potent, powerful, weighty

forebear noun ancestor, father, forefather, forerunner, predecessor

foreboding noun dread, anxiety, apprehension, apprehensiveness, chill, fear, misgiving, premonition, presentiment

forecast verb 1 predict, anticipate, augur, divine, foresee, foretell, prophesy ◆ noun 2 prediction, conjecture, guess, prognosis, prophecy

forefather noun ancestor, father, forebear, forerunner, predecessor

forefront noun lead, centre, fore, foreground, front, prominence, spearhead, vanguard

foregoing adjective preceding, above, antecedent, anterior, former, previous, prior

foreign adjective alien, exotic, external, imported, remote, strange, unfamiliar, unknown

foreigner noun alien, immigrant, incomer, stranger

foremost adjective leading, chief, highest, paramount, pre-eminent, primary, prime, principal, supreme

forerunner noun precursor, envoy, harbinger, herald, prototype

foresee verb anticipate, envisage, forecast, foretell, predict, prophesy

foreshadow verb predict, augur, forebode, indicate, portend, prefigure, presage, promise, signal

foresight noun anticipation, far-sightedness, forethought, precaution, preparedness, prescience, providence, prudence

foretell verb predict, forecast, forewarn, presage, prognosticate, prophesy

forethought noun anticipation, far-sightedness, foresight, precaution, providence, provision, prudence

forever adverb 1 evermore, always, for all time, for keeps, in perpetuity, till Doomsday, till the cows come home (informal) 2 constantly, all the time, continually, endlessly, eternally, incessantly, interminably, perpetually, unremittingly

forewarn verb caution, advise, alert, apprise, give fair warning, put on guard, tip off

forfeit noun 1 penalty, damages, fine, forfeiture, loss, mulct ♦ verb 2 lose, be deprived of, be stripped of, give up, relinquish, renounce, say goodbye to, surrender

forge verb 1 create, construct, devise, fashion, form, frame, make, mould, form, work 2 falsify, copy, counterfeit, fake, feign, imitate

forgery noun 1 fraudulence, coining, counterfeiting, falsification, fraudulent imitation 2 fake, counterfeit, falsification, imitation, phoney or phony (informal), sham

forget verb neglect, leave behind, lose sight of, omit, overlook

forgetful adjective absent-minded, careless, inattentive, neglectful, oblivious, unmindful, vague

forgive verb excuse, absolve, acquit, condone, exonerate, let bygones be bygones, let off (informal), pardon

forgiveness noun pardon, absolution, acquittal, amnesty, exoneration, mercy, remission

forgiving adjective merciful, clement, compassionate, forbearing, lenient, magnanimous, soft-hearted, tolerant

forgo verb give up, abandon, do without, relinquish, renounce, resign, surrender, waive, yield

forgotten adjective left behind, bygone, lost, omitted, past, past recall, unremembered

fork verb branch, bifurcate, diverge, divide, part, split

forked adjective branching, angled, bifurcate(d), branched, divided, pronged, split, zigzag

forlorn adjective miserable, disconsolate, down in the dumps (informal), helpless, hopeless, pathetic, pitiful, unhappy, woebegone, wretched

form noun 1 shape, appearance, configuration, formation, pattern, structure 2 type, kind, sort, style, variety 3 condition, fettle, fitness, health, shape, trim 4 procedure, convention, custom, etiquette, protocol 5 document, application, paper, sheet 6 class, grade, rank ♦ verb 7 make, build, construct, create, fashion, forge, mould, produce, shape 8 arrange, combine, draw up, organize 9 take shape, appear, become visible, come into being, crystallize, grow, materialize, rise 10 develop, acquire, contract, cultivate, pick up **11** constitute, compose, comprise, make up

formal adjective **1** official, ceremonial, ritualistic, solemn **2** conventional, affected, correct, precise, stiff, unbending

formality noun **1** convention, custom, procedure, red tape, rite, ritual **2** correctness, decorum, etiquette, protocol

format noun style, appearance, arrangement, construction, form, layout, look, make-up, plan, type

formation noun **1** establishment, constitution, development, forming, generation, genesis, manufacture, production **2** pattern, arrangement, configuration, design, grouping, structure

formative adjective developmental, influential

former adjective previous, earlier, erstwhile, one-time, prior

formerly adverb previously, at one time, before, lately, once

formidable adjective **1** intimidating, daunting, dismaying, fearful, frightful, menacing, terrifying, threatening **2** impressive, awesome, great, mighty, powerful, redoubtable, terrific, tremendous

formula noun method, blueprint, precept, principle, procedure, recipe, rule

formulate verb **1** define, detail, express, frame, give form to, set down, specify, systematize **2** devise, develop, forge, invent, map out, originate, plan, work out

forsake verb **1** desert, abandon, disown, leave in the lurch, strand **2** give up, forgo, relinquish, renounce, set aside, surrender, yield

forsaken adjective deserted, abandoned, disowned, forlorn, left in the lurch, marooned, outcast, stranded

fort noun **1** fortress, blockhouse, camp, castle, citadel, fortification, garrison, stronghold **2 hold the fort** stand in, carry on, keep things on an even keel, take over the reins

forte noun speciality, gift, long suit (informal), métier, strength, strong point, talent

forth adverb forward, ahead, away, onward, out, outward

forthcoming adjective **1** approaching, coming, expected, future, imminent, impending, prospective, upcoming **2** accessible, at hand, available, in evidence, obtainable, on tap (informal), ready **3** communicative, chatty, expansive, free, informative, open, sociable, talkative, unreserved

forthright adjective outspoken, blunt, candid, direct, frank, open, plain-spoken, straightforward, upfront (informal)

forthwith adverb at once, directly, immediately, instantly, quickly, right away, straightaway, without delay

fortification noun **1** defence, bastion, fastness, fort, fortress, protection, stronghold **2** strengthening, reinforcement

fortify verb strengthen, augment,

buttress, protect, reinforce, shore up, support

fortitude noun <u>courage</u>, backbone, bravery, fearlessness, grit, perseverance, resolution, strength, valour

fortress noun <u>castle</u>, citadel, fastness, fort, redoubt, stronghold

fortunate adjective **1** <u>lucky</u>, favoured, in luck, jammy (*Brit. slang*), successful, well-off **2** <u>favourable</u>, advantageous, convenient, expedient, felicitous, fortuitous, helpful, opportune, providential, timely

fortunately adverb <u>luckily</u>, by a happy chance, by good luck, happily, providentially

fortune noun **1** <u>wealth</u>, affluence, opulence, possessions, property, prosperity, riches, treasure **2** <u>luck</u>, chance, destiny, fate, kismet, providence **3 fortunes** <u>destiny</u>, adventures, experiences, history, lot, success

forward adjective **1** <u>leading</u>, advance, first, foremost, front, head **2** <u>presumptuous</u>, bold, brash, brazen, cheeky, familiar, impertinent, impudent, pushy (*informal*) **3** <u>well-developed</u>, advanced, precocious, premature ♦ adverb **4** <u>ahead</u>, forth, on, onward ♦ verb **5** <u>promote</u>, advance, assist, expedite, further, hasten, hurry **6** <u>send</u>, dispatch, post, send on

foster verb **1** <u>promote</u>, cultivate, encourage, feed, nurture, stimulate, support, uphold **2** <u>bring up</u>, mother, nurse, raise, rear, take care of

foul adjective **1** <u>dirty</u>, fetid, filthy, malodorous, nauseating, putrid,

repulsive, squalid, stinking, unclean **2** <u>obscene</u>, abusive, blue, coarse, indecent, lewd, profane, scurrilous, vulgar **3** <u>offensive</u>, abhorrent, despicable, detestable, disgraceful, scandalous, shameful, wicked **4** <u>unfair</u>, crooked, dishonest, fraudulent, shady (*informal*), underhand, unscrupulous ♦ verb **5** <u>pollute</u>, besmirch, contaminate, defile, dirty, stain, sully, taint

found verb <u>establish</u>, constitute, create, inaugurate, institute, organize, originate, set up, start

foundation noun **1** <u>groundwork</u>, base, basis, bedrock, bottom, footing, substructure, underpinning **2** <u>setting up</u>, endowment, establishment, inauguration, institution, organization, settlement

founder[1] noun <u>initiator</u>, architect, author, beginner, father, inventor, originator

founder[2] verb **1** <u>sink</u>, be lost, go down, go to the bottom, submerge **2** <u>fail</u>, break down, collapse, come to grief, come unstuck, fall through, miscarry, misfire **3** <u>stumble</u>, lurch, sprawl, stagger, trip

foundling noun <u>stray</u>, orphan, outcast, waif

fountain noun **1** <u>jet</u>, font, fount, reservoir, spout, spray, spring, well **2** <u>source</u>, cause, derivation, fount, fountainhead, origin, wellspring

foyer noun <u>entrance hall</u>, antechamber, anteroom, lobby, reception area, vestibule

fracas noun <u>brawl</u>, affray (*Law*),

disturbance, melee *or* mêlée, riot, rumpus, scuffle, skirmish

fraction *noun* piece, part, percentage, portion, section, segment, share, slice

fractious *adjective* irritable, captious, cross, petulant, querulous, refractory, testy, tetchy, touchy

fracture *noun* 1 break, cleft, crack, fissure, opening, rift, rupture, split ♦ *verb* 2 break, crack, rupture, splinter, split

fragile *adjective* delicate, breakable, brittle, dainty, fine, flimsy, frail, frangible, weak

fragment *noun* 1 piece, bit, chip, particle, portion, scrap, shred, sliver ♦ *verb* 2 break, break up, come apart, come to pieces, crumble, disintegrate, shatter, splinter, split up

fragmentary *adjective* incomplete, bitty, broken, disconnected, incoherent, partial, piecemeal, scattered, scrappy, sketchy

fragrance *noun* scent, aroma, balm, bouquet, fragrancy, perfume, redolence, smell, sweet odour

fragrant *adjective* perfumed, aromatic, balmy, odorous, redolent, sweet-scented, sweet-smelling

frail *adjective* weak, delicate, feeble, flimsy, fragile, infirm, insubstantial, puny, vulnerable

frailty *noun* feebleness, fallibility, frailness, infirmity, susceptibility, weakness

frame *noun* 1 casing, construction, framework, shell, structure 2 physique, anatomy, body, build, carcass 3 frame of mind mood, attitude, disposition, humour, outlook, state, temper ♦ *verb* 4 construct, assemble, build, make, manufacture, put together 5 draft, compose, devise, draw up, formulate, map out, sketch 6 mount, case, enclose, surround

framework *noun* structure, foundation, frame, groundwork, plan, shell, skeleton, the bare bones

frank *adjective* honest, blunt, candid, direct, forthright, open, outspoken, plain-spoken, sincere, straightforward, truthful

frankly *adverb* honestly, candidly, in truth, to be honest 2 openly, bluntly, directly, freely, plainly, without reserve

frankness *noun* outspokenness, bluntness, candour, forthrightness, openness, plain speaking, truthfulness

frantic *adjective* 1 furious, at the end of one's tether, berserk, beside oneself, distracted, distraught, wild 2 hectic, desperate, fraught (*informal*), frenetic, frenzied

fraternity *noun* 1 club, association, brotherhood, circle, company, guild, league, union 2 companionship, brotherhood, camaraderie, fellowship, kinship

fraternize *verb* associate, consort, cooperate, hobnob, keep company, mingle, mix, socialize

fraud *noun* 1 deception, chicanery, deceit, double-dealing, duplicity, sharp practice, swindling, treachery, trickery **2** impostor, charlatan, fake, fraudster, hoaxer, phoney or phony (informal), pretender, swindler

fraudulent adjective deceitful, crooked (informal), dishonest, double-dealing, duplicitous, sham, swindling, treacherous

fray verb wear thin, chafe, rub, wear

freak noun **1** oddity, aberration, anomaly, malformation, monstrosity, weirdo or weirdie (informal) **2** enthusiast, addict, aficionado, buff (informal), devotee, fan, fanatic, fiend (informal), nut (slang) ◆ adjective **3** abnormal, exceptional, unparalleled, unusual

free adjective **1** for nothing, complimentary, for free (informal), free of charge, gratis, gratuitous, on the house, unpaid, without charge **2** at liberty, at large, footloose, independent, liberated, loose, on the loose, unfettered **3** allowed, able, clear, permitted, unimpeded, unrestricted **4** available, empty, idle, spare, unemployed, unoccupied, unused, vacant **5** generous, lavish, liberal, unsparing, unstinting ◆ verb **6** release, deliver, let out, liberate, loose, set free, turn loose, unchain, untie **7** extricate, cut loose, disengage, disentangle, rescue

freedom noun **1** liberty, deliverance, emancipation, independence, release **2** opportunity, blank cheque, carte blanche, discretion, free rein, latitude, licence

free-for-all noun fight, brawl, dust-up (informal), fracas, melee or mêlée, riot, row, scrimmage

freely adverb **1** willingly, of one's own accord, of one's own free will, spontaneously, voluntarily, without prompting **2** openly, candidly, frankly, plainly, unreservedly, without reserve **3** abundantly, amply, copiously, extravagantly, lavishly, liberally, unstintingly

freeze verb **1** chill, harden, ice over or up, stiffen **2** suspend, fix, hold up, inhibit, peg, stop

freezing adjective icy, arctic, biting, bitter, chill, frosty, glacial, raw, wintry

freight noun **1** transportation, carriage, conveyance, shipment **2** cargo, burden, consignment, goods, load, merchandise, payload

French adjective Gallic

frenzied adjective furious, distracted, feverish, frantic, frenetic, rabid, uncontrolled, wild

frenzy noun fury, derangement, hysteria, paroxysm, passion, rage, seizure

frequent adjective **1** common, customary, everyday, familiar, habitual, persistent, recurrent, repeated, usual ◆ verb **2** visit, attend, be found at, hang out at (informal), haunt, patronize

frequently adverb often, commonly, habitually, many times, much, not infrequently, repeatedly

fresh adjective **1** new, different, modern, novel, original, recent, up-to-date **2** <u>additional</u>, added, auxiliary, extra, further, more, other, supplementary **3** <u>invigorating</u>, bracing, brisk, clean, cool, crisp, pure, refreshing, unpolluted **4** <u>lively</u>, alert, energetic, keen, refreshed, sprightly, spry, vigorous **5** <u>natural</u>, unprocessed **6** *Informal* <u>cheeky</u>, disrespectful, familiar, forward, impudent, insolent, presumptuous

freshen *verb* <u>refresh</u>, enliven, freshen up, liven up, restore, revitalize

freshness *noun* **1** <u>novelty</u>, inventiveness, newness, originality **2** <u>cleanness</u>, brightness, clearness, glow, shine, sparkle, vigour, wholesomeness

fret *verb* <u>worry</u>, agonize, brood, grieve, lose sleep over, upset *or* distress oneself

fretful *adjective* <u>irritable</u>, crotchety (*informal*), edgy, fractious, querulous, short-tempered, testy, touchy, uneasy

friction *noun* **1** <u>rubbing</u>, abrasion, chafing, grating, rasping, resistance, scraping **2** <u>hostility</u>, animosity, bad blood, conflict, disagreement, discord, dissension, resentment

friend *noun* **1** <u>companion</u>, buddy (*informal*), chum (*informal*), comrade, mate (*informal*), pal, playmate **2** <u>supporter</u>, ally, associate, patron, well-wisher

friendliness *noun* <u>kindliness</u>, affability, amiability, congeniality, conviviality, geniality, neighbourliness, sociability, warmth

friendly *adjective* <u>sociable</u>, affectionate, amicable, close, familiar, helpful, intimate, neighbourly, on good terms, pally (*informal*), sympathetic, welcoming

friendship *noun* <u>goodwill</u>, affection, amity, attachment, concord, familiarity, friendliness, harmony, intimacy

fright *noun* <u>fear</u>, alarm, consternation, dread, horror, panic, scare, shock, trepidation

frighten *verb* <u>scare</u>, alarm, intimidate, petrify, shock, startle, terrify, terrorize, unnerve

frightened *adjective* <u>afraid</u>, alarmed, petrified, scared, scared stiff, startled, terrified, terrorized, terror-stricken

frightening *adjective* <u>terrifying</u>, alarming, fearful, fearsome, horrifying, menacing, scary (*informal*), shocking, unnerving

frightful *adjective* <u>terrifying</u>, alarming, awful, dreadful, fearful, ghastly, horrendous, horrible, terrible, traumatic

frigid *adjective* **1** <u>cold</u>, arctic, frosty, frozen, glacial, icy, wintry **2** <u>forbidding</u>, aloof, austere, formal, unapproachable, unfeeling, unresponsive

frills *plural noun* <u>trimmings</u>, additions, bells and whistles, embellishments, extras, frippery, fuss, ornamentation, ostentation

fringe *noun* **1** <u>border</u>, edging, hem, trimming **2** <u>edge</u>, borderline, limits, margin, outskirts, perimeter, periphery ♦ *adjective* **3** <u>unofficial</u>, unconventional, unorthodox

frisk verb 1 frolic, caper, cavort, gambol, jump, play, prance, skip, trip 2 *Informal* search, check, inspect, run over, shake down (*U.S. slang*)

frisky adjective lively, coltish, frolicsome, high-spirited, kittenish, playful, sportive

fritter away verb waste, dissipate, idle away, misspend, run through, spend like water, squander

frivolity noun fun, flippancy, frivolousness, gaiety, levity, light-heartedness, silliness, superficiality, triviality

frivolous adjective 1 flippant, childish, foolish, idle, juvenile, puerile, silly, superficial 2 trivial, footling (*informal*), minor, petty, shallow, trifling, unimportant

frolic verb 1 play, caper, cavort, frisk, gambol, lark, make merry, romp, sport ♦ noun 2 revel, antic, game, lark, romp, spree

frolicsome adjective playful, coltish, frisky, kittenish, lively, merry, sportive

front noun 1 exterior, façade, face, foreground, frontage 2 forefront, front line, head, lead, vanguard 3 disguise, blind, cover, cover-up, façade, mask, pretext, show ♦ adjective 4 first, foremost, head, lead, leading, topmost ♦ verb 5 face onto, look over or onto, overlook

frontier noun boundary, borderline, edge, limit, perimeter, verge

frost noun hoarfrost, freeze, rime

frosty adjective 1 cold, chilly,

frozen, icy, wintry 2 unfriendly, discouraging, frigid, off-putting (*Brit. informal*), standoffish, unenthusiastic, unwelcoming

froth noun 1 foam, bubbles, effervescence, head, lather, scum, spume, suds ♦ verb 2 fizz, bubble over, come to a head, effervesce, foam, lather

frothy adjective foamy, foaming, sudsy

frown verb 1 scowl, glare, glower, knit one's brows, look daggers, lour or lower 2 frown on disapprove of, discourage, dislike, look askance at, take a dim view of

frozen adjective icy, arctic, chilled, frigid, frosted, icebound, ice-cold, ice-covered, numb

frugal adjective thrifty, abstemious, careful, economical, niggardly, parsimonious, prudent, sparing

fruit noun 1 produce, crop, harvest, product, yield 2 result, advantage, benefit, consequence, effect, end result, outcome, profit, return, reward

fruitful adjective useful, advantageous, beneficial, effective, productive, profitable, rewarding, successful, worthwhile

fruition noun maturity, attainment, completion, fulfilment, materialization, perfection, realization, ripeness

fruitless adjective useless, futile, ineffectual, pointless, profitless, unavailing, unproductive, unprofitable, unsuccessful, vain

frustrate verb thwart, balk, block, check, counter, defeat, disappoint, foil, forestall, nullify, stymie

frustrated *adjective* <u>disappointed</u>, discouraged, disheartened, embittered, resentful

frustration *noun* **1** <u>obstruction</u>, blocking, circumvention, foiling, thwarting **2** <u>annoyance</u>, disappointment, dissatisfaction, grievance, irritation, resentment, vexation

fuddy-duddy *noun* <u>conservative</u>, (old) fogey, square (*informal*), stick-in-the-mud (*informal*), stuffed shirt (*informal*)

fudge *verb* <u>hedge</u>, equivocate, flannel (*Brit. informal*), stall

fuel *noun* <u>incitement</u>, ammunition, provocation

fugitive *noun* **1** <u>runaway</u>, deserter, escapee, refugee ♦ *adjective* **2** <u>momentary</u>, brief, ephemeral, fleeting, passing, short-lived, temporary, transient, transitory

fulfil *verb* **1** <u>achieve</u>, accomplish, carry out, complete, perform, realise, satisfy **2** <u>comply with</u>, answer, conform to, fill, meet, obey, observe

fulfilment *noun* <u>achievement</u>, accomplishment, attainment, completion, consummation, implementation, realization

full *adjective* **1** <u>saturated</u>, brimming, complete, filled, loaded, replete, satiated, stocked **2** <u>plentiful</u>, abundant, adequate, ample, comprehensive, exhaustive, extensive, generous **3** <u>rich</u>, clear, deep, distinct, loud, resonant, rounded **4** <u>plump</u>, buxom, curvaceous, rounded, voluptuous **5** <u>loose</u>, baggy,

capacious, large, puffy, voluminous ♦ *noun* **6 in full** <u>completely</u>, in its entirety, in total, without exception

full-blooded *adjective* <u>vigorous</u>, hearty, lusty, red-blooded, virile

fullness *noun* **1** <u>plenty</u>, abundance, copiousness, fill, profusion, satiety, saturation, sufficiency **2** <u>richness</u>, clearness, loudness, resonance, strength

full-scale *adjective* <u>major</u>, all-out, comprehensive, exhaustive, in-depth, sweeping, thorough, thoroughgoing, wide-ranging

fully *adverb* <u>totally</u>, altogether, completely, entirely, in all respects, one hundred per cent, perfectly, thoroughly, utterly, wholly

fulsome *adjective* <u>insincere</u>, excessive, extravagant, immoderate, inordinate, sycophantic, unctuous

fumble *verb* <u>grope</u>, feel around, flounder, scrabble

fume *verb* <u>rage</u>, get hot under the collar (*informal*), rant, see red (*informal*), seethe, smoulder, storm

fumes *plural noun* <u>smoke</u>, exhaust, gas, pollution, smog, vapour

fumigate *verb* <u>disinfect</u>, clean out *or* up, cleanse, purify, sanitize, sterilize

fuming *adjective* <u>angry</u>, enraged, in a rage, incensed, on the warpath (*informal*), raging, seething, up in arms

fun *noun* **1** <u>enjoyment</u>, amusement, entertainment, jollity, merriment, mirth,

pleasure, recreation, sport
2 **make fun of** mock, lampoon, laugh at, parody, poke fun at, ridicule, satirize, send up (*Brit. informal*) ♦ *adjective* 3 enjoyable, amusing, convivial, diverting, entertaining, lively, witty

function *noun* 1 purpose, business, duty, job, mission, *raison d'être*, responsibility, role, task 2 reception, affair, do (*informal*), gathering, social occasion ♦ *verb* 3 work, act, behave, do duty, go, operate, perform, run

functional *adjective* 1 practical, hard-wearing, serviceable, useful, utilitarian 2 working, operative

fund *noun* 1 reserve, kitty, pool, stock, store, supply ♦ *verb* 2 finance, pay for, subsidize, support

fundamental *adjective* 1 essential, basic, cardinal, central, elementary, key, primary, principal, rudimentary, underlying ♦ *noun* 2 principle, axiom, cornerstone, law, rudiment, rule

fundamentally *adverb* essentially, at bottom, at heart, basically, intrinsically, primarily, radically

funds *plural noun* money, capital, cash, finance, ready money, resources, savings, the wherewithal

funeral *noun* burial, cremation, inhumation, interment, obsequies

funnel *verb* channel, conduct, convey, direct, filter, move, pass, pour

funny *adjective* 1 humorous, amusing, comic, comical, droll,

entertaining, hilarious, riotous, side-splitting, witty 2 peculiar, curious, mysterious, odd, queer, strange, suspicious, unusual, weird

furious *adjective* 1 angry, beside oneself, enraged, fuming, incensed, infuriated, livid (*informal*), raging, up in arms 2 violent, fierce, intense, savage, turbulent, unrestrained, vehement

furnish *verb* 1 decorate, equip, fit out, stock 2 supply, give, grant, hand out, offer, present, provide

furniture *noun* household goods, appliances, fittings, furnishings, goods, possessions, things (*informal*)

furore *noun* disturbance, commotion, hullabaloo, outcry, stir, to-do, uproar

furrow *noun* 1 groove, channel, crease, hollow, line, rut, seam, trench, wrinkle ♦ *verb* 2 wrinkle, corrugate, crease, draw together, knit

further *adverb* 1 in addition, additionally, also, besides, furthermore, into the bargain, moreover, to boot ♦ *adjective* 2 additional, extra, fresh, more, new, other, supplementary ♦ *verb* 3 promote, advance, assist, encourage, forward, help, lend support to, work for

furthermore *adverb* besides, additionally, as well, further, in addition, into the bargain, moreover, to boot, too

furthest *adjective* most distant, extreme, farthest, furthermost, outmost, remotest, ultimate

furtive *adjective* sly, clandestine, conspiratorial, secretive, sneaky, stealthy, surreptitious, underhand, under-the-table

fury *noun* **1** anger, frenzy, impetuosity, madness, passion, rage, wrath **2** violence, ferocity, fierceness, force, intensity, savagery, severity, vehemence

fuss *noun* **1** bother, ado, commotion, excitement, hue and cry, palaver, stir, to-do **2** argument, complaint, furore, objection, row, squabble, trouble ♦ *verb* **3** worry, fidget, flap (*informal*), fret, get worked up, take pains

fussy *adjective* **1** hard to please, choosy (*informal*), difficult, fastidious, finicky, nit-picking (*informal*), particular, pernickety, picky (*informal*) **2** overelaborate, busy, cluttered, overworked, rococo

fusty *adjective* stale, airless, damp, mildewed, mouldering, musty, stuffy

futile *adjective* useless, fruitless, ineffectual, unavailing, unprofitable, unsuccessful, vain, worthless

futility *noun* uselessness, emptiness, hollowness, ineffectiveness

future *noun* **1** hereafter, time to come **2** outlook, expectation, prospect ♦ *adjective* **3** forthcoming, approaching, coming, fated, impending, later, subsequent, to come

fuzzy *adjective* **1** fluffy, downy, frizzy, woolly **2** indistinct, bleary, blurred, distorted, ill-defined, out of focus, unclear, vague

G g

gabble *verb* **1** prattle, babble, blabber, gibber, gush, jabber, spout ♦ *noun* **2** gibberish, babble, blabber, chatter, drivel, prattle, twaddle

gadabout *noun* pleasure-seeker, gallivanter, rambler, rover, wanderer

gadget *noun* device, appliance, contraption (*informal*), contrivance, gizmo (*slang, chiefly U.S.*), instrument, invention, thing, tool

gaffe *noun* blunder, bloomer (*informal*), clanger (*informal*), faux pas, howler, indiscretion, lapse, mistake, slip, solecism

gaffer *noun* **1** *Informal* manager, boss (*informal*), foreman, overseer, superintendent, supervisor **2** old man, granddad, greybeard, old boy (*informal*), old fellow, old-timer (*U.S.*)

gag[1] *verb* **1** suppress, curb, muffle, muzzle, quiet, silence, stifle, stop up **2** retch, heave, puke (*slang*), spew, throw up (*informal*), vomit

gag[2] *noun* joke, crack (*slang*), funny (*informal*), hoax, jest, wisecrack (*informal*), witticism

gaiety *noun* **1** cheerfulness, blitheness, exhilaration, glee, high spirits, jollity, light-heartedness, merriment, mirth **2** merrymaking, conviviality, festivity, fun, jollification, revelry

gaily *adverb* **1** cheerfully, blithely,

gleefully, happily, joyfully, light-heartedly, merrily **2** colourfully, brightly, brilliantly, flamboyantly, flashily, gaudily, showily

gain verb **1** obtain, acquire, attain, capture, collect, gather, get, land, pick up, secure, win **2** reach, arrive at, attain, come to, get to **3** gain on get nearer, approach, catch up with, close, narrow the gap, overtake ♦ noun **4** profit, advantage, benefit, dividend, return, yield **5** increase, advance, growth, improvement, progress, rise

gainful adjective profitable, advantageous, beneficial, fruitful, lucrative, productive, remunerative, rewarding, useful, worthwhile

gains plural noun profits, earnings, prize, proceeds, revenue, takings, winnings

gainsay verb contradict, contravene, controvert, deny, disagree with, dispute, rebut, retract

gait noun walk, bearing, carriage, pace, step, stride, tread

gala noun festival, carnival, celebration, festivity, fête, jamboree, pageant

gale noun **1** storm, blast, cyclone, hurricane, squall, tempest, tornado, typhoon **2** Informal outburst, burst, eruption, explosion, fit, howl, outbreak, peal, shout, shriek

gall [1] noun **1** Informal impudence, brazenness, cheek (informal), chutzpah (U.S. & Canad. informal), effrontery, impertinence, insolence, nerve

(informal) **2** bitterness, acrimony, animosity, bile, hostility, rancour

gall [2] verb **1** scrape, abrade, chafe, irritate **2** annoy, exasperate, irk, irritate, provoke, rankle, vex

gallant adjective **1** brave, bold, courageous, heroic, honourable, intrepid, manly, noble, valiant **2** chivalrous, attentive, courteous, gentlemanly, gracious, noble, polite

gallantry noun **1** bravery, boldness, courage, heroism, intrepidity, manliness, spirit, valour **2** attentiveness, chivalry, courteousness, courtesy, gentlemanliness, graciousness, nobility, politeness

galling adjective annoying, bitter, exasperating, irksome, irritating, provoking, vexatious

gallivant verb wander, gad about, ramble, roam, rove

gallop verb run, bolt, career, dash, hurry, race, rush, speed, sprint

galore adverb in abundance, all over the place, aplenty, everywhere, in great quantity, in numbers, in profusion, to spare

galvanize verb stimulate, electrify, excite, inspire, invigorate, jolt, provoke, spur, stir

gamble verb **1** bet, game, have a flutter (informal), play, punt, wager **2** risk, chance, hazard, speculate, stick one's neck out (informal), take a chance ♦ noun **3** risk, chance, leap in the dark, lottery, speculation, uncertainty, venture **4** bet, flutter (informal), punt, wager

gambol verb **1** frolic, caper,

cavort, frisk, hop, jump, prance, skip ♦ *noun* 2 **frolic**, caper, hop, jump, prance, skip

game *noun* 1 **pastime**, amusement, distraction, diversion, entertainment, lark, recreation, sport 2 **match**, competition, contest, event, head-to-head, meeting, tournament 3 **wild animals**, prey, quarry 4 **scheme**, design, plan, plot, ploy, stratagem, tactic, trick ♦ *adjective* 5 **brave**, courageous, gallant, gritty, intrepid, persistent, plucky, spirited 6 **willing**, desirous, eager, interested, keen, prepared, ready

gamut *noun* **range**, area, catalogue, compass, field, scale, scope, series, sweep

gang *noun* **group**, band, clique, club, company, coterie, crowd, mob, pack, squad, team

gangling *adjective* **tall**, angular, awkward, lanky, rangy, rawboned, spindly

gangster *noun* **racketeer**, crook (*informal*), hood (*U.S. slang*), hoodlum (*chiefly U.S.*), mobster (*U.S. slang*)

gap *noun* 1 **opening**, break, chink, cleft, crack, hole, space 2 **interval**, breathing space, hiatus, interlude, intermission, interruption, lacuna, lull, pause, respite 3 **difference**, disagreement, disparity, divergence, inconsistency

gape *verb* 1 **stare**, gawk, gawp (*Brit. slang*), goggle, wonder 2 **open**, crack, split, yawn

gaping *adjective* **wide**, broad, cavernous, great, open, vast,

wide open, yawning

garbage *noun* **rubbish**, refuse, trash (*chiefly U.S.*), waste

garbled *adjective* **jumbled**, confused, distorted, double-Dutch, incomprehensible, mixed up, unintelligible

garish *adjective* **gaudy**, brash, brassy, flashy, loud, showy, tacky (*informal*), tasteless, vulgar

garland *noun* 1 **wreath**, bays, chaplet, crown, festoon, honours, laurels ♦ *verb* 2 **adorn**, crown, deck, festoon, wreathe

garments *plural noun* **clothes**, apparel, attire, clothing, costume, dress, garb, gear (*slang*), outfit, uniform

garner *verb* **collect**, accumulate, amass, gather, hoard, save, stockpile, store, stow away

garnish *verb* 1 **decorate**, adorn, embellish, enhance, ornament, set off, trim ♦ *noun* 2 **decoration**, adornment, embellishment, enhancement, ornamentation, trimming

garrison *noun* 1 **troops**, armed force, command, detachment, unit 2 **fort**, base, camp, encampment, fortification, fortress, post, station, stronghold ♦ *verb* 3 **station**, assign, position, post, put on duty

garrulous *adjective* **talkative**, chatty, gossiping, loquacious, prattling, verbose, voluble

gash *verb* 1 **cut**, gouge, lacerate, slash, slit, split, tear, wound ♦ *noun* 2 **cut**, gouge, incision, laceration, slash, slit, split, tear, wound

gasp *verb* 1 **gulp**, blow, catch

one's breath, choke, pant, puff
♦ *noun* 2 gulp, exclamation,
pant, puff, sharp intake of breath

gate *noun* barrier, door, entrance,
exit, gateway, opening, passage,
portal

gather *verb* 1 assemble,
accumulate, amass, collect,
garner, mass, muster, stockpile
2 learn, assume, conclude,
deduce, hear, infer, surmise,
understand 3 pick, cull, garner,
glean, harvest, pluck, reap,
select 4 intensify, deepen,
expand, grow, heighten,
increase, rise, swell, thicken
5 fold, pleat, tuck

gathering *noun* assembly,
company, conclave, congress,
convention, crowd, group,
meeting

gauche *adjective* awkward,
clumsy, ill-mannered, inelegant,
tactless, unsophisticated

gaudy *adjective* garish, bright,
flashy, loud, showy, tacky
(*informal*), tasteless, vulgar

gauge *verb* 1 measure, ascertain,
calculate, check, compute,
count, determine, weigh
2 judge, adjudge, appraise,
assess, estimate, evaluate, guess,
rate, reckon, value ♦ *noun*
3 indicator, criterion, guide,
guideline, measure, meter,
standard, test, touchstone,
yardstick

gaunt *adjective* thin, angular,
bony, haggard, lean, pinched,
scrawny, skinny, spare

gawky *adjective* awkward,
clumsy, gauche, loutish,
lumbering, maladroit, ungainly

gay *adjective* 1 homosexual,

lesbian, queer (*informal,
derogatory*) 2 carefree, blithe,
cheerful, jovial, light-hearted,
lively, merry, sparkling
3 colourful, bright, brilliant,
flamboyant, flashy, rich, showy,
vivid ♦ *noun* 4 homosexual,
lesbian

gaze *verb* 1 stare, gape, look,
regard, view, watch, wonder
♦ *noun* 2 stare, fixed look, look

gazette *noun* newspaper, journal,
news-sheet, paper, periodical

gear *noun* 1 cog, cogwheel,
gearwheel 2 mechanism, cogs,
machinery, works 3 equipment,
accoutrements, apparatus,
instruments, paraphernalia,
supplies, tackle, tools 4 clothing,
clothes, costume, dress,
garments, outfit, togs, wear
♦ *verb* 5 equip, adapt, adjust, fit

gelatinous *adjective* jelly-like,
glutinous, gummy, sticky, viscous

gelid *adjective* cold, arctic, chilly,
freezing, frigid, frosty, frozen,
glacial, ice-cold, icy

gem *noun* 1 precious stone,
jewel, stone 2 prize, jewel,
masterpiece, pearl, treasure

general *adjective* 1 common,
accepted, broad, extensive,
popular, prevalent, public,
universal, widespread
2 imprecise, approximate,
ill-defined, indefinite, inexact,
loose, unspecific, vague
3 universal, across-the-board,
blanket, collective,
comprehensive, indiscriminate,
miscellaneous, sweeping, total

generally *adverb* 1 usually, as a
rule, by and large, customarily,
normally, on the whole,

ordinarily, typically **2** commonly, extensively, popularly, publicly, universally, widely

generate verb produce, breed, cause, create, engender, give rise to, make, propagate

generation noun **1** production, creation, formation, genesis, propagation, reproduction **2** age group, breed, crop **3** age, epoch, era, period, time

generic adjective collective, blanket, common, comprehensive, general, inclusive, universal, wide

generosity noun **1** charity, beneficence, bounty, kindness, largesse or largess, liberality, munificence, open-handedness **2** unselfishness, goodness, high-mindedness, magnanimity, nobleness

generous adjective **1** charitable, beneficent, bountiful, hospitable, kind, lavish, liberal, open-handed, unstinting **2** unselfish, big-hearted, good, high-minded, lofty, magnanimous, noble **3** plentiful, abundant, ample, copious, full, lavish, liberal, rich, unstinting

genesis noun beginning, birth, creation, formation, inception, origin, start

genial adjective cheerful, affable, agreeable, amiable, congenial, friendly, good-natured, jovial, pleasant, warm

geniality noun cheerfulness, affability, agreeableness, amiability, conviviality, cordiality, friendliness, good cheer, joviality, warmth

genius noun **1** master, brainbox,

expert, hotshot (informal), maestro, mastermind, virtuoso, whiz (informal) **2** brilliance, ability, aptitude, bent, capacity, flair, gift, knack, talent

genre noun type, category, class, group, kind, sort, species, style

genteel adjective refined, courteous, cultured, elegant, gentlemanly, ladylike, polite, respectable, urbane, well-mannered

gentle adjective
1 sweet-tempered, compassionate, humane, kindly, meek, mild, placid, tender **2** moderate, light, mild, muted, slight, soft, soothing **3** gradual, easy, imperceptible, light, mild, moderate, slight, slow **4** tame, biddable, broken, docile, manageable, placid, tractable

gentlemanly adjective polite, civil, courteous, gallant, genteel, honourable, refined, urbane, well-mannered

gentleness noun tenderness, compassion, kindness, mildness, softness, sweetness

gentry noun nobility, aristocracy, elite, upper class, upper crust (informal)

genuine adjective **1** authentic, actual, bona fide, legitimate, real, the real McCoy, true, veritable **2** sincere, candid, earnest, frank, heartfelt, honest, unaffected, unfeigned

germ noun **1** microbe, bacterium, bug (informal), microorganism, virus **2** beginning, embryo, origin, root, rudiment, seed, source, spark

germane adjective relevant, apposite, appropriate, apropos, connected, fitting, material, pertinent, related, to the point or purpose

germinate verb sprout, bud, develop, generate, grow, originate, shoot, swell, vegetate

gesticulate verb signal, gesture, indicate, make a sign, motion, sign, wave

gesture noun 1 signal, action, gesticulation, indication, motion, sign ♦ verb 2 signal, gesticulate, indicate, motion, sign, wave

get verb 1 obtain, acquire, attain, fetch, gain, land, net, pick up, procure, receive, secure, win 2 contract, catch, come down with, fall victim to, take 3 capture, grab, lay hold of, nab (informal), seize, take 4 become, come to be, grow, turn 5 understand, catch, comprehend, fathom, follow, perceive, see, take in, work out 6 persuade, convince, induce, influence, prevail upon 7 Informal annoy, bug (informal), gall, irritate, upset, vex

get across verb 1 cross, ford, negotiate, pass over, traverse 2 communicate, bring home to, convey, impart, make clear or understood, put over, transmit

get at verb 1 gain access to, acquire, attain, come to grips with, get hold of, reach 2 imply, hint, intend, lead up to, mean, suggest 3 criticize, attack, blame, find fault with, nag, pick on

getaway noun escape, break, break-out, flight

get by verb manage, cope, exist, fare, get along, keep one's head above water, make both ends meet, survive

get off verb leave, alight, depart, descend, disembark, dismount, escape, exit

get on verb 1 board, ascend, climb, embark, mount 2 be friendly, be compatible, concur, get along, hit it off (informal)

get over verb recover from, come round, get better, mend, pull through, rally, revive, survive

ghastly adjective horrible, dreadful, frightful, gruesome, hideous, horrendous, loathsome, shocking, terrible, terrifying

ghost noun 1 spirit, apparition, phantom, soul, spectre, spook (informal), wraith 2 trace, glimmer, hint, possibility, semblance, shadow, suggestion

ghostly adjective supernatural, eerie, ghostlike, phantom, spectral, spooky (informal), unearthly, wraithlike

ghoulish adjective macabre, disgusting, grisly, gruesome, morbid, sick (informal), unwholesome

giant noun 1 ogre, colossus, monster, titan ♦ adjective 2 huge, colossal, enormous, gargantuan, gigantic, immense, mammoth, titanic, vast

gibberish noun nonsense, babble, drivel, gobbledegook (informal), mumbo jumbo, twaddle

gibe, jibe verb 1 taunt, jeer, make fun of, mock, poke fun at, ridicule, scoff, scorn, sneer

♦ *noun* **2** <u>taunt</u>, barb, crack (*slang*), dig, jeer, sarcasm, scoffing, sneer

giddiness *noun* <u>dizziness</u>, faintness, light-headedness, vertigo

giddy *adjective* <u>dizzy</u>, dizzying, faint, light-headed, reeling, unsteady, vertiginous

gift *noun* **1** <u>donation</u>, bequest, bonus, contribution, grant, hand-out, legacy, offering, present **2** <u>talent</u>, ability, capability, capacity, flair, genius, knack, power

gifted *adjective* <u>talented</u>, able, accomplished, brilliant, capable, clever, expert, ingenious, masterly, skilled

gigantic *adjective* <u>enormous</u>, colossal, giant, huge, immense, mammoth, stupendous, titanic, tremendous

giggle *verb, noun* <u>laugh</u>, cackle, chortle, chuckle, snigger, titter, twitter

gild *verb* <u>embellish</u>, adorn, beautify, brighten, coat, dress up, embroider, enhance, ornament

gimmick *noun* <u>stunt</u>, contrivance, device, dodge, ploy, scheme

gingerly *adverb* <u>cautiously</u>, carefully, charily, circumspectly, hesitantly, reluctantly, suspiciously, timidly, warily

gird *verb* <u>surround</u>, encircle, enclose, encompass, enfold, hem in, ring

girdle *noun* **1** <u>belt</u>, band, cummerbund, sash, waistband
♦ *verb* **2** <u>surround</u>, bound,

encircle, enclose, encompass, gird, ring

girl *noun* <u>female child</u>, damsel (*archaic*), daughter, lass, lassie (*informal*), maid (*archaic*), maiden (*archaic*), miss

girth *noun* <u>circumference</u>, bulk, measure, size

gist *noun* <u>point</u>, core, essence, force, idea, meaning, sense, significance, substance

give *verb* **1** <u>present</u>, award, contribute, deliver, donate, grant, hand over *or* out, provide, supply **2** <u>announce</u>, communicate, issue, notify, pronounce, transmit, utter **3** <u>concede</u>, grant, hand over, relinquish, surrender, yield **4** <u>produce</u>, cause, engender, make, occasion

give away *verb* <u>reveal</u>, betray, disclose, divulge, expose, leak, let out, let slip, uncover

give in *verb* <u>admit defeat</u>, capitulate, collapse, concede, quit, submit, succumb, surrender, yield

give off *verb* <u>emit</u>, discharge, exude, produce, release, send out, throw out

give out *verb* <u>emit</u>, discharge, exude, produce, release, send out, throw out

give up *verb* <u>abandon</u>, call it a day *or* night, cease, desist, leave off, quit, relinquish, renounce, stop, surrender

glad *adjective* **1** <u>happy</u>, contented, delighted, gratified, joyful, overjoyed, pleased **2** <u>pleasing</u>, cheerful, cheering, gratifying, pleasant

gladden verb please, cheer, delight, gratify, hearten

gladly adverb happily, cheerfully, freely, gleefully, readily, willingly, with pleasure

gladness noun happiness, cheerfulness, delight, gaiety, glee, high spirits, joy, mirth, pleasure

glamorous adjective elegant, attractive, dazzling, exciting, fascinating, glittering, glossy, prestigious, smart

glamour noun charm, allure, appeal, attraction, beauty, enchantment, fascination, prestige

glance verb 1 look, glimpse, peek, peep, scan, view 2 gleam, flash, glimmer, glint, glisten, glitter, reflect, shimmer, shine, twinkle ♦ noun 3 look, dekko (slang), glimpse, peek, peep, view

glare verb 1 scowl, frown, glower, look daggers, lour or lower 2 dazzle, blaze, flame, flare ♦ noun 3 scowl, black look, dirty look, frown, glower, lour or lower 4 dazzle, blaze, brilliance, flame, glow

glaring adjective 1 conspicuous, blatant, flagrant, gross, manifest, obvious, outrageous, unconcealed 2 dazzling, blazing, bright, garish, glowing

glassy adjective 1 transparent, clear, glossy, shiny, slippery, smooth 2 expressionless, blank, cold, dull, empty, fixed, glazed, lifeless, vacant

glaze verb 1 coat, enamel, gloss, lacquer, polish, varnish ♦ noun 2 coat, enamel, finish, gloss, lacquer, lustre, patina, polish,

shine, varnish

gleam noun 1 glow, beam, flash, glimmer, ray, sparkle 2 trace, flicker, glimmer, hint, inkling, suggestion ♦ verb 3 shine, flash, glimmer, glint, glisten, glitter, glow, shimmer, sparkle

glee noun delight, elation, exhilaration, exuberance, exultation, joy, merriment, triumph

gleeful adjective delighted, cock-a-hoop, elated, exuberant, exultant, joyful, jubilant, overjoyed, triumphant

glib adjective smooth, easy, fluent, insincere, plausible, quick, ready, slick, suave, voluble

glide verb slide, coast, drift, float, flow, roll, run, sail, skate, slip

glimmer verb 1 flicker, blink, gleam, glisten, glitter, glow, shimmer, shine, sparkle, twinkle ♦ noun 2 gleam, blink, flicker, glow, ray, shimmer, sparkle, twinkle 3 trace, flicker, gleam, hint, inkling, suggestion

glimpse noun 1 look, glance, peek, peep, sight, sighting ♦ verb 2 catch sight of, espy, sight, spot, spy, view

glint verb 1 gleam, flash, glimmer, glitter, shine, sparkle, twinkle ♦ noun 2 gleam, flash, glimmer, glitter, shine, sparkle, twinkle, twinkling

glisten verb gleam, flash, glance, glare, glimmer, glint, glitter, shimmer, shine, sparkle, twinkle

glitch noun problem, blip, difficulty, gremlin, hitch, interruption, malfunction, snag

glitter verb 1 shine, flash, glare,

gleam, glimmer, glint, glisten, shimmer, sparkle, twinkle ♦ *noun* 2 <u>shine</u>, brightness, flash, glare, gleam, radiance, sheen, shimmer, sparkle 3 <u>glamour</u>, display, gaudiness, pageantry, show, showiness, splendour, tinsel

gloat *verb* relish, crow, drool, exult, glory, revel in, rub it in (*informal*), triumph

global *adjective* 1 <u>worldwide</u>, international, universal, world 2 <u>comprehensive</u>, all-inclusive, exhaustive, general, total, unlimited

globe *noun* <u>sphere</u>, ball, earth, orb, planet, world

globule *noun* <u>droplet</u>, bead, bubble, drop, particle, pearl, pellet

gloom *noun* 1 <u>darkness</u>, blackness, dark, dusk, murk, obscurity, shade, shadow, twilight 2 <u>depression</u>, dejection, despondency, low spirits, melancholy, sorrow, unhappiness, woe

gloomy *adjective* 1 <u>dark</u>, black, dim, dismal, dreary, dull, grey, murky, sombre 2 <u>depressing</u>, bad, cheerless, disheartening, dispiriting, dreary, sad, sombre 3 <u>miserable</u>, crestfallen, dejected, dispirited, downcast, downhearted, glum, melancholy, morose, pessimistic, sad

glorify *verb* 1 <u>enhance</u>, aggrandize, dignify, elevate, ennoble, magnify 2 <u>worship</u>, adore, bless, exalt, honour, idolize, pay homage to, revere, venerate 3 <u>praise</u>, celebrate, eulogize, extol, sing *or* sound

the praises of

glorious *adjective* 1 <u>famous</u>, celebrated, distinguished, eminent, honoured, illustrious, magnificent, majestic, renowned 2 <u>splendid</u>, beautiful, brilliant, dazzling, gorgeous, shining, superb 3 <u>delightful</u>, excellent, fine, gorgeous, marvellous, wonderful

glory *noun* 1 <u>honour</u>, dignity, distinction, eminence, fame, praise, prestige, renown 2 <u>splendour</u>, grandeur, greatness, magnificence, majesty, nobility, pageantry, pomp ♦ *verb* 3 <u>triumph</u>, boast, exult, pride oneself, relish, revel, take delight

gloss[1] *noun* <u>shine</u>, brightness, gleam, lustre, patina, polish, sheen, veneer

gloss[2] *noun* 1 <u>comment</u>, annotation, commentary, elucidation, explanation, footnote, interpretation, note, translation ♦ *verb* 2 <u>interpret</u>, annotate, comment, elucidate, explain, translate

glossy *adjective* <u>shiny</u>, bright, glassy, glazed, lustrous, polished, shining, silky

glow *verb* 1 <u>shine</u>, brighten, burn, gleam, glimmer, redden, smoulder ♦ *noun* 2 <u>light</u>, burning, gleam, glimmer, luminosity, phosphorescence 3 <u>radiance</u>, brightness, brilliance, effulgence, splendour, vividness

glower *verb* 1 <u>scowl</u>, frown, give a dirty look, glare, look daggers, lour *or* lower 2 <u>scowl</u>, black look, dirty look, frown, glare, lour *or* lower

glowing adjective **1** bright, aglow, flaming, luminous, radiant **2** complimentary, adulatory, ecstatic, enthusiastic, laudatory, rave (informal), rhapsodic

glue noun **1** adhesive, cement, gum, paste ♦ verb **2** stick, affix, cement, fix, gum, paste, seal

glum adjective gloomy, crestfallen, dejected, doleful, low, morose, pessimistic, sullen

glut noun **1** surfeit, excess, oversupply, plethora, saturation, superfluity, surplus ♦ verb **2** saturate, choke, clog, deluge, flood, inundate, overload, oversupply

glutton noun gourmand, gannet (slang), pig (informal)

gluttonous adjective greedy, gormandizing, insatiable, piggish, ravenous, voracious

gluttony noun greed, gormandizing, greediness, voracity

gnarled adjective twisted, contorted, knotted, knotty, rough, rugged, weather-beaten, wrinkled

gnaw verb bite, chew, munch, nibble

go verb **1** move, advance, journey, make for, pass, proceed, set off, travel **2** leave, depart, make tracks, move out, slope off, withdraw **3** function, move, operate, perform, run, work **4** contribute, lead to, serve, tend, work towards **5** harmonize, agree, blend, chime, complement, correspond, fit, match, suit **6** elapse, expire, flow, lapse, pass, slip away

♦ noun **7** attempt, bid, crack (informal), effort, shot (informal), try, turn **8** Informal energy, drive, force, life, spirit, verve, vigour, vitality, vivacity

goad verb **1** provoke, drive, egg on, exhort, incite, prod, prompt, spur ♦ noun **2** provocation, impetus, incentive, incitement, irritation, spur, stimulus, urge

goal noun aim, ambition, end, intention, object, objective, purpose, target

gobble verb devour, bolt, cram, gorge, gulp, guzzle, stuff, swallow, wolf

gobbledegook noun nonsense, babble, cant, gabble, gibberish, hocus-pocus, jargon, mumbo jumbo, twaddle

go-between noun intermediary, agent, broker, dealer, mediator, medium, middleman

godforsaken adjective desolate, abandoned, bleak, deserted, dismal, dreary, forlorn, gloomy, lonely, remote, wretched

godlike adjective divine, celestial, heavenly, superhuman, transcendent

godly adjective devout, god-fearing, good, holy, pious, religious, righteous, saintly

godsend noun blessing, boon, manna, stroke of luck, windfall

go for verb favour, admire, be attracted to, be fond of, choose, like, prefer **2** attack, assail, assault, launch oneself at, rush upon, set about or upon, spring upon

golden adjective **1** yellow, blond or blonde, flaxen **2** successful, flourishing, glorious, halcyon, happy, prosperous, rich **3** promising, excellent, favourable, opportune

gone adjective **1** finished, elapsed, ended, over, past **2** missing, absent, astray, away, lacking, lost, vanished

good adjective **1** pleasing, acceptable, admirable, excellent, fine, first-class, first-rate, great, satisfactory, splendid, superior **2** praiseworthy, admirable, ethical, honest, honourable, moral, righteous, trustworthy, upright, virtuous, worthy **3** expert, able, accomplished, adept, adroit, clever, competent, proficient, skilled, talented **4** beneficial, advantageous, convenient, favourable, fitting, helpful, profitable, suitable, useful, wholesome **5** kind, altruistic, benevolent, charitable, friendly, humane, kind-hearted, kindly, merciful, obliging **6** valid, authentic, bona fide, genuine, legitimate, proper, real, true **7** well-behaved, dutiful, obedient, orderly, polite, well-mannered **8** full, adequate, ample, complete, considerable, extensive, large, substantial, sufficient ♦ noun **9** benefit, advantage, gain, interest, profit, use, usefulness, welfare, wellbeing **10** virtue, excellence, goodness, merit, morality, rectitude, right, righteousness, worth **11** for good permanently, finally, for ever, irrevocably, once and for all

goodbye noun farewell, adieu, leave-taking, parting

good-for-nothing noun **1** layabout, black sheep, idler, ne'er-do-well, skiver (Brit. slang), slacker (informal), waster, wastrel ♦ adjective **2** worthless, feckless, idle, irresponsible, useless

goodly adjective considerable, ample, large, significant, sizable or sizeable, substantial, tidy (informal)

goodness noun **1** excellence, merit, quality, superiority, value, worth **2** kindness, benevolence, friendliness, generosity, goodwill, humaneness, kind-heartedness, kindliness, mercy **3** virtue, honesty, honour, integrity, merit, morality, probity, rectitude, righteousness, uprightness **4** benefit, advantage, salubriousness, wholesomeness

goods plural noun **1** property, belongings, chattels, effects, gear, paraphernalia, possessions, things, trappings **2** merchandise, commodities, stock, stuff, wares

goodwill noun friendliness, amity, benevolence, friendship, heartiness, kindliness

go off verb **1** explode, blow up, detonate, fire **2** leave, decamp, depart, go away, move out, part, quit, slope off **3** Informal rot, go bad, go stale

go out verb **1** leave, depart, exit **2** be extinguished, die out, expire, fade out

go over verb examine, inspect, rehearse, reiterate, review, revise, study, work over

gore¹ noun blood, bloodshed, butchery, carnage, slaughter

gore² verb pierce, impale, transfix, wound

gorge noun 1 <u>ravine</u>, canyon, chasm, cleft, defile, fissure, pass ♦ verb 2 <u>overeat</u>, cram, devour, feed, glut, gobble, gulp, guzzle, stuff, wolf

gorgeous adjective 1 <u>beautiful</u>, dazzling, elegant, magnificent, ravishing, splendid, stunning (informal), sumptuous, superb 2 Informal <u>pleasing</u>, delightful, enjoyable, exquisite, fine, glorious, good, lovely

gory adjective <u>bloodthirsty</u>, blood-soaked, bloodstained, bloody, murderous, sanguinary

gospel noun 1 <u>truth</u>, certainty, fact, the last word 2 <u>doctrine</u>, credo, creed, message, news, revelation, tidings

gossip noun 1 <u>idle talk</u>, blether, chinwag (Brit. informal), chitchat, hearsay, scandal, small talk, tittle-tattle 2 <u>busybody</u>, chatterbox (informal), chatterer, gossipmonger, scandalmonger, tattler, telltale ♦ verb 3 <u>chat</u>, blether, gabble, jaw (slang), prate, prattle, tattle

go through verb 1 <u>suffer</u>, bear, brave, endure, experience, tolerate, undergo, withstand 2 <u>examine</u>, check, explore, forage, hunt, look, search

gouge verb 1 <u>scoop</u>, chisel, claw, cut, dig (out), hollow (out) ♦ noun 2 <u>gash</u>, cut, furrow, groove, hollow, scoop, scratch, trench

gourmet noun <u>connoisseur</u>, bon vivant, epicure, foodie (informal), gastronome

govern verb 1 <u>rule</u>, administer, command, control, direct, guide, handle, lead, manage, order 2 <u>restrain</u>, check, control, curb, discipline, hold in check, master, regulate, subdue, tame

government noun 1 <u>rule</u>, administration, authority, governance, sovereignty, statecraft 2 <u>executive</u>, administration, ministry, powers-that-be, regime

governor noun <u>leader</u>, administrator, chief, commander, controller, director, executive, head, manager, ruler

gown noun <u>dress</u>, costume, frock, garb, garment, habit, robe

grab verb <u>snatch</u>, capture, catch, catch or take hold of, clutch, grasp, grip, pluck, seize, snap up

grace noun 1 <u>elegance</u>, attractiveness, beauty, charm, comeliness, ease, gracefulness, poise, polish, refinement, tastefulness 2 <u>goodwill</u>, benefaction, benevolence, favour, generosity, goodness, kindliness, kindness 3 <u>manners</u>, consideration, decency, decorum, etiquette, propriety, tact 4 <u>indulgence</u>, mercy, pardon, reprieve 5 <u>prayer</u>, benediction, blessing, thanks, thanksgiving ♦ verb 6 <u>honour</u>, adorn, decorate, dignify, embellish, enhance, enrich, favour, ornament, set off

graceful adjective <u>elegant</u>, beautiful, charming, comely, easy, pleasing, tasteful

gracious adjective <u>kind</u>, charitable, civil, considerate, cordial, courteous, friendly, polite, well-mannered

grade noun 1 <u>level</u>, category, class, degree, echelon, group,

rank, stage ♦ *verb* **2** classify,
arrange, class, group, order,
range, rank, rate, sort

gradient *noun* slope, bank,
declivity, grade, hill, incline, rise

gradual *adjective* steady, gentle,
graduated, piecemeal,
progressive, regular, slow,
unhurried

gradually *adverb* steadily, by
degrees, gently, little by little,
progressively, slowly, step by
step, unhurriedly

graduate *verb* **1** mark off,
calibrate, grade, measure out,
proportion, regulate **2** classify,
arrange, grade, group, order,
rank, sort

graft *noun* **1** shoot, bud, implant,
scion, splice, sprout ♦ *verb*
2 transplant, affix, implant,
ingraft, insert, join, splice

grain *noun* **1** cereals, corn
2 seed, grist, kernel **3** bit,
fragment, granule, modicum,
morsel, particle, piece, scrap,
speck, trace **4** texture, fibre,
nap, pattern, surface, weave **5** *As
in* go against the grain
inclination, character,
disposition, humour, make-up,
temper

grand *adjective* **1** impressive,
dignified, grandiose, great,
imposing, large, magnificent,
regal, splendid, stately, sublime
2 excellent, fine, first-class, great
(*informal*), outstanding, smashing
(*informal*), wonderful

grandeur *noun* splendour,
dignity, magnificence, majesty,
nobility, pomp, stateliness,
sublimity

grandiose *adjective*

1 pretentious, affected,
bombastic, extravagant,
flamboyant, high-flown,
ostentatious, pompous, showy
2 imposing, grand, impressive,
lofty, magnificent, majestic,
monumental, stately

grant *verb* **1** consent to, accede
to, agree to, allow, permit
2 give, allocate, allot, assign,
award, donate, hand out,
present **3** admit, acknowledge,
concede ♦ *noun* **4** award,
allowance, donation,
endowment, gift, hand-out,
present, subsidy

granule *noun* grain, atom,
crumb, fragment, molecule,
particle, scrap, speck

graphic *adjective* **1** vivid, clear,
detailed, explicit, expressive,
lively, lucid, striking **2** pictorial,
diagrammatic, visual

grapple *verb* **1** grip, clutch, grab,
grasp, seize, wrestle **2** deal with,
address oneself to, confront, get
to grips with, struggle, tackle,
take on

grasp *verb* **1** grip, catch, clasp,
clinch, clutch, grab, grapple,
hold, lay *or* take hold of, seize,
snatch **2** understand, catch on,
catch *or* get the drift of,
comprehend, get, realize, see,
take in ♦ *noun* **3** grip, clasp,
clutches, embrace, hold,
possession, tenure **4** control,
power, reach, scope
5 understanding, awareness,
comprehension, grip,
knowledge, mastery

grasping *adjective* greedy,
acquisitive, avaricious, covetous,
rapacious

grate verb 1 shred, mince, pulverize, triturate 2 scrape, creak, grind, rasp, rub, scratch 3 annoy, exasperate, get on one's nerves (informal), irritate, jar, rankle, set one's teeth on edge

grateful adjective thankful, appreciative, beholden, indebted, obliged

gratification noun satisfaction, delight, enjoyment, fulfilment, indulgence, pleasure, relish, reward, thrill

gratify verb please, delight, give pleasure, gladden, humour, requite, satisfy

grating[1] adjective irritating, annoying, discordant, displeasing, harsh, jarring, offensive, raucous, strident, unpleasant

grating[2] noun grille, grate, grid, gridiron, lattice, trellis

gratitude noun thankfulness, appreciation, gratefulness, indebtedness, obligation, recognition, thanks

gratuitous adjective 1 free, complimentary, gratis, spontaneous, unasked-for, unpaid, unrewarded, voluntary 2 unjustified, baseless, causeless, groundless, needless, superfluous, uncalled-for, unmerited, unnecessary, unwarranted, wanton

gratuity noun tip, bonus, donation, gift, largesse or largess, reward

grave[1] noun burying place, crypt, mausoleum, pit, sepulchre, tomb, vault

grave[2] adjective 1 solemn, dignified, dour, earnest, serious, sober, sombre, unsmiling 2 important, acute, critical, dangerous, pressing, serious, severe, threatening, urgent

graveyard noun cemetery, burial ground, charnel house, churchyard, necropolis

gravity noun 1 importance, acuteness, momentousness, perilousness, seriousness, severity, significance, urgency, weightiness 2 solemnity, dignity, earnestness, gravitas, seriousness, sobriety

graze[1] verb feed, browse, crop, pasture

graze[2] verb 1 touch, brush, glance off, rub, scrape, shave, skim 2 scratch, abrade, chafe, scrape, skin ♦ noun 3 scratch, abrasion, scrape

greasy adjective fatty, oily, oleaginous, slimy, slippery

great adjective 1 large, big, enormous, gigantic, huge, immense, prodigious, vast, voluminous 2 important, crucial, momentous, serious, significant 3 famous, eminent, illustrious, noteworthy, outstanding, prominent, remarkable, renowned 4 Informal excellent, fantastic (informal), fine, marvellous (informal), superb, terrific (informal), tremendous (informal), wonderful

greatly adverb very much, considerably, enormously, exceedingly, hugely, immensely, remarkably, tremendously, vastly

greatness noun 1 immensity, enormity, hugeness, magnitude,

prodigiousness, size, vastness
2 importance, gravity,
momentousness, seriousness,
significance, urgency, weight
3 fame, celebrity, distinction,
eminence, glory, grandeur,
illustriousness, note, renown

greed, greediness noun
1 gluttony, edacity, esurience,
gormandizing, hunger, voracity
2 avarice, acquisitiveness,
avidity, covetousness, craving,
desire, longing, selfishness

greedy adjective 1 gluttonous,
gormandizing, hungry,
insatiable, piggish, ravenous,
voracious 2 grasping, acquisitive,
avaricious, avid, covetous,
craving, desirous, rapacious,
selfish

green adjective 1 leafy, grassy,
verdant 2 ecological,
conservationist,
environment-friendly,
non-polluting, ozone-friendly
3 immature, gullible,
inexperienced, naive, new, raw,
untrained, wet behind the ears
(informal) 4 jealous, covetous,
envious, grudging, resentful
♦ noun 5 lawn, common, sward,
turf

greet verb welcome, accost,
address, compliment, hail, meet,
receive, salute

greeting noun welcome, address,
reception, salutation, salute

gregarious adjective outgoing,
affable, companionable,
convivial, cordial, friendly,
sociable, social

grey adjective 1 pale, ashen,
pallid, wan 2 dismal, dark,
depressing, dim, drab, dreary,

dull, gloomy 3 characterless,
anonymous, colourless, dull

gridlock noun standstill,
deadlock, impasse, stalemate

grief noun sadness, anguish,
distress, heartache, misery,
regret, remorse, sorrow,
suffering, woe

grievance noun complaint, axe
to grind, gripe (informal), injury,
injustice

grieve verb 1 mourn, complain,
deplore, lament, regret, rue,
suffer, weep 2 sadden, afflict,
distress, hurt, injure, pain, wound

grievous adjective 1 painful,
dreadful, grave, harmful, severe
2 deplorable, atrocious, dreadful,
monstrous, offensive,
outrageous, shameful, shocking

grim adjective forbidding,
formidable, harsh, merciless,
ruthless, severe, sinister, stern,
terrible

grimace noun 1 scowl, face,
frown, sneer ♦ verb 2 scowl,
frown, lour or lower, make a face
or faces, sneer

grime noun dirt, filth, grot
(slang), smut, soot

grimy adjective dirty, filthy, foul,
grubby, soiled, sooty, unclean

grind verb 1 crush, abrade,
granulate, grate, mill, pound,
powder, pulverize, triturate
2 smooth, polish, sand, sharpen,
whet 3 scrape, gnash, grate
♦ noun 4 Informal hard work,
chore, drudgery, labour, sweat
(informal), toil

grip noun 1 clasp, hold 2 control,
clutches, domination, influence,
possession, power

3 <u>understanding</u>, command, comprehension, grasp, mastery
♦ verb 4 <u>grasp</u>, clasp, clutch, hold, seize, take hold of
5 <u>engross</u>, absorb, enthral, entrance, fascinate, hold, mesmerize, rivet

gripping adjective <u>fascinating</u>, compelling, engrossing, enthralling, entrancing, exciting, riveting, spellbinding, thrilling

grisly adjective <u>gruesome</u>, appalling, awful, dreadful, ghastly, horrible, macabre, shocking, terrifying

grit noun 1 <u>gravel</u>, dust, pebbles, sand 2 <u>courage</u>, backbone, determination, fortitude, guts (informal), perseverance, resolution, spirit, tenacity ♦ verb 3 <u>grind</u>, clench, gnash, grate

gritty adjective 1 <u>rough</u>, dusty, granular, gravelly, rasping, sandy 2 <u>courageous</u>, brave, determined, dogged, plucky, resolute, spirited, steadfast, tenacious

groan noun 1 <u>moan</u>, cry, sigh, whine 2 Informal <u>complaint</u>, gripe (informal), grouse, grumble, objection, protest ♦ verb 3 <u>moan</u>, cry, sigh, whine 4 Informal <u>complain</u>, bemoan, gripe (informal), grouse, grumble, lament, object

groggy adjective <u>dizzy</u>, confused, dazed, faint, shaky, unsteady, weak, wobbly

groom noun 1 <u>stableman</u>, hostler or ostler (archaic), stableboy ♦ verb 2 <u>smarten up</u>, clean, preen, primp, spruce up, tidy 3 <u>rub down</u>, brush, clean, curry, tend 4 <u>train</u>, coach, drill,

educate, make ready, nurture, prepare, prime, ready

groove noun <u>indentation</u>, channel, cut, flute, furrow, hollow, rut, trench, trough

grope verb <u>feel</u>, cast about, fish, flounder, forage, fumble, scrabble, search

gross adjective 1 <u>fat</u>, corpulent, hulking, obese, overweight 2 <u>total</u>, aggregate, before deductions, before tax, entire, whole 3 <u>vulgar</u>, coarse, crude, indelicate, obscene, offensive 4 <u>blatant</u>, flagrant, grievous, heinous, rank, sheer, unmitigated, utter ♦ verb 5 <u>earn</u>, bring in, make, rake in (informal), take

grotesque adjective <u>unnatural</u>, bizarre, deformed, distorted, fantastic, freakish, outlandish, preposterous, strange

ground noun 1 <u>earth</u>, dry land, land, soil, terra firma, terrain, turf 2 <u>stadium</u>, arena, field, park (informal), pitch 3 often plural <u>land</u>, estate, fields, gardens, terrain, territory 4 usually plural <u>dregs</u>, deposit, lees, sediment 5 **grounds** <u>reason</u>, basis, cause, excuse, foundation, justification, motive, occasion, pretext, rationale ♦ verb 6 <u>base</u>, establish, fix, found, set, settle 7 <u>instruct</u>, acquaint with, familiarize with, initiate, teach, train, tutor

groundless adjective <u>unjustified</u>, baseless, empty, idle, uncalled-for, unfounded, unwarranted

groundwork noun <u>preliminaries</u>, foundation, fundamentals, preparation, spadework, underpinnings

group noun **1** <u>set</u>, band, bunch, cluster, collection, crowd, gang, pack, party ♦ verb **2** <u>arrange</u>, bracket, class, classify, marshal, order, sort

grouse verb **1** <u>complain</u>, bellyache (slang), carp, gripe (informal), grumble, moan, whine, whinge (informal) ♦ noun **2** <u>complaint</u>, grievance, gripe (informal), grouch (informal), grumble, moan, objection, protest

grove noun <u>wood</u>, coppice, copse, covert, plantation, spinney, thicket

grovel verb <u>humble oneself</u>, abase oneself, bow and scrape, crawl, creep, cringe, demean oneself, fawn, kowtow, toady

grow verb **1** <u>increase</u>, develop, enlarge, expand, get bigger, multiply, spread, stretch, swell **2** <u>originate</u>, arise, issue, spring, stem **3** <u>improve</u>, advance, flourish, progress, prosper, succeed, thrive **4** <u>become</u>, come to be, get, turn **5** <u>cultivate</u>, breed, farm, nurture, produce, propagate, raise

grown-up adjective **1** <u>mature</u>, adult, fully-grown, of age ♦ noun **2** <u>adult</u>, man, woman

growth noun **1** <u>increase</u>, development, enlargement, expansion, multiplication, proliferation, stretching **2** <u>improvement</u>, advance, expansion, progress, prosperity, rise, success **3** Medical tumour, lump

grub noun **1** <u>larva</u>, caterpillar, maggot **2** Slang <u>food</u>, nosh

(slang), rations, sustenance, victuals ♦ verb **3** <u>dig up</u>, burrow, pull up, root (informal) **4** <u>search</u>, ferret, forage, hunt, rummage, scour, uncover, unearth

grubby adjective <u>dirty</u>, filthy, grimy, messy, mucky, scruffy, seedy, shabby, sordid, squalid, unwashed

grudge verb **1** <u>resent</u>, begrudge, complain, covet, envy, mind ♦ noun **2** <u>resentment</u>, animosity, antipathy, bitterness, dislike, enmity, grievance, rancour

gruelling adjective <u>exhausting</u>, arduous, backbreaking, demanding, laborious, punishing, severe, strenuous, taxing, tiring

gruesome adjective <u>horrific</u>, ghastly, grim, grisly, horrible, macabre, shocking, terrible

gruff adjective **1** <u>surly</u>, bad-tempered, brusque, churlish, grumpy, rough, rude, sullen, ungracious **2** <u>hoarse</u>, croaking, guttural, harsh, husky, low, rasping, rough, throaty

grumble verb **1** <u>complain</u>, bleat, carp, gripe (informal), grouch (informal), grouse, moan, whine, whinge (informal) **2** <u>rumble</u>, growl, gurgle, murmur, mutter, roar ♦ noun **3** <u>complaint</u>, grievance, gripe (informal), grouch (informal), grouse, moan, objection, protest **4** <u>rumble</u>, growl, gurgle, murmur, muttering, roar

grumpy adjective <u>irritable</u>, cantankerous, crotchety (informal), ill-tempered, peevish, sulky, sullen, surly, testy

guarantee noun **1** <u>assurance</u>,

bond, certainty, pledge,
promise, security, surety,
warranty, word of honour ♦ verb
2 make certain, assure, certify,
ensure, pledge, promise, secure,
vouch for, warrant

guard verb 1 watch over, defend,
mind, preserve, protect,
safeguard, secure, shield ♦ noun
2 protector, custodian, defender,
lookout, picket, sentinel, sentry,
warder, watch, watchman
3 protection, buffer, defence,
safeguard, screen, security,
shield 4 off guard unprepared,
napping, unready, unwary 5 on
guard prepared, alert, cautious,
circumspect, on the alert, on the
lookout, ready, vigilant, wary,
watchful

guarded adjective cautious, cagey
(informal), careful, circumspect,
noncommittal, prudent,
reserved, reticent, suspicious,
wary

guardian noun keeper,
champion, curator, custodian,
defender, guard, protector,
warden

guerrilla noun freedom fighter,
partisan, underground fighter

guess verb 1 estimate,
conjecture, hypothesize, predict,
speculate, work out 2 suppose,
believe, conjecture, fancy,
imagine, judge, reckon, suspect,
think ♦ noun 3 prediction,
conjecture, hypothesis, shot in
the dark, speculation,
supposition, theory

guesswork noun speculation,
conjecture, estimation,
supposition, surmise, theory

guest noun visitor, boarder,

caller, company, lodger, visitant

guidance noun advice,
counselling, direction, help,
instruction, leadership,
management, teaching

guide noun 1 escort, adviser,
conductor, counsellor, leader,
mentor, teacher, usher 2 model,
example, ideal, inspiration,
paradigm, standard 3 pointer,
beacon, guiding light, landmark,
lodestar, marker, sign, signpost
4 guidebook, Baedeker,
catalogue, directory, handbook,
instructions, key, manual ♦ verb
5 lead, accompany, conduct,
direct, escort, shepherd, show
the way, usher 6 steer,
command, control, direct,
handle, manage, manoeuvre
7 supervise, advise, counsel,
influence, instruct, oversee,
superintend, teach, train

guild noun society, association,
brotherhood, club, company,
corporation, fellowship,
fraternity, league, lodge, order,
organization, union

guile noun cunning, artifice,
cleverness, craft, deceit, slyness,
trickery, wiliness

guilt noun 1 culpability, blame,
guiltiness, misconduct,
responsibility, sinfulness,
wickedness, wrongdoing
2 remorse, contrition, guilty
conscience, regret, self-reproach,
shame, stigma

guiltless adjective innocent,
blameless, clean (slang),
irreproachable, pure, sinless,
spotless, squeaky-clean, untainted

guilty adjective 1 responsible, at
fault, blameworthy, culpable,

reprehensible, sinful, to blame, wrong 2 <u>remorseful</u>, ashamed, conscience-stricken, contrite, regretful, rueful, shamefaced, sheepish, sorry

guise noun 1 <u>form</u>, appearance, aspect, demeanour, disguise, mode, pretence, semblance, shape

gulf noun 1 <u>bay</u>, bight, sea inlet 2 <u>chasm</u>, abyss, gap, opening, rift, separation, split, void

gullibility noun <u>credulity</u>, innocence, naïveté, simplicity

gullible adjective <u>naive</u>, born yesterday, credulous, innocent, simple, trusting, unsuspecting, wet behind the ears (informal)

gully noun <u>channel</u>, ditch, gutter, watercourse

gulp verb 1 <u>swallow</u>, devour, gobble, guzzle, quaff, swig (informal), swill, wolf 2 <u>gasp</u>, choke, swallow ♦ noun 3 <u>swallow</u>, draught, mouthful, swig (informal)

gum noun 1 <u>glue</u>, adhesive, cement, paste, resin ♦ verb 2 <u>stick</u>, affix, cement, glue, paste

gumption noun <u>resourcefulness</u>, acumen, astuteness, common sense, enterprise, initiative, mother wit, savvy (slang), wit(s)

gun noun <u>firearm</u>, handgun, piece (slang), shooter (slang)

gunman noun <u>terrorist</u>, bandit, gunslinger (U.S. slang), killer

gurgle verb 1 <u>murmur</u>, babble, bubble, lap, plash, purl, ripple, splash ♦ noun 2 <u>murmur</u>, babble, purl, ripple

guru noun <u>teacher</u>, authority, leader, master, mentor, sage,

Svengali, tutor

gush verb 1 <u>flow</u>, cascade, flood, pour, run, rush, spout, spurt, stream 2 <u>enthuse</u>, babble, chatter, effervesce, effuse, overstate, spout ♦ noun 3 <u>stream</u>, cascade, flood, flow, jet, rush, spout, spurt, torrent

gust noun 1 <u>blast</u>, blow, breeze, puff, rush, squall ♦ verb 2 <u>blow</u>, blast, squall

gusto noun <u>relish</u>, delight, enjoyment, enthusiasm, fervour, pleasure, verve, zeal

gut noun 1 Informal <u>paunch</u>, belly, potbelly, spare tyre (Brit. slang) 2 **guts**: a <u>intestines</u>, belly, bowels, entrails, innards (informal), insides (informal), stomach, viscera b Informal <u>courage</u>, audacity, backbone, bottle (slang), daring, mettle, nerve, pluck, spirit ♦ verb 3 <u>disembowel</u>, clean 4 <u>ravage</u>, clean out, despoil, empty ♦ adjective 5 As in **gut reaction** <u>instinctive</u>, basic, heartfelt, intuitive, involuntary, natural, spontaneous, unthinking, visceral

gutsy adjective <u>brave</u>, bold, courageous, determined, gritty, indomitable, plucky, resolute, spirited

gutter noun <u>drain</u>, channel, conduit, ditch, sluice, trench, trough

guttural adjective <u>throaty</u>, deep, gravelly, gruff, hoarse, husky, rasping, rough, thick

guy noun Informal <u>man</u>, bloke (Brit. informal), chap, fellow, lad, person

guzzle verb <u>devour</u>, bolt, cram, drink, gobble, stuff (oneself), swill, wolf

Gypsy, Gipsy noun traveller, Bohemian, nomad, rambler, roamer, Romany, rover, wanderer

H h

habit noun 1 mannerism, custom, practice, proclivity, propensity, quirk, tendency, way 2 addiction, dependence

habitation noun 1 dwelling, abode, domicile, home, house, living quarters, lodging, quarters, residence 2 occupancy, inhabitance, occupation, tenancy

habitual adjective customary, accustomed, familiar, normal, regular, routine, standard, traditional, usual

hack[1] verb cut, chop, hew, lacerate, mangle, mutilate, slash

hack[2] noun 1 scribbler, literary hack, penny-a-liner 2 horse, crock, nag

hackneyed adjective unoriginal, clichéd, commonplace, overworked, stale, stereotyped, stock, threadbare, tired, trite

hag noun witch, crone, harridan

haggard adjective gaunt, careworn, drawn, emaciated, pinched, thin, wan

haggle verb bargain, barter, beat down

hail[1] noun 1 bombardment, barrage, downpour, rain, shower, storm, volley ♦ verb 2 rain down on, batter, beat down upon, bombard, pelt, rain, shower

hail[2] verb 1 greet, acclaim, acknowledge, applaud, cheer, honour, salute, welcome 2 flag down, signal to, wave down 3 hail from come from, be a native of, be born in, originate in

hair noun locks, head of hair, mane, mop, shock, tresses

hairdresser noun stylist, barber, coiffeur or coiffeuse

hair-raising adjective frightening, alarming, bloodcurdling, horrifying, scary, shocking, spine-chilling, terrifying

hairstyle noun haircut, coiffure, cut, hairdo, style

hairy adjective 1 shaggy, bushy, furry, hirsute, stubbly, unshaven, woolly 2 Slang dangerous, difficult, hazardous, perilous, risky

halcyon adjective 1 peaceful, calm, gentle, quiet, serene, tranquil, undisturbed 2 As in **halcyon days** happy, carefree, flourishing, golden, palmy, prosperous

hale adjective healthy, able-bodied, fit, flourishing, in the pink, robust, sound, strong, vigorous, well

half noun 1 equal part, fifty per cent, hemisphere, portion, section ♦ adjective 2 partial, halved, limited, moderate ♦ adverb 3 partially, in part, partly

half-baked adjective ill-judged, ill-conceived, impractical, poorly planned, short-sighted, unformed, unthought out or through

half-hearted adjective unenthusiastic, apathetic, indifferent, lacklustre, listless, lukewarm, perfunctory, tame

halfway adverb **1** midway, to or in the middle ♦ adjective **2** midway, central, equidistant, intermediate, mid, middle

halfwit noun fool, airhead (slang), dunderhead, idiot, imbecile (informal), moron, numbskull or numskull, simpleton, twit (informal, chiefly Brit.)

hall noun **1** entrance hall, corridor, entry, foyer, hallway, lobby, passage, passageway, vestibule **2** meeting place, assembly room, auditorium, chamber, concert hall

hallmark noun **1** seal, endorsement, mark, sign, stamp, symbol **2** indication, sure sign, telltale sign

hallucination noun illusion, apparition, delusion, dream, fantasy, figment of the imagination, mirage, vision

halo noun ring of light, aura, corona, nimbus, radiance

halt verb **1** stop, break off, cease, come to an end, desist, rest, stand still, wait **2** end, block, bring to an end, check, curb, cut short, nip in the bud, terminate ♦ noun **2** stop, close, end, pause, standstill, stoppage

halting adjective faltering, awkward, hesitant, laboured, stammering, stumbling, stuttering

halve verb bisect, cut in half, divide equally, share equally, split in two

hammer verb **1** hit, bang, beat, drive, knock, strike, tap **2** Informal defeat, beat, drub, run

rings around (informal), thrash, trounce, wipe the floor with (informal)

hamper verb hinder, frustrate, hamstring, handicap, impede, interfere with, obstruct, prevent, restrict

hand noun **1** palm, fist, mitt (slang), paw (informal) **2** hired man, artisan, craftsman, employee, labourer, operative, worker, workman **3** penmanship, calligraphy, handwriting, script **4** ovation, clap, round of applause **5 at** or **on hand nearby**, at one's fingertips, available, close, handy, near, ready, within reach ♦ verb **6** pass, deliver, hand over

handbook noun guidebook, Baedeker, guide, instruction book, manual

handcuff verb shackle, fetter, manacle

handcuffs plural noun shackles, cuffs (informal), fetters, manacles

handful noun few, small number, smattering, sprinkling

handicap noun **1** disadvantage, barrier, drawback, hindrance, impediment, limitation, obstacle, restriction, stumbling block **2** advantage, head start **3** disability, defect, impairment ♦ verb **4** restrict, burden, encumber, hamper, hamstring, hinder, hold back, impede, limit

handicraft noun craftsmanship, art, craft, handiwork, skill, workmanship

handiwork noun creation, achievement, design, invention, product, production

handle noun **1** grip, haft, hilt, stock ◆ verb **2** hold, feel, finger, grasp, pick up, touch **3** control, direct, guide, manage, manipulate, manoeuvre **4** deal with, cope with, manage

hand-out noun **1** charity, alms, dole **2** leaflet, bulletin, circular, literature (informal), mailshot, press release

handsome adjective **1** good-looking, attractive, comely, dishy (informal, chiefly Brit.), elegant, gorgeous, personable, well-proportioned **2** large, abundant, ample, considerable, generous, liberal, plentiful, sizable or sizeable

handwriting noun penmanship, calligraphy, hand, scrawl, script

handy adjective **1** available, accessible, at hand, at one's fingertips, close, convenient, nearby, on hand, within reach **2** useful, convenient, easy to use, helpful, manageable, neat, practical, serviceable, user-friendly **3** skilful, adept, adroit, deft, dexterous, expert, proficient, skilled

hang verb **1** suspend, dangle, droop **2** execute, lynch, string up (informal) ◆ noun **3** get the hang of grasp, comprehend, understand

hang back verb hesitate, be reluctant, demur, hold back, recoil

hangdog adjective guilty, cowed, cringing, defeated, downcast, furtive, shamefaced, wretched

hangover noun aftereffects, crapulence, morning after (informal)

hang-up noun preoccupation, block, difficulty, inhibition, obsession, problem, thing (informal)

hank noun coil, length, loop, piece, roll, skein

hanker verb with for or after desire, crave, hunger, itch, long, lust, pine, thirst, yearn

haphazard adjective disorganized, aimless, casual, hit or miss (informal), indiscriminate, slapdash

happen verb **1** occur, come about, come to pass, develop, result, take place, transpire (informal) **2** chance, turn out

happening noun event, affair, episode, experience, incident, occurrence, proceeding

happily adverb **1** willingly, freely, gladly, with pleasure **2** joyfully, blithely, cheerfully, gaily, gleefully, joyously, merrily **3** luckily, fortunately, opportunely, providentially

happiness noun joy, bliss, cheerfulness, contentment, delight, ecstasy, elation, jubilation, pleasure, satisfaction

happy adjective **1** joyful, blissful, cheerful, content, delighted, ecstatic, elated, glad, jubilant, merry, overjoyed, pleased, thrilled **2** fortunate, advantageous, auspicious, favourable, lucky, timely

happy-go-lucky adjective carefree, blithe, easy-going, light-hearted, nonchalant, unconcerned, untroubled

harangue verb **1** rant, address, declaim, exhort, hold forth,

lecture, spout (*informal*) ♦ *noun*
2 speech, address, declamation,
diatribe, exhortation, tirade

harass *verb* annoy, bother, harry,
hassle (*informal*), hound,
persecute, pester, plague,
trouble, vex

harassed *adjective* worried,
careworn, distraught, hassled
(*informal*), strained, tormented,
troubled, under pressure, vexed

harassment *noun* trouble,
annoyance, bother, hassle
(*informal*), irritation, nuisance,
persecution, pestering

harbour *noun* 1 port, anchorage,
haven ♦ *verb* 2 shelter, hide,
protect, provide refuge, shield
3 maintain, cling to, entertain,
foster, hold, nurse, nurture, retain

hard *adjective* 1 solid, firm,
inflexible, rigid, rocklike, stiff,
strong, tough, unyielding
2 strenuous, arduous,
backbreaking, exacting,
exhausting, laborious, rigorous,
tough 3 difficult, complicated,
intricate, involved, knotty,
perplexing, puzzling, thorny
4 unfeeling, callous, cold, cruel,
hardhearted, pitiless, stern,
unkind, unsympathetic 5 painful,
disagreeable, distressing,
grievous, intolerable, unpleasant
♦ *adverb* 6 energetically, fiercely,
forcefully, forcibly, heavily,
intensely, powerfully, severely,
sharply, strongly, vigorously,
violently, with all one's might,
with might and main
7 diligently, doggedly,
industriously, persistently,
steadily, untiringly

hard-bitten *or* **hard-boiled**

adjective tough, cynical,
hard-nosed (*informal*),
matter-of-fact, practical, realistic,
unsentimental

harden *verb* 1 solidify, anneal,
bake, cake, freeze, set, stiffen
2 accustom, habituate, inure,
season, train

hardened *adjective* 1 habitual,
chronic, incorrigible, inveterate,
shameless 2 accustomed,
habituated, inured, seasoned,
toughened

hard-headed *adjective* sensible,
level-headed, practical,
pragmatic, realistic, shrewd,
tough, unsentimental

hardhearted *adjective*
unsympathetic, callous, cold,
hard, heartless, insensitive,
uncaring, unfeeling

hardiness *noun* resilience,
resolution, robustness,
ruggedness, sturdiness, toughness

hardly *adverb* barely, just, only
just, scarcely, with difficulty

hardship *noun* suffering,
adversity, difficulty, misfortune,
need, privation, tribulation

hard up *adjective* poor, broke
(*informal*), impecunious,
impoverished, on the breadline,
out of pocket, penniless, short,
skint (*Brit. slang*), strapped for
cash (*informal*)

hardy *adjective* strong, robust,
rugged, sound, stout, sturdy,
tough

harm *verb* 1 injure, abuse,
damage, hurt, ill-treat, maltreat,
ruin, spoil, wound ♦ *noun*
2 injury, abuse, damage, hurt,
ill, loss, mischief, misfortune

harmful adjective <u>destructive</u>, damaging, deleterious, detrimental, hurtful, injurious, noxious, pernicious

harmless adjective <u>innocuous</u>, gentle, innocent, inoffensive, nontoxic, safe, unobjectionable

harmonious adjective
1 <u>melodious</u>, agreeable, concordant, consonant, dulcet, mellifluous, musical, sweet-sounding, tuneful
2 <u>friendly</u>, agreeable, amicable, compatible, congenial, cordial, sympathetic

harmonize verb <u>blend</u>, chime with, cohere, coordinate, correspond, match, tally, tone in with

harmony noun 1 <u>agreement</u>, accord, amicability, compatibility, concord, cooperation, friendship, peace, rapport, sympathy 2 <u>tunefulness</u>, euphony, melody, tune, unison

harness noun 1 <u>equipment</u>, gear, tack, tackle ♦ verb 2 <u>exploit</u>, channel, control, employ, mobilize, utilize

harrowing adjective <u>distressing</u>, agonizing, disturbing, heart-rending, nerve-racking, painful, terrifying, tormenting, traumatic

harry verb <u>pester</u>, badger, bother, chivvy, harass, hassle (informal), molest, plague

harsh adjective 1 <u>raucous</u>, discordant, dissonant, grating, guttural, rasping, rough, strident 2 <u>severe</u>, austere, cruel, Draconian, drastic, pitiless, punitive, ruthless, stern

harshly adverb <u>severely</u>, brutally, cruelly, roughly, sternly, strictly

harshness noun <u>severity</u>, asperity, austerity, brutality, rigour, roughness, sternness

harvest noun 1 <u>crop</u>, produce, yield ♦ verb 2 <u>gather</u>, mow, pick, pluck, reap

hash noun **make a hash of** Informal <u>mess up</u>, botch, bungle, make a pig's ear of (informal), mishandle, mismanage, muddle

hassle noun 1 <u>argument</u>, bickering, disagreement, dispute, fight, quarrel, row, squabble 2 <u>trouble</u>, bother, difficulty, grief (informal), inconvenience, problem ♦ verb 2 <u>bother</u>, annoy, badger, bug (informal), harass, hound, pester

haste noun 1 <u>speed</u>, alacrity, quickness, rapidity, swiftness, urgency, velocity 2 <u>rush</u>, hurry, hustle, impetuosity

hasten verb <u>rush</u>, dash, fly, hurry (up), make haste, race, scurry, speed

hastily adverb 1 <u>speedily</u>, promptly, quickly, rapidly 2 <u>hurriedly</u>, impetuously, precipitately, rashly

hasty adjective 1 <u>speedy</u>, brisk, hurried, prompt, rapid, swift, urgent 2 <u>impetuous</u>, impulsive, precipitate, rash, thoughtless

hatch verb 1 <u>incubate</u>, breed, bring forth, brood 2 <u>devise</u>, conceive, concoct, contrive, cook up (informal), design, dream up (informal), think up

hate verb 1 <u>detest</u>, abhor, despise, dislike, loathe, recoil from 2 <u>be unwilling</u>, be loath, be reluctant, be sorry, dislike,

feel disinclined, shrink from
♦ *noun* 3 dislike, animosity,
antipathy, aversion, detestation,
enmity, hatred, hostility, loathing

hateful *adjective* despicable,
abhorrent, detestable, horrible,
loathsome, obnoxious, odious,
offensive, repellent, repugnant,
repulsive

hatred *noun* dislike, animosity,
antipathy, aversion, detestation,
enmity, hate, repugnance,
revulsion

haughty *adjective* proud,
arrogant, conceited,
contemptuous, disdainful,
imperious, scornful, snooty
(*informal*), stuck-up (*informal*),
supercilious

haul *verb* 1 drag, draw, heave,
lug, pull, tug ♦ *noun* 2 gain,
booty, catch, harvest, loot,
spoils, takings, yield

haunt *verb* 1 plague, obsess,
possess, prey on, recur, stay
with, torment, trouble, weigh on
♦ *noun* 2 meeting place, hangout
(*informal*), rendezvous, stamping
ground

haunted *adjective* 1 possessed,
cursed, eerie, ghostly, jinxed,
spooky (*informal*) 2 preoccupied,
obsessed, plagued, tormented,
troubled, worried

haunting *adjective* poignant,
evocative, nostalgic, persistent,
unforgettable

have *verb* 1 possess, hold, keep,
obtain, own, retain 2 receive,
accept, acquire, gain, get,
obtain, procure, secure, take
3 experience, endure, enjoy,
feel, meet with, suffer, sustain,
undergo 4 *Slang* cheat, deceive,

dupe, fool, outwit, swindle, take
in (*informal*), trick 5 give birth
to, bear, beget, bring forth,
deliver 6 have to be obliged, be
bound, be compelled, be forced,
have got to, must, ought, should

haven *noun* sanctuary, asylum,
refuge, retreat, sanctum, shelter

have on *verb* 1 wear, be clothed
in, be dressed in 2 tease,
deceive, kid (*informal*), pull
someone's leg, take the mickey,
trick, wind up (*Brit. slang*)

havoc *noun* disorder, chaos,
confusion, disruption, mayhem,
shambles

haywire *adjective* As in go
haywire topsy-turvy, chaotic,
confused, disordered,
disorganized, mixed up, out of
order, shambolic (*informal*)

hazard *noun* 1 danger, jeopardy,
peril, pitfall, risk, threat ♦ *verb*
2 jeopardize, endanger, expose,
imperil, risk, threaten 3 As in
hazard a guess conjecture,
advance, offer, presume, throw
out, venture, volunteer

hazardous *adjective* dangerous,
dicey (*informal, chiefly Brit.*),
difficult, insecure, perilous,
precarious, risky, unsafe

haze *noun* mist, cloud, fog,
obscurity, vapour

hazy *adjective* 1 misty, cloudy,
dim, dull, foggy, overcast
2 vague, fuzzy, ill-defined,
indefinite, indistinct, muddled,
nebulous, uncertain, unclear

head *noun* 1 skull, crown, loaf
(*slang*), nut (*slang*), pate
2 leader, boss (*informal*), captain,
chief, commander, director,
manager, master, principal,

supervisor **3** top, crest, crown, peak, pinnacle, summit, tip **4 brain**, brains (*informal*), intellect, intelligence, mind, thought, understanding **5 go to one's head** excite, intoxicate, make conceited, puff up **6 head over heels** uncontrollably, completely, intensely, thoroughly, utterly, wholeheartedly ◆ *adjective* **7** chief, arch, first, leading, main, pre-eminent, premier, prime, principal, supreme ◆ *verb* **8** lead, be *or* go first, cap, crown, lead the way, precede, top **9** control, be in charge of, command, direct, govern, guide, lead, manage, run **10** make for, aim, go to, make a beeline for, point, set off for, set out, start towards, steer, turn

headache *noun* **1** migraine, head (*informal*), neuralgia **2** problem, bane, bother, inconvenience, nuisance, trouble, vexation, worry

heading *noun* title, caption, headline, name, rubric

headlong *adverb, adjective* **1** headfirst, head-on ◆ *adverb* **2** hastily, heedlessly, helter-skelter, hurriedly, pell-mell, precipitately, rashly, thoughtlessly ◆ *adjective* **3** hasty, breakneck, dangerous, impetuous, impulsive, inconsiderate, precipitate, reckless, thoughtless

headstrong *adjective* obstinate, foolhardy, heedless, impulsive, perverse, pig-headed, self-willed, stubborn, unruly, wilful

headway *noun* progress, advance, improvement,

progression, way

heady *adjective* **1** inebriating, intoxicating, potent, strong **2** exciting, exhilarating, intoxicating, stimulating, thrilling

heal *verb* cure, make well, mend, regenerate, remedy, restore, treat

health *noun* **1** wellbeing, fitness, good condition, healthiness, robustness, soundness, strength, vigour **2** condition, constitution, fettle, shape, state

healthy *adjective* **1** well, active, fit, hale and hearty, in fine fettle, in good shape (*informal*), in the pink, robust, strong **2** wholesome, beneficial, hygienic, invigorating, nourishing, nutritious, salubrious, salutary

heap *noun* **1** pile, accumulation, collection, hoard, lot, mass, mound, stack **2** *often plural* a lot, great deal, load(s) (*informal*), lots (*informal*), mass, plenty, pot's (*informal*), stack(s), tons ◆ *verb* **3** pile, accumulate, amass, collect, gather, hoard, stack **4** confer, assign, bestow, load, shower upon

hear *verb* **1** listen to, catch, overhear **2** learn, ascertain, discover, find out, gather, get wind of (*informal*), pick up **3** *Law* try, examine, investigate, judge

hearing *noun* inquiry, industrial tribunal, investigation, review, trial

hearsay *noun* rumour, gossip, idle talk, report, talk, tittle-tattle, word of mouth

heart *noun* **1** nature, character, disposition, soul, temperament **2** bravery, courage, fortitude, pluck, purpose, resolution, spirit, will 3 <u>centre</u>, core, hub, middle, nucleus, quintessence 4 **by heart** by memory, by rote, off pat, parrot-fashion (*informal*), pat, word for word

heartache *noun* <u>sorrow</u>, agony, anguish, despair, distress, grief, heartbreak, pain, remorse, suffering, torment, torture

heartbreak *noun* <u>grief</u>, anguish, desolation, despair, misery, pain, sorrow, suffering

heartbreaking *adjective* <u>tragic</u>, agonizing, distressing, harrowing, heart-rending, pitiful, poignant, sad

heartbroken *adjective* <u>miserable</u>, brokenhearted, crushed, desolate, despondent, disconsolate, dispirited, heartsick

heartfelt *adjective* <u>sincere</u>, deep, devout, earnest, genuine, honest, profound, unfeigned, wholehearted

heartily *adverb* <u>enthusiastically</u>, eagerly, earnestly, resolutely, vigorously, zealously

heartless *adjective* <u>cruel</u>, callous, cold, hard, hardhearted, merciless, pitiless, uncaring, unfeeling

heart-rending *adjective* <u>moving</u>, affecting, distressing, harrowing, heartbreaking, poignant, sad, tragic

hearty *adjective* 1 <u>friendly</u>, back-slapping, ebullient, effusive, enthusiastic, genial, jovial, warm 2 <u>substantial</u>, ample, filling, nourishing, sizable *or* sizeable, solid, square

heat *verb* 1 <u>warm up</u>, make hot,

reheat ♦*noun* 2 <u>hotness</u>, high temperature, warmth 3 <u>intensity</u>, excitement, fervour, fury, passion, vehemence

heated *adjective* <u>angry</u>, excited, fierce, frenzied, furious, impassioned, intense, passionate, stormy, vehement

heathen *noun* 1 <u>unbeliever</u>, infidel, pagan ♦*adjective* 2 <u>pagan</u>, godless, idolatrous, irreligious

heave *verb* 1 <u>lift</u>, drag (up), haul (up), hoist, pull (up), raise, tug 2 <u>throw</u>, cast, fling, hurl, pitch, send, sling, toss 3 <u>sigh</u>, groan, puff 4 <u>vomit</u>, be sick, gag, retch, spew, throw up (*informal*)

heaven *noun* 1 <u>paradise</u>, bliss, Elysium *or* Elysian fields (*Greek myth*), hereafter, life everlasting, next world, nirvana (*Buddhism, Hinduism*), Zion (*Christianity*) 2 <u>happiness</u>, bliss, ecstasy, paradise, rapture, seventh heaven, utopia 3 **the heavens** <u>sky</u>, ether, firmament

heavenly *adjective* 1 <u>beautiful</u>, blissful, delightful, divine (*informal*), exquisite, lovely, ravishing, sublime, wonderful 2 <u>celestial</u>, angelic, blessed, divine, holy, immortal

heavily *adverb* 1 <u>ponderously</u>, awkwardly, clumsily, weightily 2 <u>densely</u>, closely, compactly, thickly 3 <u>considerably</u>, a great deal, copiously, excessively, to excess, very much

heaviness *noun* <u>weight</u>, gravity, heftiness, ponderousness

heavy *adjective* 1 <u>weighty</u>, bulky, hefty, massive, ponderous 2 <u>considerable</u>, abundant, copious, excessive, large, profuse

heckle *verb* jeer, barrack (*informal*), boo, disrupt, interrupt, shout down, taunt

hectic *adjective* frantic, animated, chaotic, feverish, frenetic, heated, turbulent

hedge *noun* 1 barrier, boundary, screen, windbreak ♦ *verb* 2 dodge, duck, equivocate, evade, flannel (*Brit. informal*), prevaricate, sidestep, temporize 3 insure, cover, guard, protect, safeguard, shield

heed *noun* 1 care, attention, caution, mind, notice, regard, respect, thought ♦ *verb* 2 pay attention to, bear in mind, consider, follow, listen to, note, obey, observe, take notice of

heedless *adjective* careless, foolhardy, inattentive, oblivious, thoughtless, unmindful

heel *noun* Slang swine, bounder (*old-fashioned Brit. slang*), cad (*Brit. informal*), rotter (*slang, chiefly Brit.*)

heel over *verb* lean over, keel over, list, tilt

hefty *adjective* strong, big, burly, hulking, massive, muscular, robust, strapping

height *noun* 1 altitude, elevation, highness, loftiness, stature, tallness 2 peak, apex, crest, crown, pinnacle, summit, top, zenith 3 culmination, climax, limit, maximum, ultimate

heighten *verb* intensify, add to, amplify, enhance, improve, increase, magnify, sharpen, strengthen

heir *noun* successor, beneficiary,

heiress (*fem.*), inheritor, next in line

hell *noun* 1 underworld, abyss, fire and brimstone, Hades (*Greek myth*), hellfire, inferno, nether world 2 torment, agony, anguish, misery, nightmare, ordeal, suffering, wretchedness

hellish *adjective* devilish, damnable, diabolical, fiendish, infernal

hello *interjection* welcome, good afternoon, good evening, good morning, greetings

helm *noun* 1 tiller, rudder, wheel 2 **at the helm** in charge, at the wheel, in command, in control, in the driving seat, in the saddle

help *verb* 1 aid, abet, assist, cooperate, lend a hand, succour, support 2 improve, alleviate, ameliorate, ease, facilitate, mitigate, relieve 3 refrain from, avoid, keep from, prevent, resist ♦ *noun* 4 assistance, advice, aid, cooperation, guidance, helping hand, support

helper *noun* assistant, adjutant, aide, ally, attendant, collaborator, helpmate, mate, right-hand man, second, supporter

helpful *adjective* 1 useful, advantageous, beneficial, constructive, practical, profitable, timely 2 cooperative, accommodating, considerate, friendly, kind, neighbourly, supportive, sympathetic

helping *noun* portion, dollop (*informal*), piece, plateful, ration, serving

helpless *adjective* weak, disabled, impotent, incapable, infirm, paralysed, powerless

helter-skelter adjective
1 haphazard, confused,
disordered, higgledy-piggledy
(informal), hit-or-miss, jumbled,
muddled, random, topsy-turvy
♦ adverb **2** carelessly, anyhow,
hastily, headlong, hurriedly,
pell-mell, rashly, recklessly, wildly

hem noun **1** edge, border, fringe,
margin, trimming ♦ verb **2** hem
in surround, beset, circumscribe,
confine, enclose, restrict, shut in

hence conjunction therefore, ergo,
for this reason, on that account,
thus

henchman noun attendant,
associate, bodyguard, follower,
minder (slang), right-hand man,
sidekick (slang), subordinate,
supporter

henpecked adjective bullied,
browbeaten, dominated, meek,
subjugated, timid

herald noun **1** messenger, crier
2 forerunner, harbinger,
indication, omen, precursor,
sign, signal, token ♦ verb
3 indicate, foretoken, portend,
presage, promise, show, usher in

herd noun **1** multitude,
collection, crowd, drove, flock,
horde, mass, mob, swarm,
throng ♦ verb **2** congregate,
assemble, collect, flock, gather,
huddle, muster, rally

hereafter adverb **1** in future,
from now on, hence,
henceforth, henceforward ♦ noun
2 afterlife, life after death, next
world

hereditary adjective **1** genetic,
inborn, inbred, inheritable,
transmissible **2** inherited,

ancestral, traditional

heredity noun genetics,
constitution, genetic make-up,
inheritance

heresy noun dissidence, apostasy,
heterodoxy, iconoclasm,
unorthodoxy

heretic noun dissident, apostate,
dissenter, nonconformist,
renegade, revisionist

heretical adjective unorthodox,
heterodox, iconoclastic,
idolatrous, impious, revisionist

heritage noun inheritance,
bequest, birthright, endowment,
legacy, tradition

hermit noun recluse, anchorite,
eremite, loner (informal), monk

hero noun **1** idol, champion,
conqueror, star, superstar, victor
2 leading man, protagonist

heroic adjective courageous,
brave, daring, fearless, gallant,
intrepid, lion-hearted, valiant

heroine noun leading lady, diva,
prima donna, protagonist

heroism noun bravery, courage,
courageousness, fearlessness,
gallantry, intrepidity, spirit, valour

hesitant adjective uncertain,
diffident, doubtful, half-hearted,
halting, irresolute, reluctant,
unsure, vacillating, wavering

hesitate verb **1** waver, delay,
dither (chiefly Brit.), doubt, hum
and haw, pause, vacillate, wait
2 be reluctant, balk, be
unwilling, demur, hang back,
scruple, shrink from, think twice

hesitation noun **1** indecision,
delay, doubt, hesitancy,
irresolution, uncertainty,
vacillation **2** reluctance,

hew verb **1** cut, axe, chop, hack, lop, split **2** carve, fashion, form, make, model, sculpt, sculpture, shape, smooth

heyday noun prime, bloom, pink, prime of life, salad days

hiatus noun pause, break, discontinuity, gap, interruption, interval, respite, space

hidden adjective concealed, clandestine, covert, latent, secret, under wraps, unseen, veiled

hide¹ verb **1** conceal, secrete, stash (informal) **2** go into hiding, go to ground, go underground, hole up, lie low, take cover **3** disguise, camouflage, cloak, conceal, cover, mask, obscure, shroud, veil **4** suppress, draw a veil over, hush up, keep dark, keep secret, keep under one's hat, withhold

hide² noun skin, pelt

hidebound adjective conventional, narrow-minded, rigid, set in one's ways, strait-laced, ultraconservative

hideous adjective ugly, ghastly, grim, grisly, grotesque, gruesome, monstrous, repulsive, revolting, unsightly

hide-out noun hideaway, den, hiding place, lair, shelter

hiding noun beating, drubbing, licking (informal), spanking, thrashing, walloping (informal), whipping

hierarchy noun grading, pecking order, ranking

high adjective **1** tall, elevated,

lofty, soaring, steep, towering **2** extreme, excessive, extraordinary, great, intensified, sharp, strong **3** important, arch, chief, eminent, exalted, powerful, superior **4** Informal intoxicated, stoned (slang), tripping (informal) **5** high-pitched, acute, penetrating, piercing, piping, sharp, shrill, strident ♦ adverb **6** aloft, at great height, far up, way up

highbrow noun **1** intellectual, aesthete, egghead (informal), scholar ♦ adjective **2** intellectual, bookish, cultivated, cultured, sophisticated

high-flown adjective extravagant, elaborate, exaggerated, florid, grandiose, inflated, lofty, overblown, pretentious

high-handed adjective dictatorial, despotic, domineering, imperious, oppressive, overbearing, tyrannical, wilful

highlight noun **1** feature, climax, focal point, focus, high point, high spot, peak ♦ verb **2** emphasize, accent, accentuate, bring to the fore, show up, spotlight, stress, underline

highly adverb extremely, exceptionally, greatly, immensely, tremendously, vastly, very, very much

highly strung adjective nervous, edgy, excitable, neurotic, sensitive, stressed, temperamental, tense

hijack verb seize, commandeer, expropriate, take over

hike noun **1** walk, march, ramble, tramp, trek ♦ verb **2** walk, back-pack, ramble, tramp **3 hike up** raise, hitch up, jack up, lift, pull up

hilarious adjective funny, amusing, comical, entertaining, humorous, rollicking, side-splitting, uproarious

hilarity noun laughter, amusement, exhilaration, glee, high spirits, jollity, merriment, mirth

hill noun mount, fell, height, hillock, hilltop, knoll, mound, tor

hillock noun mound, hummock, knoll

hilly adjective mountainous, rolling, undulating

hilt noun handle, grip, haft, handgrip

hinder verb obstruct, block, check, delay, encumber, frustrate, hamper, handicap, hold up or back, impede, interrupt, stop

hindmost adjective last, final, furthest, furthest behind, rearmost, trailing

hindrance noun obstacle, barrier, deterrent, difficulty, drawback, handicap, hitch, impediment, obstruction, restriction, snag, stumbling block

hinge verb depend, be contingent, hang, pivot, rest, revolve around, turn

hint noun 1 indication, allusion, clue, implication, innuendo, insinuation, intimation, suggestion 2 advice, help, pointer, suggestion, tip 3 trace, dash, suggestion, suspicion, tinge, touch, undertone ♦ verb 4 suggest, imply, indicate,

insinuate, intimate

hippy noun bohemian, beatnik, dropout

hire verb 1 employ, appoint, commission, engage, sign up, take on 2 rent, charter, engage, lease, let ♦ noun 3 rental, charge, cost, fee, price, rent

hiss noun 1 sibilation, buzz, hissing 2 catcall, boo, jeer ♦ verb 3 whistle, sibilate, wheeze, whirr, whiz 4 jeer, boo, deride, hoot, mock

historic adjective significant, epoch-making, extraordinary, famous, ground-breaking, momentous, notable, outstanding, remarkable

historical adjective factual, actual, attested, authentic, documented, real

history noun 1 chronicle, account, annals, narrative, recital, record, story 2 the past, antiquity, olden days, yesterday, yesteryear

hit verb 1 strike, bang, beat, clout (informal), knock, slap, smack, thump, wallop (informal), whack 2 collide with, bang into, bump, clash with, crash against, run into, smash into 3 reach, accomplish, achieve, arrive at, attain, gain 4 affect, damage, devastate, impact on, influence, leave a mark on, overwhelm, touch 5 **hit it off** Informal get on (well) with, be on good terms, click (slang), get on like a house on fire (informal) ♦ noun 6 stroke, belt (informal), blow, clout (informal), knock, rap, slap, smack, wallop (informal) 7 success, sensation, smash (*informal*), triumph, winner

hit-and-miss *adjective*
haphazard, aimless, casual,
disorganized, indiscriminate,
random, undirected, uneven

hitch *noun* 1 problem, catch,
difficulty, drawback, hindrance,
hold-up, impediment, obstacle,
snag ◆ *verb* 2 fasten, attach,
connect, couple, harness, join,
tether, tie 3 *Informal* hitchhike,
thumb a lift 4 **hitch up** pull up,
jerk, tug, yank

hitherto *adverb* previously,
heretofore, so far, thus far, until
now

hit on *verb* think up, arrive at,
discover, invent, light upon,
strike upon, stumble on

hoard *noun* 1 store,
accumulation, cache, fund, pile,
reserve, stockpile, supply,
treasure-trove ◆ *verb* 2 save,
accumulate, amass, collect,
gather, lay up, put by, stash
away (*informal*), stockpile, store

hoarse *adjective* raucous, croaky,
grating, gravelly, gruff, guttural,
husky, rasping, rough, throaty

hoax *noun* 1 trick, con (*informal*),
deception, fraud, practical joke,
prank, spoof (*informal*), swindle
◆ *verb* 2 deceive, con (*slang*),
dupe, fool, hoodwink, swindle,
take in (*informal*), trick

hobby *noun* pastime, diversion,
(leisure) activity, leisure pursuit,
relaxation

hobnob *verb* socialize, associate,
consort, fraternize, hang about,
hang out (*informal*), keep
company, mingle, mix

hoist *verb* 1 raise, elevate, erect,
heave, lift ◆ *noun* 2 lift, crane,
elevator, winch

hold *verb* 1 own, have, keep,
maintain, occupy, possess, retain
2 grasp, clasp, cling, clutch,
cradle, embrace, enfold, grip
3 restrain, confine, detain,
impound, imprison 4 consider,
assume, believe, deem, judge,
presume, reckon, regard, think
5 convene, call, conduct, preside
over, run 6 accommodate,
contain, have a capacity for,
seat, take ◆ *noun* 7 grip, clasp,
grasp 8 foothold, footing,
support 9 control, influence,
mastery

holder *noun* 1 owner, bearer,
keeper, possessor, proprietor
2 case, container, cover

hold forth *verb* speak, declaim,
discourse, go on, lecture,
preach, spiel (*informal*), spout
(*informal*)

hold-up *noun* 1 delay,
bottleneck, hitch, setback, snag,
stoppage, traffic jam, wait
2 robbery, mugging (*informal*),
stick-up (*slang, chiefly U.S.*), theft

hold up *verb* 1 delay, detain,
hinder, retard, set back, slow
down, stop 2 support, prop,
shore up, sustain 3 rob, mug
(*informal*), waylay

hold with *verb* approve of, agree
to *or* with, be in favour of,
countenance, subscribe to,
support

hole *noun* 1 opening, aperture,
breach, crack, fissure, gap,
orifice, perforation, puncture,
tear, vent 2 cavity, cave, cavern,
chamber, hollow, pit 3 burrow,
den, earth, lair, shelter 4 *Informal*

holiday _noun_ **1** vacation, break, leave, recess, time off **2** festival, celebration, feast, fête, gala

holiness _noun_ divinity, godliness, piety, purity, righteousness, sacredness, saintliness, sanctity, spirituality

hollow _adjective_ **1** empty, unfilled, vacant, void **2** reverberant, deep, dull, low, muted **3** worthless, fruitless, futile, meaningless, pointless, useless, vain ♦ _noun_ **4** cavity, basin, bowl, crater, depression, hole, pit, trough **5** valley, dale, dell, dingle, glen ♦ _verb_ **6** scoop, dig, excavate, gouge

holocaust _noun_ genocide, annihilation, conflagration, destruction, devastation, massacre

holy _adjective_ **1** devout, god-fearing, godly, pious, pure, religious, righteous, saintly, virtuous **2** sacred, blessed, consecrated, hallowed, sacrosanct, sanctified, venerable

homage _noun_ respect, adoration, adulation, deference, devotion, honour, reverence, worship

home _noun_ **1** house, abode, domicile, dwelling, habitation, pad (_slang_), residence **2** birthplace, home town **3 at home: a** in, available, present **b** at ease, comfortable, familiar, relaxed **4 bring home to** make

clear, drive home, emphasize, impress upon, press home ♦ _adjective_ **5** domestic, familiar, internal, local, native

homeland _noun_ native land, country of origin, fatherland, mother country, motherland

homeless _adjective_ **1** destitute, displaced, dispossessed, down-and-out ♦ _noun_ **2 the homeless** vagrants, squatters

homely _adjective_ comfortable, cosy, friendly, homespun, modest, ordinary, plain, simple, welcoming

homespun _adjective_ unsophisticated, coarse, homely, home-made, plain, rough

homicidal _adjective_ murderous, deadly, lethal, maniacal, mortal

homicide _noun_ **1** murder, bloodshed, killing, manslaughter, slaying **2** murderer, killer, slayer

homily _noun_ sermon, address, discourse, lecture, preaching

homogeneity _noun_ uniformity, consistency, correspondence, sameness, similarity

homogeneous _adjective_ uniform, akin, alike, analogous, comparable, consistent, identical, similar, unvarying

hone _verb_ sharpen, edge, file, grind, point, polish, whet

honest _adjective_ **1** trustworthy, ethical, honourable, law-abiding, reputable, scrupulous, truthful, upright, virtuous **2** open, candid, direct, forthright, frank, plain, sincere, upfront (_informal_)

honestly _adverb_ **1** ethically, by fair means, cleanly, honourably, lawfully, legally **2** frankly, candidly, in all sincerity, plainly, straight (out), to one's face, truthfully

honesty noun 1 <u>integrity</u>, honour, incorruptibility, morality, probity, rectitude, scrupulousness, trustworthiness, truthfulness, uprightness, virtue 2 <u>frankness</u>, bluntness, candour, openness, outspokenness, sincerity, straightforwardness

honorary adjective <u>nominal</u>, complimentary, in name or title only, titular, unofficial, unpaid

honour noun 1 <u>glory</u>, credit, dignity, distinction, fame, prestige, renown, reputation 2 <u>tribute</u>, accolade, commendation, homage, praise, recognition 3 <u>fairness</u>, decency, goodness, honesty, integrity, morality, probity, rectitude 4 <u>privilege</u>, compliment, credit, pleasure ♦ verb 5 <u>respect</u>, adore, appreciate, esteem, prize, value 6 <u>fulfil</u>, be true to, carry out, discharge, keep, live up to, observe 7 <u>acclaim</u>, commemorate, commend, decorate, praise 8 <u>accept</u>, acknowledge, pass, pay, take

honourable adjective <u>respected</u>, creditable, estimable, reputable, respectable, virtuous

hoodwink verb <u>deceive</u>, con (informal), delude, dupe, fool, mislead, swindle, trick

hook noun 1 <u>fastener</u>, catch, clasp, link, peg ♦ verb 2 <u>fasten</u>, clasp, fix, secure 3 <u>catch</u>, ensnare, entrap, snare, trap

hooked adjective 1 <u>bent</u>, aquiline, curved, hook-shaped 2 <u>addicted</u>, devoted, enamoured, obsessed,

taken, turned on (slang)

hooligan noun <u>delinquent</u>, lager lout, ruffian, vandal, yob or yobbo (Brit. slang)

hooliganism noun <u>delinquency</u>, disorder, loutishness, rowdiness, vandalism, violence

hoop noun <u>ring</u>, band, circlet, girdle, loop, wheel

hoot noun 1 <u>cry</u>, call, toot 2 <u>catcall</u>, boo, hiss, jeer ♦ verb 3 <u>jeer</u>, boo, hiss, howl down

hop verb 1 <u>jump</u>, bound, caper, leap, skip, spring, trip, vault ♦ noun 2 <u>jump</u>, bounce, bound, leap, skip, spring, step, vault

hope verb 1 <u>desire</u>, aspire, cross one's fingers, long, look forward to, set one's heart on ♦ noun 2 <u>desire</u>, ambition, assumption, dream, expectation, longing

hopeful adjective 1 <u>optimistic</u>, buoyant, confident, expectant, looking forward to, sanguine 2 <u>promising</u>, auspicious, bright, encouraging, heartening, reassuring, rosy

hopefully adverb <u>optimistically</u>, confidently, expectantly

hopeless adjective <u>pointless</u>, futile, impossible, no-win, unattainable, useless, vain

horde noun <u>crowd</u>, band, drove, gang, host, mob, multitude, pack, swarm, throng

horizon noun <u>skyline</u>, vista

horizontal adjective <u>level</u>, flat, parallel

horrible adjective 1 <u>terrifying</u>, appalling, dreadful, frightful, ghastly, grim, grisly, gruesome, hideous, repulsive, revolting, shocking 2 <u>unpleasant</u>, awful,

cruel, disagreeable, dreadful,
horrid, mean, nasty, terrible

horrid adjective **1** unpleasant,
awful, disagreeable, dreadful,
horrible, terrible **2** Informal
unkind, beastly (informal), cruel,
mean, nasty

horrific adjective terrifying,
appalling, awful, dreadful,
frightful, ghastly, grisly,
horrendous, horrifying, shocking

horrify verb **1** terrify, alarm,
frighten, intimidate, make one's
hair stand on end, petrify, scare
2 shock, appal, dismay, outrage,
sicken

horror noun **1** terror, alarm,
consternation, dread, fear, fright,
panic **2** hatred, aversion,
detestation, disgust, loathing,
odium, repugnance, revulsion

horse noun nag, colt, filly,
gee-gee (slang), mare, mount,
stallion, steed (archaic or literary)

horseman noun rider, cavalier,
cavalryman, dragoon, equestrian

horseplay noun buffoonery,
clowning, fooling around, high
jinks, pranks, romping,
rough-and-tumble, skylarking
(informal)

hospitable adjective welcoming,
cordial, friendly, generous,
gracious, kind, liberal, sociable

hospitality noun welcome,
conviviality, cordiality,
friendliness, neighbourliness,
sociability, warmth

host¹ noun **1** master of
ceremonies, entertainer,
innkeeper, landlord or landlady,
proprietor **2** presenter,
anchorman or anchorwoman,

compere (Brit.) ♦ verb **3** present,
compere (Brit.), front (informal),
introduce

host² noun multitude, army,
array, drove, horde, legion,
myriad, swarm, throng

hostage noun prisoner, captive,
pawn

hostile adjective **1** opposed,
antagonistic, belligerent,
contrary, ill-disposed, rancorous
2 unfriendly, adverse,
inhospitable, unsympathetic,
unwelcoming

hostilities plural noun warfare,
conflict, fighting, war

hostility noun opposition,
animosity, antipathy, enmity,
hatred, ill will, malice,
resentment, unfriendliness

hot adjective **1** heated, boiling,
roasting, scalding, scorching,
searing, steaming, sultry,
sweltering, torrid, warm **2** spicy,
biting, peppery, piquant,
pungent, sharp **3** fierce, fiery,
intense, passionate, raging,
stormy, violent **4** recent, fresh,
just out, latest, new, up to the
minute **5** popular, approved,
favoured, in demand, in vogue,
sought-after

hot air noun empty talk,
bombast, claptrap (informal),
guff (slang), verbiage, wind

hot-blooded adjective passionate,
ardent, excitable, fiery,
impulsive, spirited,
temperamental, wild

hotchpotch noun mixture,
farrago, jumble, medley,
mélange, mess, mishmash,
potpourri

hot-headed *adjective* <u>rash</u>, fiery, foolhardy, hasty, hot-tempered, impetuous, quick-tempered, reckless, volatile

hound *verb* <u>harass</u>, badger, goad, harry, impel, persecute, pester, provoke

house *noun* **1** <u>home</u>, abode, domicile, dwelling, habitation, homestead, pad (*slang*), residence **2** <u>family</u>, household **3** <u>dynasty</u>, clan, tribe **4** <u>firm</u>, business, company, organization, outfit (*informal*) **5** <u>assembly</u>, Commons, legislative body, parliament **6 on the house** <u>free</u>, for nothing, gratis ♦ *verb* **7** <u>accommodate</u>, billet, harbour, lodge, put up, quarter, take in **8** <u>contain</u>, cover, keep, protect, sheathe, shelter, store

household *noun* <u>family</u>, home, house

householder *noun* <u>occupant</u>, homeowner, resident, tenant

housing *noun* **1** <u>accommodation</u>, dwellings, homes, houses **2** <u>case</u>, casing, container, cover, covering, enclosure, sheath

hovel *noun* <u>hut</u>, cabin, den, hole, shack, shanty, shed

hover *verb* **1** <u>float</u>, drift, flutter, fly, hang **2** <u>linger</u>, hang about **3** <u>waver</u>, dither (*chiefly Brit.*), fluctuate, oscillate, vacillate

however *adverb* <u>nevertheless</u>, after all, anyhow, but, nonetheless, notwithstanding, still, though, yet

howl *noun* **1** <u>cry</u>, bawl, bay, clamour, groan, roar, scream, shriek, wail ♦ *verb* **2** <u>cry</u>, bawl, bellow, roar, scream, shriek, wail, weep, yell

howler *noun* <u>mistake</u>, bloomer (*Brit. informal*), blunder, boob (*Brit. slang*), clanger (*informal*), error, malapropism

hub *noun* <u>centre</u>, core, focal point, focus, heart, middle, nerve centre

huddle *verb* **1** <u>crowd</u>, cluster, converge, flock, gather, press, throng **2** <u>curl up</u>, crouch, hunch up ♦ *noun* **3** *Informal* <u>conference</u>, confab (*informal*), discussion, meeting, powwow

hue *noun* <u>colour</u>, dye, shade, tinge, tint, tone

hug *verb* **1** <u>clasp</u>, cuddle, embrace, enfold, hold close, squeeze, take in one's arms ♦ *noun* **2** <u>embrace</u>, bear hug, clasp, clinch (*slang*), squeeze

huge *adjective* <u>large</u>, colossal, enormous, gigantic, immense, mammoth, massive, monumental, tremendous, vast

hulk *noun* **1** <u>wreck</u>, frame, hull, shell, shipwreck **2** <u>oaf</u>, lout, lubber, lump (*informal*)

hull *noun* <u>frame</u>, body, casing, covering, framework

hum *verb* **1** <u>murmur</u>, buzz, drone, purr, throb, thrum, vibrate, whir **2** <u>be busy</u>, bustle, buzz, pulsate, pulse, stir

human *adjective* **1** <u>mortal</u>, manlike ♦ *noun* **2** <u>human being</u>, creature, individual, man or woman, mortal, person, soul

humane *adjective* <u>kind</u>, benign, compassionate, forgiving, good-natured, merciful, sympathetic, tender, understanding

humanitarian *adjective*

1 compassionate, altruistic, benevolent, charitable, humane, philanthropic, public-spirited ♦ noun **2** philanthropist, altruist, benefactor, Good Samaritan

humanity noun **1** human race, Homo sapiens, humankind, man, mankind, people **2** human nature, mortality **3** sympathy, charity, compassion, fellow feeling, kind-heartedness, kindness, mercy, philanthropy

humanize verb civilize, educate, enlighten, improve, soften, tame

humble adjective **1** modest, meek, self-effacing, unassuming, unostentatious, unpretentious **2** lowly, mean, modest, obscure, ordinary, plebeian, poor, simple, undistinguished ♦ verb **3** humiliate, chasten, crush, disgrace, put (someone) in their place, subdue, take down a peg (informal)

humbug noun **1** fraud, charlatan, con man (informal), faker, impostor, phoney or phony (informal), swindler, trickster **2** nonsense, baloney (informal), cant, claptrap (informal), hypocrisy, quackery, rubbish

humdrum adjective dull, banal, boring, dreary, monotonous, mundane, ordinary, tedious, tiresome, uneventful

humid adjective damp, clammy, dank, moist, muggy, steamy, sticky, sultry, wet

humidity noun damp, clamminess, dampness, dankness, moistness, moisture, mugginess, wetness

humiliate verb embarrass, bring low, chasten, crush, degrade, humble, mortify, put down, put (someone) in their place, shame

humiliating adjective embarrassing, crushing, degrading, humbling, ignominious, mortifying, shaming

humiliation noun embarrassment, degradation, disgrace, dishonour, humbling, ignominy, indignity, loss of face, mortification, put-down, shame

humility noun modesty, humbleness, lowliness, meekness, submissiveness, unpretentiousness

humorist noun comedian, card (informal), comic, funny man, jester, joker, wag, wit

humorous adjective funny, amusing, comic, comical, droll, entertaining, jocular, playful, waggish, witty

humour noun **1** funniness, amusement, comedy, drollery, facetiousness, fun, jocularity, ludicrousness **2** joking, comedy, farce, jesting, pleasantry, wisecracks (informal), wit, witticisms **3** mood, disposition, frame of mind, spirits, temper ♦ verb **4** indulge, accommodate, flatter, go along with, gratify, mollify, pander to

hump noun **1** lump, bulge, bump, mound, projection, protrusion, protuberance, swelling ♦ verb **2** Slang carry, heave, hoist, lug, shoulder

hunch noun **1** feeling, idea, impression, inkling, intuition, premonition, presentiment, suspicion ♦ verb **2** draw in, arch, bend, curve

hunger noun **1** famine, starvation

2 appetite, emptiness, hungriness, ravenousness **3** desire, ache, appetite, craving, itch, lust, thirst, yearning ♦ *verb* **4** want, ache, crave, desire, hanker, itch, long, thirst, wish, yearn

hungry *adjective* **1** empty, famished, peckish (*informal, chiefly Brit.*), ravenous, starved, starving, voracious **2** eager, athirst, avid, covetous, craving, desirous, greedy, keen, yearning

hunk *noun* lump, block, chunk, mass, nugget, piece, slab, wedge

hunt *verb* **1** stalk, chase, hound, pursue, track, trail **2** search, ferret about, forage, look, scour, seek ♦ *noun* **3** search, chase, hunting, investigation, pursuit, quest

hurdle *noun* **1** fence, barricade, barrier **2** obstacle, barrier, difficulty, handicap, hazard, hindrance, impediment, obstruction, stumbling block

hurl *verb* throw, cast, fling, heave, launch, let fly, pitch, propel, sling, toss

hurricane *noun* storm, cyclone, gale, tempest, tornado, twister (*U.S. informal*), typhoon

hurried *adjective* hasty, brief, cursory, perfunctory, quick, rushed, short, speedy, swift

hurry *verb* **1** rush, dash, fly, get a move on (*informal*), make haste, scoot, scurry, step on it (*informal*) ♦ *noun* **2** urgency, flurry, haste, quickness, rush, speed

hurt *verb* **1** harm, bruise, damage, disable, impair, injure, mar, spoil, wound **2** ache, be

sore, be tender, burn, smart, sting, throb **3** sadden, annoy, distress, grieve, pain, upset, wound ♦ *noun* **4** distress, discomfort, pain, pang, soreness, suffering ♦ *adjective* **5** injured, bruised, cut, damaged, harmed, scarred, wounded **6** offended, aggrieved, crushed, wounded

hurtful *adjective* unkind, cruel, cutting, damaging, destructive, malicious, nasty, spiteful, upsetting, wounding

hurtle *verb* rush, charge, crash, fly, plunge, race, shoot, speed, stampede, tear

husband *noun* **1** partner, better half (*humorous*), mate, spouse ♦ *verb* **2** economize, budget, conserve, hoard, save, store

husbandry *noun* **1** farming, agriculture, cultivation, tillage **2** thrift, economy, frugality

hush *verb* **1** quieten, mute, muzzle, shush, silence ♦ *noun* **2** quiet, calm, peace, silence, stillness, tranquillity

hush-hush *adjective* secret, classified, confidential, restricted, top-secret, under wraps

husky *adjective* **1** hoarse, croaky, gruff, guttural, harsh, raucous, rough, throaty **2** *Informal* muscular, burly, hefty, powerful, rugged, stocky, strapping, thickset

hustle *verb* jostle, elbow, force, jog, push, shove

hut *noun* shed, cabin, den, hovel, lean-to, shanty, shelter

hybrid *noun* crossbreed, amalgam, composite, compound, cross, half-breed, mixture, mongrel

hygiene noun cleanliness, sanitation

hygienic adjective clean, aseptic, disinfected, germ-free, healthy, pure, sanitary, sterile

hymn noun anthem, carol, chant, paean, psalm

hype noun publicity, ballyhoo (informal), brouhaha, plugging (informal), promotion, razzmatazz (slang)

hypnotic adjective mesmeric, mesmerizing, sleep-inducing, soothing, soporific, spellbinding

hypnotize verb mesmerize, put in a trance, put to sleep

hypocrisy noun insincerity, cant, deceitfulness, deception, duplicity, pretence

hypocrite noun fraud, charlatan, deceiver, impostor, phoney or phony (informal), pretender

hypocritical adjective insincere, canting, deceitful, duplicitous, false, fraudulent, phoney or phony (informal), sanctimonious, two-faced

hypothesis noun assumption, postulate, premise, proposition, supposition, theory, thesis

hypothetical adjective theoretical, academic, assumed, conjectural, imaginary, putative, speculative, supposed

hysteria noun frenzy, agitation, delirium, hysterics, madness, panic

hysterical adjective 1 frenzied, crazed, distracted, distraught, frantic, overwrought, raving 2 Informal hilarious, comical, side-splitting, uproarious

I i

icy adjective 1 cold, biting, bitter, chill, chilly, freezing, frosty, ice-cold, raw 2 slippery, glassy, slippy (informal or dialect) 3 unfriendly, aloof, cold, distant, frigid, frosty, unwelcoming

idea noun 1 thought, concept, impression, perception 2 belief, conviction, notion, opinion, teaching, view 3 plan, aim, intention, object, objective, purpose

ideal adjective 1 perfect, archetypal, classic, complete, consummate, model, quintessential, supreme ♦ noun 2 model, last word, paradigm, paragon, pattern, perfection, prototype, standard

idealist noun romantic, dreamer, Utopian, visionary

idealistic adjective perfectionist, impracticable, optimistic, romantic, starry-eyed, Utopian, visionary

idealize verb romanticize, apotheosize, ennoble, exalt, glorify, magnify, put on a pedestal, worship

ideally adverb in a perfect world, all things being equal, if one had one's way

identical adjective alike, duplicate, indistinguishable, interchangeable, matching, twin

identification noun 1 recognition, naming, pinpointing 2 empathy, association, connection, fellow feeling, involvement, rapport, relationship, sympathy

identify verb 1 recognize, diagnose, make out, name, pick out, pinpoint, place, put one's finger on (informal), spot 2 **identify with** relate to, associate with, empathize with, feel for, respond to

identity noun 1 existence, individuality, personality, self 2 sameness, correspondence, unity

idiocy noun foolishness, asininity, fatuousness, imbecility, inanity, insanity, lunacy, senselessness

idiom noun 1 phrase, expression, turn of phrase 2 language, jargon, parlance, style, vernacular

idiosyncrasy noun peculiarity, characteristic, eccentricity, mannerism, oddity, quirk, trick

idiot noun fool, chump, cretin, dunderhead, halfwit, imbecile, moron, nincompoop, numbskull or numskull, simpleton, twit (informal, chiefly Brit.)

idiotic adjective foolish, asinine, crazy, daft (informal), foolhardy, harebrained, insane, moronic, senseless, stupid

idle adjective 1 inactive, redundant, unemployed, unoccupied, unused, vacant 2 lazy, good-for-nothing, indolent, lackadaisical, shiftless, slothful, sluggish 3 useless, fruitless, futile, groundless, ineffective, pointless, unavailing, unsuccessful, vain, worthless
♦ verb 4 often with **away** laze, dally, dawdle, kill time, loaf, loiter, lounge, potter

idleness noun 1 inactivity,

inaction, leisure, time on one's hands, unemployment 2 laziness, inertia, shiftlessness, sloth, sluggishness, torpor

idol noun 1 graven image, deity, god 2 hero, beloved, darling, favourite, pet, pin-up (slang)

idolatry noun adoration, adulation, exaltation, glorification

idolize verb worship, adore, dote upon, exalt, glorify, hero-worship, look up to, love, revere, venerate

idyllic adjective idealized, charming, halcyon, heavenly, ideal, picturesque, unspoiled

if conjunction provided, assuming, on condition that, providing, supposing

ignite verb 1 catch fire, burn, burst into flames, flare up, inflame, take fire 2 set fire to, kindle, light, set alight, torch

ignominious adjective humiliating, discreditable, disgraceful, dishonourable, indecorous, inglorious, shameful, sorry, undignified

ignominy noun disgrace, discredit, dishonour, disrepute, humiliation, infamy, obloquy, shame, stigma

ignorance noun unawareness, inexperience, innocence, unconsciousness, unfamiliarity

ignorant adjective 1 uninformed, benighted, inexperienced, innocent, oblivious, unaware, unconscious, unenlightened, uninitiated, unwitting 2 uneducated, illiterate 3 insensitive, crass, half-baked (informal), rude

ignore verb overlook, discount, disregard, neglect, pass over, reject, take no notice of, turn a blind eye to

ill adjective **1** unwell, ailing, diseased, indisposed, infirm, off-colour, poorly (*informal*), sick, under the weather (*informal*), unhealthy **2** harmful, bad, damaging, deleterious, detrimental, evil, foul, injurious, unfortunate ♦ noun **3** harm, affliction, hardship, hurt, injury, misery, misfortune, trouble, unpleasantness, woe ♦ adverb **4** badly, inauspiciously, poorly, unfavourably, unfortunately, unluckily **5** hardly, barely, by no means, scantily

ill-advised adjective misguided, foolhardy, ill-considered, ill-judged, imprudent, incautious, injudicious, rash, reckless, thoughtless, unwise

ill-disposed adjective unfriendly, antagonistic, disobliging, hostile, inimical, uncooperative, unwelcoming

illegal adjective unlawful, banned, criminal, felonious, forbidden, illicit, outlawed, prohibited, unauthorized, unlicensed

illegality noun crime, felony, illegitimacy, lawlessness, wrong

illegible adjective indecipherable, obscure, scrawled, unreadable

illegitimate adjective **1** unlawful, illegal, illicit, improper, unauthorized **2** born out of wedlock, bastard

ill-fated adjective doomed, hapless, ill-omened, ill-starred, luckless, star-crossed, unfortunate, unhappy, unlucky

illicit adjective **1** illegal, criminal, felonious, illegitimate, prohibited, unauthorized, unlawful, unlicensed **2** forbidden, clandestine, furtive, guilty, immoral, improper

illiterate adjective uneducated, ignorant, uncultured, untaught, untutored

ill-mannered adjective rude, badly behaved, boorish, churlish, discourteous, impolite, insolent, loutish, uncouth

illness noun disease, affliction, ailment, disorder, infirmity, malady, sickness

illogical adjective irrational, absurd, inconsistent, invalid, meaningless, senseless, unreasonable, unscientific, unsound

ill-treat verb abuse, damage, harm, injure, maltreat, mishandle, misuse, oppress

illuminate verb **1** light up, brighten **2** explain, clarify, clear up, elucidate, enlighten, interpret, make clear, shed light on

illuminating adjective informative, enlightening, explanatory, helpful, instructive, revealing

illumination noun **1** light, brightness, lighting, radiance **2** enlightenment, clarification, insight, revelation

illusion noun **1** fantasy, chimera, daydream, figment of the imagination, hallucination, mirage, will-o'-the-wisp **2** misconception, deception, delusion, error, fallacy, misapprehension

illusory adjective unreal, chimerical, deceptive, delusive, fallacious, false, hallucinatory, mistaken, sham

illustrate verb demonstrate, bring home, elucidate, emphasize, explain, point up, show

illustrated adjective pictorial, decorated, graphic

illustration noun 1 example, case, instance, specimen 2 picture, decoration, figure, plate, sketch

illustrious adjective famous, celebrated, distinguished, eminent, glorious, great, notable, prominent, renowned

ill will noun hostility, animosity, bad blood, dislike, enmity, hatred, malice, rancour, resentment, venom

image noun 1 representation, effigy, figure, icon, idol, likeness, picture, portrait, statue 2 replica, counterpart, (dead) ringer (slang), Doppelgänger, double, facsimile, spitting image (informal) 3 concept, idea, impression, mental picture, perception

imaginable adjective possible, believable, comprehensible, conceivable, credible, likely, plausible

imaginary adjective fictional, fictitious, hypothetical, illusory, imagined, invented, made-up, nonexistent, unreal

imagination noun 1 creativity, enterprise, ingenuity, invention, inventiveness, originality, resourcefulness, vision 2 unreality, illusion, supposition

imaginative adjective creative, clever, enterprising, ingenious, inspired, inventive, original

imagine verb 1 envisage, conceive, conceptualize, conjure up, picture, plan, think of, think up, visualize 2 believe, assume, conjecture, fancy, guess (informal, chiefly U.S. & Canad.), infer, suppose, surmise, suspect, take it, think

imbecile noun 1 idiot, chump, cretin, fool, halfwit, moron, numbskull or numskull, thickhead, twit (informal, chiefly Brit.) ♦ adjective 2 stupid, asinine, fatuous, feeble-minded, foolish, idiotic, moronic, thick, witless

imbibe verb 1 drink, consume, knock back (informal), quaff, sink (informal), swallow, swig (informal) 2 Literary absorb, acquire, assimilate, gain, gather, ingest, receive, take in

imbroglio noun complication, embarrassment, entanglement, involvement, misunderstanding, quandary

imitate verb copy, ape, echo, emulate, follow, mimic, mirror, repeat, simulate

imitation noun 1 mimicry, counterfeiting, duplication, likeness, resemblance, simulation 2 replica, fake, forgery, impersonation, impression, reproduction, sham, substitution ♦ adjective 3 artificial, dummy, ersatz, man-made, mock, phoney or phony (informal), reproduction, sham, simulated, synthetic

imitative adjective derivative, copycat (informal), mimetic, parrot-like, second-hand, simulated, unoriginal

imitator noun impersonator, copier, copycat (informal), impressionist, mimic, parrot

immaculate adjective 1 clean, neat, spick-and-span, spotless, spruce, squeaky-clean 2 flawless, above reproach, faultless, impeccable, perfect, unblemished, unexceptionable, untarnished

immaterial adjective irrelevant, extraneous, inconsequential, inessential, insignificant, of no importance, trivial, unimportant

immature adjective 1 young, adolescent, undeveloped, unformed, unripe 2 childish, callow, inexperienced, infantile, juvenile, puerile

immaturity noun 1 unripeness, greenness, imperfection, rawness, unpreparedness 2 childishness, callowness, inexperience, puerility

immediate adjective 1 instant, instantaneous 2 nearest, close, direct, near, next

immediately adverb at once, directly, forthwith, instantly, now, promptly, right away, straight away, this instant, without delay

immense adjective huge, colossal, enormous, extensive, gigantic, great, massive, monumental, stupendous, tremendous, vast

immensity noun size, bulk, enormity, expanse, extent, greatness, hugeness, magnitude, vastness

immerse verb 1 plunge, bathe, dip, douse, duck, dunk, sink, submerge 2 engross, absorb, busy, engage, involve, occupy, take up

immersion noun 1 dipping, dousing, ducking, dunking, plunging, submerging 2 involvement, absorption, concentration, preoccupation

immigrant noun settler, incomer, newcomer

imminent adjective near, at hand, close, coming, forthcoming, gathering, impending, in the pipeline, looming

immobile adjective stationary, at a standstill, at rest, fixed, immovable, motionless, rigid, rooted, static, still, stock still, unmoving

immobility noun stillness, fixity, inertness, motionlessness, stability, steadiness

immobilize verb paralyse, bring to a standstill, cripple, disable, freeze, halt, stop, transfix

immoderate adjective excessive, exaggerated, exorbitant, extravagant, extreme, inordinate, over the top (slang), undue, unjustified, unreasonable

immoral adjective wicked, bad, corrupt, debauched, depraved, dissolute, indecent, sinful, unethical, unprincipled, wrong

immorality noun wickedness, corruption, debauchery, depravity, dissoluteness, sin, vice, wrong

immortal adjective 1 eternal, deathless, enduring, everlasting, imperishable, lasting, perennial, undying ♦ *noun* **2** god, goddess **3** great, genius, hero

immortality *noun* **1** eternity, everlasting life, perpetuity **2** fame, celebrity, glory, greatness, renown

immortalize *verb* commemorate, celebrate, exalt, glorify

immovable *adjective* **1** fixed, firm, immutable, jammed, secure, set, stable, stationary, stuck **2** inflexible, adamant, obdurate, resolute, steadfast, unshakable, unwavering, unyielding

immune *adjective* exempt, clear, free, invulnerable, proof (against), protected, resistant, safe, unaffected

immunity *noun* **1** exemption, amnesty, freedom, indemnity, invulnerability, licence, release **2** resistance, immunization, protection

immunize *verb* vaccinate, inoculate, protect, safeguard

imp *noun* **1** demon, devil, sprite **2** rascal, brat, minx, rogue, scamp

impact *noun* **1** collision, blow, bump, contact, crash, jolt, knock, smash, stroke, thump **2** effect, consequences, impression, influence, repercussions, significance ♦ *verb* **3** hit, clash, collide, crash, crush, strike

impair *verb* worsen, blunt, damage, decrease, diminish, harm, hinder, injure, lessen, reduce, undermine, weaken

impaired *adjective* damaged,

defective, faulty, flawed, imperfect, unsound

impart *verb* **1** communicate, convey, disclose, divulge, make known, pass on, relate, reveal, tell **2** give, accord, afford, bestow, confer, grant, lend, yield

impartial *adjective* neutral, detached, disinterested, equitable, even-handed, fair, just, objective, open-minded, unbiased, unprejudiced

impartiality *noun* neutrality, detachment, disinterestedness, dispassion, equity, even-handedness, fairness, objectivity, open-mindedness

impassable *adjective* blocked, closed, impenetrable, obstructed

impasse *noun* deadlock, dead end, stalemate, standoff, standstill

impassioned *adjective* intense, animated, fervent, fiery, heated, inspired, passionate, rousing, stirring

impatience *noun* **1** haste, impetuosity, intolerance, rashness **2** restlessness, agitation, anxiety, eagerness, edginess, fretfulness, nervousness, uneasiness

impatient *adjective* **1** hasty, demanding, hot-tempered, impetuous, intolerant **2** restless, eager, edgy, fretful, straining at the leash

impeach *verb* charge, accuse, arraign, indict

impeccable *adjective* faultless, blameless, flawless, immaculate, irreproachable, perfect, unblemished, unimpeachable

impecunious *adjective* poor,

broke (*informal*), destitute, down and out, indigent, insolvent, penniless, poverty-stricken

impede *verb* hinder, block, check, disrupt, hamper, hold up, obstruct, slow (down), thwart

impediment *noun* obstacle, barrier, difficulty, encumbrance, hindrance, obstruction, snag, stumbling block

impel *verb* force, compel, constrain, drive, induce, oblige, push, require

impending *adjective* looming, approaching, coming, forthcoming, gathering, imminent, in the pipeline, near, upcoming

impenetrable *adjective* **1** solid, dense, impassable, impermeable, impervious, inviolable, thick **2** Incomprehensible, arcane, enigmatic, inscrutable, mysterious, obscure, unfathomable, unintelligible

imperative *adjective* urgent, crucial, essential, pressing, vital

imperceptible *adjective* undetectable, faint, indiscernible, microscopic, minute, slight, small, subtle, tiny

imperfect *adjective* flawed, damaged, defective, faulty, impaired, incomplete, limited, unfinished

imperfection *noun* fault, blemish, defect, deficiency, failing, flaw, frailty, shortcoming, taint, weakness

imperial *adjective* royal, kingly, majestic, princely, queenly, regal, sovereign

imperil *verb* endanger, expose, jeopardize, risk

impersonal *adjective* remote, aloof, cold, detached, dispassionate, formal, inhuman, neutral

impersonate *verb* imitate, ape, do (*informal*), masquerade as, mimic, pass oneself off as, pose as (*informal*), take off (*informal*)

impersonation *noun* imitation, caricature, impression, mimicry, parody, takeoff (*informal*)

impertinence *noun* rudeness, brazenness, cheek (*informal*), disrespect, effrontery, front, impudence, insolence, nerve (*informal*), presumption

impertinent *adjective* rude, brazen, cheeky (*informal*), disrespectful, impolite, impudent, insolent, presumptuous

imperturbable *adjective* calm, collected, composed, cool, nerveless, self-possessed, serene, unexcitable, unflappable (*informal*), unruffled

impervious *adjective* **1** sealed, impassable, impenetrable, impermeable, resistant **2** unaffected, immune, invulnerable, proof against, unmoved, untouched

impetuosity *noun* haste, impulsiveness, precipitateness, rashness

impetuous *adjective* rash, hasty, impulsive, precipitate, unthinking

impetus *noun* **1** incentive, catalyst, goad, impulse, motivation, push, spur, stimulus **2** force, energy, momentum, power

impinge verb 1 encroach, infringe, invade, obtrude, trespass, violate 2 affect, bear upon, have a bearing on, impact, influence, relate to, touch

impious adjective sacrilegious, blasphemous, godless, irreligious, irreverent, profane, sinful, ungodly, unholy, wicked

impish adjective mischievous, devilish, puckish, rascally, roguish, sportive, waggish

implacable adjective unyielding, inflexible, intractable, merciless, pitiless, unbending, uncompromising, unforgiving

implant verb 1 instil, inculcate, infuse 2 insert, fix, graft

implement verb 1 carry out, bring about, complete, effect, enforce, execute, fulfil, perform, realize ♦ noun 2 tool, apparatus, appliance, device, gadget, instrument, utensil

implicate verb incriminate, associate, embroil, entangle, include, inculpate, involve

implication noun suggestion, inference, innuendo, meaning, overtone, presumption, significance

implicit adjective 1 implied, inferred, latent, tacit, taken for granted, undeclared, understood, unspoken 2 absolute, constant, firm, fixed, full, steadfast, unqualified, unreserved, wholehearted

implied adjective unspoken, hinted at, implicit, indirect, suggested, tacit, undeclared, unexpressed, unstated

implore verb beg, beseech, entreat, importune, plead with, pray

imply verb 1 hint, insinuate, intimate, signify, suggest 2 entail, indicate, involve, mean, point to, presuppose

impolite adjective bad-mannered, discourteous, disrespectful, ill-mannered, insolent, loutish, rude, uncouth

impoliteness noun bad manners, boorishness, churlishness, discourtesy, disrespect, insolence, rudeness

import verb 1 bring in, introduce ♦ noun 2 meaning, drift, gist, implication, intention, sense, significance, thrust 3 importance, consequence, magnitude, moment, significance, substance, weight

importance noun 1 significance, concern, consequence, import, interest, moment, substance, usefulness, value, weight 2 prestige, distinction, eminence, esteem, influence, prominence, standing, status

important adjective 1 significant, far-reaching, momentous, seminal, serious, substantial, urgent, weighty 2 powerful, eminent, high-ranking, influential, noteworthy, pre-eminent, prominent

importunate adjective persistent, demanding, dogged, insistent, pressing, urgent

impose verb 1 establish, decree, fix, institute, introduce, levy, ordain 2 inflict, appoint, enforce, saddle (someone) with

imposing adjective impressive, commanding, dignified, grand, majestic, stately, striking

imposition noun **1** application, introduction, levying **2** intrusion, liberty, presumption

impossibility noun hopelessness, impracticability, inability

impossible adjective
1 unattainable, impracticable, inconceivable, out of the question, unachievable, unobtainable, unthinkable
2 absurd, ludicrous, outrageous, preposterous, unreasonable

impostor noun impersonator, charlatan, deceiver, fake, fraud, phoney or phony (informal), pretender, sham, trickster

impotence noun powerlessness, feebleness, frailty, helplessness, inability, incapacity, incompetence, ineffectiveness, paralysis, uselessness, weakness

impotent adjective powerless, feeble, frail, helpless, incapable, incapacitated, incompetent, ineffective, paralysed, weak

impoverish verb **1** bankrupt, beggar, break, ruin **2** diminish, deplete, drain, exhaust, reduce, sap, use up, wear out

impoverished adjective poor, bankrupt, destitute, impecunious, needy, on one's uppers, penurious, poverty-stricken

impracticable adjective unfeasible, impossible, out of the question, unachievable, unattainable, unworkable

impractical adjective
1 unworkable, impossible, impracticable, inoperable, nonviable, unrealistic, wild

2 idealistic, romantic, starry-eyed, unrealistic

imprecise adjective indefinite, equivocal, hazy, ill-defined, indeterminate, inexact, inexplicit, loose, rough, vague, woolly

impregnable adjective invulnerable, impenetrable, indestructible, invincible, secure, unassailable, unbeatable, unconquerable

impregnate verb **1** saturate, infuse, permeate, soak, steep, suffuse **2** fertilize, inseminate, make pregnant

impress verb **1** excite, affect, inspire, make an impression, move, stir, strike, touch **2** stress, bring home to, emphasize, fix, inculcate, instil into **3** imprint, emboss, engrave, indent, mark, print, stamp

impression noun **1** effect, feeling, impact, influence, reaction **2** idea, belief, conviction, feeling, hunch, notion, sense, suspicion **3** mark, dent, hollow, imprint, indentation, outline, stamp **4** imitation, impersonation, parody, send-up (Brit. informal), takeoff (informal)

impressionable adjective suggestible, gullible, ingenuous, open, receptive, responsive, sensitive, susceptible, vulnerable

impressive adjective grand, awesome, dramatic, exciting, moving, powerful, stirring, striking

imprint noun **1** mark, impression, indentation, sign, stamp ♦verb **2** fix, engrave, etch, impress, print, stamp

imprison verb jail, confine, detain, incarcerate, intern, lock up, put away, send down (informal)

imprisoned adjective jailed, behind bars, captive, confined, incarcerated, in jail, inside (slang), locked up, under lock and key

imprisonment noun custody, confinement, detention, incarceration, porridge (slang)

improbability noun doubt, dubiety, uncertainty, unlikelihood

improbable adjective doubtful, dubious, fanciful, far-fetched, implausible, questionable, unconvincing, unlikely, weak

impromptu adjective unprepared, ad-lib, extemporaneous, improvised, offhand, off the cuff (informal), spontaneous, unrehearsed, unscripted

improper adjective 1 indecent, risqué, smutty, suggestive, unbecoming, unseemly, untoward, vulgar 2 unwarranted, inappropriate, out of place, uncalled-for, unfit, unsuitable

impropriety noun indecency, bad taste, incongruity, vulgarity

improve verb 1 enhance, advance, better, correct, help, rectify, touch up, upgrade 2 progress, develop, make strides, pick up, rally, rise

improvement noun 1 enhancement, advancement, betterment 2 progress, development, rally, recovery, upswing

improvident adjective

imprudent, careless, negligent, prodigal, profligate, reckless, short-sighted, spendthrift, thoughtless, wasteful

improvisation noun 1 spontaneity, ad-libbing, extemporizing, invention 2 makeshift, ad-lib, expedient

improvise verb 1 extemporize, ad-lib, busk, invent, play it by ear (informal), speak off the cuff (informal), wing it (informal) 2 concoct, contrive, devise, throw together

imprudent adjective unwise, careless, foolhardy, ill-advised, ill-considered, ill-judged, injudicious, irresponsible, rash, reckless

impudence noun boldness, audacity, brazenness, cheek (informal), effrontery, impertinence, insolence, nerve (informal), presumption, shamelessness

impudent adjective bold, audacious, brazen, cheeky (informal), impertinent, insolent, presumptuous, rude, shameless

impulse noun urge, caprice, feeling, inclination, notion, whim, wish

impulsive adjective instinctive, devil-may-care, hasty, impetuous, intuitive, passionate, precipitate, rash, spontaneous

impunity noun security, dispensation, exemption, freedom, immunity, liberty, licence, permission

impure adjective 1 unrefined, adulterated, debased, mixed 2 contaminated, defiled, dirty, infected, polluted, tainted

3 immoral, corrupt, indecent, lascivious, lewd, licentious, obscene, unchaste

impurity noun contamination, defilement, dirtiness, infection, pollution, taint

imputation noun blame, accusation, aspersion, censure, insinuation, reproach, slander, slur

inability noun incapability, disability, disqualification, impotence, inadequacy, incapacity, incompetence, ineptitude, powerlessness

inaccessible adjective out of reach, impassable, out of the way, remote, unapproachable, unattainable, unreachable

inaccuracy noun error, defect, erratum, fault, lapse, mistake

inaccurate adjective incorrect, defective, erroneous, faulty, imprecise, mistaken, out, unreliable, unsound, wrong

inactive adjective unused, dormant, idle, inoperative, unemployed, unoccupied

inactivity noun immobility, dormancy, hibernation, inaction, passivity, unemployment

inadequacy noun **1** shortage, dearth, insufficiency, meagreness, paucity, poverty, scantiness **2** incompetence, deficiency, inability, incapacity, ineffectiveness **3** shortcoming, defect, failing, imperfection, weakness

inadequate adjective
1 insufficient, meagre, scant, sketchy, sparse **2** incompetent, deficient, faulty, found wanting,

incapable, not up to scratch (informal), unqualified

inadmissible adjective unacceptable, inappropriate, irrelevant, unallowable

inadvertently adverb unintentionally, accidentally, by accident, by mistake, involuntarily, mistakenly, unwittingly

inadvisable adjective unwise, ill-advised, impolitic, imprudent, inexpedient, injudicious

inane adjective senseless, empty, fatuous, frivolous, futile, idiotic, mindless, silly, stupid, vacuous

inanimate adjective lifeless, cold, dead, defunct, extinct, inert

inapplicable adjective irrelevant, inappropriate, unsuitable

inappropriate adjective unsuitable, improper, incongruous, out of place, unbecoming, unbefitting, unfitting, unseemly, untimely

inarticulate adjective faltering, halting, hesitant, poorly spoken

inattention noun neglect, absent-mindedness, carelessness, daydreaming, inattentiveness, preoccupation, thoughtlessness

inattentive adjective preoccupied, careless, distracted, dreamy, negligent, unobservant, vague

inaudible adjective indistinct, low, mumbling, out of earshot, stifled, unheard

inaugural adjective first, initial, introductory, maiden, opening

inaugurate verb launch, begin, commence, get under way, initiate, institute, introduce, set in motion **2** <u>invest</u>, induct, install

inauguration noun **1** <u>launch</u>, initiation, institution, opening, setting up **2** <u>investiture</u>, induction, installation

inauspicious adjective <u>unpromising</u>, bad, discouraging, ill-omened, ominous, unfavourable, unfortunate, unlucky, unpropitious

inborn adjective <u>natural</u>, congenital, hereditary, inbred, ingrained, inherent, innate, instinctive, intuitive, native

inbred adjective <u>innate</u>, constitutional, deep-seated, ingrained, inherent, native, natural

incalculable adjective <u>countless</u>, boundless, infinite, innumerable, limitless, numberless, untold, vast

incantation noun <u>chant</u>, charm, formula, invocation, spell

incapable adjective
1 <u>incompetent</u>, feeble, inadequate, ineffective, inept, inexpert, insufficient, unfit, unqualified, weak **2** <u>unable</u>, helpless, impotent, powerless

incapacitate verb <u>disable</u>, cripple, immobilize, lay up (informal), paralyse, put out of action (informal)

incapacitated adjective <u>indisposed</u>, hors de combat, immobilized, laid up (informal), out of action (informal), unfit

incapacity noun <u>inability</u>, impotence, inadequacy, incapability, incompetency, ineffectiveness, powerlessness, unfitness, weakness

incarcerate verb <u>imprison</u>,
confine, detain, impound, intern, jail or gaol, lock up, throw in jail

incarceration noun <u>imprisonment</u>, captivity, confinement, detention, internment

incarnate adjective <u>personified</u>, embodied, typified

incarnation noun <u>embodiment</u>, epitome, manifestation, personification, type

incense verb <u>anger</u>, enrage, inflame, infuriate, irritate, madden, make one's hackles rise, rile (informal)

incensed adjective <u>angry</u>, enraged, fuming, furious, indignant, infuriated, irate, maddened, steamed up (slang), up in arms

incentive noun <u>encouragement</u>, bait, carrot (informal), enticement, inducement, lure, motivation, spur, stimulus

inception noun <u>beginning</u>, birth, commencement, dawn, initiation, origin, outset, start

incessant adjective <u>endless</u>, ceaseless, constant, continual, eternal, interminable, never-ending, nonstop, perpetual, unceasing, unending

incessantly adverb <u>endlessly</u>, ceaselessly, constantly, continually, eternally, interminably, nonstop, perpetually, persistently

incident noun **1** <u>happening</u>, adventure, episode, event, fact, matter, occasion, occurrence **2** <u>disturbance</u>, clash, commotion, confrontation, contretemps, scene

incidental adjective secondary, ancillary, minor, nonessential, occasional, subordinate, subsidiary

incidentally adverb parenthetically, by the bye, by the way, in passing

incinerate verb burn up, carbonize, char, cremate, reduce to ashes

incipient adjective beginning, commencing, developing, embryonic, inchoate, nascent, starting

incision noun cut, gash, notch, opening, slash, slit

incisive adjective penetrating, acute, keen, perspicacious, piercing, trenchant

incite verb provoke, encourage, foment, inflame, instigate, spur, stimulate, stir up, urge, whip up

incitement noun provocation, agitation, encouragement, impetus, instigation, prompting, spur, stimulus

incivility noun rudeness, bad manners, boorishness, discourteousness, discourtesy, disrespect, ill-breeding, impoliteness

inclement adjective stormy, foul, harsh, intemperate, rough, severe, tempestuous

inclination noun 1 tendency, disposition, liking, partiality, penchant, predilection, predisposition, proclivity, proneness, propensity 2 slope, angle, gradient, incline, pitch, slant, tilt

incline verb 1 predispose, influence, persuade, prejudice,

sway 2 slope, lean, slant, tilt, tip, veer ♦ noun 3 slope, ascent, descent, dip, grade, gradient, rise

inclined adjective disposed, apt, given, liable, likely, minded, predisposed, prone, willing

include verb 1 contain, comprise, cover, embrace, encompass, incorporate, involve, subsume, take in 2 introduce, add, enter, insert

inclusion noun addition, incorporation, insertion

inclusive adjective comprehensive, across-the-board, all-embracing, blanket, general, global, sweeping, umbrella

incognito adjective in disguise, disguised, under an assumed name, unknown, unrecognized

incoherence noun unintelligibility, disjointedness, inarticulateness

incoherent adjective unintelligible, confused, disjointed, disordered, inarticulate, inconsistent, jumbled, muddled, rambling, stammering, stuttering

income noun revenue, earnings, pay, proceeds, profits, receipts, salary, takings, wages

incoming adjective arriving, approaching, entering, homeward, landing, new, returning

incomparable adjective unequalled, beyond compare, inimitable, matchless, peerless, superlative, supreme, transcendent, unmatched, unparalleled, unrivalled

incompatible adjective
inconsistent, conflicting,
contradictory, incongruous,
mismatched, unsuited

incompetence noun ineptitude,
inability, inadequacy,
incapability, incapacity,
ineffectiveness, unfitness,
uselessness

incompetent adjective inept,
bungling, floundering,
incapable, ineffectual, inexpert,
unfit, useless

incomplete adjective unfinished,
deficient, fragmentary,
imperfect, partial, wanting

incomprehensible adjective
unintelligible, baffling, beyond
one's grasp, impenetrable,
obscure, opaque, perplexing,
puzzling, unfathomable

inconceivable adjective
unimaginable, beyond belief,
incomprehensible, incredible,
mind-boggling (informal), out of
the question, unbelievable,
unheard-of, unthinkable

inconclusive adjective indecisive,
ambiguous, indeterminate,
open, unconvincing, undecided,
up in the air (informal), vague

incongruity noun
inappropriateness, conflict,
discrepancy, disparity,
incompatibility, inconsistency,
unsuitability

incongruous adjective
inappropriate, discordant,
improper, incompatible, out of
keeping, out of place,
unbecoming, unsuitable

inconsiderable adjective
insignificant, inconsequential,
minor, negligible, slight, small,

trifling, trivial, unimportant

inconsiderate adjective selfish,
indelicate, insensitive, rude,
tactless, thoughtless, unkind,
unthinking

inconsistency noun
1 incompatibility, disagreement,
discrepancy, disparity,
divergence, incongruity, variance
2 unreliability, fickleness,
instability, unpredictability,
unsteadiness

inconsistent adjective
1 incompatible, at odds,
conflicting, contradictory,
discordant, incongruous,
irreconcilable, out of step
2 changeable, capricious, erratic,
fickle, unpredictable, unstable,
unsteady, variable

inconsolable adjective
heartbroken, brokenhearted,
desolate, despairing

inconspicuous adjective
unobtrusive, camouflaged,
hidden, insignificant, ordinary,
plain, unassuming, unnoticeable,
unostentatious

incontrovertible adjective
indisputable, certain, established,
incontestable, indubitable,
irrefutable, positive, sure,
undeniable, unquestionable

inconvenience noun 1 trouble,
awkwardness, bother, difficulty,
disadvantage, disruption,
disturbance, fuss, hindrance,
nuisance ♦ verb 2 trouble,
bother, discommode, disrupt,
disturb, put out, upset

inconvenient adjective
troublesome, awkward,
bothersome, disadvantageous,
disturbing, inopportune,

unsuitable, untimely

incorporate *verb* include,
absorb, assimilate, blend,
combine, integrate, merge,
subsume

incorrect *adjective* false,
erroneous, faulty, flawed,
inaccurate, mistaken, untrue,
wrong

incorrigible *adjective* incurable,
hardened, hopeless, intractable,
inveterate, irredeemable,
unreformed

incorruptible *adjective* 1 honest,
above suspicion, straight,
trustworthy, upright
2 imperishable, everlasting,
undecaying

increase *verb* 1 grow, advance,
boost, develop, enlarge, escalate,
expand, extend, multiply, raise,
spread, swell ♦ *noun* 2 growth,
development, enlargement,
escalation, expansion, extension,
gain, increment, rise, upturn

increasingly *adverb*
progressively, more and more

incredible *adjective*
1 implausible, beyond belief,
far-fetched, improbable,
inconceivable, preposterous,
unbelievable, unimaginable,
unthinkable 2 *Informal* amazing,
astonishing, astounding,
extraordinary, prodigious,
sensational (*informal*), wonderful

incredulity *noun* disbelief,
distrust, doubt, scepticism

incredulous *adjective*
disbelieving, distrustful, doubtful,
dubious, sceptical, suspicious,
unbelieving, unconvinced

increment *noun* increase,

accrual, addition, advancement,
augmentation, enlargement,
gain, step up, supplement

incriminate *verb* implicate,
accuse, blame, charge, impeach,
inculpate, involve

incumbent *adjective* obligatory,
binding, compulsory,
mandatory, necessary

incur *verb* earn, arouse, bring
(upon oneself), draw, expose
oneself to, gain, meet with,
provoke

incurable *adjective* fatal,
inoperable, irremediable, terminal

indebted *adjective* grateful,
beholden, in debt, obligated,
obliged, under an obligation

indecency *noun* obscenity,
immodesty, impropriety,
impurity, indelicacy, lewdness,
licentiousness, pornography,
vulgarity

indecent *adjective* 1 lewd, crude,
dirty, filthy, immodest,
improper, impure, licentious,
pornographic, salacious
2 unbecoming, in bad taste,
indecorous, unseemly, vulgar

indecipherable *adjective*
illegible, indistinguishable,
unintelligible, unreadable

indecision *noun* hesitation,
dithering (*chiefly Brit.*), doubt,
indecisiveness, shilly-shallying
(*informal*), uncertainty,
vacillation, wavering

indecisive *adjective* hesitating,
dithering (*chiefly Brit.*), faltering,
in two minds (*informal*),
tentative, uncertain, undecided,
vacillating, wavering

indeed *adverb* really, actually,

certainly, in truth, truly, undoubtedly

indefensible adjective unforgivable, inexcusable, unjustifiable, unpardonable, untenable, unwarrantable, wrong

indefinable adjective inexpressible, impalpable, indescribable

indefinite adjective unclear, doubtful, equivocal, ill-defined, imprecise, indeterminate, inexact, uncertain, unfixed, vague

indefinitely adverb endlessly, ad infinitum, continually, for ever

indelible adjective permanent, enduring, indestructible, ineradicable, ingrained, lasting

indelicate adjective offensive, coarse, crude, embarrassing, immodest, risqué, rude, suggestive, tasteless, vulgar

indemnify verb 1 insure, guarantee, protect, secure, underwrite 2 compensate, reimburse, remunerate, repair, repay

indemnity noun 1 insurance, guarantee, protection, security 2 compensation, redress, reimbursement, remuneration, reparation, restitution

independence noun freedom, autonomy, liberty, self-reliance, self-rule, self-sufficiency, sovereignty

independent adjective 1 free, liberated, separate, unconstrained, uncontrolled 2 self-governing, autonomous, nonaligned, self-determining, sovereign 3 self-sufficient, liberated, self-contained, self-reliant, self-supporting

independently adverb separately, alone, autonomously, by oneself, individually, on one's own, solo, unaided

indescribable adjective unutterable, beyond description, beyond words, indefinable, inexpressible

indestructible adjective permanent, enduring, everlasting, immortal, imperishable, incorruptible, indelible, indissoluble, lasting, unbreakable

indeterminate adjective uncertain, imprecise, indefinite, inexact, undefined, unfixed, unspecified, unstipulated, vague

indicate verb 1 signify, betoken, denote, imply, manifest, point to, reveal, suggest 2 point out, designate, specify 3 show, display, express, read, record, register

indication noun sign, clue, evidence, hint, inkling, intimation, manifestation, mark, suggestion, symptom

indicative adjective suggestive, pointing to, significant, symptomatic

indicator noun sign, gauge, guide, mark, meter, pointer, signal, symbol

indict verb charge, accuse, arraign, impeach, prosecute, summon

indictment noun charge, accusation, allegation, impeachment, prosecution, summons

indifference noun disregard,

aloofness, apathy, coldness, coolness, detachment, inattention, negligence, nonchalance, unconcern

indifferent *adjective*
 1 unconcerned, aloof, callous, cold, cool, detached, impervious, inattentive, uninterested, unmoved, unsympathetic
 2 mediocre, moderate, no great shakes (*informal*), ordinary, passable, so-so (*informal*), undistinguished

indigestion *noun* heartburn, dyspepsia, upset stomach

indignant *adjective* resentful, angry, disgruntled, exasperated, incensed, irate, peeved (*informal*), riled, scornful, up in arms (*informal*)

indignation *noun* resentment, anger, exasperation, pique, rage, scorn, umbrage

indignity *noun* humiliation, affront, dishonour, disrespect, injury, insult, opprobrium, slight, snub

indirect *adjective* **1** circuitous, long-drawn-out, meandering, oblique, rambling, roundabout, tortuous, wandering
 2 incidental, secondary, subsidiary, unintended

indiscreet *adjective* tactless, impolitic, imprudent, incautious, injudicious, naive, rash, reckless, unwise

indiscretion *noun* mistake, error, faux pas, folly, foolishness, gaffe, lapse, slip

indiscriminate *adjective* random, careless, desultory, general, uncritical, undiscriminating, unsystematic, wholesale

indispensable *adjective* essential, crucial, imperative, key, necessary, needed, requisite, vital

indisposed *adjective* ill, ailing, poorly (*informal*), sick, under the weather, unwell

indisposition *noun* illness, ailment, ill health, sickness

indisputable *adjective* undeniable, beyond doubt, certain, incontestable, incontrovertible, indubitable, irrefutable, unquestionable

indistinct *adjective* unclear, blurred, faint, fuzzy, hazy, ill-defined, indeterminate, shadowy, undefined, vague

individual *adjective* **1** personal, characteristic, distinctive, exclusive, idiosyncratic, own, particular, peculiar, singular, special, specific, unique ♦ *noun* **2** person, being, character, creature, soul, unit

individualist *noun* maverick, freethinker, independent, loner, lone wolf, nonconformist, original

individuality *noun* distinctiveness, character, originality, personality, separateness, singularity, uniqueness

individually *adverb* separately, apart, independently, one at a time, one by one, singly

indoctrinate *verb* train, brainwash, drill, ground, imbue, initiate, instruct, school, teach

indoctrination *noun* training, brainwashing, drilling, grounding, inculcation, instruction, schooling

indolent *adjective* lazy, idle,

inactive, inert, languid, lethargic, listless, slothful, sluggish, workshy

indomitable *adjective* <u>invincible</u>, bold, resolute, staunch, steadfast, unbeatable, unconquerable, unflinching, unyielding

indubitable *adjective* <u>certain</u>, incontestable, incontrovertible, indisputable, irrefutable, obvious, sure, undeniable, unquestionable

induce *verb* 1 <u>persuade</u>, convince, encourage, incite, influence, instigate, prevail upon, prompt, talk into 2 <u>cause</u>, bring about, effect, engender, generate, give rise to, lead to, occasion, produce

inducement *noun* <u>incentive</u>, attraction, bait, carrot (*informal*), encouragement, incitement, lure, reward

indulge *verb* 1 <u>gratify</u>, feed, give way to, pander to, satisfy, yield to 2 <u>spoil</u>, cosset, give in to, go along with, humour, mollycoddle, pamper

indulgence *noun* 1 <u>gratification</u>, appeasement, fulfilment, satiation, satisfaction 2 <u>luxury</u>, extravagance, favour, privilege, treat 3 <u>tolerance</u>, forbearance, patience, understanding

indulgent *adjective* <u>lenient</u>, compliant, easy-going, forbearing, kindly, liberal, permissive, tolerant, understanding

industrialist *noun* <u>capitalist</u>, big businessman, captain of industry, magnate, manufacturer, tycoon

industrious *adjective* <u>hard-working</u>, busy, conscientious, diligent, energetic, persistent, purposeful, tireless, zealous

industry *noun* 1 <u>business</u>, commerce, manufacturing, production, trade 2 <u>effort</u>, activity, application, diligence, labour, tirelessness, toil, zeal

inebriated *adjective* <u>drunk</u>, half-cut (*informal*), intoxicated, legless (*informal*), merry (*Brit. informal*), paralytic (*informal*), plastered (*slang*), tight (*informal*), tipsy, under the influence (*informal*)

ineffective *adjective* <u>useless</u>, fruitless, futile, idle, impotent, inefficient, unavailing, unproductive, vain, worthless

ineffectual *adjective* <u>weak</u>, feeble, impotent, inadequate, incompetent, ineffective, inept

inefficiency *noun* <u>incompetence</u>, carelessness, disorganization, muddle, slackness, sloppiness

inefficient *adjective* <u>incompetent</u>, disorganized, ineffectual, inept, wasteful, weak

ineligible *adjective* <u>unqualified</u>, disqualified, ruled out, unacceptable, unfit, unsuitable

inept *adjective* <u>incompetent</u>, bumbling, bungling, clumsy, inexpert, maladroit

ineptitude *noun* <u>incompetence</u>, clumsiness, inexpertness, unfitness

inequality *noun* <u>disparity</u>, bias, difference, disproportion, diversity, irregularity, prejudice, unevenness

inequitable *adjective* <u>unfair</u>, biased, discriminatory, one-sided, partial, partisan, preferential, prejudiced, unjust

inert adjective <u>inactive</u>, dead, dormant, immobile, lifeless, motionless, static, still, unreactive, unresponsive

inertia noun <u>inactivity</u>, apathy, immobility, lethargy, listlessness, passivity, sloth, unresponsiveness

inescapable adjective <u>unavoidable</u>, certain, destined, fated, ineluctable, inevitable, inexorable, sure

inestimable adjective <u>incalculable</u>, immeasurable, invaluable, precious, priceless, prodigious

inevitable adjective <u>unavoidable</u>, assured, certain, destined, fixed, ineluctable, inescapable, inexorable, sure

inevitably adverb <u>unavoidably</u>, as a result, automatically, certainly, necessarily, of necessity, perforce, surely, willy-nilly

inexcusable adjective <u>unforgivable</u>, indefensible, outrageous, unjustifiable, unpardonable, unwarrantable

inexorable adjective <u>unrelenting</u>, inescapable, relentless, remorseless, unbending, unyielding

inexpensive adjective <u>cheap</u>, bargain, budget, economical, modest, reasonable

inexperience noun <u>unfamiliarity</u>, callowness, greenness, ignorance, newness, rawness

inexperienced adjective <u>immature</u>, callow, green, new, raw, unpractised, untried, unversed

inexpert adjective <u>amateurish</u>, bungling, cack-handed (informal), clumsy, inept, maladroit, unpractised, unprofessional, unskilled

inexplicable adjective <u>unaccountable</u>, baffling, enigmatic, incomprehensible, insoluble, mysterious, mystifying, strange, unfathomable, unintelligible

inextricably adverb <u>inseparably</u>, indissolubly, indistinguishably, intricately, irretrievably, totally

infallibility noun <u>perfection</u>, impeccability, omniscience, supremacy, unerringness

infallible adjective <u>foolproof</u>, certain, dependable, reliable, sure, sure-fire (informal), trustworthy, unbeatable, unfailing

infamous adjective <u>notorious</u>, disreputable, ignominious, ill-famed

infancy noun <u>beginnings</u>, cradle, dawn, inception, origins, outset, start

infant noun <u>baby</u>, babe, bairn (Scot.), child, toddler, tot

infantile adjective <u>childish</u>, babyish, immature, puerile

infatuate verb <u>obsess</u>, besot, bewitch, captivate, enchant, enrapture, fascinate

infatuated adjective <u>obsessed</u>, besotted, bewitched, captivated, carried away, enamoured, enraptured, fascinated, possessed, smitten (informal), spellbound

infatuation noun <u>obsession</u>, crush (informal), fixation, madness, passion, thing (informal)

infect verb <u>contaminate</u>, affect, blight, corrupt, defile, poison, pollute, taint

infection noun <u>contamination</u>, contagion, corruption, defilement, poison, pollution, virus

infectious adjective <u>catching</u>, communicable, contagious, spreading, transmittable, virulent

infer verb <u>deduce</u>, conclude, derive, gather, presume, surmise, understand

inference noun <u>deduction</u>, assumption, conclusion, presumption, reading, surmise

inferior adjective 1 <u>lower</u>, lesser, menial, minor, secondary, subordinate, subsidiary ♦ noun 2 <u>underling</u>, junior, menial, subordinate

inferiority noun 1 <u>inadequacy</u>, deficiency, imperfection, insignificance, mediocrity, shoddiness, worthlessness 2 <u>subservience</u>, abasement, lowliness, subordination

infernal adjective <u>devilish</u>, accursed, damnable, damned, diabolical, fiendish, hellish, satanic

infertile adjective <u>barren</u>, sterile, unfruitful, unproductive

infertility noun <u>sterility</u>, barrenness, infecundity, unproductiveness

infest verb <u>overrun</u>, beset, invade, penetrate, permeate, ravage, swarm, throng

infested adjective <u>overrun</u>, alive, crawling, ravaged, ridden, swarming, teeming

infiltrate verb <u>penetrate</u>, filter

through, insinuate oneself, make inroads (into), percolate, permeate, pervade, sneak in (informal)

infinite adjective <u>never-ending</u>, boundless, eternal, everlasting, illimitable, immeasurable, inexhaustible, limitless, measureless, unbounded

infinitesimal adjective <u>microscopic</u>, insignificant, minuscule, minute, negligible, teeny, tiny, unnoticeable

infinity noun <u>eternity</u>, boundlessness, endlessness, immensity, vastness

infirm adjective <u>frail</u>, ailing, debilitated, decrepit, doddering, enfeebled, failing, feeble, weak

infirmity noun <u>frailty</u>, decrepitude, ill health, sickliness, vulnerability

inflame verb <u>enrage</u>, anger, arouse, excite, incense, infuriate, madden, provoke, rouse, stimulate

inflamed adjective <u>sore</u>, fevered, hot, infected, red, swollen

inflammable adjective <u>flammable</u>, combustible, incendiary

inflammation noun <u>soreness</u>, painfulness, rash, redness, tenderness

inflammatory adjective <u>provocative</u>, explosive, fiery, intemperate, like a red rag to a bull, rabble-rousing

inflate verb <u>expand</u>, bloat, blow up, dilate, distend, enlarge, increase, puff up or out, pump up, swell

inflated adjective <u>exaggerated</u>,

ostentatious, overblown, swollen

inflation noun expansion, enlargement, escalation, extension, increase, rise, spread, swelling

inflexibility noun obstinacy, intransigence, obduracy

inflexible adjective **1** obstinate, implacable, intractable, obdurate, resolute, set in one's ways, steadfast, stubborn, unbending, uncompromising **2** inelastic, hard, rigid, stiff, taut

inflict verb impose, administer, apply, deliver, levy, mete or deal out, visit, wreak

infliction noun imposition, administration, perpetration, wreaking

influence noun **1** effect, authority, control, domination, magnetism, pressure, weight **2** power, clout (informal), hold, importance, leverage, prestige, pull (informal) ♦ verb **3** affect, control, direct, guide, manipulate, sway

influential adjective important, authoritative, instrumental, leading, potent, powerful, significant, telling, weighty

influx noun arrival, incursion, inrush, inundation, invasion, rush

inform verb **1** tell, advise, communicate, enlighten, instruct, notify, teach, tip off **2** incriminate, betray, blow the whistle on (informal), denounce, grass (Brit. slang), inculpate, shop (slang, chiefly Brit.), squeal (slang)

informal adjective relaxed, casual, colloquial, cosy, easy, familiar, natural, simple, unofficial

informality noun familiarity, casualness, ease, naturalness, relaxation, simplicity

information noun facts, data, intelligence, knowledge, message, news, notice, report

informative adjective instructive, chatty, communicative, edifying, educational, enlightening, forthcoming, illuminating, revealing

informed adjective knowledgeable, enlightened, erudite, expert, familiar, in the picture, learned, up to date, versed, well-read

informer noun betrayer, accuser, Judas, sneak, stool pigeon

infrequent adjective occasional, few and far between, once in a blue moon, rare, sporadic, uncommon, unusual

infringe verb break, contravene, disobey, transgress, violate

infringement noun contravention, breach, infraction, transgression, trespass, violation

infuriate verb enrage, anger, exasperate, incense, irritate, madden, provoke, rile

infuriating adjective annoying, exasperating, galling, irritating, maddening, mortifying, provoking, vexatious

ingenious adjective creative, bright, brilliant, clever, crafty, inventive, original, resourceful, shrewd

ingenuity noun originality, cleverness, flair, genius, gift, inventiveness, resourcefulness, sharpness, shrewdness

ingenuous adjective naive,

artless, guileless, honest, innocent, open, plain, simple, sincere, trusting, unsophisticated

inglorious adjective dishonourable, discreditable, disgraceful, disreputable, ignoble, ignominious, infamous, shameful, unheroic

ingratiate verb pander to, crawl, curry favour, fawn, flatter, grovel, insinuate oneself, toady

ingratiating adjective sycophantic, crawling, fawning, flattering, humble, obsequious, servile, toadying, unctuous

ingratitude noun ungratefulness, thanklessness

ingredient noun component, constituent, element, part

inhabit verb live, abide, dwell, occupy, populate, reside

inhabitant noun dweller, citizen, denizen, inmate, native, occupant, occupier, resident, tenant

inhabited adjective populated, colonized, developed, occupied, peopled, settled, tenanted

inhale verb breathe in, draw in, gasp, respire, suck in

inherent adjective innate, essential, hereditary, inborn, inbred, inbuilt, ingrained, inherited, intrinsic, native, natural

inherit verb be left, come into, fall heir to, succeed to

inheritance noun legacy, bequest, birthright, heritage, patrimony

inhibit verb restrain, check, constrain, curb, discourage, frustrate, hinder, hold back or in, impede, obstruct

inhibited adjective shy, constrained, guarded, repressed, reserved, reticent, self-conscious, subdued

inhibition noun shyness, block, hang-up (informal), reserve, restraint, reticence, self-consciousness

inhospitable adjective **1** unwelcoming, cool, uncongenial, unfriendly, unreceptive, unsociable, xenophobic **2** bleak, barren, desolate, forbidding, godforsaken, hostile

inhuman adjective cruel, barbaric, brutal, cold-blooded, heartless, merciless, pitiless, ruthless, savage, unfeeling

inhumane adjective cruel, brutal, heartless, pitiless, unfeeling, unkind, unsympathetic

inhumanity noun cruelty, atrocity, barbarism, brutality, heartlessness, pitilessness, ruthlessness, unkindness

inimical adjective hostile, adverse, antagonistic, ill-disposed, opposed, unfavourable, unfriendly, unwelcoming

inimitable adjective unique, consummate, incomparable, matchless, peerless, unparalleled, unrivalled

iniquitous adjective wicked, criminal, evil, immoral, reprehensible, sinful, unjust

iniquity noun wickedness, abomination, evil, injustice, sin, wrong

initial adjective first, beginning, incipient, introductory, opening, primary

initially adverb at first, at or in the beginning, first, firstly, originally, primarily

initiate verb 1 begin, commence, get under way, kick off (informal), launch, open, originate, set in motion, start 2 induct, indoctrinate, introduce, invest 3 instruct, acquaint with, coach, familiarize with, teach, train ♦ noun 4 novice, beginner, convert, entrant, learner, member, probationer

initiation noun introduction, debut, enrolment, entrance, inauguration, induction, installation, investiture

initiative noun 1 first step, advantage, first move, lead 2 resourcefulness, ambition, drive, dynamism, enterprise, get up and go (informal), leadership

inject verb 1 vaccinate, inoculate 2 introduce, bring in, infuse, insert, instil

injection noun 1 vaccination, inoculation, jab (informal), shot (informal) 2 introduction, dose, infusion, insertion

injudicious adjective unwise, foolish, ill-advised, ill-judged, impolitic, imprudent, incautious, inexpedient, rash, unthinking

injunction noun order, command, exhortation, instruction, mandate, precept, ruling

injure verb hurt, damage, harm, impair, ruin, spoil, undermine, wound

injured adjective hurt, broken, damaged, disabled, undermined, weakened, wounded

injury noun harm, damage, detriment, disservice, hurt, ill, trauma (Pathology), wound, wrong

injustice noun unfairness, bias, discrimination, inequality, inequity, iniquity, oppression, partisanship, prejudice, wrong

inkling noun suspicion, clue, conception, hint, idea, indication, intimation, notion, suggestion, whisper

inland adjective interior, domestic, internal, upcountry

inlet noun bay, bight, creek, firth or frith (Scot.), fjord, passage

inmost or **innermost** adjective deepest, basic, central, essential, intimate, personal, private, secret

innate adjective inborn, congenital, constitutional, essential, inbred, ingrained, inherent, instinctive, intuitive, native, natural

inner adjective 1 inside, central, interior, internal, inward, middle 2 private, hidden, intimate, personal, repressed, secret, unrevealed

innkeeper noun publican, host or hostess, hotelier, landlord or landlady, mine host

innocence noun 1 guiltlessness, blamelessness, clean hands, incorruptibility, probity, purity, uprightness, virtue 2 harmlessness, innocuousness, inoffensiveness 3 inexperience, artlessness, credulousness, gullibility, ingenuousness, naïveté, simplicity, unworldliness

innocent adjective 1 not guilty, blameless, guiltless, honest, in the clear, uninvolved **2** <u>harmless</u>, innocuous, inoffensive, unobjectionable, well-intentioned, well-meant **3** <u>naive</u>, artless, childlike, credulous, gullible, ingenuous, open, simple, unworldly

innovation noun <u>modernization</u>, alteration, change, departure, introduction, newness, novelty, variation

innuendo noun <u>insinuation</u>, aspersion, hint, implication, imputation, intimation, overtone, suggestion, whisper

innumerable adjective <u>countless</u>, beyond number, incalculable, infinite, multitudinous, myriad, numberless, numerous, unnumbered, untold

inoffensive adjective <u>harmless</u>, innocent, innocuous, mild, quiet, retiring, unobjectionable, unobtrusive

inoperative adjective <u>out of action</u>, broken, defective, ineffective, invalid, null and void, out of order, out of service, useless

inopportune adjective <u>inconvenient</u>, ill-chosen, ill-timed, inappropriate, unfavourable, unfortunate, unpropitious, unseasonable, unsuitable, untimely

inordinate adjective <u>excessive</u>, disproportionate, extravagant, immoderate, intemperate, preposterous, unconscionable, undue, unreasonable, unwarranted

inorganic adjective <u>artificial</u>, chemical, man-made

inquest noun <u>inquiry</u>, inquisition,

investigation, probe

inquire verb **1** <u>investigate</u>, examine, explore, look into, make inquiries, probe, research **2** Also **enquire** <u>ask</u>, query, question

inquiry noun **1** <u>investigation</u>, examination, exploration, inquest, interrogation, probe, research, study, survey **2** Also **enquiry** <u>question</u>, query

inquisition noun <u>investigation</u>, cross-examination, examination, grilling (informal), inquest, inquiry, questioning, third degree (informal)

inquisitive adjective <u>curious</u>, inquiring, nosy (informal), probing, prying, questioning

insane adjective **1** <u>mad</u>, crazed, crazy, demented, deranged, mentally ill, out of one's mind, unhinged **2** <u>stupid</u>, daft (informal), foolish, idiotic, impractical, irrational, irresponsible, preposterous, senseless

insanitary adjective <u>unhealthy</u>, dirty, disease-ridden, filthy, infested, insalubrious, polluted, unclean, unhygienic

insanity noun **1** <u>madness</u>, delirium, dementia, mental disorder, mental illness **2** <u>stupidity</u>, folly, irresponsibility, lunacy, senselessness

insatiable adjective <u>unquenchable</u>, greedy, intemperate, rapacious, ravenous, voracious

inscribe verb <u>carve</u>, cut, engrave, etch, impress, imprint

inscription noun <u>engraving</u>,

dedication, legend, words

inscrutable adjective
1 enigmatic, blank, deadpan, impenetrable, poker-faced (informal) **2** mysterious, hidden, incomprehensible, inexplicable, unexplainable, unfathomable, unintelligible

insecure adjective **1** anxious, afraid, uncertain, unsure
2 unsafe, defenceless, exposed, unguarded, unprotected, vulnerable, wide-open

insecurity noun anxiety, fear, uncertainty, worry

insensible adjective unaware, impervious, oblivious, unaffected, unconscious, unmindful

insensitive adjective unfeeling, callous, hardened, indifferent, thick-skinned, tough, uncaring, unconcerned

inseparable adjective
1 indivisible, indissoluble
2 devoted, bosom, close, intimate

insert verb enter, embed, implant, introduce, place, put, stick in

insertion noun inclusion, addition, implant, interpolation, introduction, supplement

inside adjective **1** inner, interior, internal, inward **2** confidential, classified, exclusive, internal, private, restricted, secret ♦ adverb **3** indoors, under cover, within ♦ noun **4** interior, contents **5** insides Informal stomach, belly, bowels, entrails, guts, innards (informal), viscera, vitals

insidious adjective stealthy,

deceptive, sly, smooth, sneaking, subtle, surreptitious

insight noun understanding, awareness, comprehension, discernment, judgment, observation, penetration, perception, perspicacity, vision

insignia noun badge, crest, emblem, symbol

insignificance noun unimportance, inconsequence, irrelevance, meaninglessness, pettiness, triviality, worthlessness

insignificant adjective unimportant, inconsequential, irrelevant, meaningless, minor, nondescript, paltry, petty, trifling, trivial

insincere adjective deceitful, dishonest, disingenuous, duplicitous, false, hollow, hypocritical, lying, two-faced, untruthful

insincerity noun deceitfulness, dishonesty, dissimulation, duplicity, hypocrisy, pretence, untruthfulness

insinuate verb **1** imply, allude, hint, indicate, intimate, suggest **2** ingratiate, curry favour, get in with, worm or work one's way in

insinuation noun implication, allusion, aspersion, hint, innuendo, slur, suggestion

insipid adjective **1** bland, anaemic, characterless, colourless, prosaic, uninteresting, vapid, wishy-washy (informal) **2** tasteless, bland, flavourless, unappetizing, watery

insist verb **1** demand, lay down the law, put one's foot down (informal), require **2** assert, aver, claim, maintain, reiterate, repeat, swear, vow

insistence noun persistence, emphasis, importunity, stress

insistent adjective persistent, dogged, emphatic, importunate, incessant, persevering, unrelenting, urgent

insolence noun rudeness, boldness, cheek (informal), disrespect, effrontery, impertinence, impudence

insolent adjective rude, bold, contemptuous, impertinent, impudent, insubordinate, insulting

insoluble adjective inexplicable, baffling, impenetrable, indecipherable, mysterious, unaccountable, unfathomable, unsolvable

insolvency noun bankruptcy, failure, liquidation, ruin

insolvent adjective bankrupt, broke (informal), failed, gone bust (informal), gone to the wall, in receivership, ruined

insomnia noun sleeplessness, wakefulness

inspect verb examine, check, go over or through, investigate, look over, scrutinize, survey, vet

inspection noun examination, check, checkup, investigation, once-over (informal), review, scrutiny, search, survey

inspector noun examiner, censor, investigator, overseer, scrutinizer, superintendent, supervisor

inspiration noun 1 influence, muse, spur, stimulus 2 revelation, creativity,

illumination, insight

inspire verb 1 stimulate, animate, encourage, enliven, galvanize, influence, spur 2 arouse, enkindle, excite, give rise to, produce

inspired adjective 1 brilliant, dazzling, impressive, memorable, outstanding, superlative, thrilling, wonderful 2 uplifted, elated, enthused, exhilarated, stimulated

inspiring adjective uplifting, exciting, exhilarating, heartening, moving, rousing, stimulating, stirring

instability noun unpredictability, changeableness, fickleness, fluctuation, impermanence, inconstancy, insecurity, unsteadiness, variability, volatility

install verb 1 set up, fix, lodge, place, position, put in, station 2 induct, establish, inaugurate, institute, introduce, invest 3 settle, ensconce, position

installation noun 1 setting up, establishment, fitting, instalment, placing, positioning 2 induction, inauguration, investiture 3 equipment, machinery, plant, system

instalment noun portion, chapter, division, episode, part, repayment, section

instance noun 1 example, case, illustration, occasion, occurrence, situation ♦ verb 2 quote, adduce, cite, mention, name, specify

instant noun 1 second, flash, jiffy (informal), moment, split second, trice, twinkling of an eye (informal) 2 juncture, moment, occasion, point, time ♦ adjective

3 immediate, direct, instantaneous, on-the-spot, prompt, quick, split-second
4 precooked, convenience, fast, ready-mixed

instantaneous adjective immediate, direct, instant, on-the-spot, prompt

instantaneously adverb immediately, at once, instantly, in the twinkling of an eye (informal), on the spot, promptly, straight away

instantly adverb immediately, at once, directly, instantaneously, now, right away, straight away, this minute

instead adverb **1** rather, alternatively, in lieu, in preference, on second thoughts, preferably **2** instead of in place of, In lieu of, rather than

instigate verb provoke, bring about, incite, influence, initiate, prompt, set off, start, stimulate, trigger

instigation noun prompting, behest, bidding, encouragement, incitement, urging

instigator noun ringleader, agitator, leader, motivator, prime mover, troublemaker

instil verb introduce, engender, imbue, implant, inculcate, infuse, insinuate

instinct noun intuition, faculty, gift, impulse, knack, predisposition, proclivity, talent, tendency

instinctive adjective inborn, automatic, inherent, innate, intuitive, involuntary, natural, reflex, spontaneous,

unpremeditated, visceral

instinctively adverb intuitively, automatically, by instinct, involuntarily, naturally, without thinking

institute noun **1** society, academy, association, college, foundation, guild, institution, school ♦ verb **2** establish, fix, found, initiate, introduce, launch, organize, originate, pioneer, set up, start

institution noun
1 establishment, academy, college, foundation, institute, school, society **2** custom, convention, law, practice, ritual, rule, tradition

institutional adjective conventional, accepted, established, formal, orthodox

instruct verb **1** order, bid, charge, command, direct, enjoin, tell **2** teach, coach, drill, educate, ground, school, train, tutor

instruction noun **1** teaching, coaching, education, grounding, guidance, lesson(s), schooling, training, tuition **2** order, command, demand, directive, injunction, mandate, ruling

instructions plural noun orders, advice, directions, guidance, information, key, recommendations, rules

instructive adjective informative, edifying, educational, enlightening, helpful, illuminating, revealing, useful

instructor noun teacher, adviser, coach, demonstrator, guide, mentor, trainer, tutor

instrument noun **1** tool, apparatus, appliance, contraption (informal), device, gadget, implement, mechanism **2** means, agency, agent, mechanism, medium, organ, vehicle

instrumental adjective active, contributory, helpful, influential, involved, useful

insubordinate adjective disobedient, defiant, disorderly, mutinous, rebellious, recalcitrant, refractory, undisciplined, ungovernable, unruly

insubordination noun disobedience, defiance, indiscipline, insurrection, mutiny, rebellion, recalcitrance, revolt

insubstantial adjective flimsy, feeble, frail, poor, slight, tenuous, thin, weak

insufferable adjective unbearable, detestable, dreadful, impossible, insupportable, intolerable, unendurable

insufficient adjective inadequate, deficient, incapable, lacking, scant, short

insular adjective narrow-minded, blinkered, circumscribed, inward-looking, limited, narrow, parochial, petty, provincial

insulate verb isolate, close off, cocoon, cushion, cut off, protect, sequester, shield

insult verb **1** offend, abuse, affront, call names, put down, slander, slight, snub ♦ noun **2** abuse, affront, aspersion, insolence, offence, put-down, slap in the face (informal), slight, snub

insulting adjective offensive, abusive, contemptuous, degrading, disparaging, insolent, rude, scurrilous

insuperable adjective insurmountable, impassable, invincible, unconquerable

insupportable adjective **1** intolerable, insufferable, unbearable, unendurable **2** unjustifiable, indefensible, untenable

insurance noun protection, assurance, cover, guarantee, indemnity, safeguard, security, warranty

insure verb protect, assure, cover, guarantee, indemnify, underwrite, warrant

insurgent noun **1** rebel, insurrectionist, mutineer, revolutionary, rioter ♦ adjective **2** rebellious, disobedient, insubordinate, mutinous, revolting, revolutionary, riotous, seditious

insurmountable adjective insuperable, hopeless, impassable, impossible, invincible, overwhelming, unconquerable

insurrection noun rebellion, coup, insurgency, mutiny, revolt, revolution, riot, uprising

intact adjective undamaged, complete, entire, perfect, sound, unbroken, unharmed, unimpaired, unscathed, whole

integral adjective essential, basic, component, constituent, fundamental, indispensable, intrinsic, necessary

integrate verb combine,

integration noun assimilation, amalgamation, blending, combining, fusing, incorporation, mixing, unification

integrity noun **1** honesty, goodness, honour, incorruptibility, principle, probity, purity, rectitude, uprightness, virtue **2** unity, coherence, cohesion, completeness, soundness, wholeness

intellect noun intelligence, brains (informal), judgment, mind, reason, sense, understanding

intellectual adjective **1** scholarly, bookish, cerebral, highbrow, intelligent, studious, thoughtful ◆ noun **2** thinker, academic, egghead (informal), highbrow

intelligence noun **1** understanding, acumen, brain power, brains (informal), cleverness, comprehension, intellect, perception, sense **2** information, data, facts, findings, knowledge, news, notification, report

intelligent adjective clever, brainy (informal), bright, enlightened, perspicacious, quick-witted, sharp, smart, well-informed

intelligentsia noun intellectuals, highbrows, literati

intelligible adjective understandable, clear, comprehensible, distinct, lucid, open, plain

intemperate adjective excessive, extreme, immoderate, profligate, self-indulgent, unbridled, unrestrained, wild

intend verb plan, aim, have in mind or view, mean, propose, purpose

intense adjective **1** extreme, acute, deep, excessive, fierce, great, powerful, profound, severe **2** passionate, ardent, fanatical, fervent, fierce, heightened, impassioned, vehement

intensify verb increase, add to, aggravate, deepen, escalate, heighten, magnify, redouble, reinforce, sharpen, strengthen

intensity noun force, ardour, emotion, fanaticism, fervour, fierceness, passion, strength, vehemence

intensive adjective concentrated, comprehensive, demanding, exhaustive, in-depth, thorough, thoroughgoing

intent noun **1** intention, aim, design, end, goal, meaning, object, objective, plan, purpose ◆ adjective **2** attentive, absorbed, determined, eager, engrossed, preoccupied, rapt, resolved, steadfast, watchful

intention noun purpose, aim, design, end, goal, idea, object, objective, point, target

intentional adjective deliberate, calculated, intended, meant, planned, premeditated, wilful

intentionally adverb deliberately, designedly, on purpose, wilfully

inter verb bury, entomb, lay to rest

intercede verb mediate, arbitrate, intervene, plead

intercept verb seize, block,

catch, cut off, head off, interrupt, obstruct, stop

interchange verb **1** switch, alternate, exchange, reciprocate, swap ♦ noun **2** junction, intersection

interchangeable adjective identical, equivalent, exchangeable, reciprocal, synonymous

intercourse noun **1** communication, commerce, contact, dealings **2** sexual intercourse, carnal knowledge, coitus, copulation, sex (informal)

interest noun **1** curiosity, attention, concern, notice, regard **2** hobby, activity, diversion, pastime, preoccupation, pursuit **3** advantage, benefit, good, profit **4** stake, claim, investment, right, share ♦ verb **5** intrigue, attract, catch one's eye, divert, engross, fascinate

interested adjective **1** curious, attracted, drawn, excited, fascinated, keen **2** involved, concerned, implicated

interesting adjective intriguing, absorbing, appealing, attractive, compelling, engaging, engrossing, gripping, stimulating, thought-provoking

interface noun connection, border, boundary, frontier, link

interfere verb **1** intrude, butt in, intervene, meddle, stick one's oar in (informal), tamper **2** often with with conflict, clash, hamper, handicap, hinder, impede, inhibit, obstruct

interference noun **1** intrusion, intervention, meddling, prying

2 conflict, clashing, collision, obstruction, opposition

interim adjective temporary, acting, caretaker, improvised, makeshift, provisional, stopgap

interior noun **1** inside, centre, core, heart ♦ adjective **2** inside, inner, internal, inward **3** mental, hidden, inner, intimate, personal, private, secret, spiritual

interloper noun trespasser, gate-crasher (informal), intruder, meddler

interlude noun interval, break, breathing space, delay, hiatus, intermission, pause, respite, rest, spell, stoppage

intermediary noun mediator, agent, broker, go-between, middleman

intermediate adjective middle, halfway, in-between (informal), intervening, mid, midway, transitional

interment noun burial, funeral

interminable adjective endless, ceaseless, everlasting, infinite, long-drawn-out, long-winded, never-ending, perpetual, protracted

intermingle verb mix, blend, combine, fuse, interlace, intermix, interweave, merge

intermission noun interval, break, interlude, pause, recess, respite, rest, stoppage

intermittent adjective periodic, broken, fitful, irregular, occasional, spasmodic, sporadic

intern verb imprison, confine, detain, hold, hold in custody

internal adjective **1** inner, inside, interior **2** domestic, civic, home, in-house, intramural

international adjective universal, cosmopolitan, global, intercontinental, worldwide

Internet noun information superhighway, cyberspace, the net (informal), the web (informal), World Wide Web

interpose verb interrupt, insert, interject, put one's oar in

interpret verb explain, construe, decipher, decode, elucidate, make sense of, render, translate

interpretation noun explanation, analysis, clarification, elucidation, exposition, portrayal, rendition, translation, version

interpreter noun translator, commentator

interrogate verb question, cross-examine, examine, grill (informal), investigate, pump, quiz

interrogation noun questioning, cross-examination, examination, grilling (informal), inquiry, inquisition, third degree (informal)

interrupt verb 1 intrude, barge in (informal), break in, butt in, disturb, heckle, interfere (with) 2 suspend, break off, cut short, delay, discontinue, hold up, lay aside, stop

interruption noun stoppage, break, disruption, disturbance, hitch, intrusion, pause, suspension

intersection noun junction, crossing, crossroads, interchange

interval noun break, delay, gap, interlude, intermission, pause, respite, rest, space, spell

intervene verb 1 involve oneself, arbitrate, intercede, interfere,

intrude, mediate, step in (informal), take a hand (informal) 2 happen, befall, come to pass, ensue, occur, take place

intervention noun mediation, agency, interference, intrusion

interview noun 1 meeting, audience, conference, consultation, dialogue, press conference, talk ♦ verb 2 question, examine, interrogate, talk to

interviewer noun questioner, examiner, interrogator, investigator, reporter

intestines plural noun guts, bowels, entrails, innards (informal), insides (informal), viscera

intimacy noun familiarity, closeness, confidentiality

intimate[1] adjective 1 close, bosom, confidential, dear, near, thick (informal) 2 personal, confidential, private, secret 3 detailed, deep, exhaustive, first-hand, immediate, in-depth, profound, thorough 4 snug, comfy (informal), cosy, friendly, warm ♦ noun 5 friend, close friend, confidant or confidante, (constant) companion, crony

intimate[2] verb 1 suggest, hint, imply, indicate, insinuate 2 announce, communicate, declare, make known, state

intimately adverb 1 confidingly, affectionately, confidentially, familiarly, personally, tenderly, warmly 2 in detail, fully, inside out, thoroughly, very well

intimation noun 1 hint, allusion, indication, inkling, insinuation, reminder, suggestion, warning

2 <u>announcement</u>, communication, declaration, notice

intimidate *verb* <u>frighten</u>, browbeat, bully, coerce, daunt, overawe, scare, subdue, terrorize, threaten

intimidation *noun* <u>bullying</u>, arm-twisting (*informal*), browbeating, coercion, menaces, pressure, terrorization, threat(s)

intolerable *adjective* <u>unbearable</u>, excruciating, impossible, insufferable, insupportable, painful, unendurable

intolerance *noun* <u>narrow-mindedness</u>, bigotry, chauvinism, discrimination, dogmatism, fanaticism, illiberality, prejudice

intolerant *adjective* <u>narrow-minded</u>, bigoted, chauvinistic, dictatorial, dogmatic, fanatical, illiberal, prejudiced, small-minded

intone *verb* <u>recite</u>, chant

intoxicated *adjective* 1 <u>drunk</u>, drunken, inebriated, legless (*informal*), paralytic (*informal*), plastered (*slang*), tipsy, under the influence 2 <u>euphoric</u>, dizzy, elated, enraptured, excited, exhilarated, high (*informal*)

intoxicating *adjective* 1 <u>alcoholic</u>, strong 2 <u>exciting</u>, exhilarating, heady, thrilling

intoxication *noun* 1 <u>drunkenness</u>, inebriation, insobriety, tipsiness 2 <u>excitement</u>, delirium, elation, euphoria, exhilaration

intransigent *adjective* <u>uncompromising</u>, hardline,

intractable, obdurate, obstinate, stiff-necked, stubborn, unbending, unyielding

intrepid *adjective* <u>fearless</u>, audacious, bold, brave, courageous, daring, gallant, plucky, stouthearted, valiant

intricacy *noun* <u>complexity</u>, complication, convolutions, elaborateness

intricate *adjective* <u>complicated</u>, complex, convoluted, elaborate, fancy, involved, labyrinthine, tangled, tortuous

intrigue *verb* 1 <u>interest</u>, attract, fascinate, rivet, titillate 2 <u>plot</u>, connive, conspire, machinate, manoeuvre, scheme ♦ *noun* 3 <u>plot</u>, chicanery, collusion, conspiracy, machination, manoeuvre, scheme, stratagem, wile 4 <u>affair</u>, amour, intimacy, liaison, romance

intriguing *adjective* <u>interesting</u>, beguiling, compelling, diverting, exciting, fascinating, tantalizing, titillating

intrinsic *adjective* <u>inborn</u>, basic, built-in, congenital, constitutional, essential, fundamental, inbred, inherent, native, natural

introduce *verb* 1 <u>present</u>, acquaint, familiarize, make known 2 <u>bring in</u>, establish, found, initiate, institute, launch, pioneer, set up, start 3 <u>bring up</u>, advance, air, broach, moot, put forward, submit 4 <u>insert</u>, add, inject, put in, throw in (*informal*)

introduction *noun* 1 <u>launch</u>, establishment, inauguration, institution, pioneering 2 <u>opening</u>, foreword, intro (*informal*), lead-in, preamble, preface, prelude, prologue

introductory *adjective* preliminary, first, inaugural, initial, opening, preparatory

introspective *adjective* inward-looking, brooding, contemplative, introverted, meditative, pensive

introverted *adjective* introspective, inner-directed, inward-looking, self-contained, withdrawn

intrude *verb* interfere, butt in, encroach, infringe, interrupt, meddle, push in, trespass

intruder *noun* trespasser, gate-crasher (*informal*), infiltrator, interloper, invader, prowler

intrusion *noun* invasion, encroachment, infringement, interference, interruption, trespass

intrusive *adjective* interfering, impertinent, importunate, meddlesome, nosy (*informal*), presumptuous, pushy (*informal*), uncalled-for, unwanted

intuition *noun* instinct, hunch, insight, perception, presentiment, sixth sense

intuitive *adjective* instinctive, innate, spontaneous, untaught

inundate *verb* flood, drown, engulf, immerse, overflow, overrun, overwhelm, submerge, swamp

invade *verb* 1 attack, assault, burst in, descend upon, encroach, infringe, make inroads, occupy, raid, violate 2 infest, overrun, permeate, pervade, swarm over

invader *noun* attacker, aggressor, plunderer, raider, trespasser

invalid[1] *adjective* 1 disabled, ailing, bedridden, frail, ill, infirm, sick ♦ *noun* 2 patient, convalescent, valetudinarian

invalid[2] *adjective* null and void, fallacious, false, illogical, inoperative, irrational, unfounded, unsound, void, worthless

invalidate *verb* nullify, annul, cancel, overthrow, undermine, undo

invaluable *adjective* precious, inestimable, priceless, valuable, worth one's or its weight in gold

invariably *adverb* consistently, always, customarily, day in, day out, habitually, perpetually, regularly, unfailingly, without exception

invasion *noun* 1 attack, assault, campaign, foray, incursion, inroad, offensive, onslaught, raid 2 intrusion, breach, encroachment, infraction, infringement, usurpation, violation

invective *noun* abuse, censure, denunciation, diatribe, tirade, tongue-lashing, vilification, vituperation

invent *verb* 1 create, coin, conceive, design, devise, discover, formulate, improvise, originate, think up 2 make up, concoct, cook up (*informal*), fabricate, feign, forge, manufacture, trump up

invention *noun* 1 creation, brainchild (*informal*), contraption, contrivance, design, device, discovery, gadget, instrument 2 <u>creativity</u>, genius, imagination, ingenuity, inventiveness, originality, resourcefulness 3 <u>fiction</u>, fabrication, falsehood, fantasy, forgery, lie, untruth, yarn

inventive adjective <u>creative</u>, fertile, imaginative, ingenious, innovative, inspired, original, resourceful

inventor noun <u>creator</u>, architect, author, coiner, designer, maker, originator

inventory noun <u>list</u>, account, catalogue, file, record, register, roll, roster

inverse adjective <u>opposite</u>, contrary, converse, reverse, reversed, transposed

invert verb <u>overturn</u>, reverse, transpose, upset, upturn

invest verb 1 <u>spend</u>, advance, devote, lay out, put in, sink 2 <u>empower</u>, authorize, charge, license, sanction, vest

investigate verb <u>examine</u>, explore, go into, inquire into, inspect, look into, probe, research, study

investigation noun <u>examination</u>, exploration, inquest, inquiry, inspection, probe, review, search, study, survey

investigator noun <u>examiner</u>, inquirer, (private) detective, private eye (informal), researcher, sleuth

investiture noun <u>installation</u>, enthronement, inauguration, induction, ordination

investment noun 1 <u>transaction</u>, speculation, venture 2 <u>stake</u>, ante (informal), contribution

inveterate adjective <u>long-standing</u>, chronic, confirmed, deep-seated, dyed-in-the-wool, entrenched, habitual, hardened, incorrigible, incurable

invidious adjective <u>undesirable</u>, hateful

invigilate verb <u>watch over</u>, conduct, keep an eye on, oversee, preside over, run, superintend, supervise

invigorate verb <u>refresh</u>, energize, enliven, exhilarate, fortify, galvanize, liven up, revitalize, stimulate

invincible adjective <u>unbeatable</u>, impregnable, indestructible, indomitable, insuperable, invulnerable, unassailable, unconquerable

inviolable adjective <u>sacrosanct</u>, hallowed, holy, inalienable, sacred, unalterable

inviolate adjective <u>intact</u>, entire, pure, unbroken, undefiled, unhurt, unpolluted, unsullied, untouched, whole

invisible adjective <u>unseen</u>, imperceptible, indiscernible

invitation noun <u>request</u>, call, invite (informal), summons

invite verb 1 <u>request</u>, ask, beg, bid, summon 2 <u>encourage</u>, ask for (informal), attract, court, entice, provoke, tempt, welcome

inviting adjective <u>tempting</u>, alluring, appealing, attractive, enticing, mouthwatering, seductive, welcoming

invocation noun <u>appeal</u>, entreaty, petition, prayer, supplication

invoke verb **1** <u>call upon</u>, appeal to, beg, beseech, entreat, implore, petition, pray, supplicate **2** <u>apply</u>, implement, initiate, put into effect, resort to, use

involuntary adjective <u>unintentional</u>, automatic, instinctive, reflex, spontaneous, unconscious, uncontrolled, unthinking

involve verb **1** <u>entail</u>, imply, mean, necessitate, presuppose, require **2** <u>concern</u>, affect, draw in, implicate, touch

involved adjective **1** <u>complicated</u>, complex, confusing, convoluted, elaborate, intricate, labyrinthine, tangled, tortuous **2** <u>concerned</u>, caught (up), implicated, mixed up in or with, participating, taking part

involvement noun <u>connection</u>, association, commitment, interest, participation

invulnerable adjective <u>safe</u>, impenetrable, indestructible, insusceptible, invincible, proof against, secure, unassailable

inward adjective **1** <u>incoming</u>, entering, inbound, ingoing **2** <u>internal</u>, inner, inside, interior **3** <u>private</u>, confidential, hidden, inmost, innermost, personal, secret

inwardly adverb <u>privately</u>, at heart, deep down, inside, secretly

irate adjective <u>angry</u>, annoyed, cross, enraged, furious, incensed, indignant, infuriated, livid

irksome adjective <u>irritating</u>, annoying, bothersome, disagreeable, exasperating, tiresome, troublesome, trying,
vexing, wearisome

iron adjective **1** <u>ferrous</u>, chalybeate, ferric **2** <u>inflexible</u>, adamant, hard, implacable, indomitable, rigid, steely, strong, tough, unbending, unyielding

ironic, ironical adjective **1** <u>sarcastic</u>, double-edged, mocking, sardonic, satirical, with tongue in cheek, wry **2** <u>paradoxical</u>, incongruous

iron out verb <u>settle</u>, clear up, get rid of, put right, reconcile, resolve, smooth over, sort out, straighten out

irony noun **1** <u>sarcasm</u>, mockery, satire **2** <u>paradox</u>, incongruity

irrational adjective <u>illogical</u>, absurd, crazy, nonsensical, preposterous, unreasonable

irrefutable adjective <u>undeniable</u>, certain, incontestable, incontrovertible, indisputable, indubitable, sure, unquestionable

irregular adjective **1** <u>variable</u>, erratic, fitful, haphazard, occasional, random, spasmodic, sporadic, unsystematic **2** <u>unconventional</u>, abnormal, exceptional, extraordinary, peculiar, unofficial, unorthodox, unusual **3** <u>uneven</u>, asymmetrical, bumpy, crooked, jagged, lopsided, ragged, rough

irregularity noun **1** <u>uncertainty</u>, desultoriness, disorganization, haphazardness **2** <u>abnormality</u>, anomaly, oddity, peculiarity, unorthodoxy **3** <u>unevenness</u>, asymmetry, bumpiness, jaggedness, lopsidedness, raggedness, roughness

irrelevant adjective <u>unconnected</u>, beside the point, extraneous, immaterial, impertinent, inapplicable, inappropriate, neither here nor there, unrelated

irreparable adjective beyond repair, incurable, irremediable, irretrievable, irreversible

irrepressible adjective ebullient, boisterous, buoyant, effervescent, unstoppable

irreproachable adjective blameless, beyond reproach, faultless, impeccable, innocent, perfect, pure, unimpeachable

irresistible adjective overwhelming, compelling, compulsive, overpowering, urgent

irresponsible adjective immature, careless, reckless, scatterbrained, shiftless, thoughtless, unreliable, untrustworthy

irreverent adjective disrespectful, cheeky (informal), flippant, iconoclastic, impertinent, impudent, mocking, tongue-in-cheek

irreversible adjective irrevocable, final, incurable, irreparable, unalterable

irrevocable adjective fixed, fated, immutable, irreversible, predestined, predetermined, settled, unalterable

irrigate verb water, flood, inundate, moisten, wet

irritability noun bad temper, ill humour, impatience, irascibility, prickliness, testiness, tetchiness, touchiness

irritable adjective bad-tempered, cantankerous, crotchety (informal), ill-tempered, irascible,

oversensitive, prickly, testy, tetchy, touchy

irritate verb 1 annoy, anger, bother, exasperate, get on one's nerves (informal), infuriate, needle (informal), nettle, rankle with, try one's patience 2 rub, chafe, inflame, pain

irritated adjective annoyed, angry, bothered, cross, exasperated, nettled, piqued, put out, vexed

irritating adjective annoying, disturbing, infuriating, irksome, maddening, nagging, troublesome, trying

irritation noun 1 annoyance, anger, displeasure, exasperation, indignation, resentment, testiness, vexation 2 nuisance, drag (informal), irritant, pain in the neck (informal), thorn in one's flesh

island noun isle, ait or eyot (dialect), atoll, cay or key, islet

isolate verb separate, cut off, detach, disconnect, insulate, segregate, set apart

isolated adjective remote, hidden, lonely, off the beaten track, outlying, out-of-the-way, secluded

isolation noun separation, detachment, remoteness, seclusion, segregation, solitude

issue noun 1 topic, bone of contention, matter, point, problem, question, subject 2 outcome, consequence, effect, end result, result, upshot 3 edition, copy, number, printing 4 children, descendants, heirs, offspring, progeny 5 take issue disagree, challenge, dispute, object, oppose, raise an objection, take exception ♦ *verb* **6** publish, announce, broadcast, circulate, deliver, distribute, give out, put out, release

isthmus *noun* strip, spit

itch *noun* **1** irritation, itchiness, prickling, tingling **2** desire, craving, hankering, hunger, longing, lust, passion, yearning, yen (*informal*) ♦ *verb* **3** prickle, irritate, tickle, tingle **4** long, ache, crave, hanker, hunger, lust, pine, yearn

itching *adjective* longing, avid, eager, impatient, mad keen (*informal*), raring, spoiling for

itchy *adjective* impatient, eager, edgy, fidgety, restive, restless, unsettled

item *noun* **1** detail, article, component, entry, matter, particular, point, thing **2** report, account, article, bulletin, dispatch, feature, note, notice, paragraph, piece

itinerant *adjective* wandering, migratory, nomadic, peripatetic, roaming, roving, travelling, vagrant

itinerary *noun* schedule, programme, route, timetable

J j

jab *verb, noun* poke, dig, lunge, nudge, prod, punch, stab, tap, thrust

jabber *verb* chatter, babble, blether, gabble, mumble, prate, rabbit (on) (*Brit. informal*), ramble, yap (*informal*)

jacket *noun* covering, case, casing, coat, sheath, skin, wrapper, wrapping

jackpot *noun* prize, award, bonanza, reward, winnings

jack up *verb* raise, elevate, hoist, lift, lift up

jaded *adjective* tired, exhausted, fatigued, spent, weary

jagged *adjective* uneven, barbed, craggy, indented, ragged, serrated, spiked, toothed

jail *noun* **1** prison, nick (*Brit. slang*), penitentiary (*U.S.*), reformatory, slammer (*slang*) ♦ *verb* **2** imprison, confine, detain, incarcerate, lock up, send down

jailer *noun* guard, keeper, warden, warder

jam *verb* **1** pack, cram, force, press, ram, squeeze, stuff, wedge **2** crowd, crush, throng **3** congest, block, clog, obstruct, stall, stick ♦ *noun* **4** predicament, deep water, fix (*informal*), hole (*slang*), hot water, pickle (*informal*), tight spot, trouble

jamboree *noun* festival, carnival, celebration, festivity, fête, revelry

jangle *verb* rattle, chime, clank, clash, clatter, jingle, vibrate

janitor *noun* caretaker, concierge, custodian, doorkeeper, porter

jar[1] *noun* pot, container, crock, jug, pitcher, urn, vase

jar[2] *verb* **1** jolt, bump, convulse, rattle, rock, shake, vibrate **2** irritate, annoy, get on one's nerves (*informal*), grate, irk, nettle, offend ♦ *noun* **3** jolt, bump, convulsion, shock, vibration

jargon *noun* parlance, argot, idiom, usage

jaundiced *adjective* 1 cynical, sceptical 2 bitter, envious, hostile, jealous, resentful, spiteful, suspicious

jaunt *noun* outing, airing, excursion, expedition, ramble, stroll, tour, trip

jaunty *adjective* sprightly, buoyant, carefree, high-spirited, lively, perky, self-confident, sparky

jaw *verb* talk, chat, chatter, gossip, spout

jaws *plural noun* opening, entrance, mouth

jazz up *verb* enliven, animate, enhance, improve

jazzy *adjective* flashy, fancy, gaudy, snazzy (*informal*)

jealous *adjective* 1 envious, covetous, desirous, green, grudging, resentful 2 wary, mistrustful, protective, suspicious, vigilant, watchful

jealousy *noun* envy, covetousness, mistrust, possessiveness, resentment, spite, suspicion

jeans *plural noun* denims, Levis (*Trademark*)

jeer *verb* 1 scoff, barrack, deride, gibe, heckle, mock, ridicule, taunt ♦ *noun* 2 taunt, abuse, boo, catcall, derision, gibe, ridicule

jell *verb* 1 solidify, congeal, harden, set, thicken 2 take shape, come together, crystallize, materialize

jeopardize *verb* endanger, chance, expose, gamble, imperil,

risk, stake, venture

jeopardy *noun* danger, insecurity, peril, risk, vulnerability

jerk *verb, noun* tug, jolt, lurch, pull, thrust, twitch, wrench, yank

jerky *adjective* bumpy, convulsive, jolting, jumpy, shaky, spasmodic, twitchy

jerry-built *adjective* ramshackle, cheap, defective, flimsy, rickety, shabby, slipshod, thrown together

jest *noun* 1 joke, bon mot, crack (*slang*), jape, pleasantry, prank, quip, wisecrack (*informal*), witticism ♦ *verb* 2 joke, kid (*informal*), mock, quip, tease

jester *noun* clown, buffoon, fool, harlequin

jet[1] *adjective* black, coal-black, ebony, inky, pitch-black, raven, sable

jet[2] *noun* 1 stream, flow, fountain, gush, spout, spray, spring 2 nozzle, atomizer, sprayer, sprinkler ♦ *verb* 3 fly, soar, zoom

jettison *verb* abandon, discard, dump, eject, expel, scrap, throw overboard, unload

jetty *noun* pier, breakwater, dock, groyne, mole, quay, wharf

jewel *noun* 1 gemstone, ornament, rock (*slang*), sparkler (*informal*) 2 rarity, collector's item, find, gem, humdinger (*slang*), pearl, treasure, wonder

jewellery *noun* jewels, finery, gems, ornaments, regalia, treasure, trinkets

jib *verb* refuse, balk, recoil, retreat, shrink, stop short

jibe *see* GIBE

jig verb skip, bob, bounce, caper, prance, wiggle

jingle noun 1 rattle, clang, clink, reverberation, ringing, tinkle 2 song, chorus, ditty, melody, tune ♦ verb 3 ring, chime, clatter, clink, jangle, rattle, tinkle

jinx noun 1 curse, hex (*U.S. & Canad. informal*), hoodoo (*informal*), nemesis ♦ verb 2 curse, bewitch, hex (*U.S. & Canad. informal*)

jitters plural noun nerves, anxiety, butterflies (in one's stomach) (*informal*), cold feet (*informal*), fidgets, nervousness, the shakes (*informal*)

jittery adjective nervous, agitated, anxious, fidgety, jumpy, shaky, trembling, twitchy (*informal*)

job noun 1 task, assignment, chore, duty, enterprise, errand, undertaking, venture 2 occupation, business, calling, career, employment, livelihood, profession, vocation

jobless adjective unemployed, idle, inactive, out of work, unoccupied

jocular adjective humorous, amusing, droll, facetious, funny, joking, jovial, playful, sportive, teasing, waggish

jog verb 1 nudge, prod, push, shake, stir 2 run, canter, lope, trot

joie de vivre noun enthusiasm, ebullience, enjoyment, gusto, relish, zest

join verb 1 connect, add, append, attach, combine, couple, fasten, link, unite 2 enrol, enlist, enter, sign up

joint adjective 1 shared, collective, combined, communal, cooperative, joined, mutual, united ♦ noun 2 junction, connection, hinge, intersection, nexus, node ♦ verb 3 divide, carve, cut up, dissect, segment, sever

jointly adverb collectively, as one, in common, in conjunction, in league, in partnership, mutually, together

joke noun 1 jest, gag (*informal*), jape, prank, pun, quip, wisecrack (*informal*), witticism 2 clown, buffoon, laughing stock ♦ verb 3 jest, banter, kid (*informal*), mock, play the fool, quip, taunt, tease

joker noun comedian, buffoon, clown, comic, humorist, jester, prankster, trickster, wag, wit

jolly adjective happy, cheerful, chirpy (*informal*), genial, jovial, merry, playful, sprightly, upbeat (*informal*)

jolt noun 1 jerk, bump, jar, jog, jump, lurch, shake, start 2 surprise, blow, bolt from the blue, bombshell, setback, shock ♦ verb 3 jerk, jar, jog, jostle, knock, push, shake, shove 4 surprise, discompose, disturb, perturb, stagger, startle, stun

jostle verb push, bump, elbow, hustle, jog, jolt, shake, shove

jot verb 1 note down, list, record, scribble ♦ noun 2 bit, fraction, grain, morsel, scrap, speck

journal noun 1 newspaper, daily, gazette, magazine, monthly, periodical, weekly 2 diary, chronicle, log, record

journalist noun reporter,

broadcaster, columnist, commentator, correspondent, hack, journo (*slang*), newsman or newswoman, pressman

journey *noun* 1 *trip*, excursion, expedition, odyssey, pilgrimage, tour, trek, voyage ♦ *verb* 2 *travel*, go, proceed, roam, rove, tour, traverse, trek, voyage, wander

jovial *adjective* *cheerful*, animated, cheery, convivial, happy, jolly, merry, mirthful

joy *noun* *delight*, bliss, ecstasy, elation, gaiety, glee, pleasure, rapture, satisfaction

joyful *adjective* *delighted*, elated, enraptured, glad, gratified, happy, jubilant, merry, pleased

joyless *adjective* *unhappy*, cheerless, depressed, dismal, dreary, gloomy, miserable, sad

joyous *adjective* *joyful*, festive, merry, rapturous

jubilant *adjective* *overjoyed*, elated, enraptured, euphoric, exuberant, exultant, thrilled, triumphant

jubilation *noun* *joy*, celebration, ecstasy, elation, excitement, exultation, festivity, triumph

jubilee *noun* *celebration*, festival, festivity, holiday

judge *noun* 1 *referee*, adjudicator, arbiter, arbitrator, moderator, umpire 2 *critic*, arbiter, assessor, authority, connoisseur, expert 3 *magistrate*, beak (*Brit. slang*), justice ♦ *verb* 4 *arbitrate*, adjudicate, decide, mediate, referee, umpire 5 *consider*, appraise, assess, esteem, estimate, evaluate, rate, value

judgment *noun* 1 *sense*, acumen, discernment, discrimination, prudence, shrewdness, understanding, wisdom 2 *verdict*, arbitration, decision, decree, finding, ruling, sentence 3 *opinion*, appraisal, assessment, belief, diagnosis, estimate, finding, valuation, view

judicial *adjective* *legal*, official

judicious *adjective* *sensible*, astute, careful, discriminating, enlightened, prudent, shrewd, thoughtful, well-judged, wise

jug *noun* *container*, carafe, crock, ewer, jar, pitcher, urn, vessel

juggle *verb* *manipulate*, alter, change, manoeuvre, modify

juice *noun* *liquid*, extract, fluid, liquor, nectar, sap

juicy *adjective* 1 *moist*, lush, succulent 2 *interesting*, colourful, provocative, racy, risqué, sensational, spicy (*informal*), suggestive, vivid

jumble *noun* 1 *muddle*, clutter, confusion, disarray, disorder, mess, mishmash, mixture ♦ *verb* 2 *mix*, confuse, disorder, disorganize, mistake, muddle, shuffle

jumbo *adjective* *giant*, gigantic, huge, immense, large, oversized

jump *verb* 1 *leap*, bounce, bound, hop, hurdle, skip, spring, vault 2 *recoil*, flinch, jerk, start, wince 3 *miss*, avoid, evade, omit, skip 4 *increase*, advance, ascend, escalate, rise, surge ♦ *noun* 5 *leap*, bound, hop, skip, spring, vault 6 *interruption*, break, gap, hiatus, lacuna, space 7 *rise*, advance, increase, increment, upsurge, upturn

jumped-up adjective <u>conceited</u>, arrogant, insolent, overbearing, pompous, presumptuous

jumper noun <u>sweater</u>, jersey, pullover, woolly

jumpy adjective <u>nervous</u>, agitated, anxious, apprehensive, fidgety, jittery (informal), on edge, restless, tense

junction noun <u>connection</u>, coupling, linking, union

juncture noun <u>moment</u>, occasion, point, time

junior adjective <u>minor</u>, inferior, lesser, lower, secondary, subordinate, younger

junk noun <u>rubbish</u>, clutter, debris, litter, odds and ends, refuse, scrap, trash, waste

jurisdiction noun 1 <u>authority</u>, command, control, influence, power, rule 2 <u>range</u>, area, bounds, compass, field, province, scope, sphere

just adverb 1 <u>exactly</u>, absolutely, completely, entirely, perfectly, precisely 2 <u>recently</u>, hardly, lately, only now, scarcely 3 <u>merely</u>, by the skin of one's teeth, only, simply, solely ♦ adjective 4 <u>fair</u>, conscientious, equitable, fair-minded, good, honest, upright, virtuous 5 <u>proper</u>, appropriate, apt, deserved, due, fitting, justified, merited, rightful

justice noun 1 <u>fairness</u>, equity, honesty, integrity, law, legality, legitimacy, right 2 <u>judge</u>, magistrate

justifiable adjective <u>reasonable</u>, acceptable, defensible, excusable, legitimate, sensible,

understandable, valid, warrantable

justification noun 1 <u>explanation</u>, defence, excuse, rationalization, vindication 2 <u>reason</u>, basis, grounds, warrant

justify verb <u>explain</u>, defend, exculpate, excuse, exonerate, support, uphold, vindicate, warrant

justly adverb <u>properly</u>, correctly, equitably, fairly, lawfully

jut verb <u>stick out</u>, bulge, extend, overhang, poke, project, protrude

juvenile adjective 1 <u>young</u>, babyish, callow, childish, immature, inexperienced, infantile, puerile, youthful ♦ noun 2 <u>child</u>, adolescent, boy, girl, infant, minor, youth

juxtaposition noun <u>proximity</u>, closeness, contact, nearness, propinquity, vicinity

K k

kamikaze adjective <u>self-destructive</u>, foolhardy, suicidal

keel over verb <u>collapse</u>, black out (informal), faint, pass out

keen adjective 1 <u>eager</u>, ardent, avid, enthusiastic, impassioned, intense, zealous 2 <u>sharp</u>, cutting, incisive, razor-like 3 <u>astute</u>, canny, clever, perceptive, quick, shrewd, wise

keenness noun <u>eagerness</u>, ardour, enthusiasm, fervour, intensity, passion, zeal, zest

keep verb 1 <u>retain</u>, conserve,

control, hold, maintain, possess, preserve 2 store, carry, deposit, hold, place, stack, stock 3 look after, care for, guard, maintain, manage, mind, protect, tend, watch over 4 support, feed, maintain, provide for, subsidize, sustain 5 detain, delay, hinder, hold back, keep back, obstruct, prevent, restrain ♦ noun 6 board, food, living, maintenance 7 tower, castle

keeper noun guardian, attendant, caretaker, curator, custodian, guard, preserver, steward, warden

keeping noun 1 care, charge, custody, guardianship, possession, protection, safekeeping 2 As in **in keeping with** agreement, accord, balance, compliance, conformity, correspondence, harmony, observance, proportion

keepsake noun souvenir, memento, relic, reminder, symbol, token

keep up verb maintain, continue, keep pace, preserve, sustain

keg noun barrel, cask, drum, vat

kernel noun essence, core, germ, gist, nub, pith, substance

key noun 1 opener, latchkey 2 answer, explanation, solution ♦ adjective 3 essential, crucial, decisive, fundamental, important, leading, main, major, pivotal, principal

key in verb type, enter, input, keyboard

keynote noun heart, centre, core, essence, gist, substance, theme

kick verb 1 boot, punt 2 Informal

give up, abandon, desist from, leave off, quit, stop ♦ noun 3 Informal thrill, buzz (slang), pleasure, stimulation

kick off verb Informal begin, commence, get the show on the road, initiate, open, start

kick out verb dismiss, eject, evict, expel, get rid of, remove, sack (informal)

kid¹ noun Informal child, baby, bairn, infant, teenager, tot, youngster, youth

kid² verb tease, delude, fool, hoax, jest, joke, pretend, trick, wind up (Brit. slang)

kidnap verb abduct, capture, hijack, hold to ransom, seize

kill verb 1 slay, assassinate, butcher, destroy, execute, exterminate, liquidate, massacre, murder, slaughter 2 suppress, extinguish, halt, quash, quell, scotch, smother, stifle, stop

killer noun assassin, butcher, cut-throat, executioner, exterminator, gunman, hit man (slang), murderer, slayer

killing adjective 1 Informal tiring, debilitating, exhausting, fatiguing, punishing 2 Informal hilarious, comical, ludicrous, uproarious ♦ noun 3 slaughter, bloodshed, carnage, extermination, homicide, manslaughter, massacre, murder, slaying 4 Informal bonanza, bomb (slang), cleanup (informal), coup, gain, profit, success, windfall

killjoy noun spoilsport, dampener, wet blanket (informal)

kin noun family, kindred, kinsfolk,

relations, relatives

kind[1] *adjective* <u>considerate</u>, benign, charitable, compassionate, courteous, friendly, generous, humane, kindly, obliging, philanthropic, tender-hearted

kind[2] *noun* <u>class</u>, brand, breed, family, set, sort, species, variety

kind-hearted *adjective* <u>sympathetic</u>, altruistic, compassionate, considerate, generous, good-natured, helpful, humane, kind, tender-hearted

kindle *verb* 1 <u>set fire to</u>, ignite, inflame, light 2 <u>arouse</u>, awaken, induce, inspire, provoke, rouse, stimulate, stir

kindliness *noun* <u>kindness</u>, amiability, benevolence, charity, compassion, friendliness, gentleness, humanity, kind-heartedness

kindly *adjective* 1 <u>good-natured</u>, benevolent, benign, compassionate, helpful, kind, pleasant, sympathetic, warm ♦ *adverb* 2 <u>politely</u>, agreeably, cordially, graciously, tenderly, thoughtfully

kindness *noun* <u>goodwill</u>, benevolence, charity, compassion, generosity, humanity, kindliness, philanthropy, understanding

kindred *adjective* 1 <u>similar</u>, akin, corresponding, like, matching, related ♦ *noun* 2 <u>family</u>, kin, kinsfolk, relations, relatives

king *noun* <u>ruler</u>, emperor, monarch, sovereign

kingdom *noun* <u>country</u>, nation, realm, state, territory

kink *noun* 1 <u>twist</u>, bend, coil, wrinkle 2 <u>quirk</u>, eccentricity, fetish, foible, idiosyncrasy, vagary, whim

kinky *adjective* 1 <u>weird</u>, eccentric, odd, outlandish, peculiar, queer, quirky, strange 2 <u>twisted</u>, coiled, curled, tangled

kinship *noun* 1 <u>relation</u>, consanguinity, kin, ties of blood 2 <u>similarity</u>, affinity, association, connection, correspondence, relationship

kiosk *noun* <u>booth</u>, bookstall, counter, newsstand, stall, stand

kiss *verb* 1 <u>osculate</u>, neck (*informal*), peck (*informal*) 2 <u>brush</u>, glance, graze, scrape, touch ♦ *noun* 3 <u>osculation</u>, peck (*informal*), smacker (*slang*)

kit *noun* <u>equipment</u>, apparatus, gear, paraphernalia, tackle, tools

kit out *verb* <u>equip</u>, accoutre, arm, deck out, fit out, fix up, furnish, provide with, supply

knack *noun* <u>skill</u>, ability, aptitude, capacity, expertise, facility, gift, propensity, talent, trick

knave *noun* <u>rogue</u>, blackguard, bounder (*old-fashioned Brit. slang*), rascal, rotter (*slang, chiefly Brit.*), scoundrel, villain

knead *verb* <u>squeeze</u>, form, manipulate, massage, mould, press, rub, shape, work

kneel *verb* <u>genuflect</u>, stoop

knell *noun* <u>ringing</u>, chime, peal, sound, toll

knickers *plural noun* <u>underwear</u>, bloomers, briefs, drawers, panties, smalls

knick-knack *noun* <u>trinket</u>, bagatelle, bauble, bric-a-brac, plaything, trifle

knife noun 1 <u>blade</u>, cutter ♦ verb 2 <u>cut</u>, lacerate, pierce, slash, stab, wound

knit verb 1 <u>join</u>, bind, fasten, intertwine, link, tie, unite, weave 2 <u>wrinkle</u>, crease, furrow, knot, pucker

knob noun <u>lump</u>, bump, hump, knot, projection, protrusion, stud

knock verb 1 <u>hit</u>, belt (informal), cuff, punch, rap, smack, strike, thump 2 Informal <u>criticize</u>, abuse, belittle, censure, condemn, denigrate, deprecate, disparage, find fault, run down ♦ noun 3 <u>blow</u>, clip, clout (informal), cuff, rap, slap, smack, thump 4 <u>setback</u>, defeat, failure, rebuff, rejection, reversal

knockabout adjective <u>boisterous</u>, farcical, riotous, rollicking, slapstick

knock about or **around** verb 1 <u>wander</u>, ramble, range, roam, rove, travel 2 <u>hit</u>, abuse, batter, beat up (informal), maltreat, manhandle, maul, mistreat, strike

knock down verb <u>demolish</u>, destroy, fell, level, raze

knock off verb 1 <u>stop work</u>, clock off, clock out, finish 2 <u>steal</u>, nick (slang, chiefly Brit.), pinch, rob, thieve

knockout noun 1 <u>killer blow</u>, coup de grâce, KO or K.O. (slang) 2 <u>success</u>, hit, sensation, smash, smash hit, triumph, winner

knot noun 1 <u>connection</u>, bond, joint, ligature, loop, tie 2 <u>cluster</u>, bunch, clump, collection ♦ verb 3 <u>tie</u>, bind, loop, secure, tether

know verb 1 <u>realize</u>,

comprehend, feel certain, notice, perceive, recognize, see, understand 2 <u>be acquainted with</u>, be familiar with, have dealings with, have knowledge of, recognize

know-how noun <u>capability</u>, ability, aptitude, expertise, ingenuity, knack, knowledge, savoir-faire, skill, talent

knowing adjective <u>meaningful</u>, expressive, significant

knowingly adverb <u>deliberately</u>, consciously, intentionally, on purpose, purposely, wilfully, wittingly

knowledge noun 1 <u>learning</u>, education, enlightenment, erudition, instruction, intelligence, scholarship, wisdom 2 <u>acquaintance</u>, familiarity, intimacy

knowledgeable adjective 1 <u>well-informed</u>, au fait, aware, clued-up (informal), cognizant, conversant, experienced, familiar, in the know (informal) 2 <u>intelligent</u>, educated, erudite, learned, scholarly

known adjective <u>famous</u>, acknowledged, avowed, celebrated, noted, recognized, well-known

L l

label noun 1 <u>tag</u>, marker, sticker, ticket ♦ verb 2 <u>mark</u>, stamp, tag

laborious adjective <u>hard</u>, arduous, backbreaking, exhausting, onerous, strenuous, tiring, tough, wearisome

labour noun **1** work, industry, toil **2** workers, employees, hands, labourers, workforce **3** childbirth, delivery, parturition ♦ verb **4** work, endeavour, slave, strive, struggle, sweat (informal), toil **5** usually with under be disadvantaged, be a victim of, be burdened by, suffer **6** overemphasize, dwell on, elaborate, overdo, strain

laboured adjective forced, awkward, difficult, heavy, stiff, strained

labourer noun worker, blue-collar worker, drudge, hand, manual worker, navvy (Brit. informal)

labyrinth noun maze, intricacy, jungle, tangle

lace noun **1** netting, filigree, openwork **2** cord, bootlace, shoelace, string, tie ♦ verb **3** fasten, bind, do up, thread, tie **4** mix in, add to, fortify, spike

lacerate verb tear, claw, cut, gash, mangle, rip, slash, wound

laceration noun cut, gash, rent, rip, slash, tear, wound

lack noun **1** shortage, absence, dearth, deficiency, need, scarcity, want ♦ verb **2** need, be deficient in, be short of, be without, miss, require, want

lackadaisical adjective **1** lethargic, apathetic, dull, half-hearted, indifferent, languid, listless **2** lazy, abstracted, dreamy, idle, indolent, inert

lackey noun **1** hanger-on, flatterer, minion, sycophant, toady, yes man **2** manservant, attendant, flunky, footman, valet

lacklustre adjective flat, drab, dull, leaden, lifeless, muted, prosaic, uninspired, vapid

laconic adjective terse, brief, concise, curt, monosyllabic, pithy, short, succinct

lad noun boy, fellow, guy (informal), juvenile, kid (informal), youngster, youth

laden adjective loaded, burdened, charged, encumbered, full, weighed down

lady noun **1** gentlewoman, dame **2** woman, female

lady-killer noun womanizer, Casanova, Don Juan, heartbreaker, ladies' man, libertine, philanderer, rake, roué

ladylike adjective refined, elegant, genteel, modest, polite, proper, respectable, sophisticated, well-bred

lag verb hang back, dawdle, delay, linger, loiter, straggle, tarry, trail

laggard noun straggler, dawdler, idler, loiterer, slowcoach (Brit. informal), sluggard, snail

laid-back adjective relaxed, casual, easy-going, free and easy, unflappable (informal), unhurried

lair noun nest, burrow, den, earth, hole

laissez faire noun nonintervention, free enterprise, free trade

lake noun pond, lagoon, loch (Scot.), lough (Irish), mere, reservoir, tarn

lame adjective **1** disabled, crippled, game, handicapped, hobbling, limping **2** unconvincing, feeble, flimsy, inadequate, pathetic, poor, thin, unsatisfactory, weak

lament verb 1 complain, bemoan, bewail, deplore, grieve, mourn, regret, sorrow, wail, weep ♦ noun 2 complaint, lamentation, moan, wailing 3 dirge, elegy, requiem, threnody

lamentable adjective regrettable, deplorable, distressing, grievous, mournful, tragic, unfortunate, woeful

lampoon noun 1 satire, burlesque, caricature, parody, send-up (Brit. informal), skit, takeoff (informal) ♦ verb 2 ridicule, caricature, make fun of, mock, parody, satirize, send up (Brit. informal), take off (informal)

land noun 1 ground, dry land, earth, terra firma 2 soil, dirt, ground, loam 3 countryside, farmland 4 property, estate, grounds, realty 5 country, district, nation, province, region, territory, tract ♦ verb 6 arrive, alight, come to rest, disembark, dock, touch down 7 end up, turn up, wind up 8 Informal obtain, acquire, gain, get, secure, win

landlord noun 1 innkeeper, host, hotelier 2 owner, freeholder, lessor, proprietor

landmark noun 1 feature, monument 2 milestone, turning point, watershed

landscape noun scenery, countryside, outlook, panorama, prospect, scene, view, vista

landslide noun 1 rockfall, avalanche, landslip ♦ adjective 2 overwhelming, conclusive, decisive, runaway

lane noun road, alley, footpath, passageway, path, pathway, street, way

language noun 1 speech, communication, discourse, expression, parlance, talk 2 tongue, dialect, patois, vernacular

languid adjective 1 lazy, indifferent, lackadaisical, languorous, listless, unenthusiastic 2 lethargic, dull, heavy, sluggish, torpid

languish verb 1 weaken, decline, droop, fade, fail, faint, flag, wilt, wither 2 often with for pine, desire, hanker, hunger, long, yearn 3 be neglected, be abandoned, rot, suffer, waste away

lank adjective 1 limp, lifeless, straggling 2 thin, emaciated, gaunt, lean, scrawny, skinny, slender, slim, spare

lanky adjective gangling, angular, bony, gaunt, rangy, spare, tall

lap[1] noun circuit, circle, loop, orbit, tour

lap[2] verb 1 ripple, gurgle, plash, purl, splash, swish, wash 2 drink, lick, sip, sup

lapse noun 1 mistake, error, failing, fault, indiscretion, negligence, omission, oversight, slip 2 interval, break, breathing space, gap, intermission, interruption, lull, pause 3 drop, decline, deterioration, fall ♦ verb 4 drop, decline, degenerate, deteriorate, fall, sink, slide, slip 5 end, expire, run out, stop, terminate

lapsed *adjective* out of date, discontinued, ended, expired, finished, invalid, run out

large *adjective* **1** big, considerable, enormous, gigantic, great, huge, immense, massive, monumental, sizable *or* sizeable, substantial, vast **2 at large: a** free, at liberty, on the loose, on the run, unconfined **b** in general, as a whole, chiefly, generally, in the main, mainly **c** at length, exhaustively, greatly, in full detail

largely *adverb* mainly, as a rule, by and large, chiefly, generally, mostly, predominantly, primarily, principally, to a great extent

large-scale *adjective* wide-ranging, broad, extensive, far-reaching, global, sweeping, vast, wholesale, wide

lark *noun* **1** prank, caper, escapade, fun, game, jape, mischief ♦ *verb* **2 lark about** play, caper, cavort, have fun, make mischief

lash[1] *noun* **1** blow, hit, stripe, stroke, swipe (*informal*) ♦ *verb* **2** whip, beat, birch, flog, scourge, thrash **3** pound, beat, buffet, dash, drum, hammer, smack, strike **4** scold, attack, blast, censure, criticize, put down, slate (*informal, chiefly Brit.*), tear into (*informal*), upbraid

lash[2] *verb* fasten, bind, make fast, secure, strap, tie

lass *noun* girl, damsel, lassie (*informal*), maid, maiden, young woman

last[1] *adjective* **1** hindmost, at the end, rearmost **2** most recent, latest **3** final, closing, concluding, terminal, ultimate ♦ *adverb* **4** in the rear, after, behind, bringing up the rear, in or at the end

last[2] *verb* continue, abide, carry on, endure, keep on, persist, remain, stand up, survive

lasting *adjective* continuing, abiding, durable, enduring, long-standing, long-term, perennial, permanent

latch *noun* **1** fastening, bar, bolt, catch, hasp, hook, lock ♦ *verb* **2** fasten, bar, bolt, make fast, secure

late *adjective* **1** overdue, behind, behindhand, belated, delayed, last-minute, tardy **2** recent, advanced, fresh, modern, new **3** dead, deceased, defunct, departed, former, past ♦ *adverb* **4** belatedly, at the last minute, behindhand, behind time, dilatorily, tardily

lately *adverb* recently, in recent times, just now, latterly, not long ago, of late

lateness *noun* delay, belatedness, tardiness

latent *adjective* hidden, concealed, dormant, invisible, potential, undeveloped, unrealized

later *adverb* afterwards, after, by and by, in a while, in time, later on, subsequently, thereafter

lateral *adjective* sideways, edgeways, flanking

latest *adjective* up-to-date, current, fashionable, modern, most recent, newest, up-to-the-minute

lather *noun* **1** froth, bubbles,

latitude noun scope, elbowroom, freedom, laxity, leeway, liberty, licence, play

latter adjective last-mentioned, closing, concluding, last, second

latterly adverb recently, lately, of late

lattice noun grid, grating, grille, trellis

laudable adjective praiseworthy, admirable, commendable, creditable, excellent, meritorious, of note, worthy

laugh verb 1 chuckle, be in stitches, chortle, giggle, guffaw, snigger, split one's sides, titter ◆ noun 2 chuckle, chortle, giggle, guffaw, snigger, titter 3 Informal clown, card (informal), entertainer, hoot (informal), scream (informal) 4 Informal joke, hoot (informal), lark, scream (informal)

laughable adjective ridiculous, absurd, derisory, farcical, ludicrous, nonsensical, preposterous, risible

laughing stock noun figure of fun, Aunt Sally (Brit.), butt, target, victim

laugh off verb disregard, brush aside, dismiss, ignore, minimize, pooh-pooh, shrug off

laughter noun amusement, glee, hilarity, merriment, mirth

launch verb 1 propel, discharge, dispatch, fire, project, send off, set in motion 2 begin, commence, embark upon, inaugurate, initiate, instigate, introduce, open, start

laurels plural noun glory, credit, distinction, fame, honour, praise, prestige, recognition, renown

lavatory noun toilet, bathroom, cloakroom (Brit.), latrine, loo (Brit. informal), powder room, (public) convenience, washroom, water closet, W.C.

lavish adjective 1 plentiful, abundant, copious, profuse, prolific 2 generous, bountiful, free, liberal, munificent, open-handed, unstinting 3 extravagant, exaggerated, excessive, immoderate, prodigal, unrestrained, wasteful, wild ◆ verb 4 spend, deluge, dissipate, expend, heap, pour, shower, squander, waste

law noun 1 constitution, charter, code 2 rule, act, command, commandment, decree, edict, order, ordinance, regulation, statute 3 principle, axiom, canon, precept

law-abiding adjective obedient, compliant, dutiful, good, honest, honourable, lawful, orderly, peaceable

law-breaker noun criminal, convict, crook (informal), culprit, delinquent, felon, miscreant, offender, villain, wrongdoer

lawful adjective legal, authorized, constitutional, legalized, legitimate, licit, permissible, rightful, valid, warranted

lawless adjective disorderly, anarchic, chaotic, rebellious, riotous, unruly, wild

lawlessness noun anarchy,

chaos, disorder, mob rule

lawsuit noun <u>case</u>, action, dispute, industrial tribunal, litigation, proceedings, prosecution, suit, trial

lawyer noun <u>legal adviser</u>, advocate, attorney, barrister, counsel, counsellor, solicitor

lax adjective <u>slack</u>, careless, casual, lenient, negligent, overindulgent, remiss, slapdash, slipshod

lay¹ verb **1** <u>place</u>, deposit, leave, plant, put, set, set down, spread **2** <u>arrange</u>, organize, position, set out **3** <u>produce</u>, bear, deposit **4** <u>put forward</u>, advance, bring forward, lodge, offer, present, submit **5** <u>attribute</u>, allocate, allot, ascribe, assign, impute **6** <u>devise</u>, concoct, contrive, design, hatch, plan, plot, prepare, work out **7** <u>bet</u>, gamble, give odds, hazard, risk, stake, wager

lay² adjective **1** <u>nonclerical</u>, secular **2** <u>nonspecialist</u>, amateur, inexpert, nonprofessional

layabout noun <u>idler</u>, couch potato (slang), good-for-nothing, loafer, lounger, ne'er-do-well, skiver (Brit. slang), wastrel

layer noun <u>tier</u>, row, seam, stratum, thickness

layman noun <u>amateur</u>, lay person, nonprofessional, outsider

lay-off noun <u>dismissal</u>, discharge, unemployment

lay off verb <u>dismiss</u>, discharge, let go, make redundant, pay off

lay on verb <u>provide</u>, cater (for), furnish, give, purvey, supply

layout noun <u>arrangement</u>, design, formation, outline, plan

lay out verb **1** <u>arrange</u>, design, display, exhibit, plan, spread out **2** Informal <u>spend</u>, disburse, expend, fork out (slang), invest, pay, shell out (informal) **3** Informal <u>knock out</u>, knock for six (informal), knock unconscious, KO or K.O. (slang)

laziness noun <u>idleness</u>, inactivity, indolence, slackness, sloth, sluggishness

lazy adjective **1** <u>idle</u>, inactive, indolent, inert, slack, slothful, slow, workshy **2** <u>lethargic</u>, drowsy, languid, languorous, sleepy, slow-moving, sluggish, somnolent, torpid

leach verb <u>extract</u>, drain, filter, percolate, seep, strain

lead verb **1** <u>guide</u>, conduct, escort, pilot, precede, show the way, steer, usher **2** <u>persuade</u>, cause, dispose, draw, incline, induce, influence, prevail, prompt **3** <u>command</u>, direct, govern, head, manage, preside over, supervise **4** <u>be ahead (of)</u>, blaze a trail, come first, exceed, excel, outdo, outstrip, surpass, transcend **5** <u>live</u>, experience, have, pass, spend, undergo **6** <u>result in</u>, bring on, cause, contribute, produce ♦ noun **7** <u>first place</u>, precedence, primacy, priority, supremacy, vanguard **8** <u>advantage</u>, edge, margin, start **9** <u>example</u>, direction, guidance, leadership, model **10** <u>clue</u>, hint, indication, suggestion **11** <u>leading role</u>, principal, protagonist, title role ♦ adjective **12** <u>main</u>, chief, first, foremost, head, leading,

premier, primary, prime, principal

leader noun <u>principal</u>, boss (informal), captain, chief, chieftain, commander, director, guide, head, ringleader, ruler

leadership noun 1 <u>guidance</u>, direction, domination, management, running, superintendency 2 <u>authority</u>, command, control, influence, initiative, pre-eminence, supremacy

leading adjective <u>main</u>, chief, dominant, first, foremost, greatest, highest, primary, principal

lead on verb <u>entice</u>, beguile, deceive, draw on, lure, seduce, string along (informal), tempt

lead up to verb <u>introduce</u>, pave the way, prepare for

leaf noun 1 <u>frond</u>, blade 2 <u>page</u>, folio, sheet ♦ verb 3 <u>leaf through</u> browse, flip, glance, riffle, skim, thumb (through)

leaflet noun <u>booklet</u>, brochure, circular, pamphlet

leafy adjective <u>green</u>, bosky (literary), shaded, shady, verdant

league noun 1 <u>association</u>, alliance, coalition, confederation, consortium, federation, fraternity, group, guild, partnership, union 2 <u>class</u>, category, level

leak noun 1 <u>hole</u>, aperture, chink, crack, crevice, fissure, opening, puncture 2 <u>drip</u>, leakage, percolation, seepage 3 <u>disclosure</u>, divulgence ♦ verb 4 <u>drip</u>, escape, exude, ooze, pass, percolate, seep, spill, trickle 5 <u>disclose</u>, divulge, give away,

let slip, make known, make public, pass on, reveal, tell

leaky adjective <u>punctured</u>, cracked, holey, leaking, perforated, porous, split

lean[1] verb 1 <u>rest</u>, be supported, prop, recline, repose 2 <u>bend</u>, heel, incline, slant, slope, tilt, tip 3 <u>tend</u>, be disposed to, be prone to, favour, prefer 4 <u>lean on</u> <u>depend on</u>, count on, have faith in, rely on, trust

lean[2] adjective 1 <u>slim</u>, angular, bony, gaunt, rangy, skinny, slender, spare, thin, wiry 2 <u>unproductive</u>, barren, meagre, poor, scanty, unfruitful

leaning noun <u>tendency</u>, bent, bias, disposition, inclination, partiality, penchant, predilection, proclivity, propensity

leap verb 1 <u>jump</u>, bounce, bound, hop, skip, spring ♦ noun 2 <u>jump</u>, bound, spring, vault 3 <u>increase</u>, escalation, rise, surge, upsurge, upswing

learn verb 1 <u>master</u>, grasp, pick up 2 <u>memorize</u>, commit to memory, get off pat, learn by heart 3 <u>discover</u>, ascertain, detect, discern, find out, gather, hear, understand

learned adjective <u>scholarly</u>, academic, erudite, highbrow, intellectual, versed, well-informed, well-read

learner noun <u>beginner</u>, apprentice, neophyte, novice, tyro

learning noun <u>knowledge</u>, culture, education, erudition, information, lore, scholarship, study, wisdom

lease verb hire, charter, let, loan, rent

leash noun lead, rein, tether

least adjective smallest, fewest, lowest, meanest, minimum, poorest, slightest, tiniest

leathery adjective tough, hard, rough

leave¹ verb 1 depart, decamp, disappear, exit, go away, make tracks, move, pull out, quit, retire, slope off, withdraw 2 forget, leave behind, mislay 3 cause, deposit, generate, produce, result in 4 give up, abandon, drop, relinquish, renounce, surrender 5 entrust, allot, assign, cede, commit, consign, give over, refer 6 bequeath, hand down, will

leave² noun 1 permission, allowance, authorization, concession, consent, dispensation, freedom, liberty, sanction 2 holiday, furlough, leave of absence, sabbatical, time off, vacation 3 parting, adieu, departure, farewell, goodbye, leave-taking, retirement, withdrawal

leave out verb omit, cast aside, disregard, exclude, ignore, neglect, overlook, reject

lecherous adjective lustful, lascivious, lewd, libidinous, licentious, prurient, randy (informal, chiefly Brit.), salacious

lecture noun 1 talk, address, discourse, instruction, lesson, speech 2 rebuke, dressing-down (informal), reprimand, reproof, scolding, talking-to (informal), telling off (informal) ♦ verb 3 talk, address, discourse, expound,

hold forth, speak, spout, teach 4 scold, admonish, berate, castigate, censure, reprimand, reprove, tell off (informal)

ledge noun shelf, mantle, projection, ridge, sill, step

leer noun, verb grin, gloat, goggle, ogle, smirk, squint, stare

lees plural noun sediment, deposit, dregs, grounds

leeway noun room, elbowroom, latitude, margin, play, scope, space

left adjective 1 left-hand, larboard (Nautical), port, sinistral 2 Of politics socialist, leftist, left-wing, radical

leftover noun remnant, oddment, scrap

left-wing adjective socialist, communist, radical, red (informal)

leg noun 1 limb, lower limb, member, pin (informal), stump (informal) 2 support, brace, prop, upright 3 stage, lap, part, portion, section, segment, stretch 4 pull someone's leg Informal tease, fool, kid (informal), make fun of, trick, wind up (Brit. slang)

legacy noun bequest, estate, gift, heirloom, inheritance

legal adjective 1 legitimate, allowed, authorized, constitutional, lawful, licit, permissible, sanctioned, valid 2 judicial, forensic, juridical

legality noun legitimacy, lawfulness, rightfulness, validity

legalize verb allow, approve, authorize, decriminalize, legitimate, legitimize, license, permit, sanction, validate

legation noun <u>delegation</u>, consulate, embassy, representation

legend noun 1 <u>myth</u>, fable, fiction, folk tale, saga, story, tale 2 <u>celebrity</u>, luminary, megastar (*informal*), phenomenon, prodigy 3 <u>inscription</u>, caption, motto

legendary adjective 1 <u>mythical</u>, apocryphal, fabled, fabulous, fictitious, romantic, traditional 2 <u>famous</u>, celebrated, famed, illustrious, immortal, renowned, well-known

legibility noun <u>clarity</u>, neatness, readability

legible adjective <u>clear</u>, decipherable, distinct, easy to read, neat, readable

legion noun 1 <u>army</u>, brigade, company, division, force, troop 2 <u>multitude</u>, drove, horde, host, mass, myriad, number, throng

legislation noun 1 <u>lawmaking</u>, enactment, prescription, regulation 2 <u>law</u>, act, bill, charter, measure, regulation, ruling, statute

legislative adjective <u>law-making</u>, judicial, law-giving

legislator noun <u>lawmaker</u>, lawgiver

legislature noun <u>parliament</u>, assembly, chamber, congress, senate

legitimate adjective 1 <u>legal</u>, authentic, authorized, genuine, kosher (*informal*), lawful, licit, rightful 2 <u>reasonable</u>, admissible, correct, justifiable, logical, sensible, valid, warranted, well-founded ♦ verb 3 <u>authorize</u>, legalize, legitimize, permit,

pronounce lawful, sanction

legitimize verb <u>legalize</u>, authorize, permit, sanction

leisure noun <u>spare time</u>, ease, freedom, free time, liberty, recreation, relaxation, rest

leisurely adjective <u>unhurried</u>, comfortable, easy, gentle, lazy, relaxed, slow

lend verb 1 <u>loan</u>, advance 2 <u>add</u>, bestow, confer, give, grant, impart, provide, supply 3 <u>lend itself to</u> suit, be appropriate, be serviceable

length noun 1 *Of linear extent* <u>distance</u>, extent, longitude, measure, reach, span 2 *Of time* <u>duration</u>, period, space, span, stretch, term 3 <u>piece</u>, measure, portion, section, segment 4 **at length: a** <u>in detail</u>, completely, fully, in depth, thoroughly, to the full **b** <u>for a long time</u>, for ages, for hours, interminably **c** <u>at last</u>, at long last, eventually, finally, in the end

lengthen verb <u>extend</u>, continue, draw out, elongate, expand, increase, prolong, protract, spin out, stretch

lengthy adjective <u>long</u>, drawn-out, extended, interminable, long-drawn-out, long-winded, prolonged, protracted, tedious

leniency noun <u>tolerance</u>, clemency, compassion, forbearance, indulgence, mercy, moderation, pity, quarter

lenient adjective <u>tolerant</u>, compassionate, forbearing, forgiving, indulgent, kind, merciful, sparing

lesbian adjective <u>homosexual</u>, gay, sapphic

less adjective **1** <u>smaller</u>, shorter ◆ preposition **2** <u>minus</u>, excepting, lacking, subtracting, without

lessen verb <u>reduce</u>, contract, decrease, diminish, ease, lower, minimize, narrow, shrink

lesser adjective <u>minor</u>, inferior, less important, lower, secondary

lesson noun **1** <u>class</u>, coaching, instruction, period, schooling, teaching, tutoring **2** <u>example</u>, deterrent, message, moral

let[1] verb **1** <u>allow</u>, authorize, entitle, give permission, give the go-ahead, permit, sanction, tolerate **2** <u>lease</u>, hire, rent

let[2] noun <u>hindrance</u>, constraint, impediment, interference, obstacle, obstruction, prohibition, restriction

letdown noun <u>disappointment</u>, anticlimax, blow, comedown (informal), setback, washout (informal)

let down verb <u>disappoint</u>, disenchant, disillusion, dissatisfy, fail, fall short, leave in the lurch, leave stranded

lethal adjective <u>deadly</u>, dangerous, destructive, devastating, fatal, mortal, murderous, virulent

lethargic adjective <u>sluggish</u>, apathetic, drowsy, dull, languid, listless, sleepy, slothful

lethargy noun <u>sluggishness</u>, apathy, drowsiness, inertia, languor, lassitude, listlessness, sleepiness, sloth

let off verb **1** <u>fire</u>, detonate, discharge, explode **2** <u>emit</u>,

exude, give off, leak, release **3** <u>excuse</u>, absolve, discharge, exempt, exonerate, forgive, pardon, release, spare

let on verb <u>reveal</u>, admit, disclose, divulge, give away, let the cat out of the bag (informal), make known, say

let out verb **1** <u>emit</u>, give vent to, produce **2** <u>release</u>, discharge, free, let go, liberate

letter noun **1** <u>character</u>, sign, symbol **2** <u>message</u>, communication, dispatch, epistle, line, missive, note

let-up noun <u>lessening</u>, break, breathing space, interval, lull, pause, remission, respite, slackening

let up verb <u>stop</u>, abate, decrease, diminish, ease (up), moderate, relax, slacken, subside

level adjective **1** <u>horizontal</u>, flat **2** <u>even</u>, consistent, plain, smooth, uniform **3** <u>equal</u>, balanced, commensurate, comparable, equivalent, even, neck and neck, on a par, proportionate ◆ verb **4** <u>flatten</u>, even off or out, plane, smooth **5** <u>equalize</u>, balance, even up **6** <u>raze</u>, bulldoze, demolish, destroy, devastate, flatten, knock down, pull down, tear down **7** <u>direct</u>, aim, focus, point, train ◆ noun **8** <u>position</u>, achievement, degree, grade, rank, stage, standard, standing, status **9 on the level** Informal <u>honest</u>, above board, fair, genuine, square, straight

level-headed adjective <u>steady</u>, balanced, calm, collected, composed, cool, sensible, unflappable (*informal*)

lever noun **1** <u>handle</u>, bar ◆verb **2** <u>prise</u>, force

leverage noun <u>influence</u>, authority, clout (*informal*), pull (*informal*), weight

levity noun <u>light-heartedness</u>, facetiousness, flippancy, frivolity, silliness, skittishness, triviality

levy verb **1** <u>impose</u>, charge, collect, demand, exact **2** <u>conscript</u>, call up, mobilize, muster, raise ◆noun **3** <u>imposition</u>, assessment, collection, exaction, gathering **4** <u>tax</u>, duty, excise, fee, tariff, toll

lewd adjective <u>indecent</u>, bawdy, lascivious, libidinous, licentious, lustful, obscene, pornographic, smutty, wanton

lewdness noun <u>indecency</u>, bawdiness, carnality, debauchery, depravity, lasciviousness, lechery, licentiousness, obscenity, pornography, wantonness

liability noun **1** <u>responsibility</u>, accountability, answerability, culpability **2** <u>debt</u>, debit, obligation **3** <u>disadvantage</u>, burden, drawback, encumbrance, handicap, hindrance, inconvenience, millstone, nuisance

liable adjective **1** <u>responsible</u>, accountable, answerable, obligated **2** <u>vulnerable</u>, exposed, open, subject, susceptible **3** <u>likely</u>, apt, disposed, inclined, prone, tending

liaise verb <u>link</u>, communicate, keep contact, mediate

liaison noun **1** <u>communication</u>, connection, contact, hook-up, interchange **2** <u>affair</u>, amour, entanglement, intrigue, love affair, romance

liar noun <u>falsifier</u>, fabricator, fibber, perjurer

libel noun **1** <u>defamation</u>, aspersion, calumny, denigration, smear ◆verb **2** <u>defame</u>, blacken, malign, revile, slur, smear, vilify

libellous adjective <u>defamatory</u>, derogatory, false, injurious, malicious, scurrilous, untrue

liberal adjective **1** <u>progressive</u>, libertarian, radical, reformist **2** <u>generous</u>, beneficent, bountiful, charitable, kind, open-handed, open-hearted, unstinting **3** <u>tolerant</u>, broad-minded, indulgent, permissive **4** <u>abundant</u>, ample, bountiful, copious, handsome, lavish, munificent, plentiful, profuse, rich

liberality noun **1** <u>generosity</u>, beneficence, benevolence, bounty, charity, kindness, largesse or largess, munificence, philanthropy **2** <u>toleration</u>, broad-mindedness, latitude, liberalism, libertarianism, permissiveness

liberalize verb <u>relax</u>, ease, loosen, moderate, modify, slacken, soften

liberate verb <u>free</u>, deliver, emancipate, let loose, let out, release, rescue, set free

liberation noun <u>deliverance</u>, emancipation, freedom, freeing, liberty, release

liberator noun <u>deliverer</u>, emancipator, freer, redeemer, rescuer, saviour

libertine noun reprobate, debauchee, lecher, profligate, rake, roué, sensualist, voluptuary, womanizer

liberty noun 1 freedom, autonomy, emancipation, immunity, independence, liberation, release, self-determination, sovereignty 2 impertinence, impropriety, impudence, insolence, presumption 3 **at liberty** free, on the loose, unrestricted

libidinous adjective lustful, carnal, debauched, lascivious, lecherous, randy (informal, chiefly Brit.), sensual, wanton

licence noun 1 certificate, charter, permit, warrant 2 permission, authority, authorization, blank cheque, carte blanche, dispensation, entitlement, exemption, immunity, leave, liberty, right 3 latitude, freedom, independence, leeway, liberty 4 laxity, excess, immoderation, indulgence, irresponsibility

license verb permit, accredit, allow, authorize, certify, empower, sanction, warrant

licentious adjective promiscuous, abandoned, debauched, dissolute, immoral, lascivious, lustful, sensual, wanton

lick verb 1 taste, lap, tongue 2 Of flames flicker, dart, flick, play over, ripple, touch 3 Slang beat, defeat, master, outdo, outstrip, overcome, rout, trounce, vanquish ♦ noun 4 dab, bit, stroke, touch 5 Informal pace, clip (informal), rate, speed

lie¹ verb 1 falsify, dissimulate, equivocate, fabricate, fib, prevaricate, tell untruths ♦ noun 2 falsehood, deceit, fabrication, fib, fiction, invention, prevarication, untruth

lie² verb 1 recline, loll, lounge, repose, rest, sprawl, stretch out 2 be situated, be, be placed, exist, remain

life noun 1 being, sentience, vitality 2 existence, being, lifetime, span, time 3 biography, autobiography, confessions, history, life story, memoirs, story 4 behaviour, conduct, life style, way of life 5 liveliness, animation, energy, high spirits, spirit, verve, vigour, vitality, vivacity, zest

lifeless adjective 1 dead, deceased, defunct, extinct, inanimate 2 dull, colourless, flat, lacklustre, lethargic, listless, sluggish, wooden 3 unconscious, comatose, dead to the world (informal), insensible

lifelike adjective realistic, authentic, exact, faithful, natural, true-to-life, vivid

lifelong adjective long-standing, enduring, lasting, long-lasting, perennial, persistent

lifetime noun existence, career, day(s), span, time

lift verb 1 raise, draw up, elevate, hoist, pick up, uplift, upraise 2 revoke, annul, cancel, countermand, end, remove, rescind, stop, terminate 3 disappear, be dispelled, disperse, dissipate, vanish ♦ noun 4 ride, drive, run 5 boost, encouragement, fillip, pick-me-up, shot in the arm *(informal)* **6** <u>elevator</u> *(chiefly U.S.)*

light[1] *noun* **1** <u>brightness</u>, brilliance, glare, gleam, glint, glow, illumination, luminosity, radiance, shine **2** <u>lamp</u>, beacon, candle, flare, lantern, taper, torch **3** <u>aspect</u>, angle, context, interpretation, point of view, slant, vantage point, viewpoint **4** <u>match</u>, flame, lighter ♦ *adjective* **5** <u>bright</u>, brilliant, illuminated, luminous, lustrous, shining, well-lit **6** <u>pale</u>, bleached, blond, faded, fair, pastel ♦ *verb* **7** <u>ignite</u>, inflame, kindle **8** <u>illuminate</u>, brighten, light up

light[2] *adjective* **1** <u>insubstantial</u>, airy, buoyant, flimsy, portable, slight, underweight **2** <u>weak</u>, faint, gentle, indistinct, mild, moderate, slight, soft **3** <u>insignificant</u>, inconsequential, inconsiderable, scanty, slight, small, trifling, trivial **4** <u>nimble</u>, agile, graceful, lithe, sprightly, sylphlike **5** <u>light-hearted</u>, amusing, entertaining, frivolous, funny, humorous, witty **6** <u>digestible</u>, frugal, modest ♦ *verb* **7** <u>settle</u>, alight, land, perch **8** <u>light on</u> or <u>upon</u> <u>come across</u>, chance upon, discover, encounter, find, happen upon, hit upon, stumble on

lighten[1] *verb* <u>brighten</u>, become light, illuminate, irradiate, light up

lighten[2] *verb* **1** <u>ease</u>, allay, alleviate, ameliorate, assuage, lessen, mitigate, reduce, relieve **2** <u>cheer</u>, brighten, buoy up, lift, perk up, revive

light-headed *adjective* <u>faint</u>, dizzy, giddy, hazy, vertiginous,

woozy *(informal)*

light-hearted *adjective* <u>carefree</u>, blithe, cheerful, happy-go-lucky, jolly, jovial, playful, upbeat *(informal)*

lightly *adverb* **1** <u>gently</u>, delicately, faintly, slightly, softly **2** <u>moderately</u>, sparingly, sparsely, thinly **3** <u>easily</u>, effortlessly, readily, simply **4** <u>carelessly</u>, breezily, flippantly, frivolously, heedlessly, thoughtlessly

lightweight *adjective* <u>unimportant</u>, inconsequential, insignificant, paltry, petty, slight, trifling, trivial, worthless

likable, likeable *adjective* <u>attractive</u>, agreeable, amiable, appealing, charming, engaging, nice, pleasant, sympathetic

like[1] *adjective* <u>similar</u>, akin, alike, analogous, corresponding, equivalent, identical, parallel, same

like[2] *verb* **1** <u>enjoy</u>, be fond of, be keen on, be partial to, delight in, go for, love, relish, revel in **2** <u>admire</u>, appreciate, approve, cherish, esteem, hold dear, prize, take to **3** <u>wish</u>, care to, choose, desire, fancy, feel inclined, prefer, want

likelihood *noun* <u>probability</u>, chance, possibility, prospect

likely *adjective* **1** <u>inclined</u>, apt, disposed, liable, prone, tending **2** <u>probable</u>, anticipated, expected, odds-on, on the cards, to be expected **3** <u>plausible</u>, believable, credible, feasible, possible, reasonable **4** <u>promising</u>, hopeful, up-and-coming

liken verb compare, equate, match, parallel, relate, set beside

likeness noun 1 resemblance, affinity, correspondence, similarity 2 portrait, depiction, effigy, image, picture, representation

likewise adverb similarly, in like manner, in the same way

liking noun fondness, affection, inclination, love, partiality, penchant, preference, soft spot, taste, weakness

limb noun 1 part, appendage, arm, extremity, leg, member, wing 2 branch, bough, offshoot, projection, spur

limelight noun publicity, attention, celebrity, fame, prominence, public eye, recognition, stardom, the spotlight

limit noun 1 breaking point, deadline, end, ultimate 2 boundary, border, edge, frontier, perimeter ♦ verb 3 restrict, bound, check, circumscribe, confine, curb, ration, restrain

limitation noun restriction, check, condition, constraint, control, curb, qualification, reservation, restraint

limited adjective restricted, bounded, checked, circumscribed, confined, constrained, controlled, curbed, finite

limitless adjective infinite, boundless, countless, endless, inexhaustible, unbounded, unlimited, untold, vast

limp¹ verb 1 hobble, falter, hop,

shamble, shuffle ♦ noun 2 lameness, hobble

limp² adjective floppy, drooping, flabby, flaccid, pliable, slack, soft

line noun 1 stroke, band, groove, mark, score, scratch, streak, stripe 2 wrinkle, crease, crow's foot, furrow, mark 3 boundary, border, borderline, edge, frontier, limit 4 string, cable, cord, rope, thread, wire 5 trajectory, course, direction, path, route, track 6 job, area, business, calling, employment, field, occupation, profession, specialization, trade 7 row, column, file, procession, queue, rank 8 in line for due for, in the running for ♦ verb 9 mark, crease, furrow, rule, score 10 border, bound, edge, fringe

lineaments plural noun features, countenance, face, physiognomy

lined adjective 1 ruled, feint 2 wrinkled, furrowed, wizened, worn

lines plural noun words, part, script

line-up noun arrangement, array, row, selection, team

linger verb 1 stay, hang around, loiter, remain, stop, tarry, wait 2 delay, dally, dawdle, drag one's feet or heels, idle, take one's time

link noun 1 component, constituent, element, member, part, piece 2 connection, affinity, association, attachment, bond, relationship, tie-up ♦ verb 3 fasten, attach, bind, connect, couple, join, tie, unite 4 associate, bracket, connect, identify, relate

lip noun **1** edge, brim, brink, margin, rim **2** Slang impudence, backchat (informal), cheek (informal), effrontery, impertinence, insolence

liquid noun **1** fluid, juice, solution ♦ adjective **2** fluid, aqueous, flowing, melted, molten, running, runny **3** Of assets convertible, negotiable

liquidate verb **1** pay, clear, discharge, honour, pay off, settle, square **2** dissolve, abolish, annul, cancel, terminate **3** kill, destroy, dispatch, eliminate, exterminate, get rid of, murder, wipe out (informal)

liquor noun **1** alcohol, booze (informal), drink, hard stuff (informal), spirits, strong drink **2** juice, broth, extract, liquid, stock

list[1] noun **1** register, catalogue, directory, index, inventory, record, roll, series, tally ♦ verb **2** tabulate, catalogue, enter, enumerate, itemize, record, register

list[2] verb **1** lean, careen, heel over, incline, tilt, tip ♦ noun **2** tilt, cant, leaning, slant

listen verb **1** hear, attend, lend an ear, prick up one's ears **2** pay attention, heed, mind, obey, observe, take notice

listless adjective languid, apathetic, indifferent, indolent, lethargic, sluggish

literacy noun education, knowledge, learning

literal adjective **1** exact, accurate, close, faithful, strict, verbatim, word for word **2** actual, bona fide, genuine, plain, real, simple, true, unvarnished

literally adverb strictly, actually, exactly, faithfully, precisely, really, to the letter, truly, verbatim, word for word

literary adjective well-read, bookish, erudite, formal, learned, scholarly

literate adjective educated, informed, knowledgeable

literature noun writings, letters, lore

lithe adjective supple, flexible, limber, lissom(e), loose-limbed, pliable

litigant noun claimant, party, plaintiff

litigate verb sue, go to court, press charges, prosecute

litigation noun lawsuit, action, case, prosecution

litter noun **1** rubbish, debris, detritus, garbage (chiefly U.S.), muck, refuse, trash **2** brood, offspring, progeny, young ♦ verb **3** clutter, derange, disarrange, disorder, mess up **4** scatter, strew

little adjective **1** small, diminutive, miniature, minute, petite, short, tiny, wee **2** young, babyish, immature, infant, junior, undeveloped ♦ adverb **3** hardly, barely **4** rarely, hardly ever, not often, scarcely, seldom ♦ noun **5** bit, fragment, hint, particle, speck, spot, touch, trace

live[1] verb **1** exist, be, be alive, breathe **2** persist, last, prevail **3** dwell, abide, inhabit, lodge, occupy, reside, settle **4** survive, endure, get along, make ends meet, subsist, support oneself **5** thrive, flourish, prosper

live² adjective **1** living, alive, animate, breathing **2** topical, burning, controversial, current, hot, pertinent, pressing, prevalent **3** burning, active, alight, blazing, glowing, hot, ignited, smouldering

livelihood noun occupation, bread and butter (informal), employment, job, living, work

liveliness noun energy, animation, boisterousness, dynamism, spirit, sprightliness, vitality, vivacity

lively adjective **1** vigorous, active, agile, alert, brisk, energetic, keen, perky, quick, sprightly **2** animated, cheerful, chirpy (informal), sparky, spirited, upbeat (informal), vivacious **3** vivid, bright, colourful, exciting, forceful, invigorating, refreshing, stimulating

liven up verb stir, animate, brighten, buck up (informal), enliven, perk up, rouse

liverish adjective **1** sick, bilious, queasy **2** irritable, crotchety (informal), crusty, disagreeable, grumpy, ill-humoured, irascible, splenetic, tetchy

livery noun costume, attire, clothing, dress, garb, regalia, suit, uniform

livid adjective **1** Informal angry, beside oneself, enraged, fuming, furious, incensed, indignant, infuriated, outraged **2** discoloured, black-and-blue, bruised, contused, purple

living adjective **1** alive, active, breathing, existing **2** current, active, contemporary, extant, in use ♦ noun **3** existence, being,

existing, life, subsistence **4** life style, way of life

load noun **1** cargo, consignment, freight, shipment **2** burden, albatross, encumbrance, millstone, onus, trouble, weight, worry ♦ verb **3** fill, cram, freight, heap, pack, pile, stack, stuff **4** burden, encumber, oppress, saddle with, weigh down, worry **5** Of firearms make ready, charge, prime

loaded adjective **1** weighted, biased, distorted **2** tricky, artful, insidious, manipulative, prejudicial **3** Slang rich, affluent, flush (informal), moneyed, wealthy, well-heeled (informal), well off, well-to-do

loaf¹ noun **1** lump, block, cake, cube, slab **2** Slang head, gumption (Brit. informal), nous (Brit. slang), sense

loaf² verb idle, laze, lie around, loiter, lounge around, take it easy

loan noun **1** advance, credit ♦ verb **2** lend, advance, let out

loath, loth adjective unwilling, averse, disinclined, opposed, reluctant

loathe verb hate, abhor, abominate, despise, detest, dislike

loathing noun hatred, abhorrence, antipathy, aversion, detestation, disgust, repugnance, repulsion, revulsion

loathsome adjective hateful, abhorrent, detestable, disgusting, nauseating, obnoxious, odious, offensive, repugnant, repulsive, revolting, vile

lobby noun **1** corridor, entrance

hall, foyer, hallway, passage, porch, vestibule **2** <u>pressure</u> <u>group</u> ♦ *verb* **3** <u>campaign</u>, influence, persuade, press, pressure, promote, push, urge

local *adjective* **1** regional, provincial **2** <u>restricted</u> (*chiefly U.S.*), confined, limited ♦ *noun* **3** <u>resident</u>, inhabitant, native

locality *noun* **1** <u>neighbourhood</u>, area, district, neck of the woods (*informal*), region, vicinity **2** <u>site</u>, locale, location, place, position, scene, setting, spot

localize *verb* <u>restrict</u>, circumscribe, confine, contain, delimit, limit

locate *verb* **1** <u>find</u>, come across, detect, discover, pin down, pinpoint, track down, unearth **2** <u>place</u>, establish, fix, put, seat, set, settle, situate

location *noun* <u>position</u>, locale, place, point, site, situation, spot, venue

lock[1] *noun* **1** <u>fastening</u>, bolt, clasp, padlock ♦ *verb* **2** <u>fasten</u>, bolt, close, seal, secure, shut **3** <u>unite</u>, clench, engage, entangle, entwine, join, link **4** <u>embrace</u>, clasp, clutch, encircle, enclose, grasp, hug, press

lock[2] *noun* <u>strand</u>, curl, ringlet, tress, tuft

lockup *noun* <u>prison</u>, cell, jail or gaol

lock up *verb* <u>imprison</u>, cage, confine, detain, incarcerate, jail, put behind bars, shut up

lodge *noun* **1** <u>cabin</u>, chalet, cottage, gatehouse, hut, shelter **2** <u>society</u>, branch, chapter, club,

group ♦ *verb* **3** <u>stay</u>, board, room **4** <u>stick</u>, come to rest, imbed, implant **5** <u>register</u>, file, put on record, submit

lodger *noun* <u>tenant</u>, boarder, paying guest, resident

lodging *noun, often plural* <u>accommodation</u>, abode, apartments, digs (*Brit. informal*), quarters, residence, rooms, shelter

lofty *adjective* **1** <u>high</u>, elevated, raised, soaring, towering **2** <u>noble</u>, dignified, distinguished, elevated, exalted, grand, illustrious, renowned **3** <u>haughty</u>, arrogant, condescending, disdainful, patronizing, proud, supercilious

log *noun* **1** <u>stump</u>, block, chunk, trunk **2** <u>record</u>, account, journal, logbook ♦ *verb* **3** <u>chop</u>, cut, fell, hew **4** <u>record</u>, chart, note, register, set down

loggerheads *plural noun* **at loggerheads** <u>quarrelling</u>, at daggers drawn, at each other's throats, at odds, feuding, in dispute, opposed

logic *noun* <u>reason</u>, good sense, sense

logical *adjective* **1** <u>rational</u>, clear, cogent, coherent, consistent, sound, valid, well-organized **2** <u>reasonable</u>, plausible, sensible, wise

loiter *verb* <u>linger</u>, dally, dawdle, dilly-dally (*informal*), hang about or around, idle, loaf, skulk

loll *verb* **1** <u>lounge</u>, loaf, recline, relax, slouch, slump, sprawl **2** <u>droop</u>, dangle, drop, flap, flop, hang, sag

lone adjective solitary, one, only, single, sole, unaccompanied

loneliness noun solitude, desolation, isolation, seclusion

lonely adjective 1 abandoned, destitute, forlorn, forsaken, friendless, lonesome 2 solitary, alone, apart, companionless, isolated, lone, single, withdrawn 3 remote, deserted, desolate, godforsaken, isolated, out-of-the-way, secluded, unfrequented, uninhabited

loner noun individualist, lone wolf, maverick, outsider, recluse

lonesome adjective lonely, companionless, desolate, dreary, forlorn, friendless, gloomy

long[1] adjective 1 elongated, expanded, extended, extensive, far-reaching, lengthy, spread out, stretched 2 prolonged, interminable, lengthy, lingering, long-drawn-out, protracted, sustained

long[2] verb desire, crave, hanker, itch, lust, pine, want, wish, yearn

longing noun desire, ambition, aspiration, craving, hope, itch, thirst, urge, wish, yearning, yen (informal)

long-lived adjective long-lasting, enduring

long shot noun outsider, dark horse

long-standing adjective established, abiding, enduring, fixed, long-established, long-lasting, time-honoured

long-suffering adjective uncomplaining, easy-going, forbearing, forgiving, patient, resigned, stoical, tolerant

long-winded adjective rambling, lengthy, long-drawn-out, prolix, prolonged, repetitious, tedious, tiresome, verbose, wordy

look verb 1 see, contemplate, examine, eye, gaze, glance, observe, scan, study, survey, view, watch 2 seem, appear, look like, strike one as 3 face, front, overlook 4 hope, anticipate, await, expect, reckon on 5 search, forage, hunt, seek ♦ noun 6 view, examination, gaze, glance, glimpse, inspection, observation, peek, sight 7 appearance, air, aspect, bearing, countenance, demeanour, expression, manner, semblance

look after verb take care of, attend to, care for, guard, keep an eye on, mind, nurse, protect, supervise, take charge of, tend

look down on verb disdain, contemn, despise, scorn, sneer, spurn

look forward to verb anticipate, await, expect, hope for, long for, look for, wait for

lookout noun 1 vigil, guard, readiness, watch 2 watchman, guard, sentinel, sentry 3 watchtower, observation post, observatory, post 4 Informal concern, business, worry

look out verb be careful, beware, keep an eye out, pay attention, watch out

look up verb 1 research, find, hunt for, search for, seek out, track down 2 improve, get better, perk up, pick up, progress, shape up (informal) 3 visit, call on, drop in on

loom (*informal*), look in on **4 look up to** respect, admire, defer to, esteem, honour, revere

loom verb appear, bulk, emerge, hover, impend, menace, take shape, threaten

loop noun **1** curve, circle, coil, curl, ring, spiral, twirl, twist, whorl ◆ verb **2** twist, coil, curl, knot, roll, spiral, turn, wind round

loophole noun let-out, escape, excuse

loose adjective **1** untied, free, insecure, unattached, unbound, unfastened, unfettered, unrestricted **2** slack, easy, relaxed, sloppy **3** vague, ill-defined, imprecise, inaccurate, indistinct, inexact, rambling, random **4** promiscuous, abandoned, debauched, dissipated, dissolute, fast, immoral, profligate ◆ verb **5** free, detach, disconnect, liberate, release, set free, unfasten, unleash, untie

loosen verb **1** untie, detach, separate, undo, unloose **2** free, liberate, release, set free **3 loosen up** relax, ease up or off, go easy (*informal*), let up, soften

loot noun **1** plunder, booty, goods, haul, prize, spoils, swag (*slang*) ◆ verb **2** plunder, despoil, pillage, raid, ransack, ravage, rifle, rob, sack

lopsided adjective crooked, askew, asymmetrical, awry, cockeyed, disproportionate, skewwhiff (*Brit. informal*), squint, unbalanced, uneven, warped

lord noun **1** master, commander,

governor, leader, liege, overlord, ruler, superior **2** nobleman, earl, noble, peer, viscount **3 Our Lord** or **the Lord** Jesus Christ, Christ, God, Jehovah, the Almighty ◆ verb **4 lord it over** order around, boss around (*informal*), domineer, pull rank, put on airs, swagger

lordly adjective proud, arrogant, condescending, disdainful, domineering, haughty, high-handed, imperious, lofty, overbearing

lore noun traditions, beliefs, doctrine, sayings, teaching, wisdom

lose verb **1** mislay, be deprived of, drop, forget, misplace **2** forfeit, miss, pass up (*informal*), yield **3** be defeated, come to grief, lose out

loser noun failure, also-ran, dud (*informal*), flop (*informal*)

loss noun **1** defeat, failure, forfeiture, mislaying, squandering, waste **2** damage, cost, destruction, harm, hurt, injury, ruin **3** sometimes plural deficit, debit, debt, deficiency, depletion **4 at a loss** confused, at one's wits' end, baffled, bewildered, helpless, nonplussed, perplexed, puzzled, stumped

lost adjective **1** missing, disappeared, mislaid, misplaced, vanished, wayward **2** off-course, adrift, astray, at sea, disoriented, off-track

lot noun **1** collection, assortment, batch, bunch (*informal*), consignment, crowd, group, quantity, set **2** destiny, accident, chance, doom, fate, fortune **3 a lot** or **lots** plenty, abundance, a great deal, heap(s), load(s) (*informal*), masses (*informal*), piles (*informal*), scores, stack(s)

loth *see* LOATH

lotion *noun* cream, balm, embrocation, liniment, salve, solution

lottery *noun* **1** raffle, draw, sweepstake **2** gamble, chance, hazard, risk, toss-up (*informal*)

loud *adjective* **1** noisy, blaring, booming, clamorous, deafening, ear-splitting, forte (*Music*), resounding, thundering, tumultuous, vociferous **2** garish, brash, flamboyant, flashy, gaudy, glaring, lurid, showy

loudly *adverb* noisily, deafeningly, fortissimo (*Music*), lustily, shrilly, uproariously, vehemently, vigorously, vociferously

lounge *verb* relax, laze, lie about, loaf, loiter, loll, sprawl, take it easy

lout *noun* oaf, boor, dolt, lummox (*informal*), yob or yobbo (*Brit. slang*)

lovable, loveable *adjective* endearing, adorable, amiable, charming, cute, delightful, enchanting, likable or likeable, lovely, sweet

love *verb* **1** adore, cherish, dote on, hold dear, idolize, prize, treasure, worship **2** enjoy, appreciate, delight in, like, relish, savour, take pleasure in ♦ *noun* **3** passion, adoration, affection, ardour, attachment, devotion, infatuation, tenderness, warmth **4** liking, devotion, enjoyment, fondness, inclination, partiality,

relish, soft spot, taste, weakness **5** beloved, darling, dear, dearest, lover, sweetheart, truelove **6 in love** enamoured, besotted, charmed, enraptured, infatuated, smitten

love affair *noun* romance, affair, amour, intrigue, liaison, relationship

lovely *adjective* **1** attractive, adorable, beautiful, charming, comely, exquisite, graceful, handsome, pretty **2** enjoyable, agreeable, delightful, engaging, nice, pleasant, pleasing

lover *noun* sweetheart, admirer, beloved, boyfriend or girlfriend, flame (*informal*), mistress, suitor

loving *adjective* affectionate, amorous, dear, devoted, doting, fond, tender, warm-hearted

low *adjective* **1** small, little, short, squat, stunted **2** inferior, deficient, inadequate, poor, second-rate, shoddy **3** coarse, common, crude, disreputable, rough, rude, undignified, vulgar **4** dejected, depressed, despondent, disheartened, downcast, down in the dumps (*informal*), fed up, gloomy, glum, miserable **5** ill, debilitated, frail, stricken, weak **6** quiet, gentle, hushed, muffled, muted, soft, subdued, whispered

lowdown *noun Informal* information, gen (*Brit. informal*), info (*informal*), inside story, intelligence

lower *adjective* **1** minor, inferior, junior, lesser, secondary, second-class, smaller, subordinate **2** reduced, curtailed, decreased, diminished, lessened

◆ *verb* **3** drop, depress, fall, let down, sink, submerge, take down **4** lessen, cut, decrease, diminish, minimize, prune, reduce, slash

low-key *adjective* subdued, muted, quiet, restrained, toned down, understated

lowly *adjective* humble, meek, mild, modest, unassuming

low-spirited *adjective* depressed, dejected, despondent, dismal, down, down-hearted, fed up, low, miserable, sad

loyal *adjective* faithful, constant, dependable, devoted, dutiful, staunch, steadfast, true, trustworthy, trusty, unwavering

loyalty *noun* faithfulness, allegiance, constancy, dependability, devotion, fidelity, staunchness, steadfastness, trustworthiness

lubricate *verb* oil, grease, smear

lucid *adjective* **1** clear, comprehensible, explicit, intelligible, transparent **2** translucent, clear, crystalline, diaphanous, glassy, limpid, pellucid, transparent **3** clear-headed, all there, *compos mentis*, in one's right mind, rational, sane

luck *noun* **1** fortune, accident, chance, destiny, fate **2** good fortune, advantage, blessing, godsend, prosperity, serendipity, success, windfall

luckily *adverb* fortunately, favourably, happily, opportunely, propitiously, providentially

luckless *adjective* ill-fated, cursed, doomed, hapless, hopeless,

jinxed, unfortunate, unlucky

lucky *adjective* fortunate, advantageous, blessed, charmed, favoured, jammy (*Brit. slang*), serendipitous, successful

lucrative *adjective* profitable, advantageous, fruitful, productive, remunerative, well-paid

lucre *noun* money, gain, mammon, pelf, profit, riches, spoils, wealth

ludicrous *adjective* ridiculous, absurd, crazy, farcical, laughable, nonsensical, outlandish, preposterous, silly

luggage *noun* baggage, bags, cases, gear, impedimenta, paraphernalia, suitcases, things

lugubrious *adjective* gloomy, doleful, melancholy, mournful, sad, serious, sombre, sorrowful, woebegone

lukewarm *adjective* **1** tepid, warm **2** half-hearted, apathetic, cool, indifferent, unenthusiastic, unresponsive

lull *verb* **1** calm, allay, pacify, quell, soothe, subdue, tranquillize ◆ *noun* **2** respite, calm, hush, let-up (*informal*), pause, quiet, silence

lumber[1] *noun* **1** junk, clutter, jumble, refuse, rubbish, trash ◆ *verb* **2** *Informal* burden, encumber, land, load, saddle

lumber[2] *verb* plod, shamble, shuffle, stump, trudge, trundle, waddle

lumbering *adjective* awkward, clumsy, heavy, hulking, ponderous, ungainly

luminous *adjective* bright,

glowing, illuminated, luminescent, lustrous, radiant, shining

lump noun 1 piece, ball, chunk, hunk, mass, nugget 2 swelling, bulge, bump, growth, hump, protrusion, tumour ♦ verb 3 group, collect, combine, conglomerate, consolidate, mass, pool

lumpy adjective bumpy, knobbly, uneven

lunacy noun 1 insanity, dementia, derangement, madness, mania, psychosis 2 foolishness, absurdity, craziness, folly, foolhardiness, madness, stupidity

lunatic adjective 1 irrational, crackbrained, crackpot (informal), crazy, daft, deranged, insane, mad ♦ noun 2 madman, maniac, nutcase (slang), psychopath

lunge noun 1 thrust, charge, jab, pounce, spring, swing ♦ verb 2 pounce, charge, dive, leap, plunge, thrust

lurch verb 1 tilt, heave, heel, lean, list, pitch, rock, roll 2 stagger, reel, stumble, sway, totter, weave

lure verb 1 tempt, allure, attract, draw, ensnare, entice, invite, seduce ♦ noun 2 temptation, allurement, attraction, bait, carrot (informal), enticement, incentive, inducement

lurid adjective 1 sensational, graphic, melodramatic, shocking, vivid 2 glaring, intense

lurk verb hide, conceal oneself, lie in wait, prowl, skulk, slink, sneak

luscious adjective delicious,

appetizing, juicy, mouth-watering, palatable, succulent, sweet, toothsome

lush adjective 1 abundant, dense, flourishing, green, rank, verdant 2 luxurious, elaborate, extravagant, grand, lavish, opulent, ornate, palatial, plush (informal), sumptuous

lust noun 1 lechery, lasciviousness, lewdness, sensuality 2 appetite, craving, desire, greed, longing, passion, thirst ♦ verb 3 desire, covet, crave, hunger for or after, want, yearn

lustre noun 1 sparkle, gleam, glint, glitter, gloss, glow, sheen, shimmer, shine 2 glory, distinction, fame, honour, prestige, renown

lusty adjective vigorous, energetic, healthy, hearty, powerful, robust, strong, sturdy, virile

luxurious adjective sumptuous, comfortable, expensive, lavish, magnificent, opulent, plush (informal), rich, splendid

luxury noun 1 opulence, affluence, hedonism, richness, splendour, sumptuousness 2 extravagance, extra, frill, indulgence, treat

lying noun 1 dishonesty, deceit, mendacity, perjury, untruthfulness ♦ adjective 2 deceitful, dishonest, false, mendacious, perfidious, treacherous, two-faced, untruthful

lyrical adjective enthusiastic, effusive, impassioned, inspired, poetic, rhapsodic

M m

macabre adjective <u>gruesome</u>, dreadful, eerie, frightening, ghastly, ghostly, ghoulish, grim, grisly, morbid

machiavellian adjective <u>scheming</u>, astute, crafty, cunning, cynical, double-dealing, opportunist, sly, underhand, unscrupulous

machine noun 1 <u>appliance</u>, apparatus, contraption, contrivance, device, engine, instrument, mechanism, tool 2 <u>system</u>, machinery, organization, setup (informal), structure

machinery noun <u>equipment</u>, apparatus, gear, instruments, tackle, tools

macho adjective <u>manly</u>, chauvinist, masculine, virile

mad adjective 1 <u>insane</u>, crazy (informal), demented, deranged, non compos mentis, nuts (slang), of unsound mind, out of one's mind, psychotic, raving, unhinged, unstable 2 <u>foolish</u>, absurd, asinine, daft (informal), foolhardy, irrational, nonsensical, preposterous, senseless, wild 3 Informal <u>angry</u>, berserk, enraged, furious, incensed, livid (informal), wild 4 <u>enthusiastic</u>, ardent, avid, crazy (informal), fanatical, impassioned, infatuated, wild 5 <u>frenzied</u>, excited, frenetic, uncontrolled, unrestrained, wild 6 <u>like mad</u> Informal <u>energetically</u>,

enthusiastically, excitedly, furiously, rapidly, speedily, violently, wildly

madcap adjective <u>reckless</u>, crazy, foolhardy, hare-brained, imprudent, impulsive, rash, thoughtless

madden verb <u>infuriate</u>, annoy, derange, drive one crazy, enrage, incense, inflame, irritate, upset

madly adverb 1 <u>insanely</u>, crazily, deliriously, distractedly, frantically, frenziedly, hysterically 2 <u>foolishly</u>, absurdly, irrationally, ludicrously, senselessly, wildly 3 <u>energetically</u>, excitedly, furiously, like mad (informal), recklessly, speedily, wildly 4 Informal <u>passionately</u>, desperately, devotedly, intensely, to distraction

madman or **madwoman** noun <u>lunatic</u>, maniac, nutcase (slang), psycho (slang), psychopath

madness noun 1 <u>insanity</u>, aberration, craziness, delusion, dementia, derangement, distraction, lunacy, mania, mental illness, psychopathy, psychosis 2 <u>foolishness</u>, absurdity, daftness (informal), folly, foolhardiness, idiocy, nonsense, preposterousness, wildness

maelstrom noun 1 <u>whirlpool</u>, vortex 2 <u>turmoil</u>, chaos, confusion, disorder, tumult, upheaval

maestro noun <u>master</u>, expert, genius, virtuoso

magazine noun 1 <u>journal</u>, pamphlet, periodical 2 <u>storehouse</u>, arsenal, depot, store, warehouse

magic noun 1 <u>sorcery</u>, black art, enchantment, necromancy, witchcraft, wizardry 2 <u>conjuring</u>, illusion, legerdemain, prestidigitation, sleight of hand, trickery 3 <u>charm</u>, allurement, enchantment, fascination, glamour, magnetism, power
♦ adjective 4 Also **magical** <u>miraculous</u>, bewitching, charming, enchanting, entrancing, fascinating, marvellous, spellbinding

magician noun <u>sorcerer</u>, conjuror or conjurer, enchanter or enchantress, illusionist, necromancer, warlock, witch, wizard

magisterial adjective <u>authoritative</u>, commanding, lordly, masterful

magistrate noun <u>judge</u>, J.P., justice, justice of the peace

magnanimity noun <u>generosity</u>, benevolence, big-heartedness, largesse or largess, nobility, selflessness, unselfishness

magnanimous adjective <u>generous</u>, big-hearted, bountiful, charitable, kind, noble, selfless, unselfish

magnate noun <u>tycoon</u>, baron, captain of industry, mogul, plutocrat

magnetic adjective <u>attractive</u>, captivating, charismatic, charming, fascinating, hypnotic, irresistible, mesmerizing, seductive

magnetism noun <u>charm</u>, allure, appeal, attraction, charisma, drawing power, magic, pull, seductiveness

magnification noun <u>increase</u>, amplification, enhancement, enlargement, expansion, heightening, intensification

magnificence noun <u>splendour</u>, brilliance, glory, grandeur, majesty, nobility, opulence, stateliness, sumptuousness

magnificent adjective 1 <u>splendid</u>, glorious, gorgeous, imposing, impressive, majestic, regal, sublime, sumptuous 2 <u>excellent</u>, brilliant, fine, outstanding, splendid, superb

magnify verb 1 <u>enlarge</u>, amplify, blow up (informal), boost, dilate, expand, heighten, increase, intensify 2 <u>overstate</u>, exaggerate, inflate, overemphasize, overplay

magnitude noun 1 <u>importance</u>, consequence, greatness, moment, note, significance, weight 2 <u>size</u>, amount, amplitude, extent, mass, quantity, volume

maid noun 1 <u>girl</u>, damsel, lass, lassie (informal), maiden, wench 2 <u>servant</u>, housemaid, maidservant, serving-maid

maiden noun 1 <u>girl</u>, damsel, lass, lassie (informal), maid, virgin, wench ♦ adjective 2 <u>unmarried</u>, unwed 3 <u>first</u>, inaugural, initial, introductory

maidenly adjective <u>modest</u>, chaste, decent, decorous, demure, pure, virginal

mail noun 1 <u>post</u>, correspondence, letters ♦ verb 2 <u>post</u>, dispatch, forward, send

maim verb <u>cripple</u>, disable, hurt, injure, mutilate, wound

main adjective 1 <u>chief</u>, central,

essential, foremost, head, leading, pre-eminent, primary, principal ♦ *noun* **2** <u>conduit</u>, cable, channel, duct, line, pipe **3 in the main** <u>on the whole</u>, for the most part, generally, in general, mainly, mostly

mainly *adverb* <u>chiefly</u>, for the most part, in the main, largely, mostly, on the whole, predominantly, primarily, principally

mainstay *noun* <u>pillar</u>, anchor, backbone, bulwark, buttress, lynchpin, prop

mainstream *adjective* <u>conventional</u>, accepted, current, established, general, orthodox, prevailing, received

maintain *verb* **1** <u>keep up</u>, carry on, continue, perpetuate, preserve, prolong, retain, sustain **2** <u>support</u>, care for, look after, provide for, supply, take care of **3** <u>assert</u>, avow, claim, contend, declare, insist, profess, state

maintenance *noun* **1** <u>continuation</u>, carrying-on, perpetuation, prolongation **2** <u>upkeep</u>, care, preservation, keeping, nurture, preservation, repairs **3** <u>allowance</u>, alimony, keep, support

majestic *adjective* <u>grand</u>, grandiose, impressive, magnificent, monumental, regal, splendid, stately, sublime, superb

majesty *noun* <u>grandeur</u>, glory, magnificence, nobility, pomp, splendour, stateliness

major *adjective* **1** <u>main</u>, bigger, chief, greater, higher, leading, senior, supreme **2** <u>important</u>, critical, crucial, great, notable, outstanding, serious, significant

majority *noun* **1** <u>preponderance</u>, best part, bulk, greater number, mass, most **2** <u>adulthood</u>, manhood *or* womanhood, maturity, seniority

make *verb* **1** <u>create</u>, assemble, build, construct, fashion, form, manufacture, produce, put together, synthesize **2** <u>produce</u>, accomplish, bring about, cause, create, effect, generate, give rise to, lead to **3** <u>force</u>, cause, compel, constrain, drive, impel, induce, oblige, prevail upon, require **4** <u>amount to</u>, add up to, compose, constitute, form **5** <u>perform</u>, carry out, do, effect, execute **6** <u>earn</u>, clear, gain, get, net, obtain, win **7 make it** *Informal* <u>succeed</u>, arrive (*informal*), crack it (*informal*), get on, prosper ♦ *noun* **8** <u>brand</u>, kind, model, sort, style, type, variety

make-believe *noun* <u>fantasy</u>, imagination, play-acting, pretence, unreality

make for *verb* <u>head for</u>, aim for, be bound for, head towards

make off *verb* **1** <u>flee</u>, bolt, clear out (*informal*), run away *or* off, take to one's heels **2 make off with** <u>steal</u>, abduct, carry off, filch, kidnap, nick (*slang, chiefly Brit.*), pinch (*informal*), run away *or* off with

make out *verb* **1** <u>see</u>, detect, discern, discover, distinguish, perceive, recognize **2** <u>understand</u>, comprehend, decipher, fathom, follow, grasp, work out **3** <u>write out</u>, complete, draw up, fill in *or* out **4** <u>pretend</u>, assert, claim, let on, make as if or though **5** fare, get on, manage

maker noun manufacturer, builder, constructor, producer

makeshift adjective temporary, expedient, provisional, stopgap, substitute

make-up noun **1** cosmetics, face (informal), greasepaint (Theatre), paint (informal), powder **2** structure, arrangement, assembly, composition, configuration, constitution, construction, format, organization **3** nature, character, constitution, disposition, temperament

make up verb **1** form, compose, comprise, constitute **2** invent, coin, compose, concoct, construct, create, devise, dream up, formulate, frame, originate **3** complete, fill, supply **4** settle, bury the hatchet, call it quits, reconcile **5** make up for compensate for, atone for, balance, make amends for, offset, recompense

making noun creation, assembly, building, composition, construction, fabrication, manufacture, production

makings plural noun beginnings, capacity, ingredients, potential

maladjusted adjective disturbed, alienated, neurotic, unstable

maladministration noun mismanagement, corruption, dishonesty, incompetence, inefficiency, malpractice, misrule

maladroit adjective clumsy, awkward, cack-handed (informal), ham-fisted or ham-handed (informal), inept,

inexpert, unskilful

malady noun disease, affliction, ailment, complaint, disorder, illness, infirmity, sickness

malaise noun unease, anxiety, depression, disquiet, melancholy

malcontent noun troublemaker, agitator, mischief-maker, rebel, stirrer (informal)

male adjective masculine, manly, virile

malefactor noun wrongdoer, criminal, delinquent, evildoer, miscreant, offender, villain

malevolence noun malice, hate, hatred, ill will, rancour, spite, vindictiveness

malevolent adjective spiteful, hostile, ill-natured, malicious, malign, vengeful, vindictive

malformation noun deformity, distortion, misshapenness

malformed adjective misshapen, abnormal, crooked, deformed, distorted, irregular, twisted

malfunction verb **1** break down, fail, go wrong ♦ noun **2** fault, breakdown, defect, failure, flaw, glitch

malice noun ill will, animosity, enmity, evil intent, hate, hatred, malevolence, spite, vindictiveness

malicious adjective spiteful, ill-disposed, ill-natured, malevolent, rancorous, resentful, vengeful

malign verb **1** disparage, abuse, defame, denigrate, libel, run down, slander, smear, vilify ♦ adjective **2** evil, bad, destructive, harmful, hostile, injurious, malevolent, malignant, pernicious, wicked

malignant adjective 1 harmful, destructive, hostile, hurtful, malevolent, malign, pernicious, spiteful 2 Medical uncontrollable, cancerous, dangerous, deadly, fatal, irremediable

malleable adjective 1 workable, ductile, plastic, soft, tensile 2 manageable, adaptable, biddable, compliant, impressionable, pliable, tractable

malodorous adjective smelly, fetid, mephitic, nauseating, noisome, offensive, putrid, reeking, stinking

malpractice noun misconduct, abuse, dereliction, mismanagement, negligence

maltreat verb abuse, bully, harm, hurt, ill-treat, injure, mistreat

mammoth adjective colossal, enormous, giant, gigantic, huge, immense, massive, monumental, mountainous, prodigious

man noun 1 male, bloke (Brit. informal), chap (informal), gentleman, guy (informal) 2 human, human being, individual, person, soul 3 mankind, Homo sapiens, humanity, humankind, human race, people 4 manservant, attendant, retainer, servant, valet ♦ verb 5 staff, crew, garrison, occupy, people

manacle noun 1 handcuff, bond, chain, fetter, iron, shackle ♦ verb 2 handcuff, bind, chain, fetter, put in chains, shackle

manage verb 1 administer, be in charge (of), command, conduct, direct, handle, run, supervise 2 succeed, accomplish, arrange, contrive, effect, engineer

3 handle, control, manipulate, operate, use 4 cope, carry on, get by (informal), make do, muddle through, survive

manageable adjective docile, amenable, compliant, easy, submissive

management noun 1 directors, administration, board, employers, executive(s) 2 administration, command, control, direction, handling, operation, running, supervision

manager noun supervisor, administrator, boss (informal), director, executive, governor, head, organizer

mandate noun command, commission, decree, directive, edict, instruction, order

mandatory adjective compulsory, binding, obligatory, required, requisite

manfully adverb bravely, boldly, courageously, determinedly, gallantly, hard, resolutely, stoutly, valiantly

mangle verb crush, deform, destroy, disfigure, distort, mutilate, ruin, spoil, tear, wreck

mangy adjective scruffy, dirty, moth-eaten, seedy, shabby, shoddy, squalid

manhandle verb rough up, knock about or around, maul, paw (informal)

manhood noun manliness, masculinity, virility

mania noun 1 madness, delirium, dementia, derangement, insanity, lunacy 2 obsession, craze, fad (informal), fetish, fixation, passion, preoccupation, thing (*informal*)

maniac noun **1** madman or madwoman, headcase (*informal*), lunatic, psycho (*slang*), psychopath **2** fanatic, enthusiast, fan, fiend (*informal*), freak (*informal*)

manifest adjective **1** obvious, apparent, blatant, clear, conspicuous, evident, glaring, noticeable, palpable, patent ♦ verb **2** display, demonstrate, exhibit, expose, express, reveal, show

manifestation noun display, demonstration, exhibition, expression, indication, mark, show, sign, symptom

manifold adjective numerous, assorted, copious, diverse, many, multifarious, multiple, varied, various

manipulate verb **1** work, handle, operate, use **2** influence, control, direct, engineer, manoeuvre

mankind noun people, Homo sapiens, humanity, humankind, human race, man

manliness noun virility, boldness, bravery, courage, fearlessness, masculinity, valour, vigour

manly adjective virile, bold, brave, courageous, fearless, manful, masculine, strapping, strong, vigorous

man-made adjective artificial, ersatz, manufactured, mock, synthetic

manner noun **1** behaviour, air, aspect, bearing, conduct, demeanour **2** style, custom, fashion, method, mode, way **3** type, brand, category, form,

kind, sort, variety

mannered adjective affected, artificial, pretentious, stilted

mannerism noun habit, characteristic, foible, idiosyncrasy, peculiarity, quirk, trait, trick

manners plural noun **1** behaviour, conduct, demeanour **2** politeness, courtesy, decorum, etiquette, p's and q's, refinement

manoeuvre noun **1** stratagem, dodge, intrigue, machination, ploy, ruse, scheme, subterfuge, tactic, trick **2** movement, exercise, operation ♦ verb **3** manipulate, contrive, engineer, machinate, pull strings, scheme, wangle (*informal*) **4** move, deploy, exercise

mansion noun residence, hall, manor, seat, villa

mantle noun **1** cloak, cape, hood, shawl, wrap **2** covering, blanket, canopy, curtain, pall, screen, shroud, veil

manual adjective **1** hand-operated, human, physical ♦ noun **2** handbook, bible, instructions

manufacture verb **1** make, assemble, build, construct, create, mass-produce, produce, put together, turn out **2** concoct, cook up (*informal*), devise, fabricate, invent, make up, think up, trump up ♦ noun **3** making, assembly, construction, creation, production

manufacturer noun maker, builder, constructor, creator, industrialist, producer

manure noun <u>compost</u>, droppings, dung, excrement, fertilizer, muck, ordure

many adjective 1 <u>numerous</u>, abundant, countless, innumerable, manifold, myriad, umpteen (informal), various ♦ noun 2 <u>a lot</u>, heaps (informal), lots (informal), plenty, scores

mar verb <u>spoil</u>, blemish, damage, detract from, disfigure, hurt, impair, ruin, scar, stain, taint, tarnish

maraud verb <u>raid</u>, forage, loot, pillage, plunder, ransack, ravage

marauder noun <u>raider</u>, bandit, brigand, buccaneer, outlaw, plunderer

march verb 1 <u>walk</u>, file, pace, parade, stride, strut ♦ noun 2 <u>walk</u>, routemarch, trek 3 <u>progress</u>, advance, development, evolution, progression

margin noun <u>edge</u>, border, boundary, brink, perimeter, periphery, rim, side, verge

marginal adjective 1 <u>borderline</u>, bordering, on the edge, peripheral 2 <u>insignificant</u>, minimal, minor, negligible, slight, small

marijuana noun <u>cannabis</u>, dope (slang), grass (slang), hemp, pot (slang)

marine adjective <u>nautical</u>, maritime, naval, seafaring, seagoing

mariner noun <u>sailor</u>, salt, sea dog, seafarer, seaman

marital adjective <u>matrimonial</u>, conjugal, connubial, nuptial

maritime adjective 1 <u>nautical</u>,

marine, naval, oceanic, seafaring 2 <u>coastal</u>, littoral, seaside

mark noun 1 <u>spot</u>, blemish, blot, line, scar, scratch, smudge, stain, streak 2 <u>sign</u>, badge, device, emblem, flag, hallmark, label, symbol, token 3 <u>criterion</u>, measure, norm, standard, yardstick 4 <u>target</u>, aim, goal, object, objective, purpose ♦ verb 5 <u>scar</u>, blemish, blot, scratch, smudge, stain, streak 6 <u>characterize</u>, brand, flag, identify, label, stamp 7 <u>distinguish</u>, denote, exemplify, illustrate, show 8 <u>observe</u>, attend, mind, note, notice, pay attention, pay heed, watch 9 <u>grade</u>, appraise, assess, correct, evaluate

marked adjective <u>noticeable</u>, blatant, clear, conspicuous, decided, distinct, obvious, patent, prominent, pronounced, striking

markedly adverb <u>noticeably</u>, clearly, considerably, conspicuously, decidedly, distinctly, obviously, strikingly

market noun 1 <u>fair</u>, bazaar, mart ♦ verb 2 <u>sell</u>, retail, vend

marketable adjective <u>sought after</u>, in demand, saleable, wanted

marksman, markswoman noun <u>sharpshooter</u>, crack shot (informal), good shot

maroon verb <u>abandon</u>, desert, leave, leave high and dry (informal), strand

marriage noun <u>wedding</u>, match, matrimony, nuptials, wedlock

marry verb 1 <u>wed</u>, get hitched (slang), tie the knot (informal)

2 unite, ally, bond, join, knit, link, merge, unify, yoke

marsh noun swamp, bog, fen, morass, quagmire, slough

marshal verb **1** arrange, align, array, deploy, draw up, group, line up, order, organize **2** conduct, escort, guide, lead, shepherd, usher

marshy adjective swampy, boggy, quaggy, waterlogged, wet

martial adjective military, bellicose, belligerent, warlike

martinet noun disciplinarian, stickler

martyrdom noun persecution, ordeal, suffering

marvel verb **1** wonder, be amazed, be awed, gape ♦ noun **2** wonder, miracle, phenomenon, portent, prodigy

marvellous adjective **1** amazing, astonishing, astounding, breathtaking, brilliant, extraordinary, miraculous, phenomenal, prodigious, spectacular, stupendous **2** excellent, fabulous (informal), fantastic (informal), great (informal), splendid, superb, terrific (informal), wonderful

masculine adjective male, manlike, manly, mannish, virile

mask noun **1** disguise, camouflage, cover, façade, front, guise, screen, veil ♦ verb **2** disguise, camouflage, cloak, conceal, cover, hide, obscure, screen, veil

masquerade noun **1** masked ball, fancy dress party, revel **2** pretence, cloak, cover-up,

deception, disguise, mask, pose, screen, subterfuge ♦ verb **3** pose, disguise, dissemble, dissimulate, impersonate, pass oneself off, pretend (to be)

mass noun **1** piece, block, chunk, hunk, lump **2** lot, bunch, collection, heap, load, pile, quantity, stack **3** size, bulk, greatness, magnitude ♦ adjective **4** large-scale, extensive, general, indiscriminate, wholesale, widespread ♦ verb **5** gather, accumulate, assemble, collect, congregate, rally, swarm, throng

massacre noun **1** slaughter, annihilation, blood bath, butchery, carnage, extermination, holocaust, murder ♦ verb **2** slaughter, butcher, cut to pieces, exterminate, kill, mow down, murder, wipe out

massage noun **1** rub-down, manipulation ♦ verb **2** rub down, knead, manipulate

massive adjective huge, big, colossal, enormous, gigantic, hefty, immense, mammoth, monumental, whopping (informal)

master noun **1** ruler, boss (informal), chief, commander, controller, director, governor, lord, manager **2** expert, ace (informal), doyen, genius, maestro, past master, virtuoso, wizard **3** teacher, guide, guru, instructor, tutor ♦ adjective **4** main, chief, foremost, leading, predominant, prime, principal ♦ verb **5** learn, get the hang of (informal), grasp **6** overcome, conquer, defeat, tame, triumph over, vanquish

masterful *adjective* **1** skilful, adroit, consummate, expert, fine, first-rate, masterly, superlative, supreme, world-class **2** domineering, arrogant, bossy (*informal*), high-handed, imperious, overbearing, overweening

masterly *adjective* skilful, adroit, consummate, crack (*informal*), expert, first-rate, masterful, supreme, world-class

mastermind *verb* **1** plan, conceive, devise, direct, manage, organize ◆ *noun* **2** organizer, architect, brain(s) (*informal*), director, engineer, manager, planner

masterpiece *noun* classic, jewel, magnum opus, *pièce de résistance, tour de force*

mastery *noun* **1** expertise, finesse, know-how (*informal*), proficiency, prowess, skill, virtuosity **2** control, ascendancy, command, domination, superiority, supremacy, upper hand, whip hand

match *noun* **1** game, bout, competition, contest, head-to-head, test, trial **2** equal, counterpart, peer, rival **3** marriage, alliance, pairing, partnership ◆ *verb* **4** correspond, accord, agree, fit, go with, harmonize, tally **5** rival, compare, compete, emulate, equal, measure up to

matching *adjective* identical, coordinating, corresponding, equivalent, like, twin

matchless *adjective* unequalled, incomparable, inimitable,

superlative, supreme, unmatched, unparalleled, unrivalled, unsurpassed

mate *noun* **1** partner, husband *or* wife, spouse **2** *Informal* friend, buddy (*informal*), chum (*informal*), comrade, crony, pal (*informal*) **3** colleague, associate, companion **4** assistant, helper, subordinate ◆ *verb* **5** pair, breed, couple

material *noun* **1** substance, matter, stuff **2** information, data, evidence, facts, notes **3** cloth, fabric ◆ *adjective* **4** physical, bodily, concrete, corporeal, palpable, substantial, tangible **5** important, essential, meaningful, momentous, serious, significant, vital, weighty **6** relevant, applicable, apposite, apropos, germane, pertinent

materialize *verb* occur, appear, come about, come to pass, happen, take shape, turn up

materially *adverb* significantly, essentially, gravely, greatly, much, seriously, substantially

maternal *adjective* motherly

maternity *noun* motherhood, motherliness

matey *adjective* friendly, chummy (*informal*), hail-fellow-well-met, intimate, pally (*informal*), sociable, thick (*informal*)

matrimonial *adjective* marital, conjugal, connubial, nuptial

matrimony *noun* marriage, nuptials, wedding ceremony, wedlock

matted *adjective* tangled, knotted, tousled, uncombed

matter *noun* **1** substance, body,

material, stuff **2** situation, affair, business, concern, event, incident, proceeding, question, subject, topic **3** As in **what's the matter?** problem, complication, difficulty, distress, trouble, worry ♦ verb **4** be important, carry weight, count, make a difference, signify

matter-of-fact adjective unsentimental, deadpan, down-to-earth, emotionless, mundane, plain, prosaic, sober, unimaginative

mature adjective **1** grown-up, adult, full-grown, fully fledged, mellow, of age, ready, ripe, seasoned ♦ verb **2** develop, age, bloom, blossom, come of age, grow up, mellow, ripen

maturity noun adulthood, experience, manhood or womanhood, ripeness, wisdom

maudlin adjective sentimental, mawkish, overemotional, slushy (informal), soppy (Brit. informal), tearful, weepy (informal)

maul verb **1** ill-treat, abuse, manhandle, molest, paw **2** tear, batter, claw, lacerate, mangle

maverick noun **1** rebel, dissenter, eccentric, heretic, iconoclast, individualist, nonconformist, protester, radical ♦ adjective **2** rebel, dissenting, eccentric, heretical, iconoclastic, individualistic, nonconformist, radical

mawkish adjective sentimental, emotional, maudlin, schmaltzy (slang), slushy (informal), soppy (Brit. informal)

maxim noun saying, adage, aphorism, axiom, dictum, motto,
proverb, rule

maximum noun **1** top, ceiling, height, peak, pinnacle, summit, upper limit, utmost, zenith ♦ adjective **2** greatest, highest, most, paramount, supreme, topmost, utmost

maybe adverb perhaps, perchance (archaic), possibly

mayhem noun chaos, commotion, confusion, destruction, disorder, fracas, havoc, trouble, violence

maze noun **1** labyrinth **2** web, confusion, imbroglio, tangle

meadow noun field, grassland, lea (poetic), pasture

meagre adjective insubstantial, inadequate, measly, paltry, poor, puny, scanty, slight, small

mean[1] verb **1** signify, convey, denote, express, imply, indicate, represent, spell, stand for, symbolize **2** intend, aim, aspire, design, desire, plan, set out, want, wish

mean[2] adjective **1** miserly, mercenary, niggardly, parsimonious, penny-pinching, stingy, tight-fisted, ungenerous **2** despicable, callous, contemptible, hard-hearted, petty, shabby, shameful, sordid, vile

mean[3] noun **1** average, balance, compromise, happy medium, middle, midpoint, norm ♦ adjective **2** average, middle, standard

meander verb **1** wind, snake, turn, zigzag **2** wander, ramble, stroll ♦ noun **3** curve, bend, coil, loop, turn, twist, zigzag

meaning noun sense, connotation, drift, gist, message, significance, substance

meaningful adjective significant, important, material, purposeful, relevant, useful, valid, worthwhile

meaningless adjective pointless, empty, futile, inane, inconsequential, insignificant, senseless, useless, vain, worthless

meanness noun 1 miserliness, niggardliness, parsimony, selfishness, stinginess 2 pettiness, disgracefulness, ignobility, narrow-mindedness, shabbiness, shamefulness

means plural noun 1 method, agency, instrument, medium, mode, process, way 2 money, affluence, capital, fortune, funds, income, resources, wealth, wherewithal 3 **by all means** certainly, definitely, doubtlessly, of course, surely 4 **by no means** in no way, definitely not, not in the least, on no account

meantime, meanwhile adverb at the same time, concurrently, in the interim, simultaneously

measly adjective meagre, miserable, paltry, pathetic, pitiful, poor, puny, scanty, skimpy

measurable adjective quantifiable, assessable, perceptible, significant

measure noun 1 quantity, allotment, allowance, amount, portion, quota, ration, share 2 gauge, metre, rule, scale, yardstick 3 action, act, deed, expedient, manoeuvre, means, procedure, step 4 law, act, bill, resolution, statute 5 rhythm, beat, cadence, metre, verse ♦ verb 6 quantify, assess, calculate, calibrate, compute, determine, evaluate, gauge, weigh

measured adjective 1 steady, dignified, even, leisurely, regular, sedate, slow, solemn, stately, unhurried 2 considered, calculated, deliberate, reasoned, sober, studied, well-thought-out

measurement noun calculation, assessment, calibration, computation, evaluation, mensuration, valuation

measure up to verb fulfil the expectations, be equal to, be suitable, come up to scratch (informal), fit or fill the bill, make the grade (informal)

meat noun flesh

meaty adjective 1 brawny, beefy (informal), burly, heavily built, heavy, muscular, solid, strapping, sturdy 2 interesting, meaningful, profound, rich, significant, substantial

mechanical adjective 1 automatic, automated 2 unthinking, automatic, cursory, impersonal, instinctive, involuntary, perfunctory, routine, unfeeling

mechanism noun 1 machine, apparatus, appliance, contrivance, device, instrument, tool 2 process, agency, means, method, operation, procedure, system, technique

meddle verb interfere, butt in, intervene, intrude, pry, tamper

meddlesome adjective interfering, intrusive, meddling, mischievous, officious, prying

mediate verb intervene, arbitrate, conciliate, intercede, reconcile, referee, step in (*informal*), umpire

mediation noun arbitration, conciliation, intercession, intervention, reconciliation

mediator noun negotiator, arbiter, arbitrator, go-between, honest broker, intermediary, middleman, peacemaker, referee, umpire

medicinal adjective therapeutic, curative, healing, medical, remedial, restorative

medicine noun remedy, cure, drug, medicament, medication, nostrum

mediocre adjective second-rate, average, indifferent, inferior, middling, ordinary, passable, pedestrian, run-of-the-mill, so so (*informal*), undistinguished

mediocrity noun insignificance, indifference, inferiority, ordinariness, unimportance

meditate verb 1 reflect, cogitate, consider, contemplate, deliberate, muse, ponder, ruminate, think 2 plan, have in mind, intend, purpose, scheme

meditation noun reflection, cogitation, contemplation, musing, pondering, rumination, study, thought

medium adjective 1 middle, average, fair, intermediate, mean, median, mediocre, middling, midway ♦ noun 2 middle, average, centre, compromise, mean, midpoint 3 means, agency, channel, instrument, mode, organ, vehicle, way 4 environment, atmosphere, conditions, milieu,

setting, surroundings 5 spiritualist

medley noun mixture, assortment, farrago, hotchpotch, jumble, *mélange*, miscellany, mishmash, mixed bag (*informal*), potpourri

meek adjective submissive, acquiescent, compliant, deferential, docile, gentle, humble, mild, modest, timid, unassuming, unpretentious

meekness noun submissiveness, acquiescence, compliance, deference, docility, gentleness, humility, mildness, modesty, timidity

meet verb 1 encounter, bump into, chance on, come across, confront, contact, find, happen on, run across, run into 2 converge, come together, connect, cross, intersect, join, link up, touch 3 satisfy, answer, discharge, fulfil, match, measure up to 4 gather, assemble, collect, come together, congregate, convene, muster 5 experience, bear, encounter, endure, face, go through, suffer, undergo

meeting noun 1 encounter, assignation, confrontation, engagement, introduction, rendezvous, tryst 2 conference, assembly, conclave, congress, convention, gathering, get-together (*informal*), reunion, session

melancholy noun 1 sadness, dejection, depression, despondency, gloom, low spirits, misery, sorrow, unhappiness ♦ adjective 2 sad, depressed,

despondent, dispirited,
downhearted, gloomy, glum,
miserable, mournful, sorrowful

melee, mêlée noun <u>fight</u>, brawl,
fracas, free-for-all (informal),
rumpus, scrimmage, scuffle,
set-to (informal), skirmish, tussle

mellifluous adjective <u>sweet</u>,
dulcet, euphonious, honeyed,
silvery, smooth, soft, soothing,
sweet-sounding

mellow adjective **1** <u>soft</u>, delicate,
full-flavoured, mature, rich, ripe,
sweet ♦ verb **2** <u>mature</u>, develop,
improve, ripen, season, soften,
sweeten

melodious adjective <u>tuneful</u>,
dulcet, euphonious, harmonious,
melodic, musical, sweet-sounding

melodramatic adjective
<u>sensational</u>, blood-and-thunder,
extravagant, histrionic,
overdramatic, overemotional,
theatrical

melody noun **1** <u>tune</u>, air, music,
song, strain, theme
2 <u>tunefulness</u>, euphony,
harmony, melodiousness,
musicality

melt verb **1** <u>dissolve</u>, fuse, liquefy,
soften, thaw **2** often with **away**
<u>disappear</u>, disperse, dissolve,
evanesce, evaporate, fade, vanish
3 <u>soften</u>, disarm, mollify, relax

member noun **1** <u>representative</u>,
associate, fellow **2** <u>limb</u>,
appendage, arm, extremity, leg,
part

membership noun **1** <u>members</u>,
associates, body, fellows
2 <u>participation</u>, belonging,
enrolment, fellowship

memento noun <u>souvenir</u>,

keepsake, memorial, relic,
remembrance, reminder, token,
trophy

memoir noun <u>account</u>,
biography, essay, journal, life,
monograph, narrative, record

memoirs plural noun
<u>autobiography</u>, diary,
experiences, journals, life story,
memories, recollections,
reminiscences

memorable adjective
<u>noteworthy</u>, celebrated, famous,
historic, momentous, notable,
remarkable, significant, striking,
unforgettable

memorandum noun <u>note</u>,
communication, jotting, memo,
message, minute, reminder

memorial noun **1** <u>monument</u>,
memento, plaque, record,
remembrance, souvenir
♦ adjective **2** <u>commemorative</u>,
monumental

memorize verb <u>remember</u>,
commit to memory, learn, learn
by heart, learn by rote

memory noun **1** <u>recall</u>,
recollection, remembrance,
reminiscence, retention
2 <u>commemoration</u>, honour,
remembrance

menace noun **1** <u>threat</u>,
intimidation, warning **2** Informal
<u>nuisance</u>, annoyance, pest,
plague, troublemaker ♦ verb
3 <u>threaten</u>, bully, frighten,
intimidate, loom, lour or lower,
terrorize

menacing adjective <u>threatening</u>,
forbidding, frightening,
intimidating, looming, louring or
lowering, ominous

mend verb **1** repair, darn, fix, patch, refit, renew, renovate, restore, retouch **2** improve, ameliorate, amend, correct, emend, rectify, reform, revise **3** heal, convalesce, get better, recover, recuperate ◆ noun **4** repair, darn, patch, stitch **5 on the mend** convalescent, getting better, improving, recovering, recuperating

mendacious adjective lying, deceitful, deceptive, dishonest, duplicitous, fallacious, false, fraudulent, insincere, untruthful

menial adjective **1** unskilled, boring, dull, humdrum, low-status, routine ◆ noun **2** servant, attendant, dogsbody (informal), drudge, flunky, lackey, skivvy (chiefly Brit.), underling

mental adjective **1** intellectual, cerebral **2** Informal insane, deranged, disturbed, mad, mentally ill, psychotic, unbalanced, unstable

mentality noun attitude, cast of mind, character, disposition, make-up, outlook, personality, psychology

mentally adverb in the mind, in one's head, intellectually, inwardly, psychologically

mention verb **1** refer to, bring up, declare, disclose, divulge, intimate, point out, reveal, state, touch upon ◆ noun **2** acknowledgment, citation, recognition, tribute **3** reference, allusion, indication, observation, remark

mentor noun guide, adviser, coach, counsellor, guru, instructor, teacher, tutor

menu noun bill of fare, carte du jour, tariff (chiefly Brit.)

mercantile adjective commercial, trading

mercenary adjective **1** greedy, acquisitive, avaricious, grasping, money-grubbing (informal), sordid, venal ◆ noun **2** hireling, soldier of fortune

merchandise noun goods, commodities, produce, products, stock, wares

merchant noun tradesman, broker, dealer, purveyor, retailer, salesman, seller, shopkeeper, supplier, trader, trafficker, vendor, wholesaler

merciful adjective compassionate, clement, forgiving, generous, gracious, humane, kind, lenient, sparing, sympathetic, tender-hearted

merciless adjective cruel, barbarous, callous, hard-hearted, harsh, heartless, pitiless, ruthless, unforgiving

mercurial adjective lively, active, capricious, changeable, impulsive, irrepressible, mobile, quicksilver, spirited, sprightly, unpredictable, volatile

mercy noun **1** compassion, clemency, forbearance, forgiveness, grace, kindness, leniency, pity **2** blessing, boon, godsend

mere adjective simple, bare, common, nothing more than, plain, pure, sheer

meretricious adjective trashy, flashy, garish, gaudy, gimcrack, showy, tawdry, tinsel

merge verb combine,

amalgamate, blend, coalesce, converge, fuse, join, meet, mingle, mix, unite

merger noun union, amalgamation, coalition, combination, consolidation, fusion, incorporation

merit noun **1** worth, advantage, asset, excellence, goodness, integrity, quality, strong point, talent, value, virtue ♦ verb **2** deserve, be entitled to, be worthy of, earn, have a right to, rate, warrant

meritorious adjective praiseworthy, admirable, commendable, creditable, deserving, excellent, good, laudable, virtuous, worthy

merriment noun fun, amusement, festivity, glee, hilarity, jollity, joviality, laughter, mirth, revelry

merry adjective **1** cheerful, blithe, carefree, convivial, festive, happy, jolly, joyous **2** Brit. informal tipsy, happy, mellow, squiffy (Brit. informal), tiddly (slang, chiefly Brit.)

mesh noun **1** net, netting, network, tracery, web ♦ verb **2** engage, combine, connect, coordinate, dovetail, harmonize, interlock, knit

mesmerize verb entrance, captivate, enthral, fascinate, grip, hold spellbound, hypnotize

mess noun **1** disorder, chaos, clutter, confusion, disarray, disorganization, hotchpotch, jumble, litter, shambles, untidiness **2** difficulty, deep water, dilemma, fix (informal), jam (informal), muddle, pickle

(informal), plight, predicament, tight spot ♦ verb **3** often with up dirty, clutter, disarrange, dishevel, muck up (Brit. slang), muddle, pollute, scramble **4** often with with interfere, fiddle (informal), meddle, play, tamper, tinker

mess about or **around** verb potter, amuse oneself, dabble, fool (about or around), muck about (informal), play about or around, trifle

message noun **1** communication, bulletin, communiqué, dispatch, letter, memorandum, note, tidings, word **2** point, idea, import, meaning, moral, purport, theme

messenger noun courier, carrier, delivery boy, emissary, envoy, errand-boy, go-between, herald, runner

messy adjective untidy, chaotic, cluttered, confused, dirty, dishevelled, disordered, disorganized, muddled, shambolic, sloppy (informal)

metamorphosis noun transformation, alteration, change, conversion, mutation, transmutation

metaphor noun figure of speech, allegory, analogy, image, symbol, trope

metaphorical adjective figurative, allegorical, emblematic, symbolic

mete verb distribute, administer, apportion, assign, deal, dispense, dole, portion

meteoric adjective spectacular, brilliant, dazzling, fast, overnight, rapid, speedy, sudden, swift

method noun 1 manner, approach, mode, modus operandi, procedure, process, routine, style, system, technique, way 2 orderliness, order, organization, pattern, planning, purpose, regularity, system

methodical adjective orderly, businesslike, deliberate, disciplined, meticulous, organized, precise, regular, structured, systematic

meticulous adjective thorough, exact, fastidious, fussy, painstaking, particular, precise, punctilious, scrupulous, strict

mettle noun courage, bravery, fortitude, gallantry, life, nerve, pluck, resolution, spirit, valour, vigour

microbe noun microorganism, bacillus, bacterium, bug (informal), germ, virus

microscopic adjective tiny, imperceptible, infinitesimal, invisible, minuscule, minute, negligible

midday noun noon, noonday, twelve o'clock

middle adjective 1 central, halfway, intermediate, intervening, mean, median, medium, mid ♦ noun 2 centre, focus, halfway point, heart, midpoint, midsection, midst

middle-class adjective bourgeois, conventional, traditional

middling adjective 1 mediocre, indifferent, run-of-the-mill, so-so (informal), tolerable, unexceptional, unremarkable 2 moderate, adequate, all right, average, fair, medium, modest, O.K. or okay (informal), ordinary, passable, serviceable

midget noun dwarf, pygmy or pigmy, shrimp (informal), Tom Thumb

midnight noun twelve o'clock, dead of night, middle of the night, the witching hour

midst noun in the midst of among, amidst, during, in the middle of, in the thick of, surrounded by

midway adjective, adverb halfway, betwixt and between, in the middle

might noun 1 power, energy, force, strength, vigour 2 with might and main forcefully, lustily, manfully, mightily, vigorously

mightily adverb 1 very, decidedly, exceedingly, extremely, greatly, highly, hugely, intensely, much 2 powerfully, energetically, forcefully, lustily, manfully, strongly, vigorously

mighty adjective powerful, forceful, lusty, robust, strapping, strong, sturdy, vigorous

migrant noun 1 wanderer, drifter, emigrant, immigrant, itinerant, nomad, rover, traveller ♦ adjective 2 travelling, drifting, immigrant, itinerant, migratory, nomadic, roving, shifting, transient, vagrant, wandering

migrate verb move, emigrate, journey, roam, rove, travel, trek, voyage, wander

migration noun wandering, emigration, journey, movement, roving, travel, trek, voyage

migratory adjective nomadic,

itinerant, migrant, peripatetic, roving, transient

mild *adjective* **1** gentle, calm, docile, easy-going, equable, meek, peaceable, placid **2** bland, smooth **3** calm, balmy, moderate, temperate, tranquil, warm

mildness *noun* gentleness, calmness, clemency, docility, moderation, placidity, tranquillity, warmth

milieu *noun* surroundings, background, element, environment, locale, location, scene, setting

militant *adjective* aggressive, active, assertive, combative, vigorous

military *adjective* warlike, armed, martial, soldierly ♦ *noun* **2** armed forces, army, forces, services

militate *verb* **militate against** counteract, be detrimental to, conflict with, counter, oppose, resist, tell against, weigh against

milk *verb* exploit, extract, pump, take advantage of

mill *noun* **1** factory, foundry, plant, works **2** grinder, crusher ♦ *verb* **3** grind, crush, grate, pound, powder **4** swarm, crowd, throng

millstone *noun* **1** grindstone, quernstone **2** burden, affliction, albatross, encumbrance, load, weight

mime *verb* act out, gesture, represent, simulate

mimic *verb* **1** imitate, ape, caricature, do (*informal*), impersonate, parody, take off

(*informal*) ♦ *noun* **2** imitator, caricaturist, copycat (*informal*), impersonator, impressionist

mimicry *noun* imitation, burlesque, caricature, impersonation, mimicking, mockery, parody, take-off (*informal*)

mince *verb* **1** cut, chop, crumble, grind, hash **2** *As in* **mince one's words** tone down, moderate, soften, spare, weaken

mincing *adjective* affected, camp (*informal*), dainty, effeminate, foppish, precious, pretentious, sissy

mind *noun* **1** intelligence, brain(s) (*informal*), grey matter (*informal*), intellect, reason, sense, understanding, wits **2** memory, recollection, remembrance **3** intention, desire, disposition, fancy, inclination, leaning, notion, urge, wish **4** sanity, judgment, marbles (*informal*), mental balance, rationality, reason, senses, wits **5** **make up one's mind** decide, choose, determine, resolve ♦ *verb* **6** take offence, be affronted, be bothered, care, disapprove, dislike, object, resent **7** pay attention, heed, listen to, mark, note, obey, observe, pay heed to, take heed **8** guard, attend to, keep an eye on, look after, take care of, tend, watch **9** be careful, be cautious, be on (one's) guard, be wary, take care, watch

mindful *adjective* aware, alert, alive to, careful, conscious, heedful, wary, watchful

mindless *adjective* stupid, foolish,

idiotic, inane, moronic,
thoughtless, unthinking, witless

mine noun **1** pit, colliery, deposit,
excavation, shaft **2** source,
abundance, fund, hoard, reserve,
stock, store, supply, treasury,
wealth ♦ verb **3** dig up, dig for,
excavate, extract, hew, quarry,
unearth

miner noun coalminer, collier
(Brit.), pitman (Brit.)

mingle verb **1** mix, blend,
combine, intermingle,
interweave, join, merge, unite
2 associate, consort, fraternize,
hang about or around, hobnob,
rub shoulders (informal), socialize

miniature adjective small,
diminutive, little, minuscule,
minute, scaled-down, tiny, toy

minimal adjective minimum,
least, least possible, nominal,
slightest, smallest, token

minimize verb **1** reduce, curtail,
decrease, diminish, miniaturize,
prune, shrink **2** play down,
belittle, decry, deprecate,
discount, disparage, make light
or little of, underrate

minimum adjective **1** least, least
possible, lowest, minimal,
slightest, smallest ♦ noun **2** least,
lowest, nadir

minion noun follower, flunky,
hanger-on, henchman, hireling,
lackey, underling, yes man

minister noun **1** clergyman,
cleric, parson, pastor, preacher,
priest, rector, vicar ♦ verb
2 attend, administer, cater to,
pander to, serve, take care of,
tend

ministry noun **1** department,

bureau, council, office, quango
2 the priesthood, holy orders,
the church

minor adjective small,
inconsequential, insignificant,
lesser, petty, slight, trivial,
unimportant

minstrel noun musician, bard,
singer, songstress, troubadour

mint verb make, cast, coin,
produce, punch, stamp, strike

minuscule adjective tiny,
diminutive, infinitesimal, little,
microscopic, miniature, minute

minute[1] noun moment, flash,
instant, jiffy (informal), second,
tick (Brit. informal), trice

minute[2] adjective **1** small,
diminutive, infinitesimal, little,
microscopic, miniature,
minuscule, tiny **2** precise, close,
critical, detailed, exact,
exhaustive, meticulous,
painstaking, punctilious

minutes plural noun record,
memorandum, notes,
proceedings, transactions,
transcript

minutiae plural noun details, finer
points, ins and outs, niceties,
particulars, subtleties, trifles, trivia

minx noun flirt, coquette, hussy

miracle noun wonder, marvel,
phenomenon, prodigy

miraculous adjective wonderful,
amazing, astonishing,
astounding, extraordinary,
incredible, phenomenal,
prodigious, unaccountable,
unbelievable

mirage noun illusion,
hallucination, optical illusion

mire noun **1** swamp, bog, marsh,

morass, quagmire **2** <u>mud</u>, dirt, muck, ooze, slime

mirror noun **1** <u>looking-glass</u>, glass, reflector ✦ verb **2** <u>reflect</u>, copy, echo, emulate, follow

mirth noun <u>merriment</u>, amusement, cheerfulness, fun, gaiety, glee, hilarity, jollity, joviality, laughter, revelry

mirthful adjective <u>merry</u>, blithe, cheerful, cheery, festive, happy, jolly, jovial, light-hearted, playful, sportive

misadventure noun <u>misfortune</u>, accident, bad luck, calamity, catastrophe, debacle, disaster, mishap, reverse, setback

misanthropic adjective <u>antisocial</u>, cynical, malevolent, unfriendly

misapprehend verb <u>misunderstand</u>, misconstrue, misinterpret, misread, mistake

misapprehension noun <u>misunderstanding</u>, delusion, error, fallacy, misconception, misinterpretation, mistake

misappropriate verb <u>steal</u>, embezzle, misspend, misuse, peculate, pocket

miscalculate verb <u>misjudge</u>, blunder, err, overestimate, overrate, slip up, underestimate, underrate

miscarriage noun <u>failure</u>, breakdown, error, mishap, perversion

miscarry verb <u>fail</u>, come to grief, fall through, go awry, go wrong, misfire

miscellaneous adjective <u>mixed</u>, assorted, diverse, jumbled, motley, sundry, varied, various

miscellany noun <u>assortment</u>, anthology, collection, hotchpotch, jumble, medley, *mélange*, mixed bag, mixture, potpourri, variety

mischance noun <u>misfortune</u>, accident, calamity, disaster, misadventure, mishap

mischief noun **1** <u>trouble</u>, impishness, misbehaviour, monkey business (*informal*), naughtiness, shenanigans (*informal*), waywardness **2** <u>harm</u>, damage, evil, hurt, injury, misfortune, trouble

mischievous adjective **1** <u>naughty</u>, impish, playful, puckish, rascally, roguish, sportive, troublesome, wayward **2** <u>malicious</u>, damaging, destructive, evil, harmful, hurtful, spiteful, vicious, wicked

misconception noun <u>delusion</u>, error, fallacy, misapprehension, misunderstanding

misconduct noun <u>immorality</u>, impropriety, malpractice, mismanagement, wrongdoing

miscreant noun <u>wrongdoer</u>, blackguard, criminal, rascal, reprobate, rogue, scoundrel, sinner, vagabond, villain

misdeed noun <u>offence</u>, crime, fault, misconduct, misdemeanour, sin, transgression, wrong

misdemeanour noun <u>offence</u>, fault, infringement, misdeed, peccadillo, transgression

miser noun <u>skinflint</u>, cheapskate (*informal*), niggard, penny-pincher (*informal*), Scrooge

miserable adjective **1** <u>unhappy</u>, dejected, depressed, despondent, disconsolate, forlorn, gloomy, sorrowful, woebegone, wretched **2** squalid, deplorable, lamentable, shameful, sordid, sorry, wretched

miserly adjective mean, avaricious, grasping, niggardly, parsimonious, penny-pinching (informal), stingy, tightfisted, ungenerous

misery noun **1** unhappiness, anguish, depression, desolation, despair, distress, gloom, grief, sorrow, suffering, torment, woe **2** Brit. informal moaner, killjoy, pessimist, prophet of doom, sourpuss (informal), spoilsport, wet blanket (informal)

misfire verb fail, fall through, go wrong, miscarry

misfit noun nonconformist, eccentric, fish out of water (informal), oddball (informal), square peg (in a round hole) (informal)

misfortune noun **1** bad luck, adversity, hard luck, ill luck, infelicity **2** mishap, affliction, calamity, disaster, reverse, setback, tragedy, tribulation, trouble

misgiving noun unease, anxiety, apprehension, distrust, doubt, qualm, reservation, suspicion, trepidation, uncertainty, worry

misguided adjective unwise, deluded, erroneous, ill-advised, imprudent, injudicious, misplaced, mistaken, unwarranted

mishandle verb mismanage, botch, bungle, make a mess of, mess up (informal), muff

mishap noun accident, calamity, misadventure, mischance, misfortune

misinform verb mislead, deceive, misdirect, misguide

misinterpret verb misunderstand, distort, misapprehend, misconceive, misconstrue, misjudge, misread, misrepresent, mistake

misjudge verb miscalculate, overestimate, overrate, underestimate, underrate

mislay verb lose, lose track of, misplace

mislead verb deceive, delude, fool, hoodwink, misdirect, misguide, misinform, take in (informal)

misleading adjective confusing, ambiguous, deceptive, disingenuous, evasive, false

mismanage verb mishandle, botch, bungle, make a mess of, mess up, misconduct, misdirect, misgovern

misplace verb lose, lose track of, mislay

misprint noun mistake, corrigendum, erratum, literal, typo (informal)

misquote verb misrepresent, falsify, twist

misrepresent verb distort, disguise, falsify, misinterpret

misrule noun disorder, anarchy, chaos, confusion, lawlessness, turmoil

miss verb **1** omit, leave out, let go, overlook, pass over, skip **2** avoid, escape, evade **3** long for, pine for, yearn for ◆ noun **4** mistake, blunder, error, failure, omission, oversight

misshapen *adjective* deformed, contorted, crooked, distorted, grotesque, malformed, twisted, warped

missile *noun* rocket, projectile, weapon

missing *adjective* absent, astray, lacking, left out, lost, mislaid, misplaced, unaccounted-for

mission *noun* task, assignment, commission, duty, errand, job, quest, undertaking, vocation

missionary *noun* evangelist, apostle, preacher

missive *noun* letter, communication, dispatch, epistle, memorandum, message, note, report

misspent *adjective* wasted, dissipated, imprudent, profitless, squandered

mist *noun* fog, cloud, film, haze, smog, spray, steam, vapour

mistake *noun* **1** error, blunder, erratum, fault, faux pas, gaffe, howler (*informal*), miscalculation, oversight, slip ♦ *verb* **2** misunderstand, misapprehend, misconstrue, misinterpret, misjudge, misread **3** confuse with, mix up with, take for

mistaken *adjective* wrong, erroneous, false, faulty, inaccurate, incorrect, misguided, unsound, wide of the mark

mistakenly *adverb* incorrectly, by mistake, erroneously, fallaciously, falsely, inaccurately, misguidedly, wrongly

mistimed *adjective* inopportune, badly timed, ill-timed, untimely

mistreat *verb* abuse, harm, ill-treat, injure, knock about *or*

around, maltreat, manhandle, misuse, molest

mistress *noun* lover, concubine, girlfriend, kept woman, paramour

mistrust *verb* **1** doubt, be wary of, distrust, fear, suspect ♦ *noun* **2** suspicion, distrust, doubt, misgiving, scepticism, uncertainty, wariness

mistrustful *adjective* suspicious, chary, cynical, distrustful, doubtful, fearful, hesitant, sceptical, uncertain, wary

misty *adjective* foggy, blurred, cloudy, dim, hazy, indistinct, murky, obscure, opaque, overcast

misunderstand *verb* misinterpret, be at cross-purposes, get the wrong end of the stick, misapprehend, misconstrue, misjudge, misread, mistake

misunderstanding *noun* mistake, error, misconception, misinterpretation, misjudgment, mix-up

misuse *noun* **1** waste, abuse, desecration, misapplication, squandering ♦ *verb* **2** waste, abuse, desecrate, misapply, prostitute, squander

mitigate *verb* ease, extenuate, lessen, lighten, moderate, soften, subdue, temper

mitigation *noun* relief, alleviation, diminution, extenuation, moderation, remission

mix *verb* **1** combine, blend, cross, fuse, intermingle, interweave, join, jumble, merge, mingle **2** socialize, associate, consort, fraternize, hang out (*informal*),

hobnob, mingle ♦ *noun*
3 mixture, alloy, amalgam,
assortment, blend, combination,
compound, fusion, medley

mixed *adjective* 1 combined,
amalgamated, blended,
composite, compound, joint,
mingled, united 2 varied,
assorted, cosmopolitan, diverse,
heterogeneous, miscellaneous,
motley

mixed-up *adjective* confused, at
sea, bewildered, distraught,
disturbed, maladjusted,
muddled, perplexed, puzzled,
upset

mixture *noun* blend, amalgam,
assortment, brew, compound,
fusion, jumble, medley, mix,
potpourri, variety

mix-up *noun* confusion, mess,
mistake, misunderstanding,
muddle, tangle

mix up *verb* 1 combine, blend,
mix 2 confuse, confound,
muddle

moan *noun* 1 groan, lament,
sigh, sob, wail, whine 2 *Informal*
grumble, complaint, gripe
(*informal*), grouch (*informal*),
grouse, protest, whine ♦ *verb*
3 groan, lament, sigh, sob,
whine 4 *Informal* grumble, bleat,
carp, complain, groan, grouse,
whine, whinge (*informal*)

mob *noun* 1 crowd, drove, flock,
horde, host, mass, multitude,
pack, swarm, throng 2 *Slang*
gang, crew (*informal*), group, lot,
set ♦ *verb* 3 surround, crowd
around, jostle, set upon, swarm
around

mobile *adjective* movable,
itinerant, moving, peripatetic,

portable, travelling, wandering

mobilize *verb* prepare, activate,
call to arms, call up, get or make
ready, marshal, organize, rally,
ready

mock *verb* 1 laugh at, deride,
jeer, make fun of, poke fun at,
ridicule, scoff, scorn, sneer,
taunt, tease 2 mimic, ape,
caricature, imitate, lampoon,
parody, satirize, send up (*Brit.
informal*) ♦ *adjective* 3 imitation,
artificial, dummy, fake, false,
feigned, phoney *or* phony
(*informal*), pretended, sham,
spurious

mockery *noun* 1 derision,
contempt, disdain, disrespect,
insults, jeering, ridicule, scoffing,
scorn 2 farce, apology (*informal*),
disappointment, joke, letdown

mocking *adjective* scornful,
contemptuous, derisive,
disdainful, disrespectful,
sarcastic, sardonic, satirical,
scoffing

mode *noun* 1 method, form,
manner, procedure, process,
style, system, technique, way
2 fashion, craze, look, rage,
style, trend, vogue

model *noun* 1 representation,
copy, dummy, facsimile, image,
imitation, miniature, mock-up,
replica 2 pattern, archetype,
example, ideal, original,
paradigm, paragon, prototype,
standard 3 sitter, poser, subject
♦ *verb* 4 shape, carve, design,
fashion, form, mould, sculpt
5 show off, display, sport
(*informal*), wear

moderate *adjective* 1 mild,
controlled, gentle, limited,

middle-of-the-road, modest, reasonable, restrained, steady **2** average, fair, indifferent, mediocre, middling, ordinary, passable, so-so (*informal*), unexceptional ♦ *verb* **3** regulate, control, curb, ease, modulate, restrain, soften, subdue, temper, tone down

moderately *adverb* reasonably, fairly, passably, quite, rather, slightly, somewhat, tolerably

moderation *noun* restraint, fairness, reasonableness, temperance

modern *adjective* current, contemporary, fresh, new, newfangled, novel, present-day, recent, up-to-date

modernity *noun* novelty, currency, freshness, innovation, newness

modernize *verb* update, make over, rejuvenate, remake, remodel, renew, renovate, revamp

modest *adjective* **1** unpretentious, bashful, coy, demure, diffident, reserved, reticent, retiring, self-effacing, shy **2** moderate, fair, limited, middling, ordinary, small, unexceptional

modesty *noun* reserve, bashfulness, coyness, demureness, diffidence, humility, reticence, shyness, timidity

modicum *noun* little, bit, crumb, drop, fragment, scrap, shred, touch

modification *noun* change, adjustment, alteration, qualification, refinement, revision, variation

modify *verb* **1** change, adapt, adjust, alter, convert, reform, remodel, revise, rework **2** tone down, ease, lessen, lower, moderate, qualify, restrain, soften, temper

modish *adjective* fashionable, contemporary, current, in, smart, stylish, trendy (*Brit. informal*), up-to-the-minute, voguish

modulate *verb* adjust, attune, balance, regulate, tune, vary

mogul *noun* tycoon, baron, big noise (*informal*), big shot (*informal*), magnate, V.I.P.

moist *adjective* damp, clammy, dewy, humid, soggy, wet

moisten *verb* dampen, damp, moisturize, soak, water, wet

moisture *noun* damp, dew, liquid, water, wetness

molecule *noun* particle, jot, speck

molest *verb* **1** annoy, badger, beset, bother, disturb, harass, persecute, pester, plague, torment, worry **2** abuse, attack, harm, hurt, ill-treat, interfere with, maltreat

mollify *verb* pacify, appease, calm, conciliate, placate, quiet, soothe, sweeten

mollycoddle *verb* pamper, baby, cosset, indulge, spoil

moment *noun* **1** instant, flash, jiffy (*informal*), second, split second, trice, twinkling **2** time, juncture, point, stage

momentarily *adverb* briefly, for a moment, temporarily

momentary *adjective* short-lived, brief, fleeting, passing, short, temporary, transitory

momentous adjective significant, critical, crucial, fateful, historic, important, pivotal, vital, weighty

momentum noun impetus, drive, energy, force, power, propulsion, push, strength, thrust

monarch noun ruler, emperor or empress, king, potentate, prince or princess, queen, sovereign

monarchy noun 1 sovereignty, autocracy, kingship, monocracy, royalism 2 kingdom, empire, principality, realm

monastery noun abbey, cloister, convent, friary, nunnery, priory

monastic adjective monkish, ascetic, cloistered, contemplative, hermit-like, reclusive, secluded, sequestered, withdrawn

monetary adjective financial, budgetary, capital, cash, fiscal, pecuniary

money noun cash, capital, coin, currency, hard cash, legal tender, readies (informal), riches, silver, wealth

mongrel noun 1 hybrid, cross, crossbreed, half-breed ♦ adjective 2 hybrid, crossbred

monitor noun 1 watchdog, guide, invigilator, prefect (Brit.), supervisor ♦ verb 2 check, follow, keep an eye on, keep tabs on, keep track of, observe, survey, watch

monk noun friar, brother

monkey noun 1 simian, primate 2 rascal, devil, imp, rogue, scamp ♦ verb 3 fool, meddle, mess, play, tinker

monolithic adjective huge, colossal, impenetrable, intractable, massive, monumental, solid

monologue noun speech, harangue, lecture, sermon, soliloquy

monopolize verb control, corner the market in, dominate, hog (slang), keep to oneself, take over

monotonous adjective tedious, boring, dull, humdrum, mind-numbing, repetitive, tiresome, unchanging, wearisome

monotony noun tedium, boredom, monotonousness, repetitiveness, routine, sameness, tediousness

monster noun 1 brute, beast, demon, devil, fiend, villain 2 freak, monstrosity, mutant 3 giant, colossus, mammoth, titan ♦ adjective 4 huge, colossal, enormous, gigantic, immense, mammoth, massive, stupendous, tremendous

monstrosity noun eyesore, freak, horror, monster

monstrous adjective 1 unnatural, fiendish, freakish, frightful, grotesque, gruesome, hideous, horrible 2 outrageous, diabolical, disgraceful, foul, inhuman, intolerable, scandalous, shocking 3 huge, colossal, enormous, immense, mammoth, massive, prodigious, stupendous, tremendous

monument noun memorial, cairn, cenotaph, commemoration, gravestone, headstone, marker, mausoleum, shrine, tombstone

monumental adjective 1 important, awesome, enormous, epoch-making, historic, majestic, memorable, significant, unforgettable **2** *Informal* immense, colossal, great, massive, staggering

mood *noun* state of mind, disposition, frame of mind, humour, spirit, temper

moody *adjective* **1** sullen, gloomy, glum, ill-tempered, irritable, morose, sad, sulky, temperamental, touchy **2** changeable, capricious, erratic, fickle, flighty, impulsive, mercurial, temperamental, unpredictable, volatile

moon *noun* **1** satellite ◆ *verb* **2** idle, daydream, languish, mope, waste time

moor[1] *noun* moorland, fell (*Brit.*), heath

moor[2] *verb* tie up, anchor, berth, dock, lash, make fast, secure

moot *adjective* **1** debatable, arguable, contestable, controversial, disputable, doubtful, undecided, unresolved, unsettled ◆ *verb* **2** bring up, broach, propose, put forward, suggest

mop *noun* **1** squeegee, sponge, swab **2** mane, shock, tangle, thatch

mope *verb* brood, fret, languish, moon, pine, pout, sulk

mop up *verb* clean up, soak up, sponge, swab, wash, wipe

moral *adjective* **1** good, decent, ethical, high-minded, honourable, just, noble, principled, right, virtuous ◆ *noun* **2** lesson, meaning, message, point, significance

morale *noun* confidence, esprit

de corps, heart, self-esteem, spirit

morality *noun* **1** integrity, decency, goodness, honesty, justice, righteousness, virtue **2** standards, conduct, ethics, manners, morals, mores, philosophy, principles

morals *plural noun* morality, behaviour, conduct, ethics, habits, integrity, manners, mores, principles, scruples, standards

morass *noun* **1** marsh, bog, fen, quagmire, slough, swamp **2** mess, confusion, mix-up, muddle, tangle

moratorium *noun* postponement, freeze, halt, standstill, suspension

morbid *adjective* **1** unwholesome, ghoulish, gloomy, melancholy, sick, sombre, unhealthy **2** gruesome, dreadful, ghastly, grisly, hideous, horrid, macabre

mordant *adjective* sarcastic, biting, caustic, cutting, incisive, pungent, scathing, stinging, trenchant

more *adjective* **1** extra, added, additional, further, new, other, supplementary ◆ *adverb* **2** to a greater extent, better, further, longer

moreover *adverb* furthermore, additionally, also, as well, besides, further, in addition, too

morgue *noun* mortuary

moribund *adjective* declining, on its last legs, stagnant, waning, weak

morning *noun* dawn, a.m., break of day, daybreak, forenoon, morn (*poetic*), sunrise

moron noun <u>fool</u>, blockhead, cretin, dunce, dunderhead, halfwit, idiot, imbecile, oaf

moronic adjective <u>idiotic</u>, cretinous, foolish, halfwitted, imbecilic, mindless, stupid, unintelligent

morose adjective <u>sullen</u>, depressed, dour, gloomy, glum, ill-tempered, moody, sour, sulky, surly, taciturn

morsel noun <u>piece</u>, bit, bite, crumb, mouthful, part, scrap, soupçon, taste, titbit

mortal adjective 1 <u>human</u>, ephemeral, impermanent, passing, temporal, transient, worldly 2 <u>fatal</u>, deadly, death-dealing, destructive, killing, lethal, murderous, terminal ♦ noun 3 <u>human being</u>, being, earthling, human, individual, man, person, woman

mortality noun 1 <u>humanity</u>, impermanence, transience 2 <u>killing</u>, bloodshed, carnage, death, destruction, fatality

mortification noun
1 <u>humiliation</u>, annoyance, chagrin, discomfiture, embarrassment, shame, vexation 2 <u>discipline</u>, abasement, chastening, control, denial, subjugation 3 Medical <u>gangrene</u>, corruption, festering

mortified adjective <u>humiliated</u>, ashamed, chagrined, chastened, crushed, deflated, embarrassed, humbled, shamed

mortify verb 1 <u>humiliate</u>, chagrin, chasten, crush, deflate, embarrass, humble, shame 2 <u>discipline</u>, abase, chasten, control, deny, subdue 3 Of flesh putrefy, deaden, die, fester

mortuary noun <u>morgue</u>, funeral parlour

mostly adverb <u>generally</u>, as a rule, chiefly, largely, mainly, on the whole, predominantly, primarily, principally, usually

moth-eaten adjective <u>decayed</u>, decrepit, dilapidated, ragged, shabby, tattered, threadbare, worn-out

mother noun 1 <u>parent</u>, dam, ma (informal), mater, mum (Brit. informal), mummy (Brit. informal) ♦ adjective 2 <u>native</u>, inborn, innate, natural ♦ verb 3 <u>nurture</u>, care for, cherish, nurse, protect, raise, rear, tend

motherly adjective <u>maternal</u>, affectionate, caring, comforting, loving, protective, sheltering

motif noun 1 <u>theme</u>, concept, idea, leitmotif, subject 2 <u>design</u>, decoration, ornament, shape

motion noun 1 <u>movement</u>, flow, locomotion, mobility, move, progress, travel 2 <u>proposal</u>, proposition, recommendation, submission, suggestion ♦ verb 3 <u>gesture</u>, beckon, direct, gesticulate, nod, signal, wave

motionless adjective <u>still</u>, fixed, frozen, immobile, paralysed, standing, static, stationary, stock-still, transfixed, unmoving

motivate verb <u>inspire</u>, arouse, cause, drive, induce, move, persuade, prompt, stimulate, stir

motivation noun <u>incentive</u>, incitement, inducement, inspiration, motive, reason, spur, stimulus

motive noun <u>reason</u>, ground(s),

incentive, inducement, inspiration, object, purpose, rationale, stimulus

motley *adjective* 1 miscellaneous, assorted, disparate, heterogeneous, mixed, varied 2 multicoloured, chequered, variegated

mottled *adjective* blotchy, dappled, flecked, piebald, speckled, spotted, stippled, streaked

motto *noun* saying, adage, dictum, maxim, precept, proverb, rule, slogan, watchword

mould¹ *noun* 1 cast, pattern, shape 2 design, build, construction, fashion, form, format, kind, pattern, shape, style 3 nature, calibre, character, kind, quality, sort, stamp, type ♦ *verb* 4 shape, construct, create, fashion, forge, form, make, model, sculpt, work 5 influence, affect, control, direct, form, make, shape

mould² *noun* fungus, blight, mildew

mouldy *adjective* stale, bad, blighted, decaying, fusty, mildewed, musty, rotten

mound *noun* 1 heap, drift, pile, rick, stack 2 hill, bank, dune, embankment, hillock, knoll, rise

mount *verb* 1 climb, ascend, clamber up, go up, scale 2 bestride, climb onto, jump on 3 increase, accumulate, build, escalate, grow, intensify, multiply, pile up, swell ♦ *noun* 4 backing, base, frame, setting, stand, support 5 horse, steed (*literary*)

mountain *noun* 1 peak, alp, fell

(*Brit.*), mount 2 heap, abundance, mass, mound, pile, stack, ton

mountainous *adjective* 1 high, alpine, highland, rocky, soaring, steep, towering, upland 2 huge, daunting, enormous, gigantic, great, immense, mammoth, mighty, monumental

mourn *verb* grieve, bemoan, bewail, deplore, lament, rue, wail, weep

mournful *adjective* 1 sad, melancholy, piteous, plaintive, sorrowful, tragic, unhappy, woeful 2 dismal, disconsolate, downcast, gloomy, grieving, heavy-hearted, lugubrious, miserable, rueful, sombre

mourning *noun* 1 grieving, bereavement, grief, lamentation, weeping, woe 2 black, sackcloth and ashes, widow's weeds

mouth *noun* 1 lips, gob (*slang, especially Brit.*), jaws, maw 2 opening, aperture, door, entrance, gateway, inlet, orifice

mouthful *noun* taste, bit, bite, little, morsel, sample, spoonful, swallow

mouthpiece *noun* spokesperson, agent, delegate, representative, spokesman *or* spokeswoman

movable *adjective* portable, detachable, mobile, transferable, transportable

move *verb* 1 go, advance, budge, proceed, progress, shift, stir 2 change, shift, switch, transfer, transpose 3 leave, migrate, pack one's bags (*informal*), quit, relocate, remove 4 drive, activate, operate, propel, shift, start, turn 5 touch, affect, excite, impress **6** <u>incite</u>, cause, induce, influence, inspire, motivate, persuade, prompt, rouse **7** <u>propose</u>, advocate, put forward, recommend, suggest, urge ♦ noun **8** <u>action</u>, manoeuvre, measure, ploy, step, stratagem, stroke, turn **9** <u>transfer</u>, relocation, removal, shift

movement noun **1** <u>motion</u>, action, activity, change, development, flow, manoeuvre, progress, stirring **2** <u>group</u>, campaign, crusade, drive, faction, front, grouping, organization, party **3** <u>workings</u>, action, machinery, mechanism, works **4** Music <u>section</u>, division, part, passage

movie noun <u>film</u>, feature, flick (slang), picture

moving adjective **1** <u>emotional</u>, affecting, inspiring, pathetic, persuasive, poignant, stirring, touching **2** <u>mobile</u>, movable, portable, running, unfixed

mow verb <u>cut</u>, crop, scythe, shear, trim

mow down verb <u>massacre</u>, butcher, cut down, cut to pieces, shoot down, slaughter

much adjective **1** <u>great</u>, abundant, a lot of, ample, considerable, copious, plenty of, sizable or sizeable, substantial ♦ noun **2** <u>a lot</u>, a good deal, a great deal, heaps (informal), loads (informal), lots (informal), plenty ♦ adverb **3** <u>greatly</u>, a great deal, a lot, considerably, decidedly, exceedingly

muck noun **1** <u>manure</u>, dung, ordure **2** <u>dirt</u>, filth, gunge

(informal), mire, mud, ooze, slime, sludge

muck up verb <u>ruin</u>, blow (slang), botch, bungle, make a mess of, make a pig's ear of (informal), mess up, muff, spoil

mucky adjective <u>dirty</u>, begrimed, filthy, grimy, messy, muddy

mud noun <u>dirt</u>, clay, mire, ooze, silt, slime, sludge

muddle verb **1** <u>jumble</u>, disarrange, disorder, disorganize, mess, scramble, spoil, tangle **2** <u>confuse</u>, befuddle, bewilder, confound, daze, disorient, perplex, stupefy ♦ noun **3** <u>confusion</u>, chaos, disarray, disorder, disorganization, jumble, mess, mix-up, predicament, tangle

muddy adjective **1** <u>dirty</u>, bespattered, grimy, mucky, mud-caked, soiled **2** <u>boggy</u>, marshy, quaggy, swampy

muffle verb **1** <u>wrap up</u>, cloak, cover, envelop, shroud, swaddle, swathe **2** <u>deaden</u>, muzzle, quieten, silence, soften, stifle, suppress

muffled adjective <u>indistinct</u>, faint, muted, stifled, strangled, subdued, suppressed

mug¹ noun <u>cup</u>, beaker, pot, tankard

mug² noun **1** <u>face</u>, countenance, features, visage **1** <u>fool</u>, chump (informal), easy or soft touch (slang), simpleton, sucker (slang) ♦ verb **2** <u>attack</u>, assault, beat up, rob, set about or upon

muggy adjective <u>humid</u>, clammy, close, moist, oppressive, sticky, stuffy, sultry

mug up verb study, bone up on (informal), burn the midnight oil (informal), cram (informal), swot (Brit. informal)

mull verb ponder, consider, contemplate, deliberate, meditate, reflect on, ruminate, think over, weigh

multifarious adjective diverse, different, legion, manifold, many, miscellaneous, multiple, numerous, sundry, varied

multiple adjective many, manifold, multitudinous, numerous, several, sundry, various

multiply verb 1 increase, build up, expand, extend, proliferate, spread 2 reproduce, breed, propagate

multitude noun mass, army, crowd, horde, host, mob, myriad, swarm, throng

munch verb chew, champ, chomp, crunch

mundane adjective 1 ordinary, banal, commonplace, day-to-day, everyday, humdrum, prosaic, routine, workaday 2 earthly, mortal, secular, temporal, terrestrial, worldly

municipal adjective civic, public, urban

municipality noun town, borough, city, district, township

munificence noun generosity, beneficence, benevolence, bounty, largesse or largess, liberality, magnanimousness, philanthropy

munificent adjective generous, beneficent, benevolent, bountiful, lavish, liberal, magnanimous, open-handed, philanthropic, unstinting

murder noun 1 killing, assassination, bloodshed, butchery, carnage, homicide, manslaughter, massacre, slaying ♦ verb 2 kill, assassinate, bump off (slang), butcher, eliminate (slang), massacre, slaughter, slay

murderer noun killer, assassin, butcher, cut-throat, hit man (slang), homicide, slaughterer, slayer

murderous adjective deadly, bloodthirsty, brutal, cruel, cut-throat, ferocious, lethal, savage

murky adjective dark, cloudy, dim, dull, gloomy, grey, misty, overcast

murmur verb 1 mumble, mutter, whisper 2 grumble, complain, moan (informal) ♦ noun 3 drone, buzzing, humming, purr, rumble, whisper

muscle noun 1 tendon, sinew 2 strength, brawn, clout (informal), forcefulness, might, power, stamina, weight ♦ verb 3 muscle in Informal impose oneself, butt in, force one's way in

muscular adjective strong, athletic, powerful, robust, sinewy, strapping, sturdy, vigorous

muse verb ponder, brood, cogitate, consider, contemplate, deliberate, meditate, mull over, reflect, ruminate

mushy adjective 1 soft, pulpy, semi-solid, slushy, squashy, squelchy, squidgy (informal) 2 Informal sentimental, maudlin, mawkish, saccharine, schmaltzy (slang), sloppy (informal), slushy (informal)

musical adjective <u>melodious</u>, dulcet, euphonious, harmonious, lyrical, melodic, sweet-sounding, tuneful

must noun <u>necessity</u>, essential, fundamental, imperative, prerequisite, requirement, requisite, sine qua non

muster verb **1** <u>assemble</u>, call together, convene, gather, marshal, mobilize, rally, summon ♦ noun **2** <u>assembly</u>, collection, congregation, convention, gathering, meeting, rally, roundup

musty adjective <u>stale</u>, airless, dank, fusty, mildewed, mouldy, old, smelly, stuffy

mutability noun <u>change</u>, alteration, evolution, metamorphosis, transition, variation, vicissitude

mutable adjective <u>changeable</u>, adaptable, alterable, fickle, inconsistent, inconstant, unsettled, unstable, variable, volatile

mutation noun <u>change</u>, alteration, evolution, metamorphosis, modification, transfiguration, transformation, variation

mute adjective <u>silent</u>, dumb, mum, speechless, unspoken, voiceless, wordless

mutilate verb **1** <u>maim</u>, amputate, cut up, damage, disfigure, dismember, injure, lacerate, mangle **2** <u>distort</u>, adulterate, bowdlerize, censor, cut, damage, expurgate

mutinous adjective <u>rebellious</u>, disobedient, insubordinate, insurgent, refractory, riotous, subversive, unmanageable, unruly

mutiny noun **1** <u>rebellion</u>, disobedience, insubordination, insurrection, revolt, revolution, riot, uprising ♦ verb **2** <u>rebel</u>, disobey, resist, revolt, rise up

mutter verb <u>grumble</u>, complain, grouse, mumble, murmur, rumble

mutual adjective <u>shared</u>, common, interchangeable, joint, reciprocal, requited, returned

muzzle noun **1** <u>jaws</u>, mouth, nose, snout **2** <u>gag</u>, guard ♦ verb **3** <u>suppress</u>, censor, curb, gag, restrain, silence, stifle

myopic adjective <u>short-sighted</u>, near-sighted

myriad adjective **1** <u>innumerable</u>, countless, immeasurable, incalculable, multitudinous, untold ♦ noun **2** <u>multitude</u>, army, horde, host, swarm

mysterious adjective <u>strange</u>, arcane, enigmatic, inexplicable, inscrutable, mystifying, perplexing, puzzling, secret, uncanny, unfathomable, weird

mystery noun <u>puzzle</u>, conundrum, enigma, problem, question, riddle, secret, teaser

mystic, mystical adjective <u>supernatural</u>, inscrutable, metaphysical, mysterious, occult, otherworldly, paranormal, preternatural, transcendental

mystify verb <u>puzzle</u>, baffle, bewilder, confound, confuse, flummox, nonplus, perplex, stump

mystique noun <u>fascination</u>, awe, charisma, charm, glamour, magic, spell

myth noun 1 <u>legend</u>, allegory, fable, fairy story, fiction, folk tale, saga, story 2 <u>illusion</u>, delusion, fancy, fantasy, figment, imagination, superstition, tall story

mythical adjective 1 <u>legendary</u>, fabled, fabulous, fairy-tale, mythological 2 <u>imaginary</u>, fictitious, invented, made-up, make-believe, nonexistent, pretended, unreal, untrue

mythological adjective <u>legendary</u>, fabulous, mythic, mythical, traditional

mythology noun <u>legend</u>, folklore, lore, tradition

N n

nab verb <u>catch</u>, apprehend, arrest, capture, collar (informal), grab, seize, snatch

nadir noun <u>bottom</u>, depths, lowest point, minimum, rock bottom

naevus noun <u>birthmark</u>, mole

naff adjective <u>bad</u>, duff (Brit. informal), inferior, low-grade, poor, rubbishy, second-rate, shabby, shoddy, worthless

nag[1] verb 1 <u>scold</u>, annoy, badger, harass, hassle (informal), henpeck, irritate, pester, plague, upbraid, worry ♦ noun 2 <u>scold</u>, harpy, shrew, tartar, virago

nag[2] noun <u>horse</u>, hack

nagging adjective <u>irritating</u>, persistent, scolding, shrewish, worrying

nail verb <u>fasten</u>, attach, fix, hammer, join, pin, secure, tack

naive adjective 1 <u>gullible</u>, callow, credulous, green, unsuspicious, wet behind the ears (informal) 2 <u>innocent</u>, artless, guileless, ingenuous, open, simple, trusting, unsophisticated, unworldly

naivety, naïveté noun 1 <u>gullibility</u>, callowness, credulity 2 <u>innocence</u>, artlessness, guilelessness, inexperience, ingenuousness, naturalness, openness, simplicity

naked adjective <u>nude</u>, bare, exposed, starkers (informal), stripped, unclothed, undressed, without a stitch on (informal)

nakedness noun <u>nudity</u>, bareness, undress

namby-pamby adjective <u>feeble</u>, insipid, sentimental, spineless, vapid, weak, weedy (informal), wimpish or wimpy (informal), wishy-washy (informal)

name noun 1 <u>title</u>, designation, epithet, handle (slang), moniker or monicker (slang), nickname, sobriquet, term 2 <u>fame</u>, distinction, eminence, esteem, honour, note, praise, renown, repute ♦ verb 3 <u>call</u>, baptize, christen, dub, entitle, label, style, term 4 <u>nominate</u>, appoint, choose, designate, select, specify

named adjective 1 <u>called</u>, baptized, christened, dubbed, entitled, known as, labelled, styled, termed 2 <u>nominated</u>, appointed, chosen, designated, mentioned, picked, selected, singled out, specified

nameless *adjective*
1 anonymous, unnamed, untitled **2** unknown, incognito, obscure, undistinguished, unheard-of, unsung **3** horrible, abominable, indescribable, unmentionable, unspeakable, unutterable

namely *adverb* specifically, to wit, viz.

nap[1] *noun* **1** sleep, catnap, forty winks (*informal*), kip (*Brit. slang*), rest, siesta ♦ *verb* **2** sleep, catnap, doze, drop off (*informal*), kip (*Brit. slang*), nod off (*informal*), rest, snooze (*informal*)

nap[2] *noun* weave, down, fibre, grain, pile

napkin *noun* serviette, cloth

narcissism *noun* egotism, self-love, vanity

narcotic *noun* **1** drug, anaesthetic, analgesic, anodyne, opiate, painkiller, sedative, tranquillizer ♦ *adjective* **2** sedative, analgesic, calming, hypnotic, painkilling, soporific

nark *verb* annoy, bother, exasperate, get on one's nerves (*informal*), irritate, nettle

narrate *verb* tell, chronicle, describe, detail, recite, recount, relate, report

narration *noun* telling, description, explanation, reading, recital, relation

narrative *noun* story, account, chronicle, history, report, statement, tale

narrator *noun* storyteller, author, chronicler, commentator, reporter, writer

narrow *adjective* **1** thin, attenuated, fine, slender, slim, spare, tapering **2** limited, close, confined, constricted, contracted, meagre, restricted, tight **3** insular, dogmatic, illiberal, intolerant, narrow-minded, partial, prejudiced, small-minded ♦ *verb* **4** tighten, constrict, limit, reduce

narrowly *adverb* just, barely, by the skin of one's teeth, only just, scarcely

narrow-minded *adjective* intolerant, bigoted, hidebound, illiberal, opinionated, parochial, prejudiced, provincial, small-minded

nastiness *noun* unpleasantness, malice, meanness, spitefulness

nasty *adjective* **1** objectionable, disagreeable, loathsome, obnoxious, offensive, unpleasant, vile **2** spiteful, despicable, disagreeable, distasteful, malicious, mean, unpleasant, vicious, vile **3** painful, bad, critical, dangerous, serious, severe

nation *noun* country, people, race, realm, society, state, tribe

national *adjective* **1** nationwide, countrywide, public, widespread ♦ *noun* **2** citizen, inhabitant, native, resident, subject

nationalism *noun* patriotism, allegiance, chauvinism, jingoism, loyalty

nationality *noun* race, birth, nation

nationwide *adjective* national, countrywide, general, widespread

native *adjective* **1** local, domestic, home, indigenous **2** inborn, congenital, hereditary, inbred, ingrained, innate, instinctive, intrinsic, natural ♦ *noun* **3** <u>inhabitant</u>, aborigine, citizen, countryman, dweller, national, resident

natter *verb* **1** <u>gossip</u>, blether, chatter, gabble, jaw (*slang*), prattle, rabbit (on) (*Brit. informal*), talk ♦ *noun* **2** <u>gossip</u>, chat, chinwag (*Brit. informal*), chitchat, conversation, gab (*informal*), jaw (*slang*), prattle, talk

natty *adjective* <u>smart</u>, dapper, elegant, fashionable, neat, snazzy (*informal*), spruce, stylish, trim

natural *adjective* **1** <u>normal</u>, common, everyday, legitimate, logical, ordinary, regular, typical, usual **2** <u>unaffected</u>, genuine, ingenuous, open, real, simple, spontaneous, unpretentious, unsophisticated **3** <u>innate</u>, characteristic, essential, inborn, inherent, instinctive, intuitive, native **4** <u>pure</u>, organic, plain, unrefined, whole

naturalist *noun* <u>biologist</u>, botanist, ecologist, zoologist

naturalistic *adjective* <u>realistic</u>, lifelike, true-to-life

naturally *adverb* **1** <u>of course</u>, certainly **2** <u>genuinely</u>, normally, simply, spontaneously, typically, unaffectedly, unpretentiously

nature *noun* **1** <u>creation</u>, cosmos, earth, environment, universe, world **2** <u>make-up</u>, character, complexion, constitution, essence **3** <u>kind</u>, category, description, sort, species, style, type, variety **4** <u>temperament</u>, disposition, humour, mood,

outlook, temper

naughty *adjective* **1** <u>disobedient</u>, bad, impish, misbehaved, mischievous, refractory, wayward, wicked, worthless **2** <u>obscene</u>, improper, lewd, ribald, risqué, smutty, vulgar

nausea *noun* <u>sickness</u>, biliousness, queasiness, retching, squeamishness, vomiting

nauseate *verb* <u>sicken</u>, disgust, offend, repel, repulse, revolt, turn one's stomach

nauseous *adjective* <u>sickening</u>, abhorrent, disgusting, distasteful, nauseating, offensive, repugnant, repulsive, revolting

nautical *adjective* <u>maritime</u>, marine, naval

naval *adjective* <u>nautical</u>, marine, maritime

navigable *adjective* **1** <u>passable</u>, clear, negotiable, unobstructed **2** <u>sailable</u>, controllable, dirigible

navigate *verb* <u>sail</u>, drive, guide, handle, manoeuvre, pilot, steer, voyage

navigation *noun* <u>sailing</u>, helmsmanship, seamanship, voyaging

navigator *noun* <u>pilot</u>, mariner, seaman

navvy *noun* <u>labourer</u>, worker, workman

navy *noun* <u>fleet</u>, armada, flotilla

near *adjective* **1** <u>close</u>, adjacent, adjoining, nearby, neighbouring **2** <u>forthcoming</u>, approaching, imminent, impending, in the offing, looming, nigh, upcoming

nearby *adjective* <u>neighbouring</u>, adjacent, adjoining, convenient, handy

nearly adverb almost, approximately, as good as, just about, practically, roughly, virtually, well-nigh

nearness noun closeness, accessibility, availability, handiness, proximity, vicinity

near-sighted adjective short-sighted, myopic

neat adjective 1 tidy, orderly, shipshape, smart, spick-and-span, systematic, trim 2 elegant, adept, adroit, deft, dexterous, efficient, graceful, nimble, skilful, stylish 3 Of alcoholic drinks straight, pure, undiluted, unmixed

neatly adverb 1 tidily, daintily, fastidiously, methodically, smartly, sprucely, systematically 2 elegantly, adeptly, adroitly, deftly, dexterously, efficiently, expertly, gracefully, nimbly, skilfully

neatness noun 1 tidiness, daintiness, orderliness, smartness, spruceness, trimness 2 elegance, adroitness, deftness, dexterity, efficiency, grace, nimbleness, skill, style

nebulous adjective vague, confused, dim, hazy, imprecise, indefinite, indistinct, shadowy, uncertain, unclear

necessarily adverb certainly, automatically, compulsorily, incontrovertibly, inevitably, inexorably, naturally, of necessity, undoubtedly

necessary adjective 1 needed, compulsory, essential, imperative, indispensable, mandatory, obligatory, required, requisite, vital 2 certain, fated, inescapable, inevitable, inexorable, unavoidable

necessitate verb compel, call for, coerce, constrain, demand, force, impel, oblige, require

necessities plural noun essentials, exigencies, fundamentals, needs, requirements

necessity noun 1 inevitability, compulsion, inexorableness, obligation 2 need, desideratum, essential, fundamental, prerequisite, requirement, requisite, sine qua non

necromancy noun magic, black magic, divination, enchantment, sorcery, witchcraft, wizardry

necropolis noun cemetery, burial ground, churchyard, graveyard

need verb 1 require, call for, demand, entail, lack, miss, necessitate, want ◆ noun 2 poverty, deprivation, destitution, inadequacy, insufficiency, lack, paucity, penury, shortage 3 requirement, demand, desideratum, essential, requisite 4 emergency, exigency, necessity, obligation, urgency, want

needed adjective necessary, called for, desired, lacked, required, wanted

needful adjective necessary, essential, indispensable, needed, required, requisite, stipulated, vital

needle verb irritate, annoy, get on one's nerves (informal), goad, harass, nag, pester, provoke, rile, taunt

needless adjective unnecessary,

gratuitous, groundless, pointless, redundant, superfluous, uncalled-for, unwanted, useless

needlework noun embroidery, needlecraft, sewing, stitching, tailoring

needy adjective poor, deprived, destitute, disadvantaged, impoverished, penniless, poverty-stricken, underprivileged

ne'er-do-well noun layabout, black sheep, good-for-nothing, idler, loafer, loser, skiver (Brit. slang), wastrel

nefarious adjective wicked, criminal, depraved, evil, foul, heinous, infernal, villainous

negate verb 1 invalidate, annul, cancel, countermand, neutralize, nullify, obviate, reverse, wipe out 2 deny, contradict, disallow, disprove, gainsay (archaic or literary), oppose, rebut, refute

negation noun 1 cancellation, neutralization, nullification 2 denial, contradiction, converse, disavowal, inverse, opposite, rejection, renunciation, reverse

negative adjective 1 contradictory, contrary, denying, dissenting, opposing, refusing, rejecting, resisting 2 pessimistic, cynical, gloomy, jaundiced, uncooperative, unenthusiastic, unwilling ♦ noun 3 contradiction, denial, refusal

neglect verb 1 disregard, disdain, ignore, overlook, rebuff, scorn, slight, spurn 2 forget, be remiss, evade, omit, pass over, shirk, skimp ♦ noun 3 disregard, disdain, inattention, indifference 4 negligence, carelessness,

derelicition, failure, laxity, oversight, slackness

neglected adjective 1 abandoned, derelict, overgrown 2 disregarded, unappreciated, underestimated, undervalued

neglectful adjective careless, heedless, inattentive, indifferent, lax, negligent, remiss, thoughtless, uncaring

negligence noun carelessness, derelicition, disregard, inattention, indifference, laxity, neglect, slackness, thoughtlessness

negligent adjective careless, forgetful, heedless, inattentive, neglectful, remiss, slack, slapdash, thoughtless, unthinking

negligible adjective insignificant, imperceptible, inconsequential, minor, minute, small, trifling, trivial, unimportant

negotiable adjective debatable, variable

negotiate verb 1 deal, arrange, bargain, conciliate, debate, discuss, mediate, transact, work out 2 get round, clear, cross, get over, get past, pass, surmount

negotiation noun bargaining, arbitration, debate, diplomacy, discussion, mediation, transaction, wheeling and dealing (informal)

negotiator noun mediator, ambassador, delegate, diplomat, honest broker, intermediary, moderator

neighbourhood noun district, community, environs, locale, locality, quarter, region, vicinity

neighbouring adjective nearby, adjacent, adjoining, bordering, connecting, near, next, surrounding

neighbourly adjective helpful, considerate, friendly, harmonious, hospitable, kind, obliging, sociable

nemesis noun retribution, destiny, destruction, fate, vengeance

nepotism noun favouritism, bias, partiality, patronage, preferential treatment

nerd, nurd noun bore, anorak (informal), dork (slang), drip (informal), geek (informal), obsessive, trainspotter (informal), wonk (informal)

nerve noun 1 bravery, bottle (Brit. slang), courage, daring, fearlessness, grit, guts (informal), pluck, resolution, will
2 impudence, audacity, boldness, brazenness, cheek (informal), impertinence, insolence, temerity ◆ verb
3 nerve oneself brace oneself, fortify oneself, steel oneself

nerveless adjective calm, composed, controlled, cool, impassive, imperturbable, self-possessed, unemotional

nerve-racking adjective tense, difficult, distressing, frightening, harrowing, stressful, trying, worrying

nerves plural noun tension, anxiety, butterflies (in one's stomach) (informal), cold feet (informal), fretfulness, nervousness, strain, stress, worry

nervous adjective apprehensive, anxious, edgy, fearful, jumpy, on edge, tense, uneasy, uptight (informal), worried

nervousness noun anxiety, agitation, disquiet, excitability, fluster, tension, touchiness, worry

nervy adjective anxious, agitated, fidgety, jittery (informal), jumpy, nervous, on edge, tense, twitchy (informal)

nest noun refuge, den, haunt, hideaway, retreat

nest egg noun reserve, cache, deposit, fall-back, fund(s), savings, store

nestle verb snuggle, cuddle, curl up, huddle, nuzzle

nestling noun chick, fledgling

net¹ noun 1 mesh, lattice, netting, network, openwork, tracery, web ◆ verb 2 catch, bag, capture, enmesh, ensnare, entangle, trap

net², nett adjective 1 final, after taxes, clear, take-home ◆ verb 2 earn, accumulate, bring in, clear, gain, make, realize, reap

nether adjective lower, below, beneath, bottom, inferior, under, underground

nettled adjective irritated, annoyed, exasperated, galled, harassed, incensed, peeved, put out, riled, vexed

network noun system, arrangement, complex, grid, labyrinth, lattice, maze, organization, structure, web

neurosis noun obsession, abnormality, affliction, derangement, instability, maladjustment, mental illness, phobia

neurotic adjective unstable,

neuter abnormal, compulsive, disturbed, maladjusted, manic, nervous, obsessive, unhealthy

neuter verb castrate, doctor (informal), emasculate, fix (informal), geld, spay

neutral adjective 1 unbiased, disinterested, even-handed, impartial, nonaligned, nonpartisan, uncommitted, uninvolved, unprejudiced 2 indeterminate, dull, indistinct, intermediate, undefined

neutrality noun impartiality, detachment, nonalignment, noninterference, noninvolvement, nonpartisanship

neutralize verb counteract, cancel, compensate for, counterbalance, frustrate, negate, nullify, offset, undo

never adverb at no time, not at all, on no account, under no circumstances

nevertheless adverb nonetheless, but, even so, (even) though, however, notwithstanding, regardless, still, yet

new adjective 1 modern, contemporary, current, fresh, ground-breaking, latest, novel, original, recent, state-of-the-art, unfamiliar, up-to-date 2 changed, altered, improved, modernized, redesigned, renewed, restored 3 extra, added, more, supplementary

newcomer noun novice, arrival, beginner, Johnny-come-lately (informal), parvenu

newfangled adjective new, contemporary, fashionable, gimmicky, modern, novel,

recent, state-of-the-art

newly adverb recently, anew, freshly, just, lately, latterly

newness noun novelty, freshness, innovation, oddity, originality, strangeness, unfamiliarity, uniqueness

news noun information, bulletin, communiqué, exposé, gossip, hearsay, intelligence, latest (informal), report, revelation, rumour, story

newsworthy adjective interesting, important, notable, noteworthy, remarkable, significant, stimulating

next adjective 1 following, consequent, ensuing, later, subsequent, succeeding 2 nearest, adjacent, adjoining, closest, neighbouring ♦ adverb 3 afterwards, following, later, subsequently, thereafter

nibble verb 1 bite, eat, gnaw, munch, nip, peck, pick at ♦ noun 2 snack, bite, crumb, morsel, peck, soupçon, taste, titbit

nice adjective 1 pleasant, agreeable, attractive, charming, delightful, good, pleasurable 2 kind, courteous, friendly, likable or likeable, polite, well-mannered 3 neat, dainty, fine, tidy, trim 4 subtle, careful, delicate, fastidious, fine, meticulous, precise, strict

nicely adverb 1 pleasantly, acceptably, agreeably, attractively, charmingly, delightfully, pleasurably, well 2 kindly, amiably, commendably, courteously, politely 3 neatly, daintily, finely, tidily, trimly

nicety noun subtlety, daintiness, delicacy, discrimination, distinction, nuance, refinement

niche noun 1 alcove, corner, hollow, nook, opening, recess 2 position, calling, pigeonhole (informal), place, slot (informal), vocation

nick verb 1 cut, chip, dent, mark, notch, scar, score, scratch, snick 2 steal, pilfer, pinch (informal), swipe (slang) ♦ noun 3 cut, chip, dent, mark, notch, scar, scratch

nickname noun pet name, diminutive, epithet, label, moniker or monicker (slang), sobriquet

nifty adjective neat, attractive, chic, deft, pleasing, smart, stylish

niggard noun miser, cheapskate (informal), Scrooge, skinflint

niggardly adjective stingy, avaricious, frugal, grudging, mean, miserly, parsimonious, tightfisted, ungenerous

niggle verb 1 worry, annoy, irritate, rankle 2 criticize, carp, cavil, find fault, fuss

niggling adjective 1 persistent, gnawing, irritating, troubling, worrying 2 petty, finicky, fussy, nit-picking (informal), pettifogging, picky (informal), quibbling

night noun darkness, dark, night-time

nightfall noun evening, dusk, sundown, sunset, twilight

nightly adjective 1 nocturnal, night-time ♦ adverb 2 every night, each night, night after night, nights (informal)

nightmare noun 1 bad dream,

hallucination 2 ordeal, horror, torment, trial, tribulation

nil noun nothing, love, naught, none, zero

nimble adjective agile, brisk, deft, dexterous, lively, quick, sprightly, spry, swift

nimbly adverb quickly, briskly, deftly, dexterously, easily, readily, smartly, spryly, swiftly

nincompoop noun idiot, blockhead, chump, fool, nitwit (informal), numbskull or numskull, twit (informal, chiefly Brit.)

nip¹ verb pinch, bite, squeeze, tweak

nip² noun dram, draught, drop, mouthful, shot (informal), sip, snifter (informal)

nipper noun Informal child, baby, boy, girl, infant, kid (informal), tot

nippy adjective 1 chilly, biting, sharp 2 Informal quick, active, agile, fast, nimble, spry

nirvana noun paradise, bliss, joy, peace, serenity, tranquillity

nit-picking adjective fussy, captious, carping, finicky, hairsplitting, pedantic, pettifogging, quibbling

nitty-gritty noun basics, brass tacks (informal), core, crux, essentials, fundamentals, gist, substance

nitwit noun Informal fool, dimwit (informal), dummy (slang), halfwit, nincompoop, oaf, simpleton

no interjection 1 never, nay, not at all, no way ♦ noun 2 refusal, denial, negation

nob noun aristocrat, bigwig

(*informal*), toff (*Brit. slang*), V.I.P.

nobble *verb* bribe, get at, influence, intimidate, win over

nobility *noun* 1 integrity, honour, incorruptibility, uprightness, virtue 2 aristocracy, elite, lords, nobles, patricians, peerage, upper class

noble *adjective* 1 worthy, generous, honourable, magnanimous, upright, virtuous 2 aristocratic, blue-blooded, highborn, lordly, patrician, titled 3 great, dignified, distinguished, grand, imposing, impressive, lofty, splendid, stately ♦ *noun* 4 lord, aristocrat, nobleman, peer

nobody *pronoun* 1 no-one ♦ *noun* 2 nonentity, cipher, lightweight (*informal*), menial

nocturnal *adjective* nightly, night-time

nod *verb* 1 acknowledge, bow, gesture, indicate, signal 2 sleep, doze, drowse, nap ♦ *noun* 3 gesture, acknowledgment, greeting, indication, sign, signal

noggin *noun* 1 cup, dram, mug, nip, tot 2 *Informal* head, block (*informal*), nut (*slang*)

no go *adjective* impossible, futile, hopeless, not on (*informal*), vain

noise *noun* sound, clamour, commotion, din, hubbub, racket, row, uproar

noiseless *adjective* silent, hushed, inaudible, mute, quiet, soundless, still

noisome *adjective* 1 poisonous, bad, harmful, pernicious, pestilential, unhealthy, unwholesome 2 offensive, disgusting, fetid, foul,

malodorous, noxious, putrid, smelly, stinking

noisy *adjective* loud, boisterous, cacophonous, clamorous, deafening, ear-splitting, strident, tumultuous, uproarious, vociferous

nomad *noun* wanderer, drifter, itinerant, migrant, rambler, rover, vagabond

nomadic *adjective* wandering, itinerant, migrant, peripatetic, roaming, roving, travelling, vagrant

nom de plume *noun* pseudonym, alias, assumed name, nom de guerre, pen name

nomenclature *noun* terminology, classification, codification, phraseology, taxonomy, vocabulary

nominal *adjective* 1 so-called, formal, ostensible, professed, puppet, purported, supposed, theoretical, titular 2 small, inconsiderable, insignificant, minimal, symbolic, token, trifling, trivial

nominate *verb* name, appoint, assign, choose, designate, elect, propose, recommend, select, suggest

nomination *noun* choice, appointment, designation, election, proposal, recommendation, selection, suggestion

nominee *noun* candidate, aspirant, contestant, entrant, protégé, runner

nonaligned *adjective* neutral, impartial, uncommitted, undecided

nonchalance noun <u>indifference</u>, calm, composure, equanimity, imperturbability, sang-froid, self-possession, unconcern

nonchalant adjective <u>casual</u>, blasé, calm, careless, indifferent, insouciant, laid-back (informal), offhand, unconcerned, unperturbed

noncombatant noun <u>civilian</u>, neutral, nonbelligerent

noncommittal adjective <u>evasive</u>, cautious, circumspect, equivocal, guarded, neutral, politic, temporizing, tentative, vague, wary

non compos mentis adjective <u>insane</u>, crazy, deranged, mentally ill, unbalanced, unhinged

nonconformist noun <u>maverick</u>, dissenter, eccentric, heretic, iconoclast, individualist, protester, radical, rebel

nonconformity noun <u>dissent</u>, eccentricity, heresy, heterodoxy

nondescript adjective <u>ordinary</u>, commonplace, dull, featureless, run-of-the-mill, undistinguished, unexceptional, unremarkable

none pronoun <u>not any</u>, nil, nobody, no-one, nothing, not one, zero

nonentity noun <u>nobody</u>, cipher, lightweight (informal), mediocrity, small fry

nonessential adjective <u>unnecessary</u>, dispensable, expendable, extraneous, inessential, peripheral, superfluous, unimportant

nonetheless adverb <u>nevertheless</u>, despite that, even so, however, in spite of that, yet

nonevent noun <u>flop</u> (informal), disappointment, dud (informal), failure, fiasco, washout

nonexistent adjective <u>imaginary</u>, chimerical, fictional, hypothetical, illusory, legendary, mythical, unreal

nonsense noun <u>rubbish</u>, balderdash, claptrap (informal), double Dutch (Brit. informal), drivel, gibberish, hot air (informal), stupidity, tripe (informal), twaddle

nonsensical adjective <u>senseless</u>, absurd, crazy, foolish, inane, incomprehensible, irrational, meaningless, ridiculous, silly

nonstarter noun <u>dead loss</u>, dud (informal), lemon (informal), loser, no-hoper (informal), turkey (informal), washout (informal)

nonstop adjective **1** <u>continuous</u>, constant, endless, incessant, interminable, relentless, unbroken, uninterrupted ♦ adverb **2** <u>continuously</u>, ceaselessly, constantly, endlessly, incessantly, interminably, perpetually, relentlessly

nook noun <u>niche</u>, alcove, corner, cubbyhole, hide-out, opening, recess, retreat

noon noun <u>midday</u>, high noon, noonday, noontide, twelve noon

norm noun <u>standard</u>, average, benchmark, criterion, par, pattern, rule, yardstick

normal adjective **1** <u>usual</u>, average, common, conventional, natural, ordinary, regular, routine, standard, typical **2** <u>sane</u>, rational, reasonable, well-adjusted

normality noun **1** regularity, conventionality, naturalness **2** sanity, balance, rationality, reason

normally adverb usually, as a rule, commonly, generally, habitually, ordinarily, regularly, typically

north adjective **1** northern, Arctic, boreal, northerly, polar ♦ adverb **2** northward(s), northerly

nose noun **1** snout, beak, bill, hooter (slang), proboscis ♦ verb **2** ease forward, nudge, nuzzle, push, shove **3** pry, meddle, snoop (informal)

nosegay noun posy, bouquet

nosey, nosy adjective inquisitive, curious, eavesdropping, interfering, intrusive, meddlesome, prying, snooping (informal)

nostalgia noun reminiscence, homesickness, longing, pining, regretfulness, remembrance, wistfulness, yearning

nostalgic adjective sentimental, emotional, homesick, longing, maudlin, regretful, wistful

nostrum noun medicine, cure, drug, elixir, panacea, potion, remedy, treatment

notability noun fame, celebrity, distinction, eminence, esteem, renown

notable adjective **1** remarkable, conspicuous, extraordinary, memorable, noteworthy, outstanding, rare, striking, uncommon, unusual ♦ noun **2** celebrity, big name, dignitary, personage, V.I.P.

notably adverb particularly, especially, outstandingly, strikingly

notation noun signs, characters, code, script, symbols, system

notch noun **1** cut, cleft, incision, indentation, mark, nick, score **2** Informal level, degree, grade, step ♦ verb **3** cut, indent, mark, nick, score, scratch

notch up verb register, achieve, gain, make, score

note noun **1** message, comment, communication, epistle, jotting, letter, memo, memorandum, minute, remark, reminder **2** symbol, indication, mark, sign, token ♦ verb **3** see, notice, observe, perceive **4** mark, denote, designate, indicate, record, register **5** mention, remark

notebook noun jotter, diary, exercise book, journal, notepad

noted adjective famous, acclaimed, celebrated, distinguished, eminent, illustrious, notable, prominent, renowned, well-known

noteworthy adjective remarkable, exceptional, extraordinary, important, notable, outstanding, significant, unusual

nothing noun nought, emptiness, nil, nothingness, nullity, void, zero

nothingness noun **1** oblivion, nonbeing, nonexistence, nullity **2** insignificance, unimportance, worthlessness

notice noun **1** observation, cognizance, consideration, heed, interest, note, regard

2 <u>attention</u>, civility, respect
3 <u>announcement</u>, advice, communication, instruction, intimation, news, notification, order, warning ◆ *verb* **4** <u>observe</u>, detect, discern, distinguish, mark, note, perceive, see, spot

noticeable *adjective* <u>obvious</u>, appreciable, clear, conspicuous, evident, manifest, perceptible, plain, striking

notification *noun* <u>announcement</u>, advice, declaration, information, intelligence, message, notice, statement, warning

notify *verb* <u>inform</u>, advise, alert, announce, declare, make known, publish, tell, warn

notion *noun* **1** <u>idea</u>, belief, concept, impression, inkling, opinion, sentiment, view
2 <u>whim</u>, caprice, desire, fancy, impulse, inclination, wish

notional *adjective* <u>speculative</u>, abstract, conceptual, hypothetical, imaginary, theoretical, unreal

notoriety *noun* <u>scandal</u>, dishonour, disrepute, infamy, obloquy, opprobrium

notorious *adjective* <u>infamous</u>, dishonourable, disreputable, opprobrious, scandalous

notoriously *adverb* <u>infamously</u>, dishonourably, disreputably, opprobriously, scandalously

notwithstanding *preposition* <u>despite</u>, in spite of

nought *noun* <u>zero</u>, nil, nothing

nourish *verb* **1** <u>feed</u>, nurse, nurture, supply, sustain, tend
2 <u>encourage</u>, comfort, cultivate,

foster, maintain, promote, support

nourishing *adjective* <u>nutritious</u>, beneficial, nutritive, wholesome

nourishment *noun* <u>food</u>, nutriment, nutrition, sustenance

novel[1] *noun* <u>story</u>, fiction, narrative, romance, tale

novel[2] *adjective* <u>new</u>, different, fresh, innovative, original, strange, uncommon, unfamiliar, unusual

novelty *noun* **1** <u>newness</u>, freshness, innovation, oddity, originality, strangeness, surprise, unfamiliarity, uniqueness
2 <u>gimmick</u>, curiosity, gadget
3 <u>knick-knack</u>, bauble, memento, souvenir, trifle, trinket

novice *noun* <u>beginner</u>, amateur, apprentice, learner, newcomer, probationer, pupil, trainee

now *adverb* **1** <u>nowadays</u>, any more, at the moment
2 <u>immediately</u>, at once, instantly, promptly, straightaway
3 **now and then** *or* **again** <u>occasionally</u>, from time to time, infrequently, intermittently, on and off, sometimes, sporadically

nowadays *adverb* <u>now</u>, any more, at the moment, in this day and age, today

noxious *adjective* <u>harmful</u>, deadly, destructive, foul, hurtful, injurious, poisonous, unhealthy, unwholesome

nuance *noun* <u>subtlety</u>, degree, distinction, gradation, nicety, refinement, shade, tinge

nubile *adjective* <u>marriageable</u>, ripe (*informal*)

nucleus *noun* <u>centre</u>, basis, core,

focus, heart, kernel, nub, pivot

nude *adjective* naked, bare, disrobed, stark-naked, stripped, unclad, unclothed, undressed, without a stitch on (*informal*)

nudge *verb* push, bump, dig, elbow, jog, poke, prod, shove, touch

nudity *noun* nakedness, bareness, deshabille, nudism, undress

nugget *noun* lump, chunk, clump, hunk, mass, piece

nuisance *noun* problem, annoyance, bother, drag (*informal*), hassle (*informal*), inconvenience, irritation, pain in the neck, pest, trouble

null *adjective* null and void, invalid, inoperative, useless, valueless, void, worthless

nullify *verb* cancel, counteract, invalidate, negate, neutralize, obviate, render null and void, veto

nullity *noun* nonexistence, invalidity, powerlessness, uselessness, worthlessness

numb *adjective* 1 unfeeling, benumbed, dead, deadened, frozen, immobilized, insensitive, paralysed, torpid ◆ *verb* 2 deaden, benumb, dull, freeze, immobilize, paralyse

number *noun* 1 numeral, character, digit, figure, integer 2 quantity, aggregate, amount, collection, crowd, horde, multitude, throng 3 issue, copy, edition, imprint, printing ◆ *verb* 4 count, account, add, calculate, compute, enumerate, include, reckon, total

numberless *adjective* infinite,

countless, endless, innumerable, multitudinous, myriad, unnumbered, untold

numbness *noun* deadness, dullness, insensitivity, paralysis, torpor

numbskull, numskull *noun* fool, blockhead, clot (*Brit. informal*), dolt, dummy (*slang*), dunce, oaf, twit (*informal*)

numeral *noun* number, digit, figure, integer

numerous *adjective* many, abundant, copious, plentiful, profuse, several, thick on the ground

nuncio *noun* ambassador, envoy, legate, messenger

nunnery *noun* convent, abbey, cloister, house

nuptial *adjective* marital, bridal, conjugal, connubial, matrimonial

nuptials *plural noun* wedding, marriage, matrimony

nurse *verb* 1 look after, care for, minister to, tend, treat 2 breast-feed, feed, nourish, nurture, suckle, wet-nurse 3 foster, cherish, cultivate, encourage, harbour, preserve, promote, succour, support

nursery *noun* creche, kindergarten, playgroup

nurture *noun* development, discipline, education, instruction, rearing, training, upbringing ◆ *verb* 2 develop, bring up, discipline, educate, instruct, rear, school, train

nut *noun* 1 *Slang* madman, crank (*informal*), lunatic, maniac, nutcase (*slang*), psycho (*slang*) 2 *Slang* head, brain, mind, reason, senses

nutrition noun <u>food</u>, nourishment, nutriment, sustenance

nutritious adjective <u>nourishing</u>, beneficial, health-giving, invigorating, nutritive, strengthening, wholesome

nuzzle verb <u>snuggle</u>, burrow, cuddle, fondle, nestle, pet

nymph noun <u>sylph</u>, dryad, girl, maiden, naiad

O o

oaf noun <u>idiot</u>, blockhead, clod, dolt, dunce, fool, goon, lout, moron, numbskull or numskull

oafish adjective <u>moronic</u>, dense, dim-witted (informal), doltish, dumb (informal), loutish, stupid, thick

oath noun 1 <u>promise</u>, affirmation, avowal, bond, pledge, vow, word 2 <u>swearword</u>, blasphemy, curse, expletive, profanity

obdurate adjective <u>stubborn</u>, dogged, hard-hearted, immovable, implacable, inflexible, obstinate, pig-headed, unyielding

obedience noun <u>respect</u>, acquiescence, compliance, docility, observance, reverence, submissiveness, subservience

obedient adjective <u>respectful</u>, acquiescent, biddable, compliant, deferential, docile, dutiful, submissive, subservient, well-trained

obelisk noun <u>column</u>, monolith, monument, needle, pillar, shaft

obese adjective <u>fat</u>, corpulent, gross, heavy, overweight, paunchy, plump, portly, rotund, stout, tubby

obesity noun <u>fatness</u>, bulk, corpulence, grossness, portliness, stoutness, tubbiness

obey verb <u>carry out</u>, abide by, act upon, adhere to, comply, conform, follow, heed, keep, observe

obfuscate verb <u>confuse</u>, befog, cloud, darken, muddy the waters, obscure, perplex

object[1] noun 1 <u>thing</u>, article, body, entity, item, phenomenon 2 <u>target</u>, focus, recipient, victim 3 <u>purpose</u>, aim, design, end, goal, idea, intention, objective, point

object[2] verb <u>protest</u>, argue against, demur, draw the line (at something), expostulate, oppose, take exception

objection noun <u>protest</u>, counter-argument, demur, doubt, opposition, remonstrance, scruple

objectionable adjective <u>unpleasant</u>, deplorable, disagreeable, intolerable, obnoxious, offensive, regrettable, repugnant, unseemly

objective noun 1 <u>purpose</u>, aim, ambition, end, goal, intention, mark, object, target ♦ adjective 2 <u>unbiased</u>, detached, disinterested, dispassionate, even-handed, fair, impartial, open-minded, unprejudiced

objectively adverb <u>impartially</u>, disinterestedly, dispassionately, even-handedly, with an open mind

objectivity noun <u>impartiality</u>, detachment, disinterestedness, dispassion

obligation noun <u>duty</u>, accountability, burden, charge, compulsion, liability, requirement, responsibility

obligatory adjective <u>compulsory</u>, binding, de rigueur, essential, imperative, mandatory, necessary, required, requisite, unavoidable

oblige verb 1 <u>compel</u>, bind, constrain, force, impel, make, necessitate, require 2 <u>indulge</u>, accommodate, benefit, gratify, please

obliged adjective 1 <u>grateful</u>, appreciative, beholden, indebted, in (someone's) debt, thankful 2 <u>bound</u>, compelled, forced, required

obliging adjective <u>cooperative</u>, accommodating, agreeable, considerate, good-natured, helpful, kind, polite, willing

oblique adjective 1 <u>slanting</u>, angled, aslant, sloping, tilted 2 <u>indirect</u>, backhanded, circuitous, implied, roundabout, sidelong

obliterate verb <u>destroy</u>, annihilate, blot out, efface, eradicate, erase, expunge, extirpate, root out, wipe out

obliteration noun <u>annihilation</u>, elimination, eradication, extirpation, wiping out

oblivion noun 1 <u>neglect</u>, abeyance, disregard, forgetfulness 2 <u>unconsciousness</u>,

insensibility, obliviousness, unawareness

oblivious adjective <u>unaware</u>, forgetful, heedless, ignorant, insensible, neglectful, negligent, regardless, unconcerned, unconscious, unmindful

obloquy noun 1 <u>abuse</u>, aspersion, attack, blame, censure, criticism, invective, reproach, slander, vilification 2 <u>discredit</u>, disgrace, dishonour, humiliation, ignominy, infamy, shame, stigma

obnoxious adjective <u>offensive</u>, disagreeable, insufferable, loathsome, nasty, nauseating, objectionable, odious, repulsive, revolting, unpleasant

obscene adjective 1 <u>indecent</u>, dirty, filthy, immoral, improper, lewd, offensive, pornographic, salacious 2 <u>sickening</u>, atrocious, disgusting, evil, heinous, loathsome, outrageous, shocking, vile, wicked

obscenity noun 1 <u>indecency</u>, coarseness, dirtiness, impropriety, lewdness, licentiousness, pornography, smut 2 <u>swearword</u>, four-letter word, profanity, vulgarism 3 <u>outrage</u>, abomination, affront, atrocity, blight, evil, offence, wrong

obscure adjective 1 <u>vague</u>, ambiguous, arcane, confusing, cryptic, enigmatic, esoteric, mysterious, opaque, recondite 2 <u>indistinct</u>, blurred, cloudy, dim, faint, gloomy, murky, shadowy 3 <u>little-known</u>, humble, lowly, out-of-the-way, remote, undistinguished, unheard-of, unknown ♦ *verb* **4** conceal, cover, disguise, hide, obfuscate, screen, veil

obscurity *noun* **1** darkness, dimness, dusk, gloom, haze, shadows **2** insignificance, lowliness, unimportance

obsequious *adjective* sycophantic, cringing, deferential, fawning, flattering, grovelling, ingratiating, servile, submissive, unctuous

observable *adjective* noticeable, apparent, detectable, discernible, evident, obvious, perceptible, recognizable, visible

observance *noun* honouring, carrying out, compliance, fulfilment, performance

observant *adjective* attentive, alert, eagle-eyed, perceptive, quick, sharp-eyed, vigilant, watchful, wide-awake

observation *noun* **1** study, examination, inspection, monitoring, review, scrutiny, surveillance, watching **2** remark, comment, note, opinion, pronouncement, reflection, thought, utterance

observe *verb* **1** see, detect, discern, discover, note, notice, perceive, spot, witness **2** watch, check, keep an eye on (*informal*), keep track of, look at, monitor, scrutinize, study, survey, view **3** remark, comment, mention, note, opine, say, state **4** honour, abide by, adhere to, comply, conform to, follow, heed, keep, obey, respect

observer *noun* spectator, beholder, bystander, eyewitness, fly on the wall, looker-on,

onlooker, viewer, watcher, witness

obsessed *adjective* preoccupied, dominated, gripped, haunted, hung up on (*slang*), infatuated, troubled

obsession *noun* preoccupation, complex, fetish, fixation, hang-up (*informal*), infatuation, mania, phobia, thing (*informal*)

obsessive *adjective* compulsive, besetting, consuming, gripping, haunting

obsolescent *adjective* waning, ageing, declining, dying out, on the wane, on the way out, past its prime

obsolete *adjective* extinct, antiquated, archaic, discarded, disused, old, old-fashioned, outmoded, out of date, passé

obstacle *noun* difficulty, bar, barrier, block, hindrance, hitch, hurdle, impediment, obstruction, snag, stumbling block

obstinacy *noun* stubbornness, doggedness, inflexibility, intransigence, obduracy, persistence, pig-headedness, tenacity, wilfulness

obstinate *adjective* stubborn, determined, dogged, inflexible, intractable, intransigent, pig-headed, refractory, self-willed, strong-minded, wilful

obstreperous *adjective* unruly, disorderly, loud, noisy, riotous, rowdy, turbulent, unmanageable, wild

obstruct *verb* block, bar, barricade, check, hamper, hinder, impede, restrict, stop, thwart

obstruction noun obstacle, bar, barricade, barrier, blockage, difficulty, hindrance, impediment

obstructive adjective uncooperative, awkward, blocking, delaying, hindering, restrictive, stalling, unhelpful

obtain verb 1 get, achieve, acquire, attain, earn, gain, land, procure, secure 2 exist, be in force, be prevalent, be the case, hold, prevail

obtainable adjective available, achievable, attainable, on tap (informal), to be had

obtrusive adjective noticeable, blatant, obvious, prominent, protruding, protuberant, sticking out

obtuse adjective slow, dense, dull, stolid, stupid, thick, uncomprehending

obviate verb preclude, avert, prevent, remove

obvious adjective evident, apparent, clear, conspicuous, distinct, indisputable, manifest, noticeable, plain, self-evident, undeniable, unmistakable

obviously adverb clearly, manifestly, of course, palpably, patently, plainly, undeniably, unmistakably, unquestionably, without doubt

occasion noun 1 time, chance, moment, opening, opportunity, window 2 event, affair, celebration, experience, happening, occurrence 3 reason, call, cause, excuse, ground(s), justification, motive, prompting, provocation ◆ verb 4 cause, bring about, engender, generate, give rise to, induce, inspire, lead to,

produce, prompt, provoke

occasional adjective infrequent, incidental, intermittent, irregular, odd, rare, sporadic, uncommon

occasionally adverb sometimes, at times, from time to time, irregularly, now and again, once in a while, periodically

occult adjective supernatural, arcane, esoteric, magical, mysterious, mystical

occupancy noun tenure, possession, residence, tenancy, use

occupant noun inhabitant, incumbent, indweller, inmate, lessee, occupier, resident, tenant

occupation noun 1 profession, business, calling, employment, job, line (of work), pursuit, trade, vocation, walk of life 2 possession, control, holding, occupancy, residence, tenancy, tenure 3 invasion, conquest, seizure, subjugation

occupied adjective 1 busy, employed, engaged, working 2 in use, engaged, full, taken, unavailable 3 inhabited, lived-in, peopled, settled, tenanted

occupy verb 1 often passive take up, divert, employ, engage, engross, involve, monopolize, preoccupy, tie up 2 live in, dwell in, inhabit, own, possess, reside in 3 fill, cover, permeate, pervade, take up 4 invade, capture, overrun, seize, take over

occur verb 1 happen, befall, come about, crop up (informal), take place, turn up (informal) 2 exist, appear, be found, be present, develop, manifest itself, show itself 3 occur to come to mind, cross one's mind, dawn on, enter one's head, spring to mind, strike one, suggest itself

occurrence noun 1 incident, adventure, affair, circumstance, episode, event, happening, instance 2 existence, appearance, development, manifestation, materialization

odd adjective 1 unusual, bizarre, extraordinary, freakish, irregular, peculiar, rare, remarkable, singular, strange 2 occasional, casual, incidental, irregular, periodic, random, sundry, various 3 spare, leftover, remaining, solitary, surplus, unmatched, unpaired

oddity noun 1 irregularity, abnormality, anomaly, eccentricity, freak, idiosyncrasy, peculiarity, quirk 2 misfit, crank (informal), maverick, oddball (informal)

oddment noun leftover, bit, fag end, fragment, off cut, remnant, scrap, snippet

odds plural noun 1 probability, chances, likelihood 2 at odds in conflict, at daggers drawn, at loggerheads, at sixes and sevens, at variance, out of line

odds and ends plural noun scraps, bits, bits and pieces, debris, oddments, remnants

odious adjective offensive, detestable, horrid, loathsome, obnoxious, repulsive, revolting, unpleasant

odour noun smell, aroma, bouquet, essence, fragrance, perfume, redolence, scent, stench, stink

odyssey noun journey, crusade, pilgrimage, quest, trek, voyage

off adverb 1 away, apart, aside, elsewhere, out ♦ adjective 2 unavailable, cancelled, finished, gone, postponed 3 bad, mouldy, rancid, rotten, sour, turned

offbeat adjective unusual, eccentric, left-field (informal), novel, outré, strange, unconventional, unorthodox, way-out (informal)

off colour adjective ill, out of sorts, peaky, poorly (informal), queasy, run down, sick, under the weather (informal), unwell

offence noun 1 crime, fault, misdeed, misdemeanour, sin, transgression, trespass, wrongdoing 2 snub, affront, hurt, indignity, injustice, insult, outrage, slight 3 annoyance, anger, displeasure, indignation, pique, resentment, umbrage, wrath

offend verb insult, affront, annoy, displease, hurt (someone's) feelings, outrage, slight, snub, upset, wound

offended adjective resentful, affronted, disgruntled, displeased, outraged, piqued, put out (informal), smarting, stung, upset

offender noun criminal, crook, culprit, delinquent, lawbreaker, miscreant, sinner, transgressor, villain, wrongdoer

offensive adjective 1 insulting, abusive, discourteous, disrespectful, impertinent, insolent, objectionable, rude 2 disagreeable, disgusting, nauseating, obnoxious, odious,

offer verb 1 **bid**, proffer, tender
2 **provide**, afford, furnish,
present 3 **propose**, advance,
submit, suggest 4 **volunteer**,
come forward, offer one's
services ♦ noun 5 **bid**, proposal,
proposition, submission,
suggestion, tender

offering noun **donation**,
contribution, gift, hand-out,
present, sacrifice, subscription

offhand adjective 1 **casual**, aloof,
brusque, careless, curt, glib
♦ adverb 2 **impromptu**, ad lib,
extempore, off the cuff (informal)

office noun **post**, function,
occupation, place, responsibility,
role, situation

officer noun **official**, agent,
appointee, executive,
functionary, office-holder,
representative

official adjective 1 **authorized**,
accredited, authentic, certified,
formal, legitimate, licensed,
proper, sanctioned ♦ noun
2 **officer**, agent, bureaucrat,
executive, functionary, office
bearer, representative

officiate verb **preside**, chair,
conduct, manage, oversee,
serve, superintend

officious adjective **interfering**,
dictatorial, intrusive,
meddlesome, obtrusive,
overzealous, pushy (informal),
self-important

offing noun **in the offing** in
prospect, imminent, on the

horizon, upcoming

off-putting adjective
discouraging, daunting,
disconcerting, dispiriting,
disturbing, formidable,
intimidating, unnerving,
unsettling

offset verb **cancel out**, balance
out, compensate for, counteract,
counterbalance, make up for,
neutralize

offshoot noun **by-product**,
adjunct, appendage,
development, spin-off

offspring noun 1 **child**,
descendant, heir, scion,
successor 2 **children**, brood,
descendants, family, heirs, issue,
progeny, young

often adverb **frequently**,
generally, repeatedly, time and
again

ogle verb **leer**, eye up (informal)

ogre noun **monster**, bogeyman,
bugbear, demon, devil, giant,
spectre

oil verb **lubricate**, grease

oily adjective **greasy**, fatty,
oleaginous

ointment noun **lotion**, balm,
cream, embrocation, emollient,
liniment, salve, unguent

O.K., okay interjection 1 **all right**,
agreed, right, roger, very good,
very well, yes ♦ adjective 2 **all
right**, acceptable, adequate, fine,
good, in order, permitted,
satisfactory, up to scratch
(informal) ♦ verb 3 **approve**, agree
to, authorize, endorse, give the
green light, rubber-stamp
(informal), sanction ♦ noun
4 **approval**, agreement, assent,

authorization, consent, go-ahead (*informal*), green light, permission, sanction, say-so (*informal*), seal of approval

old *adjective* **1** senile, aged, ancient, decrepit, elderly, mature, venerable **2** antique, antediluvian, antiquated, dated, obsolete, superannuated, timeworn **3** former, earlier, erstwhile, one-time, previous

old-fashioned *adjective* out of date, behind the times, dated, obsolescent, obsolete, old hat, outdated, outmoded, passé, unfashionable

omen *noun* sign, foreboding, indication, portent, premonition, presage, warning

ominous *adjective* sinister, fateful, foreboding, inauspicious, portentous, threatening, unpromising, unpropitious

omission *noun* exclusion, failure, lack, neglect, oversight

omit *verb* leave out, drop, eliminate, exclude, forget, neglect, overlook, pass over, skip

omnipotence *noun* supremacy, invincibility, mastery

omnipotent *adjective* almighty, all-powerful, supreme

omniscient *adjective* all-knowing, all-wise

once *adverb* **1** formerly, at one time, long ago, once upon a time, previously **2 at once: a** immediately, directly, forthwith, instantly, now, right away, straight away, this (very) minute **b** simultaneously, at the same time, together

oncoming *adjective* approaching,

advancing, forthcoming, looming, onrushing

onerous *adjective* difficult, burdensome, demanding, exacting, hard, heavy, laborious, oppressive, taxing

one-sided *adjective* biased, lopsided, partial, partisan, prejudiced, unfair, unjust

ongoing *adjective* evolving, continuous, developing, progressing, unfinished, unfolding

onlooker *noun* observer, bystander, eyewitness, looker-on, spectator, viewer, watcher, witness

only *adjective* **1** sole, exclusive, individual, lone, single, solitary, unique ♦ *adverb* **2** merely, barely, just, purely, simply

onset *noun* beginning, inception, outbreak, start

onslaught *noun* attack, assault, blitz, charge, offensive, onrush, onset

onus *noun* burden, liability, load, obligation, responsibility, task

onward, onwards *adverb* ahead, beyond, forth, forward, in front, on

ooze[1] *verb* seep, drain, dribble, drip, escape, filter, leak

ooze[2] *noun* mud, alluvium, mire, silt, slime, sludge

opaque *adjective* cloudy, dim, dull, filmy, hazy, impenetrable, muddy, murky

open *adjective* **1** unfastened, agape, ajar, gaping, uncovered, unfolded, unfurled, unlocked, yawning **2** accessible, available, free, public, unoccupied,

unrestricted, vacant
3 unresolved, arguable, debatable, moot, undecided, unsettled **4** frank, candid, guileless, honest, sincere, transparent ♦ *verb* **5** start, begin, commence, inaugurate, initiate, kick off (*informal*), launch, set in motion **6** unfasten, unblock, uncork, uncover, undo, unlock, untie, unwrap **7** unfold, expand, spread (out), unfurl, unroll

open-air *adjective* outdoor, alfresco

open-handed *adjective* generous, bountiful, free, lavish, liberal, munificent, unstinting

opening *noun* **1** hole, aperture, chink, cleft, crack, fissure, gap, orifice, perforation, slot, space **2** opportunity, chance, look-in (*informal*), occasion, vacancy **3** beginning, commencement, dawn, inception, initiation, launch, outset, start ♦ *adjective* **4** first, beginning, inaugural, initial, introductory, maiden, primary

openly *adverb* candidly, forthrightly, frankly, overtly, plainly, unhesitatingly, unreservedly

open-minded *adjective* tolerant, broad-minded, impartial, liberal, reasonable, receptive, unbiased, undogmatic, unprejudiced

operate *verb* **1** work, act, function, go, perform, run **2** handle, be in charge of, manage, manoeuvre, use, work

operation *noun* procedure, action, course, exercise, motion, movement, performance, process

operational *adjective* working,

functional, going, operative, prepared, ready, up and running, usable, viable, workable

operative *adjective* **1** in force, active, effective, functioning, in operation, operational ♦ *noun* **2** worker, artisan, employee, labourer

operator *noun* worker, conductor, driver, handler, mechanic, operative, practitioner, technician

opinion *noun* belief, assessment, feeling, idea, impression, judgment, point of view, sentiment, theory, view

opinionated *adjective* dogmatic, bigoted, cocksure, doctrinaire, overbearing, pig-headed, prejudiced, single-minded

opponent *noun* competitor, adversary, antagonist, challenger, contestant, enemy, foe, rival

opportune *adjective* timely, advantageous, appropriate, apt, auspicious, convenient, favourable, fitting, suitable, well-timed

opportunism *noun* expediency, exploitation, pragmatism, unscrupulousness

opportunity *noun* chance, moment, occasion, opening, scope, time

oppose *verb* fight, block, combat, counter, defy, resist, take issue with, take on, thwart, withstand

opposed *adjective* averse, antagonistic, clashing, conflicting, contrary, dissentient, hostile

opposing adjective hostile, conflicting, contrary, enemy, incompatible, opposite, rival

opposite adjective 1 facing, fronting 2 different, antithetical, conflicting, contrary, contrasted, reverse, unlike ♦ noun 3 reverse, antithesis, contradiction, contrary, converse, inverse

opposition noun 1 hostility, antagonism, competition, disapproval, obstruction, prevention, resistance, unfriendliness 2 opponent, antagonist, competition, foe, other side, rival

oppress verb 1 depress, afflict, burden, dispirit, harass, sadden, torment, vex 2 persecute, abuse, maltreat, subdue, subjugate, suppress, wrong

oppressed adjective downtrodden, abused, browbeaten, disadvantaged, harassed, maltreated, tyrannized, underprivileged

oppression noun persecution, abuse, brutality, cruelty, injury, injustice, maltreatment, subjection, tyranny

oppressive adjective 1 tyrannical, brutal, cruel, despotic, harsh, inhuman, repressive, severe, unjust 2 sultry, airless, close, muggy, stifling, stuffy

oppressor noun persecutor, autocrat, bully, despot, scourge, slave-driver, tormentor, tyrant

opt verb, often with for choose, decide (on), elect, go for, plump for, prefer

optimistic adjective hopeful, buoyant, cheerful, confident, encouraged, expectant, positive, rosy, sanguine

optimum adjective ideal, best, highest, optimal, peak, perfect, superlative

option noun choice, alternative, preference, selection

optional adjective voluntary, discretionary, elective, extra, open, possible

opulence noun 1 wealth, affluence, luxuriance, luxury, plenty, prosperity, riches 2 abundance, copiousness, cornucopia, fullness, profusion, richness, superabundance

opulent adjective 1 rich, affluent, lavish, luxurious, moneyed, prosperous, sumptuous, wealthy, well-off, well-to-do 2 abundant, copious, lavish, luxuriant, plentiful, profuse, prolific

opus noun work, brainchild, composition, creation, oeuvre, piece, production

oracle noun 1 prophecy, divination, prediction, prognostication, revelation 2 pundit, adviser, authority, guru, mastermind, mentor, wizard

oral adjective spoken, verbal, vocal

oration noun speech, address, discourse, harangue, homily, lecture

orator noun public speaker, declaimer, lecturer, rhetorician, speaker

oratorical adjective rhetorical, bombastic, declamatory, eloquent, grandiloquent, high-flown, magniloquent, sonorous

oratory noun eloquence,

declamation, elocution, grandiloquence, public speaking, rhetoric, speech-making

orb noun <u>sphere</u>, ball, circle, globe, ring

orbit noun 1 <u>path</u>, circle, course, cycle, revolution, rotation, trajectory 2 <u>sphere of influence</u>, ambit, compass, domain, influence, range, reach, scope, sweep ♦ verb 3 <u>circle</u>, circumnavigate, encircle, revolve around

orchestrate verb 1 <u>score</u>, arrange 2 <u>organize</u>, arrange, coordinate, put together, set up, stage-manage

ordain verb 1 <u>appoint</u>, anoint, consecrate, invest, nominate 2 <u>order</u>, decree, demand, dictate, fix, lay down, legislate, prescribe, rule, will

ordeal noun <u>hardship</u>, agony, anguish, baptism of fire, nightmare, suffering, test, torture, trial, tribulation(s)

order noun 1 <u>instruction</u>, command, decree, dictate, direction, directive, injunction, law, mandate, regulation, rule 2 <u>sequence</u>, arrangement, array, grouping, layout, line-up, progression, series, structure 3 <u>tidiness</u>, method, neatness, orderliness, organization, pattern, regularity, symmetry, system 4 <u>discipline</u>, calm, control, law, law and order, peace, quiet, tranquillity 5 <u>request</u>, application, booking, commission, requisition, reservation 6 <u>class</u>, caste, grade, position, rank, status 7 <u>kind</u>, class, family, genre, ilk, sort,

type 8 <u>society</u>, association, brotherhood, community, company, fraternity, guild, organization ♦ verb 9 <u>instruct</u>, bid, charge, command, decree, demand, direct, require 10 <u>request</u>, apply for, book, reserve, send away for 11 <u>arrange</u>, catalogue, classify, group, marshal, organize, sort out, systematize

orderly adjective 1 <u>well-organized</u>, businesslike, in order, methodical, neat, regular, scientific, shipshape, systematic, tidy 2 <u>well-behaved</u>, controlled, disciplined, law-abiding, peaceable, quiet, restrained

ordinarily adverb <u>usually</u>, as a rule, commonly, customarily, generally, habitually, in general, normally

ordinary adjective 1 <u>usual</u>, common, conventional, everyday, normal, regular, routine, standard, stock, typical 2 <u>commonplace</u>, banal, humble, humdrum, modest, mundane, plain, run-of-the-mill, unremarkable, workaday

organ noun 1 <u>part</u>, element, structure, unit 2 <u>mouthpiece</u>, forum, medium, vehicle, voice

organic adjective 1 <u>natural</u>, animate, biological, live, living 2 <u>systematic</u>, integrated, methodical, ordered, organized, structured

organism noun <u>creature</u>, animal, being, body, entity, structure

organization noun 1 <u>group</u>, association, body, company, confederation, corporation, institution, outfit (informal), syndicate **2** <u>management</u>, construction, coordination, direction, organizing, planning, running, structuring **3** <u>arrangement</u>, chemistry, composition, format, make-up, pattern, structure, unity

organize *verb* <u>arrange</u>, classify, coordinate, group, marshal, put together, run, set up, systematize, take care of

orgy *noun* **1** <u>revel</u>, bacchanalia, carousal, debauch, revelry, Saturnalia **2** <u>spree</u>, binge (*informal*), bout, excess, indulgence, overindulgence, splurge, surfeit

orient *verb* <u>familiarize</u>, acclimatize, adapt, adjust, align, get one's bearings, orientate

orientation *noun* **1** <u>position</u>, bearings, direction, location **2** <u>familiarization</u>, acclimatization, adaptation, adjustment, assimilation, introduction, settling in

orifice *noun* <u>opening</u>, aperture, cleft, hole, mouth, pore, rent, vent

origin *noun* **1** <u>root</u>, base, basis, derivation, fount, fountainhead, source, wellspring **2** <u>beginning</u>, birth, creation, emergence, foundation, genesis, inception, launch, start

original *adjective* **1** <u>first</u>, earliest, initial, introductory, maiden, primary, starting **2** <u>new</u>, fresh, ground-breaking, innovative, novel, seminal, unprecedented, unusual **3** <u>creative</u>, fertile, imaginative, ingenious, inventive, resourceful ♦ *noun* **4** <u>prototype</u>, archetype, master,

model, paradigm, pattern, precedent, standard

originality *noun* <u>novelty</u>, creativity, freshness, imagination, ingenuity, innovation, inventiveness, newness, unorthodoxy

originally *adverb* <u>initially</u>, at first, first, in the beginning, to begin with

originate *verb* **1** <u>begin</u>, arise, come, derive, emerge, result, rise, spring, start, stem **2** <u>introduce</u>, bring about, create, formulate, generate, institute, launch, pioneer

originator *noun* <u>creator</u>, architect, author, father or mother, founder, inventor, maker, pioneer

ornament *noun* **1** <u>decoration</u>, accessory, adornment, bauble, embellishment, festoon, knick-knack, trimming, trinket ♦ *verb* **2** <u>decorate</u>, adorn, beautify, embellish, festoon, grace, prettify

ornamental *adjective* <u>decorative</u>, attractive, beautifying, embellishing, for show, showy

ornamentation *noun* <u>decoration</u>, adornment, elaboration, embellishment, embroidery, frills, ornateness

ornate *adjective* <u>elaborate</u>, baroque, busy, decorated, fancy, florid, fussy, ornamented, overelaborate, rococo

orthodox *adjective* <u>established</u>, accepted, approved, conventional, customary, official, received, traditional, well-established

orthodoxy *noun* conformity, authority, conventionality, received wisdom, traditionalism

oscillate *verb* fluctuate, seesaw, sway, swing, vacillate, vary, vibrate, waver

oscillation *noun* swing, fluctuation, instability, vacillation, variation, wavering

ossify *verb* harden, fossilize, solidify, stiffen

ostensible *adjective* apparent, outward, pretended, professed, purported, seeming, so-called, superficial, supposed

ostensibly *adverb* apparently, on the face of it, professedly, seemingly, supposedly

ostentation *noun* display, affectation, exhibitionism, flamboyance, flashiness, flaunting, parade, pomp, pretentiousness, show, showing off (*informal*)

ostentatious *adjective* pretentious, brash, conspicuous, flamboyant, flashy, gaudy, loud, obtrusive, showy

ostracism *noun* exclusion, banishment, exile, isolation, rejection

ostracize *verb* exclude, banish, cast out, cold-shoulder, exile, give (someone) the cold shoulder, reject, send to Coventry, shun

other *adjective* 1 additional, added, alternative, auxiliary, extra, further, more, spare, supplementary 2 different, contrasting, dissimilar, distinct, diverse, separate, unrelated, variant

otherwise *conjunction* 1 or else, if not, or then ♦ *adverb* 2 differently, any other way, contrarily

ounce *noun* shred, atom, crumb, drop, grain, scrap, speck, trace

oust *verb* expel, depose, dislodge, displace, dispossess, eject, throw out, topple, turn out, unseat

out *adjective* 1 away, abroad, absent, elsewhere, gone, not at home, outside 2 extinguished, at an end, dead, ended, exhausted, expired, finished, used up

outbreak *noun* eruption, burst, epidemic, explosion, flare-up, outburst, rash, upsurge

outburst *noun* outpouring, eruption, explosion, flare-up, outbreak, paroxysm, spasm, surge

outcast *noun* pariah, castaway, exile, leper, *persona non grata*, refugee, vagabond, wretch

outclass *verb* surpass, eclipse, excel, leave standing (*informal*), outdo, outshine, outstrip, overshadow, run rings around (*informal*)

outcome *noun* result, conclusion, consequence, end, issue, payoff (*informal*), upshot

outcry *noun* protest, clamour, commotion, complaint, hue and cry, hullaballoo, outburst, uproar

outdated *adjective* old-fashioned, antiquated, archaic, obsolete, outmoded, out of date, passé, unfashionable

outdo *verb* surpass, beat, best, eclipse, exceed, get the better of, outclass, outmanoeuvre, overcome, top, transcend

outdoor adjective open-air, alfresco, out-of-door(s), outside

outer adjective external, exposed, exterior, outlying, outside, outward, peripheral, surface

outfit noun 1 costume, clothes, ensemble, garb, get-up (informal), kit, suit 2 Informal group, company, crew, organization, setup (informal), squad, team, unit

outgoing adjective 1 leaving, departing, former, retiring, withdrawing 2 sociable, approachable, communicative, expansive, extrovert, friendly, gregarious, open, warm

outgoings plural noun expenses, costs, expenditure, outlay, overheads

outing noun trip, excursion, expedition, jaunt, spin (informal)

outlandish adjective strange, bizarre, exotic, fantastic, far-out (slang), freakish, outré, preposterous, unheard-of, weird

outlaw noun 1 bandit, brigand, desperado, fugitive, highwayman, marauder, outcast, robber ♦ verb 2 forbid, ban, bar, disallow, exclude, prohibit, proscribe

outlay noun expenditure, cost, expenses, investment, outgoings, spending

outlet noun 1 release, avenue, channel, duct, exit, opening, vent 2 shop, market, store

outline noun 1 summary, recapitulation, résumé, rundown, synopsis, thumbnail sketch 2 shape, configuration, contour,

delineation, figure, form, profile, silhouette ♦ verb 3 summarize, adumbrate, delineate, draft, plan, rough out, sketch (in), trace

outlive verb survive, outlast

outlook noun 1 attitude, angle, frame of mind, perspective, point of view, slant, standpoint, viewpoint 2 prospect, expectations, forecast, future

outlying adjective remote, distant, far-flung, out-of-the-way, peripheral, provincial

outmoded adjective old-fashioned, anachronistic, antiquated, archaic, obsolete, out-of-date, outworn, passé, unfashionable

out-of-date adjective old-fashioned, antiquated, dated, expired, invalid, lapsed, obsolete, outmoded, outworn, passé

outpouring noun stream, cascade, effusion, flow, spate, spurt, torrent

output noun production, achievement, manufacture, productivity, yield

outrage noun 1 violation, abuse, affront, desecration, indignity, insult, offence, sacrilege, violence 2 indignation, anger, fury, hurt, resentment, shock, wrath ♦ verb 3 offend, affront, incense, infuriate, madden, scandalize, shock

outrageous adjective 1 offensive, atrocious, disgraceful, flagrant, heinous, iniquitous, nefarious, unspeakable, villainous, wicked 2 shocking, exorbitant, extravagant, immoderate, preposterous, scandalous, steep (*informal*), unreasonable

outré adjective eccentric, bizarre, fantastic, freakish, odd, off-the-wall (*slang*), outlandish, unconventional, weird

outright adjective 1 absolute, complete, out-and-out, perfect, thorough, thoroughgoing, total, unconditional, unmitigated, unqualified 2 direct, definite, flat, straightforward, unequivocal, unqualified ♦ adverb 3 absolutely, completely, openly, overtly, straightforwardly, thoroughly, to the full

outset noun beginning, commencement, inauguration, inception, kickoff (*informal*), onset, opening, start

outshine verb overshadow, eclipse, leave or put in the shade, outclass, outdo, outstrip, surpass, transcend, upstage

outside adjective 1 external, exterior, extraneous, outer, outward 2 As in **an outside chance** unlikely, distant, faint, marginal, remote, slight, slim, small ♦ noun 3 surface, exterior, façade, face, front, skin, topside

outsider noun interloper, incomer, intruder, newcomer, odd man out, stranger

outsize adjective extra-large, giant, gigantic, huge, jumbo (*informal*), mammoth, monster, oversized

outskirts plural noun edge, boundary, environs, periphery, suburbia, suburbs

outspoken adjective forthright, abrupt, blunt, explicit, frank, open, plain-spoken, unceremonious, unequivocal

outstanding adjective 1 excellent, exceptional, great, important, impressive, special, superior, superlative 2 unpaid, due, payable, pending, remaining, uncollected, unsettled

outstrip verb surpass, better, eclipse, exceed, excel, outdistance, outdo, overtake, transcend

outward adjective apparent, noticeable, observable, obvious, ostensible, perceptible, surface, visible

outwardly adverb ostensibly, apparently, externally, on the face of it, on the surface, seemingly, superficially, to all intents and purposes

outweigh verb override, cancel (out), compensate for, eclipse, prevail over, take precedence over, tip the scales

outwit verb outthink, cheat, dupe, get the better of, outfox, outmanoeuvre, outsmart (*informal*), put one over on (*informal*), swindle, take in (*informal*)

outworn adjective outdated, antiquated, discredited, disused, hackneyed, obsolete, outmoded, out-of-date, worn-out

oval adjective elliptical, egg-shaped, ovoid

ovation noun applause, acclaim, acclamation, big hand, cheers, clapping, plaudits, tribute

over preposition 1 on, above, on top of, upon 2 exceeding, above, in excess of, more than ♦ adverb 3 above, aloft, on high, overhead 4 extra, beyond, in addition, in excess, left over

♦ *adjective* **5** finished, bygone, closed, completed, concluded, done (with), ended, gone, past

overact *verb* exaggerate, ham or ham up (*informal*), overdo, overplay

overall *adjective* **1** total, all-embracing, blanket, complete, comprehensive, general, global, inclusive ♦ *adverb* **2** in general, on the whole

overawe *verb* intimidate, abash, alarm, daunt, frighten, scare, terrify

overbalance *verb* overturn, capsize, keel over, slip, tip over, topple over, tumble, turn turtle

overbearing *adjective* arrogant, bossy (*informal*), dictatorial, domineering, haughty, high handed, imperious, supercilious, superior

overblown *adjective* excessive, disproportionate, immoderate, inflated, overdone, over the top, undue

overcast *adjective* cloudy, dismal, dreary, dull, grey, leaden, louring or lowering, murky

overcharge *verb* cheat, diddle (*informal*), fleece, rip off (*slang*), short-change, sting (*informal*), surcharge

overcome *verb* **1** conquer, beat, defeat, master, overpower, overwhelm, prevail, subdue, subjugate, surmount, triumph over, vanquish ♦ *adjective* **2** affected, at a loss for words, bowled over (*informal*), overwhelmed, speechless, swept off one's feet

overconfident *adjective* brash,

cocksure, foolhardy, overweening, presumptuous

overcrowded *adjective* congested, bursting at the seams, choked, jam-packed, overloaded, overpopulated, packed (out), swarming

overdo *verb* **1** exaggerate, belabour, gild the lily, go overboard (*informal*), overindulge, overreach, overstate **2** overdo it overwork, bite off more than one can chew, burn the candle at both ends (*informal*), overload, strain or overstrain oneself, wear oneself out

overdone *adjective* **1** excessive, exaggerated, fulsome, immoderate, inordinate, overelaborate, too much, undue, unnecessary **2** overcooked, burnt, charred, dried up, spoiled

overdue *adjective* late, behindhand, behind schedule, belated, owing, tardy, unpunctual

overeat *verb* overindulge, binge (*informal*), gorge, gormandize, guzzle, pig out (*slang*), stuff oneself

overemphasize *verb* overstress, belabour, blow up out of all proportion, make a mountain out of a molehill (*informal*), overdramatize

overflow *verb* **1** spill, brim over, bubble over, pour over, run over, well over ♦ *noun* **2** surplus, overabundance, spilling over

overhang *verb* project, extend, jut, loom, protrude, stick out

overhaul *verb* **1** repair, check, do up (*informal*), examine, inspect,

recondition, restore, service
2 overtake, catch up with, get
ahead of, pass ♦ noun 3 checkup,
check, examination, going-over
(informal), inspection,
reconditioning, service

overhead adverb 1 above, aloft,
in the sky, on high, skyward, up
above, upward ♦ adjective
2 aerial, overhanging, upper

overheads plural noun running
costs, operating costs

overindulgence noun excess,
immoderation, intemperance,
overeating, surfeit

overjoyed adjective delighted,
cock-a-hoop, elated, euphoric,
jubilant, on cloud nine (informal),
over the moon (informal), thrilled

overload verb overburden,
burden, encumber, oppress,
overtax, saddle (with), strain,
weigh down

overlook verb 1 forget,
disregard, miss, neglect, omit,
pass 2 ignore, condone,
disregard, excuse, forgive, make
allowances for, pardon, turn a
blind eye to, wink at 3 have a
view of, look over or out on

overpower verb overwhelm,
conquer, crush, defeat, master,
overcome, overthrow, quell,
subdue, subjugate, vanquish

overpowering adjective
irresistible, forceful, invincible,
irrefutable, overwhelming,
powerful, strong

overrate verb overestimate,
exaggerate, overvalue

override verb overrule, annul,
cancel, countermand, nullify,
outweigh, supersede

overriding adjective ultimate,
dominant, paramount,
predominant, primary, supreme

overrule verb reverse, alter,
annul, cancel, countermand,
override, overturn, repeal,
rescind, veto

overrun verb 1 invade, occupy,
overwhelm, rout 2 infest, choke,
inundate, permeate, ravage,
spread over, swarm over
3 exceed, go beyond, overshoot,
run over or on

overseer noun supervisor, boss
(informal), chief, foreman,
master, superintendent

overshadow verb 1 outshine,
dominate, dwarf, eclipse, leave
or put in the shade, surpass,
tower above 2 spoil, blight, mar,
put a damper on, ruin, temper

oversight noun mistake, blunder,
carelessness, error, fault, lapse,
neglect, omission, slip

overt adjective open, blatant,
manifest, observable, obvious,
plain, public, unconcealed,
undisguised

overtake verb 1 pass, catch up
with, get past, leave behind,
outdistance, outdo, outstrip,
overhaul 2 befall, engulf,
happen, hit, overwhelm, strike

overthrow verb 1 defeat, bring
down, conquer, depose,
dethrone, oust, overcome,
overpower, topple, unseat,
vanquish ♦ noun 2 downfall,
defeat, destruction,
dethronement, fall, ousting,
undoing, unseating

overtone noun connotation,
hint, implication, innuendo,
intimation, nuance, sense,

suggestion, undercurrent

overture noun **1** *Music* introduction, opening, prelude **2 overtures** approach, advance, invitation, offer, proposal, proposition

overturn verb **1** tip over, capsize, keel over, overbalance, topple, upend, upturn **2** overthrow, bring down, depose, destroy, unseat

overweight adjective fat, bulky, chubby, chunky, corpulent, heavy, hefty, obese, plump, portly, stout, tubby (*informal*)

overwhelm verb **1** devastate, bowl over (*informal*), knock (someone) for six (*informal*), overcome, stagger, sweep (someone) off his or her feet, take (someone's) breath away **2** destroy, crush, cut to pieces, massacre, overpower, overrun, rout

overwhelming adjective devastating, breathtaking, crushing, irresistible, overpowering, shattering, stunning, towering

overwork verb **1** strain, burn the midnight oil, sweat (*informal*), work one's fingers to the bone **2** overuse, exhaust, exploit, fatigue, oppress, wear out, weary

overwrought adjective agitated, distracted, excited, frantic, keyed up, on edge, overexcited, tense, uptight (*informal*)

owe verb be in debt, be in arrears, be obligated or indebted

owing adjective unpaid, due, outstanding, overdue, owed, payable, unsettled

owing to preposition because of, as a result of, on account of

own adjective **1** personal, individual, particular, private ♦ pronoun **2 hold one's own** compete, keep going, keep one's end up, keep one's head above water **3 on one's own** alone, by oneself, independently, singly, unaided, unassisted, under one's own steam ♦ verb **4** possess, be in possession of, enjoy, have, hold, keep, retain **5** acknowledge, admit, allow, concede, confess, grant, recognize **6 own up** confess, admit, come clean, make a clean breast, tell the truth

owner noun possessor, holder, landlord or landlady, proprietor

ownership noun possession, dominion, title

P p

pace noun **1** step, gait, stride, tread, walk **2** speed, rate, tempo, velocity ♦ verb **3** stride, march, patrol, pound **4** pace out measure, count, mark out, step

pacifist noun peace lover, conscientious objector, dove

pacify verb calm, allay, appease, assuage, mollify, placate, propitiate, soothe

pack verb **1** package, bundle, load, store, stow **2** cram, compress, crowd, fill, jam, press, ram, stuff **3 pack off** send away, dismiss, send packing (*informal*) ♦ noun **4** bundle, back pack, burden, kitbag, knapsack, load,

package parcel, rucksack **5** packet, package **6** group, band, bunch, company, crowd, flock, gang, herd, mob, troop

package noun **1** parcel, box, carton, container, packet **2** unit, combination, whole **♦** verb **3** pack, box, parcel (up), wrap

packed adjective full, chock-a-block, chock-full, crammed, crowded, filled, jammed, jam-packed

packet noun **1** package, bag, carton, container, parcel **2** Slang fortune, bomb (Brit. slang), king's ransom (informal), pile (informal), small fortune, tidy sum (informal)

pack in verb Brit. informal stop, cease, chuck (informal), give up or give over, kick (informal)

pack up verb **1** put away, store **2** Informal stop, finish, give up, pack in (Brit. informal) **3** break down, conk out (informal), fail

pact noun agreement, alliance, bargain, covenant, deal, treaty, understanding

pad¹ noun **1** cushion, buffer, protection, stuffing, wad **2** notepad, block, jotter, writing pad **3** paw, foot, sole **4** Slang home, apartment, flat, place **♦** verb **5** pack, cushion, fill, protect, stuff **6** pad out lengthen, elaborate, fill out, flesh out, protract, spin out, stretch

pad² verb sneak, creep, go barefoot, steal

padding noun **1** filling, packing, stuffing, wadding **2** waffle (informal, chiefly Brit.), hot air (informal), verbiage, verbosity, wordiness

paddle¹ noun **1** oar, scull **♦** verb **2** row, propel, pull, scull

paddle² verb **1** wade, slop, splash (about) **2** dabble, stir

pagan adjective **1** heathen, idolatrous, infidel, polytheistic **♦** noun **2** heathen, idolater, infidel, polytheist

page¹ noun folio, leaf, sheet, side

page² noun **1** attendant, pageboy, servant, squire **♦** verb **2** call, send for, summon

pageant noun show, display, parade, procession, spectacle, tableau

pageantry noun spectacle, display, grandeur, parade, pomp, show, splendour, theatricality

pain noun **1** hurt, ache, discomfort, irritation, pang, soreness, tenderness, throb, twinge **2** suffering, agony, anguish, distress, heartache, misery, torment, torture **♦** verb **3** hurt, smart, sting, throb **4** distress, agonize, cut to the quick, grieve, hurt, sadden, torment, torture

pained adjective distressed, aggrieved, hurt, injured, offended, upset, wounded

painful adjective **1** distressing, disagreeable, distasteful, grievous, unpleasant **2** sore, aching, agonizing, smarting, tender **3** difficult, arduous, hard, laborious, troublesome, trying

painfully adverb distressingly, clearly, dreadfully, sadly, unfortunately

painkiller noun analgesic, anaesthetic, anodyne, drug

painless adjective simple, easy, effortless, fast, quick

pains plural noun trouble, bother, care, diligence, effort

painstaking adjective thorough, assiduous, careful, conscientious, diligent, meticulous, scrupulous

paint noun 1 colouring, colour, dye, pigment, stain, tint ♦ verb 2 depict, draw, picture, portray, represent, sketch 3 coat, apply, colour, cover, daub

pair noun 1 couple, brace, duo, twins ♦ verb 2 couple, bracket, join, match (up), team, twin

pal noun Informal friend, buddy (informal), chum (informal), companion, comrade, crony, mate (informal)

palatable adjective delicious, appetizing, luscious, mouthwatering, tasty

palate noun taste, appetite, stomach

palatial adjective magnificent, grand, imposing, majestic, opulent, regal, splendid, stately

palaver noun fuss, business (informal), carry on (informal, chiefly Brit.), pantomime (informal, chiefly Brit.), performance (informal), rigmarole, song and dance (Brit. informal), to-do

pale adjective 1 white, ashen, bleached, colourless, faded, light, pallid, pasty, wan ♦ verb 2 become pale, blanch, go white, lose colour, whiten

pall¹ noun 1 cloud, mantle, shadow, shroud, veil 2 gloom, check, damp, damper

pall² verb become boring, become dull, become tedious,

cloy, jade, sicken, tire, weary

pallid adjective pale, anaemic, ashen, colourless, pasty, wan

pallor noun paleness, lack of colour, pallidness, wanness, whiteness

palm off verb fob off, foist off, pass off

palpable adjective obvious, clear, conspicuous, evident, manifest, plain, unmistakable, visible

palpitate verb beat, flutter, pound, pulsate, throb, tremble

paltry adjective insignificant, contemptible, despicable, inconsiderable, meagre, mean, measly, minor, miserable, petty, poor, puny, slight, small, trifling, trivial, unimportant, worthless

pamper verb spoil, coddle, cosset, indulge, mollycoddle, pet

pamphlet noun booklet, brochure, circular, leaflet, tract

pan¹ noun 1 pot, container, saucepan ♦ verb 2 sift out, look for, search for 3 Informal criticize, censure, knock (informal), slam (slang), tear into (informal)

pan² verb move, follow, sweep, track

panacea noun cure-all, nostrum, universal cure

panache noun style, dash, élan, flamboyance

pandemonium noun uproar, bedlam, chaos, confusion, din, hullabaloo, racket, rumpus, turmoil

pander verb pander to indulge, cater to, gratify, play up to (informal), please, satisfy

pang noun twinge, ache, pain,

panic noun **1** <u>fear</u>, alarm, fright, hysteria, scare, terror ◆ verb **2** <u>go to pieces</u>, become hysterical, lose one's nerve **3** <u>alarm</u>, scare, unnerve

panic-stricken adjective <u>frightened</u>, frightened out of one's wits, hysterical, in a cold sweat (informal), panicky, scared, scared stiff, terrified

panoply noun <u>array</u>, attire, dress, garb, regalia, trappings

panorama noun <u>view</u>, prospect, vista

panoramic adjective <u>wide</u>, comprehensive, extensive, overall, sweeping

pant verb <u>puff</u>, blow, breathe, gasp, heave, wheeze

pants plural noun **1** Brit. <u>underpants</u>, boxer shorts, briefs, drawers, knickers, panties **2** U.S. <u>trousers</u>, slacks

paper noun **1** <u>newspaper</u>, daily, gazette, journal **2** <u>essay</u>, article, dissertation, report, treatise **3** papers: **a** <u>documents</u>, certificates, deeds, records **b** <u>letters</u>, archive, diaries, documents, dossier, file, records ◆ verb **4** <u>wallpaper</u>, hang

par noun <u>average</u>, level, mean, norm, standard, usual

parable noun <u>lesson</u>, allegory, fable, moral tale, story

parade noun **1** <u>procession</u>, array, cavalcade, march, pageant **2** <u>show</u>, display, spectacle ◆ verb **3** <u>flaunt</u>, display, exhibit, show off (informal) **4** <u>march</u>, process

paradigm noun <u>model</u>, example, ideal, pattern

paradise noun **1** <u>heaven</u>, Elysian fields, Happy Valley, Promised Land **2** <u>bliss</u>, delight, felicity, heaven, utopia

paradox noun <u>contradiction</u>, anomaly, enigma, oddity, puzzle

paradoxical adjective <u>contradictory</u>, baffling, confounding, enigmatic, puzzling

paragon noun <u>model</u>, epitome, exemplar, ideal, nonpareil, pattern, quintessence

paragraph noun <u>section</u>, clause, item, part, passage, subdivision

parallel adjective **1** <u>equidistant</u>, alongside, side by side **2** <u>matching</u>, analogous, corresponding, like, resembling, similar ◆ noun **3** <u>equivalent</u>, analogue, counterpart, equal, match, twin **4** <u>similarity</u>, analogy, comparison, likeness, resemblance

paralyse verb **1** <u>disable</u>, cripple, incapacitate, lame **2** <u>immobilize</u>, freeze, halt, numb, petrify, stun

paralysis noun **1** <u>immobility</u>, palsy **2** <u>standstill</u>, breakdown, halt, stoppage

paralytic adjective <u>paralysed</u>, crippled, disabled, incapacitated, lame, palsied

parameter noun Informal <u>limit</u>, framework, limitation, restriction, specification

paramount adjective <u>principal</u>, cardinal, chief, first, foremost, main, primary, prime, supreme

paranoid adjective **1** <u>mentally ill</u>, deluded, disturbed, manic, neurotic, paranoiac, psychotic **2** Informal <u>suspicious</u>, fearful, nervous, worried

paraphernalia noun equipment, apparatus, baggage, belongings, effects, gear, stuff, tackle, things, trappings

paraphrase noun 1 rewording, rephrasing, restatement ♦ verb 2 reword, express in other words or one's own words, rephrase, restate

parasite noun sponger (informal), bloodsucker (informal), hanger-on, leech, scrounger (informal)

parasitic, parasitical adjective scrounging (informal), bloodsucking (informal), sponging (informal)

parcel noun 1 package, bundle, pack ♦ verb 2 often with up wrap, do up, pack, package, tie up

parch verb dry up, dehydrate, desiccate, evaporate, shrivel, wither

parched adjective dried out or up, arid, dehydrated, dry, thirsty

pardon verb 1 forgive, absolve, acquit, excuse, exonerate, let off (informal), overlook ♦ noun 2 forgiveness, absolution, acquittal, amnesty, exoneration

pardonable adjective forgivable, excusable, minor, understandable, venial

pare verb 1 peel, clip, cut, shave, skin, trim 2 cut back, crop, cut, decrease, dock, reduce

parent noun father or mother, procreator, progenitor, sire

parentage noun family, ancestry, birth, descent, lineage, pedigree, stock

pariah noun outcast, exile, undesirable, untouchable

parish noun community, church, congregation, flock

parity noun equality, consistency, equivalence, uniformity, unity

park noun parkland, estate, garden, grounds, woodland

parlance noun language, idiom, jargon, phraseology, speech, talk, tongue

parliament noun assembly, congress, convention, council, legislature, senate

parliamentary adjective governmental, law-making, legislative

parlour noun Old-fashioned sitting room, drawing room, front room, living room, lounge

parlous adjective Archaic or humorous dangerous, hazardous, risky

parochial adjective provincial, insular, limited, narrow, narrow-minded, petty, small-minded

parody noun 1 takeoff (informal), burlesque, caricature, satire, send-up (Brit. informal), skit, spoof (informal) ♦ verb 2 take off (informal), burlesque, caricature, do a takeoff of (informal), satirize, send up (Brit. informal)

paroxysm noun outburst, attack, convulsion, fit, seizure, spasm

parrot verb repeat, copy, echo, imitate, mimic

parry verb 1 ward off, block, deflect, rebuff, repel, repulse 2 evade, avoid, dodge, sidestep

parsimonious adjective mean, close, frugal, miserly, niggardly, penny-pinching (informal), stingy, tightfisted

parson noun <u>clergyman</u>, churchman, cleric, minister, pastor, preacher, priest, vicar

part noun 1 <u>piece</u>, bit, fraction, fragment, portion, scrap, section, share 2 <u>component</u>, branch, constituent, division, member, unit 3 *Theatre* <u>role</u>, character, lines 4 <u>side</u>, behalf, cause, concern, interest 5 *often plural* <u>region</u>, area, district, neighbourhood, quarter, vicinity 6 **in good part** <u>good-naturedly</u>, cheerfully, well, without offence 7 **in part** <u>partly</u>, a little, in some measure, partially, somewhat ♦ verb 8 <u>divide</u>, break, come apart, detach, rend, separate, sever, split, tear 9 <u>separate</u>, depart, go, go away, leave, split up, withdraw

partake verb 1 **partake of** <u>consume</u>, eat, take 2 **partake in** <u>participate in</u>, engage in, share in, take part in

partial adjective 1 <u>incomplete</u>, imperfect, uncompleted, unfinished 2 <u>biased</u>, discriminatory, one-sided, partisan, prejudiced, unfair, unjust

partiality noun 1 <u>bias</u>, favouritism, preference, prejudice 2 <u>liking</u>, fondness, inclination, love, penchant, predilection, taste, weakness

partially adverb <u>partly</u>, fractionally, incompletely, in part, not wholly, somewhat

participant noun <u>participator</u>, contributor, member, player, stakeholder

participate verb <u>take part</u>, be involved in, join in, partake, perform, share

participation noun <u>taking part</u>, contribution, involvement, joining in, partaking, sharing in

particle noun <u>bit</u>, grain, iota, jot, mite, piece, scrap, shred, speck

particular adjective 1 <u>specific</u>, distinct, exact, peculiar, precise, special 2 <u>special</u>, especial, exceptional, marked, notable, noteworthy, remarkable, singular, uncommon, unusual 3 <u>fussy</u>, choosy (*informal*), demanding, fastidious, finicky, pernickety (*informal*), picky (*informal*) ♦ noun 4 *usually plural* <u>detail</u>, circumstance, fact, feature, item, specification 5 **in particular** <u>especially</u>, distinctly, exactly, particularly, specifically

particularly adverb 1 <u>especially</u>, exceptionally, notably, singularly, uncommonly, unusually 2 <u>specifically</u>, distinctly, especially, explicitly, expressly, in particular

parting noun 1 <u>going</u>, farewell, goodbye 2 <u>division</u>, breaking, rift, rupture, separation, split

partisan noun 1 <u>supporter</u>, adherent, devotee, upholder 2 <u>underground fighter</u>, guerrilla, resistance fighter ♦ adjective 3 <u>prejudiced</u>, biased, interested, one-sided, partial, sectarian

partition noun 1 <u>screen</u>, barrier, wall 2 <u>division</u>, segregation, separation 3 <u>allotment</u>, apportionment, distribution ♦ verb 4 <u>separate</u>, divide, screen

partly adverb <u>partially</u>, slightly, somewhat

partner noun 1 <u>spouse</u>, consort, husband or wife, mate, significant other (*U.S. informal*) **2** companion, ally, associate, colleague, comrade, helper, mate

partnership noun company, alliance, cooperative, firm, house, society, union

party noun **1** get-together (*informal*), celebration, do (*informal*), festivity, function, gathering, reception, social gathering **2** group, band, company, crew, gang, squad, team, unit **3** faction, camp, clique, coterie, league, set, side **4** *Informal* person, individual, someone

pass verb **1** go by or past, elapse, go, lapse, move, proceed, run **2** qualify, do, get through, graduate, succeed **3** spend, fill, occupy, while away **4** give, convey, deliver, hand, send, transfer **5** approve, accept, decree, enact, legislate, ordain, ratify **6** exceed, beat, go beyond, outdo, outstrip, surpass **7** end, blow over, cease, go ♦ noun **8** gap, canyon, gorge, ravine, route **9** licence, authorization, passport, permit, ticket, warrant

passable adjective adequate, acceptable, all right, average, fair, mediocre, so-so (*informal*), tolerable

passage noun **1** way, alley, avenue, channel, course, path, road, route **2** corridor, hall, lobby, vestibule **3** extract, excerpt, piece, quotation, reading, section, text **4** journey, crossing, trek, trip, voyage **5** safe-conduct, freedom, permission, right

passageway noun corridor, aisle, alley, hall, hallway, lane, passage

pass away verb Euphemistic die, expire, kick the bucket (*slang*), pass on, pass over, shuffle off this mortal coil, snuff it (*informal*)

passé adjective out-of-date, dated, obsolete, old-fashioned, old hat, outdated, outmoded, unfashionable

passenger noun traveller, fare, rider

passer-by noun bystander, onlooker, witness

passing adjective **1** momentary, brief, ephemeral, fleeting, short-lived, temporary, transient, transitory **2** superficial, casual, cursory, glancing, quick, short

passion noun **1** love, ardour, desire, infatuation, lust **2** emotion, ardour, excitement, feeling, fervour, fire, heat, intensity, warmth, zeal **3** rage, anger, fit, frenzy, fury, outburst, paroxysm, storm **4** mania, bug (*informal*), craving, craze, enthusiasm, fascination, obsession

passionate adjective **1** loving, amorous, ardent, erotic, hot, lustful **2** emotional, ardent, eager, fervent, fierce, heartfelt, impassioned, intense, strong

passive adjective submissive, compliant, docile, inactive, quiescent, receptive

pass off verb fake, counterfeit, make a pretence of, palm off

pass out verb Informal faint, become unconscious, black out (*informal*), lose consciousness

pass over verb disregard, ignore,

overlook, take no notice of

pass up verb Informal miss, abstain, decline, forgo, give (something) a miss (informal), let slip, neglect

password noun signal, key word, watchword

past adjective 1 former, ancient, bygone, early, olden, previous 2 over, done, ended, finished, gone ♦ noun 3 background, history, life, past life 4 **the past** former times, days gone by, long ago, olden days ♦ preposition 5 after, beyond, later than 6 beyond, across, by, over

paste noun 1 adhesive, cement, glue, gum ♦ verb 2 stick, cement, glue, gum

pastel adjective pale, delicate, light, muted, soft

pastiche noun medley, blend, hotchpotch, mélange, miscellany, mixture

pastime noun activity, amusement, diversion, entertainment, game, hobby, recreation

pastor noun clergyman, churchman, ecclesiastic, minister, parson, priest, rector, vicar

pastoral adjective 1 rustic, bucolic, country, rural 2 ecclesiastical, clerical, ministerial, priestly

pasture noun grassland, grass, grazing, meadow

pasty adjective pale, anaemic, pallid, sickly, wan

pat verb 1 stroke, caress, fondle, pet, tap, touch ♦ noun 2 stroke, clap, tap

patch noun 1 reinforcement 2 spot, bit, scrap, shred, small piece 3 plot, area, ground, land, tract ♦ verb 4 mend, cover, reinforce, repair, sew up

patchwork noun mixture, hotchpotch, jumble, medley, pastiche

patchy adjective uneven, erratic, fitful, irregular, sketchy, spotty, variable

patent noun 1 copyright, licence ♦ adjective 2 obvious, apparent, clear, evident, glaring, manifest

paternal adjective fatherly, concerned, protective, solicitous

paternity noun 1 fatherhood 2 parentage, descent, extraction, family, lineage

path noun 1 way, footpath, road, track, trail 2 course, direction, road, route, way

pathetic adjective sad, affecting, distressing, heart-rending, moving, pitiable, plaintive, poignant, tender, touching

pathos noun sadness, pitifulness, plaintiveness, poignancy

patience noun 1 forbearance, calmness, restraint, serenity, sufferance, tolerance 2 endurance, constancy, fortitude, long-suffering, perseverance, resignation, stoicism, submission

patient adjective 1 long-suffering, calm, enduring, persevering, philosophical, resigned, stoical, submissive, uncomplaining 2 forbearing, even-tempered, forgiving, indulgent, lenient, mild, tolerant, understanding ♦ noun 3 sick person, case, invalid, sufferer

patriot noun 1 <u>nationalist</u>, chauvinist, loyalist

patriotic adjective <u>nationalistic</u>, chauvinistic, jingoistic, loyal

patriotism noun <u>nationalism</u>, jingoism

patrol noun 1 <u>policing</u>, guarding, protecting, vigilance, watching 2 <u>guard</u>, patrolman, sentinel, watch, watchman ◆ verb 3 <u>police</u>, guard, inspect, keep guard, keep watch, safeguard

patron noun 1 <u>supporter</u>, backer, benefactor, champion, friend, helper, philanthropist, sponsor 2 <u>customer</u>, buyer, client, frequenter, habitué, shopper

patronage noun 1 <u>support</u>, aid, assistance, backing, help, promotion, sponsorship 2 <u>custom</u>, business, clientele, commerce, trade, trading, traffic

patronize verb 1 <u>talk down to</u>, look down on 2 <u>be a customer or client of</u>, do business with, frequent, shop at 3 <u>support</u>, back, fund, help, maintain, promote, sponsor

patronizing adjective <u>condescending</u>, disdainful, gracious, haughty, snobbish, supercilious, superior

patter¹ verb 1 <u>tap</u>, beat, pat, pitter-patter 2 <u>walk lightly</u>, scurry, scuttle, skip, trip ◆ noun 3 <u>tapping</u>, pattering, pitter-patter

patter² noun 1 <u>spiel</u> (informal), line, pitch 2 <u>chatter</u>, gabble, jabber, nattering, prattle 3 <u>jargon</u>, argot, cant, lingo (informal), patois, slang, vernacular ◆ verb 4 <u>chatter</u>,

jabber, prate, rattle on, spout (informal)

pattern noun 1 <u>design</u>, arrangement, decoration, device, figure, motif 2 <u>order</u>, method, plan, sequence, system 3 <u>plan</u>, design, diagram, guide, original, stencil, template ◆ verb 4 <u>model</u>, copy, follow, form, imitate, mould, style

paucity noun Formal <u>scarcity</u>, dearth, deficiency, lack, rarity, scantiness, shortage, sparseness

paunch noun <u>belly</u>, pot, potbelly, spare tyre (Brit. slang)

pauper noun <u>down-and-out</u>, bankrupt, beggar, mendicant, poor person

pause verb 1 <u>stop briefly</u>, break, cease, delay, halt, have a breather (informal), interrupt, rest, take a break, wait ◆ noun 2 <u>stop</u>, break, breather (informal), cessation, gap, halt, interlude, intermission, interval, lull, respite, rest, stoppage

pave verb <u>cover</u>, concrete, floor, surface, tile

paw verb Informal <u>manhandle</u>, grab, handle roughly, maul, molest

pawn¹ verb <u>hock</u> (informal, chiefly U.S.), deposit, mortgage, pledge

pawn² noun <u>tool</u>, cat's-paw, instrument, plaything, puppet, stooge (slang)

pay verb 1 <u>reimburse</u>, compensate, give, recompense, remit, remunerate, requite, reward, settle 2 <u>give</u>, bestow, extend, grant, hand out, present 3 <u>benefit</u>, be worthwhile, repay 4 <u>be profitable</u>, make a return,

payable make money 5 <u>yield</u>, bring in, produce, return ♦ *noun* 6 <u>wages</u>, allowance, earnings, fee, income, payment, recompense, reimbursement, remuneration, reward, salary, stipend

payable *adjective* <u>due</u>, outstanding, owed, owing

pay back *verb* 1 <u>repay</u>, refund, reimburse, settle up, square 2 <u>get even with</u> (*informal*), get one's own back, hit back, retaliate

payment *noun* 1 <u>paying</u>, discharge, remittance, settlement 2 <u>remittance</u>, advance, deposit, instalment, premium 3 <u>wage</u>, fee, hire, remuneration, reward

pay off *verb* 1 <u>settle</u>, clear, discharge, pay in full, square 2 <u>succeed</u>, be effective, work

pay out *verb* <u>spend</u>, disburse, expend, fork out or over or up (*slang*), shell out (*informal*)

peace *noun* 1 <u>stillness</u>, calm, calmness, hush, quiet, repose, rest, silence, tranquillity 2 <u>serenity</u>, calm, composure, contentment, repose 3 <u>harmony</u>, accord, agreement, concord 4 <u>truce</u>, armistice, treaty

peaceable *adjective* <u>peace-loving</u>, conciliatory, friendly, gentle, mild, peaceful, unwarlike

peaceful *adjective* 1 <u>at peace</u>, amicable, friendly, harmonious, nonviolent 2 <u>calm</u>, placid, quiet, restful, serene, still, tranquil, undisturbed 3 <u>peace-loving</u>, conciliatory, peaceable, unwarlike

peacemaker *noun* <u>mediator</u>, arbitrator, conciliator, pacifier

peak *noun* 1 <u>point</u>, apex, brow, crest, pinnacle, summit, tip, top 2 <u>high point</u>, acme, climax, crown, culmination, zenith ♦ *verb* 3 <u>culminate</u>, climax, come to a head

peal *noun* 1 <u>ring</u>, blast, chime, clang, clap, crash, reverberation, roar, rumble ♦ *verb* 2 <u>ring</u>, chime, crash, resound, roar, rumble

peasant *noun* <u>rustic</u>, countryman

peccadillo *noun* <u>misdeed</u>, error, indiscretion, lapse, misdemeanour, slip

peck *verb, noun* <u>pick</u>, dig, hit, jab, poke, prick, strike, tap

peculiar *adjective* 1 <u>odd</u>, abnormal, bizarre, curious, eccentric, extraordinary, freakish, funny, offbeat, outlandish, outré, quaint, queer, singular, strange, uncommon, unconventional, unusual, weird 2 <u>specific</u>, characteristic, distinctive, particular, special, unique

peculiarity *noun* 1 <u>eccentricity</u>, abnormality, foible, idiosyncrasy, mannerism, oddity, quirk 2 <u>characteristic</u>, attribute, feature, mark, particularity, property, quality, trait

pedagogue *noun* <u>teacher</u>, instructor, master or mistress, schoolmaster or schoolmistress

pedant *noun* <u>hairsplitter</u>, nit-picker (*informal*), quibbler

pedantic *adjective* <u>hairsplitting</u>, academic, bookish, donnish, formal, fussy, nit-picking (*informal*), particular, precise, punctilious

pedantry *noun* <u>hairsplitting</u>, punctiliousness, quibbling

peddle verb sell, flog (slang), hawk, market, push (informal), trade

pedestal noun support, base, foot, mounting, plinth, stand

pedestrian noun 1 walker, foot-traveller ♦ adjective 2 dull, banal, boring, commonplace, humdrum, mediocre, mundane, ordinary, prosaic, run-of-the-mill, uninspired

pedigree noun 1 lineage, ancestry, blood, breed, descent, extraction, family, family tree, genealogy, line, race, stock ♦ adjective 2 purebred, full-blooded, thoroughbred

pedlar noun seller, door-to-door salesman, hawker, huckster, vendor

peek verb 1 glance, look, peep ♦ noun 2 glance, glimpse, look, look-see (slang), peep

peel verb 1 skin, flake off, pare, scale, strip off ♦ noun 2 skin, peeling, rind

peep[1] verb 1 peek, look, sneak a look, steal a look ♦ noun 2 look, glimpse, look-see (slang), peek

peep[2] verb, noun tweet, cheep, chirp, squeak

peephole noun spyhole, aperture, chink, crack, hole, opening

peer[1] noun 1 noble, aristocrat, lord, nobleman 2 equal, compeer, fellow, like

peer[2] verb squint, gaze, inspect, peep, scan, snoop, spy

peerage noun aristocracy, lords and ladies, nobility, peers

peerless adjective unequalled, beyond compare, excellent,

incomparable, matchless, outstanding, unmatched, unparalleled, unrivalled

peevish adjective irritable, cantankerous, childish, churlish, cross, crotchety (informal), fractious, fretful, grumpy, petulant, querulous, snappy, sulky, sullen, surly

peg verb fasten, attach, fix, join, secure

pejorative adjective derogatory, deprecatory, depreciatory, disparaging, negative, uncomplimentary, unpleasant

pelt[1] verb 1 throw, batter, bombard, cast, hurl, pepper, shower, sling, strike 2 rush, belt (slang), charge, dash, hurry, run fast, shoot, speed, tear 3 pour, bucket down (informal), rain cats and dogs (informal), rain hard, teem

pelt[2] noun coat, fell, hide, skin

pen[1] verb write, compose, draft, draw up, jot down

pen[2] noun 1 enclosure, cage, coop, fold, hutch, pound, sty ♦ verb 2 enclose, cage, confine, coop up, fence in, hedge, shut up or in

penal adjective disciplinary, corrective, punitive

penalize verb punish, discipline, handicap, impose a penalty on

penalty noun punishment, fine, forfeit, handicap, price

penance noun atonement, penalty, reparation, sackcloth and ashes

penchant noun liking, bent, bias, fondness, inclination, leaning, partiality, predilection, proclivity, propensity, taste, tendency

pending adjective undecided, awaiting, imminent, impending, in the balance, undetermined, unsettled

penetrate verb 1 pierce, bore, enter, go through, prick, stab 2 grasp, comprehend, decipher, fathom, figure out (informal), get to the bottom of, suss (out) (slang), work out

penetrating adjective 1 sharp, carrying, harsh, piercing, shrill 2 perceptive, acute, astute, incisive, intelligent, keen, perspicacious, quick, sharp, sharp-witted, shrewd

penetration noun 1 piercing, entrance, entry, incision, puncturing 2 perception, acuteness, astuteness, insight, keenness, sharpness, shrewdness

penitence noun repentance, compunction, contrition, regret, remorse, shame, sorrow

penitent adjective repentant, abject, apologetic, conscience-stricken, contrite, regretful, remorseful, sorry

pen name noun pseudonym, nom de plume

pennant noun flag, banner, ensign, pennon, streamer

penniless adjective poor, broke (informal), destitute, dirt-poor (informal), down and out, flat broke (informal), impecunious, impoverished, indigent, penurious, poverty-stricken, skint (Brit. slang), stony-broke (Brit. slang)

pension noun allowance, annuity, benefit, superannuation

pensioner noun senior citizen, O.A.P., retired person

pensive adjective thoughtful, contemplative, dreamy, meditative, musing, preoccupied, reflective, sad, serious, solemn, wistful

pent-up adjective suppressed, bottled up, curbed, held back, inhibited, repressed, smothered, stifled

penury noun poverty, beggary, destitution, indigence, need, privation, want

people plural noun 1 persons, humanity, mankind, men and women, mortals 2 nation, citizens, community, folk, inhabitants, population, public 3 family, clan, race, tribe ◆verb 4 inhabit, colonize, occupy, populate, settle

pepper noun 1 seasoning, flavour, spice ◆verb 2 sprinkle, dot, fleck, spatter, speck 3 pelt, bombard, shower

perceive verb 1 see, behold, discern, discover, espy, make out, note, notice, observe, recognize, spot 2 understand, comprehend, gather, grasp, learn, realize, see, suss (out) (slang)

perceptible adjective visible, apparent, appreciable, clear, detectable, discernible, evident, noticeable, observable, obvious, recognizable, tangible

perception noun understanding, awareness, conception, consciousness, feeling, grasp, idea, impression, notion, sensation, sense

perceptive adjective observant,

acute, alert, astute, aware, percipient, perspicacious, quick, sharp

perch noun 1 <u>resting place</u>, branch, pole, post ♦ verb 2 <u>sit</u>, alight, balance, land, rest, roost, settle

percussion noun <u>impact</u>, blow, bump, clash, collision, crash, knock, smash, thump

peremptory adjective
1 <u>imperative</u>, absolute, binding, compelling, decisive, final, obligatory 2 <u>imperious</u>, authoritative, bossy (informal), dictatorial, dogmatic, domineering, overbearing

perennial adjective <u>lasting</u>, abiding, constant, continual, enduring, incessant, persistent, recurrent

perfect adjective 1 <u>complete</u>, absolute, consummate, entire, finished, full, sheer, unmitigated, utter, whole 2 <u>faultless</u>, flawless, immaculate, impeccable, pure, spotless, unblemished
3 <u>excellent</u>, ideal, splendid, sublime, superb, superlative, supreme 4 <u>exact</u>, accurate, correct, faithful, precise, true, unerring ♦ verb 5 <u>improve</u>, develop, polish, refine
6 <u>accomplish</u>, achieve, carry out, complete, finish, fulfil, perform

perfection noun 1 <u>completeness</u>, maturity 2 <u>purity</u>, integrity, perfectness, wholeness
3 <u>excellence</u>, exquisiteness, sublimity, superiority
4 <u>exactness</u>, faultlessness, precision

perfectionist noun <u>stickler</u>, precisionist, purist

perfectly adverb 1 <u>completely</u>, absolutely, altogether, fully, quite, thoroughly, totally, utterly, wholly 2 <u>flawlessly</u>, faultlessly, ideally, impeccably, superbly, supremely, wonderfully

perfidious adjective Literary <u>treacherous</u>, disloyal, double-dealing, traitorous, two-faced, unfaithful

perforate verb <u>pierce</u>, bore, drill, penetrate, punch, puncture

perform verb 1 <u>carry out</u>, accomplish, achieve, complete, discharge, do, execute, fulfil, pull off, work 2 <u>present</u>, act, enact, play, produce, put on, represent, stage

performance noun 1 <u>carrying out</u>, accomplishment, achievement, act, completion, execution, fulfilment, work
2 <u>presentation</u>, acting, appearance, exhibition, gig (informal), play, portrayal, production, show

performer noun <u>artiste</u>, actor or actress, player, Thespian, trouper

perfume noun <u>fragrance</u>, aroma, bouquet, odour, scent, smell

perfunctory adjective <u>offhand</u>, cursory, heedless, indifferent, mechanical, routine, sketchy, superficial

perhaps adverb <u>maybe</u>, conceivably, feasibly, it may be, perchance (archaic), possibly

peril noun <u>danger</u>, hazard, jeopardy, menace, risk, uncertainty

perilous adjective <u>dangerous</u>, hazardous, precarious, risky, threatening, unsafe

perimeter noun boundary, ambit, border, bounds, circumference, confines, edge, limit, margin, periphery

period noun time, interval, season, space, span, spell, stretch, term, while

periodic adjective recurrent, cyclical, intermittent, occasional, regular, repeated, sporadic

periodical noun publication, journal, magazine, monthly, paper, quarterly, weekly

peripheral adjective **1** incidental, inessential, irrelevant, marginal, minor, secondary, unimportant **2** outermost, exterior, external, outer, outside

perish verb **1** die, be killed, expire, lose one's life, pass away **2** be destroyed, collapse, decline, disappear, fall, vanish **3** rot, decay, decompose, disintegrate, moulder, waste

perishable adjective short-lived, decaying, decomposable

perjure verb perjure oneself Criminal law commit perjury, bear false witness, forswear, give false testimony, lie under oath, swear falsely

perjury noun lying under oath, bearing false witness, false statement, forswearing, giving false testimony

perk noun Brit. informal bonus, benefit, extra, fringe benefit, perquisite, plus

permanence noun continuity, constancy, continuance, durability, endurance, finality, indestructibility, perpetuity, stability

permanent adjective lasting, abiding, constant, enduring, eternal, everlasting, immutable, perpetual, persistent, stable, steadfast, unchanging

permeate verb pervade, charge, fill, imbue, impregnate, infiltrate, penetrate, saturate, spread through

permissible adjective permitted, acceptable, allowable, all right, authorized, lawful, legal, legitimate, O.K. or okay (informal)

permission noun authorization, allowance, approval, assent, consent, dispensation, go-ahead (informal), green light, leave, liberty, licence, sanction

permissive adjective tolerant, easy-going, forbearing, free, indulgent, lax, lenient, liberal

permit verb **1** allow, authorize, consent, enable, entitle, give leave or permission, give the green light to, grant, let, license, sanction ♦ noun **2** licence, authorization, pass, passport, permission, warrant

permutation noun transformation, alteration, change, transposition

pernicious adjective Formal wicked, bad, damaging, dangerous, deadly, destructive, detrimental, evil, fatal, harmful, hurtful, malign, poisonous

pernickety adjective Informal fussy, exacting, fastidious, finicky, overprecise, particular, picky (informal)

perpendicular adjective upright, at right angles to, on end, plumb, straight, vertical

perpetrate verb commit, carry out, do, enact, execute, perform, wreak

perpetual adjective 1 everlasting, endless, eternal, infinite, lasting, never-ending, perennial, permanent, unchanging, unending 2 continual, constant, continuous, endless, incessant, interminable, never-ending, persistent, recurrent, repeated

perpetuate verb maintain, immortalize, keep going, preserve

perplex verb puzzle, baffle, bewilder, confound, confuse, mystify, stump

perplexing adjective puzzling, baffling, bewildering, complex, complicated, confusing, difficult, enigmatic, hard, inexplicable, mystifying

perplexity noun 1 puzzlement, bafflement, bewilderment, confusion, incomprehension, mystification 2 puzzle, difficulty, fix (informal), mystery, paradox

perquisite noun Formal bonus, benefit, dividend, extra, perk (Brit. informal), plus

persecute verb 1 victimize, afflict, ill-treat, maltreat, oppress, torment, torture 2 harass, annoy, badger, bother, hassle (informal), pester, tease

perseverance noun persistence, determination, diligence, doggedness, endurance, pertinacity, resolution, tenacity

persevere verb keep going, carry on, continue, go on, hang on, persist, remain, stick at or to

persist verb 1 continue, carry on, keep up, last, linger, remain

2 persevere, continue, insist, stand firm

persistence noun determination, doggedness, endurance, grit, perseverance, pertinacity, resolution, tenacity, tirelessness

persistent adjective
1 continuous, constant, continual, endless, incessant, never-ending, perpetual, repeated 2 determined, dogged, obdurate, obstinate, persevering, pertinacious, steadfast, steady, stubborn, tenacious, tireless, unflagging

person noun 1 individual, being, body, human, soul 2 in person personally, bodily, in the flesh, oneself

personable adjective pleasant, agreeable, amiable, attractive, charming, good-looking, handsome, likable or likeable, nice

personage noun personality, big shot (informal), celebrity, dignitary, luminary, megastar (informal), notable, public figure, somebody, V.I.P.

personal adjective 1 private, exclusive, individual, intimate, own, particular, peculiar, special 2 offensive, derogatory, disparaging, insulting, nasty

personality noun 1 nature, character, disposition, identity, individuality, make-up, temperament 2 celebrity, famous name, household name, megastar (informal), notable, personage, star

personally adverb 1 by oneself, alone, independently, on one's own, solely 2 in one's opinion, for one's part, from one's own viewpoint, in one's books, in one's own view **3** individually, individualistically, privately, specially, subjectively

personification noun embodiment, epitome, image, incarnation, portrayal, representation

personify verb embody, epitomize, exemplify, represent, symbolize, typify

personnel noun employees, helpers, human resources, people, staff, workers, workforce

perspective noun **1** outlook, angle, attitude, context, frame of reference **2** objectivity, proportion, relation, relative importance, relativity

perspicacious adjective Formal perceptive, acute, alert, astute, discerning, keen, percipient, sharp, shrewd

perspiration noun sweat, moisture, wetness

perspire verb sweat, exude, glow, pour with sweat, secrete, swelter

persuade verb **1** talk into, bring round (informal), coax, entice, impel, incite, induce, influence, sway, urge, win over **2** convince, cause to believe, satisfy

persuasion noun **1** urging, cajolery, enticement, inducement, wheedling **2** persuasiveness, cogency, force, potency, power, pull (informal) **3** creed, belief, conviction, credo, faith, opinion, tenet, views **4** faction, camp, denomination, party, school, school of thought, side

persuasive adjective convincing, cogent, compelling, credible, effective, eloquent, forceful, influential, plausible, sound, telling, valid, weighty

pert adjective impudent, bold, cheeky, forward, impertinent, insolent, sassy (U.S. informal), saucy

pertain verb relate, apply, befit, belong, be relevant, concern, refer, regard

pertinent adjective relevant, applicable, apposite, appropriate, apt, fit, fitting, germane, material, proper, to the point

pertness noun impudence, audacity, cheek (informal), cheekiness, effrontery, forwardness, front, impertinence, insolence, sauciness

perturb verb disturb, agitate, bother, disconcert, faze, fluster, ruffle, trouble, unsettle, vex, worry

perturbed adjective disturbed, agitated, anxious, disconcerted, flustered, shaken, troubled, uncomfortable, uneasy, worried

peruse verb read, browse, check, examine, inspect, scan, scrutinize, study

pervade verb spread through, charge, fill, imbue, infuse, penetrate, permeate, suffuse

pervasive adjective widespread, common, extensive, general, omnipresent, prevalent, rife, ubiquitous, universal

perverse adjective **1** abnormal, contrary, deviant, disobedient, improper, rebellious, refractory, troublesome, unhealthy **2** wilful, contrary, dogged, headstrong, intractable, intransigent, obdurate, wrong-headed **3** stubborn, contrary, cussed (*informal*), mulish, obstinate, pig-headed, stiff-necked, wayward **4** ill-natured, churlish, cross, fractious, ill-tempered, peevish, stroppy (*Brit. slang*), surly

perversion *noun* **1** deviation, aberration, abnormality, debauchery, depravity, immorality, kink (*Brit. informal*), kinkiness (*slang*), unnaturalness, vice **2** distortion, corruption, falsification, misinterpretation, misrepresentation, twisting

perversity *noun* contrariness, contradictoriness, intransigence, obduracy, refractoriness, waywardness, wrong-headedness

pervert *verb* **1** distort, abuse, falsify, garble, misrepresent, misuse, twist, warp **2** corrupt, debase, debauch, degrade, deprave, lead astray ♦ *noun* **3** deviant, degenerate, sicko (*informal*), weirdo *or* weirdie (*informal*)

perverted *adjective* unnatural, abnormal, corrupt, debased, debauched, depraved, deviant, kinky (*slang*), pervy (*slang*), sick, twisted, unhealthy, warped

pessimism *noun* gloominess, dejection, depression, despair, despondency, distrust, gloom, hopelessness, melancholy

pessimist *noun* wet blanket (*informal*), cynic, defeatist, killjoy, prophet of doom, worrier

pessimistic *adjective* gloomy, bleak, cynical, dark, dejected, depressed, despairing, despondent, glum, hopeless, morose

pest *noun* **1** nuisance, annoyance, bane, bother, drag (*informal*), irritation, pain (*informal*), thorn in one's flesh, trial, vexation **2** infection, blight, bug, epidemic, pestilence, plague, scourge

pester *verb* annoy, badger, bedevil, be on one's back (*slang*), bother, bug (*informal*), harass, harry, hassle (*informal*), nag, plague, torment

pestilence *noun* plague, epidemic, visitation

pestilent *adjective* **1** annoying, bothersome, irksome, irritating, tiresome, vexing **2** harmful, detrimental, evil, injurious, pernicious **3** contaminated, catching, contagious, diseased, disease-ridden, infected, infectious

pestilential *adjective* deadly, dangerous, destructive, detrimental, harmful, hazardous, injurious, pernicious

pet *noun* **1** favourite, darling, idol, jewel, treasure ♦ *adjective* **2** favourite, cherished, dearest, dear to one's heart ♦ *verb* **3** pamper, baby, coddle, cosset, mollycoddle, spoil **4** fondle, caress, pat, stroke **5** *Informal* cuddle, canoodle (*slang*), kiss, neck (*informal*), smooch (*informal*), snog (*Brit. slang*)

peter out *verb* die out, dwindle, ebb, fade, fail, run out, stop, taper off, wane

petite *adjective* small, dainty, delicate, elfin, little, slight

petition noun 1 <u>appeal</u>, entreaty, plea, prayer, request, solicitation, suit, supplication ♦ verb 2 <u>appeal</u>, adjure, ask, beg, beseech, entreat, plead, pray, solicit, supplicate

petrify verb 1 <u>terrify</u>, horrify, immobilize, paralyse, stun, stupefy, transfix 2 <u>fossilize</u>, calcify, harden, turn to stone

petty adjective 1 <u>trivial</u>, contemptible, inconsiderable, insignificant, little, measly (informal), negligible, paltry, slight, small, trifling, unimportant 2 <u>small-minded</u>, mean, mean-minded, shabby, spiteful, ungenerous

petulance noun <u>sulkiness</u>, bad temper, ill humour, irritability, peevishness, pique, sullenness

petulant adjective <u>sulky</u>, bad-tempered, huffy, ill-humoured, moody, peevish, sullen

phantom noun 1 <u>spectre</u>, apparition, ghost, phantasm, shade (literary), spirit, spook (informal), wraith 2 <u>illusion</u>, figment of the imagination, hallucination, vision

phase noun <u>stage</u>, chapter, development, juncture, period, point, position, step, time

phase out verb <u>wind down</u>, close, ease off, eliminate, pull out, remove, run down, terminate, wind up, withdraw

phenomenal adjective <u>extraordinary</u>, exceptional, fantastic, marvellous, miraculous, outstanding, prodigious, remarkable, unusual

phenomenon noun 1 <u>occurrence</u>, circumstance, episode, event, fact, happening, incident 2 <u>wonder</u>, exception, marvel, miracle, prodigy, rarity, sensation

philanderer noun <u>womanizer</u> (informal), Casanova, Don Juan, flirt, ladies' man, lady-killer (informal), Lothario, playboy, stud (slang), wolf (informal)

philanthropic adjective <u>humanitarian</u>, beneficent, benevolent, charitable, humane, kind, kind-hearted, munificent, public-spirited

philanthropist noun <u>humanitarian</u>, benefactor, contributor, donor, giver, patron

philanthropy noun <u>humanitarianism</u>, almsgiving, beneficence, benevolence, brotherly love, charitableness, charity, generosity, kind-heartedness

philistine noun 1 <u>boor</u>, barbarian, ignoramus, lout, lowbrow, vulgarian, yahoo ♦ adjective 2 <u>uncultured</u>, boorish, ignorant, lowbrow, tasteless, uncultivated, uneducated, unrefined

philosopher noun <u>thinker</u>, logician, metaphysician, sage, theorist, wise man

philosophical, philosophic adjective 1 <u>wise</u>, abstract, logical, rational, sagacious, theoretical, thoughtful 2 <u>stoical</u>, calm, collected, composed, cool, serene, tranquil, unruffled

philosophy noun 1 <u>thought</u>, knowledge, logic, metaphysics, rationalism, reasoning, thinking, wisdom 2 <u>outlook</u>, beliefs, convictions, doctrine, ideology, principles, tenets, thinking, values, viewpoint, world view **3** stoicism, calmness, composure, equanimity, self-possession, serenity

phlegmatic adjective unemotional, apathetic, impassive, indifferent, placid, stoical, stolid, undemonstrative, unfeeling

phobia noun terror, aversion, detestation, dread, fear, hatred, horror, loathing, repulsion, revulsion, thing (informal)

phone noun **1** telephone, blower (informal) **2** call, ring (informal, chiefly Brit.), tinkle (Brit. informal) ◆ verb **3** call, get on the blower (informal), give someone a call, give someone a ring (informal, chiefly Brit.), give someone a tinkle (Brit. informal), make a call, ring (up) (informal, chiefly Brit.), telephone

phoney Informal ◆ adjective **1** fake, bogus, counterfeit, ersatz, false, imitation, pseudo (informal), sham ◆ noun **2** fake, counterfeit, forgery, fraud, impostor, pseud (informal), sham

photograph noun **1** picture, photo (informal), print, shot, snap (informal), snapshot, transparency ◆ verb **2** take a picture of, film, record, shoot, snap (informal), take (someone's) picture

photographic adjective **1** lifelike, graphic, natural, pictorial, realistic, visual, vivid **2** Of a person's memory accurate, exact, faithful, precise, retentive

phrase noun **1** expression, group

of words, idiom, remark, saying ◆ verb **2** express, put, put into words, say, voice, word

phraseology noun wording, choice of words, expression, idiom, language, parlance, phrase, phrasing, speech, style, syntax

physical adjective **1** bodily, corporal, corporeal, earthly, fleshly, incarnate, mortal **2** material, natural, palpable, real, solid, substantial, tangible

physician noun doctor, doc (informal), doctor of medicine, general practitioner, G.P., M.D., medic (informal), medical practitioner

physique noun build, body, constitution, figure, form, frame, shape, structure

pick verb **1** select, choose, decide upon, elect, fix upon, hand-pick, opt for, settle upon, single out **2** gather, collect, harvest, pluck, pull **3** nibble, have no appetite, peck at, play at, toy with, push the food round the plate **4** provoke, incite, instigate, start **5** open, break into, break open, crack, force ◆ noun **6** choice, decision, option, preference, selection **7** the best, crème de la crème, decant, elect, elite, the cream

picket noun **1** protester, demonstrator, picketer **2** lookout, guard, patrol, sentinel, sentry, watch **3** stake, pale, paling, post, stanchion, upright ◆ verb **4** blockade, boycott, demonstrate

pickle noun **1** Informal predicament, bind (informal), difficulty, dilemma, fix (informal), hot water (*informal*), jam (*informal*), quandary, scrape (*informal*), tight spot ♦ *verb* 2 **preserve**, marinade, steep

pick-me-up *noun Informal* tonic, bracer (*informal*), refreshment, restorative, shot in the arm (*informal*), stimulant

pick on *verb* torment, badger, bait, bully, goad, hector, tease

pick out *verb* identify, discriminate, distinguish, make out, perceive, recognize, tell apart

pick up *verb* 1 lift, gather, grasp, raise, take up, uplift 2 obtain, buy, come across, find, purchase 3 recover, be on the mend, get better, improve, mend, rally, take a turn for the better, turn the corner 4 learn, acquire, get the hang of (*informal*), master 5 collect, call for, get

pick-up *noun* improvement, change for the better, rally, recovery, revival, rise, strengthening, upswing, upturn

picnic *noun* excursion, outdoor meal, outing

pictorial *adjective* graphic, illustrated, picturesque, representational, scenic

picture *noun* 1 representation, drawing, engraving, illustration, image, likeness, painting, photograph, portrait, print, sketch 2 description, account, depiction, image, impression, report 3 double, carbon copy, copy, dead ringer (*slang*), duplicate, image, likeness, lookalike, replica, spitting image (*informal*), twin 4 personification, embodiment, epitome, essence

5 film, flick (*slang*), motion picture, movie (*U.S. informal*) ♦ *verb* 6 imagine, conceive of, envision, see, visualize 7 represent, depict, draw, illustrate, paint, photograph, show, sketch

picturesque *adjective* 1 pretty, attractive, beautiful, charming, quaint, scenic, striking 2 vivid, colourful, graphic

piebald *adjective* pied, black and white, brindled, dappled, flecked, mottled, speckled, spotted

piece *noun* 1 bit, chunk, fragment, morsel, part, portion, quantity, segment, slice 2 work, article, composition, creation, item, study, work of art

piecemeal *adverb* bit by bit, by degrees, gradually, little by little

pier *noun* 1 jetty, landing place, promenade, quay, wharf 2 pillar, buttress, column, pile, post, support, upright

pierce *verb* penetrate, bore, drill, enter, perforate, prick, puncture, spike, stab, stick into

piercing *adjective* 1 *Usually of sound* penetrating, ear-splitting, high-pitched, loud, sharp, shrill 2 keen, alert, penetrating, perceptive, perspicacious, quick-witted, sharp, shrewd 3 *Usually of weather* cold, arctic, biting, bitter, freezing, nippy, wintry 4 sharp, acute, agonizing, excruciating, intense, painful, severe, stabbing

piety *noun* holiness, faith, godliness, piousness, religion, reverence

pig *noun* 1 hog, boar, porker,

sow, swine **2** *Informal* <u>slob</u>
(*slang*), boor, brute, glutton,
swine

pigeonhole *noun*
1 <u>compartment</u>, cubbyhole,
locker, niche, place, section
♦ *verb* **2** <u>classify</u>, categorize,
characterize, compartmentalize,
ghettoize, label, slot (*informal*)
3 <u>put off</u>, defer, postpone, shelve

pig-headed *adjective* <u>stubborn</u>,
contrary, inflexible, mulish,
obstinate, self-willed,
stiff-necked, unyielding

pigment *noun* <u>colour</u>, colouring,
dye, paint, stain, tincture, tint

pile[1] *noun* **1** <u>heap</u>, accumulation,
collection, hoard, mass, mound,
mountain, stack **2** *often plural
Informal* <u>a lot</u>, great deal, ocean,
quantity, stacks **3** <u>building</u>,
edifice, erection, structure ♦ *verb*
4 <u>collect</u>, accumulate, amass,
assemble, gather, heap, hoard,
stack **5** <u>crowd</u>, crush, flock,
flood, jam, pack, rush, stream

pile[2] *noun* <u>foundation</u>, beam,
column, pillar, post, support,
upright

pile[3] *noun* <u>nap</u>, down, fibre, fur,
hair, plush

pile-up *noun Informal* <u>collision</u>,
accident, crash, multiple
collision, smash, smash-up
(*informal*)

pilfer *verb* <u>steal</u>, appropriate,
embezzle, filch, knock off (*slang*),
lift (*informal*), nick (*slang, chiefly
Brit.*), pinch (*informal*), purloin,
snaffle (*Brit. informal*), swipe
(*slang*), take

pilgrim *noun* <u>traveller</u>, wanderer,
wayfarer

pilgrimage *noun* <u>journey</u>,
excursion, expedition, mission,
tour, trip

pill *noun* **1** <u>tablet</u>, capsule, pellet
2 the pill <u>oral contraceptive</u>

pillage *verb* **1** <u>plunder</u>, despoil,
loot, maraud, raid, ransack,
ravage, sack ♦ *noun* **2** <u>plunder</u>,
marauding, robbery, sack,
spoliation

pillar *noun* **1** <u>support</u>, column,
pier, post, prop, shaft,
stanchion, upright **2** <u>supporter</u>,
leader, leading light (*informal*),
mainstay, upholder

pillory *verb* <u>ridicule</u>, brand,
denounce, stigmatize

pilot *noun* **1** <u>airman</u>, aviator, flyer
2 <u>helmsman</u>, navigator,
steersman ♦ *adjective* **3** trial,
experimental, model, test ♦ *verb*
4 <u>fly</u>, conduct, direct, drive,
guide, handle, navigate, operate,
steer

pimple *noun* <u>spot</u>, boil, plook
(*Scot.*), pustule, zit (*slang*)

pin *verb* **1** <u>fasten</u>, affix, attach,
fix, join, secure **2** <u>hold fast</u>, fix,
hold down, immobilize, pinion

pinch *verb* **1** <u>squeeze</u>, compress,
grasp, nip, press **2** <u>hurt</u>, cramp,
crush, pain **3** *Informal* <u>steal</u>, filch,
knock off (*informal*),
nick (*slang, chiefly Brit.*), pilfer,
purloin, snaffle (*Brit. informal*),
swipe (*slang*) ♦ *noun* **4** <u>squeeze</u>,
nip **5** <u>dash</u>, bit, jot, mite,
soupçon, speck **6** <u>hardship</u>, crisis,
difficulty, emergency, necessity,
plight, predicament, strait

pinched *adjective* <u>thin</u>, drawn,
gaunt, haggard, peaky, worn

pin down *verb* **1** <u>force</u>, compel,

constrain, make, press, pressurize
2 <u>determine</u>, identify, locate,
name, pinpoint, specify

pine *verb* **1** *often with* **for** <u>long</u>,
ache, crave, desire, eat one's
heart out over, hanker, hunger
for, thirst for, wish for, yearn for
2 <u>waste</u>, decline, fade, languish,
sicken

pinion *verb* <u>immobilize</u>, bind,
chain, fasten, fetter, manacle,
shackle, tie

pink *adjective* <u>rosy</u>, flushed,
reddish, rose, roseate, salmon

pinnacle *noun* <u>peak</u>, apex, crest,
crown, height, summit, top,
vertex, zenith

pinpoint *verb* <u>identify</u>, define,
distinguish, locate

pioneer *noun* **1** <u>settler</u>, colonist,
explorer **2** <u>founder</u>, developer,
innovator, leader, trailblazer
♦ *verb* **3** <u>develop</u>, create,
discover, establish, initiate,
instigate, institute, invent,
originate, show the way, start

pious *adjective* <u>religious</u>, devout,
God-fearing, godly, holy,
reverent, righteous, saintly

pipe *noun* **1** <u>tube</u>, conduit, duct,
hose, line, main, passage,
pipeline ♦ *verb* **2** <u>whistle</u>, cheep,
peep, play, sing, sound, warble
3 <u>convey</u>, channel, conduct

pipe down *verb Informal* <u>be
quiet</u>, hold one's tongue, hush,
quieten down, shush, shut one's
mouth, shut up (*informal*)

pipeline *noun* <u>tube</u>, conduit,
duct, passage, pipe

piquant *adjective* **1** <u>spicy</u>, biting,
pungent, savoury, sharp, tangy,
tart, zesty **2** <u>interesting</u>, lively,

provocative, scintillating,
sparkling, stimulating

pique *noun* **1** <u>resentment</u>,
annoyance, displeasure, huff,
hurt feelings, irritation, offence,
umbrage, wounded pride ♦ *verb*
2 <u>displease</u>, affront, annoy, get
(*informal*), irk, irritate, nettle,
offend, rile, sting **3** <u>arouse</u>,
excite, rouse, spur, stimulate,
stir, whet

piracy *noun* <u>robbery</u>,
buccaneering, freebooting,
stealing, theft

pirate *noun* **1** <u>buccaneer</u>, corsair,
freebooter, marauder, raider
2 <u>plagiarist</u>, cribber (*informal*),
infringer, plagiarizer ♦ *verb*
3 <u>copy</u>, appropriate, crib
(*informal*), plagiarize, poach,
reproduce, steal

pit *noun* **1** <u>hole</u>, abyss, cavity,
chasm, crater, dent, depression,
hollow ♦ *verb* **2** <u>scar</u>, dent,
indent, mark, pockmark

pitch *verb* **1** <u>throw</u>, cast, chuck
(*informal*), fling, heave, hurl, lob
(*informal*), sling, toss **2** <u>set up</u>,
erect, put up, raise, settle **3** <u>fall</u>,
dive, drop, topple, tumble
4 <u>toss</u>, lurch, plunge, roll ♦ *noun*
5 <u>sports field</u>, field of play,
ground, park (*U.S. & Canad.*)
6 <u>level</u>, degree, height, highest
point, point, summit **7** <u>slope</u>,
angle, dip, gradient, incline, tilt
8 <u>tone</u>, modulation, sound,
timbre **9** <u>sales talk</u>, patter, spiel
(*informal*)

pitch-black *adjective* <u>jet-black</u>,
dark, inky, pitch-dark, unlit

pitch in *verb* <u>help</u>, chip in
(*informal*), contribute, cooperate,
do one's bit, join in, lend a

hand, participate

pitch into verb Informal attack, assail, assault, get stuck into (informal), tear into (informal)

piteous adjective pathetic, affecting, distressing, harrowing, heartbreaking, heart-rending, moving, pitiable, pitiful, plaintive, poignant, sad

pitfall noun danger, catch, difficulty, drawback, hazard, peril, snag, trap

pith noun essence, core, crux, gist, heart, kernel, nub, point, quintessence, salient point

pithy adjective succinct, brief, cogent, concise, epigrammatic, laconic, pointed, short, terse, to the point, trenchant

pitiful adjective 1 pathetic, distressing, grievous, harrowing, heartbreaking, heart-rending, piteous, pitiable, sad, wretched 2 contemptible, abject, base, low, mean, miserable, paltry, shabby, sorry

pitiless adjective merciless, callous, cold-blooded, cold-hearted, cruel, hardhearted, heartless, implacable, relentless, ruthless, unmerciful

pittance noun peanuts (slang), chicken feed (slang), drop, mite, slave wages, trifle

pity noun 1 compassion, charity, clemency, fellow feeling, forbearance, kindness, mercy, sympathy 2 shame, bummer (slang), crying shame, misfortune, sin ♦ verb 3 feel sorry for, bleed for, feel for, grieve for, have compassion for, sympathize with, weep for

pivot noun 1 axis, axle, fulcrum, spindle, swivel 2 hub, centre, heart, hinge, kingpin ♦ verb 3 turn, revolve, rotate, spin, swivel, twirl 4 rely, be contingent, depend, hang, hinge

pivotal adjective crucial, central, critical, decisive, vital

pixie noun elf, brownie, fairy, sprite

placard noun notice, advertisement, bill, poster

placate verb calm, appease, assuage, conciliate, humour, mollify, pacify, propitiate, soothe

place noun 1 spot, area, location, point, position, site, venue, whereabouts 2 region, district, locale, locality, neighbourhood, quarter, vicinity 3 position, grade, rank, station, status 4 space, accommodation, room 5 home, abode, domicile, dwelling, house, pad (slang), property, residence 6 duty, affair, charge, concern, function, prerogative, responsibility, right, role 7 job, appointment, employment, position, post 8 **take place** happen, come about, go on, occur, transpire (informal) ♦ verb 9 put, deposit, install, lay, locate, position, rest, set, situate, stand, station, stick (informal) 10 classify, arrange, class, grade, group, order, rank, sort 11 identify, know, put one's finger on, recognize, remember 12 assign, allocate, appoint, charge, entrust, give

placid adjective calm, collected, composed, equable, even-tempered, imperturbable, serene, tranquil, unexcitable, unruffled, untroubled

plagiarism noun 1 copying, borrowing, cribbing (*informal*), infringement, piracy, theft

plagiarize verb copy, borrow, crib (*informal*), lift (*informal*), pirate, steal

plague noun 1 disease, epidemic, infection, pestilence 2 affliction, bane, blight, curse, evil, scourge, torment ♦ verb 3 pester, annoy, badger, bother, harass, harry, hassle (*informal*), tease, torment, torture, trouble, vex

plain adjective 1 clear, comprehensible, distinct, evident, manifest, obvious, overt, patent, unambiguous, understandable, unmistakable, visible 2 honest, blunt, candid, direct, downright, forthright, frank, open, outspoken, straightforward, upfront (*informal*) 3 unadorned, austere, bare, basic, severe, simple, Spartan, stark, unembellished, unfussy, unornamented 4 ugly, ill-favoured, no oil painting (*informal*), not beautiful, unattractive, unlovely, unprepossessing 5 ordinary, common, commonplace, everyday, simple, unaffected, unpretentious ♦ noun 6 flatland, grassland, plateau, prairie, steppe, veld

plain-spoken adjective blunt, candid, direct, downright, forthright, frank, outspoken

plaintive adjective sorrowful, heart-rending, mournful, pathetic, piteous, pitiful, sad

plan noun 1 scheme, design, method, plot, programme,

proposal, strategy, suggestion, system 2 diagram, blueprint, chart, drawing, layout, map, representation, sketch ♦ verb 3 devise, arrange, contrive, design, draft, formulate, organize, outline, plot, scheme, think out 4 intend, aim, mean, propose, purpose

plane noun 1 aeroplane, aircraft, jet 2 flat surface, level surface 3 level, condition, degree, position ♦ adjective 4 level, even, flat, horizontal, regular, smooth ♦ verb 5 skim, glide, sail, skate

plant noun 1 vegetable, bush, flower, herb, shrub, weed 2 factory, foundry, mill, shop, works, yard 3 machinery, apparatus, equipment, gear ♦ verb 4 sow, put in the ground, scatter, seed, transplant 5 place, establish, fix, found, insert, put, set

plaster noun 1 mortar, gypsum, plaster of Paris, stucco 2 bandage, adhesive plaster, dressing, Elastoplast (*Trademark*), sticking plaster ♦ verb 3 cover, coat, daub, overlay, smear, spread

plastic adjective 1 manageable, docile, malleable, pliable, receptive, responsive, tractable 2 pliant, ductile, flexible, mouldable, pliable, soft, supple

plate noun 1 platter, dish, trencher (*archaic*) 2 helping, course, dish, portion, serving 3 layer, panel, sheet, slab 4 illustration, lithograph, print ♦ verb 5 coat, cover, gild, laminate, overlay

plateau noun 1 upland,

highland, table, tableland
2 <u>levelling off</u>, level, stability,
stage

platform noun 1 <u>stage</u>, dais,
podium, rostrum, stand 2 <u>policy</u>,
manifesto, objective(s), party
line, principle, programme

platitude noun cliché, banality,
commonplace, truism

platoon noun <u>squad</u>, company,
group, outfit (informal), patrol,
squadron, team

platter noun <u>plate</u>, dish, salver,
tray, trencher (archaic)

plaudits plural noun <u>approval</u>,
acclaim, acclamation, applause,
approbation, praise

plausible adjective 1 <u>reasonable</u>,
believable, conceivable, credible,
likely, persuasive, possible,
probable, tenable 2 <u>glib</u>,
smooth, smooth-talking,
smooth-tongued, specious

play verb 1 <u>amuse oneself</u>,
entertain oneself, fool, have fun,
revel, romp, sport, trifle
2 <u>compete</u>, challenge, contend
against, participate, take on, take
part 3 <u>act</u>, act the part of,
perform, portray, represent
♦ noun 4 <u>drama</u>, comedy,
dramatic piece, farce,
pantomime, piece, show, stage
show, tragedy 5 <u>amusement</u>,
diversion, entertainment, fun,
game, pastime, recreation, sport
6 <u>fun</u>, humour, jest, joking, lark
(informal), prank, sport 7 <u>space</u>,
elbowroom, latitude, leeway,
margin, room, scope

playboy noun <u>womanizer</u>, ladies'
man, lady-killer (informal),
philanderer, rake, roué

play down verb <u>minimize</u>, gloss

over, make light of, make little
of, soft-pedal (informal),
underplay, underrate

player noun 1 <u>sportsman or
sportswoman</u>, competitor,
contestant, participant
2 <u>musician</u>, artist,
instrumentalist, performer,
virtuoso 3 <u>performer</u>, actor or
actress, entertainer, Thespian,
trouper

playful adjective <u>lively</u>, frisky,
impish, merry, mischievous,
spirited, sportive, sprightly,
vivacious

playmate noun <u>friend</u>, chum
(informal), companion, comrade,
pal (informal), playfellow

play on or **upon** verb <u>take
advantage of</u>, abuse, capitalize
on, exploit, impose on, trade on

plaything noun <u>toy</u>, amusement,
game, pastime, trifle

play up verb 1 <u>emphasize</u>,
accentuate, highlight, stress,
underline 2 Brit. informal <u>be
awkward</u>, be disobedient, be
stroppy (Brit. slang), give trouble,
misbehave 3 Brit. informal <u>hurt</u>,
be painful, be sore, bother, pain,
trouble 4 Brit. informal
<u>malfunction</u>, be on the blink
(slang), not work properly

plea noun 1 <u>appeal</u>, entreaty,
intercession, petition, prayer,
request, suit, supplication
2 <u>excuse</u>, defence, explanation,
justification

plead verb <u>appeal</u>, ask, beg,
beseech, entreat, implore,
petition, request

pleasant adjective 1 <u>pleasing</u>,
agreeable, amusing, delightful,
enjoyable, fine, lovely, nice,

pleasurable 2 nice, affable, agreeable, amiable, charming, congenial, engaging, friendly, genial, likable *or* likeable

pleasantry noun joke, badinage, banter, jest, quip, witticism

please verb delight, amuse, entertain, gladden, gratify, humour, indulge, satisfy, suit

pleased adjective happy, chuffed (*Brit. slang*), contented, delighted, euphoric, glad, gratified, over the moon (*informal*), satisfied, thrilled

pleasing adjective enjoyable, agreeable, charming, delightful, engaging, gratifying, likable *or* likeable, pleasurable, satisfying

pleasurable adjective enjoyable, agreeable, delightful, fun, good, lovely, nice, pleasant

pleasure noun happiness, amusement, bliss, delectation, delight, enjoyment, gladness, gratification, joy, satisfaction

plebeian adjective **1** common, base, coarse, low, lower-class, proletarian, uncultivated, unrefined, vulgar, working-class ◆ noun **2** commoner, common man, man in the street, pleb, prole (*derogatory slang, chiefly Brit.*), proletarian

pledge noun **1** promise, assurance, covenant, oath, undertaking, vow, warrant, word **2** guarantee, bail, collateral, deposit, pawn, security, surety ◆ verb **3** promise, contract, engage, give one's oath, give one's word, swear, vow

plentiful adjective abundant, ample, bountiful, copious, generous, lavish, liberal, overflowing, plenteous, profuse

plenty noun **1** lots (*informal*), abundance, enough, great deal, heap(s) (*informal*), masses, pile(s) (*informal*), plethora, quantity, stack(s) **2** abundance, affluence, copiousness, fertility, fruitfulness, plenitude, profusion, prosperity, wealth

plethora noun excess, glut, overabundance, profusion, superabundance, surfeit, surplus

pliable adjective **1** flexible, bendable, bendy, malleable, plastic, pliant, supple **2** impressionable, adaptable, compliant, docile, easily led, pliant, receptive, responsive, susceptible, tractable

pliant adjective **1** flexible, bendable, bendy, plastic, pliable, supple **2** impressionable, biddable, compliant, easily led, pliable, susceptible, tractable

plight noun difficulty, condition, jam (*informal*), predicament, scrape (*informal*), situation, spot (*informal*), state, trouble

plod verb **1** trudge, clump, drag, lumber, tramp, tread **2** slog, grind (*informal*), labour, persevere, plough through, plug away (*informal*), soldier on, toil

plot[1] noun **1** plan, cabal, conspiracy, intrigue, machination, scheme, stratagem **2** story, action, narrative, outline, scenario, story line, subject, theme ◆ verb **3** plan, collude, conspire, contrive, intrigue, machinate, manoeuvre, scheme **4** devise, conceive, concoct, contrive, cook up (*informal*), design, hatch, lay

5 chart, calculate, locate, map, mark, outline

plot² *noun* patch, allotment, area, ground, lot, parcel, tract

plough *verb* **1** turn over, cultivate, dig, till **2** *usually with* **through** forge, cut, drive, plunge, press, push, wade

ploy *noun* tactic, device, dodge, manoeuvre, move, ruse, scheme, stratagem, trick, wile

pluck *verb* **1** pull out or off, collect, draw, gather, harvest, pick **2** tug, catch, clutch, jerk, pull at, snatch, tweak, yank **3** strum, finger, pick, twang ♦ *noun* **4** courage, backbone, boldness, bottle (*Brit. slang*), bravery, grit, guts (*informal*), nerve

plucky *adjective* courageous, bold, brave, daring, game, gutsy (*slang*), have-a-go (*informal*), intrepid

plug *noun* **1** stopper, bung, cork, spigot **2** *Informal* mention, advert (*Brit. informal*), advertisement, hype, publicity, push ♦ *verb* **3** seal, block, bung, close, cork, fill, pack, stop, stopper, stop up, stuff **4** *Informal* mention, advertise, build up, hype, promote, publicize, push **5** plug away *Informal* slog, grind (*informal*), labour, peg away, plod, toil

plum *adjective* choice, best, first-class, prize

plumb *verb* **1** delve, explore, fathom, gauge, go into, penetrate, probe, unravel ♦ *noun* **2** weight, lead, plumb bob, plummet ♦ *adverb* **3** exactly, bang, precisely, slap, spot-on

(*Brit. informal*)

plume *noun* feather, crest, pinion, quill

plummet *verb* plunge, crash, descend, dive, drop down, fall, nose-dive, tumble

plump *adjective* chubby, corpulent, dumpy, fat, podgy, roly-poly, rotund, round, stout, tubby

plunder *verb* **1** loot, pillage, raid, ransack, rifle, rob, sack, strip ♦ *noun* **2** loot, booty, ill-gotten gains, pillage, prize, spoils, swag (*slang*)

plunge *verb* **1** throw, cast, pitch **2** hurtle, career, charge, dash, jump, rush, tear **3** descend, dip, dive, drop, fall, nose-dive, plummet, sink, tumble ♦ *noun* **4** dive, descent, drop, fall, jump

plus *preposition* **1** and, added to, coupled with ♦ *adjective* **2** additional, added, add-on, extra, supplementary ♦ *noun* **3** *Informal* advantage, asset, benefit, bonus, extra, gain, good point

plush *adjective* luxurious, de luxe, lavish, luxury, opulent, rich, sumptuous

ply *verb* **1** work at, carry on, exercise, follow, practise, pursue **2** use, employ, handle, manipulate, wield

poach *verb* encroach, appropriate, infringe, intrude, trespass

pocket *noun* **1** pouch, bag, compartment, receptacle, sack ♦ *verb* **2** steal, appropriate, filch, lift (*informal*), pilfer, purloin, take ♦ *adjective* **3** small, abridged, compact, concise, little, miniature, portable

pod noun, verb shell, hull, husk, shuck

podgy adjective tubby, chubby, dumpy, fat, plump, roly-poly, rotund, stout

podium noun platform, dais, rostrum, stage

poem noun verse, lyric, ode, rhyme, song, sonnet

poet noun bard, lyricist, rhymer, versifier

poetic adjective lyrical, elegiac, lyric, metrical

poetry noun verse, poems, rhyme, rhyming

poignancy noun 1 sadness, emotion, feeling, pathos, sentiment, tenderness 2 sharpness, bitterness, intensity, keenness

poignant adjective moving, bitter, distressing, heart-rending, intense, painful, pathetic, sad, touching

point noun 1 essence, crux, drift, gist, heart, import, meaning, nub, pith, question, subject, thrust 2 aim, end, goal, intent, intention, motive, object, objective, purpose, reason 3 item, aspect, detail, feature, particular 4 characteristic, aspect, attribute, quality, respect, trait 5 place, location, position, site, spot, stage 6 full stop, dot, mark, period, stop 7 end, apex, prong, sharp end, spike, spur, summit, tip, top 8 headland, cape, head, promontory 9 stage, circumstance, condition, degree, extent, position 10 moment, instant, juncture, time, very minute 11 unit, score, tally ♦ verb 12 indicate, call attention to, denote, designate, direct, show, signify 13 aim, direct, level, train

point-blank adjective 1 direct, blunt, downright, explicit, express, plain ♦ adverb 2 directly, bluntly, candidly, explicitly, forthrightly, frankly, openly, plainly, straight

pointed adjective 1 sharp, acute, barbed, edged 2 cutting, acute, biting, incisive, keen, penetrating, pertinent, sharp, telling

pointer noun 1 hint, advice, caution, information, recommendation, suggestion, tip 2 indicator, guide, hand, needle

pointless adjective senseless, absurd, aimless, fruitless, futile, inane, irrelevant, meaningless, silly, stupid, useless

point out verb mention, allude to, bring up, identify, indicate, show, specify

poise noun composure, aplomb, assurance, calmness, cool (slang), dignity, presence, sang-froid, self-possession

poised adjective 1 ready, all set, prepared, standing by, waiting 2 composed, calm, collected, dignified, self-confident, self-possessed, together (informal)

poison noun 1 toxin, bane, venom ♦ verb 2 murder, give (someone) poison, kill 3 contaminate, infect, pollute 4 corrupt, defile, deprave, pervert, subvert, taint, undermine, warp

poisonous adjective **1** toxic, deadly, fatal, lethal, mortal, noxious, venomous, virulent **2** evil, baleful, corrupting, malicious, noxious, pernicious

poke verb **1** jab, dig, nudge, prod, push, shove, stab, stick, thrust ◆ noun **2** jab, dig, nudge, prod, thrust

poky adjective small, confined, cramped, narrow, tiny

pole noun rod, bar, mast, post, shaft, spar, staff, stick

police noun **1** the law (informal), boys in blue (informal), constabulary, fuzz (slang), police force, the Old Bill (informal) ◆ verb **2** control, guard, patrol, protect, regulate, watch

policeman noun cop (slang), bobby (informal), constable, copper (slang), fuzz (slang), officer

policy noun procedure, action, approach, code, course, custom, plan, practice, rule, scheme

polish verb **1** shine, brighten, buff, burnish, rub, smooth, wax **2** perfect, brush up, enhance, finish, improve, refine, touch up ◆ noun **3** varnish, wax **4** sheen, brightness, finish, glaze, gloss, lustre **5** style, breeding, class (informal), elegance, finesse, finish, grace, refinement

polished adjective **1** accomplished, adept, expert, fine, masterly, professional, skilful, superlative **2** shining, bright, burnished, gleaming, glossy, smooth **3** elegant, cultivated, polite, refined, sophisticated, well-bred

polite adjective **1** mannerly, civil, complaisant, courteous, gracious, respectful, well-behaved, well-mannered **2** refined, civilized, cultured, elegant, genteel, polished, sophisticated, well-bred

politeness noun courtesy, civility, courteousness, decency, etiquette, mannerliness

politic adjective wise, advisable, diplomatic, expedient, judicious, prudent, sensible

political adjective governmental, parliamentary, policy-making

politician noun statesman, legislator, Member of Parliament, M.P., office bearer, public servant

politics noun statesmanship, affairs of state, civics, government, political science

poll noun **1** canvass, ballot, census, count, sampling, survey **2** vote, figures, returns, tally, voting ◆ verb **3** tally, register **4** question, ballot, canvass, interview, sample, survey

pollute verb **1** contaminate, dirty, foul, infect, poison, soil, spoil, stain, taint **2** defile, corrupt, debase, debauch, deprave, desecrate, dishonour, profane, sully

pollution noun contamination, corruption, defilement, dirtying, foulness, impurity, taint, uncleanness

pomp noun **1** ceremony, flourish, grandeur, magnificence, pageant, pageantry, splendour, state **2** show, display, grandiosity, ostentation

pomposity noun self-importance, affectation, airs, grandiosity, pompousness, portentousness, pretension, pretentiousness

pompous adjective
1 self-important, arrogant, grandiose, ostentatious, pretentious, puffed up, showy
2 grandiloquent, boastful, bombastic, high-flown, inflated

pond noun pool, duck pond, fish pond, millpond, small lake, tarn

ponder verb think, brood, cogitate, consider, contemplate, deliberate, meditate, mull over, muse, reflect, ruminate

ponderous adjective 1 dull, heavy, long-winded, pedantic, tedious 2 unwieldy, bulky, cumbersome, heavy, huge, massive, weighty 3 clumsy, awkward, heavy-footed, lumbering

pontificate verb expound, hold forth, lay down the law, preach, pronounce, sound off

pool[1] noun 1 pond, lake, mere, puddle, tarn 2 swimming pool, swimming bath

pool[2] noun 1 syndicate, collective, consortium, group, team, trust
2 kitty, bank, funds, jackpot, pot ◆ verb 3 combine, amalgamate, join forces, league, merge, put together, share

poor adjective 1 impoverished, broke (informal), destitute, down and out, hard up (informal), impecunious, indigent, needy, on the breadline, penniless, penurious, poverty-stricken, short, skint (Brit. slang), stony-broke (Brit. slang)
2 inadequate, deficient, incomplete, insufficient, lacking, meagre, measly, scant, scanty, skimpy 3 inferior, below par, low-grade, mediocre, not much cop (Brit. slang), rotten (informal), rubbishy, second-rate, substandard, unsatisfactory
4 unfortunate, hapless, ill-fated, luckless, pitiable, unlucky, wretched

poorly adverb 1 badly, inadequately, incompetently, inexpertly, insufficiently, unsatisfactorily, unsuccessfully ◆ adjective 2 Informal ill, below par, off colour, rotten (informal), seedy (informal), sick, under the weather (informal), unwell

pop verb 1 burst, bang, crack, explode, go off, snap 2 put, insert, push, shove, slip, stick, thrust, tuck ◆ noun 3 bang, burst, crack, explosion, noise, report

pope noun Holy Father, Bishop of Rome, pontiff, Vicar of Christ

populace noun people, general public, hoi polloi, masses, mob, multitude

popular adjective 1 well-liked, accepted, approved, fashionable, favourite, in, in demand, in favour, liked, sought-after
2 common, conventional, current, general, prevailing, prevalent, universal

popularity noun favour, acceptance, acclaim, approval, currency, esteem, regard, vogue

popularize verb make popular, disseminate, give currency to, give mass appeal, make available to all, spread, universalize

popularly adverb generally, commonly, conventionally,

customarily, ordinarily, traditionally, universally, usually, widely

populate *verb* inhabit, colonize, live in, occupy, settle

population *noun* inhabitants, community, denizens, folk, natives, people, residents, society

populous *adjective* populated, crowded, heavily populated, overpopulated, packed, swarming, teeming

pore[1] *verb* pore over study, examine, peruse, ponder, read, scrutinize

pore[2] *noun* opening, hole, orifice, outlet

pornographic *adjective* obscene, blue, dirty, filthy, indecent, lewd, salacious, smutty

pornography *noun* obscenity, dirt, filth, indecency, porn (*informal*), smut

porous *adjective* permeable, absorbent, absorptive, penetrable, spongy

port *noun* harbour, anchorage, haven, seaport

portable *adjective* light, compact, convenient, easily carried, handy, manageable, movable

portend *verb* foretell, augur, betoken, bode, foreshadow, herald, indicate, predict, prognosticate, promise, warn of

portent *noun* omen, augury, forewarning, indication, prognostication, sign, warning

portentous *adjective*
1 significant, crucial, fateful, important, menacing, momentous, ominous
2 pompous, ponderous,

self-important, solemn

porter[1] *noun* baggage attendant, bearer, carrier

porter[2] *noun* doorman, caretaker, concierge, gatekeeper, janitor

portion *noun* **1** part, bit, fragment, morsel, piece, scrap, section, segment **2** share, allocation, allotment, allowance, lot, measure, quantity, quota, ration **3** helping, piece, serving **4** destiny, fate, fortune, lot, luck ♦ *verb* **5** portion out divide, allocate, allot, apportion, deal, distribute, dole out, share out

portly *adjective* stout, burly, corpulent, fat, fleshy, heavy, large, plump

portrait *noun* **1** picture, image, likeness, painting, photograph, representation **2** description, characterization, depiction, portrayal, profile, thumbnail sketch

portray *verb* **1** represent, depict, draw, figure, illustrate, paint, picture, sketch **2** describe, characterize, depict, put in words **3** play, act the part of, represent

portrayal *noun* representation, characterization, depiction, interpretation, performance, picture

pose *verb* **1** position, model, sit **2** put on airs, posture, show off (*informal*) **3** pose as impersonate, masquerade as, pass oneself off as, pretend to be, profess to be ♦ *noun* **4** posture, attitude, bearing, position, stance **5** act, affectation, air, façade, front, mannerism, posturing, pretence

poser noun puzzle, enigma, problem, question, riddle

posh adjective Informal upper-class, classy (slang), grand, high-class, luxurious, ritzy (slang), smart, stylish, swanky (informal), swish (informal, chiefly Brit.), up-market

posit verb put forward, advance, assume, postulate, presume, propound, state

position noun 1 place, area, bearings, locale, location, point, post, situation, spot, station, whereabouts 2 posture, arrangement, attitude, pose, stance 3 attitude, belief, opinion, outlook, point of view, slant, stance, view, viewpoint 4 status, importance, place, prestige, rank, reputation, standing, station, stature 5 job, duty, employment, occupation, office, place, post, role, situation ◆ verb 6 place, arrange, lay out, locate, put, set, stand

positive adjective 1 certain, assured, confident, convinced, sure 2 definite, absolute, categorical, certain, clear, conclusive, decisive, explicit, express, firm, real 3 helpful, beneficial, constructive, practical, productive, progressive, useful 4 Informal absolute, complete, consummate, downright, out-and-out, perfect, thorough, utter

positively adverb definitely, absolutely, assuredly, categorically, certainly, emphatically, firmly, surely, unequivocally, unquestionably

possess verb 1 have, enjoy, hold, own 2 control, acquire, dominate, hold, occupy, seize, take over

possessed adjective crazed, berserk, demented, frenzied, obsessed, raving

possession noun 1 ownership, control, custody, hold, occupation, tenure, title 2 possessions property, assets, belongings, chattels, effects, estate, things

possessive adjective jealous, controlling, covetous, dominating, domineering, overprotective, selfish

possibility noun 1 feasibility, likelihood, potentiality, practicability, workableness 2 likelihood, chance, hope, liability, odds, probability, prospect, risk 3 often plural potential, capabilities, potentiality, promise, prospects, talent

possible adjective 1 conceivable, credible, hypothetical, imaginable, likely, potential 2 likely, hopeful, potential, probable, promising 3 feasible, attainable, doable, practicable, realizable, viable, workable

possibly adverb perhaps, maybe, perchance (archaic)

post[1] noun 1 mail, collection, delivery, postal service ◆ verb 2 send, dispatch, mail, transmit 3 keep someone posted notify, advise, brief, fill in on (informal), inform, report to

post[2] noun 1 support, column, picket, pillar, pole, shaft, stake, upright ◆ verb 2 put up, affix, display, pin up

post³ noun 1 job, appointment, assignment, employment, office, place, position, situation 2 station, beat, place, position ♦ verb 3 station, assign, place, position, put, situate

poster noun notice, advertisement, announcement, bill, placard, public notice, sticker

posterity noun 1 future, succeeding generations 2 descendants, children, family, heirs, issue, offspring, progeny

postpone verb put off, adjourn, defer, delay, put back, put on the back burner (informal), shelve, suspend

postponement noun delay, adjournment, deferment, deferral, stay, suspension

postscript noun P.S., addition, afterthought, supplement

postulate verb presuppose, assume, hypothesize, posit, propose, suppose, take for granted, theorize

posture noun 1 bearing, attitude, carriage, disposition, set, stance ♦ verb 2 show off (informal), affect, pose, put on airs

pot noun container, bowl, pan, vessel

potency noun power, effectiveness, force, influence, might, strength

potent adjective 1 powerful, authoritative, commanding, dominant, dynamic, influential 2 strong, forceful, mighty, powerful, vigorous

potential adjective 1 possible, dormant, future, hidden, inherent, latent, likely, promising ♦ noun 2 ability, aptitude, capability, capacity, possibility, potentiality, power, wherewithal

potion noun concoction, brew, dose, draught, elixir, mixture, philtre

potter verb mess about, dabble, footle (informal), tinker

pottery noun ceramics, earthenware, stoneware, terracotta

pouch noun bag, container, pocket, purse, sack

pounce verb 1 spring, attack, fall upon, jump, leap at, strike, swoop ♦ noun 2 spring, assault, attack, bound, jump, leap, swoop

pound¹ verb 1 beat, batter, belabour, clobber (slang), hammer, pummel, strike, thrash, thump 2 crush, powder, pulverize 3 pulsate, beat, palpitate, pulse, throb 4 stomp (informal), march, thunder, tramp

pound² noun enclosure, compound, pen, yard

pour verb 1 flow, course, emit, gush, run, rush, spew, spout, stream 2 let flow, decant, spill, splash 3 rain, bucket down (informal), pelt (down), teem 4 stream, crowd, swarm, teem, throng

pout verb 1 sulk, glower, look petulant, pull a long face ♦ noun 2 sullen look, glower, long face

poverty noun 1 pennilessness, beggary, destitution, hardship, indigence, insolvency, need, penury, privation, want 2 scarcity, dearth, deficiency, insufficiency, lack, paucity, shortage

poverty-stricken adjective penniless, broke (informal), destitute, down and out, flat broke (informal), impecunious, impoverished, indigent, poor

powder noun 1 dust, fine grains, loose particles, talc ◆ verb 2 dust, cover, dredge, scatter, sprinkle, strew

powdery adjective fine, crumbly, dry, dusty, grainy, granular

power noun 1 ability, capability, capacity, competence, competency, faculty, potential 2 control, ascendancy, authority, command, dominance, domination, dominion, influence, mastery, rule 3 authority, authorization, licence, prerogative, privilege, right, warrant 4 strength, brawn, energy, force, forcefulness, intensity, might, muscle, potency, vigour

powerful adjective 1 controlling, authoritative, commanding, dominant, influential, prevailing 2 strong, energetic, mighty, potent, strapping, sturdy, vigorous 3 persuasive, cogent, compelling, convincing, effectual, forceful, impressive, striking, telling, weighty

powerless adjective 1 defenceless, dependent, ineffective, subject, tied, unarmed, vulnerable 2 helpless, debilitated, disabled, feeble, frail, impotent, incapable, incapacitated, ineffectual, weak

practicability noun feasibility, advantage, possibility, practicality, use, usefulness, viability

practicable adjective feasible, achievable, attainable, doable, possible, viable

practical adjective 1 functional, applied, empirical, experimental, factual, pragmatic, realistic, utilitarian 2 sensible, businesslike, down-to-earth, hard-headed, matter-of-fact, ordinary, realistic 3 feasible, doable, practicable, serviceable, useful, workable 4 skilled, accomplished, efficient, experienced, proficient

practically adverb 1 almost, all but, basically, essentially, fundamentally, in effect, just about, nearly, very nearly, virtually, well-nigh 2 sensibly, clearly, matter-of-factly, rationally, realistically, reasonably

practice noun 1 custom, habit, method, mode, routine, rule, system, tradition, usage, way, wont 2 rehearsal, drill, exercise, preparation, repetition, study, training 3 profession, business, career, vocation, work 4 use, action, application, exercise, experience, operation

practise verb 1 rehearse, drill, exercise, go over, go through, prepare, repeat, study, train 2 do, apply, carry out, follow, observe, perform 3 work at, carry on, engage in, pursue

practised adjective skilled, able, accomplished, experienced, expert, proficient, seasoned, trained

pragmatic adjective practical, businesslike, down-to-earth, hard-headed, realistic, sensible, utilitarian

praise verb 1 approve, acclaim, admire, applaud, cheer, compliment, congratulate, eulogize, extol, honour, laud 2 give thanks to, adore, bless, exalt, glorify, worship ♦ noun 3 approval, acclaim, acclamation, approbation, commendation, compliment, congratulation, eulogy, plaudit, tribute 4 thanks, adoration, glory, homage, worship

praiseworthy adjective creditable, admirable, commendable, laudable, meritorious, worthy

prance verb 1 dance, caper, cavort, frisk, gambol, romp, skip 2 strut, parade, show off (informal), stalk, swagger, swank (informal)

prank noun trick, escapade, jape, lark (informal), practical joke

prattle verb chatter, babble, blather, blether, gabble, jabber, rabbit (on) (Brit. informal), waffle (informal, chiefly Brit.), witter (informal)

pray verb 1 say one's prayers, offer a prayer, recite the rosary 2 beg, adjure, ask, beseech, entreat, implore, petition, plead, request, solicit

prayer noun 1 orison, devotion, invocation, litany, supplication 2 plea, appeal, entreaty, petition, request, supplication

preach verb 1 deliver a sermon, address, evangelize 2 lecture, advocate, exhort, moralize, sermonize

preacher noun clergyman, evangelist, minister, missionary, parson

preamble noun introduction, foreword, opening statement or remarks, preface, prelude

precarious adjective dangerous, dodgy (Brit., Austral., & N.Z. informal), hazardous, insecure, perilous, risky, shaky, tricky, unreliable, unsafe, unsure

precaution noun 1 safeguard, insurance, protection, provision, safety measure 2 forethought, care, caution, providence, prudence, wariness

precede verb go before, antedate, come first, head, introduce, lead, preface

precedence noun priority, antecedence, pre-eminence, primacy, rank, seniority, superiority, supremacy

precedent noun instance, antecedent, example, model, paradigm, pattern, prototype, standard

preceding adjective previous, above, aforementioned, aforesaid, earlier, foregoing, former, past, prior

precept noun rule, canon, command, commandment, decree, instruction, law, order, principle, regulation, statute

precinct noun 1 enclosure, confine, limit 2 area, district, quarter, section, sector, zone

precious adjective 1 valuable, costly, dear, expensive, fine, invaluable, priceless, prized 2 loved, adored, beloved, cherished, darling, dear, prized, treasured 3 affected, artificial, overnice, overrefined, twee (Brit. informal)

precipice noun cliff, bluff, crag, height, rock face

precipitate verb 1 quicken, accelerate, advance, bring on, expedite, hasten, hurry, speed up, trigger 2 throw, cast, fling, hurl, launch, let fly ♦ adjective 3 hasty, heedless, impetuous, impulsive, precipitous, rash, reckless 4 swift, breakneck, headlong, rapid, rushing 5 sudden, abrupt, brief, quick, unexpected, without warning

precipitous adjective 1 sheer, abrupt, dizzy, high, perpendicular, steep 2 hasty, heedless, hurried, precipitate, rash, reckless

précis noun 1 summary, abridgment, outline, résumé, synopsis ♦ verb 2 summarize, abridge, outline, shorten, sum up

precise adjective 1 exact, absolute, accurate, correct, definite, explicit, express, particular, specific, strict 2 strict, careful, exact, fastidious, finicky, formal, meticulous, particular, punctilious, rigid, scrupulous, stiff

precisely adverb exactly, absolutely, accurately, correctly, just so, plumb (informal), smack (informal), square, squarely, strictly

precision noun exactness, accuracy, care, meticulousness, particularity, preciseness

preclude verb prevent, check, debar, exclude, forestall, inhibit, obviate, prohibit, rule out, stop

precocious adjective advanced, ahead, bright, developed, forward, quick, smart

preconceived adjective presumed, forejudged, prejudged, presupposed

preconception noun preconceived idea or notion, bias, notion, predisposition, prejudice, presupposition

precursor noun 1 herald, forerunner, harbinger, vanguard 2 forerunner, antecedent, forebear, predecessor

predatory adjective hunting, carnivorous, predacious, raptorial

predecessor noun 1 previous job holder, antecedent, forerunner, precursor 2 ancestor, antecedent, forebear, forefather

predestination noun fate, destiny, foreordainment, foreordination, predetermination

predestined adjective fated, doomed, meant, preordained

predetermined adjective prearranged, agreed, fixed, preplanned, set

predicament noun fix (informal), dilemma, hole (slang), jam (informal), mess, pinch, plight, quandary, scrape (informal), situation, spot (informal)

predict verb foretell, augur, divine, forecast, portend, prophesy

predictable adjective likely, anticipated, certain, expected, foreseeable, reliable, sure

prediction noun prophecy, augury, divination, forecast, prognosis, prognostication

predilection noun liking, bias, fondness, inclination, leaning, love, partiality, penchant, preference, propensity, taste, weakness

predispose verb incline, affect, bias, dispose, influence, lead, prejudice, prompt

predisposed adjective inclined, given, liable, minded, ready, subject, susceptible, willing

predominant adjective main, ascendant, chief, dominant, leading, paramount, prevailing, prevalent, prime, principal

predominantly adverb mainly, chiefly, for the most part, generally, largely, mostly, primarily, principally

predominate verb prevail, be most noticeable, carry weight, hold sway, outweigh, overrule, overshadow

pre-eminence noun superiority, distinction, excellence, predominance, prestige, prominence, renown, supremacy

pre-eminent adjective outstanding, chief, distinguished, excellent, foremost, incomparable, matchless, predominant, renowned, superior, supreme

pre-empt verb anticipate, appropriate, assume, usurp

preen verb 1 Of birds clean, plume 2 smarten, dress up, spruce up, titivate 3 **preen oneself (on)** pride oneself, congratulate oneself

preface noun 1 introduction, foreword, preamble, preliminary, prelude, prologue ◆ verb 2 introduce, begin, open, prefix

prefer verb like better, be partial to, choose, desire, fancy, favour, go for, incline towards, opt for, pick

preferable adjective better, best, chosen, favoured, more desirable, superior

preferably adverb rather, by choice, first, in or for preference, sooner

preference noun 1 first choice, choice, desire, favourite, option, partiality, pick, predilection, selection 2 priority, favoured treatment, favouritism, first place, precedence

preferential adjective privileged, advantageous, better, favoured, special

preferment noun promotion, advancement, elevation, exaltation, rise, upgrading

pregnant adjective 1 expectant, big or heavy with child, expecting (informal), in the club (Brit. slang), with child 2 meaningful, charged, eloquent, expressive, loaded, pointed, significant, telling, weighty

prehistoric adjective earliest, early, primeval, primitive, primordial

prejudge verb jump to conclusions, anticipate, presume, presuppose

prejudice noun 1 bias, partiality, preconceived notion, preconception, prejudgment 2 discrimination, bigotry, chauvinism, injustice, intolerance, narrow-mindedness, unfairness ◆ verb 3 bias, colour, distort, influence, poison, predispose, slant 4 harm, damage, hinder, hurt, impair, injure, mar, spoil, undermine

prejudiced adjective biased,

bigoted, influenced, intolerant, narrow-minded, one-sided, opinionated, unfair

prejudicial adjective harmful, damaging, deleterious, detrimental, disadvantageous, hurtful, injurious, unfavourable

preliminary adjective 1 first, initial, introductory, opening, pilot, prefatory, preparatory, prior, test, trial ♦ noun 2 introduction, beginning, opening, overture, preamble, preface, prelude, start

prelude noun introduction, beginning, foreword, overture, preamble, preface, prologue, start

premature adjective 1 early, forward, unseasonable, untimely 2 hasty, ill-timed, overhasty, previous (informal), rash, too soon, untimely

premeditated adjective planned, calculated, conscious, considered, deliberate, intentional, wilful

premeditation noun planning, design, forethought, intention, plotting, prearrangement, predetermination, purpose

premier noun 1 head of government, chancellor, chief minister, P.M., prime minister ♦ adjective 2 chief, first, foremost, head, highest, leading, main, primary, prime, principal

premiere noun first night, debut, opening

premise noun assumption, argument, assertion, hypothesis, postulation, presupposition, proposition, supposition

premises plural noun building,

establishment, place, property, site

premium noun 1 bonus, bounty, fee, perk (Brit. informal), perquisite, prize, reward 2 at a premium in great demand, hard to come by, in short supply, rare, scarce

premonition noun feeling, foreboding, hunch, idea, intuition, presentiment, suspicion

preoccupation noun 1 obsession, bee in one's bonnet, fixation 2 absorption, absent-mindedness, abstraction, daydreaming, engrossment, immersion, reverie, woolgathering

preoccupied adjective absorbed, absent-minded, distracted, engrossed, immersed, lost in, oblivious, rapt, wrapped up

preparation noun 1 groundwork, getting ready, preparing 2 often plural arrangement, measure, plan, provision 3 mixture, compound, concoction, medicine

preparatory adjective introductory, opening, prefatory, preliminary, primary

prepare verb make or get ready, adapt, adjust, arrange, practise, prime, train, warm up

prepared adjective 1 ready, arranged, in order, in readiness, primed, set 2 willing, disposed, inclined

preponderance noun predominance, dominance, domination, extensiveness, greater numbers, greater part, lion's share, mass, prevalence, supremacy

prepossessing *adjective*
attractive, appealing, charming, engaging, fetching, good-looking, handsome, likable or likeable, pleasing

preposterous *adjective*
ridiculous, absurd, crazy, incredible, insane, laughable, ludicrous, nonsensical, out of the question, outrageous, unthinkable

prerequisite *noun*
1 requirement, condition, essential, must, necessity, precondition, qualification, requisite, *sine qua non* ♦ *adjective* **2** required, essential, indispensable, mandatory, necessary, obligatory, requisite, vital

prerogative *noun* right, advantage, due, exemption, immunity, liberty, privilege

presage *verb* portend, augur, betoken, bode, foreshadow, foretoken, signify

prescience *noun* foresight, clairvoyance, foreknowledge, precognition, second sight

prescribe *verb* order, decree, dictate, direct, lay down, ordain, recommend, rule, set, specify, stipulate

prescription *noun* **1** instruction, direction, formula, recipe **2** medicine, drug, mixture, preparation, remedy

presence *noun* **1** being, attendance, existence, inhabitance, occupancy, residence **2** personality, air, appearance, aspect, aura, bearing, carriage, demeanour, poise, self-assurance

presence of mind *noun*
level-headedness, calmness, composure, cool (*slang*), coolness, self-possession, wits

present[1] *adjective* **1** here, at hand, near, nearby, ready, there **2** current, contemporary, existent, existing, immediate, present-day ♦ *noun* **3** the present now, here and now, the present moment, the time being, today **4 at present** just now, at the moment, now, right now **5 for the present** for now, for the moment, for the time being, in the meantime, temporarily

present[2] *noun* **1** gift, boon, donation, endowment, grant, gratuity, hand-out, offering, prezzie (*informal*) ♦ *verb* **2** introduce, acquaint with, make known **3** put on, display, exhibit, give, show, stage **4** give, award, bestow, confer, grant, hand out, hand over

presentable *adjective* decent, acceptable, becoming, fit to be seen, O.K. or okay (*informal*), passable, respectable, satisfactory, suitable

presentation *noun* **1** giving, award, bestowal, conferral, donation, offering **2** production, demonstration, display, exhibition, performance, show

presently *adverb* soon, anon (*archaic*), before long, by and by, shortly

preservation *noun* protection, conservation, maintenance, safeguarding, safekeeping, safety, salvation, support

preserve *verb* **1** save, care for, conserve, defend, keep, protect, safeguard, shelter, shield

2 <u>maintain</u>, continue, keep, keep up, perpetuate, sustain, uphold
♦ *noun* **3** <u>area</u>, domain, field, realm, sphere

preside *verb* <u>run</u>, administer, chair, conduct, control, direct, govern, head, lead, manage, officiate

press *verb* **1** <u>force down</u>, compress, crush, depress, jam, mash, push, squeeze **2** <u>hug</u>, clasp, crush, embrace, fold in one's arms, hold close, squeeze **3** <u>smooth</u>, flatten, iron **4** <u>urge</u>, beg, entreat, exhort, implore, petition, plead, pressurize **5** <u>crowd</u>, flock, gather, herd, push, seethe, surge, swarm, throng ♦ *noun* **6** <u>the press: a</u> <u>newspapers</u>, Fleet Street, fourth estate, news media, the papers **b** <u>journalists</u>, columnists, correspondents, newsmen, pressmen, reporters

pressing *adjective* <u>urgent</u>, crucial, high-priority, imperative, important, importunate, serious, vital

pressure *noun* **1** <u>force</u>, compressing, compression, crushing, squeezing, weight **2** <u>power</u>, coercion, compulsion, constraint, force, influence, sway **3** <u>stress</u>, burden, demands, hassle (*informal*), heat, load, strain, urgency

prestige *noun* <u>status</u>, credit, distinction, eminence, fame, honour, importance, kudos, renown, reputation, standing

prestigious *adjective* <u>celebrated</u>, eminent, esteemed, great, illustrious, important, notable, prominent, renowned, respected

presumably *adverb* <u>it would</u> <u>seem</u>, apparently, in all likelihood, in all probability, on the face of it, probably, seemingly

presume *verb* **1** <u>believe</u>, assume, conjecture, guess (*informal, chiefly U.S. & Canad.*), infer, postulate, suppose, surmise, take for granted, think **2** <u>dare</u>, go so far as, make so bold, take the liberty, venture

presumption *noun* **1** <u>cheek</u> (*informal*), audacity, boldness, effrontery, gall (*informal*), impudence, insolence, nerve (*informal*) **2** <u>probability</u>, basis, chance, likelihood

presumptuous *adjective* <u>pushy</u> (*informal*), audacious, bold, forward, insolent, overconfident, too big for one's boots, uppish (*Brit. informal*)

presuppose *verb* <u>presume</u>, assume, imply, posit, postulate, take as read, take for granted

presupposition *noun* <u>assumption</u>, belief, preconception, premise, presumption, supposition

pretence *noun* **1** <u>deception</u>, acting, charade, deceit, falsehood, feigning, sham, simulation, trickery **2** <u>show</u>, affectation, artifice, display, façade, veneer

pretend *verb* **1** <u>feign</u>, affect, allege, assume, fake, falsify, impersonate, profess, sham, simulate **2** <u>make believe</u>, act, imagine, make up, suppose

pretended *adjective* <u>feigned</u>, bogus, counterfeit, fake, false, phoney *or* phony (*informal*), pretend (*informal*), pseudo (*informal*), sham, so-called

pretender *noun* claimant, aspirant

pretension *noun* 1 claim, aspiration, assumption, demand, pretence, profession 2 affectation, airs, conceit, ostentation, pretentiousness, self-importance, show, snobbery, vanity

pretentious *adjective* affected, conceited, grandiloquent, grandiose, high-flown, inflated, mannered, ostentatious, pompous, puffed up, showy, snobbish

pretext *noun* guise, cloak, cover, excuse, ploy, pretence, ruse, show

pretty *adjective* 1 attractive, beautiful, bonny, charming, comely, fair, good-looking, lovely ♦ *adverb* 2 *Informal* fairly, kind of (*informal*), moderately, quite, rather, reasonably, somewhat

prevail *verb* 1 win, be victorious, overcome, overrule, succeed, triumph 2 be widespread, abound, be current, be prevalent, exist generally, predominate

prevailing *adjective* 1 widespread, common, current, customary, established, fashionable, general, in vogue, ordinary, popular, prevalent, usual 2 predominating, dominant, main, principal, ruling

prevalence *noun* commonness, currency, frequency, popularity, universality

prevalent *adjective* common, current, customary, established,

frequent, general, popular, universal, usual, widespread

prevaricate *verb* evade, beat about the bush, cavil, deceive, dodge, equivocate, flannel (*Brit. informal*), hedge

prevent *verb* stop, avert, avoid, foil, forestall, frustrate, hamper, hinder, impede, inhibit, obstruct, obviate, preclude, thwart

prevention *noun* elimination, avoidance, deterrence, precaution, safeguard, thwarting

preventive, preventative *adjective* 1 hindering, hampering, impeding, obstructive 2 protective, counteractive, deterrent, precautionary ♦ *noun* 3 hindrance, block, impediment, obstacle, obstruction 4 protection, deterrent, prevention, remedy, safeguard, shield

preview *noun* advance showing, foretaste, sneak preview, taster, trailer

previous *adjective* earlier, erstwhile, foregoing, former, past, preceding, prior

previously *adverb* before, beforehand, earlier, formerly, hitherto, in the past, once

prey *noun* 1 quarry, game, kill 2 victim, dupe, fall guy (*informal*), mug (*Brit. slang*), target

price *noun* 1 cost, amount, charge, damage (*informal*), estimate, expense, fee, figure, rate, value, worth 2 consequences, cost, penalty, toll ♦ *verb* 3 evaluate, assess, cost, estimate, rate, value

priceless *adjective* 1 valuable,

costly, dear, expensive, invaluable, precious **2** *Informal* hilarious, amusing, comic, droll, funny, rib-tickling, side-splitting

pricey, pricy *adjective* expensive, costly, dear, high-priced, steep (*informal*)

prick *verb* **1** pierce, jab, lance, perforate, punch, puncture, stab **2** sting, bite, itch, prickle, smart, tingle ♦ *noun* **3** puncture, hole, perforation, pinhole, wound

prickle *noun* **1** spike, barb, needle, point, spine, spur, thorn ♦ *verb* **2** tingle, itch, smart, sting **3** prick, jab, stick

prickly *adjective* **1** spiny, barbed, bristly, thorny **2** itchy, crawling, scratchy, sharp, smarting, stinging, tingling

pride *noun* **1** satisfaction, delight, gratification, joy, pleasure **2** self-respect, dignity, honour, self-esteem, self-worth **3** conceit, arrogance, egotism, haughtiness, pretension, pretentiousness, self-importance, self-love, superciliousness, vanity **4** gem, jewel, pride and joy, treasure

priest *noun* clergyman, cleric, curate, divine, ecclesiastic, father, minister, pastor, vicar

prig *noun* goody-goody (*informal*), prude, puritan, stuffed shirt (*informal*)

priggish *adjective* self-righteous, goody-goody (*informal*), holier-than-thou, prim, prudish, puritanical

prim *adjective* prudish, demure, fastidious, fussy, priggish, prissy (*informal*), proper, puritanical, strait-laced

prima donna *noun* diva, leading lady, star

primarily *adverb* **1** chiefly, above all, essentially, fundamentally, generally, largely, mainly, mostly, principally **2** at first, at or from the start, first and foremost, initially, in the beginning, in the first place, originally

primary *adjective* **1** chief, cardinal, first, greatest, highest, main, paramount, prime, principal **2** elementary, introductory, rudimentary, simple

prime *adjective* **1** main, chief, leading, predominant, pre-eminent, primary, principal **2** best, choice, excellent, first-class, first-rate, highest, quality, select, top ♦ *noun* **3** peak, bloom, flower, height, heyday, zenith ♦ *verb* **4** inform, brief, clue in (*informal*), fill in (*informal*), notify, tell **5** prepare, coach, get ready, make ready, train

primeval *adjective* earliest, ancient, early, first, old, prehistoric, primal, primitive, primordial

primitive *adjective* **1** early, earliest, elementary, first, original, primary, primeval, primordial **2** crude, rough, rudimentary, simple, unrefined

prince *noun* ruler, lord, monarch, sovereign

princely *adjective* **1** regal, imperial, majestic, noble, royal, sovereign **2** generous, bounteous, gracious, lavish, liberal, munificent, open-handed, rich

principal adjective 1 main, cardinal, chief, essential, first, foremost, key, leading, paramount, primary, prime ◆ noun 2 head (informal), dean, headmaster or headmistress, head teacher, master or mistress, rector 3 star, lead, leader 4 capital, assets, money

principally adverb mainly, above all, chiefly, especially, largely, mostly, predominantly, primarily

principle noun 1 rule, canon, criterion, doctrine, dogma, fundamental, law, maxim, precept, standard, truth 2 morals, conscience, integrity, probity, scruples, sense of honour 3 in principle in theory, ideally, theoretically

print verb 1 publish, engrave, impress, imprint, issue, mark, stamp ◆ noun 2 publication, book, magazine, newspaper, newsprint, periodical, printed matter 3 reproduction, copy, engraving, photo (informal), photograph, picture

prior adjective 1 earlier, foregoing, former, preceding, pre-existent, pre-existing, previous 2 prior to before, earlier than, preceding, previous to

priority noun precedence, pre-eminence, preference, rank, right of way, seniority

priory noun monastery, abbey, convent, nunnery, religious house

prison noun jail, clink (slang), confinement, cooler (slang), dungeon, jug (slang), lockup, nick (Brit. slang), penitentiary (U.S.), slammer (slang)

prisoner noun 1 convict, con (slang), jailbird, lag (slang) 2 captive, detainee, hostage, internee

prissy adjective prim, old-maidish (informal), prim and proper, prudish, strait-laced

pristine adjective new, immaculate, pure, uncorrupted, undefiled, unspoiled, unsullied, untouched, virginal

privacy noun seclusion, isolation, retirement, retreat, solitude

private adjective 1 exclusive, individual, intimate, own, personal, reserved, special 2 secret, clandestine, confidential, covert, hush-hush (informal), off the record, unofficial 3 secluded, isolated, secret, separate, sequestered, solitary

privilege noun right, advantage, claim, concession, due, entitlement, freedom, liberty, prerogative

privileged adjective special, advantaged, elite, entitled, favoured, honoured

privy adjective 1 privy to informed of, apprised of, aware of, cognizant of, in on, in the know about (informal), wise to (slang) ◆ noun 2 lavatory, latrine, outside toilet

prize[1] noun 1 reward, accolade, award, honour, trophy 2 winnings, haul, jackpot, purse, stakes ◆ adjective 3 champion, award-winning, best, first-rate, outstanding, top, winning

prize[2] verb value, cherish, esteem,

hold dear, treasure

probability noun likelihood, chance(s), expectation, liability, likeliness, odds, prospect

probable adjective likely, apparent, credible, feasible, plausible, possible, presumable, reasonable

probably adverb likely, doubtless, maybe, most likely, perchance (*archaic*), perhaps, possibly, presumably

probation noun trial period, apprenticeship, trial

probe verb 1 examine, explore, go into, investigate, look into, scrutinize, search 2 explore, feel around, poke, prod ◆ noun 3 examination, detection, exploration, inquiry, investigation, scrutiny, study

problem noun 1 difficulty, complication, dilemma, dispute, predicament, quandary, trouble 2 puzzle, conundrum, enigma, poser, question, riddle

problematic adjective tricky, debatable, doubtful, dubious, problematical, puzzling

procedure noun method, action, conduct, course, custom, modus operandi, policy, practice, process, routine, strategy, system

proceed verb 1 go on, carry on, continue, go ahead, move on, press on, progress 2 arise, come, derive, emanate, flow, issue, originate, result, spring, stem

proceeding noun 1 action, act, deed, measure, move, procedure, process, step 2 **proceedings** business, account, affairs, archives, doings,

minutes, records, report, transactions

proceeds plural noun income, earnings, gain, products, profit, returns, revenue, takings, yield

process noun 1 procedure, action, course, manner, means, measure, method, operation, performance, practice, system 2 development, advance, evolution, growth, movement, progress, progression ◆ verb 3 handle, deal with, fulfil

procession noun parade, cavalcade, cortege, file, march, train

proclaim verb declare, advertise, announce, circulate, herald, indicate, make known, profess, publish

proclamation noun declaration, announcement, decree, edict, notice, notification, pronouncement, publication

procrastinate verb delay, dally, drag one's feet (*informal*), gain time, play for time, postpone, put off, stall, temporize

procure verb obtain, acquire, buy, come by, find, gain, get, pick up, purchase, score (*slang*), secure, win

prod verb 1 poke, dig, drive, jab, nudge, push, shove 2 prompt, egg on, goad, impel, incite, motivate, move, rouse, spur, stimulate, urge ◆ noun 3 poke, dig, jab, nudge, push, shove 4 prompt, cue, reminder, signal, stimulus

prodigal adjective extravagant, excessive, immoderate, improvident, profligate, reckless, spendthrift, wasteful

prodigious adjective **1** huge, colossal, enormous, giant, gigantic, immense, massive, monstrous, vast **2** wonderful, amazing, exceptional, extraordinary, fabulous, fantastic (informal), marvellous, phenomenal, remarkable, staggering

prodigy noun **1** genius, mastermind, talent, whizz (informal), wizard **2** wonder, marvel, miracle, phenomenon, sensation

produce verb **1** cause, bring about, effect, generate, give rise to **2** bring forth, bear, beget, breed, deliver **3** show, advance, demonstrate, exhibit, offer, present **4** make, compose, construct, create, develop, fabricate, invent, manufacture **5** present, direct, do, exhibit, mount, put on, show, stage ♦ noun **6** fruit and vegetables, crop, greengrocery, harvest, product, yield

producer noun **1** director, impresario **2** maker, farmer, grower, manufacturer

product noun **1** goods, artefact, commodity, creation, invention, merchandise, produce, work **2** result, consequence, effect, outcome, upshot

production noun **1** producing, construction, creation, fabrication, formation, making, manufacture, manufacturing **2** presentation, direction, management, staging

productive adjective **1** fertile, creative, fecund, fruitful, inventive, plentiful, prolific, rich

2 useful, advantageous, beneficial, constructive, effective, profitable, rewarding, valuable, worthwhile

productivity noun output, production, work rate, yield

profane adjective **1** sacrilegious, disrespectful, godless, impious, impure, irreligious, irreverent, sinful, ungodly, wicked **2** crude, blasphemous, coarse, filthy, foul, obscene, vulgar ♦ verb **3** desecrate, commit sacrilege, debase, defile, violate

profanity noun **1** sacrilege, blasphemy, impiety, profaneness **2** swearing, curse, cursing, irreverence, obscenity

profess verb **1** claim, allege, fake, feign, make out, pretend, purport **2** state, admit, affirm, announce, assert, avow, confess, declare, proclaim, vouch

professed adjective **1** supposed, alleged, ostensible, pretended, purported, self-styled, so-called, would-be **2** declared, avowed, confessed, confirmed, proclaimed, self-acknowledged, self-confessed

profession noun **1** occupation, business, calling, career, employment, office, position, sphere, vocation **2** declaration, affirmation, assertion, avowal, claim, confession, statement

professional adjective **1** expert, adept, competent, efficient, experienced, masterly, proficient, qualified, skilled ♦ noun **2** expert, adept, maestro, master, past master, pro (informal), specialist, virtuoso

professor noun don (Brit.), fellow

(*Brit.*), prof (*informal*)

proficiency *noun* skill, ability, aptitude, competence, dexterity, expertise, knack, know-how (*informal*), mastery

proficient *adjective* skilled, able, accomplished, adept, capable, competent, efficient, expert, gifted, masterly, skilful

profile *noun* 1 outline, contour, drawing, figure, form, side view, silhouette, sketch 2 biography, characterization, sketch, thumbnail sketch, vignette

profit *noun* 1 *often plural* earnings, gain, proceeds, receipts, return, revenue, takings, yield 2 benefit, advancement, advantage, gain, good, use, value ◆ *verb* 3 benefit, be of advantage to, gain, help, improve, promote, serve 4 make money, earn, gain

profitable *adjective* 1 money-making, commercial, cost-effective, fruitful, lucrative, paying, remunerative, worthwhile 2 beneficial, advantageous, fruitful, productive, rewarding, useful, valuable, worthwhile

profiteer *noun* 1 racketeer, exploiter ◆ *verb* 2 racketeer, exploit, make a quick buck (*slang*)

profligate *adjective* 1 extravagant, immoderate, improvident, prodigal, reckless, spendthrift, wasteful 2 depraved, debauched, degenerate, dissolute, immoral, licentious, shameless, wanton, wicked, wild ◆ *noun* 3 spendthrift, squanderer, waster, wastrel 4 degenerate, debauchee, libertine, rake,

reprobate, roué

profound *adjective* 1 wise, abstruse, deep, learned, penetrating, philosophical, sagacious, sage 3 intense, acute, deeply felt, extreme, great, heartfelt, keen

profuse *adjective* plentiful, abundant, ample, bountiful, copious, luxuriant, overflowing, prolific

profusion *noun* abundance, bounty, excess, extravagance, glut, plethora, quantity, surplus, wealth

progeny *noun* children, descendants, family, issue, lineage, offspring, race, stock, young

prognosis *noun* forecast, diagnosis, prediction, prognostication, projection

programme *noun* 1 schedule, agenda, curriculum, line-up, list, listing, order of events, plan, syllabus, timetable 2 show, broadcast, performance, presentation, production

progress *noun* 1 development, advance, breakthrough, gain, growth, headway, improvement 2 movement, advance, course, passage, way 3 in progress going on, being done, happening, occurring, proceeding, taking place, under way ◆ *verb* 4 develop, advance, gain, grow, improve 5 move on, advance, continue, go forward, make headway, proceed, travel

progression *noun* 1 progress, advance, advancement, furtherance, gain, headway, movement forward 2 sequence, chain, course, cycle, series, string, succession

progressive adjective
1 underlined, advanced, avant-garde, forward-looking, liberal, modern, radical, reformist, revolutionary 2 growing, advancing, continuing, developing, increasing, ongoing

prohibit verb 1 forbid, ban, debar, disallow, outlaw, proscribe, veto 2 prevent, hamper, hinder, impede, restrict, stop

prohibition noun 1 prevention, constraint, exclusion, obstruction, restriction 2 ban, bar, boycott, embargo, injunction, interdict, proscription, veto

prohibitive adjective exorbitant, excessive, extortionate, steep (informal)

project noun 1 scheme, activity, assignment, enterprise, job, occupation, plan, task, undertaking, venture, work ♦ verb 2 forecast, calculate, estimate, extrapolate, gauge, predict, reckon 3 stick out, bulge, extend, jut, overhang, protrude, stand out

projectile noun missile, bullet, rocket, shell

projection noun 1 protrusion, bulge, ledge, overhang, protuberance, ridge, shelf 2 forecast, calculation, computation, estimate, estimation, extrapolation, reckoning

proletarian adjective
1 working-class, common,

plebeian ♦ noun 2 worker, commoner, man of the people, pleb, plebeian, prole (derogatory slang, chiefly Brit.)

proletariat noun working class, commoners, hoi polloi, labouring classes, lower classes, plebs, proles (derogatory slang, chiefly Brit.), the common people, the masses

proliferate verb increase, breed, expand, grow rapidly, multiply

proliferation noun multiplication, expansion, increase, spread

prolific adjective productive, abundant, copious, fecund, fertile, fruitful, luxuriant, profuse

prologue noun introduction, foreword, preamble, preface, prelude

prolong verb lengthen, continue, delay, drag out, draw out, extend, perpetuate, protract, spin out, stretch

promenade noun 1 walkway, esplanade, parade, prom 2 stroll, constitutional, saunter, turn, walk ♦ verb 3 stroll, perambulate, saunter, take a walk, walk

prominence noun
1 conspicuousness, markedness 2 fame, celebrity, distinction, eminence, importance, name, prestige, reputation

prominent adjective 1 noticeable, conspicuous, eye-catching, obtrusive, obvious, outstanding, pronounced 2 famous, distinguished, eminent, foremost, important, leading, main, notable, renowned, top, well-known

promiscuity noun licentiousness, debauchery, immorality, looseness, permissiveness, promiscuousness, wantonness

promiscuous adjective licentious, abandoned, debauched, fast, immoral, libertine, loose, wanton, wild

promise verb 1 guarantee, assure, contract, give an undertaking, give one's word, pledge, swear, take an oath, undertake, vow, warrant 2 seem likely, augur, betoken, indicate, look like, show signs of, suggest ♦ noun 3 guarantee, assurance, bond, commitment, oath, pledge, undertaking, vow, word 4 potential, ability, aptitude, capability, capacity, talent

promising adjective 1 encouraging, auspicious, bright, favourable, hopeful, likely, propitious, reassuring, rosy 2 talented, able, gifted, rising

promontory noun point, cape, foreland, head, headland

promote verb 1 help, advance, aid, assist, back, boost, encourage, forward, foster, support 2 raise, elevate, exalt, upgrade 3 advertise, hype, plug (informal), publicize, push, sell

promotion noun 1 rise, advancement, elevation, exaltation, honour, move up, preferment, upgrading 2 publicity, advertising, plugging (informal) 3 encouragement, advancement, boosting, furtherance, support

prompt verb 1 cause, elicit, give rise to, occasion, provoke 2 remind, assist, cue, help out

♦ adjective 3 immediate, early, instant, quick, rapid, speedy, swift, timely ♦ adverb 4 Informal exactly, on the dot, promptly, punctually, sharp

promptly adverb immediately, at once, directly, on the dot, on time, punctually, quickly, speedily, swiftly

promptness noun swiftness, briskness, eagerness, haste, punctuality, quickness, speed, willingness

promulgate verb make known, broadcast, circulate, communicate, disseminate, make public, proclaim, promote, publish, spread

prone adjective 1 liable, apt, bent, disposed, given, inclined, likely, predisposed, subject, susceptible, tending 2 face down, flat, horizontal, prostrate, recumbent

prong noun point, spike, tine

pronounce verb 1 say, accent, articulate, enunciate, sound, speak 2 declare, affirm, announce, decree, deliver, proclaim

pronounced adjective noticeable, conspicuous, decided, definite, distinct, evident, marked, obvious, striking

pronouncement noun announcement, declaration, decree, dictum, edict, judgment, proclamation, statement

pronunciation noun intonation, accent, articulation, diction, enunciation, inflection, speech, stress

proof noun 1 evidence,

authentication, confirmation, corroboration, demonstration, substantiation, testimony, verification ♦ *adjective* **2** **impervious**, impenetrable, repellent, resistant, strong

prop *verb* **1** **support**, bolster, brace, buttress, hold up, stay, sustain, uphold ♦ *noun* **2** **support**, brace, buttress, mainstay, stanchion, stay

propaganda *noun* **information**, advertising, disinformation, hype, promotion, publicity

propagate *verb* **1** **spread**, broadcast, circulate, disseminate, promote, promulgate, publish, transmit **2** **reproduce**, beget, breed, engender, generate, increase, multiply, procreate, produce

propel *verb* **drive**, force, impel, launch, push, send, shoot, shove, thrust

propensity *noun* **tendency**, bent, disposition, inclination, liability, penchant, predisposition, proclivity

proper *adjective* **1** **suitable**, appropriate, apt, becoming, befitting, fit, fitting, right **2** **correct**, accepted, conventional, established, formal, orthodox, precise, right **3** **polite**, decent, decorous, genteel, gentlemanly, ladylike, mannerly, respectable, seemly

properly *adverb* **1** **suitably**, appropriately, aptly, fittingly, rightly **2** **correctly**, accurately **3** **politely**, decently, respectably

property *noun* **1** **possessions**, assets, belongings, capital, effects, estate, goods, holdings,

riches, wealth **2** **land**, estate, freehold, holding, real estate **3** **quality**, attribute, characteristic, feature, hallmark, trait

prophecy *noun* **prediction**, augury, divination, forecast, prognostication, second sight, soothsaying

prophesy *verb* **predict**, augur, divine, forecast, foresee, foretell, prognosticate

prophet *noun* **soothsayer**, diviner, forecaster, oracle, prophesier, seer, sibyl

prophetic *adjective* **predictive**, oracular, prescient, prognostic, sibylline

propitious *adjective* **favourable**, auspicious, bright, encouraging, fortunate, happy, lucky, promising

proportion *noun* **1** **relative amount**, ratio, relationship **2** **balance**, congruity, correspondence, harmony, symmetry **3** **part**, amount, division, fraction, percentage, quota, segment, share **4** **proportions** **dimensions**, capacity, expanse, extent, size, volume

proportional, proportionate *adjective* **balanced**, commensurate, compatible, consistent, corresponding, equitable, even, in proportion

proposal *noun* **suggestion**, bid, offer, plan, presentation, programme, project, recommendation, scheme

propose *verb* **1** **put forward**, advance, present, submit, suggest **2** **nominate**, name,

present, recommend **3** intend,
aim, design, have in mind,
mean, plan, scheme **4** offer
marriage, ask for someone's
hand (in marriage), pop the
question (*informal*)

proposition *noun* **1** proposal,
plan, recommendation, scheme,
suggestion ♦ *verb* **2** make a pass
at, accost, make an improper
suggestion, solicit

propound *verb* put forward,
advance, postulate, present,
propose, submit, suggest

proprietor, proprietress *noun*
owner, landlord or landlady,
titleholder

propriety *noun* **1** correctness,
aptness, fitness, rightness,
seemliness **2** decorum, courtesy,
decency, etiquette, manners,
politeness, respectability,
seemliness

propulsion *noun* drive, impetus,
impulse, propelling force, push,
thrust

prosaic *adjective* dull, boring,
everyday, humdrum,
matter-of-fact, mundane,
ordinary, pedestrian, routine,
trite, unimaginative

proscribe *verb* **1** prohibit, ban,
embargo, forbid, interdict
2 outlaw, banish, deport,
exclude, exile, expatriate, expel,
ostracize

prosecute *verb Law* put on trial,
arraign, bring to trial, indict,
litigate, sue, take to court, try

prospect *noun* **1** expectation,
anticipation, future, hope, odds,
outlook, probability, promise
2 *sometimes plural* likelihood,
chance, possibility **3** view,

landscape, outlook, scene, sight,
spectacle, vista ♦ *verb* **4** look for,
search for, seek

prospective *adjective* future,
anticipated, coming, destined,
expected, forthcoming,
imminent, intended, likely,
possible, potential

prospectus *noun* catalogue, list,
outline, programme, syllabus,
synopsis

prosper *verb* succeed, advance,
do well, flourish, get on,
progress, thrive

prosperity *noun* success,
affluence, fortune, good fortune,
luxury, plenty, prosperousness,
riches, wealth

prosperous *adjective* **1** wealthy,
affluent, moneyed, rich,
well-heeled (*informal*), well-off,
well-to-do **2** successful,
booming, doing well,
flourishing, fortunate, lucky,
thriving

prostitute *noun* **1** whore, call
girl, fallen woman, harlot,
hooker (*U.S. slang*), loose
woman, pro (*slang*), scrubber
(*Brit. & Austral. slang*),
streetwalker, strumpet, tart
(*informal*), trollop ♦ *verb*
2 cheapen, debase, degrade,
demean, devalue, misapply,
pervert, profane

prostrate *adjective* **1** prone, flat,
horizontal **2** exhausted,
dejected, depressed, desolate,
drained, inconsolable, overcome,
spent, worn out ♦ *verb*
3 exhaust, drain, fatigue, sap,
tire, wear out, weary **4** prostrate
oneself bow down to, abase
oneself, fall at (someone's) feet,

grovel, kneel, kowtow

protagonist noun **1** supporter, advocate, champion, exponent **2** leading character, central character, hero or heroine, principal

protect verb keep safe, defend, guard, look after, preserve, safeguard, save, screen, shelter, shield, stick up for (*informal*), support, watch over

protection noun **1** safety, aegis, care, custody, defence, protecting, safeguard, safekeeping, security **2** safeguard, barrier, buffer, cover, guard, screen, shelter, shield

protective adjective protecting, defensive, fatherly, maternal, motherly, paternal, vigilant, watchful

protector noun defender, bodyguard, champion, guard, guardian, patron

protest noun **1** objection, complaint, dissent, outcry, protestation, remonstrance ♦ verb **2** object, complain, cry out, demonstrate, demur, disagree, disapprove, express disapproval, oppose, remonstrate **3** assert, affirm, attest, avow, declare, insist, maintain, profess

protestation noun declaration, affirmation, avowal, profession, vow

protester noun demonstrator, agitator, rebel

protocol noun code of behaviour, conventions, customs, decorum, etiquette, manners, propriety

prototype noun original, example, first, model, pattern, standard, type

protracted adjective extended, dragged out, drawn-out, long-drawn-out, prolonged, spun out

protrude verb stick out, bulge, come through, extend, jut, obtrude, project, stand out

protrusion noun projection, bulge, bump, lump, outgrowth, protuberance

protuberance noun bulge, bump, excrescence, hump, knob, lump, outgrowth, process, prominence, protrusion, swelling

proud adjective **1** satisfied, content, glad, gratified, pleased, well-pleased **2** conceited, arrogant, boastful, disdainful, haughty, imperious, lordly, overbearing, self-satisfied, snobbish, supercilious

prove verb **1** verify, authenticate, confirm, demonstrate, determine, establish, justify, show, substantiate **2** test, analyse, assay, check, examine, try **3** turn out, come out, end up, result

proven adjective established, attested, confirmed, definite, proved, reliable, tested, verified

proverb noun saying, adage, dictum, maxim, saw

proverbial adjective conventional, acknowledged, axiomatic, current, famed, famous, legendary, notorious, traditional, typical, well-known

provide verb **1** supply, cater, equip, furnish, outfit, purvey, stock up **2** give, add, afford, bring, impart, lend, present, produce, render, serve, yield **3** provide for or against take precautions, anticipate, forearm, plan ahead, plan for, prepare for **4** provide for support, care for, keep, maintain, sustain, take care of

providence noun fate, destiny, fortune

provident adjective **1** thrifty, economical, frugal, prudent **2** foresighted, careful, cautious, discreet, far-seeing, forearmed, shrewd, vigilant, well-prepared, wise

providential adjective lucky, fortuitous, fortunate, happy, heaven-sent, opportune, timely

provider noun **1** supplier, donor, giver, source **2** breadwinner, earner, supporter, wage earner

providing, provided conjunction on condition that, as long as, given

province noun **1** region, colony, department, district, division, domain, patch, section, zone **2** area, business, capacity, concern, duty, field, function, line, responsibility, role, sphere

provincial adjective **1** rural, country, hick (informal, chiefly U.S. & Canad.), homespun, local, rustic **2** narrow-minded, insular, inward-looking, limited, narrow, parochial, small-minded, small-town (chiefly U.S.), unsophisticated ◆ noun **3** yokel, country cousin, hayseed (U.S. & Canad. informal), hick (informal, chiefly U.S. & Canad.), rustic

provision noun **1** supplying,

catering, equipping, furnishing, providing **2** condition, clause, demand, proviso, requirement, rider, stipulation, term

provisional adjective **1** temporary, interim **2** conditional, contingent, limited, qualified, tentative

provisions plural noun food, comestibles, eatables, edibles, fare, foodstuff, rations, stores, supplies, victuals

proviso noun condition, clause, qualification, requirement, rider, stipulation

provocation noun **1** cause, grounds, incitement, motivation, reason, stimulus **2** offence, affront, annoyance, challenge, dare, grievance, indignity, injury, insult, taunt

provocative adjective offensive, annoying, galling, goading, insulting, provoking, stimulating

provoke verb **1** anger, aggravate (informal), annoy, enrage, hassle (informal), incense, infuriate, irk, irritate, madden, rile **2** cause, bring about, elicit, evoke, incite, induce, occasion, produce, promote, prompt, rouse, stir

prowess noun **1** skill, accomplishment, adeptness, aptitude, excellence, expertise, genius, mastery, talent **2** bravery, courage, daring, fearlessness, heroism, mettle, valiance, valour

prowl verb move stealthily, skulk, slink, sneak, stalk, steal

proximity noun nearness, closeness

proxy noun representative, agent,

delegate, deputy, factor, substitute

prudence *noun* <u>common sense</u>, care, caution, discretion, good sense, judgment, vigilance, wariness, wisdom

prudent *adjective* 1 <u>sensible</u>, careful, cautious, discerning, discreet, judicious, politic, shrewd, vigilant, wary, wise 2 <u>thrifty</u>, canny, careful, economical, far-sighted, frugal, provident, sparing

prudish *adjective* <u>prim</u>, old-maidish (*informal*), overmodest, priggish, prissy (*informal*), proper, puritanical, starchy (*informal*), strait-laced, stuffy, Victorian

prune *verb* <u>cut</u>, clip, dock, reduce, shape, shorten, snip, trim

pry *verb* <u>be inquisitive</u>, be nosy (*informal*), interfere, intrude, meddle, poke, snoop (*informal*)

prying *adjective* <u>inquisitive</u>, curious, interfering, meddlesome, meddling, nosy (*informal*), snooping (*informal*), spying

psalm *noun* <u>hymn</u>, chant

pseudo- *adjective* <u>false</u>, artificial, fake, imitation, mock, phoney or phony (*informal*), pretended, sham, spurious

pseudonym *noun* <u>false name</u>, alias, assumed name, incognito, nom de plume, pen name

psyche *noun* <u>soul</u>, anima, individuality, mind, personality, self, spirit

psychiatrist *noun* <u>psychotherapist</u>, analyst, headshrinker (*slang*),

psychoanalyst, psychologist, shrink (*slang*), therapist

psychic *adjective* 1 <u>supernatural</u>, mystic, occult 2 <u>mental</u>, psychological, spiritual

psychological *adjective* 1 <u>mental</u>, cerebral, intellectual 2 <u>imaginary</u>, all in the mind, irrational, psychosomatic, unreal

psychology *noun* 1 <u>behaviourism</u>, science of mind, study of personality 2 *Informal* <u>way of thinking</u>, attitude, mental make-up, mental processes, thought processes, what makes one tick

psychopath *noun* <u>madman</u>, headbanger (*informal*), headcase (*informal*), lunatic, maniac, nutcase (*slang*), nutter (*Brit. slang*), psychotic, sociopath

psychotic *adjective* <u>mad</u>, certifiable, demented, deranged, insane, lunatic, mental (*slang*), non compos mentis, unbalanced

pub *or* **public house** *noun* <u>tavern</u>, bar, inn

puberty *noun* <u>adolescence</u>, pubescence, teens

public *adjective* 1 <u>general</u>, civic, common, national, popular, social, state, universal, widespread 2 <u>communal</u>, accessible, open, unrestricted 3 <u>well-known</u>, important, prominent, respected 4 <u>plain</u>, acknowledged, known, obvious, open, overt, patent ◆ *noun* 5 <u>people</u>, citizens, community, electorate, everyone, nation, populace, society

publication *noun* 1 <u>pamphlet</u>, brochure, issue, leaflet, magazine, newspaper, periodical, title **2** <u>announcement</u>, broadcasting, declaration, disclosure, notification, proclamation, publishing, reporting

publicity noun <u>advertising</u>, attention, boost, hype, plug (informal), press, promotion

publicize verb <u>advertise</u>, hype, make known, play up, plug (informal), promote, push

public-spirited adjective <u>altruistic</u>, charitable, humanitarian, philanthropic, unselfish

publish verb **1** <u>put out</u>, issue, print, produce **2** <u>announce</u>, advertise, broadcast, circulate, disclose, divulge, proclaim, publicize, reveal, spread

pucker verb **1** <u>wrinkle</u>, contract, crease, draw together, gather, knit, purse, screw up, tighten ♦ noun **2** <u>wrinkle</u>, crease, fold

pudding noun <u>dessert</u>, afters (Brit. informal), pud (informal), sweet

puerile adjective <u>childish</u>, babyish, foolish, immature, juvenile, silly, trivial

puff noun **1** <u>blast</u>, breath, draught, gust, whiff **2** <u>smoke</u>, drag (slang), pull ♦ verb **3** <u>blow</u>, breathe, exhale, gasp, gulp, pant, wheeze **4** <u>smoke</u>, drag (slang), draw, inhale, pull at or on, suck **5** usually with **up** <u>swell</u>, bloat, dilate, distend, expand, inflate

puffy adjective <u>swollen</u>, bloated, distended, enlarged, puffed up

pugilist noun <u>boxer</u>, fighter, prizefighter

pugnacious adjective <u>aggressive</u>, belligerent, combative, hot-tempered, quarrelsome

pull verb **1** <u>draw</u>, drag, haul, jerk, tow, trail, tug, yank **2** <u>strain</u>, dislocate, rip, sprain, stretch, tear, wrench **3** <u>extract</u>, draw out, gather, pick, pluck, remove, take out, uproot **4** Informal <u>attract</u>, draw, entice, lure, magnetize ♦ noun **5** <u>tug</u>, jerk, twitch, yank **6** <u>puff</u>, drag (slang), inhalation **7** Informal <u>influence</u>, clout (informal), muscle, power, weight

pull down verb <u>demolish</u>, bulldoze, destroy, raze, remove

pull off verb <u>succeed</u>, accomplish, carry out, do the trick, manage

pull out verb <u>withdraw</u>, depart, evacuate, leave, quit, retreat

pull through verb <u>survive</u>, get better, rally, recover

pull up verb **1** <u>stop</u>, brake, halt **2** <u>reprimand</u>, admonish, bawl out (informal), rap over the knuckles, read the riot act, rebuke, reprove, slap on the wrist, tear (someone) off a strip (Brit. informal), tell off (informal)

pulp noun **1** <u>paste</u>, mash, mush **2** <u>flesh</u>, soft part ♦ verb **3** <u>crush</u>, mash, pulverize, squash ♦ adjective **4** <u>cheap</u>, lurid, rubbishy, trashy

pulsate verb <u>throb</u>, beat, palpitate, pound, pulse, quiver, thump

pulse noun **1** <u>beat</u>, beating, pulsation, rhythm, throb, throbbing, vibration ♦ verb **2** <u>beat</u>, pulsate, throb, vibrate

pulverize verb **1** <u>crush</u>,

granulate, grind, mill, pound **2** <u>defeat</u>, annihilate, crush, demolish, destroy, flatten, smash, wreck

pummel verb <u>beat</u>, batter, hammer, pound, punch, strike, thump

pump verb **1** often with <u>into</u> drive, force, inject, pour, push, send, supply **2** <u>interrogate</u>, cross-examine, probe, quiz

pun noun <u>play on words</u>, double entendre, quip, witticism

punch[1] verb **1** <u>hit</u>, belt (informal), bop (informal), box, pummel, smash, sock (slang), strike ♦ noun **2** <u>blow</u>, bop (informal), hit, jab, sock (slang), wallop (informal) **3** Informal <u>effectiveness</u>, bite, drive, forcefulness, impact, verve, vigour

punch[2] verb <u>pierce</u>, bore, cut, drill, perforate, prick, puncture, stamp

punctilious adjective <u>particular</u>, exact, finicky, formal, fussy, meticulous, nice, precise, proper, strict

punctual adjective <u>on time</u>, exact, on the dot, precise, prompt, timely

punctuality noun <u>promptness</u>, promptitude, readiness

punctuate verb **1** <u>interrupt</u>, break, intersperse, pepper, sprinkle **2** <u>emphasize</u>, accentuate, stress, underline

puncture noun **1** <u>hole</u>, break, cut, damage, leak, nick, opening, slit **2** <u>flat tyre</u>, flat ♦ verb **3** <u>pierce</u>, bore, cut, nick, penetrate, perforate, prick, rupture

pungent adjective <u>strong</u>, acrid, bitter, hot, peppery, piquant, sharp, sour, spicy, tart

punish verb <u>discipline</u>, castigate, chasten, chastise, correct, penalize, sentence

punishable adjective <u>culpable</u>, blameworthy, criminal, indictable

punishing adjective <u>hard</u>, arduous, backbreaking, exhausting, gruelling, strenuous, taxing, tiring, wearing

punishment noun <u>penalty</u>, chastening, chastisement, correction, discipline, penance, retribution

punitive adjective <u>retaliatory</u>, in reprisal, retaliative

punt verb **1** <u>bet</u>, back, gamble, lay, stake, wager ♦ noun **2** <u>bet</u>, gamble, stake, wager

punter noun **1** <u>gambler</u>, backer, better **2** Informal <u>person</u>, man in the street

puny adjective <u>feeble</u>, frail, little, sickly, stunted, tiny, weak

pupil noun <u>learner</u>, beginner, disciple, novice, schoolboy or schoolgirl, student

puppet noun **1** <u>marionette</u>, doll **2** <u>pawn</u>, cat's-paw, instrument, mouthpiece, stooge, tool

purchase verb **1** <u>buy</u>, acquire, come by, gain, get, obtain, pay for, pick up, score (slang) ♦ noun **2** <u>buy</u>, acquisition, asset, gain, investment, possession, property **3** <u>grip</u>, foothold, hold, leverage, support

pure adjective **1** <u>unmixed</u>, authentic, flawless, genuine, natural, neat, real, simple, straight, unalloyed **2** <u>clean</u>, germ-free, sanitary, spotless, squeaky-clean, sterilized, uncontaminated, unpolluted, untainted, wholesome **3** innocent, blameless, chaste, impeccable, modest, uncorrupted, unsullied, virginal, virtuous **4** complete, absolute, outright, sheer, thorough, unmitigated, unqualified, utter

purely adverb absolutely, completely, entirely, exclusively, just, merely, only, simply, solely, wholly

purge verb **1** get rid of, do away with, eradicate, expel, exterminate, remove, wipe out ♦ noun **2** removal, ejection, elimination, eradication, expulsion

purify verb **1** clean, clarify, cleanse, decontaminate, disinfect, refine, sanitize, wash **2** absolve, cleanse, redeem, sanctify

purist noun stickler, formalist, pedant

puritan noun **1** moralist, fanatic, prude, rigorist, zealot ♦ adjective **2** strict, ascetic, austere, moralistic, narrow-minded, prudish, severe, strait-laced

puritanical adjective strict, ascetic, austere, narrow-minded, proper, prudish, puritan, severe, strait-laced

purity noun **1** cleanness, cleanliness, faultlessness, immaculateness, pureness, wholesomeness **2** innocence, chasteness, chastity, decency, honesty, integrity, virginity, virtue

purloin verb steal, appropriate, filch, nick (slang, chiefly Brit.),

pilfer, pinch (informal), swipe (slang), thieve

purport verb **1** claim, allege, assert, profess ♦ noun **2** significance, drift, gist, idea, implication, import, meaning

purpose noun **1** reason, aim, idea, intention, object, point **2** aim, ambition, desire, end, goal, hope, intention, object, plan, wish **3** determination, firmness, persistence, resolution, resolve, single-mindedness, tenacity, will **4** on purpose deliberately, designedly, intentionally, knowingly, purposely

purposeless adjective pointless, aimless, empty, motiveless, needless, senseless, uncalled-for, unnecessary

purposely adverb deliberately, consciously, expressly, intentionally, knowingly, on purpose, with intent

purse noun **1** pouch, money-bag, wallet **2** money, exchequer, funds, means, resources, treasury, wealth ♦ verb **3** pucker, contract, pout, press together, tighten

pursue verb **1** follow, chase, dog, hound, hunt, hunt down, run after, shadow, stalk, tail (informal), track **2** try for, aim for, desire, seek, strive for, work towards **3** engage in, carry on, conduct, perform, practise **4** continue, carry on, keep on, maintain, persevere in, persist in, proceed

pursuit noun **1** pursuing, chase, hunt, quest, search, seeking, trailing **2** occupation, activity, hobby, interest, line, pastime, pleasure

purvey verb <u>supply</u>, cater, deal in, furnish, provide, sell, trade in

push verb 1 <u>shove</u>, depress, drive, press, propel, ram, thrust 2 <u>make or force one's way</u>, elbow, jostle, move, shoulder, shove, squeeze, thrust 3 <u>urge</u>, encourage, hurry, impel, incite, persuade, press, spur ♦ noun 4 <u>shove</u>, butt, nudge, thrust 5 Informal <u>drive</u>, ambition, dynamism, energy, enterprise, go (informal), initiative, vigour, vitality 6 **the push** Informal, chiefly Brit. <u>dismissal</u>, discharge, one's cards (informal), the boot (slang), the sack (informal)

pushed adjective, often with **for** <u>short of</u>, hurried, pressed, rushed, under pressure

pushover noun 1 <u>piece of cake</u> (Brit. informal), breeze (U.S. & Canad. informal), child's play (informal), cinch (slang), doddle (Brit. slang), picnic (informal), plain sailing, walkover (informal) 2 <u>sucker</u> (slang), easy game (informal), easy or soft mark (informal), mug (Brit. slang), soft touch (slang), walkover (informal)

pushy adjective <u>forceful</u>, ambitious, assertive, bold, brash, bumptious, obtrusive, presumptuous, self-assertive

pussyfoot verb <u>hedge</u>, beat about the bush, be noncommittal, equivocate, flannel (Brit. informal), hum and haw, prevaricate, sit on the fence

put verb 1 <u>place</u>, deposit, lay, position, rest, set, settle, situate 2 <u>express</u>, phrase, state, utter,

word 3 <u>throw</u>, cast, fling, heave, hurl, lob, pitch, toss

put across or **over** verb <u>communicate</u>, convey, explain, get across, make clear, make oneself understood

put aside or **by** verb <u>save</u>, deposit, lay by, stockpile, store

put away verb 1 <u>save</u>, deposit, keep, put by 2 <u>commit</u>, certify, institutionalize, lock up 3 <u>consume</u>, devour, eat up, gobble, wolf down 4 <u>put back</u>, replace, tidy away

put down verb 1 <u>record</u>, enter, set down, take down, write down 2 <u>stamp out</u>, crush, quash, quell, repress, suppress 3 usually with **to** <u>attribute</u>, ascribe, impute, set down 4 <u>put to sleep</u>, destroy, do away with, put out of its misery 5 Slang <u>humiliate</u>, disparage, mortify, shame, slight, snub

put forward verb <u>recommend</u>, advance, nominate, propose, submit, suggest, tender

put off verb 1 <u>postpone</u>, defer, delay, hold over, put on the back burner (informal), take a rain check on (U.S. & Canad. informal) 2 <u>disconcert</u>, confuse, discomfit, dismay, faze, nonplus, perturb, throw (informal), unsettle 3 <u>discourage</u>, dishearten, dissuade

put on verb 1 <u>don</u>, change into, dress, get dressed in, slip into 2 <u>fake</u>, affect, assume, feign, pretend, sham, simulate 3 <u>present</u>, do, mount, produce, show, stage 4 <u>add</u>, gain, increase by

put out verb 1 <u>annoy</u>, anger,

exasperate, irk, irritate, nettle, vex **2** extinguish, blow out, douse, quench **3** inconvenience, bother, discomfit, discommode, impose upon, incommode, trouble

putrid *adjective* rotten, bad, decayed, decomposed, off, putrefied, rancid, rotting, spoiled

put up *verb* **1** erect, build, construct, fabricate, raise **2** accommodate, board, house, lodge, take in **3** recommend, nominate, offer, present, propose, put forward, submit **4 put up with** *Informal* stand, abide, bear, endure, stand for, swallow, take, tolerate

puzzle *verb* **1** perplex, baffle, bewilder, confound, confuse, mystify, stump ♦ *noun* **2** problem, conundrum, enigma, mystery, paradox, poser, question, riddle

puzzled *adjective* perplexed, at a loss, at sea, baffled, bewildered, confused, lost, mystified

puzzlement *noun* perplexity, bafflement, bewilderment, confusion, doubt, mystification

puzzling *adjective* perplexing, abstruse, baffling, bewildering, enigmatic, incomprehensible, involved, mystifying

Q q

quack *noun* charlatan, fake, fraud, humbug, impostor, mountebank, phoney *or* phony (*informal*)

quaff *verb* drink, down, gulp,

imbibe, swallow, swig (*informal*)

quagmire *noun* bog, fen, marsh, mire, morass, quicksand, slough, swamp

quail *verb* shrink, blanch, blench, cower, cringe, falter, flinch, have cold feet (*informal*), recoil, shudder

quaint *adjective* **1** unusual, bizarre, curious, droll, eccentric, fanciful, odd, old-fashioned, peculiar, queer, rum (*Brit. slang*), singular, strange **2** old-fashioned, antiquated, old-world, picturesque

quake *verb* shake, move, quiver, rock, shiver, shudder, tremble, vibrate

qualification *noun* **1** attribute, ability, aptitude, capability, eligibility, fitness, quality, skill, suitability **2** condition, caveat, limitation, modification, proviso, requirement, reservation, rider, stipulation

qualified *adjective* **1** capable, able, adept, competent, efficient, experienced, expert, fit, practised, proficient, skilful, trained **2** restricted, bounded, conditional, confined, contingent, limited, modified, provisional, reserved

qualify *verb* **1** certify, empower, equip, fit, permit, prepare, ready, train **2** moderate, diminish, ease, lessen, limit, reduce, regulate, restrain, restrict, soften, temper

quality *noun* **1** excellence, calibre, distinction, grade, merit, position, rank, standing, status **2** characteristic, aspect, attribute, condition, feature, mark, property, trait **3** nature, character, kind, make, sort

qualm noun misgiving, anxiety, apprehension, compunction, disquiet, doubt, hesitation, scruple, twinge or pang of conscience, uneasiness

quandary noun difficulty, cleft stick, dilemma, impasse, plight, predicament, puzzle, strait

quantity noun **1** amount, lot, number, part, sum, total **2** size, bulk, capacity, extent, length, magnitude, mass, measure, volume

quarrel noun **1** disagreement, argument, brawl, breach, contention, controversy, dispute, dissension, feud, fight, row, squabble, tiff ♦ verb **2** disagree, argue, bicker, brawl, clash, differ, dispute, fall out (informal), fight, row, squabble

quarrelsome adjective argumentative, belligerent, combative, contentious, disputatious, pugnacious

quarry noun prey, aim, game, goal, objective, prize, victim

quarter noun **1** district, area, locality, neighbourhood, part, place, province, region, side, zone **2** mercy, clemency, compassion, forgiveness, leniency, pity ♦ verb **3** accommodate, billet, board, house, lodge, place, post, station

quarters plural noun lodgings, abode, barracks, billet, chambers, dwelling, habitation, residence, rooms

quash verb **1** annul, cancel, invalidate, overrule, overthrow, rescind, reverse, revoke

2 suppress, beat, crush, overthrow, put down, quell, repress, squash, subdue

quasi- adjective pseudo-, apparent, seeming, semi-, so-called, would-be

quaver verb **1** tremble, flicker, flutter, quake, quiver, shake, vibrate, waver ♦ noun **2** trembling, quiver, shake, tremble, tremor, vibration

queasy adjective **1** sick, bilious, green around the gills (informal), ill, nauseated, off colour, squeamish, upset **2** uneasy, anxious, fidgety, ill at ease, restless, troubled, uncertain, worried

queen noun **1** sovereign, consort, monarch, ruler **2** ideal, mistress, model, star

queer adjective **1** strange, abnormal, curious, droll, extraordinary, funny, odd, peculiar, uncommon, unusual, weird **2** faint, dizzy, giddy, light-headed, queasy

quell verb **1** suppress, conquer, crush, defeat, overcome, overpower, put down, quash, subdue, vanquish **2** assuage, allay, appease, calm, mollify, pacify, quiet, soothe

quench verb **1** satisfy, allay, appease, sate, satiate, slake **2** put out, crush, douse, extinguish, smother, stifle, suppress

querulous adjective complaining, captious, carping, critical, discontented, dissatisfied, fault-finding, grumbling, peevish, whining

query noun **1** question, doubt,

inquiry, objection, problem, suspicion ◆ *verb* **2** doubt, challenge, disbelieve, dispute, distrust, mistrust, suspect **3** ask, inquire *or* enquire, question

quest *noun* search, adventure, crusade, enterprise, expedition, hunt, journey, mission

question *noun* **1** issue, motion, point, point at issue, proposal, proposition, subject, theme, topic **2** difficulty, argument, contention, controversy, dispute, doubt, problem, query **3** in question under discussion, at issue, in doubt, open to debate **4** out of the question impossible, inconceivable, unthinkable ◆ *verb* **5** ask, cross-examine, examine, inquire, interrogate, interview, probe, quiz **6** dispute, challenge, disbelieve, doubt, mistrust, oppose, query, suspect

questionable *adjective* dubious, controversial, debatable, dodgy (*Brit., Austral., & N.Z. informal*), doubtful, iffy (*informal*), moot, suspect, suspicious

queue *noun* line, chain, file, sequence, series, string, train

quibble *verb* **1** split hairs, carp, cavil ◆ *noun* **2** objection, cavil, complaint, criticism, nicety, niggle

quick *adjective* **1** fast, brisk, express, fleet, hasty, rapid, speedy, swift **2** brief, cursory, hasty, hurried, perfunctory **3** sudden, prompt **4** intelligent, acute, alert, astute, bright (*informal*), clever, perceptive, quick-witted, sharp, shrewd, smart **5** deft, adept, adroit,

dexterous, skilful **6** excitable, irascible, irritable, passionate, testy, touchy

quicken *verb* **1** speed, accelerate, expedite, hasten, hurry, impel, precipitate **2** invigorate, arouse, energize, excite, incite, inspire, revive, stimulate, vitalize

quickly *adverb* swiftly, abruptly, apace, briskly, fast, hastily, hurriedly, promptly, pronto (*informal*), rapidly, soon, speedily

quick-tempered *adjective* hot-tempered, choleric, fiery, irascible, irritable, quarrelsome, ratty (*Brit. & N.Z. informal*), testy, tetchy

quick-witted *adjective* clever, alert, astute, bright (*informal*), keen, perceptive, sharp, shrewd, smart

quiet *adjective* **1** silent, hushed, inaudible, low, noiseless, peaceful, soft, soundless **2** calm, mild, peaceful, placid, restful, serene, smooth, tranquil **3** undisturbed, isolated, private, secluded, sequestered, unfrequented **4** reserved, gentle, meek, mild, retiring, sedate, shy ◆ *noun* **5** peace, calmness, ease, quietness, repose, rest, serenity, silence, stillness, tranquillity

quieten *verb* **1** silence, compose, hush, muffle, mute, quell, quiet, stifle, still, stop, subdue **2** soothe, allay, appease, blunt, calm, deaden, dull

quietly *adverb* **1** silently, in an undertone, inaudibly, in silence, mutely, noiselessly, softly **2** calmly, mildly, patiently, placidly, serenely

quietness *noun* peace, calm,

hush, quiet, silence, stillness, tranquillity

quilt noun bedspread, continental quilt, counterpane, coverlet, duvet, eiderdown

quintessence noun essence, distillation, soul, spirit

quintessential adjective ultimate, archetypal, definitive, prototypical, typical

quip noun joke, gibe, jest, pleasantry, retort, riposte, sally, wisecrack (informal), witticism

quirk noun peculiarity, aberration, characteristic, eccentricity, foible, habit, idiosyncrasy, kink, mannerism, oddity, trait

quirky adjective odd, eccentric, idiosyncratic, offbeat, peculiar, unusual

quit verb 1 stop, abandon, cease, discontinue, drop, end, give up, halt 2 resign, abdicate, go, leave, pull out, retire, step down (informal) 3 depart, go, leave, pull out

quite adverb 1 somewhat, fairly, moderately, rather, reasonably, relatively 2 absolutely, completely, entirely, fully, perfectly, totally, wholly 3 truly, in fact, in reality, in truth, really

quiver verb 1 shake, oscillate, quake, quaver, shiver, shudder, tremble, vibrate ♦ noun 2 shake, oscillation, shiver, shudder, tremble, tremor, vibration

quixotic adjective unrealistic, dreamy, fanciful, idealistic, impractical, romantic

quiz noun 1 examination, investigation, questioning, test ♦ verb 2 question, ask, examine,

interrogate, investigate

quizzical adjective mocking, arch, questioning, sardonic, teasing

quota noun share, allowance, assignment, part, portion, ration, slice, whack (informal)

quotation noun 1 passage, citation, excerpt, extract, quote (informal), reference 2 Commerce estimate, charge, cost, figure, price, quote (informal), rate, tender

quote verb repeat, cite, detail, instance, name, recall, recite, recollect, refer to

R r

rabble noun mob, canaille, crowd, herd, horde, swarm, throng

rabid adjective 1 fanatical, extreme, fervent, irrational, narrow-minded, zealous 2 mad, hydrophobic

race[1] noun 1 contest, chase, competition, dash, pursuit, rivalry ♦ verb 2 run, career, compete, contest, dart, dash, fly, gallop, hurry, speed, tear, zoom

race[2] noun people, blood, folk, nation, stock, tribe, type

racial adjective ethnic, ethnological, folk, genealogical, genetic, national, tribal

rack noun 1 frame, framework, stand, structure ♦ verb 2 torture, afflict, agonize, crucify, harrow, oppress, pain, torment

racket noun 1 noise, clamour, din, disturbance, fuss, outcry, pandemonium, row 2 fraud, scheme

racy adjective 1 risqué, bawdy, blue, naughty, near the knuckle (informal), smutty, suggestive 2 lively, animated, energetic, entertaining, exciting, sparkling, spirited

radiance noun 1 happiness, delight, gaiety, joy, pleasure, rapture, warmth 2 brightness, brilliance, glare, gleam, glow, light, lustre, shine

radiant adjective 1 happy, blissful, delighted, ecstatic, glowing, joyful, joyous, on cloud nine (informal), rapturous 2 bright, brilliant, gleaming, glittering, glowing, luminous, lustrous, shining

radiate verb 1 spread out, branch out, diverge, issue 2 emit, diffuse, give off or out, pour, scatter, send out, shed, spread

radical adjective 1 fundamental, basic, deep-seated, innate, natural, profound 2 extreme, complete, drastic, entire, extremist, fanatical, severe, sweeping, thorough ♦ noun 3 extremist, fanatic, militant, revolutionary

raffle noun draw, lottery, sweep, sweepstake

ragamuffin noun urchin, guttersnipe

rage noun 1 fury, anger, frenzy, ire, madness, passion, rampage, wrath 2 As in all the rage craze, enthusiasm, fad (informal), fashion, latest thing, vogue ♦ verb 3 be furious, blow one's top, blow up (informal), fly off

the handle (informal), fume, go ballistic (slang, chiefly U.S.), go up the wall (slang), lose the plot (informal), seethe, storm

ragged adjective 1 tattered, in rags, in tatters, shabby, tatty, threadbare, torn, unkempt 2 rough, jagged, rugged, serrated, uneven, unfinished

raging adjective furious, beside oneself, enraged, fuming, incensed, infuriated, mad, raving, seething

rags plural noun tatters, castoffs, old clothes, tattered clothing

raid noun 1 attack, foray, incursion, inroad, invasion, sally, sortie ♦ verb 2 attack, assault, foray, invade, pillage, plunder, sack

raider noun attacker, invader, marauder, plunderer, robber, thief

railing noun fence, balustrade, barrier, paling, rails

rain noun 1 rainfall, cloudburst, deluge, downpour, drizzle, fall, raindrops, showers ♦ verb 2 pour, bucket down (informal), come down in buckets (informal), drizzle, pelt (down), teem 3 fall, deposit, drop, shower, sprinkle

rainy adjective wet, damp, drizzly, showery

raise verb 1 lift, build, elevate, erect, heave, hoist, rear, uplift 2 increase, advance, amplify, boost, enhance, enlarge, heighten, inflate, intensify, magnify, strengthen 3 collect, assemble, form, gather, mass, obtain, rally, recruit 4 cause, create, engender, occasion, originate, produce, provoke, start 5 <u>bring up</u>, develop, nurture, rear 6 <u>suggest</u>, advance, broach, introduce, moot, put forward

rake¹ verb 1 <u>gather</u>, collect, remove 2 <u>search</u>, comb, scour, scrutinize

rake² noun <u>libertine</u>, debauchee, lecher, playboy, roué

rakish adjective <u>dashing</u>, dapper, debonair, devil-may-care, jaunty, natty (informal), raffish, smart

rally noun 1 <u>gathering</u>, assembly, congress, convention, meeting 2 <u>recovery</u>, improvement, recuperation, revival ♦ verb 3 <u>reassemble</u>, regroup, reorganize, unite 4 <u>gather</u>, assemble, collect, convene, marshal, muster, round up, unite 5 <u>recover</u>, get better, improve, recuperate, revive

ram verb 1 <u>hit</u>, butt, crash, dash, drive, force, impact, smash 2 <u>cram</u>, crowd, force, jam, stuff, thrust

ramble verb 1 <u>walk</u>, range, roam, rove, saunter, stray, stroll, wander 2 <u>babble</u>, rabbit (on) (Brit. informal), waffle (informal, chiefly Brit.), witter on (informal) ♦ noun 3 <u>walk</u>, hike, roaming, roving, saunter, stroll, tour

rambler noun <u>walker</u>, hiker, rover, wanderer, wayfarer

rambling adjective <u>long-winded</u>, circuitous, digressive, disconnected, discursive, disjointed, incoherent, wordy

ramification noun <u>ramifications</u> <u>consequences</u>, developments, results, sequel, upshot

ramp noun <u>slope</u>, gradient, incline, rise

rampage verb 1 <u>go berserk</u>, rage, run amok, run riot, storm ♦ noun 2 <u>on the rampage</u> <u>berserk</u>, amok, out of control, raging, riotous, violent, wild

rampant adjective 1 <u>widespread</u>, prevalent, profuse, rife, spreading like wildfire, unchecked, uncontrolled, unrestrained 2 Heraldry <u>upright</u>, erect, rearing, standing

rampart noun <u>defence</u>, bastion, bulwark, fence, fortification, wall

ramshackle adjective <u>rickety</u>, crumbling, decrepit, derelict, flimsy, shaky, tumbledown, unsafe, unsteady

rancid adjective <u>rotten</u>, bad, fetid, foul, off, putrid, rank, sour, stale, strong-smelling, tainted

rancour noun <u>hatred</u>, animosity, bad blood, bitterness, hate, ill feeling, ill will

random adjective 1 <u>chance</u>, accidental, adventitious, casual, fortuitous, haphazard, hit or miss, incidental ♦ noun 2 <u>at random</u> <u>haphazardly</u>, arbitrarily, by chance, randomly, unsystematically, willy-nilly

randy adjective Informal <u>aroused</u>, amorous, horny (slang), hot, lascivious, lustful, turned-on (slang)

range noun 1 <u>limits</u>, area, bounds, orbit, province, radius, reach, scope, sphere 2 <u>series</u>, assortment, collection, gamut, lot, selection, variety ♦ verb 3 <u>vary</u>, extend, reach, run, stretch 4 <u>roam</u>, ramble, rove, traverse, wander

rangy *adjective* long-limbed, gangling, lanky, leggy, long-legged

rank[1] *noun* **1** status, caste, class, degree, division, grade, level, order, position, sort, type **2** row, column, file, group, line, range, series, tier ◆ *verb* **3** arrange, align, array, dispose, line up, order, sort

rank[2] *adjective* **1** absolute, arrant, blatant, complete, downright, flagrant, gross, sheer, thorough, total, utter **2** foul, bad, disgusting, noisome, noxious, offensive, rancid, revolting, stinking **3** abundant, dense, lush, luxuriant, profuse

rank and file *noun* general public, majority, mass, masses

rankle *verb* annoy, anger, gall, get on one's nerves (*informal*), irk, irritate, rile

ransack *verb* **1** search, comb, explore, go through, rummage, scour, turn inside out **2** plunder, loot, pillage, raid, strip

ransom *noun* payment, money, payoff, price

rant *verb* shout, cry, declaim, rave, roar, yell

rap *verb* **1** hit, crack, knock, strike, tap ◆ *noun* **2** blow, clout (*informal*), crack, knock, tap **3** *Slang* punishment, blame, responsibility

rapacious *adjective* greedy, avaricious, grasping, insatiable, predatory, preying, voracious

rape *verb* **1** sexually assault, abuse, force, outrage, ravish, violate ◆ *noun* **2** sexual assault, outrage, ravishment, violation

3 desecration, abuse, defilement, violation

rapid *adjective* quick, brisk, express, fast, hasty, hurried, prompt, speedy, swift

rapidity *noun* speed, alacrity, briskness, fleetness, haste, hurry, promptness, quickness, rush, swiftness, velocity

rapidly *adverb* quickly, briskly, fast, hastily, hurriedly, in haste, promptly, pronto (*informal*), speedily, swiftly

rapport *noun* bond, affinity, empathy, harmony, link, relationship, sympathy, tie, understanding

rapprochement *noun* reconciliation, detente, reunion

rapt *adjective* spellbound, absorbed, engrossed, enthralled, entranced, fascinated, gripped

rapture *noun* ecstasy, bliss, delight, euphoria, joy, rhapsody, seventh heaven, transport

rapturous *adjective* ecstatic, blissful, euphoric, in seventh heaven, joyful, overjoyed, over the moon (*informal*), transported

rare *adjective* **1** uncommon, few, infrequent, scarce, singular, sparse, strange, unusual **2** superb, choice, excellent, fine, great, peerless, superlative

rarefied *adjective* exalted, elevated, high, lofty, noble, spiritual, sublime

rarely *adverb* seldom, hardly, hardly ever, infrequently

raring *adjective* As in **raring to** eager, desperate, enthusiastic, impatient, keen, longing, ready

rarity *noun* **1** curio, collector's

item, find, gem, treasure
2 uncommonness, infrequency,
scarcity, shortage, sparseness,
strangeness, unusualness

rascal noun rogue, blackguard,
devil, good-for-nothing, imp,
ne'er-do-well, scamp, scoundrel,
villain

rash[1] adjective reckless, careless,
foolhardy, hasty, heedless,
ill-advised, impetuous,
imprudent, impulsive, incautious

rash[2] noun **1 outbreak,** eruption
2 spate, flood, outbreak, plague,
series, wave

rashness noun recklessness,
carelessness, foolhardiness,
hastiness, heedlessness,
indiscretion, thoughtlessness

rate noun **1 speed,** pace, tempo,
velocity **2 degree,** proportion,
ratio, scale, standard **3 charge,**
cost, fee, figure, price **4 at any
rate** in any case, anyhow,
anyway, at all events ♦ verb
5 evaluate, consider, count,
estimate, grade, measure, rank,
reckon, value **6 deserve,** be
entitled to, be worthy of, merit

rather adverb **1 to some extent,** a
little, fairly, moderately, quite,
relatively, somewhat, to some
degree **2 preferably,** more
readily, more willingly, sooner

ratify verb approve, affirm,
authorize, confirm, endorse,
establish, sanction, uphold

rating noun **position,** class,
degree, grade, order, placing,
rank, rate, status

ratio noun proportion, fraction,
percentage, rate, relation

ration noun **1 allowance,**

allotment, helping, measure,
part, portion, quota, share ♦ verb
2 limit, budget, control, restrict

rational adjective sane,
intelligent, logical, lucid, realistic,
reasonable, sensible, sound, wise

rationale noun reason, grounds,
logic, motivation, philosophy,
principle, raison d'être, theory

rationalize verb justify, account
for, excuse, vindicate

rattle verb **1 clatter,** bang, jangle
2 shake, bounce, jar, jolt, vibrate
3 Informal **fluster,** disconcert,
disturb, faze, perturb, shake,
upset

raucous adjective harsh, grating,
hoarse, loud, noisy, rough,
strident

raunchy adjective Slang sexy,
coarse, earthy, lusty, sexual,
steamy (informal)

ravage verb **1 destroy,** demolish,
despoil, devastate, lay waste,
ransack, ruin, spoil ♦ noun
2 ravages damage, destruction,
devastation, havoc, ruin,
ruination, spoliation

rave verb **1 rant,** babble, be
delirious, go mad (informal),
rage, roar **2** Informal **enthuse,** be
mad about (informal), be wild
about (informal), gush, praise

ravenous adjective starving,
famished, starved

ravine noun canyon, defile,
gorge, gulch (U.S.), gully, pass

raving adjective mad, crazed,
crazy, delirious, hysterical,
insane, irrational, wild

ravish verb **1 enchant,** captivate,
charm, delight, enrapture,
entrance, fascinate, spellbind

2 **rape**, abuse, force, sexually assault, violate

ravishing *adjective* enchanting, beautiful, bewitching, charming, entrancing, gorgeous, lovely

raw *adjective* 1 uncooked, fresh, natural 2 unrefined, basic, coarse, crude, natural, rough, unfinished, unprocessed 3 inexperienced, callow, green, immature, new 4 chilly, biting, bitter, cold, freezing, parky (*Brit. informal*), piercing

ray *noun* beam, bar, flash, gleam, shaft

raze *verb* destroy, demolish, flatten, knock down, level, pull down, ruin

re *preposition* concerning, about, apropos, regarding, with reference to, with regard to

reach *verb* 1 arrive at, attain, get to, make 2 touch, contact, extend to, grasp, stretch to 3 contact, communicate with, get hold of, get in touch with, get through to ◆ *noun* 4 range, capacity, distance, extension, extent, grasp, influence, power, scope, stretch

react *verb* 1 respond, answer, reply 2 act, behave, function, operate, proceed, work

reaction *noun* 1 response, answer, reply 2 recoil, counteraction 3 conservatism, the right

reactionary *adjective* 1 conservative, right-wing ◆ *noun* 2 conservative, die-hard, right-winger

read *verb* 1 look at, peruse, pore over, scan, study 2 interpret,

comprehend, construe, decipher, discover, see, understand 3 register, display, indicate, record, show

readable *adjective* 1 enjoyable, entertaining, enthralling, gripping, interesting 2 legible, clear, comprehensible, decipherable

readily *adverb* 1 willingly, eagerly, freely, gladly, promptly, quickly 2 easily, effortlessly, quickly, smoothly, speedily, unhesitatingly

readiness *noun* 1 willingness, eagerness, keenness 2 ease, adroitness, dexterity, facility, promptness

reading *noun* 1 perusal, examination, inspection, scrutiny, study 2 recital, lesson, performance, sermon 3 interpretation, grasp, impression, version 4 learning, education, erudition, knowledge, scholarship

ready *adjective* 1 prepared, arranged, fit, organized, primed, ripe, set 2 willing, agreeable, disposed, eager, glad, happy, inclined, keen, prone 3 prompt, alert, bright, clever, intelligent, keen, perceptive, quick, sharp, smart 4 available, accessible, convenient, handy, near, present

real *adjective* genuine, actual, authentic, factual, rightful, sincere, true, unfeigned, valid

realistic *adjective* 1 practical, common-sense, down-to-earth, level-headed, matter-of-fact, real, sensible 2 lifelike, authentic, faithful, genuine, natural, true, true to life

reality noun <u>truth</u>, actuality, fact, realism, validity, verity

realization noun **1** <u>awareness</u>, cognizance, comprehension, conception, grasp, perception, recognition, understanding **2** <u>achievement</u>, accomplishment, fulfilment

realize verb **1** <u>become aware of</u>, comprehend, get the message, grasp, take in, understand **2** <u>achieve</u>, accomplish, carry out or through, complete, do, effect, fulfil, perform

really adverb <u>truly</u>, actually, certainly, genuinely, in actuality, indeed, in fact, positively, truly

realm noun **1** <u>kingdom</u>, country, domain, dominion, empire, land **2** <u>sphere</u>, area, branch, department, field, province, territory, world

reap verb **1** <u>collect</u>, bring in, cut, garner, gather, harvest **2** <u>obtain</u>, acquire, derive, gain, get

rear[1] noun **1** <u>back</u>, end, rearguard, stern, tail, tail end ♦ adjective **2** <u>back</u>, following, hind, last

rear[2] verb **1** <u>bring up</u>, breed, educate, foster, nurture, raise, train **2** <u>rise</u>, loom, soar, tower

reason noun **1** <u>cause</u>, aim, goal, grounds, incentive, intention, motive, object, purpose **2** <u>sense(s)</u>, intellect, judgment, logic, mind, rationality, sanity, soundness, understanding ♦ verb **3** <u>deduce</u>, conclude, infer, make out, think, work out **4** <u>reason with</u> <u>persuade</u>, bring round (informal), prevail upon, talk into or out of, urge, win over

reasonable adjective **1** <u>sensible</u>,

logical, plausible, practical, sane, sober, sound, tenable, wise **2** <u>moderate</u>, equitable, fair, fit, just, modest, O.K. or okay (informal), proper, right

reasoned adjective <u>sensible</u>, clear, logical, well-thought-out

reasoning noun <u>thinking</u>, analysis, logic, thought

reassure verb <u>encourage</u>, comfort, hearten, put or set one's mind at rest, restore confidence to

rebate noun <u>refund</u>, allowance, bonus, deduction, discount, reduction

rebel verb **1** <u>revolt</u>, mutiny, resist, rise up **2** <u>defy</u>, disobey, dissent ♦ noun **3** <u>revolutionary</u>, insurgent, revolutionist, secessionist **4** <u>nonconformist</u>, apostate, dissenter, heretic, schismatic ♦ adjective **5** <u>rebellious</u>, insurgent, insurrectionary, revolutionary

rebellion noun **1** <u>resistance</u>, mutiny, revolt, revolution, rising, uprising **2** <u>nonconformity</u>, defiance, heresy, schism

rebellious adjective **1** <u>revolutionary</u>, disloyal, disobedient, disorderly, insurgent, mutinous, rebel, seditious, unruly **2** <u>defiant</u>, difficult, refractory, resistant, unmanageable

rebound verb **1** <u>bounce</u>, recoil, ricochet **2** <u>misfire</u>, backfire, boomerang, recoil

rebuff verb **1** <u>reject</u>, cold-shoulder, cut, knock back (slang), refuse, repulse, slight, snub, spurn, turn down ♦ noun **2** <u>rejection</u>, cold shoulder, kick in the teeth (slang), knock-back (slang), refusal, repulse, slap in the face (informal), slight, snub

rebuke verb 1 scold, admonish, castigate, censure, chide, dress down (informal), give a rocket (Brit. & N.Z. informal), haul (someone) over the coals (informal), reprimand, reprove, tear (someone) off a strip (informal), tell off (informal) ♦ noun 2 scolding, admonition, censure, dressing down (informal), reprimand, row, telling-off (informal)

rebut verb disprove, confute, invalidate, negate, overturn, prove wrong, refute

rebuttal noun disproof, confutation, invalidation, negation, refutation

recalcitrant adjective disobedient, defiant, insubordinate, refractory, unmanageable, unruly, wayward, wilful

recall verb 1 recollect, bring or call to mind, evoke, remember 2 annul, cancel, countermand, repeal, retract, revoke, withdraw ♦ noun 3 recollection, memory, remembrance 4 annulment, cancellation, repeal, rescindment, retraction, withdrawal

recant verb withdraw, disclaim, forswear, renege, repudiate, retract, revoke, take back

recapitulate verb repeat, outline, recap (informal), recount, restate, summarize

recede verb fall back, abate, ebb, regress, retire, retreat, return, subside, withdraw

receipt noun 1 sales slip, counterfoil, proof of purchase 2 receiving, acceptance, delivery, reception

receive verb 1 get, accept, acquire, be given, collect, obtain, pick up, take 2 experience, bear, encounter, suffer, sustain, undergo 3 greet, accommodate, admit, entertain, meet, welcome

recent adjective new, current, fresh, late, modern, novel, present-day, up-to-date

recently adverb newly, currently, freshly, lately, latterly, not long ago, of late

receptacle noun container, holder, repository

reception noun 1 party, function, levee, soirée 2 welcome, acknowledgment, greeting, reaction, response, treatment

receptive adjective open, amenable, interested, open-minded, open to suggestions, susceptible, sympathetic

recess noun 1 alcove, bay, corner, hollow, niche, nook 2 break, holiday, intermission, interval, respite, rest, vacation

recession noun depression, decline, drop, slump

recipe noun 1 directions, ingredients, instructions 2 method, formula, prescription, procedure, process, technique

reciprocal adjective mutual, alternate, complementary, correlative, corresponding, equivalent, exchanged, interchangeable

reciprocate verb 1 <u>return</u>, exchange, reply, requite, respond, swap, trade

recital noun 1 <u>performance</u>, rehearsal, rendering 2 <u>recitation</u>, account, narrative, reading, relation, statement, telling

recitation noun <u>recital</u>, lecture, passage, performance, piece, reading

recite verb <u>repeat</u>, declaim, deliver, narrate, perform, speak

reckless adjective <u>careless</u>, hasty, headlong, heedless, imprudent, mindless, precipitate, rash, thoughtless, wild

reckon verb 1 <u>think</u>, assume, believe, guess (informal, chiefly U.S. & Canad.), imagine, suppose 2 <u>consider</u>, account, count, deem, esteem, judge, rate, regard 3 <u>count</u>, add up, calculate, compute, figure, number, tally, total

reckoning noun 1 <u>count</u>, addition, calculation, estimate 2 <u>bill</u>, account, charge, due, score

reclaim verb <u>regain</u>, recapture, recover, redeem, reform, retrieve, salvage

recline verb <u>lean</u>, lie (down), loll, lounge, repose, rest, sprawl

recluse noun <u>hermit</u>, anchoress, anchorite, monk, solitary

reclusive adjective <u>solitary</u>, hermit-like, isolated, retiring, withdrawn

recognition noun 1 <u>identification</u>, discovery, recollection, remembrance 2 <u>acceptance</u>, admission,

allowance, confession 3 <u>appreciation</u>, notice, respect

recognize verb 1 <u>identify</u>, know, notice, place, recall, recollect, remember, spot 2 <u>accept</u>, acknowledge, admit, allow, concede, grant 3 <u>appreciate</u>, notice, respect

recoil verb 1 <u>jerk back</u>, kick, react, rebound, spring back 2 <u>draw back</u>, falter, quail, shrink 3 <u>backfire</u>, boomerang, misfire, rebound ♦ noun 4 <u>reaction</u>, backlash, kick, rebound, repercussion

recollect verb <u>remember</u>, place, recall, summon up

recollection noun <u>memory</u>, impression, recall, remembrance, reminiscence

recommend verb 1 <u>advise</u>, advance, advocate, counsel, prescribe, propose, put forward, suggest 2 <u>praise</u>, approve, commend, endorse

recommendation noun 1 <u>advice</u>, counsel, proposal, suggestion 2 <u>praise</u>, advocacy, approval, commendation, endorsement, reference, sanction, testimonial

recompense verb 1 <u>reward</u>, pay, remunerate 2 <u>compensate</u>, make up for, pay for, redress, reimburse, repay, requite ♦ noun 3 <u>compensation</u>, amends, damages, payment, remuneration, reparation, repayment, requital, restitution 4 <u>reward</u>, payment, return, wages

reconcile verb 1 <u>resolve</u>, adjust, compose, put to rights, rectify, settle, square 2 <u>reunite</u>, appease, conciliate, make peace between, propitiate **3** accept, put up with (*informal*), resign oneself, submit, yield

reconciliation noun reunion, conciliation, pacification, reconcilement

recondite adjective obscure, arcane, concealed, dark, deep, difficult, hidden, mysterious, occult, profound, secret

recondition verb restore, do up (*informal*), overhaul, remodel, renew, renovate, repair, revamp

reconnaissance noun inspection, exploration, investigation, observation, recce (*slang*), scan, survey

reconnoitre verb inspect, case (*slang*), explore, investigate, observe, scan, spy out, survey

reconsider verb rethink, reassess, review, revise, think again

reconstruct verb **1** rebuild, recreate, regenerate, remake, remodel, renovate, restore **2** deduce, build up, piece together

record noun **1** document, account, chronicle, diary, entry, file, journal, log, register, report **2** evidence, documentation, testimony, trace, witness **3** disc, album, LP, single, vinyl **4** background, career, history, performance **5** off the record confidential, not for publication, private, unofficial ♦ verb **6** write down, chronicle, document, enter, log, minute, note, register, set down, take down **7** tape, make a recording of, tape-record, video, video-tape **8** register, give evidence of,

indicate, say, show

recorder noun chronicler, archivist, clerk, diarist, historian, scribe

recording noun record, disc, tape, video

recount verb tell, depict, describe, narrate, recite, relate, repeat, report

recoup verb **1** regain, recover, retrieve, win back **2** compensate, make up for, refund, reimburse, repay, requite

recourse noun option, alternative, choice, expedient, remedy, resort, resource, way out

recover verb **1** get better, convalesce, get well, heal, improve, mend, rally, recuperate, revive **2** regain, get back, recapture, reclaim, redeem, repossess, restore, retrieve

recovery noun **1** improvement, convalescence, healing, mending, recuperation, revival **2** retrieval, reclamation, repossession, restoration

recreation noun pastime, amusement, diversion, enjoyment, entertainment, fun, hobby, leisure activity, play, relaxation, sport

recrimination noun bickering, counterattack, mutual accusation, quarrel, squabbling

recruit verb **1** enlist, draft, enrol, levy, mobilize, muster, raise **2** win (over), engage, obtain, procure ♦ noun **3** beginner, apprentice, convert, helper, initiate, learner, novice, trainee

rectify verb correct, adjust,

emend, fix, improve, redress, remedy, repair, right

rectitude noun morality, decency, goodness, honesty, honour, integrity, principle, probity, virtue

recuperate verb recover, convalesce, get better, improve, mend

recur verb happen again, come again, persist, reappear, repeat, return, revert

recurrent adjective periodic, continued, frequent, habitual, recurring

recycle verb reprocess, reclaim, reuse, salvage, save

red adjective 1 crimson, carmine, cherry, coral, ruby, scarlet, vermilion 2 Of hair chestnut, carroty, flame-coloured, reddish, sandy, titian 3 flushed, blushing, embarrassed, florid, shamefaced ◆ noun 4 **in the red** Informal in debt, in arrears, insolvent, overdrawn 5 **see red** Informal lose one's temper, blow one's top, crack up (informal), fly off the handle (informal), go ballistic (slang, chiefly U.S.), go mad (informal)

red-blooded adjective Informal vigorous, lusty, robust, strong, virile

redden verb flush, blush, colour (up), crimson, go red

redeem verb 1 make up for, atone for, compensate for, make amends for 2 reinstate, absolve, restore to favour 3 save, deliver, emancipate, free, liberate, ransom 4 buy back, reclaim, recover, regain, repurchase, retrieve

redemption noun 1 compensation, amends, atonement, reparation 2 salvation, deliverance, emancipation, liberation, release, rescue 3 repurchase, reclamation, recovery, repossession, retrieval

red-handed adjective in the act, bang to rights (slang), (in) flagrante delicto

redolent adjective 1 reminiscent, evocative, suggestive 2 scented, aromatic, fragrant, odorous, perfumed, sweet-smelling

redoubtable adjective formidable, fearful, fearsome, mighty, powerful, strong

redress verb 1 make amends for, compensate for, make up for 2 put right, adjust, balance, correct, even up, rectify, regulate ◆ noun 3 amends, atonement, compensation, payment, recompense, reparation

reduce verb 1 lessen, abate, curtail, cut down, decrease, diminish, lower, moderate, shorten, weaken 2 degrade, break, bring low, downgrade, humble

redundancy noun unemployment, joblessness, layoff, the axe (informal), the sack (informal)

redundant adjective superfluous, extra, inessential, supernumerary, surplus, unnecessary, unwanted

reek verb 1 stink, pong (Brit. informal), smell ◆ noun 2 stink, fetor, odour, pong (Brit. informal), smell, stench

reel verb 1 stagger, lurch, pitch,

rock, roll, sway **2** whirl, revolve, spin, swirl

refer verb **1** allude, bring up, cite, mention, speak of **2** relate, apply, belong, be relevant to, concern, pertain **3** consult, apply, go, look up, turn to **4** direct, guide, point, send

referee noun **1** umpire, adjudicator, arbiter, arbitrator, judge, ref (informal) ♦ verb **2** umpire, adjudicate, arbitrate, judge, mediate

reference noun **1** citation, allusion, mention, note, quotation **2** testimonial, character, credentials, endorsement, recommendation **3** relevance, applicability, bearing, connection, relation

referendum noun public vote, plebiscite, popular vote

refine verb **1** purify, clarify, cleanse, distil, filter, process **2** improve, hone, perfect, polish

refined adjective **1** cultured, civilized, cultivated, elegant, polished, polite, well-bred **2** pure, clarified, clean, distilled, filtered, processed, purified **3** discerning, delicate, discriminating, fastidious, fine, precise, sensitive

refinement noun **1** sophistication, breeding, civility, courtesy, cultivation, culture, discrimination, gentility, good breeding, polish, taste **2** subtlety, fine point, nicety, nuance **3** purification, clarification, cleansing, distillation, filtering, processing

reflect verb **1** throw back, echo, mirror, reproduce, return **2** show, demonstrate, display, indicate, manifest, reveal **3** think, cogitate, consider, meditate, muse, ponder, ruminate, wonder

reflection noun **1** image, echo, mirror image **2** thought, cogitation, consideration, contemplation, idea, meditation, musing, observation, opinion, thinking

reflective adjective thoughtful, contemplative, meditative, pensive

reform noun **1** improvement, amendment, betterment, rehabilitation ♦ verb **2** improve, amend, correct, mend, rectify, restore **3** mend one's ways, clean up one's act (informal), go straight (informal), pull one's socks up (Brit. informal), shape up (informal), turn over a new leaf

refractory adjective unmanageable, difficult, disobedient, headstrong, intractable, uncontrollable, unruly, wilful

refrain[1] verb stop, abstain, avoid, cease, desist, forbear, leave off, renounce

refrain[2] noun chorus, melody, tune

refresh verb **1** revive, brace, enliven, freshen, reinvigorate, revitalize, stimulate **2** stimulate, jog, prompt, renew

refreshing adjective **1** stimulating, bracing, fresh, invigorating **2** new, novel, original

refreshment noun refreshments food and drink, drinks, snacks, titbits

refrigerate verb cool, chill, freeze, keep cold

refuge noun shelter, asylum, haven, hide-out, protection, retreat, sanctuary

refugee noun exile, displaced person, émigré, escapee

refund verb 1 repay, pay back, reimburse, restore, return ♦ noun 2 repayment, reimbursement, return

refurbish verb renovate, clean up, do up (informal), mend, overhaul, repair, restore, revamp

refusal noun denial, knock-back (slang), rebuff, rejection

refuse¹ verb reject, decline, deny, say no, spurn, turn down, withhold

refuse² noun rubbish, garbage, junk (informal), litter, trash, waste

refute verb disprove, discredit, negate, overthrow, prove false, rebut

regain verb 1 recover, get back, recapture, recoup, retrieve, take back, win back 2 get back to, reach again, return to

regal adjective royal, kingly or queenly, magnificent, majestic, noble, princely

regale verb entertain, amuse, delight, divert

regalia plural noun emblems, accoutrements, decorations, finery, paraphernalia, trappings

regard verb 1 consider, believe, deem, esteem, judge, rate, see, suppose, think, view 2 look at, behold, check out (informal), clock (Brit. slang), eye, gaze at, observe, scrutinize, view, watch 3 heed, attend, listen to, mind, pay attention to, take notice of 4 as regards concerning, pertaining to, regarding, relating to ♦ noun 5 heed, attention, interest, mind, notice 6 respect, care, concern, consideration, esteem, thought 7 look, gaze, glance, scrutiny, stare

regarding preposition concerning, about, as regards, in or with regard to, on the subject of, re, respecting, with reference to

regardless adjective 1 heedless, inconsiderate, indifferent, neglectful, negligent, rash, reckless, unmindful ♦ adverb 2 anyway, in any case, in spite of everything, nevertheless

regards plural noun good wishes, best wishes, compliments, greetings, respects

regenerate verb renew, breathe new life into, invigorate, reawaken, reinvigorate, rejuvenate, restore, revive

regime noun government, leadership, management, reign, rule, system

regimented adjective controlled, disciplined, ordered, organized, regulated, systematized

region noun area, district, locality, part, place, quarter, section, sector, territory, tract, zone

regional adjective local, district, parochial, provincial, zonal

register noun 1 list, archives, catalogue, chronicle, diary, file, log, record, roll, roster ♦ verb 2 record, catalogue, chronicle, enlist, enrol, enter, list, note 3 show, display, exhibit, express, indicate, manifest, mark, reveal

regress verb **revert**, backslide, degenerate, deteriorate, fall away or off, go back, lapse, relapse, return

regret verb **1** feel sorry about, bemoan, bewail, deplore, grieve, lament, miss, mourn, repent, rue ♦ noun **2** sorrow, bitterness, compunction, contrition, penitence, remorse, repentance, ruefulness

regretful adjective **sorry**, apologetic, contrite, penitent, remorseful, repentant, rueful, sad, sorrowful

regrettable adjective **unfortunate**, disappointing, distressing, lamentable, sad, shameful

regular adjective **1** normal, common, customary, habitual, ordinary, routine, typical, usual **2** even, balanced, flat, level, smooth, straight, symmetrical, uniform **3** systematic, consistent, constant, even, fixed, ordered, set, stated, steady, uniform

regulate verb **1** control, direct, govern, guide, handle, manage, rule, run, supervise **2** adjust, balance, fit, moderate, modulate, tune

regulation noun **1** rule, decree, dictate, edict, law, order, precept, statute **2** control, direction, government, management, supervision **3** adjustment, modulation, tuning

regurgitate verb **vomit**, disgorge, puke (slang), sick up (informal), spew (out or up), throw up (informal)

rehabilitate verb **1** reintegrate, adjust **2** redeem, clear, reform, restore, save

rehash verb **1** rework, refashion, rejig (informal), reuse, rewrite ♦ noun **2** reworking, new version, rearrangement, rewrite

rehearsal noun **practice**, drill, preparation, rehearsing, run-through

rehearse verb **practise**, drill, go over, prepare, recite, repeat, run through, train

reign noun **1** rule, command, control, dominion, monarchy, power ♦ verb **2** rule, be in power, command, govern, influence **3** be supreme, hold sway, predominate, prevail

reimburse verb **pay back**, compensate, recompense, refund, remunerate, repay, return

rein verb **1** control, check, curb, halt, hold back, limit, restrain, restrict ♦ noun **2** control, brake, bridle, check, curb, harness, hold, restraint

reincarnation noun **rebirth**, transmigration of souls

reinforce verb **support**, bolster, emphasize, fortify, prop, strengthen, stress, supplement, toughen

reinforcement noun **1** strengthening, augmentation, fortification, increase **2** support, brace, buttress, prop, stay **3 reinforcements** reserves, additional or fresh troops, auxiliaries, support

reinstate verb **restore**, recall, re-establish, replace, return

reiterate verb **repeat**, do again, restate, say again

reject verb **1** deny, decline, disallow, exclude, renounce, repudiate, veto **2** <u>rebuff</u>, jilt, refuse, repulse, say no to, spurn, turn down **3** <u>discard</u>, eliminate, jettison, scrap, throw away or out ♦ *noun* **4** <u>castoff</u>, discard, failure, second

rejection *noun* **1** <u>denial</u>, dismissal, exclusion, renunciation, repudiation, thumbs down, veto **2** <u>rebuff</u>, brushoff (*slang*), kick in the teeth (*slang*), knock-back (*slang*), refusal

rejig *verb* <u>rearrange</u>, alter, juggle, manipulate, reorganize, tweak

rejoice *verb* <u>be glad</u>, be happy, be overjoyed, celebrate, exult, glory

rejoicing *noun* <u>happiness</u>, celebration, elation, exultation, gladness, joy, jubilation, merrymaking

rejoin *verb* <u>reply</u>, answer, respond, retort, riposte

rejoinder *noun* <u>reply</u>, answer, comeback (*informal*), response, retort, riposte

rejuvenate *verb* <u>revitalize</u>, breathe new life into, refresh, regenerate, reinvigorate, renew, restore

relapse *verb* **1** <u>lapse</u>, backslide, degenerate, fail, regress, revert, slip back **2** <u>worsen</u>, deteriorate, fade, fail, sicken, sink, weaken ♦ *noun* **3** <u>lapse</u>, backsliding, regression, retrogression **4** <u>worsening</u>, deterioration, turn for the worse, weakening

relate *verb* **1** <u>connect</u>, associate, correlate, couple, join, link **2** <u>concern</u>, apply, be relevant to, have to do with, pertain, refer **3** <u>tell</u>, describe, detail, narrate, recite, recount, report

related *adjective* **1** <u>akin</u>, kindred **2** <u>associated</u>, affiliated, akin, connected, interconnected, joint, linked

relation *noun* **1** <u>connection</u>, bearing, bond, comparison, correlation, link **2** <u>relative</u>, kin, kinsman or kinswoman **3** <u>kinship</u>, affinity, kindred

relations *plural noun* **1** <u>dealings</u>, affairs, connections, contact, interaction, intercourse, relationship **2** <u>family</u>, clan, kin, kindred, kinsfolk, kinsmen, relatives, tribe

relationship *noun* **1** <u>association</u>, affinity, bond, connection, kinship, rapport **2** <u>affair</u>, liaison **3** <u>connection</u>, correlation, link, parallel, similarity, tie-up

relative *adjective* **1** <u>dependent</u>, allied, associated, comparative, contingent, corresponding, proportionate, related **2** <u>relevant</u>, applicable, apposite, appropriate, apropos, germane, pertinent **3** <u>relation</u>, kinsman or kinswoman, member of one's or the family

relatively *adverb* <u>comparatively</u>, rather, somewhat

relax *verb* **1** <u>be or feel at ease</u>, calm, chill out (*slang, chiefly U.S.*), lighten up (*slang*), rest, take it easy, unwind **2** <u>lessen</u>, abate, ease, ebb, let up, loosen, lower, moderate, reduce, relieve, slacken, weaken

relaxation *noun* <u>leisure</u>, enjoyment, fun, pleasure, recreation, rest

relaxed *adjective* <u>easy-going</u>, casual, comfortable, easy, free and easy, informal, laid-back (*informal*), leisurely

relay noun **1** shift, relief, turn **2** message, dispatch, transmission ♦ verb **3** pass on, broadcast, carry, communicate, send, spread, transmit

release verb **1** set free, discharge, drop, extricate, free, liberate, loose, unbridle, undo, unfasten **2** acquit, absolve, exonerate, let go, let off **3** issue, circulate, distribute, launch, make known, make public, publish, put out ♦ noun **4** liberation, deliverance, discharge, emancipation, freedom, liberty **5** acquittal, absolution, exemption, exoneration **6** issue, proclamation, publication

relegate verb demote, downgrade

relent verb be merciful, capitulate, change one's mind, come round, have pity, show mercy, soften, yield

relentless adjective **1** unremitting, incessant, nonstop, persistent, unrelenting, unrelieved **2** merciless, cruel, fierce, implacable, pitiless, remorseless, ruthless, unrelenting

relevant adjective significant, apposite, appropriate, apt, fitting, germane, pertinent, related, to the point

reliable adjective dependable, faithful, safe, sound, staunch, sure, true, trustworthy

reliance noun trust, belief, confidence, dependence, faith

relic noun remnant, fragment, keepsake, memento, souvenir, trace, vestige

relief noun **1** ease, comfort, cure, deliverance, mitigation, release, remedy, solace **2** rest, break, breather (*informal*), relaxation, respite **3** aid, assistance, help, succour, support

relieve verb **1** ease, alleviate, assuage, calm, comfort, console, cure, mitigate, relax, soften, soothe **2** help, aid, assist, succour, support, sustain

religious adjective **1** devout, devotional, faithful, godly, holy, pious, sacred, spiritual **2** conscientious, faithful, meticulous, punctilious, rigid, scrupulous

relinquish verb give up, abandon, abdicate, cede, drop, forsake, leave, let go, renounce, surrender

relish verb **1** enjoy, delight in, fancy, like, revel in, savour ♦ noun **2** enjoyment, fancy, fondness, gusto, liking, love, partiality, penchant, predilection, taste **3** condiment, sauce, seasoning **4** flavour, piquancy, smack, spice, tang, taste, trace

reluctance noun unwillingness, aversion, disinclination, dislike, distaste, loathing, repugnance

reluctant adjective unwilling, disinclined, hesitant, loath, unenthusiastic

rely verb depend, bank, bet, count, trust

remain verb **1** continue, abide, dwell, endure, go on, last, persist, stand, stay, survive **2** stay behind, be left, delay, linger, wait

remainder noun rest, balance, excess, leavings, remains, remnant, residue, surplus

remaining *adjective* <u>left-over</u>, lingering, outstanding, persisting, surviving, unfinished

remains *plural noun* 1 <u>remnants</u>, debris, dregs, leavings, leftovers, relics, residue, rest 2 <u>body</u>, cadaver, carcass, corpse

remark *verb* 1 <u>comment</u>, declare, mention, observe, pass comment, reflect, say, state 2 <u>notice</u>, espy, make out, mark, note, observe, perceive, see ♦ *noun* 3 <u>comment</u>, observation, reflection, statement, utterance

remarkable *adjective* <u>extraordinary</u>, notable, outstanding, rare, singular, striking, surprising, uncommon, unusual, wonderful

remedy *noun* 1 <u>cure</u>, medicine, nostrum, treatment ♦ *verb* 2 <u>put right</u>, correct, fix, rectify, set to rights

remember *verb* 1 <u>recall</u>, call to mind, commemorate, look back (on), recollect, reminisce, think back 2 <u>bear in mind</u>, keep in mind

remembrance *noun* 1 <u>memory</u>, recall, recollection, reminiscence, thought 2 <u>souvenir</u>, commemoration, keepsake, memento, memorial, monument, reminder, token

remind *verb* <u>call to mind</u>, jog one's memory, make (someone) remember, prompt

reminisce *verb* <u>recall</u>, hark back, look back, recollect, remember, think back

reminiscence *noun* <u>recollection</u>, anecdote, memoir, memory, recall, remembrance

reminiscent *adjective* <u>suggestive</u>, evocative, similar

remiss *adjective* <u>careless</u>, forgetful, heedless, lax, neglectful, negligent, thoughtless

remission *noun* 1 <u>pardon</u>, absolution, amnesty, discharge, exemption, release, reprieve 2 <u>lessening</u>, abatement, alleviation, ebb, lull, relaxation, respite

remit *verb* 1 <u>send</u>, dispatch, forward, mail, post, transmit 2 <u>cancel</u>, halt, repeal, rescind, stop 3 <u>postpone</u>, defer, delay, put off, shelve, suspend ♦ *noun* 4 <u>instructions</u>, brief, guidelines, orders

remittance *noun* <u>payment</u>, allowance, fee

remnant *noun* <u>remainder</u>, end, fragment, leftovers, remains, residue, rest, trace, vestige

remonstrate *verb* <u>argue</u>, dispute, dissent, object, protest, take issue

remorse *noun* <u>regret</u>, anguish, compunction, contrition, grief, guilt, penitence, repentance, shame, sorrow

remorseful *adjective* <u>regretful</u>, apologetic, ashamed, conscience-stricken, contrite, guilty, penitent, repentant, sorry

remorseless *adjective* 1 <u>pitiless</u>, callous, cruel, inhumane, merciless, ruthless 2 <u>relentless</u>, inexorable

remote *adjective* 1 <u>distant</u>, far, inaccessible, in the middle of nowhere, isolated, out-of-the-way, secluded 2 <u>aloof</u>, abstracted, cold, detached, distant, reserved, standoffish, uncommunicative, withdrawn **3** slight, doubtful, dubious, faint, outside, slender, slim, small, unlikely

removal *noun* **1** taking away or off or out, dislodgment, ejection, elimination, eradication, extraction, uprooting, withdrawal **2** dismissal, expulsion **3** move, departure, flitting (*Scot. & Northern English dialect*), relocation, transfer

remove *verb* **1** take away or off or out, abolish, delete, detach, displace, eject, eliminate, erase, excise, extract, get rid of, wipe from the face of the earth, withdraw **2** dismiss, depose, dethrone, discharge, expel, oust, throw out **3** move, depart, flit (*Scot. & Northern English dialect*), relocate

remunerate *verb* pay, compensate, recompense, reimburse, repay, requite, reward

remuneration *noun* payment, earnings, fee, income, pay, return, reward, salary, stipend, wages

remunerative *adjective* profitable, economic, lucrative, moneymaking, paying, rewarding, worthwhile

renaissance, renascence *noun* rebirth, reappearance, reawakening, renewal, restoration, resurgence, revival

rend *verb* tear, rip, rupture, separate, wrench

render *verb* **1** make, cause to become, leave **2** provide, furnish, give, hand out, pay,

present, submit, supply, tender **3** portray, act, depict, do, give, perform, play, represent

rendezvous *noun* **1** appointment, assignation, date, engagement, meeting, tryst (*archaic*) **2** meeting place, gathering point, venue ♦ *verb* **3** meet, assemble, come together, gather, join up

rendition *noun* **1** performance, arrangement, interpretation, portrayal, presentation, reading, rendering, version **2** translation, interpretation, reading, transcription, version

renegade *noun* **1** deserter, apostate, defector, traitor, turncoat ♦ *adjective* **2** rebellious, apostate, disloyal, traitorous, unfaithful

renege *verb* break one's word, back out, break a promise, default, go back

renew *verb* **1** recommence, continue, extend, reaffirm, recreate, reopen, repeat, resume **2** restore, mend, modernize, overhaul, refit, refurbish, renovate, repair **3** replace, refresh, replenish, restock

renounce *verb* give up, abjure, deny, disown, forsake, forswear, quit, recant, relinquish, waive

renovate *verb* restore, do up (*informal*), modernize, overhaul, recondition, refit, refurbish, renew, repair

renown *noun* fame, distinction, eminence, note, reputation, repute

renowned *adjective* famous, celebrated, distinguished, eminent, esteemed, notable, noted, well-known

rent[1] verb 1 hire, charter, lease, let ♦ noun 2 hire, fee, lease, payment, rental

rent[2] noun tear, gash, hole, opening, rip, slash, slit, split

renunciation noun giving up, abandonment, abdication, abjuration, denial, disavowal, forswearing, rejection, relinquishment, repudiation

reorganize verb rearrange, reshuffle, restructure

repair verb 1 mend, fix, heal, patch, patch up, renovate, restore ♦ noun 2 mend, darn, overhaul, patch, restoration 3 condition, form, shape (informal), state

reparation noun compensation, atonement, damages, recompense, restitution, satisfaction

repartee noun wit, badinage, banter, riposte, wittiness, wordplay

repast noun meal, food

repay verb 1 pay back, compensate, recompense, refund, reimburse, requite, return, square 2 get even with (informal), avenge, get one's own back on (informal), hit back, reciprocate, retaliate, revenge

repeal verb 1 abolish, annul, cancel, invalidate, nullify, recall, reverse, revoke ♦ noun 2 abolition, annulment, cancellation, invalidation, rescindment

repeat verb 1 reiterate, echo, replay, reproduce, rerun, reshow, restate, retell ♦ noun

2 repetition, echo, reiteration, replay, rerun, reshowing

repeatedly adverb over and over, frequently, many times, often

repel verb 1 disgust, gross out (U.S. slang), nauseate, offend, revolt, sicken 2 drive off, fight, hold off, parry, rebuff, repulse, resist, ward off

repellent adjective 1 disgusting, abhorrent, hateful, horrid, loathsome, nauseating, noxious, offensive, repugnant, repulsive, revolting, sickening 2 proof, impermeable, repelling, resistant

repent verb regret, be sorry, feel remorse, rue

repentance noun regret, compunction, contrition, grief, guilt, penitence, remorse

repentant adjective regretful, contrite, penitent, remorseful, rueful, sorry

repercussion noun repercussions consequences, backlash, result, sequel, side effects

repertoire noun range, collection, list, repertory, stock, store, supply

repetition noun repeating, echo, recurrence, reiteration, renewal, replication, restatement, tautology

repetitious adjective long-winded, prolix, tautological, tedious, verbose, wordy

repetitive adjective monotonous, boring, dull, mechanical, recurrent, tedious, unchanging, unvaried

rephrase verb reword, paraphrase, put differently

repine verb <u>complain</u>, fret, grumble, moan

replace verb <u>take the place of</u>, follow, oust, substitute, succeed, supersede, supplant, take over from

replacement noun <u>successor</u>, double, proxy, stand-in, substitute, surrogate, understudy

replenish verb <u>refill</u>, fill, provide, reload, replace, restore, top up

replete adjective <u>full</u>, crammed, filled, full up, glutted, gorged, stuffed

replica noun <u>duplicate</u>, carbon copy (informal), copy, facsimile, imitation, model, reproduction

replicate verb <u>copy</u>, duplicate, mimic, recreate, reduplicate, reproduce

reply verb 1 <u>answer</u>, counter, reciprocate, rejoin, respond, retaliate, retort ◆ noun 2 <u>answer</u>, counter, counterattack, reaction, rejoinder, response, retaliation, retort

report verb 1 <u>communicate</u>, broadcast, cover, describe, detail, inform of, narrate, pass on, recount, relate, state, tell 2 <u>present oneself</u>, appear, arrive, come, turn up ◆ noun 3 <u>account</u>, communication, description, narrative, news, record, statement, word 4 <u>article</u>, piece, story, write-up 5 <u>rumour</u>, buzz, gossip, hearsay, talk 6 <u>bang</u>, blast, boom, crack, detonation, discharge, explosion, noise, sound

reporter noun <u>journalist</u>, correspondent, hack (derogatory), journo (slang), pressman, writer

repose noun 1 <u>peace</u>, ease, quietness, calmness, relaxation, respite, rest, stillness, tranquillity 2 <u>composure</u>, calmness, poise, self-possession 3 <u>sleep</u>, slumber ◆ verb 4 <u>rest</u>, lie, lie down, recline, rest upon

repository noun <u>store</u>, depository, storehouse, treasury, vault

reprehensible adjective <u>blameworthy</u>, bad, culpable, disgraceful, shameful, unworthy

represent verb 1 <u>stand for</u>, act for, betoken, mean, serve as, speak for, symbolize 2 <u>symbolize</u>, embody, epitomize, exemplify, personify, typify 3 <u>portray</u>, denote, depict, describe, illustrate, outline, picture, show

representation noun <u>portrayal</u>, account, depiction, description, illustration, image, likeness, model, picture, portrait

representative noun 1 <u>delegate</u>, agent, deputy, member, proxy, spokesman or spokeswoman 2 <u>salesman</u>, agent, commercial traveller, rep ◆ adjective 3 <u>typical</u>, archetypal, characteristic, exemplary, symbolic

repress verb 1 <u>inhibit</u>, bottle up, check, control, curb, hold back, restrain, stifle, suppress 2 <u>subdue</u>, quell, subjugate

repression noun <u>subjugation</u>, constraint, control, despotism, domination, restraint, suppression, tyranny

repressive adjective <u>oppressive</u>, absolute, authoritarian, despotic, dictatorial, tyrannical

reprieve verb 1 <u>grant a stay of</u>

execution to, let off the hook (*slang*), pardon **2** relieve, abate, allay, alleviate, mitigate, palliate ♦ *noun* **3** stay of execution, amnesty, deferment, pardon, postponement, remission **4** relief, alleviation, mitigation, palliation, respite

reprimand *verb* **1** blame, censure, dress down (*informal*), haul over the coals (*informal*), rap over the knuckles, rebuke, scold, tear (someone) off a strip (*Brit. informal*) ♦ *noun* **2** blame, censure, dressing-down (*informal*), rebuke, reproach, talking-to (*informal*)

reprisal *noun* retaliation, retribution, revenge, vengeance

reproach *noun* **1** blame, censure, condemnation, disapproval, opprobrium, rebuke ♦ *verb* **2** blame, censure, condemn, criticize, lambast(e), read the riot act, rebuke, reprimand, scold, upbraid

reproachful *adjective* critical, censorious, condemnatory, disapproving, fault-finding, reproving

reprobate *noun* **1** scoundrel, bad egg (*old-fashioned informal*), blackguard, degenerate, evildoer, miscreant, ne'er-do-well, profligate, rake, rascal, villain ♦ *adjective* **2** depraved, abandoned, bad, base, corrupt, degenerate, dissolute, immoral, sinful, wicked

reproduce *verb* **1** copy, duplicate, echo, imitate, match, mirror, recreate, repeat, replicate **2** breed, multiply, procreate, propagate, spawn

reproduction *noun* **1** breeding, generation, increase, multiplication **2** copy, duplicate, facsimile, imitation, picture, print, replica

reproof *noun* rebuke, blame, censure, condemnation, criticism, reprimand, scolding

reprove *verb* rebuke, berate, blame, censure, condemn, read the riot act, reprimand, scold, tear into (*informal*), tear (someone) off a strip (*Brit. informal*), tell off (*informal*)

repudiate *verb* reject, deny, disavow, disclaim, disown, renounce

repugnance *noun* distaste, abhorrence, aversion, disgust, dislike, hatred, loathing

repugnant *adjective* distasteful, abhorrent, disgusting, loathsome, nauseating, offensive, repellent, revolting, sickening, vile

repulse *verb* **1** drive back, beat off, fight off, rebuff, repel, ward off **2** rebuff, refuse, reject, snub, spurn, turn down

repulsion *noun* distaste, abhorrence, aversion, detestation, disgust, hatred, loathing, repugnance, revulsion

repulsive *adjective* disgusting, abhorrent, foul, loathsome, nauseating, repellent, revolting, sickening, vile

reputable *adjective* respectable, creditable, excellent, good, honourable, reliable, trustworthy, well-thought-of, worthy

reputation *noun* estimation, character, esteem, name, renown, repute, standing, stature

repute noun <u>reputation</u>, celebrity, distinction, eminence, fame, name, renown, standing, stature

reputed adjective <u>supposed</u>, alleged, believed, considered, deemed, estimated, held, reckoned, regarded

reputedly adverb <u>supposedly</u>, allegedly, apparently, seemingly

request verb 1 <u>ask (for)</u>, appeal for, demand, desire, entreat, invite, seek, solicit ♦ noun 2 <u>asking</u>, appeal, call, demand, desire, entreaty, suit

require verb 1 <u>need</u>, crave, desire, lack, miss, want, wish 2 <u>demand</u>, ask, bid, call upon, compel, exact, insist upon, oblige, order

required adjective <u>needed</u>, called for, essential, necessary, obligatory, requisite

requirement noun <u>necessity</u>, demand, essential, lack, must, need, prerequisite, stipulation, want

requisite adjective 1 <u>necessary</u>, called for, essential, indispensable, needed, needful, obligatory, required ♦ noun 2 <u>necessity</u>, condition, essential, must, need, prerequisite, requirement

requisition verb 1 <u>demand</u>, call for, request ♦ noun 2 <u>demand</u>, call, request, summons

requital noun <u>return</u>, repayment

requite verb <u>return</u>, get even, give in return, pay (someone) back in his or her own coin, reciprocate, repay, respond, retaliate

rescind verb <u>annul</u>, cancel,

countermand, declare null and void, invalidate, repeal, set aside

rescue verb 1 <u>save</u>, deliver, get out, liberate, recover, redeem, release, salvage ♦ noun 2 <u>liberation</u>, deliverance, recovery, redemption, release, salvage, salvation, saving

research noun 1 <u>investigation</u>, analysis, examination, exploration, probe, study ♦ verb 2 <u>investigate</u>, analyse, examine, explore, probe, study

resemblance noun <u>similarity</u>, correspondence, kinship, likeness, parallel, sameness, similitude

resemble verb <u>be like</u>, bear a resemblance to, be similar to, look like, mirror, parallel

resent verb <u>be bitter about</u>, begrudge, grudge, object to, take exception to, take offence at

resentful adjective <u>bitter</u>, angry, embittered, grudging, indignant, miffed (informal), offended, piqued

resentment noun <u>bitterness</u>, animosity, bad blood, grudge, ill feeling, ill will, indignation, pique, rancour, umbrage

reservation noun 1 <u>doubt</u>, hesitancy, scruple 2 <u>condition</u>, proviso, qualification, rider, stipulation 3 <u>reserve</u>, preserve, sanctuary, territory

reserve verb 1 <u>keep</u>, hoard, hold, put by, retain, save, set aside, stockpile, store 2 <u>book</u>, engage, prearrange, secure ♦ noun 3 <u>store</u>, cache, fund, hoard, reservoir, savings, stock, supply 4 <u>reservation</u>, park, preserve, sanctuary, tract 5 <u>shyness</u>, constraint, reservation, restraint, reticence, secretiveness, silence, taciturnity ♦ *adjective* **6** substitute, auxiliary, extra, fall-back, secondary, spare

reserved *adjective* **1** uncommunicative, restrained, reticent, retiring, secretive, shy, silent, standoffish, taciturn, undemonstrative **2** set aside, booked, engaged, held, kept, restricted, retained, spoken for, taken

reservoir *noun* **1** lake, basin, pond, tank **2** store, pool, reserves, source, stock, supply

reshuffle *noun* **1** reorganization, change, rearrangement, redistribution, regrouping, restructuring, revision ♦ *verb* **2** reorganize, change around, rearrange, redistribute, regroup, restructure, revise

reside *verb* live, abide, dwell, inhabit, lodge, stay

residence *noun* home, abode, domicile, dwelling, flat, habitation, house, lodging, place

resident *noun* inhabitant, citizen, local, lodger, occupant, tenant

residual *adjective* remaining, leftover, unconsumed, unused, vestigial

residue *noun* remainder, dregs, excess, extra, leftovers, remains, remnant, rest, surplus

resign *verb* **1** quit, abdicate, give in one's notice, leave, step down (*informal*), vacate **2** give up, abandon, forgo, forsake, relinquish, renounce, surrender, yield **3** resign oneself accept, acquiesce, give in, submit, succumb, yield

resignation *noun* **1** leaving, abandonment, abdication, departure **2** endurance, acceptance, acquiescence, compliance, nonresistance, passivity, patience, submission, sufferance

resigned *adjective* stoical, compliant, long-suffering, patient, subdued, unresisting

resilient *adjective* **1** tough, buoyant, hardy, irrepressible, strong **2** flexible, elastic, plastic, pliable, rubbery, springy, supple

resist *verb* **1** oppose, battle, combat, defy, hinder, stand up to **2** refrain from, abstain from, avoid, forbear, forgo, keep from **3** withstand, be proof against

resistance *noun* fighting, battle, defiance, fight, hindrance, impediment, obstruction, opposition, struggle

resistant *adjective* **1** impervious, hard, proof against, strong, tough, unaffected by **2** opposed, antagonistic, hostile, intractable, intransigent, unwilling

resolute *adjective* determined, dogged, firm, fixed, immovable, inflexible, set, steadfast, strong-willed, tenacious, unshakable, unwavering

resolution *noun* **1** determination, doggedness, firmness, perseverance, purpose, resoluteness, resolve, steadfastness, tenacity, willpower **2** decision, aim, declaration, determination, intent, intention, purpose, resolve

resolve *verb* **1** decide, agree, conclude, determine, fix, intend, purpose **2** break down, analyse,

reduce, separate **3** <u>work out</u>, answer, clear up, crack, fathom
♦ *noun* **4** <u>determination</u>, firmness, resoluteness, resolution, steadfastness, willpower
5 <u>decision</u>, intention, objective, purpose, resolution

resonant *adjective* <u>echoing</u>, booming, resounding, reverberating, ringing, sonorous

resort *verb* **1** resort to <u>use</u>, employ, fall back on, have recourse to, turn to, utilize
♦ *noun* **2** <u>holiday centre</u>, haunt, retreat, spot, tourist centre
3 <u>recourse</u>, reference

resound *verb* <u>echo</u>, re-echo, resonate, reverberate, ring

resounding *adjective* <u>echoing</u>, booming, full, powerful, resonant, reverberating, ringing, sonorous

resource *noun* **1** <u>ingenuity</u>, ability, capability, cleverness, initiative, inventiveness **2** <u>means</u>, course, device, expedient, resort

resourceful *adjective* <u>ingenious</u>, able, bright, capable, clever, creative, inventive

resources *plural noun* <u>reserves</u>, assets, capital, funds, holdings, money, riches, supplies, wealth

respect *noun* **1** <u>regard</u>, admiration, consideration, deference, esteem, estimation, honour, recognition **2** <u>point</u>, aspect, characteristic, detail, feature, matter, particular, sense, way **3** <u>relation</u>, bearing, connection, reference, regard
♦ *verb* **4** <u>think highly of</u>, admire, defer to, esteem, have a good or high opinion of, honour, look up to, value **5** <u>show consideration</u>

for, abide by, adhere to, comply with, follow, heed, honour, obey, observe

respectable *adjective*
1 <u>honourable</u>, decent, estimable, good, honest, reputable, upright, worthy **2** <u>reasonable</u>, ample, appreciable, considerable, decent, fair, sizable *or* sizeable, substantial

respectful *adjective* <u>polite</u>, civil, courteous, deferential, mannerly, reverent, well-mannered

respective *adjective* <u>specific</u>, individual, own, particular, relevant

respite *noun* <u>pause</u>, break, cessation, halt, interval, lull, recess, relief, rest

resplendent *adjective* <u>brilliant</u>, bright, dazzling, glorious, radiant, shining, splendid

respond *verb* <u>answer</u>, counter, react, reciprocate, rejoin, reply, retort, return

response *noun* <u>answer</u>, counterattack, feedback, reaction, rejoinder, reply, retort, return

responsibility *noun* **1** <u>authority</u>, importance, power **2** <u>fault</u>, blame, culpability, guilt **3** <u>duty</u>, care, charge, liability, obligation, onus **4** <u>level-headedness</u>, conscientiousness, dependability, rationality, sensibleness, trustworthiness

responsible *adjective* **1** <u>in charge</u>, in authority, in control **2** to <u>blame</u>, at fault, culpable, guilty **3** <u>accountable</u>, answerable, liable **4** <u>sensible</u>, dependable, level-headed, rational, reliable, trustworthy

responsive adjective sensitive, alive, impressionable, open, reactive, receptive, susceptible

rest[1] noun 1 repose, calm, inactivity, leisure, relaxation, relief, stillness, tranquillity 2 pause, break, cessation, halt, interlude, intermission, interval, lull, respite, stop 3 support, base, holder, prop, stand ♦ verb 4 relax, be at ease, put one's feet up, sit down, take it easy 5 be supported, lean, lie, prop, recline, repose, sit

rest[2] noun remainder, balance, excess, others, remains, remnants, residue, surplus

restaurant noun bistro, café, cafeteria, diner (chiefly U.S. & Canad.), eatery, tearoom

restful adjective relaxing, calm, calming, peaceful, quiet, relaxed, serene, soothing, tranquil

restitution noun compensation, amends, recompense, reparation, requital

restive adjective restless, edgy, fidgety, impatient, jumpy, nervous, on edge

restless adjective 1 moving, nomadic, roving, transient, unsettled, unstable, wandering 2 unsettled, edgy, fidgeting, fidgety, jumpy, nervous, on edge, restive

restlessness noun 1 movement, activity, bustle, unrest, unsettledness 2 restiveness, edginess, jitters (informal), jumpiness, nervousness

restoration noun 1 repair, reconstruction, renewal, renovation, revitalization, revival 2 reinstatement,

re-establishment, replacement, restitution, return

restore verb 1 repair, fix, mend, rebuild, recondition, reconstruct, refurbish, renew, renovate 2 revive, build up, refresh, revitalize, strengthen 3 return, bring back, give back, hand back, recover, reinstate, replace, send back 4 reinstate, reintroduce

restrain verb hold back, check, constrain, contain, control, curb, curtail, hamper, hinder, inhibit, restrict

restrained adjective controlled, calm, mild, moderate, self-controlled, undemonstrative

restraint noun 1 self-control, control, inhibition, moderation, self-discipline, self-possession, self-restraint 2 limitation, ban, check, curb, embargo, interdict, limit, rein

restrict verb limit, bound, confine, contain, hamper, handicap, inhibit, regulate, restrain

restriction noun limitation, confinement, control, curb, handicap, inhibition, regulation, restraint, rule

result noun 1 consequence, effect, end, end result, outcome, product, sequel, upshot ♦ verb 2 happen, appear, arise, derive, develop, ensue, follow, issue, spring 3 result in end in, culminate in, finish with

resume verb begin again, carry on, continue, go on, proceed, reopen, restart

résumé noun summary, précis, recapitulation, rundown, synopsis

resumption noun <u>continuation</u>, carrying on, re-establishment, renewal, reopening, restart, resurgence

resurgence noun <u>revival</u>, rebirth, re-emergence, renaissance, resumption, resurrection, return

resurrect verb <u>revive</u>, bring back, reintroduce, renew

resurrection noun <u>revival</u>, reappearance, rebirth, renaissance, renewal, restoration, resurgence, return

resuscitate verb <u>revive</u>, bring round, resurrect, revitalize, save

retain verb 1 <u>keep</u>, hold, hold back, maintain, preserve, reserve, save 2 <u>hire</u>, commission, employ, engage, pay, reserve

retainer noun 1 <u>fee</u>, advance, deposit 2 <u>servant</u>, attendant, domestic

retaliate verb <u>pay (someone) back</u>, get even with (informal), get one's own back (informal), hit back, reciprocate, strike back, take revenge

retaliation noun <u>revenge</u>, an eye for an eye, counterblow, reciprocation, repayment, reprisal, requital, vengeance

retard verb <u>slow down</u>, arrest, check, delay, handicap, hinder, hold back or up, impede, set back

retch verb <u>gag</u>, be sick, heave, puke (slang), regurgitate, spew, throw up (informal), vomit

reticence noun <u>silence</u>, quietness, reserve, taciturnity

reticent adjective <u>uncommunicative</u>, close-lipped, quiet, reserved, silent, taciturn,

tight-lipped, unforthcoming

retinue noun <u>attendants</u>, aides, entourage, escort, followers, servants

retire verb 1 <u>stop working</u>, give up work 2 <u>withdraw</u>, depart, exit, go away, leave 3 <u>go to bed</u>, hit the hay (slang), hit the sack (slang), turn in (informal)

retirement noun <u>withdrawal</u>, privacy, retreat, seclusion, solitude

retiring adjective <u>shy</u>, bashful, quiet, reserved, self-effacing, timid, unassertive, unassuming

retort verb 1 <u>reply</u>, answer, come back with, counter, respond, return, riposte ♦ noun 2 <u>reply</u>, answer, comeback (informal), rejoinder, response, riposte

retract verb 1 <u>withdraw</u>, deny, disavow, disclaim, eat one's words, recant, renege, renounce, revoke, take back 2 <u>draw in</u>, pull back, pull in, sheathe

retreat verb 1 <u>withdraw</u>, back away, back off, depart, draw back, fall back, go back, leave, pull back ♦ noun 2 <u>withdrawal</u>, departure, evacuation, flight, retirement 3 <u>refuge</u>, haven, hideaway, sanctuary, seclusion, shelter

retrench verb <u>cut back</u>, economize, make economies, save, tighten one's belt

retrenchment noun <u>cutback</u>, cost-cutting, cut, economy, tightening one's belt

retribution noun <u>punishment</u>, justice, Nemesis, reckoning, reprisal, retaliation, revenge, vengeance

retrieve verb get back, recapture, recoup, recover, redeem, regain, restore, save, win back

retrograde adjective declining, backward, degenerative, deteriorating, downward, regressive, retrogressive, worsening

retrogress verb decline, backslide, deteriorate, go back, go downhill (informal), regress, relapse, worsen

retrospect noun hindsight, re-examination, review

return verb 1 come back, go back, reappear, rebound, recur, retreat, revert, turn back 2 put back, re-establish, reinstate, replace, restore 3 give back, pay back, recompense, refund, reimburse, repay 4 reply, answer, respond, retort 5 elect, choose, vote in ♦ noun 6 restoration, re-establishment, reinstatement 7 reappearance, recurrence 8 retreat, rebound, recoil 9 profit, gain, income, interest, proceeds, revenue, takings, yield 10 report, account, form, list, statement, summary 11 reply, answer, comeback (informal), rejoinder, response, retort

revamp verb renovate, do up (informal), overhaul, recondition, refurbish, restore

reveal verb 1 make known, announce, disclose, divulge, give away, impart, let out, let slip, make public, proclaim, tell 2 show, display, exhibit, manifest, uncover, unearth, unmask, unveil

revel verb 1 celebrate, carouse, live it up (informal), make merry 2 revel in enjoy, delight in, indulge in, lap up, luxuriate in, relish, take pleasure in, thrive on ♦ noun 3 often plural merrymaking, carousal, celebration, festivity, party, spree

revelation noun disclosure, exhibition, exposé, exposure, news, proclamation, publication, uncovering, unearthing, unveiling

reveller noun carouser, partygoer

revelry noun festivity, carousal, celebration, fun, jollity, merrymaking, party, spree

revenge noun 1 retaliation, an eye for an eye, reprisal, retribution, vengeance ♦ verb 2 avenge, get even, get one's own back for (informal), hit back, repay, retaliate, take revenge for

revenue noun income, gain, proceeds, profits, receipts, returns, takings, yield

reverberate verb echo, re-echo, resound, ring, vibrate

revere verb be in awe of, exalt, honour, look up to, respect, reverence, venerate, worship

reverence noun awe, admiration, high esteem, honour, respect, veneration, worship

reverent adjective respectful, awed, deferential, humble, reverential

reverie noun daydream, abstraction, brown study, woolgathering

reverse verb 1 turn round, invert, transpose, turn back, turn over, turn upside down, upend 2 change, annul, cancel, countermand, invalidate, overrule, overthrow, overturn, quash, repeal, rescind, revoke, undo **3** go backwards, back, back up, move backwards, retreat ♦ noun **4** opposite, contrary, converse, inverse **5** back, other side, rear, underside, wrong side **6** misfortune, adversity, affliction, blow, disappointment, failure, hardship, misadventure, mishap, reversal, setback ♦ adjective **7** opposite, contrary, converse

revert verb return, come back, go back, resume

review noun **1** critique, commentary, criticism, evaluation, judgment, notice **2** magazine, journal, periodical **3** survey, analysis, examination, scrutiny, study **4** Military inspection, march past, parade ♦ verb **5** assess, criticize, evaluate, judge, study **6** reconsider, reassess, re-evaluate, re-examine, rethink, revise, think over **7** look back on, recall, recollect, reflect on, remember **8** inspect, examine

reviewer noun critic, commentator, judge

revile verb malign, abuse, bad-mouth (slang, chiefly U.S. & Canad.), denigrate, knock (informal), reproach, run down, slag (off) (slang), vilify

revise verb **1** change, alter, amend, correct, edit, emend, redo, review, rework, update **2** study, go over, run through, swot up (Brit. informal)

revision noun **1** change, amendment, correction, emendation, updating

2 studying, homework, swotting (Brit. informal)

revival noun renewal, reawakening, rebirth, renaissance, resurgence, resurrection, revitalization

revive verb revitalize, awaken, bring round, come round, invigorate, reanimate, recover, refresh, rekindle, renew, restore

revoke verb cancel, annul, countermand, disclaim, invalidate, negate, nullify, obviate, quash, repeal, rescind, retract, reverse, set aside, withdraw

revolt noun **1** uprising, insurgency, insurrection, mutiny, rebellion, revolution, rising ♦ verb **2** rebel, mutiny, resist, rise **3** disgust, gross out (U.S. slang), make one's flesh creep, nauseate, repel, repulse, sicken, turn one's stomach

revolting adjective disgusting, foul, horrible, horrid, nauseating, repellent, repugnant, repulsive, sickening, yucky or yukky (slang)

revolution noun **1** revolt, insurgency, mutiny, rebellion, rising, uprising **2** transformation, innovation, reformation, sea change, shift, upheaval **3** rotation, circle, circuit, cycle, lap, orbit, spin, turn

revolutionary adjective **1** rebel, extremist, insurgent, radical, subversive **2** new, different, drastic, ground-breaking, innovative, novel, progressive, radical ♦ noun **3** rebel, insurgent, revolutionist

revolutionize verb transform, modernize, reform

revolve verb <u>rotate</u>, circle, go round, orbit, spin, turn, twist, wheel, whirl

revulsion noun <u>disgust</u>, abhorrence, detestation, loathing, repugnance, repulsion

reward noun 1 <u>payment</u>, bounty, premium, prize, recompense, repayment, return, wages 2 <u>punishment</u>, comeuppance (slang), just deserts, retribution ♦ verb 3 <u>pay</u>, compensate, recompense, remunerate, repay

rewarding adjective <u>worthwhile</u>, beneficial, enriching, fruitful, fulfilling, productive, profitable, satisfying, valuable

rhapsodize verb <u>enthuse</u>, go into ecstasies, gush, rave (informal)

rhetoric noun 1 <u>oratory</u>, eloquence 2 <u>hyperbole</u>, bombast, grandiloquence, magniloquence, verbosity, wordiness

rhetorical adjective <u>oratorical</u>, bombastic, declamatory, grandiloquent, high-flown, magniloquent, verbose

rhyme noun 1 <u>poetry</u>, ode, poem, song, verse ♦ verb 2 <u>sound like</u>, harmonize

rhythm noun <u>beat</u>, accent, cadence, lilt, metre, pulse, swing, tempo, time

rhythmic, rhythmical adjective <u>cadenced</u>, lilting, metrical, musical, periodic, pulsating, throbbing

ribald adjective <u>rude</u>, bawdy, blue, broad, coarse, earthy, naughty, near the knuckle (informal), obscene, racy, smutty, vulgar

rich adjective 1 <u>wealthy</u>, affluent, loaded (slang), moneyed, prosperous, well-heeled (informal), well-off, well-to-do 2 <u>well-stocked</u>, full, productive, well-supplied 3 <u>abundant</u>, abounding, ample, copious, fertile, fruitful, lush, luxurious, plentiful, productive, prolific 4 <u>full-bodied</u>, creamy, fatty, luscious, succulent, sweet, tasty

riches plural noun <u>wealth</u>, affluence, assets, fortune, plenty, resources, substance, treasure

richly adverb 1 <u>elaborately</u>, elegantly, expensively, exquisitely, gorgeously, lavishly, luxuriously, opulently, splendidly, sumptuously 2 <u>fully</u>, amply, appropriately, properly, suitably, thoroughly, well

rickety adjective <u>shaky</u>, insecure, precarious, ramshackle, tottering, unsound, unsteady, wobbly

rid verb 1 <u>free</u>, clear, deliver, disburden, disencumber, make free, purge, relieve, unburden 2 **get rid of** <u>dispose of</u>, dump, eject, eliminate, expel, remove, throw away or out

riddle noun <u>puzzle</u>, conundrum, enigma, mystery, poser, problem

riddled adjective <u>filled</u>, damaged, infested, permeated, pervaded, spoilt

ride verb 1 <u>control</u>, handle, manage 2 <u>travel</u>, be carried, go, move ♦ noun 3 <u>trip</u>, drive, jaunt, journey, lift, outing

ridicule noun 1 <u>mockery</u>, chaff, derision, gibe, jeer, laughter, raillery, scorn ♦ verb 2 <u>laugh at</u>, chaff, deride, jeer, make fun of, mock, poke fun at, sneer

ridiculous adjective laughable, absurd, comical, farcical, funny, ludicrous, risible, silly, stupid

rife adjective widespread, common, frequent, general, prevalent, rampant, ubiquitous, universal

riffraff noun rabble, hoi polloi, ragtag and bobtail

rifle verb ransack, burgle, go through, loot, pillage, plunder, rob, sack, strip

rift noun 1 breach, disagreement, division, falling out (informal), quarrel, separation, split 2 split, break, cleft, crack, crevice, fault, fissure, flaw, gap, opening

rig verb 1 fix (informal), arrange, engineer, gerrymander, manipulate, tamper with 2 equip, fit out, furnish, kit out, outfit, supply ♦ noun 3 apparatus, equipment, fittings, fixtures, gear, tackle

right adjective 1 just, equitable, ethical, fair, good, honest, lawful, moral, proper 2 correct, accurate, exact, factual, genuine, precise, true, valid 3 proper, appropriate, becoming, desirable, done, fit, fitting, seemly, suitable ♦ adverb 4 correctly, accurately, exactly, genuinely, precisely, truly 5 properly, appropriately, aptly, fittingly, suitably 6 straight, directly, promptly, quickly, straightaway 7 exactly, precisely, squarely ♦ noun 8 claim, authority, business, due, freedom, liberty, licence, permission, power, prerogative,

privilege ♦ verb 9 rectify, correct, fix, put right, redress, settle, sort out, straighten

right away adverb immediately, at once, directly, forthwith, instantly, now, pronto (informal), straightaway

righteous adjective virtuous, ethical, fair, good, honest, honourable, just, moral, pure, upright

righteousness noun virtue, goodness, honesty, honour, integrity, justice, morality, probity, purity, rectitude, uprightness

rightful adjective lawful, due, just, legal, legitimate, proper, real, true, valid

rigid adjective 1 strict, exact, fixed, inflexible, rigorous, set, stringent, unbending, uncompromising 2 stiff, inflexible, unyielding

rigmarole noun procedure, bother, carry-on (informal, chiefly Brit.), fuss, hassle (informal), nonsense, palaver, pantomime (informal), performance (informal)

rigorous adjective strict, demanding, exacting, hard, harsh, inflexible, severe, stern, stringent, tough

rigour noun 1 strictness, harshness, inflexibility, rigidity, sternness, stringency 2 hardship, ordeal, privation, suffering, trial

rig-out noun outfit, costume, dress, garb, gear (informal), get-up (informal), togs

rig out verb 1 dress, array, attire, clothe, costume, kit out 2 equip, fit, furnish, kit out, outfit

rig up verb set up, arrange, assemble, build, construct, erect, fix up, improvise, put together, put up

rile verb anger, aggravate (*informal*), annoy, get or put one's back up, irk, irritate

rim noun edge, border, brim, brink, lip, margin, verge

rind noun skin, crust, husk, outer layer, peel

ring[1] verb 1 chime, clang, peal, reverberate, sound, toll 2 phone, buzz (*informal*), call, telephone ♦ noun 3 chime, knell, peal 4 call, buzz (*informal*), phone call

ring[2] noun 1 circle, band, circuit, halo, hoop, loop, round 2 arena, circus, enclosure, rink 3 gang, association, band, cartel, circle, group, mob, syndicate ♦ verb 4 encircle, enclose, gird, girdle, surround

rinse verb 1 wash, bathe, clean, cleanse, dip, splash ♦ noun 2 wash, bath, dip, splash

riot noun 1 disturbance, anarchy, confusion, disorder, lawlessness, strife, tumult, turbulence, turmoil, upheaval 2 revelry, carousal, festivity, frolic, high jinks, merrymaking 3 profusion, display, extravaganza, show, splash 4 run riot: a rampage, be out of control, go wild b grow profusely, spread like wildfire ♦ verb 5 rampage, go on the rampage, run riot

riotous adjective 1 unrestrained, boisterous, loud, noisy, uproarious, wild 2 unruly, anarchic, disorderly, lawless, rebellious, rowdy, ungovernable, violent

rip verb 1 tear, burst, claw, cut, gash, lacerate, rend, slash, slit, split ♦ noun 2 tear, cut, gash, hole, laceration, rent, slash, slit, split

ripe adjective 1 mature, mellow, ready, ripened, seasoned 2 suitable, auspicious, favourable, ideal, opportune, right, timely

ripen verb mature, burgeon, develop, grow ripe, season

rip-off noun swindle, cheat, con (*informal*), con trick (*informal*), fraud, scam (*slang*), theft

rip off verb Slang swindle, cheat, con (*informal*), defraud, fleece, rob, skin (*slang*)

riposte noun 1 retort, answer, comeback (*informal*), rejoinder, reply, response, sally ♦ verb 2 retort, answer, come back, reply, respond

rise verb 1 get up, arise, get to one's feet, stand up 2 go up, ascend, climb 3 advance, get on, progress, prosper 4 get steeper, ascend, go uphill, slope upwards 5 increase, go up, grow, intensify, mount 6 rebel, mutiny, revolt 7 originate, happen, issue, occur, spring ♦ noun 8 increase, upsurge, upswing, upturn 9 advancement, climb, progress, promotion 10 upward slope, ascent, elevation, incline 11 pay increase, increment, raise (*U.S.*) 12 give rise to cause, bring about, effect, produce, result in

risk noun 1 danger, chance, gamble, hazard, jeopardy, peril, pitfall, possibility ♦ verb 2 dare, chance, endanger, gamble, hazard, imperil, jeopardize, venture

risky adjective <u>dangerous</u>, chancy (informal), dicey (informal, chiefly Brit.), dodgy (Brit., Austral., & N.Z. informal), hazardous, perilous, uncertain, unsafe

risqué adjective <u>suggestive</u>, bawdy, blue, improper, indelicate, naughty, near the knuckle (informal), racy, ribald

rite noun <u>ceremony</u>, custom, observance, practice, procedure, ritual

ritual noun 1 <u>ceremony</u>, observance, rite 2 <u>custom</u>, convention, habit, practice, procedure, protocol, routine, tradition ♦ adjective 3 <u>ceremonial</u>, conventional, customary, habitual, routine

ritzy adjective <u>luxurious</u>, de luxe, grand, high-class, luxury, plush (informal), posh (informal, chiefly Brit.), sumptuous, swanky (informal)

rival noun 1 <u>opponent</u>, adversary, competitor, contender, contestant ♦ adjective 2 <u>competing</u>, conflicting, opposing ♦ verb 3 <u>equal</u>, be a match for, come up to, compare with, compete, match

rivalry noun <u>competition</u>, conflict, contention, contest, opposition

river noun 1 <u>stream</u>, brook, burn (Scot.), creek, tributary, waterway 2 <u>flow</u>, flood, rush, spate, torrent

riveting adjective <u>enthralling</u>, absorbing, captivating, engrossing, fascinating, gripping, hypnotic, spellbinding

road noun <u>way</u>, course, highway, lane, motorway, path, pathway, roadway, route, track

roam verb <u>wander</u>, prowl, ramble, range, rove, stray, travel, walk

roar verb 1 <u>cry</u>, bawl, bay, bellow, howl, shout, yell 2 <u>guffaw</u>, hoot, laugh heartily, split one's sides (informal) ♦ noun 3 <u>cry</u>, bellow, howl, outcry, shout, yell 4 <u>guffaw</u>, hoot

rob verb <u>steal from</u>, burgle, cheat, con (informal), defraud, deprive, dispossess, do out of (informal), hold up, loot, mug (informal), pillage, plunder, raid

robber noun <u>thief</u>, bandit, brigand, burglar, cheat, con man (informal), fraud, looter, mugger (informal), plunderer, raider

robbery noun <u>theft</u>, burglary, hold-up, larceny, mugging (informal), pillage, plunder, raid, rip-off (slang), stealing, stick-up (slang, chiefly U.S.), swindle

robe noun 1 <u>gown</u>, costume, habit ♦ verb 2 <u>clothe</u>, dress, garb

robot noun <u>machine</u>, android, automaton, mechanical man

robust adjective <u>strong</u>, fit, hale, hardy, healthy, muscular, powerful, stout, strapping, sturdy, tough, vigorous

rock[1] noun <u>stone</u>, boulder

rock[2] verb 1 <u>sway</u>, lurch, pitch, reel, roll, swing, toss 2 <u>shock</u>, astonish, astound, shake, stagger, stun, surprise

rocky[1] adjective <u>rough</u>, craggy, rugged, stony

rocky[2] adjective <u>unstable</u>, rickety,

shaky, unsteady, wobbly

rod noun stick, bar, baton, cane, pole, shaft, staff, wand

rogue noun scoundrel, blackguard, crook (informal), fraud, rascal, scally (Northwest English dialect), scamp, villain

role noun 1 job, capacity, duty, function, part, position, post, task 2 part, character, portrayal, representation

roll verb 1 turn, go round, revolve, rotate, spin, swivel, trundle, twirl, wheel, whirl 2 wind, bind, enfold, envelop, furl, swathe, wrap 3 flow, run, undulate 4 level, even, flatten, press, smooth 5 tumble, lurch, reel, rock, sway, toss ♦ noun 6 turn, cycle, reel, revolution, rotation, spin, twirl, wheel, whirl 7 register, census, index, list, record 8 rumble, boom, reverberation, roar, thunder

rollicking adjective boisterous, carefree, devil-may-care, exuberant, hearty, jaunty, lively, playful

roly-poly adjective plump, buxom, chubby, fat, podgy, rounded, tubby

romance noun 1 love affair, affair, amour, attachment, liaison, relationship 2 excitement, charm, colour, fascination, glamour, mystery 3 story, fairy tale, fantasy, legend, love story, melodrama, tale

romantic adjective 1 loving, amorous, fond, passionate, sentimental, tender 2 idealistic, dreamy, impractical, starry-eyed, unrealistic 3 exciting, colourful,

fascinating, glamorous, mysterious ♦ noun 4 idealist, dreamer, sentimentalist

romp verb 1 frolic, caper, cavort, frisk, gambol, have fun, sport 2 win easily, walk it (informal), win by a mile (informal), win hands down ♦ noun 3 frolic, caper, lark (informal)

room noun 1 chamber, apartment, office 2 space, area, capacity, expanse, extent, leeway, margin, range, scope 3 opportunity, chance, occasion, scope

roomy adjective spacious, ample, broad, capacious, commodious, extensive, generous, large, sizable or sizeable, wide

root[1] noun 1 stem, rhizome, tuber 2 source, base, bottom, cause, core, foundation, heart, nucleus, origin, seat, seed 3 roots sense of belonging, birthplace, cradle, family, heritage, home, origins ♦ verb 4 establish, anchor, fasten, fix, ground, implant, moor, set, stick

root[2] verb dig, burrow, ferret

rooted adjective deep-seated, confirmed, deep, deeply felt, entrenched, established, firm, fixed, ingrained

root out verb get rid of, abolish, do away with, eliminate, eradicate, exterminate, extirpate, remove, weed out

rope noun 1 cord, cable, hawser, line, strand 2 know the ropes be experienced, be an old hand, be knowledgeable

rope in verb persuade, engage, enlist, inveigle, involve, talk into

ropey, ropy adjective Informal
1 inferior, deficient, inadequate, of poor quality, poor, substandard **2** unwell, below par, off colour, under the weather (informal)

roster noun rota, agenda, catalogue, list, register, roll, schedule, table

rostrum noun stage, dais, platform, podium, stand

rosy adjective **1** pink, red **2** glowing, blooming, healthy-looking, radiant, ruddy **3** promising, auspicious, bright, cheerful, encouraging, favourable, hopeful, optimistic

rot verb **1** decay, crumble, decompose, deteriorate, go bad, moulder, perish, putrefy, spoil **2** deteriorate, decline, waste away ◆ noun **3** decay, blight, canker, corruption, decomposition, mould, putrefaction **4** Informal nonsense, claptrap (informal), codswallop (Brit. slang), drivel, garbage (chiefly U.S.), hogwash, poppycock (informal), rubbish, stuff and nonsense, trash, tripe (informal), twaddle

rotary adjective revolving, rotating, spinning, turning

rotate verb **1** revolve, go round, gyrate, pivot, reel, spin, swivel, turn, wheel **2** take turns, alternate, switch

rotation noun **1** revolution, orbit, reel, spin, spinning, turn, turning, wheel **2** sequence, alternation, cycle, succession, switching

rotten adjective **1** decaying, bad, corrupt, crumbling, decomposing, festering, mouldy, perished, putrescent, rank, sour, stinking **2** corrupt, crooked (informal), dishonest, dishonourable, immoral, perfidious **3** Informal despicable, base, contemptible, dirty, mean, nasty **4** Informal inferior, crummy (slang), duff (Brit. informal), inadequate, lousy (slang), poor, substandard, unsatisfactory

rotter noun scoundrel, blackguard, bounder (old-fashioned Brit. slang), cad (Brit. informal), rat (informal)

rotund adjective **1** round, globular, rounded, spherical **2** plump, chubby, corpulent, fat, fleshy, podgy, portly, stout, tubby

rough adjective **1** uneven, broken, bumpy, craggy, irregular, jagged, rocky, stony **2** ungracious, blunt, brusque, coarse, impolite, rude, unceremonious, uncivil, uncouth, unmannerly **3** approximate, estimated, general, imprecise, inexact, sketchy, vague **4** stormy, choppy, squally, turbulent, wild **5** nasty, cruel, hard, harsh, tough, unfeeling, unpleasant, violent **6** basic, crude, imperfect, incomplete, rudimentary, sketchy, unfinished, unpolished, unrefined **7** unpleasant, arduous, hard, tough, uncomfortable ◆ verb **8** rough out outline, draft, plan, sketch ◆ noun **9** outline, draft, mock-up, preliminary sketch

rough-and-ready adjective makeshift, crude, improvised, provisional, sketchy, stopgap, unpolished, unrefined

round adjective **1** spherical, circular, curved, cylindrical, globular, rotund, rounded **2** plump, ample, fleshy, full, full-fleshed, rotund ♦ verb **3** go round, bypass, circle, encircle, flank, skirt, turn ♦ noun **4** sphere, ball, band, circle, disc, globe, orb, ring **5** stage, division, lap, level, period, session, turn **6** series, cycle, sequence, session, succession **7** course, beat, circuit, routine, schedule, series, tour

roundabout adjective indirect, circuitous, devious, discursive, evasive, oblique, tortuous

round off verb complete, close, conclude, finish off

roundup noun gathering, assembly, collection, herding, marshalling, muster, rally

round up verb gather, collect, drive, group, herd, marshal, muster, rally

rouse verb **1** wake up, awaken, call, rise, wake **2** excite, agitate, anger, animate, incite, inflame, move, provoke, stimulate, stir

rousing adjective lively, exciting, inspiring, moving, spirited, stimulating, stirring

rout noun **1** defeat, beating, debacle, drubbing, overthrow, pasting (slang), thrashing ♦ verb **2** defeat, beat, conquer, crush, destroy, drub, overthrow, thrash, wipe the floor with (informal)

route noun way, beat, circuit, course, direction, itinerary, journey, path, road

routine noun **1** procedure,

custom, method, order, pattern, practice, programme ♦ adjective **2** usual, customary, everyday, habitual, normal, ordinary, standard, typical **3** boring, dull, humdrum, predictable, tedious, tiresome

rove verb wander, drift, ramble, range, roam, stray, traipse (informal)

row[1] noun line, bank, column, file, range, series, string

row[2] noun **1** dispute, brawl, quarrel, squabble, tiff, trouble **2** disturbance, commotion, noise, racket, rumpus, tumult, uproar ♦ verb **3** quarrel, argue, dispute, fight, squabble, wrangle

rowdy adjective **1** disorderly, loud, noisy, rough, unruly, wild ♦ noun **2** hooligan, lout, ruffian, tearaway (Brit.), yob or yobbo (Brit. slang)

royal adjective **1** regal, imperial, kingly, princely, queenly, sovereign **2** splendid, grand, impressive, magnificent, majestic, stately

rub verb **1** polish, clean, scour, shine, wipe **2** chafe, abrade, fray, grate, scrape ♦ noun **3** polish, shine, stroke, wipe **4** massage, caress, kneading

rubbish noun **1** waste, garbage (chiefly U.S.), junk (informal), litter, lumber, refuse, scrap, trash **2** nonsense, claptrap (informal), codswallop (Brit. slang), garbage (chiefly U.S.), hogwash, hot air (informal), rot, tommyrot, trash, tripe (informal), twaddle

rub out verb erase, cancel, delete, efface, obliterate, remove, wipe out

ructions *plural noun Informal* uproar, commotion, disturbance, fracas, fuss, hue and cry, row, trouble

ruddy *adjective* rosy, blooming, fresh, glowing, healthy, radiant, red, reddish, rosy-cheeked

rude *adjective* **1** impolite, abusive, cheeky, discourteous, disrespectful, ill-mannered, impertinent, impudent, insolent, insulting, uncivil, unmannerly **2** vulgar, boorish, brutish, coarse, graceless, loutish, oafish, rough, uncivilized, uncouth, uncultured **3** unpleasant, abrupt, harsh, sharp, startling, sudden **4** roughly-made, artless, crude, inartistic, inelegant, makeshift, primitive, raw, rough, simple

rudimentary *adjective* basic, early, elementary, fundamental, initial, primitive, undeveloped

rudiments *plural noun* basics, beginnings, elements, essentials, foundation, fundamentals

rue *verb* regret, be sorry for, kick oneself for, lament, mourn, repent

rueful *adjective* regretful, contrite, mournful, penitent, remorseful, repentant, sorrowful, sorry

ruffian *noun* thug, brute, bully, heavy (*slang*), hoodlum, hooligan, rough (*informal*), tough

ruffle *verb* **1** disarrange, dishevel, disorder, mess up, rumple, tousle **2** annoy, agitate, fluster, irritate, nettle, peeve (*informal*), upset

rugged *adjective* **1** rough, broken, bumpy, craggy, difficult, irregular, jagged, ragged, rocky, uneven **2** strong-featured,

rough-hewn, weather-beaten **3** tough, brawny, burly, husky (*informal*), muscular, robust, strong, sturdy, well-built

ruin *verb* **1** destroy, crush, defeat, demolish, devastate, lay waste, smash, wreck **2** bankrupt, impoverish, pauperize **3** spoil, blow (*slang*), botch, damage, make a mess of, mess up, screw up (*informal*) ♦ *noun* **4** destruction, breakdown, collapse, defeat, devastation, downfall, fall, undoing, wreck **5** disrepair, decay, disintegration, ruination, wreckage **6** bankruptcy, destitution, insolvency

ruinous *adjective* **1** devastating, calamitous, catastrophic, destructive, dire, disastrous, shattering **2** extravagant, crippling, immoderate, wasteful

rule *noun* **1** regulation, axiom, canon, decree, direction, guideline, law, maxim, precept, principle, tenet **2** custom, convention, habit, practice, procedure, routine, tradition **3** government, authority, command, control, dominion, jurisdiction, mastery, power, regime, reign **4 as a rule** usually, generally, mainly, normally, on the whole, ordinarily ♦ *verb* **5** govern, be in authority, be in power, command, control, direct, reign **6** be prevalent, be customary, predominate, preponderate, prevail **7** decree, decide, judge, pronounce, settle

rule out *verb* exclude, ban, debar, dismiss, disqualify, eliminate, leave out, preclude, prohibit, reject

ruler noun 1 governor, commander, controller, head of state, king or queen, leader, lord, monarch, potentate, sovereign 2 measure, rule, yardstick

ruling noun 1 decision, adjudication, decree, judgment, pronouncement, verdict ♦ adjective 2 governing, commanding, controlling, reigning 3 predominant, chief, dominant, main, pre-eminent, preponderant, prevailing, principal

ruminate verb ponder, cogitate, consider, contemplate, deliberate, mull over, muse, reflect, think, turn over in one's mind

rummage verb search, delve, forage, hunt, ransack, root

rumour noun story, buzz, dirt (U.S. slang), gossip, hearsay, news, report, talk, whisper, word

rump noun buttocks, backside (informal), bottom, bum (Brit. slang), buns (U.S. slang), butt (U.S. & Canad. informal), derrière (euphemistic), hindquarters, posterior, rear, rear end, seat

rumpus noun commotion, disturbance, furore, fuss, hue and cry, noise, row, uproar

run verb 1 race, bolt, dash, gallop, hare (Brit. informal), hurry, jog, leg it (informal), lope, rush, scurry, sprint 2 flee, beat a retreat, beat it (slang), bolt, do a runner (slang), escape, leg it (informal), make a run for it, take flight, take off (informal), take to one's heels 3 move, course, glide, go, pass, roll, skim 4 work, function, go, operate, perform

5 manage, administer, be in charge of, control, direct, handle, head, lead, operate 6 continue, extend, go, proceed, reach, stretch 7 flow, discharge, go, gush, leak, pour, spill, spout, stream 8 melt, dissolve, go soft, liquefy 9 publish, display, feature, print 10 compete, be a candidate, contend, put oneself up for, stand, take part 11 smuggle, bootleg, traffic in ♦ noun 12 race, dash, gallop, jog, rush, sprint, spurt 13 ride, drive, excursion, jaunt, outing, spin (informal), trip 14 sequence, course, period, season, series, spell, stretch, string 15 enclosure, coop, pen **16 in the long run** eventually, in the end, ultimately

run across verb meet, bump into, come across, encounter, run into

runaway noun 1 fugitive, deserter, escapee, refugee, truant ♦ adjective 2 escaped, fleeing, fugitive, loose, wild

run away verb flee, abscond, bolt, do a runner (slang), escape, fly the coop (U.S. & Canad. informal), make a run for it, scram (informal), take to one's heels

run-down adjective 1 exhausted, below par, debilitated, drained, enervated, unhealthy, weak, weary, worn-out 2 dilapidated, broken-down, decrepit, ramshackle, seedy, shabby, worn-out

run down verb 1 criticize, bad-mouth (slang, chiefly U.S. & Canad.), belittle, decry, denigrate, disparage, knock (*informal*), rubbish (*informal*), slag (off) (*slang*) **2** reduce, curtail, cut, cut back, decrease, downsize, trim **3** knock down, hit, knock over, run into, run over **4** weaken, debilitate, exhaust

run into *verb* **1** meet, bump into, come across or upon, encounter, run across **2** hit, collide with, strike

runner *noun* **1** athlete, jogger, sprinter **2** messenger, courier, dispatch bearer, errand boy

running *adjective* **1** continuous, constant, incessant, perpetual, unbroken, uninterrupted **2** flowing, moving, streaming ♦ *noun* **3** management, administration, control, direction, leadership, organization, supervision **4** working, functioning, maintenance, operation, performance

runny *adjective* flowing, fluid, liquefied, liquid, melted, watery

run off *verb* flee, bolt, do a runner (*slang*), escape, fly the coop (*U.S. & Canad. informal*), make off, run away, take flight, take to one's heels

run-of-the-mill *adjective* ordinary, average, bog-standard (*Brit. & Irish slang*), mediocre, middling, passable, tolerable, undistinguished, unexceptional

run out *verb* be used up, be exhausted, dry up, end, fail, finish, give out

run over *verb* **1** knock down, hit, knock over, run down **2** go through, check, go over,

rehearse, run through

rupture *noun* **1** break, breach, burst, crack, fissure, rent, split, tear ♦ *verb* **2** break, burst, crack, separate, sever, split, tear

rural *adjective* rustic, agricultural, country, pastoral, sylvan

ruse *noun* trick, device, dodge, hoax, manoeuvre, ploy, stratagem, subterfuge

rush *verb* **1** hurry, bolt, career, dash, fly, hasten, race, run, shoot, speed, tear **2** push, hurry, hustle, press **3** attack, charge, storm ♦ *noun* **4** hurry, charge, dash, haste, race, scramble, stampede, surge **5** attack, assault, charge, onslaught ♦ *adjective* **6** hasty, fast, hurried, quick, rapid, swift, urgent

rust *noun* **1** corrosion, oxidation **2** mildew, blight, mould, must, rot ♦ *verb* **3** corrode, oxidize

rustic *adjective* **1** rural, country, pastoral, sylvan **2** uncouth, awkward, coarse, crude, rough ♦ *noun* **3** yokel, boor, bumpkin, clod, clodhopper (*informal*), hick (*informal, chiefly U.S. & Canad.*), peasant

rustle *verb* **1** crackle, crinkle, whisper ♦ *noun* **2** crackle, crinkling, rustling, whisper

rusty *adjective* **1** corroded, oxidized, rust-covered, rusted **2** reddish, chestnut, coppery, reddish-brown, russet, rust-coloured **3** out of practice, stale, unpractised, weak

rut *noun* **1** groove, furrow, indentation, track, trough, wheel mark **2** habit, dead end, pattern, routine, system

ruthless adjective merciless, brutal, callous, cruel, harsh, heartless, pitiless, relentless, remorseless

S s

sabotage noun 1 damage, destruction, disruption, subversion, wrecking ◆ verb 2 damage, destroy, disable, disrupt, incapacitate, subvert, vandalize, wreck

saccharine adjective oversweet, cloying, honeyed, nauseating, sickly

sack¹ noun 1 **the sack** dismissal, discharge, the axe (informal), the boot (slang), the push (slang) ◆ verb 2 dismiss, axe (informal), discharge, fire (informal), give (someone) the push (informal)

sack² noun 1 plundering, looting, pillage ◆ verb 2 plunder, loot, pillage, raid, rob, ruin, strip

sacred adjective 1 holy, blessed, divine, hallowed, revered, sanctified 2 religious, ecclesiastical, holy 3 inviolable, protected, sacrosanct

sacrifice noun 1 surrender, loss, renunciation 2 offering, oblation ◆ verb 3 give up, forego, forfeit, let go, lose, say goodbye to, surrender 4 offer, immolate, offer up

sacrilege noun desecration, blasphemy, heresy, impiety, irreverence, profanation, violation

sacrilegious adjective profane, blasphemous, desecrating, impious, irreligious, irreverent

sacrosanct adjective inviolable, hallowed, inviolate, sacred, sanctified, set apart, untouchable

sad adjective 1 unhappy, blue, dejected, depressed, doleful, down, low, low-spirited, melancholy, mournful, woebegone 2 tragic, depressing, dismal, grievous, harrowing, heart-rending, moving, pathetic, pitiful, poignant, upsetting 3 deplorable, bad, lamentable, sorry, wretched

sadden verb upset, deject, depress, distress, grieve, make sad

saddle verb burden, encumber, load, lumber (Brit. informal)

sadistic adjective cruel, barbarous, brutal, ruthless, vicious

sadness noun unhappiness, dejection, depression, despondency, grief, melancholy, misery, poignancy, sorrow, the blues

safe adjective 1 secure, impregnable, in safe hands, out of danger, out of harm's way, protected, safe and sound 2 unharmed, all right, intact, O.K. or okay (informal), undamaged, unhurt, unscathed 3 risk-free, certain, impregnable, secure, sound ◆ noun 4 strongbox, coffer, deposit box, repository, safe-deposit box, vault

safeguard verb 1 protect, defend, guard, look after, preserve ◆ noun 2 protection, defence, guard, security

safely adverb in safety, in one piece, safe and sound, with impunity, without risk

safety noun 1 security,

impregnability, protection
2 shelter, cover, refuge, sanctuary

sag verb **1** sink, bag, dip, droop, fall, give way, hang loosely, slump **2** tire, droop, flag, wane, weaken, wilt

saga noun tale, epic, narrative, story, yarn

sage noun **1** wise man, elder, guru, master, philosopher
◆ adjective **2** wise, judicious, sagacious, sapient, sensible

sail verb **1** embark, set sail **2** glide, drift, float, fly, skim, soar, sweep, wing **3** pilot, steer

sailor noun mariner, marine, sea dog, seafarer, seaman

saintly adjective virtuous, godly, holy, pious, religious, righteous, saintlike

sake noun **1** benefit, account, behalf, good, interest, welfare **2** purpose, aim, end, motive, objective, reason

salacious adjective lascivious, carnal, erotic, lecherous, lewd, libidinous, lustful

salary noun pay, earnings, income, wage, wages

sale noun **1** selling, deal, disposal, marketing, transaction **2 for sale** available, obtainable, on the market

salient adjective prominent, conspicuous, important, noticeable, outstanding, pronounced, striking

sallow adjective wan, anaemic, pale, pallid, pasty, sickly, unhealthy, yellowish

salt noun **1** seasoning, flavour, relish, savour, taste **2 with a grain** or **pinch of salt** sceptically,

cynically, disbelievingly, suspiciously, with reservations
◆ adjective **3** salty, brackish, briny, saline

salty adjective salt, brackish, briny, saline

salubrious adjective healthy, beneficial, good for one, health-giving, wholesome

salutary adjective beneficial, advantageous, good for one, profitable, useful, valuable

salute noun **1** greeting, address, recognition, salutation ◆ verb **2** greet, acknowledge, address, hail, welcome **3** honour, acknowledge, pay tribute or homage to, recognize

salvage verb save, recover, redeem, rescue, retrieve

salvation noun saving, deliverance, escape, preservation, redemption, rescue

salve noun ointment, balm, cream, lotion

same adjective **1** aforementioned, aforesaid **2** identical, alike, corresponding, duplicate, equal, twin **3** unchanged, changeless, consistent, constant, invariable, unaltered, unvarying

sample noun **1** specimen, example, instance, model, pattern ◆ verb **2** test, experience, inspect, taste, try ◆ adjective **3** test, representative, specimen, trial

sanctify verb consecrate, cleanse, hallow

sanctimonious adjective holier-than-thou, hypocritical, pious, self-righteous, smug

sanction noun **1** permission,

approval, authority, authorization, backing, O.K. *or* okay (*informal*), stamp *or* seal of approval **2** *often plural* ban, boycott, coercive measures, embargo, penalty ♦ *verb* **3** permit, allow, approve, authorize, endorse

sanctity *noun* **1** sacredness, inviolability **2** holiness, godliness, goodness, grace, piety

sanctuary *noun* **1** shrine, altar, church, temple **2** protection, asylum, haven, refuge, retreat, shelter **3** reserve, conservation area, national park, nature reserve

sane *adjective* **1** rational, all there (*informal*), compos mentis, in one's right mind, mentally sound, of sound mind **2** sensible, balanced, judicious, level-headed, reasonable, sound

sanguine *adjective* cheerful, buoyant, confident, hopeful, optimistic

sanitary *adjective* hygienic, clean, germ-free, healthy, wholesome

sanity *noun* **1** mental health, normality, rationality, reason, saneness **2** good sense, common sense, level-headedness, rationality, sense

sap[1] *noun* **1** vital fluid, essence, lifeblood **2** *Informal* fool, idiot, jerk (*slang, chiefly U.S. & Canad.*), ninny, simpleton, twit (*informal*), wally (*slang*)

sap[2] *verb* weaken, deplete, drain, exhaust, undermine

sarcasm *noun* irony, bitterness, cynicism, derision, mockery, satire

sarcastic *adjective* ironical, acid, biting, caustic, cutting, cynical, mocking, sardonic, sarky (*Brit. informal*), satirical

sardonic *adjective* mocking, cynical, derisive, dry, ironical, sarcastic, sneering, wry

Satan *noun* The Devil, Beelzebub, Lord of the Flies, Lucifer, Mephistopheles, Old Nick (*informal*), Prince of Darkness, The Evil One

satanic *adjective* evil, black, demonic, devilish, diabolic, fiendish, hellish, infernal, wicked

satiate *verb* **1** glut, cloy, gorge, jade, nauseate, overfill, stuff, surfeit **2** satisfy, sate, slake

satire *noun* mockery, burlesque, caricature, irony, lampoon, parody, ridicule

satirical, satiric *adjective* mocking, biting, caustic, cutting, incisive, ironical

satirize *verb* ridicule, burlesque, deride, lampoon, parody, pillory

satisfaction *noun* **1** contentment, comfort, content, enjoyment, happiness, pleasure, pride, repletion, satiety **2** fulfilment, achievement, assuaging, gratification

satisfactory *adjective* adequate, acceptable, all right, average, fair, good enough, passable, sufficient

satisfy *verb* **1** content, assuage, gratify, indulge, pacify, pander to, please, quench, sate, slake **2** fulfil, answer, do, meet, serve, suffice **3** persuade, assure, convince, reassure

saturate *verb* soak, drench, imbue, souse, steep, suffuse, waterlog, wet through

saturated *adjective* drenched, dripping, soaking (wet), sodden, sopping (wet), waterlogged, wet through

saturnine *adjective* gloomy, dour, glum, grave, morose, sombre

saucy *adjective* 1 impudent, cheeky (*informal*), forward, impertinent, insolent, pert, presumptuous, rude 2 jaunty, dashing, gay, natty (*informal*), perky

saunter *verb* 1 stroll, amble, meander, mosey (*informal*), ramble, roam, wander ♦ *noun* 2 stroll, airing, amble, ramble, turn, walk

savage *adjective* 1 wild, feral, undomesticated, untamed 2 uncultivated, rough, rugged, uncivilized 3 cruel, barbarous, bestial, bloodthirsty, brutal, ferocious, fierce, harsh, ruthless, sadistic, vicious 4 primitive, rude, unspoilt ♦ *noun* 5 lout, boor, yahoo, yob (*Brit. slang*) ♦ *verb* 6 attack, lacerate, mangle, maul

savagery *noun* cruelty, barbarity, brutality, ferocity, ruthlessness, viciousness

save *verb* 1 rescue, deliver, free, liberate, recover, redeem, salvage 2 protect, conserve, guard, keep safe, look after, preserve, safeguard 3 keep, collect, gather, hoard, hold, husband, lay by, put by, reserve, set aside, store

saving *noun* 1 economy, bargain, discount, reduction ♦ *adjective* 2 redeeming, compensatory, extenuating

savings *plural noun* nest egg, fund, reserves, resources, store

saviour *noun* rescuer, defender, deliverer, liberator, preserver, protector, redeemer

Saviour *noun* Christ, Jesus, Messiah, Redeemer

savoir-faire *noun* social know-how (*informal*), diplomacy, discretion, finesse, poise, social graces, tact, urbanity

savour *verb* 1 enjoy, appreciate, delight in, luxuriate in, relish, revel in 2 *often with* of suggest, be suggestive, show signs, smack ♦ *noun* 3 flavour, piquancy, relish, smack, smell, tang, taste

savoury *adjective* spicy, appetizing, full-flavoured, luscious, mouthwatering, palatable, piquant, rich, tasty

say *verb* 1 speak, affirm, announce, assert, declare, maintain, mention, pronounce, remark, state, utter, voice 2 suppose, assume, conjecture, estimate, guess, imagine, presume, surmise 3 express, communicate, convey, imply ♦ *noun* 4 chance to speak, voice, vote 5 influence, authority, clout (*informal*), power, weight

saying *noun* proverb, adage, aphorism, axiom, dictum, maxim

scale¹ *noun* flake, lamina, layer, plate

scale² *noun* 1 graduation, gradation, hierarchy, ladder, progression, ranking, sequence, series, steps 2 ratio, proportion 3 extent, range, reach, scope ♦ *verb* 4 climb, ascend, clamber, escalade, mount, surmount **5** <u>adjust</u>, proportion, regulate

scamp noun <u>rascal</u>, devil, imp, monkey, rogue, scallywag (informal)

scamper verb <u>run</u>, dart, dash, hasten, hurry, romp, scoot, scurry, scuttle

scan verb **1** <u>glance over</u>, check, check out (informal), examine, eye, look through, run one's eye over, run over, skim **2** <u>scrutinize</u>, investigate, scour, search, survey, sweep

scandal noun **1** <u>crime</u>, disgrace, embarrassment, offence, sin, wrongdoing **2** <u>shame</u>, defamation, discredit, disgrace, dishonour, ignominy, infamy, opprobrium, stigma **3** <u>gossip</u>, aspersion, dirt, rumours, slander, talk, tattle

scandalize verb <u>shock</u>, affront, appal, horrify, offend, outrage

scandalous adjective **1** <u>shocking</u>, disgraceful, disreputable, infamous, outrageous, shameful, unseemly **2** <u>slanderous</u>, defamatory, libellous, scurrilous, untrue

scant adjective <u>meagre</u>, barely sufficient, little, minimal, sparse

scanty adjective <u>meagre</u>, bare, deficient, inadequate, insufficient, poor, scant, short, skimpy, sparse, thin

scapegoat noun <u>whipping boy</u>, fall guy (informal)

scar noun **1** <u>mark</u>, blemish, injury, wound ♦verb **2** <u>mark</u>, damage, disfigure

scarce adjective <u>rare</u>, few, few and far between, infrequent, in short supply, insufficient, uncommon

scarcely adverb **1** <u>hardly</u>, barely **2** <u>definitely not</u>, hardly

scarcity noun <u>shortage</u>, dearth, deficiency, insufficiency, lack, paucity, rareness, want

scare verb **1** <u>frighten</u>, alarm, dismay, intimidate, panic, shock, startle, terrify ♦noun **2** <u>fright</u>, panic, shock, start, terror

scared adjective <u>frightened</u>, fearful, panicky, panic-stricken, petrified, shaken, startled, terrified

scarper verb Slang <u>run away</u>, abscond, beat it (slang), clear off (informal), disappear, flee, run for it, scram (informal), take to one's heels

scary adjective <u>frightening</u>, alarming, chilling, creepy (informal), horrifying, spine-chilling, spooky (informal), terrifying

scathing adjective <u>critical</u>, biting, caustic, cutting, harsh, sarcastic, scornful, trenchant, withering

scatter verb **1** <u>throw about</u>, diffuse, disseminate, fling, shower, spread, sprinkle, strew **2** <u>disperse</u>, disband, dispel, dissipate

scatterbrain noun <u>featherbrain</u>, butterfly, flibbertigibbet

scenario noun <u>story line</u>, outline, résumé, summary, synopsis

scene noun **1** <u>site</u>, area, locality, place, position, setting, spot **2** <u>setting</u>, backdrop, background, location, set **3** <u>show</u>, display, drama, exhibition, pageant, picture, sight, spectacle **4** act, division, episode, part **5** view, landscape, panorama, prospect, vista **6** fuss, carry-on (*informal, chiefly Brit.*), commotion, exhibition, performance, row, tantrum, to-do **7** *Informal* world, arena, business, environment

scenery *noun* **1** landscape, surroundings, terrain, view, vista **2** *Theatre* set, backdrop, flats, setting, stage set

scenic *adjective* picturesque, beautiful, panoramic, spectacular, striking

scent *noun* **1** fragrance, aroma, bouquet, odour, perfume, smell **2** trail, spoor, track ♦ *verb* **3** detect, discern, nose out, sense, smell, sniff

scented *adjective* fragrant, aromatic, odoriferous, perfumed, sweet-smelling

sceptic *noun* doubter, cynic, disbeliever, doubting Thomas

sceptical *adjective* doubtful, cynical, disbelieving, dubious, incredulous, mistrustful, unconvinced

scepticism *noun* doubt, cynicism, disbelief, incredulity, unbelief

schedule *noun* **1** plan, agenda, calendar, catalogue, inventory, list, programme, timetable ♦ *verb* **2** plan, appoint, arrange, book, organize, programme

scheme *noun* **1** plan, programme, project, proposal, strategy, system, tactics **2** diagram, blueprint, chart, draft, layout, outline, pattern **3** plot, conspiracy, intrigue, manoeuvre, ploy, ruse,

stratagem, subterfuge ♦ *verb* **4** plan, lay plans, project, work out **5** plot, collude, conspire, intrigue, machinate, manoeuvre

scheming *adjective* calculating, artful, conniving, cunning, sly, tricky, underhand, wily

schism *noun* division, breach, break, rift, rupture, separation, split

scholar *noun* **1** intellectual, academic, savant **2** student, disciple, learner, pupil, schoolboy or schoolgirl

scholarly *adjective* learned, academic, bookish, erudite, intellectual, lettered, scholastic

scholarship *noun* **1** learning, book-learning, education, erudition, knowledge **2** bursary, fellowship

scholastic *adjective* learned, academic, lettered, scholarly

school *noun* **1** academy, college, faculty, institute, institution, seminary **2** group, adherents, circle, denomination, devotees, disciples, faction, followers, set ♦ *verb* **3** train, coach, discipline, drill, educate, instruct, tutor

schooling *noun* **1** teaching, education, tuition **2** training, coaching, drill, instruction

science *noun* **1** discipline, body of knowledge, branch of knowledge **2** skill, art, technique

scientific *adjective* systematic, accurate, controlled, exact, mathematical, precise

scientist *noun* inventor, boffin (*informal*), technophile

scintillating *adjective* brilliant, animated, bright, dazzling, exciting, glittering, lively, sparkling, stimulating

scoff[1] verb scorn, belittle, deride, despise, jeer, knock (informal), laugh at, mock, pooh-pooh, ridicule, sneer

scoff[2] verb gobble (up), bolt, devour, gorge oneself on, gulp down, quzzle, wolf

scold verb 1 reprimand, berate, castigate, censure, find fault with, give (someone) a dressing-down, lecture, rebuke, reproach, reprove, tell off (informal), tick off (informal), upbraid ◆ noun 2 nag, shrew, termagant (rare)

scolding noun rebuke, dressing-down (informal), lecture, row, telling-off (informal), ticking-off (informal)

scoop noun 1 ladle, dipper, spoon 2 exclusive, exposé, revelation, sensation ◆ verb 3 often with up lift, gather up, pick up, take up 4 often with out hollow, bail, dig, empty, excavate, gouge, shovel

scope noun 1 opportunity, freedom, latitude, liberty, room, space 2 range, area, capacity, orbit, outlook, reach, span, sphere

scorch verb burn, parch, roast, sear, shrivel, singe, wither

scorching adjective burning, baking, boiling, fiery, flaming, red-hot, roasting, searing

score noun 1 points, grade, mark, outcome, record, result, total 2 grounds, basis, cause, ground, reason 3 grievance, grudge, injury, injustice, wrong 4 scores lots, hundreds, masses,

millions, multitudes, myriads, swarms ◆ verb 5 gain, achieve, chalk up (informal), make, notch up (informal), win 6 keep count, count, record, register, tally 7 cut, deface, gouge, graze, mark, scrape, scratch, slash 8 with out or through cross out, cancel, delete, obliterate, strike out 9 Music arrange, adapt, orchestrate, set

scorn noun 1 contempt, derision, disdain, disparagement, mockery, sarcasm ◆ verb 2 despise, be above, deride, disdain, flout, reject, scoff at, slight, spurn

scornful adjective contemptuous, derisive, disdainful, haughty, jeering, mocking, sarcastic, sardonic, scathing, scoffing, sneering

scoundrel noun rogue, bastard (offensive), blackguard, good-for-nothing, heel (slang), miscreant, ne'er-do-well, rascal, reprobate, rotter (slang, chiefly Brit.), scally (Northwest English dialect), scamp, swine, villain

scour[1] verb rub, abrade, buff, clean, polish, scrub, wash

scour[2] verb search, beat, comb, hunt, ransack

scourge noun 1 affliction, bane, curse, infliction, misfortune, pest, plague, terror, torment 2 whip, cat, lash, strap, switch, thong ◆ verb 3 afflict, curse, plague, terrorize, torment 4 whip, beat, cane, flog, horsewhip, lash, thrash

scout noun 1 vanguard, advance guard, lookout, outrider, precursor, reconnoitrer ◆ verb

2 reconnoitre, investigate, observe, probe, recce (slang), spy, survey, watch

scowl verb **1** glower, frown, lour or lower ♦ noun **2** glower, black look, dirty look, frown

scrabble verb scrape, claw, scramble, scratch

scraggy adjective scrawny, angular, bony, lean, skinny

scram verb go away, abscond, beat it (slang), clear off (informal), get lost (informal), leave, make oneself scarce (informal), make tracks, scarper (Brit. slang), vamoose (slang, chiefly U.S.)

scramble verb **1** struggle, climb, crawl, scrabble, swarm **2** strive, contend, jostle, push, run, rush, vie ♦ noun **3** climb, trek **4** struggle, commotion, competition, confusion, melee or mêlée, race, rush, tussle

scrap[1] noun **1** piece, bit, crumb, fragment, grain, morsel, part, particle, portion, sliver, snippet **2** waste, junk, off cuts **3** scraps leftovers, bits, leavings, remains ♦ verb **4** discard, abandon, ditch (slang), drop, jettison, throw away or out, write off

scrap[2] Informal ♦ noun **1** fight, argument, battle, disagreement, dispute, quarrel, row, squabble, wrangle ♦ verb **2** fight, argue, row, squabble, wrangle

scrape verb **1** graze, bark, rub, scratch, scuff, skin **2** rub, clean, erase, remove, scour **3** grate, grind, rasp, scratch, squeak **4** scrimp, pinch, save, skimp, stint **5** scrape through get by (informal), just make it, struggle

♦ noun **6** Informal predicament, awkward situation, difficulty, dilemma, fix (informal), mess, plight, tight spot

scrapheap noun **on the scrapheap** discarded, ditched (slang), jettisoned, put out to grass (informal), redundant, written off

scrappy adjective fragmentary, bitty, disjointed, incomplete, piecemeal, sketchy, thrown together

scratch verb **1** mark, claw, cut, damage, etch, grate, graze, lacerate, score, scrape **2** withdraw, cancel, delete, eliminate, erase, pull out ♦ noun **3** mark, blemish, claw mark, gash, graze, laceration, scrape **4 up to scratch** adequate, acceptable, satisfactory, sufficient, up to standard ♦ adjective **5** improvised, impromptu, rough-and-ready

scrawl verb scribble, doodle, squiggle, writing

scrawny adjective thin, bony, gaunt, lean, scraggy, skin-and-bones (informal), skinny, undernourished

scream verb cry, bawl, screech, shriek, yell ♦ noun cry, howl, screech, shriek, yell, yelp

screech noun, verb cry, scream, shriek

screen noun **1** cover, awning, canopy, cloak, guard, partition, room divider, shade, shelter, shield **2** mesh, net ♦ verb **3** cover, cloak, conceal, hide, mask, shade, veil **4** protect, defend, guard, shelter, shield **5** vet, evaluate, examine, filter,

gauge, scan, sift, sort
6 broadcast, present, put on,
show

screw verb **1** turn, tighten, twist
2 Informal, often with **out of**
extort, extract, wrest, wring

screw up verb **1** Informal bungle,
botch, make a mess of (informal),
make a mess of (slang), mess up,
mishandle, spoil **2** distort,
contort, pucker, wrinkle

screwy adjective crazy, crackpot
(informal), eccentric, loopy
(informal), nutty (slang), odd,
off-the-wall (slang), out to lunch
(informal), round the bend (Brit.
slang), weird

scribble verb scrawl, dash off,
jot, write

scribe noun copyist, amanuensis,
writer

scrimp verb economize, be
frugal, save, scrape, skimp, stint,
tighten one's belt

script noun **1** text, book, copy,
dialogue, libretto, lines, words
2 handwriting, calligraphy,
penmanship, writing

Scripture noun The Bible, Holy
Bible, Holy Scripture, Holy Writ,
The Good Book, The Gospels,
The Scriptures

scrounge verb Informal cadge,
beg, blag (slang), bum (informal),
freeload (slang), sponge (informal)

scrounger adjective cadger,
freeloader (slang), parasite,
sponger (informal)

scrub verb **1** scour, clean,
cleanse, rub **2** Informal cancel,
abolish, call off, delete, drop,
forget about, give up

scruffy adjective shabby,

ill-groomed, mangy, messy,
ragged, run-down, seedy, tatty,
unkempt, untidy

scrumptious adjective Informal
delicious, appetizing, delectable,
luscious, mouthwatering,
succulent, yummy (slang)

scruple noun **1** misgiving,
compunction, doubt, hesitation,
qualm, reluctance, second
thoughts, uneasiness ◆ verb
2 have misgivings about, demur,
doubt, have qualms about,
hesitate, think twice about

scrupulous adjective **1** moral,
conscientious, honourable,
principled, upright **2** careful,
exact, fastidious, meticulous,
precise, punctilious, rigorous,
strict

scrutinize verb examine, explore,
inspect, investigate, peruse, pore
over, probe, scan, search, study

scrutiny noun examination,
analysis, exploration, inspection,
investigation, perusal, search,
study

scuffle verb **1** fight, clash,
grapple, jostle, struggle, tussle
◆ noun **2** fight, brawl,
commotion, disturbance, fray,
scrimmage, skirmish, tussle

sculpture verb sculpt, carve,
chisel, fashion, form, hew,
model, mould, shape

scum noun **1** impurities, dross,
film, froth **2** rabble, dregs of
society, riffraff, trash (chiefly U.S.
& Canad.)

scupper verb Brit. slang destroy,
defeat, demolish, put paid to,
ruin, torpedo, wreck

scurrilous adjective slanderous,

abusive, defamatory, insulting, scandalous, vituperative

scurry verb 1 <u>hurry</u>, dart, dash, race, scamper, scoot, scuttle, sprint ♦ noun 2 <u>flurry</u>, scampering, whirl

scuttle verb <u>run</u>, bustle, hasten, hurry, rush, scamper, scoot, scurry

sea noun 1 <u>ocean</u>, main, the deep, the waves 2 <u>expanse</u>, abundance, mass, multitude, plethora, profusion 3 **at sea** <u>bewildered</u>, baffled, confused, lost, mystified, puzzled

seafaring adjective <u>nautical</u>, marine, maritime, naval

seal noun 1 <u>authentication</u>, confirmation, imprimatur, insignia, ratification, stamp ♦ verb 2 <u>close</u>, bung, enclose, fasten, plug, shut, stop, stopper, stop up 3 <u>authenticate</u>, confirm, ratify, stamp, validate 4 <u>settle</u>, clinch, conclude, consummate, finalize 5 **seal off** <u>isolate</u>, put out of bounds, quarantine, segregate

seam noun 1 <u>joint</u>, closure 2 <u>layer</u>, lode, stratum, vein 3 <u>ridge</u>, furrow, line, wrinkle

sear verb <u>scorch</u>, burn, sizzle

search verb 1 <u>look</u>, comb, examine, explore, hunt, inspect, investigate, ransack, scour, scrutinize ♦ noun 2 <u>look</u>, examination, exploration, hunt, inspection, investigation, pursuit, quest

searching adjective <u>keen</u>, close, intent, penetrating, piercing, probing, quizzical, sharp

season noun 1 <u>period</u>, spell, term, time ♦ verb 2 <u>flavour</u>, enliven, pep up, salt, spice

seasonable adjective <u>appropriate</u>, convenient, fit, opportune, providential, suitable, timely, well-timed

seasoned adjective <u>experienced</u>, hardened, practised, time-served, veteran

seasoning noun <u>flavouring</u>, condiment, dressing, relish, salt and pepper, sauce, spice

seat noun 1 <u>chair</u>, bench, pew, settle, stall, stool 2 <u>centre</u>, capital, heart, hub, place, site, situation, source 3 <u>residence</u>, abode, ancestral hall, house, mansion 4 <u>membership</u>, chair, constituency, incumbency, place ♦ verb 5 <u>sit</u>, fix, install, locate, place, set, settle 6 <u>hold</u>, accommodate, cater for, contain, sit, take

seating noun <u>accommodation</u>, chairs, places, room, seats

secede verb <u>withdraw</u>, break with, leave, pull out, quit, resign, split from

secluded adjective <u>private</u>, cloistered, cut off, isolated, lonely, out-of-the-way, sheltered, solitary

seclusion noun <u>privacy</u>, isolation, shelter, solitude

second[1] adjective 1 <u>next</u>, following, subsequent, succeeding 2 <u>additional</u>, alternative, extra, further, other 3 <u>inferior</u>, lesser, lower, secondary, subordinate ♦ noun 4 <u>supporter</u>, assistant, backer, helper ♦ verb 5 <u>support</u>, approve, assist, back, endorse, go along with

second² noun moment, flash, instant, jiffy (informal), minute, sec (informal), trice

secondary adjective
1 subordinate, inferior, lesser, lower, minor, unimportant
2 resultant, contingent, derived, indirect 3 backup, auxiliary, fall-back, reserve, subsidiary, supporting

second-class adjective inferior, indifferent, mediocre, second-best, second-rate, undistinguished, uninspiring

second-hand adjective 1 used, hand-me-down (informal), nearly new ♦ adverb 2 indirectly

second in command noun deputy, number two, right-hand man

secondly adverb next, in the second place, second

second-rate adjective inferior, low-grade, low-quality, mediocre, poor, rubbishy, shoddy, substandard, tacky (informal), tawdry, two-bit (U.S. & Canad. slang)

secrecy noun 1 mystery, concealment, confidentiality, privacy, silence 2 secretiveness, clandestineness, covertness, furtiveness, stealth

secret adjective 1 concealed, close, disguised, furtive, hidden, undercover, underground, undisclosed, unknown, unrevealed 2 stealthy, secretive, sly, underhand 3 mysterious, abstruse, arcane, clandestine, cryptic, occult ♦ noun 4 mystery, code, enigma, key 5 in secret secretly, slyly, surreptitiously

secrete¹ verb give off, emanate,

emit, exude

secrete² verb hide, cache, conceal, harbour, stash (informal), stow

secretive adjective reticent, close, deep, reserved, tight-lipped, uncommunicative

secretly adverb in secret, clandestinely, covertly, furtively, privately, quietly, stealthily, surreptitiously

sect noun group, camp, denomination, division, faction, party, schism

sectarian adjective
1 narrow-minded, bigoted, doctrinaire, dogmatic, factional, fanatical, limited, parochial, partisan ♦ noun 2 bigot, dogmatist, extremist, fanatic, partisan, zealot

section noun 1 part, division, fraction, instalment, passage, piece, portion, segment, slice
2 Chiefly U.S. district, area, region, sector, zone

sector noun part, area, district, division, quarter, region, zone

secular adjective worldly, civil, earthly, lay, nonspiritual, temporal

secure adjective 1 safe, immune, protected, unassailable 2 sure, assured, certain, confident, easy, reassured 3 fixed, fast, fastened, firm, immovable, stable, steady ♦ verb 4 obtain, acquire, gain, get, procure, score (slang) 5 fasten, attach, bolt, chain, fix, lock, make fast, tie up

security noun 1 precautions, defence, protection, safeguards, safety measures 2 safety, care, custody, refuge, safekeeping, sanctuary **1** <u>sureness</u>, assurance, certainty, confidence, conviction, positiveness, reliance **4** <u>pledge</u>, collateral, gage, guarantee, hostage, insurance, pawn, surety

sedate _adjective_ <u>calm</u>, collected, composed, cool, dignified, serene, tranquil

sedative _adjective_ **1** <u>calming</u>, anodyne, relaxing, soothing, tranquillizing ◆ _noun_ **2** <u>tranquillizer</u>, anodyne, downer or down (_slang_)

sedentary _adjective_ <u>inactive</u>, desk, desk-bound, seated, sitting

sediment _noun_ <u>dregs</u>, deposit, grounds, lees, residue

sedition _noun_ <u>rabble-rousing</u>, agitation, incitement to riot, subversion

seditious _adjective_ <u>revolutionary</u>, dissident, mutinous, rebellious, refractory, subversive

seduce _verb_ **1** <u>corrupt</u>, debauch, deflower, deprave, dishonour **2** <u>tempt</u>, beguile, deceive, entice, inveigle, lead astray, lure, mislead

seduction _noun_ **1** <u>corruption</u> **2** <u>temptation</u>, enticement, lure, snare

seductive _adjective_ <u>alluring</u>, attractive, bewitching, enticing, inviting, provocative, tempting

seductress _noun_ <u>temptress</u>, enchantress, _femme fatale_, siren, vamp (_informal_)

see _verb_ **1** <u>perceive</u>, behold, catch sight of, discern, distinguish, espy, glimpse, look, make out, notice, observe, sight, spot, witness **2** <u>understand</u>,

appreciate, comprehend, fathom, feel, follow, get, grasp, realize **3** <u>find out</u>, ascertain, determine, discover, learn **4** <u>make sure</u>, ensure, guarantee, make certain, see to it **5** <u>consider</u>, decide, deliberate, reflect, think over **6** <u>visit</u>, confer with, consult, interview, receive, speak to **7** <u>go out with</u>, court, date (_informal, chiefly U.S._), go steady with (_informal_) **8** <u>accompany</u>, escort, lead, show, usher, walk

seed _noun_ **1** <u>grain</u>, egg, embryo, germ, kernel, ovum, pip, spore **2** <u>origin</u>, beginning, germ, nucleus, source, start **3** <u>offspring</u>, children, descendants, issue, progeny **4** **go** or **run** **to seed** <u>decline</u>, decay, degenerate, deteriorate, go downhill (_informal_), go to pot, let oneself go

seedy _adjective_ **1** <u>shabby</u>, dilapidated, grotty (_slang_), grubby, mangy, run-down, scruffy, sleazy, squalid, tatty **2** _Informal_ <u>unwell</u>, ill, off colour, out of sorts, poorly (_informal_), under the weather (_informal_)

seeing _conjunction_ <u>since</u>, as, inasmuch as, in view of the fact that

seek _verb_ **1** <u>look for</u>, be after, follow, hunt, pursue, search for **2** <u>try</u>, aim, aspire to, attempt, endeavour, essay, strive

seem _verb_ <u>appear</u>, assume, give the impression, look

seemly _adjective_ <u>fitting</u>, appropriate, becoming, decent, decorous, fit, proper, suitable

seep _verb_ <u>ooze</u>, exude, leak,

permeate, soak, trickle, well

seer noun prophet, sibyl, soothsayer

seesaw verb alternate, fluctuate, oscillate, swing

seethe verb 1 be furious, be livid, fume, go ballistic (slang, chiefly U.S.), rage, see red (informal), simmer 2 boil, bubble, fizz, foam, froth

see through verb 1 be undeceived by, be wise to (informal), fathom, not fall for, penetrate 2 see (something) through persevere (with), keep at, persist, stick out (informal) 3 see (someone) through help out, stick by, support

segment noun section, bit, division, part, piece, portion, slice, wedge

segregate verb set apart, discriminate against, dissociate, isolate, separate

segregation noun separation, apartheid, discrimination, isolation

seize verb 1 grab, catch up, clutch, grasp, grip, lay hands on, snatch, take 2 confiscate, appropriate, commandeer, impound, take possession of 3 capture, apprehend, arrest, catch, take captive

seizure noun 1 attack, convulsion, fit, paroxysm, spasm 2 capture, apprehension, arrest 3 taking, annexation, commandeering, confiscation, grabbing

seldom adverb rarely, hardly ever, infrequently, not often

select verb 1 choose, opt for, pick, single out ♦ adjective 2 choice, excellent, first-class, hand-picked, special, superior, top-notch (informal) 3 exclusive, cliquish, elite, privileged

selection noun 1 choice, choosing, option, pick, preference 2 range, assortment, choice, collection, medley, variety

selective adjective particular, careful, discerning, discriminating

self-assurance noun confidence, assertiveness, positiveness, self-confidence, self-possession

self-centred adjective selfish, egotistic, narcissistic, self-seeking

self-confidence noun self-assurance, aplomb, confidence, nerve, poise

self-confident adjective self-assured, assured, confident, poised, sure of oneself

self-conscious adjective embarrassed, awkward, bashful, diffident, ill at ease, insecure, nervous, uncomfortable

self-control noun willpower, restraint, self-discipline, self-restraint

self-esteem noun self-respect, confidence, faith in oneself, pride, self-regard

self-evident adjective obvious, clear, incontrovertible, inescapable, undeniable

self-important adjective conceited, bigheaded, cocky, full of oneself, pompous, swollen-headed

self-indulgence noun intemperance, excess, extravagance

selfish adjective self-centred,

egoistic, egoistical, egotistic, egotistical, greedy, self-interested, ungenerous

selfless adjective unselfish, altruistic, generous, self-denying, self-sacrificing

self-possessed adjective self-assured, collected, confident, cool, poised, unruffled

self-reliant adjective independent, self-sufficient, self-supporting

self-respect noun pride, dignity, morale, self-esteem

self-restraint noun self-control, self-command, self-discipline, willpower

self-righteous adjective sanctimonious, complacent, holier-than-thou, priggish, self-satisfied, smug, superior

self-sacrifice noun selflessness, altruism, generosity, self-denial

self-satisfied adjective smug, complacent, pleased with oneself, self-congratulatory

self-seeking adjective selfish, careerist, looking out for number one (informal), out for what one can get, self-interested, self-serving

sell verb 1 trade, barter, exchange 2 deal in, handle, market, peddle, retail, stock, trade in, traffic in

seller noun dealer, agent, merchant, purveyor, retailer, salesman or saleswoman, supplier, vendor

selling noun dealing, business, trading, traffic

sell out verb 1 dispose of, be out of stock of, get rid of, run out of

2 Informal betray, double-cross (informal), sell down the river (informal), stab in the back

semblance noun appearance, aspect, façade, mask, pretence, resemblance, show, veneer

seminal adjective influential, formative, ground-breaking, important, innovative, original

send verb 1 convey, direct, dispatch, forward, remit, transmit 2 propel, cast, fire, fling, hurl, let fly, shoot

send for verb summon, call for, order, request

sendoff noun farewell, departure, leave-taking, start, valediction

send-up noun imitation, parody, satire, skit, spoof (informal), take-off (informal)

send up verb imitate, burlesque, lampoon, make fun of, mimic, mock, parody, satirize, spoof (informal), take off (informal)

senile adjective doddering, decrepit, doting, in one's dotage

senility noun dotage, decrepitude, infirmity, loss of one's faculties, senile dementia

senior adjective 1 higher ranking, superior 2 older, elder, major (Brit.)

senior citizen noun pensioner, O.A.P., old age pensioner, old or elderly person, retired person

seniority noun superiority, precedence, priority, rank

sensation noun 1 feeling, awareness, consciousness, impression, perception, sense 2 excitement, commotion, furore, stir, thrill

sensational adjective 1 dramatic,

amazing, astounding, exciting, melodramatic, shock-horror (*facetious*), shocking, thrilling **2** *Informal* excellent, fabulous (*informal*), impressive, marvellous, mean (*slang*), mind-blowing (*informal*), out of this world (*informal*), smashing (*informal*), superb

sense *noun* **1** faculty, feeling, sensation **2** feeling, atmosphere, aura, awareness, consciousness, impression, perception **3** *sometimes plural* intelligence, brains (*informal*), cleverness, common sense, judgment, reason, sagacity, sanity, sharpness, understanding, wisdom, wit(s) **4** meaning, drift, gist, implication, import, significance ♦ *verb* **5** perceive, be aware of, discern, feel, get the impression, pick up, realize, understand

senseless *adjective* **1** stupid, asinine, crazy, daft (*informal*), foolish, idiotic, illogical, inane, irrational, mad, mindless, nonsensical, pointless, ridiculous, silly **2** unconscious, insensible, out, out cold, stunned

sensibility *noun* **1** *often plural* feelings, emotions, moral sense, sentiments, susceptibilities **2** sensitivity, responsiveness, sensitiveness, susceptibility

sensible *adjective* **1** wise, canny, down-to-earth, intelligent, judicious, practical, prudent, rational, realistic, sage, sane, shrewd, sound **2** *usually with of* aware, conscious, mindful, sensitive to

sensitive *adjective* **1** easily hurt, delicate, tender **2** susceptible, easily affected, impressionable, responsive, touchy-feely (*informal*) **3** touchy, easily offended, easily upset, thin-skinned **4** responsive, acute, fine, keen, precise

sensitivity *noun* sensitiveness, delicacy, receptiveness, responsiveness, susceptibility

sensual *adjective* **1** physical, animal, bodily, carnal, fleshly, luxurious, voluptuous **2** erotic, lascivious, lecherous, lewd, lustful, raunchy (*slang*), sexual

sensuality *noun* eroticism, carnality, lasciviousness, lecherousness, lewdness, sexiness (*informal*), voluptuousness

sensuous *adjective* pleasurable, gratifying, hedonistic, sybaritic

sentence *noun* **1** punishment, condemnation, decision, decree, judgment, order, ruling, verdict ♦ *verb* **2** condemn, doom, penalize

sententious *adjective* pompous, canting, judgmental, moralistic, preachifying (*informal*), sanctimonious

sentient *adjective* feeling, conscious, living, sensitive

sentiment *noun* **1** emotion, sensibility, tenderness **2** *often plural* feeling, attitude, belief, idea, judgment, opinion, view **3** sentimentality, emotionalism, mawkishness, romanticism

sentimental *adjective* romantic, emotional, maudlin, nostalgic, overemotional, schmaltzy (*slang*), slushy (*informal*), soft-hearted, touching, weepy (*informal*)

sentimentality noun
romanticism, corniness (slang),
emotionalism, mawkishness,
nostalgia, schmaltz (slang)

sentinel noun guard, lookout,
sentry, watch, watchman

separable adjective
distinguishable, detachable,
divisible

separate verb 1 divide, come
apart, come away, detach,
disconnect, disjoin, remove,
sever, split, sunder 2 part, break
up, disunite, diverge, divorce,
estrange, part company, split up
3 isolate, segregate, single out
♦ adjective 4 unconnected,
detached, disconnected, divided,
divorced, isolated, unattached
5 individual, alone, apart,
distinct, particular, single, solitary

separated adjective
disconnected, apart,
disassociated, disunited, divided,
parted, separate, sundered

separately adverb individually,
alone, apart, severally, singly

separation noun 1 division,
break, disconnection,
dissociation, disunion, gap
2 split-up, break-up, divorce,
parting, rift, split

septic adjective infected,
festering, poisoned, putrefying,
putrid, suppurating

sepulchre noun tomb, burial
place, grave, mausoleum, vault

sequel noun 1 follow-up,
continuation, development
2 consequence, conclusion, end,
outcome, result, upshot

sequence noun succession,
arrangement, chain, course,

cycle, order, progression, series

serene adjective calm, composed,
peaceful, tranquil, unruffled,
untroubled

serenity noun calmness, calm,
composure, peace, peacefulness,
quietness, stillness, tranquillity

series noun sequence, chain,
course, order, progression, run,
set, string, succession, train

serious adjective 1 severe, acute,
critical, dangerous 2 important,
crucial, fateful, grim,
momentous, no laughing
matter, pressing, significant,
urgent, worrying 3 solemn,
grave, humourless, sober,
unsmiling 4 sincere, earnest,
genuine, honest, in earnest

seriously adverb 1 gravely,
acutely, badly, critically,
dangerously, severely 2 sincerely,
gravely, in earnest

seriousness noun 1 importance,
gravity, significance, urgency
2 solemnity, earnestness,
gravitas, gravity

sermon noun 1 homily, address
2 lecture, harangue, talking-to
(informal)

servant noun attendant,
domestic, help, maid, retainer,
skivvy (chiefly Brit.), slave

serve verb 1 work for, aid, assist,
attend to, help, minister to, wait
on 2 perform, act, complete,
discharge, do, fulfil 3 provide,
deliver, dish up, present, set out,
supply 4 be adequate, answer
the purpose, be acceptable, do,
function as, satisfy, suffice, suit

service noun 1 help, assistance,
avail, benefit, use, usefulness

2 work, business, duty, employment, labour, office **3** overhaul, check, maintenance **4** ceremony, observance, rite, worship ♦ *verb* **5** overhaul, check, fine tune, go over, maintain, tune (up)

serviceable *adjective* useful, beneficial, functional, helpful, operative, practical, profitable, usable, utilitarian

servile *adjective* subservient, abject, fawning, grovelling, obsequious, sycophantic, toadying

serving *noun* portion, helping

session *noun* meeting, assembly, conference, congress, discussion, hearing, period, sitting

set[1] *verb* **1** put, deposit, lay, locate, place, plant, position, rest, seat, situate, station, stick **2** prepare, arrange, lay, make ready, spread **3** harden, cake, congeal, crystallize, solidify, stiffen, thicken **4** arrange, appoint, decide (upon), determine, establish, fix, fix up, resolve, schedule, settle, specify **5** assign, allot, decree, impose, ordain, prescribe, specify **6** go down, decline, dip, disappear, sink, subside, vanish ♦ *noun* **7** position, attitude, bearing, carriage, posture **8** scenery, scene, setting, stage set ♦ *adjective* **9** fixed, agreed, appointed, arranged, decided, definite, established, prearranged, predetermined, scheduled, settled **10** inflexible, hard and fast, immovable, rigid, stubborn **11** conventional, stereotyped, traditional,

unspontaneous **12** set on or upon determined, bent, intent, resolute

set[2] *noun* **1** series, assortment, batch, collection, compendium **2** group, band, circle, clique, company, coterie, crowd, faction, gang

setback *noun* hold-up, blow, check, defeat, disappointment, hitch, misfortune, reverse

set back *verb* hold up, delay, hinder, impede, retard, slow

set off *verb* **1** leave, depart, embark, start out **2** detonate, explode, ignite

setting *noun* background, backdrop, context, location, scene, scenery, set, site, surroundings

settle *verb* **1** put in order, order, regulate, straighten out, work out **2** land, alight, come to rest, descend, light **3** move to, dwell, inhabit, live, make one's home, put down roots, reside, set up home, take up residence **4** colonize, people, pioneer, populate **5** calm, lull, pacify, quell, quiet, quieten, reassure, relax, relieve, soothe **6** pay, clear, discharge, square (up) **7** *often with* on *or* upon decide, agree, confirm, determine, establish, fix **8** resolve, clear up, decide, put an end to, reconcile

settlement *noun* **1** agreement, arrangement, conclusion, confirmation, establishment, working out **2** payment, clearing, discharge **3** colony, community, encampment, outpost

settler *noun* colonist

frontiersman, immigrant, pioneer

setup noun arrangement, conditions, organization, regime, structure, system

set up verb 1 build, assemble, construct, erect, put together, put up, raise 2 establish, arrange, begin, found, initiate, institute, organize, prearrange, prepare

sever verb 1 cut, cut in two, detach, disconnect, disjoin, divide, part, separate, split 2 break off, dissociate, put an end to, terminate

several adjective some, different, diverse, manifold, many, sundry, various

severe adjective 1 strict, austere, cruel, drastic, hard, harsh, oppressive, rigid, unbending 2 grim, forbidding, grave, serious, stern, tight-lipped, unsmiling 3 intense, acute, extreme, fierce 4 plain, austere, classic, restrained, simple, Spartan, unadorned, unembellished, unfussy

severely adverb 1 strictly, harshly, sharply, sternly 2 seriously, acutely, badly, extremely, gravely

severity noun strictness, hardness, harshness, severeness, sternness, toughness

sex noun 1 gender 2 Informal (sexual) intercourse, coition, coitus, copulation, fornication, lovemaking, sexual relations

sexual adjective 1 carnal, erotic, intimate, sensual, sexy 2 reproductive, genital, procreative, sex

sexual intercourse noun copulation, bonking (informal), carnal knowledge, coition, coitus, sex (informal), union

sexuality noun desire, carnality, eroticism, lust, sensuality, sexiness (informal)

sexy adjective erotic, arousing, naughty, provocative, seductive, sensual, sensuous, suggestive, titillating

shabby adjective 1 tatty, dilapidated, mean, ragged, run-down, scruffy, seedy, tattered, threadbare, worn 2 mean, cheap, contemptible, despicable, dirty, dishonourable, low, rotten (informal), scurvy

shack noun hut, cabin, shanty

shackle noun 1 often plural fetter, bond, chain, iron, leg-iron, manacle ♦ verb 2 fetter, bind, chain, manacle, put in irons

shade noun 1 dimness, dusk, gloom, gloominess, semidarkness, shadow 2 screen, blind, canopy, cover, covering, curtain, shield, veil 3 colour, hue, tinge, tint, tone 4 dash, hint, suggestion, trace 5 Literary ghost, apparition, phantom, spectre, spirit 6 put into the shade outshine, eclipse, outclass, overshadow ♦ verb 7 cover, conceal, hide, obscure, protect, screen, shield, veil 8 darken, cloud, dim, shadow

shadow noun 1 dimness, cover, darkness, dusk, gloom, shade 2 trace, hint, suggestion, suspicion 3 cloud, blight, gloom, sadness ♦ verb 4 shade, darken, overhang, screen, shield 5 follow, stalk, tail (informal), trail

shadowy adjective **1** dark, dim, dusky, gloomy, murky, shaded, shady **2** vague, dim, dreamlike, faint, ghostly, nebulous, phantom, spectral, unsubstantial

shady adjective **1** shaded, cool, dim **2** informal crooked, disreputable, dodgy (Brit., Austral., & N.Z. informal), dubious, questionable, shifty, suspect, suspicious, unethical

shaft noun **1** handle, pole, rod, shank, stem **2** ray, beam, gleam

shaggy adjective unkempt, hairy, hirsute, long-haired, rough, tousled, unshorn

shake verb **1** vibrate, bump, jar, jolt, quake, rock, shiver, totter, tremble **2** wave, brandish, flourish **3** upset, distress, disturb, frighten, rattle (informal), shock, unnerve ◆ noun **2** vibration, agitation, convulsion, jerk, jolt, quaking, shiver, shudder, trembling, tremor

shake up verb **1** stir (up), agitate, churn (up), mix **2** upset, disturb, shock, unsettle

shaky adjective **1** unsteady, faltering, precarious, quivery, rickety, trembling, unstable, weak **2** uncertain, dubious, iffy (informal), questionable, suspect

shallow adjective **1** superficial, empty, slight, surface, trivial **2** unintelligent, foolish, frivolous, ignorant, puerile, simple

sham noun **1** phoney or phony (informal), counterfeit, forgery, fraud, hoax, humbug, imitation, impostor, pretence ◆ adjective **2** false, artificial, bogus, counterfeit, feigned, imitation, mock, phoney or phony

(informal), pretended, simulated ◆ verb **3** fake, affect, assume, feign, pretend, put on, simulate

shambles noun chaos, confusion, disarray, disorder, havoc, madhouse, mess, muddle

shame noun **1** embarrassment, abashment, humiliation, ignominy, mortification **2** disgrace, blot, discredit, dishonour, disrepute, infamy, reproach, scandal, smear ◆ verb **3** embarrass, abash, disgrace, humble, humiliate, mortify **4** dishonour, blot, debase, defile, degrade, smear, stain

shamefaced adjective embarrassed, abashed, ashamed, humiliated, mortified, red-faced, sheepish

shameful adjective **1** embarrassing, cringe-making (Brit. informal), humiliating, mortifying **2** disgraceful, base, dishonourable, low, mean, outrageous, scandalous, wicked

shameless adjective brazen, audacious, barefaced, flagrant, hardened, insolent, unabashed, unashamed

shanty noun shack, cabin, hut, shed

shape noun **1** form, build, configuration, contours, figure, lines, outline, profile, silhouette **2** pattern, frame, model, mould **3** condition, fettle, health, state, trim ◆ verb **4** form, create, fashion, make, model, mould, produce **5** develop, adapt, devise, frame, modify, plan

shapeless adjective formless, amorphous, irregular, misshapen, unstructured

shapely *adjective* well-formed, curvaceous, elegant, graceful, neat, trim, well-proportioned

share *noun* 1 part, allotment, allowance, contribution, due, lot, portion, quota, ration, whack (*informal*) ♦ *verb* 2 divide, assign, distribute, partake, participate, receive, split

sharp *adjective* 1 keen, acute, jagged, pointed, serrated, spiky 2 sudden, abrupt, distinct, extreme, marked 3 clear, crisp, distinct, well-defined 4 quick-witted, alert, astute, bright, clever, discerning, knowing, penetrating, perceptive, quick 5 dishonest, artful, crafty, cunning, sly, unscrupulous, wily 6 cutting, barbed, biting, bitter, caustic, harsh, hurtful 7 sour, acid, acrid, hot, piquant, pungent, tart 8 acute, intense, painful, piercing, severe, shooting, stabbing ♦ *adverb* 9 promptly, exactly, on the dot, on time, precisely, punctually

sharpen *verb* whet, edge, grind, hone

shatter *verb* 1 smash, break, burst, crack, crush, pulverize 2 destroy, demolish, ruin, torpedo, wreck

shattered *adjective Informal* 1 exhausted, all in (*slang*), dead beat (*informal*), done in (*informal*), drained, knackered (*slang*), ready to drop, tired out, worn out 2 devastated, crushed

shave *verb* trim, crop, pare, shear

shed¹ *noun* hut, outhouse, shack

shed² *verb* 1 give out, cast, drop, emit, give, radiate, scatter,

shower, spill 2 cast off, discard, moult, slough

sheen *noun* shine, brightness, gleam, gloss, lustre, polish

sheepish *adjective* embarrassed, abashed, ashamed, mortified, self-conscious, shamefaced

sheer *adjective* 1 total, absolute, complete, downright, out-and-out, pure, unmitigated, utter 2 steep, abrupt, precipitous 3 fine, diaphanous, gauzy, gossamer, see-through, thin, transparent

sheet *noun* 1 coat, film, lamina, layer, overlay, stratum, surface, veneer 2 piece, panel, plate, slab 3 expanse, area, blanket, covering, stretch, sweep

shell *noun* 1 case, husk, pod 2 frame, framework, hull, structure ♦ *verb* 3 bomb, attack, blitz, bombard, strafe

shell out *verb* pay out, fork out (*slang*), give, hand over

shelter *noun* 1 protection, cover, defence, guard, screen 2 safety, asylum, haven, refuge, retreat, sanctuary, security ♦ *verb* 3 protect, cover, defend, guard, harbour, hide, safeguard, shield 4 take shelter, hide, seek refuge

sheltered *adjective* protected, cloistered, isolated, quiet, screened, secluded, shaded, shielded

shelve *verb* postpone, defer, freeze, put aside, put on ice, put on the back burner (*informal*), suspend, take a rain check on (*U.S. & Canad. informal*)

shepherd *verb* guide, conduct, herd, steer, usher

shield noun 1 <u>protection</u>, cover, defence, guard, safeguard, screen, shelter ◆ verb 2 <u>protect</u>, cover, defend, guard, safeguard, screen, shelter

shift verb 1 <u>move</u>, budge, displace, move around, rearrange, relocate, reposition ◆ noun 2 <u>move</u>, displacement, rearrangement, shifting

shiftless adjective <u>lazy</u>, aimless, good-for-nothing, idle, lackadaisical, slothful, unambitious, unenterprising

shifty adjective <u>untrustworthy</u>, deceitful, devious, evasive, furtive, slippery, sly, tricky, underhand

shimmer verb 1 <u>gleam</u>, glisten, scintillate, twinkle ◆ noun 2 <u>gleam</u>, iridescence

shine verb 1 <u>gleam</u>, beam, flash, glare, glisten, glitter, glow, radiate, sparkle, twinkle 2 <u>polish</u>, brush, buff, burnish 3 <u>stand out</u>, be conspicuous, excel ◆ noun 4 <u>brightness</u>, glare, gleam, light, radiance, shimmer, sparkle 5 <u>polish</u>, gloss, lustre, sheen

shining adjective <u>bright</u>, beaming, brilliant, gleaming, glistening, luminous, radiant, shimmering, sparkling

shiny adjective <u>bright</u>, gleaming, glistening, glossy, lustrous, polished

ship noun <u>vessel</u>, boat, craft

shipshape adjective <u>tidy</u>, neat, orderly, spick-and-span, trim, well-ordered, well-organized

shirk verb <u>dodge</u>, avoid, evade, get out of, skive (Brit. slang), slack

shirker noun <u>slacker</u>,

clock-watcher, dodger, idler, skiver (Brit. slang)

shiver[1] verb 1 <u>tremble</u>, quake, quiver, shake, shudder ◆ noun 2 <u>trembling</u>, flutter, quiver, shudder, tremor

shiver[2] verb <u>splinter</u>, break, crack, fragment, shatter, smash, smash to smithereens

shivery adjective <u>shaking</u>, chilled, chilly, cold, quaking, quivery

shock verb 1 <u>horrify</u>, appal, disgust, nauseate, revolt, scandalize, sicken 2 <u>astound</u>, jolt, shake, stagger, stun, stupefy ◆ noun 3 <u>impact</u>, blow, clash, collision 4 <u>upset</u>, blow, bombshell, distress, disturbance, stupefaction, stupor, trauma, turn (informal)

shocking adjective <u>dreadful</u>, appalling, atrocious, disgraceful, disgusting, ghastly, horrifying, nauseating, outrageous, revolting, scandalous, sickening

shoddy adjective <u>inferior</u>, poor, rubbishy, second-rate, slipshod, tawdry, trashy

shoot verb 1 <u>hit</u>, blast (slang), bring down, kill, open fire, plug (slang) 2 <u>fire</u>, discharge, emit, fling, hurl, launch, project, propel 3 <u>speed</u>, bolt, charge, dart, dash, fly, hurtle, race, rush, streak, tear ◆ noun 4 <u>branch</u>, bud, offshoot, sprig, sprout

shop noun <u>store</u>, boutique, emporium, hypermarket, supermarket

shore noun <u>beach</u>, coast, sands, seashore, strand (poetic)

shore up verb <u>support</u>, brace, buttress, hold, prop, reinforce, strengthen, underpin

short *adjective* **1** concise, brief, compressed, laconic, pithy, succinct, summary, terse **2** small, diminutive, dumpy, little, petite, squat **3** brief, fleeting, momentary **4** *often with of* lacking, deficient, limited, low (on), scant, scarce, wanting **5** abrupt, brusque, curt, discourteous, impolite, sharp, terse, uncivil ♦ *adverb* **6** abruptly, suddenly, without warning

shortage *noun* deficiency, dearth, insufficiency, lack, paucity, scarcity, want

shortcoming *noun* failing, defect, fault, flaw, imperfection, weakness

shorten *verb* cut, abbreviate, abridge, curtail, decrease, diminish, lessen, reduce

shortly *adverb* soon, before long, in a little while, presently

short-sighted *adjective* **1** near-sighted, myopic **2** unthinking, ill-advised, ill-considered, impolitic, impractical, improvident, imprudent, injudicious

short-tempered *adjective* quick-tempered, hot-tempered, impatient, irascible, ratty (*Brit. & N.Z. informal*), testy

shot *noun* **1** throw, discharge, lob, pot shot **2** pellet, ball, bullet, lead, projectile, slug **3** marksman, shooter **4** *Slang* attempt, effort, endeavour, go (*informal*), stab (*informal*), try, turn

shoulder *verb* **1** bear, accept, assume, be responsible for, carry, take on **2** push, elbow,

jostle, press, shove

shout *noun* **1** cry, bellow, call, roar, scream, yell ♦ *verb* **2** cry (out), bawl, bellow, call (out), holler (*informal*), roar, scream, yell

shout down *verb* silence, drown, drown out, overwhelm

shove *verb* push, drive, elbow, impel, jostle, press, propel, thrust

shovel *verb* move, dredge, heap, ladle, load, scoop, toss

shove off *verb* go away, clear off (*informal*), depart, leave, push off (*informal*), scram (*informal*)

show *verb* **1** be visible, appear **2** display, exhibit, present **3** prove, clarify, demonstrate, elucidate, point out **4** instruct, demonstrate, explain, teach **5** display, indicate, manifest, register, reveal **6** guide, accompany, attend, conduct, escort, lead ♦ *noun* **7** entertainment, presentation, production **8** exhibition, array, display, fair, pageant, parade, sight, spectacle **9** pretence, affectation, air, appearance, display, illusion, parade, pose

showdown *noun* confrontation, clash, face-off (*slang*)

shower *noun* **1** deluge, barrage, stream, torrent, volley ♦ *verb* **2** inundate, deluge, heap, lavish, pour, rain

showman *noun* performer, entertainer

show-off *noun* exhibitionist, boaster, braggart, poseur

show off *verb* **1** exhibit, demonstrate, display, flaunt, parade **2** boast, blow one's own trumpet, brag, swagger

show up verb 1 <u>stand out</u>, appear, be conspicuous, be visible 2 <u>reveal</u>, expose, highlight, lay bare 3 *Informal* <u>embarrass</u>, let down, mortify, put to shame 4 *Informal* <u>arrive</u>, appear, come, turn up

showy adjective 1 <u>ostentatious</u>, brash, flamboyant, flash (*informal*), flashy, over the top (*informal*) 2 <u>gaudy</u>, garish, loud

shred noun 1 <u>strip</u>, bit, fragment, piece, scrap, sliver, tatter 2 <u>particle</u>, atom, grain, iota, jot, scrap, trace

shrew noun <u>nag</u>, harpy, harridan, scold, spitfire, vixen

shrewd adjective <u>clever</u>, astute, calculating, canny, crafty, cunning, intelligent, keen, perceptive, perspicacious, sharp, smart

shrewdness noun <u>astuteness</u>, canniness, discernment, judgment, perspicacity, quick wits, sharpness, smartness

shriek verb, noun <u>cry</u>, scream, screech, squeal, yell

shrill adjective <u>piercing</u>, high, penetrating, sharp

shrink verb 1 <u>decrease</u>, contract, diminish, dwindle, grow smaller, lessen, narrow, shorten 2 <u>recoil</u>, cower, cringe, draw back, flinch, quail

shrivel verb <u>wither</u>, dehydrate, desiccate, shrink, wilt, wizen

shroud noun 1 <u>winding sheet</u>, grave clothes 2 <u>covering</u>, mantle, pall, screen, veil ♦ verb 3 <u>conceal</u>, blanket, cloak, cover, envelop, hide, screen, veil

shudder verb 1 <u>shiver</u>, convulse, quake, quiver, shake, tremble ♦ noun 2 <u>shiver</u>, quiver, spasm, tremor

shuffle verb 1 <u>scuffle</u>, drag, scrape, shamble 2 <u>rearrange</u>, disarrange, disorder, jumble, mix

shun verb <u>avoid</u>, keep away from, steer clear of

shut verb <u>close</u>, fasten, seal, secure, slam

shut down verb 1 <u>stop</u>, halt, switch off 2 <u>close</u>, shut up

shut out verb <u>exclude</u>, bar, debar, keep out, lock out

shuttle verb <u>go back and forth</u>, alternate, commute, go to and fro

shut up verb 1 *Informal* <u>be quiet</u>, fall silent, gag, hold one's tongue, hush, silence 2 <u>confine</u>, cage, coop up, immure, imprison, incarcerate

shy[1] adjective 1 <u>timid</u>, bashful, coy, diffident, retiring, self-conscious, self-effacing, shrinking 2 <u>cautious</u>, chary, distrustful, hesitant, suspicious, wary ♦ verb 3 *sometimes with* **off** *or* **away** <u>recoil</u>, balk, draw back, flinch, start

shy[2] verb <u>throw</u>, cast, fling, hurl, pitch, sling, toss

shyness noun <u>timidness</u>, bashfulness, diffidence, lack of confidence, self-consciousness, timidity, timorousness

sick adjective 1 <u>nauseous</u>, ill, nauseated, queasy 2 <u>unwell</u>, ailing, diseased, indisposed, poorly (*informal*), under the weather 3 *Informal* <u>morbid</u>, black, ghoulish, macabre, sadistic 4 <u>sick of</u> <u>tired</u>, bored, fed up, jaded, weary

sicken verb 1 disgust, gross out (U.S. slang), nauseate, repel, revolt, turn one's stomach 2 fall ill, ail, take sick

sickening adjective disgusting, distasteful, foul, loathsome, nauseating, offensive, repulsive, revolting, stomach-turning (informal), yukky or yucky (slang)

sickly adjective 1 unhealthy, ailing, delicate, faint, feeble, infirm, pallid, peaky, wan, weak 2 nauseating, cloying, mawkish

sickness noun 1 illness, affliction, ailment, bug (informal), complaint, disease, disorder, malady 2 nausea, queasiness, vomiting

side noun 1 border, boundary, division, edge, limit, margin, perimeter, rim, sector, verge 2 part, aspect, face, facet, flank, hand, surface, view 3 party, camp, cause, faction, sect, team 4 point of view, angle, opinion, position, slant, stand, standpoint, viewpoint 5 Brit. slang conceit, airs, arrogance ◆ adjective 6 subordinate, ancillary, incidental, lesser, marginal, minor, secondary, subsidiary ◆ verb 7 usually with with support, ally with, favour, go along with, take the part of

sidelong adjective sideways, covert, indirect, oblique

sidestep verb avoid, circumvent, dodge, duck (informal), evade, skirt

sidetrack verb divert, deflect, distract

sideways adverb 1 obliquely, edgeways, laterally, sidelong, to the side ◆ adjective 2 oblique, sidelong

sidle verb edge, creep, inch, slink, sneak, steal

siesta noun nap, catnap, doze, forty winks (informal), sleep, snooze (informal)

sieve noun 1 strainer, colander ◆ verb 2 sift, separate, strain

sift verb 1 sieve, filter, separate 2 examine, analyse, go through, investigate, research, scrutinize, work over

sight noun 1 vision, eye, eyes, eyesight, seeing 2 view, appearance, perception, range of vision, visibility 3 spectacle, display, exhibition, pageant, scene, show, vista 4 Informal eyesore, mess, monstrosity 5 catch sight of spot, espy, glimpse ◆ verb 6 spot, behold, discern, distinguish, make out, observe, perceive, see

sign noun 1 indication, clue, evidence, hint, mark, proof, signal, symptom, token 2 notice, board, placard, warning 3 symbol, badge, device, emblem, logo, mark 4 omen, augury, auspice, foreboding, portent, warning ◆ verb 5 autograph, endorse, initial, inscribe 6 gesture, beckon, gesticulate, indicate, signal

signal noun 1 sign, beacon, cue, gesture, indication, mark, token ◆ verb 2 gesture, beckon, gesticulate, indicate, motion, sign, wave

significance noun 1 importance, consequence, moment, relevance, weight 2 meaning, force, implication(s), import, message, point, purport, sense

significant adjective **1** important, critical, material, momentous, noteworthy, serious, vital, weighty **2** meaningful, eloquent, expressive, indicative, suggestive

signify verb **1** indicate, be a sign of, betoken, connote, denote, imply, intimate, mean, portend, suggest **2** Informal matter, be important, carry weight, count

silence noun **1** quiet, calm, hush, lull, peace, stillness **2** muteness, dumbness, reticence, taciturnity ♦ verb **3** quieten, cut off, cut short, deaden, gag, muffle, quiet, stifle, still, suppress

silent adjective **1** quiet, hushed, muted, noiseless, soundless, still **2** mute, dumb, speechless, taciturn, voiceless, wordless

silently adjective quietly, inaudibly, in silence, mutely, noiselessly, soundlessly, without a sound, wordlessly

silhouette noun **1** outline, form, profile, shape ♦ verb **2** outline, etch, stand out

silky adjective smooth, silken, sleek, velvety

silly adjective foolish, absurd, asinine, fatuous, idiotic, inane, ridiculous, senseless, stupid, unwise

silt noun **1** sediment, alluvium, deposit, ooze, sludge ♦ verb **2** silt up clog, choke, congest

similar adjective alike, analogous, close, comparable, like, resembling

similarity noun resemblance, affinity, agreement, analogy, closeness, comparability,

correspondence, likeness, sameness

simmer verb fume, be angry, rage, seethe, smoulder

simmer down verb calm down, control oneself, cool off or down

simper verb smile coyly, smile affectedly

simple adjective **1** easy, clear, intelligible, lucid, plain, straightforward, uncomplicated, understandable, uninvolved **2** plain, classic, natural, unembellished, unfussy **3** pure, elementary, unalloyed, uncombined, unmixed **4** artless, childlike, guileless, ingenuous, innocent, naive, natural, sincere, unaffected, unsophisticated **5** honest, bald, basic, direct, frank, naked, plain, sincere, stark **6** humble, homely, modest, unpretentious **7** feeble-minded, foolish, half-witted, moronic, slow, stupid

simple-minded adjective feeble-minded, backward, dim-witted, foolish, idiot, idiotic, moronic, retarded, simple, stupid

simpleton noun halfwit, dullard, fool, idiot, imbecile (informal), moron, numskull or numbskull

simplicity noun **1** ease, clarity, clearness, straightforwardness **2** plainness, lack of adornment, purity, restraint **3** artlessness, candour, directness, innocence, naivety, openness

simplify verb make simpler, abridge, disentangle, dumb down, reduce to essentials, streamline

simply adverb **1** plainly, clearly, directly, easily, intelligibly, naturally, straightforwardly, unpretentiously **2** just, merely, only, purely, solely **3** totally, absolutely, completely, really, utterly, wholly

simulate *verb* pretend, act, affect, feign, put on, sham

simultaneous *adjective* coinciding, at the same time, coincident, concurrent, contemporaneous, synchronous

simultaneously *adverb* at the same time, concurrently, together

sin *noun* **1** wrongdoing, crime, error, evil, guilt, iniquity, misdeed, offence, transgression ◆ *verb* **2** transgress, err, fall, go astray, lapse, offend

sincere *adjective* honest, candid, earnest, frank, genuine, guileless, heartfelt, real, serious, true, unaffected

sincerely *adverb* honestly, earnestly, genuinely, in earnest, seriously, truly, wholeheartedly

sincerity *noun* honesty, candour, frankness, genuineness, seriousness, truth

sinecure *noun* cushy number (*informal*), gravy train (*slang*), money for jam *or* old rope (*informal*), soft job (*informal*), soft option

sinful *adjective* guilty, bad, corrupt, criminal, erring, immoral, iniquitous, wicked

sing *verb* **1** warble, carol, chant, chirp, croon, pipe, trill, yodel **2** hum, buzz, purr, whine

singe *verb* burn, char, scorch, sear

singer *noun* vocalist, balladeer, chorister, crooner, minstrel, soloist

single *adjective* **1** one, distinct, individual, lone, only, separate, sole, solitary **2** individual, exclusive, separate, undivided, unshared **3** simple, unblended, unmixed **4** unmarried, free, unattached, unwed ◆ *verb* **5** *usually with* **out** pick, choose, distinguish, fix on, pick on *or* out, select, separate, set apart

single-handed *adverb* unaided, alone, by oneself, independently, on one's own, solo, unassisted, without help

single-minded *adjective* determined, dedicated, dogged, fixed, unswerving

singly *adverb* one by one, individually, one at a time, separately

singular *adjective* **1** single, individual, separate, sole **2** remarkable, eminent, exceptional, notable, noteworthy, outstanding **3** unusual, curious, eccentric, extraordinary, odd, peculiar, queer, strange

singularly *adverb* remarkably, especially, exceptionally, notably, outstandingly, particularly, uncommonly, unusually

sinister *adjective* threatening, dire, disquieting, evil, malign, menacing, ominous

sink *verb* **1** descend, dip, drop, fall, founder, go down, go under, level, plunge, submerge, subside **2** fall, abate, collapse, drop, lapse, slip, subside **3** decline, decay, deteriorate, diminish, dwindle, fade, fail, flag, lessen, weaken, worsen **4** dig, bore, drill, drive, excavate

5 stoop, be reduced to, lower oneself

sink in verb be understood, get through to, penetrate, register (informal)

sinner noun wrongdoer, evildoer, malefactor, miscreant, offender, transgressor

sip verb **1** drink, sample, sup, taste ◆ noun **2** swallow, drop, taste, thimbleful

sissy noun **1** wimp (informal), coward, jessie (Scot. slang), milksop, mummy's boy, namby-pamby, softie (informal), weakling, wet (Brit. informal)
◆ adjective **2** wimpish or wimpy (informal), cowardly, effeminate, feeble, namby-pamby, soft (informal), unmanly, weak, wet (Brit. informal)

sit verb **1** rest, perch, settle **2** convene, assemble, deliberate, meet, officiate, preside

site noun **1** location, place, plot, position, setting, spot ◆ verb **2** locate, install, place, position, set, situate

situation noun **1** state of affairs, case, circumstances, condition, plight, state **2** location, place, position, setting, site, spot **3** status, rank, station **4** job, employment, office, place, position, post

sizable, sizeable adjective large, considerable, decent, goodly, largish, respectable, substantial

size noun dimensions, amount, bulk, extent, immensity, magnitude, mass, proportions, range, volume

size up verb assess, appraise,

evaluate, take stock of

sizzle verb hiss, crackle, frizzle, fry, spit

skeleton noun framework, bare bones, draft, frame, outline, sketch, structure

sketch noun **1** drawing, delineation, design, draft, outline, plan ◆ verb **2** draw, delineate, depict, draft, outline, represent, rough out

sketchy adjective incomplete, cursory, inadequate, perfunctory, rough, scrappy, skimpy, superficial

skilful adjective expert, able, adept, adroit, clever, competent, dexterous, masterly, practised, professional, proficient, skilled

skill noun expertise, ability, art, cleverness, competence, craft, dexterity, facility, knack, proficiency, skilfulness, talent, technique

skilled adjective expert, able, masterly, professional, proficient, skilful

skim verb **1** separate, cream **2** glide, coast, float, fly, sail, soar **3** usually with **through** scan, glance, run one's eye over

skimp verb stint, be mean with, be sparing with, cut corners, scamp, scrimp

skin noun **1** hide, fell, pelt **2** coating, casing, crust, film, husk, outside, peel, rind ◆ verb **3** peel, flay, scrape

skinflint noun miser, meanie or meany (informal, chiefly Brit.), niggard, penny-pincher (informal), Scrooge

skinny adjective thin, emaciated,

lean, scrawny, undernourished

skip verb 1 hop, bob, bounce, caper, dance, flit, frisk, gambol, prance, trip 2 pass over, eschew, give (something) a miss, leave out, miss out, omit

skirmish noun 1 fight, battle, brush, clash, conflict, encounter, fracas, scrap (informal) ♦ verb 2 fight, clash, collide

skirt verb 1 border, edge, flank 2 often with around or round avoid, circumvent, evade, steer clear of

skit noun parody, burlesque, sketch, spoof (informal), takeoff (informal)

skittish adjective lively, excitable, fidgety, highly strung, jumpy, nervous, restive

skive verb slack, idle, malinger, shirk, swing the lead

skulduggery noun Informal trickery, double-dealing, duplicity, machinations, underhandedness

skulk verb lurk, creep, prowl, slink, sneak

sky noun heavens, firmament

slab noun piece, chunk, lump, portion, slice, wedge

slack adjective 1 loose, baggy, lax, limp, relaxed 2 negligent, idle, inactive, lax, lazy, neglectful, remiss, slapdash, slipshod 3 slow, dull, inactive, quiet, slow-moving, sluggish ♦ noun 4 room, excess, give (informal), leeway 5 shirk, dodge, idle, skive (Brit slang)

slacken verb, often with off lessen, abate, decrease, diminish, drop off, moderate, reduce, relax

slacker noun layabout, dodger, idler, loafer, shirker, skiver (Brit. slang)

slag off verb Slang criticize, abuse, deride, insult, malign, mock, slander, slate

slake verb satisfy, assuage, quench, sate

slam verb bang, crash, dash, fling, hurl, smash, throw

slander noun 1 defamation, calumny, libel, scandal, smear ♦ verb 2 defame, blacken (someone's) name, libel, malign, smear

slanderous adjective defamatory, damaging, libellous, malicious

slant verb 1 slope, bend, bevel, cant, heel, incline, lean, list, tilt 2 bias, angle, colour, distort, twist ♦ noun 3 slope, camber, gradient, incline, tilt 4 bias, angle, emphasis, one-sidedness, point of view, prejudice

slanting adjective sloping, angled, at an angle, bent, diagonal, inclined, oblique, tilted, tilting

slap noun 1 smack, blow, cuff, spank ♦ verb 2 smack, clap, cuff, spank

slapdash adjective careless, clumsy, hasty, hurried, messy, slipshod, sloppy (informal)

slap-up adjective luxurious, lavish, magnificent, splendid, sumptuous, superb

slash verb 1 cut, gash, hack, lacerate, rend, rip, score, slit 2 reduce, cut, drop, lower ♦ noun 3 cut, gash, incision, laceration, rent, rip, slit

slate verb Informal criticize,

censure, rebuke, scold, tear into (*informal*)

slaughter *verb* 1 murder, butcher, kill, massacre, slay ♦ *noun* 2 murder, bloodshed, butchery, carnage, killing, massacre, slaying

slaughterhouse *noun* abattoir

slave *noun* 1 servant, drudge, serf, skivvy (*chiefly Brit.*), vassal ♦ *verb* 2 toil, drudge, slog

slavery *noun* enslavement, bondage, captivity, servitude, subjugation

slavish *adjective* 1 servile, abject, base, cringing, fawning, grovelling, obsequious, submissive, sycophantic 2 imitative, second-hand, unimaginative, unoriginal

slay *verb* kill, butcher, massacre, mow down, murder, slaughter

sleaze *noun* corruption, bribery, dishonesty, extortion, fraud, unscrupulousness, venality

sleazy *adjective* sordid, disreputable, low, run-down, seedy, squalid

sleek *adjective* glossy, lustrous, shiny, smooth

sleep *noun* 1 slumber(s), doze, forty winks (*informal*), hibernation, nap, siesta, snooze (*informal*), zizz (*Brit. informal*) ♦ *verb* 2 slumber, catnap, doze, drowse, hibernate, snooze (*informal*), take a nap

sleepless *adjective* wakeful, insomniac, restless

sleepy *adjective* drowsy, dull, heavy, inactive, lethargic, sluggish

slender *adjective* 1 slim, lean,

narrow, slight, willowy 2 faint, poor, remote, slight, slim, tenuous, thin 3 meagre, little, scant, scanty, small

sleuth *noun* detective, private eye (*informal*), (private) investigator

slice *noun* 1 share, cut, helping, portion, segment, sliver, wedge ♦ *verb* 2 cut, carve, divide, sever

slick *adjective* 1 glib, plausible, polished, smooth, specious 2 skilful, adroit, deft, dexterous, polished, professional ♦ *verb* 3 smooth, plaster down, sleek

slide *verb* slip, coast, glide, skim, slither

slight *adjective* 1 small, feeble, insignificant, meagre, measly, minor, paltry, scanty, trifling, trivial, unimportant 2 slim, delicate, feeble, fragile, lightly-built, small, spare ♦ *verb* 3 snub, affront, disdain, ignore, insult, scorn ♦ *noun* 4 snub, affront, insult, neglect, rebuff, slap in the face (*informal*), (the) cold shoulder

slightly *adverb* a little, somewhat

slim *adjective* 1 slender, lean, narrow, slight, svelte, thin, trim 2 slight, faint, poor, remote, slender ♦ *verb* 3 lose weight, diet, reduce

slimy *adjective* 1 viscous, clammy, glutinous, oozy 2 obsequious, creeping, grovelling, oily, servile, smarmy (*Brit. informal*), unctuous

sling *verb* 1 throw, cast, chuck (*informal*), fling, heave, hurl, lob (*informal*), shy, toss 2 hang, dangle, suspend

slink verb creep, prowl, skulk, slip, sneak, steal

slinky adjective figure-hugging, clinging, close-fitting, skintight

slip verb 1 fall, skid 2 slide, skate, slither 3 sneak, conceal, creep, hide, steal 4 sometimes with up make a mistake, blunder, err, miscalculate 5 let slip give away, disclose, divulge, leak, reveal ◆ noun 6 mistake, blunder, error, failure, fault, lapse, omission, oversight 7 give (someone) the slip escape from, dodge, elude, evade, get away from, lose (someone)

slippery adjective 1 smooth, glassy, greasy, icy, slippy (informal or dialect), unsafe 2 devious, crafty, cunning, dishonest, evasive, shifty, tricky, untrustworthy

slipshod adjective careless, casual, slapdash, sloppy (informal), slovenly, untidy

slit noun 1 cut, gash, incision, opening, rent, split, tear ◆ verb 2 cut (open), gash, knife, lance, pierce, rip, slash

slither verb slide, glide, slink, slip, snake, undulate

sliver noun shred, fragment, paring, shaving, splinter

slobber verb drool, dribble, drivel, salivate, slaver

slobbish adjective messy, slovenly, unclean, unkempt, untidy

slog verb 1 work, labour, plod, plough through, slave, toil 2 trudge, tramp, trek 3 hit, punch, slug, sock (slang), strike, thump, wallop (informal) ◆ noun

4 labour, effort, exertion, struggle 5 trudge, hike, tramp, trek

slogan noun catch phrase, catchword, motto

slop verb spill, overflow, slosh (informal), splash

slope noun 1 inclination, gradient, incline, ramp, rise, slant, tilt ◆ verb 2 slant, drop away, fall, incline, lean, rise, tilt 3 slope off slink away, creep away, slip away

sloping adjective slanting, inclined, leaning, oblique

sloppy adjective 1 careless, messy, slipshod, slovenly, untidy 2 sentimental, gushing, mawkish, slushy (informal), soppy (Brit. informal)

slot noun 1 opening, aperture, groove, hole, slit, vent 2 Informal place, opening, position, space, time, vacancy ◆ verb 3 fit in, fit, insert

sloth noun laziness, idleness, inactivity, inertia, slackness, sluggishness, torpor

slothful adjective lazy, idle, inactive, indolent, skiving (Brit. slang), workshy

slouch verb slump, droop, loll, stoop

slovenly adjective careless, disorderly, negligent, slack, slapdash, slipshod, sloppy (informal), untidy

slow adjective 1 prolonged, gradual, lingering, long-drawn-out, protracted 2 unhurried, dawdling, lackadaisical, laggard, lazy, leisurely, ponderous, sluggish

3 late, backward, behind, delayed, tardy 4 stupid, braindead (*informal*), dense, dim, dozy (*Brit. informal*), dull-witted, obtuse, retarded, thick ♦ *verb* 5 often with **up** or **down** reduce speed, brake, decelerate, handicap, hold up, retard, slacken (off)

slowly adverb gradually, leisurely, unhurriedly

sludge noun sediment, mire, muck, mud, ooze, residue, silt, slime

sluggish adjective inactive, dull, heavy, indolent, inert, lethargic, slothful, slow, torpid

slum noun hovel, ghetto

slumber verb sleep, doze, drowse, nap, snooze (*informal*), zizz (*Brit. informal*)

slump verb 1 fall, collapse, crash, plunge, sink, slip 2 sag, droop, hunch, loll, slouch ♦ *noun* 3 fall, collapse, crash, decline, downturn, drop, reverse, trough 4 recession, depression

slur noun insult, affront, aspersion, calumny, innuendo, insinuation, smear, stain

slut noun Offensive tart, scrubber (*Brit. & Austral. slang*), slag (*Brit. slang*), slapper (*Brit. slang*), trollop

sly adjective 1 cunning, artful, clever, crafty, devious, scheming, secret, shifty, stealthy, subtle, underhand, wily 2 roguish, arch, impish, knowing, mischievous ♦ *noun 3* on the sly secretly, covertly, on the quiet, privately, surreptitiously

smack verb 1 slap, clap, cuff, hit, spank, strike ♦ *noun 2* slap, blow

♦ *adverb 3* Informal directly, exactly, precisely, right, slap (*informal*), squarely, straight

small adjective 1 little, diminutive, mini, miniature, minute, petite, pygmy or pigmy, teeny, teeny-weeny, tiny, undersized, wee 2 unimportant, insignificant, minor, negligible, paltry, petty, trifling, trivial 3 petty, base, mean, narrow 4 modest, humble, unpretentious

small-minded adjective petty, bigoted, intolerant, mean, narrow-minded, ungenerous

small-time adjective minor, insignificant, of no account, petty, unimportant

smarmy adjective Informal obsequious, crawling, ingratiating, servile, smooth, suave, sycophantic, toadying, unctuous

smart adjective 1 neat, chic, elegant, natty (*informal*), snappy, spruce, stylish, trim 2 clever, acute, astute, bright, canny, ingenious, intelligent, keen, quick, sharp, shrewd 3 brisk, lively, quick, vigorous ♦ *verb* 4 sting, burn, hurt ♦ *noun* 5 sting, pain, soreness

smart aleck noun Informal know-all (*informal*), clever-clogs (*informal*), smarty pants (*informal*), wise guy (*informal*)

smarten verb tidy, groom, put in order, put to rights, spruce up

smash verb 1 break, crush, demolish, pulverize, shatter 2 collide, crash 3 destroy, lay waste, ruin, trash (*slang*), wreck ♦ *noun 4* destruction, collapse, downfall, failure, ruin 5 collision, accident, crash

smashing adjective Informal excellent, awesome (slang), brilliant (informal), cracking (Brit. informal), fabulous (informal), fantastic (informal), great (informal), magnificent, marvellous, mean (slang), sensational (informal), super (informal), superb, terrific (informal), wonderful

smattering noun modicum, bit, rudiments

smear verb 1 spread over, bedaub, coat, cover, daub, rub on 2 dirty, smudge, soil, stain, sully 3 slander, besmirch, blacken, malign ◆ noun 4 smudge, blot, blotch, daub, splotch, streak 5 slander, calumny, defamation, libel

smell verb 1 sniff, scent 2 stink, pong (Brit. informal), reek ◆ noun 3 odour, aroma, bouquet, fragrance, perfume, scent 4 stink, fetor, pong (Brit. informal), stench

smelly adjective stinking, fetid, foul, foul-smelling, malodorous, noisome, reeking

smirk noun smug look, simper

smitten adjective 1 afflicted, laid low, plagued, struck 2 infatuated, beguiled, bewitched, captivated, charmed, enamoured

smooth adjective 1 even, flat, flush, horizontal, level, plane 2 sleek, glossy, polished, shiny, silky, soft, velvety 3 easy, effortless, well-ordered 4 flowing, regular, rhythmic, steady, uniform 5 suave, facile, glib, persuasive, slick, smarmy

(Brit. informal), unctuous, urbane 6 mellow, agreeable, mild, pleasant ◆ verb 7 flatten, iron, level, plane, press 8 calm, appease, assuage, ease, mitigate, mollify, soften

smother verb 1 suffocate, choke, stifle, strangle 2 suppress, conceal, hide, muffle, repress, stifle

smoulder verb seethe, boil, fume, rage, simmer

smudge verb 1 smear, daub, dirty, mark, smirch ◆ noun 2 smear, blemish, blot

smug adjective self-satisfied, complacent, conceited, superior

smuggler noun trafficker, bootlegger, runner

smutty adjective obscene, bawdy, blue, coarse, crude, dirty, indecent, indelicate, suggestive, vulgar

snack noun light meal, bite, refreshment(s)

snag noun 1 difficulty, catch, complication, disadvantage, downside, drawback, hitch, obstacle, problem ◆ verb 2 catch, rip, tear

snap verb 1 break, crack, separate 2 crackle, click, pop 3 bite at, bite, nip, snatch 4 speak sharply, bark, jump down (someone's) throat (informal), lash out at ◆ noun 5 crackle, pop 6 bite, grab, nip ◆ adjective 7 instant, immediate, spur-of-the-moment, sudden

snappy adjective 1 irritable, cross, edgy, ratty (Brit. & N.Z. informal), testy, tetchy, touchy 2 smart, chic, dapper, fashionable, natty (*informal*), stylish

snap up verb seize, grab, pounce upon, take advantage of

snare noun 1 trap, gin, net, noose, wire ♦ verb 2 trap, catch, entrap, net, seize, wire

snarl verb, often with **up** tangle, entangle, entwine, muddle, ravel

snarl-up noun tangle, confusion, entanglement, muddle

snatch verb 1 seize, clutch, grab, grasp, grip ♦ noun 2 bit, fragment, part, piece, snippet

sneak verb 1 slink, lurk, pad, skulk, slip, steal 2 slip, smuggle, spirit 3 *Informal* inform on, grass on (*Brit. slang*), shop (*slang, chiefly Brit.*), tell on (*informal*), tell tales ♦ noun 4 informer, telltale

sneaking adjective 1 nagging, persistent, uncomfortable, worrying 2 secret, hidden, private, undivulged, unexpressed, unvoiced

sneaky adjective sly, deceitful, devious, dishonest, double-dealing, furtive, low, mean, shifty, untrustworthy

sneer noun 1 scorn, derision, gibe, jeer, mockery, ridicule ♦ verb 2 scorn, deride, disdain, jeer, laugh, mock, ridicule

snide adjective nasty, cynical, disparaging, hurtful, ill-natured, malicious, sarcastic, scornful, sneering, spiteful

sniff verb inhale, breathe, smell

snigger noun, verb laugh, giggle, snicker, titter

snip verb 1 cut, clip, crop, dock, shave, trim ♦ noun 2 *Informal* bargain, giveaway, good buy, steal (*informal*) 3 bit, clipping,

fragment, piece, scrap, shred

snipe verb criticize, carp, denigrate, disparage, jeer, knock (*informal*), put down

snippet noun piece, fragment, part, scrap, shred

snivel verb whine, cry, grizzle (*informal, chiefly Brit.*), moan, sniffle, whimper, whinge (*informal*)

snob noun elitist, highbrow, prig

snobbery noun arrogance, airs, pretension, pride, snobbishness

snobbish adjective superior, arrogant, patronizing, pretentious, snooty (*informal*), stuck-up (*informal*)

snoop verb pry, interfere, poke one's nose in (*informal*), spy

snooper noun nosy parker (*informal*), busybody, meddler, snoop (*informal*)

snooze verb 1 doze, catnap, nap, take forty winks (*informal*) ♦ noun 2 doze, catnap, forty winks (*informal*), nap, siesta

snub verb 1 put down, cold-shoulder, cut (*informal*), humiliate, rebuff, slight ♦ noun 2 insult, affront, put-down, slap in the face

snug adjective cosy, comfortable, comfy (*informal*), warm

snuggle verb nestle, cuddle, nuzzle

soak verb 1 wet, bathe, damp, drench, immerse, moisten, saturate, steep 2 penetrate, permeate, seep 3 soak up absorb, assimilate

soaking adjective soaked, drenched, dripping, saturated, sodden, sopping, streaming, wet through, wringing wet

soar verb 1 ascend, fly, mount, rise, wing 2 rise, climb, escalate, rocket, shoot up

sob verb cry, howl, shed tears, weep

sober adjective 1 abstinent, abstemious, moderate, temperate 2 serious, composed, cool, grave, level-headed, rational, reasonable, sedate, solemn, staid, steady 3 plain, dark, drab, quiet, sombre, subdued

sobriety noun 1 abstinence, abstemiousness, moderation, nonindulgence, soberness, temperance 2 seriousness, gravity, level-headedness, solemnity, staidness, steadiness

so-called adjective alleged, pretended, professed, self-styled, supposed

sociable adjective friendly, affable, companionable, convivial, cordial, genial, gregarious, outgoing, social, warm

social adjective 1 communal, collective, common, community, general, group, public ◆ noun 2 get-together (informal), gathering, party

socialize verb mix, fraternize, get about or around, go out

society noun 1 mankind, civilization, humanity, people, the community, the public 2 organization, association, circle, club, fellowship, group, guild, institute, league, order, union 3 upper classes, beau monde, elite, gentry, high society 4 companionship,

company, fellowship, friendship

sodden adjective soaked, drenched, saturated, soggy, sopping, waterlogged

sofa noun couch, chaise longue, divan, settee

soft adjective 1 pliable, bendable, elastic, flexible, malleable, mouldable, plastic, supple 2 yielding, elastic, gelatinous, pulpy, spongy, squashy 3 velvety, downy, feathery, fleecy, silky, smooth 4 quiet, dulcet, gentle, murmured, muted, soft-toned 5 pale, bland, light, mellow, pastel, subdued 6 dim, dimmed, faint, restful 7 mild, balmy, temperate 8 lenient, easy-going, indulgent, lax, overindulgent, permissive, spineless 9 out of condition, effeminate, flabby, flaccid, limp, weak 10 Informal easy, comfortable, cushy (informal), undemanding 11 kind, compassionate, gentle, sensitive, sentimental, tenderhearted, touchy-feely (informal)

soften verb lessen, allay, appease, cushion, ease, mitigate, moderate, mollify, still, subdue, temper

softhearted adjective kind, charitable, compassionate, sentimental, sympathetic, tender, tenderhearted, warm-hearted

soggy adjective sodden, dripping, moist, saturated, soaked, sopping, waterlogged

soil[1] noun 1 earth, clay, dirt, dust, ground 2 land, country

soil[2] verb dirty, befoul, besmirch, defile, foul, pollute, spot, stain, sully, tarnish

solace noun 1 <u>comfort</u>, consolation, relief ◆ verb 2 <u>comfort</u>, console

soldier noun <u>fighter</u>, man-at-arms, serviceman, `squaddie or squaddy (Brit. slang), trooper, warrior

sole adjective <u>only</u>, alone, exclusive, individual, one, single, solitary

solely adverb <u>only</u>, alone, completely, entirely, exclusively, merely

solemn adjective 1 <u>formal</u>, ceremonial, dignified, grand, grave, momentous, stately 2 <u>serious</u>, earnest, grave, sedate, sober, staid

solemnity noun 1 <u>seriousness</u>, earnestness, gravity 2 <u>formality</u>, grandeur, impressiveness, momentousness

solicitous adjective <u>concerned</u>, anxious, attentive, careful

solicitude noun <u>concern</u>, anxiety, attentiveness, care, consideration, regard

solid adjective 1 <u>firm</u>, compact, concrete, dense, hard 2 <u>strong</u>, stable, sturdy, substantial, unshakable 3 <u>sound</u>, genuine, good, pure, real, reliable 4 <u>reliable</u>, dependable, trusty, upright, upstanding, worthy

solidarity noun <u>unity</u>, accord, cohesion, concordance, like-mindedness, team spirit, unanimity, unification

solidify verb <u>harden</u>, cake, coagulate, cohere, congeal, jell, set

solitary adjective 1 <u>unsociable</u>,

cloistered, isolated, reclusive, unsocial 2 <u>single</u>, alone, lone, sole 3 <u>lonely</u>, companionless, friendless, lonesome 4 <u>isolated</u>, hidden, out-of-the-way, remote, unfrequented

solitude noun <u>isolation</u>, loneliness, privacy, retirement, seclusion

solution noun 1 <u>answer</u>, explanation, key, result 2 Chemistry <u>mixture</u>, blend, compound, mix, solvent

solve verb <u>answer</u>, clear up, crack, decipher, disentangle, get to the bottom of, resolve, suss (out) (slang), unravel, work out

sombre adjective 1 <u>dark</u>, dim, drab, dull, gloomy, sober 2 <u>gloomy</u>, dismal, doleful, grave, joyless, lugubrious, mournful, sad, sober

somebody noun <u>celebrity</u>, dignitary, household name, luminary, megastar (informal), name, notable, personage, star

someday adverb <u>eventually</u>, one day, one of these (fine) days, sooner or later

somehow adverb <u>one way or another</u>, by fair means or foul, by hook or (by) crook, by some means or other, come hell or high water (informal), come what may

sometimes adverb <u>occasionally</u>, at times, now and then

song noun <u>ballad</u>, air, anthem, carol, chant, chorus, ditty, hymn, number, psalm, tune

soon adverb <u>before long</u>, in the near future, shortly

soothe verb 1 <u>calm</u>, allay,

appease, hush, lull, mollify, pacify, quiet, still 2 <u>relieve</u>, alleviate, assuage, ease

soothing *adjective* <u>calming</u>, emollient, palliative, relaxing, restful

soothsayer *noun* <u>prophet</u>, diviner, fortune-teller, seer, sibyl

sophisticated *adjective*
1 <u>cultured</u>, cosmopolitan, cultivated, refined, urbane, worldly 2 <u>complex</u>, advanced, complicated, delicate, elaborate, intricate, refined, subtle

sophistication *noun* <u>savoir-faire</u>, finesse, poise, urbanity, worldliness, worldly wisdom

soporific *adjective*
1 <u>sleep-inducing</u>, sedative, somnolent, tranquillizing ♦ *noun*
2 <u>sedative</u>, narcotic, opiate, tranquillizer

soppy *adjective Informal* <u>sentimental</u>, overemotional, schmaltzy (*slang*), slushy (*informal*), weepy (*informal*)

sorcerer *noun* <u>magician</u>, enchanter, necromancer, warlock, witch, wizard

sorcery *noun* <u>black magic</u>, black art, enchantment, magic, necromancy, witchcraft, wizardry

sordid *adjective* 1 <u>dirty</u>, filthy, foul, mean, seedy, sleazy, squalid, unclean 2 <u>base</u>, debauched, degenerate, low, shabby, shameful, vicious, vile 3 <u>mercenary</u>, avaricious, covetous, grasping, selfish

sore *adjective* 1 <u>painful</u>, angry, burning, inflamed, irritated, raw, sensitive, smarting, tender
2 <u>annoying</u>, severe, sharp,

troublesome 3 <u>annoyed</u>, aggrieved, angry, cross, hurt, irked, irritated, pained, resentful, stung, upset 4 <u>urgent</u>, acute, critical, desperate, dire, extreme, pressing

sorrow *noun* 1 <u>grief</u>, anguish, distress, heartache, heartbreak, misery, mourning, regret, sadness, unhappiness, woe
2 <u>affliction</u>, hardship, misfortune, trial, tribulation, trouble, woe
♦ *verb* 3 <u>grieve</u>, agonize, bemoan, be sad, bewail, lament, mourn

sorrowful *adjective* <u>sad</u>, dejected, dismal, doleful, grieving, miserable, mournful, sorry, unhappy, woebegone, woeful, wretched

sorry *adjective* 1 <u>regretful</u>, apologetic, conscience-stricken, contrite, penitent, remorseful, repentant, shamefaced
2 <u>sympathetic</u>, commiserative, compassionate, full of pity, moved 3 <u>wretched</u>, deplorable, mean, miserable, pathetic, pitiful, poor, sad

sort *noun* 1 <u>kind</u>, brand, category, class, ilk, make, nature, order, quality, style, type, variety
♦ *verb* 2 <u>arrange</u>, categorize, classify, divide, grade, group, order, put in order, rank

sort out *verb* 1 <u>resolve</u>, clarify, clear up 2 <u>organize</u>, tidy up

soul *noun* 1 <u>spirit</u>, essence, life, vital force 2 <u>personification</u>, embodiment, epitome, essence, quintessence, type 3 <u>person</u>, being, body, creature, individual, man *or* woman

sound[1] *noun* 1 <u>noise</u>, din, report,

reverberation, tone **2** impression, drift, idea, look ♦ *verb* **3** resound, echo, reverberate **4** seem, appear, look **5** pronounce, announce, articulate, declare, express, utter

sound² *adjective* **1** perfect, fit, healthy, intact, solid, unhurt, unimpaired, uninjured, whole **2** sensible, correct, logical, proper, prudent, rational, reasonable, right, trustworthy, valid, well-founded, wise **3** deep, unbroken, undisturbed, untroubled

sound³ *verb* fathom, plumb, probe

sound out *verb* probe, canvass, pump, question, see how the land lies

sour *adjective* **1** sharp, acetic, acid, bitter, pungent, tart **2** gone off, curdled, gone bad, turned **3** ill-natured, acrimonious, disagreeable, embittered, ill-tempered, peevish, tart, ungenerous, waspish

source *noun* **1** origin, author, beginning, cause, derivation, fount, originator **2** informant, authority

souvenir *noun* keepsake, memento, reminder

sovereign *noun* **1** monarch, chief, emperor *or* empress, king *or* queen, potentate, prince, ruler ♦ *adjective* **2** supreme, absolute, imperial, kingly *or* queenly, principal, royal, ruling **3** excellent, effectual, efficacious, efficient

sovereignty *noun* supreme power, domination, kingship, primacy, supremacy

sow *verb* scatter, implant, plant, seed

space *noun* **1** room, capacity, elbowroom, expanse, extent, leeway, margin, play, scope **2** gap, blank, distance, interval, omission **3** time, duration, interval, period, span, while

spacious *adjective* roomy, ample, broad, capacious, commodious, expansive, extensive, huge, large, sizable *or* sizeable

spadework *noun* preparation, donkey-work, groundwork, labour

span *noun* **1** extent, amount, distance, length, reach, spread, stretch **2** period, duration, spell, term ♦ *verb* **3** extend across, bridge, cover, cross, link, traverse

spank *verb* smack, cuff, slap

spar *verb* argue, bicker, row, scrap (*informal*), squabble, wrangle

spare *adjective* **1** extra, additional, free, leftover, odd, over, superfluous, surplus, unoccupied, unused, unwanted **2** thin, gaunt, lean, meagre, wiry ♦ *verb* **3** have mercy on, be merciful to, go easy on (*informal*), leave, let off (*informal*), pardon, save from **4** afford, do without, give, grant, let (someone) have, manage without, part with

spare time *noun* leisure, free time, odd moments

sparing *adjective* economical, careful, frugal, prudent, saving, thrifty

spark *noun* **1** flicker, flare, flash,

gleam, glint 2 trace, atom, hint, jot, scrap, vestige ♦ verb 3 often with off start, inspire, precipitate, provoke, set off, stimulate, trigger (off)

sparkle verb 1 glitter, dance, flash, gleam, glint, glisten, scintillate, shimmer, shine, twinkle ♦ noun 2 glitter, brilliance, flash, flicker, gleam, glint, twinkle 3 vivacity, dash, élan, life, spirit, vitality

sparse adjective scattered, few and far between, meagre, scanty, scarce

spartan adjective austere, ascetic, disciplined, frugal, plain, rigorous, self-denying, severe, strict

spasm noun 1 convulsion, contraction, paroxysm, twitch 2 burst, eruption, fit, frenzy, outburst, seizure

spasmodic adjective sporadic, convulsive, erratic, fitful, intermittent, irregular, jerky

spate noun flood, deluge, flow, outpouring, rush, torrent

speak verb 1 talk, articulate, converse, express, pronounce, say, state, tell, utter 2 lecture, address, declaim, discourse, hold forth

speaker noun lecturer, orator, public speaker, spokesman or spokeswoman, spokesperson

speak out or **up** verb speak one's mind, have one's say, make one's position plain

spearhead verb lead, head, initiate, launch, pioneer, set in motion, set off

special adjective 1 exceptional,

extraordinary, important, memorable, significant, uncommon, unique, unusual 2 particular, appropriate, distinctive, individual, precise, specific

specialist noun expert, authority, buff (informal), connoisseur, consultant, master, professional

speciality noun forte, bag (slang), métier, pièce de résistance, specialty

species noun kind, breed, category, class, group, sort, type, variety

specific adjective 1 particular, characteristic, distinguishing, special 2 definite, clear-cut, exact, explicit, express, precise, unequivocal

specification noun requirement, condition, detail, particular, qualification, stipulation

specify verb state, define, designate, detail, indicate, mention, name, stipulate

specimen noun sample, example, exemplification, instance, model, pattern, representative, type

speck noun 1 mark, blemish, dot, fleck, mote, speckle, spot, stain 2 particle, atom, bit, grain, iota, jot, mite, shred

speckled adjective flecked, dappled, dotted, mottled, spotted, sprinkled

spectacle noun 1 sight, curiosity, marvel, phenomenon, scene, wonder 2 show, display, event, exhibition, extravaganza, pageant, performance

spectacular adjective

1 impressive, dazzling, dramatic, grand, magnificent, sensational, splendid, striking, stunning (*informal*) ♦ *noun* **2** show, display, spectacle

spectator *noun* onlooker, bystander, looker-on, observer, viewer, watcher

spectre *noun* ghost, apparition, phantom, spirit, vision, wraith

speculate *verb* **1** conjecture, consider, guess, hypothesize, suppose, surmise, theorize, wonder **2** gamble, hazard, risk, venture

speculation *noun* **1** guesswork, conjecture, hypothesis, opinion, supposition, surmise, theory **2** gamble, hazard, risk

speculative *adjective* hypothetical, academic, conjectural, notional, suppositional, theoretical

speech *noun* **1** communication, conversation, dialogue, discussion, talk **2** talk, address, discourse, homily, lecture, oration, spiel (*informal*) **3** language, articulation, dialect, diction, enunciation, idiom, jargon, parlance, tongue

speechless *adjective* **1** mute, dumb, inarticulate, silent, wordless **2** astounded, aghast, amazed, dazed, shocked

speed *noun* **1** swiftness, haste, hurry, pace, quickness, rapidity, rush, velocity ♦ *verb* **2** race, career, gallop, hasten, hurry, make haste, rush, tear, zoom **3** help, advance, aid, assist, boost, expedite, facilitate

speed up *verb* accelerate, gather momentum, increase the tempo

speedy *adjective* quick, express, fast, hasty, headlong, hurried, immediate, precipitate, prompt, rapid, swift

spell[1] *verb* indicate, augur, imply, mean, point to, portend, signify

spell[2] *noun* **1** incantation, charm **2** fascination, allure, bewitchment, enchantment, glamour, magic

spell[3] *noun* period, bout, course, interval, season, stretch, term, time

spellbound *adjective* entranced, bewitched, captivated, charmed, enthralled, fascinated, gripped, mesmerized, rapt

spend *verb* **1** pay out, disburse, expend, fork out (*slang*) **2** pass, fill, occupy, while away **3** use up, consume, dissipate, drain, empty, exhaust, run through, squander, waste

spendthrift *noun* **1** squanderer, big spender, profligate, spender, waster ♦ *adjective* **2** wasteful, extravagant, improvident, prodigal, profligate

spew *verb* vomit, disgorge, puke (*slang*), regurgitate, throw up (*informal*)

sphere *noun* **1** ball, circle, globe, globule, orb **2** field, capacity, department, domain, function, patch, province, realm, scope, territory, turf (*U.S. slang*)

spherical *adjective* round, globe-shaped, globular, rotund

spice *noun* **1** seasoning, relish, savour **2** excitement, colour, pep, piquancy, zest, zing (*informal*)

spicy *adjective* **1** hot, aromatic,

piquant, savoury, seasoned
2 *Informal* scandalous, hot
(*informal*), indelicate, racy, ribald,
risqué, suggestive, titillating

spike *noun* 1 point, barb, prong,
spine ♦ *verb* 2 impale, spear, spit,
stick

spill *verb* 1 pour, discharge,
disgorge, overflow, slop over
♦ *noun* 2 fall, tumble

spin *verb* 1 revolve, gyrate,
pirouette, reel, rotate, turn, twirl,
whirl 2 reel, swim, whirl ♦ *noun*
3 revolution, gyration, roll, whirl
4 *Informal* drive, joy ride
(*informal*), ride

spine *noun* 1 backbone, spinal
column, vertebrae, vertebral
column 2 barb, needle, quill,
ray, spike, spur

spine-chilling *adjective*
frightening, bloodcurdling, eerie,
horrifying, scary (*informal*),
spooky (*informal*), terrifying

spineless *adjective* weak,
cowardly, faint-hearted, feeble,
gutless (*informal*), lily-livered,
soft, weak-kneed (*informal*)

spin out *verb* prolong, amplify,
delay, drag out, draw out,
extend, lengthen

spiral *noun* 1 coil, corkscrew,
helix, whorl ♦ *adjective* 2 coiled,
helical, whorled, winding

spirit *noun* 1 life force, life, soul,
vital spark 2 feeling, atmosphere,
gist, tenor, tone 3 temperament,
attitude, character, disposition,
outlook, temper 4 liveliness,
animation, brio, energy,
enthusiasm, fire, force, life,
mettle, vigour, zest 5 courage,
backbone, gameness, grit, guts
(*informal*), spunk (*informal*)

6 essence, intention, meaning,
purport, purpose, sense,
substance 7 ghost, apparition,
phantom, spectre 8 **spirits**
mood, feelings, frame of mind,
morale ♦ *verb* 9 *with* **away** *or* **off**
remove, abduct, carry,
purloin, seize, steal, whisk

spirited *adjective* lively, active,
animated, energetic, feisty
(*informal, chiefly U.S. & Canad.*),
mettlesome, vivacious

spiritual *adjective* sacred,
devotional, divine, holy, religious

spit *verb* 1 eject, expectorate,
splutter, throw out ♦ *noun*
2 saliva, dribble, drool, slaver,
spittle

spite *noun* 1 malice, animosity,
hatred, ill will, malevolence,
spitefulness, spleen, venom 2 **in
spite of** despite, (even) though,
notwithstanding, regardless of
♦ *verb* 3 hurt, annoy, harm,
injure, vex

spiteful *adjective* malicious,
bitchy (*informal*), ill-natured,
malevolent, nasty, vindictive

splash *verb* 1 scatter, shower,
slop, spatter, spray, sprinkle, wet
2 publicize, broadcast, tout,
trumpet ♦ *noun* 3 dash, burst,
patch, spattering, touch
4 *Informal* display, effect, impact,
sensation, stir

splash out *verb Informal* spend,
be extravagant, push the boat
out (*Brit. informal*), spare no
expense, splurge

splendid *adjective* 1 excellent,
cracking (*Brit. informal*), fantastic
(*informal*), first-class, glorious,
great (*informal*), marvellous,
wonderful 2 magnificent, costly,

gorgeous, impressive, lavish, luxurious, ornate, resplendent, rich, sumptuous, superb

splendour noun magnificence, brightness, brilliance, display, glory, grandeur, pomp, richness, show, spectacle, sumptuousness

splinter noun 1 sliver, chip, flake, fragment ♦ verb 2 shatter, disintegrate, fracture, split

split verb 1 break, burst, come apart, come undone, crack, give way, open, rend, rip 2 separate, branch, cleave, disband, disunite, diverge, fork, part 3 share out, allocate, allot, apportion, distribute, divide, halve, partition ♦ noun 4 crack, breach, division, fissure, gap, rent, rip, separation, slit, tear 5 division, breach, break-up, discord, dissension, estrangement, rift, rupture, schism ♦ adjective 6 divided, broken, cleft, cracked, fractured, ruptured

split up verb separate, break up, divorce, part

spoil verb 1 ruin, damage, destroy, disfigure, harm, impair, injure, mar, mess up, trash (slang), wreck 2 overindulge, coddle, cosset, indulge, mollycoddle, pamper 3 go bad, addle, curdle, decay, decompose, go off (Brit. informal), rot, turn

spoils plural noun booty, loot, plunder, prey, swag (slang)

spoilsport noun killjoy, damper, dog in the manger, misery (Brit. informal), wet blanket (informal)

spoken adjective said, expressed, oral, told, unwritten, uttered, verbal, viva voce, voiced

spokesperson noun speaker, mouthpiece, official, spin doctor (informal), spokesman or spokeswoman, voice

spongy adjective porous, absorbent

sponsor noun 1 backer, patron, promoter ♦ verb 2 back, finance, fund, patronize, promote, subsidize

spontaneous adjective unplanned, impromptu, impulsive, instinctive, natural, unprompted, voluntary, willing

spoof noun parody, burlesque, caricature, mockery, satire, send-up (Brit. informal), take-off (informal)

spooky adjective eerie, chilling, creepy (informal), frightening, scary (informal), spine-chilling, uncanny, unearthly, weird

sporadic adjective intermittent, irregular, occasional, scattered, spasmodic

sport noun 1 game, amusement, diversion, exercise, pastime, play, recreation 2 fun, badinage, banter, jest, joking, teasing ♦ verb 3 Informal wear, display, exhibit, show off

sporting adjective fair, game (informal), sportsmanlike

sporty adjective athletic, energetic, outdoor

spot noun 1 mark, blemish, blot, blotch, scar, smudge, speck, speckle, stain 2 pimple, pustule, zit (slang) 3 place, location, point, position, scene, site 4 Informal predicament, difficulty, hot water (informal), mess, plight, quandary, tight spot, trouble ♦verb **5** see, catch sight of, detect, discern, espy, make out, observe, recognize, sight **6** mark, dirty, fleck, mottle, smirch, soil, spatter, speckle, splodge, splotch, stain

spotless adjective clean, flawless, gleaming, immaculate, impeccable, pure, shining, unblemished, unstained, unsullied, untarnished

spotlight noun **1** attention, fame, limelight, public eye ♦verb **2** highlight, accentuate, draw attention to

spotted adjective speckled, dappled, dotted, flecked, mottled

spouse noun partner, consort, husband or wife, mate, significant other (U.S. informal)

spout verb stream, discharge, gush, shoot, spray, spurt, surge

sprawl verb loll, flop, lounge, slouch, slump

spray[1] noun **1** droplets, drizzle, fine mist **2** aerosol, atomizer, sprinkler ♦verb **3** scatter, diffuse, shower, sprinkle

spray[2] noun sprig, branch, corsage, floral arrangement

spread verb **1** open (out), broaden, dilate, expand, extend, sprawl, stretch, unfold, unroll, widen **2** proliferate, escalate, multiply **3** circulate, broadcast, disseminate, make known, propagate ♦noun **4** increase, advance, development, dispersal, dissemination, expansion, proliferation **5** extent, span, stretch, sweep

spree noun binge (informal),

bacchanalia, bender (informal), carousal, fling, orgy, revel

sprightly adjective lively, active, agile, brisk, energetic, nimble, spirited, spry, vivacious

spring verb **1** jump, bounce, bound, leap, vault **2** often with **from** originate, arise, come, derive, descend, issue, proceed, start, stem **3** often with **up** appear, develop, mushroom, shoot up ♦noun **4** jump, bound, leap, vault **5** elasticity, bounce, buoyancy, flexibility, resilience

springy adjective elastic, bouncy, buoyant, flexible, resilient

sprinkle verb scatter, dredge, dust, pepper, powder, shower, spray, strew

sprinkling noun scattering, dash, dusting, few, handful, sprinkle

sprint verb race, dart, dash, hare (Brit. informal), shoot, tear

sprite noun spirit, brownie, elf, fairy, goblin, imp, pixie

sprout verb grow, bud, develop, shoot, spring

spruce adjective smart, dapper, natty (informal), neat, trim, well-groomed, well turned out

spruce up verb smarten up, tidy, titivate

spry adjective active, agile, nimble, sprightly, supple

spur noun **1** stimulus, impetus, impulse, incentive, inducement, motive **2** goad, prick **3 on the spur of the moment** on impulse, impromptu, impulsively, on the spot, without planning ♦verb **4** incite, animate, drive, goad, impel, prick, prod, prompt, stimulate, urge

spurious adjective false, artificial, bogus, fake, phoney or phony (informal), pretended, sham, specious, unauthentic

spurn verb reject, despise, disdain, rebuff, repulse, scorn, slight, snub

spurt verb 1 gush, burst, erupt, shoot, squirt, surge ♦ noun 2 burst, fit, rush, spate, surge

spy noun 1 undercover agent, mole, nark (Brit., Austral., & N.Z. slang) ♦ verb 2 catch sight of, espy, glimpse, notice, observe, spot

squabble verb 1 quarrel, argue, bicker, dispute, fight, row, wrangle ♦ noun 2 quarrel, argument, disagreement, dispute, fight, row, tiff

squad noun team, band, company, crew, force, gang, group, troop

squalid adjective dirty, filthy, seedy, sleazy, slummy, sordid, unclean

squalor noun filth, foulness, sleaziness, squalidness

squander verb waste, blow (slang), expend, fritter away, misspend, misuse, spend

square adjective 1 honest, above board, ethical, fair, genuine, kosher (informal), on the level (informal), straight ♦ verb 2 even up, adjust, align, level 3 sometimes with up pay off, settle 4 often with with agree, correspond, fit, match, reconcile, tally

squash verb 1 crush, compress, distort, flatten, mash, press,

pulp, smash 2 suppress, annihilate, crush, humiliate, quell, silence

squashy adjective soft, mushy, pulpy, spongy, yielding

squawk verb cry, hoot, screech

squeak verb peep, pipe, squeal

squeal noun, verb scream, screech, shriek, wail, yell

squeamish adjective 1 delicate, fastidious, prudish, strait-laced 2 sick, nauseous, queasy

squeeze verb 1 press, clutch, compress, crush, grip, pinch, squash, wring 2 cram, crowd, force, jam, pack, press, ram, stuff 3 hug, clasp, cuddle, embrace, enfold 4 extort, milk, pressurize, wrest ♦ noun 5 hug, clasp, embrace 6 crush, congestion, crowd, jam, press, squash

squint adjective crooked, askew, aslant, awry, cockeyed, skew-whiff (informal)

squirm verb wriggle, twist, writhe

stab verb 1 pierce, impale, jab, knife, spear, stick, thrust, transfix, wound ♦ noun 2 wound, gash, incision, jab, puncture, thrust 3 twinge, ache, pang, prick 4 make or have a stab at Informal attempt, endeavour, have a go, try

stability noun firmness, solidity, soundness, steadiness, strength

stable adjective 1 firm, constant, established, fast, fixed, immovable, lasting, permanent, secure, sound, strong 2 steady, reliable, staunch, steadfast, sure

stack noun 1 pile, heap, load, mass, mound, mountain ♦ verb 2 pile, accumulate, amass, assemble, heap up, load

staff noun 1 <u>workers</u>, employees, personnel, team, workforce 2 <u>stick</u>, cane, crook, pole, rod, sceptre, stave, wand

stage noun <u>point</u>, division, juncture, lap, leg, level, period, phase, step

stagger verb 1 <u>totter</u>, lurch, reel, sway, wobble 2 <u>astound</u>, amaze, astonish, confound, overwhelm, shake, shock, stun, stupefy 3 <u>overlap</u>, alternate, step

stagnant adjective <u>stale</u>, quiet, sluggish, still

stagnate verb <u>vegetate</u>, decay, decline, idle, languish, rot, rust

staid adjective <u>sedate</u>, calm, composed, grave, serious, sober, solemn, steady

stain verb 1 <u>mark</u>, blemish, blot, dirty, discolour, smirch, soil, spot, tinge ◆ noun 2 <u>mark</u>, blemish, blot, discoloration, smirch, spot 3 <u>stigma</u>, disgrace, dishonour, shame, slur

stake[1] noun <u>pole</u>, pale, paling, palisade, picket, post, stick

stake[2] noun 1 <u>bet</u>, ante, pledge, wager 2 <u>interest</u>, concern, investment, involvement, share ◆ verb 3 <u>bet</u>, chance, gamble, hazard, risk, venture, wager

stale adjective 1 <u>old</u>, decayed, dry, flat, fusty, hard, musty, sour 2 <u>unoriginal</u>, banal, hackneyed, overused, stereotyped, threadbare, trite, worn-out

stalk verb <u>pursue</u>, follow, haunt, hunt, shadow, track

stall verb <u>play for time</u>, hedge, temporize

stalwart adjective <u>strong</u>,

staunch, stout, strapping, sturdy

stamina noun <u>staying power</u>, endurance, energy, force, power, resilience, strength

stammer verb <u>stutter</u>, falter, hesitate, pause, stumble

stamp noun 1 <u>imprint</u>, brand, earmark, hallmark, mark, signature ◆ verb 2 <u>trample</u>, crush 3 <u>identify</u>, brand, categorize, label, mark, reveal, show to be 4 <u>imprint</u>, impress, mark, print

stampede noun <u>rush</u>, charge, flight, rout

stamp out verb <u>eliminate</u>, crush, destroy, eradicate, put down, quell, scotch, suppress

stance noun 1 <u>attitude</u>, position, stand, standpoint, viewpoint 2 <u>posture</u>, bearing, carriage, deportment

stand verb 1 <u>be upright</u>, be erect, be vertical, rise 2 <u>put</u>, mount, place, position, set 3 <u>exist</u>, be valid, continue, hold, obtain, prevail, remain 4 <u>tolerate</u>, abide, allow, bear, brook, countenance, endure, handle, put up with (informal), stomach, take ◆ noun 5 <u>stall</u>, booth, table 6 <u>position</u>, attitude, determination, opinion, stance 7 <u>support</u>, base, bracket, dais, platform, rack, stage, tripod

standard noun 1 <u>benchmark</u>, average, criterion, gauge, grade, guideline, measure, model, norm, yardstick 2 often plural <u>principles</u>, ethics, ideals, morals 3 <u>flag</u>, banner, ensign ◆ adjective 4 <u>usual</u>, average, basic, customary, normal, orthodox, regular, typical 5 <u>accepted</u>, approved, authoritative, definitive, established, official, recognized

standardize verb bring into line, institutionalize, regiment

stand by verb 1 be prepared, wait 2 support, back, be loyal to, champion, take (someone's) part

stand for verb 1 represent, betoken, denote, indicate, mean, signify, symbolize 2 *Informal* tolerate, bear, brook, endure, put up with

stand-in noun substitute, deputy, locum, replacement, reserve, stopgap, surrogate, understudy

stand in for verb be a substitute for, cover for, deputize for, represent, take the place of

standing adjective 1 permanent, fixed, lasting, regular 2 upright, erect, vertical ◆noun 3 status, eminence, footing, position, rank, reputation, repute 4 duration, continuance, existence

standoffish adjective reserved, aloof, cold, distant, haughty, remote, unapproachable, unsociable

stand out verb be conspicuous, be distinct, be obvious, be prominent

standpoint noun point of view, angle, position, stance, viewpoint

stand up for verb support, champion, defend, stick up for (*informal*), uphold

staple adjective principal, basic, chief, fundamental, key, main, predominant

star noun 1 heavenly body 2 celebrity, big name, luminary,

main attraction, megastar (*informal*), name ◆adjective 3 leading, brilliant, celebrated, major, prominent, well-known

stare verb gaze, gape, gawk, gawp (*Brit. slang*), goggle, look, watch

stark adjective 1 harsh, austere, bare, barren, bleak, grim, hard, plain, severe 2 absolute, blunt, downright, out-and-out, pure, sheer, unmitigated, utter ◆adverb 3 absolutely, altogether, completely, entirely, quite, utterly, wholly

start verb 1 begin, appear, arise, commence, issue, originate 2 set about, embark upon, make a beginning, take the first step 3 set in motion, activate, get going, initiate, instigate, kick-start, open, originate, trigger 4 jump, flinch, jerk, recoil, shy 5 establish, begin, create, found, inaugurate, initiate, institute, launch, pioneer, set up ◆noun 6 beginning, birth, dawn, foundation, inception, initiation, onset, opening, outset 7 advantage, edge, head start, lead 8 jump, convulsion, spasm

startle verb surprise, frighten, make (someone) jump, scare, shock

starving adjective hungry, famished, ravenous, starved

state noun 1 condition, circumstances, position, predicament, shape, situation 2 frame of mind, attitude, humour, mood, spirits 3 country, commonwealth, federation, government, kingdom, land, nation, republic, territory **4** ceremony, display, glory, grandeur, majesty, pomp, splendour, style ♦ *verb* **5** express, affirm, articulate, assert, declare, expound, present, say, specify, utter, voice

stately *adjective* grand, august, dignified, lofty, majestic, noble, regal, royal

statement *noun* account, announcement, communication, communiqué, declaration, proclamation, report

state-of-the-art *adjective* latest, newest, up-to-date, up-to-the-minute

static *adjective* stationary, fixed, immobile, motionless, still, unmoving

station *noun* **1** headquarters, base, depot **2** place, location, position, post, seat, situation **3** position, post, rank, situation, standing, status ♦ *verb* **4** assign, establish, install, locate, post, set

stationary *adjective* motionless, fixed, parked, standing, static, stock-still, unmoving

statuesque *adjective* well-proportioned, imposing, Junoesque

stature *noun* importance, eminence, prestige, prominence, rank, standing

status *noun* position, condition, consequence, eminence, grade, prestige, rank, standing

staunch[1] *adjective* loyal, faithful, firm, sound, stalwart, steadfast, true, trusty

staunch[2] *verb* stop, check, dam, halt, stay, stem

stay *verb* **1** remain, abide, continue, halt, linger, loiter, pause, stop, tarry, wait ♦ *noun* **2** visit, holiday, sojourn, stop, stopover **3** postponement, deferment, delay, halt, stopping, suspension

steadfast *adjective* firm, faithful, fast, fixed, intent, loyal, resolute, stalwart, staunch, steady, unswerving, unwavering

steady *adjective* **1** firm, fixed, safe, stable **2** sensible, balanced, calm, dependable, equable, level-headed, reliable, sober **3** continuous, ceaseless, consistent, constant, incessant, nonstop, persistent, regular, unbroken, uninterrupted ♦ *verb* **4** stabilize, brace, secure, support

steal *verb* **1** take, appropriate, embezzle, filch, lift (*informal*), misappropriate, nick (*slang, chiefly Brit.*), pilfer, pinch (*informal*), purloin, thieve **2** sneak, creep, slink, slip, tiptoe

stealth *noun* secrecy, furtiveness, slyness, sneakiness, stealthiness, surreptitiousness, unobtrusiveness

stealthy *adjective* secret, furtive, secretive, sneaking, surreptitious

steep[1] *adjective* **1** sheer, abrupt, precipitous **2** *Informal* high, exorbitant, extortionate, extreme, overpriced, unreasonable

steep[2] *verb* **1** soak, drench, immerse, macerate, marinate (*Cookery*), moisten, souse, submerge **2** saturate, fill, imbue, infuse, permeate, pervade, suffuse

steer *verb* direct, conduct, control, guide, handle, pilot

stem[1] *noun* **1** stalk, axis, branch,

shoot, trunk ◆ *verb* **2 stem from** originate in, arise from, be caused by, derive from

stem² *verb* stop, check, curb, dam, hold back, staunch

stench *noun* stink, foul smell, pong (*Brit. informal*), reek, whiff (*Brit. slang*)

step *noun* **1** footstep, footfall, footprint, pace, print, stride, track **2** stage, move, phase, point **3** action, act, deed, expedient, means, measure, move **4** degree, level, rank ◆ *verb* **5** walk, move, pace, tread

step in *verb* intervene, become involved, take action

step up *verb* increase, intensify, raise

stereotype *noun* **1** formula, pattern ◆ *verb* **2** categorize, pigeonhole, standardize, typecast

sterile *adjective* **1** germ-free, aseptic, disinfected, sterilized **2** barren, bare, dry, empty, fruitless, unfruitful, unproductive

sterilize *verb* disinfect, fumigate, purify

sterling *adjective* excellent, fine, genuine, sound, superlative, true

stern *adjective* severe, austere, forbidding, grim, hard, harsh, inflexible, rigid, serious, strict

stick¹ *noun* **1** cane, baton, crook, pole, rod, staff, twig **2** *Brit. slang* abuse, criticism, flak (*informal*)

stick² *verb* **1** poke, dig, jab, penetrate, pierce, prod, puncture, spear, stab, thrust, transfix **2** fasten, adhere, affix, attach, bind, bond, cling, fix, glue, hold, join, paste, weld **3 with out, up,** *etc.* protrude,

bulge, extend, jut, obtrude, poke, project, show **4** *Informal* put, deposit, lay, place, set **5** stay, linger, persist, remain **6** *Slang* tolerate, abide, stand, stomach, take **7 stick up for** *Informal* defend, champion, stand up for, support

stickler *noun* perfectionist, fanatic, fusspot (*Brit. informal*), purist

sticky *adjective* **1** tacky, adhesive, clinging, gluey, glutinous, gooey (*informal*), gummy, viscid, viscous **2** *Informal* difficult, awkward, delicate, embarrassing, nasty, tricky, unpleasant **3** humid, clammy, close, muggy, oppressive, sultry, sweltering

stiff *adjective* **1** inflexible, firm, hard, inelastic, rigid, solid, taut, tense, tight, unbending, unyielding **2** awkward, clumsy, graceless, inelegant, jerky (*informal*), ungainly, ungraceful **3** difficult, arduous, exacting, hard, tough **4** severe, drastic, extreme, hard, harsh, heavy, strict **5** unrelaxed, constrained, forced, formal, stilted, unnatural

stiffen *verb* **1** brace, reinforce, tauten, tense **2** set, congeal, crystallize, harden, jell, solidify, thicken

stifle *verb* **1** suppress, check, hush, repress, restrain, silence, smother, stop **2** suffocate, asphyxiate, choke, smother, strangle

stigma *noun* disgrace, dishonour, shame, slur, smirch, stain

still *adjective* **1** motionless, calm, peaceful, restful, serene, stationary, tranquil, undisturbed

2 **silent**, hushed, quiet ♦ *verb*
3 **quieten**, allay, calm, hush, lull,
pacify, quiet, settle, silence,
soothe ♦ *conjunction* 4 **however**,
but, nevertheless,
notwithstanding, yet

stilted *adjective* **stiff**, constrained,
forced, unnatural, wooden

stimulant *noun* **pick-me-up**
(*informal*), restorative, tonic,
upper (*slang*)

stimulate *verb* **arouse**,
encourage, fire, impel, incite,
prompt, provoke, rouse, spur

stimulating *adjective* **exciting**,
exhilarating, inspiring,
provocative, rousing, stirring

stimulus *noun* **incentive**,
encouragement, fillip, goad,
impetus, incitement,
inducement, spur

sting *verb* 1 **hurt**, burn, pain,
smart, tingle, wound 2 *Informal*
cheat, defraud, do (*slang*), fleece,
overcharge, rip off (*slang*),
swindle

stingy *adjective* **mean**, miserly,
niggardly, parsimonious,
penny-pinching (*informal*),
tightfisted, ungenerous

stink *noun* 1 **stench**, fetor, foul
smell, pong (*Brit. informal*) ♦ *verb*
2 **reek**, pong (*Brit. informal*)

stint *verb* 1 **be mean**, be frugal,
be sparing, hold back, skimp on
♦ *noun* 2 **share**, period, quota,
shift, spell, stretch, term, time,
turn

stipulate *verb* **specify**, agree,
contract, covenant, insist upon,
require, settle

stipulation *noun* **specification**,
agreement, clause, condition,

precondition, proviso,
qualification, requirement

stir *verb* 1 **mix**, agitate, beat,
shake 2 **stimulate**, arouse,
awaken, excite, incite, provoke,
rouse, spur ♦ *noun* 3 **commotion**,
activity, bustle, disorder,
disturbance, excitement, flurry,
fuss

stock *noun* 1 **goods**, array,
choice, commodities,
merchandise, range, selection,
variety, wares 2 **supply**, fund,
hoard, reserve, stockpile, store
3 **property**, assets, capital, funds,
investment 4 **livestock**, beasts,
cattle, domestic animals
♦ *adjective* 5 **standard**,
conventional, customary,
ordinary, regular, routine, usual
6 **hackneyed**, banal, deal in, handle,
keep, supply, trade in 8 **provide**
with, equip, fit out, furnish,
supply 9 **stock up** store (*up*),
accumulate, amass, gather,
hoard, lay in, put away, save

stocky *adjective* **thickset**, chunky,
dumpy, solid, stubby, sturdy

stodgy *adjective* 1 **heavy**, filling,
leaden, starchy 2 **dull**, boring,
fuddy-duddy (*informal*), heavy
going, staid, stuffy, tedious,
unexciting

stoical *adjective* **resigned**,
dispassionate, impassive,
long-suffering, philosophic,
phlegmatic, stoic, stolid

stoicism *noun* **resignation**,
acceptance, forbearance,
fortitude, impassivity,
long-suffering, patience, stolidity

stolid *adjective* **apathetic**, dull,
lumpish, unemotional, wooden

stomach noun 1 <u>belly</u>, abdomen, gut (informal), pot, tummy (informal) 2 <u>inclination</u>, appetite, desire, relish, taste ◆ verb 3 <u>bear</u>, abide, endure, swallow, take, tolerate

stony adjective <u>cold</u>, blank, chilly, expressionless, hard, hostile, icy, unresponsive

stoop verb 1 <u>bend</u>, bow, crouch, duck, hunch, lean 2 **stoop to** <u>sink to</u>, descend to, lower oneself by, resort to ◆ noun 3 <u>slouch</u>, bad posture, round-shoulderedness

stop verb 1 <u>halt</u>, cease, conclude, cut short, discontinue, end, finish, pause, put an end to, quit, refrain, shut down, terminate 2 <u>prevent</u>, arrest, forestall, hinder, hold back, impede, repress, restrain 3 <u>plug</u>, block, obstruct, seal, staunch, stem 4 <u>stay</u>, lodge, rest ◆ noun 5 <u>end</u>, cessation, finish, halt, standstill 6 <u>stay</u>, break, rest 7 <u>station</u>, depot, terminus

stopgap noun <u>makeshift</u>, improvisation, resort, substitute

stoppage noun <u>stopping</u>, arrest, close, closure, cutoff, halt, hindrance, shutdown, standstill

store verb 1 <u>put by</u>, deposit, garner, hoard, keep, put aside, reserve, save, stockpile ◆ noun 2 <u>shop</u>, market, mart, outlet 3 <u>supply</u>, accumulation, cache, fund, hoard, quantity, reserve, stock, stockpile 4 <u>repository</u>, depository, storeroom, warehouse

storm noun 1 <u>tempest</u>, blizzard, gale, hurricane, squall 2 <u>outburst</u>, agitation, commotion, disturbance, furore, outbreak, outcry, row, rumpus, strife, tumult, turmoil ◆ verb 3 <u>attack</u>, assail, assault, charge, rush 4 <u>rage</u>, bluster, rant, rave, thunder 5 <u>rush</u>, flounce, fly, stamp

stormy adjective <u>wild</u>, blustery, inclement, raging, rough, squally, turbulent, windy

story noun 1 <u>tale</u>, account, anecdote, history, legend, narrative, romance, yarn 2 <u>report</u>, article, feature, news, news item, scoop

stout adjective 1 <u>fat</u>, big, bulky, burly, corpulent, fleshy, heavy, overweight, plump, portly, rotund, tubby 2 <u>strong</u>, able-bodied, brawny, muscular, robust, stalwart, strapping, sturdy 3 <u>brave</u>, bold, courageous, fearless, gallant, intrepid, plucky, resolute, valiant

stow verb <u>pack</u>, bundle, load, put away, stash (informal), store

straight adjective 1 <u>direct</u>, near, short 2 <u>level</u>, aligned, even, horizontal, right, smooth, square, true 3 <u>upright</u>, erect, plumb, vertical 4 <u>honest</u>, above board, accurate, fair, honourable, just, law-abiding, trustworthy, upright 5 <u>frank</u>, blunt, bold, candid, forthright, honest, outright, plain, straightforward 6 <u>successive</u>, consecutive, continuous, nonstop, running, solid 7 <u>undiluted</u>, neat, pure, unadulterated, unmixed 8 <u>orderly</u>, arranged, in order, neat, organized, shipshape, tidy 9 Slang <u>conventional</u>, bourgeois, conservative ◆ adverb 10 <u>directly</u>, at once, immediately, instantly

straight away *adverb* immediately, at once, directly, instantly, now, right away

straighten *verb* neaten, arrange, order, put in order, tidy (up)

straightforward *adjective*
1 honest, candid, direct, forthright, genuine, open, sincere, truthful, upfront (*informal*) **2** easy, easy-peasy (*slang*), elementary, routine, simple, uncomplicated

strain¹ *verb* **1** stretch, distend, draw tight, tauten, tighten **2** overexert, injure, overtax, overwork, pull, sprain, tax, tear, twist, wrench **3** strive, bend over backwards (*informal*), endeavour, give it one's best shot (*informal*), go for it (*informal*), knock oneself out (*informal*), labour, struggle **4** sieve, filter, purify, sift ♦ *noun* **5** stress, anxiety, burden, pressure, tension **6** exertion, effort, force, struggle **7** injury, pull, sprain, wrench

strain² *noun* **1** breed, ancestry, blood, descent, extraction, family, lineage, race **2** trace, streak, suggestion, tendency

strained *adjective* **1** forced, artificial, false, put on, unnatural **2** tense, awkward, difficult, embarrassed, stiff, uneasy

strait *noun* **1** *often plural* channel, narrows, sound **2 straits** difficulty, dilemma, extremity, hardship, plight, predicament

strait-laced *adjective* strict, moralistic, narrow-minded, prim, proper, prudish, puritanical

strand *noun* filament, fibre, string, thread

stranded *adjective* **1** beached, aground, ashore, grounded, marooned, shipwrecked **2** helpless, abandoned, high and dry

strange *adjective* **1** odd, abnormal, bizarre, curious, extraordinary, peculiar, queer, uncommon, weird, wonderful **2** unfamiliar, alien, exotic, foreign, new, novel, unknown, untried

stranger *noun* newcomer, alien, foreigner, guest, incomer, outlander, visitor

strangle *verb* **1** throttle, asphyxiate, choke, strangulate **2** suppress, inhibit, repress, stifle

strap *noun* **1** belt, thong, tie ♦ *verb* **2** fasten, bind, buckle, lash, secure, tie

strapping *adjective* well-built, big, brawny, husky (*informal*), powerful, robust, sturdy

stratagem *noun* trick, device, dodge, manoeuvre, plan, ploy, ruse, scheme, subterfuge

strategic *adjective* **1** tactical, calculated, deliberate, diplomatic, planned, political **2** crucial, cardinal, critical, decisive, important, key, vital

strategy *noun* plan, approach, policy, procedure, scheme

stray *verb* **1** wander, drift, err, go astray **2** digress, deviate, diverge, get off the point ♦ *adjective* **3** lost, abandoned, homeless, roaming, vagrant **4** random, accidental, chance

streak *noun* **1** band, layer, line, slash, strip, stripe, stroke, vein **2** trace, dash, element, strain, touch, vein ♦ *verb* 3 <u>speed</u>, dart, flash, fly, hurtle, sprint, tear, whizz (*informal*), zoom

stream *noun* 1 <u>river</u>, bayou, beck, brook, burn (*Scot.*), rivulet, tributary 2 <u>flow</u>, course, current, drift, run, rush, surge, tide, torrent ♦ *verb* 3 <u>flow</u>, cascade, flood, gush, issue, pour, run, spill, spout

streamlined *adjective* <u>efficient</u>, organized, rationalized, slick, smooth-running

street *noun* <u>road</u>, avenue, lane, roadway, row, terrace

strength *noun* 1 <u>might</u>, brawn, courage, fortitude, muscle, robustness, stamina, sturdiness, toughness 2 <u>intensity</u>, effectiveness, efficacy, force, potency, power, vigour 3 <u>advantage</u>, asset, strong point

strengthen *verb* 1 <u>fortify</u>, brace up, consolidate, harden, invigorate, restore, stiffen, toughen 2 <u>reinforce</u>, augment, bolster, brace, build up, buttress, harden, intensify, support

strenuous *adjective* <u>demanding</u>, arduous, hard, laborious, taxing, tough, uphill

stress *noun* 1 <u>strain</u>, anxiety, burden, pressure, tension, trauma, worry 2 <u>emphasis</u>, force, significance, weight 3 <u>accent</u>, accentuation, beat, emphasis ♦ *verb* 4 <u>emphasize</u>, accentuate, dwell on, underline

stretch *verb* 1 <u>extend</u>, cover, put forth, reach, spread, unroll 2 <u>pull</u>, distend, draw out, elongate, expand, strain, tighten ♦ *noun* 3 <u>expanse</u>, area, distance, extent, spread, tract 4 <u>period</u>,

space, spell, stint, term, time

strict *adjective* 1 <u>severe</u>, authoritarian, firm, harsh, stern, stringent 2 <u>exact</u>, accurate, close, faithful, meticulous, precise, scrupulous, true 3 <u>absolute</u>, total, utter

strident *adjective* <u>harsh</u>, discordant, grating, jarring, raucous, screeching, shrill

strife *noun* <u>conflict</u>, battle, clash, discord, dissension, friction, quarrel

strike *verb* 1 <u>walk out</u>, down tools, mutiny, revolt 2 <u>hit</u>, beat, clobber (*slang*), clout (*informal*), cuff, hammer, knock, punch, slap, smack, thump, wallop (*informal*) 3 <u>collide with</u>, bump into, hit, run into 4 <u>attack</u>, assail, assault, hit 5 <u>occur to</u>, come to, dawn on *or* upon, hit, register (*informal*)

striking *adjective* <u>impressive</u>, conspicuous, dramatic, noticeable, outstanding

string *noun* 1 <u>cord</u>, fibre, twine 2 <u>series</u>, chain, file, line, procession, row, sequence, succession

stringent *adjective* <u>strict</u>, inflexible, rigid, rigorous, severe, tight, tough

stringy *adjective* <u>fibrous</u>, gristly, sinewy, tough

strip¹ *verb* 1 <u>undress</u>, disrobe, unclothe 2 <u>plunder</u>, despoil, divest, empty, loot, pillage, ransack, rob, sack

strip² *noun* <u>piece</u>, band, belt, shred

strive *verb* <u>try</u>, attempt, bend over backwards (*informal*), break

stroke verb 1 caress, fondle, pet, rub ♦ noun 2 apoplexy, attack, collapse, fit, seizure 3 blow, hit, knock, pat, rap, thump

stroll verb 1 walk, amble, promenade, ramble, saunter ♦ noun 2 walk, breath of air, constitutional, promenade, ramble

strong adjective 1 powerful, athletic, brawny, burly, hardy, lusty, muscular, robust, strapping, sturdy, tough 2 durable, hard-wearing, heavy-duty, sturdy, substantial, well-built 3 persuasive, compelling, convincing, effective, potent, sound, telling, weighty, well-founded 4 intense, acute, deep, fervent, fervid, fierce, firm, keen, vehement, violent, zealous 5 extreme, drastic, forceful, severe 6 bright, bold, brilliant, dazzling

stronghold noun fortress, bastion, bulwark, castle, citadel, fort

stroppy adjective Slang awkward, bloody-minded (Brit. informal), difficult, obstreperous, quarrelsome, uncooperative

structure noun 1 building, construction, edifice, erection 2 arrangement, configuration, construction, design, form, formation, make-up, organization ♦ verb 3 arrange, assemble, build up, design, organize, shape

struggle verb 1 strive, exert oneself, give it one's best shot (informal), go all out (informal), knock oneself out (informal), labour, make an all-out effort (informal), strain, toil, work 2 fight, battle, compete, contend, grapple, wrestle ♦ noun 3 effort, exertion, labour, pains, scramble, toil, work 4 fight, battle, brush, clash, combat, conflict, contest, tussle

strut verb swagger, parade, peacock, prance

stub noun 1 butt, dog-end (informal), end, remnant, stump, tail, tail end 2 counterfoil

stubborn adjective obstinate, dogged, headstrong, inflexible, intractable, obdurate, persistent, pig-headed, recalcitrant, tenacious, unyielding

stubby adjective stocky, chunky, dumpy, short, squat, thickset

stuck adjective 1 fastened, cemented, fast, fixed, glued, joined 2 Informal baffled, beaten, stumped

stuck-up adjective snobbish, arrogant, bigheaded (informal), conceited, haughty, proud, snooty (informal), toffee-nosed (slang, chiefly Brit.)

stud verb ornament, bejewel, dot, spangle, spot

student noun learner, apprentice, disciple, pupil, scholar, trainee, undergraduate

studied adjective planned, conscious, deliberate, intentional, premeditated

studio noun workshop, atelier

studious adjective scholarly, academic, assiduous, bookish, diligent, hard-working, intellectual

study verb 1 contemplate, consider, examine, go into, ponder, pore over, read 2 learn, cram (informal), mug up (Brit. slang), read up, swot (up) (Brit. informal) 3 examine, analyse, investigate, look into, research, scrutinize, survey ◆ noun 4 learning, application, lessons, reading, research, school work, swotting (Brit. informal) 5 examination, analysis, consideration, contemplation, inquiry, inspection, investigation, review, scrutiny, survey

stuff noun 1 things, belongings, effects, equipment, gear, kit, objects, paraphernalia, possessions, tackle 2 substance, essence, matter 3 material, cloth, fabric, textile ◆ verb 4 cram, crowd, fill, force, jam, pack, push, ram, shove, squeeze

stuffing noun filling, packing, wadding

stuffy adjective 1 airless, close, frowsty, heavy, muggy, oppressive, stale, stifling, sultry, unventilated 2 Informal staid, dreary, dull, pompous, priggish, prim, stodgy

stumble verb 1 trip, fall, falter, lurch, reel, slip, stagger 2 with **across**, **on** or **upon** discover, chance upon, come across, find

stump verb baffle, bewilder, confuse, flummox, mystify, nonplus, perplex, puzzle

stumpy adjective stocky, dumpy, short, squat, stubby, thickset

stun verb overcome, astonish, astound, bewilder, confound, confuse, overpower, shock, stagger, stupefy

stunning adjective wonderful, beautiful, dazzling, gorgeous, impressive, lovely, marvellous, sensational (informal), spectacular, striking

stunt noun feat, act, deed, exploit, trick

stunted adjective undersized, diminutive, little, small, tiny

stupefy verb astound, amaze, daze, dumbfound, shock, stagger, stun

stupendous adjective 1 wonderful, amazing, astounding, breathtaking, marvellous, overwhelming, sensational (informal), staggering, superb 2 huge, colossal, enormous, gigantic, mega (slang), vast

stupid adjective 1 unintelligent, brainless, dense, dim, half-witted, moronic, obtuse, simple, simple-minded, slow, slow-witted, thick 2 foolish, asinine, daft (informal), imbecilic, inane, nonsensical, pointless, rash, senseless, unintelligent 3 dazed, groggy, insensate, semiconscious, stunned, stupefied

stupidity noun 1 lack of intelligence, brainlessness, denseness, dimness, dullness, imbecility, obtuseness, slowness, thickness 2 foolishness, absurdity, fatuousness, folly, idiocy, inanity, lunacy, madness, silliness

stupor noun daze, coma,

insensibility, stupefaction, unconsciousness

sturdy *adjective* 1 <u>robust</u>, athletic, brawny, hardy, lusty, muscular, powerful 2 <u>well-built</u>, durable, solid, substantial, well-made

stutter *verb* <u>stammer</u>, falter, hesitate, stumble

style *noun* 1 <u>design</u>, cut, form, manner 2 <u>manner</u>, approach, method, mode, technique, way 3 <u>elegance</u>, chic, élan, flair, panache, polish, smartness, sophistication, taste 4 <u>type</u>, category, genre, kind, sort, variety 5 <u>fashion</u>, mode, rage, trend, vogue 6 <u>luxury</u>, affluence, comfort, ease, elegance, grandeur ♦ *verb* 7 <u>design</u>, adapt, arrange, cut, fashion, shape, tailor 8 <u>call</u>, designate, dub, entitle, label, name, term

stylish *adjective* <u>smart</u>, chic, dressy (*informal*), fashionable, modish, trendy (*Brit. informal*), voguish

suave *adjective* <u>smooth</u>, charming, courteous, debonair, polite, sophisticated, urbane

subconscious *adjective* <u>hidden</u>, inner, intuitive, latent, repressed, subliminal

subdue *verb* 1 <u>overcome</u>, break, conquer, control, crush, defeat, master, overpower, quell, tame, vanquish 2 <u>moderate</u>, mellow, quieten down, soften, suppress, tone down

subdued *adjective* 1 <u>quiet</u>, chastened, crestfallen, dejected, downcast, down in the mouth, sad, serious 2 <u>soft</u>, dim, hushed, muted, quiet, subtle, toned down, unobtrusive

subject *noun* 1 <u>topic</u>, affair, business, issue, matter, object, point, question, substance, theme 2 <u>citizen</u>, national, subordinate ♦ *adjective* 3 <u>subordinate</u>, dependent, inferior, obedient, satellite 4 **subject to: a** <u>liable to</u>, exposed to, in danger of, open to, prone to, susceptible to, vulnerable to **b** <u>conditional on</u>, contingent on, dependent on ♦ *verb* 5 <u>put through</u>, expose, lay open, submit, treat

subjective *adjective* <u>personal</u>, biased, nonobjective, prejudiced

subjugate *verb* <u>conquer</u>, enslave, master, overcome, overpower, quell, subdue, suppress, vanquish

sublime *adjective* <u>noble</u>, elevated, exalted, glorious, grand, great, high, lofty

submerge *verb* <u>immerse</u>, deluge, dip, duck, engulf, flood, inundate, overflow, overwhelm, plunge, sink, swamp

submission *noun* 1 <u>surrender</u>, assent, capitulation, giving in, yielding 2 <u>presentation</u>, entry, handing in, tendering 3 <u>meekness</u>, compliance, deference, docility, obedience, passivity, resignation

submissive *adjective* <u>meek</u>, accommodating, acquiescent, amenable, compliant, docile, obedient, passive, pliant, tractable, unresisting, yielding

submit *verb* 1 <u>surrender</u>, accede, agree, capitulate, comply, endure, give in, succumb, tolerate, yield 2 <u>put forward</u>, hand in, present, proffer, table, tender

subordinate adjective 1 lesser, dependent, inferior, junior, lower, minor, secondary, subject ♦ noun 2 inferior, aide, assistant, attendant, junior, second

subordination noun inferiority, inferior or secondary status, servitude, subjection

subscribe verb 1 donate, contribute, give 2 support, advocate, endorse

subscription noun 1 membership fee, annual payment, dues 2 donation, contribution, gift

subsequent adjective following, after, ensuing, later, succeeding, successive

subsequently adverb later, afterwards

subservient adjective servile, abject, deferential, obsequious, slavish, submissive, sycophantic

subside verb 1 decrease, abate, diminish, ease, ebb, lessen, quieten, slacken, wane 2 sink, cave in, collapse, drop, lower, settle

subsidence noun 1 sinking, settling 2 decrease, abatement, easing off, lessening, slackening

subsidiary adjective lesser, ancillary, auxiliary, minor, secondary, subordinate, supplementary

subsidize verb fund, finance, promote, sponsor, support

subsidy noun aid, allowance, assistance, grant, help, support

substance noun 1 material, body, fabric, stuff 2 meaning, essence, gist, import, main point, significance 3 reality,

actuality, concreteness 4 wealth, assets, estate, means, property, resources

substantial adjective big, ample, considerable, important, large, significant, sizable or sizeable

substantiate verb support, authenticate, confirm, establish, prove, verify

substitute verb 1 replace, change, exchange, interchange, swap, switch ♦ noun 2 replacement, agent, deputy, locum, proxy, reserve, sub, surrogate ♦ adjective 3 replacement, alternative, fall-back, proxy, reserve, second, surrogate

substitution noun replacement, change, exchange, swap, switch

subterfuge noun trick, deception, dodge, manoeuvre, ploy, ruse, stratagem

subtle adjective 1 sophisticated, delicate, refined 2 faint, delicate, implied, slight, understated 3 crafty, artful, cunning, devious, ingenious, shrewd, sly, wily

subtlety noun 1 sophistication, delicacy, refinement 2 cunning, artfulness, cleverness, craftiness, deviousness, ingenuity, slyness, wiliness

subtract verb take away, deduct, diminish, remove, take from, take off

subversive adjective 1 seditious, riotous, treasonous ♦ noun 2 dissident, fifth columnist, saboteur, terrorist, traitor

subvert verb overturn, sabotage, undermine

succeed verb 1 make it

(*informal*), be successful, crack it (*informal*), flourish, make good, make the grade (*informal*), prosper, thrive, triumph, work **2** follow, come next, ensue, result

success noun **1** luck, fame, fortune, happiness, prosperity, triumph **2** hit (*informal*), celebrity, megastar (*informal*), sensation, smash (*informal*), star, winner

successful adjective thriving, booming, flourishing, fortunate, fruitful, lucky, profitable, prosperous, rewarding, top, victorious

successfully adverb well, favourably, victoriously, with flying colours

succession noun **1** series, chain, course, cycle, order, progression, run, sequence, train **2** taking over, accession, assumption, inheritance

successive adjective consecutive, following, in succession

succinct adjective brief, compact, concise, laconic, pithy, terse

succour noun **1** help, aid, assistance ♦ verb **2** help, aid, assist

succulent adjective juicy, luscious, lush, moist

succumb verb **1** surrender, capitulate, give in, submit, yield **2** die, fall

sucker noun Slang fool, dupe, mug (*Brit. slang*), pushover (*slang*), victim

sudden adjective quick, abrupt, hasty, hurried, rapid, rash, swift, unexpected

suddenly adverb abruptly, all of a sudden, unexpectedly

sue verb Law take (someone) to court, charge, indict, prosecute, summon

suffer verb **1** undergo, bear, endure, experience, go through, sustain **2** tolerate, put up with (*informal*)

suffering noun pain, agony, anguish, discomfort, distress, hardship, misery, ordeal, torment

suffice verb be enough, be adequate, be sufficient, do, meet requirements, serve

sufficient adjective adequate, enough, satisfactory

suffocate verb choke, asphyxiate, smother, stifle

suggest verb **1** recommend, advise, advocate, prescribe, propose **2** bring to mind, evoke **3** hint, imply, indicate, intimate

suggestion noun **1** recommendation, motion, plan, proposal, proposition **2** hint, breath, indication, intimation, trace, whisper

suggestive adjective smutty, bawdy, blue, indelicate, provocative, racy, ribald, risqué, rude

suit noun **1** outfit, clothing, costume, dress, ensemble, habit **2** lawsuit, action, case, cause, proceeding, prosecution, trial ♦ verb **3** be acceptable to, do, gratify, please, satisfy **4** befit, agree, become, go with, harmonize, match, tally

suitability noun appropriateness, aptness, fitness, rightness

suitable adjective appropriate, apt, becoming, befitting, fit, fitting, proper, right, satisfactory

suite noun rooms, apartment

suitor noun Old-fashioned admirer, beau, young man

sulk verb be sullen, be in a huff, pout

sulky adjective huffy, cross, disgruntled, in the sulks, moody, petulant, querulous, resentful, sullen

sullen adjective morose, cross, dour, glowering, moody, sour, surly, unsociable

sully verb defile, besmirch, disgrace, dishonour, smirch, stain, tarnish

sultry adjective 1 humid, close, hot, muggy, oppressive, sticky, stifling 2 seductive, provocative, sensual, sexy (informal)

sum noun total, aggregate, amount, tally, whole

summarize verb sum up, abridge, condense, encapsulate, epitomize, précis

summary noun synopsis, abridgment, outline, précis, résumé, review, rundown

summit noun peak, acme, apex, head, height, pinnacle, top, zenith

summon verb 1 send for, bid, call, invite 2 often with up gather, draw on, muster

sumptuous adjective luxurious, gorgeous, grand, lavish, opulent, splendid, superb

sum up verb summarize, put in a nutshell, recapitulate, review

sunburnt adjective tanned, bronzed, brown, burnt, peeling, red

sundry adjective various, assorted, different, miscellaneous, several, some

sunken adjective 1 hollow, drawn, haggard 2 lower, buried, recessed, submerged

sunny adjective 1 bright, clear, fine, radiant, summery, sunlit, unclouded 2 cheerful, buoyant, cheery, happy, joyful, light-hearted

sunrise noun dawn, break of day, cockcrow, daybreak

sunset noun nightfall, close of (the) day, dusk, eventide

super adjective Slang excellent, cracking (Brit. informal), glorious, magnificent, marvellous, outstanding, sensational (informal), smashing (informal), superb, terrific (informal), wonderful

superb adjective splendid, excellent, exquisite, fine, first-rate, grand, magnificent, marvellous, superior, superlative, world-class

supercilious adjective scornful, arrogant, contemptuous, disdainful, haughty, lofty, snooty (informal), stuck-up (informal)

superficial adjective 1 hasty, casual, cursory, desultory, hurried, perfunctory, sketchy, slapdash 2 shallow, empty-headed, frivolous, silly, trivial 3 surface, exterior, external, on the surface, slight

superfluous adjective excess, extra, left over, redundant, remaining, spare, supernumerary, surplus

superhuman adjective 1 heroic, phenomenal, prodigious

2 <u>supernatural</u>, paranormal

superintendence noun
<u>supervision</u>, charge, control,
direction, government,
management

superintendent noun <u>supervisor</u>,
chief, controller, director,
governor, inspector, manager,
overseer

superior adjective 1 <u>better</u>,
grander, greater, higher,
surpassing, unrivalled
2 <u>supercilious</u>, condescending,
disdainful, haughty, lofty, lordly,
patronizing, pretentious,
snobbish 3 <u>first-class</u>, choice, de
luxe, excellent, exceptional,
exclusive, first-rate ◆ noun 4 <u>boss</u>
(informal), chief, director,
manager, principal, senior,
supervisor

superiority noun <u>supremacy</u>,
advantage, ascendancy,
excellence, lead, predominance

superlative adjective
<u>outstanding</u>, excellent, supreme,
unparalleled, unrivalled,
unsurpassed

supernatural adjective
<u>paranormal</u>, ghostly, hidden,
miraculous, mystic, occult,
psychic, spectral, uncanny,
unearthly

supersede verb <u>replace</u>, displace,
oust, supplant, take the place of,
usurp

supervise verb <u>oversee</u>, control,
direct, handle, look after,
manage, run, superintend

supervision noun
<u>superintendence</u>, care, charge,
control, direction, guidance,
management

supervisor noun <u>boss</u> (informal),
administrator, chief, foreman,
inspector, manager, overseer

supplant verb <u>replace</u>, displace,
oust, supersede, take the place of

supple adjective <u>flexible</u>, limber,
lissom(e), lithe, pliable, pliant

supplement noun 1 <u>addition</u>,
add-on, appendix, extra, insert,
postscript, pull-out ◆ verb 2 <u>add</u>,
augment, extend, reinforce

supplementary adjective
<u>additional</u>, add-on, ancillary,
auxiliary, extra, secondary

supplication noun <u>plea</u>, appeal,
entreaty, petition, prayer, request

supply verb 1 <u>provide</u>,
contribute, endow, equip,
furnish, give, grant, produce,
stock, yield ◆ noun 2 <u>store</u>,
cache, fund, hoard, quantity,
reserve, source, stock 3 usually
plural <u>provisions</u>, equipment,
food, materials, necessities,
rations, stores

support verb 1 <u>bear</u>, brace,
buttress, carry, hold, prop,
reinforce, sustain 2 <u>provide for</u>,
finance, fund, keep, look after,
maintain, sustain 3 <u>help</u>, aid,
assist, back, champion, defend,
second, side with 4 <u>bear out</u>,
confirm, corroborate,
substantiate, verify ◆ noun
5 <u>help</u>, aid, assistance, backing,
encouragement, loyalty 6 <u>prop</u>,
brace, foundation, pillar, post
7 <u>supporter</u>, backer, mainstay,
prop, second, tower of strength
8 <u>upkeep</u>, keep, maintenance,
subsistence, sustenance

supporter noun <u>follower</u>,
adherent, advocate, champion,
fan, friend, helper, patron,

sponsor, well-wisher

supportive *adjective* <u>helpful</u>, encouraging, sympathetic, understanding

suppose *verb* 1 <u>presume</u>, assume, conjecture, expect, guess (*informal, chiefly U.S. & Canad.*), imagine, think 2 <u>imagine</u>, conjecture, consider, hypothesize, postulate, pretend

supposed *adjective* 1 <u>presumed</u>, accepted, alleged, assumed, professed 2 *usually with* **to** <u>meant</u>, expected, obliged, required

supposedly *adverb* <u>allegedly</u>, hypothetically, ostensibly, presumably, theoretically

supposition *noun* <u>guess</u>, conjecture, hypothesis, presumption, speculation, surmise, theory

suppress *verb* 1 <u>stop</u>, check, conquer, crush, overpower, put an end to, quash, quell, subdue 2 <u>restrain</u>, conceal, contain, curb, hold in or back, repress, silence, smother, stifle

suppression *noun* <u>elimination</u>, check, crushing, quashing, smothering

supremacy *noun* <u>domination</u>, mastery, predominance, primacy, sovereignty, supreme power, sway

supreme *adjective* <u>highest</u>, chief, foremost, greatest, head, leading, paramount, pre-eminent, prime, principal, top, ultimate

supremo *noun* <u>head</u>, boss (*informal*), commander, director, governor, leader, master, principal, ruler

sure *adjective* 1 <u>certain</u>, assured, confident, convinced, decided, definite, positive 2 <u>reliable</u>, accurate, dependable, foolproof, infallible, undeniable, undoubted, unerring, unfailing 3 <u>inevitable</u>, assured, bound, guaranteed, inescapable

surely *adverb* <u>undoubtedly</u>, certainly, definitely, doubtlessly, indubitably, unquestionably, without doubt

surface *noun* 1 <u>outside</u>, covering, exterior, face, side, top, veneer ♦ *verb* 2 <u>appear</u>, arise, come to light, come up, crop up (*informal*), emerge, materialize, transpire

surfeit *noun* <u>excess</u>, glut, plethora, superfluity

surge *noun* 1 <u>rush</u>, flood, flow, gush, outpouring 2 <u>wave</u>, billow, roller, swell ♦ *verb* 3 <u>rush</u>, gush, heave, rise, roll

surly *adjective* <u>ill-tempered</u>, churlish, cross, grouchy (*informal*), morose, sulky, sullen, uncivil, ungracious

surmise *verb* 1 <u>guess</u>, conjecture, imagine, presume, speculate, suppose ♦ *noun* 2 <u>guess</u>, assumption, conjecture, presumption, speculation, supposition

surpass *verb* <u>outdo</u>, beat, eclipse, exceed, excel, outshine, outstrip, transcend

surpassing *adjective* <u>supreme</u>, exceptional, extraordinary, incomparable, matchless, outstanding, unrivalled

surplus *noun* 1 <u>excess</u>, balance,

remainder, residue, surfeit
♦ *adjective* **2** excess, extra, odd, remaining, spare, superfluous

surprise *noun* **1** shock, bombshell, eye-opener (*informal*), jolt, revelation **2** amazement, astonishment, incredulity, wonder ♦ *verb* **3** amaze, astonish, stagger, stun, take aback **4** catch unawares or off-guard, discover, spring upon, startle

surprised *adjective* amazed, astonished, speechless, taken by surprise, thunderstruck

surprising *adjective* amazing, astonishing, extraordinary, incredible, remarkable, staggering, unexpected, unusual

surrender *verb* **1** give in, capitulate, give way, submit, succumb, yield **2** give up, abandon, cede, concede, part with, relinquish, renounce, waive, yield ♦ *noun* **3** submission, capitulation, relinquishment, renunciation, resignation

surreptitious *adjective* secret, covert, furtive, sly, stealthy, underhand

surrogate *noun* substitute, proxy, representative, stand-in

surround *verb* enclose, encircle, encompass, envelop, hem in, ring

surroundings *plural noun* environment, background, location, milieu, setting

surveillance *noun* observation, inspection, scrutiny, supervision, watch

survey *verb* **1** look over, contemplate, examine, inspect, observe, scan, scrutinize, view

2 estimate, appraise, assess, measure, plan, plot, size up ♦ *noun* **3** examination, inspection, scrutiny **4** study, inquiry, review

survive *verb* remain alive, endure, last, live on, outlast, outlive

susceptible *adjective* **1** *usually with* **to** liable, disposed, given, inclined, prone, subject, vulnerable **2** impressionable, receptive, responsive, sensitive, suggestible

suspect *verb* **1** believe, consider, feel, guess, speculate, suppose **2** distrust, doubt, mistrust ♦ *adjective* **3** dubious, doubtful, iffy (*informal*), questionable

suspend *verb* **1** hang, attach, dangle **2** postpone, cease, cut short, defer, discontinue, interrupt, put off, shelve

suspense *noun* uncertainty, anxiety, apprehension, doubt, expectation, insecurity, irresolution, tension

suspension *noun* postponement, abeyance, break, breaking off, deferment, discontinuation, interruption

suspicion *noun* **1** distrust, doubt, dubiety, misgiving, mistrust, qualm, scepticism, wariness **2** idea, guess, hunch, impression, notion **3** trace, hint, shade, soupçon, streak, suggestion, tinge, touch

suspicious *adjective* **1** distrustful, doubtful, sceptical, unbelieving, wary **2** suspect, dodgy (*Brit., Austral., & N.Z. informal*), doubtful, dubious, fishy (*informal*), questionable

sustain verb 1 <u>maintain</u>, continue, keep up, prolong, protract 2 <u>keep alive</u>, aid, assist, help, nourish 3 <u>withstand</u>, bear, endure, experience, feel, suffer, undergo 4 <u>support</u>, bear, uphold

sustained adjective <u>continuous</u>, constant, nonstop, perpetual, prolonged, steady, unremitting

swagger verb <u>show off</u> (informal), boast, brag, parade

swallow verb <u>gulp</u>, consume, devour, drink, eat, swig (informal)

swamp noun 1 <u>bog</u>, fen, marsh, mire, morass, quagmire, slough ♦ verb 2 <u>flood</u>, capsize, engulf, inundate, sink, submerge 3 <u>overwhelm</u>, flood, inundate, overload

swap, swop verb <u>exchange</u>, barter, interchange, switch, trade

swarm noun 1 <u>multitude</u>, army, crowd, flock, herd, horde, host, mass, throng ♦ verb 2 <u>crowd</u>, flock, mass, stream, throng 3 <u>teem</u>, abound, bristle, crawl

swarthy adjective <u>dark-skinned</u>, black, brown, dark, dark-complexioned, dusky

swashbuckling adjective <u>dashing</u>, bold, daredevil, flamboyant

swathe verb <u>wrap</u>, bundle up, cloak, drape, envelop, shroud

sway verb 1 <u>lean</u>, bend, rock, roll, swing 2 <u>influence</u>, affect, guide, induce, persuade ♦ noun 3 <u>power</u>, authority, clout (informal), control, influence

swear verb 1 <u>curse</u>, be foul-mouthed, blaspheme 2 <u>declare</u>, affirm, assert, promise, testify, vow

swearing noun <u>bad language</u>, blasphemy, cursing, foul language, profanity

swearword noun <u>oath</u>, curse, expletive, four-letter word, obscenity, profanity

sweat noun 1 <u>perspiration</u> 2 Informal <u>labour</u>, chore, drudgery, toil 3 Informal <u>worry</u>, agitation, anxiety, distress, panic, strain ♦ verb 4 <u>perspire</u>, glow 5 Informal <u>worry</u>, agonize, fret, suffer, torture oneself

sweaty adjective <u>perspiring</u>, clammy, sticky

sweep verb 1 <u>clear</u>, brush, clean, remove 2 <u>sail</u>, fly, glide, pass, skim, tear, zoom ♦ noun 3 <u>arc</u>, bend, curve, move, stroke, swing 4 <u>extent</u>, range, scope, stretch

sweeping adjective 1 <u>wide-ranging</u>, all-embracing, all-inclusive, broad, comprehensive, extensive, global, wide 2 <u>indiscriminate</u>, blanket, exaggerated, overstated, unqualified, wholesale

sweet adjective 1 <u>sugary</u>, cloying, saccharine 2 <u>charming</u>, agreeable, appealing, cute, delightful, engaging, kind, likable or likeable, lovable, winning 3 <u>melodious</u>, dulcet, harmonious, mellow, musical 4 <u>fragrant</u>, aromatic, clean, fresh, pure ♦ noun 5 usually plural confectionery, bonbon, candy (U.S.) 6 <u>dessert</u>, pudding

sweeten verb 1 <u>sugar</u> 2 <u>mollify</u>, appease, pacify, soothe

sweetheart noun <u>lover</u>, beloved, boyfriend or girlfriend, darling, dear, love

swell verb 1 <u>expand</u>, balloon,

bloat, bulge, dilate, distend, enlarge, grow, increase, rise
♦ *noun* **2** wave, billow, surge

swelling *noun* enlargement, bulge, bump, distension, inflammation, lump, protuberance

sweltering *adjective* hot, boiling, burning, oppressive, scorching, stifling

swerve *verb* veer, bend, deflect, deviate, diverge, stray, swing, turn, turn aside

swift *adjective* quick, fast, hurried, prompt, rapid, speedy

swiftly *adverb* quickly, fast, hurriedly, promptly, rapidly, speedily

swiftness *noun* speed, promptness, quickness, rapidity, speediness, velocity

swindle *verb* **1** cheat, con, defraud, do (*slang*), fleece, rip (someone) off (*slang*), skin (*slang*), sting (*informal*), trick
♦ *noun* **2** fraud, con trick (*informal*), deception, fiddle (*Brit. informal*), racket, rip-off (*slang*), scam (*slang*)

swindler *noun* cheat, con man (*informal*), fraud, rogue, shark, trickster

swing *verb* **1** sway, oscillate, rock, veer, wave **2** *usually with* **round** turn, curve, pivot, rotate, swivel **3** hang, dangle, suspend
♦ *noun* **4** swaying, oscillation

swingeing *adjective* severe, drastic, excessive, harsh, heavy, punishing, stringent

swipe *verb* **1** hit, lash out at, slap, strike, wallop (*informal*) **2** *Slang* steal, appropriate, filch,

lift (*informal*), nick (*slang, chiefly Brit.*), pinch (*informal*), purloin
♦ *noun* **3** blow, clout (*informal*), cuff, slap, smack, wallop (*informal*)

swirl *verb* whirl, churn, eddy, spin, twist

switch *noun* **1** change, reversal, shift **2** exchange, substitution, swap ♦ *verb* **3** change, deflect, deviate, divert, shift **4** exchange, substitute, swap

swivel *verb* turn, pivot, revolve, rotate, spin

swollen *adjective* enlarged, bloated, distended, inflamed, puffed up

swoop *verb* **1** pounce, descend, dive, rush, stoop, sweep ♦ *noun* **2** pounce, descent, drop, lunge, plunge, rush, stoop, sweep

swop *see* SWAP

swot *verb* *Informal* study, cram (*informal*), mug up (*Brit. slang*), revise

sycophant *noun* crawler, bootlicker (*informal*), fawner, flatterer, toady, yes man

sycophantic *adjective* obsequious, crawling, fawning, flattering, grovelling, ingratiating, servile, smarmy (*Brit. informal*), toadying, unctuous

syllabus *noun* course of study, curriculum

symbol *noun* sign, badge, emblem, figure, image, logo, mark, representation, token

symbolic *adjective* representative, allegorical, emblematic, figurative

symbolize *verb* represent, denote, mean, personify, signify, stand for, typify

symmetrical adjective <u>balanced</u>, in proportion, regular

symmetry noun <u>balance</u>, evenness, order, proportion, regularity

sympathetic adjective 1 <u>caring</u>, compassionate, concerned, interested, kind, pitying, supportive, understanding, warm 2 <u>like-minded</u>, agreeable, companionable, compatible, congenial, friendly

sympathize verb 1 <u>feel for</u>, commiserate, condole, pity 2 <u>agree</u>, side with, understand

sympathizer noun <u>supporter</u>, partisan, well-wisher

sympathy noun 1 <u>compassion</u>, commiseration, pity, understanding 2 <u>agreement</u>, affinity, fellow feeling, rapport

symptom noun <u>sign</u>, expression, indication, mark, token, warning

symptomatic adjective <u>indicative</u>, characteristic, suggestive

synthetic adjective <u>artificial</u>, fake, man-made

system noun 1 <u>method</u>, practice, procedure, routine, technique 2 <u>arrangement</u>, classification, organization, scheme, structure

systematic adjective <u>methodical</u>, efficient, orderly, organized

T t

table noun 1 <u>counter</u>, bench, board, stand 2 <u>list</u>, catalogue, chart, diagram, record, register,

roll, schedule, tabulation ♦ verb 3 <u>submit</u>, enter, move, propose, put forward, suggest

tableau noun <u>picture</u>, representation, scene, spectacle

taboo noun 1 <u>prohibition</u>, anathema, ban, interdict, proscription, restriction ♦ adjective 2 <u>forbidden</u>, anathema, banned, outlawed, prohibited, proscribed, unacceptable, unmentionable

tacit adjective <u>implied</u>, implicit, inferred, undeclared, understood, unexpressed, unspoken, unstated

taciturn adjective <u>uncommunicative</u>, quiet, reserved, reticent, silent, tight-lipped, unforthcoming, withdrawn

tack[1] noun 1 <u>nail</u>, drawing pin, pin ♦ verb 2 <u>fasten</u>, affix, attach, fix, nail, pin 3 <u>stitch</u>, baste 4 <u>tack on</u> append, add, attach, tag

tack[2] noun <u>course</u>, approach, direction, heading, line, method, path, plan, procedure, way

tackle verb 1 <u>deal with</u>, attempt, come or get to grips with, embark upon, get stuck into (informal), have a go at (informal), set about, undertake 2 <u>confront</u>, challenge, grab, grasp, halt, intercept, seize, stop ♦ noun 3 <u>challenge</u>, block 4 <u>equipment</u>, accoutrements, apparatus, gear, paraphernalia, tools, trappings

tacky[1] adjective <u>sticky</u>, adhesive, gluey, gummy, wet

tacky[2] adjective Informal <u>vulgar</u>, cheap, naff (Brit. slang), seedy, shabby, shoddy, sleazy, tasteless, tatty

tact noun <u>diplomacy</u>, consideration, delicacy, discretion, sensitivity, thoughtfulness, understanding

tactful adjective <u>diplomatic</u>, considerate, delicate, discreet, polite, politic, sensitive, thoughtful, understanding

tactic noun 1 <u>policy</u>, approach, manoeuvre, method, move, ploy, scheme, stratagem 2 **tactics** <u>strategy</u>, campaigning, generalship, manoeuvres, plans

tactical adjective <u>strategic</u>, cunning, diplomatic, shrewd, smart

tactician noun <u>strategist</u>, general, mastermind, planner

tactless adjective <u>insensitive</u>, impolite, impolitic, inconsiderate, indelicate, indiscreet, thoughtless, undiplomatic, unsubtle

tag noun 1 <u>label</u>, flap, identification, mark, marker, note, slip, tab, ticket ♦ verb 2 <u>label</u>, mark 3 with **along** or **on** <u>accompany</u>, attend, follow, shadow, tail (informal), trail

tail noun 1 <u>extremity</u>, appendage, end, rear end, tailpiece 2 **turn tail** <u>run away</u>, cut and run, flee, retreat, run off, take to one's heels ♦ verb 3 Informal <u>follow</u>, shadow, stalk, track, trail

tailor noun 1 <u>outfitter</u>, clothier, costumier, couturier, dressmaker, seamstress ♦ verb 2 <u>adapt</u>, adjust, alter, customize, fashion, modify, mould, shape, style

taint verb 1 <u>spoil</u>, blemish, contaminate, corrupt, damage, defile, pollute, ruin, stain, sully, tarnish ♦ noun 2 <u>stain</u>, black mark, blemish, blot, defect, demerit, fault, flaw, spot

take verb 1 <u>capture</u>, acquire, catch, get, grasp, grip, obtain, secure, seize 2 <u>accompany</u>, bring, conduct, convoy, escort, guide, lead, usher 3 <u>carry</u>, bear, bring, convey, ferry, fetch, haul, transport 4 <u>steal</u>, appropriate, misappropriate, pinch (informal), pocket, purloin 5 <u>require</u>, call for, demand, necessitate, need 6 <u>tolerate</u>, abide, bear, endure, put up with (informal), stand, stomach, withstand 7 <u>have room for</u>, accept, accommodate, contain, hold 8 <u>subtract</u>, deduct, eliminate, remove 9 <u>assume</u>, believe, consider, perceive, presume, regard, understand

take in verb 1 <u>understand</u>, absorb, assimilate, comprehend, digest, get the hang of (informal), grasp 2 <u>deceive</u>, cheat, con (informal), dupe, fool, hoodwink, mislead, swindle, trick

takeoff noun 1 <u>departure</u>, launch, liftoff 2 Informal <u>parody</u>, caricature, imitation, lampoon, satire, send-up (Brit. informal), spoof (informal)

take off verb 1 <u>remove</u>, discard, peel off, strip of 2 <u>lift off</u>, take to the air 3 Informal <u>depart</u>, abscond, decamp, disappear, go, leave, slope off 4 Informal <u>parody</u>, caricature, imitate, lampoon, mimic, mock, satirize, send up (Brit. informal)

takeover noun <u>merger</u>, coup, incorporation

take up *verb* 1 <u>occupy</u>, absorb, consume, cover, extend over, fill, use up 2 <u>start</u>, adopt, become involved in, engage in

taking *adjective* 1 <u>charming</u>, attractive, beguiling, captivating, enchanting, engaging, fetching (*informal*), likable or likeable, prepossessing ♦ *noun* 2 **takings** <u>revenue</u>, earnings, income, proceeds, profits, receipts, returns, take

tale *noun* <u>story</u>, account, anecdote, fable, legend, narrative, saga, yarn (*informal*)

talent *noun* <u>ability</u>, aptitude, capacity, flair, genius, gift, knack

talented *adjective* <u>gifted</u>, able, brilliant

talisman *noun* <u>charm</u>, amulet, fetish, lucky charm, mascot

talk *verb* 1 <u>speak</u>, chat, chatter, communicate, converse, gossip, natter, utter 2 <u>negotiate</u>, confabulate, confer, parley 3 <u>inform</u>, blab, give the game away, grass (*Brit. slang*), let the cat out of the bag, tell all ♦ *noun* 4 <u>speech</u>, address, discourse, disquisition, lecture, oration, sermon

talkative *adjective* <u>loquacious</u>, chatty, effusive, garrulous, gossipy, long-winded, mouthy, verbose, voluble, wordy

talker *noun* <u>speaker</u>, chatterbox, conversationalist, lecturer, orator

talking-to *noun* <u>reprimand</u>, criticism, dressing-down (*informal*), lecture, rebuke, reproach, reproof, scolding, telling-off (*informal*), ticking-off (*informal*)

tall *adjective* 1 <u>high</u>, big, elevated, giant, lanky, lofty, soaring, towering 2 *As in* **tall story** *Informal* <u>implausible</u>, absurd, cock-and-bull (*informal*), exaggerated, far-fetched, incredible, preposterous, unbelievable 3 *As in* **tall order** <u>difficult</u>, demanding, hard, unreasonable, well-nigh impossible

tally *verb* 1 <u>correspond</u>, accord, agree, coincide, concur, conform, fit, harmonize, match, square ♦ *noun* 2 <u>record</u>, count, mark, reckoning, running total, score, total

tame *adjective* 1 <u>domesticated</u>, amenable, broken, disciplined, docile, gentle, obedient, tractable 2 <u>submissive</u>, compliant, docile, manageable, meek, obedient, subdued, unresisting 3 <u>uninteresting</u>, bland, boring, dull, humdrum, insipid, unexciting, uninspiring, vapid ♦ *verb* 4 <u>domesticate</u>, break in, house-train, train 5 <u>discipline</u>, bring to heel, conquer, humble, master, subdue, subjugate, suppress

tamper *verb* <u>interfere</u>, alter, fiddle (*informal*), fool about (*informal*), meddle, mess about, tinker

tangible *adjective* <u>definite</u>, actual, concrete, material, palpable, perceptible, positive, real

tangle *noun* 1 <u>knot</u>, coil, entanglement, jungle, twist, web 2 <u>confusion</u>, complication, entanglement, imbroglio, jam, mess (*informal*), imbroglio, jam, mess, mix-up ♦ *verb* 3 <u>twist</u>, coil, entangle, interweave, knot, mat, mesh, ravel **4** *often with* with come into conflict, come up against, contend, contest, cross swords, dispute, lock horns

tangled *adjective* **1** twisted, entangled, jumbled, knotted, matted, messy, snarled, tousled **2** complicated, complex, confused, convoluted, involved, knotty, messy, mixed-up

tangy *adjective* sharp, piquant, pungent, spicy, tart

tantalize *verb* torment, frustrate, lead on, taunt, tease, torture

tantamount *adjective* equivalent, commensurate, equal, synonymous

tantrum *noun* outburst, fit, flare-up, hysterics, temper

tap[1] *verb* **1** knock, beat, drum, pat, rap, strike, touch ♦ *noun* **2** knock, pat, rap, touch

tap[2] *noun* **1** valve, stopcock **2 on tap: a** *Informal* available, at hand, in reserve, on hand, ready **b** on draught ♦ *verb* **3** listen in on, bug (*informal*), eavesdrop on **4** draw off, bleed, drain, siphon off

tape *noun* **1** strip, band, ribbon ♦ *verb* **2** record, tape-record, video **3** bind, seal, secure, stick, wrap

taper *verb* **1** narrow, come to a point, thin **2 taper off** lessen, decrease, die away, dwindle, fade, reduce, subside, wane, wind down

target *noun* **1** goal, aim, ambition, end, intention, mark, object, objective **2** victim, butt, scapegoat

tariff *noun* **1** tax, duty, excise, levy, toll **2** schedule, menu

tarnish *verb* **1** stain, blacken, blemish, blot, darken, discolour, sully, taint ♦ *noun* **2** stain, blemish, blot, discoloration, spot, taint

tart[1] *noun* pie, pastry, tartlet

tart[2] *adjective* sharp, acid, bitter, piquant, pungent, sour, tangy, vinegary

tart[3] *noun* slut, call girl, floozy (*slang*), prostitute, trollop, whore

task *noun* **1** job, assignment, chore, duty, enterprise, exercise, mission, undertaking **2 take to task** criticize, blame, censure, reprimand, reproach, reprove, scold, tell off (*informal*), upbraid

taste *noun* **1** flavour, relish, savour, smack, tang **2** bit, bite, dash, morsel, mouthful, sample, soupçon, spoonful, titbit **3** liking, appetite, fancy, fondness, inclination, partiality, penchant, predilection, preference **4** refinement, appreciation, discernment, discrimination, elegance, judgment, sophistication, style ♦ *verb* **5** distinguish, differentiate, discern, perceive **6** sample, savour, sip, test, try **7** have a flavour of, savour of, smack of **8** experience, encounter, know, meet with, partake of, undergo

tasteful *adjective* refined, artistic, cultivated, cultured, discriminating, elegant, exquisite, in good taste, polished, stylish

tasteless *adjective* **1** insipid, bland, boring, dull, flat, flavourless, mild, thin, weak

2 vulgar, crass, crude, gaudy, gross, inelegant, naff (*Brit. slang*), tacky (*informal*), tawdry

tasty *adjective* delicious, appetizing, delectable, full-flavoured, luscious, palatable, savoury, scrumptious (*informal*), toothsome

tatters *noun* **in tatters** ragged, down at heel, in rags, in shreds, ripped, tattered, threadbare, torn

tatty *adjective* ragged, bedraggled, dilapidated, down at heel, neglected, run-down, scruffy, shabby, threadbare, worn

taunt *verb* **1** tease, deride, insult, jeer, mock, provoke, ridicule, torment ♦ *noun* **2** jeer, derision, dig, gibe, insult, provocation, ridicule, sarcasm, teasing

taut *adjective* tight, flexed, rigid, strained, stressed, stretched, tense

tavern *noun* inn, alehouse (*archaic*), bar, hostelry, pub (*informal, chiefly Brit.*), public house

tawdry *adjective* vulgar, cheap, gaudy, gimcrack, naff (*Brit. slang*), tacky (*informal*), tasteless, tatty, tinselly

tax *noun* **1** charge, duty, excise, levy, tariff, tithe, toll ♦ *verb* **2** charge, assess, rate **3** strain, burden, exhaust, load, stretch, test, try, weaken, weary

taxing *adjective* demanding, exacting, onerous, punishing, sapping, stressful, tiring, tough, trying

teach *verb* instruct, coach, drill, educate, enlighten, guide, inform, show, train, tutor

teacher *noun* instructor, coach, educator, guide, lecturer, master or mistress, mentor, schoolteacher, trainer, tutor

team *noun* **1** group, band, body, bunch, company, gang, line-up, set, side, squad ♦ *verb* **2** often *with* **up** join, band together, cooperate, couple, get together, link, unite, work together

teamwork *noun* cooperation, collaboration, coordination, esprit de corps, fellowship, harmony, unity

tear *verb* **1** rip, claw, lacerate, mangle, mutilate, pull apart, rend, rupture, scratch, shred, split **2** rush, bolt, charge, dash, fly, hurry, race, run, speed, sprint, zoom ♦ *noun* **3** hole, laceration, rent, rip, rupture, scratch, split

tearaway *noun* hooligan, delinquent, good-for-nothing, rowdy, ruffian

tearful *adjective* weeping, blubbering, crying, in tears, lachrymose, sobbing, weepy (*informal*), whimpering

tears *plural noun* **1** crying, blubbering, sobbing, wailing, weeping **2** **in tears** crying, blubbering, distressed, sobbing, weeping

tease *verb* mock, goad, lead on, provoke, pull someone's leg (*informal*), tantalize, taunt, torment

technical *adjective* scientific, hi-tech *or* high-tech, skilled, specialist, specialized, technological

technique *noun* **1** method, approach, manner, means,

mode, procedure, style, system, way 2 **skill**, artistry, craft, craftsmanship, execution, performance, proficiency, touch

tedious adjective **boring**, drab, dreary, dull, humdrum, irksome, laborious, mind-numbing, monotonous, tiresome, wearisome

tedium noun **boredom**, drabness, dreariness, dullness, monotony, routine, sameness, tediousness

teeming[1] adjective **full**, abundant, alive, brimming, bristling, bursting, crawling, overflowing, swarming, thick

teeming[2] adjective **pouring**, bucketing down (informal), pelting

teenager noun **youth**, adolescent, boy, girl, juvenile, minor

teeter verb **wobble**, rock, seesaw, stagger, sway, totter, waver

teetotaller noun **abstainer**, nondrinker

telepathy noun **mind-reading**, sixth sense

telephone noun 1 **phone**, handset, line ♦ verb 2 **call**, dial, phone, ring (chiefly Brit.)

telescope noun 1 **glass**, spyglass ♦ verb 2 **shorten**, abbreviate, abridge, compress, condense, contract, shrink

television noun **TV**, small screen (informal), telly (Brit. informal), the box (Brit. informal), the tube (slang)

tell verb 1 **inform**, announce, communicate, disclose, divulge, express, make known, notify, proclaim, reveal, state 2 **instruct**,

bid, call upon, command, direct, order, require, summon 3 **describe**, chronicle, depict, narrate, portray, recount, relate, report 4 **distinguish**, differentiate, discern, discriminate, identify 5 **carry weight**, count, have or take effect, make its presence felt, register, take its toll, weigh

telling adjective **effective**, considerable, decisive, forceful, impressive, influential, marked, powerful, significant, striking

telling-off noun **reprimand**, criticism, dressing-down (informal), lecture, rebuke, reproach, reproof, scolding, talking-to, ticking-off (informal)

tell off verb **reprimand**, berate, censure, chide, haul over the coals (informal), lecture, read the riot act, rebuke, reproach, scold

temerity noun **boldness**, audacity, chutzpah (U.S. & Canad. informal), effrontery, front, impudence, nerve (informal), rashness, recklessness

temper noun 1 **rage**, bad mood, fury, passion, tantrum 2 **irritability**, hot-headedness, irascibility, passion, petulance, resentment, surliness 3 **self-control**, calmness, composure, cool (slang), equanimity 4 **frame of mind**, constitution, disposition, humour, mind, mood, nature, temperament ♦ verb 5 **moderate**, assuage, lessen, mitigate, mollify, restrain, soften, soothe, tone down 6 **strengthen**, anneal, harden, toughen

temperament noun 1 **nature**,

bent, character, constitution, disposition, humour, make-up, outlook, personality, temper **2** excitability, anger, hot-headedness, moodiness, petulance, volatility

temperamental adjective **1** moody, capricious, emotional, excitable, highly strung, hypersensitive, irritable, sensitive, touchy, volatile **2** unreliable, erratic, inconsistent, inconstant, unpredictable

temperance noun **1** moderation, continence, discretion, forbearance, restraint, self-control, self-discipline, self-restraint **2** teetotalism, abstemiousness, abstinence, sobriety

temperate adjective **1** mild, calm, cool, fair, gentle, moderate, pleasant **2** self-restrained, calm, composed, dispassionate, even-tempered, mild, moderate, reasonable, self-controlled, sensible

tempest noun gale, cyclone, hurricane, squall, storm, tornado, typhoon

tempestuous adjective **1** stormy, blustery, gusty, inclement, raging, squally, turbulent, windy **2** violent, boisterous, emotional, furious, heated, intense, passionate, stormy, turbulent, wild

temple noun shrine, church, sanctuary

temporarily adverb briefly, fleetingly, for the time being, momentarily, pro tem

temporary adjective

impermanent, brief, ephemeral, fleeting, interim, momentary, provisional, short-lived, transitory

tempt verb entice, allure, attract, coax, invite, lead on, lure, seduce, tantalize

temptation noun enticement, allurement, inducement, lure, pull, seduction, tantalization

tempting adjective enticing, alluring, appetizing, attractive, inviting, mouthwatering, seductive, tantalizing

tenable adjective sound, arguable, believable, defensible, justifiable, plausible, rational, reasonable, viable

tenacious adjective **1** firm, clinging, forceful, immovable, iron, strong, tight, unshakable **2** stubborn, adamant, determined, dogged, obdurate, obstinate, persistent, resolute, steadfast, unswerving, unyielding

tenacity noun perseverance, application, determination, doggedness, obduracy, persistence, resolve, steadfastness, stubbornness

tenancy noun lease, occupancy, possession, renting, residence

tenant noun leaseholder, inhabitant, lessee, occupant, occupier, renter, resident

tend[1] verb **1** be inclined, be apt, be liable, gravitate, have a tendency, incline, lean **2** go, aim, bear, head, lead, make for, point

tend[2] verb take care of, attend, cultivate, keep, look after, maintain, manage, nurture, watch over

tendency noun inclination, disposition, leaning, liability, proclivity, proneness, propensity, susceptibility

tender[1] adjective 1 gentle, affectionate, caring, compassionate, considerate, kind, loving, sympathetic, tenderhearted, warm-hearted 2 vulnerable, immature, impressionable, inexperienced, raw, sensitive, young, youthful 3 sensitive, bruised, inflamed, painful, raw, sore

tender[2] verb 1 offer, give, hand in, present, proffer, propose, put forward, submit, volunteer ♦ noun 2 offer, bid, estimate, proposal, submission 3 As in **legal tender** currency, money, payment

tenderness noun 1 gentleness, affection, care, compassion, consideration, kindness, love, sentimentality, sympathy, warmth 2 soreness, inflammation, pain, sensitivity

tense adjective 1 nervous, anxious, apprehensive, edgy, jumpy, keyed up, on edge, on tenterhooks, strained, uptight (informal) 2 stressful, exciting, nerve-racking, worrying 3 tight, rigid, strained, stretched, taut ♦ verb 4 tighten, brace, flex, strain, stretch

tension noun 1 suspense, anxiety, apprehension, hostility, nervousness, pressure, strain, stress, unease 2 tightness, pressure, rigidity, stiffness, stress, stretching, tautness

tentative adjective 1 experimental, conjectural, indefinite, provisional, speculative, unconfirmed, unsettled 2 hesitant, cautious, diffident, doubtful, faltering, timid, uncertain, undecided, unsure

tenuous adjective slight, doubtful, dubious, flimsy, insubstantial, nebulous, shaky, sketchy, weak

tepid adjective 1 lukewarm, warmish 2 half-hearted, apathetic, cool, indifferent, lukewarm, unenthusiastic

term noun 1 word, expression, name, phrase, title 2 period, duration, interval, season, span, spell, time, while ♦ verb 3 call, designate, dub, entitle, label, name, style

terminal adjective 1 deadly, fatal, incurable, killing, lethal, mortal 2 final, concluding, extreme, last, ultimate, utmost ♦ noun 3 terminus, depot, end of the line, station

terminate verb end, abort, cease, close, complete, conclude, discontinue, finish, stop

termination noun ending, abortion, cessation, completion, conclusion, discontinuation, end, finish

terminology noun language, jargon, nomenclature, phraseology, terms, vocabulary

terminus noun end of the line, depot, garage, last stop, station

terms plural noun 1 conditions, particulars, provisions, provisos, qualifications, specifications, stipulations 2 relationship, footing, relations, standing, status

terrain noun <u>ground</u>, country, going, land, landscape, topography

terrestrial adjective <u>earthly</u>, global, worldly

terrible adjective **1** <u>serious</u>, dangerous, desperate, extreme, severe **2** *Informal* <u>bad</u>, abysmal, awful, dire, dreadful, poor, rotten (*informal*) **3** <u>fearful</u>, dreadful, frightful, horrendous, horrible, horrifying, monstrous, shocking, terrifying

terribly adverb <u>extremely</u>, awfully (*informal*), decidedly, desperately, exceedingly, seriously, thoroughly, very

terrific adjective **1** <u>great</u>, enormous, fearful, gigantic, huge, intense, tremendous **2** *Informal* <u>excellent</u>, amazing, brilliant, fantastic (*informal*), magnificent, marvellous, outstanding, sensational (*informal*), stupendous, superb, wonderful

terrified adjective <u>frightened</u>, alarmed, appalled, horrified, horror-struck, panic-stricken, petrified, scared

terrify verb <u>frighten</u>, alarm, appal, horrify, make one's hair stand on end, scare, shock, terrorize

territory noun <u>district</u>, area, country, domain, land, patch, province, region, zone

terror noun **1** <u>fear</u>, alarm, anxiety, dread, fright, horror, panic, shock **2** <u>scourge</u>, bogeyman, bugbear, devil, fiend, monster

terrorize verb <u>oppress</u>, browbeat, bully, coerce, intimidate, menace, threaten

terse adjective **1** <u>concise</u>, brief, condensed, laconic, monosyllabic, pithy, short, succinct **2** <u>curt</u>, abrupt, brusque, short, snappy

test verb **1** <u>check</u>, analyse, assess, examine, experiment, investigate, put to the test, research, try out ♦ noun **2** <u>examination</u>, acid test, analysis, assessment, check, evaluation, investigation, research, trial

testament noun **1** <u>proof</u>, demonstration, evidence, testimony, tribute, witness **2** <u>will</u>, last wishes

testify verb <u>bear witness</u>, affirm, assert, attest, certify, corroborate, state, swear, vouch

testimonial noun <u>tribute</u>, commendation, endorsement, recommendation, reference

testimony noun **1** <u>evidence</u>, affidavit, deposition, statement, submission **2** <u>proof</u>, corroboration, demonstration, evidence, indication, manifestation, support, verification

testing adjective <u>difficult</u>, arduous, challenging, demanding, exacting, rigorous, searching, strenuous, taxing, tough

tether noun **1** <u>rope</u>, chain, fetter, halter, lead, leash **2** **at the end of one's tether** <u>exasperated</u>, at one's wits' end, exhausted ♦ verb **3** <u>tie</u>, bind, chain, fasten, fetter, secure

text noun **1** <u>contents</u>, body **2** <u>words</u>, wording

texture noun <u>feel</u>, consistency, grain, structure, surface, tissue

thank verb <u>say thank you</u>, show one's appreciation

thankful adjective <u>grateful</u>, appreciative, beholden, indebted, obliged, pleased, relieved

thankless adjective <u>unrewarding</u>, fruitless, unappreciated, unprofitable, unrequited

thanks plural noun 1 <u>gratitude</u>, acknowledgment, appreciation, credit, gratefulness, recognition 2 **thanks to** <u>because of</u>, as a result of, due to, owing to, through

thaw verb <u>melt</u>, defrost, dissolve, liquefy, soften, unfreeze, warm

theatrical adjective 1 <u>dramatic</u>, Thespian 2 <u>exaggerated</u>, affected, dramatic, histrionic, mannered, melodramatic, ostentatious, showy, stagy

theft noun <u>stealing</u>, embezzlement, fraud, larceny, pilfering, purloining, robbery, thieving

theme noun 1 <u>subject</u>, idea, keynote, subject matter, topic 2 <u>motif</u>, leitmotif

theological adjective <u>religious</u>, doctrinal, ecclesiastical

theoretical adjective <u>abstract</u>, academic, conjectural, hypothetical, notional, speculative

theorize verb <u>speculate</u>, conjecture, formulate, guess, hypothesize, project, propound, suppose

theory noun <u>supposition</u>, assumption, conjecture, hypothesis, presumption, speculation, surmise, thesis

therapeutic adjective <u>beneficial</u>, corrective, curative, good, healing, remedial, restorative, salutary

therapist noun <u>healer</u>, physician

therapy noun <u>remedy</u>, cure, healing, treatment

therefore adverb <u>consequently</u>, accordingly, as a result, ergo, hence, so, then, thence, thus

thesis noun 1 <u>dissertation</u>, essay, monograph, paper, treatise 2 <u>proposition</u>, contention, hypothesis, idea, opinion, proposal, theory, view

thick adjective 1 <u>wide</u>, broad, bulky, fat, solid, substantial 2 <u>dense</u>, close, compact, concentrated, condensed, heavy, impenetrable, opaque 3 Informal <u>stupid</u>, brainless, dense, dopey (informal), moronic, obtuse, slow, thickheaded 4 Informal <u>friendly</u>, close, devoted, familiar, inseparable, intimate, pally (informal) 5 <u>full</u>, brimming, bristling, bursting, covered, crawling, packed, swarming, teeming 6 **a bit thick** <u>unfair</u>, unjust, unreasonable

thicken verb <u>set</u>, clot, coagulate, condense, congeal, jell

thicket noun <u>wood</u>, brake, coppice, copse, covert, grove

thickset adjective <u>well-built</u>, bulky, burly, heavy, muscular, stocky, strong, sturdy

thief noun <u>robber</u>, burglar, embezzler, housebreaker, pickpocket, pilferer, plunderer, shoplifter, stealer

thieve verb <u>steal</u>, filch, nick

(*slang, chiefly Brit.*), pilfer, pinch (*informal*), purloin, rob, swipe (*slang*)

thin *adjective* **1** narrow, attenuated, fine **2** slim, bony, emaciated, lean, scrawny, skeletal, skinny, slender, slight, spare, spindly **3** meagre, deficient, scanty, scarce, scattered, skimpy, sparse, wispy **4** delicate, diaphanous, filmy, fine, flimsy, gossamer, sheer, unsubstantial **5** unconvincing, feeble, flimsy, inadequate, lame, poor, superficial, weak

thing *noun* **1** object, article, being, body, entity, something, substance **2** *Informal* obsession, bee in one's bonnet, fetish, fixation, hang-up (*informal*), mania, phobia, preoccupation **3** things possessions, belongings, clobber (*Brit. slang*), effects, equipment, gear, luggage, stuff

think *verb* **1** believe, consider, deem, estimate, imagine, judge, reckon, regard, suppose **2** ponder, cerebrate, cogitate, contemplate, deliberate, meditate, muse, reason, reflect, ruminate

thinker *noun* philosopher, brain (*informal*), intellect (*informal*), mastermind, sage, theorist, wise man

thinking *noun* **1** reasoning, conjecture, idea, judgment, opinion, position, theory, view ♦ *adjective* **2** thoughtful, contemplative, intelligent, meditative, philosophical, rational, reasoning, reflective

think up *verb* devise, come up

with, concoct, contrive, create, dream up, invent, visualize

thirst *noun* **1** thirstiness, drought, dryness **2** craving, appetite, desire, hankering, keenness, longing, passion, yearning

thirsty *adjective* **1** parched, arid, dehydrated, dry **2** eager, avid, craving, desirous, greedy, hungry, itching, longing, yearning

thorn *noun* prickle, barb, spike, spine

thorny *adjective* prickly, barbed, bristly, pointed, sharp, spiky, spiny

thorough *adjective* **1** careful, assiduous, conscientious, efficient, exhaustive, full, in-depth, intensive, meticulous, painstaking, sweeping **2** complete, absolute, out-and-out, outright, perfect, total, unmitigated, unqualified, utter

thoroughbred *adjective* purebred, pedigree

thoroughfare *noun* road, avenue, highway, passage, passageway, street, way

thoroughly *adverb* **1** carefully, assiduously, conscientiously, efficiently, exhaustively, from top to bottom, fully, intensively, meticulously, painstakingly, scrupulously **2** completely, absolutely, downright, perfectly, quite, totally, to the hilt, utterly

though *conjunction* **1** although, even if, even though, notwithstanding, while ♦ *adverb* **2** nevertheless, for all that, however, nonetheless, notwithstanding, still, yet

thought noun 1 thinking, brainwork, cogitation, consideration, deliberation, meditation, musing, reflection, rumination 2 idea, concept, judgment, notion, opinion, view 3 consideration, attention, heed, regard, scrutiny, study 4 intention, aim, design, idea, notion, object, plan, purpose 5 expectation, anticipation, aspiration, hope, prospect

thoughtful adjective 1 considerate, attentive, caring, helpful, kind, kindly, solicitous, unselfish 2 well-thought-out, astute, canny, prudent 3 reflective, contemplative, deliberative, meditative, pensive, ruminative, serious, studious

thoughtless adjective inconsiderate, impolite, insensitive, rude, selfish, tactless, uncaring, undiplomatic, unkind

thrash verb 1 beat, belt (informal), cane, flog, give (someone) a (good) hiding (informal), scourge, spank, whip 2 defeat, beat, crush, drub, rout, run rings around (informal), slaughter (informal), trounce, wipe the floor with (informal) 3 thresh, flail, jerk, toss and turn, writhe

thrashing noun 1 beating, belting (informal), flogging, hiding (informal), punishment, whipping 2 defeat, beating, drubbing, hammering (informal), hiding (informal), rout, trouncing

thrash out verb settle, argue out, debate, discuss, have out, resolve, solve, talk over

thread noun 1 strand, fibre, filament, line, string, yarn 2 theme, direction, drift, plot, story line, train of thought ♦ verb 3 pass, ease, pick (one's way), squeeze through

threadbare adjective 1 shabby, down at heel, frayed, old, ragged, scruffy, tattered, tatty, worn 2 hackneyed, commonplace, conventional, familiar, overused, stale, stereotyped, tired, trite, well-worn

threat noun 1 warning, foreboding, foreshadowing, omen, portent, presage, writing on the wall 2 danger, hazard, menace, peril, risk

threaten verb 1 intimidate, browbeat, bully, lean on (slang), menace, pressurize, terrorize 2 endanger, imperil, jeopardize, put at risk, put in jeopardy, put on the line 3 foreshadow, forebode, impend, portend, presage

threatening adjective 1 menacing, bullying, intimidatory 2 ominous, forbidding, grim, inauspicious, sinister

threshold noun 1 entrance, door, doorstep, doorway 2 start, beginning, brink, dawn, inception, opening, outset, verge 3 minimum, lower limit

thrift noun 1 frugality, carefulness, economy, parsimony, prudence, saving, thriftiness

thrifty adjective economical, careful, frugal, parsimonious, provident, prudent, saving, sparing

thrill noun 1 pleasure, buzz

(slang), kick (informal),
stimulation, tingle, titillation
♦ verb 2 excite, arouse, electrify,
move, stimulate, stir, titillate

thrilling adjective exciting,
electrifying, gripping, riveting,
rousing, sensational, stimulating,
stirring

thrive verb prosper, boom,
develop, do well, flourish, get
on, grow, increase, succeed

thriving adjective prosperous,
blooming, booming,
burgeoning, flourishing, healthy,
successful, well

throb verb 1 pulsate, beat,
palpitate, pound, pulse, thump,
vibrate ♦ noun 2 pulse, beat,
palpitation, pounding, pulsating,
thump, thumping, vibration

throng noun 1 crowd, crush,
horde, host, mass, mob,
multitude, pack, swarm ♦ verb
2 crowd, congregate, converge,
flock, mill around, pack, swarm
around

throttle verb strangle, choke,
garrotte, strangulate

through preposition 1 between,
by, past 2 because of, by means
of, by way of, using, via
3 during, in, throughout
♦ adjective 4 finished, completed,
done, ended ♦ adverb 5 through
and through completely,
altogether, entirely, fully,
thoroughly, totally, utterly,
wholly

throughout adverb everywhere,
all over, from start to finish,
right through

throw verb 1 hurl, cast, chuck
(informal), fling, launch, lob
(informal), pitch, send, sling, toss

2 Informal confuse, astonish,
baffle, confound, disconcert,
dumbfound, faze ♦ noun 3 toss,
fling, heave, lob (informal), pitch,
sling

throwaway adjective casual,
careless, offhand, passing,
understated

throw away verb discard,
dispense with, dispose of, ditch
(slang), dump (informal), get rid
of, jettison, reject, scrap, throw
out

thrust verb 1 push, drive, force,
jam, plunge, propel, ram, shove
♦ noun 2 push, drive, lunge,
poke, prod, shove, stab
3 momentum, impetus

thud noun, verb thump, clunk,
crash, knock, smack

thug noun ruffian, bruiser
(informal), bully boy, gangster,
heavy (slang), hooligan, tough

thump noun 1 crash, bang,
clunk, thud, thwack 2 blow,
clout (informal), knock, punch,
rap, smack, wallop (informal),
whack ♦ verb 3 strike, beat,
clobber (slang), clout (informal),
hit, knock, pound, punch,
smack, wallop (informal), whack

thunder noun 1 rumble, boom,
crash, explosion ♦ verb 2 rumble,
boom, crash, peal, resound,
reverberate, roar 3 shout, bark,
bellow, roar, yell

thunderous adjective loud,
booming, deafening,
ear-splitting, noisy, resounding,
roaring, tumultuous

thunderstruck adjective amazed,
astonished, astounded,
dumbfounded, flabbergasted
(informal), open-mouthed,

shocked, staggered, stunned, taken aback

thus *adverb* 1 <u>therefore</u>, accordingly, consequently, ergo, for this reason, hence, on that account, so, then 2 <u>in this way</u>, as follows, like this, so

thwart *verb* <u>frustrate</u>, foil, hinder, obstruct, outwit, prevent, snooker, stymie

tick¹ *noun* 1 <u>mark</u>, dash, stroke 2 <u>tapping</u>, clicking, ticktock 3 *Brit. informal* <u>moment</u>, flash, instant, minute, second, split second, trice, twinkling ♦ *verb* 4 <u>mark</u>, check off, indicate 5 <u>tap</u>, click, ticktock

tick² *noun* <u>credit</u>, account, the slate (*Brit. informal*)

ticket *noun* 1 <u>voucher</u>, card, certificate, coupon, pass, slip, token 2 <u>label</u>, card, docket, marker, slip, sticker, tab, tag

tide *noun* 1 <u>current</u>, ebb, flow, stream, tideway, undertow 2 <u>tendency</u>, direction, drift, movement, trend

tidy *adjective* 1 <u>neat</u>, clean, methodical, orderly, shipshape, spruce, well-kept, well-ordered 2 *Informal* <u>considerable</u>, ample, generous, goodly, handsome, healthy, large, sizable *or* sizeable, substantial ♦ *verb* 3 <u>neaten</u>, clean, groom, order, spruce up, straighten

tie *verb* 1 <u>fasten</u>, attach, bind, connect, join, knot, link, secure, tether 2 <u>restrict</u>, bind, confine, hamper, hinder, limit, restrain 3 <u>draw</u>, equal, match ♦ *noun* 4 <u>bond</u>, affiliation, allegiance, commitment, connection, liaison, relationship 5 <u>fastening</u>,

bond, cord, fetter, knot, ligature, link 6 <u>draw</u>, dead heat, deadlock, stalemate

tier *noun* <u>row</u>, bank, layer, level, line, rank, storey, stratum

tight *adjective* 1 <u>stretched</u>, close, constricted, cramped, narrow, rigid, snug, taut 2 *Informal* <u>miserly</u>, grasping, mean, niggardly, parsimonious, stingy, tightfisted 3 <u>close</u>, even, evenly-balanced, well-matched 4 *Informal* <u>drunk</u>, inebriated, intoxicated, paralytic (*informal*), plastered (*slang*), tipsy, under the influence (*informal*)

tighten *verb* <u>squeeze</u>, close, constrict, narrow

till¹ *verb* <u>cultivate</u>, dig, plough, work

till² *noun* <u>cash register</u>, cash box

tilt *verb* 1 <u>slant</u>, heel, incline, lean, list, slope, tip ♦ *noun* 2 <u>slope</u>, angle, inclination, incline, list, pitch, slant 3 *Medieval history* <u>joust</u>, combat, duel, fight, lists, tournament 4 <u>(at) full tilt</u> <u>full speed</u>, for dear life, headlong

timber *noun* <u>wood</u>, beams, boards, logs, planks, trees

timbre *noun* <u>tone</u>, colour, resonance, ring

time *noun* 1 <u>period</u>, duration, interval, season, space, span, spell, stretch, term 2 <u>occasion</u>, instance, juncture, point, stage 3 *Music* <u>tempo</u>, beat, measure, rhythm ♦ *verb* 4 <u>schedule</u>, set

timeless *adjective* <u>eternal</u>, ageless, changeless, enduring, everlasting, immortal, lasting, permanent

timely adjective opportune, appropriate, convenient, judicious, propitious, seasonable, suitable, well-timed

timetable noun schedule, agenda, calendar, curriculum, diary, list, programme

timid adjective fearful, apprehensive, bashful, coy, diffident, faint-hearted, shrinking, shy, timorous

timorous adjective timid, apprehensive, bashful, coy, diffident, faint-hearted, fearful, shrinking, shy

tinge noun 1 tint, colour, shade 2 bit, dash, drop, smattering, sprinkling, suggestion, touch, trace ♦ verb 3 tint, colour, imbue, suffuse

tingle verb 1 prickle, have goose pimples, itch, sting, tickle ♦ noun 2 quiver, goose pimples, itch, pins and needles (informal), prickling, shiver, thrill

tinker verb meddle, dabble, fiddle (informal), mess about, play, potter

tint noun 1 shade, colour, hue, tone 2 dye, rinse, tincture, tinge, wash ♦ verb 3 dye, colour

tiny adjective small, diminutive, infinitesimal, little, microscopic, miniature, minute, negligible, petite, slight

tip[1] noun 1 end, extremity, head, peak, pinnacle, point, summit, top ♦ verb 2 cap, crown, finish, surmount, top

tip[2] noun 1 gratuity, gift 2 hint, clue, pointer, suggestion, warning ♦ verb 3 reward, remunerate 4 advise, caution,

tip[3] verb 1 tilt, incline, lean, list, slant 2 dump, empty, pour out, unload ♦ noun 3 dump, refuse heap, rubbish heap

tipple verb 1 drink, imbibe, indulge (informal), quaff, swig, tope ♦ noun 2 alcohol, booze (informal), drink, liquor

tirade noun outburst, diatribe, fulmination, harangue, invective, lecture

tire verb 1 fatigue, drain, exhaust, wear out, weary 2 bore, exasperate, irk, irritate, weary

tired adjective 1 exhausted, drained, drowsy, fatigued, flagging, jaded, sleepy, weary, worn out 2 bored, fed up, sick, weary 3 hackneyed, clichéd, corny (slang), old, outworn, stale, threadbare, trite, well-worn

tireless adjective energetic, indefatigable, industrious, resolute, unflagging, untiring, vigorous

tiresome adjective boring, dull, irksome, irritating, tedious, trying, vexatious, wearing, wearisome

tiring adjective exhausting, arduous, demanding, exacting, laborious, strenuous, tough, wearing

titbit noun delicacy, dainty, morsel, snack, treat

titillate verb excite, arouse, interest, stimulate, tantalize, tease, thrill

titillating adjective exciting, arousing, interesting, lurid, provocative, stimulating, suggestive, teasing

title noun **1** <u>name</u>, designation, handle (*slang*), moniker or monicker (*slang*), term **2** <u>championship</u>, crown **3** <u>ownership</u>, claim, entitlement, prerogative, privilege, right

titter verb <u>laugh</u>, chortle (*informal*), chuckle, giggle, snigger

toady noun **1** <u>sycophant</u>, bootlicker (*informal*), crawler (*slang*), creep (*slang*), flatterer, flunkey, hanger-on, lackey, minion, yes man ◆ verb **2** <u>flatter</u>, crawl, creep, cringe, fawn on, grovel, kowtow to, pander to, suck up to (*informal*)

toast[1] verb <u>warm</u>, brown, grill, heat, roast

toast[2] noun **1** <u>tribute</u>, compliment, health, pledge, salutation, salute **2** <u>favourite</u>, darling, hero or heroine ◆ verb **3** <u>drink to</u>, drink (to) the health of, salute

together adverb **1** <u>collectively</u>, as one, hand in glove, in concert, in unison, jointly, mutually, shoulder to shoulder, side by side **2** <u>at the same time</u>, at one fell swoop, concurrently, contemporaneously, simultaneously ◆ adjective **3** *Informal* <u>well-organized</u>, composed, well-adjusted, well-balanced

toil noun **1** <u>hard work</u>, application, drudgery, effort, elbow grease (*informal*), exertion, graft (*informal*), slog, sweat ◆ verb **2** <u>work</u>, drudge, graft (*informal*), labour, slave, slog, strive, struggle, sweat (*informal*), work one's fingers to the bone

toilet noun <u>lavatory</u>, bathroom, convenience, gents (*Brit. informal*), ladies' room, latrine, loo (*Brit. informal*), privy, urinal, water closet, W.C.

token noun **1** <u>symbol</u>, badge, expression, indication, mark, note, representation, sign ◆ adjective **2** <u>nominal</u>, hollow, minimal, perfunctory, superficial, symbolic

tolerable adjective **1** <u>bearable</u>, acceptable, allowable, endurable, sufferable, supportable **2** <u>fair</u>, acceptable, adequate, all right, average, O.K. or okay (*informal*), passable

tolerance noun **1** <u>broad-mindedness</u>, forbearance, indulgence, open-mindedness, permissiveness **2** <u>endurance</u>, fortitude, hardiness, resilience, resistance, stamina, staying power, toughness

tolerant adjective <u>broad-minded</u>, catholic, forbearing, liberal, long-suffering, open-minded, understanding, unprejudiced

tolerate verb <u>allow</u>, accept, brook, condone, endure, permit, put up with (*informal*), stand, stomach, take

toleration noun <u>acceptance</u>, allowance, endurance, indulgence, permissiveness, sanction

toll[1] verb **1** <u>ring</u>, chime, clang, knell, peal, sound, strike ◆ noun **2** <u>ringing</u>, chime, clang, knell, peal

toll[2] noun **1** <u>charge</u>, duty, fee, levy, payment, tariff, tax **2** <u>damage</u>, cost, loss, penalty

tomb noun grave, catacomb, crypt, mausoleum, sarcophagus, sepulchre, vault

tombstone noun gravestone, headstone, marker, memorial, monument

tomfoolery noun foolishness, buffoonery, clowning, fooling around (informal), horseplay, shenanigans (informal), silliness, skylarking (informal), stupidity

tone noun 1 pitch, inflection, intonation, modulation, timbre 2 character, air, attitude, feel, manner, mood, spirit, style, temper 3 colour, hue, shade, tinge, tint ♦ verb 4 harmonize, blend, go well with, match, suit

tone down verb moderate, play down, reduce, restrain, soften, subdue, temper

tongue noun language, dialect, parlance, speech

tonic noun stimulant, boost, fillip, pick-me-up (informal), restorative, shot in the arm (informal)

too adverb 1 also, as well, besides, further, in addition, likewise, moreover, to boot 2 excessively, extremely, immoderately, inordinately, overly, unduly, unreasonably, very

tool noun 1 implement, appliance, contraption, contrivance, device, gadget, instrument, machine, utensil 2 puppet, cat's-paw, creature, flunkey, hireling, lackey, minion, pawn, stooge (slang)

top noun 1 peak, apex, crest, crown, culmination, head, height, pinnacle, summit, zenith 2 first place, head, lead 3 lid, cap, cover, stopper ♦ adjective 4 leading, best, chief, elite, finest, first, foremost, head, highest, pre-eminent, principal, uppermost ♦ verb 5 cover, cap, crown, finish, garnish 6 lead, be first, head 7 surpass, beat, better, eclipse, exceed, excel, outstrip, transcend

topic noun subject, issue, matter, point, question, subject matter, theme

topical adjective current, contemporary, newsworthy, popular, up-to-date, up-to-the-minute

topmost adjective highest, dominant, foremost, leading, paramount, principal, supreme, top, uppermost

topple verb 1 fall over, collapse, fall, keel over, overbalance, overturn, totter, tumble 2 overthrow, bring down, bring low, oust, overturn, unseat

topsy-turvy adjective confused, chaotic, disorderly, disorganized, inside-out, jumbled, messy, mixed-up, upside-down

torment verb 1 torture, crucify, distress, rack 2 tease, annoy, bother, harass, hassle (informal), irritate, nag, pester, vex ♦ noun 3 suffering, agony, anguish, distress, hell, misery, pain, torture

torn adjective 1 cut, lacerated, ragged, rent, ripped, slit, split 2 undecided, in two minds (informal), irresolute, uncertain, unsure, vacillating, wavering

tornado noun whirlwind, cyclone, gale, hurricane, squall, storm, tempest, typhoon

torpor noun inactivity, apathy, drowsiness, indolence, laziness, lethargy, listlessness, sloth, sluggishness

torrent noun stream, cascade, deluge, downpour, flood, flow, rush, spate, tide

torrid adjective **1** arid, dried, parched, scorched **2** passionate, ardent, fervent, intense, steamy (informal)

tortuous adjective **1** winding, circuitous, convoluted, indirect, mazy, meandering, serpentine, sinuous, twisting, twisty **2** complicated, ambiguous, convoluted, devious, indirect, involved, roundabout, tricky

torture verb **1** torment, afflict, crucify, distress, persecute, put on the rack, rack ♦ noun **2** agony, anguish, distress, pain, persecution, suffering, torment

toss verb **1** throw, cast, fling, flip, hurl, launch, lob (informal), pitch, sling **2** thrash, rock, roll, shake, wriggle, writhe ♦ noun **3** throw, lob (informal), pitch

tot¹ noun **1** infant, baby, child, mite, toddler **2** measure, dram, finger, nip, shot (informal), slug, snifter (informal)

tot² verb add up, calculate, count up, reckon, tally, total

total noun **1** whole, aggregate, entirety, full amount, sum, totality ♦ adjective **2** complete, absolute, comprehensive, entire, full, gross, thoroughgoing, undivided, utter, whole ♦ verb **3** amount to, come to, mount up to, reach **4** add up, reckon, tot up

totalitarian adjective dictatorial,

authoritarian, despotic, oppressive, tyrannous, undemocratic

totality noun whole, aggregate, entirety, sum, total

totally adverb completely, absolutely, comprehensively, entirely, fully, one hundred per cent, thoroughly, utterly, wholly

totter verb stagger, falter, lurch, reel, stumble, sway

touch verb **1** handle, brush, caress, contact, feel, finger, fondle, stroke, tap **2** meet, abut, adjoin, be in contact, border, contact, graze, impinge upon **3** affect, disturb, impress, influence, inspire, move, stir **4** eat, consume, drink, partake of **5** match, compare with, equal, hold a candle to (informal), parallel, rival **6** touch on refer to, allude to, bring in, cover, deal with, mention, speak of ♦ noun **7** feeling, handling, physical contact **8** tap, brush, contact, pat, stroke **9** bit, dash, drop, jot, small amount, smattering, soupçon, spot, trace **10** style, manner, method, technique, trademark, way

touch and go adjective risky, close, critical, near, nerve-racking, precarious

touching adjective moving, affecting, emotive, pathetic, pitiable, poignant, sad, stirring

touchstone noun standard, criterion, gauge, measure, norm, par, yardstick

touchy adjective oversensitive, irascible, irritable, querulous, quick-tempered, testy, tetchy, thin-skinned

tough adjective 1 resilient, durable, hard, inflexible, leathery, resistant, rugged, solid, strong, sturdy 2 strong, hardy, seasoned, stout, strapping, sturdy, vigorous 3 rough, hard-bitten, pugnacious, ruthless, violent 4 strict, firm, hard, merciless, resolute, severe, stern, unbending 5 difficult, arduous, exacting, hard, laborious, strenuous, troublesome, uphill 6 Informal unlucky, lamentable, regrettable, unfortunate ♦ noun 7 ruffian, bruiser (informal), bully, hooligan, roughneck (slang), thug

tour noun 1 journey, excursion, expedition, jaunt, outing, trip ♦ verb 2 visit, explore, go round, journey, sightsee, travel through

tourist noun traveller, excursionist, globetrotter, holiday-maker, sightseer, tripper, voyager

tournament noun competition, contest, event, meeting, series

tow verb drag, draw, haul, lug, pull, tug

towards preposition 1 in the direction of, en route for, for, on the way to, to 2 regarding, about, concerning, for, with regard to, with respect to

tower noun column, belfry, obelisk, pillar, skyscraper, steeple, turret

towering adjective high, colossal, elevated, imposing, impressive, lofty, magnificent, soaring, tall

toxic adjective poisonous, deadly, harmful, lethal, noxious, pernicious, pestilential, septic

toy noun 1 plaything, doll, game ♦ verb 2 play, amuse oneself, dally, fiddle (informal), fool (about or around), trifle

trace verb 1 find, detect, discover, ferret out, hunt down, track, unearth 2 copy, draw, outline, sketch ♦ noun 3 track, footmark, footprint, footstep, path, spoor, trail 4 bit, drop, hint, shadow, suggestion, suspicion, tinge, touch, whiff 5 indication, evidence, mark, record, remnant, sign, survival, vestige

track noun 1 path, course, line, orbit, pathway, road, trajectory, way 2 trail, footmark, footprint, footstep, mark, path, spoor, trace, wake 3 line, permanent way, rails ♦ verb 4 follow, chase, hunt down, pursue, shadow, stalk, tail (informal), trace, trail

track down verb find, dig up, discover, hunt down, run to earth or ground, sniff out, trace, unearth

tract[1] noun area, district, expanse, extent, plot, region, stretch, territory

tract[2] noun treatise, booklet, dissertation, essay, homily, monograph, pamphlet

tractable adjective manageable, amenable, biddable, compliant, docile, obedient, submissive, tame, willing, yielding

traction noun grip, friction, pull, purchase, resistance

trade noun 1 commerce, barter, business, dealing, exchange, traffic, transactions, truck 2 job, business, craft, employment, line of work, métier, occupation, profession ♦ verb 3 deal, bargain, do business, have dealings, peddle, traffic, transact, truck **4** exchange, barter, swap, switch

trader noun dealer, merchant, purveyor, seller, supplier

tradesman noun **1** craftsman, artisan, journeyman, workman **2** shopkeeper, dealer, merchant, purveyor, retailer, seller, supplier, vendor

tradition noun custom, convention, folklore, habit, institution, lore, ritual

traditional adjective customary, accustomed, conventional, established, old, time-honoured, usual

traffic noun **1** transport, freight, transportation, vehicles **2** trade, business, commerce, dealings, exchange, peddling, truck ♦ verb **3** bargain, deal, do business, exchange, have dealings, peddle

tragedy noun disaster, adversity, calamity, catastrophe, misfortune

tragic adjective disastrous, appalling, calamitous, catastrophic, deadly, dire, dreadful, miserable, pathetic, sad, unfortunate

trail noun **1** path, footpath, road, route, track, way **2** tracks, footprints, marks, path, scent, spoor, trace, wake ♦ verb **3** drag, dangle, draw, haul, pull, tow **4** lag, dawdle, follow, hang back, linger, loiter, straggle, traipse (informal) **5** follow, chase, hunt, pursue, shadow, stalk, tail (informal), trace, track

train verb **1** instruct, coach, drill, educate, guide, prepare, school, teach, tutor **2** exercise, prepare,

work out **3** aim, direct, focus, level, point ♦ noun **4** sequence, chain, progression, series, set, string, succession

trainer noun coach, handler

training noun **1** instruction, coaching, discipline, education, grounding, schooling, teaching, tuition **2** exercise, practice, preparation, working out

traipse verb trudge, drag oneself, footslog, slouch, trail, tramp

trait noun characteristic, attribute, feature, idiosyncrasy, mannerism, peculiarity, quality, quirk

traitor noun betrayer, apostate, back-stabber, defector, deserter, Judas, quisling, rebel, renegade, turncoat

trajectory noun path, course, flight path, line, route, track

tramp verb **1** hike, footslog, march, ramble, roam, rove, slog, trek, walk **2** trudge, plod, stump, toil, traipse (informal) ♦ noun **3** vagrant, derelict, down-and-out, drifter **4** hike, march, ramble, slog, trek **5** tread, footfall, footstep, stamp

trample verb crush, flatten, run over, squash, stamp, tread, walk over

trance noun daze, abstraction, dream, rapture, reverie, stupor, unconsciousness

tranquil adjective calm, peaceful, placid, quiet, restful, sedate, serene, still, undisturbed

tranquillity noun calm, hush, peace, placidity, quiet, repose, rest, serenity, stillness

tranquillize verb calm, lull, pacify, quell, quiet, relax, sedate, settle one's nerves, soothe

tranquillizer noun sedative, barbiturate, bromide, downer (slang), opiate

transaction noun deal, bargain, business, enterprise, negotiation, undertaking

transcend verb surpass, eclipse, exceed, excel, go beyond, outdo, outstrip, rise above

transcendent adjective unparalleled, consummate, incomparable, matchless, pre-eminent, sublime, unequalled, unrivalled

transcribe verb write out, copy out, reproduce, take down, transfer

transcript noun copy, duplicate, manuscript, record, reproduction, transcription

transfer verb 1 move, change, convey, hand over, pass on, relocate, shift, transplant, transport, transpose ♦ noun 2 move, change, handover, relocation, shift, transference, translation, transmission, transposition

transfix verb 1 stun, engross, fascinate, hold, hypnotize, mesmerize, paralyse 2 pierce, impale, puncture, run through, skewer, spear

transform verb change, alter, convert, remodel, revolutionize, transmute

transformation noun change, alteration, conversion, metamorphosis, revolution, sea change, transmutation

transgress verb offend, break the law, contravene, disobey, encroach, infringe, sin, trespass, violate

transgression noun offence, contravention, crime, encroachment, infraction, infringement, misdeed, misdemeanour, sin, trespass, violation

transgressor noun offender, criminal, culprit, lawbreaker, miscreant, sinner, trespasser, villain, wrongdoer

transient adjective temporary, brief, ephemeral, fleeting, impermanent, momentary, passing, short-lived, transitory

transit noun movement, carriage, conveyance, crossing, passage, transfer, transport, transportation

transition noun change, alteration, conversion, development, metamorphosis, passing, progression, shift, transmutation

transitional adjective changing, developmental, fluid, intermediate, passing, provisional, temporary, unsettled

transitory adjective short-lived, brief, ephemeral, fleeting, impermanent, momentary, passing, short, temporary, transient

translate verb interpret, construe, convert, decipher, decode, paraphrase, render

translation noun interpretation, decoding, paraphrase, rendering, rendition, version

transmission noun 1 transfer, conveyance, dissemination, sending, shipment, spread, transference 2 broadcasting, dissemination, putting out, relaying, sending, showing **3** <u>programme</u>, broadcast, show

transmit *verb* **1** <u>pass on</u>, bear, carry, convey, disseminate, hand on, impart, send, spread, transfer **2** <u>broadcast</u>, radio, relay, send out

transparency *noun* **1** <u>clarity</u>, clearness, limpidity, pellucidness, translucence **2** <u>photograph</u>, slide

transparent *adjective* **1** <u>clear</u>, crystalline, diaphanous, limpid, lucid, see-through, sheer, translucent **2** <u>plain</u>, evident, explicit, manifest, obvious, patent, recognizable, unambiguous, undisguised

transpire *verb* **1** <u>emerge</u>, become known, come out, come to light **2** *Informal* <u>happen</u>, arise, befall, chance, come about, occur, take place

transplant *verb* <u>transfer</u>, displace, relocate, remove, resettle, shift, uproot

transport *verb* **1** <u>convey</u>, bring, carry, haul, move, take, transfer **2** <u>exile</u>, banish, deport **3** <u>enrapture</u>, captivate, delight, enchant, entrance, move, ravish ♦ *noun* **4** <u>vehicle</u>, conveyance, transportation **5** <u>transference</u>, conveyance, shipment, transportation **6** <u>ecstasy</u>, bliss, delight, enchantment, euphoria, heaven, rapture, ravishment

transpose *verb* <u>interchange</u>, alter, change, exchange, move, reorder, shift, substitute, swap, switch, transfer

trap *noun* **1** <u>snare</u>, ambush, gin, net, noose, pitfall **2** <u>trick</u>,

ambush, deception, ruse, stratagem, subterfuge, wile ♦ *verb* **3** <u>catch</u>, corner, enmesh, ensnare, entrap, snare, take **4** <u>trick</u>, ambush, beguile, deceive, dupe, ensnare, inveigle

trappings *plural noun* <u>accessories</u>, accoutrements, equipment, finery, furnishings, gear, panoply, paraphernalia, things, trimmings

trash *noun* **1** <u>nonsense</u>, drivel, hogwash, moonshine, poppycock (*informal*), rot, rubbish, tripe (*informal*), twaddle **2** <u>litter</u>, dross, garbage, junk (*informal*), refuse, rubbish, waste

trashy *adjective* <u>worthless</u>, cheap, inferior, rubbishy, shabby, shoddy, tawdry

trauma *noun* <u>suffering</u>, agony, anguish, hurt, ordeal, pain, shock, torture

traumatic *adjective* <u>shocking</u>, agonizing, damaging, disturbing, hurtful, injurious, painful, scarring, upsetting, wounding

travel *verb* **1** <u>go</u>, journey, move, progress, roam, tour, trek, voyage, wander ♦ *noun* **2** *usually plural* <u>wandering</u>, excursion, expedition, globetrotting, journey, tour, trip, voyage

traveller *noun* <u>wanderer</u>, explorer, globetrotter, gypsy, holiday-maker, tourist, voyager, wayfarer

travelling *adjective* <u>mobile</u>, itinerant, migrant, nomadic, peripatetic, roaming, roving, touring, wandering, wayfaring

traverse *verb* <u>cross</u>, go over, span, travel over

travesty noun 1 mockery, burlesque, caricature, distortion, lampoon, parody, perversion ♦ verb 2 mock, burlesque, caricature, distort, lampoon, make a mockery of, parody, ridicule

treacherous adjective 1 disloyal, deceitful, double-dealing, duplicitous, faithless, false, perfidious, traitorous, unfaithful, untrustworthy 2 dangerous, deceptive, hazardous, icy, perilous, precarious, risky, slippery, unreliable, unsafe, unstable

treachery noun betrayal, disloyalty, double-dealing, duplicity, faithlessness, infidelity, perfidy, treason

tread verb 1 step, hike, march, pace, stamp, stride, walk 2 trample, crush underfoot, squash ♦ noun 3 step, footfall, footstep, gait, pace, stride, walk

treason noun disloyalty, duplicity, lese-majesty, mutiny, perfidy, sedition, traitorousness, treachery

treasonable adjective disloyal, mutinous, perfidious, seditious, subversive, traitorous, treacherous

treasure noun 1 riches, cash, fortune, gold, jewels, money, valuables, wealth 2 darling, apple of one's eye, gem, jewel, nonpareil, paragon, pride and joy ♦ verb 3 prize, adore, cherish, esteem, hold dear, idolize, love, revere, value

treasury noun storehouse, bank, cache, hoard, repository, store, vault

treat verb 1 handle, act towards, behave towards, consider, deal with, look upon, manage, regard, use 2 attend to, care for, nurse 3 entertain, lay on, provide, regale, stand (informal) ♦ noun 4 entertainment, banquet, celebration, feast, gift, party, refreshment 5 pleasure, delight, enjoyment, fun, joy, satisfaction, surprise, thrill

treatise noun essay, dissertation, monograph, pamphlet, paper, study, thesis, tract, work

treatment noun 1 care, cure, healing, medication, medicine, remedy, surgery, therapy 2 handling, action, behaviour, conduct, dealing, management, manipulation

treaty noun pact, agreement, alliance, compact, concordat, contract, convention, covenant, entente

trek noun 1 journey, expedition, hike, march, odyssey, safari, slog, tramp ♦ verb 2 journey, footslog, hike, march, rove, slog, traipse (informal), tramp, trudge

tremble verb 1 shake, quake, quiver, shiver, shudder, totter, vibrate, wobble ♦ noun 2 shake, quake, quiver, shiver, shudder, wobble

tremendous adjective 1 huge, colossal, enormous, formidable, gigantic, great, immense, stupendous, terrific 2 Informal excellent, amazing, brilliant, exceptional, extraordinary, fantastic (informal), great, marvellous, sensational (informal), wonderful

tremor noun 1 shake, quaking, quaver, quiver, shiver, trembling, wobble 2 earthquake, quake (informal), shock

trench noun ditch, channel, drain, excavation, furrow, gutter, trough

trenchant adjective 1 incisive, acerbic, caustic, cutting, penetrating, pointed, pungent, scathing 2 effective, energetic, forceful, potent, powerful, strong, vigorous

trend noun 1 tendency, bias, current, direction, drift, flow, inclination, leaning 2 fashion, craze, fad (informal), mode, rage, style, thing, vogue

trendy adjective fashionable, in fashion, in vogue, modish, stylish, voguish, with it (informal)

trepidation noun anxiety, alarm, apprehension, consternation, disquiet, dread, fear, nervousness, uneasiness, worry

trespass verb 1 intrude, encroach, infringe, invade, obtrude ◆ noun 2 intrusion, encroachment, infringement, invasion, unlawful entry

trespasser noun intruder, interloper, invader, poacher

trial noun 1 hearing, litigation, tribunal 2 test, audition, dry run (informal), experiment, probation, test-run 3 hardship, adversity, affliction, distress, ordeal, suffering, tribulation, trouble

tribe noun race, clan, family, people

tribunal noun hearing, court, trial

tribute noun 1 accolade, commendation, compliment, eulogy, panegyric, recognition, testimonial 2 tax, charge, homage, payment, ransom

trick noun 1 deception, fraud, hoax, manoeuvre, ploy, ruse, stratagem, subterfuge, swindle, trap, wile 2 joke, antic, jape, leg-pull (Brit. informal), practical joke, prank, stunt 3 secret, hang (informal), knack, know-how (informal), skill, technique 4 mannerism, characteristic, foible, habit, idiosyncrasy, peculiarity, practice, quirk, trait ◆ verb 5 deceive, cheat, con (informal), dupe, fool, hoodwink, kid (informal), mislead, swindle, take in (informal), trap

trickery noun deception, cheating, chicanery, deceit, dishonesty, guile, jiggery-pokery (informal, chiefly Brit.), monkey business (informal)

trickle verb 1 dribble, drip, drop, exude, ooze, run, seep, stream ◆ noun 2 dribble, drip, seepage

tricky adjective 1 difficult, complicated, delicate, knotty, problematic, risky, thorny, ticklish 2 crafty, artful, cunning, deceitful, devious, scheming, slippery, sly, wily

trifle noun 1 knick-knack, bagatelle, bauble, plaything, toy ◆ verb 2 toy, dally, mess about, play

trifling adjective insignificant, measly, negligible, paltry, trivial, unimportant, worthless

trigger verb set off, activate, cause, generate, produce, prompt, provoke, spark off, start

trim adjective 1 neat, dapper, natty (informal), shipshape, smart, spruce, tidy, well-groomed 2 <u>slender</u>, fit, shapely, sleek, slim, streamlined, svelte, willowy ♦ *verb* 3 <u>cut</u>, clip, crop, even up, pare, prune, shave, tidy 4 <u>decorate</u>, adorn, array, beautify, deck out, dress, embellish, ornament ♦ *noun* 5 <u>decoration</u>, adornment, border, edging, embellishment, frill, ornamentation, piping, trimming 6 <u>condition</u>, fettle, fitness, health, shape (*informal*), state 7 <u>cut</u>, clipping, crop, pruning, shave, shearing, tidying up

trimming *noun* 1 <u>decoration</u>, adornment, border, edging, embellishment, frill, ornamentation, piping 2 <u>trimmings</u> extras, accessories, accompaniments, frills, ornaments, paraphernalia, trappings

trinity *noun* <u>threesome</u>, triad, trio, triumvirate

trinket *noun* <u>ornament</u>, bagatelle, bauble, knick-knack, toy, trifle

trio *noun* <u>threesome</u>, triad, trilogy, trinity, triumvirate

trip *noun* 1 <u>journey</u>, errand, excursion, expedition, foray, jaunt, outing, run, tour, voyage 2 <u>stumble</u>, fall, misstep, slip ♦ *verb* 3 <u>stumble</u>, fall, lose one's footing, misstep, slip, tumble 4 <u>catch out</u>, trap 5 <u>skip</u>, dance, gambol, hop

triple *adjective* 1 <u>threefold</u>, three-way, tripartite ♦ *verb* 2 <u>treble</u>, increase threefold

trite *adjective* <u>unoriginal</u>, banal, clichéd, commonplace, hackneyed, stale, stereotyped,

threadbare, tired

triumph *noun* 1 <u>joy</u>, elation, exultation, happiness, jubilation, pride, rejoicing 2 <u>success</u>, accomplishment, achievement, attainment, conquest, coup, feat, victory ♦ *verb* 3 *often with* **over** <u>win</u>, overcome, prevail, prosper, succeed, vanquish 4 <u>rejoice</u>, celebrate, crow, exult, gloat, glory, revel

triumphant *adjective* <u>victorious</u>, celebratory, cock-a-hoop, conquering, elated, exultant, jubilant, proud, successful, winning

trivia *plural noun* <u>minutiae</u>, details, trifles, trivialities

trivial *adjective* <u>unimportant</u>, incidental, inconsequential, insignificant, meaningless, minor, petty, small, trifling, worthless

triviality *noun* <u>insignificance</u>, meaninglessness, pettiness, unimportance, worthlessness

trivialize *verb* <u>undervalue</u>, belittle, laugh off, make light of, minimize, play down, scoff at, underestimate, underplay

troop *noun* 1 <u>group</u>, band, body, company, crowd, horde, multitude, squad, team, unit 2 <u>troops</u> soldiers, armed forces, army, men, servicemen, soldiery ♦ *verb* 3 <u>flock</u>, march, stream, swarm, throng, traipse (*informal*)

trophy *noun* <u>prize</u>, award, booty, cup, laurels, memento, souvenir, spoils

tropical *adjective* <u>hot</u>, steamy, stifling, sultry, sweltering, torrid

trot *verb* 1 <u>run</u>, canter, jog, lope,

scamper ♦ *noun* 2 run, canter, jog, lope

trouble *noun* 1 distress, anxiety, disquiet, grief, misfortune, pain, sorrow, torment, woe, worry 2 disease, ailment, complaint, defect, disorder, failure, illness, malfunction 3 disorder, agitation, bother (*informal*), commotion, discord, disturbance, strife, tumult, unrest 4 effort, care, exertion, inconvenience, labour, pains, thought, work ♦ *verb* 5 worry, bother, disconcert, distress, disturb, pain, perturb, plague, sadden, upset 6 take pains, exert oneself, make an effort, take the time 7 inconvenience, bother, burden, disturb, impose upon, incommode, put out

troublesome *adjective* 1 worrying, annoying, demanding, difficult, inconvenient, irksome, taxing, tricky, trying, vexatious 2 disorderly, rebellious, rowdy, turbulent, uncooperative, undisciplined, unruly, violent

trough *noun* 1 manger, water trough 2 channel, canal, depression, ditch, duct, furrow, gully, gutter, trench

trounce *verb* thrash, beat, crush, drub, give a hiding (*informal*), hammer (*informal*), rout, slaughter (*informal*), wipe the floor with (*informal*)

troupe *noun* company, band, cast

truancy *noun* absence, absence without leave, malingering, shirking, skiving (*Brit. slang*)

truant *noun* absentee, malingerer, runaway, shirker,

skiver (*Brit. slang*)

truce *noun* ceasefire, armistice, cessation, let-up (*informal*), lull, moratorium, peace, respite

truculent *adjective* hostile, aggressive, bellicose, belligerent, defiant, ill-tempered, obstreperous, pugnacious

trudge *verb* 1 plod, footslog, lumber, slog, stump, traipse (*informal*), tramp, trek ♦ *noun* 2 hike, footslog, march, slog, traipse (*informal*), tramp, trek

true *adjective* 1 correct, accurate, authentic, factual, genuine, precise, real, right, truthful, veracious 2 faithful, dedicated, devoted, dutiful, loyal, reliable, staunch, steady, trustworthy 3 exact, accurate, on target, perfect, precise, spot-on (*Brit. informal*), unerring

truism *noun* cliché, axiom, bromide, commonplace, platitude

truly *adverb* 1 correctly, authentically, exactly, factually, genuinely, legitimately, precisely, rightly, truthfully 2 faithfully, devotedly, dutifully, loyally, sincerely, staunchly, steadily 3 really, extremely, greatly, indeed, of course, very

trumpet *noun* 1 horn, bugle, clarion ♦ *verb* 2 proclaim, advertise, announce, broadcast, shout from the rooftops, tout (*informal*)

trump up *verb* fabricate, concoct, contrive, cook up (*informal*), create, fake, invent, make up

truncate *verb* shorten, abbreviate, curtail, cut short, dock, lop, pare, prune, trim

truncheon noun club, baton, cudgel, staff

trunk noun 1 stem, bole, stalk 2 chest, box, case, casket, coffer, crate 3 body, torso 4 snout, proboscis

truss verb 1 tie, bind, fasten, make fast, secure, strap, tether ◆ noun 2 Medical support, bandage 3 joist, beam, brace, buttress, prop, stanchion, stay, strut, support

trust verb 1 believe in, bank on, count on, depend on, have faith in, rely upon 2 consign, assign, commit, delegate, entrust, give 3 expect, assume, hope, presume, suppose, surmise ◆ noun 4 confidence, assurance, belief, certainty, conviction, credence, credit, expectation, faith, reliance

trustful, trusting adjective unwary, credulous, gullible, naive, unsuspecting, unsuspicious

trustworthy adjective honest, dependable, honourable, principled, reliable, reputable, responsible, staunch, steadfast, trusty

trusty adjective faithful, dependable, reliable, solid, staunch, steady, strong, trustworthy

truth noun truthfulness, accuracy, exactness, fact, genuineness, legitimacy, precision, reality, validity, veracity

truthful adjective honest, candid, frank, precise, sincere, straight, true, trustworthy

try verb 1 attempt, aim, endeavour, have a go, make an effort, seek, strive, struggle 2 test, appraise, check out, evaluate, examine, investigate, put to the test, sample, taste ◆ noun 3 attempt, crack (informal), effort, go (informal), shot (informal), stab (informal), whack (informal)

trying adjective annoying, bothersome, difficult, exasperating, hard, stressful, taxing, tiresome, tough, wearisome

tubby adjective fat, chubby, corpulent, obese, overweight, plump, portly, stout

tuck verb 1 push, fold, gather, insert ◆ noun 2 fold, gather, pinch, pleat 3 Informal food, grub (slang), nosh (slang)

tuft noun clump, bunch, cluster, collection, knot, tussock

tug verb 1 pull, jerk, wrench, yank ◆ noun 2 pull, jerk, yank

tuition noun training, education, instruction, lessons, schooling, teaching, tutelage, tutoring

tumble verb 1 fall, drop, flop, plummet, stumble, topple ◆ noun 2 fall, drop, plunge, spill, stumble, trip

tumbledown adjective dilapidated, crumbling, decrepit, ramshackle, rickety, ruined

tumour noun growth, cancer, carcinoma (Pathology), lump, sarcoma (Medical), swelling

tumult noun commotion, clamour, din, hubbub, pandemonium, riot, row, turmoil, upheaval, uproar

tumultuous adjective wild, boisterous, excited, noisy, riotous, rowdy, turbulent, unruly, uproarious

tune noun **1** <u>melody</u>, air, song, strain, theme **2** <u>pitch</u>, concord, consonance, euphony, harmony ♦verb **3** <u>adjust</u>, adapt, attune, harmonize, pitch, regulate

tuneful adjective <u>melodious</u>, catchy, euphonious, harmonious, mellifluous, melodic, musical, pleasant

tuneless adjective <u>discordant</u>, atonal, cacophonous, dissonant, harsh, unmusical

tunnel noun **1** <u>passage</u>, burrow, channel, hole, passageway, shaft, subway, underpass ♦verb **2** <u>dig</u>, burrow, excavate, mine, scoop out

turbulence noun <u>confusion</u>, agitation, commotion, disorder, instability, tumult, turmoil, unrest, upheaval

turbulent adjective <u>agitated</u>, blustery, choppy, foaming, furious, raging, rough, tempestuous, tumultuous

turf noun **1** <u>grass</u>, sod, sward **2 the turf** <u>horse-racing</u>, racing, the flat

turmoil noun <u>confusion</u>, agitation, chaos, commotion, disarray, disorder, tumult, upheaval, uproar

turn verb **1** <u>change course</u>, move, shift, swerve, switch, veer, wheel **2** <u>rotate</u>, circle, go round, gyrate, pivot, revolve, roll, spin, twist, whirl **3** <u>change</u>, alter, convert, mould, mutate, remodel, shape, transform **4** <u>shape</u>, fashion, frame, make, mould **5** <u>go bad</u>, curdle, go off (Brit. informal), sour, spoil, taint ♦noun **6** <u>rotation</u>, circle, cycle,

gyration, revolution, spin, twist, whirl **7** <u>shift</u>, departure, deviation **8** <u>opportunity</u>, chance, crack (informal), go, stint, time, try **9** <u>direction</u>, drift, heading, tendency, trend **10** As in **good turn** <u>act</u>, action, deed, favour, gesture, service

turncoat noun <u>traitor</u>, apostate, backslider, defector, deserter, renegade

turn down verb **1** <u>lower</u>, lessen, muffle, mute, quieten, soften **2** <u>refuse</u>, decline, rebuff, reject, repudiate, spurn

turn in verb **1** <u>go to bed</u>, go to sleep, hit the sack (slang) **2** <u>hand in</u>, deliver, give up, hand over, return, submit, surrender, tender

turning noun <u>junction</u>, bend, crossroads, curve, side road, turn, turn-off

turning point noun <u>crossroads</u>, change, crisis, crux, moment of truth

turn off verb <u>stop</u>, cut out, put out, shut down, switch off, turn out, unplug

turn on verb **1** <u>start</u>, activate, ignite, kick-start, start up, switch on **2** <u>attack</u>, assail, assault, fall on, round on **3** Informal <u>excite</u>, arouse, attract, please, stimulate, thrill, titillate

turnout noun <u>attendance</u>, assembly, audience, congregation, crowd, gate, number, throng

turnover noun **1** <u>output</u>, business, productivity **2** <u>movement</u>, change, coming and going

turn up verb **1** <u>arrive</u>, appear,

attend, come, put in an appearance, show one's face, show up (*informal*) **2** find, dig up, disclose, discover, expose, reveal, unearth **3** come to light, crop up (*informal*), pop up **4** increase, amplify, boost, enhance, intensify, raise

tussle noun **1** fight, battle, brawl, conflict, contest, scrap (*informal*), scuffle, struggle ♦ verb **2** fight, battle, grapple, scrap (*informal*), scuffle, struggle, vie, wrestle

tutor noun **1** teacher, coach, educator, guardian, guide, guru, instructor, lecturer, mentor ♦ verb **2** teach, coach, drill, educate, guide, instruct, school, train

twaddle noun nonsense, claptrap (*informal*), drivel, garbage (*informal*), gobbledegook (*informal*), poppycock (*informal*), rubbish, waffle (*informal, chiefly Brit.*)

tweak verb, noun twist, jerk, pinch, pull, squeeze

twig noun branch, shoot, spray, sprig, stick

twilight noun dusk, dimness, evening, gloaming (*Scot. or poetic*), gloom, half-light, sundown, sunset

twin noun **1** double, clone, counterpart, duplicate, fellow, likeness, lookalike, match, mate ♦ verb **2** pair, couple, join, link, match, yoke

twine noun **1** string, cord, yarn ♦ verb **2** coil, bend, curl, encircle, loop, spiral, twist, wind

twinge noun pain, pang, prick, spasm, stab, stitch

twinkle verb **1** sparkle, blink, flash, flicker, gleam, glint, glisten, glitter, shimmer, shine ♦ noun **2** flicker, flash, gleam, glimmer, shimmer, spark, sparkle

twirl verb **1** turn, pirouette, pivot, revolve, rotate, spin, twist, wheel, whirl, wind ♦ noun **2** turn, pirouette, revolution, rotation, spin, twist, wheel, whirl

twist verb **1** wind, coil, curl, screw, spin, swivel, wrap, wring **2** distort, contort, screw up ♦ noun **3** wind, coil, curl, spin, swivel **4** development, change, revelation, slant, surprise, turn, variation **5** curve, arc, bend, meander, turn, undulation, zigzag **6** distortion, defect, deformation, flaw, imperfection, kink, warp

twit noun fool, ass, chump (*informal*), halfwit, idiot, nincompoop, numbskull or numskull, prat (*slang*), twerp or twirp (*informal*)

twitch verb **1** jerk, flutter, jump, squirm ♦ noun **2** spasm, flutter, jerk, jump, tic

two-faced adjective hypocritical, deceitful, dissembling, duplicitous, false, insincere, treacherous, untrustworthy

tycoon noun magnate, baron, capitalist, fat cat (*slang, chiefly U.S.*), financier, industrialist, mogul, plutocrat

type noun category, class, genre, group, kind, order, sort, species, style, variety

typhoon noun storm, cyclone, squall, tempest, tornado

typical adjective characteristic, archetypal, average, model, normal, orthodox, representative, standard, stock, usual

typify verb symbolize, characterize, embody, epitomize, exemplify, illustrate, personify, represent, sum up

tyrannical adjective oppressive, authoritarian, autocratic, cruel, despotic, dictatorial, domineering, high-handed, imperious, overbearing, tyrannous

tyranny noun oppression, absolutism, authoritarianism, autocracy, cruelty, despotism, dictatorship, high-handedness, imperiousness

tyrant noun dictator, absolutist, authoritarian, autocrat, bully, despot, martinet, oppressor, slave-driver

U u

ubiquitous adjective everywhere, ever-present, omnipresent, pervasive, universal

ugly adjective 1 unattractive, homely (chiefly U.S.), ill-favoured, plain, unlovely, unprepossessing, unsightly 2 unpleasant, disagreeable, distasteful, horrid, objectionable, shocking, terrible 3 ominous, baleful, dangerous, menacing, sinister

ulcer noun sore, abscess, boil, gumboil, peptic ulcer, pustule

ulterior adjective hidden, concealed, covert, secret, undisclosed

ultimate adjective 1 final, end, last 2 supreme, extreme,

greatest, highest, paramount, superlative, utmost

ultimately adverb finally, after all, at last, eventually, in due time, in the end, sooner or later

umpire noun 1 referee, arbiter, arbitrator, judge ♦ verb 2 referee, adjudicate, arbitrate, judge

unabashed adjective unembarrassed, blatant, bold, brazen

unable adjective incapable, impotent, ineffectual, powerless, unfit, unqualified

unabridged adjective uncut, complete, full-length, unexpurgated, whole

unacceptable adjective unsatisfactory, displeasing, objectionable

unaccompanied adjective 1 alone, by oneself, lone, on one's own, solo, unescorted 2 Music a cappella

unaccountable adjective 1 inexplicable, baffling, mysterious, odd, puzzling, unexplainable, unfathomable 2 not answerable, exempt, not responsible

unaccustomed adjective 1 unfamiliar, new, strange, unwonted 2 unaccustomed to not used to, inexperienced at, unfamiliar with, unused to

unaffected[1] adjective natural, artless, genuine, plain, simple, sincere, unpretentious

unaffected[2] adjective impervious, proof, unmoved, unresponsive, untouched

unafraid adjective fearless, daring, dauntless, intrepid

unalterable adjective unchangeable, fixed, immutable, permanent

unanimity noun agreement, accord, assent, concord, concurrence, consensus, harmony, like-mindedness, unison

unanimous adjective agreed, common, concerted, harmonious, in agreement, like-minded, united

unanimously adverb without exception, nem. con., with one accord

unanswerable adjective conclusive, absolute, incontestable, incontrovertible, indisputable

unanswered adjective unresolved, disputed, open, undecided

unappetizing adjective unpleasant, distasteful, off-putting (Brit. informal), repulsive, unappealing, unattractive, unpalatable

unapproachable adjective 1 unfriendly, aloof, chilly, cool, distant, remote, reserved, standoffish 2 inaccessible, out of reach, remote

unarmed adjective defenceless, exposed, helpless, open, unprotected, weak

unassailable adjective impregnable, invincible, invulnerable, secure

unassuming adjective modest, humble, quiet, reserved, retiring, self-effacing, unassertive, unobtrusive, unpretentious

unattached adjective 1 free, independent 2 single, available,

not spoken for, unengaged, unmarried

unattended adjective 1 abandoned, unguarded, unwatched 2 alone, on one's own, unaccompanied

unauthorized adjective illegal, unlawful, unofficial, unsanctioned

unavoidable adjective inevitable, certain, fated, inescapable

unaware adjective ignorant, oblivious, unconscious, uninformed, unknowing

unawares adverb 1 by surprise, off guard, suddenly, unexpectedly 2 unknowingly, accidentally, by accident, inadvertently, unwittingly

unbalanced adjective 1 biased, one-sided, partial, partisan, prejudiced, unfair 2 shaky, lopsided, uneven, unstable, wobbly 3 deranged, crazy, demented, disturbed, eccentric, insane, irrational, mad, non compos mentis, not all there, unhinged, unstable

unbearable adjective intolerable, insufferable, too much (informal), unacceptable

unbeatable adjective invincible, indomitable

unbeaten adjective undefeated, triumphant, victorious

unbecoming adjective 1 unsightly, unattractive, unbefitting, unflattering, unsuitable 2 unseemly, discreditable, improper, offensive

unbelievable adjective incredible, astonishing, far-fetched, implausible, impossible, improbable, inconceivable, preposterous, unconvincing

unbending *adjective* inflexible, firm, intractable, resolute, rigid, severe, strict, stubborn, tough, uncompromising

unbiased *adjective* fair, disinterested, equitable, impartial, just, neutral, objective, unprejudiced

unblemished *adjective* spotless, flawless, immaculate, impeccable, perfect, pure, untarnished

unborn *adjective* expected, awaited, embryonic

unbreakable *adjective* indestructible, durable, lasting, rugged, strong

unbridled *adjective* unrestrained, excessive, intemperate, licentious, riotous, unchecked, unruly, wanton

unbroken *adjective* 1 intact, complete, entire, whole 2 continuous, constant, incessant, uninterrupted

unburden *verb* confess, confide, disclose, get (something) off one's chest (*informal*), reveal

uncalled-for *adjective* unjustified, gratuitous, needless, undeserved, unnecessary, unwarranted

uncanny *adjective* 1 weird, mysterious, strange, supernatural, unearthly, unnatural 2 extraordinary, astounding, exceptional, incredible, miraculous, remarkable, unusual

unceasing *adjective* continual, constant, continuous, endless, incessant, nonstop, perpetual

uncertain *adjective*

1 unpredictable, doubtful, indefinite, questionable, risky, speculative 2 unsure, dubious, hazy, irresolute, unclear, unconfirmed, undecided, vague

uncertainty *noun* doubt, ambiguity, confusion, dubiety, hesitancy, indecision, unpredictability

unchangeable *adjective* unalterable, constant, fixed, immutable, invariable, irreversible, permanent, stable

unchanging *adjective* constant, continuing, enduring, eternal, immutable, lasting, permanent, perpetual, unvarying

uncharitable *adjective* unkind, cruel, hardhearted, unfeeling, ungenerous

uncharted *adjective* unexplored, strange, undiscovered, unfamiliar, unknown

uncivil *adjective* impolite, bad-mannered, discourteous, ill-mannered, rude, unmannerly

uncivilized *adjective* 1 primitive, barbarian, savage, wild 2 uncouth, boorish, coarse, philistine, uncultivated, uneducated

unclean *adjective* dirty, corrupt, defiled, evil, filthy, foul, impure, polluted, soiled, stained

unclear *adjective* 1 indistinct, blurred, dim, faint, fuzzy, hazy, obscure, shadowy, undefined, vague 2 doubtful, ambiguous, indefinite, indeterminate, vague

uncomfortable *adjective* 1 awkward, cramped, painful, rough 2 uneasy, awkward, discomfited, disturbed, embarrassed, troubled

uncommitted *adjective*
uninvolved, floating, free,
neutral, nonaligned, not
involved, unattached

uncommon *adjective* 1 rare,
infrequent, novel, odd, peculiar,
queer, scarce, strange, unusual
2 extraordinary, distinctive,
exceptional, notable,
outstanding, remarkable, special

uncommonly *adverb* 1 rarely,
hardly ever, infrequently,
occasionally, seldom
2 exceptionally, particularly, very

uncommunicative *adjective*
reticent, close, reserved,
secretive, silent, taciturn,
tight-lipped, unforthcoming

uncompromising *adjective*
inflexible, firm, inexorable,
intransigent, rigid, strict, tough,
unbending

unconcern *noun* indifference,
aloofness, apathy, detachment,
lack of interest, nonchalance

unconcerned *adjective*
indifferent, aloof, apathetic, cool,
detached, dispassionate, distant,
uninterested, unmoved

unconditional *adjective* absolute,
complete, entire, full, outright,
positive, total, unlimited,
unqualified, unreserved

unconnected *adjective*
1 separate, detached, divided
2 meaningless, disjointed,
illogical, incoherent, irrelevant

unconscious *adjective*
1 senseless, insensible, knocked
out, out, out cold, stunned
2 unaware, ignorant, oblivious,
unknowing 3 unintentional,

accidental, inadvertent, unwitting

uncontrollable *adjective* wild,
frantic, furious, mad, strong,
unruly, violent

uncontrolled *adjective*
unrestrained, rampant, riotous,
unbridled, unchecked,
undisciplined

unconventional *adjective*
unusual, eccentric, individual,
irregular, nonconformist, odd,
offbeat, original, outré,
unorthodox

unconvincing *adjective*
implausible, dubious, feeble,
flimsy, improbable, lame,
questionable, suspect, thin,
unlikely, weak

uncooperative *adjective*
unhelpful, awkward, difficult,
disobliging, obstructive

uncoordinated *adjective* clumsy,
awkward, bungling, graceless,
lumbering, maladroit, ungainly,
ungraceful

uncouth *adjective* coarse,
boorish, crude, graceless,
ill-mannered, loutish, oafish,
rough, rude, vulgar

uncover *verb* 1 reveal, disclose,
divulge, expose, make known
2 open, bare, show, strip,
unwrap

uncritical *adjective*
undiscriminating, indiscriminate,
undiscerning

undecided *adjective* 1 unsure,
dithering (*chiefly Brit.*), hesitant,
in two minds, irresolute, torn,
uncertain 2 unsettled, debatable,
iffy (*informal*), indefinite, moot,
open, unconcluded,
undetermined

undefined *adjective*
1 <u>unspecified</u>, imprecise, inexact, unclear 2 <u>indistinct</u>, formless, indefinite, vague

undeniable *adjective* <u>certain</u>, clear, incontrovertible, indisputable, obvious, sure, unquestionable

under *preposition* 1 <u>below</u>, beneath, underneath 2 <u>subject to</u>, governed by, secondary to, subordinate to ♦ *adverb* 3 <u>below</u>, beneath, down, lower

underclothes *plural noun* <u>underwear</u>, lingerie, undergarments, undies (*informal*)

undercover *adjective* <u>secret</u>, concealed, covert, hidden, private

undercurrent *noun* 1 <u>undertow</u>, riptide 2 <u>undertone</u>, atmosphere, feeling, hint, overtone, sense, suggestion, tendency, tinge, vibes (*slang*)

underdog *noun* <u>outsider</u>, little fellow (*informal*)

underestimate *verb* <u>underrate</u>, belittle, minimize, miscalculate, undervalue

undergo *verb* <u>experience</u>, bear, endure, go through, stand, suffer, sustain

underground *adjective*
1 <u>subterranean</u>, buried, covered 2 <u>secret</u>, clandestine, covert, hidden ♦ *noun* 3 **the underground: a** <u>the Resistance</u>, partisans **b** <u>the tube</u> (*Brit.*), the metro, the subway

undergrowth *noun* <u>scrub</u>, bracken, briars, brush, underbrush

underhand *adjective* <u>sly</u>, crafty, deceitful, devious, dishonest, furtive, secret, sneaky, stealthy

underline *verb* 1 <u>underscore</u>, mark 2 <u>emphasize</u>, accentuate, highlight, stress

underlying *adjective* <u>fundamental</u>, basic, elementary, intrinsic, primary, prime

undermine *verb* <u>weaken</u>, disable, sabotage, sap, subvert

underprivileged *adjective* <u>disadvantaged</u>, deprived, destitute, impoverished, needy, poor

underrate *verb* <u>underestimate</u>, belittle, discount, undervalue

undersized *adjective* <u>stunted</u>, dwarfish, miniature, pygmy or pigmy, small

understand *verb* 1 <u>comprehend</u>, conceive, fathom, follow, get, grasp, perceive, realize, see, take in 2 <u>believe</u>, assume, gather, presume, suppose, think

understandable *adjective* <u>reasonable</u>, justifiable, legitimate, natural, to be expected

understanding *noun*
1 <u>perception</u>, appreciation, awareness, comprehension, discernment, grasp, insight, judgment, knowledge, sense 2 <u>interpretation</u>, belief, idea, judgment, notion, opinion, perception, view 3 <u>agreement</u>, accord, pact ♦ *adjective* 4 <u>sympathetic</u>, compassionate, considerate, kind, patient, sensitive, tolerant

understood *adjective* 1 <u>implied</u>, implicit, inferred, tacit, unspoken, unstated 2 <u>assumed</u>, accepted, taken for granted

understudy *noun* <u>stand-in</u>,

replacement, reserve, substitute

undertake verb agree, bargain, contract, engage, guarantee, pledge, promise

undertaking noun 1 task, affair, attempt, business, effort, endeavour, enterprise, operation, project, venture 2 promise, assurance, commitment, pledge, vow, word

undertone noun 1 murmur, whisper 2 undercurrent, hint, suggestion, tinge, touch, trace

undervalue verb underrate, depreciate, hold cheap, minimize, misjudge, underestimate

underwater adjective submerged, submarine, sunken

under way adjective begun, going on, in progress, started

underwear noun underclothes, lingerie, undergarments, underthings, undies (informal)

underweight adjective skinny, emaciated, half-starved, puny, skin and bone (informal), undernourished, undersized

underworld noun 1 criminals, gangland (informal), gangsters, organized crime 2 nether world, Hades, nether regions

underwrite verb 1 finance, back, fund, guarantee, insure, sponsor, subsidize 2 sign, endorse, initial

undesirable adjective objectionable, disagreeable, distasteful, unacceptable, unattractive, unsuitable, unwanted, unwelcome

undeveloped adjective potential, immature, latent

undignified adjective unseemly,

improper, indecorous, inelegant, unbecoming, unsuitable

undisciplined adjective uncontrolled, obstreperous, unrestrained, unruly, wayward, wild, wilful

undisguised adjective obvious, blatant, evident, explicit, open, overt, patent, unconcealed

undisputed adjective acknowledged, accepted, certain, indisputable, recognized, unchallenged, undeniable, undoubted

undistinguished adjective ordinary, everyday, mediocre, run-of-the-mill, unexceptional, unimpressive, unremarkable

undisturbed adjective 1 quiet, tranquil 2 calm, collected, composed, placid, sedate, serene, tranquil, unfazed (informal), unperturbed, untroubled

undivided adjective complete, entire, exclusive, full, solid, thorough, undistracted, united, whole

undo verb 1 open, disentangle, loose, unbutton, unfasten, untie 2 reverse, annul, cancel, invalidate, neutralize, offset 3 ruin, defeat, destroy, overturn, quash, shatter, subvert, undermine, upset, wreck

undoing noun downfall, collapse, defeat, disgrace, overthrow, reversal, ruin, shame

undone adjective unfinished, left, neglected, omitted, unfulfilled, unperformed

undoubted adjective certain, acknowledged, definite,

indisputable, indubitable, sure, undisputed, unquestioned

undoubtedly adverb <u>certainly</u>, assuredly, definitely, doubtless, surely, without doubt

undress verb 1 <u>strip</u>, disrobe, shed, take off one's clothes ♦ noun 2 <u>nakedness</u>, nudity

undue adjective <u>excessive</u>, extreme, improper, needless, uncalled-for, unnecessary, unwarranted

unduly adverb <u>excessively</u>, overly, unnecessarily, unreasonably

undying adjective <u>eternal</u>, constant, deathless, everlasting, infinite, permanent, perpetual, unending

unearth verb 1 <u>discover</u>, expose, find, reveal, uncover 2 <u>dig up</u>, dredge up, excavate, exhume

unearthly adjective <u>eerie</u>, ghostly, phantom, spectral, spooky (informal), strange, supernatural, uncanny, weird

uneasiness noun <u>anxiety</u>, disquiet, doubt, misgiving, qualms, trepidation, worry

uneasy adjective 1 <u>anxious</u>, disturbed, edgy, nervous, on edge, perturbed, troubled, twitchy (informal), uncomfortable, worried 2 <u>awkward</u>, insecure, precarious, shaky, strained, tense, uncomfortable

uneconomic adjective <u>unprofitable</u>, loss-making, nonpaying

uneducated adjective 1 <u>ignorant</u>, illiterate, unschooled, untaught 2 <u>lowbrow</u>, uncultivated, uncultured

unemotional adjective <u>impassive</u>, apathetic, cold, cool, phlegmatic, reserved, undemonstrative, unexcitable

unemployed adjective <u>out of work</u>, idle, jobless, laid off, redundant

unending adjective <u>perpetual</u>, continual, endless, eternal, everlasting, interminable, unceasing

unendurable adjective <u>unbearable</u>, insufferable, insupportable, intolerable

unenthusiastic adjective <u>indifferent</u>, apathetic, half-hearted, nonchalant

unenviable adjective <u>unpleasant</u>, disagreeable, uncomfortable, undesirable

unequal adjective 1 <u>different</u>, differing, disparate, dissimilar, unlike, unmatched, varying 2 <u>disproportionate</u>, asymmetrical, ill-matched, irregular, unbalanced, uneven

unequalled adjective <u>incomparable</u>, matchless, paramount, peerless, supreme, unparalleled, unrivalled

unequivocal adjective <u>clear</u>, absolute, certain, definite, explicit, incontrovertible, indubitable, manifest, plain, unambiguous

unerring adjective <u>accurate</u>, exact, infallible, perfect, sure, unfailing

unethical adjective <u>dishonest</u>, disreputable, illegal, immoral, improper, shady (informal), unprincipled, unscrupulous, wrong

uneven adjective 1 rough, bumpy 2 variable, broken, fitful, irregular, jerky, patchy, spasmodic 3 unbalanced, lopsided, odd 4 unequal, ill-matched, unfair

uneventful adjective humdrum, boring, dull, ho-hum (informal), monotonous, routine, tedious, unexciting

unexceptional adjective ordinary, commonplace, conventional, mediocre, normal, pedestrian, run-of-the-mill, undistinguished, unremarkable

unexpected adjective unforeseen, abrupt, chance, fortuitous, sudden, surprising, unanticipated, unlooked-for, unpredictable

unfailing adjective 1 continuous, boundless, endless, persistent, unflagging 2 reliable, certain, dependable, faithful, loyal, staunch, sure, true

unfair adjective 1 biased, bigoted, one-sided, partial, partisan, prejudiced, unjust 2 unscrupulous, dishonest, unethical, unsporting, wrongful

unfaithful adjective 1 faithless, adulterous, two-timing (informal), untrue 2 disloyal, deceitful, faithless, false, traitorous, treacherous, untrustworthy

unfamiliar adjective strange, alien, different, new, novel, unknown, unusual

unfashionable adjective passé, antiquated, dated, obsolete, old-fashioned, old hat

unfasten verb undo, detach, let go, loosen, open, separate, untie

unfathomable adjective 1 baffling, deep, impenetrable, incomprehensible, indecipherable, inexplicable, profound 2 immeasurable, bottomless, unmeasured

unfavourable adjective 1 adverse, contrary, inauspicious, unfortunate, unlucky, unpropitious 2 hostile, inimical, negative, unfriendly

unfeeling adjective 1 hardhearted, apathetic, callous, cold, cruel, heartless, insensitive, pitiless, uncaring 2 numb, insensate, insensible

unfinished adjective 1 incomplete, half-done, uncompleted, undone 2 rough, bare, crude, natural, raw, unrefined

unfit adjective 1 incapable, inadequate, incompetent, no good, unqualified, useless 2 unsuitable, inadequate, ineffective, unsuited, useless 3 out of shape, feeble, flabby, in poor condition, unhealthy

unflappable adjective imperturbable, calm, collected, composed, cool, impassive, level-headed, self-possessed

unflattering adjective 1 blunt, candid, critical, honest 2 unattractive, plain, unbecoming

unflinching adjective determined, firm, immovable, resolute, staunch, steadfast, steady, unfaltering

unfold verb 1 open, expand, spread out, undo, unfurl, unravel, unroll, unwrap 2 reveal, disclose, divulge, make known, present, show, uncover

unforeseen *adjective*
<u>unexpected</u>, accidental, sudden, surprising, unanticipated, unpredicted

unforgettable *adjective*
<u>memorable</u>, exceptional, impressive, notable

unforgivable *adjective*
<u>inexcusable</u>, deplorable, disgraceful, shameful, unpardonable

unfortunate *adjective*
1 <u>disastrous</u>, adverse, calamitous, ill-fated 2 <u>unlucky</u>, cursed, doomed, hapless, unhappy, unsuccessful, wretched
3 <u>regrettable</u>, deplorable, lamentable, unsuitable

unfounded *adjective* <u>groundless</u>, baseless, false, idle, spurious, unjustified

unfriendly *adjective* 1 <u>hostile</u>, aloof, chilly, cold, distant, uncongenial, unsociable
2 <u>unfavourable</u>, alien, hostile, inhospitable

ungainly *adjective* <u>awkward</u>, clumsy, inelegant, lumbering, ungraceful

ungodly *adjective* 1 *Informal* <u>unreasonable</u>, dreadful, intolerable, outrageous, unearthly 2 <u>wicked</u>, corrupt, depraved, godless, immoral, impious, irreligious, profane, sinful

ungracious *adjective*
<u>bad-mannered</u>, churlish, discourteous, impolite, rude, uncivil, unmannerly

ungrateful *adjective*
<u>unappreciative</u>, unmindful, unthankful

unguarded *adjective*
1 <u>unprotected</u>, defenceless, undefended, vulnerable
2 <u>careless</u>, heedless, ill-considered, imprudent, incautious, rash, thoughtless, unthinking, unwary

unhappiness *noun* <u>sadness</u>, blues, dejection, depression, despondency, gloom, heartache, low spirits, melancholy, misery, sorrow, wretchedness

unhappy *adjective* 1 <u>sad</u>, blue, dejected, depressed, despondent, downcast, melancholy, miserable, mournful, sorrowful 2 <u>unlucky</u>, cursed, hapless, ill-fated, unfortunate, wretched

unharmed *adjective* <u>unhurt</u>, intact, safe, sound, undamaged, unscathed, whole

unhealthy *adjective* 1 <u>harmful</u>, detrimental, insalubrious, insanitary, unwholesome 2 <u>sick</u>, ailing, delicate, feeble, frail, infirm, invalid, sickly, unwell

unheard-of *adjective*
1 <u>unprecedented</u>, inconceivable, new, novel, singular, unique
2 <u>shocking</u>, disgraceful, outrageous, preposterous
3 <u>obscure</u>, unfamiliar, unknown

unhesitating *adjective* 1 <u>instant</u>, immediate, prompt, ready
2 <u>wholehearted</u>, resolute, unfaltering, unquestioning, unreserved

unholy *adjective* <u>evil</u>, corrupt, profane, sinful, ungodly, wicked

unhurried *adjective* <u>leisurely</u>, easy, sedate, slow

unidentified *adjective* <u>unnamed</u>, anonymous, nameless, unfamiliar, unrecognized

unification noun union, alliance, amalgamation, coalescence, coalition, confederation, federation, uniting

uniform noun 1 outfit, costume, dress, garb, habit, livery, regalia, suit ♦ adjective 2 unvarying, consistent, constant, even, regular, smooth, unchanging 3 alike, equal, like, same, similar

uniformity noun 1 regularity, constancy, evenness, invariability, sameness, similarity 2 monotony, dullness, flatness, sameness, tedium

unify verb unite, amalgamate, combine, confederate, consolidate, join, merge

unimaginable adjective inconceivable, fantastic, impossible, incredible, unbelievable

unimaginative adjective unoriginal, banal, derivative, dull, hackneyed, ordinary, pedestrian, predictable, prosaic, uncreative, uninspired

unimportant adjective insignificant, inconsequential, irrelevant, minor, paltry, petty, trifling, trivial, worthless

uninhabited adjective deserted, barren, desolate, empty, unpopulated, vacant

uninhibited adjective 1 unselfconscious, free, liberated, natural, open, relaxed, spontaneous, unrepressed, unreserved 2 unrestrained, free, unbridled, unchecked, unconstrained, uncontrolled, unrestricted

uninspired adjective unimaginative, banal, dull, humdrum, ordinary, prosaic, unexciting, unoriginal

unintelligent adjective stupid, braindead (informal), brainless, dense, dull, foolish, gormless (Brit. informal), obtuse, slow, thick

unintelligible adjective incomprehensible, inarticulate, incoherent, indistinct, jumbled, meaningless, muddled

unintentional adjective accidental, casual, inadvertent, involuntary, unconscious, unintended

uninterested adjective indifferent, apathetic, blasé, bored, listless, unconcerned

uninteresting adjective boring, drab, dreary, dry, dull, flat, humdrum, monotonous, tedious, unexciting

uninterrupted adjective continuous, constant, nonstop, steady, sustained, unbroken

union noun 1 joining, amalgamation, blend, combination, conjunction, fusion, mixture, uniting 2 alliance, association, coalition, confederacy, federation, league 3 agreement, accord, concord, harmony, unanimity, unison, unity

unique adjective 1 single, lone, only, solitary 2 unparalleled, incomparable, inimitable, matchless, unequalled, unmatched, unrivalled

unison noun agreement, accord, concert, concord, harmony, unity

unit noun 1 item, entity, whole

2 part, component, constituent, element, member, section, segment **3 section**, detachment, group **4 measure**, measurement, quantity

unite verb **1 join**, amalgamate, blend, combine, couple, fuse, link, merge, unify **2 cooperate**, ally, band, join forces, pool

united adjective **1 combined**, affiliated, allied, banded together, collective, concerted, pooled, unified **2 in agreement**, agreed, of one mind, of the same opinion, unanimous

unity noun **1 wholeness**, entity, integrity, oneness, singleness, union **2 agreement**, accord, assent, concord, consensus, harmony, solidarity, unison

universal adjective **widespread**, common, general, total, unlimited, whole, worldwide

universally adverb **everywhere**, always, invariably, without exception

universe noun **cosmos**, creation, macrocosm, nature

unjust adjective **unfair**, biased, one-sided, partial, partisan, prejudiced, wrong, wrongful

unjustifiable adjective **inexcusable**, indefensible, outrageous, unacceptable, unforgivable, unpardonable, wrong

unkempt adjective **1 uncombed**, shaggy, tousled **2 untidy**, dishevelled, disordered, messy, scruffy, slovenly, ungroomed

unkind adjective **cruel**, harsh, malicious, mean, nasty, spiteful, uncharitable, unfeeling,

unfriendly, unsympathetic

unknown adjective **1 hidden**, concealed, dark, mysterious, secret, unrevealed **2 strange**, alien, new **3 unidentified**, anonymous, nameless, uncharted, undiscovered, unexplored, unnamed **4 obscure**, humble, unfamiliar

unlawful adjective **illegal**, banned, criminal, forbidden, illicit, outlawed, prohibited

unleash verb **release**, free, let go, let loose

unlike adjective **different**, dissimilar, distinct, diverse, not alike, opposite, unequal

unlikely adjective **1 improbable**, doubtful, faint, remote, slight **2 unbelievable**, implausible, incredible, questionable

unlimited adjective **1 infinite**, boundless, countless, endless, extensive, great, immense, limitless, unbounded, vast **2 complete**, absolute, full, total, unqualified, unrestricted

unload verb **empty**, discharge, dump, lighten, relieve, unpack

unlock verb **open**, release, undo, unfasten, unlatch

unlooked-for adjective **unexpected**, chance, fortuitous, surprising, unanticipated, unforeseen, unpredicted

unloved adjective **neglected**, forsaken, loveless, rejected, spurned, unpopular, unwanted

unlucky adjective **1 unfortunate**, cursed, hapless, luckless, miserable, unhappy, wretched **2 ill-fated**, doomed, inauspicious, ominous, unfavourable

unmarried *adjective* single,
bachelor, maiden, unattached,
unwed

unmask *verb* reveal, disclose,
discover, expose, lay bare,
uncover

unmentionable *adjective* taboo,
forbidden, indecent, obscene,
scandalous, shameful, shocking,
unspeakable

unmerciful *adjective* merciless,
brutal, cruel, hard, implacable,
pitiless, remorseless, ruthless

unmistakable *adjective* clear,
certain, distinct, evident,
manifest, obvious, plain, sure,
unambiguous

unmitigated *adjective*
1 unrelieved, intense, persistent,
unalleviated, unbroken,
undiminished **2** complete,
absolute, arrant, downright,
outright, sheer, thorough, utter

unmoved *adjective* unaffected,
cold, impassive, indifferent,
unimpressed, unresponsive,
untouched

unnatural *adjective* **1** strange,
extraordinary, freakish,
outlandish, queer **2** abnormal,
anomalous, irregular, odd,
perverse, perverted, unusual
3 false, affected, artificial,
feigned, forced, insincere,
phoney *or* phony (*informal*), stiff,
stilted

unnecessary *adjective* needless,
expendable, inessential,
redundant, superfluous,
unneeded, unrequired

unnerve *verb* intimidate,
demoralize, discourage,
dishearten, dismay, faze, fluster,
frighten, psych out (*informal*),

rattle (*informal*), shake, upset

unnoticed *adjective* unobserved,
disregarded, ignored, neglected,
overlooked, unheeded,
unperceived, unrecognized,
unseen

unobtrusive *adjective*
inconspicuous, low-key, modest,
quiet, restrained, retiring,
self-effacing, unassuming

unoccupied *adjective* empty,
uninhabited, vacant

unofficial *adjective* unauthorized,
informal, private, unconfirmed

unorthodox *adjective*
unconventional, abnormal,
irregular, off-the-wall (*slang*),
unusual

unpaid *adjective* **1** voluntary,
honorary, unsalaried **2** owing,
due, outstanding, overdue,
payable, unsettled

unpalatable *adjective* unpleasant,
disagreeable, distasteful, horrid,
offensive, repugnant,
unappetizing, unsavoury

unparalleled *adjective*
unequalled, incomparable,
matchless, superlative, unique,
unmatched, unprecedented,
unsurpassed

unpardonable *adjective*
unforgivable, deplorable,
disgraceful, indefensible,
inexcusable

unperturbed *adjective* calm, as
cool as a cucumber, composed,
cool, placid, unfazed (*informal*),
unruffled, untroubled, unworried

unpleasant *adjective* nasty, bad,
disagreeable, displeasing,
distasteful, horrid, objectionable

unpopular *adjective* disliked,

rejected, shunned, unwanted, unwelcome

unprecedented adjective
extraordinary, abnormal, new, novel, original, remarkable, singular, unheard-of

unpredictable adjective
inconstant, chance, changeable, doubtful, erratic, random, unforeseeable, unreliable, variable

unprejudiced adjective impartial, balanced, fair, just, objective, open-minded, unbiased

unprepared adjective 1 taken off guard, surprised, unaware, unready 2 improvised, ad-lib, off the cuff (informal), spontaneous

unpretentious adjective modest, humble, plain, simple, straightforward, unaffected, unassuming, unostentatious

unprincipled adjective dishonest, amoral, crooked, devious, immoral, underhand, unethical, unscrupulous

unproductive adjective 1 useless, fruitless, futile, idle, ineffective, unprofitable, unrewarding, vain 2 barren, fruitless, sterile

unprofessional adjective
1 unethical, improper, lax, negligent, unprincipled
2 amateurish, cowboy (informal), incompetent, inefficient, inexpert

unprotected adjective vulnerable, defenceless, helpless, open, undefended

unqualified adjective 1 unfit, ill-equipped, incapable, incompetent, ineligible, unprepared 2 total, absolute, complete, downright, outright, thorough, utter

unquestionable adjective
certain, absolute, clear, conclusive, definite, incontrovertible, indisputable, sure, undeniable, unequivocal, unmistakable

unravel verb 1 undo, disentangle, free, separate, untangle, unwind 2 solve, explain, figure out (informal), resolve, work out

unreal adjective 1 imaginary, dreamlike, fabulous, fanciful, illusory, make-believe, visionary 2 insubstantial, immaterial, intangible, nebulous 3 fake, artificial, false, insincere, mock, pretended, sham

unrealistic adjective impractical, impracticable, improbable, romantic, unworkable

unreasonable adjective
1 excessive, extortionate, immoderate, undue, unfair, unjust, unwarranted 2 biased, blinkered, opinionated

unrelated adjective 1 different, unconnected, unlike 2 irrelevant, extraneous, inapplicable, inappropriate, unconnected

unreliable adjective
1 undependable, irresponsible, treacherous, untrustworthy 2 uncertain, deceptive, fallible, false, implausible, inaccurate, unsound

unrepentant adjective
impenitent, abandoned, callous, hardened, incorrigible, shameless, unremorseful

unreserved adjective 1 total, absolute, complete, entire, full, unlimited, wholehearted 2 open, demonstrative, extrovert, free, outgoing, uninhibited, unrestrained

unresolved adjective <u>undecided</u>, doubtful, moot, unanswered, undetermined, unsettled, unsolved, vague

unrest noun <u>discontent</u>, agitation, discord, dissension, protest, rebellion, sedition, strife

unrestrained adjective <u>uncontrolled</u>, abandoned, free, immoderate, intemperate, unbounded, unbridled, unchecked, uninhibited

unrestricted adjective
1 <u>unlimited</u>, absolute, free, open, unbounded, unregulated
2 <u>open</u>, public

unrivalled adjective <u>unparalleled</u>, beyond compare, incomparable, matchless, supreme, unequalled, unmatched, unsurpassed

unruly adjective <u>uncontrollable</u>, disobedient, mutinous, rebellious, wayward, wild, wilful

unsafe adjective <u>dangerous</u>, hazardous, insecure, perilous, risky, unreliable

unsatisfactory adjective <u>unacceptable</u>, deficient, disappointing, inadequate, insufficient, not good enough, not up to scratch (informal), poor

unsavoury adjective
1 <u>unpleasant</u>, distasteful, nasty, obnoxious, offensive, repellent, repulsive, revolting
2 <u>unappetizing</u>, nauseating, sickening, unpalatable

unscathed adjective <u>unharmed</u>, safe, unhurt, uninjured, unmarked, whole

unscrupulous adjective

<u>unprincipled</u>, corrupt, dishonest, dishonourable, immoral, improper, unethical

unseat verb 1 <u>throw</u>, unhorse, unsaddle 2 <u>depose</u>, dethrone, displace, oust, overthrow, remove

unseemly adjective <u>improper</u>, inappropriate, indecorous, unbecoming, undignified, unsuitable

unseen adjective <u>unobserved</u>, concealed, hidden, invisible, obscure, undetected, unnoticed

unselfish adjective <u>generous</u>, altruistic, kind, magnanimous, noble, selfless, self-sacrificing

unsettle verb <u>disturb</u>, agitate, bother, confuse, disconcert, faze, fluster, perturb, ruffle, trouble, upset

unsettled adjective 1 <u>unstable</u>, disorderly, insecure, shaky, unsteady 2 <u>restless</u>, agitated, anxious, confused, disturbed, flustered, restive, shaken, tense 3 <u>changing</u>, inconstant, uncertain, variable

unshakable adjective <u>firm</u>, absolute, fixed, immovable, staunch, steadfast, sure, unswerving, unwavering

unsightly adjective <u>ugly</u>, disagreeable, hideous, horrid, repulsive, unattractive

unskilled adjective <u>unprofessional</u>, amateurish, cowboy (informal), inexperienced, unqualified, untrained

unsociable adjective <u>unfriendly</u>, chilly, cold, distant, hostile, retiring, unforthcoming, withdrawn

unsolicited adjective
unrequested, gratuitous, unasked for, uncalled-for, uninvited, unsought

unsophisticated adjective
1 natural, artless, childlike, guileless, ingenuous, unaffected, unrefined, unspecialized 2 simple, plain, uncomplicated

unsound adjective 1 unhealthy, ailing, defective, diseased, ill, unbalanced, unstable, unwell, weak 2 unreliable, defective, fallacious, false, flawed, illogical, shaky, specious, weak

unspeakable adjective
1 indescribable, inconceivable, unbelievable, unimaginable 2 dreadful, abominable, appalling, awful, heinous, horrible, monstrous, shocking

unspoiled, unspoilt adjective
1 perfect, intact, preserved, unchanged, undamaged, untouched 2 natural, artless, innocent, unaffected

unspoken adjective tacit, implicit, implied, understood, unexpressed, unstated

unstable adjective 1 insecure, precarious, shaky, tottering, unsettled, unsteady, wobbly 2 changeable, fitful, fluctuating, inconstant, unpredictable, variable, volatile 3 unpredictable, capricious, changeable, erratic, inconsistent, irrational, temperamental

unsteady adjective 1 unstable, infirm, insecure, precarious, shaky, unsafe, wobbly 2 changeable, erratic, inconstant, temperamental, unsettled, volatile

unsuccessful adjective 1 useless, failed, fruitless, futile, unavailing, unproductive, vain 2 unlucky, hapless, luckless, unfortunate

unsuitable adjective
inappropriate, improper, inapposite, inapt, ineligible, unacceptable, unbecoming, unfit, unfitting, unseemly

unsure adjective 1 unconfident, insecure, unassured 2 doubtful, distrustful, dubious, hesitant, mistrustful, sceptical, suspicious, unconvinced

unsuspecting adjective trusting, credulous, gullible, trustful, unwary

unswerving adjective constant, firm, resolute, single-minded, staunch, steadfast, steady, true, unwavering

unsympathetic adjective hard, callous, cold, cruel, harsh, heartless, insensitive, unfeeling, unkind, unmoved

untangle verb disentangle, extricate, unravel, unsnarl

untenable adjective
unsustainable, groundless, illogical, indefensible, insupportable, shaky, unsound, weak

unthinkable adjective
1 impossible, absurd, out of the question, unreasonable 2 inconceivable, implausible, incredible, unimaginable

untidy adjective messy, chaotic, cluttered, disarrayed, disordered, jumbled, littered, muddled, shambolic, unkempt

untie verb undo, free, loosen, release, unbind, unfasten, unlace

untimely *adjective* **1** early, premature **2** ill-timed, awkward, inappropriate, inconvenient, inopportune, mistimed

untiring *adjective* tireless, constant, determined, dogged, persevering, steady, unflagging, unremitting

untold *adjective* **1** indescribable, inexpressible, undreamed of, unimaginable, unthinkable, unutterable **2** countless, incalculable, innumerable, myriad, numberless, uncountable

untouched *adjective* unharmed, intact, undamaged, unhurt, uninjured, unscathed

untoward *adjective* **1** annoying, awkward, inconvenient, irritating, troublesome, unfortunate **2** unlucky, adverse, inauspicious, inopportune, unfavourable

untrained *adjective* amateur, green, inexperienced, raw, uneducated, unqualified, unschooled, unskilled, untaught

untroubled *adjective* undisturbed, calm, cool, peaceful, placid, tranquil, unfazed (*informal*), unperturbed, unworried

untrue *adjective* **1** false, deceptive, dishonest, erroneous, inaccurate, incorrect, lying, mistaken, wrong **2** unfaithful, deceitful, disloyal, faithless, false, inconstant, treacherous, untrustworthy

untrustworthy *adjective* unreliable, deceitful, devious, dishonest, disloyal, false, slippery, treacherous, tricky

untruth *noun* lie, deceit, falsehood, fib, pork pie (*Brit. slang*), porky (*Brit. slang*), story

untruthful *adjective* dishonest, deceitful, deceptive, false, lying, mendacious

unusual *adjective* extraordinary, curious, different, exceptional, odd, queer, rare, remarkable, singular, strange, uncommon, unconventional

unveil *verb* reveal, disclose, divulge, expose, make known, uncover

unwanted *adjective* undesired, outcast, rejected, uninvited, unneeded, unsolicited, unwelcome

unwarranted *adjective* unnecessary, gratuitous, groundless, indefensible, inexcusable, uncalled for, unjustified, unprovoked

unwavering *adjective* steady, consistent, determined, immovable, resolute, staunch, steadfast, unshakable, unswerving

unwelcome *adjective* **1** unwanted, excluded, rejected, unacceptable, undesirable **2** disagreeable, displeasing, distasteful, undesirable, unpleasant

unwell *adjective* ill, ailing, sick, sickly, under the weather (*informal*), unhealthy

unwholesome *adjective* **1** harmful, deleterious, noxious, poisonous, unhealthy **2** wicked, bad, corrupting, degrading, demoralizing, evil, immoral

unwieldy *adjective* **1** awkward, cumbersome, inconvenient, unmanageable **2** bulky, clumsy, hefty, massive, ponderous

unwilling *adjective* <u>reluctant</u>, averse, disinclined, grudging, indisposed, loath, resistant, unenthusiastic

unwind *verb* **1** <u>unravel</u>, slacken, uncoil, undo, unroll, untwine, untwist **2** <u>relax</u>, loosen up, take it easy, wind down

unwise *adjective* <u>foolish</u>, foolhardy, improvident, imprudent, inadvisable, injudicious, rash, reckless, senseless, silly, stupid

unwitting *adjective*
1 <u>unintentional</u>, accidental, chance, inadvertent, involuntary, unplanned **2** <u>unknowing</u>, ignorant, innocent, unaware, unconscious, unsuspecting

unworldly *adjective* **1** <u>spiritual</u>, metaphysical, nonmaterialistic **2** <u>naive</u>, idealistic, innocent, unsophisticated

unworthy *adjective*
1 <u>undeserving</u>, not fit for, not good enough **2** <u>dishonourable</u>, base, contemptible, degrading, discreditable, disgraceful, disreputable, ignoble, shameful **3** **unworthy of** <u>unbefitting</u>, beneath, inappropriate, unbecoming, unfitting, unseemly, unsuitable

unwritten *adjective* **1** <u>oral</u>, vocal **2** <u>customary</u>, accepted, tacit, understood

unyielding *adjective* <u>firm</u>, adamant, immovable, inflexible, obdurate, obstinate, resolute, rigid, stiff-necked, stubborn, tough, uncompromising

upbeat *adjective Informal* <u>cheerful</u>, cheery, encouraging, hopeful, optimistic, positive

upbraid *verb* <u>scold</u>, admonish, berate, rebuke, reprimand, reproach, reprove

upbringing *noun* <u>education</u>, breeding, raising, rearing, training

update *verb* <u>revise</u>, amend, bring up to date, modernize, renew

upgrade *verb* <u>promote</u>, advance, better, elevate, enhance, improve, raise

upheaval *noun* <u>disturbance</u>, disorder, disruption, revolution, turmoil

uphill *adjective* **1** <u>ascending</u>, climbing, mounting, rising **2** <u>arduous</u>, difficult, exhausting, gruelling, hard, laborious, strenuous, taxing, tough

uphold *verb* <u>support</u>, advocate, aid, back, champion, defend, endorse, maintain, promote, sustain

upkeep *noun* **1** <u>maintenance</u>, keep, repair, running, subsistence **2** <u>overheads</u>, expenditure, expenses, running costs

uplift *verb* **1** <u>raise</u>, elevate, hoist, lift up **2** <u>improve</u>, advance, better, edify, inspire, raise, refine ♦ *noun* **3** <u>improvement</u>, advancement, edification, enhancement, enlightenment, enrichment, refinement

upper *adjective* **1** <u>higher</u>, high, loftier, top, topmost **2** <u>superior</u>, eminent, greater, important

upper-class *adjective* <u>aristocratic</u>, blue-blooded, highborn, high-class, noble, patrician

upper hand *noun* <u>control</u>,

advantage, ascendancy, edge, mastery, supremacy

uppermost adjective 1 top, highest, loftiest, topmost 2 supreme, chief, dominant, foremost, greatest, leading, main, principal

uppity adjective Informal conceited, bumptious, cocky, full of oneself, impertinent, self-important, uppish (Brit. informal)

upright adjective 1 vertical, erect, perpendicular, straight 2 honest, conscientious, ethical, good, honourable, just, principled, righteous, virtuous

uprising noun rebellion, disturbance, insurgence, insurrection, mutiny, revolt, revolution, rising

uproar noun commotion, din, furore, mayhem, noise, outcry, pandemonium, racket, riot, turmoil

uproarious adjective 1 hilarious, hysterical, killing (informal), rib-tickling, rip-roaring (Informal), side-splitting, very funny 2 loud, boisterous, rollicking, unrestrained

uproot verb 1 pull up, dig up, rip up, root out, weed out 2 displace, exile

upset adjective 1 sick, ill, queasy 2 distressed, agitated, bothered, dismayed, disturbed, grieved, hurt, put out, troubled, worried 3 disordered, chaotic, confused, disarrayed, in disarray, muddled 4 overturned, capsized, spilled, upside down ♦ verb 5 tip over, capsize, knock over, overturn, spill 6 mess up, change,

disorder, disorganize, disturb, spoil 7 distress, agitate, bother, disconcert, disturb, faze, fluster, grieve, perturb, ruffle, trouble ♦ noun 8 reversal, defeat, shake-up (informal) 9 illness, bug (informal), complaint, disorder, malady, sickness 10 distress, agitation, bother, disturbance, shock, trouble, worry

upshot noun result, culmination, end, end result, finale, outcome, sequel

upside down adjective 1 inverted, overturned, upturned 2 Informal confused, chaotic, disordered, higgledy-piggledy (informal), muddled, topsy-turvy

upstanding adjective honest, ethical, good, honourable, incorruptible, moral, principled, upright

upstart noun social climber, arriviste, nouveau riche, parvenu

uptight adjective Informal tense, anxious, edgy, on edge, uneasy, wired (slang)

up-to-date adjective modern, current, fashionable, in vogue, stylish, trendy (Brit. informal), up-to-the-minute

upturn noun rise, advancement, improvement, increase, recovery, revival, upsurge, upswing

urban adjective civic, city, metropolitan, municipal, town

urbane adjective sophisticated, courteous, cultivated, cultured, debonair, polished, refined, smooth, suave, well-bred

urchin noun ragamuffin, brat, gamin, waif

urge noun 1 impulse,

compulsion, desire, drive, itch, longing, thirst, wish, yearning ♦ *verb* **2** beg, beseech, entreat, exhort, implore, plead **3** advocate, advise, counsel, recommend, support **4** drive, compel, force, goad, impel, incite, induce, press, push, spur

urgency *noun* importance, extremity, gravity, hurry, necessity, need, pressure, seriousness

urgent *adjective* crucial, compelling, critical, immediate, imperative, important, pressing

usable *adjective* serviceable, available, current, functional, practical, utilizable, valid, working

usage *noun* **1** use, control, employment, handling, management, operation, running **2** practice, convention, custom, habit, method, mode, procedure, regime, routine

use *verb* **1** employ, apply, exercise, exert, operate, practise, utilize, work **2** take advantage of, exploit, manipulate **3** consume, exhaust, expend, run through, spend ♦ *noun* **4** usage, application, employment, exercise, handling, operation, practice, service **5** good, advantage, avail, benefit, help, point, profit, service, usefulness, value **6** purpose, end, object, reason

used *adjective* second-hand, cast-off, nearly new, shopsoiled

used to *adjective* accustomed to, familiar with

useful *adjective* helpful, advantageous, beneficial, effective, fruitful, practical, profitable, serviceable, valuable, worthwhile

usefulness *noun* helpfulness, benefit, convenience, effectiveness, efficacy, practicality, use, utility, value, worth

useless *adjective* **1** worthless, fruitless, futile, impractical, ineffectual, pointless, unproductive, vain, valueless **2** *Informal* inept, hopeless, incompetent, ineffectual, no good

use up *verb* consume, absorb, drain, exhaust, finish, run through

usher *noun* **1** attendant, doorkeeper, doorman, escort, guide ♦ *verb* **2** escort, conduct, direct, guide, lead

usual *adjective* normal, common, customary, everyday, general, habitual, ordinary, regular, routine, standard, typical

usually *adverb* normally, as a rule, commonly, generally, habitually, mainly, mostly, on the whole

usurp *verb* seize, appropriate, assume, commandeer, take, take over, wrest

utility *noun* usefulness, benefit, convenience, efficacy, practicality, serviceableness

utilize *verb* use, avail oneself of, employ, make use of, put to use, take advantage of, turn to account

utmost *adjective* **1** greatest, chief, highest, maximum, paramount, pre-eminent, supreme **2** farthest, extreme, final, last ◆ *noun* 3 <u>greatest</u>, best, hardest, highest

Utopia *noun* <u>paradise</u>, bliss, Eden, Garden of Eden, heaven, Shangri-la

Utopian *adjective* <u>perfect</u>, dream, fantasy, ideal, idealistic, imaginary, romantic, visionary

utter[1] *verb* <u>express</u>, articulate, pronounce, say, speak, voice

utter[2] *adjective* <u>absolute</u>, complete, downright, outright, sheer, thorough, total, unmitigated

utterance *noun* <u>speech</u>, announcement, declaration, expression, remark, statement, words

utterly *adverb* <u>totally</u>, absolutely, completely, entirely, extremely, fully, perfectly, thoroughly

V v

vacancy *noun* <u>job</u>, opening, opportunity, position, post, situation

vacant *adjective* 1 <u>unoccupied</u>, available, empty, free, idle, unfilled, untenanted, void 2 <u>vague</u>, absent-minded, abstracted, blank, dreamy, idle, inane, vacuous

vacate *verb* <u>leave</u>, evacuate, quit

vacuous *adjective* <u>unintelligent</u>, blank, inane, stupid, uncomprehending, vacant

vacuum *noun* <u>emptiness</u>, gap, nothingness, space, vacuity, void

vagabond *noun* <u>beggar</u>, down-and-out, itinerant, rover,

tramp, vagrant

vagrant *noun* 1 <u>tramp</u>, drifter, hobo (*U.S.*), itinerant, rolling stone, wanderer ◆ *adjective* 2 <u>itinerant</u>, nomadic, roaming, rootless, roving, unsettled, vagabond

vague *adjective* <u>unclear</u>, hazy, ill-defined, imprecise, indefinite, indeterminate, indistinct, loose, nebulous, uncertain, unspecified

vain *adjective* 1 <u>proud</u>, arrogant, conceited, egotistical, narcissistic, self-important, swaggering 2 <u>futile</u>, abortive, fruitless, idle, pointless, senseless, unavailing, unprofitable, useless, worthless ◆ *noun* 3 **in vain** <u>to no avail</u>, fruitless(ly), ineffectual(ly), unsuccessful(ly), useless(ly), vain(ly)

valiant *adjective* <u>brave</u>, bold, courageous, fearless, gallant, heroic, intrepid, lion-hearted

valid *adjective* 1 <u>logical</u>, cogent, convincing, good, sound, telling, well-founded, well-grounded 2 <u>legal</u>, authentic, bona fide, genuine, lawful, legitimate, official

validate *verb* <u>confirm</u>, authenticate, authorize, certify, corroborate, endorse, ratify, substantiate

validity *noun* 1 <u>soundness</u>, cogency, force, power, strength, weight 2 <u>legality</u>, authority, lawfulness, legitimacy, right

valley *noun* <u>hollow</u>, dale, dell, depression, glen, vale

valour *noun* <u>bravery</u>, boldness, courage, fearlessness, gallantry, heroism, intrepidity, spirit

valuable adjective **1** precious, costly, dear, expensive, high-priced **2** useful, beneficial, helpful, important, prized, profitable, worthwhile ♦ noun **3** valuables treasures, heirlooms

value noun **1** importance, advantage, benefit, desirability, merit, profit, usefulness, utility, worth **2** cost, market price, rate **3** values principles, ethics, (moral) standards ♦ verb **4** evaluate, appraise, assess, estimate, price, rate, set at **5** respect, appreciate, cherish, esteem, hold dear, prize, regard highly, treasure

vandal noun hooligan, delinquent, rowdy, yob or yobbo (Brit. slang)

vanguard noun forerunners, cutting edge, forefront, front line, leaders, spearhead, trailblazers, trendsetters, van

vanish verb disappear, dissolve, evanesce, evaporate, fade (away), melt (away)

vanity noun pride, arrogance, conceit, conceitedness, egotism, narcissism

vanquish verb Literary defeat, beat, conquer, crush, master, overcome, overpower, overwhelm, triumph over

vapid adjective dull, bland, boring, flat, insipid, tame, uninspiring, uninteresting, weak, wishy-washy (informal)

vapour noun mist, exhalation, fog, haze, steam

variable adjective changeable, flexible, fluctuating, inconstant, mutable, shifting, temperamental, uneven, unstable, unsteady

variance noun at variance in disagreement, at loggerheads, at odds, at sixes and sevens (informal), conflicting, out of line

variant adjective **1** different, alternative, divergent, modified ♦ noun **2** variation, alternative, development, modification

variation noun difference, change, departure, deviation, diversity, innovation, modification, novelty, variety

varied adjective different, assorted, diverse, heterogeneous, miscellaneous, mixed, motley, sundry, various

variety noun **1** diversity, change, difference, discrepancy, diversification, multifariousness, variation **2** range, array, assortment, collection, cross section, medley, miscellany, mixture **3** type, brand, breed, category, class, kind, sort, species, strain

various adjective different, assorted, disparate, distinct, diverse, miscellaneous, several, sundry, varied

varnish noun, verb polish, glaze, gloss, lacquer

vary verb change, alter, differ, disagree, diverge, fluctuate

vast adjective huge, boundless, colossal, enormous, gigantic, great, immense, massive, monumental, wide

vault[1] noun **1** strongroom, depository, repository **2** crypt, catacomb, cellar, charnel house, mausoleum, tomb, undercroft

vault[2] verb jump, bound, clear,

hurdle, leap, spring

vaulted adjective arched, cavernous, domed

veer verb swerve, change course, change direction, sheer, shift, turn

vegetate verb stagnate, deteriorate, go to seed, idle, languish, loaf

vehemence noun forcefulness, ardour, emphasis, energy, fervour, force, intensity, passion, vigour

vehement adjective strong, ardent, emphatic, fervent, fierce, forceful, impassioned, intense, passionate, powerful

vehicle noun 1 transport, conveyance, transportation 2 medium, apparatus, channel, means, mechanism, organ

veil noun 1 cover, blind, cloak, curtain, disguise, film, mask, screen, shroud ♦ verb 2 cover, cloak, conceal, disguise, hide, mask, obscure, screen, shield

veiled adjective disguised, concealed, covert, hinted at, implied, masked, suppressed

vein noun 1 blood vessel 2 seam, course, current, lode, stratum, streak, stripe 3 mood, mode, note, style, temper, tenor, tone

velocity noun speed, pace, quickness, rapidity, swiftness

velvety adjective smooth, delicate, downy, soft

vendetta noun feud, bad blood, quarrel

veneer noun mask, appearance, façade, front, guise, pretence, semblance, show

venerable adjective respected, august, esteemed, honoured, revered, sage, wise, worshipped

venerate verb respect, adore, esteem, honour, look up to, revere, reverence, worship

vengeance noun revenge, reprisal, requital, retaliation, retribution

venom noun 1 malice, acrimony, bitterness, hate, rancour, spite, spleen, virulence 2 poison, bane, toxin

venomous adjective 1 malicious, hostile, malignant, rancorous, savage, spiteful, vicious, vindictive 2 poisonous, mephitic, noxious, toxic, virulent

vent noun 1 outlet, aperture, duct, opening, orifice ♦ verb 2 express, air, discharge, emit, give vent to, pour out, release, utter, voice

venture noun 1 undertaking, adventure, endeavour, enterprise, gamble, hazard, project, risk ♦ verb 2 risk, chance, hazard, speculate, stake, wager 3 dare, hazard, make bold, presume, take the liberty, volunteer 4 go, embark on, plunge into, set out

verbal adjective spoken, oral, unwritten, word-of-mouth

verbatim adverb exactly, precisely, to the letter, word for word

verbose adjective long-winded, circumlocutory, diffuse, periphrastic, prolix, tautological, windy, wordy

verbosity noun long-windedness, loquaciousness, prolixity, verboseness, wordiness

verdant *adjective* green, flourishing, fresh, grassy, leafy, lush

verdict *noun* decision, adjudication, conclusion, finding, judgment, opinion, sentence

verge *noun* 1 border, boundary, brim, brink, edge, limit, margin, threshold ♦ *verb* 2 verge on border, approach, come near

verification *noun* proof, authentication, confirmation, corroboration, substantiation, validation

verify *verb* check, authenticate, bear out, confirm, corroborate, prove, substantiate, support, validate

vernacular *noun* dialect, idiom, parlance, patois, speech

versatile *adjective* adaptable, adjustable, all-purpose, all-round, flexible, multifaceted, resourceful, variable

versed *adjective* knowledgeable, acquainted, conversant, experienced, familiar, practised, proficient, seasoned, well informed

version *noun* 1 form, design, model, style, variant 2 account, adaptation, interpretation, portrayal, rendering

vertical *adjective* upright, erect, on end, perpendicular

vertigo *noun* dizziness, giddiness, light-headedness

verve *noun* enthusiasm, animation, energy, gusto, liveliness, sparkle, spirit, vitality

very *adverb* 1 extremely, acutely, decidedly, deeply, exceedingly, greatly, highly, profoundly, uncommonly, unusually ♦ *adjective* 2 exact, precise, selfsame

vessel *noun* 1 ship, boat, craft 2 container, pot, receptacle, utensil

vest *verb, with* in *or with* place, bestow, confer, consign, endow, entrust, invest, settle

vestibule *noun* hall, anteroom, foyer, lobby, porch, portico

vestige *noun* trace, glimmer, indication, remnant, scrap, suspicion

vet *verb* check, appraise, examine, investigate, review, scrutinize

veteran *noun* 1 old hand, old stager, past master, warhorse (*informal*) ♦ *adjective* 2 long-serving, battle-scarred, old, seasoned

veto *noun* 1 ban, boycott, embargo, interdict, prohibition ♦ *verb* 2 ban, boycott, disallow, forbid, prohibit, reject, rule out, turn down

vex *verb* annoy, bother, distress, exasperate, irritate, plague, trouble, upset, worry

vexation *noun* 1 annoyance, chagrin, displeasure, dissatisfaction, exasperation, frustration, irritation, pique 2 problem, bother, difficulty, hassle (*informal*), headache (*informal*), nuisance, trouble, worry

viable *adjective* workable, applicable, feasible, operable, practicable, usable

vibrant *adjective* energetic, alive, animated, dynamic, sparkling, spirited, vigorous, vivacious, vivid

vibrate verb shake, fluctuate, judder (*informal*), oscillate, pulsate, quiver, reverberate, sway, throb, tremble

vibration noun tremor, judder (*informal*), oscillation, pulsation, quiver, reverberation, shake, throbbing, trembling

vicarious adjective indirect, delegated, substituted, surrogate

vice noun 1 wickedness, corruption, depravity, evil, immorality, iniquity, sin, turpitude 2 fault, blemish, defect, failing, imperfection, shortcoming, weakness

vice versa adverb conversely, contrariwise, in reverse, the other way round

vicinity noun neighbourhood, area, district, environs, locality, neck of the woods (*informal*), proximity

vicious adjective 1 violent, barbarous, cruel, ferocious, savage, wicked 2 malicious, cruel, mean, spiteful, venomous, vindictive

victim noun casualty, fatality, martyr, sacrifice, scapegoat, sufferer

victimize verb persecute, discriminate against, have it in for (someone) (*informal*), pick on

victor noun winner, champion, conqueror, prizewinner, vanquisher

victorious adjective winning, champion, conquering, first, prizewinning, successful, triumphant, vanquishing

victory noun win, conquest, success, triumph

vie verb compete, contend, strive, struggle

view noun 1 sometimes plural opinion, attitude, belief, conviction, feeling, impression, point of view, sentiment 2 scene, landscape, outlook, panorama, perspective, picture, prospect, spectacle, vista 3 vision, sight ♦ verb 4 regard, consider, deem, look on

viewer noun watcher, observer, onlooker, spectator

vigilance noun watchfulness, alertness, attentiveness, carefulness, caution, circumspection, observance

vigilant adjective watchful, alert, attentive, careful, cautious, circumspect, on one's guard, on the lookout, wakeful

vigorous adjective energetic, active, dynamic, forceful, lively, lusty, powerful, spirited, strenuous, strong

vigorously adverb energetically, forcefully, hard, lustily, strenuously, strongly

vigour noun energy, animation, dynamism, forcefulness, gusto, liveliness, power, spirit, strength, verve, vitality

vile adjective 1 wicked, corrupt, degenerate, depraved, evil, nefarious, perverted 2 disgusting, foul, horrid, nasty, nauseating, offensive, repugnant, repulsive, revolting, sickening

vilify verb malign, abuse, berate, denigrate, disparage, revile, slander, smear

villain noun 1 evildoer,

villainous blackguard, criminal, miscreant, reprobate, rogue, scoundrel, wretch **2** antihero, baddy (informal)

villainous adjective wicked, bad, cruel, degenerate, depraved, evil, fiendish, nefarious, vicious, vile

villainy noun wickedness, delinquency, depravity, devilry, iniquity, turpitude, vice

vindicate verb **1** clear, absolve, acquit, exculpate, exonerate, rehabilitate **2** justify, defend, excuse

vindication noun **1** exoneration, exculpation, rehabilitation **2** justification, defence, excuse

vindictive adjective vengeful, implacable, malicious, resentful, revengeful, spiteful, unforgiving, unrelenting

vintage adjective best, choice, classic, prime, select, superior

violate verb **1** break, contravene, disobey, disregard, encroach upon, infringe, transgress **2** desecrate, abuse, befoul, defile, dishonour, pollute, profane **3** rape, abuse, assault, debauch, ravish

violation noun **1** infringement, abuse, breach, contravention, encroachment, infraction, transgression, trespass **2** desecration, defilement, profanation, sacrilege, spoliation

violence noun **1** force, bloodshed, brutality, cruelty, ferocity, fighting, savagery, terrorism **2** intensity, abandon, fervour, force, severity, vehemence

violent adjective destructive, brutal, cruel, hot-headed, murderous, riotous, savage, uncontrollable, unrestrained, vicious

V.I.P. noun celebrity, big name, luminary, somebody, star

virgin noun **1** maiden, girl ♦ adjective **2** pure, chaste, immaculate, uncorrupted, undefiled, vestal, virginal

virginity noun chastity, maidenhood

virile adjective manly, lusty, macho, manlike, masculine, red-blooded, strong, vigorous

virility noun masculinity, machismo, manhood, vigour

virtual adjective practical, essential, in all but name

virtually adverb practically, almost, as good as, in all but name, in effect, in essence, nearly

virtue noun **1** goodness, incorruptibility, integrity, morality, probity, rectitude, righteousness, uprightness, worth **2** merit, advantage, asset, attribute, credit, good point, plus (informal), strength

virtuosity noun mastery, brilliance, craft, expertise, flair, panache, polish, skill

virtuoso noun master, artist, genius, maestro, magician

virtuous adjective good, ethical, honourable, incorruptible, moral, praiseworthy, righteous, upright, worthy

virulent adjective poisonous, deadly, lethal, pernicious, toxic, venomous

viscous adjective thick,

gelatinous, sticky, syrupy

visible *adjective* apparent, clear, discernible, evident, in view, manifest, observable, perceptible, unconcealed

vision *noun* **1** sight, eyesight, perception, seeing, view **2** image, concept, conception, daydream, dream, fantasy, idea, ideal **3** hallucination, apparition, chimera, delusion, illusion, mirage, revelation **4** foresight, discernment, farsightedness, imagination, insight, intuition, penetration, prescience

visionary *adjective* **1** prophetic, mystical **2** impractical, idealistic, quixotic, romantic, speculative, starry-eyed, unrealistic, unworkable, utopian ♦ *noun* **3** prophet, mystic, seer

visit *verb* **1** call on, drop in on (*informal*), look (someone) up, stay with, stop by ♦ *noun* **2** call, sojourn, stay, stop

visitation *noun* **1** inspection, examination, visit **2** catastrophe, blight, calamity, cataclysm, disaster, ordeal, punishment, scourge

visitor *noun* guest, caller, company

vista *noun* view, panorama, perspective, prospect

visual *adjective* **1** optical, ocular, optic **2** observable, discernible, perceptible, visible

visualize *verb* picture, conceive of, envisage, imagine

vital *adjective* **1** essential, basic, fundamental, imperative, indispensable, necessary, requisite **2** important, critical,

crucial, decisive, key, life-or-death, significant, urgent **3** lively, animated, dynamic, energetic, spirited, vibrant, vigorous, vivacious, zestful

vitality *noun* energy, animation, exuberance, life, liveliness, strength, vigour, vivacity

vitriolic *adjective* bitter, acerbic, caustic, envenomed, sardonic, scathing, venomous, virulent, withering

vivacious *adjective* lively, bubbling, ebullient, high-spirited, sparkling, spirited, sprightly, upbeat (*informal*), vital

vivacity *noun* liveliness, animation, ebullience, energy, gaiety, high spirits, sparkle, spirit, sprightliness

vivid *adjective* **1** bright, brilliant, clear, colourful, glowing, intense, rich **2** lifelike, dramatic, graphic, memorable, powerful, realistic, stirring, telling, true to life

vocabulary *noun* words, dictionary, glossary, language, lexicon

vocal *adjective* **1** spoken, oral, said, uttered, voiced **2** outspoken, articulate, eloquent, expressive, forthright, frank, plain-spoken, strident, vociferous

vocation *noun* profession, calling, career, job, mission, pursuit, trade

vociferous *adjective* noisy, clamorous, loud, outspoken, strident, uproarious, vehement, vocal

vogue *noun* **1** fashion, craze,

custom, mode, style, trend, way
2 *As in* **in vogue** popularity, acceptance, currency, favour, prevalence, usage, use

voice *noun* **1** sound, articulation, tone, utterance **2** say, view, vote, will, wish ♦ *verb* **3** express, air, articulate, declare, enunciate, utter

void *noun* **1** emptiness, blankness, gap, lack, space, vacuity, vacuum ♦ *adjective* **2** invalid, ineffective, inoperative, null and void, useless, vain, worthless **3** empty, bare, free, tenantless, unfilled, unoccupied, vacant ♦ *verb* **4** invalidate, cancel, nullify, rescind **5** empty, drain, evacuate

volatile *adjective* **1** changeable, explosive, inconstant, unsettled, unstable, unsteady, variable **2** temperamental, erratic, fickle, mercurial, up and down (*informal*)

volition *noun* free will, choice, choosing, discretion, preference, will

volley *noun* barrage, blast, bombardment, burst, cannonade, fusillade, hail, salvo, shower

voluble *adjective* talkative, articulate, fluent, forthcoming, glib, loquacious

volume *noun* **1** capacity, compass, dimensions **2** amount, aggregate, body, bulk, mass, quantity, total **3** book, publication, title, tome, treatise

voluminous *adjective* large, ample, capacious, cavernous, roomy, vast

voluntarily *adverb* willingly, by choice, freely, off one's own bat,

of one's own accord

voluntary *adjective* unforced, discretionary, free, optional, spontaneous, willing

volunteer *verb* offer, step forward

voluptuous *adjective* **1** buxom, ample, curvaceous (*informal*), enticing, seductive, shapely **2** sensual, epicurean, hedonistic, licentious, luxurious, self-indulgent, sybaritic

vomit *verb* be sick, disgorge, emit, heave, regurgitate, retch, spew out *or* up, throw up (*informal*)

voracious *adjective* **1** gluttonous, greedy, hungry, insatiable, omnivorous, ravenous **2** avid, hungry, insatiable, rapacious, uncontrolled, unquenchable

vortex *noun* whirlpool, eddy, maelstrom

vote *noun* **1** poll, ballot, franchise, plebiscite, referendum, show of hands ♦ *verb* **2** elect, cast one's vote, opt

voucher *noun* ticket, coupon, token

vouch for *verb* **1** guarantee, answer for, certify, give assurance of, stand witness, swear to **2** confirm, affirm, assert, attest to, support, uphold

vow *noun* **1** promise, oath, pledge ♦ *verb* **2** promise, affirm, pledge, swear

voyage *noun* journey, crossing, cruise, passage, trip

vulgar *adjective* crude, coarse, common, impolite, indecent, ribald, risqué, rude, tasteless, uncouth, unrefined

vulgarity *noun* crudeness, bad

taste, coarseness, indelicacy, ribaldry, rudeness, tastelessness

vulnerable adjective 1 weak, sensitive, susceptible, tender, thin-skinned 2 exposed, accessible, assailable, defenceless, unprotected, wide open

W w

wad noun mass, bundle, hunk, roll

waddle verb shuffle, sway, toddle, totter, wobble

wade verb 1 walk through, ford, paddle, splash 2 **wade through** plough through, drudge at, labour at, peg away at, toil at, work one's way through

waffle verb 1 prattle, blather, jabber, prate, rabbit (on) (Brit. informal), witter on (informal) ♦ noun 2 verbosity, padding, prolixity, verbiage, wordiness

waft verb carry, bear, convey, drift, float, transport

wag verb 1 wave, bob, nod, quiver, shake, stir, vibrate, waggle, wiggle ♦ noun 2 wave, bob, nod, quiver, shake, vibration, waggle, wiggle

wage noun 1 Also **wages** payment, allowance, emolument, fee, pay, recompense, remuneration, reward, stipend ♦ verb 2 engage in, carry on, conduct, practise, proceed with, prosecute, pursue, undertake

wager noun 1 bet, flutter (Brit. informal), gamble, punt (chiefly Brit.) ♦ verb 2 bet, chance, gamble, lay, risk, speculate, stake, venture

waggle verb wag, flutter, oscillate, shake, wave, wiggle, wobble

waif noun stray, foundling, orphan

wail verb 1 cry, bawl, grieve, howl, lament, weep, yowl ♦ noun 2 cry, complaint, howl, lament, moan, weeping, yowl

wait verb 1 remain, hang fire, hold back, linger, pause, rest, stay, tarry ♦ noun 2 delay, halt, hold-up, interval, pause, rest, stay

waiter, waitress noun attendant, server, steward or stewardess

wait on or **upon** verb serve, attend, minister to, tend

waive verb set aside, abandon, dispense with, forgo, give up, relinquish, remit, renounce

wake¹ verb 1 awaken, arise, awake, bestir, come to, get up, rouse, stir 2 activate, animate, arouse, excite, fire, galvanize, kindle, provoke, stimulate, stir up ♦ noun 3 vigil, deathwatch, funeral, watch

wake² noun slipstream, aftermath, backwash, path, track, trail, train, wash, waves

wakeful adjective 1 sleepless, insomniac, restless 2 watchful, alert, alive, attentive, observant, on guard, vigilant, wary

waken verb awaken, activate, arouse, awake, rouse, stir

walk verb 1 go, amble, hike, march, move, pace, step, stride, stroll 2 escort, accompany, convoy, take ♦ noun 3 stroll, hike, march, promenade,

ramble, saunter, trek, trudge
4 gait, carriage, step **5** path,
alley, avenue, esplanade,
footpath, lane, promenade, trail
6 walk of life profession, calling,
career, field, line, trade, vocation

walker noun pedestrian, hiker,
rambler, wayfarer

walkout noun strike, industrial
action, protest, stoppage

walkover noun pushover (slang),
breeze (U.S. & Canad. informal),
cakewalk (informal), child's play
(informal), doddle (Brit. slang),
picnic (informal), piece of cake
(informal)

wall noun **1** partition, enclosure,
screen **2** barrier, fence, hedge,
impediment, obstacle,
obstruction

wallet noun holder, case,
pocketbook, pouch, purse

wallop verb **1** hit, batter, beat,
clobber (slang), pound, pummel,
strike, thrash, thump, whack
♦ noun **2** blow, bash, punch,
slug, smack, thump, thwack,
whack

wallow verb **1** revel, bask,
delight, glory, luxuriate, relish,
take pleasure **2** roll about, splash
around

wan adjective pale, anaemic,
ashen, pallid, pasty, sickly,
washed out, white

wand noun stick, baton, rod

wander verb **1** roam, drift,
meander, ramble, range, rove,
stray, stroll **2** deviate, depart,
digress, diverge, err, go astray,
swerve, veer ♦ noun **3** excursion,
cruise, meander, ramble

wanderer noun traveller, drifter,

gypsy, nomad, rambler, rover,
vagabond, voyager

wandering adjective nomadic,
itinerant, migratory, peripatetic,
rootless, roving, travelling,
vagrant, wayfaring

wane verb **1** decline, decrease,
diminish, dwindle, ebb, fade,
fail, lessen, subside, taper off,
weaken ♦ noun **2** on the wane
declining, dwindling, ebbing,
fading, obsolescent, on the
decline, tapering off, weakening

wangle verb contrive, arrange,
engineer, fiddle (informal), fix
(informal), manipulate,
manoeuvre, pull off

want verb **1** desire, covet, crave,
hanker after, hope for, hunger
for, long for, thirst for, wish
for **2** need, call for,
demand, lack, miss, require
♦ noun **3** wish, appetite, craving,
desire, longing, need,
requirement, yearning **4** lack,
absence, dearth, deficiency,
famine, insufficiency, paucity,
scarcity, shortage **5** poverty,
destitution, neediness, penury,
privation

wanting adjective **1** lacking,
absent, incomplete, missing,
short, shy **2** inadequate,
defective, deficient, faulty,
imperfect, poor, substandard,
unsound

wanton adjective **1** unprovoked,
arbitrary, gratuitous, groundless,
motiveless, needless, senseless,
uncalled-for, unjustifiable, wilful
2 promiscuous, dissipated,
dissolute, immoral, lecherous,
libidinous, loose, lustful,
shameless, unchaste

war noun 1 fighting, battle, combat, conflict, enmity, hostilities, struggle, warfare ◆verb 2 fight, battle, campaign against, clash, combat, take up arms, wage war

warble verb sing, chirp, trill, twitter

ward noun 1 room, apartment, cubicle 2 district, area, division, precinct, quarter, zone 3 dependant, charge, minor, protégé, pupil

warden noun keeper, administrator, caretaker, curator, custodian, guardian, ranger, superintendent

warder, wardress noun jailer, custodian, guard, prison officer, screw (slang)

ward off verb repel, avert, avoid, deflect, fend off, parry, stave off

wardrobe noun 1 clothes cupboard, closet 2 clothes, apparel, attire

warehouse noun store, depository, depot, stockroom, storehouse

wares plural noun goods, commodities, merchandise, produce, products, stock, stuff

warfare noun war, arms, battle, combat, conflict, fighting, hostilities

warily adverb cautiously, carefully, charily, circumspectly, distrustfully, gingerly, suspiciously, vigilantly, watchfully, with care

warlike adjective belligerent, aggressive, bellicose, bloodthirsty, hawkish, hostile, martial, warmongering

warlock noun magician, conjuror, enchanter, sorcerer, wizard

warm adjective 1 heated, balmy, lukewarm, pleasant, sunny, tepid, thermal 2 affectionate, amorous, cordial, friendly, hospitable, kindly, loving, tender ◆verb 3 heat, heat up, melt, thaw, warm up

warmonger noun hawk, belligerent, militarist, sabre-rattler

warmth noun 1 heat, hotness, warmness 2 affection, amorousness, cordiality, heartiness, kindliness, love, tenderness

warn verb notify, advise, alert, apprise, caution, forewarn, give notice, inform, make (someone) aware, tip off

warning noun caution, advice, alarm, alert, notification, omen, sign, tip-off

warp verb 1 twist, bend, contort, deform, distort ◆noun 2 twist, bend, contortion, distortion, kink

warrant noun 1 authorization, authority, licence, permission, permit, sanction ◆verb 2 call for, demand, deserve, excuse, justify, license, necessitate, permit, require, sanction 3 guarantee, affirm, attest, certify, declare, pledge, vouch for

warranty noun guarantee, assurance, bond, certificate, contract, covenant, pledge

warrior noun soldier, combatant, fighter, gladiator, man-at-arms

wary adjective cautious, alert, careful, chary, circumspect, distrustful, guarded, suspicious, vigilant, watchful

wash verb 1 <u>clean</u>, bathe, cleanse, launder, rinse, scrub 2 <u>sweep away</u>, bear away, carry off, move 3 *Informal* <u>be plausible</u>, bear scrutiny, be convincing, carry weight, hold up, hold water, stand up, stick ♦ *noun* 4 <u>cleaning</u>, cleansing, laundering, rinse, scrub 5 <u>coat</u>, coating, film, layer, overlay 6 <u>swell</u>, surge, wave

washout noun <u>failure</u>, disappointment, disaster, dud (*informal*), fiasco, flop (*informal*)

waste verb 1 <u>misuse</u>, blow (*slang*), dissipate, fritter away, lavish, squander, throw away 2 <u>waste away</u> <u>decline</u>, atrophy, crumble, decay, dwindle, fade, wane, wear out, wither ♦ *noun* 3 <u>misuse</u>, dissipation, extravagance, frittering away, prodigality, squandering, wastefulness 4 <u>rubbish</u>, debris, dross, garbage, leftovers, litter, refuse, scrap, trash 5 <u>wastes</u> <u>desert</u>, wasteland, wilderness ♦ *adjective* 6 <u>unwanted</u>, leftover, superfluous, supernumerary, unused, useless, worthless 7 <u>uncultivated</u>, bare, barren, desolate, empty, uninhabited, unproductive, wild

wasteful adjective <u>extravagant</u>, lavish, prodigal, profligate, spendthrift, thriftless, uneconomical

waster noun <u>layabout</u>, good-for-nothing, idler, loafer, ne'er-do-well, shirker, skiver (*Brit. slang*), wastrel

watch verb 1 <u>look at</u>, contemplate, eye, observe,

regard, see, view 2 <u>guard</u>, keep, look after, mind, protect, superintend, take care of, tend ♦ *noun* 3 <u>wristwatch</u>, chronometer, timepiece 4 <u>lookout</u>, observation, surveillance, vigil

watchdog noun 1 <u>guard dog</u> 2 <u>guardian</u>, custodian, monitor, protector, scrutineer

watchful adjective <u>alert</u>, attentive, observant, on the lookout, suspicious, vigilant, wary, wide awake

watchman noun <u>guard</u>, caretaker, custodian, security guard

watchword noun <u>motto</u>, battle cry, byword, catch phrase, catchword, maxim, rallying cry, slogan

water noun 1 <u>liquid</u>, H₂O ♦ *verb* 2 <u>moisten</u>, dampen, douse, drench, hose, irrigate, soak, spray

water down verb <u>dilute</u>, thin, water, weaken

waterfall noun <u>cascade</u>, cataract, fall

watertight adjective 1 <u>waterproof</u> 2 <u>foolproof</u>, airtight, flawless, impregnable, sound, unassailable

watery adjective 1 <u>wet</u>, aqueous, damp, fluid, liquid, moist, soggy 2 <u>diluted</u>, runny, thin, washy, watered-down, weak

wave verb 1 <u>signal</u>, beckon, direct, gesticulate, gesture, indicate, sign 2 <u>flap</u>, brandish, flourish, flutter, oscillate, shake, stir, swing, wag ♦ *noun* 3 <u>ripple</u>, billow, breaker, ridge, roller, swell, undulation 4 <u>outbreak</u>, flood, rash, rush, stream, surge, upsurge

waver verb **1** hesitate, dither (chiefly Brit.), falter, fluctuate, hum and haw, seesaw, vacillate **2** tremble, flicker, quiver, shake, totter, wobble

wax verb increase, develop, enlarge, expand, grow, magnify, swell

way noun **1** method, fashion, manner, means, mode, procedure, process, system, technique **2** style, custom, habit, manner, nature, personality, practice, wont **3** route, channel, course, direction, path, pathway, road, track, trail **4** journey, approach, march, passage **5** distance, length, stretch

wayfarer noun traveller, gypsy, itinerant, nomad, rover, voyager, wanderer

wayward adjective erratic, capricious, inconstant, ungovernable, unmanageable, unpredictable, unruly

weak adjective **1** feeble, debilitated, effete, fragile, frail, infirm, puny, sickly, unsteady **2** unsafe, defenceless, exposed, helpless, unguarded, unprotected, vulnerable **3** unconvincing, feeble, flimsy, hollow, lame, pathetic, unsatisfactory **4** tasteless, diluted, insipid, runny, thin, watery

weaken verb **1** lessen, diminish, dwindle, fade, flag, lower, moderate, reduce, sap, undermine, wane **2** dilute, thin out, water down

weakling noun sissy, drip

(informal), wet (Brit. informal), wimp (informal)

weakness noun **1** frailty, decrepitude, feebleness, fragility, infirmity, powerlessness, vulnerability **2** failing, blemish, defect, deficiency, fault, flaw, imperfection, lack, shortcoming **3** liking, fondness, inclination, partiality, passion, penchant, soft spot

wealth noun **1** riches, affluence, capital, fortune, money, opulence, prosperity **2** plenty, abundance, copiousness, cornucopia, fullness, profusion, richness

wealthy adjective rich, affluent, flush (informal), moneyed, opulent, prosperous, well-heeled (informal), well-off, well-to-do

wear verb **1** be dressed in, don, have on, put on, sport (informal) **2** show, display, exhibit **3** deteriorate, abrade, corrode, erode, fray, grind, rub ♦ noun **4** clothes, apparel, attire, costume, dress, garb, garments, gear (informal), things **5** damage, abrasion, attrition, corrosion, deterioration, erosion, wear and tear

weariness noun tiredness, drowsiness, exhaustion, fatigue, languor, lassitude, lethargy, listlessness

wearing adjective tiresome, exasperating, fatiguing, irksome, oppressive, trying, wearisome

wearisome adjective tedious, annoying, boring, exhausting, fatiguing, irksome, oppressive, tiresome, troublesome, trying, wearing

wear off verb subside, decrease, diminish, disappear, dwindle, fade, peter out, wane

weary adjective 1 tired, done in (informal), drained, drowsy, exhausted, fatigued, flagging, jaded, sleepy, worn out 2 tiring, arduous, laborious, tiresome, wearisome ♦ verb 3 tire, drain, enervate, fatigue, sap, take it out of (informal), tax, tire out, wear out

weather noun 1 climate, conditions ♦ verb 2 withstand, brave, come through, endure, overcome, resist, ride out, stand, survive

weave verb 1 knit, braid, entwine, interlace, intertwine, plait 2 create, build, construct, contrive, fabricate, make up, put together, spin 3 zigzag, crisscross, wind

web noun 1 spider's web, cobweb 2 network, lattice, tangle

wed verb 1 marry, get married, take the plunge (informal), tie the knot (informal) 2 unite, ally, blend, combine, interweave, join, link, merge

wedding noun marriage, nuptials, wedlock

wedge noun 1 block, chunk, lump ♦ verb 2 squeeze, cram, crowd, force, jam, lodge, pack, ram, stuff, thrust

wedlock noun marriage, matrimony

weed out verb eliminate, dispense with, eradicate, get rid of, remove, root out, uproot

weedy adjective weak, feeble, frail, ineffectual, namby-pamby, puny, skinny, thin

weep verb cry, blubber, lament, mourn, shed tears, snivel, sob, whimper

weigh verb 1 have a weight of, tip the scales at (informal) 2 consider, contemplate, deliberate upon, evaluate, examine, meditate upon, ponder, reflect upon, think over 3 matter, carry weight, count

weight noun 1 heaviness, load, mass, poundage, tonnage 2 importance, authority, consequence, impact, import, influence, power, value ♦ verb 3 load, freight 4 bias, load, slant, unbalance

weighty adjective 1 important, consequential, crucial, grave, momentous, portentous, serious, significant, solemn 2 heavy, burdensome, cumbersome, hefty (informal), massive, ponderous

weird adjective strange, bizarre, creepy (informal), eerie, freakish, mysterious, odd, queer, spooky (informal), unnatural

welcome verb 1 greet, embrace, hail, meet, receive ♦ noun 2 greeting, acceptance, hospitality, reception, salutation ♦ adjective 3 acceptable, agreeable, appreciated, delightful, desirable, gratifying, pleasant, refreshing 4 free, under no obligation

weld verb join, bind, bond, connect, fuse, link, solder, unite

welfare noun wellbeing, advantage, benefit, good, happiness, health, interest, prosperity

well¹ adverb 1 satisfactorily,

agreeably, nicely, pleasantly, smoothly, splendidly, successfully **2** skilfully, ably, adeptly, adequately, admirably, correctly, efficiently, expertly, proficiently, properly **3** prosperously, comfortably **4** suitably, fairly, fittingly, justly, properly, rightly **5** intimately, deeply, fully, profoundly, thoroughly **6** favourably, approvingly, glowingly, highly, kindly, warmly **7** considerably, abundantly, amply, fully, greatly, heartily, highly, substantially, thoroughly, very much ♦ adjective **8** healthy, fit, in fine fettle, sound **9** satisfactory, agreeable, fine, pleasing, proper, right, thriving

well² noun **1** hole, bore, pit, shaft ♦ verb **2** flow, gush, jet, pour, spout, spring, spurt, surge

well-known adjective famous, celebrated, familiar, noted, popular, renowned

well-off adjective rich, affluent, comfortable, moneyed, prosperous, wealthy, well heeled (informal), well-to-do

well-to-do adjective rich, affluent, comfortable, moneyed, prosperous, wealthy, well-heeled (informal), well-off

well-worn adjective stale, banal, commonplace, hackneyed, overused, stereotyped, trite

welt noun mark, contusion, streak, stripe, wale, weal

welter noun jumble, confusion, hotchpotch, mess, muddle, tangle, web

wet adjective **1** damp, dank, moist, saturated, soaking, sodden, soggy, sopping,

waterlogged, watery **2** rainy, drizzling, pouring, raining, showery, teeming **3** Informal feeble, effete, ineffectual, namby-pamby, soft, spineless, timorous, weak, weedy (informal) ♦ noun **4** rain, drizzle **5** Informal weakling, drip (informal), weed (informal), wimp (informal) **6** moisture, condensation, damp, dampness, humidity, liquid, water, wetness ♦ verb **7** moisten, dampen, douse, irrigate, saturate, soak, spray, water

whack verb **1** strike, bang, belt (informal), clobber (slang), hit, smack, thrash, thump, thwack, wallop (informal) ♦ noun **2** blow, bang, belt (informal), hit, smack, stroke, thump, thwack, wallop (informal) **3** Informal share, bit, cut (informal), part, portion, quota **4** As in have a whack attempt, bash (informal), crack (informal), go (informal), shot (informal), stab (informal), try, turn

wharf noun dock, jetty, landing stage, pier, quay

wheedle verb coax, cajole, entice, inveigle, persuade

wheel noun **1** circle, gyration, pivot, revolution, rotation, spin, turn ♦ verb **2** turn, gyrate, pirouette, revolve, rotate, spin, swing, swivel, twirl, whirl

wheeze verb **1** gasp, cough, hiss, rasp, whistle ♦ noun **2** gasp, cough, hiss, rasp, whistle **3** Brit. slang trick, idea, plan, ploy, ruse, scheme, stunt

whereabouts noun position, location, site, situation

wherewithal noun resources,

capital, funds, means, money, supplies

whet verb 1 As in **whet someone's appetite** stimulate, arouse, awaken, enhance, excite, kindle, quicken, rouse, stir 2 sharpen, hone

whiff noun smell, aroma, hint, odour, scent, sniff

whim noun impulse, caprice, fancy, notion, urge

whimper verb 1 cry, moan, snivel, sob, weep, whine, whinge (informal) ◆ noun 2 sob, moan, snivel, whine

whimsical adjective fanciful, curious, eccentric, freakish, funny, odd, playful, quaint, unusual

whine noun 1 cry, moan, sob, wail, whimper 2 complaint, gripe (informal), grouch (informal), grouse, grumble, moan

whinge Informal ◆ verb 1 complain, bleat, carp, gripe (informal), grouse, grumble, moan ◆ noun 2 complaint, gripe (informal), grouch, grouse, grumble, moan, whine

whip noun 1 lash, birch, cane, cat-o'-nine-tails, crop, scourge ◆ verb 2 lash, beat, birch, cane, flagellate, flog, scourge, spank, strap, thrash 3 Informal dash, dart, dive, fly, rush, shoot, tear, whisk 4 beat, whisk 5 incite, agitate, drive, foment, goad, spur, stir, work up

whirl verb 1 spin, pirouette, revolve, roll, rotate, swirl, turn, twirl, twist 2 feel dizzy, reel, spin ◆ noun 3 revolution, pirouette, roll, rotation, spin, swirl, turn,

twirl, twist 4 bustle, flurry, merry-go-round, round, series, succession 5 confusion, daze, dither (chiefly Brit.), giddiness, spin

whirlwind noun 1 tornado, waterspout ◆ adjective 2 rapid, hasty, quick, short, speedy, swift

whisk verb 1 flick, brush, sweep, whip 2 beat, fluff up, whip ◆ noun 3 flick, brush, sweep, whip 4 beater

whisper verb 1 murmur, breathe 2 rustle, hiss, sigh, swish ◆ noun 3 murmur, undertone 4 Informal rumour, gossip, innuendo, insinuation, report 5 rustle, hiss, sigh, swish

white adjective pale, ashen, pallid, pasty, wan

white-collar adjective clerical, nonmanual, professional, salaried

whiten verb pale, blanch, bleach, fade

whitewash noun 1 cover-up, camouflage, concealment, deception ◆ verb 2 cover up, camouflage, conceal, gloss over, suppress

whittle verb 1 carve, cut, hew, pare, shape, shave, trim 2 **whittle down** or **away** reduce, consume, eat away, erode, wear away

whole adjective 1 complete, entire, full, total, unabridged, uncut, undivided 2 undamaged, in one piece, intact, unbroken, unharmed, unscathed, untouched ◆ noun 3 totality, ensemble, entirety 4 **on the whole: a** all in all, all things considered, by and large **b** generally, as a rule, in general, in the main, mostly, predominantly

wholehearted *adjective* <u>sincere</u>, committed, dedicated, determined, devoted, enthusiastic, unstinting, zealous

wholesale *adjective* **1** <u>extensive</u>, broad, comprehensive, far-reaching, indiscriminate, mass, sweeping, wide-ranging ♦ *adverb* **2** <u>extensively</u>, comprehensively, indiscriminately

wholesome *adjective*
1 <u>beneficial</u>, good, healthy, nourishing, nutritious, salubrious
2 <u>moral</u>, decent, edifying, improving, respectable

wholly *adverb* <u>completely</u>, altogether, entirely, fully, in every respect, perfectly, thoroughly, totally, utterly

whopper *noun* **1** <u>giant</u>, colossus, crackerjack (*informal*), jumbo (*informal*), leviathan, mammoth, monster **2** <u>big lie</u>, fabrication, falsehood, tall story (*informal*), untruth

whopping *adjective* <u>gigantic</u>, big, enormous, giant, great, huge, mammoth, massive

whore *noun* <u>prostitute</u>, call girl, streetwalker, tart

wicked *adjective* **1** <u>bad</u>, corrupt, depraved, devilish, evil, fiendish, immoral, sinful, vicious, villainous **2** <u>mischievous</u>, impish, incorrigible, naughty, rascally, roguish

wide *adjective* **1** <u>broad</u>, expansive, extensive, far-reaching, immense, large, sweeping, vast **2** <u>spacious</u>, baggy, capacious, commodious, full, loose, roomy **3** <u>expanded</u>,

dilated, distended, outspread, outstretched **4** <u>distant</u>, off course, off target, remote ♦ *adverb* **5** <u>fully</u>, completely **6** <u>off target</u>, astray, off course, off the mark, out

widen *verb* <u>broaden</u>, dilate, enlarge, expand, extend, spread, stretch

widespread *adjective* <u>common</u>, broad, extensive, far-reaching, general, pervasive, popular, universal

width *noun* <u>breadth</u>, compass, diameter, extent, girth, scope, span, thickness

wield *verb* **1** <u>brandish</u>, employ, flourish, handle, manage, manipulate, ply, swing, use **2** *As in* **wield power** <u>exert</u>, exercise, have, maintain, possess

wife *noun* <u>spouse</u>, better half (*humorous*), bride, mate, partner

wiggle *verb, noun* <u>jerk</u>, jiggle, shake, shimmy, squirm, twitch, wag, waggle, writhe

wild *adjective* **1** <u>untamed</u>, feral, ferocious, fierce, savage, unbroken, undomesticated
2 <u>uncultivated</u>, free, natural
3 <u>uncivilized</u>, barbaric, barbarous, brutish, ferocious, fierce, primitive, savage
4 <u>uncontrolled</u>, disorderly, riotous, rowdy, turbulent, undisciplined, unfettered, unmanageable, unrestrained, unruly, wayward **5** <u>stormy</u>, blustery, choppy, raging, rough, tempestuous, violent **6** <u>excited</u>, crazy (*informal*), enthusiastic, hysterical, raving ♦ *noun* **7** <u>wilds</u> <u>wilderness</u>, back of beyond (*informal*), desert, middle of

nowhere (*informal*), wasteland

wilderness noun <u>desert</u>, jungle, wasteland, wilds

wiles plural noun <u>trickery</u>, artfulness, chicanery, craftiness, cunning, guile, slyness

wilful adjective 1 <u>obstinate</u>, determined, headstrong, inflexible, intransigent, obdurate, perverse, pig-headed, stubborn, uncompromising 2 <u>intentional</u>, conscious, deliberate, intended, purposeful, voluntary

will noun 1 <u>determination</u>, purpose, resolution, resolve, willpower 2 <u>wish</u>, desire, fancy, inclination, mind, preference, volition 3 <u>testament</u>, last wishes ♦ verb 4 <u>wish</u>, desire, prefer, see fit, want 5 <u>bequeath</u>, confer, give, leave, pass on, transfer

willing adjective <u>ready</u>, agreeable, amenable, compliant, consenting, game (*informal*), inclined, prepared

willingly adverb <u>readily</u>, by choice, cheerfully, eagerly, freely, gladly, happily, of one's own accord, voluntarily

willingness noun <u>inclination</u>, agreement, consent, volition, will, wish

willowy adjective <u>slender</u>, graceful, lithe, slim, supple, svelte, sylphlike

willpower noun <u>self-control</u>, determination, drive, grit, resolution, resolve, self-discipline, single-mindedness

wilt verb 1 <u>droop</u>, sag, shrivel, wither 2 <u>weaken</u>, fade, flag, languish, wane

wily adjective <u>cunning</u>, artful,

astute, crafty, guileful, sharp, shrewd, sly, tricky

wimp noun Informal <u>weakling</u>, coward, drip (*informal*), mouse, sissy, softy or softie

win verb 1 <u>triumph</u>, come first, conquer, overcome, prevail, succeed, sweep the board 2 <u>gain</u>, achieve, acquire, attain, earn, get, land, obtain, procure, secure ♦ noun 3 <u>victory</u>, conquest, success, triumph

wince verb 1 <u>flinch</u>, blench, cower, cringe, draw back, quail, recoil, shrink, start ♦ noun 2 <u>flinch</u>, cringe, start

wind¹ noun 1 <u>air</u>, blast, breeze, draught, gust, zephyr 2 <u>breath</u>, puff, respiration 3 <u>flatulence</u>, gas 4 <u>talk</u>, babble, blather, bluster, boasting, hot air, humbug 5 As in **get wind of** <u>hint</u>, inkling, notice, report, rumour, suggestion, warning, whisper

wind² verb 1 <u>coil</u>, curl, encircle, loop, reel, roll, spiral, twist 2 <u>meander</u>, bend, curve, ramble, snake, turn, twist, zigzag

windfall noun <u>godsend</u>, bonanza, find, jackpot, manna from heaven

wind up verb 1 <u>end</u>, close, conclude, finalize, finish, settle, terminate, wrap up 2 <u>end up</u>, be left, finish up 3 Informal <u>excite</u>, put on edge, work up

windy adjective <u>breezy</u>, blowy, blustery, gusty, squally, stormy, wild, windswept

wing noun 1 <u>faction</u>, arm, branch, group, section ♦ verb 2 <u>fly</u>, glide, soar 3 <u>wound</u>, clip, hit

wink *verb* **1** blink, bat, flutter **2** twinkle, flash, gleam, glimmer, sparkle ◆ *noun* **3** blink, flutter

winkle out *verb* extract, dig out, dislodge, draw out, extricate, force out, prise out

winner *noun* victor, champ (*informal*), champion, conqueror, master

winning *adjective* **1** victorious, conquering, successful, triumphant **2** charming, alluring, attractive, cute, disarming, enchanting, endearing, engaging, likable *or* likeable, pleasing

winnings *plural noun* spoils, gains, prize, proceeds, profits, takings

winnow *verb* separate, divide, select, sift, sort out

win over *verb* convince, bring or talk round, convert, influence, persuade, prevail upon, sway

wintry *adjective* cold, chilly, freezing, frosty, frozen, icy, snowy

wipe *verb* **1** clean, brush, mop, rub, sponge, swab **2** erase, remove ◆ *noun* **3** rub, brush

wipe out *verb* destroy, annihilate, eradicate, erase, expunge, exterminate, massacre, obliterate

wiry *adjective* lean, sinewy, strong, tough

wisdom *noun* understanding, discernment, enlightenment, erudition, insight, intelligence, judgment, knowledge, learning, sense

wise *adjective* sensible, clever, discerning, enlightened, erudite, intelligent, judicious, perceptive, prudent, sage

wisecrack *noun* **1** joke, jest, jibe, quip, witticism ◆ *verb* **2** joke, jest, jibe, quip

wish *verb* **1** want, aspire, crave, desire, hanker, hope, long, yearn ◆ *noun* **2** desire, aspiration, hope, intention, urge, want, whim, will

wispy *adjective* thin, attenuated, delicate, fine, flimsy, fragile, frail

wistful *adjective* melancholy, contemplative, dreamy, longing, meditative, pensive, reflective, thoughtful

wit *noun* **1** humour, badinage, banter, drollery, jocularity, raillery, repartee, wordplay **2** humorist, card (*informal*), comedian, joker, wag **3** cleverness, acumen, brains, common sense, ingenuity, intellect, sense, wisdom

witch *noun* enchantress, crone, hag, magician, sorceress

witchcraft *noun* magic, enchantment, necromancy, occultism, sorcery, the black art, voodoo, wizardry

withdraw *verb* remove, draw back, extract, pull out, take away, take off

withdrawal *noun* removal, extraction

withdrawn *adjective* uncommunicative, distant, introverted, reserved, retiring, shy, taciturn, unforthcoming

wither *verb* wilt, decay, decline, disintegrate, fade, perish, shrivel, waste

withering *adjective* scornful, devastating, humiliating, hurtful, mortifying, snubbing

withhold verb keep back, conceal, hide, hold back, refuse, reserve, retain, suppress

withstand verb resist, bear, cope with, endure, hold off, oppose, stand up to, suffer, tolerate

witless adjective foolish, halfwitted, idiotic, inane, moronic, senseless, silly, stupid

witness noun 1 observer, beholder, bystander, eyewitness, looker-on, onlooker, spectator, viewer, watcher 2 testifier, corroborator ♦ verb 3 see, note, notice, observe, perceive, view, watch 4 sign, countersign, endorse

wits plural noun intelligence, acumen, brains (informal), cleverness, comprehension, faculties, ingenuity, reason, sense, understanding

witter verb chatter, babble, blather, chat, gabble, jabber, prate, prattle, waffle (informal, chiefly Brit.)

witticism noun quip, bon mot, one-liner (slang), pun, riposte

witty adjective humorous, amusing, clever, droll, funny, piquant, sparkling, waggish, whimsical

wizard noun magician, conjuror, magus, necromancer, occultist, shaman, sorcerer, warlock, witch

wizardry noun magic, sorcery, voodoo, witchcraft

wizened adjective wrinkled, dried up, gnarled, lined, shrivelled, shrunken, withered

wobble verb 1 shake, rock, sway, teeter, totter, tremble ♦ noun

2 unsteadiness, shake, tremble, tremor

wobbly adjective unsteady, rickety, shaky, teetering, tottering, uneven

woe noun grief, agony, anguish, distress, gloom, misery, sadness, sorrow, unhappiness, wretchedness

woeful adjective 1 sad, deplorable, dismal, distressing, grievous, lamentable, miserable, pathetic, tragic, wretched 2 pitiful, abysmal, appalling, bad, deplorable, dreadful, feeble, pathetic, poor, sorry

woman noun lady, female, girl

womanizer noun philanderer, Casanova, Don Juan, lady-killer, lecher, seducer

womanly adjective feminine, female, ladylike, matronly, motherly, tender, warm

wonder verb 1 think, conjecture, meditate, ponder, puzzle, query, question, speculate 2 be amazed, be astonished, gape, marvel, stare ♦ noun 3 phenomenon, curiosity, marvel, miracle, prodigy, rarity, sight, spectacle 4 amazement, admiration, astonishment, awe, bewilderment, fascination, surprise, wonderment

wonderful adjective 1 excellent, brilliant, fabulous (informal), fantastic (informal), great (informal), magnificent, marvellous, outstanding, superb, terrific, tremendous 2 remarkable, amazing, astonishing, extraordinary, incredible, miraculous, phenomenal, staggering, startling, unheard-of

wonky adjective <u>shaky</u>, unsteady, wobbly

woo verb <u>court</u>, cultivate, pursue

wood noun 1 <u>timber</u> 2 <u>woodland</u>, coppice, copse, forest, grove, thicket

wooded adjective <u>tree-covered</u>, forested, sylvan (*poetic*), timbered, tree-clad

wooden adjective 1 <u>woody</u>, ligneous, timber 2 <u>expressionless</u>, deadpan, lifeless, unresponsive

wool noun <u>fleece</u>, hair, yarn

woolly adjective 1 <u>fleecy</u>, hairy, shaggy, woollen 2 <u>vague</u>, confused, hazy, ill-defined, indefinite, indistinct, muddled, unclear

word noun 1 <u>term</u>, expression, name 2 <u>chat</u>, confab (*informal*), consultation, discussion, talk, tête-à-tête 3 <u>remark</u>, comment, utterance 4 <u>message</u>, communiqué, dispatch, information, intelligence, news, notice, report 5 <u>promise</u>, assurance, guarantee, oath, pledge, vow 6 <u>command</u>, bidding, decree, mandate, order ♦ verb 7 <u>express</u>, couch, phrase, put, say, state, utter

wording noun <u>phraseology</u>, language, phrasing, terminology, words

wordy adjective <u>long-winded</u>, diffuse, prolix, rambling, verbose, windy

work noun 1 <u>effort</u>, drudgery, elbow grease (*facetious*), exertion, industry, labour, sweat, toil 2 <u>employment</u>, business, duty, job, livelihood, occupation, profession, trade 3 <u>task</u>, assignment, chore, commission, duty, job, stint, undertaking 4 <u>creation</u>, achievement, composition, handiwork, opus, piece, production ♦ verb 5 <u>labour</u>, drudge, exert oneself, peg away, slave, slog (away), sweat, toil 6 <u>be employed</u>, be in work 7 <u>operate</u>, control, drive, handle, manage, manipulate, move, use 8 <u>function</u>, go, operate, run 9 <u>cultivate</u>, dig, farm, till 10 <u>manipulate</u>, fashion, form, knead, mould, shape

workable adjective <u>viable</u>, doable, feasible, possible, practicable, practical

worker noun <u>employee</u>, artisan, craftsman, hand, labourer, tradesman, workman

working adjective 1 <u>employed</u>, active, in work 2 <u>functioning</u>, going, operative, running

workman noun <u>labourer</u>, artisan, craftsman, employee, hand, journeyman, mechanic, operative, tradesman, worker

workmanship noun <u>skill</u>, artistry, craftsmanship, expertise, handiwork, technique

workshop noun <u>studio</u>, factory,

work out verb 1 <u>solve</u>, calculate, figure out, find out 2 <u>happen</u>, develop, evolve, result, turn out 3 <u>exercise</u>, practise, train, warm up

works plural noun 1 <u>factory</u>, mill, plant, workshop 2 <u>writings</u>, canon, oeuvre, output 3 <u>mechanism</u>, action, machinery, movement, parts, workings

mill, plant, workroom

world noun **1** earth, globe **2** mankind, everybody, everyone, humanity, humankind, man, the public **3** sphere, area, domain, environment, field, realm

worldly adjective **1** earthly, physical, profane, secular, temporal, terrestrial **2** materialistic, grasping, greedy, selfish **3** worldly-wise, blasé, cosmopolitan, experienced, knowing, sophisticated, urbane

worldwide adjective global, general, international, omnipresent, pandemic, ubiquitous, universal

worn adjective ragged, frayed, shabby, tattered, tatty, the worse for wear, threadbare

worn-out adjective **1** run-down, on its last legs, ragged, shabby, threadbare, used-up, useless, worn **2** exhausted, all in (slang), done in (informal), fatigued, fit to drop, spent, tired out, weary

worried adjective anxious, afraid, apprehensive, concerned, fearful, frightened, nervous, perturbed, tense, troubled, uneasy

worry verb **1** be anxious, agonize, brood, fret **2** trouble, annoy, bother, disturb, perturb, pester, unsettle, upset, vex ◆ noun **3** anxiety, apprehension, concern, fear, misgiving, trepidation, trouble, unease **4** problem, bother, care, hassle (informal), trouble

worsen verb **1** aggravate, damage, exacerbate **2** deteriorate, decay, decline, degenerate, get worse, go

downhill (informal), sink

worship verb **1** praise, adore, exalt, glorify, honour, pray to, revere, venerate **2** love, adore, idolize, put on a pedestal ◆ noun **3** praise, adoration, adulation, devotion, glory, honour, regard, respect, reverence

worth noun **1** value, cost, price, rate, valuation **2** excellence, goodness, importance, merit, quality, usefulness, value, worthiness

worthless adjective **1** useless, ineffectual, rubbishy, unimportant, valueless **2** good-for-nothing, contemptible, despicable, vile

worthwhile adjective useful, beneficial, constructive, expedient, helpful, productive, profitable, valuable

worthy adjective praiseworthy, admirable, creditable, deserving, laudable, meritorious, valuable, virtuous, worthwhile

would-be adjective budding, self-appointed, self-styled, unfulfilled, wannabe (informal)

wound noun **1** injury, cut, gash, hurt, laceration, lesion, trauma (Pathology) **2** insult, offence, slight ◆ verb **3** injure, cut, gash, hurt, lacerate, pierce, wing **4** offend, annoy, cut (someone) to the quick, hurt, mortify, sting

wrangle verb **1** argue, bicker, contend, disagree, dispute, fight, quarrel, row, squabble ◆ noun **2** argument, altercation, bickering, dispute, quarrel, row, squabble, tiff

wrap verb **1** cover, bind, bundle up, encase, enclose, enfold,

pack, package, shroud, swathe
♦ *noun* **2** cloak, cape, mantle,
shawl, stole

wrapper *noun* cover, case,
envelope, jacket, packaging,
wrapping

wrap up *verb* **1** giftwrap, bundle
up, pack, package **2** *Informal*
end, conclude, finish off, polish
off, round off, terminate, wind up

wrath *noun* anger, displeasure,
fury, indignation, ire, rage,
resentment, temper

wreath *noun* garland, band,
chaplet, crown, festoon, ring

wreck *verb* **1** destroy, break,
demolish, devastate, ruin,
shatter, smash, spoil ♦ *noun*
2 shipwreck, hulk

wreckage *noun* remains, debris,
fragments, pieces, rubble, ruin

wrench *verb* **1** twist, force, jerk,
pull, rip, tear, tug, yank **2** sprain,
rick, strain ♦ *noun* **3** twist, jerk,
pull, rip, tug, yank **4** sprain,
strain, twist **5** blow, pang,
shock, upheaval **6** spanner,
adjustable spanner

wrest *verb* seize, extract, force,
take, win, wrench

wrestle *verb* fight, battle,
combat, grapple, scuffle,
struggle, tussle

wretch *noun* scoundrel,
good-for-nothing, miscreant,
rascal, rogue, swine, worm

wretched *adjective* **1** unhappy,
dejected, depressed,
disconsolate, downcast, forlorn,
hapless, miserable, woebegone
2 worthless, inferior, miserable,
paltry, pathetic, poor, sorry

wriggle *verb* **1** twist, jerk, jiggle,

squirm, turn, waggle, wiggle,
writhe **2** crawl, slink, snake,
worm, zigzag **3** *As in* wriggle
out of manoeuvre, dodge,
extricate oneself ♦ *noun* **4** twist,
jerk, jiggle, squirm, turn, waggle,
wiggle

wring *verb* twist, extract, force,
screw, squeeze

wrinkle *noun* **1** crease,
corrugation, crinkle, crow's-foot,
crumple, fold, furrow, line ♦ *verb*
2 crease, corrugate, crumple,
fold, furrow, gather, pucker,
rumple

writ *noun* summons, court order,
decree, document

write *verb* record, draft, draw up,
inscribe, jot down, pen, scribble,
set down

writer *noun* author, hack,
novelist, penpusher, scribbler,
scribe, wordsmith

writhe *verb* squirm, jerk,
struggle, thrash, thresh, toss,
twist, wiggle, wriggle

writing *noun* **1** script,
calligraphy, hand, handwriting,
penmanship, scrawl, scribble
2 document, book, composition,
opus, publication, work

wrong *adjective* **1** incorrect,
erroneous, fallacious, false,
inaccurate, mistaken, untrue,
wide of the mark **2** bad,
criminal, dishonest, evil, illegal,
immoral, sinful, unjust, unlawful,
wicked, wrongful
3 inappropriate, incongruous,
incorrect, unacceptable,
unbecoming, undesirable,
unseemly, unsuitable **4** defective,
amiss, askew, awry, faulty
♦ *adverb* **5** incorrectly, badly,

erroneously, inaccurately, mistakenly, wrongly **6** amiss, askew, astray, awry ♦ *noun* **7** offence, crime, error, injury, injustice, misdeed, sin, transgression, wickedness ♦ *verb* **8** mistreat, abuse, cheat, dishonour, harm, hurt, malign, oppress, take advantage of

wrongdoer *noun* offender, criminal, culprit, delinquent, lawbreaker, miscreant, sinner, villain

wrongful *adjective* improper, criminal, evil, illegal, illegitimate, immoral, unethical, unjust, unlawful, wicked

wry *adjective* **1** ironic, droll, dry, mocking, sarcastic, sardonic **2** contorted, crooked, twisted, uneven

X x

Xmas *noun* Christmas, Noel, Yule (*archaic*), Yuletide (*archaic*)

X-rays *plural noun* Röntgen rays (*old name*)

Y y

yank *verb, noun* pull, hitch, jerk, snatch, tug, wrench

yardstick *noun* standard, benchmark, criterion, gauge, measure, par, touchstone

yarn *noun* **1** thread, fibre **2** *Informal* story, anecdote, cock-and-bull story (*informal*), fable, tale, tall story

yawning *adjective* gaping, cavernous, vast, wide

yearly *adjective* **1** annual ♦ *adverb* **2** annually, every year, once a year, per annum

yearn *verb* long, ache, covet, crave, desire, hanker, hunger, itch

yell *verb* **1** scream, bawl, holler (*informal*), howl, screech, shout, shriek, squeal ♦ *noun* **2** scream, cry, howl, screech, shriek, whoop

yelp *verb* cry, yap, yowl

yen *noun* longing, ache, craving, desire, hankering, hunger, itch, passion, thirst, yearning

yes man *noun* sycophant, bootlicker (*informal*), crawler (*slang*), minion, timeserver, toady

yet *conjunction* **1** nevertheless, however, notwithstanding, still ♦ *adverb* **2** so far, as yet, thus far, until now, up to now **3** still, besides, in addition, into the bargain, to boot **4** now, just now, right now, so soon

yield *verb* **1** produce, bear, forth, earn, generate, give, net, provide, return, supply **2** surrender, bow, capitulate, give in, relinquish, resign, submit, succumb ♦ *noun* **3** profit, crop, earnings, harvest, income, output, produce, return, revenue, takings

yielding *adjective* **1** submissive, accommodating, acquiescent, biddable, compliant, docile, flexible, obedient, pliant **2** soft, elastic, pliable, spongy, springy, supple, unresisting

yob, yobbo *noun* thug, hooligan, lout, roughneck

(*slang*), ruffian

yokel *noun* peasant, (country) bumpkin, countryman, hick (*informal, chiefly U.S. & Canad.*), hillbilly, rustic

young *adjective* **1** immature, adolescent, callow, green, infant, junior, juvenile, little, youthful **2** new, early, fledgling, recent, undeveloped ♦ *plural noun* **3** offspring, babies, brood, family, issue, litter, progeny

youngster *noun* youth, boy, girl, juvenile, kid (*informal*), lad, lass, teenager

youth *noun* **1** immaturity, adolescence, boyhood, girlhood, salad days **2** boy, adolescent, kid (*informal*), lad, stripling, teenager, young man, youngster

youthful *adjective* young, boyish, childish, girlish, immature, inexperienced, juvenile

Z z

zany *adjective* comical, clownish, crazy, eccentric, goofy (*informal*), madcap, wacky (*slang*)

zeal *noun* enthusiasm, ardour, eagerness, fanaticism, fervour, gusto, keenness, passion, spirit, verve, zest

zealot *noun* fanatic, bigot, enthusiast, extremist, militant

zealous *adjective* enthusiastic, ardent, devoted, eager, fanatical, fervent, impassioned, keen, passionate

zenith *noun* height, acme, apex, apogee, climax, crest, high point, peak, pinnacle, summit, top

zero *noun* **1** nothing, nil, nought **2** bottom, nadir, rock bottom

zest *noun* **1** enjoyment, appetite, gusto, keenness, relish, zeal **2** flavour, charm, interest, piquancy, pungency, relish, spice, tang, taste

zip *noun* **1** *Informal* energy, drive, gusto, liveliness, verve, vigour, zest ♦ *verb* **2** speed, flash, fly, shoot, whizz (*informal*), zoom

zone *noun* area, belt, district, region, section, sector, sphere

zoom *verb* speed, dash, flash, fly, hurtle, pelt, rush, shoot, whizz (*informal*)